Daft/Marcic

xtra!

CONGRATULATIONS!

Your purchase of this new textbook includes complimentary access to the Daft /Marcic Xtra! Web Site (http://daftxtra.swlearning.com). This site offers a robust set of online multimedia learning tools to help you gain a deeper and richer understanding of management, including:

EXPERIENCING MANAGEMENT

Reinforces key management principles in a dynamic learning environment by exposing you to the central constructs of each topic through text, animated models or graphs, audio narration, and a variety of interactive activities and applications.

AUTHOR INSIGHT VIDEO CLIPS

Via streaming video, difficult concepts from each chapter are explained and illustrated by the textbook author, Richard Daft. These video clips can be extremely helpful review and clarification tools if you had trouble understanding an in-class lecture or if you are a visual learner.

VIDEO CASES

The videos that accompany the video cases in the text are available here for viewing, along with the discussion questions to submit for credit.

CNN VIDEO

CNN video segments and exercises let you see Management in action, in the real world, to help you learn theoretical material by applying it to current events.

XTRA! QUIZZING

You can create and take randomly-generated quizzes on whichever chapter(s) you wish to test yourself, and endlessly practice for exams.

Tear Out Card Missing?

If you did not buy a new textbook, the tear-out portion of this card may be missing, or the Access Code may not be valid. Access Codes can be used only once to register for access to Daft/Marcic Xtra!, and are not transferable. You can choose to either buy a new book or purchase access to the Daft/Marcic Xtra! site at http://daftxtra.swlearning.com.

HOW TO REGISTER YOUR SERIAL NUMBER

STEP 1 Launch a Web browser and go to http://daftxtra.swlearning.com

STEP 2 Choose the book you're using by clicking on the appropriate title.

STEP 3 Click the "Register" button to enter your serial number.

STEP 4 Enter your serial number exactly as it appears here and create a unique User ID, or enter an existing User ID if you have previously registered for a different product via a serial number.

SERIAL NUMBER: SC-00012QS4-DUMX

STEP 5 When prompted, create a password (or enter an existing password, if you have previously registered for a different product via a serial number). Submit the necessary information when prompted. Record your User ID and password in a secure location.

STEP 6 Once registered, follow the link to enter the product, or return to the URL above and select the "Enter" button. Note that the duration of

xtra!

THOMSON
SOUTH-WESTERN

For technical support, contact
1-800-423-0563
or email
support@thomsonlearning.com.

55

7+8

Understanding
Management

FOURTH EDITION

Understanding
Management

FOURTH EDITION

Richard L. Daft
Vanderbilt University

Dorothy Marcic
Vanderbilt University

THOMSON
™
SOUTH-WESTERN

Australia · Canada · Mexico · Singapore · Spain · United Kingdom · United States

Understanding Management, 4th Edition
Richard L. Daft and Dorothy Marcic

Editor-in-Chief:
Jack W. Calhoun

Vice President/Team Leader:
Michael P. Roche

Acquisitions Editor:
Joe Sabatino

Developmental Editor:
Emma F. Guttler

Senior Marketing Manager:
Rob Bloom

Production Editor:
Emily S. Gross

Manufacturing Coordinator:
Rhonda Utley

Media Developmental Editor:
Kristen Meere

Media Production Editor:
Karen L. Schaffer

Compositor:
Stratford Publishing Services, Inc.

Printer:
Quebecor World Versailles
Versailles, KY

Senior Design Project Manager:
Michelle Kunkler

Internal and Cover Designer:
Lou Ann Thesing
Cincinnati, OH

Cover Images:
© Digital Vision and
© PhotoDisc, Inc.

Photography Manager:
Deanna Ettinger

Library of Congress Control Number:
2002116835

Dedicated to Roxanne, Solange, and Elizabeth,
who light up our lives.

In memory of Gadi Harel (1940–2003),
our dear friend and colleague, whose love and
encouragement touched us deeply and who will be greatly missed.

Preface

The New Workplace

We are entering a new era, one unlike any before, and the major difference can be summed up in a word: change. The tremendous forces behind such change include the intensity of increased globalization; the movement of people around the world with its accompanying multiculturalism; and, perhaps most of all, the explosion of the information age. *Understanding Management,* Fourth Edition, was developed to help students grasp these changes and cope with the emerging world economies, and it has particular relevance for those who are interested in understanding the value and dynamics of small- and medium-sized organizations. Unlike traditional management texts, this book does not rely on abstract theories and examples from corporations that are applicable only to top managers of billion-dollar companies. Rather, our vision is to appeal to students on a practical level, and to provide insight and meaningful information for them to succeed in their futures of "working for a living." To this end, *Understanding Management* contains several distinctive elements:

- **Current Management Thinking.** The vision for the fourth edition of *Understanding Management* is to explore new management ideas in a way that is interesting and valuable to students, while retaining the best of traditional management thinking. To achieve this vision, the most recent management concepts and research are included, as well as contemporary applications of management ideas in organizations. The combination of established scholarship, new ideas, and real-life applications gives students a taste of the energy, challenge, and adventure inherent in the dynamic field of management. Examples were selected for their relevance and appeal to students interested in real management issues and how problems are being addressed in regional companies. These management concepts are especially applicable to readers with interest in small-business management and entrepreneurship.

- **Reinforcement of Management Concepts.** Case applications, boxed items, key terms, exhibits, photo captions, and end of chapter materials are heavily oriented towards middle management and explore supervisory issues being dealt with in smaller companies. *Understanding Management,* Fourth Edition, focuses on vivid illustrations of real organizations that affect people at every level, whatever the size of the company. In our view, this is not only the most interesting, up to date, and practical way to reinforce our vision of the book, but it is also a very effective way to help students identify with and fully comprehend the changing state of current management situations. Both the textual and graphic portions of the textbook help students grasp the often abstract and sometimes distant world of management.

- **Full Technology Coverage.** In recognition of the role of technology in today's world, each chapter of the text integrates coverage of the Internet and emerging technology into the various topics covered in the chapter. In addition, every chapter contains a Digital, Inc. box that features a technologically savvy company or highlights a trend that is having an impact on today's organizations. The book's technology emphasis is also reflected in the Surf the Net exercises at the end of each chapter.

Focus on the Future

The world of work is changing rapidly. And, in response, the field of management is undergoing a revolution. The result is "The New Workplace"—the theme of this edition of *Understanding Management*. Demands on today's managers go well beyond the techniques and ideas traditionally taught in management courses. The traditional world of work assumed the purpose of management was to control and limit people, enforce rules and regulations, seek stability and efficiency, design a top-down hierarchy to direct people, and achieve bottom-line results. The new workplace and emerging management paradigm recognizes that today's managers need different skills to engage workers' hearts and minds, as well as take advantage of their physical labor. The new workplace asks that managers focus on leading change, on harnessing people's creativity and enthusiasm, on finding shared vision and values, and on sharing information and power. Teamwork, collaboration, participation and learning are guiding principles that help managers and employees maneuver the difficult terrain of today's complex business environment. Managers focus on developing, not controlling, employee's skills to adapt to new technologies and extraordinary environmental shifts, and thus achieve total corporate effectiveness.

Both the new workplace and the traditional paradigm are guiding management actions in the world today. The textual portion of this book has been enhanced through an engaging, easy-to-understand writing style, and the many in-text examples and boxed items that make the concepts come alive for students. In addition to the easy-to-understand writing style of the book, many practical examples and profiles are of real people involved in real business dilemmas. The graphic component has been enhanced with several new exhibits and a new set of photo essays that illustrate specific management concepts.

Understanding Management provides a book of utmost quality that captures the excitement of organizational management, creating in students both respect for the changing field of management and confidence that they can understand and master it.

New and Improved Topic Coverage and Organization

The chapter sequence in *Understanding Management* is organized around the management functions of planning, organizing, leading, and controlling. These four functions effectively encompass both management research and characteristics of the manager's job. The fourth edition of *Understanding Management* is especially focused on the future of management education by identifying and describing emerging elements and examples of the new workplace and the changing management paradigm.

Part One introduces the world of management, including the nature of management, issues surrounding the new workplace, the learning organization, and historical perspectives on management.

- **Chapter 1** introduces the new workplace and defines the changing management paradigm. The chapter explores the growing importance of leadership and the new management competencies needed to thrive in today's business world. It also discusses the forces affecting today's organizations and managers, and includes a segment on managing during crises and unexpected events, an important skill in today's volatile workplace. Additionally, it contains a significantly expanded discussion of the behavioral sciences approach. This chapter also contains a new section on managing the technology-driven workplace, introducing the concepts of e-business (B2B, B2C, and C2C), intranets and extranets, enterprise resource planning, and knowledge management. There is continued coverage of the historical development of management and organizations.

Part Two examines the environments of management and organizations. This section includes material on the business environment and corporate culture, the global environment, ethics and social responsibility, the natural environment, and the environment of entrepreneurship and small business management.

- **Chapter 2** includes a section on culture; the four types of culture (adaptability culture, achievement culture, bureaucratic culture, and clan culture) are explored in terms of their relationship to the external environment. A complete section of this chapter is devoted to trends such as virtual teams and telecommuting that put demands on managers trying to create strong adaptive cultures.
- **Chapter 3** includes an updated and enlarged discussion of GATT and WTO.
- **Chapter 4** presents an updated and expanded exploration of environmental responsibility and how today's organizations are meeting their responsibilities in this area. This chapter also includes a new section on ethical leadership, including a new discussion of ethical issues associated with information technology.

Part Three presents two chapters on planning, including organizational goal setting and planning, strategy formulation and implementation, and the decision-making process.

- **Chapter 5** incorporates a new section on crisis management planning and also considers the impact of the Internet and e-business on strategy.
- **Chapter 6** includes a discussion of new decision approaches for the new workplace, encompassing the more active involvement required of everyone in the organization as a result. The chapter contains a new section on the Internet and e-business, including e-business strategies, discussion of e-marketplaces, using ERP and CRM to improve business operations, and knowledge management, as well. It also explores recent trends in information technology, such as the wireless Internet and instant messaging, and how they affect organizations and managers.

Part Four focuses on organizing processes. These chapters describe dimensions of structural design, the design alternatives managers can use to achieve strategic objectives, structural designs for promoting innovation and change, the design and use of the human resource function, and the ways managing diverse employees are significant to the organizing function.

- **Chapter 7** has an expanded and updated discussion of the network organization, and includes a new section on virtual organizations. Additionally, this chapter includes careful consideration of how digital technology affects structure. This chapter contains expanded coverage of innovations such as network and virtual organizations, comparing and contrasting the characteristics of traditional organizations with those of the emerging new workplace.

- **Chapter 8** has been thoroughly revised and updated to reflect the various aspects of change and development as exhibited in the new workplace.

- **Chapter 9** looks at how human resource management is changing due to globalization, information technology, and the need to build human capital. It also explores new information on trends such as telecommuting and flexible hours, virtual workers, e-recruiting, corporate universities, and new performance evaluation methods.

- **Chapter 10** includes a new section on multicultural teams and employee network groups as ways to build and support a diverse workforce, leveraging the power of diversity for the benefit of the organization. The chapter places emphasis on the challenges faced by minorities and also includes a discussion of the potential benefits and difficulties of emotional connections in the workplace.

Part Five is devoted to leadership. This section begins with a chapter on organizational behavior, providing a foundation for understanding people in organizations. This paves the way for subsequent discussion of leadership, motivating employees, communication, and team management.

- **Chapter 11** presents a new section on emotional intelligence and a discussion of both employees' and organizations' responses to stress management in today's organizations.

- **Chapter 12** includes a new discussion about leadership for the new workplace, including Level 5 leadership, male versus female methods of leading, virtual leadership, and servant leadership. It also has a brief new discussion of visionary leadership.

- **Chapter 13** contains an added discussion of the Q12—a Gallup Organization survey of the factors that influence employee motivation.

- **Chapter 14** has a new section on feedback and learning as important components of the communication process.

- **Chapter 15** considers global and virtual teams.

Part Six describes the controlling function of management, including basic principles of total quality management, the design of control systems, information technology, and techniques for control of operations management.

- **Chapter 16** presents a new section on basic financial statements and the use of the balanced scorecard as a basis for control of the organization. This chapter also includes new information on six sigma quality control measurements and market value-added financial control measurements.

Appendices include video cases, continuing cases, and a section on entrepreneurship and small business management. The latter explores various aspects of running a business, the entrepreneurial role, and topics such as the elements of a strong business plan, personality traits of entrepreneurs, and case studies of entrepreneurial firms and the environments that entrepreneurs tend to create.

Distinguishing Features

One major goal of this book is to offer better ways of using the textbook medium to convey management knowledge to the reader. To this end, the book includes several special features:

Chapter Outline and Learning Objectives.   Each chapter begins with a clear statement of its learning objectives and an outline of its contents. These devices provide an overview of what is to come and can also be used by students to guide their study and test their understanding and retention of important points.

Management Challenge and Solution.   The text portion of each chapter begins with a real-life problem faced by an organization manager. The problem pertains to the topic of the chapter and will heighten students' interest in chapter concepts. The questions posed in the Management Challenge are resolved in the Summary and Management Solution at the end of the chapter, where chapter concepts guiding the management's actions are highlighted.

Photo Essays.   A key feature of the book is the use of photographs accompanied by detailed captions that describe management events and how they relate to chapter material. The well-chosen photographs provide vivid illustrations and intimate glimpses of concrete management scenes, events, and people. The photos are captioned with brief essays that explain specific management concepts.

Contemporary Examples.   Every chapter of the text contains a large number of written examples of management incidents. They are placed at strategic points in the chapter and are designed to demonstrate the application of concepts to specific companies. These in-text examples—indicated by an icon in the margin—include well-known entrepreneurs and companies such as David Bowie, Oprah, Alicia Keyes, and India.Arie. These examples put students in touch with the real world of organizations so that they can appreciate the value of management concepts.

Boxed Features.   *Understanding Management*, Fourth Edition, contains a unique set of pedagogy addressing topics straight from the field of management that are of special interest to students, thus heightening their interest in the subject matter and providing an auxiliary view of management issues not typically available in textbooks. These features may describe a contemporary topic or problem that is relevant to chapter content, or they may contain a diagnostic questionnaire or a special example of how managers handle a problem: **Best Practices** boxes feature companies that make ethical decision regarding their business practices and their employees' well being; **Digital, Inc.** boxes focus on technology as used by companies to achieve their business goals; **Focus On . . .** boxes cover company practices as they relate to issues of diversity, cooperation, and entrepreneurship.

Exhibits.   Many aspects of management are research based, and some concepts tend to be abstract and theoretical. To enhance students' awareness and understanding of these concepts, many exhibits have been included throughout the book. These exhibits consolidate key points, indicate relationships among variables, and visually illustrate concepts. They also make effective use of color to enhance the text's imagery and appeal.

Glossaries.   Learning the management vocabulary is essential to understanding contemporary management. This process is facilitated in three ways. First, key concepts are boldfaced and completely defined where they first appear in the text. Second, brief definitions are set out in the margins for easy review and follow-up. Third, a glossary summarizing all key terms and definitions appears at the end of the book for handy reference.

Chapter Summary and Discussion Questions.   Each chapter closes with a summary of key points that students should retain. The discussion questions are a complementary learning tool that will enable students to check their understanding of key issues, to think beyond basic concepts, and to determine areas that require further study. The summary and discussion questions help students discriminate between main and supporting points and provide mechanisms for self-teaching.

Management Exercises.   End-of-chapter exercises, called "Management in Practice: Ethical Dilemma," "Manager's Workbook," and "Manager's Workshop" provide self-tests for students and an opportunity to experience management issues in a personal way. These exercises take the form of questionnaires, scenarios, and activities, and many also provide an opportunity for students to work in teams.

Surf the Net.   Each chapter contains three Internet exercises to involve students in the high-tech world of cyberspace. Students are asked to explore the Web for research into topics related to each chapter. This hands-on experience helps them develop Internet, research, and management skills.

Cases for Critical Analysis.   Also appearing at the end of each chapter is a brief but substantive case that provides an opportunity for student analysis and class discussion. Many of these cases are about companies whose names students will recognize; others are based on real management events with the identities of companies and managers disguised. These cases allow students to sharpen their diagnostic skills for management problem solving.

Video Cases.   Appendix A comprises 22 "Video Cases" that can enhance class discussion, because students can see the direct application of the management theories they have learned. Each video case explores the issues covered in the video, allowing students to synthesize the material they've just viewed. The video cases culminate with several questions that can be used to launch classroom discussion or as homework. Suggested answers are provided in the Instructor's Manual.

Continuing Case.   Appendix B presents a "Continuing Case," corresponding with Parts One through Six and providing a running discussion of management topics as experienced by one company as they relate to the material discussed in each part. Focusing on one company, Ford Motor Company, allows students to follow the managers' and the organization's problems and solutions in a long-term context.

Supplemental Materials—Leading by Example

The fourth edition's ancillary package, another market innovation from Richard L. Daft and Dorothy Marcic, is loaded with powerful resources for students and instructor alike. Combining the latest technology with proven teaching tools, the package enables students to put chapter concepts into action and gain valuable insights into real-world practices. In addition, an expansive collection of supplemental teaching materials offers support to instructors—from the novice to the most seasoned professor.

Completely integrated with the text, this comprehensive package continues to lead the market with its innovative and real-world management applications. Many new, cutting-edge features have been added to create an unrivaled support system.

Instructor Resources Include:

- **Instructor's Manual** (0-324-26053-9) Designed to provide support for instructors new to the course, as well as innovative materials for experienced instructors, the Instructor's Manual includes Chapter Outlines, annotated Learning Objectives, Lecture Notes, and sample Lecture Outlines. Additionally, the Instructor's Manual includes answers and teaching notes to end-of-chapter materials, including the video cases and continuing case in Appendixes A and B. The Instructor's Manual is available in print form, as well as electronically on both the instructor's Web site and the Instructor's Resource CD-ROM.

- **Instructor's Resource CD-ROM** (0-324-26055-5) Key instructor ancillaries (Instructor's Manual, Test Bank, ExamView and PowerPoint slides) are provided on CD-ROM, giving instructors the ultimate tool for customizing lectures and presentations.

- **Test Bank** (0-324-26054-7) Scrutinized for accuracy, the Test Bank includes more than 2,000 true/false, multiple choice, short answer, and essay questions. Each question has been rated for level of difficulty and is designated either as factual or application so that instructors can provide a balanced set of questions for student exams.

- **ExamView** Available on the Instructor's Resource CD-ROM, ExamView contains all of the questions in the printed Test Bank. This program is an easy-to-use test creation software compatible with Microsoft Windows. Instructors can add or edit questions, instructions, and answers, and select questions (randomly or numerically) by previewing them on the screen. Instructors can also create and administer quizzes online, whether over the Internet, a local area network (LAN), or a wide area network (WAN).

- **PowerPoint Lecture Presentation** Available on the Instructor's Resource CD-ROM and the Web site, the PowerPoint Lecture Presentation enables instructors to customize their own multimedia classroom presentation. Containing approximately 350 slides, the package includes figures and tables from the text, as well as outside materials to supplement chapter concepts. Approximately one Web site URL is included per chapter, allowing instructors to simply click on links to move from the PowerPoints to pertinent Web sites. Material is organized by chapter, and can be modified or expanded for individual classroom use. PowerPoints are also easily printed to create customized transparency masters.

- **Overhead Transparency Acetates** (0-324-26058-X) Created from artwork in the text, as well as outside materials, the full-color acetates are available with this text. These transparencies can supplement lectures by displaying the key concepts from the text.

- **WebTutor™** (0-324-27467-X on WebCT, or 0-324-27468-8 on BlackBoard) WebTutor is an interactive, Web-based, student supplement on WebCT and/or BlackBoard that harnesses the power of the Internet to deliver innovative learning aids that actively engage students. The instructor can incorporate Web Tutor as an integral part of the course, or the students can use it on their own as a study guide. Benefits to students include automatic and immediate feedback from quizzes and exams; interactive, multimedia-rich explanation of concepts; online exercises that reinforce what they've learned; flashcards that include audio support; and greater interaction and involvement through online discussion forums.

- **Management Videos** (0-324-26056-3) These videos utilize real-world companies to illustrate management concepts as outlined in the text. Focusing on both small and large business, the videos give students an inside perspective on the situations and issues that corporations face. Video cases in Appendix A reinforce what the student has seen in the text, and provide an opportunity for critical analysis and discussion.

- **Turner Learning/CNN, Management and Organizations Video** (0-324-13495-9) Bring the news gathering and programming power of CNN into your classroom with this VHS cassette of high-interest clips from the world's leading 24-hour global news network. Short segments—perfect for introducing key concepts—cover a range of issues, from online anonymity to workplace privacy, affirmative action, compulsory overtime, biotechnology, and more.

- **Web Site** (*http://daft.swlearning.com*) The *Understanding Management* Web site is a comprehensive, resource-rich location for both instructors and students to find pertinent information. It includes a complete listing of URLs from the text, case links, interactive quizzes, InfoTrac exercises, PowerPoint Lecture Presentations, and Search the Web features with links to additional sources. The Instructor Resources section contains an IM download, full Test Bank download, PowerPoint download, case material, and PDF files of one chapter. The Interactive Study Center includes Interactive Quizzes, complete text glossary, and key end-of-chapter materials for online reference.

- **TextChoice: Management Exercises and Cases** TextChoice is the home of Thomson Learning's online digital content. TextChoice provides the fastest, easiest way for you to create your own learning materials. South-Western's Management Exercises and Cases database includes a variety of experiential exercises, classroom activities, management in film exercises, and cases to enhance any management course. Choose as many exercises as you like and even add your own material to create a supplement tailor fitted to your course. Contact your South-Western/Thomson Learning sales representative for more information.

Student Resources Include:

- **Xtra!** (0-324-26057-1) Each new text includes one semester's free access to interactive quizzes, digitized versions of the *Understanding Management* videos, *Experiencing Management* by Dennis Middlemist, and additional activities. Xtra! is also available for purchase with used textbooks at *http://daftxtra.swlearning.com.*

- **InfoTrac** Free with the purchase of each textbook, this online database of articles gives students access to full-text articles from hundreds of scholarly and popular periodicals such as *Newsweek, Time,* and *USA Today.* Updated daily, this tool allows students to research topics pertinent to classroom discussion and to keep up with current events.

- **Study Guide** (0-324-27346-0) Packed with real-world examples and additional applications for helping students master management concepts, this learning supplement is an excellent resource. For each chapter of the text, the Study Guide includes a summary and completion exercise; a review with multiple-choice, true/false and short answer questions; a mini-case with multiple-choice questions; management applications; and an experiential exercise that can be assigned as homework or used in class.

- **Music for Management CD-ROM** (0-03-033451-9) A CD of more than 10 songs related to such topics as goal setting, leadership, management history, diversity, internal/external focus of control, and so on. Dr. Marcic sings the songs that were original chart toppers by Shania Twain, The Dixie Chicks, Mariah Carey, Gloria Estefan, and others. Exercises related to the songs will be available as well as teaching notes for instructors.

- *Bottom Line* **Business Novel** (0-03-029311-1) Written by Dorothy Marcic, this unique addition to the ancillary package is an intriguing, contemporary novel about murder, greed, and betrayal in the workplace. *Bottom Line* is not only a great read, but offers opportunities for students to interact with the ideas and issues explored in the story.

Acknowledgments

It was a gratifying experience to work with the team of dedicated professionals at South-Western who were committed to the vision of producing the best management text ever. We are grateful to Joe Sabatino, Acquisitions Editor, whose enthusiasm, creative ideas, assistance, and vision kept this book's spirit alive. Rob Bloom, Senior Marketing Strategist, provided keen market knowledge and innovative ideas for instructional support. Emma Guttler, Developmental Editor, provided superb project coordination and offered excellent ideas and suggestions to help the team meet a demanding and sometimes arduous schedule. Emily Gross, Production Editor, cheerfully and expertly guided us through the production process. Molly Flynn, Editorial Assistant, and Anna Hasselo, Marketing Assistant, skillfully pitched in to help keep the project on track.

Here at Vanderbilt I want to extend special appreciation to my assistant, May Woods. May provided excellent support and assistance on a variety of projects, which allowed me time to write. I also want to acknowledge an intellectual debt to my colleagues: Bruce Barry, Ray Friedman, Barry Gerhart, Tom Mahoney, Neta Moye, Rich Oliver, David Owens, and Bart Victor. Thanks also to Dean Bill Christie, who has supported my writing projects and maintained a positive scholarly atmosphere in the school.—*R.L.D.*

Working on this book has been so gratifying and fun. I want to thank my assistant, Tracy Moor, who was there whenever I needed her. Don Cusic of Belmont University was of enormous help in writing the music business introductions, as was Lori Kampa. Bill Geisler was always there, supplying new ideas, and his wife Diti provided spiritual sustenance. My good friend and colleague, Jennie Carter Thomas of Belmont, is a breath of fresh air and a wonderful companion. Other friends and colleagues who gave their support include: Peter Vaill, Mary Watson, Joe Seltzer, Judi Neal, Bob Marks, Joe Garcia, Susan Susanne Fest, Nan Allison, Amy Lynch, Holly Tashien, Susan Schorr, Leslie Asplund, Danielle Locke, Ron Browning, and Shidan Majidi, as well as my agent, John Willig, and my manager, Andy Barton.

How can one undertake such a project without family love and support? My sister, Janet Mittelsteadt, is a true friend, as are my cousins: Marilyn Nowak is a bright light, Michael Shoemaker is the geneologist who has helped me find my own roots, and Katherine Runde is so precious. My Aunt Babe is forever a link to the past. There is no way to imagine my life without my three beautiful daughters, Roxanne, Solange and Elizabeth, who have taught me more than all my degrees combined. And, finally, my husband and partner, Dick Daft, whose collaboration on this book indicates just one aspect of our unity and connection.—*D.M.*

Other people who made major contributions to the textbook are the management experts who provided advice, reviews, answers to our questions, and suggestions for changes, insertions, and clarification. We thank these colleagues for their valuable feedback and suggestions:

David C. Adams
Manhattanville College

Hal Babson
Columbus State Community College

Kristin Backhaus
SUNY—New Paltz

Jan Beyer
University of Texas

Katharine Bohley
University of Indianapolis

Bonnie Chavez
Santa Barbara Community College

Sally Dresdow
University of Wisconsin, Green Bay

Diane Duca
Central Washington University

Janice Edwards
College of the Rockies

John C. Edwards
Southern Illinois University—Carbondale

Mary Beth Klinger
College of Southern Maryland

Martin Lecker
Rockland Community College

Susan Leshnower
Midland College

Don Lisnerski
University of North Carolina—Asheville

Joseph Martelli
University of Findlay

Rachel Mather
Adelphi University

Susan Smith Nash
University of Oklahoma

Stephen Peters
Walla Walla Community College

Brian Porter
Hope College

Gerald D. Ramsey
Indiana University Southeast

Amit Shah
Frostburg State University

Jessica Simmons
University of Texas

H. Daniel Stage
Loyola Marymount

Kent Zimmerman
James Madison University

About the Authors

Richard L. Daft, Ph.D., is Associate Dean for Academic Programs and the Brownlee O. Currey, Jr. Professor in Management in the Owen Graduate School of Management at Vanderbilt University. Professor Daft specializes in the study of organization theory and leadership, and enjoys applying these ideas in his role as Associate Dean. Dr. Daft is a Fellow of the Academy of Management and has served on the editorial boards of *Academy of Management Journal, Administrative Science Quarterly,* and *Journal of Management Education.* He was the Associate Editor-in-Chief of *Organization Science* and served for three years as associate editor of *Administrative Science Quarterly.*

Professor Daft has authored or co-authored 12 books, including *Organization Theory and Design* (South-Western College Publishing, 2001), *The Leadership Experience* (South-Western College Publishing, 2001) and *What to Study: Generating and Developing Research Questions* (Sage, 1982). He recently published *Fusion Leadership: Unlocking the Subtle Forces That Change People and Organizations* (Berrett-Koehler, 2000, with Robert Lengel). He has also authored dozens of scholarly articles, papers, and chapters. His work has been published in *Administrative Science Quarterly, Academy of Management Journal, Academy of Management Review, Strategic Management Journal, Journal of Management, Accounting Organizations and Society, Management Science, MIS Quarterly, California Management Review,* and *Organizational Behavior Teaching Review.* Professor Daft has been awarded several government research grants to pursue studies of organization design, organizational innovation and change, strategy implementation, and organizational information processing.

Dr. Daft also is an active teacher and consultant. He has taught management, leadership, organizational change, organizational behavior, organizational theory, and organizational behavior. He has been involved in management development and consulting for many companies and government organizations, including the American Banking Association, Bell Canada, National Transportation Research Board, NL Baroid, Nortel, TVA, Pratt & Whitney, State Farm Insurance, Tenneco, the United States Air Force, The U.S. Army, J. C. Bradford & Co., Central Parking System, Entergy Sales and Service, Bristol-Meyers Squibb, First American National Bank, and the Vanderbilt University Medical Center.

Dorothy Marcic, Ed.D and M.P.H, is a faculty member at Vanderbilt University. Dr. Marcic is a former Fulbright Scholar at the University of Economics in Prague and the Czech Management Center, where she taught courses and did research in leadership, organizational behavior, and cross-cultural management. She also teaches courses at the Monterrey Institute of International Studies and the University of Economics in Prague, and has taught courses or given presentations at the Helsinki School of Economics, Slovenia Management Center, College of Trade in Bulgaria, City University of Slovakia, Landegg Institute in Switzerland, the Swedish Management Association, Technion University in Israel, and the London School of Economics. Other international work includes projects at the Autonomous University in Guadalajara, Mexico, and a training program for the World Health Organization in Guatemala. She has served on the boards of the Organizational Teaching Society, the Health

Administration Section of the American Public Health Association, and the Journal of Applied Business Research.

Dr. Marcic has authored 12 books, including *Organizational Behavior: Experiences and Cases* (South-Western Publishing, Sixth Edition, 2001), *Management International* (West Publishing, 1984), *Women and Men in Organizations* (George Washington University, 1984), and *Managing with the Wisdom of Love: Uncovering Virtue in People and Organizations* (Jossey-Bass, 1997), which was rated one of the top 10 business books of 1997 by *Management General*. In addition, she has had dozens of articles printed in such publications as *Journal of Management Development, International Quarterly of Community Health Education, Psychological Reports*, and *Executive Development*. She has recently been exploring how to use the arts in the teaching of leadership and has a new book, *RESPECT: Women and Popular Music* (Texere, 2002).

Professor Marcic has conducted hundreds of seminars on various business topics and consulted for executives at AT&T Bell Labs; the Governor and Cabinet of North Dakota; the U.S. Air Force; Slovak Management Association; Eurotel; Czech Ministry of Finance; the Cattaraugus Center; USAA Insurance; State Farm Insurance; and the Salt River-Pima Indian Tribe in Arizona.

Brief Contents

Contents

■ PART 3   PLANNING 143

Chapter 5   **Organizational Planning and Goal Setting 144**

Chapter 6   **Managerial Decision Making 184**

■ **PART 4**   ORGANIZING   231

Chapter 7   **Fundamentals of Organizing 232**

■ **PART 5**   LEADERSHIP 373

Understanding Management

FOURTH EDITION

PART ONE

Managers in Learning Organizations

The music business is roughly divided between "creative" and "business," with the "creative" element including singers, musicians, and songwriters, and the "business" element consists of those who market, promote, publicize, organize, or manage an artist's career. This gives an idea of the depth and breadth of the music business, which includes companies that publish songs, market recordings, and stage live shows. The recording company is the economic engine in the music industry, and the success of the record company's efforts affects all other aspects of the music industry.

The leader of a recording company must work with all of these aspects because the label is the "hub" of the wheel, the center around which all parts of an artist's career revolve. The leader of the label interacts with others from different aspects of the music industry with one major goal in mind: the success of an artist selling recordings. If the artist is commercially successful, then the publishers, booking agents, artist's manager, concert promoters, merchandisers, and others connected to that artist have the opportunity to be successful.

The key is communicating information so that the artist and those connected with his or her career can act quickly and effectively to take advantage of opportunities as the record label works to promote a recording.

Managing the New Workplace

LEARNING OBJECTIVES

After studying this chapter, you should be able to

1. Explain the difference between efficiency and effectiveness and their importance for organizational performance.

2. Define ten roles that managers perform in organizations.

3. Discuss the transition to a new workplace and the management competencies needed to deal with issues such as diversity, globalization, and rapid change.

4. Describe the learning organization and the changes in structure, empowerment, and information sharing that managers make to support it.

5. Understand how historical forces influence the practice of management.

6. Identify and explain major developments in the history of management thought.

7. Describe the major components of the classical and humanistic management perspectives.

8. Discuss the management science perspective and its current use in organizations.

9. Explain the major concepts of total quality management.

10. Explain the leadership skills needed for effective crisis management.

Management Challenge

When former St. Louis cheerleader Charlene Pedrolie started her new job as manufacturing chief of West Virginia's Rowe Furniture in 1995, she had never lived in a town where people displayed confederate flags on pickup truck decals. Not only that, but this was an industry with older male bosses and here she was a young, 30-ish *woman*, born after some of the other managers were already working at Rowe.

The plant was built in another era, and the factory windows were now painted dark to save on cooling costs. People worked mechanistically, almost like robots, with identical motions all day long, with one person cutting, another gluing, another sewing, while others either labeled, loaded, or inspected the high-quality sofas, easy chairs, and love seats. Pay was high, but the work horribly boring, and it was getting harder to keep the newer employees motivated under these conditions. Another problem was that furniture took weeks to complete after the customer's order.

Because of Rowe's quality and lower cost, it got exposure in some of the best showrooms in the country. Still, sales had become flat in recent years. Pedrolie's research found that customers wanted custom-designed furniture with a wider selection than was available on the floor, but they did not want to wait forever. In fact, some were not even buying furniture because of long delays. Pedrolie realized she had to move fast to recapture the market.[1]

If you were Pedrolie, what would you do to get custom furniture to customers sooner and, at the same time, make the work more interesting for the employees?

Charlene Pedrolie is being challenged by forces greater than she is. Changing customer tastes for greater speed in furniture delivery, plus workers wanting more than mechanistic tasks, require new behaviors. For the past decade or so, managers have been talking about how their organizations struggle to keep pace in an uncertain world that changes faster than ever.

Managers are constantly dealing with uncertainty and unexpected events, whether it be something as small as the sudden loss of a major customer, flat sales, or something as large and dramatic as what happened on September 11, 2001. Solid management skills and actions are the key to helping any organization weather a crisis and remain healthy, inspired, and productive. Today's organizations are coping with diverse and far-reaching challenges. They must keep pace with ever-advancing technology, find ways to incorporate the Internet and e-business into their strategies and business models, and strive to remain competitive in the face of increasingly tough global competition, uncertain environments, cutbacks in personnel and resources, and massive worldwide economic, political, and social shifts. The growing diversity of the workforce creates other dynamics: How does the company maintain a strong corporate culture while supporting diversity; balancing work and family concerns; and coping with conflicting demands of all employees for a fair shot at power and responsibility. Workers are asking that managers share rather than hoard power. Organizational structures are becoming flatter, with power and information pushed down and out among fewer layers and with teams of front-line workers playing new roles as decision makers. New ways of working, such as virtual teams and telecommuting, put additional demands on managers.

Because of these changes, a revolution is taking place in the field of management. A new kind of leader is needed who can guide businesses through this turbulence—a strong leader who recognizes the complexity of today's world and realizes there are no perfect answers.[2] The revolution asks managers to do more with less, to engage whole employees, to see change rather than stability as the nature of things, and to create vision and cultural values that allow people to create a truly collaborative workplace. This new management approach is very different from a traditional mindset that emphasizes tight top-down control, employee separation and specialization, and management by impersonal measurements and analysis. In a situation such as the one Charlene Pedrolie is facing at Rowe Furniture, a totally different approach is needed to save the company.

Making a difference as a manager today and tomorrow requires integrating solid, tried-and-true management skills with new approaches that emphasize the human touch, enhance flexibility, and involve employees' hearts and minds as well as their bodies. Successful departments and organizations don't just happen—they are managed to be that way. Managers in every organization today face major challenges and have the opportunity to make a difference. For example, Lorraine Monroe made a difference at Harlem's Frederick Douglass Academy when she transformed it from one of the worst to one of the best schools in New York City. Stephen Quesnelle, head of quality programs at Mitel Corp. in Ottawa, Canada, made a difference when he organized "sacred cow hunts" to encourage employees to track down and do away with outdated policies and procedures that were holding the company back. Today, signs of energy, change, and renewal are everywhere at Mitel.[3]

These managers are not unusual. Every day, managers solve difficult problems, turn organizations around, and achieve astonishing performances. To be successful, every organization needs skilled managers.

This textbook introduces and explains the process of management and the changing ways of thinking about and perceiving the world that are becoming increasingly critical for managers of today and tomorrow. By reviewing the actions of some successful and not-so-successful managers, you will learn the fundamentals of management. By the end of this chapter, you will already recognize some of the skills that managers use to keep organizations on track. By the end of this book, you will understand fundamental management skills for planning, organizing, leading, and controlling a department or an entire organization. In this chapter, we will define management and look at the ways in which roles and activities are changing for today's managers. Another section of the chapter talks about a new kind of workplace that has evolved as a result of changes in technology, globalization, and other forces, and examines how managers can meet the challenges of this new environment and manage unexpected events. Finally, the chapter will look at historical trends in management.

The Definition of Management

What do managers such as Charlene Pedrolie, Stephen Quesnelle, and Lorraine Monroe have in common? They get things done through their organizations. Managers create the conditions and environment that enable organizations to survive and thrive beyond the tenure of any specific supervisor or manager. For example, members of the Grateful Dead rock band created and managed a successful business, Grateful Dead Productions, which continues to thrive even though band member Jerry Garcia has been dead for more than five years and the band no longer regularly performs together. Grateful Dead Productions remains active in merchandise sales, CD releases, and Internet projects, bringing in about $70 million annually. The band members, who shared top management duties and responsibilities, created an organization with a powerful culture, a strong vision, and the motivation and human energy that set great organizations apart and help them survive over the long haul.[4]

A key aspect of managing is recognizing the role and importance of others. Good managers know that the only way they can accomplish anything at all is through the people of the organization. Early twentieth-century management scholar Mary Parker Follett defined management as "the art of getting things done through people."[5] More recently, noted management theorist Peter Drucker stated that the job of managers is to give direction to their organizations, provide leadership, and decide how to use organizational resources to accomplish goals.[6] Getting things done through people and other resources and providing leadership and direction are what managers do. These activities apply not only to top executives such as Charlene Pedrolie, but also to the leader of a security team, a supervisor of an accounting department, or a director of marketing. Moreover, management often is considered universal because it uses organizational resources to accomplish goals and attain high performance in all types of profit and not-for-profit organizations. Thus, **management** is the attainment of organizational goals in an effective and efficient manner through planning, organizing, leading, and controlling organizational resources.

There are two important ideas in this definition: (1) the four functions of planning, organizing, leading, and controlling, and (2) the attainment of organizational goals in an effective and efficient manner. Managers use a multitude of skills to perform these functions. Management's conceptual, human, and technical skills are discussed later in the chapter. Exhibit 1.1 illustrates the

management

The attainment of organizational goals in an effective and efficient manner through planning, organizing, leading, and controlling organizational resources.

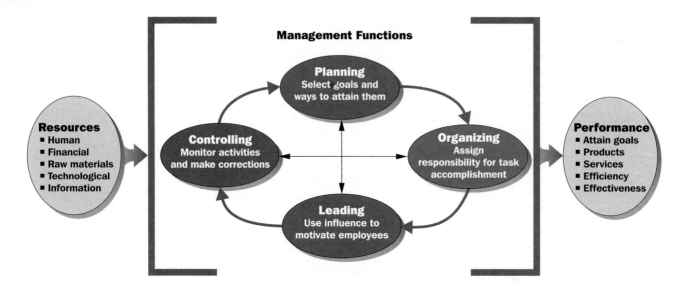

Management Functions

Resources
- Human
- Financial
- Raw materials
- Technological
- Information

Planning
Select goals and ways to attain them

Controlling
Monitor activities and make corrections

Organizing
Assign responsibility for task accomplishment

Leading
Use influence to motivate employees

Performance
- Attain goals
- Products
- Services
- Efficiency
- Effectiveness

EXHIBIT 1.1

The Process of Management

process of how managers use resources to attain organizational goals. Although some management theorists identify additional management functions, such as staffing, communicating, or decision making, those additional functions will be discussed as subsets of the four primary functions in Exhibit 1.1. Chapters of this book are devoted to the multiple activities and skills associated with each function, as well as to the environment, global competitiveness, and ethics, which influence how managers perform these functions.

Organizational Performance

The other part of our definition of management is the attainment of organizational goals in an efficient and effective manner. Management is so important because organizations are so important. In an industrialized society where complex technologies dominate, organizations bring together knowledge, people, and raw materials to perform tasks no individual could do alone. Without organizations, how could technology be provided that enables us to share information around the world in an instant, electricity be produced from huge dams and nuclear power plants, and thousands of videos and DVDs be made available for our entertainment? Organizations pervade our society. Most college students will work in an organization—perhaps Sun Microsystems, Cinergy, or Hollywood Video. College students already are members of several organizations, such as a university, junior college, YMCA, church, fraternity, or sorority. College students also deal with organizations every day: to renew a driver's license, be treated in a hospital emergency room, buy food from a supermarket, eat in a restaurant, or buy new clothes. Managers are responsible for these organizations and for seeing that resources are used wisely to attain organizational goals.

organization

A social entity that is goal directed and deliberately structured.

This definition applies to all **organizations**, including both profit and not-for-profit. Vickery Stoughton runs Toronto General Hospital and manages a $200 million budget. He endures intense public scrutiny, heavy government regulation, and daily crises of life and death. Bob Stein founded Night Kitchen to provide authors with e-publishing tools for creating e-books and multimedia texts. Eleanor Josaitis worked with her parish priest, the late Father William

BEST PRACTICES

How Joe Torre Brings Out the Best in His Players

Joe Torre was fired three times in a 15-year management career before signing on as manager of the New York Yankees. But since then, everything he's touched has seemed to turn to gold. The Yankees haven't missed the playoffs since Torre took over, and during his tenure they've won four out of five World Series. Although Torre himself is the first to point out that the team's success depends on a combination of factors, it is clear that his management approach plays a big role.

Torre believes his years of dedication, learning, and growing as a manager finally paid off. One of the biggest lessons he learned is that success and winning aren't the same thing. Success, says Torre, is "playing—or working—to the best of your ability." His philosophy is that people should strive every day to fulfill their potential as individuals and as members of a team, and to help them do so requires a management approach that puts the needs and feelings of people first. Torre's approach is based on knowing his team members as individuals and treating everyone with fairness, respect, and trust, the three elements he considers essential for productive work relationships. Torre doesn't give a lot of big motivational speeches. Instead, he relies on one-to-one communication. He watches, listens, and tries to understand the needs, motivations, and problems of each person, recognizing that what's going on in players' lives off the field affects their perfor-

mance. When Torre needs to sort out a problem with a player, he does it in private. He never uses fear, manipulation, or public humiliation to motivate or control players.

In addition, Torre understands that every player sometimes hits a slump, and he doesn't treat players differently just because they're not playing well. "I've worked for organizations in the past that are real quick to jump off the bandwagon when things aren't going well. . . ." says pitcher Mike Stanton. "With Joe, you don't really have to look over your shoulder, because you'll lose confidence in yourself a long time before Joe loses confidence in you." Torre sticks by his players, and he absorbs the flak from upper management without passing it on to the team. He also doesn't burden players with a lot of strict rules, preferring to treat them as responsible adults who are all working toward a shared goal.

Torre's emphasis on people and relationships has created a high-performance workplace where mistakes and failure are routinely accepted. It's the kind of workplace most organizations need in today's volatile environment. They can achieve it, Torre says, by handling their jobs based on the values of "respect, trust, integrity, and commitment to our work and the people we work with."

SOURCES: Joe Torre with Henry Dreher, *Joe Torre's Ground Rules for Winners: 12 Keys to Managing Team Players, Tough Bosses, Setbacks, and Success* (New York: Hyperion, 1999); Jerry Useem, "A Manager for All Seasons," *Fortune* (April 30, 2001), 66–72; and Malcolm Moran, "Conflict Resolution, the Joe Torre Way," *The New York Times* (July 14, 1997), C5.

Cunningham, to establish an organization in Detroit called Focus: Hope, which feeds 48,000 hungry people a day, runs a training program in precision machining and metalworking, sponsors a day-care center, and runs several for-profit manufacturing companies, whose plants and equipment are worth more than $100 million.[7] Small, offbeat, and not-for-profit organizations are more numerous than large, visible corporations—and just as important to society.

Based on our definition of management, the manager's responsibility is to coordinate resources in an effective and efficient manner to accomplish the organization's goals. Organizational **effectiveness** is the degree to which the organization achieves a stated goal. It means that the organization succeeds in accomplishing what it tries to do. Organizational effectiveness means providing a product or service that customers value. Organizational **efficiency** refers to the amount of resources used to achieve an organizational goal. It is based on how much raw materials, money, and people are necessary for producing a given volume of output. Efficiency can be calculated as the amount of resources used to produce a product or service.

Sometimes, however, managers' efforts to improve efficiency can hurt organizational effectiveness. This is especially true in relation to severe cost cutting. At Delta Airlines, former CEO Robert W. Allen dramatically increased cost efficiency by cutting spending on personnel, food, cleaning, and maintenance.

effectiveness
The degree to which the organization achieves a stated goal.

efficiency
The use of minimal resources—raw materials, money, and people—to produce a desired volume of output.

Allen believed the moves were needed to rescue the company from a financial tailspin, but Delta fell to last place among major carriers in on-time performance, the morale of employees sank, and customer complaints about dirty planes and long lines at ticket counters increased by more than 75 percent.[8] Current CEO Leo Mullin is striving to maintain the efficiencies instituted by Allen, but also improve organizational effectiveness.

The ultimate responsibility of managers is to achieve high **performance**, which is the attainment of organizational goals by using resources in an efficient and effective manner.

performance

The organization's ability to attain its goals by using resources in an efficient and effective manner.

Management Skills

A manager's job is complex and multidimensional and, as we shall see throughout this book, requires a range of skills. Although some management theorists propose a long list of skills, the necessary skills for managing a department or an organization can be summarized in three categories: conceptual, human, and technical.[9] As illustrated in Exhibit 1.2, the application of these skills changes as managers move up in the organization. Though the degree of each skill necessary at different levels of an organization may vary, all managers must possess skills in each of these important areas to perform effectively.

Management Types

Managers use conceptual, human, and technical skills to perform the four management functions of planning, organizing, leading, and controlling in all organizations—large and small, manufacturing and service, profit and not-for-profit, traditional and Internet-based. But not all managers' jobs are the same. Managers are responsible for different departments, work at different levels in the hierarchy, and meet different requirements for achieving high performance. Kevin Kurtz is a middle manager at Lucasfilm, where he works with employees to develop marketing campaigns for some of the entertainment company's hottest properties, including the next *Star Wars* episode.[10] Domenic Antonellis is CEO of the New England Confectionary Co. (Necco), the company that makes those tiny pastel candy hearts stamped with phrases such as "Be Mine" and "Kiss Me."[11] Both are managers, and both must contribute to planning, organizing, leading, and controlling their organizations—but in different amounts and ways.

E X H I B I T *1.2*

Relationship of Conceptual, Human, and Technical Skills to Management Level

Management Level
Top Managers

Middle Managers

First-Line Managers

Nonmanagers (Individual Contributors)

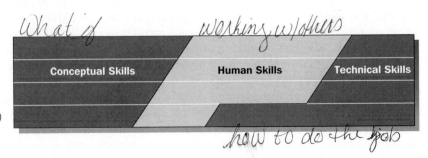

What Is It Like to Be a Manager?

So far we have described how managers at various levels perform four basic functions that help ensure that organizational resources are used to attain high levels of performance. These tasks require conceptual, human, and technical skills. Unless someone has actually performed managerial work, it is hard to understand exactly what managers do on an hour-by-hour, day-to-day basis. The manager's job is so diverse that a number of studies have been undertaken in an attempt to describe exactly what happens. The question of what managers actually do to plan, organize, lead, and control was answered by Henry Mintzberg, who followed managers around and recorded all their activities.[12] He developed a description of managerial work that included three general characteristics and ten roles. These characteristics and roles have been supported in subsequent research.[13]

Leonard Riggio, chief executive of Barnes & Noble Inc., whose book sales total $2.8 billion, is positioning his organization to achieve high performance. Riggio has set a goal to become the largest retailer for online book sales. Although Barnesandnoble.com got a late start in the world of online book sales, Riggio's goal is to outsell Amazon, the world's largest online bookseller.

Manager Activities

One of the most interesting findings about managerial activities is how busy managers are and how hectic the average workday can be. Bruce Nelson, CEO of Office Depot, works 14-hour days and is constantly tracking operations at 947 stores in eight time zones. A typical week for Nelson found him answering e-mails on his laptop while flying to stores in three different states, checking the competition by posing as a customer at an OfficeMax store, dining with the board of a major customer to give them a briefing about the office products industry, meeting with managers throughout headquarters in 15-minute back-to-back sessions to get updates and offer advice, talking with media representatives to outline his plan for reviving the troubled company, and accepting an award recognizing Office Depot's information technology performance.[14]

Managerial Activity Is Characterized by Variety, Fragmentation, and Brevity.[15] The manager's involvements are so widespread and voluminous that there is little time for quiet reflection. The average time spent on any one activity is less than nine minutes. Managers shift gears quickly. Significant crises are interspersed with trivial events in no predictable sequence. One example of just two typical hours for general manager, Janet Howard, follows. Note the frequent interruptions and the brevity and variety of tasks.

7:30 AM Janet arrives at work and begins to plan her day.

7:37 AM A subordinate, Morgan Cook, stops in Janet's office to discuss a dinner party the previous night and to review the cost-benefit analysis for a proposed microcomputer.

7:45 AM Janet's secretary, Pat, motions for Janet to pick up the telephone. "Janet, they had serious water damage at the downtown office last night. A pipe broke, causing about $50,000 damage. Everything will be back in shape in three days. Thought you should know."

8:00 AM Pat brings in the mail. She also asks for instructions for typing a report Janet gave her yesterday.

8:14 AM   Janet gets a phone call from the accounting manager, who is returning a call from the day before. They talk about an accounting report.

8:25 AM   A Mr. Nance is ushered in. Mr. Nance complains that a sales manager mistreats his employees and something must be done. Janet rearranges her schedule to investigate this claim.

9:00 AM   Janet returns to the mail. One letter is from an irate customer. Janet dictates a helpful, restrained reply. Pat brings in phone messages.

9:15 AM   Janet receives an urgent phone call from Larry Baldwin. They discuss lost business, unhappy subordinates, and a potential promotion.[16]

The Manager Performs a Great Deal of Work at an Unrelenting Pace.[17] Managers' work is fast paced and requires great energy. The managers observed by Mintzberg processed 36 pieces of mail each day, attended eight meetings, and took a tour through the building or plant. As soon as a manager's daily calendar is set, unexpected disturbances erupt. New meetings are required. During time away from the office, executives catch up on work-related reading, paperwork, and e-mail.

At O'Hare International Airport, an unofficial count one Friday found operations manager Hugh Murphy interacting with about 45 airport employees. In addition, he listened to complaints from local residents about airport noise, met with disgruntled executives of a French firm who built the airport's new $128 million people-mover system, attempted to soothe a Hispanic city alderman who complained that Mexicana Airlines passengers were being singled out by overzealous tow-truck operators, toured the airport's new fire station, and visited the construction site for the new $20 million tower—and that was *before* the events of September 11, 2001, changed airport operations, making them even more complex. Hugh Murphy's unrelenting pace is typical for managers.[18] Management can be rewarding, but it can also be frustrating and stressful, as discussed in the Focus on Skills box.

Manager Roles

Mintzberg's observations and subsequent research indicate that diverse manager activities can be organized into ten roles.[19] A **role** is a set of expectations for a manager's behavior. Exhibit 1.3 provides examples of each of the ten roles. These roles are divided into three conceptual categories: informational (managing by information); interpersonal (managing through people); and decisional (managing through action). Each role represents activities that managers undertake to ultimately accomplish the functions of planning, organizing, leading, and controlling. Although it is necessary to separate the components of the manager's job to understand the different roles and activities of a manager, it is important to remember that the real job of management cannot be practiced as a set of independent parts; all the roles interact in the real world of management. As Mintzberg says, "The manager who only communicates or only conceives never gets anything done, while the manager who only 'does' ends up doing it all alone."[20]

role

A set of expectations for one's behavior.

Category	Role	Activity
Informational	**Monitor**	Seek and receive information, scan periodicals and reports, maintain personal contacts.
	Disseminator	Forward information to other organization members; send memos and reports, make phone calls.
	Spokesperson	Transmit information to outsiders through speeches, reports, memos.
Interpersonal	**Figurehead**	Perform ceremonial and symbolic duties such as greeting visitors, signing legal documents.
	Leader	Direct and motivate subordinates; train, counsel, and communicate with subordinates.
	Liaison	Maintain information links both inside and outside organization; use mail, phone calls, meetings.
Decisional	**Entrepreneur**	Initiate improvement projects; identify new ideas, delegate idea responsibility to others.
	Disturbance handler	Take corrective action during disputes or crises; resolve conflicts among subordinates; adapt to environmental crises.
	Resource allocator	Decide who gets resources; schedule, budget, set priorities.
	Negotiator	Represent department during negotiation of union contracts, sales, purchases, budgets; represent departmental interests.

EXHIBIT 1.3

Ten Manager Roles

[handwritten margin notes:] Resource Allocator Entrepreneur disturbance handler

SOURCES: Adapted from Henry Mintzberg, *The Nature of Managerial Work* (New York: Harper & Row, 1973), 92–93; and Henry Mintzberg, "Managerial Work: Analysis from Observation," *Management Science* 18 (1971), B97–B110.

Managing in Small Businesses and Not-For-Profit Organizations

Small businesses are growing in importance. Hundreds of small businesses are opened every month by people who have found themselves squeezed out of the corporation due to downsizing or who voluntarily leave the corporate world to seek a slower pace and a healthier balance between work and family life. Many small businesses are opened by women or minorities who found limited opportunities for advancement in large corporations. In addition, the Internet has opened new avenues for small business formation. The huge wave of dot-com start-ups in the late 1990s was driven not just by dreams of wealth, but also by the desire of people to get out of big corporations and start something new and exciting.

The environment for small business has become increasingly complicated due to technology, globalization, government regulation, and increasing customer demands. Solid management is critical to success, but small companies sometimes have difficulty developing the managerial dexterity needed to survive in a complex environment. One survey on trends and future developments in small business found that nearly half of respondents saw inadequate management skills as a threat to their companies, as compared to less than 25 percent in larger organizations.[21]

FOCUS ON SKILLS

Do You Really Want to Be a Manager?

The first training course that aspiring managers at FedEx take is called "Is Management for Me?" Becoming a manager is considered by most people to be a positive, forward-looking career move. Indeed, there are lots of appealing aspects to life as a manager. However, there are also many challenges, and not every person will be happy and fulfilled in a management position. Here are some of the issues would-be managers in the new workplace should consider before deciding they want to pursue a management career:

The increased workload. It isn't unusual for managers to work 70- 80-hour weeks, and some work even longer hours. A manager's job always starts before a shift and ends hours after the shift is over. Matt Scott, a software engineer promoted to management at Fore Systems, Inc., found himself frustrated by the increasing paperwork and crowded meeting schedule.

The unrelenting sense of obligation. A manager's work is never done. Nancy Carreon, an associate partner for an architectural firm, sometimes wakes up in the middle of the night thinking about something she needs to do—so she gets up and does it. George Pollard, a senior human resources official at FedEx, says, "Managers are always on the clock. We're representatives of [the company] even when we're not at work."

The headache of responsibility for other people. A lot of people get into management because they like the idea of having power, but the reality is that many managers feel overwhelmed by the responsibility of supervising and disciplining others. Laura Kelso, who today thrives on the fast pace and responsibility of being a manager, says that the first time she had to fire someone, she agonized for weeks over how to do it. New managers are often astonished at the amount of time it takes to handle "people problems." Kelly Cannell, who quit her job as a manager, puts it this way: "What's the big

deal [about managing people]? The big deal is that people are human. . . . To be a good manager, you have to mentor them, listen to their problems, counsel them, and at the end of the day you still have your own work on your plate. . . . Don't take the responsibility lightly, because no matter what you think, managing people is not easy."

Being caught in the middle. For many people, this is the most difficult aspect of management. Except for those in the top echelons, managers find themselves acting as a backstop, caught between upper management and the workforce. A computer software designer explains why she wanted out of management: "I didn't feel comfortable touting the company line in organizational policies and technical decisions I disagreed with. It was very hard asking folks to do things I wouldn't like to do myself, like put in gobs of overtime or travel at the drop of a hat." Even when managers disagree with the decisions of top executives, they are responsible for implementing them.

For some people, the frustrations of management aren't worth it. For others, management is a fulfilling and satisfying career choice and the emotional rewards can be great. One key to being happy as a manager may be carefully evaluating whether you can answer yes to the question, "Do I really want to be a manager?"

SOURCES: Heath Row, "Is Management for Me? *That* is the Question," *Fast Company* (February–March 1998), 50–52; Timothy D. Schellhardt, "Want to Be a Manager? Many People Say No, Calling Job Miserable," *The Wall Street Journal* (April 4, 1997), A1, A4; Matt Murray, "A Software Engineer Becomes a Manager, with Many Regrets," *The Wall Street Journal*, May 14, 1997, A1, A14; Hal Lancaster, "Managing Your Career: Nancy Carreon Works Long, Hard Weeks. Does She Need To?" *The Wall Street Journal* (May 13, 1997), B1; and Matt Murray, "Managing Your Career—The Midcareer Crisis: Am I in This Business to Become a Manager?" *The Wall Street Journal* (July 25, 2000), B1.

One interesting finding is that managers in small businesses tend to emphasize roles different from those of managers in large corporations. Managers in small companies often see their most important role as spokesperson, because they must promote the small, growing company to the outside world. The entrepreneur role is also very important in small businesses, because managers must be creative and help their organizations develop new ideas to be competitive. Small-business managers tend to rate lower on the leader role and on information-processing roles compared with counterparts in large corporations.

Not-for-profit organizations also represent a major application of management talent. The Red Cross, the Girl Scouts, universities, city governments, hospitals, public schools, symphonies, and art museums all require excellent management. The functions of planning, organizing, leading, and controlling apply to not-for-profits just as they do to business organizations, and managers in not-for-profits use similar skills and perform similar activities. The primary

DIGITAL, INC.

Dating in Bytes

After breaking up with his girlfriend, Wei-Li Tjong needed an ego boost and a way to meet new women. On a whim, he went to Nerve.com and posted his Johnny Depp look-alike picture with a description of himself as "passionate and sexy." He got 12 responses that day. Within a few months, he had dated 70 women, most for after-dinner drinks of low commitment. He says that about one-third of the women went home with him. Maybe that's why customers are more willing to open their wallets for online dating services: The geographic reach is large, and the results are immediate.

Some of the dating services are subsidiaries of larger companies. For example, match.com is owned by Ticketmaster and brings in about $60 million yearly revenues for their parent company.

Nerve.com, on the other hand, protects its small and funky market, appealing to on-the-edge urban professionals. Fearing it will lose its base, nerve.com has resisted merging with other companies. It gained attention during the 1990s with publication of steamy bohemian literature and spun off its personal ads into Spring Street Networks, hiring a Wall Streeter as CEO.

The issues these companies face are ethical and strategic. Do they allow married people to post ads? Yahoo! does, if the people are truthful about their marital status, as Yahoo!'s strategy is not to be "paternalistic." Since almost one-third of visitors to some sites are married, this is an important question. Some sites, such as match.com, screen the application before they will post an ad, hoping to limit their customers to "singles only." Strategic decisions involve how far to take this dating service. Matchmaker.com holds periodic gatherings where people can meet each other face-to-face and is considering offering customers help with flowers, restaurants, and so on.

People keep signing up. Personal ads are more acceptable to the younger crowd, who see it as an opportunity to meet lots of potential dates. Older folks are not as likely to fork over the cash, as they tend to see personal ads as a last resort for losers. Still, even with the 20-somethings, there are problems. Mr. Tjong found out that people are not always truthful. One woman had gained a "significant" amount of weight since her photo was taken. Others did not always live up to their descriptions. And, not surprisingly, the rate of second dates is quite low.

For Mr. Tjong, it took 70 dates to fall in love. Some people might find that more exhausting than fun.

SOURCES: Warren St. John, "Young, Single and Dating at Hyperspeed," *The New York Times* (April 21, 2002), 9–10; Bod Tedeschi, "Online Matchmakers Are Helping to Bolster the Finances of Their Corporate Parents As They Raise the Romantic Hopes of Clients," *The New York Times* (February 4, 2002), C6; Brad Reagan, "E-Commerce: Openers—Bored of the Rings," *The Wall Street Journal* (April 15, 2002), R4.

difference is that managers in businesses direct their activities toward earning money for the company, while managers in not-for-profits direct their efforts toward generating some kind of social impact. The unique characteristics and needs of not-for-profit organizations created by this distinction present unique challenges for managers.[22]

Financial resources for not-for-profits typically come from government appropriations, grants, and donations rather than from the sale of products or services to customers. In businesses, managers focus on improving the organization's products and services to increase sales revenues. In not-for-profits, however, services are typically provided to nonpaying clients, and a major problem for many organizations is securing a steady stream of funds to continue operating. Not-for-profit managers, committed to serving clients with limited resources, must focus on keeping organizational costs as low as possible.[23] Donors generally want their money to go directly to helping clients rather than for overhead costs. If not-for-profit managers can't demonstrate a highly efficient use of resources, they might have a hard time securing additional donations or government appropriations.

In addition, since not-for-profit organizations do not have a conventional *bottom line*, managers may struggle with the question of what constitutes results and effectiveness. Whereas it is easy to measure dollars and cents, not-for-profits have to measure intangibles such as "improve public health" or "make a difference in the lives of the disenfranchised." It is more difficult to gauge the performance of employees and managers when the goal is providing a public service rather than increasing sales and profits. Managers in not-for-profits must market their services to attract not only clients but also the volunteers and donors on whom they depend. However, these volunteers cannot be supervised and controlled in the same way a business manager deals with employees.

The roles defined by Mintzberg also apply to not-for-profit managers, but these may differ somewhat. We might expect managers in not-for-profits to place more emphasis on the roles of spokesperson (to "sell" the organization to donors and the public), leader (to build a mission-driven community of employees and volunteers), and resource allocator (to distribute government resources or grant funds that are often assigned top-down).

Managers in all organizations—large corporations, small businesses, and not-for-profit organizations—carefully integrate and adjust the management functions and roles to meet new challenges within their own circumstances and keep their organizations healthy. One way in which many organizations are meeting new challenges is through increased use of the Internet. Some government agencies are using the Web to cut bureaucracy, improve efficiency, and save money.

Management and the New Workplace

The world of organizations and management is changing. Rapid environmental shifts are causing fundamental transformations that have a dramatic impact on the manager's job. These transformations are reflected in the transition to a new workplace, as illustrated in Exhibit 1.4. The primary characteristic of the new workplace is that it is centered around bits rather than atoms—*information* and ideas rather than machines and physical assets. The shift from an industrial age to an information age has altered the nature of work, employees, and the work-

EXHIBIT 1.4

The Transition to a New Workplace

New Competencies

1. good communication skills
   a. motivate
   b. retain talent
2. team building skills

Continuous learning

1. team based structure
2. open information
3. employee empowerment

	The Old Workplace	The New Workplace
Characteristics		
Resources	Atoms—physical assets	Bits—information
Work	Structured, localized	Flexible, virtual
Workers	Dependable employees	Empowered employees, free agents
Forces on Organizations		
Technology	Mechanical	Digital, e-business
Markets	Local, domestic	Global, including Internet
Workforce	Homogenous	Diverse
Values	Stability, efficiency	Change, speed
Events	Calm, predictable	Turbulent, more frequent crises
Management Competencies		
Leadership	Autocratic	Dispersed, empowering
Focus	Profits	Connection to customers, employees
Doing Work	By individuals	By teams
Relationships	Conflict, competition	Collaboration
Design	Efficient performance	Experimentation, learning organization

place itself.[24] The old workplace was characterized by routine, specialized tasks and standardized control procedures. Employees typically perform their jobs in one specific company facility, such as an automobile factory located in Detroit or an insurance agency located in Des Moines. The organization is coordinated and controlled through the vertical hierarchy, with decision-making authority residing with upper-level managers.

In the new workplace, by contrast, work is free-flowing and *flexible*. The shift is most obvious in e-commerce and Internet-based organizations, which have to respond to changing markets and competition at a second's notice. However, all organizations are facing the need for greater speed and flexibility. *Empowered employees* are expected to seize opportunities and solve problems as they emerge. The workplace is organized around networks rather than rigid hierarchies, and work is often *virtual*. Thanks to modern information and communications technology, employees can often perform their jobs from home or another remote location, at any time of the day or night. Flexible hours, telecommuting, and virtual teams are increasingly popular ways of working that require new skills from managers. There are an estimated 9 million telecommuters in the United States, for example, and the number is expected to increase over the next few years. AT&T has 7,500 fully mobile workers.[25]

Lincoln Electric
http://www.lincolnelectric.com

It used to be that when you showed up for work, you knew where to go and what to do. Not any more. Increasingly in the new workplace, companies such as Cleveland's Lincoln Electric move employees around and change salaried workers, for example, to hourly clerical tasks, paying them differently for each assignment. Some places even keep a roster of on-call employees who stick by the phone, waiting to hear if they are needed that day.

At Lincoln Electric, employees are required to cross-train in a number of jobs; that way, needs can be filled in one area as another has surplus labor. This has allowed Lincoln Electric to offer long-term employment to its workers, as well as operating with a lean workforce, which helps increase productivity. This commitment to employees includes taking back workers whose subsidiary was sold.

Rick Willard had worked in a Regal motor plant in Arkansas for 30 years. When Lincoln sold Regal, the 56-year-old knew he would have a job back in Cleveland with Lincoln Electric, but he just didn't know what kind of job. In fact, since he's returned, he's had four jobs, most recently making circuit boards and then learning to make welding harnesses. Clocking 50 hours a week, he still earns only half of what he did at Regal, where his work as a machinist paid better. On the positive side, Willard keeps his complete benefits and will be eligible to retire with full benefits at age 60.

Willard doesn't agree with complainers who want steady, predictable pay, because then perhaps the job would disappear. "It's good for the company and sometimes good for the employee. You still have a place to go."[26]

Teams in today's organizations may also include outside contractors, suppliers, customers, competitors, and *free agents* who are not affiliated with a specific organization but work on a project-by-project basis. The valued worker is one who learns quickly, shares knowledge, and is comfortable with risk, change, and ambiguity.

Forces on Organizations

The most striking change now affecting organizations and management is *technology*. In 1995, there were about 238 million computers in use and 39 million Internet users on a global basis. Five years later, the numbers had expanded to an estimated 530 million computers and more than 316 million Internet users.[27] There's a global technology explosion, and its impact on organizations and management is astonishing. Organizations are increasingly using *digital networking* technologies to tie together employees and company partners in far-flung operations. The growing use of *wireless technology* is expanding options even further, truly enabling people to work from practically anywhere, not just from a computer hooked to a company network. Wireless remote access to the Internet, for example, already enables salespeople to send and receive instant messages on hand-held devices from any location, helping them quickly close deals.[28]

One of the biggest technological advances is the *Internet*, which is transforming the way business is done. Only a few years ago, the Internet was still little more than a curiosity to many managers, but how things have changed. In January 1999, Jack Welch urged managers at General Electric to "destroyyourbusiness. com," and since then GE has been using the Web to cut layers of management, promote teamwork, improve customer service, and save money.[29] Companies develop *intranets* and *extranets*, communication systems that use Internet technology and tie employees, managers, free agents, customers, suppliers, partners, subcontractors, and shareholders together in a seamless information flow. Organizations are turning to *e-business* ideas and models to increase speed, cut costs, improve quality, and better serve customers. Some believe the Internet will continue to bring sweeping changes to the music business, as described below.

Bowie Bonds

http://www.davidbowie.com

When David Bowie was a huge rock star in the 1970s, complete with flaming groupies, or a reformed punk artist in the 1980s, he was never slated to become the smartest entrepreneur in the rock business. Of course, he admits that back then he was abusing drugs, which didn't leave him much brainpower for the kinds of deals he is working now. Currently he is so clean he won't even take Advil, because, as he says, "I have such an addictive personality." With his newly clear intelligence and his own ability to be just ahead of the times, he has secured continued success. Influenced by the IPS craze, he raised $55 million by becoming the first big music star to take his music catalog/song royalties public, through 1997's Bowie Bonds. In 1998 he started the high-tech company Ultrastar and his own Internet service provider that also happens to be his fan club (davidbowie.com). Recently he started his own record label, Iso, and has a short-term distribution agreement with Sony while he gets the label up and running.

His keen sense of music's business environment makes him uneasy about the future. Uncertain whether he even wants to be on a label in a few years, he thinks the business won't work anymore by the rules of labels and distribution. "The absolute transformation of everything we ever thought about music will take place within 10 years, and nothing is going to be able to stop it . . . I'm truly confident that copyright, for instance, will no longer exist in 10 years, and authorship and intellectual property is in for such a smashing." He believes he has to take advantage of these last years of the music business as it has been. "You'd better be prepared for doing a lot of touring because that's the only unique situation that's going to be left." Even with all the changes he expects, he's still looking forward to it. "It's terribly exciting," he says.[30]

The Internet and other new technologies are also tied closely to *globalization,* another force that is significantly affecting organizations. People around the world are connected in the flow of information, money, ideas, and products, and interdependencies are increasing. The French tire manufacturer Michelin gets 35 percent of its revenues in the United States, while U.S.-based Johnson & Johnson does 43 percent of its business abroad.[31] Schering AG, the German pharmaceuticals company, employees 56 percent of its 22,000 workers outside its home country.[32] Customers today operate globally and they expect organizations to provide worldwide service.

Managers have to understand cross-cultural patterns, and they often work with virtual team members from many different countries. *Diversity* of the population and the workforce has become a fact of life for all organizations. Talented, educated knowledge workers seek opportunities all over the world, just as organizations search the world for the best minds to help them compete in a global economy. The general population of the United States, and thus of the workforce, is also growing more ethnically and racially diverse. Generational diversity is another powerful force in today's workplace, with employees of all ages working together on teams and projects in a way rarely seen in the past. Although the workforce in general is growing older with the aging of the baby boomers and there is a trend toward staying in the workforce longer, Generation X employees, now in their late 20s and 30s, are having a profound impact on the workplace. And members of the next generation, Generation Y, which rivals the baby boomers in size, are beginning to enter the workforce.

In the face of these transformations, organizations are learning to value *change* and *speed* over stability and efficiency. The fundamental paradigm during much of the twentieth century was a belief that things can be stable. In contrast, the new paradigm recognizes change and chaos as the natural order of things.[33] Events in today's world are *turbulent* and *unpredictable,* with both small and large crises occurring on a more frequent basis.

In the face of these transitions, managers must rethink their approach to organizing, directing, and motivating workers. According to one consultant, many managers who have grown accustomed to the old workplace complain that employees no longer play by the rules. The consultant's response: "Why should they play by the rules? The rules are dead."[34]

New Management Competencies

As discussed earlier in the chapter, not all managers' jobs are the same. Managers rely on varied skills and perform different activities, depending on hierarchical level and job responsibilities. For all managers, however, human skills are becoming increasingly important.[35] In a survey of managers on their views of how the Internet has affected management, for example, the majority considered communicating effectively, retaining talented employees, and motivating workers to be essential management skills for the Internet world.[36] Although these abilities have always been important to managers, they take on added significance today, particularly when employees are dispersed and working in a virtual environment.

Today's best managers give up their command-and-control mindset to embrace ambiguity and create organizations that are fast, flexible, adaptable, and relationship-oriented. *Leadership* is dispersed throughout the organization, and managers empower others to gain the benefit of their ideas and creativity. The model of managers controlling workers no longer applies in a workplace where employee brainpower is more important than physical assets.[37] More-over, managers often supervise employees who are scattered in various locations, requiring a new approach to leadership that focuses more on mentoring and providing direction and support than on giving orders and ensuring that they are followed.

Rather than a single-minded focus on profits, today's managers must recognize the critical importance of staying *connected to employees* and *customers*. The Internet has given increased knowledge and power to customers, so organizations have to remain flexible and adaptable to respond quickly to changing demands or competition. In some e-commerce organizations, managers have almost totally ignored profits in favor of building customer relationships. Although all organizations have to be concerned with profits sooner or later, as managers of numerous failed dot-coms learned, the emphasis these companies put on developing customers and relationships is a reflection of trends affecting all organizations.

Team-building skills are crucial for today's managers. Teams of front-line employees who work directly with customers have become the basic building block of organizations. Instead of managing a department of employees, many managers act as team leaders of ever-shifting, temporary projects. At SEI Investments, all work is distributed among 140 teams. Some are permanent, such as those that serve major customers or focus on specific markets, but many are designed to work on short-term projects or problems. Computer linkups, called *pythons*, drop from the ceiling. As people change assignments, they just unplug their pythons, move their desks and chairs to a new location, plug into a new python, and get to work on the next project.[38]

Success in the new workplace depends on the strength and quality of collaborative *relationships*. Partnerships, both within the organization and with outside customers, suppliers, and even competitors, are recognized as the key to a winning organization. New ways of working emphasize collaboration across functions and hierarchical levels as well as with other companies. E-business models that digitally link customers, suppliers, partners, and other stakeholders require managers to assess and manage relationships far beyond the confines of the traditional organization.

An important management challenge in the new workplace is to build a *learning organization* by creating an organizational climate that values experimentation and risk taking, applies current technology, tolerates mistakes and failure, and rewards nontraditional thinking and the sharing of knowledge. Everyone in the organization participates in identifying and solving problems, enabling the organization to continuously experiment, improve, and increase its capability. The role of managers is not to make decisions, but to create learning capability, where everyone is free to experiment and learn what works best.

Application: Managing Crises and Unexpected Events

Many managers may dream of working in an organization and a world where life seems relatively calm, orderly, and predictable. Today's world, though, is marked by increasing turbulence and disorder. Organizations face various levels of crisis every day—everything from the loss of computer data, to charges of racial discrimination, to a factory fire, to a flu epidemic. However, these organizational crises have been compounded by crises on a more global level. Consider a few of the major events that have affected U.S. companies within the last few years: an energy crisis in California that led to a virtual state takeover of the energy market; the massacre at Columbine High School, which prompted schools all over the country to form crisis teams to deal with school violence; the grounding of Concorde jets for 14 months after the fiery crash of an Air France Concorde in Paris. And then the U.S. was hit with the most devastating and far-reaching event of the twenty-first century to date: the September 11, 2001, terrorist attacks in New York and Washington that destroyed the World Trade Center, seriously damaged the Pentagon, killed thousands of people, and interrupted business around the world. The subsequent bombings in Afghanistan, continuing uncertainty over terrorist activities, and a deepening recession continue to affect companies worldwide. Anthrax scares altered companies' advertising and marketing plans as they weighed the public's perceptions of the U.S. mail. Organizations scrambled to implement videoconferencing as airport security checks stretched travel time beyond the point where business flights made economic sense.

Dealing with the unexpected has always been part of the manager's job, but our world has become so fast, interconnected, and complex that unexpected events happen more frequently and often with greater and more painful consequences. All of the new management skills and competencies we have discussed are important to managers in such an environment. In addition, crisis management is an emerging need that places further demands on today's managers. As California Governor Gray Davis put it, "Extraordinary times . . . require extraordinary leadership."[39] Some of the most recent thinking on crisis management suggests the importance of five leadership skills.[40]

1. Stay calm.

2. Be visible.

3. Put people before business.

4. Tell the truth.

5. Know when to get back to business.

Stay Calm. A leader's emotions are contagious, so leaders have to stay calm, focused, and optimistic about the future. Perhaps the most important part of a manager's job in a crisis situation is to absorb people's fears and uncertainties. Leaders have to suppress their own fears, doubts, and pain to comfort others. Although they acknowledge the danger and difficulties, they remain rock-steady and hopeful, which gives comfort, inspiration, and hope to others.

Be Visible. When people's worlds have become ambiguous and uncertain, they need to feel that someone is in control. George W. Bush got off to a shaky start as a crisis leader following the September 11 terrorist attacks because people didn't know where he was. As soon as he became visible, practically the entire country rallied behind him.

Put People before Business. The companies that weather a crisis best, whether the crisis is large or small, are those in which managers make people and human feelings their top priority. Top managers of Thomson Financial, which had about 200 employees in the World Trade Center and 1,800 elsewhere in downtown Manhattan, spent little to no time at all on business issues for the first few days after September 11, concentrating instead on the physical and emotional needs of employees and helping the families of the 11 Thomson workers lost in the attacks.[41]

Tell the Truth. Following the 2001 collapse of Enron Corp. and charges of unethical and possibly illegal activities, top managers at Enron compounded the crisis by destroying documents, refusing to be straightforward with employees and the media, and stonewalling investigators by pleading the fifth amendment. Managers at Arthur Andersen, Enron's accounting firm, also reportedly handled the crisis by destroying documents and pleading the fifth.

Know When to Get Back to Business. Although managers should first deal with the physical and emotional needs of people, they also need to get back to business as soon as possible. The company has to keep going, and most people want to be a part of the rebuilding process, to feel that they have a home with the company and something to look forward to. The rejuvenation of the

FOCUS ON LEADERSHIP

American Express Reacts

Kenneth Chenault had just been hired for his dream job as chairman and CEO of American Express Co., becoming one of the few African Americans ever to head a major U.S. corporation. He knew he would face challenges, but he never imagined in his worst nightmares anything like what happened.

While he was on a business trip to Salt Lake City, and talking on the telephone with a colleague back in New York, terrorists crashed airplanes into the twin towers of the World Trade Center, just across the street from American Express headquarters. Chenault immediately telephoned security and instructed them to begin evacuation procedures. Over the next two days Chenault set up a command center in Salt Lake City and held hourly conference calls with top executives to keep tabs on what was happening and to deal with immediate problems. He learned that the attacks had left 11 American Express employees dead or missing. "He was there, and he was in the middle of it," said one manager.

American Express was already going through some difficult times before the September 11, 2001, terrorist attacks. In his first year on the job, Chenault twice reported disappointing financial results and announced layoffs of almost 7,000 jobs. Now, as the number one issuer of credit cards and the number one travel agency, he knew American Express would be at the center of an economic storm. Chenault knew that everyone—from the lowest-ranking employee of the company to the biggest shareholder—would be looking to him for leadership.

Even while he stayed in Salt Lake City, Chenault took control, gathering information and taking steps to ensure the safety of employees. From the moment the crisis began, Chenault remained calm, steady, and focused, dealing with personal losses, refusing to complain about his company's

problems, listening to employees and sharing their grief, taking care of customers, doing favors for other companies, and getting the company back to business as quickly as possible. Every decision he made was guided by his concerns for employees and customer service. After ordering the evacuation, his next move was to have the call center track down each and every employee. Then he turned to customers, helping 560,000 stranded American Express cardholders get home, waiving delinquent fees on late payments, and increasing credit limits if customers needed it.

When he returned to New York, Chenault gathered his employees at the Paramount Theater, where he expressed his own despair, anger, and sadness and gave employees a chance to do the same. At the end, he told them, "I represent the best company and the best people in the world. In fact, you are my strength, and I love you." Thus began the long healing process. Chenault continued to be a highly visible leader. In his visits to the various temporary offices, he exchanged hugs and handshakes, tears and laughter. When President Bush visited New York, Chenault was there, stressing the need for greater airport security, joining with New York mayor Rudolph Giuliani and Governor George Pataki to ask for more aid, and meeting with other business leaders to support the president's plan for economic recovery. During all this time, Chenault was also studying his company's financial problems and how to help the organization survive this extremely difficult period in its history. "If you're the leader, you've got to feel you're the person where the decisions rest," he says. "This is no time for excuses."

SOURCES: John A. Byrne and Heather Timmons, "Tough Times for a New CEO," *Business Week* (October 29, 2001), 64–70; and Patrick McGeehan, "Sailing into a Sea of Troubles," *The New York Times* (October 5, 2001), C1, C4.

business is a sign of hope and an inspiration to employees. Moments of crisis also present excellent opportunities for looking forward and using the emotional energy that has emerged to build a better company.

Crisis management is an important aspect of any manager's job, particularly in today's turbulent times. This is a challenging time to be entering the field of management. Throughout this book, you will learn much more about the new workplace, about the new and dynamic roles managers are playing in the twenty-first century, and about how you can be an effective manager in a complex, ever-changing world. One manager found out through horrors just how important a leader is during a crisis, as shown in the Focus on Leadership box.

The Learning Organization

Managers began thinking about the concept of the learning organization after the publication of Peter Senge's book, *The Fifth Discipline: The Art and Practice of Learning Organizations.*[42] Senge described the kind of changes managers needed to undergo to help their organizations adapt to an increasingly chaotic world. These ideas gradually evolved to describe characteristics of the organization itself. There is no single view of what the learning organization looks like. The learning organization is an attitude or philosophy about what an organization can become.

The **learning organization** can be defined as one in which everyone is engaged in identifying and solving problems, enabling the organization to continuously experiment, change, and improve, thus increasing its capacity to grow, learn, and achieve its purpose. The essential idea is problem solving, in contrast to the traditional organization designed for efficiency. In the learning organization all employees look for problems, such as understanding special customer needs. Employees also solve problems, which means putting things together in unique ways to meet a customer's needs.

To develop a learning organization, managers make changes in all the subsystems of the organization. Three important adjustments to promote continuous learning are shifting to a team-based structure, empowering employees, and sharing information. These three characteristics are illustrated in Exhibit 1.5 and each is described here.

Team-Based Structure. An important value in a learning organization is collaboration and communication across departmental and hierarchical boundaries. Self-directed teams are the basic building block of the structure. These

learning organization

An organization in which everyone is engaged in identifying and solving problems, enabling the organization to continuously experiment, improve, and increase its capability.

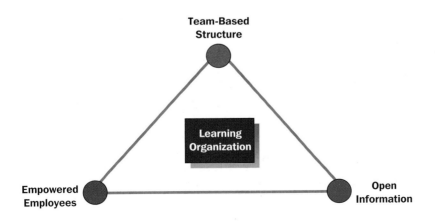

Elements of a Learning Organization

teams are made up of employees with different skills who share or rotate jobs to produce an entire product or service. Traditional management tasks are pushed down to lower levels of the organization, with teams often taking responsibility for training, safety, scheduling, and decisions about work methods, pay and reward systems, and coordination with other teams. Although team leadership is critical, in learning organizations the traditional boss is practically eliminated. People on the team are given the skills, information, tools, motivation, and authority to make decisions central to the team's performance and to respond creatively and flexibly to new challenges or opportunities that arise.

Employee Empowerment. *Empowerment* means unleashing the power and creativity of employees by giving them the freedom, resources, information, and skills to make decisions and perform effectively. Traditional management tries to limit employees, while empowerment expands their behavior. Empowerment may be reflected in self-directed work teams, quality circles, job enrichment, and employee participation groups as well as through decision-making authority, training, and information so that people can perform jobs without close supervision.

In learning organizations, people are a manager's primary source of strength, not a cost to be minimized. Companies that adopt this perspective believe in treating employees well by providing competitive wages, good working conditions, and opportunities for personal and professional development. In addition, they often provide a sense of employee ownership by sharing gains in productivity and profits.[43]

Open Information.   A learning organization is flooded with information. To identify needs and solve problems, people have to be aware of what's going on. They must understand the whole organization as well as their part in it. Formal data about budgets, profits, and departmental expenses are available to everyone. At Solectron Corp., the world's largest and fastest-growing contract manufacturer, managers widely share information to carry out the company's guiding principles: superior customer service and respect for individual workers. "If you really want to respect individuals," says Winston Chen, "you've got to let them know how they're doing—and let them know soon enough so they can do something about it."[44] Open information becomes extraordinarily important in organizations that deal with ideas rather than material goods. Managers know that providing too much information is better than providing too little. In addition, managers encourage people throughout the organization to share information. At Viant Inc., which helps companies build and maintain Web-based businesses, people are rewarded for their willingness to absorb and share knowledge. Rather than encouraging consultants to hoard specialized knowledge, CEO Bob Gett says, "We value you more for how much information you've given to the guy next to you."[45]

Managing the Technology-Driven Workplace

The shift to the learning organization goes hand-in-hand with the current transition to a technology-driven workplace. Today's organizations can't be managed and controlled in the same way organizations were managed 100 years ago—or perhaps even 20 years ago.

The physical world that Frederick Taylor and other proponents of scientific management measured determines less and less of what is valued in organizations and society. Our lives and organizations have been engulfed by informa-

As president and chief operating officer at oil company Unocal, Tim Ling is among the young executives who are eschewing the oil industry's traditional closed, old-economy methods to embrace open information and communication. Ling prodded Unocal employees, from drillers to managers, to share information and become financially sophisticated. To extend the benefits of this open information culture, Ling also wants to get expert analysis from outside the company by feeding seismic data via broadband to geologists around the world.

tion technology. Ideas, information, and relationships are becoming more important than production machinery, physical products, and structured jobs.[46] Many employees perform much of their work on computers and may work in virtual teams, connected electronically to colleagues around the world. Even in factories that produce physical goods, machines have taken over much of the routine and uniform work, freeing workers to use more of their minds and abilities. Managers and employees in today's companies focus on opportunities rather than efficiencies, which requires that they be flexible, creative, and unconstrained by rigid rules and structured tasks.

In addition to employees being connected electronically, organizations are becoming enmeshed in electronic networks. The world of e-business is booming as more and more business takes place by digital processes over a computer network rather than in physical space. **E-business** refers to the work an organization does by using electronic linkages (including the Internet) with customers, partners, suppliers, employees, or other key constituents. For example, organizations that use the Internet or other electronic linkages to communicate with employees or customers are engaged in e-business. A company might set up an **intranet**, an internal communications system that uses the technology and standards of the Internet but is accessible only to people within the company. The intranet looks and acts like a Web site, but it is cordoned off from the public with the use of software programs known as *firewalls*.[47] Some companies extend the communication system's function with an **extranet**, which gives access to key suppliers, partners, customers, or others outside the organization.

E-commerce is a narrower term referring specifically to business exchanges or transactions that occur electronically. E-commerce replaces or enhances the exchange of money and products with the exchange of data and information from one computer to another. Three types of e-commerce—business-to-consumer, business-to-business, and consumer-to-consumer—are illustrated in Exhibit 1.6. Today, most e-commerce takes place on the Internet. Companies

e-business

Work an organization does by using electronic linkages.

intranet

An internal communications system that uses the technology and standards of the Internet but is accessible only within the company.

extranet

A company communications system that gives access to suppliers, partners, and others outside the company.

e-commerce

Business exchanges or transactions that occur electronically.

EXHIBIT *1.6*

Three Types of E-commerce

Business-to-Consumer (B2C)
Selling Products and Services Online

TYPES OF E-COMMERCE

Business-to-Business (B2B)
Transactions between Organizations

Consumer-to-Consumer (C2C)
Electronic Markets Created by Web-Based Intermediaries

such as Gateway, Amazon.com, 800-Flowers, Expedia.com, and Progressive are engaged in what is referred to as *business-to-consumer e-commerce (B2C)*, because they sell products and services to consumers over the Internet. Consumers can log onto Internet Web sites and purchase computers, books, CDs, flowers and gifts, airline tickets, insurance policies, or practically anything else they desire. In addition, they can pay bills online, chat with consultants about business opportunities or with doctors about medical problems, shop for the lowest-priced refrigerator directly from the manufacturer, or check the history of a used car.

Although this is probably the most visible expression of e-commerce to the public, the fastest growing area of e-commerce is *business-to-business e-commerce (B2B)*, which refers to electronic transactions between organizations. Many companies handle B2B commerce over private *electronic data interchange (EDI)* networks. For example, Wal-Mart has used a private network to transmit sales data to suppliers such as Procter & Gamble, where the network can automatically trigger a shipment of new products as they're needed to restock Wal-Mart's shelves.

More and more companies are using Web-based technology because the Internet systems are easier to use than EDI and are accessible to a larger number of suppliers and vendors.[48] Large organizations such as General Electric, Carrier Corp., and Ford Motor Company purchase billions of dollars worth of goods and services a year electronically via Internet or private computer linkages to supplier companies.[49] GE is focused on "digitizing" every function it possibly can, from buying airline tickets to paying suppliers. For example, GE used to process more than 3 million paper invoices a year. Now, most of GE's purchasing and payments are handled digitally. GE managers predict that automating transactions with suppliers will save the company well over a billion dollars a year.[50] Ford Motor Company purchases a large portion of the steel it uses to build cars through e-Steel. Rather than Ford managers having to go through a maze of processes and paperwork before steel ends up on the assembly line, e-Steel software automatically tracks steel movements on an Internet-based system.[51]

Some companies have taken e-commerce to very high levels to achieve amazing performance. Dell Computer pioneered the use of end-to-end digital supply-chain networks to keep in touch with customers, take orders, buy components from suppliers, coordinate with manufacturing partners, and ship customized products directly to consumers. This trend is affecting every industry, prompting a group of consultants at a Harvard University conference to conclude that businesses today must either "Dell or be Delled."[52] These advances mean managers not only need to be technologically savvy, but they become responsible for managing a web of relationships that reaches far beyond the boundaries of the physical organization, building flexible e-links between a company and its employees, suppliers, partners, and customers.[53]

The third area of e-commerce, *consumer-to-consumer (C2C)*, is made possible when an Internet-based business acts as an intermediary between and among consumers. One of the best-known examples of C2C e-commerce is Web-based auctions such as those made possible by eBay or QXL. Internet auctions have created a large electronic marketplace where consumers can buy and sell directly with one another, often handling practically the entire transaction via the Web. Another popular area of C2C commerce is peer-to-peer file-sharing networks. Companies such as Napster, BearShare, and Morpheus provide the technology for swapping music files, video clips, software, and other files. This area of e-commerce will likely grow in coming years.

In an increasingly digital world, many organizations and employees deal almost entirely with intangibles such as ideas and information. Consider Frederick Taylor's comment about the kind of worker needed in the iron business a century ago: "Now one of the first requirements for a man who is fit to handle pig iron as a regular occupation is that he shall be so stupid and so phlegmatic that he more nearly resembles in his mental makeup the ox than any other type."[54] The philosophy of scientific management was that managers structured and controlled jobs so carefully that thinking on the part of employees wasn't required—indeed, it was usually discouraged. How different things are today! Companies such as Microsoft or Ipswitch that develop software and Internet applications depend on employees' minds more than their physical bodies. In companies where the power of an idea determines success, managers' primary goal is to tap into the creativity and knowledge of every employee.

New electronic technologies also shape the organization itself and how it is managed. Technology provides the architecture that supports and reinforces the new workplace. For example, one approach to information management is **enterprise resource planning (ERP)** systems, which unite all of a company's major business functions, such as order processing, product design, purchasing, inventory, manufacturing, distribution, human resources, receipt of payments, and forecasting of future demand. Because ERP weaves together all of the company's systems, managers anywhere in the organization can see the big picture and act quickly, based on up-to-the-minute information.[55] ERP prompts a new approach to management—a companywide management system in which everyone, from the CEO down to a machine operator on the factory floor, has instant access to critical information. Thus, ERP also supports management attempts to harness and leverage organizational *knowledge*.

Peter Drucker coined the term *knowledge work* more than 40 years ago,[56] but it is only in recent years that managers have genuinely recognized knowledge as an important organizational resource that should be managed just as they manage cash flow or raw materials. **Knowledge management** refers to the efforts to systematically find, organize, and make available a company's intellectual capital and to foster a culture of continuous learning and knowledge sharing so that a company's activities build on what is already known.[57] Information technology plays an important role by enabling the storage and dissemination of data and information across the organization, but technology is only one part of a larger management system.[58] A complete knowledge management system includes not only the technology for capturing and storing knowledge for easy access, but also new management values that support risk-taking, learning, and collaboration. Rather than seeing employees as factors of production and looking for ways to use human and material resources for greatest efficiency, today's most successful managers cherish people for their ability to think, create, share knowledge, and build relationships.

enterprise resource planning (ERP)

Systems that unite a company's major business functions—order processing, product design, purchasing, inventory, etc.

knowledge management

The efforts to systematically find, organize, and make available a company's intellectual capital and to foster a culture of continuous learning and knowledge sharing.

Management and Organization

Management philosophies and organizational forms change over time to meet new needs. The workplace of today is very different from what it was 50 years ago—indeed, from what it was even 10 years ago. Yet there are ideas and practices from the past that are still highly relevant and applicable to management today. Many students wonder why history matters to managers. A historical perspective provides a broader way of thinking, a way of searching for patterns and determining whether they recur across time periods. For example, certain management techniques that seem modern, such as employee stock-ownership programs, have repeatedly gained and lost popularity since the early 20th century because of historical forces.[59] William Cooper Procter, grandson of the co-founder of Procter & Gamble, introduced a profit-sharing plan in 1887, and expanded it by tying it to stock ownership a few years later. Sam Walton opened Wal-Mart's financial records, including salaries, to all employees in the 1960s, long before business magazines were touting the value of *open-book management.*[60]

A study of the past contributes to understanding both the present and the future. It is a way of learning from others' mistakes so as not to repeat them; learning from others' successes so as to repeat them in the appropriate situation; and most of all, learning to understand why things happen to improve our organizations in the future.

A historical perspective on management provides a context or environment in which to interpret current opportunities and problems. However, studying history does not mean merely arranging events in chronological order; it means developing an understanding of the impact of societal forces on organizations. Studying history is a way to achieve strategic thinking, see the big picture, and improve conceptual skills. We will start by examining how social, political, and economic forces have influenced organizations and the practice of management.[61]

Social forces refer to those aspects of a culture that guide and influence relationships among people. What do people value? What do people need? What are the standards of behavior among people? These forces shape what is known as the *social contract,* which refers to the unwritten, common rules and perceptions about relationships among people and between employees and management.

social forces

The aspects of a culture that guide and influence relationships among people—their values, needs, and standards of behavior.

A significant social force today is the changing attitudes, ideas, and values of Generation X and Generation Y employees. Generation X workers, those now in their late 20s and 30s, have had a profound impact on the workplace over the past decade or so, and Generation Y promises to have an even greater one.[62] People born between the years of 1980 and 1995 make up a whopping 26 percent of the population, and the older members are entering the workforce now. These young workers, the most educated generation in the history of the United States, grew up technologically adept and globally conscious. Some trends sparked by Generation X and Y workers are completely reshaping the social contract. Career life cycles are getting shorter, with workers typically changing jobs every few years and changing careers several times during their lifetime.[63] Young workers also expect to have access to cutting-edge technology, opportunities to learn and further their career and personal goals, and the power to make substantive decisions and changes in the workplace. Finally, there is a growing focus on work/life balance, reflected in trends such as telecommuting, flextime, shared jobs, and organization-sponsored sabbaticals.

political forces

The influence of political and legal institutions on people and organizations.

Political forces refer to the influence of political and legal institutions on people and organizations. Political forces include basic assumptions underlying the political system, such as the desirability of self-government, property rights, contract rights, the definition of justice, and the determination of innocence or guilt of a crime. The spread of capitalism throughout the world has dramatically altered the business landscape. The dominance of the free-market system and growing interdependencies among the world's countries require organizations to operate differently and managers to think in new ways. At the same time, growing anti-American sentiments in many parts of the world create challenges for U.S. companies and managers. Another strong political force is the empowerment of citizens throughout the world. Power is being diffused both within and among countries as never before.[64] People are demanding empowerment, participation, and responsibility in all areas of their lives, including their work.

Economic forces pertain to the availability, production, and distribution of resources in a society. Governments, military agencies, churches, schools, and business organizations in every society require resources to achieve their goals, and economic forces influence the allocation of scarce resources. The economy of the United States and other developed countries is shifting dramatically, with the sources of wealth, the fundamentals of distribution, and the nature of economic decision making undergoing significant changes.[65] The emerging new economy is based largely on ideas, information, and knowledge rather than material resources. Supply chains and distribution of resources have been revolutionized by digital technology. Inventories, which once could trigger recessions, are declining or completely disappearing. Another economic trend is the booming importance of small and mid-sized businesses, including start-ups, which early in the twenty-first century grew at three times the rate of the national economy. "I call it 'the invisible economy,' yet it is *the* economy," says David Birch of Cognetics Inc., a Cambridge, Massachusetts, firm that tracks business formation.[66] A massive shift in the economy is not without its upheavals, of course. Years of seemingly endless growth ground to a halt as stock prices fell, particularly for dot-com and technology companies. Numerous Internet-based companies went out of business, and organizations throughout the U.S. and Canada began laying off hundreds of thousands of workers. However, this economic downturn may also be a stimulus for even greater technological innovation and small business vitality.

Management practices and perspectives vary in response to these social, political, and economic forces in the larger society. Exhibit 1.7 illustrates the

economic forces

Forces that affect the availability, production, and distribution of a society's resources among competing users.

EXHIBIT 1.7

Management Perspectives over Time

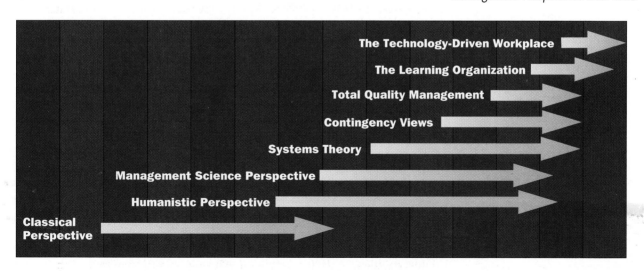

evolution of significant management perspectives over time, each of which will be examined in the remainder of this chapter.

Classical Perspective

classical perspective

A management perspective that emerged during the nineteenth and early twentieth centuries that emphasized a rational, scientific approach to the study of management and sought to make organizations efficient operating machines.

The practice of management can be traced to 3000 B.C. to the first government organizations developed by the Sumerians and Egyptians, but the formal study of management is relatively recent.[67] The early study of management as we know it today began with what is now called the *classical perspective*.

The **classical perspective** on management emerged during the nineteenth and early twentieth centuries. The factory system that began to appear in the 1800s posed challenges that earlier organizations had not encountered. Problems arose in tooling the plants, organizing managerial structure, training employees (many of them non-English-speaking immigrants), scheduling complex manufacturing operations, and dealing with increased labor dissatisfaction and resulting strikes.

These myriad new problems and the development of large, complex organizations demanded a new approach to coordination and control, and a "new subspecies of economic man—the salaried manager"[68]—was born. Between 1880 and 1920, the number of professional managers in the United States grew from 161,000 to more than a million.[69] These professional managers began developing and testing solutions to the mounting challenges of organizing, coordinating, and controlling large numbers of people and increasing worker productivity. Thus began the evolution of modern management with the classical perspective.

This perspective contains three subfields, each with a slightly different emphasis: scientific management, bureaucratic organizations, and administrative principles.[70]

scientific management

A subfield of the classical management perspective that emphasized scientifically determined changes in management practices as the solution to improving labor productivity.

Scientific Management

Organizations' somewhat limited success in achieving improvements in labor productivity led a young engineer to suggest that the problem lay more in poor management practices than in labor. Frederick Winslow Taylor (1856–1915) insisted that management itself would have to change and, further, that the manner of change could be determined only by scientific study; hence, the label **scientific management** emerged. Taylor suggested that decisions based on rules of thumb and tradition be replaced with precise procedures developed after careful study of individual situations.[71]

Taylor's philosophy is encapsulated in his statement, "In the past the man has been first. In the future, the system must be first."[72] The scientific management approach is illustrated by the unloading of iron from rail cars and reloading finished steel for the Bethlehem Steel plant in 1898. Taylor calculated that with correct movements, tools, and sequencing, each man was capable of loading 47.5 tons per day instead of the typical 12.5 tons. He also worked out an incentive system that paid each man $1.85 a day for meeting the new standard, an increase from the previous rate of $1.15. Productivity at Bethlehem Steel shot up overnight.

Although known as the "father of scientific management," Taylor was not alone in this area. Henry Gantt, an associate of Taylor's, developed the *Gantt Chart*—a bar graph that measures planned and completed work along each

Frederick Winslow Taylor (1856–1915) Taylor's theory that labor productivity could be improved by scientifically determined management practices earned him the status of "father of scientific management."

stage of production by time elapsed. Two other important pioneers in this area were the husband-and-wife team of Frank B. and Lillian M. Gilbreth. Frank B. Gilbreth (1868–1924) pioneered *time and motion study* and arrived at many of his management techniques independently of Taylor. He stressed efficiency and was known for his quest for the "one best way" to do work. Although Gilbreth is known for his early work with bricklayers, his work had great impact on medical surgery by drastically reducing the time patients spent on the operating table. Surgeons were able to save countless lives through the application of time and motion study. Lillian M. Gilbreth (1878–1972) was more interested in the human aspect of work. When her husband died at the age of 56, she had 12 children ages 2 to 19. The undaunted "first lady of management" went right on with her work. She presented a paper in place of her late husband, continued their seminars and consulting, lectured, and eventually became a professor at Purdue University.[73] She pioneered in the field of industrial psychology and made substantial contributions to human resource management.

The basic ideas of scientific management are shown in Exhibit 1.8. To use this approach, managers should develop standard methods for doing each job, select workers with the appropriate abilities, train workers in the standard methods, support workers and eliminate interruptions, and provide wage incentives.

The ideas of scientific management that began with Taylor dramatically increased productivity across all industries, and they are still important today. Indeed, the concept of arranging work based on careful analysis of tasks for maximum productivity is deeply embedded in our organizations.[74] However, because scientific management ignored the social context and workers' needs, it led to increased conflict and sometimes violent clashes between managers and employees. Under this system, workers often felt exploited. This was in sharp contrast to the harmony and cooperation that Taylor and his followers had envisioned.

Lillian M. Gilbreth (1878–1972)
Frank B. Gilbreth (1868–1924)
Shown here using a "motion study" device, this husband-and-wife team contributed to the principles of scientific management. His development of time and motion studies and her work in industrial psychology pioneered many of today's management and human resource techniques.

Bureaucratic Organizations

A systematic approach developed in Europe that looked at the organization as a whole is the **bureaucratic organizations** approach, a subfield within the classical perspective. Max Weber (1864–1920), a German theorist, introduced most of the concepts on bureaucratic organizations.[75]

bureaucratic organizations
A subfield of the classical management perspective that emphasized management on an impersonal, rational basis through such elements as clearly defined authority and responsibility, formal recordkeeping, and separation of management and ownership.

EXHIBIT 1.8

Characteristics of Scientific Management

General Approach
- Developed standard method for performing each job.
- Selected workers with appropriate abilities for each job.
- Trained workers in standard methods.
- Supported workers by planning their work and eliminating interruptions.
- Provided wage incentives to workers for increased output.

Contributions
- Demonstrated the importance of compensation for performance.
- Initiated the careful study of tasks and jobs.
- Demonstrated the importance of personnel selection and training.

Criticisms
- Did not appreciate the social context of work and higher needs of workers.
- Did not acknowledge variance among individuals.
- Tended to regard workers as uninformed and ignored their ideas and suggestions.

EXHIBIT 1.9

Characteristics of Weberian Bureaucracy

SOURCE: Adapted from Max Weber, *The Theory of Social and Economic Organizations,* ed. and trans. A.M. Henderson and Talcott Parsons (New York: Free Press, 1947), 328–337.

Elements of Bureaucracy

1. Labor is divided with clear definitions of authority and responsibility that are legitimized as official duties.
2. Positions are organized in a hierarchy of authority, with each position under the authority of a higher one.
3. All personnel are selected and promoted based on technical qualifications, which are assessed by examination or according to training and experience.
4. Administrative acts and decisions are recorded in writing. Recordkeeping provides organizational memory and continuity over time.
5. Management is separate from the ownership of the organization.
6. Managers are subject to rules and procedures that will ensure reliable, predictable behavior. Rules are impersonal and uniformly applied to all employees.

During the late 1800s, many European organizations were managed on a personal, family-like basis. Employees were loyal to a single individual rather than to the organization or its mission. The dysfunctional consequence of this management practice was that resources were used to realize individual desires rather than organizational goals. Employees in effect owned the organization and used resources for their own gain rather than to serve customers. Weber envisioned organizations that would be managed on an impersonal, rational basis. This form of organization was called a *bureaucracy.* Exhibit 1.9 summarizes the six characteristics of bureaucracy as specified by Weber.

Weber believed that an organization based on rational authority would be more efficient and adaptable to change because continuity is related to formal structure and positions rather than to a particular person, who may leave or die. To Weber, rationality in organizations meant employee selection and advancement based on competence rather than on "whom you know." The organization relies on rules and written records for continuity. The manager depends not on his or her personality for successfully giving orders but on the legal power invested in the managerial position.

The term *bureaucracy* has taken on a negative meaning in today's organizations and is associated with endless rules and red tape. We have all been frustrated by waiting in long lines or following seemingly silly procedures. On the other hand, rules and other bureaucratic procedures provide a standard way of dealing with employees. Everyone gets equal treatment, and everyone knows what the rules are. This has enabled many organizations to become extremely efficient. Consider United Parcel Service (UPS), also called the "Brown Giant."

United Parcel Service

http://www.ups.com

United Parcel Service took on the U.S. Postal Service at its own game—and won. UPS specializes in the delivery of small packages. Why has the Brown Giant been so successful? One important reason is the concept of bureaucracy. UPS is bound up in rules and regulations. There are safety rules for drivers, loaders, clerks, and managers. Strict dress codes are enforced—no beards; hair cannot touch the collar; mustaches must be trimmed evenly; and no sideburns. Rules specify cleanliness standards for buildings and other properties. No eating or drinking is permitted at employee desks. Every manager is given bound copies of policy books and expected to use them regularly.

UPS also has a well-defined division of labor. Each plant consists of specialized drivers, loaders, clerks, washers, sorters, and maintenance personnel. UPS thrives on written records. Daily worksheets specify performance goals and work output. Daily employee quotas and achievements are reported on a weekly and monthly basis.

Technical qualification is the criterion for hiring and promotion. The UPS policy book says the leader is expected to have the knowledge and capacity to justify the position of leadership. Favoritism is forbidden. The bureaucratic model works just fine at UPS, "the tightest ship in the shipping business."[76]

Administrative Principles

Another major subfield within the classical perspective is known as the **administrative principles** approach. Whereas scientific management focused on the productivity of the individual worker, the administrative principles approach focused on the total organization. The contributors to this approach included Henri Fayol, Mary Parker Follett, and Chester I. Barnard.

Henri Fayol (1841–1925) was a French mining engineer who worked his way up to become head of a major mining group known as Comambault. Comambault survives today as part of Le Creusot-Loire, the largest mining and metallurgical group in central France. In his later years, Fayol wrote down his concepts on administration, based largely on his own management experiences.[77]

In his most significant work, *General and Industrial Management,* Fayol discussed 14 general principles of management, several of which are part of management philosophy today. For example:

- *Unity of command.* Each subordinate receives orders from one—and only one—superior.

- *Division of work.* Managerial and technical work are amenable to specialization to produce more and better work with the same amount of effort.

- *Unity of direction.* Similar activities in an organization should be grouped together under one manager.

- *Scalar chain.* A chain of authority extends from the top to the bottom of the organization and should include every employee.

Fayol felt that these principles could be applied in any organizational setting. He also identified five basic functions or elements of management: planning, organizing, commanding, coordinating, and controlling. These functions underlie much of the general approach to today's management theory.

Mary Parker Follett (1868–1933) was trained in philosophy and political science at what today is Radcliffe College. She applied herself in many fields, including social psychology and management. She wrote of the importance of common superordinate goals for reducing conflict in organizations.[78] Her work was popular with businesspeople of her day but was often overlooked by management scholars.[79] Follett's ideas served as a contrast to scientific management and are reemerging as applicable for modern managers dealing with rapid changes in today's global environment. Her approach to leadership stressed the importance of people rather than engineering techniques. She offered the pithy admonition, "Don't hug your blueprints," and analyzed the dynamics of management-organization interactions. Follett addressed issues that are timely today, such as ethics, power, and how to lead in a way that encourages employees to give their best. The concepts of empowerment, facilitating rather than controlling employees, and allowing employees to act depending on the

administrative principles

A subfield of the classical management perspective that focused on the total organization rather than the individual worker, delineating the management functions of planning, organizing, commanding, coordinating, and controlling.

Courtesy of Ronald G. Greenwood

Mary Parker Follett (1868–1933) Follett was a major contributor to the administrative principles approach to management. Her emphasis on worker participation and shared goals among managers was embraced by many businesspeople of the day and has been recently "rediscovered" by corporate America.

authority of the situation opened new areas for theoretical study by Chester Barnard and others.[80] Harbor Sweets is one company Mary Parker Follet would have no doubt admired.

Harbor Sweets

Benneville Strohecker created Harbor Sweets candy company in his Salem, Massachusetts, basement in 1973. Today it is a $3 million dollar business, and Strohecker is proud to have built a company that ignores convention. Increasingly, most of the workforce is part-time, with flexible hours, and is composed of a diverse group of teenagers, old-timers, the handicapped, and immigrants from countries ranging from Laos to the Dominican Republic.

Strohecker paid his 150 employees wages similar to those at McDonald's, and with no benefits except paid vacation, but they are part of a company profit-sharing plan and receive discounted candy. In a seasonal business centered around holidays, summer layoffs are common.

If you think these workers feel like exploited stepchildren, think again. Harbor Sweets attracts smart, dedicated people who stay around. Strohecker sums up the key to the company's success and the essence of his management style: "Trust still remains the most important ingredient in our recipes. But I believe it is not just being nice. Relying on trust is good business." He believed in those ideas so much, in fact, that when he was ready to let go of some responsibility and sell part of the business, he chose a former part-time worker, Phyllis LeBlanc, who had earned an MBA and moved up, first to marketing manager and then chief operating officer.

This is a lofty sentiment, and Strohecker means it. In an age of background checks and integrity profiles, he "hired by gut." Trust extended to allowing employees to fill out their own time cards. Only recently, at the request of employees, were time clocks installed at Harbor Sweets.

On occasion, Strohecker deviated from reliance on trust. He once brought in a consultant group to increase plant efficiency. What at first seemed prudent and reasonable turned out to be self-defeating, and the system was discarded. "The very fact that we were measuring is not the culture of Harbor Sweets," says Strohecker. Instead, he told his employees to work as hard as they could; they responded with many suggestions of their own, and the former sense of freedom was restored. A similar scenario evolved when a financial consultant wanted to present Strohecker some benefit options, but the boss suggested going directly to the employees. The astonished consultant was certain Strohecker has lost his mind and that the employees would plunder him. He was wrong on both counts. They decided on a package that was probably more conservative than even Strohecker would have chosen.

LeBlanc made some mistakes early on, such as investing in an expensive machine to replace handwork in making candies. The machine made a mess and the candies are once again made by hand. These mistakes resulted in poor profits, so LeBlanc introduced another efficiency effort and now shift managers have production goals. Some of the workers whisper "factory" under their breath as an accusation.

Even though the world is changing, LeBlanc is trying to hold on to Harbor's culture and its quality products. When another machine failed to wrap a candy properly, a meeting was called to get ideas from workers and the new CEO told them, comfortably, "We've had an awful lot of changes this year. And although we *are* trying to produce more candy and be more efficient, we don't want to ruin our best product!"[81]

Chester I. Barnard (1886–1961) studied economics at Harvard but failed to receive a degree because he lacked a course in laboratory science. He began his career work in the statistical department of AT&T and in 1927 became president of New Jersey Bell. One of Barnard's significant contributions was the concept of the informal organization. The *informal organization* occurs in all formal organizations and includes cliques and naturally occurring social groupings. Barnard argued that organizations are not machines and informal relationships are powerful forces that can help the organization if properly managed. Another significant contribution was the *acceptance theory of authority,* which states that people have free will and can choose whether to follow management orders. People typically follow orders because they perceive positive benefit to themselves, but they do have a choice. Managers should treat employees properly because their acceptance of authority may be critical to organization success in important situations.[82]

This 1914 photograph shows the initiation of a new arrival at a Nebraska planting camp. This initiation was not part of the formal rules and illustrates the significance of the informal organization *described by Barnard. Social values and behaviors were powerful forces that could help or hurt the planting organization depending on how they were managed.*

The overall classical perspective as an approach to management was very powerful and gave companies fundamental new skills for establishing high productivity and effective treatment of employees. Indeed, America surged ahead of the world in management techniques, and other countries, especially Japan, borrowed heavily from American ideas.

Humanistic Perspective

Mary Parker Follett and Chester Barnard were early advocates of a more **humanistic perspective** on management that emphasized the importance of understanding human behaviors, needs, and attitudes in the workplace as well as social interactions and group processes.[83] We will discuss three subfields based on the humanistic perspective: the human relations movement, the human resources perspective, and the behavioral sciences approach.

humanistic perspective

A management perspective that emerged around the late nineteenth century that emphasized understanding human behavior, needs, and attitudes in the workplace.

The Human Relations Movement

America has always espoused the spirit of human equality. However, this spirit has not always been translated into practice when it comes to power sharing between managers and workers. The human relations school of thought considers that truly effective control comes from within the individual worker rather than from strict, authoritarian control.[84] This school of thought recognized and directly responded to social pressures for enlightened treatment of employees. The early work on industrial psychology and personnel selection received little attention because of the prominence of scientific management. Then a series of studies at a Chicago electric company, which came to be known as the **Hawthorne studies**, changed all that.

Beginning about 1895, a struggle developed between manufacturers of gas and electric lighting fixtures for control of the residential and industrial market.[85] By 1909 electric lighting had begun to win, but the increasingly efficient electric fixtures used less total power. The electric companies began a campaign to convince industrial users that they needed more light to get more productivity. When advertising did not work, the industry began using experimental tests to demonstrate their argument. Managers were skeptical about the results, so the Committee on Industrial Lighting (CIL) was set up to run the tests. To further add to the tests' credibility, Thomas Edison was made honorary chairman of the CIL. In one test location—the Hawthorne plant of the Western Electric Company—some interesting events occurred.

Hawthorne studies

A series of experiments on worker productivity begun in 1924 at the Hawthorne plant of Western Electric Company in Illinois; attributed employees' increased output to managers' better treatment of them during the study.

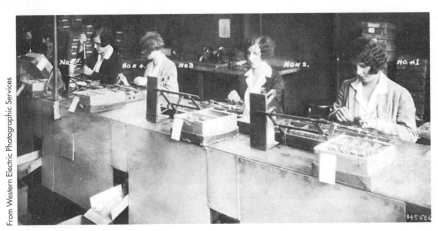

From Western Electric Photographic Services

This is the Relay Room of the Western Electric Hawthorne, Illinois, plant in 1927. Six women worked in this relay assembly test room during the controversial experiment on employee productivity. Professors Mayo and Roethlisberger evaluated conditions such as rest breaks and workday length, physical health, amount of sleep, and diet. Experimental changes were fully discussed with the women and were abandoned if they disapproved. Gradually the researchers began to realize they had created a change in supervisory style and human relations, which they believed was the true cause of the increased productivity.

human relations movement

A movement in management thinking and practice that emphasized satisfaction of employees' basic needs as the key to increased worker productivity.

The major part of this work involved four experimental and three control groups. In all, five different "tests" were conducted. These pointed to the importance of factors *other* than illumination in affecting productivity. To more carefully examine these factors, numerous other experiments were conducted.[86] The results of the most famous study, the first Relay Assembly Test Room (RATR) experiment, were extremely controversial. Under the guidance of two Harvard professors, Elton Mayo and Fritz Roethlisberger, the RATR studies lasted nearly six years (May 10, 1927, to May 4, 1933) and involved 24 separate experimental periods. So many factors were changed and so many unforeseen factors remained uncontrolled that scholars disagree on the factors that truly contributed to the general increase in performance over that period. Most early interpretations, however, agreed on one thing: Money was not the cause of the increased output.[87] It was believed that the factor that best explained increased output was "human relations." Employees performed better when managers treated them in a positive manner. However, recent reanalyses of the experiments have revealed that a number of factors were different for the workers involved, and some suggest that money may well have been the single most important factor.[88] An interview with one of the original participants revealed that just getting into the experimental group had meant a huge increase in income.[89]

These new data clearly show that money mattered a great deal at Hawthorne. In addition, worker productivity increased partly as a result of the increased feelings of importance and group pride employees felt by virtue of being selected for this important project.[90] One unintended contribution of the experiments was a rethinking of field research practices. Researchers and scholars realized that the researcher can influence the outcome of an experiment by being too closely involved with research subjects. This has come to be known as the *Hawthorne effect* in research methodology. Subjects behaved differently because of the active participation of researchers in the Hawthorne experiments.[91]

From a historical perspective, whether the studies were academically sound is of less importance than the fact that they stimulated an increased interest in looking at employees as more than extensions of production machinery. The interpretation that employees' output increased when managers treated them in a positive manner started a revolution in worker treatment for improving organizational productivity. Despite flawed methodology or inaccurate conclusions, the findings provided the impetus for the **human relations movement**. IBM was one of the earliest proponents of a human relations approach. This approach shaped management theory and practice for well over a quarter-century, and the belief that human relations is the best approach for increasing productivity persists today.

The Human Resources Perspective

The human relations movement initially espoused a "dairy farm" view of management—contented cows give more milk, so satisfied workers will give more work. Gradually, views with deeper content began to emerge. The human resources perspective maintained an interest in worker participation and considerate leadership but shifted the emphasis to consider the daily tasks that people perform. The **human resources perspective** combines prescriptions for design of job tasks with theories of motivation.[92] In the human resources view, jobs should be designed so that tasks are not perceived as dehumanizing or demeaning but instead allow workers to use their full potential. Two of the best-known contributors to the human resources perspective were Abraham Maslow and Douglas McGregor.

Abraham Maslow (1908–1970), a practicing psychologist, observed that his patients' problems usually stemmed from an inability to satisfy their needs. Thus, he generalized his work and suggested a hierarchy of needs. Maslow's hierarchy started with physiological needs and progressed to safety, belongingness, esteem, and, finally, self-actualization needs. Chapter 13 discusses his ideas in more detail.

Douglas McGregor (1906–1964) had become frustrated with the early simplistic human relations notions while president of Antioch College in Ohio. He challenged both the classical perspective and the early human relations assumptions about human behavior. Based on his experiences as a manager and consultant, his training as a psychologist, and the work of Maslow, McGregor formulated his Theory X and Theory Y, which are explained in Exhibit 1.10.[93] McGregor believed that the classical perspective was based on Theory X assumptions about workers. He also felt that a slightly modified version of Theory X fit early human relations ideas. In other words, human relations ideas did not go far enough. McGregor proposed Theory Y as a more realistic view of workers for guiding management thinking.

The point of Theory Y is that organizations can take advantage of the imagination and intellect of all their employees. Employees will exercise self-control and will contribute to organizational goals when given the opportunity. A few

human resources perspective
A management perspective that suggests jobs should be designed to meet higher-level needs by allowing workers to use their full potential.

[handwritten margin note: Self acualization / esteem / social / safety / phisiclited]

Assumptions of Theory X
- The average human being has an inherent dislike of work and will avoid it if possible....
- Because of the human characteristic of dislike for work, most people must be coerced, controlled, directed, or threatened with punishment to get them to put forth adequate effort toward the achievement of organizational objectives....
- The average human being prefers to be directed, wishes to avoid responsibility, has relatively little ambition, wants security above all.

Assumptions of Theory Y
- The expenditure of physical and mental effort in work is as natural as play or rest. The average human being does not inherently dislike work....
- External control and the threat of punishment are not the only means for bringing about effort toward organizational objectives. A person will exercise self-direction and self-control in the service of objectives to which he or she is committed....
- The average human being learns, under proper conditions, not only to accept but to seek responsibility....
- The capacity to exercise a relatively high degree of imagination, ingenuity, and creativity in the solution of organizational problems is widely, not narrowly, distributed in the population.
- Under the conditions of modern industrial life, the intellectual potentialities of the average human being are only partially utilized.

EXHIBIT 1.10

Theory X and Theory Y

SOURCE: Douglas McGregor, *The Human Side of Enterprise* (New York: McGraw-Hill, 1960), 33–48.

companies today still use Theory X management, but many are trying Theory Y techniques. One organization that taps into the full potential of every worker by operating from Theory Y assumptions is Finland's SOL Cleaning Service.

SOL Cleaning Service

http://www.sol.fi

They work in one of the world's least glamorous industries, but employees at SOL love their jobs. The industrial cleaning business is characterized by back-breaking labor, low wages, high turnover, and lousy service. SOL, however, presents a different picture—that of a fast-paced, high-energy, knowledge-driven company with happy employees and superior customer service. Each SOL supervisor leads a team of up to 50 cleaners who cheerfully fan out across Finland each morning wearing bright red-and-yellow jumpsuits. The company headquarters in Helsinki explodes with color and creativity. Employees wander the halls talking on bright-yellow cordless phones and meet in rooms that look more like playgrounds than offices. In Finland, and increasingly across Europe, SOL is known as an icon of what it takes to win in today's tough business environment.

Part of SOL's success is its management approach based on Theory Y assumptions. There are no job titles, executive perks, or assigned parking spaces and other status symbols at SOL. Everyone is considered equal, and each employee's contribution is valued. In addition, SOL has no individual offices and no set working hours. All work is performed by self-directed teams that create their own budgets, do their own hiring, set their own performance goals, and negotiate their own arrangements with customers. Employees actively and enthusiastically strive toward meeting goals and solving customer problems. If a team builds up enough business, it can set up its own satellite office and run it like a minibusiness. SOL also has a training program that would be the envy of any high-tech corporation, providing training in topics such as time management, budgeting, relationship skills, and customer service.

By operating from Theory Y principles, SOL has turned cleaners into entrepreneurs and changed the perception of the industrial cleaning industry in Finland. Few people grow up dreaming of becoming an industrial cleaner, but at SOL employees are motivated and fulfilled, committed to doing their best for the team, the company, and the customer.[94]

The Behavioral Sciences Approach

behavioral sciences approach

A subfield of the humanistic management perspective that applies social science in an organizational context, drawing from economics, psychology, sociology, and other disciplines.

The **behavioral sciences approach** develops theories about human behavior based on scientific methods and study. Behavioral science draws from sociology, psychology, anthropology, economics, and other disciplines to understand employee behavior and interaction in an organizational setting. The approach can be seen in practically every organization. When General Electric conducts research to determine the best set of tests, interviews, and employee profiles to use when selecting new employees, it is employing behavioral science techniques. When Gap clothing stores train new managers in the techniques of employee motivation, most of the theories and findings are rooted in behavioral science research. Behavioral science can help us understand how people work and how work systems develop, such as the use of paper in the history of organizations, as described in the Best Practices box.

All of the remaining chapters of this book contain research findings and management applications that can be attributed to the behavioral sciences approach.

BEST PRACTICES

What Happened to Paperless?

The next time you take an airplane trip, think of this: As the plane takes off, the flight information (type of plane, requested altitude, destination, radar ID) is printed on a stiff piece of paper called a flight strip. As the plane flies up and down, goes through different air sectors, changes speeds, and so on, the air traffic controller jots down notes and moves the flight strip around on his or her desk. This is all done while also watching a large radar console, talking with up to 25 different planes, and jotting down notes on those other 24 flight strips. Air traffic control depends not only on technology, but also on good old-fashioned paper and pencil. In this era of high-tech breakthroughs, why must airplane handling be managed like breakfast orders at an all-night diner?

Several years ago, Apple studied the phenomenon of paper on desks and found that it has great significance. Office workers can wax eloquent about each pile of papers and how important it is. The team found that papers represent active and ongoing thinking, that knowledge workers use desk space to organize their thoughts and to separate out the items that they haven't yet figured out how to categorize. Messy desks might, in fact, be a sign of complex work and thinking.

Large organizations where complex reports are developed find that paper is more efficient than electronic documents. Professionals at the International Monetary Fund work on each sheet and lay the paper out in front of the group. Pieces are passed around, annotated, and later reassembled; tasks that are more cumbersome are done on computers.

How did we get to this situation, anyway? The paper proliferation began at the end of the nineteenth century with the advent of large corporations and scientific management. Coping with the new complexities of the industrial economy meant weekly sales reports, company newsletters, and office manuals. The typewriter was an innovation back then, which made it possible to create documents quickly, especially when carbon paper arrived soon after. A secretary in a railroad company, for example, could type up 10 copies of the railroad schedule and send them to stations on the rail line. This was efficiency and control, but what could be done with all this paper? Papers were stored in cumbersome cases or in pigeonholes in secretaries' desks.

Melvil Dewey devoted his life work to cataloging information. He is renowned for founding the Dewey decimal system for organizing library books, but he also developed the vertical file, a place where all those pieces of paper could be put and not become lost—such as filing railroad schedules under "S."

Modern knowledge work is characterized by the pile rather than the file. People who pressure others to keep their desks clean are harking back to the values of the nineteenth-century, when paper was considered best put away. Who needs files anyway, when computers are much more efficient information storers? The issue for modern workers is not to use less paper, but to keep less. If the purpose of paper nowadays is to help promote creative thinking, then once that thinking is expressed, the paper has served its purpose and is ready for the round file—the recycling bin.

SOURCE: Malcom Gladwell, "The Social Life of Paper," *The New Yorker* (March 25, 2002), 92–96; Abigail Sellen and Richard Harper, *The Myth of the Paperless Office* (Cambridge, Mass.: MIT Press, 2002).

Management Science Perspective

World War II caused many management changes. The massive and complicated problems associated with modern global warfare presented managerial decision makers with the need for more sophisticated tools than ever before. The **management science perspective** emerged to address those problems. This view is distinguished for its application of mathematics, statistics, and other quantitative techniques to management decision making and problem solving. During World War II, groups of mathematicians, physicists, and other scientists were formed to solve military problems. Because those problems frequently involved moving massive amounts of materials and large numbers of people quickly and efficiently, the techniques had obvious applications to large-scale business firms.[95]

Operations research grew directly out of the World War II groups (called *operational research teams* in Great Britain and *operations research teams* in the

management science perspective

A management perspective that emerged after World War II and applied mathematics, statistics, and other quantitative techniques to managerial problems.

United States).[96] It consists of mathematical model building and other applications of quantitative techniques to managerial problems.

Operations management refers to the field of management that specializes in the physical production of goods or services. Operations management specialists use quantitative techniques to solve manufacturing problems. Some of the commonly used methods are forecasting, inventory modeling, linear and nonlinear programming, queuing theory, scheduling, simulation, and break-even analysis.

Information technology (IT) is the most recent subfield of the management science perspective, which is often reflected in management information systems. These systems are designed to provide relevant information to managers in a timely and cost-efficient manner. More recently, information technology within organizations has evolved to include intranets and extranets, as well as various software programs that help managers estimate costs, plan and track production, manage projects, allocate resources, or schedule employees. When Weyerhaeuser Company's door factory implemented an intranet combined with software to track inventory, calculate estimates, schedule production, and automate order-taking, it was applying information technology to cut both manufacturing costs and production time.[97]

Most of today's organizations have departments of information technology specialists to help them apply management science techniques to complex organizational problems. IT specialists helped Turner Industries, a large-scale construction company, develop a system that combines project estimating and control systems with planning and scheduling software that can automatically calculate the cost of a project down to the last nail and then track costs and construction progress on a daily basis.[98]

Total Quality Management

The quality movement in Japan emerged partly as a result of American influence after World War II. The ideas of W. Edwards Deming, known as the "father of the quality movement," were initially scoffed at in America, but the Japanese embraced his theories and modified them to help rebuild their industries into world powers.[99] Japanese companies achieved a significant departure from the American model by gradually shifting from an inspection-oriented approach to quality control toward an approach emphasizing employee involvement in the prevention of quality problems.[100]

total quality management (TQM)

A concept that focuses on managing the total organization to deliver quality to customers. Four significant elements of TQM are employee involvement, focus on the customer, benchmarking, and continuous improvement.

During the 1980s and into the 1990s, **total quality management (TQM)**, which focuses on managing the total organization to deliver quality to customers, was at the forefront in helping managers deal with global competition. The approach infuses quality values throughout every activity within a company, with front-line workers intimately involved in the process. Four significant elements of quality management are employee involvement, focus on the customer, benchmarking, and continuous improvement.

Employee involvement means that TQM requires companywide participation in quality control. All employees are *focused on the customer;* TQM companies find out what customers want and try to meet their needs and expectations. *Benchmarking* refers to a process whereby companies find out how others do something better than they do and then try to imitate or improve on it. *Continuous improvement* is the implementation of small, incremental improvements in all areas of the organization on an ongoing basis. TQM is not a quick fix, but companies such as Motorola, Procter & Gamble, and DuPont have achieved astonishing results in efficiency, quality, and customer satisfaction through total quality management.[101] TQM is still an important part of today's organizations, and many companies pursue challenging quality goals to demonstrate their commitment to improving quality. For example, *Six Sigma* is a highly ambitious quality standard popularized by Motorola that specifies a goal of no more than 3.4 defects per million parts. Numerous companies, including DuPont, Texas Instruments, General Electric, and Nokia, pursue Six Sigma quality standards.

■ Summary and Management Solution

This chapter introduced a number of important concepts and described the changing nature of management. High performance requires the efficient and effective use of organizational resources through the four management functions of planning, organizing, leading, and controlling. To perform the four functions, managers need three skills—conceptual, human, and technical. Conceptual skills are more important at the top of the hierarchy; human skills are important at all levels; and technical skills are most important for first-line managers.

Two characteristics of managerial work also were explained in the chapter: (1) Managerial activities involve variety, fragmentation, and brevity and (2) Managers perform a great deal of work at an unrelenting pace. Managers are expected to perform activities associated with ten roles: the informational roles of monitor, disseminator, and spokesperson; the interpersonal roles of figurehead, leader, and liaison; and the decisional roles of entrepreneur, disturbance handler, resource allocator, and negotiator.

These management characteristics apply to small businesses, entrepreneurial start-ups, and not-for-profit organizations just as they do in large corporations. In addition, they are being applied in a new workplace and a rapidly changing world. In the new workplace, work is free-flowing and flexible to encourage speed and adaptation, and empowered employees are expected to seize opportunities and solve problems. The workplace is organized around networks rather than vertical hierarchies, and work is often virtual. These changing characteristics have resulted from forces such as advances in technology and e-business, globalization, increased diversity, and a growing emphasis on change and speed over stability and efficiency. Managers need new skills and competencies in this new environment. Leadership is dispersed and empowering. Customer relationships are critical, and most work is done by teams that work directly with customers. In the new workplace, managers focus on building relationships, which may include customers, partners, and suppliers. In addition, they strive to build learning capability throughout the organization. An emerging need is for leadership during crises and unexpected events. Managers in crisis situations should stay calm, be visible, put people before business, tell the truth, and know when to get back to business.

Many managers are redesigning their companies toward the learning organization, which fully engages all employees in identifying and solving problems. The learning organization is characterized by a team-based structure, empowered employees, and open information. The learning organization represents a substantial departure from the traditional management hierarchy.

The shift to a learning organization goes hand-in-hand with today's transition to a technology-driven workplace. Ideas, information, and relationships are becoming more important than production machinery and physical assets, which requires new approaches to management. E-commerce is burgeoning as more economic activity takes place over digital computer networks rather than in physical space. Two specific management tools that support the digital workplace are enterprise resource planning and knowledge management. Both require managers to think in new ways about the role of employees in the organization. Managers value employees for their ability to think, build relationships, and share knowledge, which is quite different from the scientific management perspective of a century ago.

The three major perspectives on management that have evolved since the late 1800s are the classical perspective, the humanistic perspective, and the management science perspective. Each perspective has several specialized subfields. A recent extension of management perspectives is total quality management. The most recent thinking about organizations has been brought about by the shift to a new workplace.

An excellent example of a leader during difficult times is Charlene Pedrolie, the manufacturing chief of

Rowe Furniture described at the beginning of the chapter. The company was losing sales because of slow turnaround time for custom goods and workers were stuck in boring and dead-end jobs. The first goal was to develop an online ordering system in showrooms throughout the country, to get orders in quicker. But the system of manufacturing had to change too. Here's where Pedrolie's abilities were shown. Trained as a chemical engineer, she had supervised a soap line for Lever Brothers and understood some of the more innovative techniques in manufacturing. But Pedrolie knew it needed more than that. It needed the collective wisdom of many competent people, those employees who did the sewing, gluing, cutting, and so on. She brought them together and used their knowledge to redesign the process. She cross-trained them in other skills, so that cutters learned gluing and stapling. Entire departments were eliminated as people learned a set of various skills, while the 500 employees were organized into units called clusters, or "cells." Each cell started from ground zero and designed the most efficient process they could. It was confusing at first, once the new system was in place, as people were bumping into each other. But Pedrolie pushed forward. She gave everyone access to whatever information they needed on the spot, and she encouraged people to talk across normal boundaries, including from production workers to retailers. The result: a new culture of innovation in the plant, which also resulted in an on-site day-care center and a company concierge, which saved the plant 784 hours of lost worker time in the first six months. Plus no more bored workers. Turnaround time for orders is now at 30 days and quality has increased. Pedrolie brought about a company turnaround.[102]

■ Discussion Questions

1. How do you feel about having a manager's responsibility in today's world characterized by uncertainty, ambiguity, and sudden changes or threats from the environment? Describe some skills and qualities that are important to managers under these conditions.

2. What is the difference between efficiency and effectiveness? Which is more important for performance? Can an organization succeed in both simultaneously?

3. What changes in management functions and skills might occur as one is promoted up the management hierarchy? How can managers acquire the new skills?

4. If managerial work is characterized by variety, fragmentation, and brevity, how do managers perform basic management functions such as planning, which would seem to require reflection and analysis?

5. A college professor told her students, "The purpose of a management course is to teach students *about* management, not to teach them to be managers." Do you agree or disagree with this statement? Discuss.

6. Describe the characteristics of the new workplace. How do these characteristics compare to those of an organization in which you have worked?

7. Why is it important to understand the different perspectives and approaches to management theory that have evolved throughout the history of organizations?

8. How do societal forces influence the practice and theory of management? Do you think management techniques are a response to these forces?

9. Based on your experience at work or school, describe some ways in which the principles of scientific management and bureaucracy are still used in organizations. Do you believe these characteristics will ever cease to be a part of organizational life? Discuss.

10. A management professor once said that for successful management, studying the present was most important, studying the past was next, and studying the future was least important. Do you agree? Why?

11. Which of the three characteristics of learning organizations do you find most appealing? Which would be hardest for you to adopt?

12. As organizations become more technology-driven, which do you think will become more important—the management of the human element of the organization or the management of technology? Discuss.

13. What is the behavioral sciences approach? How does it differ from earlier approaches to management?

14. Why can an event such as the Hawthorne studies be a major turning point in the history of management even if the idea is later shown to be in error? Discuss.

15. Do you think management theory will ever be as precise as theories in the fields of physics, chemistry, or experimental psychology? Why or why not?

16. Many e-commerce companies have gone out of business and others are struggling. Would you consider a career in e-commerce at this time? Why or why not?

■ Manager's Workbook

Management Aptitude Questionnaire

Rate each of the following questions according to the following scale:

	1 I never am like this.	2 I rarely am like this.	3 I some-times am like this.	4 I often am like this.	5 I always am like this.
1. When I have a number of tasks or homework to do, I set priorities and organize the work around deadlines.	1	2	3	4	5
2. Most people would describe me as a good listener.	1	2	3	4	5
3. When I am deciding on a particular course of action for myself (such as hobbies to pursue, languages to study, which job to take, special projects to be involved in), I typically consider the long-term (three years or more) implications of what I would choose to do.	1	2	3	4	5
4. I prefer technical or quantitative courses rather than those involving literature, psychology, or sociology.	1	2	3	4	5
5. When I have a disagreement with someone, I hang in there and talk it out until it is completely resolved.	1	2	3	4	5
6. When I have a project or assignment, I really get into the details rather than the "big picture" issues.*	5	4	3	2	1
7. I would rather sit in front of my computer than spend a lot of time with people.	1	2	3	4	5
8. I try to include others in activities or discussions.	1	2	3	4	5
9. When I take a course, I relate what I am learning to other courses I have taken or concepts I have learned elsewhere.	1	2	3	4	5
10. When somebody makes a mistake, I want to correct the person and let her or him know the proper answer or approach.*	5	4	3	2	1
11. I think it is better to be efficient with my time when talking with someone, rather than worry about the other person's needs, so that I can get on with my real work.	1	2	3	4	5
12. I know my long-term vision of career, family, and other activities and have thought it over carefully.	1	2	3	4	5
13. When solving problems, I would much rather analyze some data or statistics than meet with a group of people.	1	2	3	4	5
14. When I am working on a group project and someone doesn't pull a fair share of the load, I am more likely to complain to my friends than to confront the slacker.*	5	4	3	2	1
15. Talking about ideas or concepts can get me really enthused or excited.	1	2	3	4	5
16. The type of management course for which this book is used is really a waste of time.	1	2	3	4	5
17. I think it is better to be polite and not to hurt people's feelings.*	5	4	3	2	1
18. Data or things interest me more than people.	1	2	3	4	5

*reverse scoring item

Scoring key

Add the total points for the following sections. Note that starred * items are reverse scored, as such:

1 I always am like this.
2 I often am like this.

3 I sometimes am like this.
4 I rarely am like this.
5 I never am like this.

1, 3, 6, 9, 12, 15   Conceptual skills total score _____
2, 5, 8, 10, 14, 17   **H**uman skills total score _____
4, 7, 11, 13, 16, 18 **T**echnical skills total score _____

These skills are three abilities needed to be a good manager. Ideally, a manager should be strong (though not necessarily equal) in all three. Anyone noticeably weaker in any of the skills should take courses and read to build up that skill. For further background on the three skills, please refer to the model on page 10.

Note: This exercise was contributed by Dorothy Marcic.

■ Manager's Workshop

The Absolute Worst Manager

1. By yourself, think of two managers you have had—the best and the worst. Write down a few sentences to describe each.

The best manager I ever had was . . .

The worst manager I ever had was . . .

2. Divide into groups of five to seven members. Share your experiences. Each group should choose a couple of examples to share with the whole group. Complete the table below as a group.

	Management principle followed or broken	Skills evident or missing	Lessons to be learned	Advice you would give managers
The best managers				
The worst managers				

3. What are the common problems managers have?

4. Prepare a list of "words of wisdom" you would give as a presentation to a group of managers. What are some basic principles they should use to be effective?

■ Management in Practice: Ethical Dilemma

Can Management Afford to Look the Other Way?

Harry Rull had been with Shellington Pharmaceuticals for 30 years. After a tour of duty in the various plants and 7 years overseas, Harry was back at headquarters, looking forward to his new role as vice president of U.S. Marketing.

Two weeks into his new job, Harry received some unsettling news about one of the managers under his supervision. During casual lunch conversation, the director of human resources mentioned that Harry should expect a phone call about Roger Jacobs, Manager of New Product Development. Jacobs had a history of being "pretty horrible" to his subordinates, she said, and one disgruntled employee had asked to speak to someone in senior management. After lunch, Harry did some follow-up work. Jacobs's performance reviews had been stellar, but his personnel file also contained a large number of notes documenting charges of Jacobs's mistreatment of subordinates. The complaints ranged from "inappropriate and derogatory remarks" to subsequently dropped charges of sexual harassment. What was more disturbing was that the amount as well as the severity of complaints had increased with each of Jacobs's ten years with Shellington.

When Harry questioned the company president about the issue, he was told, "Yeah, he's had some problems, but you can't just replace someone with an eye for new products. You're a bottom-line guy; you understand why we let these things slide." Not sure how to handle the situation, Harry met briefly with Jacobs and reminded him to "keep the team's morale up." Just after the meeting, Sally Barton from HR called to let him know the problem she'd mentioned over lunch had been worked out. However, she warned, another employee had now come forward demanding that her complaints be addressed by senior management.

What Do You Do?

1. Ignore the problem. Jacobs's contributions to new product development are too valuable to risk losing him, and the problems over the past ten years have always worked them- selves out anyway. No sense starting something that could make you look bad.

2. Launch a full-scale investigation of employee complaints about Jacobs, and make Jacobs aware that the documented history over the past ten years has put him on thin ice.

3. Meet with Jacobs and the employee to try to resolve the cur- rent issue, then start working with Sally Barton and other senior managers to develop stronger policies regarding sex- ual harassment and treatment of employees, including clear-cut procedures for handling complaints.

SOURCE: Based on Doug Wallace, "A Talent for Mismanagement," *What Would You Do? Business Ethics*, Vol. II (November–December 1992), 3–4.

■ Surf the Net

1. **Web Research.** You will be asked in many of the "Surf the Net" exercises throughout the text to locate information on the Web. This exercise is designed to help you improve your Web research skills. After spending some time at one of the Web Tutorial links listed below, outline three new ideas you discovered that would help you to find what you are looking for on the Web.
   UC Berkeley's Teaching Library Internet Workshops:
   http://www.lib.berkeley.edu/TeachingLib/Guides/Internet/FindInfo.html
   University of South Carolina's Basic Tutorial on Searching the Web:
   http://www.sc.edu/beaufort/library/bones.html

2. **Management Occupations.** The U.S. Department of Labor's Bureau of Labor Statistics uses the Standard Occu- pational Classification (SOC) system to classify workers into one of more than 820 occupations according to their occupational definition. To facilitate classification, occu- pations requiring similar job duties, skills, education, or experience are combined to form 23 major groups.
   Go to *http://stats.bls.gov/soc/soc_majo.htm* to see the 23 major groups; choose the link for "Management Occupa- tions." Select one management occupation of interest to you under each of the four minor groups (11-1000 Top Executives; 11-2000 Advertising, Marketing, Promotions, Public Relations, and Sales Managers; 11-3000 Operations Specialties Managers; and 11-9000 Other Management Occupations). List the SOC number, occupation title, and description for the four occupations you selected.

3. **Ten Manager Roles.** Find and read a feature story on a current leader of an organization. Look for examples of the leader performing activities from those listed in Exhibit 1.3, "Ten Manager Roles." On your sheet of paper, identify the source of your article, the leader featured, and the roles you identified the individual fulfilling, along with a brief description of the activity the individual performed. Use any of the links below to access current issues of busi- ness periodicals that often include feature stories on orga- nizational leaders.
   http://www.business2.com
   http://www.businessweek.com
   http://www.fastcompany.com
   http://www.forbes.com
   http://www.fortune.com
   http://www.inc.com
   http://www.redherring.com

■ Case for Critical Analysis

Electra-Quik

Barbara Russell, a manufacturing vice president, walked into the monthly companywide meeting with a light step and a hopefulness she hadn't felt in a long time. The company's new, dynamic CEO was going to announce a new era of empower- ment at Electra-Quik, an 80-year-old, publicly held company that had once been a leading manufacturer and retailer of elec- trical products and supplies. In recent years, the company experienced a host of problems: market share was declining in the face of increased foreign and domestic competition; new product ideas were few and far between; departments such as manufacturing and sales barely spoke to one another; morale was at an all-time low, and many employees were actively seeking other jobs. Everyone needed a dose of hope.

Martin Griffin, who had been hired to revive the failing company, briskly opened the meeting with a challenge: "As we face increasing competition, we need new ideas, new energy, new spirit to make this company great. And the source for this change is you—each one of you." He then went on to explain that under the new empowerment campaign, employees would be getting more information about how the company was run and would be able to work with their fellow employees in new and creative ways. Martin proclaimed a new era of trust and cooperation at Electra-Quik. Barbara felt the excitement stirring within her; but as she looked around the room, she saw many of the other employees, including her friend Harry, rolling their eyes. "Just another pile of corporate crap," Harry said later. "One minute they try downsizing, the next re-engineering. Then they dabble in restructuring. Now Martin wants to push empowerment. Garbage like empowerment isn't a substitute for hard work and a little faith in the people who have been with this company for years. We made it great once, and we can do it again. Just get out of our way." Harry had been a manufacturing engineer with Electra-Quik for more than 20 years. Barbara knew he was extremely loyal to the company, but he—and a lot of others like him—were going to be an obstacle to the empowerment efforts.

Top management assigned selected managers to several problem-solving teams to come up with ideas for implementing the empowerment campaign. Barbara loved her assignment as team leader of the manufacturing team, working on ideas to improve how retail stores got the merchandise they needed when they needed it. The team thrived, and trust blossomed among the members. They even spent nights and weekends working to complete their report. They were proud of their ideas, which they believed were innovative but easily achievable: permit a manager to follow a product from design through sales to customers; allow salespeople to refund up to $500 worth of merchandise on the spot; make information available to salespeople about future products; and swap sales and manufacturing personnel for short periods to let them get to know one another's jobs.

When the team presented its report to department heads, Martin Griffin was enthusiastic. But shortly into the meeting he had to excuse himself because of a late-breaking deal with a major hardware store chain. With Martin absent, the department heads rapidly formed a wall of resistance. The director of human resources complained that the ideas for personnel changes would destroy the carefully crafted job categories that had just been completed. The finance department argued that allowing salespeople to make $500 refunds would create a gold mine for unethical customers and salespeople. The legal department warned that providing information to salespeople about future products would invite industrial spying.

The team members were stunned. As Barbara mulled over the latest turn of events, she considered her options: keep her mouth shut, take a chance and confront Martin about her sincerity in making empowerment work, push slowly for reform and work for gradual support from the other teams, or look for another job and leave a company she really cared about. Barbara realized there would be no easy choices and no easy answers.

Questions

1. How might top management have done a better job changing Electra-Quik into a new kind of organization? What might they do now to get the empowerment process back on track?
2. Can you think of ways Barbara could have avoided the problems her team faced in the meeting with department heads?
3. If you were Barbara Russell, what would you do now? Why?

SOURCE: Based on Lawrence R. Rothstein, "The Empowerment Effort That Came Undone," *Harvard Business Review* (January–February 1995), 20–31.

The Environment of Management

A good leader knows there is nothing as constant as change in the music business. It is an intensely competitive industry where a relative handful of gatekeepers must decide which creative endeavors enter the marketplace. After that decision is made, the public decides what is a hit or who is a star. The leader of a recording label develops and maintains good relationships with the gatekeepers so that the label's artists will have every opportunity to be heard by fans and consumers. Positive relationships between leaders at a label and radio programmers, retailers, distributors, concert promoters, publishing agents, and booking agents create a positive environment for an artist's work to be received.

There is a great deal of uncertainty in the music industry but, at the same time, there are basic patterns that often lead to success. For example, a major label has distribution, so the recordings will be available to stores; the label will have a promotional department to keep in touch with radio stations; and if a recording is a "hit," the print and TV media will want to interview and present the artist, and consumers will want to purchase the recording and attend a show.

The Environment and Corporate Culture

LEARNING OBJECTIVES

After studying this chapter, you should be able to

1 Describe the general and task environments and the dimensions of each.

2 Explain the strategies managers use to help organizations adapt to an uncertain environment.

3 Define corporate culture and give organizational examples.

4 Explain organizational symbols, stories, heroes, slogans, and ceremonies and their relationship to corporate culture.

5 Describe how corporate culture relates to the environment.

6 Define a cultural leader and explain the tools a cultural leader uses to change corporate culture.

Management Challenge

When the economy is strong, building a business doesn't necessarily take as much discipline as when times are bad. Ask Rick Sapio. When he started his Dallas-based mutuals.com to provide direct sales mutual-fund advisory services, as well as account management, for a flat fee, he found it easy to raise money.

It all started back when Rick was watching a television interview with the founder of flowers.com, and Rick wondered why Charles Schwab never thought of opening a similar service. Before you could say dial 1–800, Rick had a new telephone number: 1-800-MUTUALS. Not long after, he dropped everything, quit his engineering job, and began to pursue a longtime dream—to start a financial company. He moved from Hackensack, New Jersey, to Dallas, Texas, in a U-Haul, and began to look for investors.

Sapio raised $14 million during those early years. Raising so much money was not necessarily a good thing, because he became accustomed to spending high, as well. Even though revenues were increasing by 114 percent a year, mutuals.com was consistently in debt. Maybe it was because of the extra office the CEO—Sapio—wanted in lower Manhattan. Or perhaps it was because the company sponsored gym memberships, expensive parking spaces, and membership dues to professional organizations for its employees. Not to mention that Sapio paid himself generously (wasn't he worth it?). Then there was $400,000 spent on television advertising, which resulted in very few new customers. Employees spent freely, too. And why not? They were bringing in plenty of money from accounts and investors.

None of this spending was a problem until the stock market crashed in 2000. A great number of dot-com businesses went into bankruptcy as investments dwindled. Sapio's company was headed on a downward spiral and the future was not rosy.[1]

If you were Sapio, how would you keep the company afloat at a time when investors and other sources of revenue were fleeing for the hills?

Rick Sapio is being challenged by forces greater than he is—first a booming economy that perhaps led to unhealthy growth, and then a collapsed stock market, threatening the livelihood of the entire company.

Even in a seemingly simple, low-tech industry such as manufacturing baby food, challenges from the environment can wreak havoc on an organization's reputation, sales, and profits, as Gerber's found when some if its baby foods were criticized for using genetically altered corn, which some environmental groups claimed contained toxins.[2] In high-tech industries, environmental conditions are even more volatile. Xerox, one of the original high-tech companies emerging after World War II, once owned the copier market, but has suffered huge losses in recent years, partly because managers misread cues from the environment and changes in technology needs.

Dialog Corp., the pioneer of the data-retrieval industry founded by Lockheed in 1963, is now fighting for its life after managers missed an opportunity to become a leader of the Internet revolution. "Dialog had a chance at the inception of the Web to index it, in essence to be a Yahoo!," says Jeffrey Gault, former head of the business. "But we passed on it because we couldn't see how we could make money on it."[3] The environment surprises many companies. Bookstores such as Barnes & Noble and Borders were caught napping when a new approach to bookselling emerged. Amazon.com was ringing up sales on the Internet for a year before Barnes & Noble managers even began thinking about selling online, and the company had a whopping three-year head start over Borders' online site.[4]

Government actions and red tape can also affect an organization's environment and foment a crisis. Deregulation of the electric utilities industry is forcing a massive restructuring of power companies in states such as California, Texas, and Massachusetts, and will eventually impact companies all across the United States. Changes in Medicaid are hurting hospitals such as La Rabida, on Chicago's South Side, which is dedicated to serving the poor.[5]

The study of management traditionally has focused on factors within the organization—a closed systems view—such as leading, motivating, and controlling employees. The classical, behavioral, and management science schools described in Chapter 1 focused on internal aspects of organizations over which managers have direct control. These views are accurate but incomplete. Globalization and the trend toward a borderless world affect companies in new ways. Even for those companies that try to operate solely on the domestic stage, events that have greatest impact typically originate in the external environment. To be effective, managers must monitor and respond to the environment—an open systems view. This chapter explores in detail components of the external environment and how they affect the organization. We will also examine a major part of the organization's internal environment—corporate culture. Corporate culture is shaped by the external environment and is an important part of the context within which managers do their jobs.

The External Environment

organizational environment

All elements existing outside the organization's boundaries that have the potential to affect the organization.

The world as we know it is undergoing tremendous and far-reaching changes. These changes can be understood by defining and examining components of the external environment.

The external **organizational environment** includes all elements existing outside the boundary of the organization that have the potential to affect the

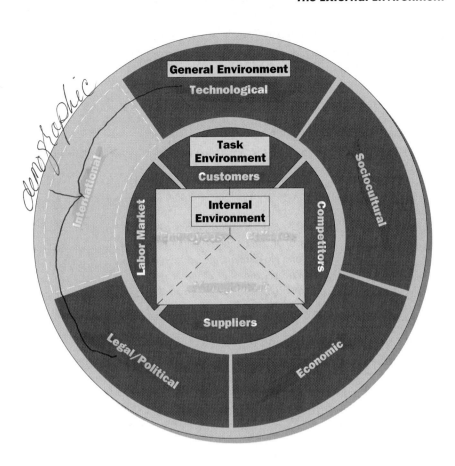

EXHIBIT *2.1*

Location of the Organization's General, Task, and Internal Environments

organization.[6] The environment includes competitors, resources, technology, and economic conditions that influence the organization. It does not include those events so far removed from the organization that their impact is not perceived.

The organization's external environment can be further conceptualized as having two layers: general and task environments, as illustrated in Exhibit 2.1.[7]

The **general environment** is the outer layer that is widely dispersed and affects organizations indirectly. It includes social, demographic, and economic factors that influence all organizations about equally. Increases in the inflation rate or the percentage of dual-career couples in the workforce are part of the organization's general environment. These events do not directly change day-to-day operations, but they do affect all organizations eventually. One way they impact is by creating parents who have more demands for educating their young children, a situation one company is capitalizing on, as shown in the example below.

general environment

The layer of the external environment that affects the organization indirectly.

Talk about looking for trouble. The U.S. toy industry is dominated by giants: Mattel, Hasbro, Fisher Price, Little Tykes, and so on. With so many failed start-ups in recent years (anyone remember Purple Moon?), it would be foolish for a new company to introduce a toy that would compete with the big guys, wouldn't it? Not to mention that educational toys don't usually make money.

Luckily, Mike Wood and Jim Marggraff at LeapFrog didn't know that. When high-paid law partner Wood became frustrated looking for materials to teach his three-year-old to read, he started building an electronic toy to help children

LeapFrog

http://www.leapfrog.com

make the sounds that correspond to the letters of the alphabet. With a clumsy prototype in hand, he got an order for 40,000 units from Toys 'R' Us. That was enough for him to bid the law firm goodbye, raise $800,000 from friends and family, and start his own company, LeapFrog. After developing a series of follow-up toys, Wood offered $40 million for a majority stake in his company to Knowledge Universe, owned by Michael Milken (former junk-bond king of the 1980s) and others.

That's when Jim Marggraff entered the picture. He had left a lucrative job at Cisco Systems to launch an innovative globe with an interactive pen-like pointer. Marggraff's pointer combined with Wood's unit ultimately evolved into Leap-Pad, a paper book placed on top of an electronic pad. When a child touches the pen to a word in the book, the pad "speaks" that word.

Still, there were all those big toy companies to worry about. Few small companies have lived to tell about competing with the giants. In a market dominated by GameBoy, Pokémon, and PlayStation, the odds were against LeapFrog. Nevertheless, its $49.99 LeapPad became the best-selling plaything in 2000, outperforming even the red-hot Razor Skooter®. Good things just kept happening. Revenues for 2001 were $314 million, almost a 100 percent increase over 2000. With Wal-Mart and Toys 'R' Us its biggest customers, LeapFrog is now trying to increase sales to schools.

Leapfrog has also developed a prototype for an interactive adult magazine, a sort of *Time* magazine with electronic games. Marggraff says he's gotten some positive responses from publishers. Perhaps he'll try management textbooks next.[8]

task environment

The layer of the external environment that directly influences the organization's operations and performance.

internal environment

The environment within the organization's boundaries.

The **task environment** is closer to the organization and includes the sectors that conduct day-to-day transactions with the organization and directly influence its basic operations and performance. It is generally considered to include competitors, suppliers, and customers.

The organization also has an **internal environment**, which includes the elements within the organization's boundaries. The internal environment is composed of current employees, management, and especially corporate culture, which defines employee behavior in the internal environment and how well the organization will adapt to the external environment. Exhibit 2.1 illustrates the relationship among the general, task, and internal environments. As an open system, the organization draws resources from the external environment and releases goods and services back to it. We will now discuss the two layers of the external environment in more detail. Then we will discuss corporate culture, the key element in the internal environment. Other aspects of the internal environment, such as structure and technology, will be covered in Parts Four and Five of this book.

General Environment

The general environment represents the outer layer of the environment. These dimensions influence the organization over time but often are not involved in day-to-day transactions with it. The dimensions of the general environment include international, technological, sociocultural, economic, and legal–political.

international dimension

Portion of the external environment that represents events originating in foreign countries as well as opportunities for American companies in other countries.

International. The **international dimension** of the external environment represents events originating in foreign countries as well as opportunities for American companies in other countries. Note in Exhibit 2.1 that the international dimension represents a context that influences all other aspects of the external environment. The international environment provides new competitors, customers, and suppliers and shapes social, technological, and economic trends, as well.

Today, every company has to compete on a global basis. Dixon Ticonderoga Co., which makes pencils, is in trouble because of increased foreign competition, especially from low-cost pencil companies in China. Today, about 50 percent of the pencils bought in the United States come from overseas, compared to 16 percent a decade ago.[9] High-quality, low-priced automobiles from Japan and Korea have permanently changed the American automobile industry. With the development of the Internet as a place for doing business, even the smallest companies can look at the whole world as their market. When operating globally, managers have to consider legal, political, sociocultural, and economic factors not only in their home country but in various other countries as well. For example, a drop in the U.S. dollar's foreign exchange rate lowers the price of U.S. products overseas, increasing export competitiveness.

China's membership in the World Trade Organization will dramatically change the international dimension of the external environment. With 1.3 billion people, China is already an attractive market, but WTO membership will spur economic growth even more. For U.S. construction companies such as Caterpillar, and sales representative Anny Wong, pictured here, China is a dream market, with highways, dams, and buildings springing up everywhere. However, doing business in this new market also presents many challenges, such as setting up distribution chains, service centers, and dealer networks.

Many companies have had to cut prices to remain competitive in the new global economy. Economic problems in other parts of the world now have a tremendous impact on U.S. companies. Companies such as Coca-Cola, which get a large percentage of sales from Asia, are feeling the pinch of the Asian economic crisis. Russia's economic woes also are affecting U.S. companies. For example, a small distributor of vitamins and sports supplements near Nashville, Tennessee, gets 20 percent of its sales from Russia. The economic turmoil in that country, however, has left U.S.A. Laboratories struggling to get paid and make up for lost orders.[10]

The global environment represents an ever-changing and uneven playing field compared with the domestic environment. Changes in the international domain can abruptly turn the domestic environment upside down. The mad-cow epidemic in Europe affected U.S. companies in numerous ways because of concerns about the spread of the disease to the United States. The Red Cross adopted a rule against blood donations from persons who have spent six months or more in mad-cow countries, even though there's no evidence the human form of the disease is transmitted this way. The ruling has decreased the already declining supply of blood, affecting hospitals, insurance companies, and consumers, who must cope with higher health care costs.

Technological. The **technological dimension** includes scientific and technological advancements in a specific industry as well as in society at large. In recent years, this dimension has created massive and far-reaching changes for organizations in all industries. Fifteen years ago, many organizations didn't even use desktop computers. Today, computer networks, Internet access, videoconferencing capabilities, cell phones, fax machines, pagers, and laptops are practically taken for granted as the minimum tools for doing business. Technological advancements that make the Internet accessible to nearly everyone have changed the nature of competition and of organizations' relationships

technological dimension

The dimension of the general environment that includes scientific and technological advancements in the industry and society at large.

MSNBC, the cable and online television news network, was begun by Microsoft Corp. and General Electric Co.'s NBC unit in recognition of the technological dimension of the company's general environment. MSNBC positions NBC for a high-tech future where TV and the Internet are combined. With high-tech appeal beamed out of a converted warehouse in hues of metallic orange-tinted blue, MSNBC draws the affluent 25–54 age group, viewers that advertisers covet.

© Douglas Levere

to customers. Many companies are adopting technologically sophisticated e-business methods that use private networks or the Internet to handle practically all their operations. Wireless technology and new software applications are making the Internet easily accessible from a cell phone or other hand-held devices. Communications and computing devices are getting smaller, more powerful, and more affordable. A technology research firm reports that more than half of all U.S. households have a cell phone, and in eight European countries, including Finland, Portugal, and Italy, the number of cell phones is now greater than the number of fixed-line telephones.[11]

Other technological advances will also affect organizations and managers. The recent decoding of the human genome could lead to revolutionary medical advances. Cloning technology and stem cell research are raising both scientific and ethical concerns. Scientists interpreting the secrets of matter at the level of the atom have been able to create amazing new materials, such as "smart gels" that mold to human needs on cue. Shoes made with smart gels in the soles conform to the wearer's feet to achieve a perfect fit. High-tech composites, embedded with sensors that enable them to think for themselves, are being used to earthquake-proof bridges and highways as well as build better airplanes and railcars.[12] Cellular telephone technology has helped change the culture in some organizations, as shown in Digital, Inc.

sociocultural dimension

The dimension of the general environment representing the demographic characteristics, norms, customs, and values of the population within which the organization operates.

Sociocultural. The **sociocultural dimension** of the general environment represents the demographic characteristics as well as the norms, customs, and values of the general population. Important sociocultural characteristics are geographical distribution and population density, age, and education levels. Today's demographic profiles are the foundation of tomorrow's workforce and consumers. Forecasters see increased globalization of both consumer markets and the labor supply, with increasing diversity both within organizations and consumer markets.[13] Consider the following key demographic trends in the United States:

DIGITAL, INC.

Unplugged Conversations

When mobility is the key word in communications, you can't beat cell phones. North America is behind European cities, some of which have more cell phones than land lines. Changing to a cell-phone-based business communication system can change the culture of an organization. At the Swedish Postal Service's Postnet Internet subsidiary, being wireless is more than a technological advance: It is now part of the culture. There are no desks or even what might be called offices. Rooms contain a number of tables with electrical and data-connection cables. Almost no one sits at the same table each day; instead, an employee finds a spot, hooks up his or her laptop, and makes calls on the cell phone. At night, all that's left are the cables.

CEO Lisbeth Gustafsson spends most of her day walking around, making calls on her mobile phone, which is connected to the main switchboard of the postal system. "If I had a fixed phone, I would have to be in a fixed place, and that's not part of the concept. The concept here is mobility," she says. If people want to work at home, it's no sweat for the company, and the customer never knows the difference.

Cell phones are also offering new perks for business travelers. Next time you are at Helsinki airport, you will be able to call a toll-free number, order a Coca-Cola from the nearby vending machine, and have the cost posted to your cell-phone account. That kind of freedom is the "real thing" in technology.

SOURCE: Janet Guyon, "The World Is Your Office," *Fortune* (June 12, 2000), 227–234.

1. By 2050, non-Hispanic whites will make up only about half of the population, down from 74 percent in 1995. Hispanics are expected to make up nearly a quarter of the U.S. population.[14]

2. The huge post–World War II baby-boom generation is aging and losing its interest in high-cost goods. Meanwhile, their sons and daughters, sometimes called Generation Y, rival the baby boomers in size and will soon rival them in buying power.

3. The fastest-growing type of living arrangement is single-father households, which rose 62 percent in 10 years, even though two-parent and single-mother households are still much more numerous.[15]

4. The U.S. will continue to receive a flood of immigrants, largely from Asia and Mexico.

The sociocultural dimension also includes societal norms and values. A groundswell of interest in spirituality in the U.S. since the mid-1990s is beginning to affect organizations. In 1999, 78 percent of Americans reported feeling a need to experience spiritual growth, compared to only 20 percent five years earlier. Sales of books and other materials related to religion and spirituality are booming, and some companies are openly bringing spiritual values and ideas into the workplace.[16] Other sociocultural trends also affect organizations. Handgun manufacturers struggled as public acceptance and support of guns in the home fell in the wake of tragic school shootings, and then witnessed a surge in buying following the September 11, 2001, terrorist attacks. The anti-cholesterol and low-fat fervor of a few years back has cooled, hurting the profit margins of companies manufacturing healthy food products.

American consumers' growing taste for international foods reflects a change in the sociocultural dimension of the environment. Interest in Italian cuisine, for example, has been growing rapidly. Gourmet pasta maker Monterey Pasta was recently ranked as Number 26 on Fortune magazine's list of the 100 fastest-growing companies, based partly on an annual earnings-per-share growth rate of 147 percent.

© Meredith Heuer

Economic. The **economic dimension** represents the general economic health of the country or region in which the organization operates. Consumer purchasing power, the unemployment rate, and interest rates are part of an organization's economic environment. Because organizations today are operating in a global environment, the economic dimension has become exceedingly

economic dimension

The dimension of the general environment representing the overall economic health of the country or region in which the organization functions.

complex and creates even more uncertainty for managers. The economies of countries are more closely tied together now. For example, an economic recession and the decline of consumer confidence in the U.S. following the September 11 terrorist attacks affected economies and organizations around the world. Similarly, economic problems in Asia and Europe have had a tremendous impact on companies and the stock market in the United States.

One significant recent trend in the economic environment is the frequency of mergers and acquisitions. Citibank and Travelers merged to form Citigroup, Glaxo Wellcome bought out SmithKline Beecham, and Wal-Mart purchased Britain's ASDA Group. In the toy industry, the three largest toy makers—Hasbro, Mattel, and Tyco—gobbled up at least a dozen smaller competitors within a few years. At the same time, however, there is a tremendous vitality in the small business sector of the economy.

legal–political dimension

The dimension of the general environment that includes federal, state, and local government regulations and political activities designed to influence company behavior.

Legal–Political.   The **legal–political dimension** includes government regulations at the local, state, and federal levels as well as political activities designed to influence company behavior. The U.S. political system encourages capitalism, and the government tries not to overregulate business. However, government laws do specify rules of the game. The federal government influences organizations through the Occupational Safety and Health Administration (OSHA), Environmental Protection Agency (EPA), fair trade practices, libel statutes allowing lawsuits against business, consumer protection legislation, product safety requirements, import and export restrictions, and information and labeling requirements. Litigation and regulation can create big problems for companies. Microsoft Corporation has been involved in a long, expensive, and exhausting antitrust battle with the U.S. Department of Justice. Microsoft managers have learned the huge impact this environmental sector can have on an organization. Many organizations also have to contend with government and legal issues in other countries. Coca-Cola came under government regulatory surveillance in parts of Europe because of alleged unsanitary conditions in some of its bottling plants. General Electric's attempted $41 billion purchase of Honeywell International won regulatory approval in the U.S., but was squashed by European Union (EU) regulators on the grounds that it would severely reduce competition and raise prices for consumers.

pressure group

An interest group that works within the legal–political framework to influence companies to behave in socially responsible ways.

Managers must recognize a variety of **pressure groups** that work within the legal–political framework to influence companies to behave in socially responsible ways. Automobile manufacturers, toy makers, and airlines have been targeted by Ralph Nader's Center for Responsive Law. Tobacco companies today are certainly feeling the far-reaching power of antismoking groups. Middle-aged activists who once protested the Vietnam War have gone to battle to keep Wal-Mart from "destroying the quality of small-town life." Some groups have also attacked the giant retailer on environmental issues, which likely will be one of the strongest pressure points in the coming years.[17] Two of the hottest current issues for pressure groups that are also related to environmental concerns are biotechnology, as illustrated by this chapter's opening case, and world trade. Environmental and human rights protesters have disrupted World Trade Organization meetings and meetings of the World Bank and the International Monetary Fund to protest a system of worldwide integration that has food, goods, people, and capital freely moving across borders. This current international issue will be discussed in more detail in Chapter 3.

Task Environment

As described earlier, the task environment includes those sectors that have a direct working relationship with the organization, among them customers, competitors, suppliers, and the labor market.

Customers. Those people and organizations in the environment who acquire goods or services from the organization are **customers**. As recipients of the organization's output, customers are important because they determine the organization's success. Patients are the customers of hospitals, students the customers of schools, and travelers the customers of airlines. Clothing companies have to stay constantly in touch with shifting customer tastes. Levi Strauss's fortunes have faded faster than a pair of new jeans in recent years because of the company's failure to respond quickly to fashion trends such as flared legs, cargo pockets, and baggy pants. Young, fashion-conscious consumers think of Levi's as "for the older generation, like middle-aged people."[18] Abercrombie & Fitch picked up on the trends, making its clothes the hottest fashion among college-age students a few years back, but now the company is also having trouble coming up with fresh, new styles to boost sagging sales. Marketers are hoping the controversial magazine-style catalog, featuring racy photographs of teenagers, will revive Abercrombie's image among youth, but parents are rebelling against what many consider pornographic displays of children.

One concern for managers today is that the Internet has given increased power to customers and enabled them to directly impact the organization. For example, gripe sites such as walmartsucks.org, where customers and sales associates cyber-vent about the nation's largest retailer, and untied.com, where United Airlines employees and disgruntled fliers rail against the air carrier, can quickly damage a company's reputation and sales. "In this new information environment," says Kyle Shannon, CEO of e-commerce consultancy Agency.com, "you've got to assume everyone knows everything."[19] However, smart managers and companies are also tapping into the power of the Internet to learn all they can about customers as well, as described in the example below.

customers
People and organizations in the environment who acquire goods or services from the organization.

Managers in companies all over the world are discovering how the Internet keeps customers informed and interconnected. Some are also using the power of the Internet to learn everything they can about customers, as well. Managers in many companies regularly monitor gripe sites to see what is being said about them so they can make changes and respond to problems. Keeping tabs on gripe sites provides a kind of free focus group for companies.

Now, a new market research company, Look-Look, headquartered in Hollywood, is taking a further step toward helping companies use the Web to tap into the needs and interests of the coveted youth market. Look-Look uses the Web to monitor rapidly changing youth market trends and provides the information to apparel companies, beverage firms, cosmetics companies, and movie studios. However, the most innovative aspect of Look-Look is its global corps of teen correspondents, who are paid to e-mail information about their styles, trends, opinions, and ideas. Look-Look's clients pay an annual fee of about $20,000 to instantly reach a virtual, worldwide focus group, 24/7. The company's founders, DeeDee Gordon and Sharon Lee, read and study everything their correspondents tell them about, from J. K. Rowling's series of Harry Potter books to Web sites such as *Ain't It Cool,* to spot trends, make connections, and give their clients predictions about what will sell and what won't.

Look-Look

http://www.look-look.com

We want to be as close as possible to what's going on with kids," says Gordon, "so we get it from the kids themselves." Look-Look's online approach enables their company to deliver up-to-the-minute market research with the speed and accuracy that companies need. With youth spending estimated at $140 billion a year and growing, companies that target the youth market are logging on fast.[20]

Competitors. Other organizations in the same industry or type of business that provide goods or services to the same set of customers are referred to as **competitors**. Each industry is characterized by specific competitive issues. The recording industry differs from the steel industry and the pharmaceutical industry.

competitors

Other organizations in the same industry or type of business that provide goods or services to the same set of customers.

FOCUS ON COLLABORATION

The New Golden Rule: Cooperate!

News flash: Companies all over the world are sleeping with the enemy. A decade ago, many managers would have considered it heresy to collaborate with competitors, but today they are finding that collaboration is necessary to compete in a rapidly changing environment. Worldwide, research and development budgets are shrinking even as technological complexity grows by leaps and bounds. Collaboration in product development is sweeping every field from autos to aircraft to biotechnology. Archrivals GE Aircraft Engines and Pratt & Whitney teamed up to share the $1 billion cost of developing a new jet engine. Bayer, Germany's $28-billion-a-year drug company, partnered with CuraGen, a tiny U.S. genomics company, to search for new obesity and diabetes drugs. What's remarkable about the partnership is that the unequal partners will split profits from any products they develop 50–50.

Suppliers are also a part of this new collaborative business model. Speed is essential in today's economy, which requires a seamless integration between a company and its suppliers. Volkswagen, Europe's biggest automaker, has stretched the supplier relationship to new limits at its revolutionary plant in Brazil. Twelve international suppliers work directly in Volkswagen's factory, making their own components and then fastening them together into finished trucks and buses. Although few have stretched the supplier relationship as far as VW, other auto companies, including Ford, DaimlerChrysler, and General Motors, are also experimenting with this *modular approach*, in which suppliers provide premade chunks of a vehicle that can be quickly assembled into a finished car or truck by a handful of workers. Manufacturers win with lower costs, while suppliers gain in higher volume, and transaction costs go down for everyone. In the quest for speed and efficiency, collaboration is a trend that is likely to go even further in coming years.

Experts have looked at the key elements that help make collaborative relationships successful and offer the following tips:

- *Enter the relationship with a spirit of true partnership.* An arm's length, semiadversarial, no-trust, "dump-them-tomorrow-if-we-get-a-better-deal" mindset guarantees failure. Successful partnerships are based on openness, trust, and long-term commitment.

- *Outline what each partner is expected to bring to the relationship from the beginning to the end of the collaborative project.* This enables managers to determine where there are gaps and how to fill them. It also establishes what the partners expect from one another to help maintain good relationships throughout the life of the partnership.

- *Clarify the responsibilities of all partnership members.* This includes defining those who will lead the project, how decisions will be made, review and oversight responsibilities, and who has final authority regarding any negotiations, contract approvals, and so forth.

- *Determine how the risks and profits will be shared.* Include the stake expected from each member and how profits will be divided.

- *Put it in writing.* An open, trusting relationship does not mean there should not be a legal contract and clear, written guidelines for how the partnership will conduct business. A legal contract prevents misunderstandings and provides continuity through changes in personnel and management.

SOURCES: Based on information in Lee Berton, "Shall We Dance?" *CFO* (January 1998), 28–35; Brian O'Reilly, "There's Still Gold in Them Thar Pills," *Fortune* (July 23, 2001), 58–70; David Woodruff with Ian Katz and Keith Naughton, "VW's Factory of the Future," *Business Week* (October 7, 1996), 52–56; Diana Jean Schemo, "Is VW's New Plant Lean, or Just Mean?" *The New York Times* (November 19, 1996), D1; Philip Siekman, "Building 'Em Better in Brazil," *Fortune* (September 6, 1999), 246(c)–246(v); Oren Harari, "The Logistics of Success," *Management Review* (June 1999), 24–26; and Gail Dutton, "The New Consortiums," *Management Review* (January 1999), 46–50.

Competitive wars are being waged worldwide in all industries. Coke and Pepsi continue to battle it out for the soft-drink market. UPS and FedEx are fighting the overnight delivery wars. In the home improvement market, competition between Home Depot and Lowe's is getting sharper than a buzz saw. Home Depot revolutionized the home improvement retail industry with its immense orange warehouse stores and well-trained sales force. But in recent years, the industry's Number 2 retailer, Lowe's, has been building even larger stores on Home Depot's turf and slowly stealing market share. To fight back, Home Depot recently announced that it will begin selling appliances to compete with Lowe's appliance business.[21] Part of the new workplace involves competitors working together, in ways unheard of previously, as shown in the Focus on Collaboration box.

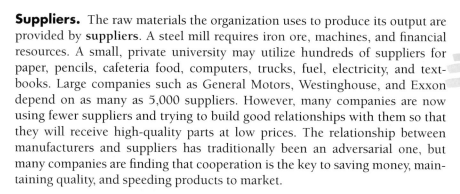

Suppliers. The raw materials the organization uses to produce its output are provided by **suppliers**. A steel mill requires iron ore, machines, and financial resources. A small, private university may utilize hundreds of suppliers for paper, pencils, cafeteria food, computers, trucks, fuel, electricity, and textbooks. Large companies such as General Motors, Westinghouse, and Exxon depend on as many as 5,000 suppliers. However, many companies are now using fewer suppliers and trying to build good relationships with them so that they will receive high-quality parts at low prices. The relationship between manufacturers and suppliers has traditionally been an adversarial one, but many companies are finding that cooperation is the key to saving money, maintaining quality, and speeding products to market.

suppliers
People and organizations who provide the raw materials the organization uses to produce its output.

Labor Market. The **labor market** represents people in the environment who can be hired to work for the organization. Every organization needs a supply of trained, qualified personnel. Unions, employee associations, and the availability of certain classes of employees can influence the organization's labor market. Labor market forces affecting organizations right now include (1) the growing need for computer-literate information technology workers; (2) the necessity for continuous investment in human resources through recruitment, education, and training to meet the competitive demands of the borderless world; and (3) the effects of international trading blocs, automation, and shifting plant location upon labor dislocations, creating unused labor pools in some areas and labor shortages in others.

labor market
The people available for hire by the organization.

The Organization–Environment Relationship

Why do organizations care so much about factors in the external environment? The reason is that the environment creates uncertainty for organization managers, and they must respond by designing the organization to adapt to the environment.

Environmental Uncertainty

Organizations must manage environmental uncertainty to be effective. *Uncertainty* means that managers do not have sufficient information about environmental factors to understand and predict environmental needs and changes.[22] As indicated in Exhibit 2.2, environmental characteristics that influence uncertainty are the number of factors that affect the organization and the extent to

EXHIBIT 2.2

The External Environment and Uncertainty

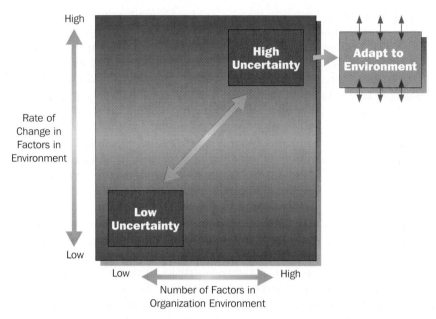

which those factors change. A large multinational like Nortel Networks has thousands of factors in the external environment creating uncertainty for managers. When external factors change rapidly, the organization experiences very high uncertainty; examples are telecommunications and aerospace firms, computer and electronics companies, and e-commerce organizations that sell products and services over the Internet. Companies have to make an effort to adapt to the rapid changes in the environment. When an organization deals with only a few external factors and these factors are relatively stable, such as for soft-drink bottlers or food processors, managers experience low uncertainty and can devote less attention to external issues.

Adapting to the Environment

If an organization faces increased uncertainty with respect to competition, customers, suppliers, or government regulation, managers can use several strategies to adapt to these changes, including boundary-spanning roles, interorganizational partnerships, mergers or joint ventures, and flexible structure.

Organic organizations create many teams to handle changes in raw materials, new products, government regulations, or marketing. Fleet Financial Group found flexible groups helped some important productivity problems, as described in the example below.

Fleet Financial Group

http://www.fleet.com

"If businesses in America want to face the global challenges of a world economy," heard CEO Terry Murray at a business meeting, "they need to redesign work so it enhances both productivity and family life." Even though the Radcliffe Public Policy Center's Paula Rayman spoke with certainty, the Fleet Financial Group CEO was skeptical.

Fleet had grown from one bank in Rhode Island in the 1980s to 75 banks by the late 1990s, and then to 1,500 by 2002 after some mergers. In order to remain "fighting trim," layoffs and extended hours were common. The company was anything but family-friendly. Turnover was running at 30 percent, costing hundreds of thousands of dollars each year. Happy employees are more productive, noted Rayman, but unhappy employees end up being expensive. Murray's response: "Prove it! Prove that what's good for work and family is good for the bottom line." And he gave her a year and a budget to prove it.

Rayman and MIT professor Lotte Bailyn embarked on a project that put under a microscope two Fleet units—a 20-person group that had recently moved from Framingham, Massachusetts, to Boston and a Providence, Rhode Island, 35-employee group. Though the leaders feared griping, initial brainstorming sessions with employees uncovered their main concerns, how they knew if they were productive, and how they balanced (or didn't) work and family. Small groups of employees further brainstormed solutions to both productivity and family issues.

How to prove this would work? Employees completed before and after questionnaires, as well as detailed diaries of work, productivity, and family. In the "before" responses, two-thirds were not satisfied with the work/family balance, some having severe conflicts at home that even caused physical illnesses from the stress.

The Framingham unit wanted to reduce their long commutes, and they realized there was too much work piled on the underwriters, which resulted in backups and overtime. The team came up with ways to redistribute the work more equitably, including the hiring of two administrative assistants to write loan commitment letters. "The quality of our lives improved tremendously," said underwriter David Bengston. At the same time, the Providence group was feeling overloaded due to new accounting and computer systems and felt they were about to burn out. So they asked for flextime and some telecommuting to relieve pressure, as well as offering ways to streamline the work itself. Half of the employees ended up telecommuting a few days a week and two-thirds went on flextime. An added bonus: the flexible environment required more communication, meaning they all learned more about what others were doing.

The final piece in making it work was a breakdown of the computer network in Providence. The programmers at home were the only ones who could hook into their work. So manager Maria Barry told the employees, "Go home and we'll tell you when to come back."

Employees rated the experiment a success, flextime workers reported feeling more control over their jobs, productivity was up, and family members who were interviewed noted that loved ones worked fewer hours. Even skeptic CEO Murray now sees that it doesn't matter *how* the work is completed. If employees are happy, results are better. "What impresses me is how enthusiastic our employees are," he says. "Morale is good and the work is getting done."[23]

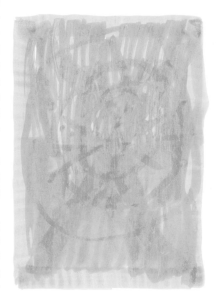

The Internal Environment: Corporate Culture

The internal environment within which managers work includes corporate culture, production technology, organization structure, and physical facilities. Of these, corporate culture has surfaced as extremely important to competitive advantage. The internal culture must fit the needs of the external environment and company strategy. When this fit occurs, highly committed employees create a high-performance organization that is tough to beat.[24] **Culture** can be defined as the set of key values, beliefs, understandings, and norms shared by members of an organization.[25] The concept of culture helps managers understand the hidden, complex aspects of organizational life. Culture is a pattern of shared values and assumptions about how things are done within the organization.

culture

The set of key values, beliefs, understandings, and norms that members of an organization share.

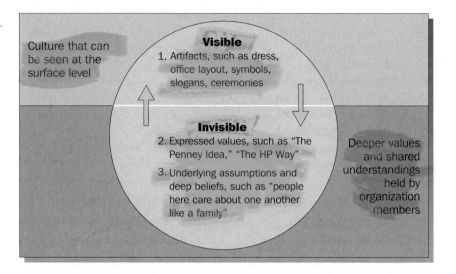

Culture that can be seen at the surface level

Visible
1. Artifacts, such as dress, office layout, symbols, slogans, ceremonies

Invisible
2. Expressed values, such as "The Penney Idea," "The HP Way"

3. Underlying assumptions and deep beliefs, such as "people here care about one another like a family"

Deeper values and shared understandings held by organization members

© Robbie McClaren/SABA

Tom Loutzenheiser, technology president of software company Apexx Technology, appreciates the many positive attributes of the company's Boise, Idaho location, including affordable housing, short commutes, and the opportunity to kayak on the Boise River just minutes away. Employees at Apexx also appreciate the company's corporate culture, which values the individual and believes in giving employees freedom, privacy, and responsibility. Apexx Technology's office layout reflects its cultural values by offering employees more personal space, offices with real windows, and solid walls that rise all the way to the ceiling. "It's not a cube farm," says employee Jennifer Bedford, reflecting her approval.

This pattern is learned by members as they cope with external and internal problems and taught to new members as the correct way to perceive, think, and feel. Culture can be analyzed at three levels, as illustrated in Exhibit 2.3, with each level becoming less obvious.[26] At the surface level are visible artifacts, which include such things as manner of dress, patterns of behavior, physical symbols, organizational ceremonies, and office layout. Visible artifacts are all the things one can see, hear, and observe by watching members of the organization. At a deeper level are the expressed values and beliefs, which are not observable but can be discerned from how people explain and justify what they do. These are values that members of the organization hold at a conscious level. They can be interpreted from the stories, language, and symbols organization members use to represent them. Some values become so deeply embedded in a culture that members are no longer consciously aware of them. These basic, underlying assumptions and beliefs are the essence of culture and subconsciously guide behavior and decisions. In some organizations, a basic assumption might be that people are essentially lazy and will shirk their duties whenever possible; thus, employees are closely supervised and given little freedom, and colleagues are frequently suspicious of one another. More enlightened organizations operate on the basic assumption that people want to do a good job; in these organizations, employees are given more freedom and responsibility, and colleagues trust one another and work cooperatively. Basic assumptions in an organization's culture often begin with strongly held values espoused by a founder or early leader.

One of the most important things leaders do is create and influence organizational culture because it has a significant impact on performance. In comparing 18 companies that have experienced long-term success with 18 similar companies that have not done so well, James C. Collins and Jerry I. Porras found the key determining factor in successful companies to be a culture in which employees share such a strong vision that they know in their hearts what is right for the company. Their book, *Built to Last: Successful Habits of Visionary Companies*, describes how companies such as Disney and Procter & Gamble have successfully adapted to a changing world without losing sight of the core values that guide the organization.[27] Some companies put values in writing so they can be passed on to new generations of employees. PSS World Medical, a specialty marketer and distributor of medical products, gives every employee a booklet titled *The Blue Ribbon Scorecard—A Foundation for PSS Culture.*[28] Companies known for their strong, distinctive cultures, such as Southwest Airlines, the Container Store, and SAS Institute, regularly show up on *Fortune* magazine's list of the best companies to work for in America.

The fundamental values that characterize cultures at these and other companies can be understood through the visible manifestations of symbols, stories, heroes, slogans, and ceremonies. Any company's culture can be interpreted by observing these factors.

Symbols

A **symbol** is an object, act, or event that conveys meaning to others. Symbols associated with corporate culture convey the organization's important values. For example, managers at WorldNow, a New York–based start-up that provides Internet solutions to local television broadcasters, wanted a way to symbolize the company's unofficial mantra of "drilling down to solve problems." They bought a dented old drill for $2 and dubbed it The Team Drill. Each month, the drill is presented to a different employee in recognition of exceptional work, and the employee personalizes the drill in some way before passing it on to the next winner.[29]

At Siebel Systems in San Mateo, California, employees are surrounded by symbolic reminders that the customer always comes first. Every conference room is named after a major Siebel customer. All the artwork on office walls comes from customer ads or annual reports. "The cornerstone of our corporate culture," says CEO Tom Siebel, "is that we are committed to do whatever it takes to make sure that each and every one of our customers succeeds."[30]

symbol
An object, act, or event that conveys meaning to others.

Stories

A **story** is a narrative based on true events that is repeated frequently and shared among organizational employees. Stories are told to new employees to keep the organization's primary values alive. One of Nordstrom's primary means of emphasizing the importance of customer service is through corporate storytelling. An example is the story about men's clothing salesman Van Mensah, who received a letter explaining that a customer had mistakenly washed his 12 new shirts in hot water, causing the shirts to shrink. The customer wanted to know whether Mensah had any suggestions to help him out of his predicament. Mensah immediately called the customer in Sweden and informed him that a dozen new shirts—in the same size, style, and colors—were being mailed out that day, compliments of the company.[31] A frequently-told story at UPS concerns an employee who, without authorization, ordered an extra Boeing 737 to ensure timely delivery of a load of Christmas packages that had been left behind in the holiday rush. As the story goes, rather than punishing the worker, UPS rewarded his initiative. By telling this story, UPS workers communicate that the company stands behind its commitment to worker autonomy and customer service.[32]

story
A narrative based on true events that is repeated frequently and shared by organizational employees.

Heroes

A **hero** is a figure who exemplifies the deeds, character, and attributes of a strong culture. Heroes are role models for employees to follow. Sometimes heroes are real, such as Lee Iacocca, who proved the courage of his convictions

hero
A figure who exemplifies the deeds, character, and attributes of a strong corporate culture.

by working for $1 a year when he first went to Chrysler. Other times they are symbolic, such as the mythical sales representative at Robinson Jewelers who delivered a wedding ring directly to the church because the ring had been ordered late. The deeds of heroes are out of the ordinary, but not so far out as to be unattainable by other employees. Heroes show how to do the right thing in the organization. Companies with strong cultures take advantage of achievements to define heroes who uphold key values.

At Minnesota Mining and Manufacturing (3M), top managers keep alive the heroes who developed projects that were killed by top management. One hero was a vice president who was fired earlier in his career for persisting with a new product even after his boss had told him, "That's a stupid idea. Stop!" After the worker was fired, he would not leave. He stayed in an unused office, working without a salary on the new product idea. Eventually he was rehired, the idea succeeded, and he was promoted to vice president. The lesson of this hero as a major element in 3M's culture is to persist at what you believe in.[33]

Slogans

slogan

A phrase or sentence that succinctly expresses a key corporate value.

A **slogan** is a phrase or sentence that succinctly expresses a key corporate value. Many companies use a slogan or saying to convey special meaning to employees. H. Ross Perot of Electronic Data Systems established the philosophy of hiring the best people he could find and noted how difficult it was to find them. His motto was, "Eagles don't flock. You gather them one at a time." At Sequins International, where 80 percent of the employees are Hispanic, words from W. Edwards Deming, "You don't have to please the boss; you have to please the customer," are embroidered in Spanish on the pockets of workers' jackets.[34] Cultural values can also be discerned in written public statements, such as corporate mission statements or other formal statements that express the core values of the organization. The mission statement for Hallmark Cards, for example, emphasizes values of excellence, ethical and moral conduct in all relationships, business innovation, and corporate social responsibility.[35]

Ceremonies

ceremony

A planned activity that makes up a special event and is conducted for the benefit of an audience.

A **ceremony** is a planned activity that makes up a special event and is conducted for the benefit of an audience. Managers hold ceremonies to provide dramatic examples of company values. Ceremonies are special occasions that reinforce valued accomplishments, create a bond among people by allowing them to share an important event, and anoint and celebrate heroes.[36]

The value of a ceremony can be illustrated by the presentation of a major award. Mary Kay Cosmetics Company holds elaborate awards ceremonies, presenting gold and diamond pins, furs, and luxury cars to high-achieving sales consultants. The setting is typically an auditorium, in front of a large, cheering audience, and everyone dresses in glamorous evening clothes. The most successful consultants are introduced by film clips, like the kind used to present award nominees in the entertainment industry. These ceremonies recognize and celebrate high-performing employees and emphasize the rewards for performance.[37] An award can also be bestowed secretly by mailing it to the employee's home or, if a check, by depositing it in a bank. But such procedures would not make the bestowal of rewards a significant organizational event and would be less meaningful to the employee.

In summary, organizational culture represents the values, norms, understandings, and basic assumptions that employees share, and these values are signified by symbols, stories, heroes, slogans, and ceremonies. Managers help define important symbols, stories, and heroes to shape the culture.

Environment and Culture

A big influence on internal corporate culture is the external environment. Cultures can vary widely across organizations; however, organizations within the same industry may often reveal similar cultural characteristics because they are operating in similar environments.[38] The internal culture should embody what it takes to succeed in the environment. If the external environment requires extraordinary customer service, the culture should encourage good service; if it calls for careful technical decision making, cultural values should reinforce managerial decision making.

Adaptive Cultures

Research at Harvard on 207 U.S. firms illustrated the critical relationship between corporate culture and the external environment. The study found that a strong corporate culture alone did not ensure business success unless the culture encouraged healthy adaptation to the external environment. As illustrated in Exhibit 2.4, adaptive corporate cultures have different values and behavior from unadaptive corporate cultures. In adaptive cultures, managers are concerned about customers and those internal people and processes that bring about useful change. In the unadaptive corporate cultures, managers are concerned about themselves, and their values tend to discourage risk taking and change. Thus a strong culture alone is not enough, because an unhealthy culture may encourage the organization to march resolutely in the wrong direction. Healthy cultures help companies adapt to the environment.[39]

	Adaptive Corporate Cultures	**Unadaptive Corporate Cultures**
Visible Behavior	Managers pay close attention to all their constituencies, especially customers, and initiate change when needed to serve their legitimate interests, even if it entails taking some risks.	Managers tend to behave somewhat insularly, politically, and bureaucratically. As a result, they do not change their strategies quickly to adjust to or take advantage of changes in their business environments.
Expressed Values	Managers care deeply about customers, stockholders, and employees. They also strongly value people and processes that can create useful change (e.g., leadership initiatives up and down the management hierarchy).	Managers care mainly about themselves, their immediate work group, or some product (or technology) associated with that work group. They value the orderly and risk-reducing management process much more highly than leadership initiatives.

EXHIBIT *2.4*

Environmentally Adaptive versus Unadaptive Corporate Cultures

Types of Cultures

In considering what cultural values are important for the organization, managers consider the external environment as well as the company's strategy and goals. Studies have suggested that the right fit between culture, strategy, and the environment is associated with four categories or types of culture, as illustrated in Exhibit 2.5. These categories are based on two dimensions: (1) the extent to which the external environment requires flexibility or stability; and (2) the extent to which a company's strategic focus is internal or external. The four categories associated with these differences are adaptability, achievement, clan, and bureaucratic.[40]

The *adaptability culture* emerges in an environment that requires fast response and high-risk decision making. Managers encourage values that support the company's ability to rapidly detect, interpret, and translate signals from the environment into new behavior responses. Employees have autonomy to make decisions and act freely to meet new needs, and responsiveness to customers is highly valued. Managers also actively create change by encouraging and rewarding creativity, experimentation, and risk taking. One good example of an adaptability culture is 3M, the maker of Post-it notes, Scotch-Brite scrubbing pads, and hundreds of other innovative products. All employees attend a class on risk taking and are encouraged to use 15 percent of their time working on projects of their own choosing, without management approval. Most e-commerce companies, as well as companies in the electronics, cosmetics, and fashion industries, use this type of culture because they must move quickly to respond to changes in the environment.

The *achievement culture* is suited to organizations that are concerned with serving specific customers in the external environment but without the intense need for flexibility and rapid change. This is a results-oriented culture that values competitiveness, aggressiveness, personal initiative, and willingness to work long and hard to achieve results. An emphasis on winning and achieving specific ambitious goals is the glue that holds the organization together.[41] Siebel Systems, which sells complex software systems, has thrived on an achievement

Exhibit *2.5*

Four Types of Corporate Cultures

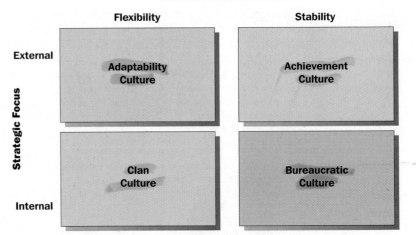

SOURCES: Based on Daniel R. Denison and Aneil K. Mishra, "Toward a Theory of Organizational Culture and Effectiveness," *Organization Science* 6, no. 2 (March–April 1995): 204–223; Robert Hooijberg and Frank Petrock, "On Cultural Change: Using the Competing Values Framework to Help Leaders Execute a Transformational Strategy," *Human Resource Management* 32, no. 1 (1993): 29–50; and R.E. Quinn, *Beyond Rational Management: Mastering the Paradoxes and Competing Demands of High Performance* (San Francisco: Jossey-Bass, 1988).

culture. Employees who succeed at Siebel are intense, competitive, and driven to win. Those who perform and meet stringent goals are handsomely rewarded; those who don't are fired. Nearly every employee at Siebel is given a ranking within each department, and every six months the bottom 5 percent are axed. Employees who thrive on the competitive culture helped Siebel's revenues grow rapidly.[42]

The *clan culture* has an internal focus on the involvement and participation of employees to rapidly meet changing needs from the environment. This culture places high value on meeting the needs of employees, and the organization may be characterized by a caring, family-like atmosphere. Managers emphasize values such as cooperation, consideration of both employees and customers, and avoiding status differences. One company that achieves success with a clan culture is SAS Institute, based in Cary, North Carolina.

SAS Institute
http://www.sas.com

SAS, which stands for statistical analysis software, writes software that makes it possible to gather and understand data, producing products that set the industry standard in the world of knowledge management. It is a competitive field with high stakes, but the atmosphere at SAS headquarters in Cary, North Carolina, is relaxed, almost serene. Jim Goodnight, co-founder of SAS, created a caring corporate culture where employees are respected and given the freedom and information they need to perform at the top of their abilities.

The most important value is taking care of employees and making sure they have whatever they need to be satisfied and productive. Employees are encouraged to lead a balanced life rather than to work long hours and express a hard-charging, competitive spirit. The company even adopted a seven-hour workday to give employees more personal time. SAS also offers amazing benefits, including two Montessori day-care centers, a 36,000 square foot fitness center, unlimited sick days, an on-site health clinic, elder care advice and referrals, and live music in the cafeteria, where employees may eat with their families. Other key values at SAS are equality, fairness, and cooperation.

SAS's culture places a high value on people and human relationships. Managers at the company trust employees to do their jobs to the best of their ability—and then they expect them to go home and enjoy their friends and families. As one employee put it, "Because you're treated well, you treat the company well."[43]

Thanks to SAS's clan culture, employees care about one another and about the company, a focus that has helped SAS adapt to stiff competition and changing markets.

The final category of culture, the *bureaucratic culture,* has an internal focus and a consistency orientation for a stable environment. Following the rules and being thrifty are valued, and the culture supports and rewards a methodical, rational, orderly way of doing things. In today's fast-changing world, few companies operate in a stable environment, and most managers are shifting away from bureaucratic cultures because of a need for greater flexibility. However, one thriving new company, Pacific Edge Software, has successfully implemented some elements of a bureaucratic culture, ensuring that all their projects are on time and on budget. The husband-and-wife team of Lisa Hjorten and Scott Fuller implanted a culture of order, discipline, and control from the moment they founded the company. The emphasis on order and focus means employees can generally go home by 6:00 PM rather than working all night to finish an important project. Hjorten insists that the company's culture isn't rigid or uptight, just *careful*. Although sometimes being careful means being slow, so far Pacific Edge has managed to keep pace with the demands of the external environment.[44]

Each of these four categories of culture can be successful. The relative emphasis on various cultural values depends on the needs of the environment and the organization's focus. Managers are responsible for instilling the cultural values the organization needs to be successful in its environment.

Shaping Corporate Culture for the New Workplace

Research conducted over the last decade by a Stanford University professor indicates that the one factor that increases a company's value the most is people and how they are treated.[45] In addition, a recent *Fortune* magazine survey found that CEOs cite organizational culture as their most important mechanism for attracting, motivating, and retaining talented employees, a capability they consider the single best predictor of overall organizational excellence.[46] At Athene Software, managers created a strong, people-oriented culture to keep talented engineers happy and productive, as described in the Best Practices box. However, managers face new challenges in shaping and maintaining strong, adaptive corporate cultures because of changes in the nature of work and the workplace.

BEST PRACTICES

Athene's Culture Nurtures Loyalty and Excellence

At Athene Software, a Boulder, Colorado–based developer of software for communications service providers, ISPs, and other e-businesses, managers deliberately created an "engineer-friendly" culture that has helped the small company keep good employees and compete in a tough, changing industry.

They began with the basic assumption that creating great software is all about people joyfully working together. To make that happen meant treating people with care and respect. Athene's culture depends first and foremost on hiring the right people. The hiring process begins with phone interviews with the company's technical advisors and background checks to screen candidates for technical qualifications. These are followed by a series of interviews with key managers and potential colleagues. Finally, candidates are required to "audition" before a voluntary group of company employees by demonstrating something about themselves that shows how they will fit in at Athene. The audition process serves an added function of helping to retain current employees because they have a chance to help select top-quality people who strive for excellence and want to be part of building a great company.

After people are hired, Athene makes sure they have whatever they need to perform. Managers have built an environment that adapts to people's needs rather than expecting the opposite. "A big part of our culture is balance," says CEO Eric Johnson. "Everyone has a hierarchy of things that are important to them. . . . We want to support [the employee] as a whole person." Whenever employees have to work extra hours, their contribution is recognized with monetary bonuses, public thank-yous, and extra time off that they are required to take. Athene also ensures that its people get to work on leading-edge technology, have the tools and equipment they need, and have opportunities for training and career development. The company gives all engineers private offices, spends around $10,000 on each for hardware and software, and offers in-house training classes once a week. That commitment leads directly to higher job satisfaction and higher retention rates. "A technology business is all about people," says Johnson. "It is suicide not to treat people with compassion and integrity."

SOURCE: Mark Gordon, "Corporate Culture Manifesto," *CIO* (March 15, 2001), 62–66.

New Demands for Managing Corporate Culture

In today's increasingly global and virtual organizations, shared cultural values are what holds far-flung people and operations together. Culture can provide the glue that gives people a sense of belonging, serves as a compass for employee behavior, and enables dispersed employees to work in concert toward shared goals that meet changing needs from the environment.[47] But how do managers create and maintain a strong culture in a workplace where some employees may never even see one another? Trends such as virtual teams, networks, flexible hours, and telecommuting, in addition to global dispersion, mean that the traditional mechanisms for transmitting culture may be lost. Employees have little opportunity to learn about the values of the organization from observing others and sharing in activities such as stories and cultural symbolism on a regular basis.

One way managers are addressing this issue is by putting increased emphasis on *selection and socialization* of new employees. Dale Pratt, director of human resources for Nortel Networks, described earlier in the chapter, manages a virtual team with colleagues as far away as Europe and China.[48] She and other managers emphasize that success in the new workplace begins with selecting the right people. For example, at Microsoft, the interview process is designed to find employees who "fit" the company's culture and already share many of the values the organization promotes. The interview consists of a grueling ritual in which job candidates are grilled by their prospective colleagues with questions such as, "Why are manhole covers round?" and, "Given a gold bar that can be cut exactly twice and a contractor who must be paid one-seventh of a gold bar a day for seven days, what do you do?" The correct answers aren't as important as how candidates handle the pressure and think on their feet. Microsoft wants employees who are smart, passionate, and unconventional. Those who make it through the process feel like members of a special club. The mystique of the entrance exam is only one element that reinforces Microsoft's esprit de corps.[49] But it is an important one because it ensures that people who join the company are likely to fit the company's distinctive corporate culture.

Other companies also have strenuous interviewing and hiring practices. PSS World Medical doesn't call candidates back for follow-up interviews. Requiring the candidate to take the initiative through every step of the hiring process, which takes six to eight weeks, ensures that PSS hires people with the right values and attitudes to fit its culture.[50]

After employees are hired, socializing them into the culture is also important. Putting the company's values in writing and distributing them in various forms—through newsletters and magazines, videos, intranets, in training classes—is important when people are working in far-flung locations, but people generally need more than that to begin to internalize the values. Many companies that have global and virtual employees bring people together with longtime employees early in their employment so they can learn the culture. Nokia, the mobile phone supplier, has all new employees take a cultural awareness class, where they learn how the Swedish company's culture and management style is different from many American companies. Costco, a discount warehouse operator, brings new overseas managers to the United States for up to 10 weeks to work side-by-side with longtime employees so they can learn about the company's values.[51] One company uses a company song to transmit its culture, as described in the Focus on Leadership box.

FOCUS ON LEADERSHIP

Lennar Corporation

Not many CEOs lead corporate meetings by reading Dr. Suess books. Or call themselves "Dr. Stuess" and pen company songs such as "Scratchings from the Little Red Hen." Meet 43-year-old Stuart Miller, CEO of Lennar Corporation, a fast-growing company that has recently become the number two home builder in the U.S.

What may seem like peculiar practices have actually helped the upstart company maintain its unity and strength as it went through explosive growth in recent years. Begun by Miller's father in 1954 with a $10,000 investment, Lennar acquired so many companies, the rate of growth was dizzying. Still, something worked. Even during a recent economic downturn, profits soared by 32 percent.

Outsiders may not know much about the Little Red Hen, but the company song is printed on little cards and distributed to all workers, who often recite lines to one another at meetings and gatherings.

Recently hired Chief Financial Officer Bruce Gross thought the Little Red Hen was a little too weird and tried to talk executives out of reciting it in front of a banker's meeting, worried it would hurt the credibility of the company. But the bankers loved it.

Lennar also made some smart strategic decisions. Several years ago, subdivision home builders offered houses with customized floor plans. Wanting to be more efficient, Lennar cut down on the number of options available in tiles, appliances, and moldings, despite warnings against this strategy. But the practice paid off, helping to trim costs and appealing to mid- and low-price home shoppers.

Some people think that wacky culture means no discipline. On the contrary, units are held to high standards and every month each of the 50 division heads sends a one-page report to Miller on their status in meeting financial goals.

At a recent seminar for 150 employees, the company met in a hotel convention space decorated in a jungle theme and simulated the "Survivor" show under a banner that read "In Search of RONA" (return on net assets), where participants were grilled on financial goals, as well as being taught responses to tough media questions and how to handle crisis situations.

It's a company that "Yertle, the Turtle" would be proud of.

SOURCE: Evan Perez, "Lennar Corp. Thrives as Residential Builder with Oddball Culture," *The Wall Street Journal* (July 27, 2001), A1, A4.

Few organizations have yet adequately addressed the problem of transmitting culture to virtual workers. In the late 1990s, Hewlett-Packard created a training and development program for managers called "Managing Remotely." The forums addressed such issues as work/life balance, communication processes, and how to orient virtual employees to HP's culture.[52] However, most companies do not have anything so extensive. Many companies that use virtual workers require that people work on-site for a period of time in the beginning to allow the culture to sink in. Some also require periodic office visits or occasional face-to-face forums where the culture is reinforced.[53] As the number of virtual teams and telecommuters grows, managers will face the growing challenge of building and maintaining a unifying culture. Managers can learn to create a sense of connectedness that binds virtual employees together and brings them into the cultural fold.[54] One key aspect of shaping culture in all organizations is cultural leadership.

Cultural Leadership

One way managers change norms and values toward what is adaptive to the external environment or for smooth internal integration is through *cultural leadership*. Managers must *overcommunicate* to ensure that employees understand the new culture values, and they signal these values in actions as well as words.

A **cultural leader** defines and uses signals and symbols to influence corporate culture. Cultural leaders influence culture in two key areas:

cultural leader

A manager who uses signals and symbols to influence corporate culture.

1. *The cultural leader articulates a vision for the organizational culture that employees can believe in and that generates excitement.* This means the leader defines and communicates central values that employees believe in and will rally around.

2. *The cultural leader heeds the day-to-day activities that reinforce the cultural vision.* The leader makes sure that work procedures and reward systems match and reinforce the values. Actions speak louder than words, so cultural leaders "walk their talk."[55]

One way leaders create a culture that everyone can believe in is by directly involving employees in determining what the company's values should be. Managers at United Stationers built a new, adaptive culture from the ground up by asking all 6,000 globally dispersed employees to help define the values that would be the building blocks of the culture.[56]

Managers also widely communicate the cultural values through words and actions. At Starbucks, CEO Howard Schultz welcomes all new employees by video, where he tells about the company's history and culture and shares some stories of his own personal experiences. Each employee also receives 24 hours of initial training, during which they talk with managers and other employees about Starbucks's mission and values.[57] Starbucks managers use these mechanisms as a way to maintain the culture as the company expands internationally. At MTW Corp., managers work with every new employee to create an "expectations agreement," an ever-evolving document that ensures that actions and work procedures that reinforce the company's cultural values will be adhered to

BEST PRACTICES

Eileen Fisher

Simple, elegant, and natural: This describes not only Eileen Fisher's clothing designs, but also the way the $130 million, 400-employee, company is run. It began when graphics-designer Fisher felt overwhelmed while getting dressed every morning for work. Why couldn't women clothing be attractive and yet as simple and unchanging as men's? She bought a $350 terry-cloth remnant in 1984, stitched up four garments, took them to a trade show, and got $3,000 in orders, with $40,000 in orders the following month. Eileen Fisher Inc. was born.

Eileen Fisher designs are simple and elegant, made from natural fabrics such as cotton, wool, and silk. Each piece can be mixed and matched with other pieces, much like a Lego system, which simplifies a woman's wardrobe. Fisher says she was inspired by her parochial school uniforms, which made getting dressed in the morning so easy. The goal is to help customers achieve a simple and joyful life.

The company, too, has developed a culture that might be called simple, elegant, and natural. A few years ago she moved her company to Irvington, New York, where employees could get to work without using cars. The Hudson River location gives a sense of calm to workers. Her values call for the development of the "natural woman" in customers and the same kind of natural-person philosophy for employees. "It's not about money," she said. "It's about people, friends, family, and community and how people treat each other. There has to be natural growth. It can't be something you force."

Natural growth requires wellness, says Fisher. Wanting not only company growth, but also growth of every worker, several years ago Fisher offered each employee $1,000 for self-care activities, such as yoga, massage, voice lessons, and so on. Recently Susan Schor joined as vice-president of people and culture, and she brings self-care activities into the work-site, making it easier for employees to participate. This focus on wellness helps create an energized and creative workforce.

Eileen Fisher is designing her strategy to reinforce the culture. Goals include creating wellness in the business development process, nurturing relationships with customers and employees, and helping people to tell the truth to one another. "You must love the product—and the people," says Fisher.

SOURCES: Claudia Z. Carlin, "Eileen Fisher Simplifies," *Westchester Magazine* (May 2002), 44–45+; and Merri Rosenberg, "A Designer Who Lives Like Her Clients," *The New York Times* (Sept. 10, 2000), 8.

by both managers and workers.[58] Top executives at Weirton Steel act as cultural leaders by participating in every team training session to symbolize their commitment to a team-based culture—a significant commitment in an 8,000-employee organization.[59] Eileen Fisher is one CEO who lives her values in the workplace, as described in the Best Practices box.

Some companies also directly tie compensation to how well people live their values. Gillette Co., based in Boston, Massachusetts, and Germany's Siemens both consider managers' and employees' commitment to the cultural values as part of their overall performance during salary reviews, a powerful reminder that culture is important.[60] Creating and maintaining a strong, adaptive culture is not easy in today's changing workplace, but through their words—and particularly their actions—cultural leaders let everyone in the organization know what really counts.

■ Summary and Management Solution

This chapter discussed several important ideas about internal and external organizational environments. Events in the external environment are considered important influences on organizational behavior and performance. The external environment consists of two layers: the task environment and the general environment. The task environment includes customers, competitors, suppliers, and the labor market. The general environment includes technological, sociocultural, economic, legal-political, and international dimensions. Management techniques for helping the organization adapt to the environment include boundary-spanning roles, interorganizational partnerships, and mergers and joint ventures.

A good example of a leader flexible to unexpected circumstances is Rick Sapio, described at the beginning of the chapter. Rick Sapio realized changing conditions required different approaches, both in strategy and in financial focus. He learned an important lesson in business: that profits equal revenues minus expenses. In the stock-market boom years, he worried more about revenues and less about expenses. But now he no longer had that luxury. The first thing he did was to look carefully at all expenses. He started a practice where the books are closed every day, to get a real-time view of the company's true revenue and expenses.

Every day at 4:37 PM, after the stock market closes, he huddles with his managers and they look at all the expenses to see if any are out of whack, looking for ways to reduce costs in areas that are getting bloated. If employees overspend without approval, they pay out of their own pockets. Sapio closed the Manhattan office; it was just too costly. The company quit paying for his gym and parking. Plus Sapio slashed his own salary by $20,000 and asked employees to take some pay in stock options,

which resulted in savings of $70,000. They agreed to stop TV ads and focus on print and Internet ads, saving $1 million. Finally, Sapio realized he needed to change his business model to suit the changing times. The company went from direct sales to selling through large institutional investors. Reports had shown that 85 percent of revenues came from 35 percent of customers, so they fired 65 percent of the customers and saved 90 percent of their expenses. Sapio learned that by reducing expenses, profits are maximized, which becomes its own marketing tool.[61]

Even companies in relatively simple, stable industries may face significant challenges from the external environment, as illustrated by the opening story of the Gerber baby-food company. Managers at Gerber and its parent company, Norvartis AG, responded quickly to activists' allegation that Gerber baby food contained ingredients that could be harmful. While maintaining their stand that genetically altered products are not dangerous, Gerber is dropping some of its existing corn and soybean suppliers in favor of ones that produce crops that are not genetically altered. Plans for labeling changes to indicate if some products may contain minuscule amounts of genetically altered ingredients are being discussed. Gerber's rapid response was made at considerable cost and inconvenience, but managers knew the repercussions of ignoring this threat from the environment could be much more expensive in the long run. "I have got to listen to my customers," says Al Piergallini, president and CEO of Novartis's U.S. consumer health operations. "If there is an issue, or even an inkling of an issue, I am going to make amends." To keep in touch with this growing environmental issue, Gerber is consulting with various non–Greenpeace-affiliated environmentalists and consumer groups. Managers want to anticipate future problems from the external environment and be ready with a rapid response.[62]

One internal organizational factor that enabled Gerber to respond so quickly is the company's adaptive culture. Corporate culture is a major element of the internal organizational environment and includes the key values, beliefs, understandings, and norms that organization members share. Organizational activities that illustrate corporate culture include symbols, stories, heroes, slogans, and ceremonies. For the organization to be effective, corporate culture should be aligned with the needs of the external environment.

Four types of culture are adaptability, achievement, clan, and bureaucratic. Strong cultures are effective when they enable an organization to adapt to changes in the external environment. Shared cultural values are important for binding people together in today's changing workplace where employees may be dispersed. Managers are putting greater emphasis on selection and socialization of employees so that employees fit the cultural values of the organization. In addition, cultural leaders strengthen or change corporate culture by (1) communicating a compelling vision to employees and (2) reinforcing the vision through day-to-day activities, work procedures, and reward systems.

■ Discussion Questions

1. Some scientists predict major changes in the earth's climate, including a temperature rise of 8°F over the next 60 years. Should any companies be paying attention to this possible long-range environmental trend? Explain.
2. Would the task environment for a bank contain the same elements as that for a government welfare agency? Discuss.
3. What do you think are the most important forces in the external environment creating uncertainty for organizations today? Do the forces you identified typically arise in the task environment or the general environment?
4. Contemporary best-selling management books often argue that customers are the most important element in the external environment. Do you agree? Are there company situations for which this may not be true?
5. American Airlines was thriving until the September 11, 2001, terrorist attacks against the United States, when fear of flying, general uncertainty, and a worldwide recession stunned the airline. Discuss the type

of response American Airlines managers might make to this change in the environment.
6. Why are interorganizational partnerships becoming so important for today's companies? Do you think the terrorist attacks against the United States will likely contribute to an increase or decrease in interorganizational collaboration? Why?
7. Define corporate culture and explain its importance for managers.
8. Why are symbols important to a corporate culture? Do stories, heroes, slogans, and ceremonies also have symbolic value? Discuss.
9. Describe the cultural values of a company for which you have worked. Did those values fit the needs of the external environment? Of employees?
10. What type of environmental situation is associated with an adaptability culture? How does this culture differ from the clan culture?
11. Do you think a corporate culture with strong values is better for organizational effectiveness than a culture with weak values? Are there times when a strong culture might reduce effectiveness? Discuss.

■ Manager's Workbook

What Is a Strong Corporate Culture?

Think about an organization with which you are familiar, such as your school or a company for which you have worked.

Answer the questions below based on whether you agree that they describe the organization.

	Disagree Strongly				Agree Strongly
1. Virtually all managers and most employees can describe the company's values, purpose, and customer importance.	1	2	3	4	5
2. There is clarity among organization members about how their jobs contribute to organizational goals.	1	2	3	4	5

	Disagree Strongly				Agree Strongly
3. It is very seldom that a manager will act in a way contrary to the company's espoused values.	1	2	3	4	5
4. Warmth and support of other employees is a valued norm, even across departments.	1	2	3	4	5
5. The company and its managers value what's best for the company over the long term more than short-term results.	1	2	3	4	5
6. Leaders make it a point to develop and mentor others.	1	2	3	4	5
7. Recruiting is taken very seriously, with multiple interviews in an effort to find traits that fit the culture.	1	2	3	4	5
8. Recruits are given negative as well as positive information about the company so they can freely choose whether to join.	1	2	3	4	5
9. Employees are expected to acquire real knowledge and mastery—not political alliances—before they can be promoted.	1	2	3	4	5
10. Company values emphasize what the company must do well to succeed in a changing environment.	1	2	3	4	5
11. Conformity to company mission and values is more important than conformity to procedures and dress.	1	2	3	4	5
12. You have heard stories about the company's leaders or "heroes" who helped make the company great.	1	2	3	4	5
13. Ceremonies and special events are used to recognize and reward individuals who contribute to the company in significant ways.	1	2	3	4	5

Total Score _____

Compute your score. If your total score is 52 or above, your organization has a strong culture, similar to a Procter & Gamble or IBM. A score from 26 to 51 suggests a culture of medium strength, which is positive for the organization, such as for American Airlines, Coca-Cola, and Citigroup. A score of 25 or below indicates a weak culture, which is probably not helping the company adapt to the external environment or meet the needs of organization members. Discuss the pros and cons of a strong culture. Does a strong culture mean everyone has to be alike?

SOURCES: Adapted from Richard Pascale, "The Paradox of 'Corporate Culture': Reconciling Ourselves to Socialization," *California Management Review* 27, no. 2 (1985); and David A. Kolb, Joyce S. Osland, and Irwin M. Rubin, *Organizational Behavior: An Experiential Approach,* 6th ed. (Englewood Cliffs, N.J.: Prentice-Hall, 1995), 346–347.

◆ Manager's Workshop

Organizational Graffiti
Needed:

a) 2 x 2 Post-it Notes, or blank sheets of paper (optional)
b) Colored sticky-dots (optional)
  1. Each person creates a graffito on the Post-it or paper. The topics should relate to the following questions (your instructor may choose different questions): (5–10 min) What are the norms of behavior in most of your courses? What types of norms would you prefer instead?
  2. All notes are stuck up on a large board (or pages are taped on the blackboard). (5 min)
  3. The whole group works together to organize graffiti into theme categories, reducing to the least number of categories without sacrificing substance. (5–10 min)
  4. Each grouping is given a title by group. (5–10 min)
  5. Each person is given three sticky-dots, which are used to "vote" for most important title. (If no sticky-dots are available, each person puts three check-marks by titles.) All dots can be placed on one title, if desired. (5 min)
  6. The top two titles are discussed as action plans. What does the group plan to do? Who will do it? When? How? How will the group know how well it is doing? What is the first step? How can this information benefit the whole company? (10–20 min)
  7. Final discussion. What did you learn about cultures and norms? How can it be helpful to make the implicit explicit? (5–10 min)

Optional method: small groups develop their own group graffiti and present it to the entire class.

SOURCE: Adapted from Christopher Taylor, "Organizational Graffiti: A Different Approach to Uncovering Issues," *Journal of Management Education* (June 1999), 290–296.

■ Management in Practice: Ethical Dilemma

Competitive Intelligence Predicament

Miquel Vasquez was proud of his job as a new product manager for a biotechnology start-up, and he loved the high stakes and tough decisions that went along with the job. But as he sat in his den after a long day, he was troubled, struggling over what had happened earlier that day and the information he now possessed.

Just before lunch, Miquel's boss had handed him a stack of private strategic documents from their closest competitor. It was a competitive intelligence gold mine—product plans, pricing strategies, partnership agreements, and other documents, most clearly marked "proprietary and confidential." When Miquel asked where the documents came from, his boss told him with a touch of pride that he had taken them right off the competing firm's server. "I got into a private section of their intranet and downloaded everything that looked interesting," he said. Later, realizing that Miquel was suspicious, the boss would say only that he had obtained "electronic access" via a colleague and had not personally broken any passwords. Maybe not, Miquel thought to himself, but this wouldn't pass the *60 Minutes* test. If this ever got out to the press, the company's reputation would be ruined.

Miquel didn't feel good about using these materials. He spent the afternoon searching for answers to his dilemma, but found no clear company policies or regulations that offered any guidance. His sense of fair play told him this was unethical, if not downright illegal. What bothered him even more was the knowledge that this kind of thing might happen again. Using this confidential information would certainly give him and his company a competitive advantage, but Miquel wasn't sure he wanted to work for a firm that would stoop to such tactics.

What Do You Do?

1. Go ahead and use the documents to the company's benefit, but make clear to your boss that you don't want him passing confidential information to you in the future. If he threatens to fire you, threaten to leak the news to the press.

2. Confront your boss privately and let him know you're uncomfortable with how the documents were obtained and what this says about the company's culture. In addition to the question of the legality of using the information, point out that it is a public relations nightmare waiting to happen.

3. Talk to the company's legal counsel and contact the Society of Competitive Intelligence Professionals for guidance. Then, with their opinions and facts to back you up, go to your boss.

SOURCE: Adapted from Kent Weber, "Gold Mine or Fool's Gold?" *Business Ethics* (January–February 2001), 18.

■ Surf the Net

1. **Monitor the Environment.** A comprehensive informational Web site designed especially for executives is at *http://www.ceoexpress.com*. After familiarizing yourself with this site, send an e-mail message to your instructor. Your instructor will play the role of your boss, who is currently unaware that CEOExpress® exists. In your e-mail, present evidence to convince your "boss" that the information at this site would help him or her monitor the environment and, therefore, is a site worthy of bookmarking and visiting regularly.

2. **Mergers and Acquisitions.** To learn more about merger and acquisition activity that affects the economic environment, locate and record the merger and acquisition announcements made in the past two weeks. Use a search engine to locate this information that can be found at such sites as *http://www.theonlineinvestor.com/*.

3. **Corporate Culture.** Select two sites from the list below. Print out the information the organization presents about its corporate culture. On your printouts, try to identify one aspect of the organization's culture at each of the three levels described in Exhibit 2.3. Be prepared to present your findings in a class discussion on corporate culture.
   AES Corporation: *http://www.aesc.com/culture/*
   Galileo International: *http://www.galileo.com/careers/carcorpc.htm*
   Gore: *http://www.gore.com/corp/about/index.html*
   J.D. Edwards: *http://www.jdedwards.com/*; click on Company, then on Careers
   LMI: *http://www.lmi.org/Careers.htm*
   Motorola: *http://www.motorolacareers.com/ufsd2/corporate.cfm*
   Mutual of Omaha: *http://www.careerlink.org/emp/mut/corp.htm*
   Pella: *http://www.pella.com/careers*
   Sony: *http://sel.newjobs.com/Corporate.html*

■ Case for Critical Analysis

Society of Equals

Ted Shelby doesn't make very many mistakes, but . . .

"Hey Stanley," says Ted Shelby, leaning in through the door, "you got a minute? I've just restructured my office. Come on and take a look. I've been implementing some great new concepts!"

Stanley is always interested in Ted Shelby's new ideas, for if there is anyone Stanley wants to do as well as, it is Edward W. Shelby IV. Stanley follows Ted back to his office and stops, non-plussed.

Restructured is right! Gone are Ted's size B (Junior Executive) walnut veneer desk and furniture, and his telephone table. In fact, the room is practically empty save for a large, round, stark white cafeteria table and the half-dozen padded vinyl swivel chairs that surround it.

"Isn't it a beauty! As far as I know, I'm the first executive in the plant to innovate this. The shape is the crucial factor here—no front or rear, no status problems. We can all sit here and communicate more effectively."

We? Communicate? Effectively? Well, it seems that Ted has been attending a series of Executive Development Seminars given by Dr. Faust. The theme of the seminars was—you guessed it—*participative management*. Edward W. Shelby IV has always liked to think of himself as a truly democratic person.

"You see, Stanley," says Ted, managing his best sincere/intense attitude, "the main thing wrong with our culture is that most of the communication is top-down. We in the executive suite send our messages down the line, but we never ask for ideas and suggestions from the rest of the company. Just because we have more status and responsibility doesn't mean that we are necessarily (Stanley duly noted the word *necessarily*) better than the people below us. In fact, with our customers' needs changing so fast these days, we need all the ideas we can get. We've got to shift to a culture of participation and employee involvement if we want to keep up with today's fast pace of business."

"So that's what the cafeteria table is for?" Stanley asks.

"Yes!" says Ted. "We need better two-way communication—up the line as well as down the line. We managers don't have all the answers, and I don't know why I never realized it before that seminar. Why, for example, the folks who run those machines out there. I'll bet any one of them knows a thing or two about how to speed up our manufacturing process that I've never thought of. So I've transformed my office into a full-feedback communication net."

"That certainly is an innovation around here," says Stanley.

A few days later Stanley passed by Ted Shelby's office and was surprised that Ted's desk, furniture, and telephone table were back where they used to be.

Stanley, curious about the unrestructuring, went to Bonnie for enlightenment. "What," he asked, "happened to Shelby's round table?"

"That table we were supposed to sit around and input things?" she said. "All I know is, about two days after he had it put in, Mr. Drake came walking through here. He looked in that office, and then he sort of stopped and went back—and he looked in there for a long time. Then he came over to me, and you know how his face sort of gets red when he's really mad? Well, this time he was so mad that his face was absolutely white. And when he talked to me, I don't think he actually opened his mouth; and I could barely hear him, he was talking so low. And he said, 'Have that removed. Now. Have Mr. Shelby's furniture put back in his office. Have Mr. Shelby see me.'"

My, my. You would think Ted would have known better, wouldn't you? But then, by now you should have a pretty firm idea of just why it is those offices are set up as they are.

Questions

1. How would you characterize the culture in this company? What are the dominant values?
2. Why did Ted Shelby's change experiment fail? To what extent did Ted use the appropriate change tools to increase employee communication and participation?
3. What would you recommend Ted do to change his relationship with subordinates? Is it possible for a manager to change cultural values if the rest of the organization, especially top management, does not agree?

SOURCE: R. Richard Ritti and G. Ray Funkhouser, *The Ropes to Skip & The Ropes to Know*, 3d. ed. (New York: Wiley, 1987), 176–177. This material is used by permission of John Wiley & Sons, Inc.

Managing in a Global Environment

LEARNING OBJECTIVES

After studying this chapter, you should be able to

1 Describe the emerging borderless world.

2 Define international management and explain how it differs from the management of domestic business operations.

3 Indicate how dissimilarities in the economic, sociocultural, and legal-political environments throughout the world can affect business operations.

4 Describe market entry strategies that businesses use to develop foreign markets.

5 Describe the characteristics of a multinational corporation.

6 Explain the challenges of managing in a global environment.

Management Challenge

By using computers and cakes, Edwin San Roman and his wife, Maria del Carmen Vucetich, came up with an idea to service a waiting market: Peruvian expatriates around the world, particularly in the U.S. For example, Pedro Sanchez in Los Angeles could visit the Tortas Peru website (*http://www.tortasperu.com*) and order a home-baked cake, as a way of showing his love to family members living in Peru. Finding women to bake the cakes was no problem. Vucetich found women all over the country, most of whom needed to earn extra money, but found it difficult to work outside the home. Orders would be sent to the women from the Web site via e-mail. Even though few people in Peru have computers, the country is well-covered with Internet cafes, where women can access their own e-mail accounts. These women would make the cake to order and personally deliver it to the Peruvian loved one of the customer. Average cost: $20. Because a large percentage of the customers were Peruvians living in the U.S., payment was made by having them send a check to an American address. However, it took several days for the check to clear and sometimes the cake arrived too late for the special event. Customers were losing interest. Yet, other means of payment, such as credit cards, were not common in Peru. Roman and Vucetich realized if they did not figure out some other solution that would meet customers' needs and that could be implemented in Peru, their short-lived business would turn to crumbs.[1]

If you were Roman and Vucetich, what would you recommend doing?

Not only small international companies, but also large ones have struggles going global. As you'll see later, Wal-Mart is a well-established company facing enormous challenges in developing a successful international business. Other large, successful U.S. companies, including Federal Express and Nike, also have found that "the rest of the world is not the United States of America," as one FedEx competitor put it. However, all of these companies recognize that international expansion is necessary, despite the risks. Companies such as McDonald's, IBM, Coca-Cola, Kellogg, Texas Instruments, and Gillette all rely on international business for a substantial portion of sales and profits. Internet-based companies headquartered in the United States, such as Amazon, Yahoo, and America Online, are also rapidly expanding internationally and finding that, even on the Web, going global is fraught with difficulties. These and other online companies have encountered problems ranging from cultural blunders to violations of foreign laws. All organizations face special problems in trying to tailor their products and business management to the unique needs of foreign countries—but if they succeed, the whole world is their marketplace.

How important is international business to the study of management? *If you are not thinking international, you are not thinking business management.* It's that serious. As you read this page, ideas, takeover plans, capital investments, business strategies, products, and services are traveling around the planet by telephone, computer, fax, and overnight mail. The events of September 11, 2001, when terrorists attacked New York and Washington, underscored the point that isolation is impossible. The future of our businesses and our societies will be determined by global rather than local relationships. The warning Andrew Grove, chairman of Intel, issued to business leaders in a 1995 *Fortune* magazine article has struck home with full force: "[There is] no choice but to operate in a world shaped by globalization."[2]

Rapid advances in technology and communications have made the international dimension an important part of the external environment that is discussed in Chapter 2. Companies can locate different parts of the organization wherever it makes the most business sense—top leadership in one place, technical brainpower and production in other locales. Virtual connections enable close, rapid coordination and communication among people working in different parts of the world, so it is no longer necessary to keep all operations in one place. Samsung, the Korean electronics giant, moved its semiconductor-making facilities to the Silicon Valley to be closer to the best scientific brains in the industry. Canada's Nortel Networks selected a location in the southwest of England as its world manufacturing center for a new fixed-access radio product. Siemens of Germany has moved its electronic ultrasound division to the United States, while the U.S. company DuPont shifted its electronic operations headquarters to Japan.[3]

If you think you are isolated from global influence, think again. Even if you do not budge from your home-

Contract manufacturers such as Taiwan's Quanta Computer Inc., the world's No. 1 maker of notebook PCs, operate in a global environment. Taiwan makes about 60 percent of the world's notebook PCs, and one out of every seven notebooks comes from Quanta, whose U.S. customers include Dell, Gateway, Hewlett-Packard, Apple, and Compaq. A recent international management challenge for Quanta occurred when the U.S. halted air traffic for three days after the September 11 terrorist attacks. Finished computers began to pile up in Quanta's cavernous warehouse in Linkou. So managers improvised, loading thousands of notebooks on a plane leased by Dell, which flew them to Texas.

© David Hartung/Liaison Agency

town, your company may be purchased tomorrow by the English, Japanese, or Germans. People working for Ben & Jerry's Ice Cream, Dr. Pepper, Pillsbury, Carnation, Shell Oil, and Burger King already work for foreign bosses.

All this means that the environment for companies is becoming extremely complex and extremely competitive. Less-developed countries are challenging mature countries in a number of industries. India has become a major player in software development, and electronics manufacture is rapidly leaving Japan for other countries in Asia.

This chapter introduces basic concepts about the global environment and international management. First, we consider the difficulty managers have operating in an increasingly borderless world. We will address challenges— economic, legal-political, and sociocultural—facing companies within the global business environment. Then we will discuss multinational corporations and touch upon the various types of strategies and techniques needed for entering and succeeding in foreign markets.

A Borderless World

Why do companies such as Wal-Mart, Federal Express, and America Online want to pursue a global strategy, despite failures and losses? They recognize that business is becoming a unified global field as trade barriers fall, communication becomes faster and cheaper, and consumer tastes in everything from clothing to cellular phones converge. Thomas Middelhoff of Germany's Bertelsmann AG, which purchased U.S. publisher Random House, put it this way: "There are no German and American companies. There are only successful and unsuccessful companies."[4]

Companies that think globally have a competitive edge. Consider Hong Kong's Johnson Electric Holdings Ltd., a large producer of micromotors that power hair dryers, blenders, and automobile power windows and door locks. With factories in South China and a research and development lab in Hong Kong, Johnson is thousands of miles away from a leading automaker. Yet the company has cornered the market for electric gizmos in U.S. automobiles by using new information technology. Via videoconferencing, Johnson design teams meet "face-to-face" for two hours each morning with their customers in the United States and Europe. The company's processes and procedures are so streamlined that Johnson can take a concept and deliver a prototype to the United States in six weeks.[5]

In addition, domestic markets are saturated for many companies. The only potential for significant growth lies overseas. Kimberly-Clark and Procter & Gamble, which spent years slugging it out in the flat U.S. diaper market, are targeting new markets such as China, India, Israel, Russia, and Brazil. The demand for steel in China, India, and Brazil together is expected to grow 10 percent annually in the coming years—three times the U.S. rate, providing opportunities for companies such as Nucor and North Star Steel.[6] For online companies, too, going global is a key to growth. Predictions are that within a few years two-thirds of the world's Internet users will be outside the United States, and Western Europe and Japan together will account for almost half of the world's e-commerce revenue.[7]

The reality of today's borderless companies also means consumers can no longer tell from which country they're buying. Your Mercury Marauder may have come from Ontario, while a neighbor's Nissan may have been built in

Tennessee. A Gap polo shirt may be made from cloth cut in the United States but sewn in Honduras. Eat an all-American Whopper and you've just purchased from a British company.

Corporations can participate in the international arena on a variety of levels, and the process of globalization typically passes through four distinct stages, as illustrated in Exhibit 3.1.

As the number of stateless corporations increases, so too the awareness of national borders decreases, as reflected by the frequency of foreign participation at the management level. Rising managers are expected to know a second or third language and to have international experience. The need for global managers with cross-cultural sensitivity is intense, as discussed in the Focus on Diversity box. The need for global managers is intense. Corporations around the world want the brightest and best candidates for global management, and young managers who want their careers to move forward recognize the importance of global experience. According to Harvard Business School professor Christopher Bartlett, author of *Managing Across Borders*, people should try to get global exposure when they are young in order to start building skills and networks that will grow throughout their careers.[8]

The International Business Environment

international management

The management of business operations conducted in more than one country.

International management is the management of business operations conducted in more than one country. The fundamental tasks of business management, including the financing, production, and distribution of products and services, do not change in any substantive way when a firm is transacting business across international borders. The basic management functions of planning, organizing, leading, and controlling are the same whether a company operates domestically or internationally. However, managers will experience greater difficulties and risks when performing these management functions on an international scale. For example:

- When Coors Beer tried to translate a slogan with the phrase "Turn it Loose" into Spanish, it came out as "Drink Coors and Get Diarrhea." Budweiser goofed when its Spanish ad promoted Bud Light as "Filling, less delicious."[9]
- It took McDonald's more than a year to figure out that Hindus in India do not eat beef. The company's sales took off only after McDonald's started making burgers sold in India out of lamb.[10]

EXHIBIT 3.1

Four Stages of Globalization

	1. Domestic	2. International	3. Multinational	4. Global
Strategic Orientation	Domestically oriented	Export-oriented, multidomestic	Multinational	Global
Stage of Development	Initial foreign involvement	Competitive positioning	Explosion of international operations	Global
Cultural Sensitivity	Of little importance	Very important	Somewhat important	Critically important
Manager Assumptions	"One best way"	"Many good ways"	"The least-cost way"	"Many good ways"

SOURCE: Based on Nancy J. Adler, *International Dimensions of Organizational Behavior*, 4th ed. (Cincinnati, Ohio: South-Western, 2002), 8–9.

FOCUS ON DIVERSITY

Cross-Cultural Communication

American managers are often at a disadvantage when doing business overseas. Part of this is the lack of foreign language skills, as well as inexperience in dealing with other cultures and less-than-ideal living conditions. Consequently, many mistakes are made—mistakes that could easily be avoided.

The manager's attitude is perhaps the single most important factor in success. Those who go abroad with a sense of "wonder" about the new culture are better off than those with a judgemental view of "If it is different, then my culture must be better." Seeing differences as new and interesting is more productive than being critical. Such evaluations lead to an "us versus them" approach, which never sits well with the locals.

Though every culture has its own way of communicating, here are some basic principles to follow in international business relations:

1. Always show respect and listen carefully. Don't be in a hurry to finish the "business." Many other cultures value the social component of these interactions.

2. Try to gain an appreciation for the differences between "masculine" and "feminine" cultures, as described by Geert Hofsede in *Motivation, Leadership, and Achievement.* American masculine business behaviors include high achievement, acquisition of material goods, and efficiency, while other, more "feminine" cultures value relationships, leisure time with family, and developing a sense of community. Don't mistake this more feminine approach with a lack of motivation. Similarly, cultures that value "being and inner spiritual development" rather than compulsive "doing," are not necessarily inferior.

3. Try hard not to feel that your way is the best way. This can come across as arrogance and rubs salt in deep wounds in some lesser-developed countries.

4. Emphasize points of agreement.

5. When there are disagreements, check on the perceived definitions of words. Often there may be a huge or subtle shade of meaning that is causing the problem. You may actually both be trying to say the same thing.

6. Save face and "give" face as well, for this can be a way of showing honor to others.

7. Don't embarrass anyone in front of others. Even if you mean it as a "joke," it likely won't be taken that way.

8. Don't go alone. Take someone who knows the culture or language better than you. If you are discussing in English and your counterparts speak it only as a second language, you might be surprised how much they miss. Taking an excellent translator along is often a good investment.

9. Don't assume the other country views leadership the same way that you do. In many other cultures, "empowerment" seems more like anarchy and the result of an ineffectual manager.

10. Don't lose your temper.

11. Avoid clique-building and try to interact with the locals as much as possible. Americans tend to travel or spend time together in packs or tribes, which is not welcoming to the locals.

12. Always show respect.

13. Leave the common American task-oriented, fast-paced style at home. Effective transfer of skills to other cultures requires a patient nonjudgmentalism. Hasty criticisms of the foreigner's ideas only serve to shut that person down and close the door to meaningful interactions.

14. Keep in mind, however, that some countries, such as Israel, are even more fast-paced than the United States. People in these countries can be impatient with Americans' small talk.

15. Also be sensitive to the difference between the North American low-context culture—where employees are encouraged to be self-reliant—and high-context cultures (much of Asia, Africa, South America), where workers expect warmly supportive relationships with their supervisors and coworkers.

16. If you travel to the increasingly visited out-of-the-way locations, learn to tolerate unpredictability and go without what you may consider basic amenities. Avoid complaining to business clients about poor telephone service, lack of hot (or any, for that matter) water, erratic availability of electricity, or unsavory food. Just remember that you are the visitor and should act with the grace that goes along with that role.

SOURCE: Lalita Khosla, "You Say Tomato," *Forbes* (May 21, 2001), 36; Hari Bedi, "A Little Respect Can Bridge the Divide," *Asian Business* (January 1997), 50; Lorna Wright, "Building Cultural Competence," *Canadian Business Review* (Spring 1996), 29–33; and Geert Hofstede, "Motivation, Leadership and Organization: Do American Theories Apply Abroad?" *Organizational Dynamics* (Summer 1980), 42–63.

- In Africa, the labels on bottles show pictures of what is inside so illiterate shoppers can know what they're buying. When a baby-food company showed a picture of an infant on its label, the product didn't sell very well.[11]

- United Airlines discovered that even colors can doom a product. The airline handed out white carnations when it started flying from Hong Kong, only to discover that to many Asians such flowers represent death and bad luck.[12]

Some of these examples might seem humorous, but there's nothing funny about them to managers trying to operate in a competitive global environment. Companies seeking to expand their international presence on the Internet also can run into cross-cultural problems. What should managers of emerging global companies look for to avoid obvious international mistakes? When they are comparing one country with another, the economic, legal-political, and sociocultural sectors present the greatest difficulties. Key factors to understand in the international environment are summarized in Exhibit 3.2.

The Economic Environment

The economic environment represents the economic conditions in the country where the international organization operates. This part of the environment includes such factors as economic development; infrastructure; resource and product markets; exchange rates; and inflation, interest rates, and economic growth.

EXHIBIT 3.2

Key Factors in the International Environment

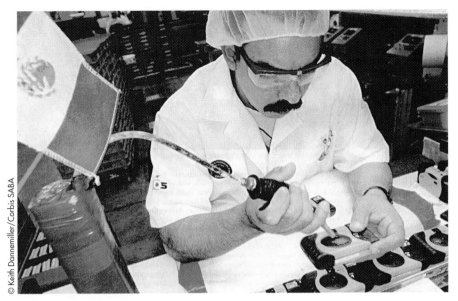

A solid infrastructure, *including decent highways, a Pacific port, and nonstop air service to the U.S., helps make Guadalajara a favorite factory town for U.S. companies such as IBM, Hewlett-Packard, and Siemens. Guadalajara and surrounding areas in the Mexican state of Jalisco boast the world's largest concentration of electronic contract manufacturers. Factories are bright, shining, and sophisticated, and the annual worker turnover rate is less than 5 percent. Single-use Kodaks, like the one being manufactured in the photo, are made with film coated in Rochester, New York, but assembled and packaged in Mexico.*

Economic Development. Economic development differs widely among the countries and regions of the world. Countries can be categorized as either *developing* or *developed*. Developing countries are referred to as *less-developed countries (LDCs)*. The criterion traditionally used to classify countries as developed or developing is *per capita income*, which is the income generated by the nation's production of goods and services divided by total population. The developing countries have low per capita incomes. LDCs generally are located in Asia, Africa, and South America. Developed countries are generally located in North America, Europe, and East Asia. Today, developing countries in Southeast Asia, Latin America, and Eastern Europe are driving global growth.[13]

Most international business firms are headquartered in the wealthier, economically advanced countries. However, smart companies are investing heavily in Asia, Eastern Europe, and Latin America. For example, the number of Internet users in Latin America is expected to grow to 19 million by 2003, up from only 4.8 million in 1998, and e-commerce sales are expected to zoom to $8 billion.[14] Both Compaq and Dell have launched online stores for Latin American customers to buy computers over the Internet. America Online sees Latin America as crucial to expanding its global presence, even though Universo Online International (UOL), based in Brazil, got a tremendous head start over AOL.[15] These companies face risks and challenges today, but they stand to reap huge benefits in the future.

Infrastructure. A country's physical facilities that support economic activities make up its **infrastructure**, which includes transportation facilities such as airports, highways, and railroads; energy-producing facilities such as utilities and power plants; and communication facilities such as telephone lines and radio stations. Companies operating in LDCs must contend with lower levels of technology and perplexing logistical, distribution, and communication problems. Undeveloped infrastructures represent opportunities for some firms, such as United Technologies Corporation, based in Hartford, Connecticut, whose businesses include jet engines, air-conditioning and heating systems, and elevators. As countries such as China, Russia, and Vietnam open their

infrastructure
A country's physical facilities that support economic activities.

DIGITAL, INC.

World Bank

Like so many other developing countries, Pakistan has crumbling roads and even worse finances. The country asked the World Bank for help in rating a cheap paving method. Two years ago, it would have taken bank experts nine months to research the problem. Using the Internet, it was solved in one day. After posting a query on its Web site, the bank received a reply from one of its employees in Argentina, who had written a book on the subject.

The Web is helping the World Bank to be a leader in knowledge management, unleashing the human expertise that is available in its ranks worldwide. Its Web site acts as a giant chat room, covering topics and data relating to concepts such as health care, education, or urban planning, and forging expert communities across borders. A recent project linked experts from 10 Latin American cities, with competencies in solid waste, municipal engineering, and transport. "Knowledge sharing will allow us to really have an impact on poverty," says Robert Chavez, a World Bank urban planner.

Instead of shuffling money from richer nations to poorer ones and hoping that the needy are actually helped, this new way of doing business fundamentally changes the agency's operations. Timely know-how can be given, allowing funds to be used more wisely. It creates a "different vision," says knowledge-management director Stephen Denning. As the new knowledge management keeps moving ahead, Third World countries just might be on a well-built road to economic gains.

SOURCE: Catherine Yang, "Sharing Knowledge Globally," *Business Week* (September 18, 2000), 102.

markets, new buildings need elevators and air and heat systems; opening remote regions for commerce requires more jet engines and helicopters.[16] Helping countries develop their infrastructure often falls on the shoulders of international agencies such as the World Bank, which discovered the Web as a major asset, as described in the Digital, Inc. box.

Resource and Product Markets. When operating in another country, company managers must evaluate the market demand for their products. If market demand is high, managers may choose to export products to that country. To develop plants, however, resource markets for providing needed raw materials and labor must also be available. For example, the greatest challenge for McDonald's, which now sells Big Macs on every continent except Antarctica, is to obtain supplies of everything from potatoes to hamburger buns to plastic straws. At McDonald's in Cracow, the burgers come from a Polish plant, partly owned by Chicago-based OSI Industries; the onions come from Fresno, California; the buns come from a production and distribution center near Moscow; and the potatoes come from a plant in Aldrup, Germany. McDonald's tries to contract with local suppliers when possible. In Thailand, McDonald's actually helped farmers cultivate Idaho russet potatoes of sufficient quality to produce their golden french fries.[17]

Exchange Rates. *Exchange rate* is the rate at which one country's currency is exchanged for another country's. Changes in the exchange rate can have major implications for the profitability of international operations that exchange millions of dollars into other currencies every day.[18] For example, assume that the U.S. dollar is exchanged for 0.8 euros. If the dollar increases in value to 0.9 euros, U.S. goods will be more expensive in France because it will take more euros to buy a dollar's worth of U.S. goods. It will be more difficult to export U.S. goods to France, and profits will be slim. If the dollar drops to a value of 0.7 euros, on the other hand, U.S. goods will be cheaper in France and can be exported at a profit.

The Legal–Political Environment

Businesses must deal with unfamiliar political systems when they go international, as well as with more government supervision and regulation. Government officials and the general public often view foreign companies as outsiders or even intruders and are suspicious of their impact on economic independence and political sovereignty. Some of the major legal–political concerns affecting international business are political risk, political instability, and laws and regulations.

Political Risk and Instability. A company's political risk is defined as its risk of loss of assets, earning power, or managerial control due to politically based events or actions by host governments.[19] Political risk includes government takeovers of property and acts of violence directed against a firm's properties or employees. Because such acts are not uncommon, companies must formulate special plans and programs to guard against unexpected losses. For example, Hercules, Inc., a large chemical company, increased the number of security guards at several of its European plants. Some companies buy political risk insurance, especially as they move into high-risk areas such as Eastern Europe, China, and Brazil. Political risk analysis has emerged as a critical component of environmental assessment for multinational organizations.[20]

U.S. firms or companies linked to the United States often are subject to major threats in countries characterized by **political instability**. For example, when barricades and tear gas blocked thousands of protesters in Pakistan from storming the U.S. consulate in Karachi on the first Muslim holy day after the U.S. began bombings in Afghanistan, the demonstrators turned instead to KFC, where they set fire to the restaurant, which is viewed as a symbol of America.[21]

Laws and Regulations. Government laws and regulations differ from country to country and make doing business a true challenge for international firms. Host governments have myriad laws concerning libel statutes, consumer protection, information and labeling, employment and safety, and wages. International companies must learn these rules and regulations and abide by them. For example, When Yahoo's Web site hosted an auction of Nazi paraphernalia, a French court ruled that the company must block access to French users because selling such items violates French law.[22] Sometimes dealing with another country's laws can be unexpectedly helpful, as Iqbal Quadir found in Bangladesh, described in the Focus on Collaboration box.

The most visible changes in legal-political factors grow out of international trade agreements and the emerging international trade alliance system. Consider, for example, the impact of the General Agreement on Tariffs and Trade (GATT), the European Union (EU), and the North American Free Trade Agreement (NAFTA).

GATT and the World Trade Organization

The General Agreement on Tariffs and Trade (GATT), signed by 23 nations in 1947, started as a set of rules to ensure nondiscrimination, clear procedures, the negotiation of disputes, and the participation of lesser developed countries in international trade. GATT and its successor, the World Trade Organization (WTO), primarily use tariff concessions as a tool to increase trade. Member

---

political risk

A company's risk of loss of assets, earning power, or managerial control due to politically based events or actions by host governments.

political instability

Events such as riots, revolutions, or government upheavals that affect the operations of an international company.

FOCUS ON COLLABORATION

GrameenPhone

Ten years ago, when Iqbal S. Quadir tried to get investors for a mobile phone network in Bangladesh, he received a lot of rejections, such as the one from a New York cell phone executive who said, "We're not the Red Cross." That's precisely the kind of thinking that keeps countries poor, says Harvard lecturer Quadir, because companies don't see the possibilities for profit in underdeveloped areas.

Proving the naysayers wrong, Quadir's GrameenPhone posted profits of $27 million last year, after only five years in operation. No one thought that possible—not even business-mogul-turned philanthropist Bill Gates, who has said there is no market for such electronic devices in poor and remote areas. Certainly the government did not think it would take off, either. They didn't even charge Quadir an up-front licensing fee, as they held the common belief that cell phones would be a marginal business for only the rich. But Quadir managed to pull together a group of private individuals with some government loans, as well.

One of Quadir's early investors was Bangladesh's Grameen Bank, world-famous for its microloans to small businesses in poor countries. Grameen bank follows a similar model. It offers normal cellular service to urban customers, and also has another tier, Village Phone. That's where people in areas with no phone service get small loans to buy a phone and air time, turning around and selling time on their phones to people in their village. GrameenPhone boasts 575,000 subscribers in over 12,000 villages—more even than the national telecom.

Quadir is now on the board of many organizations, including DigitalDivide.com, devoted to this system of public and private funding to aid entrepreneurs in poor countries. His next venture might prove to be even more challenging: Setting up a cell phone company in Afghanistan, a country with no visible banking or telecommunications. Undaunted, he pushes forward. "I've done it before."

SOURCE: Susan E. Reed, "Helping the Poor, Phone by Phone," *The New York Times* (May 26, 2002), 3.2.

---

most favored nation

A term describing a GATT clause that calls for member countries to grant other member countries the most favorable treatment they accord any country concerning imports and exports.

countries agree to limit the level of tariffs they will impose on imports from other members, and the **most favored nation** clause, which calls for each member country to grant to every other member country the most favorable treatment it accords to any country with respect to imports and exports.[23]

The goal of the WTO is to guide—and sometimes urge—the nations of the world toward free trade and open markets.[24] However, the power of the WTO is partly responsible for a growing backlash against global trade. An increasing number of individuals and public interest groups are protesting that global trade locks poor people into poverty and harms wages, jobs, and the environment.

European Union

Formed in 1958 to improve economic and social conditions among its members, the European Economic Community, now called the European Union (EU), has expanded to a 15-nation alliance illustrated in Exhibit 3.3. Poland, Hungary, the Czech Republic, Cyprus, Slovenia, and Estonia are in negotiations to join the EU, and at least seven other countries are considering opening membership negotiations.

euro

A single European currency that replaced the currencies of 11 European nations.

Another aspect of significance to countries operating globally is the EU's monetary revolution and the introduction of the **euro**. In January 2002, the euro, a single European currency, replaced 11 national currencies and unified a huge marketplace, creating a competitive economy second only to the United States.[25] Germany, France, Spain, Italy, Ireland, the Netherlands, Austria, Belgium, Finland, Portugal, and Luxembourg traded their deutschemarks, francs, lira, and other currencies to adopt the euro, a currency with a single exchange rate. The United Kingdom has thus far refused to accept the euro, in part because of a sense of nationalism, but many believe that the United Kingdom will eventually adopt the currency.

EXHIBIT 3.3

The Fifteen Nations within the EU

Although building alliances among countries is difficult, the benefits of doing so are overcoming divisions and disagreements. Canada, Mexico, and the United States have established what is expected to be an equally powerful alliance.

North American Free Trade Agreement (NAFTA)

The North American Free Trade Agreement, which went into effect on January 1, 1994, merged the United States, Canada, and Mexico into a megamarket with more than 360 million consumers. The agreement breaks down tariffs and trade restrictions on most agricultural and manufactured products over a 15-year period. The treaty builds on the 1989 U.S.–Canada agreement and is expected to spur growth and investment, increase exports, and expand jobs in all three nations.[26]

Between 1994, when NAFTA went into effect, and 1998, U.S. trade with Mexico increased a whopping 113 percent to $173.4 billion, while trade with Canada rose 63 percent, to $329.9 billion.[27]

The Sociocultural Environment

A nation's **culture** includes the shared knowledge, beliefs, and values, as well as the common modes of behavior and ways of thinking, among members of a society. Cultural factors are more perplexing than political and economic factors in foreign countries. Culture is intangible, pervasive, and difficult to learn.

culture

The shared knowledge, beliefs, values, behaviors and ways of thinking among members of a society.

It is absolutely imperative that international businesses and managers comprehend the significance of local cultures and deal with them effectively. Cultural clashes can show themselves in unusual ways, as described in the example below.

Miss Pakistan Earth

Neelam Nourani won the Miss Pakistani Earth competition in 2002 without wearing a bathing suit, so as not to offend Muslim sensibilities about revealing women's bodies. Judges were told to speculate whether the contestants had "nice healthy bodies" underneath their roomy trouser-and-tunic costumes. Now Nourani will have to buy a swimsuit to compete in the international Miss Earth contest.

Along with other concerns in Muslim countries, there has been some pressure to "develop." Along with fast food, beauty contests have become a measure of Westernization, which is shunned by countries such as Malaysia and Indonesia, which have the world's largest Muslim populations. Others try to adapt contests to the Muslim way. That was Muhammed Usman's idea in 1994 when he saw rival India take the Miss World and Miss Universe crowns. Both India and Pakistan have nuclear weapons, reasoned Usman, so "Why not beauty queens?" He hooked up with the 2002 Miss Earth contest, which has a "green theme" and features "beauties for a cause."

Usman, using family and friends as investors, held the first Pakistani contest in 2002. Seventy-three people showed up to watch 18 contestants sing and dance or recite Urdu poetry. Britney Spears fan Nourani based her energetic performance on a disco Pakistani song.

Winner Nourani had to hire bodyguards for her promotional tour to protect herself from Islamic extremists. "In Pakistan, if you take part in beauty contests," she says, you're considered a scandalous woman. Afghani Zohra Yusof Daoud would like to see that changed. An activist for women's rights in California, she was Miss Afghanistan in 1972. She wants the world to see Afghani women are more than faceless burka-wearers. But the contest would have to "incorporate Muslim values," she notes, and is not sure how that could be done. Having spent some of her formative years in the U.S., Nourani has a Western frankness that made her an outcast amongst the contestants. "We are Allah's creation," she says. "We have a right to represent womanhood."[28]

Social Values

Research done by Geert Hofstede on 116,000 IBM employees in 40 countries identified four dimensions of national value systems that influence organizational and employee working relationships.[29] Examples of how countries rate on the four dimensions are shown in Exhibit 3.4.

power distance

The degree to which people accept inequality in power among institutions, organizations, and people.

uncertainty avoidance

A value characterized by people's intolerance for uncertainty and ambiguity and resulting support for beliefs that promise certainty and conformity.

1. *Power distance*. High **power distance** means that people accept inequality in power among institutions, organizations, and people. Low power distance means that people expect equality in power. Countries that value high power distance are Malaysia, the Philippines, and Panama. Countries that value low power distance are Denmark, Austria, and Israel.

2. *Uncertainty avoidance*. High **uncertainty avoidance** means that members of a society feel uncomfortable with uncertainty and ambiguity and thus support beliefs that promise certainty and conformity. Low uncertainty avoidance means that people have high tolerance for the unstructured, the

Country	Power Distance[a]	Uncertainty Avoidance[b]	Individualism[c]	Masculinity[d]
Australia	7	7	2	5
Costa Rica	8 (tie)	2 (tie)	10	9
France	3	2 (tie)	4	7
West Germany	8 (tie)	5	5	3
India	2	9	6	6
Japan	5	1	7	1
Mexico	1	4	8	2
Sweden	10	10	3	10
Thailand	4	6	9	8
United States	6	8	1	4

[a] 1=highest power distance
10=lowest power distance
[b] 1=highest uncertainty avoidance
10=lowest uncertainty avoidance
[c] 1=highest individualism
10=highest collectivisim
[d] 1=highest masculinity
10=highest femininity

EXHIBIT 3.4

Rank Orderings of Ten Countries along Four Dimensions of National Value Systems

SOURCE: From Dorothy Marcic, *Organizational Behavior and Cases*, 4th ed. (St. Paul, Minn.: West, 1995). Based on Geert Hofstede, *Culture's Consequences* (London: Sage Publications, 1984); and *Cultures and Organizations: Software of the Mind* (New York: McGraw-Hill, 1991).

unclear, and the unpredictable. High uncertainty avoidance countries include Greece, Portugal, and Uruguay. Countries with low uncertainty avoidance values are Singapore and Jamaica.

3. *Individualism and collectivism.* **Individualism** reflects a value for a loosely knit social framework in which individuals are expected to take care of themselves. **Collectivism** means a preference for a tightly knit social framework in which individuals look after one another and organizations protect their members' interests. Countries with individualist values include the United States, Canada, Great Britain, and Australia. Countries with collectivist values are Guatemala, Ecuador, and China.

4. *Masculinity/femininity.* **Masculinity** stands for preference for achievement, heroism, assertiveness, work centrality (with resultant high stress), and material success. **Femininity** reflects the values of relationships, cooperation, group decision making, and quality of life. Societies with strong masculine values are Japan, Austria, Mexico, and Germany. Countries with feminine values are Sweden, Norway, Denmark, and France. Both men and women subscribe to the dominant value in masculine and feminine cultures.

Hofstede and his colleagues later identified a fifth dimension, **long-term orientation** versus **short-term orientation**. The long-term orientation, found in China and other Asian countries, includes a greater concern for the future and highly values thrift and perseverance. A short-term orientation, found in Russia and West Africa, is more concerned with the past and the present and places a high value on tradition and meeting social obligations.[30]

Social values influence organizational functioning and management styles. For example, managers attempting to implement self-directed work teams in Mexico have run into problems because Mexico is characterized by very high power distance and a relatively low tolerance for uncertainty. These characteristics often conflict with the American concept of teamwork, which emphasizes shared power and authority, with team members working on a variety of problems without formal guidelines, rules, and structure. Many workers in Mexico, as well as France and Mediterranean countries, expect organizations to be hierarchical. Germany and other central European countries have organizations

individualism

A preference for a loosely knit social framework in which individuals are expected to take care of themselves.

collectivism

A preference for a tightly knit social framework in which individuals look after one another and organizations protect their members' interests.

masculinity

A cultural preference for achievement, heroism, assertiveness, work centrality, and material success.

femininity

A cultural preference for cooperation, group decision making, and quality of life.

long-term orientation

A greater concern for the future and high value on thrift and perseverance.

short-term orientation

A concern with the past and present and a high value on meeting social obligations.

that strive to be impersonal, well-oiled machines. In India, Asia, and Africa, organizations are viewed as large families. Effective management styles differ in each country, depending on cultural characteristics.[31]

Other Cultural Characteristics

Other cultural characteristics that influence international organizations are language, religion, attitudes, social organization, and education. Some countries, such as India, are characterized by *linguistic pluralism*, meaning that several languages exist there. Other countries rely heavily on spoken versus written language. Religion includes sacred objects, philosophical attitudes toward life, taboos, and rituals. Attitudes toward achievement, work, and time can all affect organizational productivity. An attitude called **ethnocentrism** means that people have a tendency to regard their own culture as superior and to downgrade other cultures. Ethnocentrism within a country makes it difficult for foreign firms to operate there. Social organization includes status systems, kinship and families, social institutions, and opportunities for social mobility. Education influences the literacy level, the availability of qualified employees, and the predominance of primary or secondary degrees.

American managers are regularly accused of an ethnocentric attitude that assumes the American way is the best way. At an executive training seminar at IMD, a business school in Lausanne, Switzerland, managers from Europe expressed a mixture of admiration and disdain for U.S. managers. "They admire the financial results," says J. Peter Killing, an IMD professor, "but when they meet managers from the U.S. they see that even these educated, affluent Americans don't speak any language besides English, don't know how or when to eat and drink properly, and don't know anything about European history, let alone geography."[32] As business grows increasingly global, U.S. managers are learning that cultural differences cannot be ignored if international operations are to succeed. For example, Coke withdrew its two-liter bottle from the Spanish market after discovering that compartments of Spanish refrigerators were too small for it.[33] McDonald's hasn't even tried to market Egg McMuffins in Brazil because of the deeply ingrained tradition of eating breakfast at home. On the other hand, Kellogg introduced breakfast cereal into Brazil through carefully chosen advertising. Although the traditional breakfast is coffee and a roll, many Brazilians have been won over to the American breakfast and now start their day with Kellogg's Sucrilhos (Frosted Flakes) and Crokinhos (Cocoa Krispies).[34]

Organizations that recognize and manage cultural differences report major successes. Consider the cultural challenges managers of Bob's Big Boy face in Thailand.

ethnocentrism

A cultural attitude marked by the tendency to regard one's own culture as superior to others.

Bob's Big Boy

http://www.bigboy.com

McDonald's and Burger King have taken American fast food worldwide, and now a host of smaller companies, including A&W, Shakey's, and Dairy Queen, are heading overseas to serve customers who are hungry for more. But one adventurous franchiser who opened a Big Boy restaurant in Thailand learned quickly that there are plenty of barriers to overcome. Peter Smythe first began scouting for a franchise on behalf of a Thailand arms dealer who wanted to start a business for his daughters to run. When he met the owners of Big Boy, Elias Brothers of Warren, Michigan, Smythe knew he'd found a match. Big Boy, with 600 restaurants worldwide, seemed a natural for further global expansion. Its 1950s-roadside decor, diverse menu, and famous Big Boy icon all added up to a great American brand. "All you have to do is open the door and they will come," 78-year-old Louis Elias told Smythe. But when Smythe opened the door in Thailand, no one came (not even the arms dealer and his daughters, who showed no interest in running the business).

Smythe was left on his own to save Big Boy in Thailand, so he began talking to people about why they were not coming to the restaurant. The reasons were many and varied, ranging from feelings that the restaurant had bad "room energy" to the cost of the food. Many people told Smythe they'd rather get a bowl of noofles or sweet satay from a street vendor for one-fifth what they'd have to pay for a greasy American burger. And one of the biggest reasons was that Thai customers found the pudgy, grinning Big Boy statue just a little creepy. They couldn't figure out what the icon meant. A few eventually decided it was a religious figure and began laying bowls of rice and incense at his feet.

Smythe realized the attempt to transport a 65-year-old brand and food to a 3,500-year-old culture without making any adjustments wasn't going to fly. He began adding a few inexpensive Thai dishes to the menu, and customers began trickling in. He added sugar and chili powder to the burger recipe to better match Thai taste buds. The Big Boy statue stayed, but by educating employees, who pass what they learn on to friends and family, Smythe has persuaded customers to take the icon in stride. Smythe also took the comments about room energy seriously, even though he hasn't completely solved the problem.

And he still has plenty of other hurdles to contend with, as well. All the bakers he contacted told him the buns he wanted were "too complicated," so Smythe had to make his own bun molds. When small suppliers go out of business, he has to scramble to find replacements. And one of the biggest problems he's encountered is that at the peak of lunch hour the entire staff disappears into the back to eat their lunch of noodles and soup. "I asked them to take turns eating," Smythe says. "They say, 'No, we all have to eat at the same time.'" Smythe just has to do the best he can to work around the problem. His five-year adventure in Thailand has not been easy, but by listening to the local people and making adjustments to meet cultural differences, Smythe has now opened three additional—and highly profitable—Big Boy franchises in the country.[35]

Getting Started Internationally

Small and medium-sized companies have a couple of ways to become involved internationally. One is to seek cheaper sources of supply offshore, which is called *outsourcing*. Another is to develop markets for finished products outside their home country, which may include exporting, licensing, and direct investing. These are called **market entry strategies** because they represent alternative ways to sell products and services in foreign markets. Most firms begin with exporting and work up to direct investment. Exhibit 3.5 shows the strategies companies can use to enter foreign markets.

market entry strategy
An organizational strategy for entering a foreign market.

Outsourcing

Global outsourcing, sometimes called *global sourcing*, means engaging in the international division of labor so that manufacturing can be done in countries with the cheapest sources of labor and supplies. A company may take away a contract from a domestic supplier and place it with a company in the Far East, 8,000 miles away. Manufacturers in Asia and Latin America are rapidly getting

global outsourcing
Engaging in the international division of labor so as to obtain the cheapest sources of labor and supplies regardless of country; also called *global sourcing*.

EXHIBIT 3.5

*Strategies for Entering
International Markets*

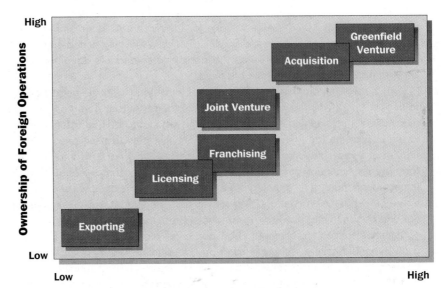

wired into the Internet to help them compete in an e-business world. Large companies outsource to companies all over Asia, and they like the convenience, speed, and efficiency of handling business by electronic transactions. Singapore-based Advanced Manufacturing Online uses a system that enables both suppliers and clients to send orders and solicit price quotes over the Web.[36] Another outsourcing company is Hong Kong-based Li & Fung, as described in the Best Practices box.

A unique variation of global outsourcing is the *Maquiladora* industry along the Texas–Mexico border. In the beginning, twin plants were set up, with the U.S. plant manufacturing components with sophisticated machinery and the Mexican plant assembling components using cheap labor. With increasing sophistication in Mexico, new factories with sophisticated equipment are being built farther south of the border, with assembled products imported into the United States at highly competitive prices. General Electric, for example, employs more than 30,000 people in appliance factories in Mexico, and is now shifting some of its engineering work to that country as well as to India, Brazil, and Turkey. And service companies are taking advantage of the *maquiladora* concept as well. U.S. data-processing companies use high-speed data lines to ship document images to Mexico and India, where 45,000 workers do everything from processing airline tickets to screening U.S. credit-card applications.[37]

Exporting

exporting

An entry strategy in which the organization maintains its production facilities within its home country and transfers its products for sale in foreign countries.

With **exporting**, the corporation maintains its production facilities within the home nation and transfers its products for sale in foreign countries.[38] Exporting enables a country to market its products in other countries at modest resource cost and with limited risk. U.S. exports are on the rise, and small to mid-size companies are benefiting. Multiplex Co., a St. Louis manufacturer of beverage-dispensing equipment for fast-food service, exports about 40 percent of its products. National Graphics, a specialty coater of papers and films, ships 60 percent of its products overseas, and National's CEO believes exports helped to save the company.[39]

Real Time Garments by Li & Fung

If you buy a shirt at Guess or Limited, chances are it was out-sourced through Li & Fung in Hong Kong. Run by Harvard graduates and Hong Kong natives William and Victor Fung, Li & Fung has no machines, no factories, and no fabrics. The Fungs deal only in information. They work with 7,500 suppliers in 37 countries, taking orders from companies such as Ambercrombie & Fitch, Disney, Levi Strauss, and American Eagle Outfitters. "There are no secrets to manufacturing," says Managing Director William. "A shirt is a shirt." Instead of manufacturing clothing, they build on proprietary information, such as how to make a shirt faster or more efficiently.

When an order comes in, the Fungs use personalized Web sites to fine-tune the specifications with the customer. Taking that information and feeding it into their own intranet, they are able to find the best supplier of raw materials and the best factories to assemble the garments. An order for pants from an American brand followed this course: the fabric was woven in China, because the supplier used dark green dyes; fasteners came from Hong Kong and Korea, chosen for durability; sup-plies were then shipped to Guatemala for sewing. "For simple things like pants with four seams, Guatemala is great," says division manager Ada Liu. With its proximity to the U.S., it takes only a few days for delivery from Guatemala. If production problems occur, Li & Fung can tap into an extensive database to find another supplier. As the order progresses, customers can make last-minute changes on Li & Fung's Web site.

As recently as five years ago, when the company was run by phone and fax, Li & Fung would get an order of 50,000 cargo pants and have it delivered five months later, instead of within the few weeks that it takes today. Now, with customers online making adjustments to color or cutting right before those are done, there are fewer mistakes and fewer unhappy customers.

Until a few years ago, clothing stores changed their stock four times a year, for each season. In the new economy, some stores rotate their clothes every week. This makes the name of the store Express take on a new meaning.

SOURCE: Joanne Lee-Young and Megan Barnett, "Furiously Fast Fashions," *The Industry Standard* (June 11, 2001), 72–79.

Licensing

The next stage in pursuing international markets is licensing and franchising, which are similar approaches. With **licensing**, a corporation (the licensor) in one country makes certain resources available to companies in another country (the licensee). These resources include technology, managerial skills, and/or patent and trademark rights. They enable the licensee to produce and market a product similar to what the licensor has been producing. This arrangement gives the licensor an opportunity to participate in the production and sale of products outside its home country at relatively low cost. Hasbro has licensing agreements with companies in several Latin American countries and Japan. Hasbro builds brand identity and consumer awareness by contracting with toy companies in other countries to manufacture products locally. Heineken, which has been called the world's first truly global brand of beer, usually begins by exporting to help boost familiarity with its product; if the market looks enticing enough, Heineken then licenses its brands to a local brewer.

Franchising is a special form of licensing that occurs when the franchisee buys a complete package of materials and services, including equipment, prod-ucts, product ingredients, trademark and trade name rights, managerial advice, and a standardized operating system. Whereas with licensing, a licensee gener-ally keeps its own company name and operating systems, a franchise takes the name and systems of the franchisor. For example, Anheuser-Busch licenses the right to brew and distribute Budweiser beer to several breweries, including Labatt in Canada and Kirin in Japan, but these breweries retain their own company names, identities, and autonomy. On the other hand, a Burger King

licensing
An entry strategy in which an organization in one country makes certain resources available to companies in another in order to participate in the production and sale of its products abroad.

franchising
A form of licensing in which an organization provides its foreign franchisees with a complete package of materials and services.

© Chris Brown/SABA

Daewoo Campus Advisers at U.S. universities? Through exporting, Korea's Daewoo Motor Co. sold 30,000 vehicles in its first year in the U.S. market. The Campus Advisers, a group of 2,000 college students at some 200 campuses, run Daewoo events and direct potential buyers to the nearest Daewoo sales showroom. The advisers receive $300 to $500 per car sold and an all-expense-paid seven-day trip to Korea, plus free use of a car for 3 months and the option to buy it at a discount.

direct investing

An entry strategy in which the organization is involved in managing its production facilities in a foreign country.

joint venture

A variation of direct involvement in which an organization shares costs and risks with another firm to build a manufacturing facility, develop new products, or set up a sales and distribution network.

franchise anywhere in the world is a Burger King, and managers use standard procedures designed by the franchisor. The fast-food chains are some of the best-known franchisors. KFC, Burger King, Wendy's, and McDonald's outlets are found in almost every large city in the world. The story is often told of the Japanese child visiting Los Angeles who excitedly pointed out to his parents, "They have McDonald's in America."

Licensing and franchising offer a business firm relatively easy access to international markets at low cost, but they limit its participation in and control over the development of those markets.

Direct Investing

A higher level of involvement in international trade is direct investment in manufacturing facilities in a foreign country. **Direct investing** means that the company is involved in managing the productive assets, which distinguishes it from other entry strategies that permit less managerial control.

Currently, the most popular type of direct investment is to engage in strategic alliances and partnerships. In a **joint venture**, a company shares costs and risks with another firm, typically in the host country, to develop new products, build a manufacturing facility, or set up a sales and distribution network.[40] A partnership is often the fastest, cheapest, and least risky way to get into the global game. Entrepreneurial companies such as Molex, a manufacturer of connectors, and Nypro, a maker of industrial components, have used partnerships to gain overseas access to several countries. Heineken Breweries has entered into a joint venture with Singapore's Asia Pacific Breweries, makers of Tiger Beer, and Ci-Co S.A. Auburn Farms, a Sacramento, California, manufacturer of all-natural snack foods, recently entered into a joint venture with South Africa's Beacon Sweets & Chocolates.[41] Internet companies have also used joint ventures as a way to expand. AOL created a joint venture with Venezuela's Cisneros Group to smooth its entry into Latin America.[42]

Multinational Corporations

multinational corporation (MNC)

An organization that receives more than 25 percent of its total sales revenues from operations outside the parent company's home country; also called *global corporation* or *transnational corporation*.

The size and volume of international business are so large that they are hard to comprehend. The revenue of General Motors is comparable to the gross domestic product (GDP) of Finland, that of General Electric is comparable in size to Israel's GDP, Toyota revenues to Hong Kong's GDP, and those of the Royal Dutch/Shell Group to the GDP of Norway.[43] As discussed earlier in this chapter, a large volume of international business is being carried out in a seemingly borderless world by very large international businesses that can be thought of as *global corporations, stateless corporations,* or *transnational corporations.* In the business world, these large international firms typically are called **multinational corporations (MNCs)**, which have been the subject of enormous attention. MNCs can move a wealth of assets from country to country and influence national economies, politics, and cultures.

The truly global companies that transcend national boundaries are growing in number. These companies no longer see themselves as American, Chinese, or German; they are totally globally operating and serve a global market.

Managing in a Global Environment

Managing in a foreign country is particularly challenging. Before undertaking a foreign assignment, managers must understand that they will face great personal challenges. Managers working in foreign countries must be sensitive to cultural subtleties and understand that the ways to provide proper leadership, decision making, motivation, and control vary in different cultures. When companies operate internationally, the need for personal learning and growth is critical. Sometimes that learning doesn't come too easily, as Wal-Mart learned the hard way.

Wal-Mart

http://www.wal-mart.com

Wal-Mart's first blunder was stocking its shelves with footballs in a country where soccer rules. In the suburbs of São Paulo, Brazil, the highly successful U.S. company discovered that its merchandise, tactics, and attitudes don't always translate well internationally. With opportunities for growth dwindling at home, Wal-Mart has embarked on a crusade to bring "everyday low prices" to the emerging markets of Brazil, Argentina, China, and Indonesia. But doing business internationally is a learning—and sometimes a losing—process. In its first two years in South America, Wal-Mart lost an estimated $48 million. Part of the difficulty is due to stiff competition from companies such as Brazil's Grupo Pao de Acucar SA and France's Carrefour SA, which have much stronger footholds in the region. However, analysts also blame Wal-Mart. By failing to do its homework, Wal-Mart made mistakes such as stocking footballs instead of soccer balls, live trout instead of sushi, and leaf blowers that are useless in the concrete world of São Paulo. It brought in stock-handling equipment that didn't work with standardized local pallets and installed a computerized bookkeeping system that didn't take Brazil's complicated tax system into account. Perhaps most damaging, the company's insistence on doing things "the Wal-Mart way" has alienated some local suppliers and employees.

To resolve these issues, the company has revised its merchandising and changed some of its tactics to better suit local cultures in Brazil and China. In Brazil, for example, it has scaled back the size of stores and moved to mid-size cities where competition is less fierce. Wal-Mart is trying to work with local partners who can help the company translate its business cross-culturally. Despite problems, the company is opening more stores in both Brazil and Argentina. Bob Martin, Wal-Mart's head of international operations, believes the international market is worth the risks. "The market is ripe and wide open for us."[44]

Personal Challenges for Global Managers

Managers will be most successful in foreign assignments if they are culturally flexible and easily adapt to new situations and ways of doing things. A tendency to be ethnocentric—to believe that your own country's cultural values and ways of doing things are superior—is a natural human condition. Managers can learn to break down those prejudices and appreciate another culture. As one Swedish executive of a large multinational corporation put it, "We Swedes are so content with . . . the Swedish way, that we forget that 99 percent of the rest of the world isn't Swedish."[45] Managers working in foreign countries may never come to understand the local culture like a native; the key is to be sensitive to cultural differences and understand that other ways of thinking and doing are also valid.

Most managers in foreign assignments face a period of homesickness, loneliness, and culture shock from being suddenly immersed in a culture with completely different languages, foods, values, beliefs, and ways of doing things. **Culture shock** refers to the frustration and anxiety that result from constantly being subjected to strange and unfamiliar cues about what to do and how to do it. Even simple, daily events can become sources of stress.[46]

Preparing managers to work in foreign cultures is essential. Some companies try to give future managers exposure to foreign cultures early in their careers. American Express Company's Travel-Related Services unit gives American business-school students summer jobs in which they work outside the United States for up to 10 weeks. Colgate-Palmolive selects 15 recent graduates each year and then provides up to 24 months of training prior to multiple overseas job stints.[47]

culture shock

Feelings of confusion, disorientation, and anxiety that result from being immersed in a foreign culture.

Managing Cross-Culturally

To be effective on an international level, managers can first understand their own cultural values and assumptions, as discussed in Chapter 2; then they can interpret the culture of the country and organization in which they are working and develop the sensitivity required to avoid making costly cultural blunders.[48]

In the United States, cross-cultural training is a popular way of helping managers prepare for overseas assignments. Sixty-three percent of global companies now offer managers at least one full day of cultural training about the foreign country where they have been assigned. "Americans tend to think everyone's the same," says Steven Jones of East–West Business Strategies in San Francisco. "It's a dangerous assumption."[49] One way managers prepare for foreign assignments is to understand how the country differs in terms of Hofstede's social values (power distance, individualism, uncertainty avoidance, masculinity, and orientation) as discussed earlier in this chapter. These values greatly influence how a manager should interact with subordinates and colleagues in the new assignment. For example, the United States scores extremely high on individualism, and a U.S. manager working in a country such as Japan, which scores very high on collectivism, will have to modify his or her approach to leading and controlling in order to be successful. The following examples illustrate how cultural differences can be significant for expatriate managers.

Leading. In relationship-oriented societies that rank high on collectivism, such as those in Asia, the Arab world, and Latin America, leaders should use a warm, personalized approach with employees. One of the greatest difficulties U.S. leaders have had doing business in China, for example, is failing to recognize that to the Chinese any relationship is a personal relationship.[50] Managers are expected to have periodic social visits with workers, inquiring about morale and health. Leaders should be especially careful about criticizing others. To Asians, Africans, Arabs, and Latin Americans, the loss of self-respect brings dishonor to themselves and their families. One researcher tells of a Dutch doctor managing a company clinic who had what he considered a "frank discussion" with a Chinese subordinate. The subordinate, who perceived the doctor as a father figure, took the criticism as a "savage indictment" and committed suicide.[51] Though this is an extreme example, the principle of *saving face* is highly important in some cultures.

Decision Making. In the United States, mid-level managers may discuss a problem and give the boss a recommendation. German managers, on the other hand, expect the boss to issue specific instructions. In Mexico, employees often don't understand participatory decision making. Mexico ranks extremely high on power distance, and many workers expect managers to exercise their power in making decisions and issuing orders. American managers working in Mexico have been advised to rarely explain a decision, lest workers perceive this as a sign of weakness.[52] In contrast, managers in Arab and African nations are expected to use consultative decision making in the extreme.

Motivating. Motivation must fit the incentives within the culture. In Japan, employees are motivated to satisfy the company. A financial bonus for star performance would be humiliating to employees from Japan, China, or Ecuador. An American executive in Japan offered a holiday trip to the top salesperson, but employees were not interested. After he realized that Japanese are motivated in groups, he changed the reward to a trip for everyone if together they achieved the sales target. They did. Managers in Latin America, Africa, and the Middle East must show respect for employees as individuals with needs and interests outside of work.[53]

Controlling. When things go wrong, managers in foreign countries often are unable to get rid of employees who do not work out. In Europe, Mexico, and Indonesia, to hire and fire based on performance seems unnaturally brutal. Workers are protected by strong labor laws and union rules.

In foreign cultures, managers also should not control the wrong things. A Sears manager in Hong Kong insisted that employees come to work on time instead of 15 minutes late. The employees did exactly as they were told, but they also left on time instead of working into the evening as they had previously. A lot of work was left unfinished. The manager eventually told the employees to go back to their old ways. His attempt at control had a negative effect.

Global Learning

Managing across borders calls for organizations to learn across borders. One reason Japanese companies have been so successful internationally is that their culture encourages learning and adaptability. In Asia generally, teaching and learning are highly regarded, and the role of managers is seen as one of teaching or facilitating—of helping those around them to learn.[54] It is partly this emphasis on continuous learning that has helped Matsushita Electric master markets and diverse cultures in 38 countries, from Malaysia to Brazil, from Austria to China, from Iran to Tanzania. One of Matsushita's top lessons for going global is to be a good corporate citizen in every country, respecting cultures, customs, and languages. In countries with Muslim religious practices, for example, Matsushita provides special prayer rooms and allows two prayer sessions per shift.[55] Doing global business on the Web requires continuous learning about other cultures and conditions elsewhere, as described in the Best Practices box.

BEST PRACTICES

Virtual Reality: Negotiating the Cross-Cultural Web

With worldwide acceptance of the Internet ballooning, going global has the green light. But technological and cultural issues are so tightly interwoven that there are a multitude of new ways to offend or alienate customers in other nations. For instance, certain gestures, colors, and phrases don't translate well or are considered offensive. A thumbs-up sign means approval or encouragement to Americans and many Europeans, but the gesture is considered an obscenity in Greece. Purple is a sign of royalty in some parts of the world, but in others it is associated with death. Credit cards are the backbone of e-commerce in the United States, but they are still a rarity in many countries, causing all sorts of payment problems. And consumers in Germany view credit as a crutch for people who cannot control their finances.

Managers should also consider that many online shoppers want to buy from sites that cater to their native language—for example, research has found that Japanese managers are much more likely to conduct an online transaction when addressed in Japanese. Unfortunately, although just 6 percent of the world's people speak English as a first language, 96 percent of all e-commerce sites are written in English. In fact, less than half of U.S. companies have even attempted to pattern their Web sites to the culture or language of foreign users. This complacent attitude adds up to lost opportunities and negative attitudes toward U.S. Internet companies.

Some companies are leading the way in overcoming global challenges on the Internet. Autobytel.com, an online car buying and information site, relies on partnerships. These regional partners help navigate through a myriad of social laws and European online privacy laws. As Autobytel pushes into Japan, it has teamed up with six Japan-based corporations, hoping to tap into their expertise. Josh McCarter, vice president of international development, says, "You have to understand how cars are built and sold" in any market you enter. For example, in the U.S., most vehicles have only a few option packages available. By contrast, in Japan and most of Europe, it is usual for customers to spec out a vehicle. Local partners can help companies surmount these differences by developing a Web site that can offer numerous configurations.

QXL.com, based in London, is battling to become the dominant online auctioneer in Europe. QXL's home-field advantage makes it easier to go international, but leaders also credit their European mindset, which readily accepts cultural and linguistic differences. This openness to other cultures and ways of doing things has given American managers at eBay a run for their money. Another Internet auction site, Baazee.com, based in Bombay, India, has also found innovative ways to adapt to local cultures. Baazee's managers have found that most Indians associate auctions with bankruptcy liquidations. In addition, they don't place trust in buying without seeing the merchandise. To solve this problem, managers set up "exchange centers," where the seller and winning bidder can complete their business in person after the buyer is satisfied with the item.

The Internet might someday build its own global Web culture, but so far, the "virtual reality" for managers is a need to shape their Web sites to reach local communities.

SOURCES: Steve Ulfelder, "All the Web's a Stage," *CIO* (October 1, 2000), 133–142; Daniel Pearl, "Lost in the Translation," *The Wall Street Journal* (February 12, 2001), R12, R14; and Adam Lincoln, "Lost in Translation," *eCFO* (Spring 2001), 38–43.

■ Summary and Management Solution

This chapter has emphasized the growing importance of an international perspective on management. Successful companies are expanding their business overseas and successfully competing with foreign companies on their home turf. Business in the global arena involves special risks and difficulties because of complicated economic, legal-political, and sociocultural forces. Moreover, the global environment changes rapidly, as illustrated by the emergence of the European Union, the North American Free Trade Agreement, and the shift in Eastern Europe to democratic forms of government. Major alternatives for serving foreign markets are exporting, licensing, fran-

chising, and direct investing through joint ventures or wholly owned subsidiaries.

International markets provide many opportunities but are also fraught with difficulty, as Tortas Peru, described at the beginning of this chapter, discovered. Roman was asked to speak at a virtual seminar on tourism in Peru. One of the other speakers was using a credit card system that was workable in Peru, so Roman immediately signed up that service. In addition, they still take personal checks sent to the U.S. address or do bank transfers. With a way to collect money, Tortas Peru was able to expand to seven Peruvian cities and promises to deliver a cake to any of those cities within 72 hours of the order. Plus they take a digital picture of the cake being delivered and send it back to the customer in the U.S. Tortas Peru is such a successful business model that when it entered the 2001 Stockholm Challenge with 62 other contenders for the New Economy Award, it was the only winner. More importantly, it not only provides a service to Peruvian expatriates, but also provides much-needed income to Peruvian housewives who don't have to leave their homes—or their cake pans.[56]

Much of the growth in international business has been carried out by large businesses called *MNCs*. These large companies exist in an almost borderless world, encouraging the free flow of ideas, products, manufacturing, and marketing among countries to achieve the greatest efficiencies. Managers in *MNCs* as well as those in much smaller companies doing business internationally face many challenges. Managers often experience culture shock when transferred to foreign countries. They must learn to be sensitive to cultural differences and tailor their management style to the culture. For managers and organizations in an increasingly borderless world, learning across borders is critical.

As a means of learning across borders, here is a poem that addresses cultural differences.

An Asian View of Cultural Differences

We live in time. You live in space.
We are always at rest. You are always on the move.
We are passive. You are aggressive.
We like to contemplate. You like to act.
We accept the world as it is. You try to change the world according to your blueprint.
We live in peace with nature. You try to impose your will on her.
Religion is our first love. Technology is your passion.
We delight to think about the meaning of life. You delight in physics.
We believe in freedom of silence. You believe in freedom of speech.
We lapse into meditation. You strive for articulation.
We marry first, then love. You love first, then marry.
Our marriage is the beginning of a love affair. Your marriage is the happy end of a romance.
It is an indissoluble bond. It is a contract.
Our love is mute. Your love is vocal.
We try to conceal it from the world. You delight in showing it to others.
Self-denial is the secret to our survival. Self-assertiveness is the key to your success.
We are taught from the cradle to want less and less. You are urged every day to want more and more.
We glorify austerity and renunciation. You emphasize gracious living and enjoyment.
In the sunset years of life we renounce the world and prepare for the hereafter. You retire to enjoy the fruits of your labor.

—Dr. Mai Van Trang

■ Discussion Questions

1. Why do you think international businesses traditionally prefer to operate in industrialized countries? Discuss.
2. What might be some long-term ramifications of the war on terrorism for U.S. managers and companies operating internationally?
3. What policies or actions would you recommend to an e-commerce company wanting to do business internationally?
4. What steps could a company take to avoid making product design and marketing mistakes when introducing new products into a foreign country?
5. Compare the advantages associated with the foreign-market entry strategies of exporting, licensing, and wholly owned subsidiaries.
6. What does it mean to say that the world is becoming "borderless"? That large companies are "stateless"?
7. What might managers do to avoid making mistakes concerning control and decision making when operating in a foreign culture?
8. What is meant by the cultural values of individualism and power distance? How might these values affect organization design and management processes?
9. How do you think trade alliances such as NAFTA and the EU may affect you as a future manager?

■ Manager's Workbook

State of the World Test

How aware are you of the rest of the planet? If you will be working internationally, the better you know about the world, the more successful you are likely to be.

1. Which six countries make up over half of the world's population?

   a. _____

   b. _____

   c. _____

   d. _____

   e. _____

   f. _____

2. Which six most commonly spoken first languages account for one-third of the total world population:

   a. _____

   b. _____

   c. _____

   d. _____

   e. _____

   f. _____

3. How many living languages (those still spoken) are there in the world?
   a. 683
   b. 2,600
   c. 6,800

4. How many nations were there in 2001?
   a. 291
   b. 191
   c. 91

5. The proportion of people in the world over age 60 will increase _____ percent by 2050.

6. The number of people immigrating from poorer countries to developed ones will be _____ per year in coming years.

7. Between 1970 and 2000, the number of people in the world suffering from malnutrition:
   a. declined
   b. remained about the same
   c. increased

8. Between 1960 and 1987, the world spent approximately $10 trillion on health care. How much did the world spend on military?
   a. $7 trillion
   b. $10 trillion
   c. $17 trillion
   d. $25 trillion

9. According to the United Nations, what percentage of the world's work (paid and unpaid) is done by women?
   a. one-third
   b. one-half
   c. two-thirds
   d. three-fourths

10. Women make up _____ percent of the world's illiterates.

11. In some African countries, _____ percent of women have suffered female genital mutilation.

12. According to the United Nations, what percentage of the world's income is earned by women?
    a. one-tenth
    b. three-tenths
    c. one-half
    d. seven-tenths

13. The nations of Africa, Asia, Latin America, and the Middle East, often referred to as the Third World, contain about 78 percent of the world's population. What percentage of the world's monetary income do they possess?
    a. 10 percent
    b. 20 percent
    c. 30 percent
    d. 40 percent

14. Americans constitute approximately 5 percent of the world's population. What percentage of the world's resources do Americans consume?
    a. 15 percent
    b. 25 percent
    c. 35 percent
    d. 45 percent

15. Which city has the worst air pollution: New York, Mexico City, or Moscow?

16. The total output of the world economy was $6.3 trillion in 1950. What was it in 2000?

17. The number of host computers on the internet grew by _____ percent from 1990 to 2000.

18. Which three countries have the highest rate of HIV infection?

19. If the world were represented by 100 people, fill in the blanks below to indicate what percentage of people are the following:

    _____ would be Asian

    _____ would be non-White

    _____ would be non-Christian

    _____ would live in substandard housing

    _____ would be illiterate

    _____ would have a college education

    _____ would own a computer

SOURCE: Reka Balu, "Please Don't Forward This E-mail!" *Fast Company* (June 2001), 58–59; World Watch Institute, *World Watch 2002*, W.W. Norton; *http://www.un.org*, 2002.

■ Manager's Workshop

Global Showcase

1. Divide into groups of four or five. Each person is assigned a country by the instructor. It should be a country the person is not familiar with, someplace entirely new.
2. Outside of class, individually prepare a report on your country, including where it is located (maps are helpful—use PowerPoint or an overhead slide); characteristics of the population and economy; health and education levels; roles within families, how children are viewed; how achievement, group harmony, and independence are viewed. Also describe the three things you value most in that country and the three things that are difficult for you to understand.
3. Groups meet, either in or out of class, to compare their results. Discuss similarities and differences in types of

behavior expected, how work is viewed, and the value of work in that culture.
4. Each group prepares a five-minute presentation to the whole class, extracting the most important information on each country, along with similarities and differences among the countries.
5. The instructor leads a discussion on cultural differences. What did you learn from this exercise? What is the relationship between behaviors and ways of thinking?

SOURCE: Adapted from Uzoamaka P. Anakwe, "The Art of Dialogue in Building Cross-Cultural Sensitivity in the Classroom," *Journal of Management Education* 26, no. 3 (2002), 291–306.

■ Manager's Workshop

Global Economy Scavenger Hunt

In order to get a perspective on the pervasiveness of the global economy, you will be asked to find a number of things and bring them back to class.

1. Divide into teams of four to six members.
2. Each team should bring items to a future class from the list below.
3. On the designated day in class, each team will give a two-minute presentation on the items that were the most difficult or the most interesting to find.
4. How many countries did your team get items from? How many for the entire class?

List for scavenger hunt:

1. Brochures of annual reports of four multinational corporations.
2. Evidence from three local businesses to show they do business internationally.
3. Locate a retail store that sells only "Made in America."
4. Ten toys or games that originated in other countries.
5. Five toys or games that had components from one country and assembled in another—or somehow developed in more than one country.

6. Food items from 25 different countries.
7. Articles of clothing from 15 different countries.
8. List books sold in your town from authors of 12 different countries. Where were the books published? Who translated them?
9. List of 12 films in the past five years that starred someone from another country.
10. List of five films in the past five years that had multinational crews and locations. Include at least one that was coproduced by two or more countries.
11. Descriptions of interviews from five foreigners (not from your team or the class) asking them what are six things they like about the U.S. and six things they don't like.
12. A list of eight places where a language other than English is displayed (on a bulletin board, poster, etc.).
13. Two maps of the world drawn before 1900.
14. Five items in your town that were manufactured in another country that were not made in that country six years ago.

SOURCE: Adapted from Jan Drum, Steve Hughes, and George Otere, "Global Scavenger Hunt," in *Global Winners* (Yarmouth, Maine: Intercultural Press, 1994), 21–23.

■ Management in Practice: Ethical Dilemma

The Problem in Asia

Cindy Wilkinson should have been smiling as she stared out the window of the plane headed toward Illinois. She had just successfully completed three challenging years in Asia for Axcor Inc. and was now headed home to a plum assignment at

headquarters and a chance to have Thanksgiving dinner with her family again.

But Cindy's thoughts kept turning to what she had come to think of as The Problem. She knew she'd be debriefed upon her return to headquarters, and she was either going to have to hide an ugly matter or reveal a serious problem in the Asian operations, a move that could threaten her career with Axcor. The ugliness centered on Wang Zing, who had been Axcor's director of Asian operations for the past five years. It hadn't taken Cindy long to realize that Zing consistently undermined people's confidence and caused them to suffer undeserved shame. He seemed to have an uncanny ability to spot people's weaknesses and use them to manipulate staff members. One of his favorite activities was humiliating employees in public. Cindy had learned in her cross-cultural training prior to her assignment that obedience was highly valued in Asian cultures, along with the concept of saving face. Zing abused those cultural values, his position, and the staff, resulting in an inefficient operation that wasn't meeting its potential. Yet, because top managers had never clearly defined goals for the Asian operation, evaluating Zing was tricky. Whenever the corporate comptroller made his annual visit, Zing would lavish him with hospitality and the executive would leave thinking everything in Asia was going just grand.

Cindy knew the comptroller liked Zing and influenced the views of other top executives, but she felt that she needed to describe the degradation of employees that she had witnessed. Even if she simply identified some basic changes that could increase productivity, it would end up pointing the finger at Zing. Possible retribution could sidetrack or even destroy her career.

What Do You Do?

1. Keep your mouth shut. This is the comptroller's responsibility. You've just gotten the job you wanted at headquarters, and to rock the boat now could do more harm to your career than it would do good for the company.
2. Tell top executives straight out that Zing is mistreating employees and creating an environment that is detrimental to productivity and performance.
3. Frame your remarks in terms of the inefficiencies you witnessed in the Asian operation, with specific details to back you up. Recommend that clear, high standards be established for the Asian business and suggest some elements of those standards, including treatment of employees.

SOURCE: Adapted from Doug Wallace, "When Being Right Isn't Enough," *BusinessEthics* (March–April 1999), 18.

■ Surf the Net

1. **Largest Companies in the World.** *Fortune* magazine, in its annual listing called the "Global 500," ranks the world's largest companies based on sales revenue. Go to *http://www.fortune.com* and locate the Global 500. Fill in the chart below:
Global 500 Ranking for _____ (Year)

Ranking	Company	Headquarters (Country)
1		
2		
3		
4		
5		
6		
7		
8		
9		
10		

2. **World Trade Organization.** Visit the WTO at *http://www.wto.org* and answer the following questions:
   • Where is the WTO located?
   • When was it established?
   • How many countries are members?
   • What are the WTO's main functions?
3. **The World Fact Book.** You will find fascinating information is available at *http://www.odci.gov/cia/publications/factbook/index.html*. Access the "Field Listing" option for "GDP—per capita." On a separate sheet of paper list how much the per capita GDP is for the United States and countries with a higher per capita GDP than the United States. Next, identify two or three countries with per capita GDP closest to that of the United States. Finally, indicate the country with the lowest per capita GDP, including the amount.

■ Case for Critical Analysis

Unocal Corporation

Unocal Corporation seemed an unlikely candidate for a high-risk global rampage. Consumers everywhere recognized the ubiquitous 76 logo of this quintessential California oil company. They knew it as a large petroleum retailer, with a prestigious downtown headquarters and important role as a Los Angeles civic booster. Casting aside its reputation as a conservative company with tightly defined domestic markets and focused petroleum interests in California, Unocal spent the 1990s transforming itself into an international company with major investments in some of the world's least-developed economies.

In 1995, immediately after becoming chairman of Unocal, Roger Beach began to sell off domestic retail assets and eliminate exploration and refining activities in the United States. Resources shifted to unlikely places where few other major oil producers had risked operations—places such as Myanmar (formerly known as Burma), Turkmenistan, Uzbekistan, and the strife-ridden Balkans. Beach turned up the heat on company investments in Indonesian oil fields, launched full-service energy subsidiaries through government alliances in Thailand, broadened holdings in Malaysia, and began negotiations for an integrated refining/retailing enterprise in Pakistan. Nearly 40 percent of Unocal's exploration and extraction budget was thrown into these emerging markets, much of it pinpointed for very-high-risk locations in the former Soviet republics and the Persian subcontinent.

Why take these risks? Beach answers that Unocal, unable to compete head-to-head with the oil industry giants for capital markets, decided to create an extremely attractive strategic package of full-service energy production in countries grasping to develop infrastructure. "What every government likes about Unocal's strategy is one-stop shopping; one group able to take the whole project from development to the marketing end," Beach said. "We have become partners in their development and as important to them as they are to us." The Unocal strategy defies normal industry trends based on distributing huge capital investments to tie up oil reserves and mineral rights, then cutting deals for operations. Instead, Unocal comes in the front door with packaged energy services ranging from turning the first spade of dirt on exploration to delivering power to the end user, and that proposal includes oil, gas, or electric power generation.

Beach sees far less risk than industry analysts perceive in the emerging markets. The dangers of war, political upheaval, and currency fluctuations are clear and present, yet the company says it has hedged against these threats by diversifying investments. However, according to Beach, success will depend on creating a globally managed company capable of understanding and participating in foreign market environments. Consequently, in 1996, he initiated a major transformation in Unocal's management systems, beginning by relocating its headquarters from its stately downtown offices to a small, highly efficient suite near the Los Angeles International Airport. Mid-level managers were either repositioned in regional offices, such as

Singapore, Istanbul, or Jakarta, or they left the company. The executive core, which had been distinctly Los Angeleno in character, gained a multicultural character, representing Eastern European and Asian group alliances. Subsidiaries in Jakarta, Thailand, and Myanmar took on local names and corporate identities, shedding their American profiles, and Unocal's many foreign alliances have made it part of the communities in which it operates.

In Thailand, Unocal worked on the country's privatization plan to convert its Petroleum Authority of Thailand (PTT) operations into privately owned and operated international oil services. Unocal and the PTT have begun to build pipelines in the Gulf of Thailand linking Unocal's hydrocarbon fields in the nation's rugged peninsula, and a joint venture in Malaysia has begun to open regional energy markets from Myanmar to the Philippines. Surface evaluations have hailed this consortium as a master stroke of strategy; however, related activities have exposed Unocal to strong criticism. Unocal became the largest single U.S. investor in Myanmar as part of the expansion, but Myanmar's military government has languished in political and economic isolation as a result of U.S. legislation aimed at boycotting the country for its unacceptable human-rights practices. Political activists in more than a dozen U.S. states have won passage of legislation barring imports from Myanmar and outlawing private investments there by U.S. firms. Municipal governments in five states have passed boycott laws, as well, and Unocal, together with PepsiCo and several other American companies operating in Myanmar, have become major targets for international pressure groups. PepsiCo bowed to the pressure and moved out of Myanmar, but Unocal has flatly refused to budge.

The company's insistence on remaining in Myanmar, however, is not a vote in support of the country's human-rights record. Indeed, Unocal would find it difficult to withdraw, because it has formed an equity agreement with the giant French petrochemical company Total, which also has substantial pipeline investments with Unocal in the Persian Gulf and southern Asia. Unocal's contracts with Total make it a *de facto* partner of the French government. Moreover, Unocal has invested in public and private interests in Myanmar that spread to five other major Southeast Asian states. But a Unocal representative cites the importance of the company's role in helping the nation's development. "To withdraw and isolate [Myanmar] would have no effect. Questionable human-rights leadership and political practices would continue and perhaps proliferate," she said. "On the other hand, our strength and the fact that we can provide meaningful jobs and ethical international business, encourages changes for the good. Even if every American firm vacated, firms from other nations would welcome the chance to develop [Myanmar] without American competition."

That position doesn't relieve the political or financial risk to Unocal. Ethics and U.S. policies aside, Myanmar lacks a strong track record for keeping its promises. As a closed military state, self-isolated for ideological reasons since the end of World War II, it has few friends anywhere in the world. For years, it was linked to the Soviet Union for aid and military support, and it backed insurgent forces in several neighboring civil conflicts. These situations did not endear the government to potential regional economic allies. However, the country is strategically positioned within the Southeast Asian theater, and it has attracted consideration, with much controversy, for membership in ASEAN.

Unocal holds a rather exposed position in the country, as it does in Uzbekistan, Turkmenistan, and the Balkans. An American company without the legal or political support of its home government can expect little help should the host government decide to freeze its assets, bar currency repatriation, or resort to outright expropriation. Meanwhile, Unocal has tied up several billion dollars in the region while maintaining no safety net at home. Indeed, it faces potentially costly threats from home, and if the company is pushed to the wall by legislation, the chairman says, he will take Unocal out of U.S. control.

Questions

1. What market entry strategies has Unocal used, based on the activities described in the case? Would you classify Unocal as a multinational corporation (MNC)? Why or why not?

2. Identify and discuss the various types of risks faced by Unocal in emerging markets (consider the economic, legal-political, and sociocultural environment). Which risks seem most threatening to the company?

3. What do you think of the Unocal representative's statement that "to withdraw and isolate Myanmar would have no effect" regarding that country's poor human-rights record? Do you believe U.S. companies should stay in such countries in the hope of improving the ethical climate? Discuss.

SOURCE: "Unocal Corporation," from *International Management: Text and Cases*, 143–145, David H. Holt, First Edition © 1998 by Holt. Reprinted with permission of South-Western, a division of Thomson Learning: www.thomsonrights.com. Fax 800-730-2215.

Managerial Ethics and Corporate Social Responsibility

LEARNING OBJECTIVES

After studying this chapter, you should be able to

1 Define ethics and explain how ethical behavior relates to behavior governed by law and free choice.

2 Explain the utilitarian, individualism, moral-rights, and justice approaches for evaluating ethical behavior.

3 Describe how both individual and organizational factors shape ethical decision making.

4 Define corporate social responsibility and how to evaluate it along economic, legal, ethical, and discretionary criteria.

5 Describe four organizational approaches to environmental responsibility.

6 Explain the concept of stakeholder and identify important stakeholders for organizations.

7 Discuss how ethical organizations are created through ethical leadership and organizational structures and systems.

Management Challenge

The global AIDS crisis has trapped several large U.S. drug companies in an ethical quandary. They want to be seen as helping to fight this global tragedy, but international activists portray the drug companies as arrogant and greedy. They charge that the companies are putting their own profits above the value of human lives by keeping patented life-saving medicines beyond the reach of the world's poor. A lawsuit filed by 40 drug makers against the South African government has reinforced the Scrooge-like image. When Nelson Mandela was president of South Africa, he signed a law allowing the country to import cheap generic versions of patented medicines without first getting permission from the patent owners. Concerned with the spread of AIDS, the U.S. government agreed to "look the other way" if poor nations make and import generic drugs. However, the pharmaceutical companies framed the issue as a fight over intellectual property rights, attempting to avoid the question of how it might affect the treatment and spread of AIDS. A widening circle of activist organizations, including Doctors Without Borders and Oxfam, have attacked the patents of U.S. drug companies as a direct threat to the health and well-being of the world's poor. Some activist groups have gone so far as to accuse the companies of genocide.[1]

Do you believe it is unethical for U.S. drug companies to file suit against poor nations that cannot afford name-brand drugs? Where should managers draw the line between protecting their organization's intellectual property and bending the rules to alleviate human suffering?

This situation illustrates how difficult ethical issues can be and symbolizes the growing importance of discussing ethics and social responsibility. Corporations are rushing to adopt codes of ethics and develop socially responsible policies: Ethics consultants are doing a land-office business. Unfortunately, the trend is necessary. In recent years, numerous companies, including Sears, Archer-Daniels-Midland, and Tyson Foods, have been charged with major breaches of ethical or legal standards. Bridgestone/Firestone and the Ford Motor Company spent months blaming each other for a series of deadly tire failures. And Enron, America's seventh-largest corporation in mid-2000, was essentially destroyed by a combination of deceit, arrogance, shady financial dealings, and inappropriate accounting practices that inflated earnings and hid debt. The world of cyberspace is opening new avenues for potential ethical lapses. Alibris, an online bookseller specializing in rare books, pled guilty to a charge of intercepting e-mail messages sent by Amazon.com to customers. Former iVillage executives have accused that company of cheating employees out of promised stock options.[2]

On the other hand, there also is positive news to report. The toy maker Mattel conducts social audits of its policies and practices to make sure its factories are adhering to ethical and socially responsible guidelines. Managers at American Electric Power Company are spending $5.5 million on a reforestation program in Bolivia in an effort to offset the carbon dioxide the company releases into the environment.[3] Internet start-ups such as eBay and Infoseek have made significant donations to charitable causes.[4] And Eastman Kodak Company took an unprecedented step several years ago by tying a percentage of managers' pay to factors such as how well they treat their employees.[5]

This chapter expands on the ideas about environment, corporate culture, and the international environment discussed in Chapters 2 and 3. We will first focus on specific ethical values that build on the idea of corporate culture. Then we will examine corporate relationships to the external environment as reflected in social responsibility. Ethics and social responsibility are hot topics in corporate America. This chapter discusses fundamental approaches that help managers think through ethical issues. Understanding ethical approaches helps managers build a solid foundation on which to base future decision making.

What Is Managerial Ethics?

ethics

The code of moral principles and values that govern the behaviors of a person or group with respect to what is right or wrong.

human behavior influenc-
ed by:
1. law
2. free choice
3. ethics

Ethics is difficult to define in a precise way. In a general sense, **ethics** is the code of moral principles and values that govern the behaviors of a person or group with respect to what is right or wrong. Ethics sets standards as to what is good or bad in conduct and decision making.[6] Ethics deals with internal values that are a part of corporate culture and shapes decisions concerning social responsibility with respect to the external environment. An ethical issue is present in a situation when the actions of a person or organization may harm or benefit others.[7]

Ethics can be more clearly understood when compared with behaviors governed by laws and by free choice. Exhibit 4.1 illustrates that human behavior falls into three categories. The first is codified law, in which values and standards are written into the legal system and enforceable in the courts. In this area, lawmakers have ruled that people and corporations must behave in a certain way, such as obtaining licenses for cars or paying corporate taxes. The Internet revolution has raised new legal issues, such as how copyrights are interpreted in cyberspace. For example, the courts ruled that Napster, the file-

EXHIBIT *4.1*

Three Domains of Human Action

swapping service that enabled people to download music for free, was guilty of music piracy and must stop letting users exchange copyrighted material.[8] The domain of free choice is at the opposite end of the scale and pertains to behavior about which law has no say and for which an individual or organization enjoys complete freedom. An individual's choice of religion or a music company's choice of the number of artists to sign or CDs to release are examples of free choice.

Between these domains lies the area of ethics. This domain has no specific laws, yet it does have standards of conduct based on shared principles and values about moral conduct that guide an individual or company. In the domain of free choice, obedience is strictly to oneself. In the domain of codified law, obedience is to laws prescribed by the legal system. In the domain of ethical behavior, obedience is to unenforceable norms and standards about which the individual or company is aware. An ethically acceptable decision is both legally and morally acceptable to the larger community.

Many companies and individuals get into trouble with the simplified view that choices are governed by either law or free choice. It leads people to mistakenly assume that "If it's not illegal, it must be ethical," as if there were no third domain.[9] A better option is to recognize the domain of ethics and accept moral values as a powerful force for good that can regulate behaviors both inside and outside corporations. As principles of ethics and social responsibility are more widely recognized, companies can use codes of ethics and their corporate cultures to govern behavior, thereby eliminating the need for additional laws and avoiding the problems of unfettered choice. Sometimes deregulation of an industry has removed laws and increased unethical behavior where companies did not have socially responsible cultures, as in the case of radio, described below.

Radio Payola

The big 1950s scandal was about payola, where radio disc jockeys took money to play certain songs. Outlawed by Congress in 1960, payment for airplay was forbidden unless financial transactions were aired publicly.

In recent years, though, a new and quasi-legal kind of payola has emerged, partly as a result of the 1996 deregulation of radio, which was supposed to let the market determine the rules. The problem is, deregulation hasn't worked as well in the area of payola. In order to skirt the law, payment is not made directly to disc jockeys to play particular songs. Instead, promoters—or middlemen—pay radio owners large fees—as high as $1 million dollars—to have exclusive first access to that station's playlist for a period of time. The promotor then notes which songs will be aired and collects as much as $4,000 per song from the record labels that he or she represents.

Critics charge that this system has led to a homogenization of the airwaves and artists complain that they are hurt if they don't go with the program. One promoter allegedly retaliated against Britney Spears and other artists who refused to use their concert promotion services.

> Another result of deregulation has been the consolidation of the radio industry. Under the regulated system, there was a limit to the number of stations anyone could own. Now that limit is gone, and while there were 5,133 owners of radio stations in 1966, in 2002 there were primarily four radio station groups—Clear Channel, Chancellor, Infinity, and Capstart—controlling access to 63 percent of 41 million listeners. This consolidation has increased the power of the promoters and encouraged the new payola system.
>
> Profit pressure from both radio stations and record companies has "pushed the economics and ethics of radio promotion beyond the point where labels can police themselves," says music industry executive Tim Dubois of the Universal South label. "We need a new set of rules," he says. "We have to know where the line is drawn, and it has to be brighter than it is now."[10]

ethical dilemma

A situation that arises when all alternative choices or behaviors have been deemed undesirable because of potentially negative consequence, making it difficult to distinguish right from wrong.

Because ethical standards are not codified, disagreements and dilemmas about proper behavior often occur. An **ethical dilemma** arises in a situation when each alternative choice or behavior is undesirable because of potentially harmful consequences. Right or wrong cannot be clearly identified.

The individual who must make an ethical choice in an organization is the *moral agent*.[11] Consider the dilemmas facing a moral agent in the following situations:

- A top employee at your small company tells you he needs some time off because he has AIDS. You know the employee needs the job as well as the health insurance benefits. Providing health insurance has already stretched the company's budget, and this will send premiums through the roof. You recently read of a case in which federal courts upheld the right of an employer to modify health plans by putting a cap on AIDS benefits. Should you investigate whether this is a legal possibility for your company?

- As a sales manager for a major pharmaceuticals company, you've been asked to promote a new drug that costs $2,500 per dose. You've read the reports saying the drug is only 1 percent more effective than an alternate drug that costs less than one-fourth as much. Can you in good conscience aggressively promote the $2,500-per-dose drug? If you don't, could lives be lost that might have been saved with that 1 percent increase in effectiveness?

- Your company has been asked to pay a gratuity in India to speed the processing of an import permit. This is standard procedure, and your company will suffer if you do not pay the gratuity. Is this different from tipping a maître d' in a nice restaurant?

- You are the accounting manager of a division that is $15,000 below profit targets. Approximately $20,000 of office supplies were delivered on December 21. The accounting rule is to pay expenses when incurred. The division general manager asks you not to record the invoice until February.

- Your boss says he cannot give you a raise this year because of budget constraints, but he will look the other way if your expense accounts come in a little high because of your good work this past year.

These are the kinds of dilemmas and issues with which managers must deal that fall squarely in the domain of ethics. Now let's turn to approaches to ethical decision making that provide criteria for understanding and resolving these difficult issues.

© Thomas Broening

Discovered in 1998, human embryonic stem cells have the potential to revolutionize medical practice and improve the quality and length of life, but they present an ethical dilemma for many people. Embryonic stem cells come from in vitro fertilization clinics, and human fetal stem cells are drawn from aborted fetuses, putting them in the middle of America's reproductive rights debate. Federal funding for human fetal-cell research was banned from 1987 to 1993, and a five-year ban on federal funding of human embryonic-cell research was lifted only recently. Because his son was diagnosed with a brain tumor, Richard Garr, CEO of NeuralStem Biopharmaceuticals, is diligent with his company's research. He hopes that stem cells will be able to replace neurons lost to otherwise incurable brain disorders.

Criteria for Ethical Decision Making

Most ethical dilemmas involve a conflict between the needs of the part and the whole—the individual versus the organization or the organization versus society as a whole. For example, should a company install mandatory alcohol and drug testing for employees, which might benefit the organization as a whole but reduce the individual freedom of employees? Or should products that fail to meet tough FDA standards be exported to other countries where government standards are lower, benefiting the company but being potentially harmful to world citizens? Sometimes ethical decisions entail a conflict between two groups. For example, should the potential for local health problems resulting from a company's effluents take precedence over the jobs it creates as the town's leading employer?

Managers faced with these kinds of tough ethical choices often benefit from a normative approach—one based on norms and values—to guide their decision making. Normative ethics uses several approaches to describe values for guiding ethical decision making. Four of these that are relevant to managers are the utilitarian approach, individualism approach, moral-rights approach, and justice approach.[12] Guidelines for ethical decision-making are shown in the Focus on Ethics box.

Utilitarian Approach

The **utilitarian approach**, espoused by the nineteenth-century philosophers Jeremy Bentham and John Stuart Mill, holds that moral behavior produces the

utilitarian approach
The ethical concept that moral behaviors produce the greatest good for the greatest number.

FOCUS ON ETHICS

Guidelines for Ethical Decision Making

If a *60 Minutes* crew were waiting on your doorstep one morning, would you feel comfortable justifying your actions to the camera? One young manager, when confronted with ethical dilemmas, tries to find the answers with this *60 Minutes* test. Others say they use such criteria as whether they would be proud to tell their parents or grandparents about their decision, or whether they could sleep well at night and face themselves in the mirror in the morning. Managers often rely on their own personal integrity in making ethical decisions. But knowing what to do is not always easy. As a future manager, you will almost surely face ethical dilemmas one day. The following guidelines will not tell you exactly what to do, but, taken in the context of the text discussion, they will help you evaluate the situation more clearly by examining your own values and those of your organization. The answers to these questions will force you to think hard about the social and ethical consequences of your behavior.

1. Is the problem/dilemma really what it appears to be? If you are not sure, *find out.*

2. Is the action you are considering legal? Ethical? If you are not sure, *find out.*

3. Do you understand the position of those who oppose the action you are considering? Is it reasonable?

4. Whom does the action benefit? Harm? How much? How long?

5. Would you be willing to allow everyone to do what you are considering doing?

6. Have you sought the opinion of others who are knowledgeable on the subject and who would be objective?

7. Would your action be embarrassing to you if it were made known to your family, friends, coworkers, or superiors?

8. Even if you are sure the decision is reasonable and that you could defend it to others, does your gut instinct tell you it is the right thing to do?

There are no correct answers to these questions in an absolute sense. Yet if you determine that an action is potentially harmful to someone or would be embarrassing to you, or if you do not know the ethical or legal consequences, these guidelines will help you clarify whether the action is socially responsible.

SOURCES: Anthony M. Pagano and Jo Ann Verdin, *The External Environment of Business* (New York: Wiley, 1988), Chapter 5; Joseph L. Badaracco, Jr., and Allen P. Webb, "Business Ethics: A View from the Trenches," *California Management Review* 37, no. 2 (Winter 1995), 8–28; and Sherry Baker, "Ethical Judgment," *Executive Excellence* (March 1992), 7–8.

greatest good for the greatest number. Under this approach, a decision maker is expected to consider the effect of each decision alternative on all parties and select the one that optimizes the satisfaction for the greatest number of people. Because actual computations can be very complex, simplifying them is considered appropriate. For example, a simple economic frame of reference could be used by calculating dollar costs and dollar benefits. Also, a decision could be made that considers only the people who are directly affected by the decision, not those who are indirectly affected. The utilitarian ethic is cited as the basis for the recent trend among companies to police employee personal habits such as alcohol and tobacco consumption on the job, and in some cases after hours as well, because such behavior affects the entire workplace. Similarly, many companies argue that monitoring how employees spend their time on the Internet is necessary to maintain the company's ethical climate and workplace productivity. If employees are viewing pornographic sites, visiting racist chat rooms, or spending hours shopping or day-trading online, the entire organization ultimately suffers.[13]

individualism approach

The ethical concept that acts are moral when they promote the individual's best long-term interests, which ultimately leads to the greater good.

Individualism Approach

The **individualism approach** contends that acts are moral when they promote the individual's best long-term interests. Individual self-direction is paramount, and external forces that restrict self-direction should be severely limited.[14] Individuals calculate the best long-term advantage to themselves as a measure of a decision's goodness. The action that is intended to produce a greater ratio of good to bad for the individual compared with other alternatives is the right one to perform. In theory, with everyone pursuing self-direction, the greater good is ultimately served because people learn to accommodate each other in their own long-term interest. Individualism is believed to lead to honesty and integrity because that works best in the long run. Lying and cheating for immediate self-interest just causes business associates to lie and cheat in return. Thus, individualism ultimately leads to behavior toward others that fits standards of behavior people want toward themselves.[15] Individualism is closest to the domain of free choice described in Exhibit 4.1

Moral-Rights Approach

The **moral-rights approach** asserts that human beings have fundamental rights and liberties that cannot be taken away by an individual's decision. Thus, an ethically correct decision is one that best maintains the rights of those people affected by it.

Six moral rights should be considered during decision making:

1. *The right of free consent.* Individuals are to be treated only as they knowingly and freely consent to be treated.

2. *The right to privacy.* Individuals can choose to do as they please away from work and have control of information about their private life.

3. *The right of freedom of conscience.* Individuals may refrain from carrying out any order that violates their moral or religious norms.

4. *The right of free speech.* Individuals may criticize truthfully the ethics or legality of actions of others.

5. *The right to due process.* Individuals have a right to an impartial hearing and fair treatment.

6. *The right to life and safety.* Individuals have a right to live without endangerment or violation of their health and safety.

To make ethical decisions, managers need to avoid interfering with the fundamental rights of others. For example, a decision to eavesdrop on employees violates the right to privacy. Sexual harassment is unethical because it violates the right to freedom of conscience. The right of free speech would support whistle-blowers who call attention to illegal or inappropriate action within a company. Reebok wanted to move away from its image as a sweatshop owner to one doing right by employees, as shown in the example below.

> During 1998 and 1999, the Indonesian consulting firm Insan Hitawasana Sejahtera (IHS) spent 1,400 hours studying labor conditions and interviewing factory workers at two contract factories in Indonesia that manufacture 75 percent of the footwear sold by U.S.-based Reebok. The final report, "Peduli Hak" ("Caring for Rights" in Indonesian) outlined some disturbing facts, including problems with health and safety procedures and worker–manager communication.
>
> Disturbing conditions in overseas factories is nothing new. What was new about this study was that Reebok asked for it and then candidly discussed the negative findings in the press. Reebok wanted an independent evaluation of

moral-rights approach
The ethical concept that moral decisions are those that best maintain the rights of those people affected by them.

Reebok

http://www.reebok.com

working conditions so managers could make improvements and meet their ethical responsibilities toward Indonesian factory workers. One project that came out of the report was a pilot project conducted by an arm of the AFL-CIO to strengthen the union's role as an advocate for workers in five Indonesian factories. Although unions were already in place in the factories, they had little power compared to unions in the United States.

A corporation training its employees in how to make their union stronger might seem hard to believe, but Reebok considered it an ethical duty. Because most factory workers in Indonesia are functionally illiterate and often cannot understand or defend their rights, the union must be powerful enough to be an advocate for them. Reebok also has an innovative worker communication system that provides a secure way for employees to report their concerns. Drop boxes are placed not only in factories and dormitories, but also in places where privacy is assured, such as public bathrooms and mosques. Each location has forms in the local language, with Reebok's human rights standards printed on the back.

Doug Cahn, Reebok's vice president of human rights programs, recently visited Indonesian factories to see if the efforts had made a difference. "I saw specially designed chairs for pregnant women. I saw job rotation systems, and signs posted in Indonesian encouraging workers to take water breaks as frequently as they wished," he said. "I saw seminars on how to use fire safety equipment, saw scrubbers on smokestacks, saw procedures for [safe] chemical handling. It was a sea change in what I'd seen beginning to take place a year ago."[16]

Justice Approach

The **justice approach** holds that moral decisions must be based on standards of equity, fairness, and impartiality. It requires that different treatment of people not be based on arbitrary characteristics. Individuals who are similar in respects relevant to a decision should be treated similarly. Thus, men and women should not receive different salaries if they are performing the same job. However, people who differ in a substantive way, such as job skills or job responsibility, can be treated differently in proportion to the differences in skills or responsibility among them. This difference should have a clear relationship to organizational goals and tasks.

The justice approach is closest to the thinking underlying the domain of codified law in Exhibit 4.1, because it assumes that justice is applied through rules and regulations. This theory does not require complex calculations such as those demanded by a utilitarian approach, nor does it justify self-interest as the individualism approach does. Most of the laws guiding human resource management (Chapter 9) are based on the justice approach.

These various approaches offer general principles that managers can recognize as useful in making ethical decisions. However, understanding the approaches is only a first step; managers still have to consider how to apply them.

Factors Affecting Ethical Choices

When managers are accused of lying, cheating, or stealing, the blame is usually placed on the individual or on the company situation. Most people believe that individuals make ethical choices because of individual integrity, which is true, but it is not the whole story. Ethical or unethical business practices usually reflect the values, attitudes, beliefs, and behavior patterns of the organizational culture; thus, ethics is as much an organizational as a personal issue.[17] Let's examine how both the manager and the organization shape ethical decision making.[18]

The Manager

Managers bring specific personality and behavioral traits to the job. Personal needs, family influence, and religious background all shape a manager's value system. Specific personality characteristics, such as ego strength, self-confidence, and a strong sense of independence may enable managers to make ethical decisions.

One important personal trait is the stage of moral development.[19] A simplified version of one model of personal moral development is shown in Exhibit 4.2. At the *preconventional level,* individuals are concerned with external rewards and punishments and obey authority to avoid detrimental personal consequences. In an organizational context, this level may be associated with managers who use an autocratic or coercive leadership style, with employees oriented toward dependable accomplishment of specific tasks. At level two, called the *conventional level,* people learn to conform to the expectations of good behavior as defined by colleagues, family, friends, and society. Meeting social and interpersonal obligations is important. Work group collaboration is the preferred manner for accomplishment of organizational goals, and managers use a leadership style that encourages interpersonal relationships and cooperation. At the *postconventional,* or *principled* level, individuals are guided by an internal set of values and standards and will even disobey rules or laws that violate these principles. Internal values become more important than the expectations of significant others. For example, when the *USS Indianapolis* sank after being torpedoed during World War II, one Navy pilot disobeyed orders and risked his life to save men who were being picked off by sharks. The

EXHIBIT 4.2

Three Levels of Personal Moral Development

Level 3: Postconventional

Follows self-chosen principles of justice and right. Aware that people hold different values and seeks creative solutions to ethical dilemmas. Balances concern for individual with concern for common good.

Level 2: Conventional

Lives up to expectations of others. Fulfills duties and obligations of social system. Upholds laws.

Level 1: Preconventional

Follows rules to avoid punishment. Acts in own interest. Obedience for its own sake.

Leadership Style:	Autocratic/coercive	Guiding/encouraging, team oriented	Transforming, or servant leadership
Employee Behavior:	Task accomplishment	Work group collaboration	Empowered employees, full participation

SOURCES: Based on L. Kohlberg, "Moral Stages and Moralization: The Cognitive-Developmental Approach," in *Moral Development and Behavior: Theory, Research, and Social Issues,* ed. T. Lickona (New York: Holt, Rinehart, and Winston, 1976), 31–53; and Jill W. Graham, "Leadership, Moral Development and Citizenship Behavior," *Business Ethics Quarterly* 5, no. 1 (January 1995), 43–54.

Julius Walls Jr., chief executive of Greyston Bakery, demonstrates the postconventional level of moral development. Greyston makes gourmet brownies, cakes, and tarts. Walls hires employees off the street, first come, first served, because he thinks everyone deserves a chance at a job. He also helps workers with problems whether or not they're job related. Greyston serves the poor by feeding the rich. Much of its $4 million in annual sales are generated by selling bits of brownies to Ben & Jerry's for its chocolate fudge brownie ice cream and frozen yogurt, and the company donates all profits to the needy.

© Michael Lewis

pilot was operating from the highest level of moral development in attempting the rescue despite a direct order from superiors. When managers operate from this highest level of development, they use transformative or servant leadership, focusing on the needs of followers and encouraging others to think for themselves and to engage in higher levels of moral reasoning. Employees are empowered and given opportunities for constructive participation in governance of the organization.

The great majority of managers operate at level two. A few have not advanced beyond level one. Only about 20 percent of American adults reach the level-three stage of moral development. People at level three are able to act in an independent, ethical manner regardless of expectations from others inside or outside the organization. Managers at level three of moral development will make ethical decisions whatever the organizational consequences for them.

One interesting study indicates that most researchers have failed to account for the different ways in which women view social reality and develop psychologically and have thus consistently classified women as being stuck at lower levels of development. Researcher Carol Gilligan has suggested that the moral domain be enlarged to include responsibility and care in relationships. Women may, in general, perceive moral complexities more astutely than men and make moral decisions based not on a set of absolute rights and wrongs but on principles of not causing harm to others.[20]

One reason higher levels of ethical conduct are increasingly important is the impact of globalization on organizational ethics and corporate culture. Globalization has made ethical issues even more complicated for today's managers.[21] American managers working in foreign countries need sensitivity and an openness to other systems, as well as mature ethical judgment to work out differences. For example, although tolerance for bribery is waning, it is still an accepted way of doing business in many countries. Foreign managers sometimes resent Americans' "holier-than-thou" attitudes and the stereotypical belief that all foreign managers are corrupt.[22] It is not always easy to resolve international issues. There are, however, increasing calls for the development of global standards for ethical business conduct, which may help managers negotiate the difficult terrain of international ethics. In 1999, the United Nations completed a nine-point Global Compact that outlines global ethical principles in the areas of human rights, labor standards, and the environment. So far, 44 major corporations have made a commitment to incorporate the guidelines into their business practices.[23]

The Organization

The values adopted within the organization are important, especially when we understand that most people are at the level-two stage of moral development, which means they believe their duty is to fulfill obligations and expectations of others. All ethical decisions are made within the context of our interactions with other people, and the social networks within an organization play an important role in guiding people's actions. For example, for most of us, doing something we know is wrong becomes easier when "everyone else is doing it." In organizations, an important influence on ethical behavior is the norms and values of the team, department, or organization as a whole. Research has shown that these values strongly influence employee actions and decision making.[24] Consider the business of major league baseball, where some players use steroids because the practice is so widespread, as described in the example below.

Baseball, Inc.

"At least half the guys are using steroids," says 1996 National League Most Valuable Player Ken Caminiti, becoming the first high-profile player to admit to a long-whispered-about practice. That estimate had been earlier affirmed by Arizona Diamondbacks pitcher Curt Schilling, who also added, "Is that a problem? It depends on what you consider a problem. It certainly has tainted records, there's no doubt about that." The very next day, Caminiti backtracked so fast, some thought he'd found a horse head in his bed.

Just after that, though, retired slugger Jose Canseco not only admitted to steroid use, but promised to name names if he gets a book deal. What gets overlooked is that steroids only benefit the players who use them, as opposed to reducing the size of ballparks or using a lower mound, changes that benefit all players equally.

Unlike basketball, football, and hockey, major league baseball does no drug testing. But with so many record-breaking players, many assume that steroids are being used freely. Their use is associated with health risks, increasing heart and liver damage, and even strokes. NFL star Lyle Alzado went public in 1992 about contracting brain cancer from longtime steroid use.

So why take the risks? Players use steroids because they increase muscle mass and can lead to better performance and hence to higher contract dollars. Replying to concerns, Schilling said, "If you can get an advantage somewhere, even if it involves crossing an ethical line, people will do it. Home runs are money."

Caminiti said that the practice is so prevalent that players who don't use steroids put themselves at a disadvantage. One of the biggest hurdles in the way

> of drug testing has been the baseball players themselves, through their union. The tide may be turning, though. Diamondback first-baseman Mark Grace says that players are finally getting fed up with inflated statistics and record breaking: "I personally would love to see it banned."[25]

Corporate culture serves to let employees know what beliefs and behaviors the company supports and those it will not tolerate. If unethical behavior is tolerated or even encouraged, it will become routine. For example, an investigation of thefts and kickbacks in the oil business found that the cause was the historical acceptance of thefts and kickbacks. Employees were socialized into those values and adopted them as appropriate. In most companies, employees believe that if they do not go along with the ethical values expressed, their jobs will be in jeopardy or they will not fit in.[26]

Culture can be examined to see the kinds of ethical signals given to employees. Exhibit 4.3 indicates questions to ask to understand the cultural system. High ethical standards can be affirmed and communicated through public awards and ceremonies. Heroes provide role models that can either support or refute ethical decision making. For example, Wendy's founder, Dave Thomas, stood for integrity and was a highly effective salesman for the company. People viewed Wendy's food favorably in part because they liked Dave's down-to-earth, honest, and friendly manner. When he died in January 2002, Wendy's signs across the country bid farewell to "our founder and friend."

Culture is not the only aspect of an organization that influences ethics, but it is a major force because it defines company values. Other aspects of the organization, such as explicit rules and policies, the reward system, the extent to which the company cares for its people, the selection system, emphasis on legal and professional standards, and leadership and decision processes, can also have an impact on ethical values and manager decision making.[27] At Levi Strauss, for example, the selection system is aimed at promoting diversity of background and thought among workers, a set of "corporate aspirations" written by top management is to guide all major decisions, and one-third of a manager's raise can depend on how well he or she toes the values line.[28]

EXHIBIT 4.3

Questions for Analyzing a Company's Cultural Impact on Ethics

SOURCE: Linda Klebe Treviño, "A Cultural Perspective on Changing and Developing Organizational Ethics," in *Research in Organizational Change and Development,* ed. R. Woodman and W. Pasmore (Greenwich, Conn.: JAI Press, 1990), 4.

1. Identify the organization's heroes. What values do they represent? Given an ambiguous ethical dilemma, what decision would they make and why?
2. What are some important organizational rituals? How do they encourage or discourage ethical behavior? Who gets the awards, people of integrity or individuals who use unethical methods to attain success?
3. What are the ethical messages sent to new entrants into the organization—must they obey authority at all costs, or is questioning authority acceptable or even desirable?
4. Does analysis of organizational stories and myths reveal individuals who stand up for what's right, or is conformity the valued characteristic? Do people get fired or promoted in these stories?
5. Does language exist for discussing ethical concerns? Is this language routinely incorporated and encouraged in business decision making?
6. What informal socialization processes exist, and what norms for ethical/unethical behavior do they promote?

What Is Social Responsibility?

Now let's turn to the issue of **social responsibility**. In one sense, the concept of corporate social responsibility, like ethics, is easy to understand: It means distinguishing right from wrong and doing right. It means being a good corporate citizen. The formal definition of social responsibility is management's obligation to make choices and take actions that will contribute to the welfare and interests of society as well as the organization.[29] For more in-depth information on social responsibility, the Digital, Inc. box lists a number of Web sites for social responsibility associations.

> **social responsibility**
>
> The obligation of organization management to make decisions and take actions that will enhance the welfare and interests of society as well as the organization.

DIGITAL, INC.

Resources for Social Responsibility

Want to do some more extensive research on corporate social responsibility (CSR)? The Web has many resources that give you an in-depth look at current issues and practices.

Best Practices

1. *http://www.bsr.org* One of the best sites on CSR, it gives practical advice on how to set up social programs; it also gives many "best practice" examples in its various reports on different topics regarding CSR.

2. *http://www.csreurope.org* This is more or less BSR Europe, as it gives the same kinds of information as the BSR site, but does so for European companies.

3. *http://www.worldcsr.com* With a mix of examples from the United States and Europe, this is a one-stop shopping for information on the United States and Europe. Also, one of the links on the site, *http://www.business-impact.org*, is a databank of links to such related organizations as Global Reporting Institute, World Business Council for Sustainable Development, and Institute for Global Ethics.

4. *http://www.responsibleshopper.com* Helps you find enlightened companies that don't dump toxic waste or employ children in Honduras.

Social Investing

1. *http://www.socialfunds.com* Arguably the best social investing site, it is run by SRI World Group, which has a staff of reporters posting information without charge.

2. *http://www.socialinvest.org* Run by the nonprofit Social Investment Forum, this is a good companion to the site listed above.

3. *http://www.goodmoney.com* Showcases Good Money Industrial Average, a socially responsible index that outperformed the Dow 2000. Also provides social profiles and performance data for 400 companies in the Domini Social Index.

Corporate Watchdog

1. *http://www.corpwatch.org* A great site for activists that identifies human rights abuses abroad, environmental news, and places to participate in letter-writing campaigns.

Labor and Human Rights

1. *http://oracle02.ilo.org/vpi/welcome* Sponsored by the International Labor Relations Organization, this site offers extensive information on private-sector initiatives on labor and social workplace issues.

Progressive Economics

1. *http://www.movingideas.org* Offers the best thinking on progressive economic policy and is sponsored by *The American Prospect* magazine.

2. *http://www.neweconomics.org* Focused on constructing a new economy based on people and environment, this site is run by the U.K. thinktank The New Economics Forum Foundation (NEF).

Employee Ownership

1. *http://cog.kent.edu* A treasure-trove of research and papers from academics and practitioners on employee ownership.

Sustainability

1. *http://www.GreenBiz.com* Run by *The Green Business Letter*, this is an excellent site on businesses following the Green, or environmentally aware, path.

Ethics

1. *http://www.depaul.edu/ethics* Run by DePaul University's Institute for Business and Professional Ethics, this offers a huge compilation of ethics materials.

SOURCE: Karen McNichol, "Best Resources for Corporate Social Responsibility," *Business Ethics* (Summer 2001), 16–19. Reprinted with the permission of *Business Ethics*, P.O. Box 8439, Minneapolis, MN (tel: 612-879-0695).

Organizational Stakeholders

One reason for the difficulty understanding social responsibility is that managers must confront the question "responsibility to whom?" Recall from Chapter 2 that the organization's environment consists of several sectors in both the task and general environment. From a social responsibility perspective, enlightened organizations view the internal and external environment as a variety of stakeholders.

A **stakeholder** is any group within or outside the organization that has a stake in the organization's performance. Each stakeholder has a different criterion of responsiveness, because it has a different interest in the organization.[30] For example, Wal-Mart uses aggressive bargaining tactics with suppliers so that it is able to provide low prices for customers. Some stakeholders see this as socially responsible behavior because it benefits customers and forces suppliers to be more efficient. Others, however, argue that the aggressive tactics are an abuse of power and may prevent suppliers from even paying their own employees a decent wage.[31]

Exhibit 4.4 illustrates important stakeholders for a software company. Investors and shareholders, employees, customers, and suppliers are considered primary stakeholders, without whom the organization cannot survive. Investors, shareholders, and suppliers' interests are served by managerial efficiency—that is, use of resources to achieve profits. Employees expect work satisfaction, pay, and good supervision. Customers are concerned with decisions

stakeholder

Any group within or outside the organization that has a stake in the organization's performance.

EXHIBIT 4.4

Stakeholders Relevant to a Software Company

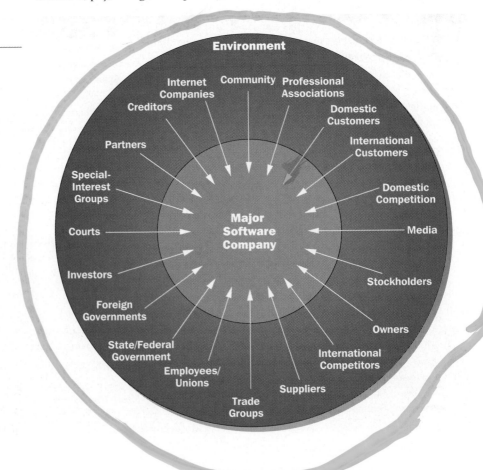

about the quality, safety, and availability of goods and services. When any primary stakeholder group becomes seriously dissatisfied, the organization's viability is threatened.[32]

Other important stakeholders are the government and the community. Cisco Systems learned the importance of investing in its local community school, as shown in the Focus on Collaboration box.

Socially responsible organizations consider the effects of their actions on all stakeholder groups and may invest in a number of philanthropic causes that benefit stakeholders. For example, Engage Media, an online marketing company, participates in blood drives and clothing drives for the needy, and employees recently joined a breast cancer walk in San Francisco. The company gives employees one day off per quarter for volunteer activities.[33] The Body Shop weaves social responsibility and environmental protection into every facet of company operations. For example, the Body Shop buys cocoa butter directly from farmers in poor countries rather than purchasing it on the commodities market. Then the company sets up a social fund in the communities where it conducts trade so that needed schools or health clinics can be built.[34] These companies are acting in a socially responsible way by helping stakeholders.

Today, special-interest groups continue to be one of the largest stakeholder concerns that companies face. Environmental responsibility has become a primary issue as both business and the public acknowledge the damage that has been done to our natural environment.

FOCUS ON COLLABORATION

Executives Volunteer to Educate

Vandalism. Poverty. High crime rate. Not a recipe for success in isolated bay-side East Palo Alto, California. Sitting in the shadow of richer Palo Alto, this area has a smaller tax base and spends half as much as Palo Alto on its schools. Teachers were overwhelmed with the problems and had few resources to solve them. Around 1990 engineers from the then-fledgling Cisco Systems started visiting Costano Public School. At first, they just played basketball with the students. Then they started tutoring math. Pretty soon they got a visit from Cisco CEO John Morgridge, who was committed to education. If the school needed computers, Cisco provided them. More tutors came. Employees even showed up on Saturdays to paint dingy walls. After more than ten years, the investment has paid off. Local students—mostly African American, Latino, and Pacific Islanders—respect each other and show enthusiasm in the classroom. Standardized test scores show the students moving up from the bottom tenth to the median for California students.

Lots of businesspeople get excited about fixing public schools. But after the initial excitement wears off and results don't come as fast as hoped, the investors disappear. Educa-

tion doesn't work like a company. Executives can't call a meeting, set goals, and then demand deliverables on time. It's not easy to unravel social problems, such as poor health care, gangs, substandard housing, and multiple languages, all of which have an impact on schooling.

Despite these hurdles, network equipment company Cisco has stayed in for the long haul and made positive effects on the school. It installed a computer lab and sent its own engineers to network the machines, while training the computer teacher so that he could maintain it. Cisco also upgraded the school library, and sent a dental van to fix the teeth of students who rarely or never see a dentist. Cisco staff donated almost 100 school uniforms and even a washing machine so that even the poorest parents could wash them.

Even after Cisco moved its location, making it inconvenient for staff to stop by, the company maintained its commitment. Morgridge himself serves as "principal for a day" once a year. "If you want to make an impact," he says, "you need to invest your time every bit as much as your money."

SOURCE: George Anders, "The Reeducation of Silicon Valley," *Fast Company* (April 2002), 101, 108.

The Natural Environment

When the first Earth Day celebration was held in 1970, most managers considered environmentalists to be an extremist fringe group and felt little need to respond to environmental concerns.[35] Today environmental issues have become a hot topic among business leaders, and managers and organizations in all industries are jumping on the environmental bandwagon by "going green." Environmentalism has become an integral part of organizational strategy for many companies. The relationship between corporations and environmental activist groups has shifted from one of adversity to one of collaboration. Forty-eight companies, including Ford Motor Company, Bristol-Myers Squibb, Procter & Gamble, General Motors, and Royal Dutch/Shell, volunteered to respond to guidelines set up by the Coalition for Environmentally Responsible Economies.[36]

Huge corporations are joining the fight against global warming by counting greenhouse gases and changing business policies to cut emissions. Pratt & Whitney, a division of United Technologies Corp., now uses computers to simulate some tests of its jet engines instead of running the turbines. And at BP Amoco PLC, managers are now evaluated not just on their division's financial results but also on how well they cut emissions in their unit.[37]

Ford Motor Company has pledged to improve the average fuel economy of its sport-utility vehicles by 25 percent over five years. Managers voluntarily reported that Ford's plants and vehicles alone emit the equivalent of 1.7 percent of the world's carbon dioxide emissions, and they promised that the company's response to environmental problems will be a top criterion for evaluating corporate performance over the next decade.[38] In addition, in January 2002 the federal government announced a partnership with U.S. automakers to develop a car that runs on hydrogen fuel cells. GM President and CEO Rick Wagoner said, "If this works, this is the holy grail, this is the breakthrough."[39]

One model uses the phrase *shades of green* to evaluate a company's commitment to environmental responsibility.[40] The various shades, which represent a company's approach to addressing environmental concerns, are illustrated in Exhibit 4.5. Under the *legal approach,* an organization does just what is necessary to satisfy legal requirements. In general, managers and the company show little concern for environmental issues. For example, Willamette Industries of Portland, Oregon, agreed to install $7.4 million worth of pollution control equipment in its 13 factories to comply with Environmental Protection Agency requirements. The move came only after Willamette was fined a whopping $11.2 million for violating emissions standards.[41] The next shade, the *market approach,* represents a growing awareness of and sensitivity to environmental concerns, primarily to satisfy customers. A company might provide environmentally friendly products because customers want them, for instance, not necessarily because of strong management commitment to the environment.

A further step is to respond to multiple demands from the environment. The *stakeholder approach* means that companies attempt to answer the environmental concerns of various stakeholder groups, such as customers, the local community, business partners, and special interest groups. Ontario Power Generation, DuPont, Shell, and Alcan Aluminum are among the large companies that are partnering with Environmental Defense to reduce greenhouse gases.[42] The move comes in response to growing concerns among customers, communities where the companies operate, and environmental groups, as well as a recognition that emissions are likely to be regulated by government actions.

EXHIBIT 4.5

The Shades of Corporate Green

SOURCE: Based on R.E. Freeman, J. Pierce, and R. Dodd, *Shades of Green: Ethics and the Environment* (New York: Oxford University Press, 1995).

Finally, at the highest level of green, organizations take an *activist approach* to environmental issues by actively searching for ways to conserve the Earth's resources. Interface, a leader in the floor-covering industry, provides an excellent illustration of a manager and a company taking an activist approach.

Ray Anderson spent most of his life as an environmental glutton. His company, Interface, Inc., an Atlanta-based business with 7,300 employees, turns petrochemicals into textiles. The petroleum the company uses took millions of years to make and is irreplaceable; the carpets that come from it last forever—and most of them end up in landfills after only a decade of use.

But Ray Anderson had a revelation when he came across a book called *The Ecology of Commerce,* by Paul Hawken. As he read about the breadth of toxins accumulating in humans from one generation to the next and the speed at which natural resources were being depleted, the captain of industrial capitalism thought of his grandchildren and wept. Today, Ray Anderson is becoming a radical environmentalist who makes the folks from Greenpeace look timid. He has embraced the concept of sustainability, which calls for mimicking nature—everything's waste is something else's food. Anderson's goal for Interface: Create zero waste and consume zero oil while making a healthy profit. It took Anderson a year to convince the rest of his company (the largest maker of commercial carpeting and upholstery for office cubicles) that Interface could save the earth and still make money. Today, however, from the factory floor to the R&D lab, sustainability has become as important a consideration in every business decision as profitability.

Interface's performance shatters the idea that social responsibility and profits can't go hand in hand. Over a one-year period, sales grew from $800 million to $1 billion. During that time, the amount of raw materials used by the company dropped almost 20 percent per dollar of sales. That means, Anderson points out, "$200 million of sustainable business." The company's latest innovation is an "Evergreen Lease," with building owners renting rather than buying carpet. Interface installs, maintains, replaces, carries away, and recycles carpet tiles as

Interface Inc.

http://www.interfaceinc.com

they wear out. The old tiles become new carpet. Interface also hopes to soon offer commercial hemp carpet, which can be composted completely when its use is over.

Ray Anderson is not timid about explaining why he is instituting all these changes. He wants to save the world—and make sure his grandchildren will still have one.[43]

Evaluating Corporate Social Performance

A model for evaluating corporate social performance is presented in Exhibit 4.6. The model indicates that total corporate social responsibility can be subdivided into four criteria—economic, legal, ethical, and discretionary responsibilities.[44] Managers and organizations are typically involved in several issues at the same time, and a company's ethical and discretionary responsibilities are increasingly considered as important as economic and legal issues. These four criteria fit together to form the whole of a company's social responsiveness.

Note the similarity between the categories in Exhibit 4.6 and those in Exhibit 4.1. In both cases, ethical issues are located between the areas of legal and freely discretionary responsibilities. Exhibit 4.6 also has an economic category, because profits are a major reason for corporations' existence.

Economic Responsibilities

The first criterion of social responsibility is *economic responsibility*. The business institution is, above all, the basic economic unit of society. Its responsibility is to produce the goods and services that society wants and to maximize profits for its owners and shareholders. Economic responsibility, carried to the extreme, is called the *profit-maximizing* view, advocated by Nobel economist Milton Friedman. This view argues that the corporation should be operated on a profit-oriented basis, with its sole mission to increase its profits so long as it stays within the rules of the game.[45]

The purely profit-maximizing view is no longer considered an adequate criterion of performance in Canada, the United States, and Europe. This approach means that economic gain is the only social responsibility and can lead companies into trouble.

E X H I B I T *4.6*

Criteria of Corporate Social Performance

Legal Responsibilities

All modern societies lay down ground rules, laws, and regulations that businesses are expected to follow. *Legal responsibility* defines what society deems as

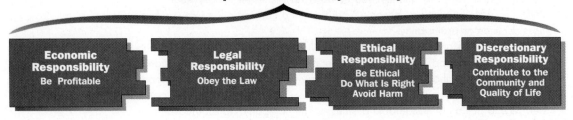

Total Corporate Social Responsibility

Economic Responsibility	Legal Responsibility	Ethical Responsibility	Discretionary Responsibility
Be Profitable	Obey the Law	Be Ethical / Do What Is Right / Avoid Harm	Contribute to the Community and Quality of Life

SOURCES: Based on Archie B. Carroll, "A Three-Dimensional Conceptual Model of Corporate Performance," *Academy of Management Review* 4 (1979), 499; and "The Pyramid of Corporate Social Responsibility: Toward the Moral Management of Corporate Stakeholders," *Business Horizons* 34 (July–August 1991), 42.

important with respect to appropriate corporate behavior.[46] Businesses are expected to fulfill their economic goals within the legal framework. Legal requirements are imposed by local town councils, state legislators, and federal regulatory agencies.

Organizations that knowingly break the law are poor performers in this category. Intentionally manufacturing defective goods or billing a client for work not done is illegal. Organizations ultimately pay for ignoring their legal responsibilities. An example of the punishment given to one company that broke the law is described in the press release shown in Exhibit 4.7.

Ethical Responsibilities

Ethical responsibility includes behaviors that are not necessarily codified into law and may not serve the corporation's direct economic interests. As described earlier in this chapter, to be *ethical*, organization decision makers should act with equity, fairness, and impartiality, respect the rights of individuals, and provide different treatment of individuals only when relevant to the organization's goals and tasks.[47] *Unethical* behavior occurs when decisions enable an individual or company to gain at the expense of other people or society as a whole. For example, investigation of the Enron scandal revealed that some managers forged business deals that were not always in the best interest of the company in order to earn sizable brokering commissions. In addition, top Enron executives profited by selling their stock when they realized the company was sliding

© David J. Phillip—AP/Wide World Photos

For businesses, the first criterion of corporate social responsibility is economic responsibility. Recently, companies such as Enron, Lucent, and Nortel have failed to carry out their economic responsibility, especially when the value of the company stock plummeted. Not only have Enron employees such as those in the photo lost their jobs, but some lost most of their 401(k) retirement plans. One 61-year-old administrative assistant, who had dutifully placed 15 percent of her salary into a 401(k) plan, invested the entire amount in the company's rapidly climbing stock. She amassed close to $500,000, only to be forced out of work with a 401(k) worth only $22,000 when Enron collapsed.

♻EPA United States
Environmental Protection Agency

Headquarters Press Release
Washington, DC

Date Published:	07/12/2001
Title:	WASHINGTON STATE/ALASKA COMPANY SENTENCED IN ASBESTOS CASE

FOR RELEASE: THURSDAY, JULY 12, 2001
WASHINGTON STATE/ALASKA COMPANY SENTENCED IN ASBESTOS CASE

Luke C. Hester 202-564-7818 / hester.luke@epa.gov

On June 27, Great Pacific Seafood, a Washington State corporation operating in Alaska, and its General Manager, Roger D. Stiles, were sentenced for violations of the Clean Air Act. Great Pacific Seafood was sentenced to serve five years probation, pay a $75,000 fine, pay $7,000 in restitution, publish a public apology statement in the local newspaper and adopt an environmental management program. Stiles was sentenced to pay a $5,000 fine, perform 120 hours of community service, and serve two to three years probation. Great Pacific Seafood and Stiles pleaded guilty to having five of its employees directly or indirectly exposed to asbestos fibers without the proper training, equipment or protective clothing. The hazardous nature of abatement was never disclosed to two of the employees. Failure to follow asbestos work practices can expose workers to the inhalation of airborne asbestos fibers which can cause lung cancer, a lung disease known as "asbestosis" and mesothelioma, a cancer of the chest and abdominal cavities. This case was investigated by the EPA Criminal Investigation Division, the FBI and the Alaska State Occupational Safety and Health Administration. Technical assistance was provided by the EPA Office of Air Quality. The case was prosecuted by the U.S. Attorney's Office in Anchorage.

R-105 ###

EXHIBIT 4.7

One Company's Punishment for Breaking the Law

BEST PRACTICES

Natural Step

"**G**ood guys in business doing the wrong thing for the right purpose, we can't afford that," states Dr. Karl-Henrik Robert, cancer doctor turned environmentalist and founder of Sweden-based Natural Step. Begun in 1989, Natural Step is a consortium of associations and businesses all aimed at creating sustainability, and poses these guidelines: that fossil fuels, metals, and plastics not be used faster than they can be reintegrated into the earth's crust; that the diversity of nature not be compromised; and that resources be used fairly and efficiently.

One of the first companies to come on board was IKEA, the giant furniture builder. At first, executives thought they would go broke making items with no metal or persistent glues and from sustainable forest wood. However, the furniture proved so profitable that they increased its production. Money-losing Scandic hospitals joined Natural Step, asking employees how they could be more environmentally friendly. Employee responses helped the company do things such as replace shampoo bottles with refillable containers and suggest that customers choose a change of linens every few days instead of daily. Scandic reduced is use of plastic by 70 percent and metal by 50 percent. Not only were costs reduced, but the morale of its 4,225 employees increased due to their involvement. Today Scandia says its profitability can be traced to its sustainability policies.

Electrolux joined when one large client demanded more environmentally friendly supplies. The company began using water- and powder-based paints, which are better than the more common solvent-based paints, and also produced the first refrigerators free of chlorofluorocarbons.

Natural Step tries to overcome the incorrect assumption that good economics cannot coexist with good ecology. Dr. Robert began the organization with a model of collaboration: using dialog and seeking to understand, and building coalitions and networks, rather than conflict and contention. That model has shown success, as Natural Step now has branches in 11 countries. In the United States, 3M's pollution prevention has saved the company $360 million; Interface (described elsewhere in this chapter) seeks to eliminate waste; and Xerox's Lakes project in Rochester, New York, has saved $1 billion using a "zero to landfill" strategy. As well-known ecologist Paul Hawkins said, "Sustainability means leaving the world better than you found it, taking no more than you need, trying not to harm life or the environment, making amends if you do."

SOURCE: Brian Back, "Swedish Father Talks Environment," *The Business Journal* (October 13, 2000), 16–17; Hilary Bradbury and Judith A. Clair, "Promoting Sustainable Organizations with Sweden's Natural Step," *Academy of Management Executive* 13, no. 4, 1999, 63–74.

toward bankruptcy, while unsuspecting employees and other investors lost billions. Reebok provides an example of ethical action by making a firm commitment to human rights in its overseas factories.

Discretionary Responsibilities

discretionary responsibility

Organizational responsibility that is voluntary and guided by the organization's desire to make social contributions not mandated by economics, law, or ethics.

Discretionary responsibility is purely voluntary and is guided by a company's desire to make social contributions not mandated by economics, law, or ethics. Discretionary activities include generous philanthropic contributions that offer no payback to the company and are not expected. An example of discretionary behavior occurred when Pittsburgh Brewing Company helped laid-off steelworkers by establishing and contributing to food banks in the Pittsburgh area. Discretionary responsibility is the highest criterion of social responsibility, because it goes beyond societal expectations to contribute to the community's welfare. The Natural Step organization has brought together corporate need for profits with a desire to do the right thing, to make a positive contribution to society, as described in the Best Practices box.

Managing Company Ethics and Social Responsibility

Many managers are concerned with improving the ethical climate and social responsiveness of their companies. As one expert on the topic of ethics said, "Management is responsible for creating and sustaining conditions in which people are likely to behave themselves."[48] Managers must take active steps to ensure that the company stays on an ethical footing. As we discussed earlier in this chapter, ethical business practices depend on both individual managers and the organization's values, policies, and practices. Exhibit 4.8 illustrates the three pillars that support an ethical organization.[49]

Ethical Individuals

Managers who are essentially ethical individuals make up the first pillar. These individuals possess honesty and integrity, which is reflected in their behavior and decisions. People inside and outside the organization trust them because they can be relied upon to follow the standards of fairness, treat people right, and be ethical in their dealings with others. Ethical individuals strive for a high level of moral development, as discussed earlier in the chapter.

However, being a moral person and making ethical decisions is not enough. Managers must also create a strong ethical climate for others. They find ways to focus the entire organization's attention on ethical values and create an organizational environment that encourages, guides, and supports the ethical behavior of all employees. Two additional pillars are needed to provide a strong foundation for an ethical organization: ethical leadership and organizational structures and systems.

Ethical Leadership

In a study of ethics policy and practice in successful, ethical companies such as Boeing, Chemical Bank, General Mills, GTE, Xerox, and Johnson & Johnson,

EXHIBIT 4.8

The Three Pillars of an Ethical Organization

SOURCE: Adapted from Linda Klebe Treviño, Laura Pincus Hartman, and Michael Brown, "Moral Person and Moral Manager," *California Management Review* 42, No. 4 (Summer 2000), 128–142.

no point emerged more clearly than the crucial role of leadership.[50] For example, a survey of readers of *The Secretary* magazine found that employees are acutely aware of their bosses' ethical lapses.[51] The company grapevine quickly communicates situations in which top managers choose an expedient action over an ethical one.[52] The primary way in which leaders set the tone for an organization's ethics is through their own actions. In addition, leaders make a commitment to ethical values and help others throughout the organization embody and reflect those values.[53]

If people don't hear about values from top leadership, they get the idea that ethical values are not important in the organization. Peter Holt, CEO of the Holt Companies, sees himself as the company's chief ethics officer. Ethical values are woven into the organizational culture, and Holt continually works to renew the values and signal his total commitment to them. Most importantly, he visits each of the firm's locations twice a year to meet with employees, answer questions, and talk about the importance of each employee upholding Holt's core values every day in every action. Holt's evaluation and reward systems are also tied to how well managers and employees live the values in their everyday actions.[54] Using performance reviews and rewards effectively is a powerful way for managers to signal that ethics counts. Consistently rewarding ethical behavior and disciplining unethical conduct at all levels of the company is a critical component of providing ethical leadership.[55]

Organizational Structures and Systems

The third pillar of ethical organizations is the set of tools that managers use to shape values and promote ethical behavior throughout the organization. Three of these tools are codes of ethics, ethical structures, and supporting whistle-blowers.

code of ethics

A formal statement of the organization's values regarding ethics and social issues.

Code of Ethics. A code of ethics is a formal statement of the company's values concerning ethics and social issues; it communicates to employees what the company stands for. Codes of ethics tend to exist in two types: principle-based statements and policy-based statements. *Principle-based statements* are designed to affect corporate culture; they define fundamental values and contain general language about company responsibilities, quality of products, and treatment of employees. General statements of principle are often called *corporate credos*. Examples are GTE's "Vision and Values" and Johnson & Johnson's "The Credo."[56]

Codes of ethics state the values or behaviors that are expected and those that will not be tolerated, backed up by management's action. A recent survey of *Fortune* 1,000 companies found that 98 percent address issues of ethics and business conduct in formal corporate documents, and 78 percent of those have separate codes of ethics that are widely distributed.[57] When top management supports and enforces these codes, including rewards for compliance and discipline for violation, ethics codes can uplift a company's ethical climate.[58] The code of ethics at Lockheed Martin reflects the theme "Setting the Standard."

Lockheed Martin

http://www.lockheedmartin.com

Lockheed Martin's board of directors adopted a booklet called *Setting the Standard* as the company's complete code of ethics and business conduct. The directors emphasize that ethical conduct requires more than complying with laws and regulations. An abbreviated version of the ethics code is included in the letter that accompanies the booklet sent to all employees:

"While maintaining sensitivity to the diverse social and cultural settings in which we conduct our business, Lockheed Martin aims to *set the standard* for ethical conduct at all of our localities throughout the world. We will achieve this through behavior in accordance with six virtues: Honesty, Integrity, Respect, Trust, Responsibility, and Citizenship.

- **Honesty:** to be truthful in all our endeavors; to be honest and forthright with one another and with our customers, communities, suppliers, and shareholders.
- **Integrity:** to say what we mean, to deliver what we promise, and to stand for what is right.
- **Respect:** to treat one another with dignity and fairness, appreciating the diversity of our workforce and the uniqueness of each employee.
- **Trust:** to build confidence through teamwork and open, candid communication.
- **Responsibility:** to speak up—without fear of retribution—and report concerns in the workplace, including violations of laws, regulations, and company policies, and seek clarification and guidance whenever there is doubt.
- **Citizenship:** to obey all the laws of the countries in which we do business and to do our part to make the communities in which we live and work better.

There are numerous resources available to assist you in meeting the challenge of performing your duties and responsibilities. . . .

We are proud of our employees and the leadership role we play in making the world a better place to live. Thank you for doing your part to create and maintain an ethical work environment . . . and for *Setting the Standard.*"[59]

An area of growing concern for companies doing business internationally is developing ethics codes that focus on the issue of human rights. Responding to the public outcry against sweatshops in the garment industry, a New York nonprofit organization and a number of influential companies have proposed a set of global labor standards to deal with issues such as child labor, low wages, and unsafe working environments. The group has come up with a scheme called Social Accountability 8000, or SA 8000, which is designed to work like the ISO 9000 quality-auditing system of the International Standards Organization. The SA 8000 is the first auditable social standard in the world. Fashion designer and retailer Eileen Fisher has taken steps to ensure that every factory supplying her $100 million business is in compliance with SA 8000. Fisher has set a standard for corporate social responsibility by training suppliers to prepare for certification and even footing the bill for their audits. Other companies, including Avon and Toys 'R' Us, are also certifying their factories and requiring their suppliers to do likewise.[60]

Ethical Structures. Ethical structures represent the various systems, positions, and programs a company can undertake to implement ethical behavior. An **ethics committee** is a group of executives appointed to oversee company ethics. The committee provides rulings on questionable ethical issues. The ethics committee assumes responsibility for disciplining wrongdoers, which is essential if the organization is to directly influence employee behavior. For example, Motorola has an Ethics Compliance Committee that is charged with interpreting, clarifying, and communicating the company's code of ethics and

ethics committee
A group of executives assigned to oversee the organization's ethics by ruling on questionable issues and disciplining violators.

with adjudicating suspected code violations. Many companies, such as Sears, Northup Grumman, and Columbia/HCA Healthcare, have set up ethics offices with full-time staff to ensure that ethical standards are an integral part of company operations. These offices are headed by a **chief ethics officer**, a company executive who oversees all aspects of ethics and legal compliance, including establishing and broadly communicating standards, ethics training, dealing with exceptions or problems, and advising senior managers in the ethical and compliance aspects of decisions.[61] The title of *chief ethics officer* was almost unheard of a decade ago, but there is a growing demand for these ethics specialists because of highly publicized ethical and legal problems faced by companies in recent years. The Ethics Officer Association, a trade group, reports that membership has soared to more than 700 companies, up from only 12 in 1992.[62] Most ethics offices also work as counseling centers to help employees resolve difficult ethical issues. A toll-free confidential hotline allows employees to report questionable behavior as well as seek guidance concerning ethical dilemmas.

Ethics training programs also help employees deal with ethical questions and translate the values stated in a code of ethics into everyday behavior.[63] Training programs are an important supplement to a written code of ethics. The Boeing Corporation requires all employees to go through at least one hour of ethical training a year; senior managers have to participate in at least five hours. At McMurray Publishing Company in Phoenix, all employees attend a *weekly* meeting on workplace ethics, where they discuss how to handle ethical dilemmas and how to resolve conflicting values.[64]

A strong ethics program is important, but it is no guarantee against lapses. Dow Corning, whose faulty silicone breast implants shocked the business community, pioneered an ethics program that was looked upon as a model. Established in the mid-1970s, Dow's ambitious ethics program included the Business Conduct committee, training programs, regular reviews and audits to monitor compliance, and reports to the Audit and Social Responsibility committee. What went wrong? The ethics program dealt with the overall environment, but specific programs such as product safety were handled through normal channels—in this case the Medical Device Business Board, which slowed further safety studies.[65] Dow Corning's problems sent a warning to other industries. It is not enough to *have* an impressive ethics program. The ethics program must be merged with day-to-day operations, encouraging ethical decisions to be made throughout the company.

Whistle-Blowing. Employee disclosure of illegal, immoral, or illegitimate practices on the employer's part is called **whistle-blowing**.[66] No organization can rely exclusively on codes of conduct and ethical structures to prevent all unethical behavior. Holding organizations accountable depends to some degree on individuals who are willing to blow the whistle if they detect illegal, dangerous, or unethical activities. Whistle-blowers often report wrongdoing to outsiders, such as regulatory agencies, senators, or newspaper reporters. Some firms have instituted innovative programs and confidential hotlines to encourage and support internal whistle-blowing. For this to be an effective ethical safeguard, however, companies must view whistle-blowing as a benefit to the company and make dedicated efforts to protect whistle-blowers.[67]

When there are no effective protective measures, whistle-blowers suffer. Although whistle-blowing has become widespread in recent years, it is still

chief ethics officer
A company executive who oversees ethics and legal compliance.

ethics training
Training programs to help employees deal with ethical questions and values.

whistle-blowing
The disclosure by an employee of illegal, immoral, or illegitimate practices by the organization.

risky for employees, who can lose their jobs, be ostracized by coworkers, or be transferred to lower-level positions. For example, when Judith Neal blew the whistle at Honeywell's munitions plant in Joliet, Illinois, she ended up feeling as if she were the one being punished. Neal discovered that plant managers were falsifying test data to meet production goals, allowing substandard and potentially dangerous ammunition that Air Force and Army pilots and soldiers staked their lives on to pass inspection. Honeywell eventually settled with the federal government and two of the wrongdoers were punished, but Neal herself may have suffered the most. She heard rumors that a high-level manager was referring to her as "dead meat." In fact, there were credible threats against her physical person, saying they would "break both the legs of the whistle blower." She reported the rumors to Honeywell officials, but no action was taken. Eventually, the manager was promoted to a job at another plant, while Neal was asked to stay home for a month "for her own protection." When she returned, Neal found that most of her job responsibilities had been transferred to other employees, and she eventually quit in frustration. She filed suit years later and was awarded a financial settlement, but Neal emphasizes that money can never compensate for "the loss of privacy, the humiliation of having your personal life dredged up. Or for the nightmares, the anxiety of wondering if something is going to happen to you because you've spoken out."[68]

Managers can be trained to view whistle-blowing as a benefit rather than a threat, and systems can be set up to effectively protect employees who report illegal or unethical activities.

Ethics and the New Workplace

Many of today's best companies realize that success can be measured in many ways, not all of which show up on the financial statement. However, the relationship of a corporation's ethics and social responsibility to its financial performance concerns both managers and management scholars and has generated a lively debate.[69] One concern of managers is whether good citizenship will hurt performance—after all, ethics programs cost money. A number of studies have been undertaken to determine whether heightened ethical and social responsiveness increases or decreases financial performance. Studies have provided varying results but generally have found that there is a small positive relationship between social responsibility and financial performance.[70] For example, the Domini Social Index, created in 1989 to track the stock performance of socially responsible companies, indicates that they perform as well as or better than companies that are not socially responsible.[71] A recent study by Walker Research found that when price and quality are equal, two-thirds of customers say they would switch brands to do business with a company that is ethical and socially responsible.[72] Although results from these studies are not proof, they do provide an indication that use of resources for ethics and social responsibility does not hurt companies.[73] Enlightened companies realize that integrity and trust are essential elements in sustaining successful and profitable business relationships with an increasingly connected web of employees, customers, suppliers, and partners. Although doing the right thing might not always be profitable in the short run, it develops a level of trust that money cannot buy and that will ultimately benefit the company.

© Alcoa

With funding by the Davenport Works division of Alcoa, the world's largest producer of aluminum, college student and commercial fisherman Chad Pregracke is leading a group of volunteers in an attempt to rid the Mississippi River banks of trash and debris in the Quad cities area. Pregracke, who was named the Illinois Wildlife Federation's Environmental Citizen of the Year, has cleared the shores of 30,000 pounds of debris, including 92 metal barrels, 153 tires, 3 refrigerators, a stove, and a television. By funding such a program, Alcoa enhances its reputation as a socially responsible company.

In the world of fast-moving Internet companies, ethics sometimes takes a back seat as managers and employees do whatever it takes to get the most business in the least amount of time. However, smart managers are finding that old-fashioned integrity pays off. Managers at one Silicon Valley start-up, CenterBeam Inc., have made integrity the guiding principle of their corporate culture, and employees routinely tell stories that signify the "make-or-break" importance the company puts on keeping its promises. One, for example, concerns an employee who was offered a job just before a résumé from a positively dazzling candidate arrived. At many fast-moving start-ups, the job offer to the first candidate would have been rescinded, but CenterBeam had made a commitment and stuck to it. Another story concerns a similar situation with a supplier, when CenterBeam managers honored their promise even though it cost the company thousands of dollars. Both decisions ultimately served the company well because they built trust among employees, suppliers, and partners, as well as customers.[74]

Changes in the workplace have brought other new ethical issues for managers. Options such as telecommuting, virtual work, and flexible hours open the door to employee abuse of the flexibility offered by the organization, but the success of these new ways of working depends on mutual trust. New information technology provides tools for managers to keep an even tighter rein on workers. Managers can choose to closely monitor when employees are logged on to the network and what they are doing, as well as where they are spending their time on the Internet. The American Management Association's survey of electronic monitoring and surveillance of employees found that nearly 74 percent of large U.S. businesses record and review employees' communications and activities on the job, a figure that nearly doubled between 1997 and 2000.[75] Although most companies have a policy that lets employees know they're subject to being watched, some do not. In addition, some ethical managers believe such close monitoring not only wastes time and money but is just downright wrong because it invades employees' privacy.

Companies need effective ways to investigate sexual harassment or other illegal and inappropriate workplace activities. However, snooping for snooping's sake is ethically questionable. Showing distrust of virtual workers and telecommuters can also backfire by weakening the employee's trust and commitment. "If you hire great people and you engage them in the business and they really have that passion and they know that you care, you shouldn't be sitting around babysitting or monitoring them," said one manager.[76] Another issue of growing concern in the new workplace is the privacy of customers on the Internet. Companies are compiling vast portfolios of personal information on their Web site visitors. This information is marketing gold for organizations, but critics argue that it is a serious violation of the individual's right to privacy.[77] A recent survey found that 71 percent of Americans polled are either very concerned or somewhat concerned about threats to their personal privacy over the Web. To head off the passage of new privacy laws now being debated in Washington, many companies are developing their own ways to protect individual privacy on the Internet.[78]

These are complicated ethical issues, and they become even more complicated because of the increasing globalization of business. However, companies that make an unwavering commitment to maintaining high standards of ethics and social responsibility will lead the way toward a brighter future for both business and society.

■ Summary and Management Solution

Ethics and social responsibility are hot topics for today's managers. The ethical domain of behavior pertains to values of right and wrong. Ethical decisions and behavior are typically guided by a value system. Four value-based approaches that serve as criteria for ethical decision making are utilitarian, individualism, moral-rights, and justice. For an individual manager, the ability to make correct ethical choices will depend on both individual and organizational characteristics. An important individual characteristic is level of moral development. Corporate culture is an organizational characteristic that influences ethical behavior.

Corporate social responsibility concerns a company's values toward society. How can organizations be good corporate citizens? The model for evaluating social performance uses four criteria: economic, legal, ethical, and discretionary. Evaluating corporate social behavior often requires assessing its impact on organizational stakeholders. One issue of growing concern is environmental responsibility. Organizations may take a legal, market, stakeholder, or activist approach to addressing environmental concerns.

Ethical organizations are supported by three pillars: ethical individuals, ethical leadership, and organizational structures and systems, including codes of ethics, ethics committees, chief ethics officers, training programs, and mechanisms to protect whistle-blowers. Companies that are ethical and socially responsible perform as well as—and often better than—those that are not socially responsible. However, changes in the workplace are raising new ethical issues for managers and organizations, such as ethical use of technology for monitoring employees, trust among business partners, and the privacy of individuals on the Internet.

Returning to our management challenge at the beginning of the chapter, there are no easy right-or-wrong answers to the drug companies' dilemma. Protecting intellectual property rights (drug patents) is a legitimate right of organizations, and the drug companies would argue that it is also a responsibility to their employees and shareholders, as well as customers. Managers who take a utilitarian approach to ethics, for example, might argue that protecting their patents ultimately provides the most good for the most people, since patents are the foundation of research and development of new drugs. However, those who take a justice approach might argue that this decision doesn't take into account the concept of justice toward the unfortunate victims of AIDS in poor countries. In response to bad publicity and public outcry over the South Africa dispute, companies are taking some action, going beyond purely economic and legal responsibilities to take ethical issues into consideration. One response to social demands is to reduce the prices of AIDS drugs to Africa and other developing areas of the world. Merck, for example, says it will make no profit from the AIDS drugs it sells in developing countries. Officials with Doctors Without Borders welcomed the announcement, but warned that it might still leave drugs out of the reach of many poor AIDS sufferers in the developing world.[79] Most activists would like to see the drug companies take a further step toward *discretionary responsibility* by ensuring that anyone who needs HIV and AIDS medicines has access to them.

■ Discussion Questions

1. Dr. Martin Luther King, Jr., said, "As long as there is poverty in the world, I can never be rich. . . . As long as diseases are rampant, I can never be healthy. . . . I can never be what I ought to be until you are what you ought to be." Discuss this quote with respect to the material in this chapter. Would this be true for corporations, too?

2. Environmentalists are trying to pass laws for oil spills that would remove all liability limits for the oil companies. This would punish corporations financially. Is this the best way to influence companies to be socially responsible?

3. Compare and contrast the utilitarian approach with the moral-rights approach to ethical decision making. Which do you believe is the best for managers to follow? Why?

4. Imagine yourself in a situation of being encouraged to inflate your expense account. Do you think your choice would be more affected by your individual moral development or by the cultural values of the company for which you worked? Explain.

5. Is it socially responsible for organizations to undertake political activity or join with others in a trade association to influence the government? Discuss.

6. The criteria of corporate social responsibility suggest that economic responsibilities are of the greatest magnitude, followed by legal, ethical, and discretionary responsibilities. Do you agree? Discuss.

7. What are some current ethical issues in the business news? Identify one company that seems to be handling an issue in an ethical and socially responsible manner and one that appears to be unethical or socially irresponsible.

8. Do you believe it is ethical for companies to compile portfolios of personal information on their Web site

visitors without informing them? How about for organizations to monitor their employees' use of the Web? Discuss.

9. Which do you think would be more effective for shaping long-term ethical behavior in an organization: a written code of ethics combined with ethics training or strong ethical leadership? Why?

10. Lincoln Electric considers customers and employees to be more important stakeholders than shareholders. Is it appropriate for management to define some stakeholders as more important than others? Should all stakeholders be considered equal?

■ Manager's Workbook

The spread of technology into the workplace has raised a variety of new ethical questions, and many old ones still linger. Compare your answers with those of other Americans surveyed in questions 1–16. Questions 17–20 test your knowledge of ethics programs in organizations.

Office Technology

1. Is it wrong to use company e-mail for personal reasons?   Yes   No
2. Is it wrong to use office equipment to help your children or spouse do schoolwork?   Yes   No
3. Is it wrong to play computer games on office equipment during the workday?   Yes   No
4. Is it wrong to use office equipment to do Internet shopping?   Yes   No
5. Is it unethical to blame an error you made on a technological glitch?   Yes   No
6. Is it unethical to visit pornographic Web sites using office equipment?   Yes   No

Gifts and Entertainment

7. What's the value at which a gift from a supplier or client becomes troubling? $25 $50 $100
8. Is a $50 gift to a boss unacceptable?   Yes   No
9. Is a $50 gift *from* the boss unacceptable?   Yes   No
10. Of gifts from suppliers: Is it OK to accept a $200 pair of football tickets?   Yes   No
11. Is it OK to accept a $120 pair of theater tickets?   Yes   No
12. Is it OK to accept a $100 holiday food basket? Yes   No

13. Is it OK to accept a $25 gift certificate?   Yes   No
14. Can you accept a $75 prize won at a raffle at a supplier's conference?   Yes   No

Truth and Lies

15. Due to on-the-job pressure, have you ever abused or lied about sick days?   Yes   No
16. Due to on-the-job pressure, have you ever taken credit for someone else's work or idea? Yes   No
17. What percentage of Fortune 500 companies and what percentage of all corporations have codes of ethics that apply to employees?
18. The three "C's" of business ethics are:
    a. compliance, contributions, and consequences
    b. camaraderie, candor, clear-sightedness
    c. consideration, coexistence, counsel
19. The proper role of companies in promoting business ethics is:
    a. covering up unethical practices so no one gets caught
    b. clarifying, forcing, and role-modeling expectations about ethical behaviors
    c. leave employees to figure it out on their own
20. An ethical stance is a position:
    a. to increase profits
    b. taken consistently for a long time
    c. taken to impress stockholders

SOURCES: "Taking the High Road," *Buildings* (February 2002), 57–58; Ethics Officer Association, Belmont, Massachusetts; Ethical Leadership Group, Wilmette, Illinois; surveys sampled a cross section of workers at large companies and nationwide.

■ Manager's Workshop

1. In groups of four to seven students, discuss the case below, rank-ordering the four choices for strategies.
2. As a group, determine which of the ethical approaches (utilitarian, individualism, moral-rights, and justice) relate to each of the four choices.

3. Groups report their rankings to the large class and instructor facilitates discussion on ethical frameworks.

Case Study

You are the head seismologist of one of the top research institutions in the country. A new machine that you helped develop has determined that a damaging earthquake is imminent in a nearby state in three days. Your new equipment can predict earthquakes with an 80 percent reliability. The area that the earthquake is likely to strike has a great population density and many bridges and tall buildings, some of which are so-called projects.

You reported your findings to the director of your institute, but nothing has been done. You now have two days until the earthquake and you must decide what to do. Here are the given options:

1. You should be careful about your findings. After all, there is a 20 percent chance you are wrong and you could create unnecessary chaos—not to mention the fact that your career is at stake.

2. You must immediately inform all of the media. Everyone should know and be able to prepare for the possible disaster.

3. Calculate the costs of damage expected from the quake, both in damaged buildings and lost lives. Compare this with the cost of falsely predicting the quake and all the costs associated with the chaos that would result. Compare these two figures and decide which is greater.

4. Look back and see how other earthquake threats have been treated. Was there bias in terms of warning people in richer versus poorer regions? What is the fair thing to do in this less-than-affluent area?

SOURCE: Adapted from Mark Mallinger, "Decisive Decision-Making: An Exercise Using Ethical Frameworks," *Journal of Management Education* 21, no. 3, 1997, 411–417.

■ Management in Practice: Ethical Dilemma

What Is Right?

It is often hard for a manager to determine what is "right" and even more difficult to put ethical behavior into practice. A manager's ethical orientation often brings him or her into conflict with people, policies, customers, or bosses. Consider the following dilemmas. How would you handle them?

1. A well-liked member of your staff with an excellent record confides to you that he has Acquired Immune Deficiency Syndrome (AIDS). Although his illness has not affected his performance, you're concerned about his future health and about the reactions of his coworkers. You
   a. tell him to keep you informed about his health and say nothing to his coworkers.
   b. arrange for him to transfer to an area of the organization where he can work alone.
   c. hold a staff meeting to inform his coworkers and ask them how they feel about his continued presence on your team.
   d. consult your human resources officer on how to proceed.

2. During a reorganization, you're told to reduce staff in the department you manage. After analyzing staffing requirements, you realize the job would be a lot easier if two professionals, who are both over age 60, would retire. You
   a. say nothing and determine layoffs based purely on performance and length of service.
   b. schedule a meeting with both employees and ask if they'd consider early retirement.
   c. schedule a meeting with all staff and ask if anyone is interested in severance or early retirement.
   d. lay off the older workers.

3. One of your colleagues has recently experienced two personal tragedies—her husband filed for divorce and her mother died. Although you feel genuine sympathy for her, her work is suffering. A report you completed, based on inaccurate data she provided, has been criticized by management. Your manager asks you for an explanation. You

   a. apologize for the inaccuracies and correct the data.
   b. tell your manager that the data supplied by your colleague was the source of the problem.
   c. say your colleague has a problem and needs support.
   d. tell your manager that because of your work load, you didn't have time to check the figures in the report.

4. Your firm recently hired a new manager who is at the same level you are. You do not like the man personally and consider him a rival professionally. You run into a friend who knows your rival well. You discover this man did not attend Harvard as he stated on his résumé and, in fact, has not graduated from any college. You know his supposed Harvard background was instrumental in getting him hired. You
   a. expose the lie to your superiors.
   b. without naming names, consult your human resources officer on how to proceed.
   c. say nothing. The company obviously failed to check him out, and the lie probably will surface on its own.
   d. confront the man with the information and let him decide what to do.

5. During a changeover in the accounting department, you discover your company has been routinely overcharging members of the public for services provided to them. Your superiors say repayment of charges would wreak havoc on company profits. Your company is federally regulated, and the oversight commission has not noticed the mistake. Your bosses say the problem will never come to light and they will take steps to correct the problem so it never happens again. You
   a. contact the oversight commission.
   b. take the matter public, anonymously or otherwise.
   c. say nothing. It is now in the hands of the bosses.
   d. work with the bosses on a plan to recognize the company's error and set up a schedule of rebates that would not unduly penalize the company.

Questions

1. Use the guidelines described in the Focus on Ethics "Guidelines for Ethical Decision Making" to determine the appropriate behavior in these cases. Do you have all the information you need to make an ethical decision? How would family or friends react to each alternative if you were in these situations?

2. Which approach to ethical decision making—utilitarian, individualism, justice, or moral-rights—seems most appropriate for handling each situation?

SOURCES: Game developed by Katherine Nelson, "Board Games," *Owen Manager* (Spring 1990), 14–16; Craig Dreilinger and Dan Rice, "Office Ethics," *Working Woman* (December 1991), 35–39, and Kevin Kelly and Joseph Weber, "When a Rival's Trade Secret Crosses Your Desk. . . ," *Business Week* (May 20, 1991), 18.

■ Surf the Net

1. **Ethics Quiz.** The Internet contains many interactive sites where you can learn more about ethical decision making. Visit one of the sites below or find one of your own that will allow you to gain further insight about ethical issues.
   http://www.nevada.edu/~pernellj/quiz.html
   http://www.confessonline.com/quiz.asp
   http://library.humboldt.edu/infoservices/OWLS/OWL8-Test.htm
   http://www.ethicsandbusiness.org/stylequiz.htm
   http://www.ai.org/ethics/pubs/newsarticles/Quiz.html

2. **The Global Compact.** To learn more about the Nine Principles of the Global Compact Network, find answers to the following questions at *http://www.unglobalcompact.org/*
   a. What are the Nine Principles?
   b. How does a company participate in the Global Compact?

3. **Internet Legal Issues.** An Internet law library that provides extensive summaries of court decisions shaping the law of the Web can be found at
   http://www.phillipsnizer.com/internetlib.htm

Topics addressed include copyright, trademark, dilution and other intellectual property issues, jurisdiction, linking, framing, meta tags, clip-art, defamation, domain name, e-mail, encryption, gambling, click-wrap agreements, shrink-wrap licenses, spamming, and many other subjects (50+ topics are linked from the home page at this site). Select a topic of interest, print out the summary, and bring it to class.

■ Case for Critical Analysis

Massengill's Department Store

Massengill's Department Store had been a fixture in small and mid-sized cities across the Southeast for 75 years. But for the past couple of decades, the Atlanta-based chain had been slowly going downhill. Once a cutting-edge retailer, Massengill's had come to be known primarily for its dilapidated stores and dowdy-looking clothes. Everyone knew the chain was on the verge of bankruptcy. But that was before Marv Heimler. Heimler had been lured away from his job running a nationwide chain based in Dallas–Fort Worth to rescue Massengill's. And rescue it he had. Massengill's was now the talk of the retail industry, thanks to its soaring sales and accompanying surge in stock price.

Heimler had been offered a generous compensation package that was tied to his performance in leading Massengill's through a rapid turnaround. And, indeed, Heimler realized he had no time to lose if Massengill's was to survive. He came in with an aggressive plan for change that included remodeling shabby stores, cutting overhead costs, and offering modern, trendy merchandise sold by sophisticated, knowledgeable sales associates. "Link selling," in which shoppers enter the store looking for one item but end up leaving with three or four, was an important part of the new strategy. Unfortunately, the new

strategy also meant that layoffs were inevitable. Massengill's had long been run by old-fashioned, patriarchal managers who had held fast to their no-layoffs policy. However, to save the company meant aggressively slashing costs and investing the savings in remodeling, new merchandise, and training programs. Closing the in-store snack bars and consolidating distribution centers were the first steps, which eliminated about 500 jobs. In addition, many of the long-time salespeople had neither the abilities required for link-selling nor a feel for the chic, sophisticated clothing Massengill's was now offering. Heimler knew he had to cut out the "deadwood" (a term he was careful to never use in public) to make room for a new breed of modern, energized sales associates.

Layoff notices went out to more than 500 floor supervisors and longtime salespeople on Friday before lunch. That would give people time to clean out their desks and say goodbye to their colleagues before the end of the day. And most of the survivors would have a weekend to process what had happened before returning to work.

Heimler had expected people to be upset about the layoffs, but the severity of the reaction surprised him. Even the new employees he had brought in seemed to be upset. An article in a recent industry magazine had speculated that Massengill's success would be short-lived if morale continued to decline. "There's no trust at Massengill's," the article had said. "People feel like senior management isn't honest with its people. They just want to fix up the company fast and mop up the damage later."

Claire Sparkes, his head of human resources, confirmed that the article was on target. "People are really angry," she told him. "They think you should have held meetings to explain what was happening with the company and give people some warning."

"Everybody knew Massengill's was on the verge of financial collapse," Heimler snapped back. "When a new CEO is brought in to turn things around, everybody knows layoffs are coming. Why rub their noses in it? And if I hadn't moved quickly, nobody here would have a job! The whole chain would have gone down the tubes, and instead of 1,000 or so jobs being lost there would have been 5,000 people out of work! How would people have liked that?"

When Claire left his office, Heimler evaluated his situation. Massengill's was clearly soaring again. Customers were flocking in, sales and profits were going up, and Heimler was a hero on Wall Street. His compensation package is already worth more than $1 million, and his contract has just been renewed for two more years, with an increased salary and more stock options. He knows he has transformed Massengill's from an outdated chain that catered to older women to a hip, fun place for affluent young customers. Heimler reviewed last quarter's results and saw that sales and profits are still going up. So why does everyone keep telling him morale is going down?

Questions

1. What approach to ethical decision making (utilitarian, individualism, moral-rights, or justice) seems to best describe Marv Heimler's turnaround strategy at Massengill's?

2. At what level of moral development would you place Heimler? Why?

3. How could Heimler have handled the layoffs to avoid the problems he's now facing? If you were in his position, what would you do now?

SOURCE: Based on Suzy Wetlaufer, "After the Layoffs, What Next?" *Harvard Business Review* (September–October 1998), 24–42.

PART THREE

Planning

Before a recording is released into the market, a great deal of planning has taken place—primarily by the artist's manager. First, the artist and manager must develop a career plan, or road map, for the artist to follow. The manager and booking agent will plan in which cities an act should appear; and the marketing department at a record label will develop a marketing plan and a publicity plan to make sure that both the recording and the artist receive maximum exposure in the marketplace.

These plans must all be flexible and serve as guiding lights rather than as fixed paths. A big hit puts increased demands on an artist almost overnight, and a plan must be able to adapt to that success; but a recording that fails to hit means that the artist, manager, and his or her artist development team must alter the original plan in order to maximize the opportunities they do have, as well as to create new opportunities for the artist and recording. Their efforts must lead to media exposure so that consumers can become aware and, hopefully, purchase the recording or attend a show.

Planning is absolutely essential in the music business, but a fixed plan is generally useless because no outcome can be determined. A basic plan of where the artist is going is essential, but allowances must be made for constant reappraisal, alteration, or fine-tuning of this plan.

Organizational Planning and Goal Setting

LEARNING OBJECTIVES

After studying this chapter, you should be able to

1 Define goals and plans and explain the relationship between them.

2 Explain the concept of organizational mission and how it influences goal setting and planning.

3 Describe the types of goals an organization should have and why they resemble a hierarchy.

4 Define the characteristics of effective goals.

5 Describe the four essential steps in the MBO process.

6 Describe and explain the importance of the three stages of crisis management planning.

7 Discuss how planning in the new workplace differs from traditional approaches to planning.

8 Define the components of strategic management.

9 Describe the strategic planning process and SWOT analysis.

10 Describe business-level strategies, including Porter's competitive forces and strategies and partnership strategies.

11 Explain the major considerations in formulating functional strategies.

12 Enumerate the considerations used for implementing strategy.

Everyone is familiar with the little plastic strings used to attach price tags to garments. These were made in a Boston plant that was near collapse some years ago. When young engineer Gordon Lankton bought one-half of the middling company Nypro (Nylon Products) in 1962, it had 40 employees and brought in $870,000 in yearly revenue. The previous CEO did not want it to grow past $2 million. But after he left, Lankton took over. The main problem with the strings was that they easily became tangled, so Lankton invented a connector that kept them from snarling. With patent in hand, he grew the business $10 million per year, with the strings accounting for half of the business. "We were making 10 million strings a day," he says, "and I could visualize 10 million people swearing every day as they tried to remove them from the items they bought." Even with its success, though, the company nearly went bankrupt in the early 1980s when interest rates soared to 20 percent. Lankton saw his profits eaten up by interest rates. In fact, he was losing money and ready to go under. He needed a dramatic strategy to survive.[1]

If you were Gordon Lankton, what would you do?

One of the primary responsibilities of managers is to decide where the organization should go in the future and how to get it there. But how do managers plan for the future in an uncertain and constantly changing environment? As we discussed in Chapter 1 of this textbook, most organizations are facing growing uncertainty. The September 11, 2001, terrorist attacks in the United States and subsequent events have left many managers wondering how to cope and have sparked a renewed interest in organizational planning, particularly planning for unexpected problems and events.

In some organizations, typically small ones, planning is informal. In others, managers follow a well-defined planning framework. The company establishes a basic mission and develops formal goals and strategic plans for carrying it out. Companies such as Royal Dutch/Shell, IBM, Mazda, and United Way undertake a strategic planning exercise each year—reviewing their missions, goals, and plans to meet environmental changes or the expectations of important stakeholders such as the community, owners, or stockholders. Many of these companies also develop *contingency plans* for unexpected circumstances and disaster recovery plans for what the organization would do in the event of a major disaster such as a hurricane, earthquake, or other crisis.

Of the four management functions—planning, organizing, leading, and controlling—described in Chapter 1, planning is considered the most fundamental. Everything else stems from planning. Yet planning also is the most controversial management function. Planning cannot read an uncertain future. Planning cannot tame a turbulent environment. A statement by General Colin Powell, now U.S. Secretary of State, offers a warning for managers: "No battle plan survives contact with the enemy."[2]

In this chapter, we will explore the process of planning and consider how managers develop effective plans that can grow and change to meet new conditions. Special attention is given to goal setting, for that is where planning starts. Then, the various types of plans that managers use to help the organization achieve those goals are discussed, with special attention paid to crisis management planning. Finally, we will examine new approaches to planning that emphasize the involvement of employees, customers, partners, and other stakeholders in strategic thinking and execution. Chapter 5 will look at strategic planning in depth and examine a number of strategic options managers can use in a competitive environment. In Chapter 6, we look at management decision making. Proper decision-making techniques are crucial to selecting the organization's goals, plans, and strategic options.

Overview of Goals and Plans

goal
A desired future state that the organization attempts to realize.

plan
A blueprint specifying the resource allocations, schedules, and other actions necessary for attaining goals.

planning
The act of determining the organization's goals and the means for achieving them.

Goals and plans have become general concepts in our society. A **goal** is a desired future state that the organization attempts to realize. Goals are important because organizations exist for a purpose, and goals define and state that purpose. A **plan** is a blueprint for goal achievement and specifies the necessary resource allocations, schedules, tasks, and other actions. Goals specify future ends; plans specify today's means. The word **planning** usually incorporates both ideas; it means determining the organization's goals and defining the means for achieving them.[3]

Exhibit 5.1 illustrates the levels of goals and plans in an organization. The planning process starts with a formal mission statement that defines the basic purpose of the organization, especially for external audiences. The mission

EXHIBIT *5.1*

Levels of Goals/Plans and Their Importance

statement is the basis for the strategic (company) level of goals and plans, which in turn shapes the tactical (divisional) level and the operational (departmental) level.[4] Top managers are typically responsible for establishing *strategic* goals and plans that reflect a commitment to both organizational efficiency and effectiveness, as described in Chapter 1. *Tactical* goals and plans are the responsibility of middle managers, such as the heads of major divisions or functional units. A division manager will formulate tactical plans that focus on the major actions the division must take to fulfill its part in the strategic plan set by top management. *Operational* plans identify the specific procedures or processes needed at lower levels of the organization, such as individual departments and employees. Front-line managers and supervisors develop operational plans that focus on specific tasks and processes and that help to meet tactical and strategic goals. Planning at each level supports the other levels.

Purposes of Goals and Plans

The complexity of today's environment and uncertainty about the future overwhelm many managers and lead them to focus on operational issues and short-term results rather than long-term goals and plans. However, planning generally positively affects a company's performance.[5] In addition to improving financial and operational performance, developing explicit goals and plans at each level illustrated in Exhibit 5.1 is important because of the external and internal messages they send. These messages go to both external and internal audiences and provide important benefits for the organization.[6]

- *Legitimacy.* An organization's mission describes what the organization stands for and its reason for existence. It symbolizes legitimacy to external audiences such as investors, customers, and suppliers. The mission helps them and the local community look on the company in a favorable light and, hence, accept its existence. A strong mission also has an impact on employees, enabling them to become committed to the organization because they can identify with its overall purpose and reason for existence. One of the traits often cited by employees in *Fortune* magazine's list of the "100 Best Companies to Work For in America" is a sense of purpose and meaning. For example, at Medtronic, a medical products company, employees are inspired by the mission to "alleviate pain, restore health, and extend life."[7]

- *Source of Motivation and Commitment.* Goals and plans facilitate employees' identification with the organization and help motivate them by reducing uncertainty and clarifying what they should accomplish. Lack of a clear goal can damage employee motivation and commitment. When Main Street Muffins lost sight of its goal and began branching into new lines of business, morale sank so low that bakers were calling in sick at 3 AM or walking off the job with no notice. The company took a nosedive toward bankruptcy before the owners developed a statement to remind everyone that the primary goal of Main Street Muffins was "to profitably improve an organization that overwhelms the food industry with its devotion to high-quality products and services." With the new goal statement as a guide, employee commitment and motivation gradually improved, and the company became profitable again within three months.[8] Whereas a goal provides the "why" of an organization or subunit's existence, a plan tells the "how." A plan lets employees know what actions to undertake to achieve the goal.

- *Guides to Action.* Goals and plans provide a sense of direction. They focus attention on specific targets and direct employee efforts toward important outcomes. Hartford Technology Services Co., for example, set goals to establish a customer profile database, survey customer satisfaction, and secure service agreements with ten new customers.[9]

- *Rationale for Decisions.* Through goal setting and planning, managers learn what the organization is trying to accomplish. They can make decisions to ensure that internal policies, roles, performance, structure, products, and expenditures will be made in accordance with desired outcomes. Decisions throughout the organization will be in alignment with the plan.

- *Standard of Performance.* Because goals define desired outcomes for the organization, they also serve as performance criteria. They provide a standard of assessment. If an organization wishes to grow by 15 percent, and actual growth is 17 percent, managers will have exceeded their prescribed standard. Top managers at Procter & Gamble have set a goal to double consumer products sales to $70 billion by 2006.[10]

The overall planning process prevents managers from thinking merely in terms of day-to-day activities. When organizations drift away from goals and plans, they typically get into trouble. This occurred at Amex Life Assurance, an American Express subsidiary based in San Rafael, California. A new president implemented a strong planning system that illustrates the power of planning to improve organizational performance.

Amex Life Assurance

Sarah Nolan knew that the chairman of American Express was a self-professed maniac on quality. But when Nolan arrived as the new president of Amex Life Assurance, she found a paperwork assembly line that served customers at a snail's pace. A simple change of address took two days; sending out a new insurance policy took at least ten days. Nolan's primary goal was to get everyone at Amex working together while keeping the focus on the customer. She sent five managers representing different specialties to an empty office park and told them to imagine they were setting up an entirely new business. Nolan gave the group only three rules to follow in their task of planning a new operation:

1. Put the customer first.

2. Don't copy anything we do here.

3. Be ready to process applications yourselves in six months.

When the planning group returned, ten layers of personnel had been collapsed into three, each of which would deal directly with the public. Fewer employees were needed, so more than one-third were transferred to other divisions. Expenses were cut in half and profitability increased sixfold. Nolan used planning to help managers break out of their focus on day-to-day activities and reorient the company toward its strategic goal of customer satisfaction.[11]

Goals in Organizations

Setting goals starts with top managers. The overall planning process begins with a mission statement and strategic goals for the organization as a whole.

Organizational Mission

At the top of the goal hierarchy is the **mission**—the organization's reason for existence. The mission describes the organization's values, aspirations, and reason for being. A well-defined mission is the basis for development of all subsequent goals and plans. Without a clear mission, goals and plans may be developed haphazardly and not take the organization in the direction it needs to go.

The formal **mission statement** is a broadly stated definition of basic business scope and operations that distinguishes the organization from others of a similar type.[12] The content of a mission statement often focuses on the market and customers and identifies desired fields of endeavor. Some mission statements describe company characteristics such as corporate values, product quality, location of facilities, and attitude toward employees. Mission statements often reveal the company's philosophy as well as its purpose. One example is the mission statement for the franchise Mail Boxes Etc., presented in Exhibit 5.2.

mission
The organization's reason for existence.

mission statement
A broadly stated definition of the organization's basic business scope and operations that distinguishes it from similar types of organizations.

E X H I B I T 5.2

Mission Statement for Mail Boxes Etc.

Mission Statement for Mail Boxes Etc.
Our Mission
Making Business Easier Worldwide Through Our Service and Distribution Network, Delivering Personalized and Convenient Business Solutions With World-Class Customer Service.
Our Core Values
Caring   Honesty   Fairness Integrity   Trust   Respect Commitment   Accountability

SOURCE: Mail Boxes Etc. Web site, *http://www.mbe.com,* accessed on August 29, 2001.

Mail Boxes Etc. devised its concise mission statement to express its commitment to ethical considerations as well as good business practices. Such short, straightforward mission statements describe basic business activities and purposes, as well as the values that guide the company. Another example of this type of mission statement is that of Bertucci's, a chain of full-service pizza restaurants with headquarters in Wakefield, Massachusetts:

> Bertucci's is committed to serving our customers as guests in an atmosphere that reflects the traditional welcome, warmth, and abundance of an Italian Home.
>
> To this we add value, quality, and service as the restaurant cornerstones upon which we have built and will continue to build our futures.
>
> We are dedicated to provide the best experience for our guests so that our entire family of team members, stockholders, suppliers, and, in addition, our communities benefit.[13]

Because of mission statements such as those of Mail Boxes Etc. and Bertucci's, employees as well as customers, suppliers, and stockholders know the company's stated purpose and values. Mission can come from a deeper sense of values and social responsibility, as it did for Jackie Danforth, described in the Focus on Ethics box.

FOCUS ON ETHICS

New Horizons

As a teenager, Jacqueline Danforth was out of control: drinking, taking drugs, sneaking out at night to party at New York's famous Studio 54, and even running away. She knew her adopted parents loved her, but their high-powered lifestyle didn't fit with a girl who wanted to be on a farm milking cows. It didn't help that her mother was celebrity newswoman Barbara Walters, because she had to worry whether people liked her for herself. At age 14, Walters knew something had to be done, so she took Danforth, kicking and screaming, to a rugged emotional-growth boarding school in Idaho, where she stayed for three years. "It saved my life," Danforth now says.

Danforth was inspired to help other troubled teens, and in 2001 started her own company, the Maine-based wilderness program New Horizons, where girls aged 12 to 18 spend nine weeks camping out with trained therapists and wilderness guides, learning about themselves and gaining self-esteem and self-control. Its mission is to inspire adolescent females— using the combined resources of the natural environment, caring, knowledgeable professionals, and the power of self-discovery—to enhance their individual mental, physical, social, and spiritual well-being.

Danforth spent months getting licenses and insurance, building a Web site, developing curriculum, buying land, hiring staff, and flying around the country to educational conferences to get the word out to teachers who could refer girls to New Horizons.

You'd think Danforth would call on her mom for seed money, but the daughter wanted to do it on her own and found her own group of investors. So determined was she to do it alone, that "she didn't want my accountants or lawyer," says Walters. The tuition of $2,800 per week covers all staff salaries, food, medical staff, and even high-quality all-weather gear for the girls. Danforth doesn't yet pay herself a salary.

While some other wilderness programs operate like army boot camps, with strict discipline and severe punishments, New Horizons has firm boundaries, but operates on the philosophy that "these girls are good at heart," says Danforth.

Most of the girls arrive in Bangor, Maine, angry and scared, but within a few weeks begin to change. "It's not like you just work on your own problems," reports a girl who, when drunk, crashed her mother's car en route to a drug rehab program.

Danforth knows there are many struggles ahead as the organization develops. But it is worth it. "Now I have a mission in life," she says. "My mother is a hard act to follow," she admits, because Walters has influenced so many people. Even though Danforth may not reach as many people, she is content with her goals. "I do want to feel that I'm giving back."

SOURCE: Beth Johnson, "Finding Her Own Path," *Good Housekeeping* (April 2002), 102–106.

Goals and Plans

Broad statements describing where the organization wants to be in the future are called **strategic goals**. They pertain to the organization as a whole rather than to specific divisions or departments. Strategic goals are often called *official goals,* because they are the stated intentions of what the organization wants to achieve. For example, five years after he started Physician Sales and Service, Pat Kelly set a strategic goal for PSS to become the first national physician supply chain, a goal he soon reached. Now, Kelly wants the company to become a world distributor of medical products.[14] E.piphany has a strategic goal to become the No. 2 provider of customer relationship management software, as described in this chapter's Best Practices box.

Strategic plans define the action steps by which the company intends to attain strategic goals. The strategic plan is the blueprint that defines the organizational activities and resource allocations—in the form of cash, personnel, space, and facilities—required for meeting these targets. Strategic planning tends to be long term and may define organizational action steps from two to five years in the future. The purpose of strategic plans is to turn organizational goals into realities within that time period.

As an example, a small company wanted to improve its market share from 15 percent to 20 percent over the next three years. This strategic goal was pursued through the following strategic plans: (1) allocate resources for the development of new, competitive products with high growth potential; (2) improve production methods to achieve higher output at lower costs; and (3) conduct research to develop alternative uses for current products and services.[15]

The results that major divisions and departments within the organization intend to achieve are defined as **tactical goals**. These goals apply to middle management and describe what major subunits must do in order for the organization to achieve its overall goals.

Tactical plans are designed to help execute major strategic plans and to accomplish a specific part of the company's strategy.[16] Tactical plans typically have a shorter time horizon than strategic plans—over the next year or so. The word *tactical* originally comes from the military. In a business organization, tactical plans define what major departments and organizational subunits will do to implement the organization's strategic plan. For example, the overall strategic plan of a florist such as 1-800-Flowers might involve becoming a leading telephone and Internet-based purveyor of flowers, which requires high-volume sales during peak seasons such as Valentine's Day and Mother's Day. Human resources managers at 1-800-Flowers developed tactical plans to ensure that the company has the dedicated order takers and customer service representatives it needs during this critical period. Tactical plans include cross-training employees so they can switch to different jobs as departmental needs change, allowing order takers to transfer to jobs at headquarters during off-peak times to prevent burnout, and using regular order takers to train and supervise temporary workers during peak seasons.[17] These actions help top managers implement their overall strategic plan. Normally, it is the middle manager's job to take the broad strategic plan and identify specific tactical plans.

© Rich Frishman

Boeing's strategic goal *is to remain an aerospace industry giant despite a drop in air travel and resulting decrease in demand for airplanes. To meet this challenge, the* strategic plan *includes cutting production in its airplane manufacturing division and reassigning financial resources. Boeing is slicing its commercial aircraft business by 15 percent, cutting 10,000 to 15,000 manufacturing jobs. The change meant closing one of the three assembly lines for 737 jets at the company's Renton, Washington, plant shown here.*

strategic goals

Broad statements of where the organization wants to be in the future; pertain to the organization as a whole rather than to specific divisions or departments.

strategic plans

The action steps by which an organization intends to attain strategic goals.

tactical goals

Goals that define the outcomes that major divisions and departments must achieve in order for the organization to reach its overall goals.

tactical plans

Plans designed to help execute major strategic plans and to accomplish a specific part of the company's strategy.

BEST PRACTICES

Start-Up E.piphany Plans to "Grow Up" Fast

CEO Roger Siboni proudly proclaims that E.piphany is not a start-up anymore. "We're a grown-up," he says. He may be stretching things a bit, but few competitors doubt that Siboni's company is becoming a force to be reckoned with. E.piphany has made a name for itself by pulling ahead of scores of companies vying for a share of the $9 billion market for customer relationship management (CRM) software that works with the Internet. The young company still has a long way to go to meet Siboni's strategic goal of becoming No. 2 (after Siebel Systems) in CRM, but many observers think Siboni is right on track.

The first focus of Siboni's plan is on turning a profit, and he has salespeople busily courting new customers while making sure everyone throughout the company keeps costs in line. E.piphany relies on industry buzz and customer recommendations to help attract new customers, rather than spending millions on marketing blitzes. For example, the company spent just $400,000 on targeted advertising in 1999, while other companies burned through millions. He urges his staff to watch their pennies and let the dollars take care of themselves. Every decision in the company is made with a consideration of the bottom line. Even with this careful approach, E.piphany has been able to attract some major clients, including about 20 percent of the top 100 U.S. companies and some of the leading technology and dot-com businesses.

Another aspect of Siboni's plan is to nurture relationships with people and organizations that can help E.piphany reach its goals. As a former deputy chairman at KPMG, Siboni has established many key relationships, and today nearly every KPMG customer, executive, and partner is somehow linked to E.piphany. Even when relationships have turned form collegial to competitive, such as Siboni's relationship with Tom Siebel of rival Siebel Systems, he still tends to them with care and respect. "It's the power of the Rolodex," says Karen Richardson, who left her job to join E.piphany. "I wouldn't have come if I hadn't known who the CEO was," she adds.

Siboni's careful attention to costs, customers, and relationships has E.piphany on target to meet his short-term goal of increasing revenue by 100 percent and becoming profitable by the end of 2002. And as for the long-term plan? Oracle's CEO Larry Ellison has seen the upstart gaining ground, and he doesn't like it. As for Siebel Systems, the giant is so far ahead in market share that managers barely acknowledge E.piphany as a competitor. They might regret that. Taking a four-year-old company into battle against Oracle and Siebel will not be easy, but Siboni is determined to meet his enemies head on to reach his strategic goals.

SOURCES: Kim Cross, "Captain Connected," *Business 2.0* (April 17, 2001), 31–33; and Joy D. Russell, "E.piphany Aims at Siebel's Market—Company Says Its New Generation of CRM Software Will Give Siebel a Run for Its Money," *VARbusiness* (January 7, 2002), 26.

---

operational goals

Specific, measurable results expected from departments, work groups, and individuals within the organization.

operational plans

Plans developed at the organization's lower levels that specify action steps toward achieving operational goals and that support tactical planning activities.

The specific results expected from departments, work groups, and individuals are the **operational goals**. They are precise and measurable. "Process 150 sales applications each week," "achieve 90 percent of deliveries on time," "reduce overtime by 10 percent next month," and "develop two new elective courses in accounting" are examples of operational goals.

Operational plans are developed at the lower levels of the organization to specify action steps toward achieving operational goals and to support tactical plans. The operational plan is the department manager's tool for daily and weekly operations. Goals are stated in quantitative terms, and the department plan describes how goals will be achieved. Operational planning specifies plans for supervisors, department managers, and individual employees.

Schedules are an important component of operational planning. Schedules define precise time frames for the completion of each operational goal required for the organization's tactical and strategic goals. Operational planning also must be coordinated with the budget, because resources must be allocated for desired activities. For example, Apogee Enterprises, a window and glass fabricator with 150 small divisions, is fanatical about operational planning and budgeting. Committees are set up that require inter- as well as intradivisional review and challenge of budgets, profit plans, and proposed capital expenditures. Assigning the dollars makes the operational plan work for everything from hiring new salespeople to increasing travel expenses.

Hierarchy of Goals

Effectively designed organizational goals fit into a hierarchy; that is, the achievement of goals at low levels permits the attainment of high-level goals.

Criteria for Effective Goals

To ensure goal-setting benefits for the organization, certain characteristics and guidelines should be adopted. The characteristics of both goals and the goal-setting process are listed in Exhibit 5.3. These characteristics pertain to organizational goals at the strategic, tactical, and operational levels:

- *Specific and measurable.* When possible, goals should be expressed in quantitative terms, such as increasing profits by 2 percent, decreasing scrap by 1 percent, or increasing average teacher effectiveness ratings from 3.5 to 3.7. A team at Sealed Air Corporation, a manufacturer of packaging materials, was motivated by a goal to reduce by two hours the average time needed to change machine settings.[18] Not all goals can be expressed in numerical terms, but vague goals have little motivating power for employees. By necessity, goals are qualitative as well as quantitative, especially at the top of the organization. The important point is that the goals be precisely defined and allow for measurable progress. For example, Liisa Joronen, chairman of SOL Cleaning Service, believes in giving teams the right to set their own performance goals; however, she's a stickler for accountability. "The more we free our people from rules," she says, "the more we need good measurements." Every time SOL lands a contract, the salesperson works at the new customer's site along with the SOL team that will do the future cleaning. Together they establish performance goals. Every month, customers rate the team's performance based on the goals.[19]

- *Cover key result areas.* Goals cannot be set for every aspect of employee behavior or organizational performance; if they were, their sheer number would render them meaningless. Instead, managers should identify a few key result areas—perhaps up to four or five for any organizational department or job. Key result areas are those activities that contribute most to company performance.[20] Most companies use a balanced approach to goal setting. For example, Northern States Power Co. tracks measurements in four key areas: financial performance, customer service and satisfaction, internal processes, and innovation and learning.[21]

- *Challenging but realistic.* Goals should be challenging but not unreasonably difficult. One newly hired manager discovered that his staff would have to work 100-hour weeks to accomplish everything expected of them. When goals are unrealistic, they set employees up for failure and lead to decreasing employee morale.[22] However, if goals are too easy, employees may not feel motivated. *Stretch goals* are extremely ambitious but realistic goals that challenge employees to meet high standards. For example, top managers at 3M set a goal that 30 percent of sales must come from products introduced in the past four years; the old standard was 25 percent. Setting ambitious goals helps to keep 3M churning out innovative new products—more than 500 in one recent year alone—and has entrenched the company as a leader in some of today's most dynamic markets.[23] The key to effective stretch goals is ensuring that goals are set within the existing resource base, not beyond departments' time, equipment, or financial resources.

EXHIBIT 5.3

Characteristics of Effective Goal Setting

Goal Characteristics
- Specific and measurable
- Cover key result areas
- Challenging but realistic
- Defined time period
- Linked to rewards

- *Defined time period.* Goals should specify the time period over which they will be achieved. A time period is a deadline stating the date on which goal attainment will be measured. A goal of launching a company intranet, for example, might have a deadline such as June 30, 2003. If a strategic goal involves a two-to-three-year time horizon, specific dates for achieving parts of it can be set up. For example, strategic sales goals could be established on a three-year time horizon, with a $100 million target in year one, a $129 million target in year two, and a $165 million target in year three.

- *Linked to rewards.* The ultimate impact of goals depends on the extent to which salary increases, promotions, and awards are based on goal achievement. People who attain goals should be rewarded. Rewards give meaning and significance to goals and help commit employees to achieving goals. Failure to attain goals often is due to factors outside employees' control. For example, failure to achieve a financial goal may be associated with a drop in market demand due to industry recession; thus, an employee could not be expected to reach it. Nevertheless, a reward may be appropriate if the employee partially achieved goals under difficult circumstances.[24]

Planning Types and Performance

The purpose of planning and goal setting is to help the organization achieve high performance. Managers use strategic, tactical, and operational goals to direct employees and resources toward achieving specific outcomes that enable the organization to perform efficiently and effectively. Overall organizational performance depends on achieving outcomes identified by the planning process. Managers use a number of planning approaches to focus the organization toward high performance. Among the most popular are management by objectives, single-use plans, standing plans, and contingency (or scenario) plans.

Management by Objectives

management by objectives
A method of management whereby managers and employees define goals for every department, project, and person and use them to monitor subsequent performance.

Management by objectives (MBO) is a method whereby managers and employees define goals for every department, project, and person and use them to monitor subsequent performance.[25] A model of the essential steps of the MBO process is presented in Exhibit 5.4. Four major activities must occur in order for MBO to be successful:[26]

1. *Set goals.* This is the most difficult step in MBO. Setting goals involves employees at all levels and looks beyond day-to-day activities to answer the question "What are we trying to accomplish?" A good goal should be concrete and realistic, provide a specific target and time frame, and assign responsibility. Goals may be quantitative or qualitative, depending on whether outcomes are measurable. Quantitative goals are described in numerical terms, such as "Salesperson Jones will obtain 16 new accounts in December." Qualitative goals use statements such as "Marketing will reduce complaints by improving customer service next year." Goals should be jointly derived. Mutual agreement between employee and supervisor creates the strongest commitment to achieving goals. In the case of teams, all team members may participate in setting goals.

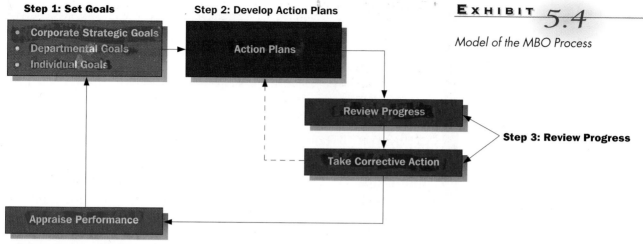

Step 1: Set Goals

- Corporate Strategic Goals
- Departmental Goals
- Individual Goals

Step 2: Develop Action Plans

Action Plans

Review Progress

Step 3: Review Progress

Take Corrective Action

Appraise Performance

Step 4: Appraise Overall Performance

E X H I B I T 5.4

Model of the MBO Process

2. *Develop action plans.* An *action plan* defines the course of action needed to achieve the stated goals. Action plans are made for both individuals and departments.

3. *Review progress.* A periodic progress review is important to ensure that action plans are working. These reviews can occur informally between managers and subordinates, where the organization may wish to conduct three-, six-, or nine-month reviews during the year. This periodic checkup allows managers and employees to see whether they are on target or whether corrective action is necessary. Managers and employees should not be locked into predefined behavior and must be willing to take whatever steps are necessary to produce meaningful results. The point of MBO is to achieve goals. The action plan can be changed whenever goals are not being met.

4. *Appraise overall performance.* The final step in MBO is to carefully evaluate whether annual goals have been achieved for both individuals and departments. Success or failure to achieve goals can become part of the performance appraisal system and the designation of salary increases and other rewards. The appraisal of departmental and overall corporate performance shapes goals for the next year. The MBO cycle repeats itself on an annual basis. The specific application of MBO must fit the needs of each company.

Like any system, MBO achieves benefits when used properly but results in problems when used improperly. Benefits and problems are summarized in Exhibit 5.5.

The benefits of the MBO process can be many. Corporate goals are more likely to be achieved when they focus manager and employee efforts. Performance is improved because employees are committed to attaining the goal, are motivated because they help decide what is expected, and are free to be resourceful. Goals at lower levels are aligned with and enable the attainment of goals at top management levels.

Problems with MBO occur when the company faces rapid change. The environment and internal activities must have some stability for performance to be measured and compared against goals. When new goals must be set every few

EXHIBIT 5.5

MBO Benefits and Problems

Benefits of MBO	Problems with MBO
1. Manager and employee efforts are focused on activities that will lead to goal attainment.	1. Constant change prevents MBO from taking hold.
2. Performance can be improved at all company levels.	2. An environment of poor employer–employee relations reduces MBO effectiveness.
3. Employees are motivated.	3. Strategic goals may be displaced by operational goals.
4. Departmental and individual goals are aligned with company goals.	4. Mechanistic organizations and values that discourage participation can harm the MBO process.
	5. Too much paperwork saps MBO energy.

months, there is no time for action plans and appraisal to take effect. Also, poor employer-employee relations reduce effectiveness because there is an element of distrust between managers and workers. Sometimes goal "displacement" occurs if employees focus exclusively on their operational goals to the detriment of other teams or departments. Overemphasis on operational goals can harm the attainment of overall goals. Another problem arises in mechanistic organizations characterized by rigidly defined tasks and rules that may not be compatible with MBO's emphasis on mutual determination of goals by employee and supervisor. In addition, when participation is discouraged, employees will lack the training and values to jointly set goals with employers. Finally, if MBO becomes a process of filling out annual paperwork rather than energizing employees to achieve goals, it becomes an empty exercise. Once the paperwork is completed, employees forget about the goals, perhaps even resenting the paperwork in the first place.

Single-Use and Standing Plans

Single-use plans are developed to achieve a set of goals that are not likely to be repeated in the future. Standing plans are ongoing plans that are used to provide guidance for tasks performed repeatedly within the organization. Exhibit 5.6 outlines the major types of single-use and standing plans. Single-use plans typically include both programs and projects. The primary standing plans are organizational policies, rules, and procedures. Standing plans generally pertain to such matters as employee illness, absences, smoking, discipline, hiring, and dismissal. Many companies are discovering a need to develop standing plans regarding the use of e-mail, as discussed in the Focus on Leadership box.

Contingency Plans

When organizations are operating in a highly uncertain environment or dealing with long time horizons, sometimes planning can seem like a waste of time. In fact, strict plans may even hinder rather than help an organization's performance in the face of rapid technological, social, economic, or other environmental change. In these cases, managers can develop multiple future scenarios to help them form more flexible plans. **Contingency plans**, sometimes referred to as *scenarios*, define company responses to be taken in the case of emergencies, setbacks, unexpected conditions. To develop contingency plans, managers identify uncontrollable factors, such as recession, inflation, technological

contingency plans

Plans that define company responses to specific situations, such as emergencies, setbacks, or unexpected conditions.

Single-Use Plans	Standing Plans
Program • Plans for attaining a one-time organizational goal • Major undertaking that may take several years to complete • Large in scope; may be associated with several projects **Examples:** Building a new headquarters Converting all paper files to digital	**Policy** • Broad in scope—a general guide to action • Based on organization's overall goals/strategic plan • Defines boundaries within which to make decisions **Examples:** Drug-free workplace policies Sexual harassment policies
Project • Also a set of plans for attaining a one-time goal • Smaller in scope and complexity than a program; shorter time horizon • Often one part of a larger program **Examples:** Renovating the office Setting up a company intranet	**Rule** • Narrow in scope • Describes how a specific action is to be performed • May apply to specific setting **Example:** No-smoking rule in areas of plant where hazardous materials are stored
	Procedure • Sometimes called a standard operating procedure • Defines a precise series of steps to attain certain goals **Examples:** Procedures for issuing refunds Procedures for handling employee grievances

EXHIBIT 5.6

Major Types of Single-Use and Standing Plans

developments, or safety accidents. To minimize the impact of these potential factors, managers can forecast the worst-case scenarios. For example, if sales fall 20 percent and prices drop 8 percent, what will the company do? Managers can develop contingency plans that might include layoffs, emergency budgets, or new sales efforts.[27] As another example, top managers at Duke Energy Corp., which has invested heavily in building new power plants to meet increasing demand, developed contingency plans for what the company would do if U.S. economic growth slowed to 1 percent a year, leaving the company with too much capacity amid weakening prices.[28]

Crisis Management Planning

A special type of contingency planning is crisis management planning. Sometimes, events are so sudden and devastating that they require immediate response. Consider events such as the November 12, 2001, crash of American Airlines Flight 587 in a New York neighborhood already devastated by terrorist attacks, the 1982 Tylenol crisis, when four people died after taking cyanide-laced capsules, the 1993 deaths due to e-coli bacteria from Jack-in-the-Box hamburgers, or the 1986 Challenger space shuttle explosion. Companies also face many smaller crises that call for rapid response, such as recent allegations of tainted Coca-Cola in Belgium or charges of child labor abuse against Kathy

FOCUS ON LEADERSHIP

Regulating E-mail in the Workplace

Top executives around the globe are discovering that casual e-mail messages can come back to haunt them—in court. Messages dashed off years ago by Bill Gates became digital "smoking guns" in the Justice Department's antitrust case against Microsoft. Chevron Corp. had to pay female employees $2.2 million to settle a sexual harassment lawsuit arising from inappropriate e-mail circulated by male co-workers.

As with any powerful tool, e-mail has the potential to be hazardous, backfiring not only on the employee but on the organization as well. One study found that "potentially dangerous or nonproductive" messages account for fully 31 percent of all company e-mail . Experts say a formal written policy is the best way for companies to protect themselves, and they offer some tips for managers on developing effective policies governing the use of e-mail.

- *Make clear that all e-mail and its contents are the property of the company.* Many experts recommend warning employees that the company reserves the right to read any messages transmitted over its system. "Employees need to understand that a company can access employees' e-mail at any time without advance notice or consent," says lawyer Pam Reeves. This helps to discourage frivolous e-mails or those that might be considered crude and offensive.

- *Tie the policy to the company's sexual harassment policy or other polices governing employee behavior on the job.* In almost all sexual harassment cases, judges have ruled that the use of e-mail was considered part of the workplace environment.

- *Establish clear guidelines on matters such as the use of e-mail for jokes and other non–work related communications, the sending of confidential messages, and how to handle junk e-mail.* At Prudential Insurance, for example, employees are prohibited from using company e-mail to share jokes, photographs, or any kind of nonbusiness information.

- *Set a time limit for how long messages will be saved before they are automatically deleted by network managers.* Retention periods of 30 to 90 days are typical. Most organizations also set up a centralized archive for retaining essential e-mail messages.

- *Require that all employees read updates from the company's network and security managers.*

A solid e-mail policy is no guarantee that e-mail won't someday be used against the company in a lawsuit. For example. even deleted e-mails can usually be tracked down by a computer-forensics expert. However, an effective policy is the best step companies can take to manage the potential risks of e-mail abuse.

SOURCES: Marcia Stepanek with Steve Hamm, "When the Devil Is in the E-mails," *BusinessWeek* (June 8, 1998), 72–74; and Joseph McCafferty, "The Phantom Menace," *CFO* (June 1999), 89–91.

Lee Gifford's clothing company. Crises have become integral features of our organizations and our everyday lives.[29] For managers to respond appropriately, they need carefully thought-out and coordinated plans. Although crises may vary, a good crisis management plan can be used to respond to any disaster at any time of the day or night.

Exhibit 5.7 outlines the three essential stages of crisis management.[30] The prevention stage involves activities managers undertake to try to prevent crises from occurring and to detect warning signs of potential crises. The preparation stage includes all the detailed planning to handle a crises when it occurs. Containment focuses on the organization's response to an actual crisis and any follow-up concerns.

Prevention. Although unexpected events and disasters will happen, managers should do everything they can to prevent crises. One critical part of the prevention stage is building relationships with key stakeholders such as employees, customers, suppliers, governments, unions, and the community. By developing favorable relationships, managers can often prevent crises from happening. Similarly, organizations that build a reputation as a solid, reputable company are able to avert many crises and respond more effectively to those that cannot be avoided.

Prevention
- Build relationships.
- Detect signals from environment.

Preparation
- Designate crisis management team and spokesperson.
- Create detailed crisis management plan.
- Set up effective communications system.

Containment
- Rapid response: Activate the crisis management plan.
- Get the awful truth out.
- Meet safety and emotional needs.
- Return to business.

EXHIBIT 5.7

Three Stages of Crisis Management

SOURCE: Based on information in W. Timothy Coombs, *Ongoing Crisis Communication: Planning, Managing, and Responding* (Thousand Oaks, Calif.: Sage Publications, 1999)

Open communication with employees, customers, and all stakeholders enables the organization and stakeholder groups to better understand one another and develop mutual respect. For example, organizations that have open, trusting relationships with employees and unions may avoid crippling labor strikes. Open communication also helps managers identify problems early so they do not turn into major issues. For example, Nike had early warning from distributors in the Middle East that its flame logo on a basketball shoe looked like the word *Allah* in Arabic script and would be considered offensive to Muslims. Although the company made some minor changes, managers failed to take the warning seriously. Eventually, Nike had to recall nearly 40,000 pairs of the shoes and issue an apology to Muslims.[31] Similarly, Coca-Cola suffered a major crisis in Europe because it failed to respond quickly to reports of "foul-smelling" Coke in Belgium. CEO Douglas Daft recently observed that every problem the company has faced in recent years "can be traced to a singular cause: We neglected our relationships."[32]

Preparation. Three steps in the preparation stage are: designating a crisis management team and spokesperson, creating a detailed crisis management plan, and setting up an effective communications system. The crisis management team is a cross-functional group of people who are designated to swing into action if a crisis occurs. They are closely involved in creating the crisis management plan, and they'll be called upon to implement the plan if a disaster hits. The U.S. Office of Personnel Management in Washington, D.C., has nearly 200 people assigned and trained to take immediate action if a disaster occurs, including 8 employees assigned to each of 10 floors to handle an evacuation.[33]

The organization should also designate a spokesperson who will be the voice of the company during the crisis. The spokesperson in many cases is the top leader of the organization. After the terrorist attacks on the World Trade Center, Mayor Rudolph Guiliani was the spokesperson for the city of New York. Donald Carty, CEO of American Airlines, was the spokesperson following the crash of Flight 587. However, organizations typically assign more than one spokesperson so that someone else will be prepared if the top leader is not available.

The crisis management plan (CMP) should be a detailed, written plan that specifies the steps to be taken, and by whom, if a crisis occurs. The CMP should list complete contact information for

Ever since the great Chicago fire of 1871, the city of Chicago has emphasized crisis management planning *to prepare for fires, floods, chemical spills, or other disasters. Following the events of September 11, 2001, and the subsequent anthrax attacks in the U.S., officials such as Fire Chief James Joyce and Mayor Richard Daley, pictured here, adapted crisis plans to deal with the threat of bioterrorism. The city's crisis management team spent four days and nights at the Emergency Communications Center, smoothly deploying police and paramedics to investigate sightings of suspicious powder and updating the press twice daily. "We calmed people because we spoke with one voice," said Police Superintendent Terry Hillard.*

© Chris Volk

members of the crisis management team, as well as for outside agencies such as emergency personnel, insurance companies, and so forth. It should include plans for ensuring the safety of employees and customers, procedures for back-up and recovery of computer systems and protecting proprietary information, details on where people should go if they need to be evacuated, plans for alternative work sites if needed, and guidelines for handling media and other outside communications. Some firms hand out wallet-sized cards that inform employees about evacuation procedures and what to do following an evacuation.[34] Morgan Stanley Dean Witter, the World Trade Center's largest tenant with 3,700 employees, adopted a crisis management plan after bomb threats during the Persian Gulf War in 1991. Top managers credit its detailed evacuation procedures for saving the lives of all but six employees during the September 11 attack. "Everybody knew about the . . . plan," said a spokesman. "We met constantly to talk about it."[35] A key point is that a crisis management plan should be a living, changing document that is regularly reviewed, practiced, and updated as needed.

A major part of the CMP is a communications plan that designates a crisis command center and sets up a complete communications and messaging system. The command center serves as a place for the crisis management team to meet, gather data and monitor incoming information, and disseminate information to the media and the public. The plan should designate alternate communication centers in case the main center is disrupted and should include plans for varied communication methods, such as toll-free call centers, Internet and intranet communications, and plans for rerouting data traffic if necessary. All employees should have multiple ways to get in touch with the organization and report their whereabouts and status after a disaster. The organization should also have varied ways to contact employees and notify them of changing circumstances and plans.

Containment. Some crises are inevitable no matter how well prepared an organization is. When a crisis hits, a rapid response is crucial. The team should be able to immediately implement the crisis management plan, so training and practice are important. In addition, the organization should "get the awful truth out" to employees and the public as soon as possible.[36] This is the stage where it becomes critical for the organization to speak with one voice so that employees, customers, and the public do not get conflicting stories about what happened and what the organization is doing about it. The crisis team gathers as much information as possible and the designated spokesperson presents the facts as they are known. Failing to get the truth out quickly lowers an organization's chances of recovering from the crisis. After the Exxon Valdez oil spill in Prince William Sound, it took CEO Lawrence Rawls more than a week to comment on the disaster, which left employees and the public bitter and angry.[37] When he did speak out, Rawls tried to minimize the disaster by implying that the death of 30,000 birds in the oil spill was not very significant. His inability to understand and respond to people's emotions damaged his and the company's reputation.

Likewise, when anthrax-laced letters contaminated the Hart Senate office building in 2001, Capitol Hill staffers were tested and placed on antibiotics, but the U.S. Postal Service (USPS) was not as quick to respond. Two postal workers died and several others were infected by the deadly spores, and the American Postal Workers Union was vocal in its anger. The USPS, relying on bad information about anthrax and not wanting to bring mail service to a halt, downplayed the dangers to the mail handlers and to the public. The crisis ended with no further postal worker deaths, but the slow reaction of the USPS to protect its employees left a bitter taste in the mouths of postal workers.[38]

After ensuring the physical safety of people (and in some cases, animal life) the next focus should be on responding to the emotional needs of employees, customers, and the public. Giving facts and statistics to try to downplay the disaster always backfires because it does not meet people's emotional need to feel that someone cares about them and what the disaster has meant to their lives. After a crisis as devastating as the World Trade Center attacks or the Columbine school shootings, companies may provide counseling and other services to help people cope.

Organizations also strive to give people a sense of security and belonging. Getting back to business quickly is essential because it helps people believe that things can return to normal. Companies that cannot get up and running within 10 days after any major crisis are not likely to stay in business.[39] People want to feel that they are going to have a job and be able to take care of their families. Taking steps to protect people from danger during future disasters is important at this stage also. In this sense, crisis management planning comes full circle, because managers use the crisis to strengthen their prevention abilities and be better prepared in the future. A crisis is an important time for companies to strengthen their stakeholder relationships. By being open and honest about the crisis and putting people first, organizations build stronger bonds with employees, customers, and other stakeholders, and gain a reputation as a trustworthy company. Although layoffs might be necessary in some situations, experts on crisis management suggest they should be a last resort following a major crisis because they damage trust, morale, and the company's reputation.

Planning in the New Workplace

The process of planning is changing. Traditionally, strategy and planning have been the domain of top managers. However, in today's workplace, top managers no longer control the planning process; everyone becomes involved. In some companies, planning is being taken out of the executive boardroom and central planning department to become a part of everyday work throughout the organization. We will first discuss traditional, top-down approaches to planning and then examine some of the newer approaches that emphasize bottom-up planning and the involvement of stakeholders in the planning process.

Top down ↓

Traditional Approaches to Planning

Traditionally, corporate planning has been done entirely by top executives, by consulting firms, or, most commonly, by central planning departments. **Central planning departments** are groups of planning specialists who report directly to the CEO or president. This approach was popular during the 1970s. Planning specialists were hired to gather data and develop detailed strategic plans for the corporation as a whole. This planning approach was top down because goals and plans were assigned to major divisions and departments from the planning department after approval by the president. This approach worked well in many applications.

Although traditional approaches to planning still are popular with some companies, formal planning increasingly is being criticized as inappropriate for

central planning department

A group of planning specialists who develop plans for the organization as a whole and its major divisions and departments and typically report directly to the president or CEO.

today's fast-paced environment. Central planning departments may be out of touch with the constantly changing realities faced by front-line employees, which may leave employees struggling to follow a plan that no longer fits the environment and customer needs. In addition, formal plans dictated by top mangers and central planning departments inhibit creativity and learning because employees have less incentive to think for themselves and come up with new ideas. In the new workplace, managers take a different approach to planning.

New Workplace Approaches to Planning

A new approach to planning is to involve everyone in the organization, and sometimes outside stakeholders as well, in the planning process. The evolution to a new approach began with a shift to **decentralized planning**, which means that planning experts work with managers in major divisions or departments to develop their own goals and plans. This enabled managers throughout the company to come up with their own creative solutions to problems and become more committed to following through on the plans. As the environment became even more volatile, top executives saw the benefits of pushing decentralized planning even further, by having planning experts work directly with line managers and front-line workers to develop dynamic plans that meet fast-changing needs.

In a complex and competitive business environment, traditional planning done by a select few no longer works. Strategic thinking and execution become the expectation of every employee.[40] For an example of a company that is finding hidden sources of ideas and innovation by involving all its workers in planning, consider Springfield Remanufacturing, described in the example below.

decentralized planning

Managers work with planning experts to develop their own goals and plans.

SRC Holdings Corporation

Jack Stack and twelve other former International Harvester managers started Springfield Remanufacturing Corporation on a shoestring in 1983. The company still exists, but today it is part of SRC Holdings Corporation, a group of 22 semiautonomous companies located in the Springfield, Missouri area. Stack, CEO of SRC Holdings, has built this amazingly successful corporation by tapping into people's universal desire to win. Stack's philosophy is that "the best, most efficient, most profitable way to operate a business is to give everybody a voice in how the company is run and a stake in the financial outcome, good or bad."

SRC involves everyone in the planning process and uses a bonus system based on hitting the plan's targets. Top managers meet with middle managers, supervisors, and front-line employees throughout their divisions to develop and sell their long-range plans. If a manager's plan is beyond the plant's capacity, the workers feel free to suggest workable alternatives. By the time managers present their plans to the top brass, everyone in the various divisions has had a say and has thus developed a sense of ownership in the plan.

All SRC businesses make their operating and financial performance numbers freely available so employees can compare performance to the plan. People "huddle" at least weekly around mural-sized charts in the employee cafeteria to talk about the numbers and what needs to be done to meet the targets. Employees take the company's success personally because they all own shares in the company through employee stock ownership plans (ESOPs). SRC has invested heavily in financial education for all workers so that everyone understands what is at stake and what is to be gained. "What we're doing . . ." Stack says, "is showing people how to get through life without fear. Once people understand what it takes to be a businessperson, not just a cog in the system but someone on the brighter side of capitalism, then their lives can change forever."[41]

Planning comes alive when employees are involved in setting goals and determining the means to reach them. Here are some guidelines for planning in the new workplace.

Start with a Strong Mission. Planning in the new workplace requires flexibility to meet ever-changing demands from the environment. Employees may have to constantly adapt plans to meet new needs. E-commerce organizations, for example, operate second-to-second rather than year-to-year, so traditional plans can serve only as a general guideline. In such an environment, a powerful sense of purpose and direction becomes even more important. Without a strong mission to guide employee thinking and behavior, the resources of a fast-moving company such as an e-commerce business can quickly become uncoordinated, with employees pursuing radically different plans and activities. A compelling mission can also serve to increase employee commitment and motivation, which are critical to helping organizations compete in a fast-shifting environment.[42]

Set Stretch Goals. Stretch goals are highly ambitious goals that are so clear, compelling, and imaginative that they fire up employees and fuel progress. As we discussed earlier in the chapter, an important criterion for effective goals is that they be challenging, yet realistic. In today's workplace, stretch goals are extremely important because things are moving so fast. A company that focuses on gradual, incremental improvements in products, processes, or systems will get left behind. Managers can use stretch goals to compel employees to think in new ways that can lead to bold, innovative breakthroughs. Motorola used stretch goals to achieve *six sigma* quality, as described in Chapter 1, which has now become the standard for numerous companies. Managers first set a goal of a tenfold increase in quality over a two-year period. After this goal was met, they set a new stretch goal of a hundredfold improvement over a four-year period.[43]

Create a Culture that Encourages Learning. In the new workplace, managers create a culture that celebrates diversity, supports risk-taking, and encourages constant experimentation and learning. An important value is questioning the status quo. Tomorrow's opportunities might come from very different directions than the basis of today's success. For example, soft-drink makers missed out on huge opportunities for new drinks such as chilled teas, sports drinks, and New Age beverages because they were focused on continuing the status quo rather than experimenting with new products.[44] Managers in the new workplace might have to change plans at the drop of a hat, which requires a mindset that embraces ambiguity, risk taking, making mistakes, and learning.

Design New Roles for Planning Staff. Companies transform the conventional planner's job.[45] Planning specialists serve as facilitators and supporters; they do not decide on the substance of goals and plans. Planning experts can be very helpful in gathering data, performing statistical analyses, and doing other specialized tasks. The key difference is that, rather than looking for the *right answers,* they supply information in order to broaden the consideration of issues and support strategic thinking.

planning task force

A group of managers and employees who develop a strategic plan.

Use Temporary Task Forces. A planning task force is a temporary group of managers and employees who take responsibility for developing a strategic plan. Many of today's companies use interdepartmental task forces to help establish goals and make plans for achieving them. In the new workplace, the task force often includes outside stakeholders as well, such as customers, suppliers, strategic partners, investors, or even members of the general community. Today's companies are highly focused on satisfying the needs and interests of all stakeholder groups, so they bring these stakeholders into the planning and goal-setting process.[46] LendLease, an Australian real estate and financial services company, for example, includes numerous stakeholders, including community advocates and potential customers, in the planning process for every new project it undertakes.[47]

Planning Still Starts and Stops at the Top. Top managers create a mission that is worthy of employees' best efforts and provide a framework for planning and goal setting. Even though planning is decentralized, top managers must show support and commitment to the planning process. Top managers also accept responsibility when planning and goal setting are ineffective, rather than blaming the failure on lower-level managers or workers.

Thinking Strategically

So far, this chapter has provided an overview of the types of goals and plans that organizations use. Now we will explore strategic management, which is considered one specific type of planning. Strategic planning in for-profit business organizations typically pertains to competitive actions in the marketplace. In not-for-profit organizations such as the Red Cross, strategic planning pertains to events in the external environment. The final responsibility for strategy rests with top managers and the chief executive. For an organization to succeed, the CEO must be actively involved in making the tough choices and trade-offs that define and support strategy.[48] However, senior executives at such companies as General Electric, 3M, and Johnson & Johnson want middle- and low-level managers to think strategically. Some companies also are finding ways to get front-line workers involved in strategic thinking and planning. Strategic thinking means to take the long-term view and to see the big picture, including the organization and the competitive environment, and to consider how they fit together. Understanding the strategy concept, the levels of strategy, and strategy formulation versus implementation is an important start toward strategic thinking.

strategic management

The set of decisions and actions used to formulate and implement strategies that will provide a competitively superior fit between the organization and its environment so as to achieve organizational goals.

What Is Strategic Management?

Strategic management is the set of decisions and actions used to formulate and implement strategies that will provide a competitively superior fit between the organization and its environment so as to achieve organizational goals.[49] Managers ask questions such as, "What changes and trends are occurring in the competitive environment? Who are our customers? What products or services should we offer? How can we offer those products and services most efficiently?" Answers to these questions help managers make choices about how to position their organization in the environment with respect to rival companies.[50] Superior organizational performance is not a matter of luck. It is determined by the choices that managers make. Top executives use strategic management to define an overall direction for the organization, which is the firm's **grand strategy**. Sometimes that grand strategy is one of growth, as is eBay's, described in the Digital, Inc. box.

Other companies decide to have a strategy of staying small, thereby insuring success, as described below.

> **grand strategy**
> The general plan of major action by which an organization intends to achieve its long-term goals.

> **Enterprise Telecommunications**

Talk about making the most of your assets! Lisa Hong was a born gabber and practiced her gift with gusto in high school. But she didn't stop there. Within eight years, she had a six-figure business with 100 clients, doing what she had enjoyed for so long: talking on the telephone.

It all started when she was a teenager. A real estate agent asked Lisa to be his secretary while he was out of town. Lisa had a phone installed in her bedroom and his calls were forwarded. She realized she was on to something and started a phone-answering business called Enterprise. Callers have the impression that Enterprise is the front office of a large corporation, when, in reality, most of her clients are small businesses with only a handful of employees. In this high-tech age of impersonal e-mails and random marketing calls, Hong adopted a strategy of high "touch" for the 1,200 calls received daily. Her operators take messages and sales orders, as well as screen calls.

A second-generation Korean who spends her free time on aerobics and bellydancing, Hong still clings to the old-country values of hard work and family. Two siblings answer phones and her parents do the bookkeeping. While other entrepreneurs want to grow as large as possible, Hong sees this as the road to ruin. She has looked at other phone-answering services with scores of employees and has chosen instead a strategy of differentiation, to stay small and personable. Her plan is to stop taking in new customers when her list reaches 150.

Her clients like it that way. Therapist John Fishbein likes not only the reasonable monthly rates of about $250 (much cheaper than $1,200 for a full-time receptionist), but also Enterprise's ability to connect with his patients. "My patients have the feeling that Lisa's right in the office. Sometimes patients come in my office and ask, 'Where's Lisa?'"[51]

Purpose of Strategy

Within the overall grand strategy of an organization, executives define an explicit **strategy**, which is the plan of action that describes resource allocation and activities for dealing with the environment and attaining the organization's goals. The essence of formulating strategy is choosing how the organization will be different.[52] Managers make decisions about whether the company will perform different activities or will execute similar activities differently than competitors do. Strategy necessarily changes over time to fit environmental conditions, but to remain competitive, companies develop strategies that focus on core competencies, develop synergy, and create value for customers.

> **strategy**
> The plan of action that prescribes resource allocation and other activities for dealing with the environment and helping the organization attain its goals.

DIGITAL, INC.

EBay: Building on Success

At a time when almost every Internet and technology company is handing out pink slips, the scene is quite different within the walls of San Jose, California-based eBay. In fact, the online auction company is planning to add to its work force of 2,400. EBay, which began as a site for selling collectibles, is pursuing a growth strategy, successfully molding itself into a platform for selling everything from computers to clothes. Every 60 minutes on the site, 120 PCs, 10 diamond rings, and 1,200 articles of clothing are sold, and someone buys a Corvette every three hours.

EBay CEO Meg Whitman sees her biggest job as keeping the company nimble and maintaining community spirit as the organization grows. From day one, eBay has been profitable, and in the second quarter of 2001, the company reported profits of $24.6 million, more than triple those reported a year earlier. Part of the reason for the success is because top managers have kept their focus on the community of buyers and sellers even as they have invested steadily in the company's growth.

There are several elements to eBay's strategic plan for growth. First, to branch out from its auction format, the company purchased Half.com, a site where new and used items can be listed at a fixed price. In addition, the company added a new feature called "Buy It Now," which allows users to acquire an item immediately, omitting the time-consuming auction process altogether. About 35 percent of all items listed by sellers on eBay now offer that option, which speeds up the rate of trading on the site. Another approach has been to allow businesses such as J. C. Penney, IBM, and Sun Microsystems to set up virtual storefronts. Ebay expected to attract around 2,000 businesses, but nearly 10 times that number wanted a piece of the action, recognizing the inexpensive potential for reaching millions of consumers. On the global front, eBay has acquired iBazar, a European trading site, and invested in the growth of its German, Canadian, and U.K. operations.

Mark Goldstein, former CEO of BlueLight.com, the online unit of Kmart, says, "eBay is what all of us wanted our Internet businesses to be." Even as e-commerce stalls in today's declining economy, online shoppers-turned-bargain-hunters surf the value-priced aisles of eBay, finding anything and everything. In fact, eBay is rapidly becoming "the Wal-Mart of the Internet."

SOURCE: Miguel Helft, "What Makes eBay Unstoppable?" *The Industry Standard* (August 6–13, 2001), 32–37.

---

core competence

A business activity that an organization does particularly well in comparison to competitors.

Core Competence. A company's **core competence** is something the organization does especially well in comparison to its competitors. A core competence represents a competitive advantage because the company acquires expertise that competitors do not have. A core competence may be in the area of superior research and development, expert technological know-how, process efficiency, or exceptional customer service.[53] At Amgen, a pharmaceutical company, strategy focuses on the company's core competence of high-quality scientific research. Rather than starting with a specific disease and working backward, Amgen takes brilliant science and finds unique uses for it.[54] Boeing Corporation has a core competence in flexible design and assembly of aircraft.[55] And Home Depot thrives because of a strategy focused on superior customer service. Managers stress to all employees that listening to customers and helping them solve their do-it-yourself worries takes precedence over just making a sale.[56] In each case, leaders identified what their company does particularly well and built strategy around it. Dell Computer has succeeded with its core competencies of speed and cost efficiency.

Dell Computer

http://www.dell.com

Dell Computer is constantly changing, adapting, and finding new ways to master its environment, but one thing hasn't changed from the days when Michael Dell first began building computers in his dorm room: the focus on speed and low cost. Most observers agree that a major factor in Dell's success is that it has retained a clear image of what it does best. The company spent years developing a core competence in speedy delivery by squeezing time lags and inefficiencies out of the manufacturing and assembly process, then extended the same brutal standards to the supply chain. Good relationships with a few key suppliers and precise coordination mean that Dell can sometimes receive parts in minutes rather than days.

The system is most evident at Dell's new OptiPlex factory in Austin, Texas, where Dell first introduced a new way of making PCs, called Metric 12, that combines just-in-time inventory delivery with a complicated, integrated computer system that practically hands a worker the right part—whether it be any of a dozen different microprocessors or a combination of software—at just the right time. The goal of the new system is not only to cut costs, but also to save time by decreasing the number of worker touches per machine. Rather than building computers in progressive, assembly-line fashion, small teams of workers at Opti-Plex build a complete machine by following precise guidelines and using the components that arrive in carefully indicated racks in front of them. A small glassed-in office above the factory floor functions as a control tower, where employees take orders, alert suppliers, order parts, and arrange shipping, much of this handled over the Internet. By using sophisticated supply-chain software, Dell can keep a few hours' worth of parts on hand and replenish only what it needs throughout the day. Dell's just-in-time system works so smoothly that nearly 85 percent of orders are built, customized, and shipped within eight hours.

Dell's fixation with speed and thrift comes directly from the top. Michael Dell believes the core competencies that made Dell a star in PCs and servers can also make the company a winner as it moves into developing low-cost storage systems and Internet services. To anyone who doubts that Dell can compete in this new market, he says, "Bring them on. We're coming right at them."[57]

Synergy. When organizational parts interact to produce a joint effect that is greater than the sum of the parts acting alone, **synergy** occurs. The organization may attain a special advantage with respect to cost, market power, technology, or management skill. When properly managed, synergy can create additional value with existing resources, providing a big boost to the bottom line.[58] A good example is PepsiCo's new "Power of One" strategy, which is aimed at leveraging the synergies of its soft drink and snack-food divisions to achieve greater market power. PepsiCo CEO Roger Enrico has used the company's clout with supermarkets to move Pepsi drinks next to Frito-Lay snacks on store shelves, increasing the chance that when shoppers pick up chips and soda, the soda of choice will be a Pepsi product. Managers are betting that the strength of Frito-Lay, which enjoys near-total dominance of the snack-food market, will gain not only greater shelf space for Pepsi, but increased market share as well.[59]

> **synergy**
> The condition that exists when the organization's parts interact to produce a joint effect that is greater than the sum of the parts acting alone.

Synergy can also be obtained by good relations with suppliers, as at Dell Computer, or by strong alliances among companies. Sweden's appliance giant Electrolux partnered with Ericsson, the Swedish telecommunications giant, in a joint venture called *e2 Home* to create a new way to make and sell appliances. Together, Electrolux and Ericsson are offering products such as the Screen-fridge, a refrigerator with Internet connections that enables users to check traffic conditions, order take-out, or buy groceries, and an experimental *pay-per-use* washing machine. Neither company could have offered these revolutionary products on its own. "The technology was there, the appliances were there, but we needed a way to connect those two elements—to add value for consumers," said Per Grunewald, e2 Home's president.[60]

Value Creation. Delivering value to the customer should be at the heart of strategy. Value can be defined as the combination of benefits received and costs paid by the customer. Managers help their companies create value by devising strategies that exploit core competencies and attain synergy. Managers at California's Gallo Winery are finding new ways to use core competencies to create better value. Gallo, long-famous for its inexpensive wines, produces one of every four bottles of wine sold in the U.S. Today, the company is pouring $100 million into Gallo of Sonoma, a line of upscale wines with value prices. As the low-cost producer, Gallo is able to sell upscale wines for $1 to $30 less per bottle than comparable-quality competitors.[61] Likewise, McDonald's made a thorough study of how to use its core competencies to create better value for customers, resulting in the introduction of "Extra Value Meals" and the decision to open restaurants in different locations, such as inside Wal-Mart and Sears stores.[62]

The Strategic Management Process

The overall strategic management process is illustrated in Exhibit 5.8. It begins when executives evaluate their current position with respect to mission, goals, and strategies. They then scan the organization's internal and external environments and identify strategic factors that might require change. Internal or external events might indicate a need to redefine the mission or goals or to formulate a new strategy at either the corporate, business, or functional level. The final stage in the strategic management process is implementation of the new strategy.

Strategy Formulation versus Implementation

strategy formulation

The stage of strategic management that involves the planning and decision making that lead to the establishment of the organization's goals and of a specific strategic plan.

Strategy formulation includes the planning and decision making that lead to the establishment of the firm's goals and the development of a specific strategic plan.[63] Strategy formulation may include assessing the external environment and internal problems and integrating the results into goals and strategy. This is in contrast to **strategy implementation**, which is the use of managerial and organizational tools to direct resources toward accomplishing strategic results.[64] Strategy implementation is the administration and execution of the strategic plan. Managers may use persuasion, new equipment, changes in organization structure, or a reward system to ensure that employees and resources are used to make formulated strategy a reality.

strategy implementation

The stage of strategic management that involves the use of managerial and organizational tools to direct resources toward achieving strategic outcomes.

Situation Analysis

situation analysis

Analysis of the strengths, weaknesses, opportunities, and threats (SWOT) that affect organizational performance.

Formulating strategy often begins with an assessment of the internal and external factors that will affect the organization's competitive situation. **Situation analysis** typically includes a search for SWOT—strengths, weaknesses, opportunities, and threats that affect organizational performance. Situation analysis is important to all companies but is crucial to those considering globalization because of the diverse environments in which they will operate. External information about opportunities and threats may be obtained from a variety of sources, including customers, government reports, professional journals, suppliers, bankers, friends in other organizations, consultants, or association meetings. Many firms hire special scanning organizations to provide them with newspaper clippings, Internet research, and analyses of relevant domestic and global trends. Some firms use more subtle techniques to learn about competitors, such as asking potential recruits about their visits to other companies, hir-

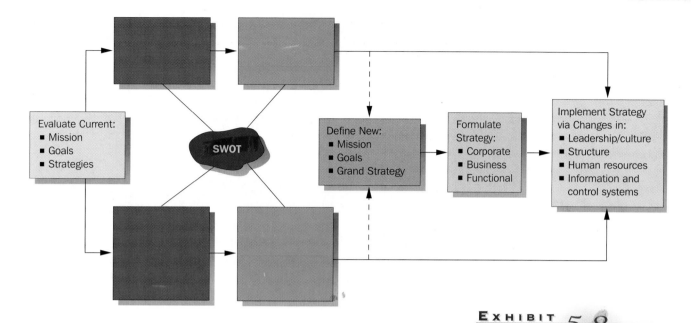

E X H I B I T 5.8

The Strategic Management Process

ing people away from competitors, debriefing former employees or customers of competitors, taking plant tours posing as "innocent" visitors, and even buying competitors' garbage.[65] In addition, many companies are hiring competitive intelligence professionals to scope out competitors.

Executives acquire information about internal strengths and weaknesses from a variety of reports, including budgets, financial ratios, profit and loss statements, and surveys of employee attitudes and satisfaction. Managers spend 80 percent of their time giving and receiving information. Through frequent face-to-face discussions and meetings with people at all levels of the hierarchy, executives build an understanding of the company's internal strengths and weaknesses.

Internal Strengths and Weaknesses. *Strengths* are positive internal characteristics that the organization can exploit to achieve its strategic performance goals. *Weaknesses* are internal characteristics that might inhibit or restrict the organization's performance. Some examples of what executives evaluate to interpret strengths and weaknesses are given in Exhibit 5.9. The information sought typically pertains to specific functions such as marketing, finance, production, and R & D. Internal analysis also examines overall organization structure, management competence and quality, and human resource characteristics. Based on their understanding of these areas, managers can determine their strengths or weaknesses vis-à-vis other companies. For example, Citigroup has been able to grow rapidly because of its financial strength and reliable business processes. The company has developed sophisticated financial and product know-how in the United States and was able to leverage that knowledge to support its global strategy and provide more than 100 million customers worldwide with any financial service, in any currency, reliably and at a low cost.[66]

Planning tools
Break even any.
Gantt chart
Pert

Management and Organization	Marketing	Human Resources
Management quality	Distribution channels	Employee experience, education
Staff quality	Market share	Union status
Degree of centralization	Advertising efficiency	Turnover, absenteeism
Organization charts	Customer satisfaction	Work satisfaction
Planning, information, control systems	Product quality	Grievances
	Service reputation	
	Sales force turnover	

Finance	Production	Research and Development
Profit margin	Plant location	Basic applied research
Debt-equity ratio	Machinery obsolescence	Laboratory capabilities
Inventory ratio	Purchasing system	Research programs
Return on investment	Quality control	New-product innovations
Credit rating	Productivity/efficiency	Technology innovations

External Opportunities and Threats. *Threats* are characteristics of the external environment that may prevent the organization from achieving its strategic goals. *Opportunities* are characteristics of the external environment that have the potential to help the organization achieve or exceed its strategic goals. The task environment sectors are the most relevant to strategic behavior and include the behavior of competitors, customers, suppliers, and the labor supply. The general environment contains those sectors that have an indirect influence on the organization but nevertheless must be understood and incorporated into strategic behavior. The general environment includes technological developments, the economy, legal-political and international events, and sociocultural changes. Additional areas that might reveal opportunities or threats include pressure groups, interest groups, creditors, natural resources, and potentially competitive industries.

An example of how external analysis can uncover a threat occurred in Kellogg Company's cereal business. Scanning the environment revealed that Kellogg's once-formidable share of the U.S. cold-cereal market had dropped nearly 10 percent. Information from the competitor and customer sectors indicated that major rivals were stepping up new-product innovations and cutting prices. In addition, private-label versions of such standbys as cornflakes were cutting into Kellogg's sales. Kellogg executives used knowledge of this threat as a basis for a strategic response.

The value of situation analysis in helping executives formulate the correct strategy is illustrated by Toys 'R' Us.

Toys 'R' Us

http://www.toysrus.com

Toys 'R' Us was started in a bicycle shop more than 50 years ago and grew to become the hottest toy store around during the 1980s. But by the mid-1990s, the once high-flying company was struggling just to stay aloft. John Eyler is the third CEO since 1994 to try to fix the company's massive problems. He has developed a new strategic direction for Toys 'R' Us that can be explained with SWOT analysis.

One of the company's greatest *strengths* is its reputation for carrying the widest selection of toys around. No other store carries the broad variety of toys and games found on Toys 'R' Us shelves. In addition, the company has tremendous market presence. With more than 700 U.S. stores, most people have a Toys 'R' Us store within easy reach—and many still think of Toys 'R' Us as *the* place to go if they are shopping specifically for toys. Unfortunately, the company's *weaknesses* far outweigh these strengths, including deplorable customer service, dirty and dilapidated stores, crowded aisles and poor product displays, and weak inventory management that puts too many slow-selling toys in stores and too few of the latest "must-have" products.

The biggest *threat* to the company is increased competition. A few years ago, Wal-Mart overtook Toys 'R' Us as the No. 1 U.S. toy seller. Other discount chains have also increased their toy selection and become more sophisticated toy retailers. In addition, online toy sellers hurt the company's sales during the late 1990s. However, Eyler and other managers also see a tremendous *opportunity* to become a unique kind of toy store.

To capitalize on the company's strengths and opportunities, Eyler has formulated a business-level strategy that attempts to provide the magic of upscale toy vendor FAO Schwarz at a reasonable Toys 'R' Us price. Rather than trying to compete with discount competitors on price, Toys 'R' Us will focus on superior customer service and creating a unique shopping environment. Eyler is remodeling and reorganizing stores, revamping inventory management, beefing up staffing and training, and increasing the percentage of private-label proprietary toys that will be sold exclusively at Toys 'R' Us. The new look of Toys 'R' Us does away with the warehouse-style aisles and replaces them with toys clustered by interest groups in cul-de-sacs and bright, interesting displays that are determined by factors such as age level and gender. Proprietary products, such as the Animal Planet line of animatronic wild animals and the new collection of licensed *E.T.* toys and gizmos, will be displayed in cubby holes close to the entrance to make them more visible and to give Toys 'R' Us a hit product that discount competitors cannot match.[67]

Formulating Business-Level Strategy

Now we turn to strategy formulation within the strategic business unit, in which the concern is how to compete. The same three generic strategies—growth, stability, and retrenchment—apply at the business level, but they are accomplished through competitive actions rather than the acquisition or divestment of business divisions. One model for formulating strategy is Porter's competitive strategies, which provides a framework for business unit competitive action.

Porter's Competitive Forces and Strategies

Michael E. Porter studied a number of business organizations and proposed that business-level strategies are the result of five competitive forces in the company's environment.[68] More recently, Porter has examined the impact of the Internet on business-level strategy.[69] New Web-based technology is influencing industries in both positive and negative ways, and understanding this impact is essential for managers to accurately analyze their competitive environments and design appropriate strategic actions.

Five Competitive Forces. Exhibit 5.10 illustrates the competitive forces that exist in a company's environment and indicates some ways Internet technology

Exhibit 5.10

The Five Forces Affecting Industry Competition

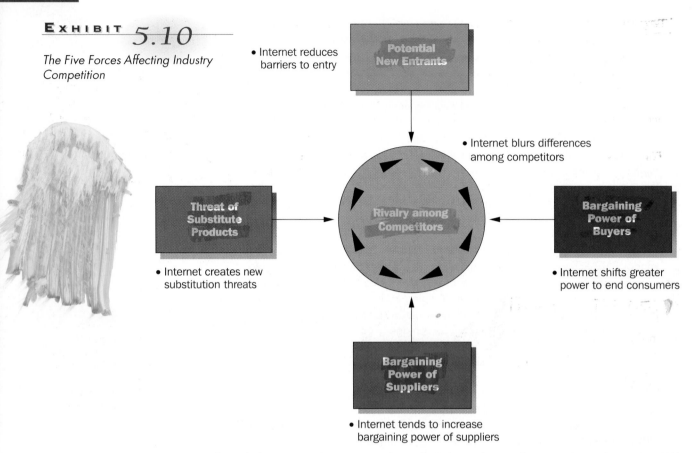

- Internet reduces barriers to entry

- Internet blurs differences among competitors

- Internet creates new substitution threats

- Internet shifts greater power to end consumers

- Internet tends to increase bargaining power of suppliers

SOURCES: Based on Michael E. Porter, *Competitive Strategy: Techniques for Analyzing Industries and Competitors* (New York: Free Press, 1980); and Michael E. Porter, "Strategy and the Internet," *Harvard Business Review* (March, 2001), 63–78.

is affecting each area. These forces help determine a company's position vis-à-vis competitors in the industry environment.

1. *Potential new entrants.* Capital requirements and economies of scale are examples of two potential barriers to entry that can keep out new competitors. It is far more costly to enter the automobile industry, for example, than to start a specialized mail-order business. In general, Internet technology has made it much easier for new companies to enter an industry, for example, by curtailing the need for such organizational elements as an established sales force, physical assets such as buildings and machinery, or access to existing supplier and sales channels.

2. *Bargaining power of buyers.* Informed customers become empowered customers. The Internet provides easy access to a wide array of information about products, services, and competitors, thereby greatly increasing the bargaining power of end consumers. For example, a customer shopping for a car can gather extensive information about various options, such as wholesale prices for new cars or average value for used vehicles, detailed specifications, repair records, and even whether a used car has ever been involved in an accident.

3. *Bargaining power of suppliers.* The concentration of suppliers and the availability of substitute suppliers are significant factors in determining supplier power. The sole supplier of engines to a manufacturer of small airplanes will have great power, for example. The impact of the Internet in this area can be both positive and negative. That is, procurement over the Web tends to give a company greater power over suppliers, but the Web also gives suppliers access to a greater number of customers, as well as the ability to reach end users. Overall, the Internet tends to raise the bargaining power of suppliers.

4. *Threat of substitute products.* The power of alternatives and substitutes for a company's product may be affected by cost changes or trends such as increased health consciousness that will deflect buyer loyalty to companies. Companies in the sugar industry suffered from the growth of sugar substitutes; manufacturers of aerosol spray cans lost business as environmentally conscious consumers chose other products. The Internet has created a greater threat of new substitutes by enabling new approaches to meeting customer needs. For example, traditional travel agencies have been hurt by the offering of low-cost airline tickets over the Internet.

5. *Rivalry among competitors.* As illustrated in Exhibit 5.10, rivalry among competitors is influenced by the preceding four forces, as well as by cost and product differentiation. With the leveling force of the Internet and information technology, it has become more difficult for many companies to find ways to distinguish themselves from their competitors, so rivalry has intensified.

Porter referred to the "advertising slugfest" when describing the scrambling and jockeying for position that often occurs among fierce rivals within an industry. Famous examples include the competitive rivalry between Pepsi and Coke and between UPS and FedEx. IBM and Oracle Corp. are currently involved in a fight for the No. 1 spot in the $50 billion corporate-software market. IBM recently rented a billboard near Oracle's headquarters proclaiming a "search for intelligent software." A few days later, Oracle fired the next shot with a competing billboard retorting, "Then you've come to the right place."[70]

Competitive Strategies. In finding its competitive edge within these five forces, Porter suggests that a company can adopt one of three strategies: differentiation, cost leadership, and focus. Companies can use the Internet to support and strengthen the strategic approach they choose. The organizational characteristics typically associated with each strategy are summarized in Exhibit 5.11.

1. *Differentiation.* The **differentiation** strategy involves an attempt to distinguish the firm's products or services from others in the industry. The organization may use advertising, distinctive product features, exceptional service, or new technology to achieve a product perceived as unique. The differentiation strategy can be profitable because customers are loyal and will pay high prices for the product. Examples of products that have benefited from a differentiation strategy include Mercedes-Benz automobiles, Maytag appliances, and Tommy Hilfiger clothing, all of which are perceived as distinctive in their markets. Service companies, such as American Express and Hilton Hotels, can also use a differentiation strategy. The Harleysville Group uses its corporate culture to differentiate itself in the insurance industry, as described below.

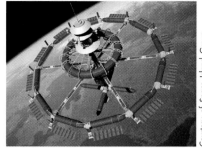

Courtesy of Space Island Group, West Covina, CA

Talk about a differentiation strategy! By 2007, entrepreneurs at Space Island Group plan to offer tourists a trip to a privately funded space station, complete with hotels, restaurants, and attractions. Founder and president Gene Meyers is enlisting the help of more than 150 high-level engineers, many of whom worked on the original NASA space shuttle program. Space Island plans on building a fleet of 50 commercial shuttles at a cost of $300 million each over the next ten years. The first should be up and running by 2005, with the first commercial station scheduled for full operations by 2007. Space Island will rely on superior technological know-how, employee creativity, and strong marketing abilities to make its unique project a success.

differentiation

A type of competitive strategy with which the organization seeks to distinguish its products or services from competitors.

Harleysville Group

http://harleysvillegroup.com

The Harleysville Group is not your average, run-of-the-mill insurance company, and employees as well as customers know it. At Harleysville, managers strive to provide their employees with an appealing atmosphere and plenty of perks. The goal is to create a work environment that makes people want to stay. They must be doing things right, because the Harleysville Group boasts a 95 percent retention rate over the past several years. That translates into experienced, knowledgeable employees who can provide top-quality service. Customers who have grown tired of working with companies where the staff is constantly changing can appreciate the difference that comes from working with people who are happy and knowledgeable.

Harleysville does plenty to keep employees happy. Besides an impressive vacation plan, extensive medical benefits, a cafeteria that serves freshly made food, and snack carts that go about the building selling coffee and pastries, the company also provides onsite ATMs and a clothes-cleaning service that includes pick-up and delivery. A massage therapist comes in once a week, and employees pay 10 dollars for a 15-minute session, far below the market rate. The CEO pays for a 15-minute session each week and often gives it away to an employee as a way to say thanks for some extra effort. Two other, highly important perks are the company's project bonuses and matching 401(k) investments. It is not unusual for the company to hand out checks for $1,500 or $2,000 to reward people for excellent work on a team project. For the 401(k) plan, Harleysville will match an employee's contribution anywhere from 25 percent to 100 percent, depending on company performance. In the last four years, the company has matched contributions one-to-one. For example, if an employee put in $5,000, the company would add that amount.

Other perks are aimed at increasing employees' knowledge and career skills. Tech-savvy workers are critical to the Harleysville Group, so the company spends more than $600,000 every year in technical training for the IS department alone. And that doesn't include the corporate funding for employees who are taking college courses and working toward higher degrees. To make it even easier, the company brings community college professors to the company campus so employees can take some courses without having to travel at the end of their work day.

Harleysville refuses to pay sky-high salaries, but the extensive benefits and the people-friendly work environment help the company stand out in the insurance industry. Inevitably, some employees do leave, but it usually isn't for a $5,000 raise, notes CEO Wayne Ratz. "It's more for an extravagant opportunity or for a lifestyle change."[71]

Companies that pursue a differentiation strategy typically need strong marketing abilities, a creative flair, and a reputation for leadership.[72] A differentiation strategy can reduce rivalry with competitors if buyers are loyal to a company's brand. Consider the example of online company eBay, described earlier in the chapter. Rather than cutting prices when Amazon.com and other rivals entered the online auction business, eBay continued to focus on building a distinctive community, offering customers services and experiences they could not get on other sites. Customers stayed loyal to eBay rather than switching to low-cost rivals. Successful differentiation can also reduce the bargaining power of large buyers because other products are less attractive, and this also helps the firm fight off threats of substitute products. In addition, differentia-

Strategy	Organizational Characteristics
Differentiation	Acts in a flexible, loosely knit way, with strong coordination among departments
	Strong capability in basic research
	Creative flair, thinks "out of the box"
	Strong marketing abilities
	Rewards employee innovation
	Corporate reputation for quality or technological leadership
Cost Leadership	Strong central authority; tight cost controls
	Maintains standard operating procedures
	Easy-to-use manufacturing technologies
	Highly efficient procurement and distribution systems
	Close supervision; finite employee empowerment
	Frequent, detailed control reports
Focus	May use combination of above policies directed at particular strategic target
	Values and rewards flexibility and customer intimacy
	Measures cost of providing service and maintaining customer loyalty
	Pushes empowerment to employees with customer contact

SOURCE: Based on Michael E. Porter, *Competitive Strategy: Techniques for Analyzing Industries and Competitors* (New York: The Free Press, 1980); Michael Treacy and Fred Wiersema, "How Market Leaders Keep Their Edge," *Fortune*, February 6, 1995, 88–89; and Michael A. Hitt, R. Duane Ireland, and Robert E. Hoskisson, *Strategic Management* (St. Paul, Minn.: West, 1995), 100–113.

EXHIBIT *5.11*

Organizational Characteristics of Porter's Competitive Strategies

tion erects entry barriers in the form of customer loyalty that a new entrant into the market would have difficulty overcoming.

2. *Cost Leadership.* With a **cost leadership** strategy, the organization aggressively seeks efficient facilities, pursues cost reductions, and uses tight cost controls to produce products more efficiently than competitors. A low-cost position means that the company can undercut competitors' prices and still offer comparable quality and earn a reasonable profit. Comfort Inn and Motel 6 are low-priced alternatives to Holiday Inn and Ramada Inn. Dell Computer, described earlier in the chapter, has squeezed every cent possible out of the cost of building and selling PCs, making it the undisputed low-cost leader and the number-one maker of personal computers.

Being a low-cost producer provides a successful strategy to defend against the five competitive forces in Exhibit 5.10. For example, the most efficient, low-cost company is in the best position to succeed in a price war while still making a profit. For example, Dell declared a brutal price war in mid-2001, just as the PC industry entered its worst slump ever. The result? Dell racked up $361 million in profits while the rest of the industry reported losses of $1.1 billion. Likewise, the low-cost producer is protected from powerful customers and suppliers, because customers cannot find lower prices elsewhere, and other buyers would have less slack for price negotiation with suppliers. If substitute products or potential new entrants occur, the low-cost producer is better positioned than higher-cost rivals to prevent loss of market share. The low price acts as a barrier against new entrants and substitute products.[73]

3. *Focus.* With a **focus** strategy, the organization concentrates on a specific regional market or buyer group. The company will use either a differentiation or low-cost approach, but only for a narrow target market. Enterprise Rent-A-Car has made its mark by focusing on a market the major companies such as

cost leadership

A type of competitive strategy with which the organization aggressively seeks efficient facilities, cuts costs, and employs tight cost controls to be more efficient than competitors.

focus

A type of competitive strategy that emphasizes concentration on a specific regional market or buyer group.

Hertz and Avis don't even play in—the low-budget insurance replacement market. Drivers whose cars have been wrecked or stolen have one less thing to worry about when Enterprise delivers a car right to their driveway. By using a focus strategy, Enterprise has been able to grow rapidly.[74]

Managers think carefully about which strategy will provide their company with its competitive advantage. Gibson Guitar Corp., famous in the music world for its innovative, high-quality products, found that switching to a low-cost strategy to compete against Japanese rivals such as Yamaha and Ibanez actually hurt the company. When managers realized people wanted Gibson products because of their reputation, not their price, they went back to a differentiation strategy and invested in new technology and marketing.[75] In his studies, Porter found that some businesses did not consciously adopt one of these three strategies and were stuck with no strategic advantage. Without a strategic advantage, businesses earned below-average profits compared with those that used differentiation, cost leadership, or focus strategies. In addition, because the Internet is having such a profound impact on the competitive environment in all industries, it is more important than ever that companies distinguish themselves through careful strategic positioning in the marketplace.[76]

Partnership Strategies

So far, we have been discussing strategies that are based on how to compete with other companies. An alternative approach to strategy emphasizes collaboration. In some situations, companies can achieve competitive advantages by cooperating with other firms rather than competing. Partnership strategies are becoming increasingly popular as firms in all industries join with other organizations to promote innovation, expand markets, and pursue joint goals. Partnering was once a strategy adopted primarily by small firms that needed greater marketing muscle or international access. Today, however, it has become a way of life for most companies, large and small. The question is no longer whether to collaborate, but rather where, how much, and with whom to collaborate.[77] Competition and cooperation often exist at the same time. In New York City, Time Warner (now AOL Time Warner) refused to carry Fox's 24-hour news channel on its New York City cable systems. The two companies engaged in all-out war that included court lawsuits and front-page headlines. This conflict, however, masked a simple fact: the two companies can't live without each other. Fox and Time Warner are wedded to one another in separate business deals around the world. They will never let the local competition in New York upset their larger cooperation on a global scale.[78]

The Internet is both driving and supporting the move toward partnership thinking. The ability to rapidly and smoothly conduct transactions, communicate information, exchange ideas, and collaborate on complex projects via the Internet means that companies such as Citigroup, Dow Chemical, and Herman Miller have been able to enter entirely new businesses by partnering in business areas that were previously unimaginable. IBM is collaborating with numerous partners around the world on the Internet, including competitors such as Dell and Hewlett-Packard, to develop, enhance, and market Linux-based software and services.[79]

Mutual dependencies and partnerships have become a fact of life, but the degree of collaboration varies. Organizations can choose to build cooperative relationships in many ways, such as through preferred suppliers, strategic business partnering, joint ventures, or mergers and acquisitions. Exhibit 5.12 illus-

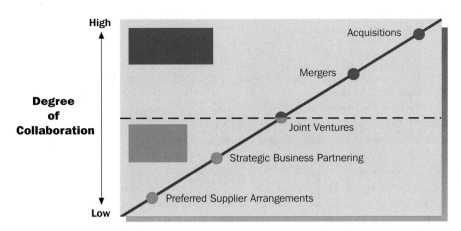

E X H I B I T *5.12*

A Continuum of Partnership Strategies

SOURCE: Adapted from Roberta Maynard, "Striking the Right Match," *Nation's Business* (May 1996), 18–28.

trates these major types of strategic business relationships according to the degree of collaboration involved. With preferred supplier relationships, a company such as Wal-Mart, for example, develops a special relationship with a key supplier such as Procter & Gamble that eliminates middlemen by sharing complete information and reducing the costs of salespeople and distributors. Preferred supplier arrangements provide long-term security for both organizations, but the level of collaboration is relatively low. Strategic business partnering requires a higher level of collaboration. Toys 'R' Us and Amazon.com have negotiated a strategic partnership to sell toys online. Amazon agreed to provide warehousing, order fulfillment, and site design, and in return got warrants to purchase 5 percent of toysrus.com, plus up-front payments and a share of the site's sales.[80]

Today's companies simultaneously embrace both competition and cooperation. Few companies can go it alone under a constant onslaught of international competition, changing technology, and new regulations. In this new environment, businesses choose a combination of competitive and partnership strategies that add to their overall sustainable advantage.[81]

Putting Strategy into Action

The final step in the strategic management process is *implementation*—how strategy is put into action. Some people argue that strategy implementation is the most difficult and important part of strategic management.[82] No matter how creative the formulated strategy, the organization will not benefit if it is incorrectly implemented. In today's competitive environment, there is an increasing recognition of the need for more dynamic approaches to formulating as well as implementing strategies. Strategy is not a static, analytical process; it requires vision, intuition, and employee participation.[83] Many organizations are abandoning central planning departments, and strategy is becoming an everyday part of the job for workers at all levels. Strategy implementation involves using several tools—parts of the firm that can be adjusted to put strategy into action—as illustrated in Exhibit 5.13. Once a new strategy is selected, it is implemented through changes in leadership, structure, information and control systems, and human resources.[84] For strategy to be implemented successfully, all aspects of the organization need to be in congruence with the strategy. Implementation involves regularly making difficult decisions about doing

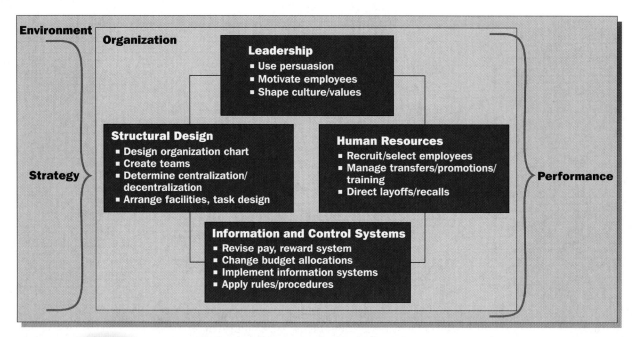

EXHIBIT *5.13*

Tools for Putting Strategy into Action

SOURCE: Adapted from Jay R. Galbraith and Robert K. Kazanjian, *Strategy Implementation: Structure, Systems, and Process*, 2d ed. (St. Paul, Minn.: West, 1986), 115. Used with permission.

things in a way that supports rather than undermines the organization's chosen strategy. Remaining chapters of this book examine in detail topics such as leadership, organizational structure, information and control systems, and human resource management.

Leadership

The primary key to successful strategy implementation is leadership. *Leadership* is the ability to influence people to adopt the new behaviors needed for strategy implementation. An important part of implementing strategy is building consensus. People throughout the organization have to believe in the new strategy and have a strong commitment to achieving the vision and goals. Leadership means using persuasion, motivating employees, and shaping culture and values to support the new strategy. Managers may make speeches to employees, build coalitions of people who support the new strategic direction, and persuade middle managers to go along with their vision for the company. Michael Dell of Dell Computer is a master of strategic leadership. Dell builds support for his vision and strategy at each year's employee meeting, where he has a chance to tell employees face-to-face exactly where he wants them to take the company in the year ahead. Dell's charisma and persuasive leadership keep employees fired up about his goals for the company.[85] With a clear sense of direction and a shared purpose, employees feel motivated, challenged, and empowered to pursue new strategic goals. Another way leaders build consensus and commitment is through broad participation. When people participate in strategy formulation, implementation is easier because managers and employees already understand the reasons for the new strategy and feel more committed to it.

Human Resources

The organization's *human resources* are its employees. The human resource function recruits, selects, trains, transfers, promotes, and lays off employees to achieve strategic goals. For example, training employees can help them understand the purpose and importance of a new strategy or help them develop the necessary specific skills and behaviors. Sometimes employees may have to be let go and replaced. One newspaper shifted its strategy from an evening to a morning paper to compete with a large newspaper from a nearby city. The new strategy fostered resentment and resistance among department heads. In order to implement it, 80 percent of the department heads had to be let go because they refused to cooperate. New people were recruited and placed in those positions, and the morning newspaper strategy was a resounding success.[86]

Mannie Jackson revived the Harlem Globetrotters, an organization on the brink of bankruptcy and irrelevancy, by recruiting new players who could recapture the glory the Globetrotters enjoyed in the 1960s and 1970s. Jackson rates potential players on their skill, charisma, punctuality, and attitude. He wants only top athletes who can promote the Globetrotter brand and are willing to be role models.[87]

In summary, strategy implementation is essential for effective strategic management. Managers implement strategy through the tools of leadership, structural design, information and control systems, and human resources. Without effective implementation, even the most creative strategy will fail.

■ Summary and Management Solution

This chapter focused on organizational planning. Organizational planning involves defining goals and developing a plan with which to achieve them. An organization exists for a single, overriding purpose known as its mission—the basis for strategic goals and plans. Goals within the organization are defined in a hierarchical fashion, beginning with strategic goals followed by tactical and operational goals. Plans are defined similarly, with strategic, tactical, and operational plans used to achieve the goals. Other goal concepts include characteristics of effective goals and goal-setting behavior.

Several types of plans were described, including strategic, tactical, operational, single-use, standing, and contingency plans, as well as management by objectives. A special type of contingency planning is crisis management planning, which involves the stages of prevention, preparation, and containment.

In the past, planning was almost always done entirely by top managers, by consultants, or by central planning departments. In the new workplace, planning is decentralized and people throughout the organization are involved in establishing dynamic plans that can meet fast-changing needs from the environment. Some guidelines for planning in the new workplace include starting with a powerful mission, setting stretch goals, creating a culture that encourages learning, designing new roles for

planning staff, and using temporary task forces that may include outside stakeholders. In the new workplace, employees on the front lines may constantly be adapting plans to meet new needs. However, top managers are still responsible for providing a guiding mission and a solid framework for planning and goal setting.

Also described were important concepts of strategic management. Strategic management begins with an evaluation of the organization's current mission, goals, and strategy. This evaluation is followed by situation analysis (called SWOT analysis), which examines opportunities and threats in the external environment as well as strengths and weaknesses within the organization. Situation analysis leads to the formulation of explicit strategic plans, which then must be implemented.

Ken Lankton analyzed his failing company and changed the strategy, because he saw his successful plastics manufacturing business almost go bankrupt due to high interest rates. While most plastics manufacturers served only a limited area, Lankton decided the world was his market. He focused on superior quality and quick delivery to customers. As long as a customer would promise $10 million per year in business, Lankton would build a factory right next to theirs. His strategy worked and the company grew like Jack's beanstalk. For Abbott Laboratories in Chicago, Lankton built a factory to make disposable blood analyzers and syringes. Hewlett-Packard got a plant in Corvalis, Oregon, that made printer parts. By 2001 sales had exploded to $682 million. In 1999, Lankton decided to make the company employee-owned. Previously, he had given 30 percent of the stock to 130 employees for exceptional performance, but now they all would own it.[88]

■ Discussion Questions

1. To what extent would planning have helped the U.S. Postal Service respond more quickly and effectively to the crisis of anthrax-tainted letters being sent through the mail? What types of planning would be appropriate for unexpected events?

2. Write a brief mission statement for a local business with which you are familiar. How might having a clear, written mission statement benefit a small organization?

3. What strategies could the college or university at which you are taking this management course adopt to compete for students in the marketplace? Would these strategies depend on the school's goals?

4. If you were a top manager of a medium-sized real estate sales agency, would you use MBO? If so, give examples of goals you might set for managers and sales agents.

5. How is planning changing in the new workplace? Do you think planning becomes more important or less important in a world where everything is changing fast and crises have become a regular part of organizational life? Why?

6. Assume Southern University decides to (1) raise its admission standards and (2) initiate a business fair to which local townspeople will be invited. What types of plans would it use to carry out these two activities?

7. Perform a situation (SWOT) analysis for the university you attend. Do you think university administrators consider these factors when devising their strategy?

8. What is meant by the core competence and synergy components of strategy? Give examples.

9. Using Porter's competitive strategies, how would you describe the strategies of Wal-Mart, Bloomingdale's, and Target? Do any of these companies also use partnership strategies? Discuss.

■ Manager's Workbook

Goal Setting

Consider goals for yourself in order to do well in this course. What do you need to do in order to get a good grade? Goals should be according to the "Criteria for Effective Goals" on pages 153–4. In addition, you need a system to monitor your progress, such as the table below, which shows the types of goals you may choose to select for yourself.

Goals   Class Weeks

	First week (from now)	Second week	Third week	Fourth week
1. 100% attendance				
2. Class notes				
3. Read assigned chapters				
4. Outline chapters				
5. Define vocabulary words				
6. Answer end of chapter questions				
7. Complete "Workbook" assignments				
8. Class participation				
9.				
10.				

Your instructor may ask you to turn in your monitor sheets at the end of the course.

1. According to goal-setting theory, using and monitoring goals is supposed to help performance. Did you do better as a result of your goals?

2. What did you learn from this that could help you in other classes?

Source: Adapted from Nancy C. Morey, "Applying Goal Setting in the Classroom," *The Organizational Behavior Teaching Review*, 11, no. 4 (1986–87), 53–59.

■ Manager's Workshop

Developing Strategy for a Small Business

Instructions: In groups of 4–6, select a local business with which you (or group members) are familiar. Complete the following activities.

Activity 1. Perform a SWOT analysis for the business.

SWOT Analysis for _____ (name of company)

	Internal (within company)	External (outside company)
Positive	Strengths:	Opportunities:
Negative	Weaknesses:	Threats:

Activity 2. Write a statement of the business's current strategy.
Activity 3. Decide on a goal you would like the business to achieve in two years, and write a statement of proposed strategy for achieving that goal.

Activity 4. Write a statement describing how the proposed strategy will be implemented.
Activity 5. What have you learned from this exercise?

■ Management in Practice: Ethical Dilemma

Completing Project WebFirst

After two years with HealthFirst, Mary Palmer was handed her first big assignment, Project WebFirst. HealthFirst, a marketer of health products and services, was pushing hard to reposition itself on the Internet, and she was going to play a major role. Mary remembered with pride the rush she felt when the senior vice president of operations had explained that she'd been chosen to lead the project because of her reputation for getting results. "Put together a team that can do the job fast," he had said.

Mary had never been one to let any grass grow under her feet. She quickly put together a skeleton team and got down to business. Mary worked with the others to carefully develop goals and plans for every step of the project and set a clear timeline for meeting them. As the project progressed, more people were added to the team and things moved along nicely. But, unexpectedly, HealthFirst announced to senior managers a major acquisition that would mean at least a 20 percent reduction in the work force. Mary was informed that the employees working on Project WebFirst would be affected, and that the work force reduction timetable was aggressive. "You've done a great job managing the project so far," the senior VP of operations told her. "We know you'll manage this aspect just as well. We've got to keep things moving and get the Web strategy up and rolling."

Mary knew what that meant—she couldn't afford to lose the commitment and motivation of even one team member, or the carefully laid plans would fall to pieces. As word about the

acquisition and possible layoffs spread through the company, team members began asking if they would be affected. Mary knows her employees want the truth, but she fears that telling them some of them will lose their jobs will delay the project. The company wants results *now*, and Mary wants the successful completion of Project WebFirst on her résumé.

What Do You Do?

1. Level with the Project WebFirst team members that some of them will probably be let go. Emphasize, however, that the success of the project will benefit each one of them, whether they stay with HealthFirst or need to find another job, so they need to stay focused.
2. Tell the team members that their jobs are not in jeopardy. Keeping the project moving to a successful completion is your first priority.
3. Get as much specific information as you can from top management about the merger and impending job reductions. Put together a group to develop an action plan, including a severance package that can help cushion the loss of jobs. Then, meet with your team and be as honest as you can about what is going on with the company.

SOURCE: Based on Doug Wallace, "Ripping Away a Curtain of Denial," *BusinessEthics* (Millennium-End Double Issue, 1999), 26.

■ Surf the Net

1. **Mission Statement.** Select a company you are interested in, or choose one from the Company Index at the back of this text. Using a search engine such as *http://www. alltheweb.com,* locate the company's Web site. Because not all companies include their mission statement at their Web site, be prepared to look at more than one company's Web site until you find a site that does publish the company's mission statement. Complete this exercise by submitting to your instructor a printout similar to the following for the company you selected:

> **Example** Chapter 5, Surf the Net Exercise 1. I went to Dell Computer's Web site at *http://www.dell.com* and selected the following links to locate the mission statement: "About Dell," "Dell Vision," and "Mission Statement." Printed below is Dell's mission statement:
>
> **Mission Statement**
> Dell's mission is to be the most successful computer company in the world at delivering the best customer experience in markets we serve. In doing so, Dell will meet customer expectations of:
>
> 1. Highest quality
> 2. Leading technology
> 3. Competitive pricing
> 4. Individual and company accountability
> 5. Best-in-class service and support
> 6. Flexible customization capability
> 7. Superior corporate citizenship
> 8. Financial stability

2. **Goal Setting.** You've learned in this chapter about organizational goal setting. Many similarities exist between organizational and personal goal setting. The goal-setting skills you develop in setting personal goals will easily transfer to an organizational setting. Therefore, this exercise allows you to practice personal goal setting. Use one of the following sites or locate one of your own that will help you write a personal goal statement. Your goal statement should reflect specific ideas you learned about goal statements from the Web site.
   http://www.topachievement.com/goalsetting.html
   http://www.about-goal-setting.com
   http://www.bodyresults.com/E2SMARTgoals.htm
3. **Contingency Plans.** The Federal Emergency Management Agency (FEMA), founded in 1979, is an independent agency of the federal government that reports to the president. Its mission is "to reduce loss of life and property and protect our nation's critical infrastructure from all types of hazards, through a comprehensive, risk-based emergency management program of mitigation, preparedness, response, and recovery." In this exercise you will focus on FEMA's preparedness information located at *http://www.fema.gov*

   FEMA encourages the use of contingency plans by stating on this site: "Disasters take many forms. They're caused by gale force winds, sudden floods, releases of deadly chemicals, fire, ice, even upheavals of the earth itself. When disaster strikes, the best protection is knowing what to do." Select a natural or technological disaster, read the preparedness information provided and write a brief outline of a contingency plan for what an organization should do before, during, and after the disaster.

■ Case for Critical Analysis

H.I.D.

Dave Collins, president of H.I.D., sat down at the conference table with his management team members, Karen Setz, Tony Briggs, Dave King, and Art Johnson. H.I.D. owns ten Holiday Inns in Georgia, eight hotels of different types in Canada, and one property in the Caribbean. It also owns two Quality Inns in Georgia. Dave Collins and his managers got together to define their mission and goals and to set strategic plans. As they began their strategic planning session, the consultant they had hired suggested that each describe what he or she wanted for the company's domestic operations in the next 10 years—how many hotels it should own, where to locate them, and who the target market was. Another question he asked them to consider

was what the driving force of the company should be—that is, the single characteristic that would separate H.I.D. from other companies.

The team members wrote their answers on flip charts, and the consultant summarized the results. Dave Collins's goal included 50 hotels in 10 years, with the number increasing to 26 or 27 in 5 years. All the other members saw no more than 20 hotels in 10 years and a maximum of 15 or 16 within 5 years. Clearly there was disagreement among the top managers about long-term goals and the desirable growth rate.

With the consultant's direction, the team members began to critique their growth targets. Dave King, director of operations and development, observed, "We just can't build that many hotels in that time period, certainly not given our current staffing, or any reasonable staffing we could afford. I don't see how we could achieve that goal." Art Johnson, the accountant, agreed. Karen Setz then asked, "Could we build them all in Georgia? You know we've centered on the medium-priced hotel in smaller towns. Do we need to move to bigger towns now, such as Jacksonville, or add another to the one we have in Atlanta?" Dave Collins responded, "We have an opportunity out in California, we may have one in New Jersey, and we are looking at the possibility of going to Jacksonville."

The consultant attempted to refocus the discussion: "Well, how does this all fit with your mission? Where are you willing to locate geographically? Most of your operation is in Georgia. Can you adequately support a national building effort?"

Tony Briggs responded, "Well, you know we have always looked at the smaller-town hotels as being our niche, although we deviated from that for the hotel in Atlanta. But we generally stay in smaller towns where we don't have much competition. Now we are talking about an expensive hotel in California."

Dave Collins suggested, "Maybe it's time we changed our target market, changed our pricing strategy, and went for larger hotels in urban areas across the whole country. Maybe we need to change a lot of factors about our company."

Questions

1. What is H.I.D.'s mission at present? How may this mission change?

2. What do you think H.I.D.'s mission, strategic goals, and strategic plans are likely to be at the end of this planning session? Why?

3. What goal-setting behavior is being used here to reach agreement among H.I.D.'s managers? Do managers typically disagree about the direction of their organization?

SOURCE: This case was provided by James Higgins.

Managerial Decision Making

LEARNING OBJECTIVES

After studying this chapter, you should be able to

1 Explain why decision making is an important component of good management.

2 Explain the difference between programmed and nonprogrammed decisions and the decision characteristics of risk, uncertainty, and ambiguity.

3 Describe the classical, administrative, and political models of decision making and their applications.

4 Identify the six steps used in managerial decision making.

5 Explain four personal decision styles used by managers.

6 Discuss the advantages and disadvantages of participative decision making.

7 Identify techniques for improving decision making in today's fast-moving and uncertain environment

8 Describe the importance of information technology for organizations and the attributes of quality information.

Management Challenge

In the early morning of April 18, 2002, President Bush and some key advisors met in the Oval Office to make a decision regarding a new disturbing intelligence report. It said a suicide bomber might attack a U.S. bank. The advisors differed on what to do. The assistant attorney general as well as FBI Chief Robert Mueller wanted to warn banks, in order to prepare for potential victims. Publicity brings prevention, they argued. Well aware of the FBI agent's report in August 2001 warning that Osama bin Laden was using U.S. flight schools to train suicide bombers, which never was acted on, these two powerful men did not want to make the same mistake. On the other side were two men: The deputy treasury secretary and the homeland security director, Tom Ridge, who argued that the threat wasn't credible enough and that the fragile economy could not sustain banks closing. They also knew that most intelligence reports are never shared with the public. Some reports go to law enforcement officials so they can be on high alert, but many of the warnings just don't pan out. Just four days previously, 150 banks in Washington, D.C. had been closed because of a telephone threat that seemed credible, but it turned out to come from a 14-year-old boy in the Netherlands, who was quickly arrested. There were many issues to consider. Here were some of the most powerful people in the world, having a difficult time making what could be a life-and-death decision. Compounding the difficulty of decision making was the fact that world finance ministers and central bankers were arriving for a semiannual meeting at the World Bank.

President Bush is not one to allow indecision at top ranks, so he turned to the four advisors and said, "You ought to talk about it."[1]

If you were one of the advisors, what would you recommend doing so that the group could reach a decision?

The president's advisors met for the next 36 hours, making decisions that could have serious impacts on many people. So much hung in the balance and the stakes were so high that the quality of the decision-making process was crucial.

Managers often are referred to as *decision makers*. Although many of their important decisions are strategic, managers also make decisions about every other aspect of an organization, including structure, control systems, responses to the environment, and human resources. Managers scout for problems, make decisions for solving them, and monitor the consequences to see whether additional decisions are required. Good decision making is a vital part of good management, because decisions determine how the organization solves its problems, allocates resources, and accomplishes its goals.

Consider the case of Encyclopedia Britannica. For most of its 230-year history, the *Encyclopedia Britannica* has been viewed as an illustrious repository of cultural and historical knowledge—almost a national treasure. Generations of students and librarians relied on the Britannica to research everything from the Aleutian Islands to the history of zydeco—but that was before CD-ROMs and the Internet became the study tools of choice. Suddenly, the 32-volume collection of encyclopedias seemed destined to fade into history. Britannica was slow to move into electronic media and practically ceded the market to upstarts such as Microsoft's *Encarta*. Managers made a serious blunder in 1993 when they sold the company's Compton unit, a CD-ROM pioneer now being used by millions of consumers. Even when Britannica finally introduced a CD-ROM, it was priced at a staggering $1,200, while Microsoft was offering cut-rate deals or giving *Encarta* away free with personal computers. When Jacob Safra and a Swiss investment group bought Britannica, new top executives immediately began installing managers who could lead the company into the digital age. Safra believed Britannica could once again be the quality leader. However, decisions had to be made about how to compete with rivals such as Compton's and Microsoft's *Encarta,* as well as the numerous free options available on the Internet.[2]

Problem recognition was easy: the venerable old company was about to go under. In diagnosing the causes, new owners determined that a major factor was an ossified management culture dominated by book salesmen, leading to years of squabbling over new product development and thus hindering the move into electronic media. One of the first decisions Jacob Safra made was to bring in a new management team. The team then considered various alternatives for reviving the faltering company. The first decisions were to rush out a revamped, lower-cost CD-ROM package, targeted particularly to schools, and to launch the Britannica.com Web site, which allows users to call up encyclopedia entries online, as well as get a list of links to other Web sites related to the topic. Top executives also decided to create a separate digital media division to focus on new product development for the digital world. Managers in this new division quickly focused on the wireless Web as the route to the future. After evaluating alternatives for how to establish Britannica as the wireless Web's brand-name information source, they decided not to go it alone, but to create alliances with wireless carriers and license Britannica's content to other Web sites. Impressed with Britannica's content, companies have so far been glad to establish partnerships. These decisions have helped the company cross the bridge to the digital era, but so far the wireless Web has not proven to be much of a money maker. Managers are in the process of evaluation to determine what new decisions need to be made.

Top executives at Encyclopedia Britannica Holding SA made and implemented early decisions that kept Britannica alive and kicking. More recently, the new managers, including a new senior vice president for product development, had to sharpen their skills to make important decisions that would affect the future of their business. Every organization grows, prospers, or fails as a result of decisions by its managers.

Decision making is not easy. It must be done amid ever-changing factors, unclear information, and conflicting points of view. For example, launching a separate Internet company named Cozone that expanded CompUSA's product line and market seemed a good idea when managers made the decision in 1999, but the spinoff fell apart after only six months. Managers and board members had conflicting views about establishing an entirely new and distinct brand online. Other decisions, such as the confusing name, the failure to take advantage of cooperative marketing, and the refusal to allow merchandise bought online to be returned at CompUSA retail stores, helped to doom the new business.[3] Both Mattel and Hasbro, the top U.S. toymakers, passed on the Ninja Turtles idea in the late 1980s, and the action figures went on to sell billions. Coca-Cola pumped some $30 million into developing the Break-Mate, a miniature soda fountain, but the product flopped in the marketplace and Break-Mate fountains now sit gathering dust in storage sheds.[4]

The business world is also full of evidence of good decisions. Andy Grove, former CEO of Intel Corporation, decided to get out of the DRAM memory-chip business in the mid-1980s and focus relentlessly on microprocessors. The decision was a risky one, and many Intel executives opposed it, but it set Intel on course to become one of the richest and most powerful companies in the world.[5] Nokia became a $10 billion leader in the cellular phone industry because managers at the company decided to sell off unrelated businesses such as paper, tires, and aluminum and concentrate the company's resources on electronics.[6]

Chapter 5 described strategic planning. This chapter explores the decision process that underlies strategic planning. Plans and strategies are arrived at through decision making; the better the decision making, the better the strategic planning. First we will examine decision characteristics. Then we will look at decision-making models and the steps executives should take when making important decisions. We will also examine participative decision making and discuss techniques for improving decision making in today's organizations.

Types of Decisions and Problems

A **decision** is a choice made from available alternatives. For example, an accounting manager's selection among Bill, Tasha, and Jennifer for the position of junior auditor is a decision. Many people assume that making a choice is the major part of decision making, but it is only a part.

Decision making is the process of identifying problems and opportunities and then resolving them.[7] Decision making involves effort both before and after the actual choice. Thus, the decision as to whether to select Bill, Tasha, or Jennifer requires the accounting manager to ascertain whether a new junior auditor is needed, determine the availability of potential job candidates, interview candidates to acquire necessary information, select one candidate, and follow up with the socialization of the new employee into the organization to ensure the decision's success.

decision
A choice made from available alternatives.

decision making
The process of identifying problems and opportunities and then resolving them.

Programmed and Nonprogrammed Decisions

Management decisions typically fall into one of two categories: programmed and nonprogrammed. Programmed decisions involve situations that have

DIGITAL, INC.

Starbucks Makes a New Connection

Starbucks has made its presence known in the physical world for quite some time, but two years ago managers set out on a mission to connect with their customers in a different way: by means of the Internet. Top executives wanted to leverage the power of the Starbucks brand to build a presence in cyberspace, and they moved swiftly with plans to set up Starbucks X, a Web site where they dreamed of being involved in the online merchandising of everything from furniture to videocassettes.

But the decision to redefine the business in radical ways proved to be unwise, and the company stumbled badly in the online world. In addition, the complexity and uncertainty of the venture caused the company to lose its balance, and Starbucks' physical stores also began reporting disappointing sales and earnings. Starbucks' chairman Howard Schultz and other top executives pulled back to analyze the complex problem, evaluate alternatives, and make a choice about how to successfully make a connection between Starbucks' physical stores and the realm of the Internet. Eventually, they decided to tie their Web site closely to the company's central mission and goals. Combining an online store with the company's small catalog division, together known as Starbucks Direct, was a smart move; Starbucks Direct now brings in about $20 million

a year—a welcome revenue stream. Rather than trying to expand its business into new areas, Starbucks now runs a simple, easy-to-use Web site that sells coffee beans, brewing machines, and mugs, and has online hosts that offer coffee history and lore to interested visitors.

However, with the Internet such a major part of people's lives, managers faced other decisions about connecting to the new technology. They did not want to create cybercafés, which tend to be dimly lit with people hunched over machines. In addition, they were concerned about cluttering up the cozy café atmosphere with cumbersome computer gear. With the proliferation of PDAs and affordable laptops, Starbucks' managers began to see a way to provide high-speed wireless Internet connections in stores without damaging the traditional café experience and scaring away customers. When asked about the risk of people coming in, using the Internet, and not buying anything, Darren Huston, senior vice president for new initiatives, said he was not worried about loitering. "The reality is exactly the opposite. Our most successful stores turn out to be the ones with the most loitering. We think it's great if people want to stay awhile. It creates a sense of community."

SOURCE: George Anders, "Starbucks Brews a New Strategy," *Fast Company* (August, 2001), 145–146.

---

programmed decision

A decision made in response to a situation that has occurred often enough to enable decision rules to be developed and applied in the future.

nonprogrammed decision

A decision made in response to a situation that is unique, is poorly defined and largely unstructured, and has important consequences for the organization.

occurred often enough to enable decision rules to be developed and applied in the future.[8] **Programmed decisions** are made in response to recurring organizational problems. The decision to reorder paper and other office supplies when inventories drop to a certain level is a programmed decision. Other programmed decisions concern the types of skills required to fill certain jobs, the reorder point for manufacturing inventory, exception reporting for expenditures 10 percent or more over budget, and selection of freight routes for product deliveries. Once managers formulate decision rules, subordinates and others can make the decision, freeing managers for other tasks.

Nonprogrammed decisions are made in response to situations that are unique, are poorly defined and largely unstructured, and have important consequences for the organization. Many nonprogrammed decisions involve strategic planning, because uncertainty is great and decisions are complex. Decisions to build a new factory, develop a new product or service, enter a new geographical market, or relocate headquarters to another city are all nonprogrammed decisions. Starbucks's decision to incorporate the Internet as part of its growth strategy, described in the Digital, Inc. box, is a good example of the complexity and uncertainty of nonprogrammed decisions. Another example of a nonprogrammed decision was when Ronald Zarrella, president of General Motors North American operations, shelved plans to introduce a new design for the company's best-selling car, the Chevrolet Cavalier. He delayed building new factories and invested the millions of dollars saved in getting innovative new models of trucks and sport-utility vehicles on the market quickly. Zarrella and his top executives had to analyze complex problems, evaluate alternatives, and make a decision about the best way to reverse GM's declining market share.[9]

Certainty, Risk, Uncertainty, and Ambiguity

One primary difference between programmed and nonprogrammed decisions relates to the degree of certainty or uncertainty managers deal with in making the decision. In a perfect world, managers would have all the information necessary for making decisions. In reality, however, some things are unknowable; thus, some decisions will fail to solve the problem or attain the desired outcome. Managers try to obtain information about decision alternatives that will reduce decision uncertainty. Every decision situation can be organized on a scale according to the availability of information and the possibility of failure. The four positions on the scale are certainty, risk, uncertainty, and ambiguity, as illustrated in Exhibit 6.1. Whereas programmed decisions can be made in situations involving certainty, many situations that managers deal with every day involve at least some degree of uncertainty and require nonprogrammed decision making.

Certainty. Certainty means that all the information the decision maker needs is fully available.[10] Managers have information on operating conditions, resource costs or constraints, and each course of action and possible outcome. For example, if a company considers a $10,000 investment in new equipment that it knows for certain will yield $4,000 in cost savings per year over the next five years, managers can calculate a before-tax rate of return of about 40 percent. If managers compare this investment with one that will yield only $3,000 per year in cost savings, they can confidently select the 40 percent return. However, few decisions are certain in the real world. Most contain risk or uncertainty.

Risk. Risk means that a decision has clear-cut goals and that good information is available, but the future outcomes associated with each alternative are subject to chance. However, enough information is available to allow the

certainty

All the information the decision maker needs is fully available.

risk

A decision has clear-cut goals and good information is available, but the future outcomes associated with each alternative are subject to chance.

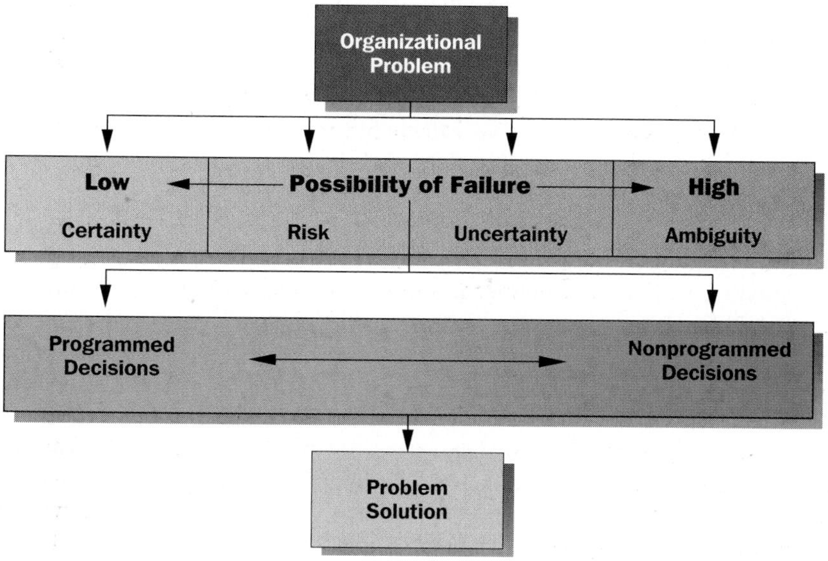

EXHIBIT *6.1*

Conditions That Affect the Possibility of Decision Failure

Courtesy of mptv.com

Federal Express took a big risk when it decided to become an integral part of the movie Cast Away. Product integration goes beyond displaying a product in the background of a movie scene—with integration, products actually become part of the script. FedEx had to weigh the downside of linking its services with an unrelated and volatile film industry against the positive exposure it could possibly gain by being associated with celebrity star Tom Hanks and a blockbuster movie.

uncertainty
Managers know which goal they wish to achieve, but information about alternatives and future events is incomplete.

ambiguity
The goals to be achieved or the problem to be solved is unclear, alternatives are difficult to define, and information about outcomes is unavailable.

probability of a successful outcome for each alternative to be estimated.[11] Statistical analysis might be used to calculate the probabilities of success or failure. The measure of risk captures the possibility that future events will render the alternative unsuccessful. Some oil companies use a quantitative simulation approach to estimate hydrocarbon reserves, enabling oil executives to evaluate the variation in risk at each stage of exploration and production and make better decisions. Saturn took a risk with the introduction of a mid-sized car to compete with the Toyota Camry and Honda's Accord. Managers had information that indicated the new L-series would sell well, based on the strength of the Saturn brand. However, they underestimated the extent to which people perceived Saturn as a "small-car" company and failed to put the emphasis they needed into marketing the new vehicle.[12]

Uncertainty. Uncertainty means that managers know which goals they wish to achieve, but information about alternatives and future events is incomplete.[13] Managers do not have enough information to be clear about alternatives or to estimate their risk. Factors that may affect a decision, such as price, production costs, volume, or future interest rates, are difficult to analyze and predict. Managers may have to make assumptions from which to forge the decision even though it will be wrong if the assumptions are incorrect. Managers may have to come up with creative approaches to alternatives and use personal judgment to determine which alternative is best.

Mary Hadar, an assistant managing editor of the *Washington Post*, faces uncertainty every day as she has to make quick decisions about which stories will run in one of the world's most influential newspapers. Although she has a base of knowledge and experience to rely on, Hadar often has to make many assumptions and use personal judgment and intuition to make decisions such as whether to run a controversial story or when to cut back on coverage of certain issues.[14]

Many decisions made under uncertainty do not produce the desired results, but managers face uncertainty every day. They must find creative ways to cope with uncertainty in order to make effective decisions.

Ambiguity. Ambiguity is by far the most difficult decision situation. Ambiguity means that the goals to be achieved or the problem to be solved is unclear, alternatives are difficult to define, and information about outcomes is unavailable.[15] Ambiguity is what students would feel if an instructor created student groups, told each group to complete a project, but gave the groups no topic, direction, or guidelines whatsoever. Ambiguity has been called a "wicked" decision problem. Managers have a difficult time coming to grips with the issues. Wicked problems are associated with manager conflicts over goals and decision alternatives, rapidly changing circumstances, fuzzy information, and unclear linkages among decision elements.[16] Sometimes managers will come up with a "solution" only to realize that they hadn't clearly defined the real problem to begin with.[17] A recent example of a wicked decision problem was when managers at Ford Motor Company and Firestone confronted the problem of tires used on the Ford Explorer coming apart on the road, causing deadly blowouts and rollovers. Just defining the problem and whether the tire itself or the design of the Explorer was at fault was the first hurdle. Information was fuzzy and fast-changing, and managers were in conflict over how to handle the problem. Neither side has dealt with this ongoing decision situation very effectively, and the reputations of both companies have suffered as a result. Fortunately, most decisions are not characterized by ambiguity. But when they are, managers must conjure up goals and develop reasonable scenarios for decision alternatives in the absence of information.

Decision-Making Models

The approach managers use to make decisions usually falls into one of three types—the classical model, the administrative model, or the political model. The choice of model depends on the manager's personal preference, whether the decision is programmed or nonprogrammed, and the extent to which the decision is characterized by risk, uncertainty, or ambiguity.

Classical Model

The **classical model** of decision making is based on economic assumptions. This model has arisen within the management literature because managers are expected to make decisions that are economically sensible and in the organization's best economic interests. The assumptions underlying this model are as follows:

classical model

A decision-making model based on the assumption that managers should make logical decisions that will be in the organization's best economic interests.

1. The decision maker operates to accomplish goals that are known and agreed upon. Problems are precisely formulated and defined.

2. The decision maker strives for conditions of certainty, gathering complete information. All alternatives and the potential results of each are calculated.

3. Criteria for evaluating alternatives are known. The decision maker selects the alternative that will maximize the economic return to the organization.

4. The decision maker is rational and uses logic to assign values, order preferences, evaluate alternatives, and make the decision that will maximize the attainment of organizational goals.

The classical model of decision making is considered to be **normative**, which means it defines how a decision maker *should* make decisions. It does not describe how managers actually make decisions so much as it provides guidelines on how to reach an ideal outcome for the organization. The value of the classical model has been its ability to help decision makers be more rational. For example, many senior managers rely solely on intuition and personal preferences for making decisions.[18] In recent years, the classical approach has been given wider application because of the growth of quantitative decision techniques that use computers. Quantitative techniques include such things as decision trees, payoff matrices, break-even analysis, linear programming, forecasting, and operations research models. The use of computerized information systems and databases has increased the power of the classical approach.

normative

An approach that defines how a decision maker should make decisions and provides guidelines for reaching an ideal outcome for the organization.

In many respects, the classical model represents an "ideal" model of decision making that is often unattainable by real people in real organizations. It is most valuable when applied to programmed decisions and to decisions characterized by certainty or risk, because relevant information is available and probabilities can be calculated. For example, new analytical software programs for front-line decision making can automate many programmed decisions, such as freezing the account of a customer who has failed to make payments.[19] GE Capital Mortgage uses a decision software program called Loss Mitigation Optimizer to improve the decision making of loss management representatives. These employees have to decide whether the company can "cure" loans for customers who have stopped making payments or whether it will have to recommend foreclosure. By analyzing and measuring relevant variables, the program helped GE Capital Mortgage improve its cure rates from 30 percent of cases to more than 50 percent, while representatives were taking about 40 percent less time per deal.[20] Another organization that makes extensive use of the classical approach is the SABRE Group, which began as a system for keeping track of reservations for American Airlines.

The SABRE Group

http://www.sabre.com

Originally developed as a system for tracking airline reservations, the SABRE Group is today made up of a number of companies that provide information technology solutions to a wide variety of businesses.

The power of SABRE is illustrated by its yield management system for American Airlines. American operates more than 4,000 flights a day, each one offering multiple fare classes, and begins taking reservations 330 days prior to each departure. The job of yield management is to forecast demand by inventory class and to optimize the decision of whether to sell at a lower price than the customer is willing to pay now or wait for higher-value, late-arriving demand. SABRE has estimated that the use of its computer-based system generates almost $1 billion in annual incremental revenue for American Airlines.

Another problem for airlines is scheduling. For a large carrier such as American, scheduling is an extremely complex problem with thousands of decision constraints and millions of variables. Some of those variables include where to fly, how often to serve a specific market, what time of day to fly, what type of aircraft to assign to each route, and what flights to designate as through-flights. SABRE designed a system that relies on sophisticated forecasting models and optimization models that make these complex decisions. The system added millions of dollars to American's bottom line each year and SABRE has now succeeded in selling it to such airlines as Delta, Lufthansa, Swissair, Northwest, Air France, US Air, and Air New Zealand.[21]

Administrative Model

administrative model

A decision-making model that describes how managers actually make decisions in situations characterized by nonprogrammed decisions, uncertainty, and ambiguity.

The **administrative model** of decision making describes how managers actually make decisions in difficult situations, such as those characterized by nonprogrammed decisions, uncertainty, and ambiguity. Many management decisions are not sufficiently programmable to lend themselves to any degree of quantification. Managers are unable to make economically rational decisions even if they want to.[22]

Bounded Rationality and Satisficing. The administrative model of decision making is based on the work of Herbert A. Simon. Simon proposed two concepts that were instrumental in shaping the administrative model: bounded rationality and satisficing. **Bounded rationality** means that people have limits, or boundaries, on how rational they can be. The organization is incredibly complex, and managers have the time and ability to process only a limited amount of information with which to make decisions.[23] Because managers do not have the time or cognitive ability to process complete information about complex decisions, they must satisfice. **Satisficing** means that decision makers choose the first solution alternative that satisfies minimal decision criteria. Rather than pursuing all alternatives to identify the single solution that will maximize economic returns, managers will opt for the first solution that appears to solve the problem, even if better solutions are presumed to exist. The decision maker cannot justify the time and expense of obtaining complete information.[24]

An example of both bounded rationality and satisficing occurs when a junior executive on a business trip spills coffee on her blouse just before an important meeting. She will run to a nearby clothing store and buy the first satisfactory replacement she finds. Having neither the time nor the opportunity to explore all the blouses in town, she satisfices by choosing a blouse that will solve the immediate problem. In a similar fashion, managers generate alternatives for complex problems only until they find one they believe will work. For example, several years ago then-Disney chairman Ray Watson and chief operating officer Ron Miller attempted to thwart takeover attempts, but they had limited options. They satisficed with a quick decision to acquire Arivda Realty and Gibson Court Company. The acquisition of these companies had the potential to solve the problem at hand; thus, they looked no further for possibly better alternatives.[25]

The administrative model relies on assumptions different from those of the classical model and focuses on organizational factors that influence individual decisions. It is more realistic than the classical model for complex, nonprogrammed decisions. According to the administrative model,

1. Decision goals often are vague, conflicting, and lack consensus among managers. Managers often are unaware of problems or opportunities that exist in the organization.

2. Rational procedures are not always used, and, when they are, they are confined to a simplistic view of the problem that does not capture the complexity of real organizational events.

3. Managers' search for alternatives is limited because of human, information, and resource constraints.

4. Most managers settle for a satisficing rather than a maximizing solution. This is partly because they have limited information and partly because they have only vague criteria for what constitutes a maximizing solution.

The administrative model is considered to be **descriptive**, meaning that it describes how managers actually make decisions in complex situations rather than dictating how they *should* make decisions according to a theoretical ideal. The administrative model recognizes the human and environmental limitations that affect the degree to which managers can pursue a rational decision-making process.

Intuition. Another aspect of administrative decision making is **intuition**. Intuition represents a quick apprehension of a decision situation based on past

bounded rationality

The concept that people have the time and cognitive ability to process only a limited amount of information on which to base decisions.

satisficing

To choose the first solution alternative that satisfies minimal decision criteria regardless of whether better solutions are presumed to exist.

descriptive

An approach that describes how managers actually make decisions rather than how they should.

intuition

The immediate comprehension of a decision situation based on past experience but without conscious thought.

experience but without conscious thought.[26] Intuitive decision making is not arbitrary or irrational, because it is based on years of practice and hands-on experience that enable managers to quickly identify solutions without going through painstaking computations. In today's fast-paced, uncertain business environment, intuition plays an increasingly important role in decision making. A study of 60 business professionals from a variety of industries, for example, found that nearly half said they relied on intuition often in making decisions in the workplace, while another 30 percent reported using intuition sometimes.[27]

Cognitive psychologist Gary Klein has studied how people make good decisions using their intuition under extreme time pressure and uncertainty.[28] Klein has found that intuition begins with *recognition*. When people build a depth of experience and knowledge in a particular area, the right decision often comes quickly and effortlessly as a recognition of information that has been largely forgotten by the conscious mind. For example, firefighters make decisions by recognizing what is typical or abnormal about a fire, based on their experience, as described in the Best Practices box.

Similarly, in the business world, managers are continuously perceiving and processing information that they may not consciously be aware of, and their base of knowledge and experience helps them make decisions that may be characterized by uncertainty and ambiguity.

The Dodge Viper, which became a smashing success for Chrysler (now DaimlerChrysler) in the 1990s, would never have been made if Bob Lutz, then the company's president, had not followed his gut instinct despite opposition and criticism. In explaining one of the most critical decisions of his career, Lutz says that "it just felt right."[29] Another example comes from the Fox television

BEST PRACTICES

Wildland Firefighters

If you ever fall from a highway overpass onto the metal struts of a sign, just hope you get rescue workers who practice good decision-making on the spot. In such a case, the wrong kind of rescue gear, even a seemingly good position for the victim, can spell disaster. Traditional thinking argues that the rescue worker should carefully consider the many options available. Unfortunately, these situations don't allow for the luxury of decision analysis. According to cognitive psychologist Gary Klein, only novices need to be burdened by the practice of evaluating every possible course of action. Experienced workers know the various consequences so well that they intuitively make the right choice.

Klein's best decision makers are wildland firefighters, who work in the Western U.S., as well as Australia and New Zealand, and are constantly putting out scorching fires. Thereby, they build a rich reservoir of experience to draw upon. Obsessive about learning from experience, they are always doing an after-action-review to see what could have been done better. As for leadership, the top people started at the bottom, so they know what it means to be in the midst of a killer fire. One fire commander claimed he had ESP. During a raging house fire, he ordered the hose team into the house, but the fire blazed on, baffling the commander with its persistence. Then, his so-called "sixth sense" kicked in and he suddenly ordered everyone out of the house. Just as they vacated, the house collapsed. Rather than ESP, Klein says the commander's experience made him see that the fire was not matching his expectations. The fire was burning through the floor, so the sound was quieter than usual and it was hotter than normal, indicating other more treacherous conditions.

What can companies learn from this? Decision-making in times of uncertainty, risk and time pressure requires experience, which allows the person to look for clues or patterns to help guide the course of action. It's the ability to size up a situation quickly. Novices need the decision-making models, but real experience is the best teacher.

SOURCE: Bill Breen, "What's Your Intuition?" *Fast Company* (September 2000), 290–300.

network, where prime time ratings were dismal until Steven Chao came up with "America's Most Wanted" and "Cops." Initially, everyone hated the idea for these raw, crime-oriented shows, but Chao and his boss Barry Diller stuck with their gut feelings and pushed the projects.[30]

Political Model

The third model of decision making is useful for making nonprogrammed decisions when conditions are uncertain, information is limited, and there is disagreement among managers about what goals to pursue or what course of action to take. Most organizational decisions involve many managers who are pursuing different goals, and they have to talk with one another to share information and reach an agreement. Managers often engage in coalition building for making complex organizational decisions. A **coalition** is an informal alliance among managers who support a specific goal. *Coalition building* is the process of forming alliances among managers. In other words, a manager who supports a specific alternative, such as increasing the corporation's growth by acquiring another company, talks informally to other executives and tries to persuade them to support the decision. When the outcomes are not predictable, managers gain support through discussion, negotiation, and bargaining. Without a coalition, a powerful individual or group could derail the decision-making process. Coalition building gives several managers an opportunity to contribute to decision making, enhancing their commitment to the alternative that is ultimately adopted.[31]

> **coalition**
> An informal alliance among managers who support a specific goal.

The political model closely resembles the real environment in which most managers and decision makers operate. Decisions are complex and involve many people, information is often ambiguous, and disagreement and conflict over problems and solutions are normal. There are four basic assumptions of the political model:

1. Organizations are made up of groups with diverse interests, goals, and values. Managers disagree about problem priorities and may not understand or share the goals and interests of other managers.

2. Information is ambiguous and incomplete. The attempt to be rational is limited by the complexity of many problems as well as personal and organizational constraints.

3. Managers do not have the time, resources, or mental capacity to identify all dimensions of the problem and process all relevant information. Managers talk to each other and exchange viewpoints to gather information and reduce ambiguity.

4. Managers engage in the push and pull of debate to decide goals and discuss alternatives. Decisions are the result of bargaining and discussion among coalition members.

One of today's most visible coalition leaders is President George W. Bush, who, following terrorist bombings in the United States, successfully built a coalition of world leaders to support a U.S.-led campaign against terrorism. The inability of leaders to build coalitions often makes it difficult or impossible for managers to see their decisions implemented. Hershell Ezrin resigned as CEO of Canada's Speedy Muffler King because he was unable to build a coalition of managers who supported his decisions for change at the troubled company.

Classical Model	**Administrative Model**	**Political Model**
Clear-cut problem and goals	Vague problem and goals	Pluralistic; conflicting goals
Condition of certainty	Condition of uncertainty	Condition of uncertainty/ambiguity
Full information about alternatives and their outcomes	Limited information about alternatives and their outcomes	Inconsistent viewpoints; ambiguous information
Rational choice by individual for maximizing outcomes	Satisficing choice for resolving problem using intuition	Bargaining and discussion among coalition members

EXHIBIT 6.2

Characteristics of Classical, Administrative, and Political Decision-Making Models

Many senior-level executives resented Ezrin's appointment and refused to go along with his ideas for reviving the company.[32]

The key dimensions of the classical, administrative, and political models are listed in Exhibit 6.2. Recent research into decision-making procedures has found rational, classical procedures to be associated with high performance for organizations in stable environments. However, administrative and political decision-making procedures and intuition have been associated with high performance in unstable environments in which decisions must be made rapidly and under more difficult conditions.[33]

Decision-Making Steps

Whether a decision is programmed or nonprogrammed and regardless of managers' choice of the classical, administrative, or political model of decision making, six steps typically are associated with effective decision processes. These are summarized in Exhibit 6.3.

EXHIBIT 6.3

Six Steps in the Managerial Decision-Making Process

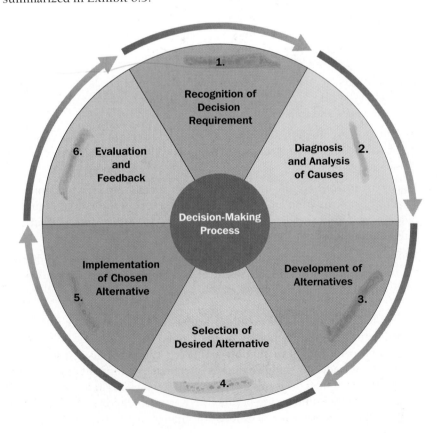

1. Recognition of Decision Requirement
2. Diagnosis and Analysis of Causes
3. Development of Alternatives
4. Selection of Desired Alternative
5. Implementation of Chosen Alternative
6. Evaluation and Feedback

Decision-Making Process

Recognition of Decision Requirement

Managers confront a decision requirement in the form of either a problem or an opportunity. A **problem** occurs when organizational accomplishment is less than established goals. Some aspect of performance is unsatisfactory. An **opportunity** exists when managers see potential accomplishment that exceeds specified current goals. Managers see the possibility of enhancing performance beyond current levels. Oprah Winfrey's agent saw opportunities for her that she never dreamed of, as described in the Focus on Collaboration box.

Awareness of a problem or opportunity is the first step in the decision sequence and requires surveillance of the internal and external environment for issues that merit executive attention.[34] This resembles the military concept of gathering intelligence. Managers scan the world around them to determine whether the organization is satisfactorily progressing toward its goals.

Some information comes from periodic financial reports, performance reports, and other sources that are designed to discover problems before they become too serious. For example, sharply declining sales figures in the Oldsmobile and Buick divisions of General Motors signaled a problem that needed to be addressed. Managers could see that Oldsmobile and Buick had been on a downhill slide for years as the loyal buyers of these brands were aging and the cars failed to appeal to younger buyers.[35] Recognition of the problem led managers to focus on decisions about the fate of these two divisions in their overall efforts to lead GM out of the downturn. Managers also take advantage of informal sources. They talk to other managers, gather opinions on how things are going, and seek advice on which problems should be tackled or which opportunities embraced.[36]

Recognizing decision requirements is difficult, because it often means integrating bits and pieces of information in novel ways.

problem
A situation in which organizational accomplishments have failed to meet established goals.

opportunity
A situation in which managers see potential organizational accomplishments that exceed current goals.

FOCUS ON COLLABORATION

Oprah, Inc.

With her Oprah Brand designed around the mantra "You are responsible for your own life," it might seem strange that Oprah Winfrey describes her decision making as "leaps of faith" and that she embraces a management-by-instinct style. But that's not the whole story. The other part of the picture is about her business manager, Jeff Jacobs, who is president of Oprah's company, Harpo, Inc. He was a young entertainment lawyer when the T-shirt- and flip-flop-wearing Oprah asked for help in 1984 with a new contract. With an instinct for business potential, Jacobs convinced her to invest in herself, rather than remaining an actor-for-hire, which is how most entertainers are employed.

While Oprah develops her themes and images, Jacobs works behind the scenes keeping the business running and making tough decisions. Every gut instinct that Oprah has is backed up with Jacobs's realistic business experience, which includes knowing when to "multipurpose the content," for example. That means that Dr. Phil appears on Oprah, writes a column in Harpo's *O Magazine*, and will also be spun off with his own Harpo-produced TV show. Oprah still has a strong sense of her mission, and her decisions follow her purpose and values. Sometimes her wishes clash with business concerns. She decided to place the *O Magazine* table of contents on page 2, rather than the more common page 22. Advertisers prefer that people wade through their glossy ads before finding the contents. But Oprah wouldn't have it. "Let's put the readers first," she commanded.

Oprah tries to live up to her message—to be strong, courageous, and a good role model. She has yet to make the decision to give up control of her brand—Oprah—unlike Martha Stewart, who sold her name rights to now-bankrupt Kmart, and also took her company public. Oprah feels strongly about maintaining her individuality in the process. "If I lost control of the business, I'd lose myself or at least the ability to be myself. Owning is a way to be myself." She deeply regrets her decision, based on financial gain, to sell rights to Oprah reruns. "It's not a commodity. It's my soul. It's who I am."

SOURCE: Patricia Sellers, "The Business of Being Oprah," *Fortune* (April 1, 2002) 50–64.

Diagnosis and Analysis

diagnosis

The step in the decision-making process in which managers analyze underlying causal factors associated with the decision situation.

Once a problem or opportunity has come to a manager's attention, the understanding of the situation should be refined. **Diagnosis** is the step in the decision-making process in which managers analyze underlying causal factors associated with the decision situation. Managers make a mistake here if they jump right into generating alternatives without first exploring the cause of the problem more deeply.

Kepner and Tregoe, who have conducted extensive studies of manager decision making, recommend that managers ask a series of questions to specify underlying causes, including the following:

- What is the state of disequilibrium affecting us?
- When did it occur?
- Where did it occur?
- How did it occur?
- To whom did it occur?
- What is the urgency of the problem?
- What is the interconnectedness of events?
- What result came from which activity?[37]

Such questions help specify what actually happened and why. Managers at Yahoo! are struggling to diagnose the underlying factors in the company's recent troubles. The problem is an urgent one, as the stock price has fallen dramatically, advertising sales have plunged, and numerous executives, including the heads of four international units, have resigned. As Yahoo! scrambles to remain an important part of the Internet, managers are looking at the interconnectedness of issues such as the dot-com crash and declining economy, the failure of top executives to delegate responsibility as the company grew larger, aggressive and arrogant sales tactics that alienated "old economy" clients, the lack of effective control systems, and an insular culture that caused Yahoo! to lose experienced executives from acquired companies and miss out on some important opportunities.[38]

© Sian Kennedy

More than 100 customers recently reported fraudulent charges to their credit cards immediately after placing an order with UltiMutt, a $300,000 Web-based business that designs and sells posters combining dogs and motivational quotes. Diagnosis of the problem for business owners Ron Johnson and Lori Scherping involved understanding how hackers gained access to their site. Further analysis led Johnson and Scherping to discover that international hackers had stolen UltiMutt's on-line customer database. Within hours, software engineers updated the site's shopping cart software and security was reinstated. "Whatever doesn't kill me makes me stronger," states Johnson, who is now working on a way to eliminate the need to store customer data on his server.

Development of Alternatives

Once the problem or opportunity has been recognized and analyzed, decision makers begin to consider taking action. The next stage is to generate possible alternative solutions that will respond to the needs of the situation and correct the underlying causes. One study found that limiting the search for alternatives is a primary cause of decision failure in organizations.[39]

For a programmed decision, feasible alternatives are easy to identify and in fact usually are already available within the organization's rules and procedures. Nonprogrammed decisions, however, require developing new courses of action that will meet the company's needs. For decisions made under conditions of high uncertainty, managers may develop only one or two custom solutions that will satisfice for handling the problem.

Decision alternatives can be thought of as the tools for reducing the difference between the organization's current and desired performance. At General Motors, executives considered alternatives such as attempting to revive the Oldsmobile and Buick divisions through increased marketing, closing down one or both divisions, or taking the risk of authorizing one of the divisions to bring out a bold new vehicle model. Eventually, GM decided to pull the plug on its 103-year-old Oldsmobile line and bring out a different kind of Buick, a "crossover" that looks like a sport-utility vehicle, drives like a car, and is Buick's first departure from its line of stodgy sedans. Buick and GM managers hope the contemporary, thoughtful design of the Rendezvous will appeal to younger drivers, especially women, who represent a growing percentage of new car buyers.[40]

Selection of Desired Alternative

Once feasible alternatives have been developed, one must be selected. The decision choice is the selection of the most promising of several alternative courses of action. The best alternative is one in which the solution best fits the overall goals and values of the organization and achieves the desired results using the fewest resources.[41] The manager tries to select the choice with the least amount of risk and uncertainty. Because some risk is inherent for most nonprogrammed decisions, managers try to gauge prospects for success. Under conditions of uncertainty, they might have to rely on their intuition and experience to estimate whether a given course of action is likely to succeed. Basing choices on overall goals and values can also effectively guide selection of alternatives. For example, stockbroker Edward Jones was hit hard by the gloomy stock market and the declining economy following the September 11, 2001 terrorist attacks in the United States. To make decisions about how to cope, managers relied on the company's values and goals of treating employees right and building long-term relationships. Not a single employee was laid off, and although bonuses were reduced, the company issued them a week early to help employees who were hurt by the trading decline. Edward Jones's values-based decision making helped win the company the Number 1 spot on *Fortune* magazine's 2001 list of best companies to work for.[42]

Making choices depends on managers' personality factors and willingness to accept risk and uncertainty. For example, **risk propensity** is the willingness to undertake risk with the opportunity of gaining an increased payoff. The level of risk a manager is willing to accept will influence the analysis of cost and benefits to be derived from any decision. Consider the situations in Exhibit 6.4: Which alternative would you choose? A person with a low risk propensity would tend to take assured moderate returns by going for a tie score, building a domestic plant, or pursuing a career as a physician. A risk taker would go for the victory, build a plant in a foreign country, or embark on an acting career.

risk propensity
The willingness to undertake risk with the opportunity of gaining an increased payoff.

For each of the following decisions, which alternative would you choose?
1. In the final seconds of a game with the college's traditional rival, the coach of a college football team may choose a play that has a 95 percent chance of producing a tie score or one with a 30 percent chance of leading to victory or to sure defeat if it fails.
2. The president of a Canadian company must decide whether to build a new plant within Canada that has a 90 percent chance of producing a modest return on investment or to build it in a foreign country with an unstable political history. The latter alternative has a 40 percent chance of failing, but the returns would be enormous if it succeeded.
3. A college senior with considerable acting talent must choose a career. She has the opportunity to go on to medical school and become a physician, a career in which she is 80 percent likely to succeed. She would rather be an actress but realizes that the opportunity for success is only 20 percent.

EXHIBIT 6.4

Decision Alternatives with Different Levels of Risk

Implementation of Chosen Alternative

The **implementation** stage involves the use of managerial, administrative, and persuasive abilities to ensure that the chosen alternative is carried out. This is similar to the idea of strategic implementation described in Chapter 5. The ultimate success of the chosen alternative depends on whether it can be translated into action. Sometimes an alternative never becomes reality because managers lack the resources or energy needed to make things happen. Implementation may require discussion with people affected by the decision. Communication, motivation, and leadership skills must be used to see that the decision is carried out.

At General Motors, Chief Executive Rick Wagoner has hired new top executives, including Bob Lutz, former product development chief at Chrysler, who share his vision and can help to implement his decisions for livening up GM's global product portfolio. Paul J. Liska, executive vice president and CFO at the St. Paul Cos., a commercial insurer, successfully implemented decisions that led to annual cost savings of about $500 million and kept the company competitive in the cutthroat insurance industry. For example, Liska revised incentive plans to persuade managers to go along with some of the cost-reduction decisions.[43] If managers lack the ability or desire to implement decisions, the chosen alternative cannot be carried out to benefit the organization.

Evaluation and Feedback

In the evaluation stage of the decision process, decision makers gather information that tells them how well the decision was implemented and whether it was effective in achieving its goals. For example, Tandy executives evaluated their decision to open computer centers for business and feedback revealed poor sales performance. Feedback indicated that implementation was unsuccessful, and computer centers were closed so Tandy could focus on its successful Radio Shack retail stores.

Feedback is important because decision making is a continuous, never-ending process. Decision making is not completed when an executive or board of directors votes yes or no. Feedback provides decision makers with information that can precipitate a new decision cycle. The decision may fail, thus generating a new analysis of the problem, evaluation of alternatives, and selection of a new alternative. Many big problems are solved by trying several alternatives in sequence, each providing modest improvement. Feedback is the part of monitoring that assesses whether a new decision needs to be made.

An illustration of the overall decision-making process, including evaluation and feedback, was the decision to introduce a new deodorant at Tom's of Maine.

Tom's of Maine

http://www.tomsofmaine.com

Tom's of Maine, known for its all-natural personal hygiene products, saw an opportunity to expand its line with a new natural deodorant. However, the opportunity quickly became a problem when the deodorant worked only half of the time with half of the customers who used it, and its all-recyclable plastic dials were prone to breakage.

The problem of the failed deodorant led founder Tom Chappell and other managers to analyze and diagnose what went wrong. They finally determined that the company's product development process had run amok. The same group of merry product developers was responsible from conception to launch of the product. They were so attached to the product that they failed to test it properly or consider potential problems, becoming instead "a mutual admiration society." Managers considered several alternatives for solving the problem. The decision to publicly admit the problem and recall the deodorant was an easy one for Chappell, who runs his company on principles of fairness and honesty. Not only did the company apologize to customers, but it also listened to their complaints and suggestions. Chappell himself helped answer calls and letters. Although the recall cost $400,000 and led to a stream of negative publicity, it ultimately helped the company improve relationships with customers.

Evaluation and feedback also led Tom's of Maine to set up "acorn groups," from which it hopes mighty oaks of successful products will grow. Acorn groups are cross-departmental teams that will shepherd new products from beginning to end. The cross-functional teams are a mechanism for catching problems—and new opportunities—that ordinarily would be missed. They pass on their ideas and findings to senior managers and the product-development team.

Tom's was able to turn a problem into an opportunity, thanks to evaluation and feedback. Not only did the disaster ultimately help the company solidify relationships with customers, but it also led to a formal mechanism for learning and sharing ideas—something the company did not have before.[44]

Tom's of Maine's decision illustrates all the decision steps, and the process ultimately ended in success. Strategic decisions always contain some risk, but feedback and follow-up decisions can help get companies back on track. By learning from their decision mistakes, managers and companies can turn problems into opportunities.

Personal Decision Framework

Imagine you were a manager at Tom's of Maine, Yahoo!, a local movie theater, or the public library. How would you go about making important decisions that might shape the future of your department or company? So far we have discussed a number of factors that affect how managers make decisions. For example, decisions may be programmed or nonprogrammed, situations are characterized by various levels of uncertainty, and managers may use the classical, administrative, or political model of decision making. In addition, there are six recognized steps to take in the decision-making process.

However, not all managers go about making decisions in the same way. In fact, there are significant differences in the ways individual managers may approach problems and make decisions concerning them. These differences can be explained by the concept of personal decision styles. Exhibit 6.5 illustrates the role of personal style in the decision-making process. Personal **decision style** refers to differences among people with respect to how they perceive problems

decision style
Differences among people with respect to how they perceive problems and make decisions.

EXHIBIT 6.5

Personal Decision Framework

Situation	Personal Decision Style	Decision Choice
• Programmed/nonprogrammed • Classical, administrative, political • Decision steps	• Directive • Analytical • Conceptual • Behavioral	• Best solution to problem

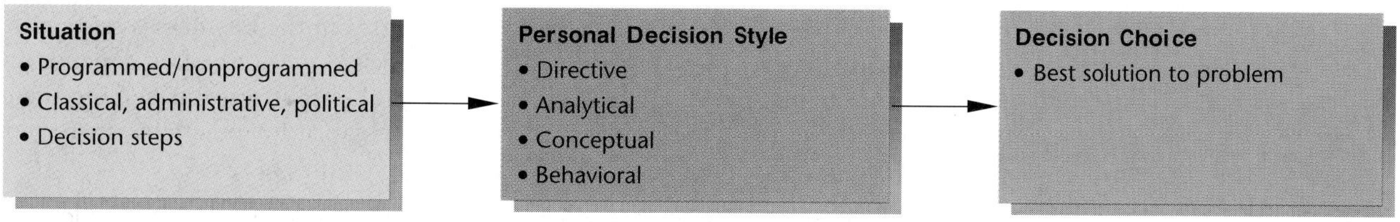

and make decisions. Research has identified four major decision styles: directive, analytical, conceptual, and behavioral.[45]

1. The *directive style* is used by people who prefer simple, clear-cut solutions to problems. Managers who use this style often make decisions quickly because they do not like to deal with a lot of information and may consider only one or two alternatives. People who prefer the directive style generally are efficient and rational and prefer to rely on existing rules or procedures for making decisions.

2. Managers with an *analytical style* like to consider complex solutions based on as much data as they can gather. These individuals carefully consider alternatives and often base their decisions on objective, rational data from management control systems and other sources. They search for the best possible decision based on the information available.

3. People who tend toward a *conceptual style* also like to consider a broad amount of information. However, they are more socially oriented than those with an analytical style and like to talk to others about the problem and possible alternatives for solving it. Managers using a conceptual style consider many broad alternatives, rely on information from both people and systems, and like to solve problems creatively.

4. The *behavioral style* is often the style adopted by managers having a deep concern for others as individuals. Managers using this style like to talk to people one-on-one and understand their feelings about the problem and the effect of a given decision upon them. People with a behavioral style usually are concerned with the personal development of others and may make decisions that help others achieve their goals.

Most managers have a dominant decision style. For example, every Friday, Richard Scrushy, founder and CEO of HealthSouth, reviews a stack of computer printouts concerning every detail of the performance of each facility in his chain of outpatient orthopedic clinics.[46] Scrushy likes to have as much data as he can to help him make decisions regarding the $4 billion company. However, managers frequently use several different styles or a combination of styles in making the varied decisions they confront daily. For example, a manager might use a directive style for deciding on which printing company to use for new business cards, yet shift to a more conceptual style when handling an interdepartmental conflict. The most effective managers are able to shift among styles as needed to meet the situation. Being aware of one's dominant decision style can help a manager avoid making critical mistakes when his or her usual style may be inappropriate to the problem at hand.

Increasing Participation in Decision Making

Managers do make some decisions as individuals, but decision makers more often are part of a group. Indeed, major decisions in the business world rarely are made entirely by an individual. Effective decision making often depends on whether managers involve the right people in the right ways in helping them solve problems.[47] One model that provides guidance for practicing managers was originally developed by Victor Vroom and Arthur Jago.[48]

1 Better decisions
2 more support
3 faster implementation

The Vroom-Jago Model

The **Vroom-Jago model** helps a manager gauge the appropriate amount of participation by subordinates in making a specific decision. The model has three major components: leader participation styles, a set of diagnostic questions with which to analyze a decision situation, and a series of decision rules.

Vroom-Jago model

A model designed to help managers gauge the amount of subordinate participation in decision making.

Leader Participation Styles. The model employs five levels of subordinate participation in decision making ranging from highly autocratic (leader decides alone) to highly democratic (leader delegates to group), as illustrated in Exhibit 6.6.[49] The exhibit shows five decision styles, starting with the leader making the decision alone (Decide); presenting the problem to subordinates individually for their suggestions and then making the decision (Consult Individually); presenting the problem to subordinates as a group, collectively obtaining their ideas and suggestions, then making the decision (Consult Group); sharing the problem with subordinates as a group and acting as a facilitator to help the group arrive at a decision (Facilitate); or delegating the problem and permitting the group to make the decision within prescribed limits (Delegate).

Diagnostic Questions. How does a manager decide which of the five decision styles to use? The appropriate degree of decision participation depends on a number of situational factors, such as the required level of decision quality, the level of leader or subordinate expertise, and the importance of having

EXHIBIT *6.6*

Five Leader Participation Styles

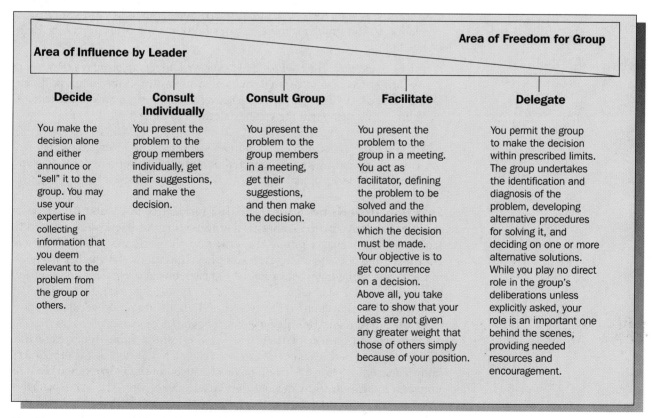

SOURCE: Victor H. Vroom, "Leadership and the Decision Making Process," *Organizational Dynamics* 28, 4 (Spring 2000), 82–94. This is Vroom's adaptation of Tannenbaum and Schmidt's Taxonomy. Used with permission.

subordinates commit to the decision. Leaders can analyze the appropriate degree of participation by answering seven diagnostic questions.

1. *Decision Significance: How significant is this decision for the project or organization?* If the quality of the decision is highly important to the success of the project or organization, the leader has to be actively involved.

2. *Importance of Commitment: How important is subordinate commitment to carrying out the decision?* If implementation requires a high level of commitment to the decision, leaders should involve subordinates in the decision process.

3. *Leader Expertise: What is the level of the leader's expertise in relation to the problem?* If the leader does not have a high amount of information, knowledge, or expertise, the leader should involve subordinates to obtain it.

4. *Likelihood of Commitment: If the leader were to make the decision alone, would subordinates have high or low commitment to the decision?* If subordinates typically go along with whatever the leader decides, their involvement in the decision-making process will be less important.

5. *Group Support for Goals: What is the degree of subordinate support for the team's or organization's objectives at stake in this decision?* If subordinates have low support for the goals of the organization, the leader should not allow the group to make the decision alone.

6. *Group Expertise: What is the level of group members' knowledge and expertise in relation to the problem?* If subordinates have a high level of expertise in relation to the problem, more responsibility for the decision can be delegated to them.

7. *Team Competence: How skilled and committed are group members to working together as a team to solve problems?* When subordinates have high skills and high desire to work together cooperatively to solve problems, more responsibility for decision making can be delegated to them.

These questions seem detailed, but considering these seven situational factors can quickly narrow the options and point to the appropriate level of group participation in decision making.

Selecting a Decision Style. The decision matrix in Exhibit 6.7 allows a manager to adopt a participation style by answering the diagnostic questions in sequence. The manager enters the matrix at the left-hand side, at Problem Statement, and considers the seven situational questions in sequence from left to right, answering high (H) or low (L) to each one and avoiding crossing any horizontal lines. The first question would be: *How significant is this decision for the project or organization?* If the answer is High, the leader proceeds to importance of commitment: *How important is subordinate commitment to carrying out the decision?* An answer of High leads to a question about leader expertise: *What is the level of the leader's expertise in relation to the problem?* If the leader's knowledge and expertise is High, the leader next considers likelihood of commitment: *If the leader were to make the decision alone, how likely is it that subordinates would be committed to the decision?* If there is a high likelihood that subordinates would be committed, the decision matrix leads directly to the Decide style of decision making, in which the leader makes the decision alone and presents it to the group.

EXHIBIT 6.7

Vroom-Jago Decision Model for Determining an Appropriate Decision-Making Style— Group Problems

Instructions: The matrix operates like a funnel. You start at the left with a specific decision problem in mind. The column headings denote situational factors which may or may not be present in that problem. You progress by selecting High or Low (H or L) for each relevant situational factor. Proceed down the funnel, judging only those situational factors for which a judgement is called for, until you reach the recommended process.

	Decision Significance?	Importance of Commitment?	Leader Expertise?	Likelihood of Commitment?	Group Support?	Group Expertise?	Team Competence?	
P R O B L E M S T A T E M E N T	H	H	H	H	–	–	–	Decide
				L	H	H	H	Delegate
							L	Consult (Group)
						L	–	Consult (Group)
					L	–	–	Consult (Group)
			L	H	H	H	H	Facilitate
							L	Consult (Individually)
						L	–	Consult (Individually)
					L	–	–	Consult (Individually)
				L	H	H	H	Facilitate
							L	Consult (Group)
						L	–	Consult (Group)
					L	–	–	Consult (Group)
		L	H	–	–	–	–	Decide
			L	–	H	H	H	Facilitate
							L	Consult (Individually)
						L	–	Consult (Individually)
					L	–	–	Consult (Individually)
	L	H	–	H	–	–	–	Decide
				L	–	–	H	Delegate
							L	Facilitate
		L	–	–	–	–	–	Decide

SOURCE: Victor H. Vroom, "Leadership and the Decision-Making Process," *Organizational Dynamics* 28, no. 4 (Spring 2000), 82–94. Used with permission.

The Vroom-Jago model has been criticized as being less than perfect,[50] but it is useful to managers, and the body of supportive research is growing.[51] Managers can use the model to make timely, high-quality decisions. Consider the application of the model to a problem at Madison Manufacturing.

Madison Manufacturing

When Madison Manufacturing won a coveted contract from a large auto manufacturer to produce an engine to power their flagship sports car, Dave Robbins was thrilled to be selected as project manager. This project has dramatically enhanced the reputation of Madison, and Robbins and his team of engineers have taken great pride in their work. However, their enthusiasm was dashed by a recent report of serious engine problems in cars delivered to customers. Taking quick action, the auto manufacturer suspended sales of the sports car, halted current production, and notified owners of the current model not to drive the car. Everyone involved knows this is a disaster. Unless the engine problem is solved quickly, Madison Manufacturing could be exposed to extended litigation. In addition, Madison's valued relationship with one of the world's largest auto manufacturers would likely be lost forever.

As the project manager, Robbins has spent two weeks in the field inspecting the seized engines and the auto plant where they were installed. Based on this extensive research, Robbins has some pretty good ideas about what is causing the problem, but he knows there are members of his team who may have stronger expertise for solving it. In addition, while he has been in the field, other team members have been carefully evaluating the operations and practices in Madison's plant where the engine is manufactured. Therefore, Robbins chooses to get the team together and discuss the problem before making his final decision. The group meets for several hours, discussing the problem in detail and sharing their varied perspectives, including the information Robbins and team members have gathered. Following the group session, Robbins makes his decision, which will be presented at the team meeting the following morning, after which testing and correction of the engine problem will begin.[52]

The Vroom-Jago model in Exhibit 6.7 shows that Robbins used the correct decision style. Moving from left to right in Exhibit 6.7, the questions and answers are as follows: *How significant is the decision?* Definitely high. The company's future might be at stake. *How important is subordinate commitment to the decision?* Also high. The team members must support and implement Robbins's solution. *What is the level of Robbins's information and expertise?* Probably low. Even though he has spent several weeks researching the seized engines, other team members have additional information and expertise that needs to be considered. *If Robbins makes the decision on his own, would team members have high or low commitment to it?* The answer to this question is probably also low. Even though team members respect Robbins, they take pride in their work as a team and know Robbins does not have complete information. This leads to the question, *What is the degree of subordinate support for the team's or organization's objectives at stake in this decision?* Definitely high. This leads to the question, *What is the level of group members' knowledge and expertise in relation to the problem?* The answer to this question is low, which leads to the Consult Group decision style, as described earlier in Exhibit 6.6. Thus, Robbins used the style that would be recommended by the Vroom-Jago model.

In many situations, several decision styles might be equally acceptable. However, in today's workplace, managers are encouraging greater employee participation in solving problems whenever possible. Broad participation often leads to better decisions. Involving others in decision making also contributes to individual and organizational learning, which is critical for rapid decision making in the new workplace.

New Decision Approaches for the New Workplace

The ability to make fast, widely supported, high-quality decisions on a frequent basis is a critical skill in today's fast-moving organizations.[53] In many industries, the rate of competitive and technological change is so extreme that opportunities are fleeting, clear and complete information is seldom available, and the cost of a slow decision means lost business or even company failure. Does this mean managers in today's workplace should make the majority of decisions on their own? No. The rapid pace of today's business environment calls for just the opposite—that is, for people throughout the organization to be involved in decision making and have the information, skills, and freedom they need to respond immediately to problems and questions. Managers—as well as employees throughout the organization—often have to act first and analyze later.[54] There is no time for top managers to evaluate options, conduct research, develop alternatives, and tell people what to do and how to do it. When speed matters, a slow decision may be as ineffective as the wrong decision, and companies can learn to make decisions fast. Effective decision making in today's fast-moving businesses relies on the following guidelines.

Learn, Don't Punish. Decisions made under conditions of uncertainty and time pressure produce many errors, but managers in the new workplace are willing to take the risk in the spirit of trial and error. If a chosen decision alternative fails, the organization can learn from it and try another alternative that better fits the situation. Each failure provides new information and learning. People throughout the organization are encouraged to take risks and learn from their mistakes. Good managers know that every time a person makes a decision, whether it turns out to have positive or negative consequences, it helps the employee learn and be a better decision maker the next time around. By making mistakes, people go through the process of *decision learning,* which means that they gain valuable experience and knowledge to perform more effectively in the future.

When people are afraid to make mistakes, the company is stuck. For example, when Robert Crandall led American Airlines, he built a culture in which any problem that caused a flight delay was followed by finding someone to blame. People became so scared of making a mistake that whenever something went wrong, no one was willing to jump in and try to fix the problem. In contrast, Southwest Airlines uses what it calls *team delay,* which means a flight delay is everyone's problem. This puts the emphasis on fixing the problem rather than on finding an individual to blame.[55] In the new workplace, managers do not use mistakes and failure to create a climate of fear. Instead, they encourage people to take risks and move ahead with the decision process, despite the potential for errors. At the Brady Corporation, described in this chapter's Focus on Collaboration box, managers used humor to break down a culture of fear and mistrust.

Know When to Bail. Even though the new workplace encourages risk taking and learning from mistakes, it also teaches people to know when to pull the plug on something that is not working. Research has found that organizations often continue to invest time and money in a solution despite strong evidence that it is not appropriate. This tendency is referred to as **escalating commitment.** Managers might block or distort negative information because they don't want to be responsible for a bad decision, or they might simply refuse to accept that their solution is wrong. In today's successful companies, people don't get so attached to their own ideas that they're unwilling to recognize when to move on. According to Stanford University professor Robert Sutton, the key to successful creative decision making is to "fail early, fail often, and pull the plug early."[56]

escalating commitment
Continuing to invest time and resources in a failing decision.

Practice the Five Whys. One way to encourage good decision making under high uncertainty is to get people to think more broadly and deeply about problems rather than going with a superficial understanding and a first response. However, this doesn't mean people have to spend hours analyzing a problem and gathering research. One simple procedure adopted by a number of leading companies is known as the *five whys.*[57] For every problem, employees learn to ask "Why?" not just once, but five times. The first *why* generally produces

FOCUS ON COLLABORATION

At Brady: "From No to Yo"

The Brady Corporation was founded in 1914 as a maker of advertising calendars and tin road signs. The founder, William H. Brady, Jr., who served as CEO for 30 years, instilled a patriarchal, conservative, and cautious culture that became entrenched in the organization. In fact, Brady Corp. took business so seriously that coffee was not even allowed at employees' desks until 1989. No wonder that, when Katherine M. Hudson came to Brady as president and CEO in 1994, employees seemed exceptionally uptight and guarded.

Hudson also discovered that the uptight culture had led to some serious problems at the company, which now had 3,200 employees, ran operations in 20 countries, and sold about 50,000 different products. For example, she found that local managers of two Canadian units had barely communicated with one another for 15 years due to old conflicts and mistrust. Then, the cautious side of the culture became apparent to Hudson on a trip to Asia, when a manager timidly asked if he could "hire another half person." The manager was shocked when Hudson told him he could hire five more people if he could give her a business justification for it.

Hudson began referring to the reluctance to collaborate and the fear of taking risks as a *culture of no*. She was determined to get people to say yes to information sharing, yes to cooperation, and yes to risk-taking and learning. To encourage an open, collaborative, reliable, can-do climate, Hudson coined an official corporate motto, "from no to yo." To give manufacturing workers more power and flexibility, she instituted flextime and began treating blue-collar employees like salaried workers. This approach empowered workers and gave them more authority and responsibility for making decisions, enabling them to get the job done without managers looking over their shoulders. Now, an employee needs to juggle his schedule, he works it out with team members rather than going to a manager. The company also emphasizes honesty with employees, customers, and the community to build trust and encourage flexible behavior. Hudson wants employees to feel confident enough to take risks, acknowledge mistakes, and share their experience with co-workers.

Another way to get people to go from no to yo was to get everyone to loosen up and enjoy themselves. Hudson set out to make fun a fundamental part of Brady's new culture—and she had solid business reasons for doing so. The benefits of the new, more relaxed approach are many. Jealously guarded turf boundaries have broken down, and a company-wide *esprit de corps* has taken their place. Hudson also believes humor helps people make better decisions because it relieves stress, promotes creativity, opens people up to new ideas, and encourages people to take action. Fear limits decision making power, and a fun, friendly work environment overcomes fear. "Our performance is a sign that a company can be fun and friendly for its employees and fierce with its competitors," Hudson says. In fact, the fun has made us fiercer, by making the organization more flexible and dynamic and our people more creative and enthusiastic," Needless to say, it has probably also made Brady a more enjoyable place to work.

SOURCE: Katherine M. Hudson, "One Laugh at a Time," *Harvard Business Review* (July–August 2001), 45–54.

---

a superficial explanation for the problem, and each subsequent *why* probes deeper into the causes of the problem and potential solutions. The point of the *five whys* is to improve how people think about problems and generate alternatives for solving them.

Build Collective Intuition. Earlier in the chapter, we discussed the role of intuition in decision making. Managers in the new workplace encourage people to develop and use their intuition on an individual level as they make rapid decisions to serve customers. However, they also build what has been called *collective intuition* for making complex, uncertain organizational decisions.[58] Just as an individual develops his or her intuition based on knowledge and experience, collective intuition comes from the combined knowledge, experience, and understanding of the group.

Managers may hold frequent "don't miss" meetings at which they discuss real-time information that helps them perceive problems and opportunities sooner and more completely. For example, top managers at one highly successful computer company are known for being able to respond to threats or opportunities at the drop of a hat. They do it by constantly tracking internal and external information and then discussing it in regular, intensive meetings. The broad sharing of information and interplay of diverse ideas at group meetings develop a deeper understanding of problems and ensure that people consider different sides of an issue before developing alternatives and reaching solutions. Research has shown that bringing people together to discuss problems and decision alternatives in a group leads to more effective decision making than having a manager consult with each member individually.[59] One reason for this is the collective intuition of the group.

Engage in Constructive Conflict. A technique for better group decision making is to encourage constructive conflict. Managers in today's successful companies recognize that conflict based on divergent points of view can bring a problem into focus, stimulate creative thinking, create a broader understanding of issues and alternatives, and improve decision quality.[60] Constructive conflict means that the conflict is related to the work and the issue or problem at hand, not to personal or political rivalries.

There are several ways to stimulate constructive conflict. One way is by ensuring that the group is diverse in terms of age and gender, functional area of expertise, hierarchical level, and experience with the business. Some groups assign a **devil's advocate**, who has the role of challenging the assumptions and assertions made by the group.[61] The devil's advocate may force the group to rethink its approach to the problem and avoid reaching premature conclusions. Another approach is to have group members develop as many alternatives as they can as quickly as they can.[62] This allows the team to work with multiple alternatives and encourages people to advocate ideas they might not prefer simply to encourage debate. Still another way to encourage constructive conflict is to use a technique called **point-counterpoint**, which breaks a decision-making group into two subgroups and assigns them different, often competing responsibilities.[63] The groups then develop proposals and discuss and debate the various options until they arrive at a common set of understandings and recommendations.

Decision making in today's high-speed, complex environment is one of the most important—and most challenging—responsibilities for managers. By involving others, learning from mistakes rather than assigning blame, knowing when to bail, practicing the *five whys*, building collective intuition, and engaging in constructive conflict, managers can improve the quality and effectiveness of decision making.

devil's advocate

A decision-making technique in which an individual is assigned the role of challenging the assumptions and assertions made by the group to prevent premature consensus.

point-counterpoint

A decision-making technique in which people are assigned to express competing points of view.

Using Information Technology for Decision Making

Almost every company uses some form of information technology. Indeed, the strategic use of information technology is one of the defining aspects of organizational success in today's world. A classic example is the success of Wal-Mart, which can be traced partly to the extensive use of technology to manage every aspect of the business. Managers use information systems that rely on a massive data warehouse to make decisions about what to stock, how to price and promote it, and when to reorder or discontinue items. Handheld scanners enable managers to keep close tabs on inventory and monitor sales; at the end of each workday, orders for new merchandise are sent by computer to headquarters, where they are automatically organized and sent to regional distribution centers, which have electronic linkages with key suppliers for reordering. Back at headquarters, top executives analyze buying patterns and other information, enabling them to spot problems or opportunities and convey the information to stores.[64] Many other companies, in industries from manufacturing to entertainment, are using information technology to get closer to customers, enter new markets, and streamline business processes.

Information technology and e-business have changed the way people and organizations work and thus present new challenges for managers. We begin by developing a basic understanding of information technology and the types of information systems frequently used in organizations. Then, we will look at the growing use of the Internet and e-business, including a discussion of fundamental e-business strategies, business-to-business marketplaces, use of information technology in business operations, and the importance of knowledge management. The following section will discuss the management implications of using new information technology. Finally, we will briefly examine some emerging information technology trends.

Information Technology

information technology

The hardware, software, telecommunications, database management, and other technologies used to store, process, and distribute information.

An organization's **information technology** consists of the hardware, software, telecommunications, database management, and other technologies it uses to store data and make them available in the form of information for organizational decision making.

By providing managers with more information more quickly than ever before, modern information technology improves efficiency and effectiveness at each stage of the strategic decision-making process. Whether through computer-aided manufacturing, information sharing with customers, or international inventory control, information technology aids operational processes and decision making. Consider the case of American Greetings Corporation, which sells greeting cards in about 35,000 retail locations in the United States. The company uses information technology to gather and analyze data to test the popularity of new card designs, automate production of cards, identify which kinds of cards will sell best at particular stores, fill orders, and report to retailers on the performance of American Greetings' displays in their stores. By combining efficiency through automation with a precisely targeted and well-tested product line, American Greetings stays profitable and helps its customers, the retailers, to be profitable as well.[65]

Data versus Information

data

Raw, unsummarized, and unanalyzed facts and figures.

information

Data that have been converted into a meaningful and useful context for the receiver.

The ability to generate more data with technology presents a serious challenge to information technicians, managers, and other users of information. They must sort through overwhelming amounts of data to identify only that which is necessary for a particular purpose. **Data** are raw facts and figures that in and of themselves may not be useful. To be useful, data must be processed into finished **information**—that is, data that have been converted into a meaningful and useful context for specific users. An increasing challenge for managers is being able to effectively identify and access useful information. American Greetings, for example, might gather *data* about demographics in various parts of the country. These data are then translated into *information;* for example, stores in Florida require an enormous assortment of greeting cards directed at grandson, granddaughter, niece, and nephew, while stores in some other parts of the country might need a larger percentage of slightly irreverent, youth-oriented products.

The magnitude of the job of transforming data into useful information is reflected in organizations' introduction of the chief information officer (CIO) position. CIOs are responsible for managing organizational databases and implementing new information technology. As they make decisions involving the adoption of new technologies, CIOs integrate old and new technologies to support organizational decision making, operations, and communication. Effective CIOs not only manage the technology infrastructure but also focus on information design, so that managers have high-quality information to improve decision making, problem solving, and performance.[66] Ideally, the CIO combines knowledge of information technology with the ability to help managers and employees identify their information needs, as well as ways the organization can use its IT capabilities to support its strategy. An important part of the CIO's job is shaping disjointed data into clear, meaningful, and useful information.

Characteristics of Useful Information

Organizations depend on high-quality information to develop strategic plans, identify problems, and interact with other organizations. Information is of high quality if it has characteristics that make it useful for these tasks. The characteristics of useful information fall into three broad categories, as illustrated in Exhibit 6.8.

1. *Time.* Information should be available and provided when needed, up to date, and related to the appropriate time period (past, present, or future).

2. *Content.* Useful information is error free, suited to the user's needs, complete, concise, relevant (that is, it excludes unnecessary data), and an accurate measure of performance.

3. *Form.* The information should be provided in a form that is easy for the user to understand and that meets the user's needs for the level of detail. The presentation should be ordered and use the combination of words, numbers, and diagrams that is most helpful to the user. Also, information should be presented in a useful medium (printed documents, video display, sound).

You may live in the United States, but it is possible for you to access your financial information at this Citibank facility in Budapest, Hungary. Due to advances in information technology, the banking industry has developed complex databases to provide financial information globally, and it is estimated that by the year 2010, four to five billion people worldwide will be active users of a vast range of financial products and services. Today, Citibank's business is as much information and communications as financial services.

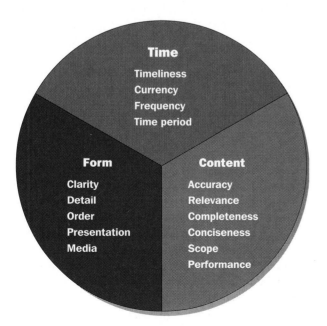

E X H I B I T **6.8**

Characteristics of High-Quality Information

SOURCE: Adapted from James A. O'Brien, *Introduction to Information Systems,* 8th ed. (Burr Ridge, IL: Irwin, 1997), 284–285.

Types of Information Systems

Most managers today appreciate the value of making information readily available in some kind of formal, computer-based information system. Such a system combines hardware, software, and human resources to support organizational information and communication needs. One way to distinguish among the many types of information systems is to focus on the functions they perform and the people they serve in an organization. Two broad categories of information systems widely used today are shown in Exhibit 6.9. Operations information systems support information-processing needs of a business's day-to-day operations, as well as low-level operations management functions. Management information systems typically support the strategic decision-making needs of higher-level managers.

Operations Information Systems

operations information system
A computer-based information system that supports a company's day-to-day operations.

A variety of systems, called **operations information systems**, support the information-processing needs related to a business's day-to-day operations. Types of operations information systems include transaction-processing systems, process control systems, and office automation systems. Each of these supports daily operations and decisions that typically are made by nonmanagement employees or lower-level managers.

transaction-processing system
A type of operations information system that records and processes data resulting from routine business transactions such as sales, purchases, and payroll.

Transaction-processing systems (TPSs) record and process data resulting from business operations. They include information systems that record sales to customers, purchases from suppliers, inventory changes, and wages to employees. A TPS collects data from these transactions and stores them in a database. Employees use information from the database to produce reports and other information, such as customer statements and employee paychecks. Most of an organization's reports are generated from these databases. Transaction-processing systems identify, collect, and organize the fundamental information from which an organization operates.

office automation systems
Systems that combine modern hardware and software to handle the tasks of publishing and distributing information.

Office automation systems combine modern hardware and software such as word processors, desktop publishers, e-mail, and teleconferencing to handle the tasks of publishing and distributing information. Office automation systems also are used to transform manual accounting procedures to electronic media. Companies such as Wal-Mart, Chevron, and American Airlines send thousands of electronic payments a month to suppliers, eliminating the need for writing and mailing checks. Merrill Lynch uses office automation to electronically manage consultants' travel and entertainment expenses, cutting the time it takes to process a report and issue reimbursement from six weeks to four days and slashing the average cost of processing a report from $25 to only

EXHIBIT 6.9

Types of Information Systems

Operations Information Systems
- Transaction-processing systems
- Process control systems
- Office automation systems

Management Information Systems
- Information-reporting systems
- Decision support systems
- Executive information systems
- Groupware

a few bucks.[67] These systems enable businesses to streamline office tasks, reduce errors, and improve customer service. In this way, office automation systems support the other kinds of information systems.

Operations information systems aid organizational decision makers in many ways and across various settings. For example, Enterprise Rent-A-Car's Computer Assisted Rental System (Ecars) provides front-line employees with up-to-the-minute information that enables them to provide exceptional service to each customer. The computer-based system helps Enterprise keep track of the 1.4 million transactions the company logs every hour. If a customer visits a branch office and requests a certain kind of car, the agent can immediately determine if one is available anywhere in the city. Insurance companies such as Geico can also link their claims systems directly to Enterprise's automated rental system, book a reservation, and send payments electronically, eliminating the need for paper invoices and checks.[68] Similarly, when Tim Doreck learned to use an information system, his business improved.

When Tim Doreck relied on his answering machine, he lost business. Not long ago a group of 12 people wanted to hire his dive boat. By the time he called them back, they already had found another boat. His loss: $1,000.

That was a lesson he won't forget. Now, Doreck's Monterey Express Diving Charters uses the Web-based reservation system Time-Trade, enabling customers to book their own charters. After they log on, they can see what's available and reserve immediately, receiving both an online confirmation and an e-mail. Is it worth the $49.95 he pays each month as a sole proprietor? Doreck says his phone and cellular bills have been cut dramatically and he spends 70 percent less time sending e-mails to inquiring customers, while his business is up 30 percent. Customers seem to like the online booking. "They are more inclined to book trips further ahead," he notes, "and they're more inclined to book when they just think of it."[69]

Monterey Express

http://www.montereyexpress.com

Management Information Systems

Until the 1960s, information systems were used primarily for transaction processing, accounting, and record keeping. Then the introduction of computers using silicon chip circuitry allowed for more processing power per dollar. As computer manufacturers promoted these systems and managers began visualizing ways in which the computers could help them make important decisions, management information systems were born. A **management information system** (MIS) is a computer-based system that provides information and support for effective managerial decision making. The basic elements of a management information system are illustrated in Exhibit 6.10. The MIS is supported by the organization's operations information systems and by organizational databases (and frequently databases of external data as well). Management information systems typically include reporting systems, decision support systems, executive information systems, and groupware.

MISs typically support strategic decision-making needs of mid-level and top management. However, as technology becomes more widely accessible, more employees are wired into networks, and organizations push decision making downward in the hierarchy, these kinds of systems are seeing use at all levels of the organization.

management information system (MIS)

A computer-based system that provides information and support for effective managerial decision making.

SOURCE: Adapted from Ralph M. Stair and George W. Reynolds, *Principles of Information Systems: A Managerial Approach*, 4th ed. (Cambridge, Mass.: Course Technology, 1999), 391.

The Internet and E-Business

Internet

A global collection of computer networks linked together for the exchange of data and information.

World Wide Web (WWW)

A collection of central servers for accessing information on the Internet.

e-business

Any business that takes place by digital processes over a computer network rather than in physical space.

e-commerce

Business exchanges that occur electronically.

In recent years, most organizations have incorporated the Internet as part of their information technology strategy.[70] The **Internet** is a global collection of computer networks linked together for the exchange of data and information. The **World Wide Web (WWW)** is a collection of central servers for accessing information on the Internet. Originally developed for use by the U.S. military, the Internet and the World Wide Web have become household words and an important part of our personal and work lives. Exhibit 6.11 shows the opening Web page for Herman Miller Inc., the first office furniture maker to design and sell a line of products over the Internet. Both business and nonprofit organizations quickly realized the potential of the Internet for expanding their operations globally, improving business processes, reaching new customers, and making the most of their resources. E-business began to boom. **E-business** can be defined as any business that takes place by digital processes over a computer network rather than in physical space. Most commonly today, it refers to electronic linkages over the Internet with customers, partners, suppliers, employees, or other key constituents. **E-commerce** is a more limited term that refers specifically to business exchanges or transactions that occur electronically.

Some organizations are set up as e-businesses that are run completely over the Internet, such as eBay, Amazon.com, and Yahoo. These companies would not exist without the Internet. However, most established organizations, including General Electric, Wal-Mart, and the U.S. Postal Service, also make extensive use of the Internet, and we will focus on these types of companies in the remainder of this section. The goal of e-business for established organizations is to digitalize as much of the business as possible to make the organization more efficient and effective. Companies are using the Internet and the Web for everything from filing expense reports and calculating daily sales to connecting directly with suppliers for the exchange of information and ordering of parts.[71] Exhibit 6.12 illustrates the key components of e-business for two organizations, a manufacturing company and a retail chain. First, each organi-

E X H I B I T *6.11*

Opening Page of the Web Site for Herman Miller, Inc.

zation uses an **intranet**, an internal communications system that uses the technology and standards of the Internet but is accessible only to people within the company. The next component is a system that allows the separate companies to share data and information. Two options are an electronic data interchange network or an extranet. **Electronic data interchange (EDI)** networks link the computer systems of buyers and sellers to allow the transmission of structured data primarily for ordering, distribution, and payables and receivables.[72] An **extranet** is an external communications system that uses the Internet and is shared by two or more organizations. Each organization moves certain data outside of its private intranet, but makes the data available only to the other companies sharing the extranet. The final piece of the overall system is the Internet, which is accessible to the general public. Organizations make some information available to the public through their Web sites, which may include products or services offered for sale. For example, at the Web site of Herman

intranet

An internal communications system that uses the technology and standards of the Internet but is accessible only to people within the organization.

electronic data interchange (EDI)

A network that links the computer systems of buyers and sellers to allow the transmission of structured data primarily for ordering, distribution, and payables and receivables.

extranet

An external communications system that uses the Internet and is shared by two or more organizations.

E X H I B I T *6.12*

The Key Components of E-Business for Two Traditional Organizations

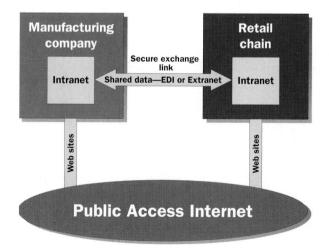

SOURCE: Based on Jim Turcotte, Bob Silveri, and Tom Jobson, "Are You Ready for the E-Supply Chain?" *APICS—The Performance Advantage* (August 1998), 56–59.

Miller, shown earlier in Exhibit 6.11, dealers and consumers can place orders for furniture online and also check order status or make changes with just a few mouse clicks.

E-Business Strategies

Traditional organizations such as Herman Miller that want to establish an Internet division have to decide how best to integrate *bricks and clicks*—that is, how to blend their traditional operations with an Internet initiative. The range of basic strategies for setting up an Internet operation are illustrated in Exhibit 6.13. At one end of the spectrum, companies can set up an in-house division that is closely integrated with the traditional business. The opposite approach is to create a spin-off company that is totally separate from the traditional organization. Many companies also take a middle road, by forging strategic partnerships with other organizations to go online. Each of these presents distinct advantages and disadvantages.[73]

In-House Internet Division. Setting up an in-house dot-com division offers tight integration between the Internet operation and the organization's traditional operation. The organization creates a separate department or unit within the company that functions within the structure and guidance of the traditional organization. This approach gives the new division several advantages by piggybacking on the established company, including brand recognition, purchasing leverage with suppliers, shared customer information and marketing opportunities, and distribution efficiencies. Office Depot launched its online business as a tightly integrated in-house part of its overall retail operation. A potential problem with an in-house division is that the new operation doesn't have the flexibility and autonomy needed to move quickly in the Internet world. In some cases, the traditional business's focus on protecting current customers and fear of cannibalization by the dot-com division can suffocate the new division and prevent it from succeeding.

Spin-Off. To give the Internet operation greater organizational focus, autonomy, and flexibility, some organizations choose to create a separate spin-off company. For example, Barnes & Noble created a separate division, barnesandnoble.com, which it ultimately spun off as a stand-alone company to compete with Amazon. Whirlpool created a spin-off called Brandwise.com, a site designed to

SOURCE: Based on Ranjay Gulati and Jason Garino, "Get the Right Mix of Bricks and Clicks," *Harvard Business Review* (May–June 2000), 107–114.

EXHIBIT 6.13

The Range of Strategies for Integrating Bricks and Clicks

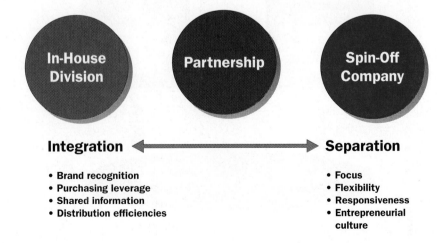

help consumers find the best products and value—even if that means from other manufacturers. Advantages of a spin-off include faster decision making, increased flexibility and responsiveness to changing market conditions, an entrepreneurial culture, and management that is totally focused on the success of the online operation. Potential disadvantages are the loss of brand recognition and marketing opportunities, higher start-up costs, and loss of leverage with suppliers.

Strategic Partnership. Partnerships, whether through joint ventures or alliances, enable organizations to attain some of the advantages and overcome some of the disadvantages of the purely in-house or spin-off options. For example, after initially blundering in the online world, Toys 'R' Us partnered with an established e-commerce company, Amazon.com, to capitalize on the advantages of both integration and separation. Partner Amazon brought e-commerce experience and an entrepreneurial mindset, while Toys 'R' Us provided purchasing leverage, brand recognition in the toy industry, and an established customer base. Each company can provide its core strengths—Amazon handles customer service, warehousing, order fulfillment, and maintenance of the Web site, while Toys 'R' Us does all inventory management, merchandising, purchasing, and marketing for the co-branded site.[74] The primary disadvantages of partnerships are time spent managing relationships, potential conflicts between partners, and a possibility that one company will fail to deliver as promised or go out of business. For example, if Amazon.com should fail, it would take toysrus.com's entire business with it.

E-Marketplaces

The biggest boom in e-commerce is in business-to-business (B2B) transactions, or buying and selling between companies. Using the Internet helps companies cut their costs, broaden their supplier base, and streamline their purchasing processes.[75] A significant trend is the development of **B2B marketplaces**, in which an intermediary sets up an electronic marketplace where buyers and

B2B marketplace

An electronic marketplace set up by an intermediary where buyers and sellers meet.

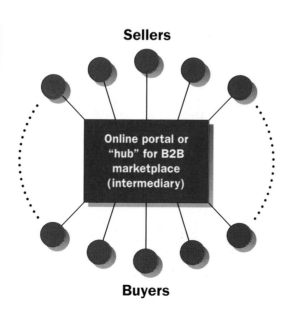

Many sellers offer products and services through an intermediary to many buyers.

Sellers

Online portal or "hub" for B2B marketplace (intermediary)

Buyers

EXHIBIT 6.14

B2B Marketplace Model

sellers meet, acting as a hub for B2B commerce. Exhibit 6.14 illustrates a B2B marketplace, where many different sellers offer products and services to many different buyers through a *hub,* or online portal. Conducting business through a Web marketplace can mean lower transaction costs, more favorable negotiations, and productivity gains for both buyers and sellers. For example, defense contractor United Technologies bought $450 million worth of metals, motors, and other products via an e-marketplace in 2000 and got prices about 15 percent less than what it usually pays.[76] Transactions on e-marketplaces are expected to reach $2.8 trillion by 2004, according to AMR Research.[77]

Open, public marketplaces include Covisint, an auto-parts marketplace, Onvia, a marketplace for office supplies, and e2open, which links buyers and sellers in the high-tech industry. In addition, some companies set up private marketplaces to link with a specially invited group of suppliers and partners.[78] For example, General Motors spent $96 billion in 2001 on raw materials and parts purchased through Covisint, but GM also operates its own private marketplace, GMSupplyPower, to share proprietary information with thousands of its parts suppliers. E-marketplaces can bring efficiencies to many operations, but some companies find that they don't offer the personal touch their business needs, as described in the Focus on Collaboration box.

FOCUS ON COLLABORATION

Grant J. Hunt Co. Likes the Personal Touch

For five generations, family-owned Grant J. Hunt Co. has reached out for new technology to speed up its food distribution business. So, when sales crews began pitching the concept of an online produce marketplace, 47-year-old Grant Hunt listened. One executive from a B2B marketplace start-up assured Hunt he could lay off half his sales staff because of the efficiencies gained. Others pointed out the potential for gaining new customers all over the world and getting higher prices by advertising produce to the highest bidder.

Yet today, Hunt's salespeople are working the way they have for years, buying and selling produce using the telephone and the fax machine. Although the B2B marketplaces put Hunt in touch with a host of potential new customers, most of them were marginal operations with shaky credit histories. In addition, Hunt was a little leery about the public nature of the exchanges, which meant that all sorts of confidential information could get out to customers and competitors. However, the biggest drawback was that the online marketplace couldn't provide personal attention to customers or to constantly shifting marketplace conditions. "No B-to-B site can say to a buyer at a supermarket, 'How about a special this weekend on tomatoes, because we are coming into a lot of them right now,'" Hunt points out.

The Hunt Co. has always tried to develop close, personalized relationships with its suppliers and customers, negotiating

deals on a individual basis. Hunt prides himself on the fact that customers trust him to provide accurate and honest information. He or his salespeople make daily visits to large growers and the local produce markets, shaking hands and talking small talk. The rest of the time they spend glued to the telephone, matching farmers' crops with buyers such as regional supermarket chains, wholesalers, and restaurant supply outfits, often varying their prices as needed with each customer to close a deal. "The Internet is very good at taking one message and sending it out to the whole world," he says. "That's not how our world works."

Hunt found that the relationships he had developed and the processes he had in place were so efficient that he had little to gain from joining the B2B marketplace craze. In fact, over time, many of the start-ups have also realized that the produce business doesn't fit well with the online marketplace concept. BuyProduce.com, for example, has closed its Web site and shifted its emphasis to helping produce companies such as Hunt improve their own in-house systems. Hunt is careful to point out that he is not anti-technology. "If they provided something that would be of real value, I would use it in a heartbeat."

SOURCE: Lee Gomes, "How Lower-Tech Gear Beat Web 'Exchanges' at Their Own Game," *The Wall Street Journal* (March 16, 2001), A11.

Customer Relationship Management

In addition to better internal information management and information sharing with suppliers and other organizations, companies are using e-business solutions to build stronger customer relationships. One approach is **customer relationship management (CRM) systems** that help companies track customers' interactions with the firm and allow employees to call up a customer's past sales and service records, outstanding orders, or unresolved problems.[79] CRM stashes away in a database all the customer information that small-town store owners would keep in their heads—the names of customers, what they bought, what problems they've had with their purchases, and so forth. CRM helps to coordinate sales, marketing, and customer service departments so that all smoothly work together to best serve customer needs. For example, when a customer places an order, the salesperson enters the order into the CRM software, which updates the database. Whenever the customer calls with a question or problem, CRM automatically brings up the customer's record so that the customer service or technical support representative has all pertinent information right in front of him and is able to provide personalized service, make additional sales pitches based on the customer's purchasing history, and update the database with information related to the call. Data from Web site customer contacts is also automatically entered into the database. Marketing can use the detailed customer information to implement tailored marketing programs. Best Buy marketers track typical buying patterns and market bundled product offerings to the right customers, which has led to increased sales.[80] In addition, executives can analyze CRM data to solve persistent problems and anticipate new ones.

Increasingly, what distinguishes an organization from its competitors are its knowledge resources, such as product ideas and the ability to identify and find solutions to customers' problems. Exhibit 6.15 lists examples of how CRM and other information technology can shorten the distance between customers and the organization, contributing to organizational success through customer loyalty, superior service, better information gathering, and organizational learning.

customer relationship management (CRM) systems

Systems that help companies track customers' interactions with the firm and allow employees to call up information on past transactions.

Management Implications of Information Technology

Information technology and e-business can enable managers to be better connected with employees, the environment, and each other. In general, information technology has positive implications for the practice of management, although it can also present problems. Some specific implications of information technology for managers include improved employee effectiveness, increased efficiency, empowered employees, information overload, enhanced collaboration, and organizational learning.

Improved Employee Effectiveness.

Information technology can provide employees with all kinds of data about their customers, competitors, markets, and service, as well as enable them to share information or insights with others. In addition, time and geographic boundaries are dissolving. A management team can work throughout the day on a project in Switzerland and, while they sleep, a team in the United States can continue where the Swiss team left off. Employees all over the world have instant access to databases at any time of the day or night and the ability to

EXHIBIT **6.15**

Competitive Advantages Gained from Customer Relationship Management (CRM) Systems

Competitive Advantage	Example
• Increase in customer loyalty	Full information about customer profile and previous requests or preferences is instantly available to sales and service representatives when a customer calls.
• Superior service	Customer representatives can provide personalized service, offer new products and services based on customer's purchasing history.
• Superior information gathering and knowledge sharing	The system is updated each time a customer contacts the organization, whether the contact is in person, by phone, or via the Web. Sales, marketing, service, and technical support have access to shared database.
• Organizational learning	Managers can analyze patterns to solve problems and anticipate new ones.

share information via the intranet. Advanced information technology allows managers and employees to work whenever and wherever they are most needed and most productive.

In general, information technology enables managers to design jobs to provide employees with more intellectual engagement and more challenging work. The availability of information technology does not guarantee increased job performance, but when implemented and used appropriately, it can have a dramatic influence on employee effectiveness.

Increased Efficiency

New information technology offers significant promise for speeding work processes, cutting costs, and increasing efficiency. For example, at IBM, automating customer service helped reduce the number of call center employees and saved $750 million in 2001. Companies like IBM are also moving all aspects of purchasing to the Web, helping to slash costs and wring deeper discounts from suppliers.

Sweeping away administrative paperwork and automating mundane tasks is another advantage of new technology. At EZRider, a Massachusetts-based retailer of snowboards, whenever a salesperson keys in a purchase, the company's computer system records the amount of the sale; at the end of the pay period, the system automatically computes the salesperson's commission in a matter of seconds.[81] The Michigan Department of Transportation used a management information system (MIS) to increase efficiency for its employees, as described below.

Michigan DOT

Next time you drive down a new highway, remember that it took more than asphalt and concrete to build it. It requires lots of people to make decisions and others to inspect the work. A few years ago, that meant that field technicians were driving to road construction sites with so many boxes of paper in the car they could barely move. Bill Young remembers the days when he visited a site with a printout of the Inspector's Daily Report, which he filled out by hand to track thousands of work items and materials. At the end of the day, he'd turn in the report and someone else would tally the information onto another form, which would be copied and sent to five people—all before the contractor got paid. The Department of Transportation (DOT) needed a battalion of people to verify contractors' work, including as many as 20 inspectors daily for larger projects. Furthermore, the manual system generated a lot of errors.

The new workplace has changed all that. Now Young travels with only his laptop and is usually the only inspector required at any site. He enters data on the laptop, then uploads it to a new software program called FieldManager. Back in the office, technicians use that information to cut checks to contractors, while inspectors take the data and are able to amend contracts, settle contract disputes, or check budget statuses. FieldManager also gives Michigan taxpayers a break: less money is used on bureaucratic overhead and more on high-quality highways. The program has helped DOT adjust to an increase in its budget from $500 million in 1993 to $1.5 billion today, while reducing staff from 5,000 to 3,000.

Private consultants who oversee DOT projects have been helped, too. Engineering specialist Stuart Laasko, whose company pays $15,000 for the FieldManager license, is grateful. "My background is civil engineering. It's not bookkeeping," he says, noting he no longer has to spend time adding and transferring numbers from one report to another. "The amount of work you can push through with this is amazing."[82]

Empowered Employees

Information technology is profoundly affecting the way organizations are structured. Through implementing IT, organizations change the locus of knowledge by providing information to people who would not otherwise receive it. Low-level employees are increasingly challenged with more information and are expected to make decisions previously made by supervisors.[83]

These changes support the objectives of knowledge management by enabling decisions to be made by the employees who are in the best position to implement the decisions and see their effects. For example, the U.S. Army is beginning to use new information technology that pushes information about battlefield conditions, the latest intelligence on the enemy, and so forth, down the line to the lowest-ranking troops. Armed with better data and trained to see patterns in the barrage of information, lieutenants in the field will be making more of the tough decisions once made by commanders.[84]

Information Overload

One problem associated with advances in technology is that the company can become a quagmire of information, with employees so overwhelmed by the sheer volume that they are unable to sort out the valuable from the useless.

In many cases, the ability to produce data and information is outstripping employees' ability to process it. One British psychologist claims to have identified a new mental disorder caused by too much information; he has termed it Information Fatigue Syndrome.[85] Information technology is a primary culprit in contributing to this new "disease." However, managers have the ability to alleviate the problem and improve information quality. The first step is to ensure that suppliers of information technology and CIOs work closely with employees to identify the kinds of questions they must answer and the kinds of information they really need. Specialists often are enamored with the volume of data a system can produce and overlook the need to provide small amounts of quality information in a timely and useful manner for decision making. Top executives should be actively involved in setting limits by focusing the organization on key strategies and on the critical questions that must be answered to pursue those strategies.[86]

Enhanced Collaboration

Information technology enhances collaboration both within the organization and with customers, suppliers, and other organizations. Intranets and other networks can connect employees around the world for the sharing and exchange of information and ideas. Information technology can also improve communication and collaboration with external parties such as customers. For example, ESAB Welding and Cutting Products regained its market leadership by offering customers a way to check product and pricing information, place orders, and track shipments online.[87]

Extranets are increasingly important for linking companies with contract manufacturers and outsourcers, supporting the development of network and virtual organizations as will be described in Chapter 7. For example, Hong Kong's Li & Fung is one of the biggest providers of clothing for retailers such as Abercrombie & Fitch, Guess, Ann Taylor, the Limited, and Disney, but the company doesn't own any factories, machines, or fabrics. Li & Fung specializes in managing information, relying on an electronically connected web of 7,500 supply and manufacturing partners in 37 different countries to provide raw materials and assemble the clothes. Using an extranet to stay in immediate touch with worldwide partners enables Li & Fung to move new items quickly from factories to retailers. When data indicate that there's a backlog at a factory in Madagascar, a job can instantly be moved to a partner in Sri Lanka or Spain. In addition, retailers can use the extranet to track orders as they move through production and make last-minute changes and additions.[88]

Organizational Learning

Information technology is an important part of today's learning organizations because it contributes to more rapid identification of problems and opportunities, faster decision making, and greater learning capacity from widely shared information and knowledge.

IT enables the accumulation and widespread communication of a larger volume as well as a wider range of information. For example, organizations can purchase access to hundreds of databases about industry, financial, and demographic trends in their environments, helping managers stay on top of important trends that will impact their business. Managers can provide key information to employees to help them make better decisions and continuously find ways to improve operations and customer service. In addition, when used appropriately, IT helps break down barriers and create a sense of team spirit that is essential for learning, change, and growth.

IT Trends in the New Workplace

Information technology continues to evolve, and new concepts and applications are emerging every day. Some recent trends in information technology that are having the greatest impact in the new workplace are instant messaging, wireless applications, and peer-to-peer technology.

Instant Messaging

instant messaging
Technology that provides a way to send quick notes from PC to PC over the Internet so two people who are online at the same time can communicate instantly.

The current rage in communication is interactive, real-time communication known as instant messaging. **Instant messaging** technology provides a way to zap quick notes from PC to PC over the Internet so that two people who are online at the same time can communicate instantaneously.[89] Companies such as America Online and Yahoo! provide instant messaging services to their customers, and the technology is being expanded to work on interactive televisions and mobile phones. For businesses, instant messaging can enable remote employees—those who work from home or in the field—to communicate with one another and with headquarters more efficiently than ever before. For example, a salesman might use his laptop to chat with his supervisor on the other side of the country through instant messaging and clarify a new pricing policy before going on a sales call. In addition, when used within the organization, instant messaging decreases the time spent playing phone tag and untangling crossed e-mail messages.[90]

Wireless Internet

Another popular new technology is the wireless Internet. It is estimated that in 2002, 225 million people will use wireless services that bypass the Web and serve up information any place at any time.[91] That means employees can gain access to bits of data and information over handheld devices exactly when and where they need it, bypassing the cumbersome pages of the Web, which can be extremely slow over a mobile device. Because much of today's workforce is highly mobile, wireless technologies that don't require using a PC are critical for helping people be more efficient and effective outside of the office. Celanese Chemicals' remote sales force and customer service employees can access real-time company information from the company's ERP system via mobile phones, Palm devices, and other wireless gadgets.[92] For example, a saleswoman can get instant confirmation on the availability of a specific chemical, allowing her to promise immediate shipment and close a lucrative sale. "If the system saves just one order," says William Schmitt, a senior IT executive at Celanese, "it will practically pay for itself."

The major providers of wireless phone service are introducing a new generation of mobile phones with services including wireless Internet access and text messaging. Miss Teen USA Marissa Whitley, who lives and works in New York City and takes frequent trips all over the country, uses wireless Internet services to keep in touch with friends and family. Her first text message was from her best friend: "Don't forget about me in the Big Apple." Whitley, who does not own a computer, finds text messaging and wireless Internet access 'really quick and easy."

© Charlie Samuels

Peer-to-Peer File Sharing

Napster, the music-sharing service that was wildly popular a few years back, got into trouble for illegally distributing copyrighted music. However, the technology behind Napster is finding a variety of uses in legitimate business. Napster's software enabled one person to locate and download music directly from another person's personal computer. This cutting-edge technology, called **peer-to-peer (P2P) file sharing**, allows PCs to communicate directly with one another over the Internet, bypassing central databases, servers, control points, and Web pages.[93] Peer-to-peer software lets any individual's computer "talk" directly to another PC without an intermediary, enhancing the opportunities for information sharing and collaboration. Personal computers today have enormous storage capacity. Peer-to-peer technology improves efficiency by allowing for the sharing of PC files directly between two PCs, eliminating the need for setting up and managing huge central storage systems. GlaxoSmithKline uses P2P technology to enable its 10,000 employees and researchers outside the company to share their drug test data digitally and work collaboratively on new research. Law firm Baker & McKenzie uses it to allow major clients to tap directly into its attorney's files stored on computers worldwide. For example, clients closing a merger can monitor the progress of the deal without attorneys having to keep files in one place or send lengthy electronic documents, improving organizational speed and efficiency.[94]

peer-to-peer (P2P) file sharing

File sharing that allows PCs to communicate directly with one another over the Internet, bypassing central databases, servers, control points, and Web pages.

■ Summary and Management Solution

This chapter made several important points about the process of organizational decision making. The study of decision making is important because it describes how managers make successful strategic and operational decisions. Managers must confront many types of decisions, including programmed and nonprogrammed, and these decisions differ according to the amount of risk, uncertainty, and ambiguity in the environment.

Three decision-making approaches were described: the classical model, the administrative model, and the political model. The classical model explains how managers should make decisions so as to maximize economic efficiency. The administrative model describes how managers actually make nonprogrammed, uncertain decisions with skills that include intuition. The political model relates to making nonprogrammed decisions when conditions are uncertain, information is limited and ambiguous, and there is conflict among managers about what goals to pursue or what course of action to take. Managers have to engage in discussion and coalition building to reach agreement for decisions.

Decision making should involve six basic steps: problem recognition, diagnosis of causes, development of alternatives, choice of an alternative, implementation of the alternative, and feedback and evaluation. Consider how President Bush's advisors analyzed the problem mentioned at the beginning of the chapter and created an ongoing dialogue for about 36 hours on how to choose the best alternative.

After receiving President Bush's command to "talk about it," the advisors talked on the phone and huddled in hallways for 24 hours, each helping to sift through all available data. Still no consensus was achieved. They were using their intuition in times of risk and uncertainty, and were also relying on building collective intuition, as described in this chapter, which makes use of dialogue on external and internal information. Because they were striving collectively for the best solution, they were very open to two new pieces of data that emerged. At 3 AM the following morning, the CIA turned in its daily "threat matrix" update, gleaned from interrogation and electronic surveillance around the world. One piece of data said that the Taliban and al-Qaida were talking about a U.S. bank being bombed. Some hours later another intelligence report showed that a top Taliban prisoner mentioned an Eastern Seaboard bank being the target of suicide bombers. It was all the advisors needed. They warned the banks to go on high alert, asking them not to close, as the information was too sketchy. "The

thing that's amazing is decisions like this happen every day," says one advisor. Noting the desire to get back to normal for most people, he continues, "For government officials . . . that deal with threat information, there's not going to be any getting back to normal for a long time."[95]

Another factor affecting decision making is the manager's personal decision style. The four major decision styles are directive, analytical, conceptual, and behavioral. The chapter also explained the Vroom-Jago model, which managers can use to determine when a decision calls for group participation. Involving others in decision making contributes to individual and organizational learning, which is critical in today's fast-paced environment. In the new workplace, decisions often have to be made quickly and with limited information. To improve the effectiveness of decision making in fast-moving organizations, managers use the following guidelines: learn, don't punish; know when to bail; practice the five whys; build collective intuition; and engage in constructive conflict.

Information technology and e-business are changing the way today's people and organizations work. Organizations are evolving into information cultures in which managers and employees can share information and knowledge across boundaries of time and geography. In addition, customers, partners, and suppliers are brought into the information network.

Modern information technology gathers huge amounts of data and transforms them into useful information for decision makers. The systems that use this technology should be designed to generate information with appropriate time, content, and form attributes. The array of information systems available and the multitude of data they produce can be overwhelming. Many organizations hire a chief information officer to help manage decisions regarding technology infrastructure and information design.

Most organizations have incorporated the Internet and e-business as part of their information technology strategy. To set up an Internet division, traditional organizations may choose to establish an in-house dot-com division, create a separate spin-off company, or enter into a partnership. Companies are also benefitting from participation in electronic marketplaces, where many different sellers offer products and services to many different buyers through an online hub.

Information technology and e-business have a number of specific implications for managers and organizations, including greater employee effectiveness, increased efficiency, empowered employees, information overload, enhanced collaboration, and increased potential for learning, change, and growth. Information technology continues to evolve. Some recent trends having significant impact in the workplace are instant messaging, wireless Internet applications, and peer-to-peer technology.

■ Discussion Questions

1. Why is decision making considered a fundamental part of management effectiveness?
2. Explain the difference between risk and ambiguity. How might decision making differ for each situation?
3. Analyze three decisions you made over the past six months. Which of these were programmed and which were nonprogrammed?
4. Why are many decisions made by groups rather than by individuals?
5. The Vroom-Jago model describes five decision styles. How should a manager go about choosing which style to use?
6. What are the major differences between the administrative and political models of decision making?
7. List some possible advantages and disadvantages to using computer technology for managerial decision making.
8. Do you think intuition is a valid approach to making decisions in an organization? Why or why not? How might intuition be combined with a rational decision approach?
9. Do you see a conflict between the new workplace emphasis on risk taking and decision learning and the six steps in Exhibit 6.3 that are associated with effective decision making? Discuss.
10. How might constructive conflict contribute to better decision making?
11. Why is it important for managers to understand the difference between data and information?
12. What types of information technology do you use as a student on a regular basis? How might your life be different if this technology was not available to you?
13. In what ways might access to an MIS change the way decisions are made at a large package-delivery company?
14. Do you believe information overload is a problem for today's students? For employees? What could you do to deal more effectively with information overload?
15. How is e-business affecting the way organizations are structured and the way jobs are designed?

■ Manager's Workbook

What's Your Personal Decision Style?

Read each of the following questions and circle the answer that *best* describes you. Think about how you typically act in a work or school situation and mark the answer that first comes to mind. There are no right or wrong answers.

1. In performing my job or class work, I look for:
   a. practical results
   b. the best solution
   c. creative approaches or ideas
   d. good working conditions
2. I enjoy jobs that:
   a. are technical and well-defined
   b. have a lot of variety
   c. allow me to be independent and creative
   d. involve working closely with others
3. The people I most enjoy working with are:
   a. energetic and ambitious
   b. capable and organized
   c. open to new ideas
   d. agreeable and trusting

4. When I have a problem, I usually:
   a. rely on what has worked in the past
   b. apply careful analysis
   c. consider a variety of creative approaches
   d. seek consensus with others
5. I am especially good at:
   a. remembering dates and facts
   b. solving complex problems
   c. seeing many possible solutions
   d. getting along with others
6. When I don't have much time, I:
   a. make decisions and act quickly
   b. follow established plans or priorities
   c. take my time and refuse to be pressured
   d. ask others for guidance and support
7. In social situations, I generally:
   a. talk to others
   b. think about what's being discussed
   c. observe
   d. listen to the conversation

8. Other people consider me:
   a. aggressive
   b. disciplined
   c. creative
   d. supportive
9. What I dislike most is:
   a. not being in control
   b. doing boring work
   c. following rules
   d. being rejected by others
10. The decisions I make are usually:
    a. direct and practical
    b. systematic or abstract
    c. broad and flexible
    d. sensitive to others' needs

Scoring: These questions rate your personal decision style, as described in the text and listed in Exhibit 6.5. Count the number of *a* answers. This is your *directive* score.
Count the number of *b* answers for your *analytical* score.
The number of *c* answers is your *conceptual* score.
The number of *d* answers is your *behavioral* score.

What is your dominant decision style? Are you surprised, or does this reflect the style you thought you used most often?

SOURCE: Adapted from Alan J. Rowe and Richard O. Mason, *Managing with Style: A Guide to Understanding, Assessing, and Improving Decision Making* (San Francisco: Jossey-Bass, 1987), 40–41.

■ Manager's Workshop

Whom Do You Choose?

1. You are the member of a medical selection committee. Take five minutes to individually fill out the table below with your rank orderings. Dilemma: A group of well-known people have all applied for a liver transplant. Without the transplant, they can expect to die in anywhere from six months to two years, depending on other factors. A number of donor livers are expected in the next few weeks. You are on the medical selection committee that decides who gets the transplants. Of course, you cannot know who will match up with the livers that arrive. So your job is just to choose the five who you recommend, then rank-order those five people below in terms of whom you think is most deserving of the transplant. Give "1" as the first one to get it, "2" as the next, and so on. List your reasons in the appropriate box.

2. Form groups of four to six. Using the classical and administrative models of decision-making, answer the following

dilemma by rank-ordering in the table below. You will first need to choose your top five as a group, then rank-order those five.

3. Each group shares its top five and the rankings with the whole class. Describe how and when you used the classical or administrative models in your decision making.

People who applied for liver transplant: Michael Jackson, Britney Spears, Alicia Keyes, Justin Timberlake, Nelson Mandela, Dale Earnhart, Jr., Julia Roberts, Brad Pitt, Stephen Spielberg, President Bush, Jennifer Lopez, Reese Witherspoon, Monica Lewinsky, Halle Berry, President Clinton, Bill Gates, Denzel Washington, Elton John, Harry Potter author J. K. Rowling, Oprah Winfrey, TV producer David E. Kelley, the Pope, Mark McGuire, Madonna, Shaquille O'Neill, Michael Jordan, Michelle Kwan.

Name	Rank order you assigned	Group ranking	Classical or administrative model? Why?	Reason for your ranking

Discussion Questions

1. How can a decision model help in the process of making a decision?
2. Did the models help explain any of the conflict you had? Did they help explain how to deal with the conflict?
3. Did the models help you understand how difficult decision-making can sometimes be?

■ Management in Practice: Ethical Dilemma

The No-Show Consultant

Jeffrey Moses was facing one of the toughest decisions of his short career as a manager with International Consulting. Andrew Carpenter, one of his best consultants, was clearly in trouble, and his problems were affecting his work. International Consulting designs, installs, and implements complex back-office software systems for companies all over the world. About half the consultants work out of the main office, while the rest, including Andrew, work primarily from home.

This Monday morning, Moses had gotten an irate call from a major New York client saying Andrew never showed up at the company's headquarters, where the client had been expecting his new computer system to go live for the first time. In calling around to other customers on the East Coast trying to locate the missing consultant, Moses heard other stories. Andrew had also missed a few other appointments—all on Monday mornings—but no one had felt the need to report it since he had called to reschedule. In addition, he had practically come to blows with an employee who challenged him about the capabilities of the new system, and he had inexplicably walked out of one customer's office in the middle of the day without a word to anyone. Another client reported that the last time he saw Andrew he appeared to have a serious hangover. Most of the clients liked Andrew, but they were concerned that his behavior was increasingly erratic. One client suggested that she would prefer to work with someone else. As for the major New York customer, they preferred that Andrew rather than a new consultant finish the project, but they were also demanding that International eat half the $250,000 consultant's fee.

After Moses finally located Andrew by calling his next-door neighbor, Andrew confessed that he'd had a "lost weekend" and been too drunk to get on the plane. He then told Moses that his wife had left and taken their two-year-old son with her. He admitted that he had been drinking a little more than usual lately, but insisted that he was getting himself under control and promised there would be no more problems. "I'm really not an alcoholic or anything," he said. "I've just been upset about Brenda leaving, and I let it get out of hand this weekend." Moses told Andrew that if he would get to New York and complete the project, all would be forgiven.

Now, however, he wondered if he should really just let things slide. Moses talked to Andrew's team leader about the situation and was told that the leader was aware of Andrew's recent problems but thought everything would smooth itself over. "Consultants with his knowledge, level of skill, and willingness to travel are hard to find. He's well-liked among all the customers; he'll get his act together." However, when Moses discussed the problem with Carolyn Walter, vice president of operations, she argued that Andrew should be dismissed. "You're under no obligation to keep him just because you said you would," she pointed out. "This was a major screw-up, and it's perfectly legal to fire someone for absenteeism. Your calls to customers should make clear that this was not a one-time thing. Get rid of him now before things get worse. If you think eating half that $250,000 fee hurts now, just think what could happen if this behavior continues."

What Do You Do?

1. Give him a month's notice and terminate. He's known as a good consultant, so he probably won't have any trouble finding a new job, and you'll avoid any further problems associated with his emotional difficulties and his possible alcohol problem.
2. Let it slide. Missing the New York appointment is Andrew's first big mistake. He says he is getting things under control and you believe he should be given a chance to get himself back on track.
3. Let Andrew know that you care about what he's going through, but insist that he take a short paid leave and get counseling to deal with his emotional difficulties and evaluate the seriousness of his problems with alcohol. If the alcohol abuse continues, require him to attend a treatment program or find another job.

Source: Based on Jeffrey L. Seglin, "The Savior Complex," *Inc.* (February 1999), 67–69; and Nora Johnson, "'He's Been Beating Me,' She Confided," *Business Ethics* (Summer 2001), 21.

■ Surf the Net

1. **Brain Teasers.** Problem solving is part of the decision-making process. The purpose of many decisions is to determine the best alternative for solving a problem. Just for fun, visit one of the sites listed below, and try your hand at solving some of the brain teasers. Be prepared to share during class your favorite brain teaser and the way you solved the problem.
   http://www.billsgames.com/brain-teasers
   http://www.afunzone.com/brainteaserzone.html
   http://www.ed.uiuc.edu/courses/satex/sp97/projects/ PickYourBrain/BrainTeasers/

2. **Decision Making.** Use one of the sites listed or conduct your own Web search for information on management decision making. Identify the most informative site on the subject and submit to your instructor the Web address, along with a summary of the information you found that would prove helpful to anyone making management decisions.
   http://www.ubmail.ubalt.edu/~harsham/opre640/opre640.htm
   http://www.mapnp.org/library/prsn_prd/decision.htm
   http://horizon.unc.edu/courses/papers/ AnticipatoryManagement.asp

3. **Mindmapping.** Go to one of the sites listed, or locate your own site, to learn about mindmapping: *http://www.thinksmart.com/mission/workout/mindmapping_intro.html*

http://home.snafu.de/h.nauheimer/cp_03.htm
Go to Exhibit 6.3 and suggest where in the managerial decision-making process mindmapping might be useful.

■ ## Case for Critical Analysis

The Merger

Peter Lundgren poured his fifth cup of coffee down the drain and checked his watch. More caffeine was just going to make matters worse at this point. He needed to be calm for the meeting with Ashton if they were going to reach any sort of agreement at all. Stanley Ashton and Peter Lundgren were trying something new by serving as co-CEOs of Arlington Inc., which resulted from a merger of Arlington Oil with Dunsford Petroleum Co.

The merger, announced as a marriage of equals, created a corporation with nearly $40 billion in assets better able to compete with huge corporations in the rough-and-tumble oil industry. It was expected that the merger would result in significant cost savings in refining, marketing, and transportation, as well as more capital to fund worldwide exploration and production. The media and stock market had both responded favorably, but the euphoria had faded and the hard work of integrating the two organizations had begun. The most difficult aspect was proving to be merging the two cultures and creating an effective human resource integration strategy. It had been widely reported in the press that cost savings would come from operating efficiencies rather than widespread job cuts, but that told only part of the story. The merger had left Arlington with two managers for almost every available position at upper and middle management levels. The very top levels had been selected prior to the merger, with Lundgren and Ashton negotiating so that each could keep his most trusted executives on board. Ashton has brought the director of HR, head of global marketing, and chief information officer from Dunsford. Lundgren kept his chief operating officer, chief financial officer, and head of R & D. Both Lundgren and Ashton knew they were facing some tough decisions concerning the other positions. Of course, the managers knew it too, and several of the best from both companies had already taken other jobs because of the uncertainty.

Peter has always preferred making personnel decisions based largely on gut instinct. He likes to talk to people face-to-face, look them in the eye, find out what they care about and what their personal and professional goals are, and decide if they would be a good fit with the organization. He is naturally biased toward some of his own executives because he knows them, but he is more than willing to negotiate just as he did with the top slots. In fact, there are several managers he would just as soon get rid of, and this presents a good opportunity. Ashton, on the other hand, except for the few high-level positions he's already argued for, doesn't seem to have much of a personal interest in whether Dunsford managers stay on. He wants to put all the executives through an outside evaluation and appraisal process that includes personality testing, IQ and emotional intelligence testing, and all sorts of other tests, in addition to looking at their performance and business results. Peter realizes an objective process would take the bias and emotion out of the decision making, but he is concerned that Ashton's plan will take too long and that the best executives will leave the company rather than go through all the testing and evaluation. In addition, it has been his experience that the best managers are those who just "feel right" for the company, rather than those who look good on paper. He can feel a headache coming on as the time for meeting with Ashton nears.

Questions

1. Is the decision facing Lundgren and Ashton programmed or nonprogrammed? Why?
2. Based on the information in this case, what is Lundgren's dominant decision style according to the personal decision framework? What is Ashton's dominant style? Can the two executives effectively co-lead the company considering their different perspectives and approaches?
3. Which model of decision making—classical, administrative, or political—do you think would be most appropriate to make personnel decisions for the new company? Discuss.

SOURCE: Based on David A. Light, "Who Goes, Who Stays?" *Harvard Business Review* (January 2001), 35–44.

PART FOUR

Organizing

The artist's manager is the key person for organizing an artist's career. The manager will develop an artist development team, comprising those who have a direct stake in the success of an artist and who will benefit financially when the artist succeeds. For example, on this team will be the record label and the people involved in radio promotion, sales, publicity, and product development within that company. Other members of the team may include songwriters, song publishers, concert promoters, booking agents, musicians, public relations consultants, hairstylists, set designers, wardrobe consultants, merchandisers—those who design and manufacture T-shirts, baseball caps, belt buckles, and other items sold at performances—as well as a myriad of other people who play a role in helping an artist to have a successful career.

The artist's manager must understand all aspects of the music business and have a close, personal relationship with a given artist, based on mutual trust and understanding. The manager must be able to motivate the individuals on an artist's development team as well as the artist. He or she must be a "big picture" person who at the same time exercises constant attention to details.

Fundamentals of Organizing

LEARNING OBJECTIVES

After studying this chapter, you should be able to

1 Discuss the fundamental characteristics of organizing, including such concepts as work specialization, chain of command, line and staff, centralization, and span of management.

2 Explain the contemporary team and network structures and why they are being adopted by organizations.

3 Discuss the advantages and disadvantages of the new virtual approach to organizing.

4 Describe mechanisms for achieving coordination and when they may be applied.

5 Explain the major differences between traditional vertical organizations and the new workplace learning organization.

6 Describe how organization structure can be designed to fit environmental uncertainty.

7 Define production technology (manufacturing, service, and digital) and explain how it influences organization structure.

Management Challenge

Christopher B. Galvin was watching the company his grandfather had founded more than 70 years ago slowly fall apart. How had the mighty Motorola come to this? The company that had invented the cellular telephone industry was being hammered by rivals such as Finland's Nokia. Neglect of the Internet and failure to develop cutting-edge wireless network gear, combined with an arrogant sales approach, was hurting sales, profits, and the stock price. And, perhaps worst of all, rivals were ridiculing the company that once won the Malcolm Baldrige National Quality Award for its now-shoddy products. Employee morale was sinking with the company's fortunes. Galvin inherited this mess in 1997—and he knew he needed to do something fast or Motorola would fade into history. Galvin wanted to transform Motorola into a major Internet player, but intense internal competition and slow product development was hindering the company's efforts to compete in the fast-paced Internet world. For Motorola to once again be a world-class competitor, Galvin had to find ways to cut costs, increase innovation, build employee morale, and serve customers better and faster.[1]

If you were Christopher Galvin, how would you transform Motorola to speed up innovative product development for the Internet? What advice would you give him about using organization structure to achieve this goal?

Managers in companies like Motorola frequently must rethink structure and may reorganize to meet new competitive conditions in the environment. In recent years, many corporations, including American Express, Apple, IBM, Microsoft, and Ford Motor Co, have realigned departmental groupings, chains of command, and teams and task forces to attain new strategic goals. Structure is a powerful tool for reaching strategic goals, and a strategy's success often is determined by its fit with organization structure.

Every firm wrestles with the problem of how to organize. Reorganization often is necessary to reflect a new strategy, changing market conditions, or innovative technology. Today, many companies have found a need to make structural changes that are compatible with use of the Internet for e-business. For example, Brady Corporation, a Milwaukee-based manufacturer of identification and safety products, is reorganizing to increase cross-functional collaboration in connection with the rollout of a new system that links customers, distributors, and suppliers over the Internet.[2] Hewlett-Packard consolidated its 83 independently run units into four major divisions to increase internal collaboration and enhance flexibility.[3] A growing number of companies operate as network organizations, limiting themselves to a few core activities and letting outside specialists handle the rest. Others function as virtual organizations, groups of people or companies that come together for a specific purpose or project and then disband when the project is complete.

Each of these organizations is using fundamental concepts of organizing. **Organizing** is the deployment of organizational resources to achieve strategic goals. The deployment of resources is reflected in the organization's division of labor into specific departments and jobs, formal lines of authority, and mechanisms for coordinating diverse organization tasks.

Organizing is important because it follows from strategy. Strategy defines *what* to do; organizing defines *how* to do it. Organization structure is a tool that managers use to harness resources for getting things done. Part 4 explains the variety of organizing principles and concepts used by managers. This chapter covers fundamental concepts that apply to all organizations and departments, and also looks at how structural designs are tailored to the organization's situation. Chapter 8 discusses how organizations can be structured to facilitate innovation and change. Chapters 9 and 10 examine how to utilize human resources to the best advantage within the organization's structure.

organizing

The deployment of organizational resources to achieve strategic goals.

Organizing the Vertical Structure

organization structure

The framework in which the organization defines how tasks are divided, resources are deployed, and departments are coordinated.

The organizing process leads to the creation of organization structure, which defines how tasks are divided and resources deployed. **Organization structure** is defined as (1) the set of formal tasks assigned to individuals and departments; (2) formal reporting relationships, including lines of authority, decision responsibility, number of hierarchical levels, and span of managers' control; and (3) the design of systems to ensure effective coordination of employees across departments.[4]

The set of formal tasks and formal reporting relationships provides a framework for vertical control of the organization. The characteristics of vertical structure are portrayed in the **organization chart**, which is the visual representation of an organization's structure.

A sample organization chart for a soda bottling plant is illustrated in Exhibit 7.1. The plant has four major departments—accounting, human resources,

organization chart

The visual representation of an organization's structure.

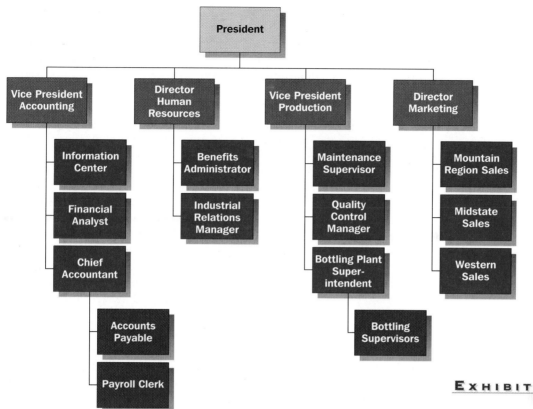

Organization Chart for a Soda Bottling Plant

production, and marketing. The organization chart delineates the chain of command, indicates departmental tasks and how they fit together, and provides order and logic for the organization. Every employee has an appointed task, line of authority, and decision responsibility. The following sections discuss several important features of vertical structure in more detail.

Work Specialization

Organizations perform a wide variety of tasks. A fundamental principle is that work can be performed more efficiently if employees are allowed to specialize.[5] **Work specialization**, sometimes called *division of labor,* is the degree to which organizational tasks are subdivided into separate jobs. Work specialization in Exhibit 7.1 is illustrated by the separation of production tasks into bottling, quality control, and maintenance. Employees within each department perform only the tasks relevant to their specialized function. When work specialization is extensive, employees specialize in a single task. Jobs tend to be small, but they can be performed efficiently. Work specialization is readily visible on an automobile assembly line where each employee performs the same task over and over again. It would not be efficient to have a single employee build the entire automobile or even perform a large number of unrelated jobs.

Despite the apparent advantages of specialization, many organizations are moving away from this principle. With too much specialization, employees are isolated and do only a single, boring job. Many companies are enlarging jobs to provide greater challenges or assigning teams to tasks so that employees can rotate among the several jobs performed by the team. For example, at BHP

work specialization

The degree to which organizational tasks are subdivided into individual jobs; also called division of labor.

Copper Metals in San Manuel, Arizona, managers disbanded the traditional assembly line and cross-trained teams of workers to handle all the steps in the copper-refining process. After shifting to the team approach, production increased 20 percent and the unit's safety record improved dramatically.[6] The team approach to organization design will be discussed later in this chapter, and approaches to designing jobs to fit employee needs are described in Chapters 13 and 15.

Chain of Command

chain of command
An unbroken line of authority that links all individuals in the organization and specifies who reports to whom.

The **chain of command** is an unbroken line of authority that links all persons in an organization and shows who reports to whom. It is associated with two underlying principles. *Unity of command* means that each employee is held accountable to only one supervisor. The *scalar principle* refers to a clearly defined line of authority in the organization that includes all employees. Authority and responsibility for different tasks should be distinct. All persons in the organization should know to whom they report as well as the successive management levels all the way to the top. In Exhibit 7.1, the payroll clerk reports to the chief accountant, who in turn reports to the vice president, who in turn reports to the company president.

authority
The formal and legitimate right of a manager to make decisions, issue orders, and allocate resources to achieve organizationally desired outcomes.

Authority, Responsibility, and Delegation   The chain of command illustrates the authority structure of the organization. **Authority** is the formal and legitimate right of a manager to make decisions, issue orders, and allocate resources to achieve organizationally desired outcomes. Authority is distinguished by three characteristics:[7]

1. *Authority is vested in organizational positions, not people.* Managers have authority because of the positions they hold, and other people in the same positions would have the same authority.

2. *Authority is accepted by subordinates.* Although authority flows top-down through the organization's hierarchy, subordinates comply because they believe that managers have a legitimate right to issue orders. The *acceptance theory of authority* argues that a manager has authority only if subordinates choose to accept his or her commands. If subordinates refuse to obey because the order is outside their zone of acceptance, a manager's authority disappears.[8] For example, Richard Ferris, the former chairman of United Airlines, resigned because few people accepted his strategy of acquiring hotels, a car rental company, and other organizations to build a travel empire. When key people refused to accept his direction, his authority was lost, and he resigned.

3. *Authority flows down the vertical hierarchy.* Positions at the top of the hierarchy are vested with more formal authority than are positions at the bottom.

responsibility
The duty to perform the task or activity an employee has been assigned.

Responsibility is the flip side of the authority coin. **Responsibility** is the duty to perform the task or activity an employee has been assigned. Typically, managers are assigned authority commensurate with responsibility. When managers have responsibility for task outcomes but little authority, the job is possible but difficult. They rely on persuasion and luck. When managers have authority exceeding responsibility, they may become tyrants, using authority toward frivolous outcomes.[9]

Accountability is the mechanism through which authority and responsibility are brought into alignment. **Accountability** means that the people with authority and responsibility are subject to reporting and justifying task outcomes to those above them in the chain of command.[10] Subordinates must be aware that they are accountable for a task and accept the responsibility and authority for performing it. Accountability can be built into the organization structure. For example, at Whirlpool incentive programs provide strict accountability. Performance of all managers is monitored, and bonus payments are tied to successful outcomes.

Another concept related to authority is delegation.[11] **Delegation** is the process managers use to transfer authority and responsibility to positions below them in the hierarchy. Most organizations today encourage managers to delegate authority to the lowest possible level to provide maximum flexibility to meet customer needs and adapt to the environment. Managers are encouraged to delegate authority, although they often find it difficult. Techniques for delegation are discussed in the Focus on Skills box.

Line and Staff Authority. An important distinction in many organizations is between line authority and staff authority, reflecting whether managers work in line or staff departments in the organization's structure. *Line departments* perform tasks that reflect the organization's primary goal and mission. In a software company, line departments make and sell the product. In an Internet-based company, line departments would be those that develop and manage online offerings and sales. *Staff departments* include all those that provide specialized skills in support of line departments. Staff departments have an advisory relationship with line departments and typically include marketing, labor relations, research, accounting, and human resources.

Line authority means that people in management positions have formal authority to direct and control immediate subordinates. **Staff authority** is narrower and includes the right to advise, recommend, and counsel in the staff specialists' area of expertise. Staff authority is a communication relationship; staff specialists advise managers in technical areas. For example, the finance department of a manufacturing firm would have staff authority to coordinate with line departments about which accounting forms to use to facilitate equipment purchases and standardize payroll services.

Span of Management

The **span of management** is the number of employees reporting to a supervisor. Sometimes called the *span of control,* this characteristic of structure determines how closely a supervisor can monitor subordinates. Traditional views of organization design recommended a span of management of about seven subordinates per manager. However, many lean organizations today have spans of management as high as 30, 40, and even higher. For example, at Consolidated Diesel's team-based engine assembly plant, the span of management is 100.[12] Research on the Lockheed Missile and Space Company and other manufacturing companies has suggested that span of management can vary widely and that several factors influence the span.[13] Generally, when supervisors must be closely involved with subordinates, the span should be small, and when supervisors need little involvement with subordinates, it can be large. The following factors are associated with less supervisor involvement and thus larger spans of control:

accountability
The fact that the people with authority and responsibility are subject to reporting and justifying task outcomes to those above them in the chain of command.

delegation
The process managers use to transfer authority and responsibility to positions below them in the hierarchy.

line authority
A form of authority in which individuals in management positions have the formal power to direct and control immediate subordinates.

staff authority
A form of authority granted to staff specialists in their areas of expertise.

span of management
The number of employees who report to a supervisor; also called *span of control.*

FOCUS ON SKILLS

How to Delegate

The attempt by top management to decentralize decision making often gets bogged down because middle managers are unable to delegate. Managers may cling tightly to their decision-making and task responsibilities. Failure to delegate occurs for a number of reasons: Managers are most comfortable making familiar decisions; they feel they will lose personal status by delegating tasks; they believe they can do a better job themselves; or they have an aversion to risk—they will not take a chance on delegating because performance responsibility ultimately rests with them.

Yet decentralization offers an organization many advantages. Decisions are made at the right level, lower-level employees are motivated, and employees have the opportunity to develop decision-making skills. Overcoming barriers to delegation in order to gain these advantages is a major challenge. The following approach can help each manager delegate more effectively:

1. *Delegate the whole task.* A manager should delegate an entire task to one person rather than dividing it among several people. This gives the individual complete responsibility and increases his or her initiative while giving the manager some control over the results.

2. *Select the right person.* Not all employees have the same capabilities and degree of motivation. Managers must match talent to task if delegation is to be effective. They should identify subordinates who have made independent decisions in the past and have shown a desire for more responsibility.

3. *Ensure that authority equals responsibility.* Merely assigning a task is not effective delegation. Managers often load subordinates with increased responsibility but do not extend their decision-making range. In addition to having responsibility for completing a task, the worker must be given the authority to make decisions about how best to do the job.

4. *Give thorough instruction.* Successful delegation includes information on what, when, why, where, who, and how.

The subordinate must clearly understand the task and the expected results. It is a good idea to write down all provisions discussed, including required resources and when and how the results will be reported.

5. *Maintain feedback.* Feedback means keeping open lines of communication with the subordinate to answer questions and provide advice, but without exerting too much control. Open lines of communication make it easier to trust subordinates. Feedback keeps the subordinate on the right track.

6. *Evaluate and reward performance.* Once the task is completed, the manager should evaluate results, not methods. When results do not meet expectations, the manager must assess the consequences. When they do meet expectations, the manager should reward employees for a job well done with praise, financial rewards when appropriate, and delegation of future assignments.

Are You a Positive Delegator?

Positive delegation is the way an organization implements decentralization. Do you help or hinder the decentralization process? If you answer yes to more than three of the following questions, you may have a problem delegating:

- I tend to be a perfectionist.

- My boss expects me to know all the details of my job.

- I don't have the time to explain clearly and concisely how a task should be accomplished.

- I often end up doing tasks myself.

- My subordinates typically are not as committed as I am.

- I get upset when other people don't do the task right.

- I really enjoy doing the details of my job to the best of my ability.

- I like to be in control of task outcomes.

SOURCES: Thomas R. Horton, "Delegation and Team Building: No Solo Acts Please," *Management Review* (September 1992), 58–61; Andrew E. Schwartz, "The Why, What, and to Whom of Delegation," *Management Solutions* (June 1987), 31–38; "Delegation," *Small Business Report* (June 1986), 38–43; and Russell Wild, "Clone Yourself," *Working Woman* (May 2000), 79–80.

1. Work performed by subordinates is stable and routine.

2. Subordinates perform similar work tasks.

3. Subordinates are concentrated in a single location.

4. Subordinates are highly trained and need little direction in performing tasks.

© Dennis Kleiman

Ian Adamson is a businessman and adventure racer whose team won the Eco-Challenge in Borneo, which involves 320 miles of hiking, running, swimming, biking, canoeing, and rappelling. The flat structure of his sports team is highly efficient for meeting such challenges. It has no leader; instead, members gather on the course and make decisions collectively as quickly as possible or spontaneously defer to someone who has expert knowledge. Teammates pitch in to help one another. For a fee, Adamson's recently formed company, Colorado Adventure Training, shows managers from companies such as Starbucks how to benefit from this non-hierarchical approach.

5. Rules and procedures defining task activities are available.

6. Support systems and personnel are available for the manager.

7. Little time is required in nonsupervisory activities such as coordination with other departments or planning.

8. Managers' personal preferences and styles favor a large span.

The average span of control used in an organization determines whether the structure is tall or flat. A **tall structure** has an overall narrow span and more hierarchical levels. A **flat structure** has a wide span, is horizontally dispersed, and has fewer hierarchical levels.

The trend in recent years has been toward wider spans of control as a way to facilitate delegation.[14] Exhibit 7.2 illustrates how an international metals company was reorganized. The multilevel set of managers shown in panel *a* was replaced with ten operating managers and nine staff specialists reporting directly to the CEO, as shown in panel *b*. The CEO welcomed this wide span of 19 management subordinates because it fit his style, his management team was top quality and needed little supervision, and they were all located on the same floor of an office building.

tall structure
A management structure characterized by an overall narrow span of management and a relatively large number of hierarchical levels.

flat structure
A management structure characterized by an overall broad span of control and relatively few hierarchical levels.

Centralization and Decentralization

Centralization and decentralization pertain to the hierarchical level at which decisions are made. **Centralization** means that decision authority is located near the top of the organization. With **decentralization**, decision authority is pushed downward to lower organization levels. Organizations may have to experiment to find the correct hierarchical level at which to make decisions.

In the United States and Canada, the trend over the past 30 years has been toward greater decentralization of organizations. Decentralization is believed

centralization
The location of decision authority near top organizational levels.

decentralization
The location of decision authority near lower organizational levels.

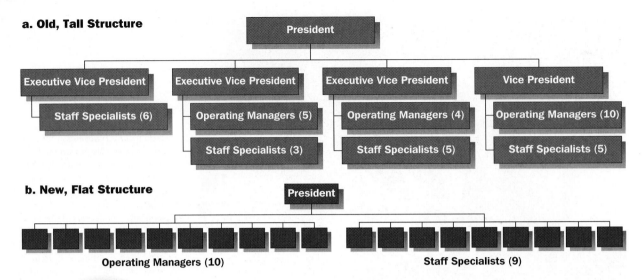

a. Old, Tall Structure

President

Executive Vice President — Staff Specialists (6)

Executive Vice President — Operating Managers (5) — Staff Specialists (3)

Executive Vice President — Operating Managers (4) — Staff Specialists (5)

Vice President — Operating Managers (10) — Staff Specialists (5)

b. New, Flat Structure

President

Operating Managers (10)   Staff Specialists (9)

EXHIBIT 7.2

Reorganization to Increase Span of Management for President of an International Metals Company

to relieve the burden on top managers, make greater use of workers' skills and abilities, ensure that decisions are made close to the action by well-informed people, and permit more rapid response to external changes.

However, this trend does not mean that every organization should decentralize all decisions. Managers should diagnose the organizational situation and select the decision-making level that will best meet the organization's needs. Factors that typically influence centralization versus decentralization are as follows:

1. Greater change and uncertainty in the environment are usually associated with decentralization. A good example of how decentralization can help cope with rapid change and uncertainty occurred following the September 11, 2001, attacks on the World Trade Center. UPS trucks, which carry 7 percent of the country's gross domestic product on any given day, were able to keep running on time, thanks largely to a decentralized management system that gives local managers authority to make key decisions. "I've learned to stay out of the way and let our folks run the system," says UPS Vice-Chairman Michael L. Eskew.[15] Today, most companies feel greater uncertainty because of intense global competition; hence, many have decentralized. The changing environment relating to defense has caused the U.S. Army to go through major restructuring and decentralization in recent years, as shown in the Focus on Skills box.

2. The amount of centralization or decentralization should fit the firm's strategy. For example, Johnson & Johnson gives almost complete authority to its 180 operating companies to develop and market their own products. Decentralization fits the corporate strategy of empowerment that gets each division close to customers so it can speedily adapt to their needs.[16] Taking the opposite approach, Larry Ellison at Oracle used the Internet to centralize operations in order to cut costs and focus everyone on the goal of providing global Internet systems for customers.

3. In times of crisis or risk of company failure, authority may be centralized at the top. When Honda could not get agreement among divisions about new car models, President Nobuhiko Kawamoto made the decision himself.[17]

FOCUS ON SKILLS

Delta Forces

Part of the job interview is a 20-hour 50-mile march, carrying a 70-pound load. The exercise "revealed clearly those candidates who had character—real determination, self-discipline, and self-sacrifice—and those who did not," said Delta Forces founder Army Col. Charles Beckwith, former Vietnam Green Beret. Created in 1977 to rescue hostages, one of its first missions was the 1980 botched rescue of the 53 hostages held by Iran, where not only were the hostages not saved, but eight U.S. soldiers were killed.

Realizing the unit was not functioning correctly, the army restructured Delta Forces, which has since carried out successful operations in Grenada, in Panama capturing dictator Noriega, and in the Gulf War destroying Scud missile launchers.

Unlike the regular army, with its hierarchical structure and authority, Delta Forces are much more team-based and composed of small units. Recruiting is very selective and based not only on endurance, but also on language skills and the ability to adapt or blend into another culture. To reduce hierarchy, soldiers call each other primarily by nicknames, rather than the normal military titles, and plans are not made high above, but instead by the noncommissioned officers in the unit.

Even though the job requires tough behavior, it is not just brawn they are looking for, which is why the 50-mile march is such an important selection criterion. "A lot of really physically strong guys try out for Delta," Beckwith said, "but the guys who make an impression are the ones that don't give up, even after they've attained the minimum requirement."

SOURCE: "Delta Forces' Secret Wielders of Death," *Veterans of Foreign Wars Magazine* (March 2002), 16–18; "Covert U.S. Military Units Att . . ." *The Washington Post* (April 28, 2002), A3.

Departmentalization

Another fundamental characteristic of organization structure is **departmentalization**, which is the basis for grouping positions into departments and departments into the total organization. Managers make choices about how to use the chain of command to group people together to perform their work. There are five approaches to structural design that reflect different uses of the chain of command in departmentalization. The functional, divisional, and matrix are traditional approaches that rely on the chain of command to define departmental groupings and reporting relationships along the hierarchy. Two contemporary approaches are the use of teams and networks. A brief illustration of the five structural alternatives is presented in Exhibit 7.3. In addition, some companies are using a *virtual* approach to organization, which we will describe at the end of this chapter. Newer approaches such as teams, networks, and virtual organizations have emerged to meet changing organizational needs in an increasingly global, knowledge-based business environment.

> **departmentalization**
>
> The basis on which individuals are grouped into departments and departments into the total organization.

1. *Vertical functional approach.* People are grouped together in departments by common skills and work activities, such as in an engineering department and an accounting department.

2. *Divisional approach.* Departments are grouped together into separate, self-contained divisions based on a common product, program, or geographical region. Diverse skills rather than similar skills are the basis of departmentalization.

3. *Matrix approach.* Functional and divisional chains of command are implemented simultaneously and overlay one another in the same departments. Two chains of command exist, and some employees report to two bosses.

4. *Team-based approach.* The organization creates a series of teams to accomplish specific tasks and to coordinate major departments. Teams can exist from the office of the president all the way down to the shop floor.

EXHIBIT 7.3

Five Approaches to Structural Design

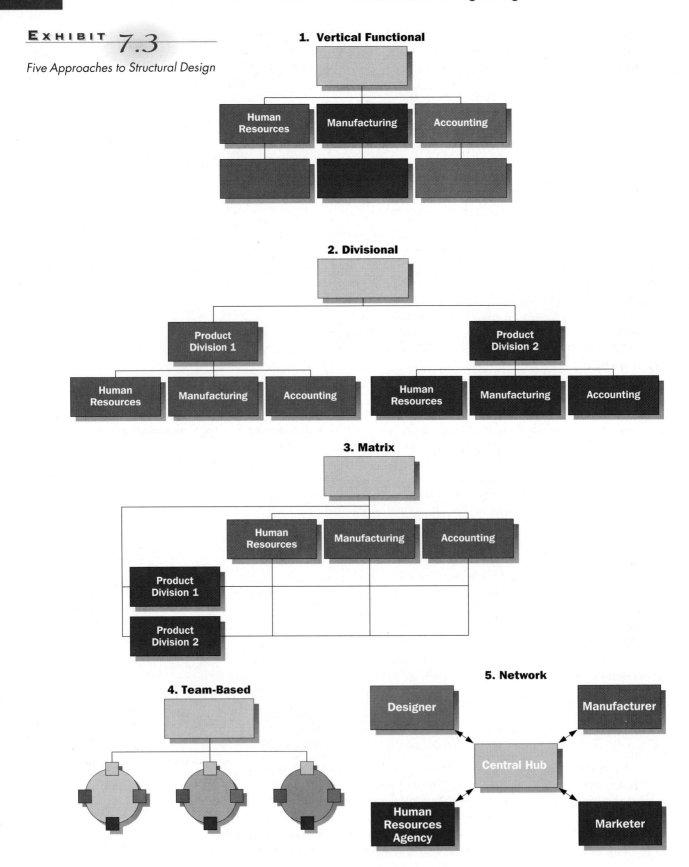

1. **Vertical Functional**

Human Resources | Manufacturing | Accounting

2. **Divisional**

Product Division 1 — Human Resources | Manufacturing | Accounting

Product Division 2 — Human Resources | Manufacturing | Accounting

3. **Matrix**

Human Resources | Manufacturing | Accounting

Product Division 1

Product Division 2

4. **Team-Based**

5. **Network**

Designer

Manufacturer

Central Hub

Human Resources Agency

Marketer

5. *Network approach.* The organization becomes a small, central hub electronically connected to other organizations that perform vital functions. Departments are independent, contracting services to the central hub for a profit. Departments can be located anywhere in the world.

Each approach to structure serves a distinct purpose for the organization, and each has advantages and disadvantages. The basic difference among structures is the way in which employees are departmentalized and to whom they report. The differences in structure illustrated in Exhibit 7.3 have major consequences for employee goals and motivation. Let us now turn to some of the five structural designs and examine their implications for managers.[18]

Team Approach

Probably the most widespread trend in departmentalization has been the effort by companies to implement team concepts. The vertical chain of command is a powerful means of control, but passing all decisions up the hierarchy takes too long and keeps responsibility at the top. Today, companies are trying to find ways to delegate authority, push responsibility to low levels, and create participative teams that engage the commitment of workers. This approach enables organizations to be more flexible and responsive in the competitive global environment. Chapter 15 will discuss teams in detail.

How It Works. There are two ways to think about using teams in organizations. **Cross-functional** teams consist of employees from various functional departments who are responsible to meet as a team and resolve mutual problems. Team members typically still report to their functional departments, but they also report to the team, one member of whom may be the leader. For example, Coca-Cola Fountain Manufacturing's Baltimore Syrup Operation used cross-functional teams to work on policies for vacation and compensation.[19]

Hallmark uses teams made up of artists, writers, lithographers, designers, and photographers to develop new greeting cards, with each team empowered to make decisions about cards for a particular holiday or season. The team approach cut in half the time it takes for Hallmark to get new cards to market.[20] With cross-functional teams, teams are used to provide needed horizontal coordination to complement an existing divisional or functional structure.

The second approach is to use **permanent teams**, groups of employees who are brought together similar to a formal department. Each team brings together employees from all functional areas focused on a specific task or project, such as parts supply and logistics for an automobile plant. Emphasis is on horizontal communication and information sharing because representatives from all functions are coordinating their work and skills to complete a specific organizational task. Authority is pushed down to lower levels, and front-line employees are often given the freedom to make decisions and take action on their own. Team members may share or rotate team leadership. With a **team-based structure**, the entire organization is made up of teams that coordinate their work and work directly with customers to accomplish the organization's goals. Imagination Ltd., Britain's largest design firm, is based entirely on teamwork. Imagination puts together a diverse team at the beginning of each new project it undertakes, whether it be creating the lighting for Disney cruise ships or redesigning the packaging for Ericsson's cell-phone products. The team then works closely with the client throughout the project. "Teamwork is a harder way of doing the work," says Ralph Ardill, director of marketing and strategic planning. "But when it clicks, the result is a seamless experience."[21] Imagination

cross-functional team
A group of employees from various departments that meets as a team to resolve mutual problems.

permanent team
A group of participants from several functions who are permanently assigned to solve ongoing problems of common interest.

team-based structure
Structure in which the entire organization is made up of teams that coordinate their work and work directly with customers to accomplish the organization's goals.

Courtesy of Avery Dennison Corp.

These members of the Avery Hi-Liter® EverBold™ marker team, part of the North American consumer products division at Avery Dennison Corporation, collaborated as a cross-functional team to launch a new pen-style highlighter product. Avery Dennison is a company committed to using the team-based approach to maintain and grow their market leadership. The company empowers multi-functional teams of employees to develop and launch new consumer products.

Ltd. has managed to make it click every time by building a culture that supports teamwork, as described in the Focus on Collaboration box.

Advantages and Disadvantages. Designing team relationships often helps overcome shortcomings in a functional, top-down approach to organizing. With cross-functional teams, the organization is able to retain some advantages of a functional structure, such as economies of scale and in-depth training, while gaining the benefits of team relationships. The team concept breaks down barriers across departments. Team members know one another's problems and compromise rather than blindly pursue their own goals. The team concept also allows the organization to more quickly adapt to customer requests and environmental changes and speeds decision making because decisions need not go to the top of the hierarchy for approval. Another big advantage is the morale boost. Employees are enthusiastic about their involvement in bigger projects rather than narrow departmental tasks. Jobs are enriched. The creation of teams also enables responsibility and authority to be pushed down the hierarchy, requiring fewer managers for supervision.

But the team approach has disadvantages as well. Employees may be enthusiastic about team participation, but they may also experience conflicts and dual loyalties. A cross-functional team may make different demands on members than do their department managers, and members who participate in more than one team must resolve these conflicts. A large amount of time is devoted to meetings, thus increasing coordination time. Unless the organization truly needs teams to coordinate complex projects and adapt to the environment, it will lose production efficiency with them. Finally, the team approach may cause too much decentralization. Senior department managers who traditionally made decisions might feel left out when a team moves ahead on its own. Team members often do not see the big picture of the corporation and may make decisions that are good for their group but bad for the organization as a whole. Top management can help keep the team in alignment with corporate goals.

The advantages and disadvantages of the team structure are summarized in Exhibit 7.4.

EXHIBIT 7.4

Advantages and Disadvantages of Team Structure

Advantages	Disadvantages
• Some advantages of functional structure	• Dual loyalties and conflict
• Reduced barriers among departments, increased compromise	• Time and resources spent on meetings
• Less response time, quicker decisions	• Unplanned decentralization
• Better morale, enthusiasm from employee involvement	
• Reduced administrative overhead	

FOCUS ON COLLABORATION

Imagination Ltd.

The essence of teamwork is that people contribute selflessly, putting the good of the whole above their own individual interests. It doesn't always work that way, but Imagination Ltd. seems to have found the secret ingredient to seamless teamwork. According to Adrian Caddy, Imagination's creative director: "The culture at Imagination is this: You can articulate your ideas without fear."

Imagination Ltd. has put together a company made up of teams of designers, architects, lighting experts, writers, theater people, film directors, and artists, in addition to IT specialists, marketing experts, and other functional specialties. By having employees with a wide range of skills, the company is able to put together a diverse team to provide each client with a new approach to its design problems. Imagination is deliberately nonhierarchical; only four people have formal titles, and on most project teams, no one is really in charge. Teams meet weekly, and everyone participates in every meeting from the very beginning, so there is no perception that any particular talent is primary—or secondary. Information technology specialists, production people, and client-contact personnel are just as much a part of the team as the creative types. In addition, each person is expected to come up with ideas outside his or her area of expertise. The philosophy is that people at Imagination must be willing to *make* all kinds of suggestions and also to *take* all kinds of suggestions. So many ideas get batted around, revised, and adapted at the weekly meetings that no one can ever really claim ownership of a particular element of the project. The team also works closely with the client as a source of ideas and inspiration.

Talent and respect help to make the system work. Imagination hires its employees carefully, based not only on the quality of their work but also on their open-mindedness and curiosity about the world beyond their functional area of expertise. Then, the company makes sure everyone's work is so closely integrated that people gain an understanding and respect for what others do. "The integrated approach breeds respect for one another," says writer Chris White. "When you work alone, or in isolation within your discipline, you can get an overblown sense of your own importance to a project."

SOURCE: Charles Fishman, "Total Teamwork: Imagination Ltd.," *Fast Company* (April 2000), 156–168.

Network Approach

The most recent approach to departmentalization extends the idea of horizontal coordination and collaboration beyond the boundaries of the organization. The **network structure** means that the firm subcontracts many of its major functions to separate companies and coordinates their activities from a small headquarters organization.[22]

How It Works. The organization may be viewed as a central hub surrounded by a network of outside specialists, as illustrated in Exhibit 7.5. Rather than being housed under one roof, services such as accounting, design, manufacturing, and distribution are outsourced to separate organizations that are connected

network structure

An organization structure that disaggregates major functions into separate companies that are brokered by a small headquarters organization.

EXHIBIT 7.5

Network Approach to Departmentalization

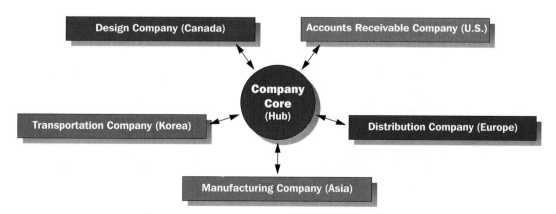

electronically to the central office.[23] Networked computer systems and the Internet enable organizations to exchange data and information so rapidly and smoothly that a loosely connected network of suppliers, manufacturers, assemblers, and distributors can look and act like one seamless company.

The idea behind networks is that a company can concentrate on what it does best and contract out other activities to companies with distinctive competence in those specific areas. This enables a company to do more with less.[24] For example, R & D Laboratories develops specialized vitamin and mineral supplements for dialysis patients, but the products are manufactured and packaged by subcontracted pharmaceutical companies and warehoused and distributed by 200 wholesalers. When R & D has a promising new product, it can ramp up production just by making a few phone calls to its network partners.[25] Three former Compaq Computer managers, Doug Johns, David Hocker, and Nicholas Forlenza, started a computer company that ran from 1995 to 2002 using the network approach.

Monorail

http://www.monorail.com

When Doug Johns left Compaq Computer Corporation, he was managing 6 million square feet of warehouse and office space. He and his partners David Hocker and Nicholas Forlenza wanted to start a different kind of computer company, one that had only a few core employees and relied on partnerships to accomplish its goals. The three believed there were only two things that couldn't be outsourced: world-class management expertise and a knack for establishing the right partnerships.

Monorail was able to succeed and grow rapidly by using a network structure. The company, based in Marietta, Georgia, operated from a single leased floor of an office building. It had no factories, no warehouses, no credit departments, and no help desks or call centers. The company's 50 core employees focused on product design and marketing and outsourced everything else. Here's how the Monorail system worked: When a retailer such as CompUSA ordered a computer from Monorail, the order was transmitted electronically through FedEx Logistics Services to one of Monorail's many contract manufacturers, who assembled the PC and shipped it directly to the retailer. Meanwhile, FedEx wired an invoice to Sun Trust bank in Atlanta, whose factoring department handled billing and credit approvals. All other functions were also outsourced, which meant Johns, Hocker, and Forlenza spent much of their time managing relationships to maintain seamless integration with their network partners.

In January 2002, facing a shrinking market for personal computers, the founders of Monorail decided to close its doors and pursue other opportunities. However, the partners remain convinced that the network model was a primary reason their company was able to succeed for as long as it did in the tough PC industry.[26]

With a network structure, it is difficult to answer the question "Where is the organization?" in traditional terms. For example, a firm might contract for expensive services such as training, transportation, legal, and engineering, so these functions are no longer part of the organization. Or consider a piece of ice hockey equipment that is designed in Scandinavia, engineered in the United States, manufactured in Korea, and distributed in Canada by a Japanese sales organization. These pieces are drawn together contractually and coordinated electronically, creating a new form of organization. Much like building blocks, parts of the network can be added or taken away to meet changing needs.[27] The ability to arrange and rearrange resources gives the network organization greater flexibility and rapid response. However, relationships with subcontractors are the glue that holds the organization together, so these ties are not taken lightly.

A similar approach to networking is called the **modular approach**, in which a manufacturing company uses outside suppliers to provide entire chunks of a product, which are then assembled into a final product by a handful of workers. Computer companies such as Dell and Gateway purchase premade pieces of computers and handle only the final assembly. Automobile plants, including General Motors, Ford, Volkswagen, and DaimlerChrysler, are leaders in using the modular approach. GM has a modular factory in Brazil and plans to open several more to replace inefficient plants in the United States. The modular approach hands off responsibility for engineering and production of entire sections of an automobile, such as the chassis or interior, to outside suppliers. Suppliers design a module, making some of the parts themselves and subcontracting others. These modules are delivered right to the assembly line, where a handful of GM employees bolt them together into a finished vehicle.[28]

Advantages and Disadvantages. The biggest advantage to the network structure seems to be competitiveness on a global scale. Network organizations, even small ones, can be truly global. A network organization can draw on resources worldwide to achieve the best quality and price and can sell its products and services worldwide. A second advantage is work force flexibility and challenge. Flexibility comes from the ability to hire whatever services are needed, such as engineering design or maintenance, and to change a few months later without constraints from owning plant, equipment, and facilities. The organization can continually redefine itself to fit new product and market opportunities. For those employees who are a permanent part of the organization, the challenge comes from greater job variety and job satisfaction from working within the lean structure. Finally, this structure is perhaps the leanest of all organization forms because little supervision is required. Large teams of staff specialists and administrators are not needed. A network organization may have only two or three levels of hierarchy compared with ten or more in traditional organizations.[29] These advantages of a network structure, along with the disadvantages, are summarized in Exhibit 7.6.

One of the major disadvantages is lack of hands-on control.[30] Managers do not have all operations under one roof and must rely on contracts, coordination, negotiation, and electronic linkages to hold things together. A problem of equal importance is the possibility of losing an organizational part. If a subcontractor fails to deliver, goes out of business, or has a plant burn down, the headquarters organization can be put out of business. Uncertainty is higher because necessary services are not under one roof and under direct management control. Finally, in this type of organization, employee loyalty can weaken. Employees may feel they can be replaced by contract services. A cohesive corporate culture is less likely to develop, and turnover tends to be higher because emotional commitment between organization and employee is weak. With

modular approach

A manufacturing company uses outside suppliers to provide large components of the product, which are then assembled into a final product by a few workers.

Advantages	Disadvantages
• Global competitiveness	• No hands-on control
• Workforce flexibility/challenge	• Can lose organizational part
• Reduced administrative overhead	• Employee loyalty weakened

EXHIBIT 7.6

Advantages and Disadvantages of Network Structure

changing products and markets, the organization may need to reshuffle employees at any time to acquire the correct mix of skills.

The Virtual Organization Approach

As illustrated by the discussion of networks, ways of organizing are changing quite dramatically. In a variety of industries, vertically integrated hierarchical organizations are giving way to loosely interconnected groups of companies with permeable boundaries.[31] An extension of the network approach is the **virtual organization**, which brings together people temporarily to exploit specific opportunities, then disbands when objectives are met.[32]

virtual organization
An organization that has few on-site employees and does most of its interactions online.

How It Works. The virtual organization will have few full-time employees, choosing instead to temporarily hire outside specialists to complete a specific project, such as a major advertising campaign or a new software application. These people do not become a part of the organization, but join together as a separate entity for a specific purpose. Companies use a virtual approach to harness the talents and energies of the best people for a particular job, rather than trying to develop those capabilities in-house.[33] For example, Host Universal, an advertising agency, is based entirely on a virtual approach. Rather than running an agency full of employees, founders Robin Smith and Steven Hess contract work out to small ad hoc teams of creative professionals that offer the best combination of talent for each particular project. The "organization" itself consists only of Smith and Hess. Everyone else is a freelance professional hired on a project-by-project basis. Then, the team works directly for and is paid directly by the client. Host Universal takes a percentage off the top for finding clients and matching them with the right combination of talent for the project.[34]

When an organization uses a virtual approach, the virtual group typically has full authority to make decisions and take action within certain predefined boundaries and goals. In addition, the group itself monitors and controls performance and members' behavior.

Most virtual organizations use electronic connections for the sharing of data and information. Collaborative software enables virtual members such as those at Host Universal to work simultaneously on the same document in cyberspace, for example.[35] However, participants may also meet face to face to coordinate their work. Some organizations have redesigned offices to provide temporary space for virtual workers to meet or work on-site. Recent workplace design trends such as hoteling, which means multiple workers serially share a single space, and free-address offices, where employees choose a desk each day on a first-come, first-served basis, are in response to the growing use of virtual workers. Virtual workers use laptops and cell phones, which they set up on work tables at the client's office and then pack everything up at night.

Advantages and Disadvantages. The virtual approach enables a company to put together a collection of the most-skilled professionals for a particular project on an as-needed basis. As such, virtual organizations are incredibly responsive and flexible. Like network organizations, virtual organizations can be truly global and draw on resources and expertise worldwide. The virtual form also enables a company to take advantage of world-class talent on a temporary basis without having to hire these people as full-time employees. Many knowledge professionals value personal time and autonomy over a stable job and income, and the virtual form gives them opportunities to work on projects that are of particular interest to them.

One of the major disadvantages is the lack of control. The boundaries of a virtual organization are weak and ambiguous. Thus, top managers have to provide a strong definition of project goals to keep the group focused, but they then turn day-to-day decision making over to the people participating directly in the virtual project.[36] Virtual teams also place new demands on managers, who are constantly working with new people, new ideas, and new problems. Not only must managers be technologically adept, they also face enormous communication and motivation challenges. The potential for misunderstanding is tremendous when people are communicating primarily via phone and e-mail. In addition, people working in a virtual environment lose the motivation that comes from regular interaction with others and the development of close relationships in the workplace.[37] The advantages and disadvantages of the virtual approach are summarized in Exhibit 7.7.

The Horizontal Organization

Many companies are recognizing that traditional vertical organization structures are ineffective in today's fast-shifting environment, which is one reason for the growing use of teams, networks, and virtual approaches, as described earlier in the chapter. Managers are looking for ways to transform their organizations into more flexible systems that emphasize rapid response and customer focus. Particularly for companies using the Internet to conduct business, a tight vertical approach such as a traditional functional structure does not work. In general, the trend is toward breaking down barriers between departments, and many companies are moving toward horizontal structures based on work processes rather than departmental functions.[38] Regardless of the type of structure, all organizations need mechanisms for horizontal coordination.

The Need for Coordination

As organizations grow and evolve, two things happen. First, new positions and departments are added to deal with factors in the external environment or with new strategic needs.[39] For example, many organizations have established Information Technology departments to cope with the proliferation of new information systems, or *chief knowledge officers* to find ways to leverage organizational knowledge in today's information-based economy. The executive search firm Russell Reynolds Associates created the position of *chief experience officer* to be in charge of the customer's total experience with the firm.[40] Many of today's organizations, particularly Internet and technology-based companies, are using

Advantages	Disadvantages
• Can draw on expertise worldwide	• Lack of control, weak boundaries
• Highly flexible and responsive	• Greater demands on managers
• Reduced overhead costs	• Communication difficulties and potential for misunderstanding

E X H I B I T 7.7

Advantages and Disadvantages of the Virtual Approach

unique job titles to reflect new needs. For example, Impact Online created a title of *chief imagination officer* for its Volunteer-Match Web site. The job reflects the need to imagine the possibilities for matching enthusiastic people with nonprofit organizations that need volunteers.[41] As companies add positions and departments to meet changing needs, they grow more complex, with hundreds of positions and departments performing incredibly diverse activities.

Second, senior managers have to find a way to tie all of these departments together. The formal chain of command and the supervision it provides is effective, but it is not enough. The organization needs systems to process information and enable communication among people in different departments and at different levels. **Coordination** refers to the quality of collaboration across departments. Without coordination, a company's left hand will not act in concert with the right hand, causing problems and conflicts. Coordination is required regardless of whether the organization has a functional, divisional, or team structure. Employees identify with their immediate department or team, taking its interest to heart, and may not want to compromise with other units for the good of the organization as a whole.

Without a major effort at coordination, an organization may be like Chrysler Corporation in the 1980s when Lee Iacocca took over:

> What I found at Chrysler were 35 vice presidents, each with his own turf. . . . I couldn't believe, for example, that the guy running engineering departments wasn't in constant touch with his counterpart in manufacturing. But that's how it was. Everybody worked independently. I took one look at that system and I almost threw up. That's when I knew I was in really deep trouble.
>
> I'd call in a guy from engineering, and he'd stand there dumbfounded when I'd explain to him that we had a design problem or some other hitch in the engineering-manufacturing relationship. He might have the ability to invent a brilliant piece of engineering that would save us a lot of money. He might come up with a terrific new design. There was only one problem: he didn't know that the manufacturing people couldn't build it. Why? Because he had never talked to them about it. Nobody at Chrysler seemed to understand that interaction among the different functions in a company is absolutely critical. People in engineering and manufacturing almost have to be sleeping together. These guys weren't even flirting![42]

If one thing changed at Chrysler (now DaimlerChrysler) in the years before Iacocca retired, it was improved coordination. Cooperation among engineering, marketing, and manufacturing enabled the rapid design and production of the Chrysler PT Cruiser, for example.

In the international arena, coordination is especially important. How can managers ensure that needed coordination will take place in their company, both domestically and globally? Coordination is the outcome of information and cooperation. Managers can design systems and structures to promote horizontal coordination. Exhibit 7.8 illustrates the evolution of organizational structures, with a growing emphasis on horizontal coordination and communication. The vertical functional structure, discussed in the previous chapter, dates back nearly a century and was the first to be widely used by large organizations.[43] Although the structure is effective in stable environments, it does not provide the horizontal coordination needed in times of rapid change. Innova-

---

coordination

The quality of collaboration across departments.

Jo DeMars is president of DeMars & Associates Ltd., a company that manages warranty dispute arbitration programs for major automakers. DeMars had grown her business, now 13 years old, by meticulously managing every aspect of the company's operations. "I found myself getting so wrapped up in the day-to-day tasks that I couldn't be strategic," states DeMars. One day she went out to lunch and didn't come back to the office for four months. She spent the time setting up systems to improve horizontal coordination at DeMars. She hired an interim CEO and an operations manager, who helped DeMars improve communication and coordination among the company's 17 employees, 36 independent contractors, and 300 volunteer arbitrators.

Source: Erica Freudenstein

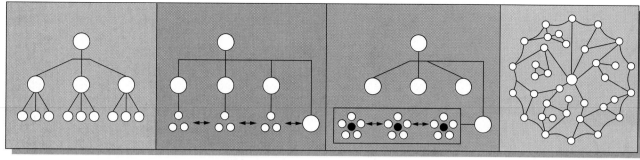

| Traditional Vertical Structure | Teams and Project Managers for Horizontal Coordination | Reengineering to Horizontal Processes | New Workplace Learning Organization |

EXHIBIT 7.8

Evolution of Organization Structures

tions such as teams, task forces, and project managers work within the vertical structure but provide a means to increase cross-functional communication and cooperation. The next stage involves reengineering to structure the organization around horizontal processes rather than vertical functions. The vertical hierarchy is flattened, with perhaps only a few senior executives in traditional support functions such as finance and human resources. Some organizations have taken a further step to the learning organization, doing away with all vestiges of an organizational hierarchy. The learning organization represents the ultimate in horizontal coordination. The following sections examine in more detail these methods for achieving horizontal coordination.

Task Forces, Teams, and Project Management

A **task force** is a temporary team or committee designed to solve a short-term problem involving several departments.[44] Task force members represent their departments and share information that enables coordination.

For example, the Shawmut National Corporation created two task forces in the human resources department to consolidate all employment services into a single area. The task force looked at job banks, referral programs, employment procedures, and applicant tracking systems; found ways to perform these functions for all Shawmut's divisions in one human resource department; and then disbanded.[45] General Motors uses task forces to solve temporary problems in its manufacturing plants. When a shipment of car doors arrived from a fabricating plant with surface imperfections, the plant manager immediately created a task force to solve the problem. He got everybody together on the factory floor to examine the part that was causing the trouble, and the task force resolved the problem in about two hours.[46]

In addition to creating task forces, companies also set up teams. As used for coordination, a **team** is a group of participants from several departments who meet regularly to solve ongoing problems of common interest.[47] The permanent team is similar to a task force except that it works with continuing rather than temporary problems and might exist for several years. Teams used for coordination are like the cross-functional teams described earlier in this chapter. For example, to improve coordination at Simplicity Pattern Company, CEO Louis Morris set up a Creative Committee, made up of the heads of the sales, finance, marketing, and creative departments. DaimlerChrysler sent managers and engineers to a three-day seminar held by Performance Learning Inc. to help them work better in teams. The seminar includes having team members

task force

A temporary team or committee formed to solve a specific short-term problem involving several departments.

team

A group of participants from several departments who meet regularly to solve ongoing problems of common interest.

participate in a relay race, driving high-speed race cars around a course of orange traffic cones. The exercise is designed to help team members think in terms of working together for the good of the whole rather than just for their own department.[48]

Companies also use project managers to increase coordination between functional departments. A **project manager** is a person who is responsible for coordinating the activities of several departments for the completion of a specific project.[49] Project managers are critical today because many organizations are almost constantly reinventing themselves, creating flexible structures, and working on projects with an ever-changing assortment of people and organizations.[50] Project managers might work on several different projects at one time and might have to move in and out of new projects at a moment's notice.

The distinctive feature of the project manager position is that the person is not a member of one of the departments being coordinated. Project managers are located outside of the departments and have responsibility for coordinating several departments to achieve desired project outcomes. For example, General Mills, Procter & Gamble, and General Foods all use product managers to coordinate their product lines. A manager is assigned to each line, such as Cheerios, Bisquick, and Hamburger Helper. Product managers set budget goals, marketing targets, and strategies and obtain the cooperation from advertising, production, and sales personnel needed for implementing product strategy.

In some organizations, project managers are included on the organization chart, as illustrated in Exhibit 7.9. The project manager is drawn to one side of the chart to indicate authority over the project but not over the people assigned to it. Dashed lines to the project manager indicate responsibility for coordination and communication with assigned team members, but department managers retain line authority over functional employees.

Project managers might also have titles such as product manager, integrator, program manager, or process owner. Project managers need excellent people skills. They use expertise and persuasion to achieve coordination among various departments, and their jobs involve getting people together, listening, building trust, confronting problems, and resolving conflicts and disputes in the best interest of the project and the organization. Consider the role of Hugh Hoffman at American Standard Companies.

project manager

A person responsible for coordinating the activities of several departments on a full-time basis for the completion of a specific project.

American Standard Companies

http://www.amstd-comfort.com

Hugh J. Hoffman began working at American Standard as a ceramic engineer in 1970. Today, he works as a full-time project manager in the company's chinaware business, which makes toilets and bidets. Hoffman, whose official title is *process owner, chinaware order fulfillment,* coordinates all the activities that ensure that American Standard's factories turn out the products customers order and deliver them on time. Hoffman's job requires that he think about everything that happens between the time an order comes in and the time it gets paid for, including design, manufacturing, painting, sales, shipping and receiving, and numerous other tasks. Project managers such as Hoffman have to act as if they are running their own business, setting goals, and developing strategies for achieving them. It is not always easy because Hoffman works outside the boundaries and authority structure of traditional departments. His years of expertise and good people skills help him motivate others and coordinate the work of many departments and geographically dispersed factories. "I move behind the scenes," Hoffman says. "I understand the workings of the company and know how to get things done."[51]

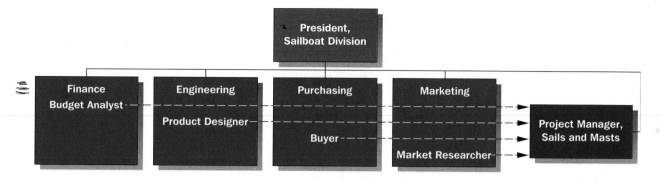

EXHIBIT 7.9

Example of Project Manager Relationships to Other Departments

Using project managers has helped American Standard do things faster, better, and cheaper than competitors. Many organizations move to a stronger horizontal approach such as the use of permanent teams, project managers, or process owners after going through a redesign procedure called reengineering.

Reengineering

Reengineering, sometimes called *business process reengineering,* is the radical redesign of business processes to achieve dramatic improvements in cost, quality, service, and speed.[52] Because the focus of reengineering is on process rather than function, reengineering generally leads to a shift away from a strong vertical structure to one emphasizing stronger horizontal coordination and greater flexibility in responding to changes in the environment.

Reengineering changes the way managers think about how work is done in their organizations. Rather than focusing on narrow jobs structured into distinct, functional departments, they emphasize core processes that cut horizontally across the company and involve teams of employees working to provide value directly to customers.[53] A **process** is an organized group of related tasks and activities that work together to transform inputs into outputs and create value. Common examples of processes include new product development, order fulfilment, and customer service.[54]

Reengineering frequently involves a shift to a horizontal structure based on teams. For example, reengineering at Texas Instruments led to the formation of product development teams that became the fundamental organizational unit. Each team is made up of people drawn from engineering, marketing, and other departments and takes full responsibility for a product from conception through launch. Functional departments still exist, but their responsibility is no longer to do the work but to train people in the skills required to work in horizontal teams.[55]

Reengineering basically means starting over, throwing out all the notions of how work *was* done and deciding how it can best be done now. It requires identifying customer needs and then designing processes and aligning people to meet those needs. Several years ago, IBM went through business process reengineering in order to standardize its operations worldwide and better serve customers who were operating on a global basis. Today, the company is once again going through a rapid redesign of processes to make them compatible with e-business and the Internet.[56] Reengineering can also squeeze out the dead space and time lags in work flows, as illustrated by reengineering of the travel system at the U.S. Department of Defense.

reengineering
The radical redesign of business processes to achieve dramatic improvements in cost, quality, service, and speed.

process
An organized group of related tasks and activities that work together to transform inputs into outputs and create value.

U.S. Department of Defense

http://www.dod.gov

The Pentagon can act quickly to move thousands of tons of humanitarian aid material or hundreds of thousands of troops, but until recently, sending employees on routine travel has been a different story. Before Pentagon travelers could even board a bus, they had to secure numerous approvals and fill out reams of paperwork. Coming home wasn't any easier—the average traveler spent six hours preparing vouchers for reimbursement following a trip.

The Department of Defense set up a task force to reengineer the cumbersome travel system, aiming to make it cheaper, more efficient, and more customer friendly. The reengineered system reduces the steps in the pretravel process from an astounding 13 to only 4, as shown in Exhibit 7.10. Travel budgets and authority to approve travel requests and vouchers, which have traditionally rested in the budget channels of the various service commands, was transferred to local supervisors. Travelers make all their arrangements through a commercial travel office, which prepares a "should-cost" estimate for each trip. This document is all a traveler needs before, during, and after a trip: With a supervisor's signature, it becomes a travel authorization; during travel, it serves as an itinerary; after amendments to reflect variations from plans, it becomes an expense report. Other travel expenses and needed cash or travelers' checks can be charged to a government-issued travel card, with payment made directly to the travel card company through electronic funds transfer.[57]

As illustrated by this example, reengineering can lead to stunning results, but, like all business ideas, it has its drawbacks. Simply defining the organization's key business processes can be mind-boggling. AT&T's Network Systems division started with a list of 130 processes and then began working to pare them down to 13 core ones.[58] Organizations often have difficulty realigning power relationships and management processes to support work redesign, and thus do not reap the intended benefits of reengineering. According to some estimates, 70 percent of reengineering efforts fail to reach their intended goals.[59] Because reengineering is expensive, time consuming, and usually

EXHIBIT 7.10

Reengineering the Travel System— U.S. Department of Defense

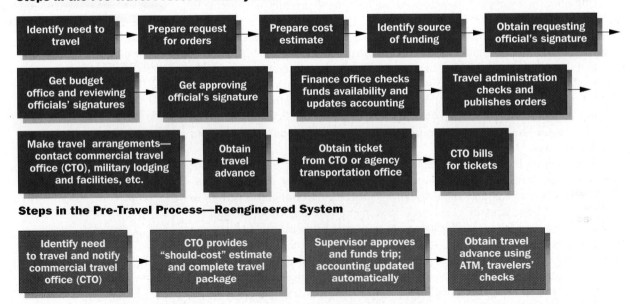

Steps in the Pre-Travel Process—Old System

Identify need to travel → Prepare request for orders → Prepare cost estimate → Identify source of funding → Obtain requesting official's signature →

Get budget office and reviewing officials' signatures → Get approving official's signature → Finance office checks funds availability and updates accounting → Travel administration checks and publishes orders →

Make travel arrangements—contact commercial travel office (CTO), military lodging and facilities, etc. → Obtain travel advance → Obtain ticket from CTO or agency transportation office → CTO bills for tickets

Steps in the Pre-Travel Process—Reengineered System

Identify need to travel and notify commercial travel office (CTO) → CTO provides "should-cost" estimate and complete travel package → Supervisor approves and funds trip; accounting updated automatically → Obtain travel advance using ATM, travelers' checks

SOURCE: Richard Koonce, "Reengineering the Travel Game," *Government Executive* (May 1995), 28–34, 69–70.

painful, it seems best suited to companies that are facing serious competitive threats.

Traditional Organizations versus the New Workplace

Recall that the purpose of structure is to organize resources to accomplish organizational goals. Elements of structure such as chain of command, centralization/decentralization, formal authority, teams, and coordination devices fit together to form an overall structural approach. In some organizations, the formal, vertical hierarchy is emphasized as the way to achieve control and coordination. In other organizations, decision making is decentralized, cross-functional teams are implemented, and employees are given great freedom to pursue their tasks as they see fit.

The increasing shift toward more horizontal versus vertical structures reflects the trend toward greater employee empowerment, broad information sharing, and decentralized decision making. At the apex of this movement is a type of organization called the *learning organization*. There is no single view of what the learning organization looks like. It is an attitude or philosophy about what an organization can become. Exhibit 7.11 compares characteristics of the new workplace learning organization with the traditional vertical organization.

In the traditional organization, the vertical structure predominates, with few task forces, teams, or project managers for horizontal coordination. Information is formally communicated up and down the organizational hierarchy and is not widely shared. In addition, jobs are broken down into narrow, specialized tasks, and employees generally have little say over how they do their work. The culture is rigid and does not encourage risk taking and change, and decision making is centralized. At the opposite end of the scale is the learning organization. The **learning organization** can be defined as one in which everyone is engaged in identifying and solving problems, enabling the organization to continuously experiment, change, and improve, thus increasing its capacity to grow, learn, and achieve its purpose. The learning organization is characterized by a horizontal team-based structure, open information, decentralized decision making, empowered employees, and a strong adaptive culture.

learning organization

An organization in which everyone is engaged in identifying and solving problems, enabling the organization to continuously experiment, improve, and increase its capability.

EXHIBIT 7.11

Differences in Traditional versus Learning Organizations

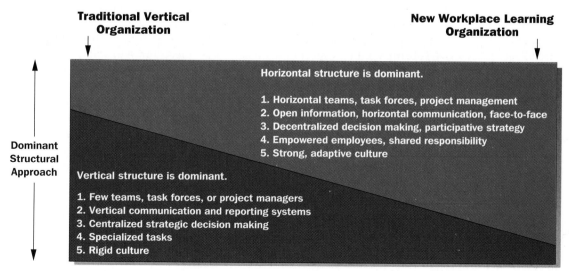

Horizontal Structure

In the new workplace learning organization, the vertical structure that created distance between the top and bottom of the organization is disbanded. Structure is created around workflows or core processes rather than departmental functions. All the people who work on a particular process, such as new product development or order fulfillment, have access to one another so they can easily communicate and coordinate their efforts, share knowledge, and provide value directly to customers.[60] Self-directed teams are the fundamental unit in a learning organization. Self-directed teams are made up of employees with different skills who rotate jobs to produce an entire product or service, and they deal directly with customers, making changes and improvements as they go along. Team members have the authority to make decisions about new ways of doing things, including taking responsibility for training, safety, scheduling vacations, and decisions about work methods, pay and reward systems, and coordination with other teams. Teams are discussed in detail in Chapter 15.

Learning organizations also strive to break down boundaries with other companies. New organizational forms such as the network organization, described earlier in this chapter, are horizontal teams of companies rather than teams of individuals. Learning organizations may use a combination of self-directed teams, virtual teams, alliances and partnerships, virtual organizations, and other structural innovations to support collaboration within and between organizations.

Open Information

In the new workplace learning organization, information is widely shared. To identify needs and solve problems, people have to be aware of what's going on. They must understand the whole organization as well as their part in it. Formal data about budgets, profits, and departmental expenses are available to everyone. This approach, which will be described in Chapter 16, is called *open-book management*. Every employee is free to look at the books and exchange information with anyone in the company. At Whole Foods Markets, for example, employees are trained to understand financial and operational information. Even sensitive data such as salaries and bonuses are available to any employee. Managers at Solectron Corp., the world's largest contract manufacturer, emphasize open sharing of information as a way to carry out the company's two primary values: superior customer service and respect for individual workers. "If you really want to respect individuals," says Solectron's Winston Chen, "you've got to let them know how they're doing—and let them know soon enough so they can do something about it."[61]

Electronic communication is essential to information and knowledge sharing in a learning organization. Networks of computers, Internet technology, and the use of intranets and extranets change the locus of knowledge by getting information to the people who really need it and enabling employees to stay constantly in touch with one another. However, the learning organization also recognizes the importance of getting people communicating face-to-face, with the emphasis on listening. Some companies are using *dialogue*, which takes people away from work in groups of 30 or 40 to communicate deeply and honestly. Open communication and information sharing are discussed in detail in Chapters 14 and 16.

Decentralized Decision Making and Participative Strategy

In traditional organizations, decisions are passed up the hierarchy for approval. In a learning organization, the people closest to the problem are given the authority and responsibility for decision making. Because people at all levels are intimately involved in making decisions, this allows strategy to emerge bottom up as well as top down. In traditional vertical organizations, top executives are responsible for strategy because only they have the big picture, knowledge, and expertise to direct the corporation. In the learning organization, leaders still influence overall vision and direction, but they do not control or direct strategy alone. Everyone helps. Information is gathered by employees who work directly with customers, suppliers, and other organizations. Perhaps thousands of people are in touch with the environment, providing data about external changes in technology and customer needs. They are the ones to identify needs and solutions, passing these ideas into the organization for discussion.[62]

Participative strategy relies on an experimental mindset. People are encouraged to try new things, and failure is accepted. Managers realize that problems and decisions present new learning opportunities, and they encourage employees to step outside their comfort zone and take risks. Strategy in learning organizations also may emerge from partnership linkages with suppliers, customers, and even competitors. Learning organizations have permeable boundaries and often are linked with other companies, giving each organization greater access to information about new strategic needs and directions.[63] Instead of looking at customers or suppliers at arm's length, the new workplace learning organization brings them into the company as partners working together to provide benefits for all. Onvia.com, for example, which sells to small businesses, asked its customers to help determine how the organization should stock its virtual shelves.[64]

Empowered Employees and Shared Responsibility

Learning organizations empower employees to an extraordinary degree, giving them the authority and responsibility to use their own discretion and ability to achieve an outcome. *Empowerment* means giving employees the power, freedom, knowledge, and skills to make decisions and perform effectively. Rather than dividing jobs into rigidly defined, specialized tasks, learning organizations allow people the freedom and opportunity to react quickly to changing conditions. There are few rules and procedures, and knowledge and control of tasks are located with workers rather than top managers. Individuals are encouraged to experiment, learn, and solve problems within the team. How do companies implement empowerment? It starts by promoting the decentralization of decision making and broader worker participation. For example, there are very few rules for teams at SEI Investments. Teams have as few as 2 members or as many as 30, and the various teams are structured differently. The teams themselves make the decisions about what roles each worker plays, how the team will operate, when it is time to disband, and so forth. The company's CEO calls it "fluid leadership."[65]

In learning organizations, people are considered a primary source of strength, not a cost to be minimized. Firms that adopt this perspective often employ the following practices: Treat employees well. Provide employment security and good wages. Provide a sense of employee ownership by sharing

Larry Gaynor, founder, president, and CEO of The Nailco Group (TNG), a beauty salon products distribution company located in Farmington Hills, Michigan, attributes his company's success to its strong, adaptive culture. At TNG's annual meeting in 1994, Goynor boldly invited his 65 employees to push sales from $18 million per year to $50 million— and they reached the goal in 5 years. TNG's culture includes "sales-enthusiastic [values], a learning friendly environment, and incredible customer service." Almost as soon as new employees arrive, they are introduced to TNG's winning team spirit. As Maureen Mann, vice president of sales for the Industry Source division, states, "You have to want to play on the team, and you have to want to win."

© Jon Mureson

gains in productivity and profits. Commit to education for all members' growth and development. Help employees become world-renowned experts. Cross-train to help people acquire multiple skills. Promote from within.[66]

Strong, Adaptive Culture

Corporate culture is the set of key values, beliefs, understandings, and norms shared by members of the organization. The culture is the foundation of a learning organization. The culture of a learning organization is strong and typically includes strong values in the following three areas:

1. *The whole is more important than the part, and boundaries between parts are minimized.*[67] People in the new workplace learning organization are aware of the whole system and how parts fit together. The emphasis on the whole reduces boundaries. People no longer hoard information or ideas for themselves. The move toward a *boundaryless organization* means reducing barriers among departments, divisions, and external organizations. The free flow of people, ideas, and information allows coordinated action to occur in an uncertain and changing environment.

2. *The culture is egalitarian.* The culture of a learning organization creates a sense of community, compassion, and caring for one another. People count. Every person has value. The learning organization becomes a place for creating a web of relationships that nurtures and develops each person to his or her maximum potential. Executive perks such as private dining rooms or reserved parking spots are eliminated. For example, the igus Inc. manufacturing company in Cologne, Germany, built a new plant to foster an open and egalitarian work environment. Walls separating the office area from the factory floor are transparent, to eliminate perceived barriers between employees and managers. There are no designated parking spaces for managers, and everyone comes in the same entrance, uses the same restrooms, and eats in the same cafeteria.[68] In learning organizations, everyone may share in stock options or performance bonuses, too. The orientation toward people provides safety for experimentation, frequent mistakes, and failures that enable learning. People are treated with respect and thereby contribute their best to the company.

3. *The culture values change, risk-taking, and improvement.* A basic value is to question the status quo, the current way of doing things. Can we do this any better? Why do we do this job that way? Constant questioning of assumptions and challenging the status quo open the gates to creativity and improvement. The organization learns to do things faster and to improve everything on an ongoing basis. An adaptive culture means that people care about important stakeholders, including employees, customers, and stockholders. Managers pay close attention to stakeholders and initiate change when needed. The culture also celebrates and rewards the creators of new ideas, products, and work processes.

In the learning organization, the culture encourages openness, boundarylessness, equality, continuous improvement, and change. The learning organization is always moving forward. Although no company represents a perfect example of a learning organization, one excellent example is Chaparral Steel, which has been called a learning laboratory.

Chaparral Steel

http://www.chaparralsteel.com

The tenth-largest U.S. steel producer, Chaparral Steel has won international recognition for quality and productivity. Chaparral produces 1,100 tons of steel each year compared to the U.S. average of 350 tons. It has become an experimental laboratory for the latest techniques of learning organizations.

What makes Chaparral so effective? Managers articulate a clear vision—to lead the world in the low-cost, safe production of high-quality steel—along with the cultural values of egalitarianism and respect for the individual. Everyone participates. Everyone is empowered to solve problems. When a cooling hose burst, a group of operators—a welder, a foreman, and a buyer—all responded because they saw the problem. There is no assumption that other people are expected to do a job. Since employees know the vision and values, supervisors do not micromanage. Chaparral has few supervisors, and only two levels of hierarchy separate the CEO from operators in the rolling mill.

Employees are rewarded for learning new skills and for performance. Ideas are contributed by just about everyone. Employees are paid a salary rather than an hourly wage—hence, everyone acts like an owner and a manager. People are also rewarded with bonuses from company profits, which are shared with everyone, including janitors and secretaries.

All employees contribute to sharing information and knowledge. A steel plant is deliberately held to fewer than 1,000 employees so that people can communicate easily. An employee experimenting with new equipment will tell other people how it works. Employees who visit a competitor's plant will explain to others what they learned. There are no staff people and no boundaries among departments because there are few departments. Everyone is considered a salesperson and is free to communicate with customers and potential customers. There is no research and development department because employees on the line are responsible for innovation in new techniques and products. To reinforce continuous learning, employees are encouraged to attend school, and many are teachers of other employees in formal classes. The culture values ideas that benefit the whole company rather than individual ownership of ideas, so new knowledge is shared liberally.

Experimentation is rampant. The cultural value is: If you have an idea, try it. First-level managers can authorize thousands of dollars for employee experiments. Everyone is encouraged to push beyond current knowledge. This involves risk, which is another cultural value. Employees tolerate, even welcome, risk on a production line that is very expensive to shut down.

Strategy emerges from employee contacts outside the organization. Employees travel constantly, scanning for new ideas at trade shows and other companies. Teams of employees that include vice-presidents and shop people travel together to investigate a new technology.

Chaparral is so good at what it does that it welcomes competitors to visit the plant. A competitor can be shown everything Chaparral does and yet take away nothing, because a learning organization is created by leadership, culture, and empowered people. Most other steelmakers have been unable to achieve this, because they don't have the commitment or the vision.[69]

Chaparral Steel is becoming a true learning organization. The leadership provides a flat, team-based design, a shared vision, and an attitude of serving employees. The culture stresses egalitarian values, providing support for risk taking. There are no boundaries separating departments. People are empowered to the point where no one has to take orders if he or she feels the order is wrong. The strategy emerges through the experiences of employees who work with customers and new technologies. Chaparral is flooded with information from experiments and travel, which is liberally shared.

Factors Shaping Structure

How do managers know whether to design a structure that emphasizes the formal, vertical hierarchy or one with an emphasis on horizontal communication and collaboration? The answer lies in the contingency factors that influence organization structure. Recall from Chapter 1 that *contingency* pertains to those factors on which structure depends. Research on organization structure shows that the emphasis given to a rigid or flexible structure depends on the contingency factors of strategy, environment, production technology, and departmental interdependence. The right structure is designed to "fit" the contingency factors as illustrated in Exhibit 7.12. Let us look at the relationship between some contingency factors and organization structure in more detail. The four contingency factors affect whether an organization should have a traditional vertical structure or a new workplace horizontal structure. These four areas are changing quite dramatically for most organizations, creating a need for stronger horizontal coordination.

Structure Follows Strategy

In Chapter 5, we discussed several strategies that business firms can adopt. Two strategies proposed by Michael E. Porter are differentiation and cost leadership.[70] With a differentiation strategy, the organization attempts to develop innovative products unique to the market, which is MTV International's strategy, as described below.

MTV

http://www.mtv.com

MTV was there first internationally. Since expanding into the Russian Market in 1993, it has been ahead of the competition for 24-hour music channels in nearly every market. In some of the markets, it has adopted the strategy of taking on local partners. And if strategy determines structure, MTV has found it needs to be more decentralized in these situations, giving up control so that 70 percent of programming is local content.

Sometimes that causes problems, such as the nude wrestling program that cropped up in Taiwan (MTV central pulled it off the air), or the early programmers in India who thought Bollywood music (from India's vast movie industry) was uncool. After viewers left en masse, local programmers got the message and reinstated Bollywood music. Since then, its ratings have soared 700 percent.

Following this strategy can be time consuming. MTV Networks International president Bill Roedy spent an entire evening listening to Chinese opera and participating in endless karaoke sessions; he tried desperately to cultivate relationships in China. It worked, because MTV Mandarin is seen in 60 million homes and last year over 10,000 Chinese teens competed to become the next MTV Mandarin veejay. Some of the local programming could only happen in that country. Take Italy's *MTV Kitchen,* where singers and songwriters chat while cooking, or the one in Brazil: *Rockgol* is a soccer championship pitting Brazilian musicians against recording industry executives. It's like having Lenny Kravitz and Michael Jackson on a football team against Tommy Mottola and David Geffen.[71]

Contingency Factors

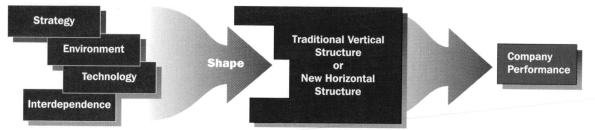

With a cost leadership strategy, the organization strives for internal efficiency. The strategies of cost leadership versus differentiation typically require different structural approaches, so managers try to pick strategies and structures that are congruent.

Exhibit 7.13 shows a simplified continuum that illustrates how structural approaches are associated with strategic goals. The pure functional structure is appropriate for achieving internal efficiency goals. The vertical functional structure uses task specialization and a strict chain of command to gain efficient use of scarce resources, but it does not enable the organization to be flexible or innovative. In contrast, the learning organization is appropriate when the primary goal is innovation and flexibility. Each team is small, is able to be responsive, and has the people and resources necessary for performing its task. The flexible horizontal structure enables organizations to differentiate themselves and respond quickly to the demands of a shifting environment but at the expense of efficient resource use. Changing strategy and environmental conditions also shape structure in government organizations. For example, under financial pressure to cut costs and political pressure to keep customers happy, Departments of Motor Vehicles in some states are farming out DMV business whenever possible, by building strong partnerships with other companies. For example, in several states, including Illinois, Oregon, and Tennessee, auto dealers register new cars on site when they are sold.[72]

Exhibit 7.13 also illustrates how other forms of structure described in this chapter—decentralized with horizontal coordination, divisional, and team—represent intermediate steps on the organization's path to efficiency and/or innovation. The functional structure with horizontal teams and integrating managers provides greater coordination and flexibility than the pure functional

EXHIBIT 7.12

Contingency Factors that Influence Organization Structure

EXHIBIT 7.13

Relationship of Strategic Goals to Structural Approach

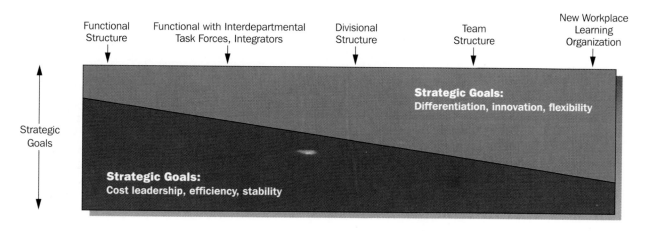

structure. The divisional structure promotes differentiation because each division can focus on specific products and customers, although divisions tend to be larger and less flexible than small teams. Exhibit 7.13 does not include all possible structures, but it illustrates how structures can be used to facilitate the strategic goals of cost leadership or differentiation.

Structure Reflects the Environment

In Chapter 2, we discussed the nature of environmental uncertainty. Environmental uncertainty means that decision makers have difficulty acquiring good information and predicting external changes. Uncertainty occurs when the external environment is rapidly changing and complex. An uncertain environment causes three things to happen within an organization.

1. *Increased differences occur among departments.* In an uncertain environment, each major department—marketing, manufacturing, research and development—focuses on the task and environmental sectors for which it is responsible and hence distinguishes itself from the others with respect to goals, task orientation, and time horizon.[73] Departments work autonomously. These factors create barriers among departments.

2. *The organization needs increased coordination to keep departments working together.* Additional differences require more emphasis on horizontal coordination to link departments and overcome differences in departmental goals and orientations. The Salvation Army finds its needs for coordination increase during some disasters, as described in the Best Practices box.

3. *The organization must adapt to change.* The organization must maintain a flexible, responsive posture toward the environment. Changes in products and technology require cooperation among departments, which means additional emphasis on coordination through the use of teams, project managers, and horizontal information processing.[74]

The contingency relationship between environmental uncertainty and structural approach is illustrated in Exhibit 7.14. When the external environment is more stable, the organization can succeed with a traditional structure that emphasizes vertical control. There is little need for change, flexibility, or

EXHIBIT 7.14

Relationship between Environment and Structure

	STRUCTURE	
	Vertical	Horizontal
Uncertain (Unstable)	**Incorrect Fit:** Vertical structure in uncertain environment Structure too tight	**Correct Fit:** Horizontal structure in uncertain environment
Certain (Stable)	**Correct Fit:** Vertical structure in certain environment	**Incorrect Fit:** Horizontal structure in certain environment Structure too loose

ENVIRONMENT

BEST PRACTICES

Salvation Army

The Salvation Army is a frugal organization. Nobody makes much money and accounting practices demand strict accountability for every penny spent. So imagine the possible panic that could occur when they step in to help with an emergency and commit to spending $250,000 without even knowing where the money will come from. Without a flexible structure, the organization would find itself either conflicted or else with one side—either strict financial controls or generous donations—winning out. Salvation Army has figured out how to have it both ways by having several organizations in one. Their day-to-day financial accountability reputation allows them to raise emergency funds quickly.

At the same time, they need to organize for emergencies using the Incident Command Model used by government and relief agencies. It is a highly structured, command-and-control formula that allows anyone to know exactly who is in charge of what. But other circumstances require a more entrepreneurial approach and the Army has the flexibility to allow that. During the 1997 upper Midwest floods, for example, Major Dahlberg (they go by military titles) brought in real estate specialist–Salvation Army people, who were given general guidelines and then allowed to go off on their own to acquire properties and find rental units. There wasn't time for supervisors to sign off on every transaction, so the specialists were given authority to make deals on the spot, under the agreed-upon format. Other Army people focused on networking, working the horizontal relationships to enhance their service. During that time, Wal-Mart helped them assess logistical needs, then sent in 26 experienced warehouse staff to help them organize the distribution of clothing, food, and household items. As a result, they reduced the wait time in the distribution centers to 45 minutes, down from 2.5 hours.

The Salvation Army has a flexible structure that allows various units to adapt to the work being done, or to environmental conditions. Some workers are almost independent contractors, cleaning houses and preparing food, while office workers are given more guidelines and supervision. The structure is driven by the mission of a particular unit, as well. A risk is developing too many "hero" types who love to save people during disasters, but who aren't as likely to spend their time in staff development, organization design, or planning. Without organization, however, disasters will be just that—disasters. Over years of experience, the Salvation Army has learned how to replace people who crave adrenaline and excitement more than a chance to serve. Such a model allows for organizational flexibility. It's about good management.

SOURCE: Robert A. Watson and Ben Brown, *The Most Effective Organization in the US: Leadership Secrets of the Salvation Army* (New York: Crown Business, 2001).

intense coordination. The structure can emphasize specialization, centralized decision making, and wide spans of control. When environmental uncertainty is high, a horizontal structure that emphasizes lateral relationships such as teams and horizontal projects is appropriate. Vertical structure characteristics such as specialization, centralization, and formalized procedures should be downplayed. In an uncertain environment, the organization figures things out as it goes along, departments must cooperate, and decisions should be decentralized to the teams and task forces working on specific problems. The flight deck of the USS *Dwight D. Eisenhower,* a nuclear-powered aircraft carrier, provides an excellent example of the relationship between structure and the environment.

The USS *Dwight D. Eisenhower*

On an aircraft carrier such as the USS *Dwight D. Eisenhower,* there are thousands of disastrous accidents just waiting to happen. Launching or landing a plane from the oil-slicked deck of a nuclear-powered carrier is a tricky, finely balanced procedure. A sudden wind shift, a mechanical breakdown, or the slightest of miscommunications could spell disaster. Yet, surprisingly, flight deck operations generally run as smooth as silk, and accidents are quite rare. The reason has a lot to do with organizational structure.

At first glance, a nuclear aircraft carrier is structured in a rigid, hierarchical way—the captain issues orders to commanders, who direct lieutenants, who pass orders on to ensigns, and on down the hierarchy. There is a strict chain of command, and people are expected to follow orders promptly and without question. Formalization is high, with manuals detailing standard operating procedures for everything. But an interesting thing happens in times of high demand, such as the launching and recovery of planes during real or simulated wartime. In this different environment, the hierarchy dissolves and a loosely organized, collaborative structure in which sailors and officers work together as colleagues takes its place. People discuss and negotiate the best procedure to use, and everyone typically follows the lead of whoever has the most experience and knowledge in a particular area, no matter the person's rank or job title. During this time, no one is thinking about job descriptions, authority, or chain of command; they are just thinking about getting the job done safely. With planes landing every 60 seconds, there is no time to send messages up the chain of command and wait for decisions to come down from the top. Anyone who notices a problem is expected to respond quickly, and each member of the crew has the power—and the obligation—to shut down flight operations immediately if the circumstances warrant it.[75]

Researchers have studied this ability to glide smoothly from a rigid, hierarchical structure to a loosely structured, horizontal one, not only on aircraft carriers but in other organizations that have to be exceptionally responsive to environmental changes—for example, air-traffic controllers or nuclear power plants. The hierarchical side helps keep discipline and ensure adherence to rules that have been developed and tested over many years to cope with expected and well-understood problems and situations. However, during times of complexity and high uncertainty, the most effective structure is one that loosens the lines of command and enables people to work across departmental and hierarchical lines to anticipate and avoid problems.[76]

Structure Fits the Technology

technology

The knowledge, tools, techniques, and activities used to transform the organization's inputs into outputs.

Technology includes the knowledge, tools, techniques, and activities used to transform organizational inputs into outputs.[77] Technology includes machinery, employee skills, and work procedures. A useful way to think about technology is as production activities. The production activities may be to produce steel castings, television programs, or computer software.

Production technology is significant because it has direct influence on the organization structure. Structure must be designed to fit the technology as well as to accommodate the external environment. Technologies vary between manufacturing and service organizations. In addition, new digital technology has an impact on structure as well. In the following paragraphs, we discuss each characteristic of technology and the structure that best fits it.

Woodward's Manufacturing Technology. The most influential research into the relationship between manufacturing technology and organization structure was conducted by Joan Woodward, a British industrial sociologist.[78] She gathered data from 100 British firms to determine whether basic structural characteristics, such as administrative overhead, span of control, centralization, and formalization, were different across firms. She found that manufacturing firms could be categorized according to three basic types of production technology:

1. *Small-batch and unit production.* **Small-batch production** firms produce goods in batches of one or a few products designed to customer specification. Each customer orders a unique product. This technology also is used to make large, one-of-a-kind products, such as computer-controlled machines. Small-batch manufacturing is close to traditional skilled-craft work, because human beings are a large part of the process; they run machines to make the product. Examples of items produced through small-batch manufacturing include custom clothing, special-order machine tools, space capsules, satellites, and submarines.

small-batch production

A type of technology that involves the production of goods in batches of one or a few products designed to customer specifications.

2. *Large-batch and mass production.* **Mass production** technology is distinguished by standardized production runs. A large volume of products is produced, and all customers receive the same product. Standard products go into inventory for sale as customers need them. This technology makes greater use of machines than does small-batch production. Machines are designed to do most of the physical work, and employees complement the machinery. Examples of mass production are automobile assembly lines and the large-batch techniques used to produce computers, tobacco products, and textiles.

mass production

A type of technology characterized by the production of a large volume of products with the same specifications.

3. *Continuous process production.* In **continuous process production**, the entire work flow is mechanized. This is the most sophisticated and complex form of production technology. Because the process runs continuously, there is no starting and stopping. Human operators are not part of actual production because machinery does all of the work. Human operators simply read dials, fix machines that break down, and manage the production process. Examples of continuous process technologies are chemical plants, distilleries, petroleum refineries, and nuclear power plants.

continuous process production

A type of technology involving mechanization of the entire work flow and nonstop production.

The difference among the three manufacturing technologies is called technical complexity. **Technical complexity** means the degree to which machinery is involved in the production to the exclusion of people. With a complex technology, employees are hardly needed except to monitor the machines.

technical complexity

The degree to which complex machinery is involved in the production process to the exclusion of people.

The structural characteristics associated with each type of manufacturing technology are illustrated in Exhibit 7.15. Note that formalization and centralization are high for mass production technology and low for continuous process.

	Manufacturing Technology		
	Small Batch	Mass Production	Continuous Process
Technical Complexity of Production Technology	Low	Medium	High
Organization structure:			
Formalization	Low	High	Low
Centralization	Low	High	Low
Top administrator ratio	Low	Medium	High
Indirect/direct labor ratio	1/9	1/4	1/1
Supervisor span of control	23	48	15
Communication:			
Written (vertical)	Low	High	Low
Verbal (horizontal)	High	Low	High
Overall structure	Flexible	Rigid	Flexible

EXHIBIT 7.15

Relationship between Manufacturing Technology and Organization Structure

SOURCE: Based on Joan Woodward, *Industrial Organizations: Theory and Practice* (London: Oxford University Press, 1965).

Unlike small-batch and continuous process, standardized mass production machinery requires centralized decision making and well-defined rules and procedures. The administrative ratio and the percentage of indirect labor required also increase with technological complexity. Because the production process is nonroutine, closer supervision is needed. More indirect labor in the form of maintenance people is required because of the machinery's complexity; thus, the indirect/direct labor ratio is high. Span of control for first-line supervisors is greatest for mass production. On an assembly line, jobs are so routinized that a supervisor can handle an average of 48 employees. The number of employees per supervisor in small-batch and continuous process production is lower because closer supervision is needed. Overall, small-batch and continuous process firms have somewhat loose, flexible structures, and mass production firms have tight, vertical structures.

The important conclusion about manufacturing technology was described by Woodward as follows: "Different technologies impose different kinds of demands on individuals and organizations, and these demands have to be met through an appropriate structure."[79] Woodward found that the relationship between structure and technology was directly related to company performance. Low-performing firms tended to deviate from the preferred structural form, often adopting a structure appropriate for another type of technology. High-performing organizations had characteristics very similar to those listed in Exhibit 7.15.

Service Technology. Service organizations are becoming increasingly important in North America. For the past two decades, more people have been employed in service organizations than in manufacturing organizations. Thus, research has been undertaken to understand the structural characteristics of service organizations. Examples of service organizations include consulting companies, law firms, brokerage houses, airlines, hotels, advertising firms, amusement parks, and educational organizations. In addition, service technology characterizes many departments in large corporations, even manufacturing firms. In a manufacturing company such as Ford Motor Company, the legal, human resources, finance, and market research departments all provide service. Thus, the structure and design of these departments reflect their own service technology rather than the manufacturing plant's technology. **Service technology** can be defined as follows:

service technology

Technology characterized by intangible outputs and direct contact between employees and customers.

1. *Intangible output.* The output of a service firm is intangible. Services are perishable and, unlike physical products, cannot be stored in inventory. The service is either consumed immediately or lost forever. Manufactured products are produced at one point in time and can be stored until sold at another time.

2. *Direct contact with customers.* Employees and customers interact directly to provide and purchase the service. Production and consumption are simultaneous. Service firm employees have direct contact with customers. In a manufacturing firm, technical employees are separated from customers, and hence no direct interactions occur.[80]

One distinct feature of service technology that directly influences structure is the need for employees to be close to the customer.[81] Structural characteristics are similar to those for continuous manufacturing technology, shown in Exhibit 7.15. Service firms tend to be flexible, informal, and decentralized. Horizontal communication is high because employees must share information and resources to serve customers and solve problems. Services also are dispersed; hence each unit is often small and located geographically close to customers. For example, banks, hotels, fast-food franchises, and doctors' offices disperse their facilities into regional and local offices to provide faster and better service to customers.

Some services can be broken down into explicit steps, so that employees can follow set rules and procedures. For example, McDonald's has standard procedures for serving customers and Marriott has standard procedures for cleaning hotel rooms. When services can be standardized, a tight centralized structure can be effective, but service firms in general tend to be more flexible and decentralized.

Digital Technology. Digital technology is characterized by use of the Internet and other digital processes to conduct or support business online. E-commerce organizations such as Amazon.com, which sells books and other products to consumers over the Internet, eBay, an online auction site, Yahoo!, an Internet search engine, and Priceline.com, which allows consumers to name their own price and then negotiates electronically with its partner organizations on behalf of the consumer, are all examples of firms based on digital technology. In addition, large companies such as General Electric, Dell Computer, and Ford Motor Company are involved in business-to-business commerce, using digital technology to conduct transactions with suppliers and partners.

Like service firms, organizations based on digital technology tend to be flexible and decentralized. The fast-paced digital world practically demands a focus on horizontal processes rather than departmental functions. Horizontal communication and collaboration are typically very high, and these companies may frequently be involved in network and virtual arrangements. Digital technology is driving the move toward horizontal forms that link customers, suppliers, and partners into the organizational network, with everyone working together as if they were one organization, such as practiced by Noosh, Inc., described in the Digital, Inc. box.

People may use electronic connections to link themselves together into teams. For example, an employee may send an e-mail to people both within and outside the organization who can help with a particular customer problem and quickly form a virtual team to develop a solution.[82] In other words, digital technology encourages boundarylessness, where information and work activities flow freely among various organizational participants. Formalization and centralization are low, and employees are empowered to work in teams to meet fast-changing needs. Verbal and electronic communication is high, both up and down as well as across the organization because up-to-the minute information is essential. In the digital world, advantage comes from seeing first and moving fastest, which requires extraordinary openness and flexibility.[83]

digital technology
Technology characterized by use of the Internet and other digital processes to conduct or support business operations.

DIGITAL, INC.

Noosh, Inc.

Think of all those orders that go out each day for business stationery. Or how about those little key rings with a company's logo on them? Or sales kits? To design, develop, and order these items requires the collaboration of creative services units, printers, electronic media shops, and direct mailers. It can be a nightmare of miscommunication and conflict. Dave Hannbrink saw this as a business opportunity and launched Palo Alto–based Noosh, Inc., to provide a "collaborative commerce service" in order to improve the management process of procuring these collateral materials.

Noosh clients range from large corporate customers to printers and they all can log onto *http://www.noosh.com* and pay for services by transaction. They can inspect or change orders, send instant messages to everyone else involved in the project, and look up past communications regarding that particular project. Because mistakes can cost hundreds of thousands of dollars in this business, the smoother the communication, the more efficient the operation. In this complex world, businesses have more and more interactions outside their

doors. As an employee at Goldman Sachs said, "The biggest inefficiency a business faces is dealing with everyone else."

Deciding not to compete with online printers, Noosh found its niche in becoming the central information storehouse for collateral materials procurement. This ultimately leads to better relationships, because all the information is stored in the central location. It even helps certain vendors get more business. San Francisco commercial printer ColorGraphics started using Noosh at the request of several large customers. Because of the ease of sharing information, "it made some customers more comfortable giving us jobs," says ColorGraphics representative James Fucillo. Another Noosh customer, U.K. publisher The Stationery House, uses the system to allow its 200 suppliers to be involved in the design and manufacturing process when needed. Says stationery store manager Keith Burbage, "Noosh is a true collaborative system and a major breakthrough for the publishing industry."

SOURCE: Beth Stackpole, "Channel Crossing," *CIO* (February 15, 2001), 148–156.

■ Summary and Management Solution

This chapter introduced a number of important organizing concepts. Fundamental characteristics of organization structure include work specialization, chain of command, authority and responsibility, span of management, and centralization and decentralization. These dimensions of organization represent the vertical hierarchy and indicate how authority and responsibility are distributed along the hierarchy.

The other major concept is departmentalization, which describes how organization employees are grouped. Three traditional approaches are functional, divisional, and matrix; contemporary approaches are team and network structures. The most recent trend in organizing is the virtual approach. The functional approach groups employees by common skills and tasks. The opposite structure is divisional, which groups people by organizational output such that each division has a mix of functional skills and tasks. The matrix structure uses two chains of command simultaneously, and some employees have two bosses. The two chains of command in a domestic organization typically are functional and product division, and, for international firms, the two chains of command typically are product and geographic regions. The team approach uses permanent teams and

cross-functional teams to achieve better coordination and employee commitment than is possible with a pure functional structure. The network approach means that a firm concentrates on what it does best and subcontracts other functions to separate organizations that are connected to the headquarters electronically. The virtual approach brings together a group of specialists to complete a specific project, and the group disbands when objectives are met. Each organization form has advantages and disadvantages and can be used by managers to meet the needs of the competitive situation. In addition, managers adjust elements of the vertical structure, such as the degree of centralization or decentralization, to meet changing needs.

At Motorola, described at the beginning of the chapter, a lack of horizontal communication and collaboration was turning the company once admired around the world into a has-been. Galvin worked with other top managers to initiate a complete overhaul of the company and transform Motorola into a new kind of organization that could adapt to the rapid changes of the digital era. To increase horizontal communication and collaboration, they combined all of the 30 different units that make cell phone, wireless equipment, satellite, and cable modem products into one large communications division. Managers are paid based on their ability to work collaboratively to give customers easy-to-use ways to stay tapped into the Internet, whether it be via cell phone, pager, modem, or something no one has even invented yet. Furthermore, two horizontal coordination units were put in place: one charged with coordinating all the communication businesses to meet customer needs and the second charged with coordinating Internet strategies across all of Motorola's operations. Galvin's primary goal was to break down the intensely competitive culture that had developed within Motorola and replace it with one in which everyone puts the good of the whole above their individual business units.

After putting the new structure in place, managers began to work on external relationships. Motorola has developed strategic alliances with some of the most important players in the Internet world, including Cisco Systems, Yahoo!, America Online, and Amazon.com. In addition, the company is bringing major customers into the information network so they can also help shape the strategic direction Motorola will take. Motorola's shift to a more flexible, horizontal structure reflects its strategy of differentiating itself with innovative, Net-ready wireless products, the need to respond to rapid environmental changes, and the complexity and fast pace of digital technology. So far, the results of the shift have been dramatic. Motorola was able to bring out innovative phones embedded with Web browsers ahead of competitors, and customers are impressed with the quality and technological sophistication of the new equipment.[84] The increased horizontal communication and collaboration, both within the company and with outside organizations, have made Motorola mighty once again.

■ Discussion Questions

1. Many experts note that organizations have been making greater use of teams in recent years. What factors might account for this trend?
2. What is the network approach to structure? Is the use of authority and responsibility different compared with other forms of departmentalization? Explain.
3. How is a virtual organization different from a network organization? When might a company choose to use a virtual approach rather than a network structure?
4. A few of today's organizations pride themselves on the fact that they have no organization charts. What do you think this says about a company's structure?
5. What types of skills does a person need to be an effective project manager? Why do you think so many of today's companies are organizing around projects?
6. Discuss why an organization in an uncertain environment requires more horizontal relationships than one in a certain environment.
7. Why are empowered employees, open information, and cultural values of minimal boundaries and equality important in a new workplace learning organization as opposed to a traditional, vertical organization?
8. What is the difference between manufacturing and service technology? How would you classify a university, a local discount store, a nursery school? How would you expect the structure of a service organization to differ from that of a manufacturing organization?
9. What impact does the growing use of digital technology have on organizational structure? Would you expect the structure of an Internet-based organization such as eBay, which operates almost entirely online, to be different from a bricks-and-mortar company such as Aramark (a food-service company), which uses the Internet for business-to-business transactions with vendors? Why or why not?

■ Manager's Workbook

Loose versus Tight Organization Structure

Interview an employee at your university, such as a department head or secretary. Have the employee answer the following questions about his or her job and organizational conditions.

	Strongly Disagree			Strongly Agree	
1. Your work would be considered routine.	5	4	3	2	1
2. There is a clearly known way to do the major tasks you encounter.	5	4	3	2	1
3. Your work has high variety and frequent exceptions.	1	2	3	4	5

	Strongly Disagree				Strongly Agree
4. Communications from above consist of information and advice rather than instructions and directions.	1	2	3	4	5
5. You have the support of peers and supervisor to do your job well.	1	2	3	4	5
6. You seldom exchange ideas or information with people doing other kinds of jobs.	5	4	3	2	1
7. Decisions relevant to your work are made above you and passed down.	5	4	3	2	1
8. People at your level frequently have to figure out for themselves what their jobs are for the day.	1	2	3	4	5
9. Lines of authority are clear and precisely defined.	5	4	3	2	1
10. Leadership tends to be democratic rather than autocratic in style.	1	2	3	4	5
11. Job descriptions are written and up-to-date for each job.	5	4	3	2	1
12. People understand each other's jobs and often do different tasks.	1	2	3	4	5
13. A manual of policies and procedures is available to use when a problem arises.	5	4	3	2	1

Total Score _____

A score of 52 or above suggests that the employee is working in a "loosely structured" organization. The score reflects a flexible structure that is often associated with uncertain environments and small-batch technology. People working in this structure feel empowered. Many organizations today are moving in the direction of flexible structures and empowerment.

A score of 26 or below suggests a "tight structure." This structure utilizes traditional control and functional specializa-tion, which often occurs in a certain environment, a stable organization, and routine or mass-production technology. People in this structure may feel controlled and constrained.

Discuss the pros and cons of loose versus tight structure. Does the structure of the employee you interviewed fit the nature of the organization's environment, strategic goals, and technology? How might you redesign the structure to make the work organization more effective?

■ Manager's Workshop

Bistro Technology

You will be analyzing the technology used in three different restaurants: McDonald's, Burger King, and a typical family restaurant. Your instructor will tell you whether to do this assignment as individuals or in a group.

You must visit all three restaurants and infer how the work is done, according to the criteria below. However, you are not allowed to "interview" any employees, but must instead be only an observer. Take lots of notes while you are there.

	McDonald's	Burger King	Family restaurant
Organization goals: Speed, service, atmosphere, etc.			
Authority structure			
Type of technology, based on Woodward's model			
Organization structure: Mechanistic or organic			
Team vs. individual: Do people work together or alone?			
Tasks: Routine versus non-routine			
Specialization of tasks by employees (division of labor)			
Expertise required: Technical versus social			
Decision-making: Centralized versus decentralized			

1. Is the technology used the best one for each restaurant, considering its goals and environment?
2. From the data above, determine if the structure and other characteristics fit the technology.
3. If you were part of a consulting team assigned to improve the operations of each organization, what recommendations would you make?

SOURCE: Adapted from "Hamburger Technology," in Douglas T. Hall et al., *Experiences in Management and Organizational Behavior,* 2e. New York: John Wiley & Sons, 1982, pp. 244–247; and "Behavior, Technology, and Work Design," in A.B. Shani and James B. Lau, *Behavior in Organizations.* Chicago: Irwin, 1996, pp. M16–23 to M16–26.

■ Management in Practice: Ethical Dilemma

Caught in the Middle

Tom Harrington loved his job as an assistant quality control officer for Rockingham Toys. After six months of unemployment, he was anxious to make a good impression on his boss, Frank Golopolus. One of the responsibilities of his boss was ensuring that new product lines met federal safety guidelines. Rockingham had made several manufacturing changes over the past year. Golopolus and the rest of the quality control team had been working 60-hour weeks to troubleshoot the new production process.

While sorting incoming mail during the past weeks, Harrington had become aware of numerous changes in product safety guidelines that he knew would impact the new Rockingham toys. Golopolus was taking no action to implement new guidelines, and he didn't seem to understand or care about them. Harrington, who avoided the questions he received from the floor to cover for his boss, was beginning to wonder if Rockingham would have time to make changes with the Christmas season rapidly approaching.

Harrington knew it was not his job to order the changes, and he didn't want to alienate Golopolus by interfering, but he was beginning to worry what might happen if he didn't act. Rockingham had a fine product safety reputation and was rarely challenged on matters of quality. He felt loyalty to Golopolus for giving him a job, but he worried Golopolus was in over his head.

What Do You Do?

1. Prepare a memo to Golopolus, summarizing the new safety guidelines that affect the Rockingham product line and recommending implementation.
2. Mind your own business. You do not have authority to monitor the federal regulations. Besides, you've been unemployed and need this job.
3. Send copies of the reports anonymously to the operations manager, who is Golopolus's boss.

SOURCE: Based on Doug Wallace, "The Man Who Knew Too Much," *What Would You Do? Business Ethics,* vol. II (March–April 1993), 7–8.

■ Surf the Net

1. **Organization Structure.** Using the search phrase "organization chart," locate an organization chart for a government agency, print it out, analyze it based on what you have learned in the chapter about the various organization structures, and be prepared to discuss your example during class.
2. **Team-based Approach.** Go to the "Career" section of any of the following companies' Web sites to locate how the company presents a discussion of the team-based emphasis the company uses.
   Merck: *http://www.merck.com/*
   Pizza Hut: *http://www.pizzahut.com/*
   Reliant Energy: *http://www.reliantenergy.com*

3. **Team Player Analysis.** Go to the following site, carefully read the exercise instructions, and then go to the exercise (where you will be asked to complete a free registration process to gain access to the exercise).
   http://www.managementlearning.com/inv/begiwti/index.html

   After completing the exercise, print your result profile, along with the description of the eight team strengths (producer, diplomat, driver, inventor, judge, scout, supporter, and inspector). Bring your printouts to class and be prepared to discuss your results.

■ Case for Critical Analysis

Tucker Company

In 1993 the Tucker Company underwent an extensive reorganization that divided the company into three major divisions. These new divisions represented Tucker's three principal product lines. Mr. Harnett, Tucker's president, explained the basis for the new organization in a memo to the board of directors as follows:

The diversity of our products requires that we reorganize along our major product lines. Toward this end I have established three new divisions: commercial jet engines, military jet engines, and utility turbines. Each division will be headed by a new vice president who will report directly to me. I believe that this new approach will enhance our performance through the commitment of individual managers. It should also help us to identify unprofitable areas where the special attention of management may be required.

For the most part, each division will be able to operate independently. That is, each will have its own engineering, manufacturing, accounting departments, etc. In some cases, however, it will be necessary for a division to utilize the services of other divisions or departments. This is necessary because the complete servicing with individual divisional staffs would result in unjustifiable additional staffing and facilities.

The old companywide laboratory was one such service department. Functionally, it continued to support all of the major divisions. Administratively, however, the manager of the laboratory reported to the manager of manufacturing in the military jet engine division.

From the time the new organization was initiated until February 1999, when the laboratory manager Mr. Garfield retired, there was little evidence of interdepartmental or interdivisional conflict. His replacement, Ms. Hodge, unlike Mr. Garfield, was always eager to gain the attention of management. Many of Hodge's peers perceived her as an empire builder who was interested in her own advancement rather than the company's well-being. After about six months in the new position, Hodge became involved in several interdepartmental conflicts over work that was being conducted in her laboratory.

Historically, the engineering departments had used the laboratory as a testing facility to determine the properties of materials selected by the design engineers. Hodge felt that the laboratory should be more involved in the selection of these materials and in the design of experiments and subsequent evaluations of the experimental data. Hodge discussed this with Mr. Franklin of the engineering department of the utility turbine division. Franklin offered to consult with Hodge but stated that the final responsibility for the selection of materials was charged to his department.

In the months that followed, Hodge and Franklin had several disagreements over the implementation of the results. Franklin told Hodge that, because of her position at the testing lab, she was unable to appreciate the detailed design considerations that affected the final decision on materials selection. Hodge claimed that Franklin lacked the materials expertise that she, as a metallurgist, had.

Franklin also noted that the handling of his requests, which had been prompt under Garfield's management, was taking longer and longer under Hodge's management. Hodge explained that military jet engine divisional problems had to be assigned first priority because of the administrative reporting structure. She also said that if she were more involved in Franklin's problems, she could perhaps appreciate when a true sense of urgency existed and could revise priorities.

The tensions between Franklin and Hodge reached a peak when one of Franklin's critical projects failed to receive the scheduling that he considered necessary. Franklin phoned Hodge to discuss the need for a schedule change. Hodge suggested that they have a meeting to review the need for the work. Franklin then told Hodge that this was not a matter of her concern and that her function was merely to perform the tests as requested. He further stated that he was not satisfied with the low-priority rating that his division's work received. Hodge reminded Franklin that when Hodge had suggested a means for resolving this problem, Franklin was not receptive. At this point, Franklin lost his temper and hung up on Hodge.

Questions

1. Sketch out a simple organization chart showing Tucker Company's three divisions, including the location of the laboratory. Why would the laboratory be located in the military jet engine division?

2. Analyze the conflict between Ms. Hodge and Mr. Franklin. Do you think the conflict is based on personalities or on the way in which the organization is structured?

3. Sketch out a new organization chart showing how you would restructure Tucker Company so that the laboratory would provide equal services to all divisions. What advantages and disadvantages do you see in the new structure compared to the previous one?

SOURCE: Reprinted with permission of Macmillan Publishing Company from "The Laboratory," *Organizational Behavior: Readings and Cases,* 2d ed., 385–387, by L. Katz, prepared under the supervision of Theodore T. Herbert. Copyright © 1981 by Theodore T. Herbert.

CHAPTER

8

Change and Development

LEARNING OBJECTIVES

After studying this chapter, you should be able to

1 Define organizational change and explain the forces for change.

2 Describe the sequence of four change activities that must be performed in order for change to be successful.

3 Explain the techniques managers can use to facilitate the initiation of change in organizations, including idea champions, new-venture teams, and idea incubators.

4 Define sources of resistance to change.

5 Explain force field analysis and other implementation tactics that can be used to overcome resistance to change.

6 Explain the difference among technology, product, structure, and culture/people changes.

7 Explain the change process—bottom up, top down, horizontal—associated with each type of change.

8 Define organizational development and large-group interventions.

When Harvard Business School student Andrew Ive realized his dorm room had no fire escape, he bought one and it splintered under his weight. He got fellow HBS student Aldo DiBelardino, who had an engineering background, to design a spiffy and safe ladder, while Ive polished the X-It Products business plan. Within three years, X-It had an innovative product—a lightweight ladder that could collapse to a shoebox size. After showing the product for a couple of years at Chicago's National Hardware Show to giants such as Wal-Mart and Lowe's, it was also selling to the Southwest market of Home Depot, as well as through Amway and Kmart. They were even approached by market leader British Kidde Safety with an offer to buy out X-It. But later, at a trade show, Ive noticed a ladder almost exactly like theirs being sold at the Kidde booth. Ive screamed foul, but Kidde said X-It's patent was only pending. X-It filed suit, a case that took two years to win and cost $3 million in legal fees, and at the same time the company's revenues slumped 31 percent to $248,000. Not only was the company deteriorating financially, but the two founders had opposite ideas on how to save the company. Ive wanted to add to infrastructure with extensive customer service and a new and more convenient office. DiBelardino, on the other hand, saw cost-cutting as the only salvation. The investors decided to take DiBelardino's proposal, which meant the exit of Ive.[1]

If you were DiBelardino, what would you do now to keep X-It from collapsing?

forces
customer
competitor
technology
economic
international
political

Ive, DiBelardino, and X-It are not alone. Every organization sometimes faces the need to change quickly and dramatically to survive in a changing environment. Sometimes, changes are brought about by forces outside the organization. Other times, managers within the company want to initiate major changes but don't know how. Lack of innovation from within is widely recognized as one of the critical problems facing business today in the United States and Canada. To be successful, organizations must embrace many types of change. Businesses must develop improved production technologies, create new products desired in the marketplace, implement new administrative systems, and upgrade employees' skills. Companies such as Whirlpool, Black & Decker, and Merck implement all of these changes and more.

How important is organizational change? Consider this: The parents of today's college students grew up without digital cameras, e-mail, laptop computers, DVDs, Web-access cell phones, and online shopping. Companies that produce the new products and services have prospered, but many companies caught with outdated products and technologies have failed. Today's successful companies are constantly striving to come up with new products and services. For example, Kyocera Wireless Corp. developed a device that combines a high-end mobile phone with a Palm OS digital assistant in a stylish package barely bigger than a deck of playing cards. Even at a list price of $500, the demand for the Smartphone was so great that Kyocera could barely keep up.[2] Engineers at automakers such as DaimlerChrysler, General Motors, and Toyota are perfecting fuel-cell power systems that could make today's internal combustion engine as obsolete as the steam locomotive. Pharmaceutical companies and biotechnology firms around the world are searching for new drugs and vaccines to fight diseases such as AIDS and cancer.[3] Organizations that change successfully are both profitable and admired.

organizational change
The adoption of a new idea or behavior by an organization.

Organizational change is defined as the adoption of a new idea or behavior by an organization.[4] In this chapter, we will look at how organizations can be designed to respond to the environment through internal change and development. First we will examine the basic forces for organizational change. Then we will look closely at how managers facilitate two change requirements: initiation and implementation. Finally, we will discuss the four major types of change—technology, new product, structure, and culture/people—and how the organization can be designed to facilitate each.

Change and the New Workplace

Today's organizations need to continuously adapt to new situations if they are to survive and prosper. As we discussed in Chapter 1, one of the most dramatic elements of change is the shift to a technology-driven workplace in which ideas, information, and relationships are becoming critically important. Many changes are being driven by advances in information technology and the Internet. New trends such as e-business, enterprise resource planning, and knowledge management require profound changes in the organization. These shifts are frequently linked to development of the *learning organization*, which is the epitome of continuous organizational learning and change.

As described in Chapter 7, the new workplace learning organization involves everyone in problem solving and continuous improvement based on the lessons of experience.[5] The various elements of the learning organization discussed in Chapter 7 interact with one another in such a way that each element responds to and influences every other element toward changing the organization to keep pace with today's digital world. For example, a *horizontal structure* breaks down boundaries within the organization, as well as with other companies, to promote collaboration for learning and change, which requires changes in employee empowerment, information sharing, and culture. *Empowerment* liberates employees but also places upon them the added responsibilities of working collaboratively, initiating changes, and participating in strategy to benefit the entire company. Redefining *culture* demands the rethinking of roles, processes, and values, breaking down barriers that have separated departments so that everyone shares information and works together. *Information sharing* requires adjustments on the part of managers for the inclusion of employees, suppliers, and customers, often necessitating cultural and structural changes. *Strategy* is likewise linked to structure and culture as the organization changes its fundamental way of doing business and allows change initiatives to flow bottom up as well as top down and to emerge from linkages with customers and partner organizations.

© Shelly Harrison

After years of wowing investors with stories of laboratory developments rather than predictable earnings, many biotechnology firms are undergoing transformational change to redesign and renew their entire organizations and show concrete evidence of growth. For example, Millennium Pharmaceuticals Inc., in the photo, is buying COR Therapeutics to get its experienced sales force and an established anticlotting drug. To compete with huge pharmaceutical companies such as Pfizer, biotech companies need to expand their product lines and make changes in systems, structures, and culture to promote growth.

The learning organization simultaneously embraces two types of planned change: *incremental change,* which refers to organizational efforts to gradually improve basic operational and work processes in different parts of the company, and *transformational change,* which involves redesigning and renewing the entire organization.[6] Change, particularly transformational change, does not happen easily. However, managers can learn to anticipate and facilitate change to help their organizations keep pace with the rapid changes in the external environment.

Model of Planned Organizational Change

Change can be managed. By observing external trends, patterns, and needs, managers use planned change to help the organization adapt to external problems and opportunities.[7] When organizations are caught flat-footed, failing to anticipate or respond to new needs, management is at fault.

An overall model for planned change is presented in Exhibit 8.1. Four events make up the change sequence: (1) Internal and external forces for change exist; (2) organization managers monitor these forces and become aware of a need for change; and (3) the perceived need triggers the initiation of change, which (4) is then implemented. How each of these activities is handled depends on the organization and managers' styles.

We now turn to a brief discussion of the specific activities associated with the first two events—forces for change and the perceived need for the organization to respond.

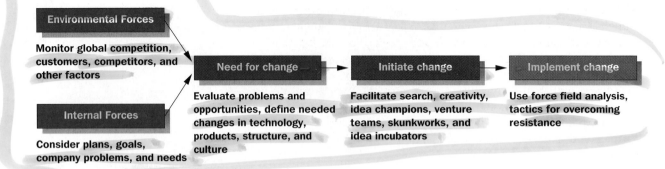

EXHIBIT *8.1*

Model of Change Sequence of Events

Forces for Change

Forces for organizational change exist both in the external environment and within the organization.

Environmental Forces. As described in Chapters 2 and 3, external forces originate in all environmental sectors, including customers, competitors, technology, economic forces, and the international arena.

Internal Forces. Internal forces for change arise from internal activities and decisions. If top managers select a goal of rapid company growth, internal actions will have to be changed to meet that growth. New departments or technologies will be created. Demands by employees, labor unions, and production inefficiencies all can generate a force to which management must respond with change. At the New York law firm of Cadwalader, Wickersham, and Taft, for example, growing complaints from younger partners about the firm's outmoded ways of doing business led to changes such as ending money-losing practices, revising pay systems that generated rivalries among partners, and changing archaic and time-consuming procedures. The changes helped turn the declining organization into one of the hottest firms on Wall Street.[8]

Need for Change

As indicated in Exhibit 8.1, external or internal forces translate into a perceived need for change within the organization. Many people are not willing to change unless they perceive a problem or a crisis. For example, many U.S. companies have changed how they conduct business as a result of the terrorist attacks of September 11, 2001. Top managers at E Commerce Group, a company that processes payments by phone and online, had been trying to find ways to promote teamwork and collaboration, but they kept running into resistance. However, after the hijacked planes struck the World Trade Center, across the street from E Commerce's offices, employees immediately began pitching in to help one another any way they could, and the new spirit of collaboration and teamwork has continued. "This crisis broke down the barriers," said Marc Mehl, cofounder and chief operating officer.[9]

In many cases, there is no crisis that prompts change. Most problems are subtle, so managers have to recognize and then make others aware of the need for change.[10] One way managers sense a need for change is when there is a **performance gap**—a disparity between existing and desired performance levels. They then try to create a sense of urgency so that others in the organization will recognize and understand the need for change. For example, the chief component-purchasing manager at Nokia noticed that order numbers for some

performance gap

A disparity between existing and desired performance levels.

of the computer chips it purchased from Philips Electronics weren't adding up, and he discovered that a fire at Philips' Albuquerque, New Mexico, plant had delayed production. The manager moved quickly to alert top managers, engineers, and others throughout the company that Nokia could be caught short of chips unless it took action. Within weeks, a crisis team had redesigned chips, found new suppliers, and restored the chip supply line. In contrast, managers at Ericsson, a competitor that also purchased chips from Philips, had the same information but failed to recognize or create a sense of crisis for change, which left the company millions of chips short of what it needed to produce a key product.[11]

Google.com founders realized there was a gap between where they were and where they wanted to be and are changing the organization to increase its potential, as shown in the Digital, Inc. box.

Recall from Chapter 5 the discussion of SWOT analysis. Managers are responsible for monitoring threats and opportunities in the external environment as well as strengths and weaknesses within the organization to determine whether a need for change exists.

Managers in every company must be alert to problems and opportunities, because the perceived need for change is what sets the stage for subsequent actions that create a new product or technology. Big problems are easy to spot. Sensitive monitoring systems are needed to detect gradual changes that can fool managers into thinking their company is doing fine. An organization may be in greater danger when the environment changes slowly, because managers may fail to trigger an organizational response. Failing to use planned change to

DIGITAL, INC.

Google.com

Where do you go after your small company earns $50 million in one year, after being in business only five years? Twentysomethings Sergey Brin and Larry Page started google.com as Stanford University computer science graduate students and dropped out of school to run it full-time in 1998. Currently, its business is split evenly between advertising on the Web site and offering its services to corporations. But it was run rather loosely in the beginning, which is something it can no longer afford, as its revenues continue to grow. Veteran Novell CEO Eric Schmidt was hired to help turn google.com into a tightly managed ship, including moving from small-business software to a heavy-duty financial product. Schmidt already has a new mission: to maximize Google's search technology through entering new markets.

The search engine's approach has been unique. Not only does it search for keywords inside Web pages, but it rank orders them by relevance, and caches most pages, in case some of them later disappear. Google is now the most-used search engine on the Internet, with 150 million searches daily. While other engines are losing advertising dollars, Google is adding them, mostly because its ads are unobtrusive lines above each listing.

Google is now trying to innovate its mission and business practices. Going after corporate customers, it offers the same basic service. For example, marthastewart.com hires it to trawl its own Web site when customers are searching for particular items. Though it operates in 66 languages and half its traffic comes from overseas, Google has yet to see much advertising from other countries. Schmidt plans to fix that by setting up a network of offices around the world that can forge relationships with potential advertisers.

All of this won't be enough if Google doesn't keep innovating its technology. It has to stay ahead of the pack, or it could go the way of the once-beloved Netscape browser. One thing in its favor: About half of its 300 employees are computer-science engineers, many with Ph.D.s, giving the company the brainpower to keep its lead. In order to keep innovation coming, Google treats employees well, offering massage therapists, parking-lot roller-hockey games, and free gourmet lunches cooked by private chefs, who prepare sushi, Hindu, and Thai food.

SOURCE: Jessica Guyn, "Dilbert Cartoon Graces Google Home Page for a Week," *Knight Ridder Tribune Business News* (May 21, 2002), 1; Ben Elgin and Kim Kerstetter, "Why They're Agog over Google," *Business Week* (September 24, 2001), 83–85.

meet small needs can place the organization in hot water, as illustrated in the following passage:

> When frogs are placed in a boiling pail of water, they jump out—they don't want to boil to death. However, when frogs are placed in a cold pail of water, and the pail is placed on a stove with the heat turned very low, over time the frogs will boil to death.[12]

Initiating Change

After the need for change has been perceived and communicated, change must be implemented. This is a critical phase of change management—the stage where the ideas that solve perceived needs are developed. Responses that an organization can make are to search for or create a change to adopt.

Search

search

The process of learning about current developments inside or outside the organization that can be used to meet a perceived need for change.

Search is the process of learning about current developments inside or outside the organization that can be used to meet the perceived need for change. Search typically uncovers existing knowledge that can be applied or adopted within the organization. Managers talk to friends and colleagues, read professional reports, or hire consultants to learn about ideas used elsewhere.

Many needs, however, cannot be resolved through existing knowledge but require that the organization develop a new response. Initiating a new response means that managers must design the organization so as to facilitate creativity of both individuals and departments, encourage innovative people to initiate new ideas, or create structural elements such as new venture departments, skunkworks, and idea incubators.

Creativity

creativity

The generation of novel ideas that may meet perceived needs or offer opportunities for the organization.

Creativity is the generation of novel ideas that may meet perceived needs or respond to opportunities for the organization. Creativity is the essential first step in innovation, which is vital to long-term organizational success.[13] People noted for their creativity include Edwin Land, who invented the Polaroid camera; Frederick Smith, who came up with the idea for Federal Express's overnight delivery service during an undergraduate class at Yale; and Swiss engineer George de Mestral, who created Velcro after noticing the tiny hooks on the burrs caught on his wool socks. Each of these people saw unique and creative opportunities in a familiar situation.

Each of us has the capacity to be creative. Characteristics of highly creative people are illustrated in the left-hand column of Exhibit 8.2. Creative people often are known for originality, open-mindedness, curiosity, a focused approach to problem solving, persistence, a relaxed and playful attitude, and receptivity to new ideas.[14]

Creativity can also be designed into organizations. Companies or departments within companies can be organized to be creative and initiate changes. Most companies want more highly creative employees and often seek to hire creative individuals. However, the individual is only part of the story, and everyone has some potential for creativity. Managers are responsible for creating a work environment that allows creativity to flourish.[15] The characteristics

The Creative Individual	The Creative Organization or Department

1. Conceptual fluency
   Open-mindedness
	1. Open channels of communication
	   Contact with outside sources
	   Overlapping territories
	   Suggestion systems, brainstorming, group
	   techniques

2. Originality	2. Assigning nonspecialists to problems
	   Eccentricity allowed
	   Hiring people who make you uncomfortable

3. Less authority
   Independence
   Self-confidence
	3. Decentralization, loosely defined positions, loose
	   control
	   Acceptance of mistakes
	   People encouraged to defy their bosses

4. Playfulness
   Undisciplined exploration
   Curiosity
	4. Freedom to choose and pursue problems
	   Not a tight ship, playful culture, doing the
	   impractical
	   Freedom to discuss ideas, long time horizon

5. Persistence
   Commitment
   Focused approach
	5. Resources allocated to creative personnel and
	   projects without immediate payoff
	   Reward system encourages innovation
	   Absolution of peripheral responsibilities

EXHIBIT 8.2

Characteristics of Creative People and Organizations

SOURCES: Based on Gary A. Steiner, ed., *The Creative Organization* (Chicago: University of Chicago Press, 1965), 16–18; Rosabeth Moss Kanter, "The Middle Manager as Innovator," *Harvard Business Review* (July–August 1982), 104–105; James Brian Quinn, "Managing Innovation: Controlled Chaos," *Harvard Business Review* (May–June 1985), 73–84; and Robert I. Sutton, "The Weird Rules of Creativity," *Harvard Business Review* (September 2001), 94–103.

of creative organizations correspond to those of individuals, as illustrated in the right-hand column of Exhibit 8.2. Creative organizations are loosely structured. People find themselves in a situation of ambiguity, assignments are vague, territories overlap, tasks are poorly defined, and much work is done through teams.[16] Creative organizations have an internal culture of playfulness, freedom, challenge, and grass-roots participation.[17] They harness all potential sources of new ideas from within. Many participative management programs are born out of the desire to enhance creativity for initiating changes. People are not stuck in the rhythm of routine jobs.

To keep creativity alive at MaMaMedia.com, a New York-based company that provides Web-based "playful learning" for kids, top managers hold weekly meetings called *thought provoking sessions*.[18] Each week, a different team hosts the meeting and sets the format, but the guiding principle is to learn by having fun. One team, for example, had everyone make peanut butter and jelly sandwiches by following simple programming-like instructions. The goal was to show people how explicit programmers need to be when they are writing code, thus increasing cross-functional understanding and collaboration. These weekly meetings keep MaMaMedia's playful, creative culture alive even as employees deal with day-to-day deadlines and demands.

The most creative companies embrace risk and encourage employees to make mistakes. Jim Read, president of the Read Corporation, says, "When my employees make mistakes trying to improve something, I give them a round of applause. No mistakes mean no new products. If they ever become afraid to make one, my company is doomed."[19] Similarly, former Time Warner chairman Steve Ross believed people who didn't make enough mistakes should be fired.[20]

Idea Champions and New-Venture Teams

If creative conditions are successful, new ideas will be generated that must be carried forward for acceptance and implementation. This is where idea champions come in. The formal definition of an **idea champion** is a person who sees

idea champion

A person who sees the need for and champions productive change within the organization.

the need for and champions productive change within the organization. For example, Wendy Black of Best Western International championed the idea of coordinating the corporate mailings to the company's 2,800 hoteliers into a single packet every two weeks. Some hotels were receiving three special mailings a day from different departments. Her idea saved $600,000 a year in postage alone.[21]

Remember: Change does not occur by itself. Personal energy and effort are required to successfully promote a new idea. Often a new idea is rejected by management. Champions are passionately committed to a new product or idea despite rejection by others. At Kyocera Wireless, lead engineer Gary Koerper was a champion for the Smartphone. When he could not get his company's testing department to validate the new product, he had an outside firm do the testing for him—at a cost of about $30,000—without approval from Kyocera management.[22]

Managers can directly influence whether champions will flourish. When Texas Instruments studied 50 of its new-product introductions, a surprising fact emerged: Without exception, every new product that had failed had lacked a zealous champion. In contrast, most of the new products that succeeded had a champion. Texas Instruments' managers made an immediate decision: No new product would be approved unless someone championed it. Researchers have also found that the new ideas that succeed are generally those that are backed by someone who believes in the idea wholeheartedly and is determined to convince others of its value.[23]

Another way to facilitate corporate innovation is through a new-venture team. A **new-venture team** is a unit separate from the rest of the organization that is responsible for developing and initiating a major innovation.[24] New-venture teams give free reign to members' creativity because their separate facilities and location free them from organizational rules and procedures. These teams typically are small, loosely structured, and flexible, reflecting the characteristics of creative organizations described in Exhibit 8.2. Some companies outsource rather than coming up with their own separate unit, as shown in the Focus on Innovation box. Peter Drucker advises organizations that wish to innovate to use a separate team or department:

> For the existing business to be capable of innovation, it has to create a structure that allows people to be entrepreneurial. . . . This means, first, that the entrepreneurial, the new, has to be organized separately from the old and the existing. Whenever we have tried to make an existing unit the carrier of the entrepreneurial project, we have failed.[25]

One variation of a new venture team is called a *skunkworks*.[26] A **skunkworks** is a separate small, informal, highly autonomous, and often secretive group that focuses on breakthrough ideas for the business. The original skunkworks, which still exists, was created by Lockheed Martin more than 50 years ago. The essence of a skunkworks is that highly talented people are given the time and freedom to let creativity reign.[27] The laser printer was invented by a Xerox researcher who was transferred to the Xerox Palo Alto Research Center (PARC) after his ideas about using lasers were stifled within the company for being "too impractical and expensive."[28]

Another recent popular way to facilitate the development of new ideas in-house is the *idea incubator*. An **idea incubator** is run entirely in-house but provides a safe harbor where ideas from employees throughout the organization can be developed without interference from company bureaucracy or politics.[29]

new-venture team

A unit separate from the mainstream of the organization that is responsible for developing and initiating innovations.

skunkworks

A separate small, informal, highly autonomous, and often secretive group that focuses on breakthrough ideas for the business.

idea incubator

An in-house program that provides a safe harbor where ideas from employees throughout the organization can be developed without interference from company bureaucracy or politics.

FOCUS ON INNOVATION

Frog Design

From the front, it looks like Captain Hook's eye patch. From the side, it might be Madonna's headset microphone, being worn too close to her eye. It is a tiny computer, a cross between a laptop and a handheld device. Only this one is worn on the head, with a movable eyepiece that projects a small computer screen image. Right now, it's clunky, but the design team is working toward a version that will look like sleek eyeglasses.

Hitachi Corp. got the idea for the headset from crowded Japanese subway cars, where space is so limited that people can't move their arms enough to work a handheld computer. So why not create something that is hands-free and worn over the eyes? Hitachi presented Frog Design in San Francisco with their prototype, which resembled a Sumo wrestler's headband combined with a miner's headlamp. The awkward design kept slipping down, or caused headaches.

Frog Design decided to start again from zero. "Sometimes its better to start from scratch," said designer Gray Holland. Hitachi's partner in this venture, Xybernaut, of Fairfax, Virginia, had lots of experience building computerized headgear, having marketed head-mounted computers for electrical linemen. But going from industrial to consumer use was a big leap. "No one wants the cyborg look," said another designer, Mark Olson.

Frog went through its normal innovation process: (1) *phase zero:* understand the problem; (2) *ideation:* brainstorm with or without the client and generate many rough ideas, followed by interdisciplinary team's prototype design; (3) *refinement:* polish the idea, making it sound; (4) *engineering:* figure out how to make it; (5) *integration:* make sure the design works with the product; and (6) *production:* work with the manufacturer. Through these processes, the team decided the eyeglass design was best and figured out how to make adjustable eye and ear pieces, as well as coming up with a design that wouldn't slip or be ergonomically incorrect and cause neck pain. It was decided that color was important, too, and the team chose warm champagne tones to humanize the headware.

At $1,500 a pop, people need to be persuaded that the relatively uncool headset will be worth the cost, so Frog is trying to minimize geekiness and maximize fashion. Olson thinks fashion will lose out here. "The technology is still the biggest turn-on," he says.

SOURCE: Ann Grimes, "You Can Have the Greatest Product Imaginable, But If It Isn't Designed Well, Forget It," *The Wall Street Journal* (October 15, 2001), R11.

One value of an internal incubator is that an employee with a good idea has somewhere to go with it, rather than having to shop the idea all over the company and hope someone pays attention. Companies as diverse as Boeing, Adobe Systems, Ball Aerospace, United Parcel Service, and Ziff Davis are using incubators to quickly produce products and services related to the company's core business.[30]

Implementing Change

Creative culture, idea champions, new-venture teams, and idea incubators are ways to facilitate the initiation and development of new ideas. The other step to be managed in the change process is implementation. A new, creative idea will not benefit the organization until it is in place and being fully utilized. One frustration for managers is that employees often seem to resist change for no apparent reason. To effectively manage the implementation process, managers should be aware of the reasons for employee resistance and be prepared to use techniques for obtaining employee cooperation. Major, corporate-wide changes can be particularly difficult, as discussed in the Focus on Collaboration box.

Resistance to Change

Idea champions often discover that other employees are unenthusiastic about their new ideas. Members of a new-venture group may be surprised when

FOCUS ON COLLABORATION

Making Change Stick

Employees are not always receptive to change. A combination of factors can lead to rejection of, or even outright rebellion against, management's "new and better ideas."

Land's End, Inc., of Dodgeville, Wisconsin, began as a small mail-order business specializing in sailing gear. Employees enjoyed the family-like atmosphere and uncomplicated work environment. By the mid 1990s, the company had mushroomed into a $1 billion company with several overseas outlets and had passed giant L. L. Bean as number one in specialty catalog sales in the United States.

Such success encouraged founder and chairman Gary Comer to embark on a dramatic management experiment incorporating many of today's trends—teams, 401 (k) plans, peer reviews, and the elimination of guards and time clocks. Comer brought in top talent, including former L. L. Bean executive William T. End as CEO, to implement the changes.

But employees balked. Weekly production meetings became a nuisance. "We spent so much time in meetings that we were getting away from the basic stuff of taking care of business," says one employee. Even a much-ballyhooed new mission statement seemed "pushy." One long-time employee complained that "we don't need anything hanging over our heads telling us to do something we're already doing."

Confusion and frustration reigned at Land's End and was reflected in an earnings drop of 17 percent. Eventually, End left the company, and a new CEO initiated a return to the familiar "Land's End Way" of doing things. Teams were disbanded, and many of the once-promising initiatives were shelved as workers embraced what was familiar and uncomplicated.

The inability of people to adapt to change is not new. Neither is the failure of management to sufficiently lay the groundwork to prepare employees for change. Harvard professor John P. Kotter established an eight-step plan for implementing change that can provide a greater potential for successful transformation of a company:

1. Establish a sense of urgency through careful examination of the market and identification of opportunities and potential crises.

2. Form a powerful coalition of managers able to lead the change.

3. Create a vision to direct the change and the strategies for achieving that vision.

4. Communicate the vision throughout the organization.

5. Empower others to act on the vision by removing barriers, changing systems, and encouraging risk taking.

6. Plan for visible, short-term performance improvements and create those improvements.

7. Consolidate improvements, reassess changes, and make necessary adjustments in the new programs.

8. Articulate the relationship between new behaviors and organizational success.

Major change efforts can be messy and full of surprises, but following these guidelines can break down resistance and mean the difference between success and failure.

SOURCES: Gregory A. Patterson, "Land's End Kicks Out Modern New Managers, Rejecting a Makeover," *The Wall Street Journal* (April 3, 1995), A1, A6; and John P. Kotter, "Leading Changes: Why Transformation Efforts Fail," *Harvard Business Review* (March–April 1995), 59–67.

---

managers in the regular organization do not support or approve their innovations. Managers and employees not involved in an innovation often seem to prefer the status quo. Employees appear to resist change for several reasons, and understanding them helps managers implement change more effectively.

Self-Interest. Employees typically resist a change they believe will take away something of value. A proposed change in job design, structure, or technology may lead to a perceived loss of power, prestige, pay, or company benefits. The fear of personal loss is perhaps the biggest obstacle to organizational change.[31] When Federated Department Stores announced in 2002 that it was closing Fingerhut, a division it had acquired in 1999, Fingerhut employees were so outraged that they staged a demonstration outside Federated's Cincinnati, Ohio, headquarters. Employees at Fingerhut argued that the company had three prospective buyers, but that Federated was interested only in liquidating Fingerhut. In this case, the interests of Fingerhut's employees were definitely at odds with those of Federated's management.[32]

Lack of Understanding and Trust. Employees often do not understand the intended purpose of a change or distrust the intentions behind it. If previous working relationships with an idea champion have been negative, resistance may occur. One manager had a habit of initiating a change in the financial reporting system about every 12 months and then losing interest and not following through. After the third time, employees no longer went along with the change because they did not trust the manager's intention to follow through to their benefit.

Uncertainty. *Uncertainty* is the lack of information about future events. It represents a fear of the unknown. Uncertainty is especially threatening for employees who have a low tolerance for change and fear the novel and unusual. They do not know how a change will affect them and worry about whether they will be able to meet the demands of a new procedure or technology.[33] Union leaders at General Motors' Steering Gear Division in Saginaw, Michigan, resisted the introduction of employee participation programs. They were uncertain about how the program would affect their status and thus initially opposed it.

Different Assessments and Goals. Another reason for resistance to change is that people who will be affected by innovation may assess the situation differently from an idea champion or new-venture group. Often critics voice legitimate disagreements over the proposed benefits of a change. Managers in each department pursue different goals, and an innovation may detract from performance and goal achievement for some departments. For example, if marketing gets the new product it wants for its customers, the cost of manufacturing may increase, and the manufacturing superintendent thus will resist. Resistance may call attention to problems with the innovation. At a consumer products company in Racine, Wisconsin, middle managers resisted the introduction of a new employee program that turned out to be a bad idea. The managers truly believed that the program would do more harm than good.[34]

These reasons for resistance are legitimate in the eyes of employees affected by the change. The best procedure for managers is not to ignore resistance but to diagnose the reasons and design strategies to gain acceptance by users.[35] Strategies for overcoming resistance to change typically involve two approaches: the analysis of resistance through the force-field technique and the use of selective implementation tactics to overcome resistance.

Force-Field Analysis

Force-field analysis grew from the work of Kurt Lewin, who proposed that change was a result of the competition between *driving* and *restraining forces*.[36] Driving forces can be thought of as problems or opportunities that provide motivation for change within the organization. Restraining forces are the various barriers to change, such as a lack of resources, resistance from middle managers, or inadequate employee skills. When a change is introduced, management should analyze both the forces that drive change (problems and opportunities) as well as the forces that resist it (barriers to change). By selectively

force-field analysis
The process of determining which forces drive and which resist a proposed change.

removing forces that restrain change, the driving forces will be strong enough to enable implementation, as illustrated by the move from A to B in Exhibit 8.3. As barriers are reduced or removed, behavior will shift to incorporate the desired changes.

Just-in-time (JIT) inventory control systems schedule materials to arrive at a company just as they are needed on the production line. In an Ohio manufacturing company, management's analysis showed that the driving forces (opportunities) associated with the implementation of JIT were (1) the large cost savings from reduced inventories, (2) savings from needing fewer workers to handle the inventory, and (3) a quicker, more competitive market response for the company. Restraining forces (barriers) discovered by managers were (1) a freight system that was too slow to deliver inventory on time, (2) a facility layout that emphasized inventory maintenance over new deliveries, (3) worker skills inappropriate for handling rapid inventory deployment, and (4) union resistance to loss of jobs. The driving forces were not sufficient to overcome the restraining forces.

To shift the behavior to JIT, managers attacked the barriers. An analysis of the freight system showed that delivery by truck provided the flexibility and quickness needed to schedule inventory arrival at a specific time each day. The problem with facility layout was met by adding four new loading docks. Inappropriate worker skills were attacked with a training program to instruct workers in JIT methods and in assembling products with uninspected parts. Union resistance was overcome by agreeing to reassign workers no longer needed for maintaining inventory to jobs in another plant. With the restraining forces reduced, the driving forces were sufficient to allow the JIT system to be implemented.

Implementation Tactics

The other approach to managing implementation is to adopt specific tactics to overcome employee resistance. For example, resistance to change may be overcome by educating employees or inviting them to participate in implementing the change. Researchers have studied various methods for dealing with resistance to change. The following five tactics, summarized in Exhibit 8.4, have proven successful.[37]

Communication and Education. *Communication* and *education* are used when solid information about the change is needed by users and others who

EXHIBIT 8.3

Using Force-Field Analysis to Change from Traditional to Just-in-Time Inventory System

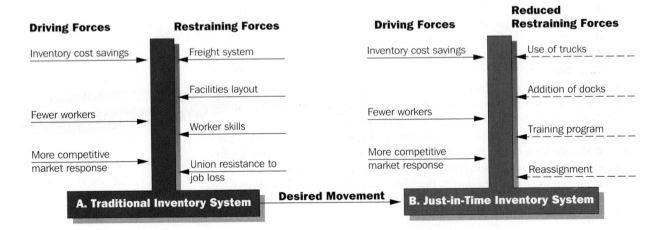

Driving Forces

Inventory cost savings

Fewer workers

More competitive market response

Restraining Forces

Freight system

Facilities layout

Worker skills

Union resistance to job loss

A. Traditional Inventory System

Desired Movement

Driving Forces

Inventory cost savings

Fewer workers

More competitive market response

Reduced Restraining Forces

Use of trucks

Addition of docks

Training program

Reassignment

B. Just-in-Time Inventory System

Approach	When to Use
Communication, education	• Change is technical. • Users need accurate information and analysis to understand change.
Participation	• Users need to feel involved. • Design requires information from others. • Users have power to resist.
Negotiation	• Group has power over implementation. • Group will lose out in the change.
Coercion	• A crisis exists. • Initiators clearly have power. • Other implementation techniques have failed.
Top management support	• Change involves multiple departments or reallocation of resources. • Users doubt legitimacy of change.

EXHIBIT 8.4

Tactics for Overcoming Resistance to Change

SOURCE: Based on J.P. Kotter and L.A. Schlesinger, "Choosing Strategies for Change," *Harvard Business Review* 57 (March–April 1979), 106–114.

may resist implementation. Education is especially important when the change involves new technical knowledge or users are unfamiliar with the idea. Canadian Airlines International spent a year and a half preparing and training employees before changing its entire reservations, airport, cargo, and financial systems as part of a new "Service Quality" strategy. Smooth implementation resulted from this intensive training and communications effort, which involved 50,000 tasks, 12,000 people, and 26 classrooms around the world.[38]

Participation. *Participation* involves users and potential resisters in designing the change. This approach is time-consuming, but it pays off because users understand and become committed to the change. Participation also helps managers determine potential problems and understand the differences in perceptions of change among employees.[39] When General Motors tried to implement a new management appraisal system for supervisors in its Adrian, Michigan, plant, it met with immediate resistance. Rebuffed by the lack of cooperation, top managers proceeded more slowly, involving supervisors in the design of the new appraisal system. Through participation in system design, managers understood what the new approach was all about and dropped their resistance to it.

Negotiation. Negotiation is a more formal means of achieving cooperation. *Negotiation* uses formal bargaining to win acceptance and approval of a desired change. For example, if the marketing department fears losing power if a new management structure is implemented, top managers may negotiate with marketing to reach a resolution. Companies that have strong unions frequently must formally negotiate change with the unions. The change may become part of the union contract reflecting the agreement of both parties. For example, when General Motors changed the way it runs Saturn, a part of implementation involved negotiating new labor rules with the United Auto Workers union local.

Coercion. *Coercion* means that managers use formal power to force employees to change. Resisters are told to accept the change or lose rewards or even their jobs. In most cases, this approach should not be used because employees feel like victims, are angry at change managers, and may even sabotage the changes. However, coercion may be necessary in crisis situations when a rapid response is urgent. For example, a number of top managers at Coca-Cola were reassigned or forced out after they refused to go along with new CEO Douglas Daft's changes for revitalizing the sluggish corporation.[40]

Herman Wright, PruCare of Austin's director of sales and marketing, shown here with his sales and service staff, knows that top management support is essential to overcoming resistance to change. In PruCare's thrust toward customer satisfaction, Wright used the implementation tactics of communication and participation. He communicated his desire to build customer relationships based on trust and then pushed responsibility down to everyone in the organization: "We stopped telling people what to do and started listening."

© 1994 Bill Albrecht

Top Management Support. The visible support of top management also helps overcome resistance to change. *Top management support* symbolizes to all employees that the change is important for the organization. Top management support is especially important when a change involves multiple departments or when resources are being reallocated among departments. Without top management support, these changes can get bogged down in squabbling among departments. Moreover, when top managers fail to support a project, they can inadvertently undercut it by issuing contradictory orders. This happened at Flying Tiger Lines before it was acquired by Federal Express. The airborne freight hauler came up with a plan to eliminate excessive paperwork by changing the layout of offices so that two agents rather than four could handle each shipment. No sooner had part of the change been implemented than top management ordered another system; thus, the office layout was changed again. The new layout was not as efficient, but it was the one that top management supported. Had middle managers informed top managers and obtained their support earlier, the initial change would not have been defeated by a new priority.[41]

The following example illustrates how smart implementation techniques can smooth the change process.

General Stair Corporation
http://www.generalstair.com

General Stair Corp., a maker of prefabricated stairs and railings, was facing a desperate situation in the mid-1990s. Competition was increasing, and the Opa-Locka, Florida, company's profit and market share were declining. General Stair found itself dealing with a constant price war. To distinguish his company from the competition, founder Saby Behar decided General Stair should start offering a money-back delivery guarantee, something he knew his customers (who often worked on 30 or more buildings at a time) would appreciate. However, managers and other employees were aghast at the suggestion. Workers weren't sure they could meet the requirements for such a guarantee and were concerned that it might require more overtime. Managers worried about the cost of upgrading communications systems for field reps to stay in touch with headquarters as well as builders and contractors.

Implementation of the change involved several steps. To combat the initial resistance among his managers, Behar held several meetings explaining his reasons for making the change and answering managers' questions. This at least got people talking about whether and how such a guarantee could actually work. Next, managers brought in the rest of the employees to discuss the proposed change and how to put it into action. They knew they had to revamp communications, but discussions with employees led them to realize other systems, such as distribution and compensation, needed to change as well. In addition, rather than a complete money-back guarantee, the group eventually settled on a fine of $50 per day for late deliveries. Although the company already had a good on-time delivery record, employees were trained in new procedures that would help assure consistent performance.

Because top management involved employees from the early stages, the changes went smoothly. Labor costs were slashed by 30 percent, even though employees were earning up to 60 percent more money because of a new piece-rate system. Productivity was up 300 percent. And, within the first year, the company had to pay out only a few $50 vouchers for late deliveries. General Stair's market share and profits are once again looking healthy.[42]

Types of Planned Change

Now that we have explored how the initiation and implementation of change can be carried out, let us look at the different types of change that occur in organizations. We will address two issues: what parts of the organization can be changed and how managers can apply the initiation and implementation ideas to each type of change.

The types of organizational change are strategy, technology, products, structure, and culture/people, as illustrated in Exhibit 8.5. Organizations may innovate in one or more areas, depending on internal and external forces for change. In the rapidly changing toy industry, a manufacturer has to introduce new products frequently. In a mature, competitive industry, production technology changes are adopted to improve efficiency. The arrows connecting the types of change in Exhibit 8.5 show that a change in one part may affect other parts of the organization: A new product may require changes in technology, and a new technology may require new people skills or a new structure. For example, when Shenandoah Life Insurance Company computerized processing and claims operations, the structure had to be decentralized, employees required intensive training, and a more participative culture was needed. Related changes were required for the new technology to increase efficiency.

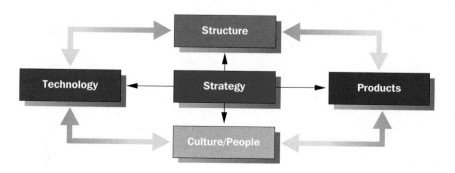

EXHIBIT 8.5

Types of Organizational Change

SOURCE: Based on Harold J. Leavitt, "Applied Organizational Change in Industry: Structural, Technical, and Human Approaches," in *New Perspectives in Organization Research*, ed. W. W. Cooper, H. J. Leavitt, and M. W. Shelly II (New York: Wiley, 1964), 55–74.

Technology Changes

technology change

A change that pertains to the organization's production process.

A **technology change** is related to the organization's production process—how the organization does its work. Technology changes are designed to make the production of a product or service more efficient. The adoption of automatic mail-sorting machines by the U.S. Postal Service is an example of a technology change, as is the adoption by supermarkets of laser scanning checkout systems linked to computers that provide instant inventory information.

How can managers encourage technology change? The general rule is that technology change is bottom up.[43] The *bottom-up* approach means that ideas are initiated at lower organization levels and channeled upward for approval. Lower-level technical experts act as idea champions—they invent and champion technological changes. Employees at lower levels understand the technology and have the expertise needed to propose changes.

Great Harvest Bread Company encourages bottom-up change among its franchisees by giving them almost complete freedom to run their businesses as they see fit. This freedom inspires new and better ways of doing things that quickly spread to other stores by phone, fax, and e-mail.[44] Bottom up doesn't mean much if you are the lone entrepreneur. John Bloor saw a change in the environment—customers once again interested in Triumph motorcycles—but he soon realized he needed new technology for his company to succeed, as described in the Best Practices box.

New-Product Changes

product change

A change in the organization's product or service output.

A **product change** is a change in the organization's product or service output. New-product innovations have major implications for an organization, because they often are an outcome of a new strategy and may define a new market.[45] In addition, product life cycles are getting shorter, so that companies need to continuously come up with innovative ideas for new products and services that

BEST PRACTICES

Triumph Motorcycles

John Bloor began by looking for an abandoned factory to buy, but he instead ended up buying an abandoned motorcycle company. England's motorcycle manufacturing went belly-up in the early 1980s, and Bloor was taking on a big challenge with the $200,000 purchase price of the Triumph company. Japan's Suzuki and Honda motorcycles, and the U.S.'s Harley-Davidson, were ruling the globe. But Bloor was betting on his own ingenuity and the nostalgic power of the Triumph image. Triumph had been a premier brand in the 1950s and 1960s; Marlon Brando rode one in his motorcycle flick, *The Wild Ones.*

Realizing that technology was the key to success, Bloor first hired three former Triumph employees, who had helped develop new models. Next he hopped on a plane to Japan and managed to visit Kawasaki, Yamaha, and Suzuki plants. (The companies didn't think he was serious competition, so why not let him in?) These visits helped Bloor to resolve to start from scratch with new models and new factory processes. When he opened the new factory in 1991, he had state-of-the-art equipment from Japan and had enlisted the brainpower of local engineers who build race cars. The decision to keep a three-cylinder engine from the original Triumph lineup has given the company a distinctive calling card—and has contributed to the company's rebirth, with sales in 2001 of $245 million.

A former home builder, Bloor didn't know exactly what he was getting into, or how complex the design and manufacturing of motorcycles would be. "You need to multiply by two or three whatever money you think you will need," he says. And hope you don't hit a lot of speed bumps in the process.

SOURCE: Stuart K. Brown, "A Sweet Triumph," *Fortune Small Business* (April 2002), 49–54.

meet needs in the marketplace. Product innovation is the primary way in which many organizations adapt to changes in markets, technologies, and competition.[46] Examples of new products include Mountain Dew Code Red, the Buick Rendezvous, and Gillette's Venus razor for women.

Introducing a new product is not easy, but hundreds of new products are introduced every day. Even though the cost of successfully launching a new product is $20 million to $50 million, approximately 25,000 new products appeared in one recent year, including 5,000 new toys.[47] Many of those products will fail in the marketplace. Estimates are that between 33 and 60 percent of all new products that reach the marketplace never generate an economic return.[48] Consider such flops as the Apple Newton, Procter & Gamble's Fit Produce wash, or Gerber's "Singles," a line of meals for adults. Product development is a risky, high-stakes game for organizations. Companies that successfully develop new products usually have the following characteristics:

1. People in marketing have a good understanding of customer needs.

2. Technical specialists are aware of recent technological developments and make effective use of new technology.

3. Members from key departments—research, manufacturing, marketing—cooperate in the development of the new product.[49]

These findings mean that the ideas for new products typically originate at the lower levels of the organization just as they do for technology changes. The difference is that new-product ideas flow horizontally among departments. Product innovation requires expertise from several departments simultaneously. A new-product failure is often the result of failed cooperation.[50]

Innovation is becoming a major strategic weapon in the global marketplace. One example of innovation is the use of **time-based competition**, which means delivering products and services faster than competitors, giving companies a significant strategic advantage. For example, by using the Internet to collaborate on new designs with suppliers, Moen teams take a new kitchen or bath faucet from drawing board to store shelf in only 16 months. The time savings means engineers can work on three times as many projects and introduce up to 15 new designs a year for today's fashion-conscious consumers, helping Moen move from number three in market share to a tie for number one with rival Delta Faucet Co.[51] Dillard's department stores went to an automatic reorder system that replenishes stocks in 12 days rather than 30, providing retail goods to customers more quickly.[52]

time-based competition
A strategy of competition based on the ability to deliver products and services faster than competitors.

Structural Changes

Structural changes involve the hierarchy of authority, goals, structural characteristics, administrative procedures, and management systems.[53] Almost any change in how the organization is managed falls under the category of structural change. For example, to revitalize consumer-goods giant Procter & Gamble, managers reorganized into seven global business units based on product categories, spent billions on new information technology systems, and decentralized the IT staff so that IT employees now work in P&G's individual product, market, and business teams.[54]

Other examples of structural or administrative change include shifting to a team-based structure, implementing no-smoking policies, and centralizing

structural changes
Any changes in the way in which the organization is designed and managed.

information and accounting systems. Successful structural change is accomplished through a top-down approach, which is distinct from technology change (bottom up) and new products (horizontal).[55]

The top-down process does not mean that coercion is the best implementation tactic. Implementation tactics include education, participation, and negotiation with employees. Unless there is an emergency, managers should not force structural change on employees. They may hit a resistance wall, and the change will fail. Andrea Jung, CEO of Avon, is keeping this in mind as she attempts to take the cosmetics company onto the Web and into retail stores, moves that could seriously threaten the sales and profits of the company's independent sales representatives. When the company first printed its Web site address on the catalog, many reps covered it up with their own stickers and complained so forcefully that the company quickly removed it. Now, Jung is trying to involve sales reps closely in every step the company takes toward a new way of doing business. The emphasis she puts on the importance of the independent sales force has more "Avon Ladies" signing up than ever before.[56]

Top-down change means that initiation of the idea occurs at upper levels and is implemented downward. It does not mean that lower-level employees are not educated about the change or allowed to participate in it.

Culture/People Changes

culture/people change

A change in employees' values, norms, attitudes, beliefs, and behavior.

A **culture/people change** refers to a change in employees' values, norms, attitudes, beliefs, and behavior. Changes in culture and people pertain to how employees think; these are changes in mindset rather than technology, structure, or products and services. *People change* pertains to just a few employees, such as when a handful of middle managers is sent to a training course to improve their leadership skills. *Culture change* pertains to the organization as a whole, such as when Union Pacific Railroad changed its basic mindset by becoming less bureaucratic and focusing employees on customer service and quality through teamwork and employee participation.[57] Two specific tools for changing people and culture are training and development programs and organizational development (OD).

Training and Development

Training is one of the most frequently used approaches to changing the organization's mindset. A company might offer training programs to large blocks of employees on subjects such as teamwork, diversity, emotional intelligence, quality circles, communication skills, or participative management. Training and development programs aimed at changing individual behavior and interpersonal skills have become a big business for consultants, universities, and training firms.

Some companies particularly emphasize training and development for managers, with the idea that the behavior and attitudes of managers will influence people throughout the organization and lead to culture change. A number of Silicon Valley companies, including Intel, Sun Microsystems, and Netscape, regularly send managers to the Growth and Leadership Center (GLC), where they learn to use emotional intelligence to build better relationships. Nick Kepler, director of technology development at Advanced Micro Devices Inc., was surprised to learn how his emotionless approach to work was intimidating people and destroying the rapport needed to shift to a culture based on collaborative teamwork.[58]

Organizational Development

Organizational development (OD) is a planned, systematic process of change that uses behavioral science knowledge and techniques to improve an organization's health and effectiveness through its ability to adapt to the environment, improve internal relationships, and increase learning and problem-solving capabilities.[59] OD focuses on the human and social aspects of the organization and works to change individual attitudes and relationships among employees.[60]

The following are three types of current problems that OD can help managers address.[61]

1. *Mergers/acquisitions.* The disappointing financial results of many mergers and acquisitions are caused by the failure of executives to determine whether the administrative style and corporate culture of the two companies fit, and OD experts can be used to smooth the integration of two firms.

2. *Organizational decline/revitalization.* Organizations undergoing a period of decline and revitalization experience a variety of problems, including a low level of trust, lack of innovation, high turnover, and high levels of conflict and stress. The period of transition requires opposite behaviors, including confronting stress, creating open communication, and fostering creative innovation to emerge with high levels of productivity. OD techniques can contribute greatly to cultural revitalization by managing conflicts, fostering commitment, and facilitating communication.

3. *Conflict management.* Conflict can occur at any time and place within a healthy organization. For example, a product team for the introduction of a new software package was formed at a computer company. Made up of strong-willed individuals, the team made little progress because members could not agree on project goals. At a manufacturing firm, salespeople promised delivery dates to customers that were in conflict with shop supervisor priorities for assembling customer orders. In a publishing company, two managers disliked each other intensely. They argued at meetings, lobbied politically against each other, and hurt the achievement of both departments. Organizational development efforts can help solve these kinds of conflicts.

Organizational development can be used to solve the types of problems just described and many others. However, to be truly valuable to companies and employees, organizational development practitioners go beyond looking at ways to solve specific problems. Instead, they become involved in broader issues that contribute to improving organizational life, such as encouraging a sense

organizational development (OD)

The application of behavioral science techniques to improve an organization's health and effectiveness through its ability to cope with environmental changes, improve internal relationships, and increase problem-solving capabilities.

Lincoln Electric in Cleveland, Ohio, has one of the oldest and most radical pay-for-performance incentive programs in the country. The Lincoln Electric system paid employees up to 100 percent of their wages in annual performance bonuses. However, due to recent global competition and an increase in institutional shareholders, workers' bonuses have decreased while revenues reached $1 billion. Many workers are concerned about future bonus reductions. As managers struggle to meet new competitive threats, they may use organizational development techniques to adapt to current conditions without sacrificing employee goodwill.

© Daniel Levin

of community, pushing for an organizational climate of openness and trust, and making sure the company provides employees with opportunities for personal growth and development.[62] Specialized techniques have been developed to help meet OD goals.

OD Activities. A number of OD activities have emerged in recent years. Three of the most popular and effective are as follows.

1. *Team-building activities.* **Team building** enhances the cohesiveness and success of organizational groups and teams. For example, a series of OD exercises can be used with members of cross-departmental teams to help them learn to act and function as a team. An OD expert can work with team members to increase their communication skills, facilitate their ability to confront one another, and accept common goals.

2. *Survey-feedback activities.* **Survey feedback** begins with a questionnaire distributed to employees on values, climate, participation, leadership, and group cohesion within their organization. After the survey is completed, an OD consultant meets with groups of employees to provide feedback about their responses and the problems identified. Employees are engaged in problem solving based on the data.

3. *Large-Group Interventions.* In recent years, there has been a growing interest in applications of OD techniques to large group settings, which are more attuned to bringing about fundamental organizational change in today's complex, fast-changing world.[63] The **large-group intervention** approach brings together participants from all parts of the organization—often including key stakeholders from outside the organization as well—to discuss problems or opportunities and plan for change. A large-group intervention might involve 50 to 500 people and last several days. The idea is to include everyone who has a stake in the change, gather perspectives from all parts of the system, and enable people to create a collective future through sustained, guided conversation and dialogue.

Large-group interventions reflect a significant shift in the approach to organizational change from earlier OD concepts and approaches. Exhibit 8.6 lists the primary differences between the traditional OD model and the large-scale intervention model of organizational change.[64] In the newer approach, the focus is on the entire system, which takes into account the organization's interaction with its environment. The source of information for discussion is expanded to include customers, suppliers, community members, even com-

---

team building

A type of OD intervention that enhances the cohesiveness of departments by helping members learn to function as a team.

survey feedback

A type of OD intervention in which questionnaires on organizational climate and other factors are distributed among employees and the results reported back to them by a change agent.

large-group intervention

An approach that brings together participants from all parts of the organization (and may include key outside stakeholders as well) to discuss problems or opportunities and plan for major change.

EXHIBIT *8.6*

OD Approaches to Culture Change

	Traditional Organizational Development Model	Large-Group Intervention Model
Focus for action:	Specific problem or group	Entire system
Information Source:	Organization	Organization and environment
Distribution:	Limited	Widely shared
Time frame:	Gradual	Fast
Learning:	Individual, small group	Whole organization
Change process:	Incremental change	Rapid transformation

SOURCE: Adapted from Barbara Benedict Bunker and Billie T. Alban, "Conclusion: What Makes Large Group Interventions Effective," *The Journal of Applied Behavioral Science* 28, no. 4 (December 1992), 579–591.

petitors, and this information is shared widely so that everyone has the same picture of the organization and its environment. The acceleration of change when the entire system is involved can be remarkable. In addition, learning occurs across all parts of the organization simultaneously, rather than in individuals, small groups, or business units. The end result is that the large-group approach offers greater possibilities for fundamental, radical transformation of the entire culture, whereas the traditional approach creates incremental change in a few individuals or small groups at a time. General Electric's Work Out Program provides an excellent example of the large-group intervention approach.

General Electric
http://www.ge.com

GE's Work Out began in large-scale off-site meetings facilitated by a combination of top leaders, outside consultants, and human resources specialists. In each business unit, the basic pattern was the same. Hourly and salaried workers came together from many different parts of the organization in an informal three-day meeting to discuss and solve problems. Gradually, the Work Out events began to include external stakeholders such as suppliers and customers as well as employees. Today, Work Out is not an event, but a process of how work is done and problems are solved at GE.

The format for Work Out includes seven steps:

1. Choose a work process or problem for discussion.

2. Select an appropriate cross-functional team, to include external stakeholders.

3. Assign a "champion" to follow through on recommendations.

4. Meet for several days and come up with recommendations to improve processes or solve problems.

5. Meet with leaders, who are asked to respond to recommendations on the spot.

6. Hold additional meetings as needed to implement the recommendations.

7. Start the process all over again with a new process or problem.

GE's Work Out process not only solves problems and improves productivity for the company but also gives employees the experience of openly and honestly interacting with one another without regard to vertical or horizontal differences. By doing so, the process has helped to create a "culture of boundarylessness" that is critical for continuous learning and improvement.[65]

Large-group interventions represent a significant shift in the way leaders think about change and reflect an increasing awareness of the importance of dealing with the entire system, including external stakeholders, in any significant change effort.

OD Steps. Consider the culture change at Rowe Furniture Corporation, which reduced the time for making and delivering custom-made pieces from six months to an amazing 10 days. A major aspect was a change in mindset of both managers and employees to give front-line employees more authority and responsibility, as well as open access to company information. Rather than waiting for supervisors to make decisions, every Rowe team now has instant access to up-to-date information about order flows, output, productivity, and quality and is empowered to make decisions and take action as needed to meet schedules and deadlines set by the teams themselves.[66]

Organizational development experts acknowledge that corporate culture and human behavior are relatively stable and that companywide changes, such as those at Rowe Furniture, require major effort. The theory underlying organizational development proposes three distinct stages for achieving behavioral and attitudinal change: (1) unfreezing, (2) changing, and (3) refreezing.[67] The example below describes how Alberto-Culver created a new employee-focused culture that helped turn the business around by following the stages of unfreezing, changing, and refreezing.

Alberto-Culver

http://www.alberto.com

"Do we make people happy and then the business gets better; or do we fix the business, which will make people happier?" That's the question top executives were asking Carol Lavin Bernick, president of Alberto-Culver North America. It became clear to Bernick that the company was facing a cultural crisis. For years, Alberto-Culver had suffered from general overall employee dissatisfaction, a turnover rate that was double the national average, deflated sales and slipping margins on their most popular brands, and an organization that was not equal to the challenge of an emerging competitive environment. Bernick wanted to make culture change a priority, but she had to find a way to get everyone throughout the organization committed to change.

She began the change process with a companywide meeting aimed at letting everyone know where the company stood and where it needed to go in the future (unfreezing). Before the meeting began, Bernick scattered pennies around the floor and observed employees as they entered the room—no one attempted to pick up a cent. "Can anyone name our best-selling product?" she asked. "VO5 shampoo!" came the resounding response. "Look around you on the floor, and if you see a penny, pick it up," Bernick continued. "That penny represents our total profit on a bottle of Alberto VO5 shampoo." Employees were already aware of many problems in the business, but this was an eye-opener. Thus began the process of creating a culture of honesty and shared ownership, where employees think like business people and act like team players.

The next stage (changing) involved creating a specific plan for change. One step was to develop a list of 10 cultural imperatives: honesty, ownership, trust, customer orientation, commitment, fun, innovation, risk taking, speed and urgency, and teamwork. Another was to create a specific role called the *growth development leader* (GDL). Each handpicked GDL mentors about a dozen people, helping to bring about culture change at the individual and small-group level. GDLs work to build team spirit and help people understand how their work fits into the big picture. One specific task is helping to spell out *Individual Economic Values,* or IEVs, short statements that describe how each individual contributes to the organization's productivity and profitability. With the IEVs, managers have given employees greater freedom and power to drive the success of the company. Growth development leaders also get intimately involved in people's lives and careers. For example, they help people set personal and professional goals that achieve the right balance for the individual, reinforcing the idea that Alberto-Culver is a company that respects and values its employees as individuals with lives outside of work.

Finally, Bernick needed to find ways to make the changes stick (refreezing). At every opportunity, managers reinforce the central cultural tenet that individuals can make a difference, and that companies don't succeed—people do. Managers regularly measure individual and organizational progress against the cultural goals. "I'm a firm believer that you change what you measure," says

Bernick. "Once a year, we do an all-employee survey to assess our progress against cultural goals and to gather feedback." Managers also celebrate every success and reward people for exhibiting the attitudes and behaviors that fit the new culture, such as through stock options, Business Builder Awards, and People's Choice Awards. "If you want something to grow," claims Bernick, "pour champagne on it."[68]

The first stage, **unfreezing**, means that people throughout the organization are made aware of problems and the need for change. This stage creates the motivation for people to change their attitudes and behaviors. Unfreezing may begin when managers present information that shows discrepancies between desired behaviors or performance and the current state of affairs. In addition, as we discussed earlier in the chapter, managers need to establish a sense of urgency to unfreeze people throughout the organization and create an openness and willingness to change. The unfreezing stage is often associated with *diagnosis*, which uses an outside expert called a change agent. The **change agent** is an OD specialist who performs a systematic diagnosis of the organization and identifies work-related problems. He or she gathers and analyzes data through personal interviews, questionnaires, and observations of meetings. The diagnosis helps determine the extent of organizational problems and helps unfreeze managers by making them aware of problems in their behavior.

The second stage, **changing**, occurs when individuals experiment with new behavior and learn new skills to be used in the workplace. This is sometimes known as intervention, during which the change agent implements a specific plan for training managers and employees. The changing stage might involve a number of specific steps.[69] Recall the eight steps for leading change from the Focus on Collaboration box earlier in this chapter. For example, managers put together a coalition of people with the will and power to guide the change, create a vision for change that everyone can believe in, and widely communicate the vision and plans for change throughout the company. In addition, successful change involves empowering employees throughout the organization to act on the plan to accomplish the desired changes.

The third stage, **refreezing**, occurs when individuals acquire new attitudes or values and are rewarded for them by the organization. The impact of new behaviors is evaluated and reinforced. The change agent supplies new data that show positive changes in performance. Managers may provide updated data to employees that demonstrate positive changes in individual and organizational performance. Top executives celebrate successes and reward positive behavioral changes. This is the stage where changes are institutionalized in the organizational culture, so that employees begin to view the changes as a normal, integral part of how the organization operates. Employees may also participate in refresher courses to maintain and reinforce the new behaviors.

unfreezing
The stage of organizational development in which participants are made aware of problems in order to increase their willingness to change their behavior.

change agent
An OD specialist who contracts with an organization to facilitate change.

changing
The intervention stage of organizational development in which individuals experiment with new workplace behavior.

refreezing
The reinforcement stage of organizational development in which individuals acquire a desired new skill or attitude and are rewarded for it by the organization.

■ Summary and Management Solution

Change is inevitable in organizations. This chapter discussed the techniques available for managing the change process. One of the most dramatic elements of change for today's organizations is the shift to a technology-driven workplace and an emphasis on information and relationships. Current trends such as e-business require profound changes in the organization and may be associated with a shift to the learning organization, which embraces continuous learning and change. Managers should think of change as having four elements—the forces for change, the perceived need for change, the initiation of change, and the implementation of change. Forces for change can originate either within or outside the firm, and managers are responsible for monitoring events that may require a planned organizational response. Techniques for initiating changes include designing the organization for creativity, encouraging change agents, and establishing new-venture teams and idea incubators. The final step is implementation. Force-field analysis is one technique for diagnosing barriers, which often can be removed. Managers also should draw on the implementation tactics of communication, participation, negotiation, coercion, or top management support.

This chapter also discussed specific types of change. Technology changes are accomplished through a bottom-up approach that utilizes experts close to the technology. Successful new-product introduction requires horizontal linkage among marketing, research and development, manufacturing, and perhaps other departments or customers, partners, and suppliers. Structural changes tend to be initiated in a top-down fashion, because upper managers are the administrative experts and champion these ideas for approval and implementation. Culture/people change pertains to the skills, behaviors, and attitudes of employees. Training and organizational development are important approaches to change people's mindset and corporate culture. The OD process entails three steps—unfreezing (diagnosis of the problem), the actual change (intervention), and refreezing (reinforcement of new attitudes and behaviors). Popular OD techniques include team building, survey feedback, and large-group interventions.

As described in the beginning of the chapter, Aldo DiBelardino had many challenges ahead to pull the struggling X-It out of the gutter, to essentially save his innovation of the ladder. As the new CEO, he realized he had to act fast, to bring necessary changes to the company. First up was to straighten out the relationship with important customers, such as Hohman. To send more ladders to Hohman, DiBelardino needed cash to order them from China. And cash was nowhere in sight. He approached several investors and asked for small, short-term loans, not only to get cash, but also to re-establish trust with the investors. By using negotiation and because of his concern for people, he had developed a positive relationship with a Chinese shipper, who extended credit to him, allowing transport of the ladders. He saw the performance gap between existing and desired performance levels and executed major cutbacks, reducing expenses from $25,000 per month to $9,000 by giving up the Manhattan office and the contract with an expensive PR firm that Ive had contracted. Ive leaving meant lower costs, as no salary for him was needed anymore. An old school friend rented DiBelardino a cheap warehouse near Chesapeake Bay where he also set up an office with a $300 computer. Using other hometown relationships, he was able to contract cheap labor. In the meantime, the jury awarded X-It over $21 million in compensatory damages, a ruling that Kidde is expected to appeal. DiBelardino learned a lot about himself and the company through the whole process and, as a result, company sales rose 23 percent in 2001, up to $320,000.[70]

■ Discussion Questions

1. The September 11, 2001, terrorist attack on the World Trade Center led many companies that had been bitter rivals to put their competitive spirit aside and focus on cooperation and courtesy. Do you believe this type of change will be a lasting one? Discuss.

2. A manager of an international chemical company said that very few new products in her company were successful. What would you advise the manager to do to help increase the company's success rate?

3. What are internal and external forces for change? Which force do you think is the major cause of organizational change in a university? In a pharmaceuticals firm?

4. Carefully planned change often is assumed to be effective. Do you think unplanned change can sometimes be beneficial to an organization? Discuss.

5. Why do organizations experience resistance to change? What techniques can managers use to overcome resistance?

6. Explain force-field analysis. Analyze the driving and restraining forces for a change with which you have been associated.

7. Define the roles associated with an idea champion. Why do you think idea champions are so essential to the initiation of change?

8. To what extent would changes in technology affect new products, and vice versa? Compare the process for changing technology and that for product change.

9. Given that structural change is often made top down, should coercive implementation techniques be used? Discuss.

10. Do the underlying values of organizational development differ from assumptions associated with other types of change? Discuss.

11. How do large-group interventions differ from OD techniques such as team building and survey feedback?

■ Manager's Workbook

Innovation Climate

In order to examine differences in level of innovation encouragement in organizations, you will be asked to rate two different organizations. You may choose one in which you have worked, or the university where you are studying. The other should be someone else's workplace, either a family member, friend, or acquaintance. Therefore, you will have to interview that person to answer the questions below. You should put your own answers in column A, your interviewee's answers in column B, and finally, what you think would be the "ideal" in column C.

Use the following scale of 1–5:
1 = don't agree at all to 5 = agree completely

Item of measure	Column A Your organization	Column B Other organization	Column C Your ideal
1. Creativity is encouraged here.*			
2. People are allowed to solve the same problems in different ways.*			
3. I get free time to pursue creative ideas.#			
4. The organization publicly recognizes and also rewards those who are innovative.#			
5. Our organization is flexible and always open to change.*			

Below, score items on the opposite scale:
1 = agree completely to 5 = don't agree at all

6. The primary job of people here is to follow orders which come from the top.*			
7. The best way to get along here is to think and act like the others.*			
8. This place seems to be more concerned with the status quo than with change.*			
9. People are rewarded more if they don't rock the boat.#			
10. New ideas are great, but we don't have enough people or money to carry them out.#			

Note: * starred items indicate the organization's innovation climate
pound sign items show "resource support"

1. What comparisons about innovative climates can you make from these two organizations?
2. How might productivity differ when there is a climate that supports versus a climate that does not support innovation?
3. Which type of place would you rather work? Why?

SOURCE: Adapted from Susanne G. Scott and Reginald A. Bruce, "Determinants of Innovative Behavior: A Path Model of Individual Innovation in the Workplace," *Academy of Management Journal,* 37, no. 3 (1994), 580–607.

■ Manager's Workshop

An Ancient Tale

1. Read the introduction and case study and answer the questions.
2. In groups of 3–4, discuss your answers.
3. Groups report to the whole class and the instructor leads a discussion on the issues raised.

Introduction

To understand, analyze, and improve organizations, we must carefully think through the issue of who is responsible for what activities in different organizational settings. Often we hold responsible someone who has no control over the outcome, or we fail to teach or train someone who could make the vital difference.

To explore this issue, the following exercise could be conducted on either an individual or group basis. It provides an opportunity to see how different individuals assign responsibility for an event. It is also a good opportunity to discuss the concept of organizational boundaries (what is the organization, who is in or out, etc.).

Case Study

You should read the short story and respond quickly to the first three questions. Then take a little more time on questions four through six. The results, criteria, and implications could then be discussed in groups.

Long ago in an ancient kingdom there lived a princess who was very young and very beautiful. The princess, recently married, lived in a large and luxurious castle with her husband, a powerful and wealthy lord. The young princess was not content, however, to sit and eat strawberries by herself while her husband took frequent and long journeys to neighboring kingdoms. She felt neglected and soon became quite unhappy. One day, while she was alone in the castle gardens, a handsome vagabond rode out of the forest bordering the castle. He spied the beautiful princess, quickly won her heart, and carried her away with him.

Following a day of dalliance, the young princess found herself ruthlessly abandoned by the vagabond. She then discovered that the only way back to the castle led through the bewitched forest of the wicked sorcerer. Fearing to venture into the forest alone, she sought out her kind and wise godfather. She explained her plight, begged forgiveness of the godfather, and asked his assistance in returning home before her husband returned. The godfather, however, surprised and shocked at her behavior, refused forgiveness and denied her any assistance. Discouraged but still determined, the princess disguised her identity and sought the help of the most noble of all the kingdom's knights. After hearing the sad story, the knight pledged his unfailing aid—for a modest fee. But alas, the princess had no money and the knight rode away to save other damsels.

The beautiful princess had no one else from whom she might seek help, and decided to brave the great peril alone. She followed the safest path she knew, but when she was almost through the forest, the wicked sorcerer spied her and caused her to be devoured by the fire-breathing dragon.

1. Who was inside the organization and who was outside? Where were the boundaries?
2. Who is most responsible for the death of the beautiful princess?
3. Who is next most responsible? Least responsible?
4. What is your criterion for the above decisions?
5. What interventions would you suggest to prevent a recurrence?
6. What are the implications for *organizational development and change*?

Character	Most Responsible	Next Most Responsible	Least Responsible
Princess			
Husband			
Vagabond			
Godfather			
Knight			
Sorcerer			

Check one character in each column.

SOURCE: Adapted from J. B. Ritchie and Paul Thompson. Reprinted with permission from *Organization and People: Readings, Cases and Exercises in Organizational Behavior.* Copyright 1980 by West Publishing, pp. 68–70. All rights reserved, in Dorothy Marcic, *Organizational Behavior: Experiences and Cases,* 4th ed., pp. 378–79.

■ Management in Practice: Ethical Dilemma

Research for Sale

Lucinda Jackson walked slowly back to R & D Laboratory 4 at Reed Pharmaceuticals. She was stunned. Top management was planning to sell her entire team project to Trichem Industries in an effort to raise the capital Reed needed to buy a small, competing drug company. Two years ago, when she was named project administrator for the cancer treatment program, Jackson was assured that the program was the highest priority at Reed. She was allowed to recruit the best and the brightest in the research center in their hunt for an effective drug to treat lung cancer. There had been press releases and personal appearances at stockholder meetings.

When she first approached a colleague, Len Rosen, to become head chemist on the project, he asked her whether Reed was in cancer research for the long haul or if they were just grabbing headlines. Based on what she had been told by the vice president in charge of R & D, Jackson assured him that their project was protected for as long as it took. Now, a short two years later, she learned that not only was Reed backing out but also that the project was being sold as a package to an out-of-state firm. There were no jobs at Reed being offered as alternatives for the team. They were only guaranteed jobs if they moved with the project to Trichem.

Jackson felt betrayed, but she knew it was nothing compared to what the other team members would feel. Rosen was a ten-year veteran at Reed, and his wife and family had deep roots in the local community. A move would be devastating to them. Jackson had a few friends in top management, but she didn't know if any would back her if she fought the planned sale.

In groups of 4–6, answer the questions below. Afterwards, the instructor will lead a group discussion on your responses.

What Do You Do?

1. Approach top management with the alternative of selling the project and sending the team temporarily to train staff at Trichem but allowing them to return to different projects at Reed after the transition. After all, they promised a commitment to the project.
2. Wait for the announcement of the sale of the project and then try to secure as much support as possible for the staff and families in their relocation: moving expense reimbursement, job placement for spouses, and so on.
3. Tell a few people, such as Rosen, and then combine forces with them and threaten to quit if the project is sold. Make attempts to scuttle the sale to Trichem before it happens, and perhaps even leak the news to the press. Perhaps the threat of negative publicity will cause top management to reconsider.

SOURCE: Adapted from Doug Wallace, "Promises Made, Promises Broken," in *What Would You Do?* vol. 1 (March–April 1990), 16–18. Reprinted with the permission of Business Ethics, P.O. Box 8439, Minneapolis, MN 55408, (612) 879–0695.

■ Surf the Net

1. **Technological Change**. Check out three well-known technology news sites and write a note or e-mail to your professor concerning the site you think would help you most to stay current on technology trends. After visiting the three sites listed, choose the site you prefer and give two reasons you selected one site over the other two.
   http://techupdate.zdnet.com
   http://www.techreview.com
   http://www.cnet.com
2. **Creativity.** Using information found at the sites listed or at another site with creativity information, prepare a three-to five-minute oral presentation on any aspect of creativity that interests you and that you could make interesting to your professor and classmates. Remember that both content and creative presentation format will contribute to your success on this assignment.
   http://www.jvdcreativity.com/info.htm
   http://members.ozemail.com.au/~caveman/Creative/Admin/crbigpic.htm
   http://www.creativityatwork.com/
3. **Negotiation.** Type in the search phrase "negotiation articles" in a search engine such as *http://www.wisenut.com*. Select one article, print it out, read and highlight relevant points, and be prepared to share a thought or two from your article during a class discussion on negotiation.

◆ Case for Critical Analysis

Southern Discomfort

Jim Malesckowski remembers the call of two weeks ago as if he just put down the telephone receiver. "I just read your analysis and I want you to get down to Mexico right away," Jack Ripon, his boss and chief executive officer, had blurted in his ear. "You know we can't make the plant in Oconomo work anymore—the costs are just too high. So go down there, check out what our operational costs would be if we move, and report back to me in a week."

At that moment, Jim felt as if a shiv had been stuck in his side, just below the rib cage. As president of the Wisconsin Specialty Products Division of Lamprey, Inc., he knew quite well the challenge of dealing with high-cost labor in a third-generation, unionized U.S. manufacturing plant. And although he had done the analysis that led to his boss's knee-jerk response, the call still stunned him. There were 520 people who made a living at Lamprey's Oconomo facility, and if it closed, most of them wouldn't have a journeyman's prayer of finding another job in the town of 9,000 people.

Instead of the $16-per-hour average wage paid at the Oconomo plant, the wages paid to the Mexican workers—who lived in a town without sanitation and with an unbelievably toxic effluent from industrial pollution—would amount to about $1.60 an hour on average. That's a savings of nearly $15 million a year for Lamprey, to be offset in part by increased costs for training, transportation, and other matters.

After two days of talking with Mexican government representatives and managers of other companies in the town, Jim had enough information to develop a set of comparative figures of production and shipping costs. On the way home, he started to outline the report, knowing full well that unless some miracle occurred, he would be ushering in a blizzard of pink slips for people he had come to appreciate.

The plant in Oconomo had been in operation since 1921, making special apparel for persons suffering injuries and other medical conditions. Jim had often talked with employees who would recount stories about their fathers or grandfathers working in the same Lamprey company plant—the last of the original manufacturing operations in town.

But friendship aside, competitors had already edged past Lamprey in terms of price and were dangerously close to overtaking it in product quality. Although both Jim and the plant manager had tried to convince the union to accept lower wages,

union leaders resisted. In fact, on one occasion when Jim and the plant manager tried to discuss a cell manufacturing approach, which would cross-train employees to perform up to three different jobs, local union leaders could barely restrain their anger. Yet probing beyond the fray, Jim sensed the fear that lurked under the union reps' gruff exterior. He sensed their vulnerability, but could not break through the reactionary bark that protected it.

A week has passed and Jim just submitted his report to his boss. Although he didn't specifically bring up the point, it was apparent that Lamprey could put its investment dollars in a bank and receive a better return than what its Oconomo operation is currently producing.

Tomorrow, he'll discuss the report with the CEO. Jim doesn't want to be responsible for the plant's dismantling, an act he personally believes would be wrong as long as there's a chance its costs can be lowered. "But Ripon's right," he says to himself. "The costs are too high, the union's unwilling to cooperate, and the company needs to make a better return on its investment if it's to continue at all. It sounds right but feels wrong. What should I do?"

Questions

1. Assume you want to lead the change to save the Oconomo plant. Describe how you would proceed, using the four stages of the change process described in the chapter—forces, need, initiation, and implementation.

2. What is the primary type of change needed—technology, product, structure, or people/culture? To what extent will the primary change have secondary effects on other types of change at the Oconomo factory?

3. What techniques would you use to overcome union resistance and implement change?

SOURCE: Doug Wallace, "What Would You Do?" *Business Ethics* (March/April 1996), 52–53. Reprinted with permission.

Human Resource Management

LEARNING OBJECTIVES

After studying this chapter, you should be able to

1 Explain the role of human resource management in organizational strategic planning.

2 Describe federal legislation and societal trends that influence human resource management.

3 Explain what the changing social contract between organizations and employees means for workers and human resource managers.

4 Explain how organizations determine their future staffing needs through human resource planning.

5 Describe the tools managers use to recruit and select employees.

6 Describe how organizations develop an effective workforce through training and performance appraisal.

7 Explain how organizations maintain a workforce through the administration of wages and salaries, benefits, and terminations.

Management Challenge

Jack Butler was a 23-year-old Boston University graduate hoping to go to law school when his father was diagnosed with cancer. Butler's father asked him to take over the family business in Pittsburgh. The only good news was that the younger Butler would be able to prepare for his new role. "My father taught me the business while I watched him die," he says.

Two years later, Butler found himself CEO of a small company, Butler Gas Products, which manufactures and sells gases and equipment for medical and industrial use. Though the company had done reasonably well under Butler's father, the early 1980s brought new challenges. Sales fell 50 percent as the steel industry declined, cutting into the business of Butler's customers: scrap yards, mechanical contractors, and fabricating shops. At the same time that steel was declining, the high-technology and medical sectors were on the upswing. Butler saw business potential: In the future, an aging population would have growing needs for medical equipment that uses various gases. Butler started Qualtech Specialty Gases to test gas purity, and later he entered the gas-cylinder business. But the problem was that these were totally new areas for Butler Gas Products' workers. Butler knew his new ventures depended on the ability of 30 employees to grow into new skills. Or perhaps he needed to clean house and start with new employees.[1]

If you were Jack Butler and knew you needed a new type of employee to make the business a success, what would you do?

Photo by Michael Maurey. Courtesy of Walgreens Co.

Walgreens Co., the leader in the chain drugstore industry in both sales and profits, recognizes the strategic role of human resource management. In its Annual Report, the company states, "Well-trained pharmacy technicians like Celeste Burgess (photo) are pivotal to both patient service and the efficient operation of Walgreens Intercom Plus workflow system. Approximately 2,000 technicians passed a national certification exam during 1998, enhancing their pay and pharmacy knowledge."

human resource management (HRM)

Activities undertaken to attract, develop, and maintain an effective workforce within an organization.

The situation at Butler Gas Products provides a dramatic example of the challenges that human resource managers face every day. The people who make up an organization give that organization its primary source of competitive advantage, and human resource management plays a key role in finding and developing the organization's people as human resources that contribute to and directly affect company success. The term **human resource management (HRM)** refers to the design and application of formal systems in an organization to ensure the effective and efficient use of human talent to accomplish organizational goals.[2] This includes activities undertaken to attract, develop, and maintain an effective workforce.

Companies such as Southwest Airlines, Disney, and Dell Computer have become famous for their philosophy about human resource management, which is the foundation of their success. HRM is equally important for government and nonprofit organizations. For example, public schools in the United States are facing a severe teacher shortage, with HRM directors struggling with how to fill an estimated 2.2 million teacher vacancies over the next decade. Many are trying innovative programs such as recruiting in foreign countries, establishing relationships with leaders at top universities, and having their most motivated and enthusiastic teachers work with university students considering teaching careers.[3]

Over the past decade, human resource management has shed its old "personnel" image and gained recognition as a vital player in corporate strategy. Research has found that effective human resource management has a positive impact on organizational performance, including higher employee productivity and stronger financial performance.[4] Human resource personnel are considered key players on the management team. In addition, today's flatter organizations often require that managers throughout the organization play an active role in human resource management. Activities and tasks that were once handled by HRM professionals, such as recruiting and selecting the right personnel, developing effective training programs, or creating appropriate performance appraisal systems, may be pushed out to managers across the organization. Thus, all managers need to be skilled in the basics of human resource management.

The Strategic Role of Human Resource Management

The strategic approach to human resource management recognizes three key elements. First, as we just discussed, all managers are human resource managers. For example, at IBM every manager is expected to pay attention to the development and satisfaction of subordinates. Line managers use surveys, career planning, performance appraisal, and compensation to encourage commitment to IBM.[5] Second, employees are viewed as assets. Employees, not buildings and machinery, give a company a competitive advantage. How a company manages its workforce may be the single most important factor in sustained competitive success.[6] Third, human resource management is a matching process, integrating the organization's strategy and goals with the correct approach to managing the firm's human resources.[7] Some current strategic issues of particular concern to managers include becoming more competitive on a global basis; improving quality, productivity, and customer service; managing mergers and acquisitions; and applying new information technology for e-business. All of these strategic decisions determine a company's need for skills and employees.

This chapter examines the three primary goals of HRM as illustrated in Exhibit 9.1. HRM activities and goals do not take place inside a vacuum but within the context of issues and factors affecting the entire organization, such as increasing globalization, changing technology and the shift to knowledge work, rapid shifts in markets and the external environment, societal trends, government regulations, and changes in the organization's culture, structure, strategy, and goals.

The three broad HR activities outlined in Exhibit 9.1 are to attract an effective workforce to the organization, develop the workforce to its potential, and maintain the workforce over the long term.[8] Achieving these goals requires skills in planning, training, performance appraisal, wage and salary administration, benefit programs, and even termination. Each of the activities in Exhibit 9.1 will be discussed in this chapter.

EXHIBIT 9.1

Strategic Human Resource Management

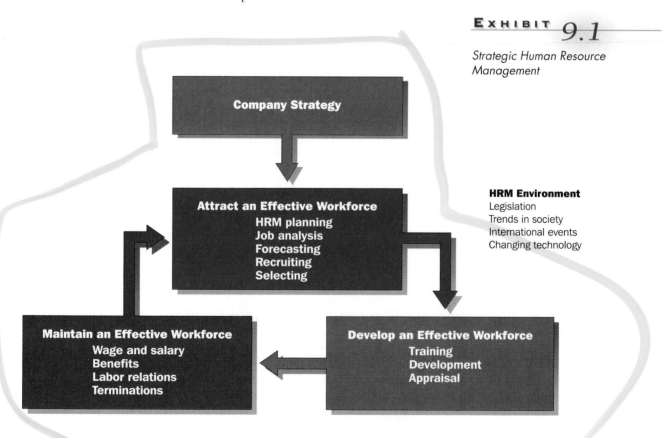

HRM Environment
Legislation
Trends in society
International events
Changing technology

Company Strategy

Attract an Effective Workforce
HRM planning
Job analysis
Forecasting
Recruiting
Selecting

Maintain an Effective Workforce
Wage and salary
Benefits
Labor relations
Terminations

Develop an Effective Workforce
Training
Development
Appraisal

Environmental Influences on HRM

"Our strength is the quality of our people."

"Our people are our most important resource."

These often-repeated statements by executives emphasize the importance of HRM. Human resource managers must find, recruit, train, nurture, and retain the best people. [9] Without the proper personnel, the brightest idea or management trend—whether virtual teams, e-business, telecommuting, or flexible compensation—is doomed to failure. In addition, when employees don't feel valued, usually they are not willing to give their best to the company and often leave to find a more supportive work environment. For these reasons, it is important that human resource executives be involved in competitive strategy. Human resource executives also interpret federal legislation and respond to the changing nature of careers and work relationships.

Competitive Strategy

HRM contributes directly to the bottom line through its appreciation that it is the organization's human assets—its people—that meet or fail to meet strategic goals. To keep companies competitive, HRM is changing in three primary ways: focusing on building human capital; developing global HR strategies; and using information technology.

human capital

The economic value of the knowledge, experience, skills, and capabilities of employees.

Building Human Capital. Today, more than ever, strategic decisions are related to human resource considerations. For example, in an information- and knowledge-based economy, success depends on an organization's ability to manage *human capital*.[10] **Human capital** refers to the economic value of the knowledge, experience, skills, and capabilities of employees.[11] To build human capital, HRM develops strategies for ensuring a workforce with superior knowledge and skills. This means recruiting to find the best talent, enhancing their skills and knowledge with training programs and opportunities for personal and professional development, and providing compensation and benefits that enhance the sharing of knowledge and appropriately reward people for their contributions to the organization. Human resource managers also help create an environment that gives highly talented people compelling reasons to stay with the company. Judy Lyles of DET Distributing Company in Nashville, Tennessee, sees the human resource department not just as the keeper of the rules, but as the "keeper of workers' hearts—the keeper of why they want to come to work every day."[12] Another person who has taken up this mantle is Judith Neal, who felt so strongly about helping companies build heart and spirit, she quit her job and started an organization to achieve this, as described below.

Spirit at Work

The grief and threats that she suffered as a whistle-blower (see Ethics section, Chapter 3) encouraged Judith Neal to become a college teacher, to positively influence the next generation of managers. Her dream was to help them take on more socially responsible roles, thereby reducing the numbers of demotivated and disenfranchised workers. After finding her own spiritual path, she began to see her life's work as helping organizations create uplifting work environments, where human dignity could be nurtured and expressed.

After several years of teaching at the University of New Haven, her calling became too intense for only part-time work. "I wanted to do something more profound and under my control," she said. With the help of the small settlement she eventually received as a result of the whistle-blower trial, Neal set about to help bring spirit to corporations. In the process, she discovered she had become an entrepreneur.

Instead of spending long hours working with managers, Neal found herself in front of her computer, often doing clerical tasks for up to 14 hours a day: answering e-mails, filling out financial reports, answering the phone, and creating mailings. Like many other entrepreneurs, she didn't realize she would need skills in accounting, strategic planning, fund-raising, managing a board, Web site management, database management, and so on. Neal didn't even consider the financial aspect of her nonprofit organization: "I had some vague, unrealistic ideas about how I would bring money in, but because I am not a fund-raiser, I was never able to bring in enough money to pay me a salary." At the same time, other part-time staff members were receiving regular paychecks for their work. Neal was somehow able to support herself and the business through consulting, speaking, and freelance writing, but the inequality of the rewards for her work remained.

After two years with all work and no social life, Neal accepted an offer to merge with Spirit in Business, a company that will take over all the drudgery of paperwork and leave Neal free to do what she most enjoys: working directly with leaders to create more empowered organizations.

Her advice to others: Choose work that you are passionate about, because it will take lots of hours; hire or rope-in volunteers to help with the more mundane tasks or the things you're not good at, such as fund-raising; and have enough money to live on for two years while the business is building, because everything will cost twice as much as you think. Would Neal do it again? Absolutely: She learned so much about herself. "But I would have set aside more time to play music and be with friends. Life is short, and it's foolish to bury yourself in work 100 percent of the time."[13]

Globalization. Another issue for today's organizations is competing on a global basis, which brings tremendous new challenges for human resource management. Most companies are still in the early stages of developing effective HRM policies, structures, and services that respond to the current reality of globalization.[14] In a study of more than 200 global companies, including Eli Lilly, PPG Industries, and UPS, managers reported that the biggest challenge for HRM is leadership development and training for the international arena. Companies in all industries report a growing need for capable global leaders, people who not only have good leadership abilities but can also manage across geographical and cultural boundaries. HRM departments are busily developing policies and procedures for recruiting and training people for global leadership. In addition, HRM is responsible for recruitment, training, and performance management of employees who might have to work across geographical, technical, and cultural boundaries to help the organization achieve its goals. The success of global business strategies is closely tied to the effectiveness of the organization's global HR strategies.[15]

Information Technology. Information technology is helping HRM meet these and other challenges. A **human resource information system** is an

human resource information system

An integrated computer system designed to provide data and information used in HR planning and decision making.

integrated computer system designed to provide data and information used in HR planning and decision making. The most basic use is the automation of payroll and benefits activities. However, new software programs and Web-based human resource service providers such as ManCom Team Inc. (*http://www.mancom.com*) allow companies to automate practically the entire human resources function, from recruiting and hiring, to orientation and training, to payroll and benefits administration. Some leading organizations are coming close to a paperless HR system, which saves time and money as well as frees HRM staff from mundane chores so they can focus on more strategic issues.[16] For example, by simplifying the task of analyzing vast amounts of data, human resource information systems can dramatically improve the effectiveness of long-term HR planning.

Federal Legislation

Over the past 40 years, several federal laws have been passed to ensure equal employment opportunity (EEO). Some of the most significant legislation and executive orders are summarized in Exhibit 9.2. The point of the laws is to stop discriminatory practices that are unfair to specific groups and to define enforcement agencies for these laws. EEO legislation attempts to balance the pay given to men and women; provide employment opportunities without regard to race, religion, national origin, and sex; ensure fair treatment for employees of all ages; and avoid discrimination against disabled individuals.

The Equal Employment Opportunity Commission (EEOC) created by the Civil Rights Act of 1964 initiates investigations in response to complaints concerning discrimination. The EEOC is the major agency involved with employment discrimination. **Discrimination** occurs when some applicants are hired or promoted based on criteria that are not job relevant. For example, refusing to hire a black applicant for a job he is qualified to fill or paying a woman a lower wage than a man for the same work are discriminatory acts. When discrimination is found, remedies include providing back pay and taking affirmative action. **Affirmative action** requires that an employer take positive steps to guarantee equal employment opportunities for people within protected groups. An affirmative action plan is a formal document that can be reviewed by employees and enforcement agencies. The goal of organizational affirmative action is to reduce or eliminate internal inequities among affected employee groups.

Failure to comply with equal employment opportunity legislation can result in substantial fines and penalties for employers. For example, Shoney's was accused of discrimination against black employees and job applicants. The class-action suit charged that company policy conspired to limit the number of black employees working in public areas of the restaurant. In 1992 the company agreed to pay $105 million to victims of its hiring, promotion, and firing policies, dating back to 1985.[17] Suits for discriminatory practices can cover a broad range of employee complaints. One issue of growing concern is *sexual harassment,* which is also a violation of Title VII of the Civil Rights Act. The EEOC guidelines specify that behavior such as unwelcome advances, requests for sexual favors, and other verbal and physical conduct of a sexual nature becomes sexual harassment when submission to the conduct is tied to continued employment or advancement or when the behavior creates an intimidating, hostile, or offensive work environment.[18] Sexual harassment will be discussed in detail in Chapter 10.

discrimination

The hiring or promoting of applicants based on criteria that are not job relevant.

affirmative action

A policy requiring employers to take positive steps to guarantee equal employment opportunities for people within protected groups.

Federal Law	Year	Provisions
Equal Opportunity/ Discrimination Laws		
Civil Rights Act	1991	Provides for possible compensatory and punitive damages plus traditional back pay for cases of intentional discrimination brought under Title VII of the 1964 Civil Rights Act. Shifts the burden of proof to the employer.
Americans with Disabilities Act	1990	Prohibits discrimination against qualified individuals by employers on the basis of disability and demands that "reasonable accommodations" be provided for the disabled to allow performance of duties.
Vocational Rehabilitation Act	1973	Prohibits discrimination based on physical or mental disability and requires that employees be informed about affirmative action plans.
Age Discrimination in Employment Act (ADEA)	1967 (amended 1978, 1986)	Prohibits age discrimination and restricts mandatory retirement.
Civil Rights Act, Title VII	1964	Prohibits discrimination in employment on the basis of race, religion, color, sex, or national origin.
Compensation/Benefits Laws		
Health Insurance Portability and Accountability Act (HIPPA)	1996	Allows employees to switch health insurance plans when changing jobs and get the new coverage regardless of preexisting health conditions; prohibits group plans from dropping a sick employee.
Family and Medical Leave Act	1993	Requires employers to provide up to 12 weeks unpaid leave for childbirth, adoption, or family emergencies.
Equal Pay Act	1963	Prohibits sex differences in pay for substantially equal work.
Health/Safety Laws		
Consolidated Omnibus Budget Reconciliation Act (COBRA)	1985	Requires continued health insurance coverage (paid by employee) following termination.
Occupational Safety and Health Act (OSHA)	1970	Establishes mandatory safety and health standards in organizations.

EXHIBIT 9.2

Major Federal Laws Related to Human Resource Management

Exhibit 9.2 also lists the major federal laws related to compensation and benefits and health and safety issues. The scope of human resource legislation is increasing at federal, state, and municipal levels. The Personal Responsibility and Work Opportunity Reconciliation Act of 1998, otherwise known as the Welfare Reform Act, is another federal law impacting employers. Some of them, such as Young Electric Sign, have used outsourced software to comply with federal regulations, as described in the following example.

Young Electric Sign

http://www.yesco.com

When a Las Vegas company starts getting telephone messages saying, "You know what we want. Give it to us now—or else!" many people would think that thugs were making those demands. Not so. The calls were from Utah state officials demanding information about employees of family-owned Young Electric Sign. As required by the Welfare Reform Act, bosses must file a New Hire Reporting form within 20 days, so that bureaucrats in other states can see whether a new employee owes child support. A new hire who turns up as a "deadbeat" gets his or her pay docked by the employer, who sends that sum to the state.

HRM chief Paul Bradley just about went crazy trying to fill out the appropriate paperwork for all the relevant 1,200 employees, but often did not get the documents filed on time. He spent 80 hours trying to electronically file the reports, but was even more frustrated when the reports kept bouncing back from Utah's state computer. That's when Bradley started getting those ugly telephone calls from government officials.

Finally, in desperation, Bradley outsourced the work to an HR firm, Ceridian, Ltd., paying $90,000 for hardware and software and a yearly fee of $39,000. Young Electric is not the only company to do so. About 30 percent of HR directors use outside services for their new hire reports. Bradley is now able to get back to his other work, helping the company meet customer needs, and doesn't regret the cost of the program. "Well worth it," he says.[19]

The working rights and conditions of women, minorities, older employees, and the disabled will probably receive increasing legislative attention in the future.

The Changing Nature of Careers

Another current issue is the changing nature of careers. HRM can benefit employees and organizations by responding to recent changes in the relationship between employers and employees and new ways of working, such as telecommuting, job sharing, and virtual organizations.

The Changing Social Contract

In the old social contract between organization and employee, the employee could contribute ability, education, loyalty, and commitment and expect in return the company would provide wages and benefits, work, advancement, and training throughout the employee's working life. But the volatile changes in the environment have disrupted this contract. Many organizations have been downsized, eliminating many employees. Employees who are left may feel little stability. In a fast-moving company, a person is hired and assigned to a project. The project changes over time, as do the person's tasks. Then the person is assigned to another project and then to still another. These new projects require working with different groups and leaders and schedules, and people may be working in a virtual environment, where they rarely see their colleagues face to face. Workers often have no place to call their own.[20] Careers no longer progress up a vertical hierarchy but move across jobs horizontally. People succeed only if the organization succeeds, and they might lose their jobs. Particularly in learning organizations, everyone is expected to be a self-motivated worker who has excellent interpersonal relationships and is continuously acquiring new skills. Part of the phenomenon is the growth of self-employed, or contingent workers, some of whom form loose alliances, as described in the Focus on Collaboration box.

Exhibit 9.3 lists some elements of the new social contract. The new contract is based on the concept of employability rather than lifetime employment. Individuals manage their own careers; the organization no longer takes care of them or guarantees employment. Companies agree to pay somewhat higher wages and invest in creative training and development opportunities so that people will be more employable when the company no longer needs their services. Employees take more responsibility and control in their jobs, becoming partners in business improvement rather than cogs in a machine. In return, the organization provides challenging work assignments as well as information and resources to enable workers to continuously learn new skills. The new contract can provide many opportunities for employees to be more involved and express new aspects of themselves.

However, many employees are not prepared for new levels of cooperation or responsibility on the job. Employment insecurity is stressful for most employees, and it is harder than it was in the past to gain an employee's full commitment and enthusiasm. In addition, one study found that while most workers today feel they are contributing to their companies' success, they are increasingly skeptical that their hard work is being fully recognized.[21] Some companies are finding it difficult to keep good workers because employee trust has been destroyed. To respond to these problems, HRM departments can help organizations develop a mix of training, career development opportunities, compensation packages, and rewards and incentives. They can provide career information and assessment, combined with career coaching, to help employees determine new career directions.[22]

The New Workplace

What company boasts of being America's largest employer in the opening years of the twenty-first century? It's not General Motors, McDonald's, or even the still-growing Wal-Mart, with more than a million employees.[23] The answer is that America's largest employer is a temporary agency, Manpower Inc.[24] Temporary employment agencies such as Manpower grew rapidly during the 1980s and 1990s, and by 2001, more than 3.3 million workers were in temporary firm placements. People in these temporary jobs do everything from data entry to becoming the interim CEO. Although in the past, most temporary workers were in clerical and manufacturing positions, in recent years, demand has grown for professionals, particularly financial analysts, information technology specialists, accountants, product managers, and operations experts.[25]

	New Contract	Old Contract
Employee	Employability, personal responsibility	Job security
	Partner in business improvement	A cog in the machine
	Learning	Knowing
Employer	Continuous learning, lateral career movement, incentive compensation	Traditional compensation package
	Creative development opportunities	Standard training programs
	Challenging assignments	Routine jobs
	Information and resources	Limited information

EXHIBIT 9.3

The Changing Social Contract

SOURCES: Based on Louisa Wah, "The New Workplace Paradox," *Management Review*, January 1998, 7; and Douglas T. Hall and Jonathan E. Moss, "The New Protean Career Contract: Helping Organizations and Employees Adapt," *Organizational Dynamics* (Winter, 1998), 22–37.

FOCUS ON COLLABORATION

Home-Based Businesses

Josh Ostroff has a ten-minute morning commute: from his bedroom downstairs to his computer, stopping on the way to brew coffee. After getting laid off from an advertising agency in the Boston area, he started his own media consulting firm, Virtual Media Resources. Instead of losing time in traffic, he is on the phone, Internet, or e-mail, gathering data and talking to clients—or spending time with his family.

Jennifer Overholt, an admitted night owl, does much of her work in the still of the night. While the streets are dark and quiet, she pores over reports and information, helping clients form strategic and marketing analyses. Sometimes she sends a middle-of-the-night e-mail to one of her five partners, some of whom are working at that time, too, and all of whom work from their homes. California-based Indigo Partners is a loose confederation of solo consultants who cooperate on projects while retaining the autonomy of freelancers. There is no hierarchy and there are no regular meetings: Small teams are formed to take on each project. Any partner can take time off for as long as desired and for any reason. One partner took off a year to help with a start-up, and another left for the summer to join her husband in London.

"Flying solo" used to refer to pilots. Nowadays it can also describe the nearly 20 million self-employed or contract workers in the United States. Gone are the days when magazines for entrepreneurs advertised audiotapes with background "office noises," to be played while talking on the phone. Back then it was considered an embarrassment to be working from home. People also used other tactics, such as typing "Suite 201" after their street address, renting post office boxes, adding "& Associates" after their last names, or recording a telephone greeting that said "All our lines are currently occupied."

The downsides of working solo include lack of a steady paycheck; no co-workers with whom to brainstorm; and difficulty in scheduling both work and family time, as projects may come in waves. Overholt says that all the Indigo partners have talked about someday returning to "corporate America." But she doesn't appear to be in a hurry: "The thing is, this is a great life. Why would I want to give it up?"

SOURCES: Marcelo Prince, "On Their Own: Freelance Workers," *The Wall Street Journal* (March 27, 2002), R14; Julie Bick, "Solo: The New Age of Self-Employment," *Inc.* (November 1, 2001), 86–91; John Grossman, "Meeting's at 9, I'll Be the One in Slippers," *Inc.* (May 19, 1998), 47–48.

In addition to the growth of temporary placement agencies, other changes in the workplace and workforce are occurring on a massive, global scale.[26] Not since the advent of mass production and modern organizations has a redefinition of work and career been so profound. The emergence of the *virtual organization,* as described in Chapter 7, means that many or even most of a company's workforce is made up of people who are hired on a project-by-project basis. **Contingent workers** are people who work for an organization, but not on a permanent or full-time basis. This may include temporary placements, contracted professionals, leased employees, or part-time workers. One estimate is that contingent workers make up at least 25 percent of the U.S. workforce.[27] The use of contingent workers means reduced payroll and benefit costs, as well as increased flexibility for both employers and employees.

A related trend is telecommuting. **Telecommuting** means using computers and telecommunications equipment to do work without going to an office. TeleService Resources has more than 25 telephone agents who work entirely from home, using state-of-the-art call-center technology that provides seamless interaction with TSR's Dallas-Fort Worth call center.[28] In 2000, an estimated 24 million people in the United States telecommuted on a regular or occasional basis, and Europe reported an estimated 10 million telecommuters.[29] Wireless Internet devices, laptops, cell phones, and fax machines make it possible for people to work just about anywhere. There's a growth of what is called *extreme telecommuting,* which means that people live and work in countries far away from the organization's physical location. For example, Paolo Concini works from his home in Bali, Indonesia, even though his company's offices are located

contingent workers

People who work for an organization, but not on a permanent or full-time basis, including temporary placements, contracted professionals, or leased employees.

telecommuting

Using computers and telecommunications equipment to perform work from home or another remote location.

in China and Europe.[30] Virtual workers and managers can live and work anywhere they want, untethered to any office or specific location. *Flexible scheduling* for regular employees is also important in today's workplace. Approximately 27 percent of the workforce has flexible hours. When and where an employee does the job is becoming less important.[31]

The advent of *teams* and *project management* is another significant trend in the new workplace. People who used to work alone on the shop floor, in the advertising department, or in middle management are now thrown into teams and succeed as part of a group. Each member of the team acts like a manager, becoming responsible for quality standards, scheduling, and even hiring and firing other team members. With the emphasis on projects, the distinctions between job categories and descriptions are collapsing. Many of today's workers straddle functional and departmental boundaries and handle multiple tasks and responsibilities.[32]

These new ways of working bring many advantages, but they also present many challenges for organizations and human resource management, such as new ways of recruiting and compensation that address the interests and needs of contingent and virtual workers, or new training methods that help people work cross-functionally. All human resource managers, whether in traditional organizations or new virtual organizations, have to achieve the three primary goals described earlier: attracting, developing, and maintaining an effective workforce.

Attracting an Effective Workforce

The first goal of HRM is to attract individuals who show signs of becoming valued, productive, and satisfied employees. The first step in attracting an effective workforce involves human resource planning, in which managers or HRM professionals predict the need for new employees based on the types of vacancies that exist, as illustrated in Exhibit 9.4. The second step is to use recruiting

EXHIBIT 9.4

Attracting an Effective Workforce

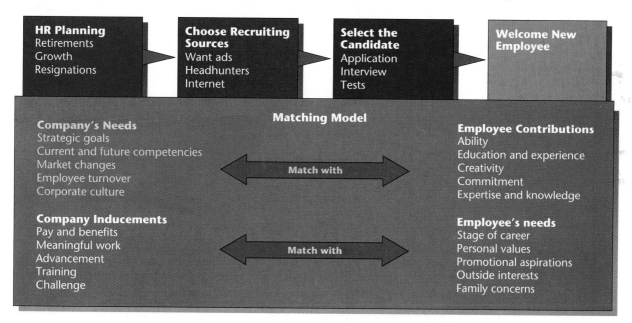

procedures to communicate with potential applicants. The third step is to select from the applicants those persons believed to be the best potential contributors to the organization. Finally, the new employee is welcomed into the organization.

Underlying the organization's effort to attract employees is a matching model. With the **matching model**, the organization and the individual attempt to match the needs, interests, and values that they offer each other.[33] HRM professionals attempt to identify a correct match. For example, a small software developer might require long hours from creative, technically skilled employees. In return, it can offer freedom from bureaucracy, tolerance of idiosyncrasies, and potentially high pay. A large manufacturer can offer employment security and stability, but it might have more rules and regulations and require greater skills for "getting approval from the higher-ups." The individual who would thrive working for the software developer might feel stymied and unhappy working for a large manufacturer. Both the company and the employee are interested in finding a good match. A new approach, called *job sculpting*, attempts to match people to jobs that enable them to fulfill deeply embedded life interests.[34] This often requires that HR managers play detective to find out what really makes a person happy. The idea is that people can fulfill deep-seated needs and interests on the job, which will induce them to stay with the organization.

Human Resource Planning

Human resource planning is the forecasting of human resource needs and the projected matching of individuals with expected vacancies. Human resource planning begins with several questions:

- What new technologies are emerging, and how will these affect the work system?
- What is the volume of the business likely to be in the next five to ten years?
- What is the turnover rate, and how much, if any, is avoidable?

The responses to these questions are used to formulate specific questions pertaining to HR activities, such as the following:

- How many senior managers will we need during this time period?
- What types of engineers will we need, and how many?
- Are persons with adequate computer skills available for meeting our projected needs?
- How many administrative personnel—technicians, IT specialists—will we need to support the additional managers and engineers?[35]
- Can we use temporary, contingent, or virtual workers to handle some tasks?

Answers to these questions help define the direction for the organization's HRM strategy. For example, if forecasting suggests that there will be a strong need for more technically trained individuals, the organization can (1) define the jobs and skills needed in some detail, (2) hire and train recruiters to look for the specified skills, and/or (3) provide new training for existing employees. By anticipating future HRM needs, the organization can prepare itself to meet

---

matching model
An employee selection approach in which the organization and the applicant attempt to match each other's needs, interests, and values.

human resource planning
The forecasting of human resource needs and the projected matching of individuals with expected job vacancies.

competitive challenges more effectively than organizations that react to problems only as they arise.

One of the most successful applications of human resource planning is the Tennessee Valley Authority's development of an eight-step system.

In the confusion and uncertainty following a period of reorganization and downsizing, a crucial role for HRM is balancing the need for future workforce planning with the creation of a climate of stability for the remaining workers. TVA created an eight-step plan that assesses future HR needs and formulates actions to meet those needs. The first step is laying the groundwork for later implementation of the program by creating planning and oversight teams within each business unit. Step two involves assessing processes and functions that can be benchmarked. Step three involves the projection of skills and employee numbers (demand data) necessary to reach goals within each business unit. Once these numbers are in place, step four involves projection of the current employee numbers (supply data) over the "planning horizon" without new hires and taking into consideration the normal attrition of staff through death, retirement, resignation, and so forth. Comparison of the difference between supply and demand (step five) gives the "future gap" or "surplus situation." This knowledge enables HR to develop strategies and operational plans (step six). Step seven involves communication of the action plan to employees. The final step is to periodically evaluate and update the plan as the organization's needs change.

Although, in a small organization, developing demand and supply data could be handled with a pad and a calculator, TVA uses a sophisticated automated system to update and revise the plan as needed to meet new competitive situations. Determining skills-gap and surplus information (step five) helped TVA develop a workforce plan to implement cross-organizational placement and retraining as alternatives to further employee cutbacks in the individual business units, thereby providing a greater sense of stability for workers. If needs change and TVA faces a demand for additional employees, this process will enable the company to recruit workers with the skills needed to help meet organizational goals.[36]

TVA

http://www.tva.com

Recruiting

Recruiting is defined as "activities or practices that define the characteristics of applicants to whom selection procedures are ultimately applied."[37] Although we frequently think of campus recruiting as a typical recruiting activity, many organizations use *internal recruiting*, or "promote-from-within" policies, to fill their high-level positions.[38] At Mellon Bank, for example, current employees are given preference when a position opens. Internal recruiting has several advantages: It is less costly than an external search, and it generates higher employee commitment, development, and satisfaction because it offers opportunities for career advancement to employees rather than outsiders.

Frequently, however, *external recruiting*—recruiting newcomers from outside the organization—is advantageous. Applicants are provided by a variety of outside sources including advertising, state employment services, private employment agencies (*headhunters*), job fairs, and employee referrals.

recruiting
The activities or practices that define the desired characteristics of applicants for specific jobs.

Assessing Organizational Needs. An important step in recruiting is to get a clear picture of what kinds of people the organization needs. Basic

© Robert Holmgren

Craig Johnson (standing, with some of his recruits) is the founder of Venture Law Group, a firm that redefined what a law firm can do by seizing a unique niche for itself. The firm helps launch successful start-up companies using services that include external recruiting. Joseph Grundfest, a Stanford University professor, called Johnson with the vaguest glimmer of a business idea. Johnson recognized the elements of a successful start-up and used his expertise to get the business off the ground. "What we needed was somebody who could act as a coach and a team builder, who could bring to the table the right mix of people early on," comments Grundfest, who compares Johnson's role in Silicon Valley to that of a talent agent in Hollywood.

job analysis

The systematic process of gathering and interpreting information about the essential duties, tasks, and responsibilities of a job.

job description

A concise summary of the specific tasks and responsibilities of a particular job.

job specification

An outline of the knowledge, skills, education, and physical abilities needed to adequately perform a job.

realistic job preview (RJP)

A recruiting approach that gives applicants all pertinent and realistic information about the job and the organization.

building blocks of human resource management include job analysis, job descriptions, and job specifications. **Job analysis** is a systematic process of gathering and interpreting information about the essential duties, tasks, and responsibilities of a job, as well as about the context within which the job is performed.[39] To perform job analysis, managers or specialists ask about work activities and work flow, the degree of supervision given and received in the job, knowledge and skills needed, performance standards, working conditions, and so forth. The manager then prepares a written **job description**, which is a clear and concise summary of the specific tasks, duties, and responsibilities, and **job specification**, which outlines the knowledge, skills, education, physical abilities, and other characteristics needed to adequately perform the job.

Job analysis helps organizations recruit the right kind of people and match them to appropriate jobs. For example, to enhance internal recruiting, Sara Lee Corporation identified six functional areas and 24 significant skills that it wants its finance executives to develop, as illustrated in Exhibit 9.5. Managers are tracked on their development and moved into other positions to help them acquire the needed skills.[40]

Realistic Job Previews. Job analysis also helps enhance recruiting effectiveness by enabling the creation of realistic job previews. A **realistic job preview (RJP)** gives applicants all pertinent and realistic information—positive and negative—about the job and the organization.[41] RJPs enhance employee satisfaction and reduce turnover, because they facilitate matching individuals, jobs, and organizations. Individuals have a better basis on which to determine their suitability to the organization and "self-select" into or out of positions based on full information.

Legal Considerations. Organizations must ensure that their recruiting practices conform to the law. As discussed earlier in this chapter, equal employment opportunity (EEO) laws stipulate that recruiting and hiring decisions cannot discriminate on the basis of race, national origin, religion, or sex. The Americans with Disabilities Act underscored the need for well-written job descriptions and specifications that accurately reflect the mental and physical

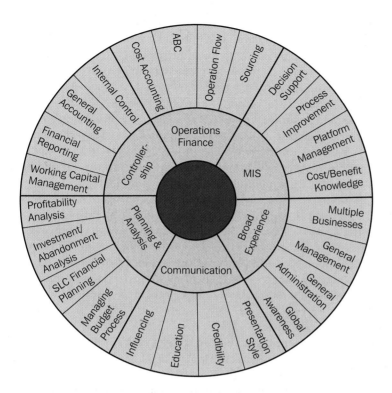

EXHIBIT 9.5

Sara Lee's Required Skills for Finance Executives

SOURCE: Adapted from Victoria Griffith, "When Only Internal Expertise Will Do," *CFO* (October 1998), 95–96, 102.

dimensions of jobs. *Affirmative action* refers to the use of goals, timetables, or other methods in recruiting to promote the hiring, development, and retention of *protected groups*—persons historically underrepresented in the workplace. For example, a city might establish a goal of recruiting one black firefighter for every white firefighter until the proportion of black firefighters is commensurate with the black population in the community.

Most large companies try to comply with affirmative action and EEO guidelines. Prudential Insurance Company's policy is presented in Exhibit 9.6. Prudential actively recruits employees and takes affirmative action steps to recruit individuals from all walks of life.

E-cruiting. One of the fastest-growing approaches to recruiting today is use of the Internet, which dramatically extends an organization's recruiting reach.[42] Although traditional recruiting methods such as print advertisements and job

EXHIBIT 9.6

Prudential's Corporate Recruiting Policy

An Equal Opportunity Employer

Prudential recruits, hires, trains, promotes, and compensates individuals without regard to race, color, religion or creed, age, sex, marital status, national origin, ancestry, liability for service in the armed forces of the United States, status as a special disabled veteran or veteran of the Vietnam era, or physical or mental handicap.

This is official company policy because:
- we believe it is right
- it makes good business sense
- it is the law

We are also committed to an ongoing program of affirmative action in which members of under-represented groups are actively sought out and employed for opportunities in all parts and at all levels of the company. In employing people from all walks of life, Prudential gains access to the full experience of our diverse society.

SOURCE: Prudential Insurance Company.

Choose a big co.'s web site now do they recruit & hire?

e-cruiting

Recruiting job applicants online.

fairs work quite well for many companies, **e-cruiting**, or recruiting job applicants online, offers access to a wider pool of applicants and can save time and money. In addition to posting job openings on company Web sites, many organizations use commercial recruiting sites such as Monster.com, CareerPath, HotJobs.com, and Career Mosaic, where job seekers can post their resumes and companies can search for qualified applicants. Forrester Research reports that approximately 2.5 million resumes are posted online, and the number is growing.[43]

Companies as diverse as Prudential Insurance, Cisco Systems, and Atkinsson Congregational Church have used the Web for recruiting. Cisco, which gets about 66 percent of new hires from the Web, claims that e-cruiting has cut the time it takes to fill a job from 113 days down to 45 days.[44] Costs go down, too. The Employee Management Association estimates that the cost per hire using Internet recruiting is $377, versus $3,295 per hire using print media.[45] Organizations have not given up their traditional recruiting strategies, but the Internet has given HRM managers new tools for searching the world to find the best available talent. One kind of e-cruiting is done by the project, as a contract worker. A young computer programmer saw a business opportunity with helping people recruit computer programming talent, as described in the Digital, Inc., box.

Other Recent Approaches to Recruiting. Organizations are also finding other ways to enhance their recruiting success. Most companies are putting renewed emphasis on referrals from current employees. A company's employees often know of someone who would be qualified for a position and fit in

DIGITAL, INC.

2 Rent a Coder

Ian Ippolito became frustrated while trying to find Web development sourcecode, so in 1997 he started *http://www.planet-source-code.com* (PSC), which exploded into 1.2 million monthly coder visits. Before the dot-com bubble burst, its $10,000–15,000 monthly advertising fees helped to fuel generous offers to buy PSC.

After the fall of the dot-coms, advertisers left in droves, many of them bankrupt. With no income and huge bills, Ippolito kicked himself for not taking one of those attractive offers. However, PSC's success also brought him numerous requests to write programs, which made him realize that his PSC audience was an undervalued asset. He had a real, live opportunity on his hands and needed to monetize the audience fast, or he would bite the dust like his colleagues.

In July 2001 he started *http://www.2rentacoder.com* (RAC), which connects the PSC programmers with people who need programmers. A coding customer asks for help on the site. Within 24 hours, five to six e-mail bids arrive from qualified programmers. The customer can review each programmer's profile. When selecting a coder, the customer places the fee (via credit card) in an escrow account that passes to the coder only after successful completion of the project.

When setting up the site, Ippolito had to decide whether he would include international coders. Many Americans encouraged him to stay in the country, where fees are $40–50 per hour, allowing RAC's 15 percent fee (paid by the programmer) to net more income. A coder in India makes $4–5 per hour (the average worker in India earns 40 cents per hour). Ippolito finally followed his conscience, going with free market forces rather than protectionism. Now, most of his 20,000 programmers are based in India and Romania.

RAC has become the eBay of sourcecode, with 1,200 monthly transactions. In the first month, the site brought in $30; the second month, $600; the third month, $2,700; and the fourth month, $6,000. It keeps growing, and so do the services on the site. Ippolito has customer feedback ratings, leading to a listing of the top ten coders, who work hard to maintain their status.

Ippolito says that he copes with all the ups and downs by not taking the highs too seriously, because that can make the lows worse. "The only thing you can control is your attitude," he says.

SOURCES: Lee Gomes, "Mani and Me: Hearing 'Mister I Work Cheap' From Across the Globe," *The Wall Street Journal* (June 3, 2002), B1; Ian Ippolito, personal communication, June 2002.

with the organization's culture. Many organizations offer cash awards to employees who submit names of people who subsequently accept employment, because referral by current employees is one of the cheapest and most reliable methods of external recruiting.[46] The professional service firm Deloitte & Touche has shelled out more than $3.5 million in cash awards to employees who refer candidates through the "Refer Potential Movers and Shakers" program, the firm's single best source of high-talent hires.[47]

In addition, some companies turn to nontraditional sources to find dedicated employees, particularly when there is a tight labor market. Manufacturer Dee Zee, which makes aluminum truck accessories in a factory in Des Moines, Iowa, found a source of loyal, hard-working employees among refugees from Bosnia, Vietnam, and Kosovo.[48] Since 1998, Bank of America has hired and trained more than 3,000 former welfare recipients in positions that offer the potential for promotions and long-term careers.[49] Days Inn has experimented with hiring the homeless, offering them wages plus a room for a small fee.[50] Recruiting on a global basis is on the rise, as well. Public schools are recruiting teachers from overseas. High-tech companies are looking for qualified workers in foreign countries because they cannot find people with the right skills in the United States.[51]

Selecting

The next step for managers is to select desired employees from the pool of recruited applicants. In the **selection** process, employers assess applicants' characteristics in an attempt to determine the "fit" between the job and applicant characteristics. Several selection devices are used for assessing applicant qualifications. The most frequently used are the application form, interview, employment test, and assessment center. Human resource professionals may use a combination of these devices to obtain a valid prediction of employee job performance. **Validity** refers to the relationship between one's score on a selection device and one's future job performance. A valid selection procedure will provide high scores that correspond to subsequent high job performance.

Application Form. The **application form** is used to collect information about the applicant's education, previous job experience, and other background characteristics. Research in the life insurance industry shows that biographical information inventories can validly predict future job success.[52]

One pitfall to be avoided is the inclusion of questions that are irrelevant to job success. In line with affirmative action, the application form should not ask questions that will create an adverse impact on protected groups unless the questions are clearly related to the job.[53] For example, employers should not ask whether the applicant rents or owns his or her own home because (1) an applicant's response might adversely affect his or her chances at the job, (2) minorities and women may be less likely to own a home, and (3) home ownership is probably unrelated to job performance. On the other hand, the CPA exam is relevant to job performance in a CPA firm; thus, it is appropriate to ask whether an applicant for employment has passed the CPA exam, even if only one-half of all female or minority applicants have done so versus nine-tenths of male applicants.

Interview. The interview is used in the hiring process in almost every job category in virtually every organization. The *interview* serves as a two-way

selection
The process of determining the skills, abilities, and other attributes a person needs to perform a particular job.

validity
The relationship between an applicant's score on a selection device and his or her future job performance.

application form
A device for collecting information about an applicant's education, previous job experience, and other background characteristics.

communication channel that allows both the organization and the applicant to collect information that would otherwise be difficult to obtain.

This is another area where the organization can get into legal trouble if the interviewer asks questions that violate EEO guidelines. Exhibit 9.7 lists some examples of appropriate and inappropriate interview questions.

Although widely used, the interview is not generally a valid predictor of job performance. However, it has high *face validity*. That is, it seems valid to employers, and managers prefer to hire someone only after they have been through some form of interview, preferably face-to-face. The Focus on Skills box offers some tips for effective interviewing.

Today's organizations are trying different approaches to overcome the limitations of the interview. Some put candidates through a series of interviews, each one conducted by a different person and each one probing a different aspect of the candidate. Companies such as Virginia Power and Philip Morris USA use *panel interviews,* in which the candidate meets with several interviewers who take turns asking questions, to increase interview validity.[54]

FOCUS ON SKILLS

The Right Way to Interview a Job Applicant

A so-so interview usually nets a so-so employee. Many hiring mistakes can be prevented during the interview. The following techniques will ensure a successful interview:

1. *Know what you want.* Before the interview, prepare questions based on your knowledge of the job to be filled.

2. *Prepare a road map.* Develop questions that will reveal whether the candidate has the correct background and qualifications. The questions should focus on previous experiences that are relevant to the current job.

3. *Use open-ended questions in which the right answer is not obvious.* Ask the applicant to give specific examples of previous work experiences. For example, don't ask, "Are you a hard worker?" or "Tell me about yourself." Instead ask, "Can you give me examples from your previous work history that reflect your level of motivation?" or "How did you go about getting your current job?"

4. *Do not ask questions that are irrelevant to the job.* This is particularly important when the irrelevant questions might adversely affect minorities or women.

5. *Listen; don't talk.* You should spend most of the interview listening. If you talk too much, the focus will shift to you, and you might miss important cues. One expert actually recommends stating all your questions right at the beginning of the interview. This forces you to sit back and listen and also gives you a chance to watch a candidate's behavior and body language.

6. *Allow enough time so that the interview will not be rushed.* Leave time for the candidate to ask questions about the job.

The types of questions the candidate asks can be an important clue to his or her interest in the job.

7. *Avoid reliance on your memory.* Request the applicant's permission to take notes; then do so unobtrusively during the interview or immediately after.

Even a well-planned interview may be disrupted by the unexpected. Robert Half asked vice presidents and human resource directors at 100 major American corporations to describe the most unusual thing that they were aware of ever happening during a job interview. Various applicants reportedly:

- "Wore a Walkman and said she could listen to me and the music at the same time."

- "Announced she hadn't had lunch and proceeded to eat a hamburger and french fries in the interviewer's office."

- "A balding candidate abruptly excused himself. He returned to the office a few minutes later wearing a hairpiece."

- "Not only did he ignore the 'No Smoking' sign in my office, he lit up the wrong end of several filter-tip cigarettes."

- "She chewed bubble gum and constantly blew bubbles."

- "Job applicant challenged the interviewer to arm wrestle."

- "He interrupted to telephone his therapist for advice on answering specific interview questions."

- "He dozed off and started snoring during the interview."

SOURCES: James M. Jenks and Brian L. P. Zevnik, "ABCs of Job Interviewing," *Harvard Business Review* (July–August 1989), 38–42; Dr. Pierre Mornell, "Zero Defect Hiring," *Inc.* (March 1998), 75–83; and Martha H. Peak, "What Color Is Your Bumbershoot?" Reprinted by permission of publisher from *Management Review* (October 1989), 63, ©1989. American Management Association, New York. All rights reserved.

Category	Okay to Ask	Inappropriate or Illegal to Ask
National origin	• The applicant's name • If applicant has ever worked under a different name	• The origin of applicant's name • Applicant's ancestry/ethnicity
Race	• Nothing	• Race or color of skin
Disabilities	• Whether applicant has any disabilities that might inhibit performance of job	• If applicant has any physical or mental defects • If applicant has ever filed workers' compensation claim
Age	• If applicant is over 18	• Applicant's age • When applicant graduated from high school
Religion	• Nothing	• Applicant's religious affiliation • What religious holidays applicant observes
Criminal record	• If applicant has ever been convicted of a crime	• If applicant has ever been arrested
Marital/family status	• Nothing	• Marital status, number of children or planned children • Child care arrangements
Education and Experience	• Where applicant went to school • Prior work experience	• When applicant graduated • Hobbies
Citizenship	• If applicant has a legal right to work in the United States	• If applicant is a citizen of another country

SOURCE: Based on "Appropriate and Inappropriate Interview Questions," in George Bohlander, Scott Snell, and Arthur Sherman, *Managing Human Resources*, 12th ed. (Cincinnati, Ohio: South-Western College Publishing, 2001), 207; and "Guidelines to Lawful and Unlawful Preemployment Inquiries," Appendix E, in Robert L. Mathis and John H. Jackson, *Human Resource Management*, 2nd ed. (Cincinnati, Ohio: South-Western, 2002), 189-190.

EXHIBIT 9.7

Employment Applications and Interviews: What Can You Ask?

Some organizations are also using *computer-based interviews* to complement traditional interviewing information. These typically require a candidate to answer a series of multiple-choice questions tailored to the specific job. The answers are compared to an ideal profile or to a profile developed on the basis of other candidates. Companies such as Pinkerton Security, Coopers & Lybrand, and Pic 'n Pay Shoe Stores have found computer-based interviews to be valuable for searching out information regarding the applicant's honesty, work attitude, drug history, candor, dependability, and self-motivation.[55]

Employment Test. Employment tests may include intelligence tests, aptitude and ability tests, and personality inventories, particularly those shown to be valid predictors. Many companies today are particularly interested in personality inventories that measure such characteristics as openness to learning, initiative, responsibility, creativity, and emotional stability.

employment test
A written or computer-based test designed to measure a particular attribute such as intelligence or aptitude.

Assessment Center. First developed by psychologists at AT&T, assessment centers are used to select individuals with high potential for managerial careers by such organizations as IBM, General Electric, and J.C. Penney.[56] Assessment centers present a series of managerial situations to groups of applicants over, say, a two- or three-day period. One technique is the *in-basket simulation*, which requires the applicant to play the role of a manager who must decide how to respond to ten memos in his or her in-basket within a two-hour period.

assessment center
A technique for selecting individuals with high managerial potential based on their performance on a series of simulated managerial tasks.

Panels of two or three trained judges observe the applicant's decisions and assess the extent to which they reflect interpersonal, communication, and problem-solving skills.

Assessment centers have proven to be valid predictors of managerial success, and some organizations now use them for hiring front-line workers, as well. Mercury Communications in England uses an assessment center to select telecommunications customer assistants. Applicants participate in simulated exercises with customers and in various other exercises designed to assess their listening skills, customer sensitivity, and ability to cope under pressure.[57]

Developing an Effective Workforce

Following selection, the major goal of HRM is to develop employees into an effective workforce. Development includes training and performance appraisal.

Training and Development

Training and development represent a planned effort by an organization to facilitate employees' learning of job-related behaviors.[58] Organizations spend nearly $100 billion each year on training. Training may occur in a variety of forms. The most common method is on-the-job training. In **on-the-job training (OJT)**, an experienced employee is asked to take a new employee "under his or her wing" and show the newcomer how to perform job duties. OJT has many advantages, such as few out-of-pocket costs for training facilities, materials, or instructor fees and easy transfer of learning back to the job. When implemented well, OJT is considered the fastest and most effective means of facilitating learning in the workplace.[59] One type of on-the-job training involves moving people to various types of jobs within the organization, where they work with experienced employees to learn different tasks. This *cross-training* may place an employee in a new position for as short as a few hours or for as long as a year, enabling the employee to develop new skills and giving the organization greater flexibility.

Another type of on-the-job training is *mentoring*, which means a more experienced employee is paired with a newcomer or a less-experienced worker to provide guidance, support, and learning opportunities. An innovative program at General Electric has turned the mentoring relationship upside down, pairing older, senior executives with little or no computer knowledge and expertise with young, computer- and Internet-savvy employees to help the old-timers learn about the world of e-business.[60] Pret A Manger uses on-the-job training and weekly information and pep sessions to keep employees on the right track for performance. It also uses a mentor program for managers, as described in the Best Practices box.

Other frequently used training methods include:

- *Orientation training,* in which newcomers are introduced to the organization's culture, standards, and goals

- *Classroom training,* including lectures, films, audiovisual techniques, and simulations

- *Self-directed learning,* also called programmed instruction, which involves the use of books, manuals, or computers to provide subject matter in highly

on-the-job training (OJT)

A type of training in which an experienced employee "adopts" a new employee to teach him or her how to perform job duties.

BEST PRACTICES

Pret A Manger

Think of American fast food and what comes to mind? Conformity of products, bland food, marginalized employees. Pret A Manger (faux French for "ready to eat") wants to change that. Founded in 1986 by two college buddies who saw an opportunity to combine French care regarding food and American-style service in London, it has grown to 118 shops in England and expanded to Hong Kong and to the home of the Whopper, initially opening a shop in New York City.

Each shop offers freshly prepared sandwiches, served up with an earnest discipline just shy of snootiness. Malt-grain bread with one or two inches of filling is all packed neatly into a cardboard and cellophane box; none of those famous New York oversized, impossible-to-bite sandwiches. Pret A Manger fits into the new $2.5 billion dining category called "fast-casual" or "adult limited-service," the fastest growing restaurant segment. It's now possible to "own" the $6 sandwich, just as Starbucks "owns" the $3 cup of coffee: The stakes are high.

Pret A Manger knows it takes more to succeed than good sandwiches, and has one potent insight: You can structure a mass-market business with innovation rather than rote standardization. The firm is constantly tweaking its menu, last year introducing 111 new items, most of which didn't last long. The company doesn't believe in focus groups. Their one principle: If people don't buy it, they stop selling it.

Nor are their employees mass produced. No one is pigeonholed into repetitive tasks, nor are they given scripts to memorize. Instead, they get a weekly pub night, organized by the company. Managers can earn equity in the company and rarely work during weekends or nights. When managers are first hired, they become part of Pret's "Buddy System," and continue to work in a specified "buddy store" periodically. It's a way to keep communication flowing both up and down, but mostly up, as the headquarters is hungry for feedback from the ground level. New Chairman and CEO Andrew Wolfe, a refugee from PepsiCo., has also introduced some organizational tools, such as IT systems and new training manuals.

Pret A Manger sold a 33 percent share to McDonald's in 2002, and some employees feared corruption of Pret's values or its dedication to wholesome, healthy food. For now, Wolfe is holding fast to the Pret culture. "I took this job because my personal values and the company values match," he says. "I wanted to be myself and make decisions based on what's right. There's no reason I'd allow anything to change that."

SOURCES: Ian Parker, "Faster Food," *The New Yorker* (May 27, 2002), 70–75; Scott Kirsner, "Recipe for Reinvention," *Fast Company* (April 2002), 38–42.

organized and logical sequences that require employees to answer a series of questions about the material

- *Computer-based training*, including computer-assisted instruction, Web-based training, and teletraining. (As with self-directed learning, the employee works at his or her own pace and instruction is individualized, but the training program is interactive and more complex, nonstructured information can be communicated.) Exhibit 9.8 shows the most frequently used types and methods of training in today's organizations.

Corporate Universities. A recent popular approach to training and development is the corporate university. The number of corporate universities has ballooned over the past decade, with more than 2,000 now in operation.[61] Perhaps the most well-known example is Hamburger University, McDonald's worldwide training center, which has been in existence for almost 40 years. A **corporate university** is an in-house training and education facility that offers broad-based learning opportunities for employees—and frequently for customers, suppliers, and strategic partners as well—throughout their careers.[62] For example, tens of thousands of FedEx employees, from couriers to top executives, have attended training at the company's Leadership Institute located near Memphis, Tennessee.[63] FedEx demonstrates a commitment to continuous learning by spending 3 percent of its total expenses on training, about six times that of most companies. Corporate universities have also extended their reach with new technology that enables distance learning via videoconferencing and online educational opportunities.

corporate university

An in-house training and education facility that offers broad learning opportunities for employees.

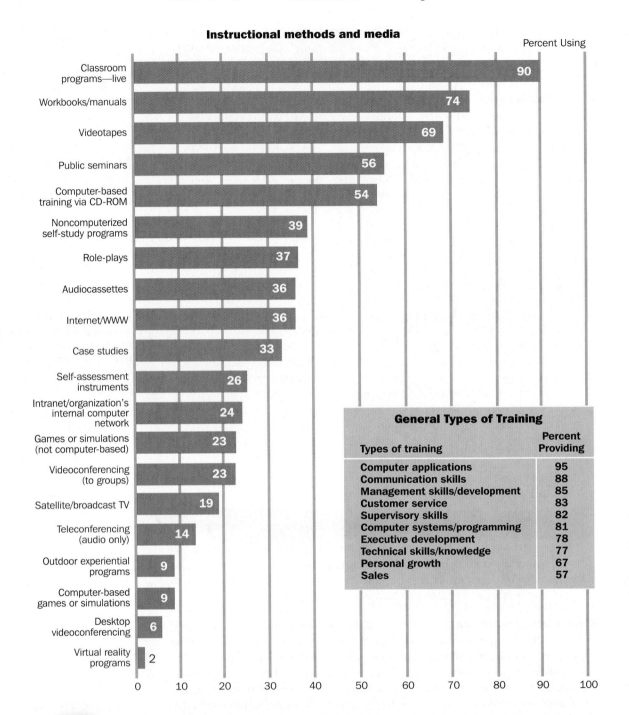

Instructional methods and media

Percent Using

- Classroom programs—live: 90
- Workbooks/manuals: 74
- Videotapes: 69
- Public seminars: 56
- Computer-based training via CD-ROM: 54
- Noncomputerized self-study programs: 39
- Role-plays: 37
- Audiocassettes: 36
- Internet/WWW: 36
- Case studies: 33
- Self-assessment instruments: 26
- Intranet/organization's internal computer network: 24
- Games or simulations (not computer-based): 23
- Videoconferencing (to groups): 23
- Satellite/broadcast TV: 19
- Teleconferencing (audio only): 14
- Outdoor experiential programs: 9
- Computer-based games or simulations: 9
- Desktop videoconferencing: 6
- Virtual reality programs: 2

General Types of Training	
Types of training	Percent Providing
Computer applications	95
Communication skills	88
Management skills/development	85
Customer service	83
Supervisory skills	82
Computer systems/programming	81
Executive development	78
Technical skills/knowledge	77
Personal growth	67
Sales	57

EXHIBIT 9.8

Types and Methods of Training

SOURCE: Data from "Industry Report 1999," *Training 36* (October 1999), 54, 56. Reprinted with permission from the October 1999 issue of *Training* magazine. Copyright 1999, Bill Communications, Minneapolis, Minn. All rights reserved. Not for resale.

The growth of corporate universities, as well as new approaches such as computer-assisted and online programs, reflects a shift in mindset from *training* as something provided to employees to *learning* that employees initiate on their own to enhance their knowledge and skills and further their own career development.[64] For example, J.C. Penney has created a completely virtual corporate university, called The Learning Place, that offers ongoing educational opportunities to all of Penney's 200,000 employees.[65]

Promotion from Within. Another way to further employee development is through promotion from within, which can help companies retain valuable employees. This provides challenging assignments, prescribes new responsibilities, and helps employees grow by expanding and developing their abilities.

One approach to promotion from within is *job posting,* which means that positions are announced on bulletin boards, on the intranet, or in company publications as openings occur. Interested employees notify the human resource department, which then helps make the fit between employees and positions.

Performance Appraisal

Performance appraisal is another important technique for developing an effective workforce. **Performance appraisal** comprises the steps of observing and assessing employee performance, recording the assessment, and providing feedback to the employee. During performance appraisal, skillful managers give feedback and praise concerning the acceptable elements of the employee's performance. They also describe performance areas that need improvement. Employees can use this information to change their job performance.

Performance appraisal can also reward high performers with merit pay, recognition, and other rewards. However, the most recent thinking is that linking performance appraisal to rewards has unintended consequences. The idea is that performance appraisal should be ongoing, not something that is done once a year as part of a consideration of raises.

Generally, HRM professionals concentrate on two things to make performance appraisal a positive force in their organization: (1) the accurate assessment of performance through the development and application of assessment systems such as rating scales and (2) training managers to effectively use the performance appraisal interview, so managers can provide feedback that will reinforce good performance and motivate employee development.

Assessing Performance Accurately. To obtain an accurate performance rating, managers must acknowledge that jobs are multidimensional and performance thus may be multidimensional as well. For example, a sports broadcaster may perform well on the job-knowledge dimension; that is, she or he may be able to report facts and figures about the players and describe which rule applies when there is a questionable play on the field. But the same sports broadcaster may not perform as well on another dimension, such as communication. She or he may be unable to express the information in a colorful way that interests the audience or may interrupt the other broadcasters.

If performance is to be rated accurately, the performance appraisal system should require the rater to assess each relevant performance dimension. A multidimensional form increases the usefulness of the performance appraisal and facilitates employee growth and development.

A recent trend in performance appraisal is called **360-degree feedback,** a process that uses multiple raters, including self-rating, as a way to increase awareness of strengths and weaknesses and guide employee development.

performance appraisal
The process of observing and evaluating an employee's performance, recording the assessment, and providing feedback to the employee.

360-degree feedback
A process that uses multiple raters, including self-rating, to appraise employee performance and guide development.

Members of the appraisal group may include supervisors, coworkers, and customers, as well as the individual, thus providing appraisal of the employee from a variety of perspectives.[66] A recent study found that 26 percent of companies used some type of multirater performance appraisal in 2000, up from 11 percent in 1995.[67] At PhotoDisc, a Seattle digital-imaging company, employees participate in selecting the people who will evaluate them, and reviewers can enter their comments and evaluations into a computer-based program at any time. Managers still conduct year-end reviews, but they use the 360-degree feedback as a guide.[68]

Other alternative performance-evaluation methods have also been gaining ground. One controversial method, which is nevertheless growing in popularity, is the *performance review ranking*.[69] As most commonly used, a manager evaluates his or her direct reports relative to one another and categorizes each on a scale, such as A = outstanding performance, B = high-middle performance, or C = in need of improvement. Many companies routinely fire those people falling in the bottom 10 percent of the ranking. Ford Motor Company, Intel, Hewlett-Packard, Sun Microsystems, and Microsoft all use versions of the ranking system.[70] Proponents say the ranking technique provides an effective way to assess performance and offer guidance for employee development. But critics of these systems, sometimes called *rank and yank,* argue that they are based on subjective judgments, produce skewed results, and discriminate against workers who are "different" from the mainstream. A class-action lawsuit charges that Ford's ranking system discriminates against older workers. Use of the system has also triggered employee lawsuits at Conoco and Microsoft, and employment lawyers warn that other lawsuits will follow.[71]

Performance Evaluation Errors. Although we would like to believe that every manager assesses employees' performance in a careful and bias-free manner, researchers have identified several rating problems.[72] One of the most dangerous is **stereotyping**, which occurs when a rater places an employee into a class or category based on one or a few traits or characteristics—for example, stereotyping an older worker as slower and more difficult to train. Another rating error is the **halo effect**, in which a manager gives an employee the same rating on all dimensions even if his or her performance is good on some dimensions and poor on others.

One approach to overcome management performance evaluation errors is to use a behavior-based rating technique, such as the behaviorally anchored rating scale. The **behaviorally anchored rating scale (BARS)** is developed from critical incidents pertaining to job performance. Each job performance scale is anchored with specific behavioral statements that describe varying degrees of performance. By relating employee performance to specific incidents, raters can more accurately evaluate an employee's performance.[73]

Exhibit 9.9 illustrates the BARS method for evaluating a production line supervisor. The production supervisor's job can be broken down into several dimensions, such as equipment maintenance, employee training, or work scheduling. A behaviorally anchored rating scale should be developed for each dimension. The dimension in Exhibit 9.9 is work scheduling. Good performance is represented by a 7, 8, or 9 on the scale and unacceptable performance as a 1, 2, or 3. If a production supervisor's job has eight dimensions, the total performance evaluation will be the sum of the scores for each of eight scales.

---

stereotyping

Placing an employee into a class or category based on one or a few traits or characteristics.

halo effect

A type of rating error that occurs when an employee receives the same rating on all dimensions regardless of his or her performance on individual ones.

behaviorally anchored rating scale (BARS)

A rating technique that relates an employee's performance to specific job-related incidents.

Job: Production Line Supervisor
Work Dimension: Work Scheduling

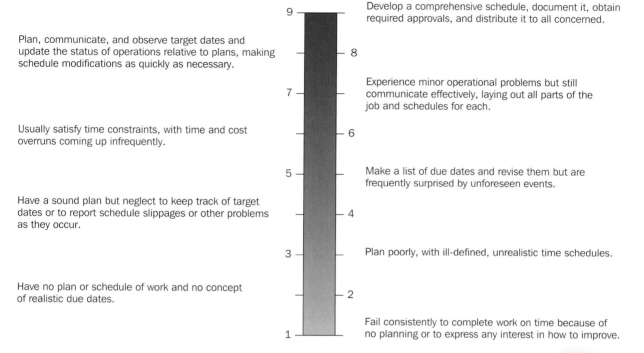

Develop a comprehensive schedule, document it, obtain required approvals, and distribute it to all concerned. — 9

Plan, communicate, and observe target dates and update the status of operations relative to plans, making schedule modifications as quickly as necessary. — 8

Experience minor operational problems but still communicate effectively, laying out all parts of the job and schedules for each. — 7

Usually satisfy time constraints, with time and cost overruns coming up infrequently. — 6

Make a list of due dates and revise them but are frequently surprised by unforeseen events. — 5

Have a sound plan but neglect to keep track of target dates or to report schedule slippages or other problems as they occur. — 4

Plan poorly, with ill-defined, unrealistic time schedules. — 3

Have no plan or schedule of work and no concept of realistic due dates. — 2

Fail consistently to complete work on time because of no planning or to express any interest in how to improve. — 1

SOURCES: Based on J. P. Campbell, M. D. Dunnette, R. D. Arvey, and L. V. Hellervik, "The Development and Evaluation of Behaviorally Based Rating Scales," *Journal of Applied Psychology* 57 (1973), 15–22; and Francine Alexander, "Performance Appraisals," *Small Business Reports* (March 1989), 20–29.

EXHIBIT 9.9

Example of a Behaviorally Anchored Rating Scale

Maintaining an Effective Workforce

Now we turn to the topic of how managers and HRM professionals maintain a workforce that has been recruited and developed. Maintenance of the current workforce involves compensation, wage and salary systems, benefits, and occasional terminations.

Compensation

The term **compensation** refers to (1) all monetary payments and (2) all goods or commodities used in lieu of money to reward employees.[74] An organization's compensation structure includes wages and/or salaries and benefits such as health insurance, paid vacations, or employee fitness centers. Developing an effective compensation system is an important part of human resource management because it helps to attract and retain talented workers. In addition, a company's compensation system has an impact on strategic performance.[75] Human resource managers design the pay and benefits systems to fit company strategy and to provide compensation equity.

compensation
Monetary payments (wages, salaries) and nonmonetary goods/commodities (benefits, vacations) used to reward employees.

Wage and Salary Systems. Ideally, management's strategy for the organization should be a critical determinant of the features and operations of the pay system.[76] For example, managers may have the goal of maintaining or improving profitability or market share by stimulating employee performance. Thus, they should design and use a merit pay system rather than a system based on other criteria such as seniority.

The most common approach to employee compensation is *job-based pay,* which means linking compensation to the specific tasks an employee performs. However, these systems present several problems. For one thing, job-based pay may fail to reward the type of learning behavior needed for the organization to adapt and survive in today's environment. In addition, these systems reinforce an emphasis on organizational hierarchy and centralized decision making and control, which are inconsistent with the growing emphasis on employee participation and increased responsibility.[77]

Skill-based pay systems are becoming increasingly popular in both large and small companies, including Sherwin-Williams, Au Bon Pain, and Quaker Oats. Employees with higher skill levels receive higher pay than those with lower skill levels. At Quaker Oats pet food plant in Topeka, Kansas, for example, employees start at $8.75 per hour but can reach a top hourly rate of $14.50 when they master a series of skills.[78] Also called *competency-based pay,* skill-based pay systems encourage employees to develop their skills and competencies, thus making them more valuable to the organization as well as more employable if they leave their current job.

Compensation Equity. Whether the organization uses job-based pay or skill-based pay, good managers strive to maintain a sense of fairness and equity within the pay structure and thereby fortify employee morale. **Job evaluation** refers to the process of determining the value or worth of jobs within an organization through an examination of job content. Job evaluation techniques enable managers to compare similar and dissimilar jobs and to determine internally equitable pay rates—that is, pay rates that employees believe are fair compared with those for other jobs in the organization.

Organizations also want to make sure their pay rates are fair compared to other companies. HRM managers may obtain **wage and salary surveys** that show what other organizations pay incumbents in jobs that match a sample of "key" jobs selected by the organization. These surveys are available from a number of sources, including the U.S. Bureau of Labor Statistics National Compensation Survey.

Pay for Performance. Most of today's organizations develop compensation plans based on a *pay-for-performance standard* to raise productivity and cut labor costs in a competitive global environment. **Pay-for-performance**, also called *incentive pay,* means tying at least part of compensation to employee effort and performance, whether it be through merit-based pay, bonuses, team incentives, or various gainsharing or profit-sharing plans. Data show that growth in base wages is slowing in many industries, and the use of pay-for-performance has steadily increased since the early 1990s, with approximately 70 percent of companies now offering some form of incentive pay.[79] Incentives are aligned with the behaviors needed to help the organization achieve its strategic goals. Employees have an incentive to make the company more efficient and profitable because if goals are not met, no bonuses are paid.

Benefits

The best human resource managers know that a compensation package requires more than money. Although wage and salary is an important compo-

---

job evaluation

The process of determining the value of jobs within an organization through an examination of job content.

wage and salary surveys

Surveys that show what other organizations pay incumbents in jobs that match a sample of "key" jobs selected by the organization.

pay-for-performance

Incentive pay that ties at least part of compensation to employee effort and performance.

nent, it is only a part. Equally important are the benefits offered by the organization. Benefits make up 40 percent of labor costs in the U.S.[80]

Some benefits are required by law, such as Social Security, unemployment compensation, and worker's compensation. In addition, companies with 50 or more employees are required by the Family and Medical Leave Act of 1993 to give up to 12 weeks of unpaid leave for such things as the birth or adoption of a child, the serious illness of a spouse or family member, or an employee's serious illness. Other types of benefits, such as health insurance, vacations, and such things as on-site day care or fitness centers are not required by law but are provided by organizations to maintain an effective workforce.

One reason that benefits make up such a large portion of the compensation package is that health-care costs have been increasing so quickly. Many organizations require employees to absorb some of the cost of medical benefits, such as through copayments or higher deductibles.

Besides the actual cost of benefits, there remains the expense of administering them. Computerization can cut the time and expense tremendously; thus, benefits administration is the most technologically advanced area of HRM. At companies such as Wells Fargo and LG&E Energy, employees access their benefits package through an intranet, creating a "self-service" benefits administration.[81] This also enables employees to change their benefits selections easily. Today's organizations realize that the "one-size-fits-all" benefits package is no longer appropriate, so they frequently offer *cafeteria-plan benefits packages* that allow employees to select the benefits of greatest value to them.[82] Other companies use surveys to determine which combination of fixed benefits is most desirable. The benefits packages provided by large companies attempt to meet the needs of all employees.

Termination

Despite the best efforts of line managers and HRM professionals, the organization will lose employees. Some will retire, others will depart voluntarily for other jobs, and still others will be forced out through mergers and cutbacks or for poor performance. The value of termination for maintaining an effective workforce is twofold. First, employees who are poor performers can be dismissed. Productive employees often resent disruptive, low-performing employees who are allowed to stay with the company and receive pay and benefits comparable to theirs. Second, employers can use exit interviews as a valuable HR tool, regardless of whether the employee leaves voluntarily or is forced out. An **exit interview** is an interview conducted with departing employees to determine why they are leaving.[83] The value of the exit interview is to provide an excellent and inexpensive way to learn about pockets of dissatisfaction within the organization and hence reduce future turnover.

When companies experience downsizing through mergers or because of global competition or a shifting economy, often a large number of managers and workers are terminated at the same time. In these cases, enlightened companies try to find a smooth transition for departing employees. For example, General Electric laid off employees in three gradual steps. It also set up a reemployment center to assist employees in finding new jobs or in learning new skills. It provided counseling in how to write a résumé and conduct a job search. Additionally, General Electric placed an advertisement in local newspapers saying that these employees were available.[84]

exit interview
An interview conducted with departing employees to determine the reasons for their termination.

Managers at Agilent Technologies, an $8.3 billion technology spin-off from Hewlett-Packard, have worked hard to gain employees' trust. When downsizing became necessary and managers had to terminate a large number of workers, they made the layoffs easier by showing empathy and respect for employees. As a result, after the workers at this Agilent plant in Newark, California, were told their plant was closing, they upped production higher than ever before—out of respect for their managers and concern for co-workers in other plants. Agilent's humane approach helped the company attain a spot on Fortune magazine's list of Best Companies to Work For even in the midst of downsizing and cost-cutting.

© Elena Dorfman—Matrix

By showing genuine concern in helping place laid-off employees, a company communicates the value of human resources and helps maintain a positive corporate culture, as shown below.

Hunt Tractor

Imagine you are laid off—due to downsizing—and your employer hires a grief counselor to help you deal with the trauma.

Then imagine a company that never lays off anyone. Construction-equipment dealership Hunt Tractor's president, Frank Miske, Jr., says he doesn't even "fantasize" about axing workers. "We don't lay people off because we don't want to lose them. Besides that, it's not morally right to lay them off because loyal employees built this company," which has been profitable since it began in 1969.

Hunt Tractor belongs to a rare group of businesses that have never laid off anyone. During down times, chairman and World War II naval hero Roy Hunt keeps workers busy with painting, roofing, building renovation, training, machine repairs, and tidying up. What does the company see as the benefits? High rates of retention of its highly skilled workers, increased productivity, lower recruiting costs, superior customer service due to extremely loyal and satisfied employees, and costs savings because of lower turnover and absenteeism. Not a bad deal.

Roy Hunt knows all too well the difficulties of layoffs and then rehiring later when business picks up. "Our people are not robots," he says. "You can't just take somebody from off the street and expect them to do the job." He gets tired of reading all the headlines about cold and uncaring companies that eliminate thousands of jobs at will. "Our business isn't run like that," he adds. "I'd like to dispel the notion that we're all only interested in the bottom line."[85]

Summary and Management Solution

This chapter described several important points about human resource management in organizations. All managers are responsible for human resources, and most organizations have a human resource department that works with line managers to ensure a productive workforce. Human resource management plays a key strategic role in today's organizations. HRM is changing in three ways to keep today's organizations competitive—focusing on human capital; globalizing HR systems, policies, and structures; and using information technology to help achieve strategic goals. The HR department must also implement procedures to reflect federal and state legislation and respond to changes in working relationships and career directions. The old social contract of the employee being loyal to the company and the company taking care of the employee until retirement no longer holds. Employees are responsible for managing their own careers. Although many people still follow a traditional management career path, others look for new opportunities as contingent workers, telecommuters, team players, and virtual employees.

The HR department strives to achieve three goals for the organization. The first goal of the human resource department is to attract an effective workforce through human resource planning, recruiting, and employee selection. The second is to develop an effective workforce. Newcomers are introduced to the organization and to their jobs through orientation and training programs. Moreover, employees are evaluated through performance appraisal programs. The third goal is to maintain an effective workforce. Human resource managers retain employees with wage and salary systems, benefits packages, and termination procedures. In many organizations, information technology is being used to more effectively meet all three of these important HR goals.

With regard to the case of Butler Gas Products, from the beginning of the chapter, Jack Butler decided he had good employees and wanted to help them grow into their new jobs. "My father taught me in the beginning to surround myself with good people, people who are smarter than you," he says. Two of those people were his sisters: Barb Glessner as VP and sales coordinator and Debi Butler as VP of new business development. They told Jack the future of the business was in the 30 employees, not in merely offering the best prices to customers. "We sell a commodity," says Glessner, so price is not the issue. What will make the company a success, she says, is making sure employees exceed customer expectations. That means workers need to be happy and well trained. Butler Gas Products now spends $50,000 to $70,000 per year on training for every single employee. And they get what they pay for, because the company now does $3 million per year. But training is not enough. Butler pays well, and offers great benefits and a generous retirement package. They want employees to keep growing. Each worker has a personal development plan, to help them align their own goals with that of helping make the company successful. If desired, each person can select a mentor from anywhere in the company. One thing you can't criticize the company for is scrimping on training. Messner says "sometimes the company overdoes it." But it's still worth it. "We found that investment in people pays off," she says.[86]

Discussion Questions

1. It is the year 2010. In your company, central planning has given way to frontline decision making, and bureaucracy has given way to teamwork. Shop floor workers use computers and robots. There is a labor shortage for many job openings, and the few applicants lack skills to work in teams, make decisions, or use sophisticated technology. As vice-president of human resource management since 2000, what should you have done to prepare for this problem?

2. If you were asked to advise a private company about its equal employment opportunity responsibilities, what two points would you emphasize as most important?

3. How can the human resource activities of recruiting, performance appraisal, and compensation be related to corporate strategy?

4. Think back to your own job experience. What human resource management activities described in this chapter were performed for the job you filled? Which ones were absent?

5. How "valid" do you think the information obtained from a personal interview versus an employment test versus an assessment center would be for predicting effective job performance for a college professor? An assembly-line worker in a team-oriented plant? Discuss.

6. How will the growing use of telecommuters, contingent workers, and virtual teams affect human resource management? How can managers improve recruiting and retention of these new kinds of employees?

7. Do you see any conflict between the current emphasis on computerizing HR and the growing focus on building human capital? Discuss.

8. Why is mentoring such a powerful means of developing an effective workforce?

9. What is the role of compensation in maintaining an effective workforce? When would benefits play an important part in compensation? When might they not be important?

10. What purpose do exit interviews serve for human resource management?

■ Manager's Workbook

Test Your Human Resources Knowledge

This quiz will test your knowledge of human resources issues affecting today's workplace. The quiz was designed by the Council on Education in Management, a Walnut Creek, California, firm that conducts human resources and employment law seminars nationwide.

1. If you receive an unsolicited résumé in the mail, you must keep it for two years.   T   F

2. Time-management principles are pretty much the same in any administrative job.   T   F

3. Regardless of the type of business or the various laws that may apply, there is a core of common practices for keeping personnel records and files that makes sense for almost any organization.   T   F

4. Every employer must have an affirmative action plan.   T   F

5. An employer must investigate an allegation of sexual harassment even if the victim asks to remain anonymous.   T   F

6. An employer is not obligated to pay overtime to a nonexempt employee who works more than 40 hours in a week after being asked not to put in overtime.   T   F

7. If your company is found guilty of discrimination, the Equal Employment Opportunity Commission will be more lenient if your records show that the violation was unintentional.   T   F

8. Americans with Disabilities Act regulations require companies to maintain written job descriptions.   T   F

9. Reference checking is an important procedure, despite the fact that many companies won't release this information.   T   F

10. Your employee orientation and handbook should help assure new employees that they will be a part of the team as long as they do a good job.   T   F

■ Manager's Workshop

Hiring and Evaluating Using Core Competencies

1. Form groups of 4–7 members. Develop a list of "core competencies" for the job of student in this course. (Or alternately, you may choose a job in one of the group members' organizations.) List the core competencies below.

1. _____   5. _____

2. _____   6. _____

3. _____   7. _____

4. _____   8. _____

2. Which of the above are the most important four?

1. _____   3. _____

2. _____   4. _____

3. What questions would you ask a potential employee/ student to determine if that person could be successful in this class, based on the four most important core competencies? (interviewing)

1. _____

2. _____

3. _____

4. _____

4. What learning experiences would you develop to enhance those core competencies? (training and development)

1. _____

2. _____

3. _____

4. _____

5. How would you evaluate or measure the success of a student in this class, based on the four core competencies? (performance evaluation)

1. _____

2. _____

3. _____

4. _____

■ Management in Practice: Ethical Dilemma

A Conflict of Responsibilities

As director of human resources, Tess Danville was asked to negotiate a severance deal with Terry Winston, the Midwest regional sales manager for Cyn-Com Systems. Winston's problems with drugs and alcohol had become severe enough to precipitate his dismissal. His customers were devoted to him, but top management was reluctant to continue gambling on his reliability. Lives depended on his work as the salesman and installer of Cyn-Com's respiratory diagnostic technology. Winston had been warned twice to clean up his act, but had never succeeded. Only his unique blend of technical knowledge and high-powered sales ability had saved him before.

But now the vice president of sales asked Danville to offer Winston the option of resigning rather than be fired if he would sign a noncompete agreement and agree to go into rehabilitation. Cyn-Com would also extend a guarantee of confidentiality on the abuse issue and a good work reference as thanks for the millions of dollars of business that Winston had brought to Cyn-Com. Winston agreed to take the deal. After his departure, a series of near disasters was uncovered as a result of Winston's mismanagement. Some of his maneuvers to cover up his mistakes bordered on fraud.

Today Danville received a message to call the human resources director at a cardiopulmonary technology company to give a personal reference on Terry Winston. From the area code, Danville could see that he was not in violation of the noncompete agreement. She had also heard that Winston had completed a 30-day treatment program as promised. Danville knew she was expected to honor the confidentiality agreement, but she also knew that if his shady dealings had been discovered before his departure, he would have been fired without any agreement. Now she was being asked to give Winston a reference for another medical sales position.

What Do You Do?

1. Honor the agreement, trusting Winston's rehabilitation is complete on all levels and that he is now ready for a responsible position. Give a good recommendation.
2. Contact the vice-president of sales and ask him to release you from the agreement or to give the reference himself. After all, he made the agreement. You don't want to lie.
3. Without mentioning specifics, give Winston such an unenthusiastic reference that you hope the other human resources director can read between the lines and believe that Winston will be a poor choice.

■ Surf the Net

1. **100 Great Places to Work** Go to *http://www. greatplacetowork.com.* Locate these two items at the site:
   Great Place to Work® Model©
   Benefits of Being a Great Place to Work®
   Print out both pages, read and highlight sections of particular interest to you, and then submit your highlighted printouts to your instructor to show you've completed this assignment.
2. **Internet Recruiting** Select the tab "For Employers" located at the top of the following site:
   http://www.wetfeet.com
   At this site you will learn more about how employers are using the Internet to help them in the recruiting process. Locate information on recruitment technologies and the featured "Recruitment Website of the Month." Summarize your findings in a printed note or e-mail to your instructor.
3. **Compensation** Fill in the following information about yourself: After receiving the college degree you're currently pursuing,

   (a) what kind of job do you see yourself doing?

   (b) where, geographically, do you wish to work? (For this assignment, you will need to select a U.S. location.)

   Now find the "Salary Wizard" at *http://www.salary.com.* Provide the information requested and then select "Create salary report." Print out the report, write your name at the top, and submit it to your instructor.

■ Case for Critical Analysis

Waterway Industries

Waterway Industries was founded in the late 1960s as a small manufacturer of high-quality canoes. Based in Lake Placid, New York, the company quickly gained a solid reputation throughout the Northeast and began building a small customer base in the Pacific Northwest as well. By the late 1980s, Waterway was comfortably ensconced in the canoe market. Although earnings growth was fairly steady, CEO Cyrus Maher was persuaded by a friend to venture into kayaks. After Waterway began selling its own line of compact, inexpensive kayaks in 1998, Maher quickly learned that the decision was a good one. Most of Waterway's existing canoe customers placed sizable kayak orders, and a number of private-label companies also began contacting Maher about making kayaks for their companies. When Lee Carter was hired to establish a formal marketing department at Waterway, things really took off. Carter began bringing in so many large orders that the company had to contract with other manufacturers to keep up.

Managers began to envision the day when Waterway would be a major player in water sports equipment. They developed a long-range strategic plan that called for aggressive growth, new product designs, and nationwide marketing and distribution by 2003. Maher believes most employees are adjusting well to the faster pace at the company. Many of the shop-floor employees are outdoor enthusiasts who like making quality products that they and their friends use. Waterway has always had a relaxed, informal working atmosphere, where employees get along well, enjoy their jobs, and get their work completed on time. However, the greater work load means people have less time for horsing around, and they can no longer leave by 3 PM to enjoy canoeing or kayaking when the weather is good.

Maher thinks workers have been given adequate raises to compensate for the faster work pace, but he has recently been hearing complaints from the shop floor about inadequate pay. He recently turned down a request from the plant supervisor for additional hourly wage increases for top performers, insisting that wages were in line with what other local manufacturers were paying. Unfortunately, a new automotive parts plant offering a slightly higher wage recently lured away three of his best workers.

Several managers have also approached Maher about salary adjustments. Waterway's two designers suggested that they would be interested in equity (part ownership) in the company, whereby they would receive a share of the profits if their designs did well. Maher's response was to give the senior designer a modest pay raise and extra vacation and to increase the bonuses for both designers. Both seemed satisfied with the new arrangement. Waterway's CFO, on the other hand, recently left the company to take a position with a power boat manufacturer after Maher twice refused his request for a redesigned compensation package to include equity. Now, on a trip to the cafeteria to get a cup of coffee, Maher has just overheard Lee Carter discussing a possible job opportunity with another company. He is well aware of the lucrative packages being offered to sales and marketing managers in the sporting goods industry, and he doesn't want to lose Carter. He would like to find a way to recognize her hard work and keep her at Waterway for at least a few more years.

Maher has asked you, the company's sole human resource manager, for advice about changing the company's compensation system. In the past, he has handled things informally, giving employees annual salary increases and bonuses, and dealing with employees one-on-one (as he did with the designers) when they have concerns about their current compensation. Now, Maher is wondering if his company has grown to the point where he needs to establish some kind of formal compensation system that can recognize employees who make outstanding contributions to the company's success.

Questions

1. Does Waterway's current compensation system seem to fit the company's strategy of aggressive growth and product innovation? How might it be changed to achieve a better fit?

2. How would you gather the data and design a competitive compensation system for Waterway? Would your approach be different for hourly workers versus managers?

3. How can nonfinancial incentives play a role in helping Waterway retain hourly shop workers? Aggressive and ambitious managers like Lee Carter?

SOURCE: Based on Robert D. Nicoson, "Growing Pains," *Harvard Business Review* (July–August 1996), 20–36.

Managing Diverse Employees

LEARNING OBJECTIVES

After studying this chapter, you should be able to

1 Explain the dimensions of employee diversity and why ethnorelativism is the appropriate attitude for today's corporations.

2 Discuss the changing workplace and the management activities required for a culturally diverse workforce.

3 Understand the challenges minority employees face daily.

4 Explain affirmative action and why factors such as the glass ceiling have kept it from being more successful.

5 Describe how to change the corporate culture, structure, and policies and how to use diversity awareness training to meet the needs of diverse employees.

6 Explain the importance of addressing sexual harassment in the workplace.

7 Define the importance of multicultural teams and employee networks groups for today's globally diverse organizations.

When African-American employees at Texaco filed a racial discrimination lawsuit against the company several years ago, top executives took quick action to defend the company against the charges and try to save Texaco's reputation. But as the drama unfolded, it soon became clear that Texaco's lawyers were facing an impossible task. A top official had secretly taped meetings of managers freely using racial epithets and discussing how to make incriminating documents "disappear." One of the key plaintiffs published a book detailing the humiliations she and other black employees had suffered for years. In addition to exposing blatant acts of racism by Texaco managers and employees, the lawsuit revealed several examples of institutional racism, such as hundreds of minority employees being paid less than the minimum salary for their job category. With mounting evidence staring him in the face, CEO Peter Bijur reached for the white flag. Texaco settled the case for a whopping $175 million, a portion of which would set up an independent task force to monitor Texaco's diversity efforts. Bijur and other top leaders knew the settlement was just the beginning of the pain. The real challenge would be to root out and destroy the racism that permeated the organization. Modest diversity efforts and promises weren't going to cut it. Top executives had to come up with solid plans to make supporting and valuing diverse employees a key element of Texaco's culture.[1]

If you were a top manager at Texaco, what steps would you take to make Texaco a company where minority employees feel valued and supported?

Texaco is not the only company that has faced difficulties with issues of diversity. In recent years, high-profile racial discrimination or harassment lawsuits have been filed against Lockheed Martin, Coca-Cola, and Boeing. Mitsubishi is still reeling from the effects of the largest sexual harassment lawsuit in history, which was brought by the Equal Employment Opportunity Commission in 1996 after hundreds of women charged that Mitsubishi ignored complaints that they were regularly groped on the factory floor and made to endure crude jokes and lewd photographs.[2]

Diversity in the population, the workforce, and the marketplace is a fact of life no manager can afford to ignore today. All managers daily face the challenge of managing employee diversity. The management of employee diversity entails recruiting, training, and fully utilizing workers who reflect the broad spectrum of society in all areas—gender, race, age, disability, ethnicity, religion, sexual orientation, education, and economic level.

Companies such IBM, Fannie Mae, Allstate Insurance, and Hewlett-Packard all have established programs for increasing diversity. These programs teach current employees to value ethnic, racial, and gender differences, direct their recruiting efforts, and provide development training for women and minorities. These companies value diversity and are enforcing this value in day-to-day recruitment and promotion decisions.

Companies are beginning to reflect the U.S. image as a melting pot, but with a difference. In the past, the United States was a place where people of different national origins, ethnicities, races, and religions came together and blended to resemble one another. Opportunities for advancement were limited to those workers who fit easily into the mainstream of the larger culture. Some immigrants chose desperate measures to fit in, such as abandoning their native language, changing their last name, and sacrificing their own unique cultures. In essence, everyone in workplace organizations was encouraged to share similar beliefs, values, and lifestyles despite differences in gender, race, and ethnicity.[3]

Now organizations recognize that everyone is not the same and that the differences people bring to the workplace are valuable.[4] Rather than expecting all employees to adopt similar attitudes and values, companies are learning that these differences enable them to compete globally and to acquire rich sources of new talent. Although diversity in North America has been a reality for some time, genuine efforts to accept and *manage* diverse people began only in recent years.

This chapter introduces the topic of diversity, its causes and consequences. We will look at some of the challenges minorities face, ways managers deal with workforce diversity, and organizational responses to create an environment that welcomes and values diverse employees. The chapter will also look at issues of sexual harassment, global diversity, and new approaches to managing diversity in today's workplace.

Valuing Diversity

At 3Com's modem factory in Morton Grove, Illinois, the 1,200 workers speak 20 different native languages.[5] Such astonishing diversity is becoming typical in many companies all across the United States. Projections are that by 2010, almost half of the nation's new workers will be people traditionally classified as minorities.[6] Top managers say their companies value diversity for a number of reasons, such as to give the organization access to a broader range of opinions

In college, Ken Chenault spent endless hours arguing that the African-American cause was best served in the long run by rising to power within the Establishment instead of assailing it from the outside. Today he has the chance to prove his point as CEO of American Express Company, one of the most respected companies in the United States. Although the weak economy and the decline in travel after the September 11, 2001, terrorist attacks have seriously hurt the company's revenues, earnings, and stock price, Chenault has been praised for his strong leadership during a difficult time. He's shown here with former chairman and CEO Harvey Golub, who counted on Chenault (then president and chief operating officer) for both his business skills and his efforts to improve workforce diversity at the company.

and viewpoints, to reflect an increasingly diverse customer base, and to demonstrate the company's commitment to "doing the right thing."[7] Moreover, a survey by the Society for Human Resource Management found that 62 percent of job seekers prefer to work for organizations that show a commitment to diversity.[8]

However, many managers are ill-prepared to handle diversity issues. Many Americans grew up in racially unmixed neighborhoods and had little exposure to people substantially different from themselves.[9] The challenge is particularly great when working with people from other countries and cultures. A typical American manager, schooled in traditional management training, could easily make the following mistakes:[10]

- To reward a Vietnamese employee's high performance, her manager promoted her, placing her at the same level as her husband, who also worked at the factory. Rather than being pleased, the worker became upset and declined the promotion because Vietnamese husbands are expected to have a higher status than their wives.

- A manager, having learned that a friendly pat on the arm or back would make workers feel good, took every chance to touch his subordinates. His Asian employees hated being touched and thus started avoiding him, and several asked for transfers.

- A manager declined a gift offered by a new employee, an immigrant who wanted to show gratitude for her job. He was concerned about ethics and explained the company's policy about not accepting gifts. The employee was so insulted she quit.

These issues related to cultural diversity are difficult and real. But before discussing how companies handle them, let's define *diversity* and explore people's attitudes toward it.

Dimensions of Diversity

Workforce diversity means an inclusive workforce made up of people with different human qualities or who belong to various cultural groups. From the

workforce diversity
Hiring people with different human qualities who belong to various cultural groups.

EXHIBIT *10.1*

*Primary and Secondary
Dimensions of Diversity*

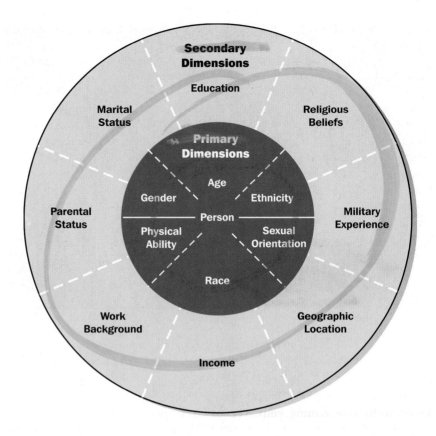

SOURCE: Adapted from Marilyn Loden and Judy B. Rosener, *Workforce America!* (Homewood, IL: Business One Irwin 1991), 20. Used with permission of the McGraw Hill Companies.

perspective of individuals, diversity means including people different from themselves along dimensions such as age, ethnicity, gender, or race. It is important to remember that diversity includes everyone, not just minorities.

Key dimensions of diversity are illustrated in Exhibit 10.1. The inner circle represents primary dimensions of diversity, which include inborn differences or differences that have an impact throughout one's life.[11] Secondary dimensions, shown in the outer ring of Exhibit 10.1, can be acquired or changed throughout one's lifetime. The challenge for today's managers is to recognize that each person can bring value and strengths to the workplace based on his or her own unique combination of diversity characteristics.

Attitudes toward Diversity

Valuing diversity by recognizing, welcoming, and cultivating differences among people so they can develop their unique talents and be effective organizational members is difficult to achieve. **Ethnocentrism** is the belief that one's own group and subculture are inherently superior to other groups and cultures. Ethnocentrism makes it difficult to value diversity. Viewing one's own culture as the best culture is a natural tendency among most people. Moreover, the business world tends to reflect the values, behaviors, and assumptions based on the experiences of a rather homogeneous, white, middle-class, male workforce.[12] Indeed, most theories of management presume that workers share similar values, beliefs, motivations, and attitudes about work and life in general. These theories presume there is one set of behaviors that best help an organization to be productive and effective and therefore should be adopted by all employees.[13] This one-best-way approach explains why a manager may cause a problem by

ethnocentrism

The belief that one's own group or subculture is inherently superior to other groups or cultures.

touching Asian employees or by not knowing how to handle a gift from an immigrant.

Ethnocentric viewpoints and a standard set of cultural practices produce a **monoculture**, a culture that accepts only one way of doing things and one set of values and beliefs, which can cause problems for minority employees. People of color, women, gay people, the disabled, the elderly, and other diverse employees may feel undue pressure to conform, may be victims of stereotyping attitudes, and may be presumed deficient because they are different. White, heterosexual men, many of whom themselves do not fit the notions of the "ideal" employee, may also feel uncomfortable with the monoculture and resent stereotypes that label white males as racists and sexists. Valuing diversity means ensuring that all people are given equal opportunities in the workplace.[14]

The goal for organizations seeking cultural diversity is pluralism rather than a monoculture and ethnorelativism rather than ethnocentrism. **Ethnorelativism** is the belief that groups and subcultures are inherently equal. **Pluralism** means that an organization accommodates several subcultures. Movement toward pluralism seeks to fully integrate into the organization the employees who otherwise would feel isolated and ignored.

Most organizations must undertake conscious efforts to shift from a monoculture perspective to one of pluralism. An important first step is examining the attitudes and assumptions that characterize the organization, as described in the Focus on Collaboration box. Employees in a monoculture may not be aware of culture differences, or they may have acquired negative stereotypes toward other cultural values and assume that their own culture is superior. Through effective training, employees can be helped to accept different ways of thinking and behaving, the first step away from narrow, ethnocentric thinking. Ultimately, employees are able to integrate diverse cultures, which means that judgments of appropriateness, goodness, badness, and morality are no longer applied to cultural differences. Cultural differences are experienced as essential,

monoculture

A culture that accepts only one way of doing things and one set of values and beliefs.

ethnorelativism

The belief that groups and subcultures are inherently equal.

pluralism

The organization accommodates several subcultures, including employees who would otherwise feel isolated and ignored.

FOCUS ON COLLABORATION

Shifting Attitudes

To capitalize on the strengths of diversity and shift toward a more pluralistic organizational culture, managers should consider their own and other organization members' attitudes and assumptions about diversity. Here are some common misperceptions, along with perceptions that are more appropriate for today's workplace:

- *The melting-pot myth:* People desire to mold their behavior after the dominant culture so they will fit in better.
  More appropriate—cultural pluralism: We are not all the same; groups within society and the organization differ across cultures.

- *The similarity myth:* "They" are all just like me.
  More appropriate—acceptance of differences: They are not just like me; many people differ from me culturally, and most people exhibit both similarities and differences when compared to me.

- *The only-one-way myth:* Our way is the only way. We do not recognize or accept any other way of living or working.
  More Appropriate—multiple ways: There are many culturally distinct ways of reaching one's goals, of working, and of living one's life.

- *The one-best-way myth:* Our way is still the best way. All other approaches are inferior.
  More appropriate—several possible ways: There are many different and equally good ways to reach the same goal. The best way depends on a variety of factors, including the cultures of the people involved.

SOURCE: Adapted from "Cultural Assumptions and Their Implications for Management," by Nancy J. Adler, Exhibit 4.3 in *International Dimensions of Organizational Behavior*, 4th ed. (Cincinnati, Ohio: South-Western Publishing, 2002), 117, based on Nancy J. Adler, "Domestic Multiculturalism: Cross-Cultural Management in the Public Sector," in William Eddy, ed., *Handbook of Organization Management*. Copyright Marcel Dekker, Inc., New York.

natural, and joyful, enabling an organization to enjoy true pluralism and take advantage of diverse human resources.[15]

For example, IBM has made a firm commitment to break out of monoculture thinking. Ted Childs, an African American who serves as IBM's vice president of global diversity, has led a corporate-wide campaign to integrate diversity into every facet of the company's management and technical operations. Eight executive task forces—one each for African Americans, Asians, disabled people, gays and lesbians, Hispanics, Native Americans, white males, and women—are charged with making recommendations from their varied perspectives for how to make IBM a better place to work. The face of IBM is changing as the company takes proactive steps to hire, develop, and promote women, racial and ethnic minorities, and other under-represented groups. Between January 1996 and December 1999, the number of women executives at IBM worldwide soared from 185 to 508, and the number of minority executives in the United States rose from 117 to 270.[16] In addition, 57 percent of IBM's board of directors are women, multicultural, or non-U.S.-born individuals.[17]

The Changing Workplace

The importance of cultural diversity and employee attitudes that welcome cultural differences will result from the inevitable changes taking place in the workplace, in our society, and in the economic environment. These changes include globalization and the changing workforce.[18] Earlier chapters described the impact of global competition on business in North America. Competition is intense. About 70 percent of all U.S. businesses are engaged directly in competition with companies overseas. Companies that succeed in this environment need to adopt radical new ways of doing business, with sensitivity toward the needs of different cultural practices. Consider the consulting firm McKinsey & Co. In the 1970s, most consultants were American, but by 1999, McKinsey's chief partner was a foreign national (Rajat Gupta from India), only 40 percent of consultants were American, and the firm's foreign-born consultants came from 40 different countries.[19] Companies that ignore diversity have a hard time competing in today's global marketplace.

The other significant challenge is the changing composition of the workforce. The average worker is older now, and many more women, people of color, and immigrants are seeking job and advancement opportunities. The demographics of the U.S. population are shifting dramatically. According to the 2000 census, non-Hispanic whites are now the *minority* population in the 100 largest U.S. cities. The number of immigrant workers jumped 17 percent to 15.7 million in 1999, and immigrants now make up 12 percent of the total U.S. workforce. Minorities are expected to make up 40 percent of people entering the workforce during the first decade of the twenty-first century; many will be first-generation immigrants and almost two-thirds of them will be female. By 2020, it is estimated that fully half of the total full-time U.S. workforce will be women. Already, white males, the majority of workers in the past, represent less than half of the workforce.[20] So far, the ability of organizations to manage diversity has not kept pace with these demographic trends, which has created a number of significant challenges for minority workers and managers. Some smaller companies, such as Lopez Negrete Communications, described in the Focus on Skills box, have capitalized on the difficulties of multiculturalism and are helping large companies to understand the issues.

FOCUS ON SKILLS

Lopez Negrete Communications

"He quit his job? Oh boy," was Alex Lopez Negrete's mother's not-exactly-thrilled response when she heard that her son had quit his job as head of a successful advertising agency to start his own company. The 43-year-old Mexican immigrant always knew what he wanted to do. And when he came to live in America, he still relished his own culture, as many new immigrants do. And that is part of the secret of his success.

Over 90 percent of his advertising business is based on helping clients market more effectively to the growing Hispanic market. His firm's clients include some of the top U.S. companies, such as Wal-Mart and Tyson Chicken, which are finally taking note of the tremendous buying power of African and Hispanic markets. He has learned a lot working with both big clients and small, and he especially urges small business owners to adopt a multicultural strategy. "It's not just advertising," he says, but a whole way of thinking and doing business that becomes "in-language" and "in-culture." Here are some tips he offers:

1. Don't use stereotyped portrayals of ethnic groups—this will drive away your intended ethnic market

2. Don't skimp on ads for an ethnic market—this will turn off potential customers, who may feel put-down

3. If your Spanish is less-than-perfect, hire someone else to do voice-overs for commercials.

Lopez Negrete has received offers but refuses to sell his agency. Because of his firm's greater intimacy with the client's needs, his business has rapidly expanded to $45 million in revenues. This also demonstrates how the marketplace has changed. As fellow entrepreneur and African American Byron Lewis says, "Diversity represents an opportunity to increase profits for many advertisers."

SOURCES: Mary Sit-Duvall, "Houston Advertising Guru Helps U.S. Companies Appeal to Hispanic Market," *Knight Ridder Tribune Business News* (May 19, 2002), 1; Chris Sandlund, "There's a New Face to America," *Success* (April 1999), 38–45.

Challenges Minorities Face

The one-best-way approach discussed in the previous section leads to a mind-set that views difference as deficiency or dysfunction. For many career women and minorities, their experience suggests that no matter how many college degrees they earn, how many hours they work, how they dress, or how much effort and enthusiasm they invest, they are never perceived as "having the right stuff." If the standard of quality were based, for instance, on being white and male, anything else would be seen as deficient. This dilemma often is difficult for white men to understand because most of them are not intentionally racist and sexist. As one observer points out, you would need to be nonwhite to understand what it is like to have people assume your subordinate is your superior simply because he is white, or to lose a sale after the customer sees you in person and finds out you're not Caucasian.[21]

Bias in the workplace often shows up in subtle ways—a lack of choice assignments; the disregard by a subordinate of a minority manager's directions; or the ignoring of comments made by women and minorities at meetings. A recent survey by Korn Ferry International found that 59 percent of minority managers surveyed had observed a racially motivated double standard in the delegation of assignments.[22] Their perceptions are supported by a study conducted by Harvard Business School professor David Thomas, who found that minority managers spend more time in the "bullpen" waiting for their chance and then have to prove themselves over and over again with each new assignment. Minority employees typically feel that they have to put in longer hours and extra effort to achieve the same status as their white colleagues. "It's not enough to be as good as the next person," says Bruce Gordon, president of Bell Atlantic's enterprise group. "We have to be better."[23]

biculturalism

The sociocultural skills and attitudes used by racial minorities to move back and forth between the dominant culture and their own ethnic or racial culture.

Another problem is that many minority workers feel they have to become bicultural in order to succeed. **Biculturalism** can be defined as the sociocultural skills and attitudes used by racial minorities as they move back and forth between the dominant culture and their own ethnic or racial culture.[24] Research on differences between whites and blacks has focused on issues of biculturalism and how it affects employees' access to information, level of respect and appreciation, and relation to superiors and subordinates. In general, African Americans, as well as other racial minorities, feel less accepted in their organizations, perceive themselves to have less discretion on their jobs, receive lower ratings on job performance, experience lower levels of job satisfaction, and reach career plateaus earlier than whites. They find themselves striving to adopt behaviors and attitudes that will help them be successful in the white-dominated corporate world while at the same time maintaining their ties to the black community and culture. This chapter's Digital, Inc. box describes a company with a goal of helping African Americans achieve career success and stay connected to black culture and lifestyle.

Other minority groups struggle with biculturalism as well. For example, Asian Americans who aspire to management positions are often frustrated by the stereotype that they are hardworking but not executive material because they are too quiet and deferential. Assertiveness and pressing your views in a group is seen as a characteristic of leadership in American culture, but Asians

DIGITAL, INC.

BETting on the Internet: BET.com

Robert L. Johnson started the Black Entertainment Television (BET) network 22 years ago with little more than a good idea—a cable channel for black viewers. Today, BET is the leading African-American-owned and -operated media and entertainment company in the United States. The core BET network reaches into more than 65 million homes and is worth over $2 billion; 90 percent of African-American households with cable regularly tune in. Johnson has also leveraged the brand to establish a successful book company for African-American titles, a film company that produces and markets African-American-themed films, documentaries, and made-for-television movies, and, most recently, a successful Web site.

As the premier multimedia company for African Americans, it only made sense for BET to expand into the Internet world. Johnson worked out partnerships with Microsoft, Liberty Digital Media, News Corporation, and USA Networks to launch BET.com. Although there are dozens of community portals and sites targeting African Americans, BET is rapidly emerging as the leading online destination. Part of that is thanks to BET's emphasis on building an online community for African Americans who want to stay in touch with black music, lifestyle, and culture. Everything is tailored to the preferences and needs of the black community. For example, the news channel provides the latest news from around the world, with specific emphasis on how it affects the African-American community. Other channels include Health, Music, Money, Relationships, and Style. The career center lists thousands of job postings and offers advice, resources, and networking opportunities for African-American professionals and entrepreneurs. Some of the most popular aspects of BET.com, however, are the message boards, chat rooms, and community sections, where members can participate with others in the GetFit Club, the Movie Club, a spirituality area, professional groups, or other areas of special interest.

This rich community life helped BET.com get voted "Best African American Community Site 2001" by Yahoo! Internet Life magazine. Although blacks continue to lag behind whites in Internet access, the digital divide is narrowing. Today, African Americans are going online at a rate twice that of the general population and will soon make up around 40 percent of the total U.S. Internet population. BET.com is ready, giving African Americans a place where they can be part of a thriving online community, explore new areas of interest, take advantage of opportunities for economic advancement, and obtain information related to virtually any aspects of their lives.

SOURCES: http://www.BET.com, accessed on November 15, 2001; David Whitford, "BET's Johnson: On the Air and in the Air," *Fortune* (July 24, 2000), 50; T. J. DeGroat, "Blacks Make Most Out of Internet," DiversityInc.com, Career Center; and Jason McKay, "African American Websites Are Hooking People Up in More Ways Than One," *Black Enterprise* (October 2000), http://www.blackenterprise.com.

typically view this behavior as inappropriate and immature.[25] Some Asian Americans feel they have a chance for career advancement only by becoming bicultural or abandoning their native cultures altogether.

Management Challenges

What does this mean for managers who are responsible for creating a workplace that offers fulfilling work, opportunities for professional development and career advancement, and respect for all individuals? Inappropriate behavior by employees lands squarely at the door of the organization's top executives. Managers can look at different areas of the organization to see how well they are doing in creating a workplace that values and supports diversity. Exhibit 10.2 illustrates some of the key areas of management challenge for dealing with a culturally diverse workforce. Managers focus on these issues to see how well they are addressing the needs and concerns of diverse employees.

For example, consider the increased career involvement of women. This change represents an enormous opportunity to organizations, but it also means that organizations must deal with issues such as work-family conflicts, dual-career couples, and sexual harassment. Moreover, managers must ensure that their organization's human resources systems are designed to be bias-free, dropping the perception of the middle-aged white male as the ideal employee. The growing immigrant population presents other challenges. Whereas in

EXHIBIT *10.2*

Management Challenges for a Culturally Diverse Workforce

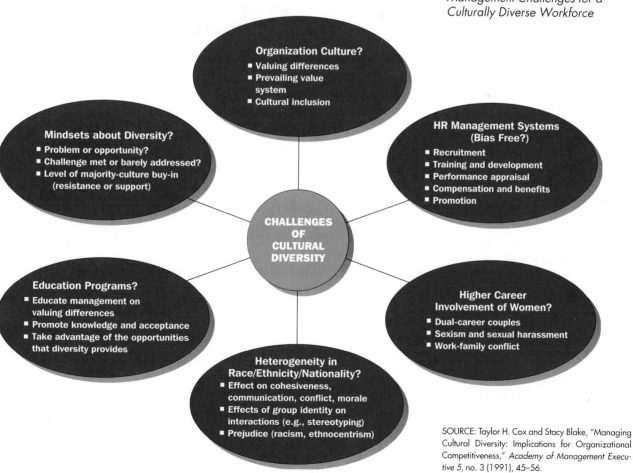

SOURCE: Taylor H. Cox and Stacy Blake, "Managing Cultural Diversity: Implications for Organizational Competitiveness," *Academy of Management Executive 5*, no. 3 (1991), 45–56.

previous generations most foreign-born immigrants came from Western Europe, 84 percent of recent immigrants come from Asia and Latin America.[26] These immigrants come to the United States with a wide range of backgrounds, often without adequate skills in using English. Organizations must face not only the issues of dealing with race, ethnicity, and nationality to provide a prejudice-free workplace but also develop sufficient educational programs to help immigrants acquire the technical and customer service skills required in a service economy.

Another human resources issue is developing performance appraisal and reward systems that support a diverse workforce. Allstate Insurance developed a system that rates all managers on how well they handle diversity issues.

Allstate Insurance Company

http://www.allstate.com

Allstate Insurance doesn't just talk about the importance of diversity; the company actually tracks support for diversity at every level of management. As the largest property insurer for African Americans and Hispanics, Allstate has made diversity a priority since 1993. The company already had a working affirmative action program and had tried several approaches to diversity training. However, Jerry Choate, CEO, and Carlton Yearwood, director of Allstate's diversity team, believed the company needed a way to track its success on supporting diversity. Its new system gives top executives feedback that they can use continually to make the workplace more comfortable and satisfying for all employees. Today, Allstate surveys all 50,000 workers each quarter on how well it is meeting its commitments to employees and customers, including recruiting, developing, and promoting employees regardless of race or gender. A "diversity index" probes how well workers feel their managers "walk the talk" about bias-free service, respect for the individual, and a culturally sensitive workplace. Performance on these indexes determines 25 percent of a manager's bonus pay.

Overall, Allstate is doing pretty well on the diversity index. Some 40 percent of Allstate's executives and managers are women. Twenty-one percent are minorities, compared to the national average of 10 percent. The company has earned a string of awards, such as the "1999 Best Companies for Hispanics to Work," the "1998 Top 10 Companies for Minority Managers," and the "Best Companies for Working Mothers." Allstate believes its tracking system has created a more productive work environment where all employees feel valued. "What you measure is what people focus on," says Karleen Zuzich, assistant vice president of human resources. "This really sends a clear signal that management of [diverse] people . . . is really important."[28]

Top managers at Allstate and other companies that value diversity look for ways to bring diverse people into the organization and shape organizational values to accept and appreciate cultural differences. In addition, training programs can promote knowledge and acceptance of diverse cultures and educate managers on valuing diversity as a competitive advantage.

Affirmative Action

Since 1964, civil legislation has prohibited discrimination in hiring based on race, religion, sex, or national origin. As described in Chapter 9, these policies were designed to facilitate recruitment, retention, and promotion of minorities and women. To some extent, these policies have been successful, opening organization doors to women and minorities. However, despite the job opportunities, few women and minorities have succeeded in getting into top management posts.

Current Debates about Affirmative Action

Affirmative action was developed in response to conditions 40 years ago. Adult white males dominated the workforce, and economic conditions were stable and improving. Because of widespread prejudice and discrimination, legal and social coercion were necessary to allow women, people of color, immigrants, and other minorities to become part of the economic system.[28]

Today, the situation has changed. More than half the U.S. workforce consists of women and minorities; the economic situation is changing rapidly as a result of international competition.

Many companies actively recruit women and minorities to comply with affirmative action guidelines. Companies often succeeded in identifying a few select individuals who were recruited, trained, and given special consideration. These people carried great expectations and pressure. They were highly visible role models for the newly recruited groups. It was generally expected that these individuals would march right to the top of the corporate ladder.

Within a few years, it became clear that few of these people would reach the top. Management typically was frustrated and upset because of the money poured into the affirmative action programs. The individuals were disillusioned by token programs that offered limited advancement. Managers were unhappy with the program failures and may have doubted the qualifications of people they recruited. Did they deserve the jobs at all? Were women and minority candidates to blame for the failure of the affirmative action program? Should companies be required to meet federally mandated minority-hiring targets?

Even the intended beneficiaries of affirmative action programs often disagree as to their value, and some believe these programs do more harm than good. One reason for this may be the stigma of incompetence that often is associated with affirmative action hires. One study found that both working managers and students consistently rated people portrayed as affirmative action hires as less competent and recommended lower salary increases than for those not associated with affirmative action.[29]

In recent years, outspoken opponents of affirmative action have brought the debate into the public consciousness. The courts have upheld recent challenges to affirmative action, and referenda in several states have limited its use for hiring and college admissions practices. The emphasis today is more on diversity programs that seek to include everyone, rather than affirmative action and compliance programs that tend to spotlight race, which many claim leads to tensions and divisiveness.[30] For example, efforts at Federated Department Stores once focused specifically on minorities and women, but the diversity program has now broadened to include 26 groups, including seniors, the disabled, homosexuals, atheists, the devout, and so on.[31]

While many welcome the broader diversity emphasis, many social justice activists argue that it is simply a way for companies to put on a show of virtue without having to do anything concrete about affirmative action issues. Al Jackson, director of diversity and staff development at *Scholastic Magazine*, echoes the sentiments of many when he notes that most firms do not hire and promote women and minorities as readily as they do white males, no matter how much they talk about valuing diversity.[32]

© Alyson Aliano

Colleen Barrett broke through corporate America's glass ceiling when she became president of Southwest Airlines after the retirement of Herb Kelleher. "Some CEOs will still introduce me as Herb's secretary," she says. The now highest-ranking woman in the U.S. airline industry did indeed begin her career 34 years ago as Kelleher's secretary at his San Antonio law firm. Today, Barrett just laughs when people mistake her for a secretary, but she knows there are still too many barriers to women moving into higher-level positions. As Southwest's president, Barrett oversees the airline's marketing, advertising, customer service, and human resources. She is also chiefly responsible for safeguarding Southwest's famed esprit de corps.

glass ceiling

Invisible barrier that separates women and minorities from top management positions.

Ultimately, the problem boils down to an unspoken and often unintended sexism and racism in organizations. The affirmative action cycle fails when women, people of color, and immigrants are brought into a monoculture system and the burden of adaptation falls on the candidates coming through the system rather than on the organization itself. Part of the reason for the failure may be attributed to what is called the *glass ceiling.*

The Glass Ceiling

The **glass ceiling** is an invisible barrier that separates women and minorities from top management positions. They can look up through the ceiling and see top management, but prevailing attitudes are invisible obstacles to their own advancement.

Evidence of the glass ceiling is the distribution of women and minorities, who are clustered at the bottom levels of the corporate hierarchy. Women make up less than 4 percent and nonwhite minorities less than 3 percent of all *Fortune* 500 executives.[33] Overall, African Americans hold only 8 percent of all executive positions and Hispanics about 5 percent.[34] Women of color fare the worst. While they make up 23 percent of the total U.S. women's workforce, they account for only 14 percent of the women in all management positions in the United States.[35]

Women and minorities also earn substantially less. As shown in Exhibit 10.3, black male employees earn about 20 percent less and Hispanic male employees 37 percent less than their white counterparts. Women earn considerably less than men, with Hispanic women faring the worst. As illustrated in the exhibit, black women earn 35 percent less and Hispanic women 47 percent less than white men.[36]

In particular, women who leave the corporate world to care for young children have a difficult time moving up the hierarchy when they return. One term used to describe this is the *mommy track,* which implies that women's commitment to their children limits their commitment to the company or their ability to handle the rigors of corporate management. These women risk being treated as beginners when they return, no matter how vast their skills and experience, and they continue to lag behind in salary, title, and responsibility.[37] One estimate is that a woman who quits or reduces her involvement in a corporate job to raise children sacrifices about $1 million in lost income, a figure former *New York Times* economics reporter Ann Crittenden refers to as the *mommy tax.*[38] Some women are taking the situation into their own hands, as described in the Best Practices box.

Another sensitive issue related to the glass ceiling is homosexuals in the workplace. Many gay men and lesbians believe they will not be accepted as they are and risk losing their jobs or their chances for advancement. The director of human resources for a large Midwestern hospital would like to be honest about her lesbianism but says she knows of almost no one at her level of the corporate hierarchy who has taken that step—"It's just not done here."[39] Thus, gays and lesbians often fabricate heterosexual identities to keep their jobs or avoid running into the glass ceiling they see other employees encounter.

Why does the glass ceiling persist? The monoculture at top levels is the most frequent explanation. Top-level corporate culture evolves around white, heterosexual, American males, who tend to hire and promote people who look,

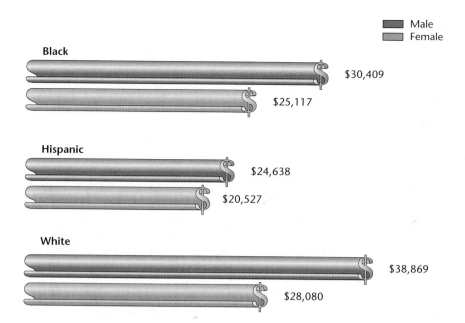

Male
Female

Black
$30,409
$25,117

Hispanic
$24,638
$20,527

White
$38,869
$28,080

EXHIBIT 10.3

The Wage Gap

SOURCE: "2000 Median Annual Earnings by Race and Sex," reported by the National Committee on Pay Equity, *http://www.infoplease.com.*

act, and think like them.[40] Compatibility in thought and behavior plays an important role at higher levels of organizations.[41] For example, in a survey of women who have managed to break through the glass ceiling, fully 96 percent said adapting to a predominantly white male culture was an important factor in their success.[42]

Another reason for the persistent glass ceiling is the relegation of women and minorities to less visible positions and projects so that their work fails to come to the attention of top executives. Recent research has suggested the existence of *glass walls* that serve as invisible barriers to important lateral movement within the organization. Glass walls bar experience in areas such as line supervision or general management that would enable women and minorities to advance vertically.[43]

In general, women and minorities think that they must work harder and perform at higher levels than their white male counterparts to be noticed, recognized, and promoted. For example, a recent book distilling advice for women from the experiences of top female executives indicates that women have to invest significant effort to make sure their work is recognized and rewarded.[44]

Current Responses to Diversity

Affirmative action opened the doors of organizations in this country to women and minorities. However, the path toward promotion to top ranks has remained closed for the most part, with many women and minorities hitting the glass ceiling.[45] Although the federal government responded to this problem with the Civil Rights Act of 1991 to amend and strengthen the Civil Rights Act of 1964, affirmative action currently is under attack. As the debate over affirmative action continues, companies need to find new ways to deal with the obstacles that prevent women and minorities from advancing to senior management positions in the future. For example, Texas Instruments CEO Thomas Engibous admits that his company needs to do a better job of placing women and minorities in key positions. "We do a good job hiring women, African Americans, and Hispanics," Engibous says. "But we have too many high-ranking women in

BEST PRACTICES

Women Entrepreneurs

Can you hear the thunder of the stampede? It's the sound of 8 million women starting their own businesses. While half were top-level executives who wanted to prove they could do something extraordinary, almost one-fourth say it was because they experienced the glass ceiling while working for former employers, who wouldn't, or couldn't, allow women to reach their desired potential. This newly unleashed potential is exploding into the economy. One out of five U.S. employees works for a female-owned firm, while the number of female-headed companies has more than doubled in the past ten years, to where they now account for one-third of all businesses and earn annually about $1.5 trillion. Minority women are becoming entrepreneurs at even faster rates. And businesses started by women are more likely to stay in business than those started by a male. What are the trends?

1. Women used to start service businesses, but now there is more variety. Technology companies are often started by women. Asian Women in Business's Bonnie Wong sees Asian women becoming manufacturers and lumber company owners.

2. Women have an easier time getting credit. Gone are the days when the husband had to cosign the loan.

3. Businesses are being started by women of all ages, some from their dorm rooms, and 50 percent of all owners started their firms before they hit 35.

   What's needed?

- Lots of networking, especially outside your normal interactions.

- A strong vision—and staying true to it.

- Hard work.

- Creativity.

- Willingness to try new approaches. For example, when Oregonian Barbara Todd started her catalog-based business, she needed only $50,000—one-tenth the usual amount—for start-up costs. Instead of buying wholesale and selling through the catalog, she charged each client $5,000 to list products in her catalog.

- Seeing the opportunities. Eloise Blackmon started her Gary, Indiana, F&B Transport company when she saw the difficulty people were having getting off welfare because of lack of transportation. Now her vans deliver 100 adults and children to work and day care. Her clients, she says, "are dedicated and want to work." They just need some help.

- Seeing employees as a resource. Patty Dominic's PDQ Personnel Services was growing so fast she had a cash flow problem and could not meet payroll. So she brought her employees together and told them the truth. The next day, a woman brought in a check for $5,000 as a loan, and other women offered the services of their husbands, who were investment bankers, CPA's and management consultants. They helped her put together a sound business plan and to secure financing.

- Value yourself and your product. New Orleans cab driver Jacquelyn Hughes Mooney's hobby was sewing decorative pillows. She gave up her secure income to push her pillows full time at craft fairs and did so well that she went on to designer quilts, some selling for as much as $6,000 to celebrities such as Oprah Winfrey and Bryant Gumbel. After a woman complained about spending $200 on a quilt, Mooney realized how important it is for women to place value on their work. "No one else will think my work is significant until I do," she says of her company, named Rhythm and Hughes.

A real attraction in starting a business is the chance to be one's own boss, and to be able to build one's own vision. When biotech entrepreneur Nancy Levy was asked by her husband why she was putting so much on the line, she answered, "I like to create things . . . I took a huge risk."

SOURCES: Diane E. Lewis, "Study Shows Rise in Number of Private Firms Owned by Women," *Knight Ridder Tribune Business News* (February 5, 2002), 2; Paulette Thomas, "Closing the Gender Gap," *The Wall Street Journal* (May 24, 1999), R12; Steven J. Stark, "Breaking In," *Success* (January 1999), 39; Sharon Nelton, "Women's Firms Thrive," *Nation's Business* (August 1998), 37–40.

peripheral areas. We need a better mix in the business's line management if we're going to have a woman or minority as TI's CEO someday."[46]

In addition, to prepare for and respond to an increasingly diverse business climate, managers in most companies are expanding the organization's emphasis on diversity beyond race and gender to consider such factors as ethnicity, age, physical ability, religion, and sexual orientation. One reason age is important is because younger workers are often more technically skilled than older ones, which can create tensions as companies try to utilize skills of very young workers. An example of teenage Web skill that led to a new business is described below.

> Lots of 15-year-old girls hang out at the mall or worry about which nail color is right . . . but not Ashley Power. When she picked up *HTML for Dummies*, she never thought it would lead to having a Hollywood publicist, a talent agent, and a book, *Goosehead Guide to Life*—in other words, a new life. As founder and CEO of the 300,000 daily-hit site Goosehead.com, the California high school sophomore was more likely to fly off to Japan to meet potential investors than attend a local basketball game.
>
> Ashley's first Web site, posted when she was a seventh grader, was simply e-mail plus movie ratings and photographs, with a teen chat room and homework help added later. The name "Goosehead" came from a childhood experience with a broken lawn ornament. In 1998, Ashley heard about streaming media and broadband. Her dreams for the site grew with the traffic, but she didn't know much about the new technology. That had never stopped her before. Sending messages to the Webmasters of her favorite sites, she solicited assistance from them. Some of these early advisors later became part of Ashley's 27-person workforce.
>
> Goosehead never became profitable. Funded by outside partners, but mostly by Ashley's stepfather, Mark Schilder, the site required $20,000 per month to pay for staff salaries, content development, and its Web entertainment series, *Whatever,* starring Ashley as her alter ego, Skye Warner.
>
> During the summer, Ashley worked 50 hours a week on the site. She dreamed about the good old days—a few years ago—when the Web was about fellowship, not money. "That's how it has to be," she said, "It's a business." And it was also about a business that finally could not succeed. Several poor management decisions, such as a contract paying $5,000 monthly for bandwidth and supporting a drag racing tournament, ultimately led to investors demanding that the assets be liquidated. At least Ashley can now be a role model for other teens to take risks and try starting a business.[47]

Once managers create and define a vision for a diverse workplace, they can analyze and assess the current culture and systems within the organization. This assessment is followed by a willingness to change the status quo in order to modify current systems and ways of thinking. Throughout this process, people need support in dealing with the many challenges and inevitable conflicts they will face. Training and support are important for the people in pioneering roles. Finally, managers should not de-emphasize affirmative action programs, because these are critical for giving minorities and women access to jobs in the organization. Once managers accept the need for a program to develop a truly diverse workplace, action can begin. A program to implement such a change involves three major steps: (1) building a corporate culture that values diversity; (2) changing structures, policies, and systems to support diversity; and (3) providing diversity awareness training.

Changing the Corporate Culture

When the underlying culture of an organization does not change, all the other efforts to support diversity fail, as managers at Mitsubishi have learned. Even though the company settled a sexual harassment suit filed by women at the

Normal, Illinois, plant, established a zero tolerance policy, and fired workers who were guilty of blatant harassment, workers describe a work environment that remains deeply hostile to women and minorities. Although the incidents of harassment have decreased, women and minority workers still feel threatened and powerless because the culture and environment that allowed the harassment to occur hasn't changed. Mitsubishi managers are still struggling with these difficult issues.[48]

Chapters 2 and 8 described approaches for changing corporate culture. Managers can start by actively using symbols for the new values, such as encouraging and celebrating the promotion of minorities and disciplining employees who display behavior that does not fit a diverse workplace. Managers should take care that workers who complain are not treated like the wrongdoers. To promote positive change, managers have to first change their own assumptions and attitudes. It is managers who lead the way from a white male monoculture to a multiculture in which differences are valued and all people are respected. Culture change starts at the top, and most organizations recognized as diversity leaders have CEOs and other top leaders who demonstrate a strong commitment to making diversity part of the organizational mission.[49]

Advantica, the owner of Denny's Restaurants, which was hit with a series of discrimination lawsuits in the early 1990s, has been changing structures and policies to promote and support diversity. The company responded to the discrimination charges with aggressive minority hiring and supplier-diversity efforts. In 2001, for the second year in a row, Advantica was awarded first place in Fortune magazine's list of "America's 50 Best Companies for Minorities." Four of the company's eleven board members, 31 percent of top officials and managers, and 48 percent of new hires are members of minority groups.

© Sarah A. Friedman

Managers throughout the company can be educated to help transform the culture. For one thing, they can examine the unwritten rules and assumptions. What are the myths about minorities? What are the values that exemplify the existing culture? Are unwritten rules communicated from one person to another in a way that excludes women and minorities? For example, many men may not discuss unwritten rules with women and minorities because they assume everyone is aware of them and they do not want to seem patronizing.[50]

Companies are addressing the issue of changing culture in a variety of ways. Some are using surveys, interviews, and focus groups to identify how the cultural values affect minorities and women. Others have set up structured networks of people of color, women, and other minority groups to explore the issues they face in the workplace and to recommend changes to senior management.

Many companies have discovered that people will choose companies that are accepting, inviting, and friendly and that help them meet personal goals.[51] Successful companies carefully assess their cultures and make changes from the top down because the key to productivity is a loyal, trained, capable workforce. New cultural values mean that the exclusionary practices of the past must come to an end.

Changing Structures and Policies

Many policies within organizations originally were designed to fit the stereotypical male employee. Now leading companies are changing structures and policies to facilitate and support a diverse workforce. A survey of *Fortune* 1000 companies conducted by the Center for Creative Leadership found that 85 percent of companies surveyed have formal policies against racism and sexism, and 76 percent have structured grievance procedures and complaint review processes.[52] Companies are also developing policies to support the recruitment and career advancement of diverse employees. At least half of *Fortune* 1000 compa-

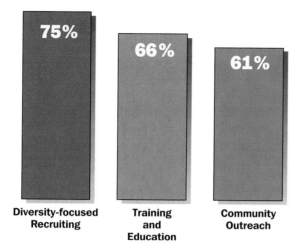

EXHIBIT *10.4*

The Most Common Diversity Initiatives: Percentage of Fortune 1000 Respondents

SOURCE: Data reported in "Impact of Diversity Initiatives on the Bottom Line: A SHRM Survey of the Fortune 1000," pp. S12–S14, in *Fortune*, special advertising section, "Keeping Your Edge: Managing a Diverse Corporate Culture," produced in association with the Society for Human Resource Management, *http://www.fortune.com/sections*.

nies have staff dedicated exclusively to encouraging diversity. Exhibit 10.4 illustrates the most common diversity initiatives.

Recruitment. A good way to revitalize the recruiting process is for the company to examine employee demographics, the composition of the labor pool in the area, and the composition of the customer base. Managers then can work toward a workforce composition that reflects the labor pool and the customer base.

For many organizations, a new approach to recruitment will mean recruiting more effectively than today. This could mean making better use of formal recruiting strategies, offering internship programs to give people opportunities, and developing creative ways to draw upon previously unused labor markets.

For example, Nationwide's Scholars Program brings in Hispanic and African American college students for a three-year program that includes summer internships and year-long mentoring.[53] Marathon Ashland Petroleum has created a six-point recruiting strategy to increase diversity, including: (1) recruiting corporate-wide and cross-functionally; (2) building relationships with first- and second-tiered schools to recruit minority students; (3) offering internships for racial and ethnic minorities; (4) offering minority scholarships; (5) establishing informal mentoring programs; and (6) forming affiliations with minority organizations.[54]

Career Advancement. The successful advancement of diverse group members means that organizations must find ways to eliminate the glass ceiling. One of the most successful structures to accomplish this is the mentoring relationship. A **mentor** is a higher ranking, senior organizational member who is committed to providing upward mobility and support to a protégé's professional career.[55] Mentoring provides minorities and women with direct training and inside information on the norms and expectations of the organization. A mentor also acts as a friend or counselor, enabling the employee to feel more confident and capable.

One researcher who has studied the career progress of high-potential minorities has found that those who advance the furthest all share one characteristic—a strong mentor or network of mentors who nurtured their professional development.[56] However, research also indicates that minorities, as well as women, are much less likely than men to develop mentoring relationships.[57]

mentor

A higher-ranking, senior organizational member who is committed to providing upward mobility and support to a protégé's professional career.

Women and minorities may not seek mentors because they feel that job competency should be enough to succeed, or they may feel uncomfortable seeking out a mentor when most of the senior executives are white males. Women may fear that initiating a mentoring relationship could be misunderstood as a romantic overture, whereas male mentors may think of women as mothers, wives, or sisters rather than as executive material. Cross-race mentoring relationships may leave both parties uncomfortable, but the mentoring of minority employees must often be across race since there are few minorities in upper-level positions. The few minorities and women who have reached the upper ranks often are overwhelmed with mentoring requests from people like themselves, and they may feel uncomfortable in highly visible minority-minority or female-female mentoring relationships, which isolate them from the white male status quo.

The solution is for organizations to overcome some of the barriers to mentor relationships between white males and minorities. When organizations can institutionalize the value of white males actively seeking women and minority protégés, the benefits will mean that women and minorities will be steered into pivotal jobs and positions critical to advancement. Mentoring programs also are consistent with the Civil Rights Act of 1991 that requires the diversification of middle and upper management.

Accommodating Special Needs. Many people have special needs of which top managers are unaware. For example, if a number of people entering the organization at the lower level are single parents, the company can reassess job scheduling and opportunities for child care. If a substantial labor pool is non-English-speaking, training materials and information packets can be provided in another language.

In many families today, both parents work, which means that the company may provide structures to deal with child care, maternity or paternity leave, flexible work schedules, home-based employment, and perhaps part-time employment or seasonal hours that reflect the school year. The key to attracting and keeping elderly or disabled workers may include long-term-care insurance and special health or life benefits. Alternative work scheduling also may be important for these groups of workers. Many organizations are struggling with generational diversity, striving to meet the needs of workers at different ages and life cycles. Pitney Bowes created the Life Balance Resources program to help employees in different generations cope with life cycle issues, such as helping Generation Y workers find their first apartment or car, assisting Generation X employees in locating child care or getting a home loan, and helping baby boomers plan for retirement or find elder care for aging parents.[58]

Another issue for U.S. companies is that racial/ethnic minorities and immigrants have often had fewer educational opportunities than other groups. Some companies have worked with high schools to provide fundamental skills in literacy and arithmetic, or they provide these programs within the company to upgrade employees to appropriate educational levels. The movement toward increasing educational services for employees can be expected to increase for immigrants and the economically disadvantaged in the years to come.

Changing organizational structures and policies is important because it demonstrates a concrete commitment to supporting diversity. If managers talk about the value of a diverse workforce but do not do anything to ensure that diverse workers have opportunities and support in the workplace, employees are not likely to trust that the company truly values diversity. Ernst & Young

LLP has become a diversity leader by changing structures and policies to bolster the recruitment, retention, and advancement of women and minorities.

Ernst & Young LLP
http://www.ey.com

The accounting and consulting services firm Ernst & Young once viewed diversity primarily in terms of complying with EEO and affirmative action guidelines. However, even though managers worked hard to bring women and minorities into the organization, they began to realize that the company was losing female and minority professionals at a much higher rate than white males.

Top executives authorized a two-year study to help them understand the pressures and challenges that minority groups were feeling and how to address them. Then, they made a firm commitment to diversity by creating two new departments: the Office of Minority Recruitment and Retention, headed by Allen Boston, an African-American partner, and the Office for Retention, directed by Deborah K. Holmes, a lawyer who had been involved in the diversity study. Assigning resources directly to diversity efforts has significantly increased the recruitment and retention of women and minorities. By 1999, 7 percent of Ernst & Young's partners and senior managers were members of minority groups, and the percentage of minorities recruited each year had risen from around 10 percent to around 24 percent. The number of women in senior positions is also edging up.

Now, Ernst & Young is pushing even further, allocating resources for training and mentoring programs, work-life balance initiatives, and other efforts designed to meet the needs of diverse employees. Even more significantly, the company is providing for minority scholarships and programs at both undergraduate and graduate institutions and sponsoring organizations that give minority high school students a chance to get an inside look at the accounting and engineering professions. E & Y also recently started an innovative program called Your Master Plan (YMP), which gives recent college graduates a chance to work at Ernst & Young while pursuing a master's degree in accounting, paid for by the firm. These initiatives give young minority individuals opportunities they otherwise might not have—and they give Ernst & Young access to high-quality minority employees. According to Miriam Nalumansi, who began the YMP program last year, "One of the things that attracted me to Ernst & Young was the firm's commitment to diversity. I'm black, I'm female—those are things I have to consider."[59]

Diversity Awareness Training

Many organizations, including Monsanto, Xerox, and Mobil Oil, provide special training, called **diversity awareness training**, to help people become aware of their own cultural boundaries, their prejudices and stereotypes, so they can learn to work and live together. Working or living within a multicultural context requires a person to use interaction skills that transcend the skills typically effective when dealing with others from one's own in-group.[60] Diversity awareness programs help people learn how to handle conflict in a constructive manner, which tends to reduce stress and negative energy in diverse work teams.

People vary in their sensitivity and openness to other cultures. Exhibit 10.5 shows a model of six stages of diversity awareness. The continuum ranges from a total lack of awareness to a complete understanding and acceptance of people's differences. This model is useful in helping diversity awareness trainers assess participants' openness to change. People at different stages might

diversity awareness training
Special training designed to make people aware of their own prejudices and stereotypes.

E X H I B I T   *10.5*

Stages of Diversity Awareness

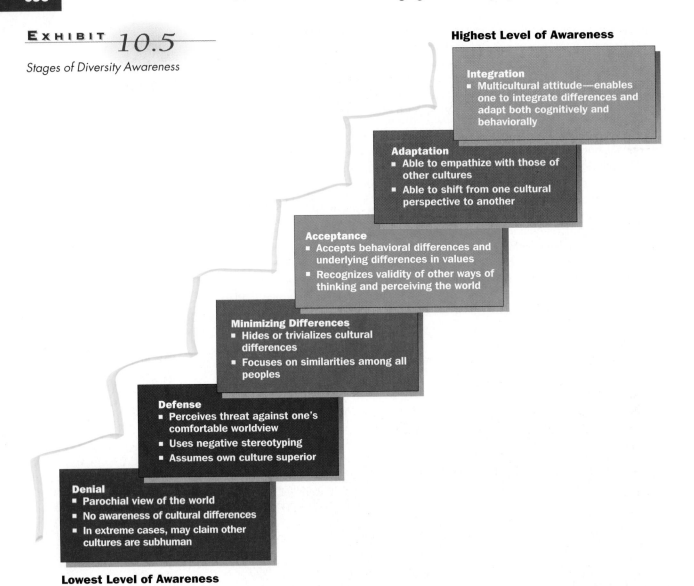

E X H I B I T   *10.5*

Stages of Diversity Awareness

Highest Level of Awareness

Integration
- Multicultural attitude—enables one to integrate differences and adapt both cognitively and behaviorally

Adaptation
- Able to empathize with those of other cultures
- Able to shift from one cultural perspective to another

Acceptance
- Accepts behavioral differences and underlying differences in values
- Recognizes validity of other ways of thinking and perceiving the world

Minimizing Differences
- Hides or trivializes cultural differences
- Focuses on similarities among all peoples

Defense
- Perceives threat against one's comfortable worldview
- Uses negative stereotyping
- Assumes own culture superior

Denial
- Parochial view of the world
- No awareness of cultural differences
- In extreme cases, may claim other cultures are subhuman

Lowest Level of Awareness

SOURCE: Based on M. Bennett, "A Developmental Approach to Training for Intercultural Sensitivity," *International Journal of Intercultural Relations* 10 (1986), 179–196.

require different kinds of training. A basic aim of awareness training is to help people recognize that hidden and overt biases direct their thinking about specific individuals and groups. If people can come away from a training session recognizing that they prejudge people and that this needs to be consciously addressed in communications with and treatment of others, an important goal of diversity awareness training has been reached.

Many diversity awareness programs used today are designed to help people of varying backgrounds communicate effectively with one another and to understand the language and context used in dealing with people from other groups. The point of this training is to help people be more flexible in their communications with others, to treat each person as an individual, and not to rely on stereotypes. Effective programs move people toward being open in their relationships with others. For example, if you were a part of such a program, it would help you develop an explicit awareness of your own cultural values, your own cultural boundaries, and your own cultural behaviors. Then you would be provided the same information about other groups, and you would be given the opportunity to learn about and communicate with people from other groups. One of the most important elements in diversity training is to bring together people of differing perspectives so that they can engage in learning new interpersonal communication skills with one another.

Defining New Relationships in Organizations

One outcome of diversity is an increased incidence of close personal relationships in the workplace, which can have both positive and negative results for employees as well as the organization. Two issues of concern are emotional intimacy and sexual harassment.

Emotional Intimacy

Close relationships between men and women often have been discouraged in companies for fear that they would disrupt the balance of power and threaten organizational stability.[61] This opinion grew out of the assumption that organizations are designed for rationality and efficiency, which were best achieved in a nonemotional environment.

However, a recent study of friendships in organizations sheds interesting light on this issue.[62] Managers and workers responded to a survey about emotionally intimate relationships with both male and female coworkers. Many men and women reported having close relationships with an opposite-sex coworker. Called *nonromantic love relationships*, the friendships resulted in trust, respect, constructive feedback, and support in achieving work goals. Intimate friendships did not necessarily become romantic, and they affected each person's job and career in a positive way. Rather than causing problems, nonromantic love relationships, according to the study, affected work teams in a positive manner because conflict was reduced. Indeed, men reported somewhat greater benefit than women from these relationships, perhaps because the men had fewer close relationships outside the workplace upon which to depend.

However, when such relationships *do* become romantic or sexual in nature real problems can result. Office romance is on the rise, with more than 30 percent of employees reporting they have been involved with a coworker at some time in their careers. Although not all office romances lead to trouble, usually they create difficulties for managers.

Romances that require the most attention from managers are those that arise between a supervisor and a subordinate. These relationships often lead to morale problems among other staff members, complaints of favoritism, and questions about the supervisor's intentions or judgment. Although few companies have written policies about workplace romance in general, 70 percent of companies surveyed have policies prohibiting romantic relationships between a superior and a subordinate,[63] as described in the example below. At IBM, training programs and written policies emphasize that a manager can become romantically involved with a subordinate only if he or she agrees to stop supervising the subordinate, by transferring to another job within or outside the company. The onus is on the manager rather than the subordinate to take action.[64]

Office Romances

After eight years of working alongside a female colleague at Primus Financial in Franklin, Tennessee, Gary Gaulke realized he wanted more out of the relationship. Because the company was small back then, Gary felt it important to keep strict boundaries. So he and Donna began a relationship they kept secret from Primus. The family-friendly company was supportive of husbands and wives working there, but Gary and Donna were in a gray zone, not married and uncertain of where the relationship would go. "We needed to make sure we'd still be able to remain good friends if things didn't work out," says Donna. After a year, they came out of the closet with their relationship and let people at work know what was going on.

Most managers and HR professionals discourage workplace romances, having experienced the organizational fallout that can be caused by breakups. In fact, most companies forbid dating between bosses and subordinates. Of the roughly 20 percent that do have policies on office romances, most grudgingly tolerate them. It's a good thing, too, because one study estimates that 8 million of these relationships are initiated each year. Here are some tips for those considering an office romance:

- Date equals; don't go after a subordinate or a boss.

- Make sure expectations are similar: if one person wants a relationship and the other a fling, both are asking for trouble.

- Couples should agree to not flirt at work, not send lovey-dovey e-mails, and not bring disagreements into the office.

- Develop a friendship first to see if the relationship has staying power.

About 30 percent of respondents in one study said they were still dating or married to someone they met at work . . . just like the Gaulkes. After falling in love three years ago, they decided to marry and now live "happily ever after," while both still work at Primus.[65]

Sexual Harassment

While psychological closeness between men and women in the workplace may be a positive experience, sexual harassment is not. Sexual harassment is illegal. As a form of sexual discrimination, sexual harassment in the workplace is a violation of Title VII of the 1964 Civil Rights Act. Sexual harassment in the classroom is a violation of Title VIII of the Education Amendment of 1972. The following categorize various forms of sexual harassment as defined by one university:

- *Generalized.* This form involves sexual remarks and actions that are not intended to lead to sexual activity but that are directed toward a coworker based solely on gender and reflect on the entire group.

- *Inappropriate/offensive.* Though not sexually threatening, it causes discomfort in a coworker, whose reaction in avoiding the harasser may limit his or her freedom and ability to function in the workplace.

- *Solicitation with promise of reward.* This action treads a fine line as an attempt to "purchase" sex, with the potential for criminal prosecution.

- *Coercion with threat of punishment.* The harasser coerces a coworker into sexual activity by using the threat of power (through recommendations, grades, promotions, and so on) to jeopardize the victim's career.

- *Sexual crimes and misdemeanors.* The highest level of sexual harassment, these acts would, if reported to the police, be considered felony crimes and misdemeanors.[66]

Over the past decade, the number of sexual harassment cases filed annually in the United States has more than doubled. About 17,000 complaints were filed in 1998 alone, up from 6,883 in 1991.[67] About 10 percent of those were filed by males. The Supreme Court has held that same-sex harassment as well as harassment of men by female coworkers is just as illegal as the harassment of women by men. In the suit that prompted the Court's decision, a male oil-rig worker claimed he was singled out by other members of the all-male crew for crude sex play, unwanted touching, and threats of rape.[68] Eight men, former employees of Jenny Craig Inc., sued the company, charging that female bosses made lewd comments or that they were denied promotions because of their sex. A male worker at a hot tub manufacturer won a $1 million court decision after claiming that his female boss made sexual overtures to him almost daily. These are among a growing number of men urging recognition that sexual harassment is not just a woman's problem.[69]

Because the corporate world is dominated by a male culture, however, sexual harassment affects women to a much greater extent. Women who are moving up the corporate hierarchy by entering male-dominated industries report a high frequency of harassment. Surveys report an increase in sexual harassment programs, but female employees also report a lack of prompt and just action by executives to incidents of sexual harassment. However, companies are discovering that "an ounce of prevention really is worth a pound of cure." Top executives are seeking to address problems of harassment through company diversity programs, revised complaint systems and grievance procedures, written policy statements, workshops, lectures, and role-playing exercises to increase employee sensitivity and awareness to the issue.[70]

Global Diversity

Globalization is a reality for today's companies. As stated in a recent report from the Hudson Institute, *Workforce 2020*, "The rest of the world matters to a degree that it never did in the past."[71] Even small companies that do not do business in other countries are affected by global diversity issues. However, large multinational companies that hire employees in many countries face tremendous challenges because they must apply diversity management across a broader stage than North America. Managers must develop new skills and awareness to handle the unique challenges of global diversity: cross-cultural understanding, the ability to build networks, and the understanding of geopolitical forces. Two significant aspects of global diversity programs involve employee selection and training and the understanding of the communication context.

Selection and Training

Expatriates are employees who live and work in a country other than their own. Careful screening, selection, and training of employees to serve overseas increase the potential for corporate global success. Human resource managers consider global skills in the selection process. In addition, expatriates receive

expatriates
Employees who live and work in a country other than their own.

Exhibit *10.6*

Arrangement of High- and Low-Context Cultures

High Context	Chinese
	Korean
	Japanese
	Vietnamese
	Arab
	Greek
	Spanish
	Italian
	English
	North American
	Scandinavian
Low Context	Swiss
	German

SOURCES: Edward T. Hall, *Beyond Culture* (Garden City, N.Y.: Anchor Press/Doubleday, 1976); and J. Kennedy and A. Everest, "Put Diversity in Context," *Personnel Journal* (September 1991), 50–54.

high-context culture

A culture in which communication is used to enhance personal relationships.

low-context culture

A culture in which communication is used to exchange facts and information.

cross-cultural training that develops language skills and cultural and historical orientation. Career-path counseling often is available.[72] Texaco set up its Executive Business Analyst (EBA) program to develop a pool of diverse leaders who have the global management skills to work anywhere in the world.[73] Through the program, recent recruits or current employees complete rotational assignments, including some outside the United States and on global teams. Global diversity training, cultural sensitivity training, and mentoring are also provided through the EBA program.

Equally important, however, is honest self-analysis by overseas candidates and their families. Before seeking or accepting an assignment in another country, a candidate should ask himself or herself such questions as the following:

- Is your spouse interrupting his or her own career path to support your career? Is that acceptable to both of you?

- Is family separation for long periods involved?

- Can you initiate social contacts in a foreign culture?

- Can you adjust well to different environments and changes in personal comfort or quality of living, such as the lack of television, gasoline at $5 per gallon, limited hot water, varied cuisine, and national phone strikes?

- Can you manage your future reentry into the job market by networking and maintaining contacts in your home country?[74]

Employees working overseas must adjust to all of these conditions. Managers going global might find that their own management style needs adjustment to succeed in a foreign country. One aspect of this adjustment is learning the communication context of a foreign location.

Communication Differences

People from some cultures tend to pay more attention to the social context (social setting, nonverbal behavior, social status) of their verbal communication than Americans do. For example, American managers working in China have discovered that social context is considerably more important in that culture, and they have learned to suppress their impatience and devote the time needed to establish personal and social relationships.

Exhibit 10.6 indicates how the emphasis on social context varies among countries. In a **high-context culture**, people are sensitive to circumstances surrounding social exchanges. People use communication primarily to build personal social relationships; meaning is derived from context—setting, status, nonverbal behavior—more than from explicit words; relationships and trust are more important than business; and the welfare and harmony of the group are valued. In a **low-context culture**, people use communication primarily to exchange facts and information; meaning is derived primarily from words; business transactions are more important than building relationships and trust; and individual welfare and achievement are more important than the group.[75]

To understand how differences in cultural context affect communications, consider the U.S. expression "The squeaky wheel gets the oil." It means that the loudest person will get the most attention, and attention is assumed to be favorable. Equivalent sayings in China and Japan are "Quacking ducks get shot," and "The nail that sticks up gets hammered down," respectively. Standing out as an individual in these cultures clearly merits unfavorable attention.

High-context cultures include Asian and Arab countries. Low-context cultures tend to be American and Northern European. Even within North America, cultural subgroups vary in the extent to which context counts, explaining why differences among groups make successful communication difficult. White females, Native Americans, and African Americans all tend to prefer higher context communication than do white males. A high-context interaction requires more time because a relationship has to be developed, and trust and friendship must be established. Furthermore, most male managers and most people doing the hiring in organizations are from low-context cultures, which conflicts with people entering the organization from a background in a higher context culture. Overcoming these differences in communication is a major goal of diversity awareness training.

Diversity in the New Workplace

Organizations use the approaches discussed in this chapter to create an environment that welcomes and supports diverse individuals. Ninety-one percent of companies responding to a survey by the Society for Human Resource Management believe that diversity initiatives help maintain a competitive advantage. Some specific benefits include improving employee morale, decreasing interpersonal conflict, facilitating progress into new markets, and increasing the organization's creativity.[76] Some of today's companies are also pushing into new territory to support a globally diverse workforce. Two popular mechanisms for leveraging diversity in today's organizations are multicultural teams and employee network groups.

Multicultural Teams

Companies have long known that putting together teams made up of members from different functional areas results in better problem solving and decision making. Now, they are recognizing that **multicultural teams**—teams made up of members from diverse national, racial, ethnic, and cultural backgrounds—provide even greater potential for enhanced creativity, innovation, and value in today's global marketplace.[77] Research has found that diverse teams generate more and better alternatives to problems and produce more innovative solutions than homogeneous teams.[78] A team made up of people with different perspectives, backgrounds, and cultural values creates a healthy mix of ideas, which sometimes encourages more reluctant people to speak out. In addition, diversity can stimulate a healthy level of conflict that leads to greater creativity and better decisions.

multicultural teams
Teams made up of members from diverse national, racial, ethnic, and cultural backgrounds.

Some organizations, such as RhonePoulenc Rorer (RPR), based in Collegeville, Pennsylvania, are committed to mixing people from diverse countries and cultures from the top to the bottom of the organization. There are 15 nationalities represented in RPR's top management teams, including a French CEO, an Austrian head of operations, an American general counsel, an Egyptian head of human resources, and an Italian director of corporate communications.[79] The top management team at Redwood City, California–based Obongo includes members from India, the United States, Brazil, Ireland, and Bulgaria. Obongo was started by people from two different countries who have woven cultural diversity into the technology start-up's DNA. Today, Obongo has teams made up of people from 12 countries and 18 different cultures.[80]

Multicultural teams are becoming common in both U.S. and Canadian organizations. One consultant notes that the workforce of many Canadian organizations is often jokingly referred to as the *United Nations* because companies have so many different nationalities working together on project teams.[81] The U.N. approach appears in many U.S. companies, as well. For example, Radha Basu manages a team of Hewlett-Packard software writers who stretch across six countries and 15 time zones.[82]

Despite their many advantages,[83] multicultural teams are more difficult to manage because of the increased potential for miscommunication and misunderstanding. Multicultural teams typically have more difficulty learning to communicate and work well together, but with effective cross-cultural training and good management, the problems seem to dissipate over time.[84] One management team videotaped its meetings so members could see how their body language reflects cultural differences. An American manager remarked, "I couldn't believe how even my physical movements dominated the table, while Ron [a Filipino American] . . . actually worked his way off-camera within the first five minutes."[85] The goal of talking about team members' cultural differences is not to minimize them for the sake of team harmony but to better understand how they affect team interaction and performance. Many organizations that use multicultural teams want to help people enhance and retain their varied cultural identities. One of the most popular mechanisms is employee network groups.

Employee Network Groups

employee network groups

Groups based on social identity, such as race or gender, and organized by employees to focus on concerns of employees from that group.

Employee network groups are based on social identity, such as gender or race, and are organized by employees to focus on concerns of employees from that group.[86] For example, at Visteon Corp., a global automotive systems producer, the women's network group develops the leadership and technical skills of female employees, designs strategies for how members can contribute to Visteon's business and diversity goals, and works to keep top managers informed of members' contributions, concerns, and needs.[87] The idea behind network groups is that minority employees can join together across traditional organizational boundaries for mutual support and to extend member influence in the organization. Network groups pursue a variety of activities, such as meetings to educate top managers, mentoring programs, networking events, training sessions and skills seminars, minority intern programs, and community volunteer activities. Network groups give people a chance to meet, interact with, and develop social and professional ties to others throughout the organization, which may include key decision makers. Network groups are a powerful way to reduce social isolation for women and minorities, help these employees be more effective, and enable members to achieve greater career advancement.

An important characteristic of network groups is that they are formed by employees, not the organization, and membership is voluntary. However, successful organizations support and encourage network groups by making clear that such groups are welcome, helping members who want to form groups contact other organizations for assistance, and perhaps providing financial assistance for programs. Although at first glance the proliferation of employee network groups seems to be in direct opposition to the trend toward multicultural teams, the two mechanisms actually work quite well together. At Kraft Foods, networks are considered critical to the success of multicultural teams because they build awareness and acceptance of cultural differences and help people feel more comfortable working together.[88] Visteon has credited the Visteon African American Network's mentoring program for strengthening the company's retention and development of talented black employees.

There has been a rapid growth of employee network groups for minorities who have faced barriers to advancement in organizations, including African Americans, Hispanics, American Indians, Asian Americans, women, gays and lesbians, and disabled employees. Network groups offer significant potential for supporting a workplace that values diversity. In general, female and minority employees who participate in a network group feel more pride about their work and are more optimistic about their careers than those who do not have the support of a network.[89]

■ Summary and Management Solution

Several important ideas pertain to workforce diversity, which is the inclusion of people with different human qualities and from different cultural groups. Dimensions of diversity are both primary, such as age, gender, and race, and secondary, such as education, marital status, and income. Ethnocentric attitudes generally produce a monoculture that accepts only one way of doing things and one set of values and beliefs, thereby excluding nontraditional employees from full participation. Minority employees face several significant challenges in the workplace.

Acceptance of diversity is becoming especially important because of sociocultural changes and the changing workforce. Diversity in the workplace reflects diversity in the larger environment.

Affirmative action programs have been successful in gaining employment for women and minorities, but the glass ceiling has kept many women and minorities from obtaining top management positions

Breaking the glass ceiling ultimately means changing the corporate culture within organizations; changing internal structures and policies toward employees, including accommodating special needs; and providing diversity awareness training to help people become aware of their own cultural boundaries and prejudices. This training also helps employees learn to communicate with people from other cultural contexts.

The increased diversity in organizations has provided opportunities for emotional intimacy and friendships between men and women that are beneficial to all parties. However, when these relationships become romantic or sexual, they can present problems for managers. Increasing diversity also means that organizations must develop programs to deal with global as well as domestic diversity and with potential conflicts, such as sexual harassment, that arise.

Two recent approaches to supporting and leveraging the power of diversity in organizations are multicultural teams and employee network groups. Multicultural teams can provide a broader and deeper base of experience and ideas for enhanced problem solving, creativity, and innovation. Organizations that value diversity also encourage and support network groups to enable minority organization members to reduce their social isolation, be more effective in their jobs, have a greater impact on the organization, and achieve greater opportunities for career advancement. Minority employees who participate in networks typically feel more pride in their work and are more optimistic about their careers.

Returning to the opening example of Texaco, CEO Peter Bijur knew that nothing less than a total overhaul of the corporate culture could begin to erase Texaco's image as the embodiment of corporate racism. Exhibit 10.7 lists the major elements of Texaco's culture change program, which was hammered out in collaboration with members on the independent task force required by the lawsuit. Today, Texaco is in the midst of a remarkable transformation, which some experts believe could make the company a model for diversity. All employees are required to attend a two-day diversity training program, and managers are sent to change-management and communication courses as well. Bijur has also set specific diversity goals with specific timetables and has made it clear to top executives as well as managers and supervisors throughout the company that their future career advancement will be determined by how well they implemented the new diversity initiatives. These initiatives include recruiting minority candidates, developing in-house minority talent through mentoring programs, increasing the use of minority suppliers, monitoring employee attitudes, appropriately addressing grievances, and improving relationships with minority organizations.

EXHIBIT 10.7

Major Elements of Texaco's Culture Change Initiative

Recruitment and Hiring
- Ask search firms to identify wider arrays of candidates
- Enhance the interviewing, selection, and hiring skills of managers
- Expand college recruitment at historically minority colleges

Identifying and Developing Talent
- Form a partnership with INROADS, a nationwide internship program that targets minority students for management careers
- Establish a mentoring process
- Refine the company's global succession planning system to improve identification of talent
- Improve the selection and development of managers and leaders to help ensure that they are capable of maximizing team performance

Ensuring Fair Treatment
- Conduct extensive diversity training
- Implement an alternative dispute resolution process
- Include women and minorities on all human resources committees throughout the company

Holding Managers Accountable
- Link managers' compensation to their success in creating "openness and inclusion in the workplace"
- Implement 360-degree feedback for all managers and supervisors
- Redesign the company's employee attitude survey and begin using it annually to monitor employee attitudes

Improve Relationships with External Stakeholders
- Broaden the company's base of vendors and suppliers to incorporate more minority- and women-owned businesses
- Increase banking, investment, and insurance business with minority- and women-owned firms
- Add more independent, minority retailers and increase the number of minority managers in company-owned gas stations and Xpress Lube outlets

SOURCE: Don Hellriegel, Susan E. Jackson, and John W. Slocum, Jr., *Management,* 8th ed. (Cincinnati, Ohio: South-Western Publishing, 1999). Used with permission. Originally adapted from V. C. Smith, "Texaco Outlines Comprehensive Initiatives," *Human Resource Executive* (February 1997), 13; A. Bryant, "How Much Has Texaco Changed? A Mixed Report Card on Anti-bias Efforts," *New York Times* (November 2, 1997), 3–1, 3–16, 3–17; and "Texaco's Workforce Diversity Plan," as reprinted in *Workforce* (March 1997, suppl.).

Compensation is also tied to how effectively managers "create openness and inclusion in the workplace." To further spur culture change, Bijur recruited several eminent African Americans to join Texaco's top ranks.

Recruiting African-American executives wasn't easy in the wake of the racial discrimination scandal, but Bijur's ardent personal commitment to changing Texaco's culture convinced them to join in the quest.[90]

■ Discussion Questions

1. If you were a senior manager at a company such as Mitsubishi, Allstate Insurance, or Texaco, how would you address the challenges faced by minority employees?

2. Some people argue that social class is a major source of cultural differences, yet social class is not listed as a primary or secondary dimension in Exhibit 10.1. Discuss reasons for this.

3. Have you been associated with an organization that made assumptions associated with a monoculture? Describe the culture.

4. What is the glass ceiling, and why do you think it has proved to be such a barrier to women and minorities?

5. How might employee network groups contribute to the advancement of women and minorities to higher-level positions in an organization?

6. In preparing an organization to accept diversity, do you think it is more important to change the corporate culture or to change structures and policies? Explain.

7. If a North American corporation could choose either high-context or low-context communications, which do you think would be best for the company's long-term health? Discuss.

8. Many single people meet and date people from their work organization because the organization provides a context within which to know and trust

another person. How do you think this practice affects the potential for emotional intimacy? Sexual harassment?

9. As a manager, how would you accommodate the special needs of different groups—such as single parents, older workers, or employees with poor English language skills—without appearing to show favoritism?

10. Discuss the advantages and disadvantages of multicultural teams. Why might an organization that plans to implement multicultural teams want to provide encouragement and support diverse employee network groups?

■ Manager's Workbook

Diversity and Work Quiz

1. Women account for 46 percent of the total U.S. workforce.   T   F

2. By 2006, women will account for 50 percent of the total growth in the labor force.   T   F

3. Of divorced women, 75 percent are in the labor force, while 52 percent of married women work.   T   F

4. The largest occupational group for women is secretaries, while the second largest is cashiers.   T   F

5. About 4 million women hold more than one job.   T   F

6. Women's 1999 median earnings working full-time, year-round: $28,324.   T   F

7. In families with a working wife, the median income is $68,000, while a family without a wife in the paid labor force is $40,000.   T   F

8. Over the age of 65, 14 percent of women live below the poverty line, while only 7 percent of men do.   T   F

9. The number of working women has doubled since 1970—from 30 million to 60 million.   T   F

10. Fifty-nine percent of women with infants under the age of one are in the labor force.   T   F

11. Women earn 80 cents on the dollar compared to men.   T   F

12. The highest weekly earnings for women come from which group? Lawyers, engineers, or physicians? _____

13. By the year 2050, what percentage of the total U.S. population will be Asians, Hispanics, blacks, or other non-whites? _____

14. Of the 43 million people in the U.S. with disabilities, how many are of working age (16–64)? _____
How many are employed? _____
How many unemployed want to work? _____

15. What percentage of the total U.S. population speaks a language other than English at home? _____ What percentage of those speaks Spanish? _____

16. Of the 8.7 million immigrants who arrived in the U.S. between 1980–1990, what percentage has college degrees? _____ What percentage of U.S. natives has college degrees? _____ What percentage of male vs. female? _____ women age 25 and older? _____ men age 25 and older? _____

17. According to a recent *Newsweek* poll, what percentage of U.S. people believes gays and lesbians should be given equal rights and opportunities in the workplace? _____

18. What are the two most racially and ethnically diverse states in the U.S.? _____ The two least? _____ By 2020, what percentage of U.S. population will be 65 or older? _____ Between 1998–2008, what is the percentage increase of workers 55 and older? _____

■ Manager's Workshop

Globian Exercise

Background

In another galaxy, far, far away, there is a planet called "Globe." The inhabitants on this planet are physically very similar to the people on Earth and differ from one another, just as Earthlings do. There is one major difference, however, between Globians and Earthlings: on Globe there is no conflict.

Word has spread to Globe that Earth is a planet on which there is conflict that pervades relationships between individuals, groups, nations, and many other aspects of life. So the Glo-

bian Governing Council has decided to send a team of anthropologists/sociologists to Earth to learn about conflict. Their instructions are to determine whether it would be advantageous to bring conflict, whatever it is, back to their home planet.

The Globians work in pairs as they meet with small groups of Earthlings to carry out their study.

1. Selection of Globians and Earthlings
   The class is divided into small groups of 6–8, from which two persons will be identified as Globians and one to two as observers, and with the rest as Earthlings.

2. Each group of Earthlings and pair of Globians meets separately to discuss their assignment and get into role. Role assignments are below. Read *only* the roles for your group.
3. Meetings between Groups of Earthlings (3–4 people) and Globian Pairs (2 people)
   Purpose: to explore the nature and purpose of conflict. Come up with (1) a definition of conflict and (2) what the purpose of conflict is. Make sure both sides agree with these. Write them down on a sheet of paper.
4. Debriefing in Groups
   Each Earthling group and Globian pair meets separately to discuss what happened during the preceding meeting.
5. Fishbowl with Globians in the Center
   Meeting in the center of the fishbowl, Globians report on what happened in their meetings with Earthlings, discuss what they learned about conflict, and explore the pros and cons of taking conflict back home to Globe.
6. Total class discussion on cultural differences, cross-cultural communication, and assumption sets.

ROLES
Instructions for Globians

You have been sent to Earth by the governing council of the planet Globe to study the Earthly phenomenon known as "conflict." You do not understand what is meant by the term and are completely ignorant about conflict in any form. The behavior known on Earth as conflict does not exist on Globe. The term "conflict" is not in the vocabulary or language of Globe. Other terms associated with conflict on Earth are also unfamiliar to you. Peace and harmony is the norm on your planet; difference and diversity are accepted and treated with appreciation. The concept of conflict is like a totally unfamiliar foreign language to you.

You are to function with a sincere attitude of inquiry. You have a serious job to perform and much depends on your ability to carry out this assignment. You enter into contact with Earthlings with a genuine curiosity about this unfamiliar phenomenon. You are prepared to ask questions, seek explanations, gather information, make observations, and in every way possible to determine what "conflict" is and to be prepared to take this information back to your planet.

It is entirely possible that, despite the Earthlings' best efforts to help you, it will turn out that "conflict" makes no sense to you. No matter; you remain within your accustomed state of peace and harmony even though you cannot make sense of what the Earthlings say or do in their efforts to explain.

Instructions for Earthlings

As representatives of Earth, you have agreed to help the Globians. You are experts on conflict, having experienced, observed, and lived with it all your lives. Your visitors want to know what conflict is and what purposes it serves, if any. Your job is to do whatever you can to educate the Globians about conflict. Because you take conflict for granted and probably experience it almost on a daily basis, it may be difficult for you to understand how any society of intelligent, thinking beings can exist without experiencing conflict or understanding what is meant by the term. Using your skills in conflict, which you have been developing throughout your lives, you want to provide the Globians with the unique opportunity to learn and understand as much about this Earthly phenomenon as possible.

You may use whatever methods you deem appropriate to convey this concept to your guests. It is important, however, to keep in mind that it is not part of your job to persuade the Globians that conflict already exists on their planet. Their question is whether or not conflict is worth importing into their home planet. Do your best to help them understand what conflict is and what purposes it serves on Earth.

Instructions for Observers

The task of the observer is to watch the behavior of group members and note how the group works together. Guidelines on what to look for include, but aren't limited to, the following:
1. Who speaks most and least? In what order do people talk?
2. Does everyone contribute? What happens to the contributions of different members?
3. What occurs when the Globians arrive? To what extent does the group stick to its original plan for interacting with the visitors? Does the plan change? If so, how does the change occur?
4. What is the level of tension in the group: before the Globians arrive? after they join the group?
5. What kinds of emotions are expressed by group members and exhibited in their posture, facial expressions, and actions?

SOURCE: By Carole Parker and Donald Klein. The original version of the Globe Exercise was created by Donald Klein in June 1984 for use in the Beyond Conflict Training Laboratory in Bethel, Maine, conducted by NTL Institute for Applied Behavioral Science.

■ Management in Practice: Ethical Dilemma

A Man's World?

Jana Mercer has been working for Crown Industries for nearly 20 years, first as a clerical worker and later as an accountant. As a division of a national forest products company, Crown offers good salaries and benefits in a part of the southern United States where unemployment is typically high and wages are low. Jana, a single mother of two, has always felt lucky to have the job.

However, recently a young accountant, Tommy Thompson, had suddenly been promoted to a job that Jana—and everyone else in the department—thought she was better qualified for.

The job had never been advertised inside or outside the company. Instead, top managers had suddenly boosted the position's pay scale five grades and given the job to Tommy. All the supervisors in the unit thought Jana should have been given the job, and they took their complaints to the comptroller, who promptly told them to mind their own business. After nights of lying awake fuming, Jana finally decided to take some steps of her own. She went to the comptroller and applied for the position, insisting that she be given an interview. Weeks went by with no word, until Jana requested a meeting with the comptroller and general manager. The comptroller tried to pacify her by saying he had not interviewed her because he knew she wouldn't be happy in the position. "You'd get bored in a week, Jana," he said. "The job isn't nearly as interesting or challenging as what you're doing now." Jana disagreed and pointed out that the pay was much higher. In addition, the higher profile would give her a better chance for future promotions. "Look, honey," the GM soothed, putting his hand on her shoulder. "The decision has already been made. Tommy's a good man, and he fits in well with the other top guys around here. You just have to understand it's a man's world. My wife goes through the same thing at her company."

Jana was so stunned she didn't know how to respond. As she slowly walked back to her office, she wondered what she should do next.

What Do You Do?

1. Let it go. After all, it is a man's world at Crown, and you need to accept it. You've got a good job making a decent salary and you can't afford to lose it.
2. Go to the division president, and if he doesn't do anything, keep moving up the hierarchy of the national company, making enough noise until you find someone who will take action.
3. Document everything in writing, including letters of support from people inside the unit, and go to the Equal Employment Opportunity Commission. This is a clear case of discrimination, and it is evident that Crown's corporate culture supports this type of abuse.

SOURCE: Based on Doug Wallace, "It's (Still) a Man's World," *BusinessEthics* (July–August 1998), 16.

■ Surf the Net

1. **Diversity Recruiting.** Assume you are a Human Resources Director who is interested in enhancing your organization's diversity recruiting efforts. To increase the diversity of the workforce, you are becoming informed on the subject of increasing college enrollment of minorities. Research the following two organizations that coordinate with corporations to support minority students interested in business careers. Write a brief recommendation to your instructor outlining which of the two organizations you would prefer to work with and include two or three factors that influenced your decision.
   a. LEAD (Leadership Education and Development Program in Business, Inc.) at *http://www.leadnational.org*
   b. INROADS at *http://www.inroads.org*
2. **50 Most Powerful Women in Business.** *Fortune* magazine updates its "50 Most Powerful Women in Business" list every year. Go to *http://www.fortune.com* to locate the most recent list and complete the chart based on what you find at the site.

Rank	Name	Title	Company
1			
2			
3			
4			
5			

3. **Sexual Harassment.** To help determine how well you understand sexual harassment laws, complete the Sexual Harassment Quiz at *http://www.hrtools.com/etoolsapplets/ SEXHARASSIQtest/shiqtest.asp.*

   After selecting your answers, choose the "Submit Quiz" option. Choose "View Correct Answers" to see how you scored and learn the reasoning behind each correct answer. Print out the "View Correct Answers" page, write your name at the top of the printout, and submit it to your instructor.

■ Case for Critical Analysis

Draper Manufacturing

You have just been hired as a diversity consultant by Draper Manufacturing. Ralph Draper, chairman and CEO, and other top managers feel a need to resolve some racial issues that have been growing over the past several years at their plant in Nashville, Tennessee. Draper Manufacturing is a small, family-owned company that manufactures mattresses. It employs 90 people full-time, including African Americans, Asians, and His-

panics. About 75 percent of the workforce is female. The company also occasionally hires part-time workers, most of whom are Hispanic women. Most of these part-timers are hired for periods of a few months at a time, when production is falling behind schedule.

To begin your orientation to the company, Draper has asked his production manager, Wallace Burns, to take you around the plant. As Burns points out the various areas responsible for each stage of the production process, you overhear several different languages being spoken. In the shipping and receiving department, you notice that most workers are black men. Burns confirms that 90 percent of the workers in shipping and receiving are African American and points out that the manager of that department, Adam Fox, is also African American.

Later in the afternoon you attend a regular meeting of top managers to meet everyone and get a feel for the organizational culture. Draper introduces you as a diversity consultant and notes that several of his managers have expressed concerns about festering racial tensions in the company. He notes that "Each of the minority groups sticks together. The blacks and Orientals rarely mix, and most of the Mexicans stick together and speak only in Spanish. It seems that some of our workers are just downright lazy sometimes. We keep falling behind in our production schedule and having to hire part-time workers, but then we generally have to fire two or three of those a month for goofing off on the job." He closes his introduction by saying that you have been hired to help the company solve their growing diversity problems.

Draper then turns toward the management committee's routine daily business. The others present are the general manager, human resources manager (the only woman), sales manager, quality control manager, plant manager (Wallace Burns), and shipping and receiving manager (Adam Fox, the only non-

white manager). Soon an angry debate begins between Fox and the sales manager. The sales manager says that orders are not being shipped on time, and several complaints have been received about the quality of the product. Fox argues that he needs more workers in shipping and receiving to do the job right, and he adds that the quality of incoming supplies is lousy. While this debate continues, the other managers remain silent and seem quite uncomfortable. Finally, the quality control manager attempts to calm things down with a joke about his wife. Most of the men in the group laugh loudly, and the conversation shifts to other topics on the agenda.

Questions

1. What suggestions would you make to Draper's managers to help them move toward successfully managing diversity issues?
2. If you were the shipping and receiving or human resources manager, how do you think you would feel about working at Draper? What are some of the challenges you might face at this company?
3. Based on the information in the case, at what stage of diversity awareness (Exhibit 10.5) do managers at Draper Manufacturing seem to be? Discuss.

SOURCE: Based on "Northern Industries," a case prepared by Rae Andre of Northeastern University.

PART FIVE

Leadership

In the music industry, successful leadership requires desire, ambition, intelligence, social skills, a strong work ethic, a desire to lead, and an in-depth knowledge of the field. Because the recording labels are the economic engines of the music business, strong leadership is essential. Leadership must focus internally—within the company—as well as externally, or outside the company. The leader creates the "personality" of a company, sets a visible example, communicates the vision and goals of the company, and oversees the execution of the tasks required to achieve these goals. Leadership at the head of a record company requires a strong belief in the potential of an artist and the ability to translate that belief into action so that all the elements are working toward the success of an artist and the recordings he or she produces. Externally, the leader must be cognizant of the business trends and forces that affect his or her industry.

Foundations of Behavior in Organizations

LEARNING OBJECTIVES

After studying this chapter, you should be able to

1 Define attitudes, including their major components, and explain their relationship to personality, perception, and behavior.

2 Discuss the importance of work-related attitudes.

3 Identify major personality traits and describe how personality can influence workplace attitudes and behaviors.

4 Define the five components of emotional intelligence and explain why they are important for managers in today's organizations.

5 Explain how people learn in general and in terms of individual learning styles.

6 Discuss the effects of stress and identify ways individuals and organizations can manage stress to improve employee health, satisfaction, and productivity.

Management Challenge

Vinita Gupta never expected running a company to be easy, but she was not prepared for this. Gupta had founded the networking equipment-maker Quick Eagle Networks in 1985 under the name Digital Link, took it public ten years later, and then stepped out for a couple of years. After sales plummeted, she returned as CEO to try to turn things around. Sales and profits improved, but employee morale kept getting worse. Employees were quitting in droves, with annual turnover hitting 30 percent. Spirits were so low that even key executives were jumping ship, leaving profitable Quick Eagle to join profitless competitors. When Gupta tried to determine what was going on, she uncovered an unnerving possibility—could it be that her own personality and attitudes were part of the problem? Introverted, soft-spoken, and highly focused on work, Gupta had always depended on other managers to be the cheerleaders and coaches in the company. But now, she was hearing through the grapevine that people found her aloof and unapproachable, and that the stiff, serious atmosphere she created made Quick Eagle . . . well, just not a very fun place to work. Gupta was accustomed to focusing on the details of the business and making necessary changes to keep quality, sales, and profits high. But maybe boosting morale and stemming the tide of talented workers walking out the door meant she now had to make some changes in herself.[1]

If you were Vinita Gupta, how would you gain a better understanding of yourself, your employees, and the changes you need to make to improve morale at Quick Eagle Networks? Do you believe the personality of a company's CEO affects organizational performance?

People differ in many ways. Some are quiet and shy while others are gregarious; some are thoughtful and serious while others are impulsive and fun-loving. Employees—and managers—bring their individual differences to work each day. These differences in attitudes, values, personality, and so forth influence how people interpret an assignment, whether they like to be told what to do, how they handle challenges, and how they interact with others. Managers' personalities and attitudes, as well as their ability to understand individual differences among employees, can profoundly affect the workplace and influence employee motivation, morale, and job performance. People are an organization's most valuable resource—and the source of some of the most difficult problems. Three basic leadership skills are at the core of identifying and solving people problems: (1) diagnosing, or gaining insight into the situation a manager is trying to influence; (2) adapting individual behavior and resources to meet the needs of the situation; and (3) communicating in a way that others can understand and accept. Thus, managers need insight about individual differences to understand what a behavioral situation is now and what it may be in the future.

To handle this responsibility, managers need to understand the principles of organizational behavior—that is, the ways individuals and groups tend to act in organizations. By increasing their knowledge of individual differences in the areas of attitudes, personality, perception, learning, and stress management, managers can understand and lead employees and colleagues through many workplace challenges. This chapter introduces basic principles of organizational behavior in each of these areas.

Organizational Behavior

organizational behavior

An interdisciplinary field dedicated to the study of how individuals and groups tend to act in organizations.

Organizational behavior, commonly called OB, is an interdisciplinary field dedicated to the study of human attitudes, behavior, and performance in organizations. OB draws concepts from many disciplines, including psychology, sociology, cultural anthropology, industrial engineering, economics, ethics, and vocational counseling, as well as the discipline of management. The concepts and principles of organizational behavior are important to managers because in every organization human beings ultimately make the decisions that control how the organization will acquire and use resources. Those people may cooperate with, compete with, support, or undermine one another. Their beliefs and feelings about themselves, their coworkers, and the organization shape what they do and how well they do it. People can distract the organization from its strategy by engaging in conflict and misunderstandings, or they can pool their diverse talents and perspectives to accomplish much more as a group than they could ever do as individuals.

By understanding what causes people to behave as they do, managers can exercise leadership to achieve positive outcomes. They can foster behaviors such as **organizational citizenship**, that is, work behavior that goes beyond job requirements and contributes as needed to the organization's success. An employee demonstrates organizational citizenship by being helpful to coworkers and customers, doing extra work when necessary, and looking for ways to improve products and procedures. Managers can encourage organizational citizenship by applying their knowledge of human behavior in many ways, such as selecting people with positive attitudes and personalities, helping them see how they can contribute, and enabling them to learn from and cope with work-

organizational citizenship

Work behavior that goes beyond job requirements and contributes as needed to the organization's success.

place challenges. Andy Law encourages not only organizational citizenship within his company, St. Luke's, but also corporate citizenship toward society, as described in the Focus on Ethics box.

Attitudes

Most students have probably heard the expression that someone "has an attitude problem," which means there is some consistent quality about the person that affects his or her behavior in a negative way. An employee with an attitude problem might be hard to get along with, might constantly gripe and cause problems, and might persistently resist new ideas. We all seem to know intuitively what an attitude is, but we do not consciously think about how strongly attitudes affect behavior. Defined formally, an **attitude** is an evaluation—either positive or negative—that predisposes a person to act in a certain way. Understanding

attitude

A cognitive and affective evaluation that predisposes a person to act in a certain way.

FOCUS ON ETHICS

St. Luke's

Integrity is not typically expected in advertising. A recent Gallup poll placed advertising near the bottom of ethical professions, with only congresspeople and used-car salespeople ranking lower. A relatively new advertising agency in London is out to change that. St. Luke's offers a completely new model of what it believes the industry must come to be known for: "honest, ethical advertising that represents a company's Total Role in Society (TRS)," which includes an evaluation of the organization among the totality of its stakeholders: employees, customers, shareholders, the community, the environment, vendors, competitors, the families of employees, and so on.

This is partly manifested in the corporate mission statement: "Profit is like health; you need it, but it is not what you live for." The founders' ideas of a company's TRS include a company seeing itself as a force for social good, with the purpose to "benefit society," where profits are a requirement, but not the purpose, and where a company must come to be seen as a "trusted social citizen" before it will be able to sell or advertise productively. These ideas cannot be dismissed as naive when they are expressed by the fastest-growing advertising agency in London, with first-year revenues at $72 million. Though geared toward the future, some of the company's inspiration can be traced back thousands of years to Aristotle and the Gospel of St. Luke.

The agency preaches and practices a gospel of total ethics and common ownership. St. Luke's employees own the company—all of it; every employee holds equal shares, from the person who answers the telephone to the creative director.

St. Luke's was once the London office of Chiat/Day, the agency known for the Energizer bunny. When communications conglomerate Omnicom bought the struggling agency

and announced plans to merge Chiat/Day with a larger agency, Andy Law, managing director, bought the London office and then called in all the employees to let them decide their own future. The employees' response was that they wanted to work for a company that embodied their own personal values. Further, they wanted a concrete mechanism for universal commitment and contribution.

The physical layout of St. Luke's reflects the company's cultural values. Employees have traded desks and personal work spaces for "brand rooms"—large, client-specific, glass-enclosed conference rooms where teams meet for each account to generate ideas and store work-in-progress. Between meetings and visits to clients, employees take a seat at any one of dozens of computers that they share communally. Employees eat lunch together, play Ping-Pong™, or crawl out the window to enjoy a moment of sunshine on the rooftop. There are no trophies or awards lining the walls and shelves at St. Luke's. The company has never won any advertising awards for the simple reason that it refuses to enter any contests.

In a recent survey asking London's art directors and copywriters where they would most like to work, tiny St. Luke's came in third. Law believes people want to work for a company they can be proud of, and he and his employees have created a distinctive culture at St. Luke's that emphasizes self-motivation, personal growth, and integrity in all actions. "We've created this company to live beyond us," says Law. "We're just renting resources. Remember that we're a collective here—everybody is equal. What's disappeared are ego and greed. . . ."

SOURCE: Sarah Ellison, "UK Ad Titan St. Luke's Is Still Different," *The Wall Street Journal* (December 6, 2000); Stevan Alburty, "The Ad Agency to End All Ad Agencies," *Fast Company* (December–January 1997), 116–124.

employee attitudes is important to managers because attitudes determine how people perceive the work environment, interact with others, and behave on the job. A person who has the attitude "I love my work; it's challenging and fun" probably will tackle work-related problems cheerfully, while one who comes to work with the attitude "I hate my job" is not likely to exhibit much enthusiasm or commitment to solving problems. Managers strive to develop and reinforce positive attitudes among employees.

Managers should recognize that negative attitudes can be both the result of underlying problems in the workplace as well as a contributor to forthcoming problems.[2] For example, top executives at Federated Department Stores appointed a young, computer whiz-kid as chief operating officer for its e-commerce division. Older managers with years of experience in retailing had negative attitudes about this guy they considered still wet behind the ears, while the new COO had negative attitudes about older workers, whom he considered slow to accept new ideas or learn new methods. Soon, experienced managers started leaving the company. Federated's top leaders realized that the company needed to do a better job of handling generational diversity, as discussed in the previous chapter, to help employees develop more positive attitudes.[3]

Components of Attitudes

One important step for managers is recognizing and understanding the *components* of attitudes, which is particularly important when attempting to change attitudes.

Behavioral scientists consider attitudes to have three components: cognitions (thoughts), affect (feelings), and behavior.[4] The cognitive component of an attitude includes the beliefs, opinions, and information the person has about the object of the attitude, such as knowledge of what a job entails and opinions about personal abilities. The affective component is the person's emotions or feelings about the object of the attitude, such as enjoying or hating a job. The behavioral component of an attitude is the person's intention to behave toward the object of the attitude in a certain way. Exhibit 11.1 illustrates the three components of a positive attitude toward one's job. The cognitive element is the conscious thought that "my job is interesting and challenging." The affective element is the feeling that "I love this job." These, in turn, are related to the behavioral component—an employee might choose to arrive at work early because he or she is happy with the job.

Often, when we think about attitudes, we focus on the cognitive component. However, it is important for managers to remember the other components as well. When people feel strongly about something, the affective component may predispose them to act, no matter what someone does to change their opinions. For example, if an employee is passionate about a new idea, that employee may go to great lengths to implement it. Likewise, an employee who is furious about being asked to work overtime on his birthday may act on that anger—by failing to cooperate, lashing out at coworkers, or even quitting—no matter what arguments the employee's manager presents about the need to work. In cases such as these, effective leadership includes addressing the affect (emotions) associated with the attitude. Are employees so excited that their judgment may be clouded, or so discouraged that they have given up trying? If nothing else, the manager probably needs to be aware of situations that involve strong emotions and give employees a chance to vent their feelings safely. Leaders, too, can allow emotions to cloud their judgment, as

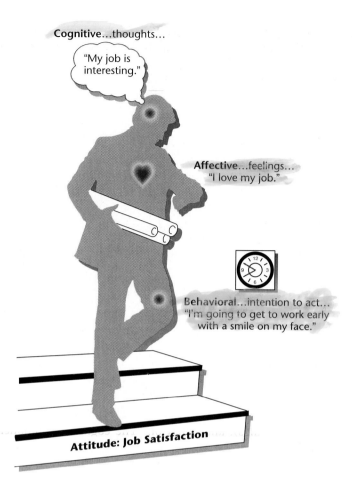

EXHIBIT *11.1*

Components of an Attitude

Umang Gupta did when he started his company. He paid dearly for his overrated self-assessment, as described in the Digital, Inc. box.

As a general rule, changing one component of an attitude—cognitions, affect, or behavior—can contribute to an overall change in attitude. Suppose a manager concludes that some employees have the attitude that the manager should make all the decisions affecting the department, but the manager prefers that employees assume more decision-making responsibility. To change the underlying attitude, the manager would consider whether to educate employees about the areas in which they can make good decisions (changing the cognitive component), build enthusiasm with pep talks about the satisfaction of employee empowerment (changing the affective component), or simply insist that employees make their own decisions (behavioral component) with the expectation that, once they experience the advantages of decision-making authority, they will begin to like it.

Work-Related Attitudes

The attitudes of most interest to managers are those related to work, especially attitudes that influence how well employees perform. To lead employees effectively, managers logically seek to cultivate the kinds of attitudes that are associated with high performance. Two attitudes that might relate to high performance are satisfaction with one's job and commitment to the organization.

DIGITAL, INC.

Gupta Corporation

Umang Gupta had a dream. Ever since moving from India to the U.S. in 1980, he wanted to start his own computer company. Realizing that Silicon Valley was a good place for training, he first worked at IBM and then moved to the start-up Oracle, helping to write its business plan.

But his dream persisted, and in 1984 he launched Gupta Corp., sparsely financed from fees of early customers, such as Lotus Corp. This is a riskier strategy than venture-capital financing, because it demands a lengthy technological lead in order to withstand competition from later and better-financed rivals. But the strategy worked—for a while, anyway. Gupta's vision of creating software to manage databases brought in enough revenue to peak at $400 million, allowing Gupta to have a net worth of $100 million "for a few days." He had a mission to change the world, and, because of the power of his mission, he was cramming in as many meetings as he could each day.

Then the bottom fell out. Powerful, new, well-financed competitors jumped into the market and Gupta Corp. suffered through seven quarters of losses. Stock prices plummeted. Gupta resigned as CEO and the company changed its name to Centura Software.

Gupta now realizes he made a number of mistakes. First, he was undercapitalized and could not withstand later compe-

tition. Then he rode the company on only one technology, making it too vulnerable. But the root of these problems, he says, was his own ego, or the "hubris danger zone." He felt so certain of his own ideas that he did not listen enough to others. One result of that was that he did not anticipate the importance of the Internet. "The company wasn't a company, but a cause. We were going to change the world," he said. That attitude can motivate young employees, but it also can blind leaders and employees to market realities.

In his new position as CEO of Keynote Systems, which measures the performance of commercial Web sites, he is careful to construct the business around several technologies and technological services. He also delegates strategic information-gathering to a number of employees, who keep their minds and eyes open to new developments outside. Rather than cramming meetings together, he now blocks out time to roam the halls and brainstorm with employees. And he regularly attends venture capital conferences. "I'm making sure my peripheral vision remains intact so I'm not blindsided again," he says.

SOURCE: Bob Brown, "Q&A: Gupta Touts Network Services," *Network World* (April 8, 2002), 31–32; Hal Lancaster, "A Founder's Lesson: Market Reality Matters More than a Mission," *The Wall Street Journal* (November 2, 1999), B1.

---

job satisfaction
A positive attitude toward one's job.

Job Satisfaction. A positive attitude toward one's job is called **job satisfaction**. In general, people experience this attitude when their work matches their needs and interests, when working conditions and rewards (such as pay) are satisfactory, and when the employees like their coworkers.

Many managers believe job satisfaction is important because they think satisfied employees will do better work. In fact, research shows that the link between satisfaction and performance is generally small and is affected by other factors.[5] The importance of satisfaction varies according to the amount of control the employee has; an employee doing routine tasks may produce about the same output no matter how he or she feels about the job. However, an internal study at Sears recently found a clear link between employee satisfaction, customer satisfaction, and revenue. In particular, employees' attitudes about whether their workloads were manageable and well-organized ranked among the top-10 indicators of company performance.[6]

Managers of today's knowledge workers often rely on job satisfaction to keep motivation and enthusiasm for the organization high. Organizations don't want to lose talented, highly skilled workers. In addition, most managers care about their employees and simply want them to feel good about their work— and almost everyone prefers being around people who have positive attitudes. Managers play an important role in whether employees have positive or negative attitudes toward their jobs.[7]

Organizational Commitment. Another important attitude is **organizational commitment**, which is loyalty to and heavy involvement in the organization. An employee with a high degree of organizational commitment is likely to say *we* when talking about the organization. Such a person tries to contribute to the organization's success and wishes to remain with the organization. This attitude is common at the A.W. Chesterton Company, a Massachusetts company that produces mechanical seals and pumps. CEO James D. Chesterton takes a personal interest in his employees, and they in turn are very loyal to him and to the organization. When two Chesterton pumps that supply water on Navy ship USS *John F. Kennedy* failed on a Saturday night just before the ship's scheduled departure, Todd Robinson, the leader of the team that produces the seals, swung into action. He and his fiancée, who also works for Chesterton, worked through the night to make new seals and deliver them to be installed before the ship left port.[8]

Most managers want to enjoy the benefits of loyal, committed employees, including low turnover and willingness to do more than the job's basic requirements. Organizational commitment is especially important in a tight labor market which forces employers to compete harder to attract and keep good workers. Also, in recent years many employees have expressed more distrust and less commitment to their employers. As shown in Exhibit 11.2, a survey of 450,000 employees found that although most executives believe employees respect management, their employees' attitudes are in fact quite different.[9] The percentage of workers who say management is respected by employees has been steadily declining since 1991. In the most recent available year of the survey (1997), about 50 percent of employees reported that management generally is respected, as compared with about 70 percent of top managers who believed that.

Managers can take action to promote organizational commitment by keeping employees informed, giving them a say in decisions, providing the necessary training and other resources that enable them to succeed, treating them fairly, and offering rewards they value. For example, recent studies suggest that employee commitment in today's workplace is strongly correlated with initiatives and benefits that help employees to balance their work time and personal lives.[10]

organizational commitment
Loyalty to and heavy involvement in one's organization.

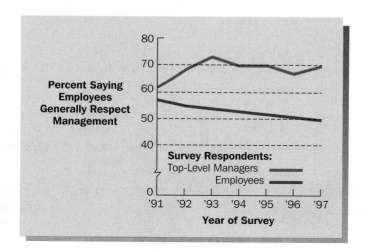

Percent Saying Employees Generally Respect Management

Survey Respondents:
Top-Level Managers
Employees

Year of Survey

EXHIBIT 11.2

Changing Attitudes: Employees' Respect for Management

SOURCE: Adapted from Aaron Bernstein, "We Want You to Stay. Really," *Business Week* (June 22, 1998), 67–68+ (citing data from an annual survey of 450,000 employees and managers by the International Survey Research Corporation).

Conflicts among Attitudes

Sometimes a person may discover that his or her attitudes conflict with one another or are not reflected in his or her behavior. For example, a person's high level of organizational commitment might conflict with that person's commitment to family members. If employees routinely work evenings and weekends, their long hours and dedication to the job may conflict with their belief that family ties are important. This can create a state of **cognitive dissonance**, a psychological discomfort that occurs when individuals recognize inconsistencies in their own attitudes and behaviors.[11] The theory of cognitive dissonance, developed by social psychologist Leon Festinger in the 1950s, says that people want to behave in accordance with their attitudes and usually will take corrective action to alleviate the dissonance and achieve balance.

In the case of working overtime, people who control their hours might restructure responsibilities so that they have time for both work and family. In contrast, those who are unable to restructure workloads might develop an unfavorable attitude toward the employer, reducing their organizational commitment. They might resolve their dissonance by saying they would like to spend more time with their kids but their unreasonable employer demands that they work too many hours.

cognitive dissonance

A condition in which two attitudes or a behavior and an attitude conflict.

Perception

perception

The cognitive process people use to make sense out of the environment by selecting, organizing, and interpreting information.

Another critical aspect of understanding behavior is perception. **Perception** is the cognitive process people use to make sense out of the environment by selecting, organizing, and interpreting information from the environment. Attitudes affect perceptions, and vice versa. For example, a person might have developed the attitude that managers are insensitive and arrogant, based on a pattern of perceiving arrogant and insensitive behavior from managers over a period of time. If the person moves to a new job, this attitude will continue to affect the way he or she perceives superiors in the new environment, even though managers in the new workplace might take great pains to understand and respond to employees' needs.

Because of individual differences in attitudes, personality, values, interests, and so forth, people often "see" the same thing in different ways. A class that is boring to one student might be fascinating to another. One student might perceive an assignment to be challenging and stimulating, whereas another might find it a silly waste of time. Referring back to the topic of diversity discussed in Chapter 10, many African Americans perceive that blacks are regularly discriminated against, whereas many white employees perceive that blacks are given special opportunities in the workplace.[12]

We can think of perception as a step-by-step process, as shown in Exhibit 11.3. First, we observe information (sensory data) from the environment through our senses: taste, smell, hearing, sight, and touch. Next, our mind screens the data and will select only the items we will process further. Third,

EXHIBIT 11.3

The Perception Process

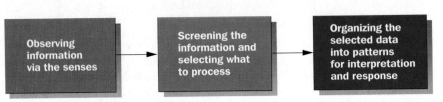

we organize the selected data into meaningful patterns for interpretation and response. Most differences in perception among people at work are related to how they select and organize sensory data.

Perceptual Selectivity

We all are aware of our environment, but not everything in it is equally important to our perception of it. We tune in to some data (e.g., a familiar voice off in the distance) and tune out other data (e.g., paper shuffling next to us). People are bombarded by so much sensory data that it is impossible to process it all. The brain's solution is to run the data through a perceptual filter that retains some parts (selective attention) and eliminates others. **Perceptual selectivity** is the process by which individuals screen and select the various objects and stimuli that vie for their attention. Certain stimuli catch their attention, and others do not.

People typically focus on stimuli that satisfy their needs and that are consistent with their attitudes, values, and personality. For example, an employee who has a need for positive feedback on her performance to feel good about herself may pick up on positive statements made by her supervisor but tune out most negative comments. A supervisor could use this understanding to tailor his feedback in a positive way to help the employee improve her work. The influence of needs on perception has been studied in laboratory experiments and found to have a strong impact on what people perceive.[13]

Characteristics of the stimuli itself also affect perceptual selectivity. People tend to notice stimuli that stand out against other stimuli or that are more intense than surrounding stimuli. Examples would be a loud noise in a quiet room or a bright red dress at a party where most women are wearing basic black. People also tend to notice things that are familiar to them, such as a familiar voice in a crowd, as well as things that are new or different from their previous experiences. In addition, *primacy* and *recency* are important to perceptual selectivity. People pay relatively greater attention to sensory data that occur toward the beginning of an event or toward the end. Primacy supports the old truism that first impressions really do count, whether it be on a job interview, meeting a date's parents, or participating in a new social group. Recency reflects the reality that the last impression might be a lasting impression. For example, Malaysian Airlines has discovered its value in building customer loyalty. A woman traveling with a nine-month-old might find the flight itself an exhausting blur, but one such traveler enthusiastically told people for years how Malaysian Airlines flight attendants helped her with baggage collection and ground transportation.[14]

As these examples show, perceptual selectivity is a complex filtering process. Managers can use an understanding of perceptual selectivity to obtain clues about why one person "sees" things differently from others, and they can apply the principles to their own communications and actions, especially when they want to attract or focus attention.

Perceptual Distortions

Once people have selected the sensory data to be perceived, they begin grouping the data into recognizable patterns. Perceptual organization is the process by which people organize or categorize stimuli according to their own frame of reference. Of particular concern in the work environment are **perceptual distortions**,

perceptual selectivity

The process by which individuals screen and select the various stimuli that vie for their attention.

perceptual distortions

Errors in perceptual judgment that arise from inaccuracies in any part of the perception process.

errors in perceptual judgment that arise from inaccuracies in any part of the perceptual process.

Some types of errors are so common that managers should become familiar with them. These include stereotyping, the halo effect, projection, and perceptual defense. Managers who recognize these perceptual distortions can better adjust their perceptions to more closely match objective reality.

Stereotyping is the tendency to assign an individual to a group or broad category (e.g., female, black, elderly or male, white, disabled) and then to attribute widely held generalizations about the group to the individual. Thus, someone meets a new colleague, sees he is in a wheelchair, assigns him to the category "physically disabled," and attributes to this colleague generalizations she believes about people with disabilities, which may include a belief that he is less able than other coworkers. However, the person's inability to walk should not be seen as indicative of lesser abilities in other areas. Indeed, the assumption of limitations may not only offend him, it also prevents the person making the stereotypical judgment from benefiting from the many ways in which this person can contribute. Stereotyping prevents people from truly knowing those they classify in this way. In addition, negative stereotypes can prevent talented people from advancing in an organization and fully contributing their talents to the organization's success. Dr. Bill Thomas is creating a new kind of nursing home. Seeking to overcome stereotypes toward the elderly, he sees these perceptions contributing to poor living conditions in the homes, as described in the Focus on Collaboration box.

The **halo effect** occurs when the perceiver develops an overall impression of a person or situation based on one attribute, either favorable or unfavorable. In

stereotyping

The tendency to assign an individual to a group or broad category and then attribute generalizations about the group to the individual.

halo effect

An overall impression of a person or situation based on one attribute, either favorable or unfavorable.

FOCUS ON COLLABORATION

Eden Alternative

Does anyone want to leave his home and live in a nursing home?" asks physician-actor-novelist and Harvard grad Dr. Bill Thomas. The question is rhetorical; and the answer is almost always a resounding "NO." "That's why we're turning the industry upside down," says Thomas. Believing humans are not meant to live in cold, impersonal institutions, but rather in an Eden-like garden designed for growth, Thomas first wrote about his vision of nurturing nursing homes that respect "elders," and then took his one-man show on the road in 1999. Finding that nursing home patients suffer from the three plagues of boredom, helplessness, and loneliness, Thomas and his wife Jude decided to put their ideas into practical action and launched a new nursing home venture, Eden Alternative.

The next step was to turn the Thomas's farm into a nonprofit organization that has so far "Edenized" 300 nursing homes: turned them into warm and nurturing environments, with more satisfied patients—and a better bottom line. Several states are so impressed that they have offered grants to Eden, paid for by fines levied on poorly run institutions for the elderly.

Ideas about nursing homes are entrenched, so change takes time and involves huge organizational and social

reforms regarding the care of elders, priorities for resources, and general habits in the homes. For example, Eden encourages input from the residents and staff on how to make a better facility. Such behaviors are difficult for more traditional administrators to swallow.

Thomas found that Edenizing works better in some environments than others: "Warm" cultures are more open to change, because residents and employees have trust in and generosity for one another, while "cold" cultures are characterized by cynicism and pessimism. Eden surveys new nursing homes for their "temperature," and then proceeds to "warm the soil" by having administrators hold potlucks where no work is discussed and employees are encouraged to begin doing good deeds for one another. "You open people's minds by opening their hearts," Thomas says.

When not in his office, Thomas is out spreading the word about Eden's philosophy, realizing that changes in nursing homes will be a long time in coming. While trying to be a realist, he is still the optimist: As his business card states, "It can be different."

SOURCE: Chuck Salter, "(Not) the Same Old Story," *Fast Company* (February 2002), 78–84.

other words, a halo blinds the perceiver to other attributes that should be used in generating a more complete assessment. The halo effect can play a significant role in performance appraisal. For example, a person with an outstanding attendance record may be assessed as responsible, industrious, and highly productive; another person with less-than-average attendance may be assessed as a poor performer. Either assessment may be true, but it is the manager's job to be sure the assessment is based on complete information about all job-related attributes and not just his or her preferences for good attendance.

Projection is the tendency of perceivers to see their own personal traits in other people; that is, they project their own needs, feelings, values, and attitudes into their judgment of others. For example, a manager who is achievement oriented might assume that subordinates are as well. This might cause the manager to restructure jobs to be less routine and more challenging, without regard for employees' actual satisfaction. The best guards against errors based on projection are self-awareness and empathy.

Perceptual defense is the tendency of perceivers to protect themselves against ideas, objects, or people that are threatening. People perceive things that are satisfying and pleasant but tend to disregard things that are disturbing and unpleasant. In essence, people develop blind spots in the perceptual process so that negative sensory data do not hurt them. For example, the director of a nonprofit educational organization in Tennessee hated dealing with conflict because he had grown up with parents who constantly argued and often put him in the middle of their arguments. The director consistently overlooked discord among staff members until things would reach a boiling point. When the blow-up occurred, the director would be shocked and dismayed, because he had truly perceived that everything was going smoothly among the staff. Recognizing perceptual blind spots can help people develop a clearer picture of reality.

projection
The tendency to see one's own personal traits in other people.

perceptual defense
The tendency of perceivers to protect themselves by disregarding ideas, objects, or people that are threatening to them.

Attributions

As people organize what they perceive, they often draw conclusions about the stimuli. For example, stereotyping involves assigning a number of traits to a person. Among the judgments people make as part of the perceptual process are attributions. **Attributions** are judgments about what caused a person's behavior—something about the person or something about the situation. An *internal attribution* says characteristics of the person led to the behavior ("My boss yelled at me because he's impatient and doesn't listen"). An *external attribution* says something about the situation caused the person's behavior ("My boss yelled at me because I missed the deadline and the customer is upset"). Attributions are important because they help people decide how to handle a situation. In the case of the boss yelling, a person who blames the yelling on the boss's personality will view the boss as the problem and might cope by avoiding the boss. In contrast, someone who blames the yelling on the situation might try to help prevent such situations in the future.

Social scientists have studied the attributions people make and identified three factors that influence whether an attribution will be external or internal.[15] These three factors are illustrated in Exhibit 11.4:

attributions
Judgments about what caused a person's behavior—either characteristics of the person or of the situation.

1. *Distinctiveness*—whether the behavior is unusual for that person (in contrast to a person displaying the same kind of behavior in many situations). If the behavior is distinctive, the perceiver probably will make an *external* attribution.

EXHIBIT 11.4

EXHIBIT *11.4*

Factors Influencing Whether Attributions Are Internal or External

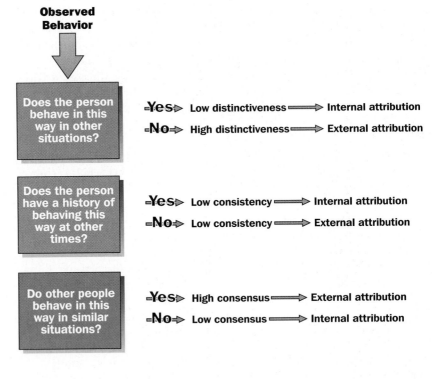

2. *Consistency*—whether the person being observed has a history of behaving in the same way. People generally make *internal* attributions about consistent behavior.

3. *Consensus*—whether other people tend to respond to similar situations in the same way. A person who has observed others handle similar situations in the same way will likely make an external attribution; that is, it will seem that the situation produces the type of behavior observed.

In addition to these general rules, people tend to have biases that they apply when making attributions. When evaluating others, we tend to underestimate the influence of external factors and overestimate the influence of internal factors. This tendency is called the **fundamental attribution error**. For example, when someone has been promoted to chief executive officer, people generally consider the characteristics of the person that allowed him or her to achieve the promotion. In reality, however, the selection of that person may have been heavily influenced by external factors, such as business conditions creating a need for someone with a strong financial or marketing background at that particular time.

Another bias that distorts attributions involves attributions we make about our own behavior. People tend to overestimate the contribution of internal factors to their successes and overestimate the contribution of external factors to their failures. This tendency, called the **self-serving bias**, means people give themselves too much credit for what they do well and give external forces too much blame when they fail. Thus, if your manager says you don't communicate well enough, and you think your manager doesn't listen well enough, the truth may actually lie somewhere in between.

fundamental attribution error

The tendency to underestimate the influence of external factors on another's behavior and to overestimate the influence of internal factors.

self-serving bias

The tendency to overestimate the contribution of internal factors to one's successes and the contribution of external factors to one's failures.

Personality and Behavior

Another area of particular interest to organizational behavior is personality. In the workplace, we find people whose behavior is consistently pleasant or aggressive or stubborn in a variety of situations. To explain that behavior, we may say, "He has a pleasant personality" or "She has an aggressive personality." An individual's **personality** is the set of characteristics that underlie a relatively stable pattern of behavior in response to ideas, objects, or people in the environment. Understanding an individual's personality can help managers predict how that person will act in a particular situation. Managers who appreciate the ways their employees' personalities differ have insight into what kinds of leadership behavior will be most influential.

personality
The set of characteristics that underlie a relatively stable pattern of behavior in response to ideas, objects, or people in the environment.

Personality Traits

In common usage, people think of personality in terms of traits, or relatively stable characteristics of a person. Researchers have investigated whether any traits stand up to scientific scrutiny. Although investigators have examined thousands of traits over the years, their findings have been distilled into five general dimensions that describe personality. These often are called the "Big Five" personality factors, as illustrated in Exhibit 11.5.[16] Each factor may contain a wide range of specific traits. The **Big Five personality factors** describe an individual's extroversion, agreeableness, conscientiousness, emotional stability, and openness to experience:

Big Five personality factors
Dimensions that describe an individual's extroversion, agreeableness, conscientiousness, emotional stability, and openness to experience.

1. *Extroversion.* The degree to which a person is sociable, talkative, assertive, and comfortable with interpersonal relationships.
2. *Agreeableness.* The degree to which a person is able to get along with others by being good-natured, cooperative, forgiving, understanding, and trusting.

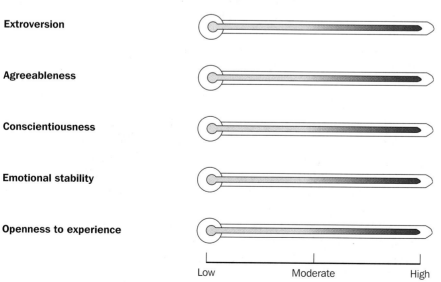

A person may have a low, moderate, or high degree of each of these factors:

Extroversion

Agreeableness

Conscientiousness

Emotional stability

Openness to experience

Low   Moderate   High

E X H I B I T 11.5

The "Big Five" Personality Factors

3. *Conscientiousness.* The degree to which a person is focused on a few goals, thus behaving in ways that are responsible, dependable, persistent, and achievement oriented.

4. *Emotional stability.* The degree to which a person is calm, enthusiastic, and secure, rather than tense, nervous, depressed, moody, or insecure.

5. *Openness to experience.* The degree to which a person has a broad range of interests and is imaginative, creative, artistically sensitive, and willing to consider new ideas.

As illustrated in the exhibit, these factors represent a continuum. That is, any individual may exhibit a low, moderate, or high degree of each quality. A person who has an extremely high degree of agreeableness would likely be described as warm, friendly, and good-natured, while one at the opposite extreme might be described as cold, rude, or hard to get along with. In general, having a moderate-to-high degree of each of the personality factors is considered desirable for a wide range of employees. In addition, certain factors may be particularly important for specific kinds of work. For example, Nancy Naatz works for Aramark, an organization that handles many transactions online, but she needs a high degree of extroversion and agreeableness to build the relationships that are critical to her success, as described in the example below. These traits might not be as important for an employee who has little need to interact with others.

ARAMARK

http://www.aramark.com

Nancy Naatz's employer, Aramark Corp., is a champion of business-to-business (B2B) e-commerce. In fact, the company uses the Internet to order more than 85 percent of the food and supplies it needs to cater special events and run cafeterias for large corporate clients. But that doesn't mean Naatz sits in a comfy chair pointing and clicking all day. She has to be comfortable not just with technology but also with meeting and talking to all kinds of people face to face. Naatz spends much of her time meeting with local food vendors or patrolling the cafeteria, talking with employees, and consulting with executives at Sears Roebuck & Co., one of Aramark's major clients. Naatz, whose title at Aramark is resident district manager, business services, has discovered that not everything can be handled online. Even in the B2B world, a smile and a handshake is still sometimes the best route to success.

Although Aramark is a Web-savvy company that uses software that allows its managers to draw from a national database of distributors to make online purchases, managers are given the freedom to do whatever it takes to make the client happy. Keeping in close touch with the needs of customers is an important aspect of the job. On Naatz's daily jaunts into the bustling Sears cafeteria she pays close attention to the length of lines at each food counter, helping her quickly zero in on employee trends and alter the menu and her food orders accordingly. Naatz frequently has to make judgment calls, something a computer cannot do. She knows that Sears executives, for example, want their formal awards dinners to be nice but not too "stuffy." She selects a menu that she believes fits well with the company's casual corporate style.

Cultivating a relationship with local or regional vendors is also an essential part of the job because clients often have special needs that can be hard to come by among the commodities of the Web. For example, Sears employees wanted sushi added to the cafeteria menu and top executives wanted fresh, New York-style bagels for their daily continental breakfasts. "When I meet with a local supplier, it's generally not because they have better pricing," Naatz says. "I often meet with them because we want to make sure we get items fresh and quick." Naatz often sizes up potential contacts with an old-fashioned face-to-face meeting before she begins the business of haggling over details, negotiating terms, and striking deals.

After Sears moved out of the Sears Tower in 1992, vendors from far and wide came to court the company in hopes of landing the food and guest services contract for the new location. The Aramark bid won. Why? Because Aramark promised to have a live human being on hand to solve problems for Sears as they arose.[17]

Many companies, including J.C. Penney, Toys 'R' Us, and the Union Pacific Railroad, use personality testing to hire, evaluate, or promote employees. For example, American MultiCinema (AMC), one of the largest theater chains in the United States, looks for front-line workers with high conscientiousness and high emotional stability.[18] Marriott Hotels looks for people who score high on conscientiousness and agreeableness because they believe these individuals will provide better service to guests.[19] Companies also use personality testing for managers. Hewlett-Packard, Dell Computer, and General Electric all put candidates for top positions through testing, interviews with psychologists, or both to see if they have the "right stuff" for the job.[20]

However, despite growing use, there is little evidence that personality tests are a valid predictor of job success. In addition, the Big Five dimensions have been criticized because they are difficult to measure precisely. Because each dimension is made up of a number of specific traits, a person might score high on some traits but low on others. For example, considering the dimension of conscientiousness, a person might score high on a trait such as dependability, but score low on achievement orientation. Furthermore, research on the Big Five has mostly been limited to the United States, so there are dangers in applying the theory cross-culturally.

Emotional Intelligence

In recent years, new insights into personality have been gained through research in the area of *emotional intelligence.* Emotional intelligence (EQ) includes five basic components:[21]

1. *Self-awareness.* The basis for all the other components; being aware of what you are feeling. People who are in touch with their feelings are better able to guide their own lives and actions.

2. *Managing emotions.* The ability to balance one's moods so that worry, anxiety, fear, or anger do not cloud thinking and get in the way of what needs to be done.

3. *Motivating oneself.* The ability to be hopeful and to persist in the face of obstacles, setbacks, and even outright failure. This ability is crucial for pursuing long-term goals. For example, MetLife found that applicants who failed the regular sales aptitude test but scored high on optimism made 21 percent more sales in their first year and 57 percent more in their second year than those who passed the sales test but scored high on pessimism.[22]

4. *Empathy.* Being able to put yourself in someone else's shoes, to recognize what others are feeling without them needing to tell you. People frequently

© Marc Asnin—Corbis SABA

Harvard Law School's Program on Negotiation offers seminars that help small business owners develop their emotional intelligence and be more effective leaders. "People [wrongly] assume that you check your feelings at the door when you go to work," says Sheila Heen, a Harvard Law School lecturer. The program offers training in topics such as Improving Your Listening Skills, Managing Anger at Work, Managing Your Feelings, and Getting Straight on Purposes. In the photo, participants practice expressing their emotions without becoming "emotional."

don't say how they feel in words, but rather in tone of voice, body language, and facial expression.

5. *Social skill.* The ability to connect to others, build positive relationships, respond to the emotions of others, and influence others.

Studies have found a positive relationship between job performance and high degrees of emotional intelligence in a variety of jobs. Numerous organizations, including the U.S. Air Force and Canada Life, have used EQ tests to measure such things as self-awareness, ability to empathize, and capacity to build positive relationships.[23] EQ seems to be particularly important for jobs that require a high degree of social interaction, which includes managers, who are responsible for influencing others and building positive attitudes and relationships in the organization. For example, Paul Wieand became president of Bucks County Bank at the age of 33, then masterminded mergers that tripled its size and turned it into a major regional institution. Yet only a few years later, he was forced to resign. Wieand's arrogance and insensitivity led to such poor morale and negative attitudes that the board felt he was a threat to the company's continued success. After he was forced out, Weiand began reading extensively to help him understand why running a bank was so easy intellectually but so hard emotionally. Eventually, he developed a new philosophy of management based on the belief that everyone "wants the same things in life: to be recognized, to be cared for, and to be given an opportunity to grow."[24] Weiand's personal turnaround illustrates an important point: Emotional intelligence is not an in-born personality characteristic, but something that can be learned and developed throughout one's lifetime.[25]

At times of great change or crisis, managers need a higher EQ level to help employees cope with the anxiety and stress they may be experiencing. For example, following the September 11, 2001, terrorist attacks in the United States and amid continuing fears of anthrax, a declining economy, and aviation safety, an important role for managers was meeting the psychological and emotional needs of employees. The Focus on Skills box outlines some elements of emotional intelligence that are particularly important in times of crisis.

Attitudes and Behaviors Influenced by Personality

An individual's personality influences a wide variety of work-related attitudes and behaviors. Among those that are of particular interest to managers are locus of control, authoritarianism, Machiavellianism, and problem-solving styles.

Locus of Control. People differ in terms of what they tend to attribute as the cause of their success or failure. Their **locus of control** defines whether they place the primary responsibility within themselves or on outside forces.[26] Some people believe that their actions can strongly influence what happens to them. They feel in control of their own fate. These individuals have a high *internal*

locus of control

The tendency to place the primary responsibility for one's success or failure either within oneself (internally) or on outside forces (externally).

FOCUS ON SKILLS

What's Your Crisis EQ?

The September 11, 2001, terrorist attacks on the Pentagon and the World Trade Center left lingering psychological and emotional damage in workplaces all across the United States and even the rest of the world. Numerous companies, some in places far removed from the scene of the actual attacks, called upon crisis counselors to help their employees cope with the trauma. However, outside counseling is not enough in such an environment. Managers also need the skills to help people deal with their emotions and return to a more normal work routine. Although managers cannot take the place of professional counselors, they can use patience, flexibility, and understanding to assist people through a crisis. Here are some important elements of crisis EQ for managers:

- Be visible and provide as much up-to-date, accurate information as possible about what is going on in the company and the industry. Rumor control is critical.

- Find simple ways to get employees together. Order pizza for the entire staff. Invite telecommuters to come in to the office so they can connect with others and have a chance to share their emotions.

- Give employees room to be human. It is natural for people to feel anger and other strong emotions, so allow those feelings to be expressed as long as they are not directed at other employees.

- Publicize the company's charitable endeavors and make employees aware of the various opportunities both within and outside the organization to volunteer and donate to charity.

- Thank employees in person and with handwritten notes when they go above and beyond the call of duty during a difficult time.

- Recognize that routine, structured work can help people heal. Postpone major, long-term projects and decisions to the extent possible and break work into shorter, more manageable tasks. Listen to employees and determine what they need to help them return to a normal work life.

- Provide professional counseling services for people who need it. Those with a history of alcohol abuse, trouble at home, or previous mental or emotional problems are especially at risk, but anyone who has trouble gradually returning to his or her previous level of work may need outside counseling.

SOURCES: Based on Matthew Boyle, "Nothing Really Matters," *Fortune* (October 15, 2001), 261–264; and Sue Shellenbarger, "Readers Face Dilemma Over How Far to Alter Post-Attack Workplace," (Work & Family column), *The Wall Street Journal* (October 31, 2001), B1.

locus of control. Other people believe that events in their lives occur because of chance, luck, or outside people and events. They feel more like pawns of their fate. These individuals have a high *external* locus of control. Many top leaders of e-commerce and high-tech organizations exhibit a high internal locus of control. These managers have to cope with rapid change and uncertainty associated with Internet business. They must believe that they and their employees can counter the negative impact of outside forces and events. John Chambers, CEO of Cisco Systems, is a good example. Despite today's tough economy and a drastically diminished stock price, Chambers has not lost his belief that Cisco can defeat any challenge thrown its way.[27] A person with a high external locus of control would likely feel overwhelmed trying to make the rapid decisions and changes needed to keep pace with the industry, particularly in the current environment of uncertainty.

Research on locus of control has shown real differences in behavior across a wide range of settings. People with an internal locus of control are easier to motivate because they believe the rewards are the result of their behavior. They are better able to handle complex information and problem solving, are more achievement oriented, but are also more independent and therefore more difficult to lead. On the other hand, people with an external locus of control are harder to motivate, less involved in their jobs, more likely to blame others when faced with a poor performance evaluation, but more compliant and conforming and, therefore, easier to lead.[28]

The questionnaire below is designed to measure locus-of-control beliefs. Researchers using this questionnaire in a study of college students found a mean of 51.8 for men and 52.2 for women, with a standard deviation of 6 for each. The higher your score on this questionnaire, the more you tend to believe that you are generally responsible for what happens to you; in other words, higher scores are associated with internal locus of control. Low scores are associated with external locus of control. Scoring low indicates that you tend to believe that forces beyond your control, such as powerful other people, fate, or chance, are responsible for what happens to you.

For each of these 10 questions, indicate the extent to which you agree or disagree using the following scale:

1 = strongly disagree   5 = slightly agree
2 = disagree   6 = agree
3 = slightly disagree   7 = strongly agree
4 = neither disagree nor agree

_____ 1. When I get what I want, it is usually because I worked hard for it.
_____ 2. When I make plans, I am almost certain to make them work.
_____ 3. I prefer games involving some luck over games requiring pure skill.
_____ 4. I can learn almost anything if I set my mind to it.
_____ 5. My major accomplishments are entirely due to my hard work and ability.
_____ 6. I usually don't set goals, because I have a hard time following through on them.
_____ 7. Competition discourages excellence.
_____ 8. Often people get ahead just by being lucky.
_____ 9. On any sort of exam or competition, I like to know how well I do relative to everyone else.
_____ 10. It's pointless to keep working on something that's too difficult for me.

To determine your score, reverse the values you selected for questions 3, 6, 7, 8, and 10 (1 = 7, 2 = 6, 3 = 5, 4 = 4, 5 = 3, 6 = 2, 7 = 1). For example, if you strongly disagree with the statement in question 3, you would have given it a value of 1. Change this value to a 7. Reverse the scores in a similar manner for questions 6, 7, 8, and 10. Now add the point values from all 10 questions together.

Your score: _____

EXHIBIT 11.6

Measuring Locus of Control

SOURCE: Adapted from J. M. Burger, *Personality: Theory and Research* (Belmont, Calif.: Wadsworth, 1986), 400–401, cited in D. Hellriegel, J. W. Slocum, Jr., and R. W. Woodman, *Organizational Behavior*, 6th ed. (St. Paul, Minn.: West, 1992), 97–100. Original Source: "Sphere-Specific Measures of Perceived Control," by D. L. Paulhus, *Journal of Personality and Social Psychology*, 44, 1253–1265.

Do you believe luck plays an important role in your life, or do you feel that you control your own fate? To find out more about your locus of control, read the instructions and complete the questionnaire in Exhibit 11.6.

authoritarianism

The belief that power and status differences *should* exist within the organization.

Authoritarianism. Authoritarianism is the belief that power and status differences *should* exist within the organization.[29] Individuals high in authoritarianism tend to be concerned with power and toughness, obey recognized authority above them, stick to conventional values, critically judge others, and oppose the use of subjective feelings. The degree to which managers possess authoritarianism will influence how they wield and share power. The degree to which employees possess authoritarianism will influence how they react to their managers. If a manager and employees differ in their degree of authoritarianism, the manager may have difficulty leading effectively. The trend toward empowerment and shifts in expectations among younger employees for more equitable relationships have contributed to a decline in strict authoritarianism in many organizations. The shift can be seen in the National Football League, where a rising number of coaches put more emphasis on communication and building relationships than on ruling with an iron hand. Coaches like Steve Mariucci (San Francisco 49ers), Tony Dungy (Indianapolis Colts), and Jeff Fisher (Tennessee Titans) are aware that today's players have different expectations than those of previous generations. "This is not old Rome with gladiators," says San Francisco's Mariucci. "This is modern-day football. . . . If you cannot relate to today's player, you are through as a coach."[30]

Machiavellianism. Another personality dimension that is helpful in understanding work behavior is **Machiavellianism**, which is characterized by the acquisition of power and the manipulation of other people for purely personal gain. Machiavellianism is named after Niccolo Machiavelli, a sixteenth-century author who wrote *The Prince,* a book for noblemen of the day on how to acquire and use power.[31] Psychologists have developed instruments to measure a person's Machiavellianism (Mach) orientation.[32] Research shows that high Machs are predisposed to being pragmatic, capable of lying to achieve personal goals, more likely to win in win-lose situations, and more likely to persuade than be persuaded.[33]

Different situations may require people who exhibit one or the other type of behavior. In loosely structured situations, high Machs actively take control, while low Machs accept the direction given by others. Low Machs thrive in highly structured situations, while high Machs perform in a detached, disinterested way. High Machs are particularly good in jobs that require bargaining skills or that involve substantial rewards for winning.[34]

Problem-Solving Styles. Managers also need to understand that individuals differ in the way they go about gathering and evaluating information for problem solving and decision making. Psychologist Carl Jung has identified four functions related to this process: sensation, intuition, thinking, and feeling.[35] According to Jung, gathering information and evaluating information are separate activities. People gather information either by *sensation* or *intuition,* but not by both simultaneously. Sensation-type people would rather work with known facts and hard data and prefer routine and order in gathering information. Intuitive-type people would rather look for possibilities than work with facts and prefer solving new problems and using abstract concepts.

Information evaluation involves making judgments about the information a person has gathered. People evaluate information by *thinking* or *feeling.* These represent the extremes in orientation. Thinking-type individuals base their judgments on impersonal analysis, using reason and logic rather than personal values or emotional aspects of the situation. Feeling-type individuals base their judgments more on personal feelings such as harmony and tend to make decisions that result in approval from others.

According to Jung, only one of the four functions—sensation, intuition, thinking, or feeling—is dominant in an individual. However, the dominant function usually is backed up by one of the functions from the other set of paired opposites. Exhibit 11.7 shows the four problem-solving styles that result from these matchups, as well as occupations that people with each style tend to prefer.

Studies show that the sensation-thinking combination characterizes many managers in Western industrialized societies. However, as shown in Exhibit 11.7, the intuitive-thinking style is useful for top executives who have to deal with many complex problems and make fast decisions. Carly Fiorina, CEO of Hewlett-Packard, might be considered an intuitive-thinking type. Fiorina is a creative thinker who is able to see the big picture and broad possibilities for HP's future. Although she cares about employees, Fiorina doesn't flinch from getting rid of people who don't support her vision for change.[36]

Machiavellianism
The tendency to direct much of one's behavior toward the acquisition of power and the manipulation of others for personal gain.

Personal Style	Action Tendencies	Likely Occupations
Sensation–thinking	• Emphasizes details, facts, certainty • Is a decisive, applied thinker • Focuses on short-term, realistic goals • Develops rules and regulations for judging performance	• Accounting • Production • Computer programming • Market research • Engineering
Intuitive–thinking	• Prefers dealing with theoretical or technical problems • Is a creative, progressive, perceptive thinker • Focuses on possibilities using impersonal analysis • Is able to consider a number of options and problems simultaneously	• Systems design • Systems analysis • Law • Middle/top management • Teaching business, economics
Sensation–feeling	• Shows concern for current, real-life human problems • Is pragmatic, analytical, methodical, and conscientious • Emphasizes detailed facts about people rather than tasks • Focuses on structuring organizations for the benefit of people	• Directing supervisor • Counseling • Negotiating • Selling • Interviewing
Intuitive–feeling	• Avoids specifics • Is charismatic, participative, people oriented, and helpful • Focuses on general views, broad themes, and feelings • Decentralizes decision making, develops few rules and regulations	• Public relations • Advertising • Human Resources • Politics • Customer service

EXHIBIT 11.7

Four Problem-Solving Styles

person-job fit

The extent to which a person's ability and personality match the requirements of a job.

Person-Job Fit

Given the wide variation among personalities and among jobs, an important responsibility of managers is to try to match employee and job characteristics so that work is done by people who are well suited to do it. This requires that managers be clear about what they expect employees to do. They should have a sense of the kinds of people who would succeed at the work that must be done. The extent to which a person's ability and personality match the requirements of a job is called **person-job fit**. When hiring and leading employees, managers should try to achieve person-job fit, so that employees are more likely to contribute and be satisfied.[37] When dot-com companies exploded out of the gate in the late 1990s, the importance of person-job fit became very apparent. People who had rushed to Internet companies in hopes of finding a new challenge—or making a quick buck—found themselves floundering in jobs for which they were unsuited. One manager recruited by a leading executive search firm lasted less than two hours at his new job. The search firm, a division of Russell Reynolds Associates, later developed a "Web Factor" diagnostic to help determine whether people have the right personality for the Internet, including such things as a tolerance for risk and uncertainty, an obsession with learning, and a willingness to do whatever needs doing, regardless of job title.[38]

A related concern is *person-environment fit*, which looks not only at whether the person and job are suited to one another but also how well the individual will fit in the overall organizational environment. An employee who is by nature strongly authoritarian, for example, would have a hard time in an organization such as W. L. Gore and Associates, where there are few rules, no hierarchy, no fixed or assigned authority, and no bosses. Many of today's organizations pay attention to person–environment fit from the beginning of the recruitment process. Texas Instruments' Web page includes an area called Fit Check that evaluates personality types anonymously and gives prospective job candidates a chance to evaluate for themselves whether they would be a good match with the company.[39]

Learning

Years of schooling have conditioned many of us to think that learning is something students do in response to teachers in a classroom. With this view, in the managerial world of time deadlines and concrete action, learning seems remote—even irrelevant. However, today's successful managers need specific knowledge and skills as well as the ability to adapt to changes in the world around them. Managers have to learn.

Learning is a change in behavior or performance that occurs as the result of experience. Experience may take the form of observing others, reading or listening to sources of information, or experiencing the consequences of one's own behavior. This important way of adapting to events is linked to individual differences in attitudes, perception, and personality.

Two individuals who undergo similar experiences—for example, a business transfer to a foreign country—probably will differ in how they adapt their behaviors to (that is, learn from) the experience. In other words, each person learns in a different way.

learning
A change in behavior or performance that occurs as a result of experience.

The Learning Process

One model of the learning process, shown in Exhibit 11.8, depicts learning as a four-stage cycle.[40] First, a person encounters a concrete experience. This is followed by thinking and reflective observation, which lead to abstract conceptualization and, in turn, to active experimentation. The results of the experimentation generate new experiences, and the cycle repeats.

The Best Buy chain of consumer electronics superstores owes its birth to the learning process of its founder, Richard M. Schulze. In the 1960s, Schulze built a stereo store called Sound of Music into a chain of nine stores in and near St. Paul, Minnesota. However, a tornado destroyed his largest and most profitable store, so he held a massive clearance sale in the parking lot. So many shoppers descended on the lot that they caused traffic to back up for two miles. Reflecting on this experience, Schulze decided there was great demand for a store featuring large selection and low prices, backed by heavy advertising. He tried out his idea by launching his first Best Buy superstore. Today there are more than

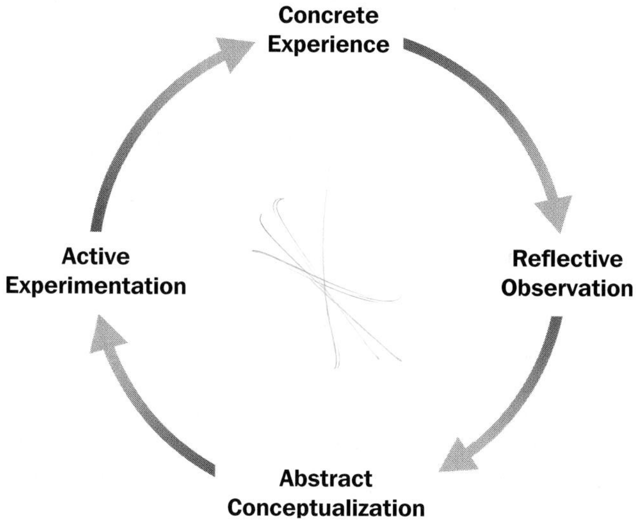

Concrete Experience → Reflective Observation → Abstract Conceptualization → Active Experimentation

EXHIBIT 11.8

Experiential Learning Cycle

400 Best Buy outlets as well as a thriving online division, and the chain's profits are in the billions of dollars.[41]

The arrows in the model of the learning process imply that this process is a recurring cycle. People continually test their conceptualizations and adapt them as a result of their personal reflections and observations about their experiences.

Learning Styles

Individuals develop personal learning styles that vary in terms of how much they emphasize each stage of the learning cycle. These differences occur because the learning process is directed by individual needs and goals. For example, an engineer might place greater emphasis on abstract concepts, while a salesperson might emphasize concrete experiences. Because of these preferences, personal learning styles typically have strong and weak points.

To assess a person's strong and weak points as a learner in the learning cycle, questionnaires have been developed to measure the relative emphasis the person places on each of the four learning stages shown in Exhibit 11.8: concrete experience, reflective observation, abstract conceptualization, and active experimentation. Some people have a tendency to overemphasize one stage of the learning process, or to avoid some aspects of learning. Not many people have totally balanced profiles, but the key to effective learning is competence in each of the four stages when it is needed.

Each person's learning style is a combination of the emphasis placed on the four stages. Researchers have identified four fundamental learning styles that combine elements of the four stages.[42] Exhibit 11.9 summarizes the characteristics and dominant learning abilities of these four learning styles, labeled

EXHIBIT 11.9

Learning Style Types

Learning Style Type	Dominant Learning Abilities	Learning Characteristics	Likely Occupations
Diverger	• Concrete experience • Reflective observation	• Is good at generating ideas, seeing a situation from multiple perspectives, and being aware of meaning and value • Tends to be interested in people, culture, and the arts	• Human resource management • Counseling • Organization development specialist
Assimilator	• Abstract conceptualization • Reflective observation	• Is good at inductive reasoning, creating theoretical models, and combining disparate observations into an integrated explanation • Tends to be less concerned with people than ideas and abstract concepts	• Research • Strategic planning
Converger	• Abstract conceptualization • Active experimentation	• Is good at decisiveness, practical application of ideas, and hypothetical deductive reasoning • Prefers dealing with technical tasks rather than interpersonal issues	• Engineering • Production
Accommodator	• Concrete experience • Active experimentation	• Is good at implementing decisions, carrying out plans, and getting involved in new experiences • Tends to be at ease with people but may be seen as impatient or pushy	• Marketing • Sales

Diverger, Assimilator, Converger, and Accommodator. The exhibit also lists occupations that frequently attract individuals with each of the learning styles. For example, people whose dominant style is *Assimilator* do well in research and strategic planning. *Accommodators* are often drawn to sales and marketing. A good example of the Accommodator learning style is Gertrude Boyle, who took over Columbia Sportswear after the death of her husband. She and her son, Tim, propelled the company from sales of $13 million in 1984 to $358 million in 1997 by observing what competitors were doing and actively experimenting to find a novel sales approach. The 74-year-old Gert Boyle decided to star in her own "Tough Mother" ads as a way to distinguish the company from competitors who advertised their products worn by fit, young models. Boyle believes in constantly pushing herself and her company, questioning everything, and trying new ideas.[43] Exhibit 11.9 lists other likely occupations for Divergers, Assimilators, Convergers, and Accommodators.

Through awareness of their learning style, managers can understand how they approach problems and issues, their learning strengths and weaknesses, and how they react to employees or coworkers who have different learning styles. Roberta Pearle Lamb, as a diverger, knew she needed the help of her converger husband to help her focus goals and create practical solutions as she started a new business, as described below.

Opera Aperta

http://www.opera-aperta.org

How is starting an opera company like starting a business? Ask opera singer Roberta Pearle Lamb, whose entrepreneur husband became her advisor when she founded Opera Aperta in Boston. "Raising money and lining up good employees are universal challenges for start-ups," says Chris Lamb. But there are differences, he notes: "In her business, hiring is easy and funding is difficult, and in my business hiring is hard and the funding is easier." He should know. He and his business partner recently raised $6 million in venture capital, while Mrs. Lamb thinks she could get by with $60,000. Yet both are involved in risky ventures.

Mrs. Lamb decided to follow in her husband's footsteps and become an entrepreneur after noticing the need for more opera companies in Boston, especially during the summer. She estimated that $38,000 would be enough to stage an English-language version of a Mozart opera. Because performers were eager for experience, she was able to save on salaries. By fund-raising with family and friends, she was also able to have cut-rate costumes made.

She learned to keep focusing her vision, to sharply define what she wanted. Her goals: To showcase local talent and fill every seat. Mr. Lamb gave her this advise on business discipline: "Keep it simple, and don't overreach your first time out. As a start-up you have to be ruthlessly pragmatic." He advised her to create supply and demand by booking a smaller venue and limiting the number of performances so that people would be eager for the next season. Her password became "sellout."

The advice worked. The infant company (Boston's only summer opera house) had a sellout two-date summer run at a 500-seat Boston University location. But the critics were stinging, particularly about Mrs. Lamb's performance. Rather than quitting, she is still learning. Next year she plans to sit out and not overpower the rest of the opera company. She felt it was tough to be held to the same standards as longstanding opera companies, but she has no regrets as the four-year-old company continues to grow. "I don't have any debt. I paid everybody and I'm happy about that," she says.[44]

Continuous Learning

To thrive or even to survive in today's fast-changing business climate, individuals and organizations must be continuous learners. For individuals, continuous learning entails looking for opportunities to learn from classes, reading, and talking to others, as well as looking for the lessons in life's experiences. One manager who embodies the spirit of continuous learning is Larry Ricciardi, senior vice president and corporate counsel at IBM. Ricciardi is an avid traveler and voracious reader who likes to study art, literature, and history. In addition, Ricciardi likes to add supermarket tabloids to his daily fare of *The Wall Street Journal*. On business trips, he scouts out side trips to exotic or interesting sites so he can learn something new.[45] Ricciardi never knows when he might be able to apply a new idea or understanding to improve his life, his job, or his organization.

For organizations, continuous learning involves the processes and systems through which the organization enables its people to learn, share their growing knowledge, and apply it to their work. In an organization in which continuous learning is taking place, employees actively apply comments from customers, news about competitors, training programs, and more to increase their knowledge and improve the organization's practices. For example, at the Mayo Clinic, doctors are expected to consult with doctors in other departments, with the patient, and with anyone else inside or outside the clinic who might help with any aspect of the patient's problem.[46] The emphasis on teamwork, openness, and collaboration keeps learning strong at Mayo.

Managers can foster continuous learning by consciously stopping from time to time and asking, "What can we learn from this experience?" They can allow employees time to attend training and reflect on their experiences. Recognizing that experience can be the best teacher, managers should focus on how they and their employees can learn from mistakes, rather than fostering a climate in which employees hide mistakes because they fear being punished for them. Managers also encourage organizational learning by establishing information systems that enable employees to share knowledge and learn in new ways. See Chapter 6 for a discussion on information technology. As individuals, managers can help themselves and set an example for their employees by being continuous learners, listening to others, reading widely, and reflecting on what they observe.

Can leaders really learn and change their own behavior? Marshall Goldsmith shows they can. He helps managers listen to feedback and self-reflect, causing real behavior changes, as shown in the Best Practices box.

Stress and Stress Management

stress

A physiological and emotional response to stimuli that place physical or psychological demands on an individual.

Just as organizations can support or discourage learning, many other organizational characteristics interact with individual differences to influence behavior in the organization. In every organization, these characteristics include sources of stress. Formally defined, **stress** is an individual's physiological and emotional response to stimuli that place physical or psychological demands on the individual and create uncertainty and lack of personal control when important outcomes are at stake.[47] These stimuli, called stressors, produce some combination of frustration (the inability to achieve a goal, such as the inability to meet a deadline because of inadequate resources) and anxiety (such as the fear of being disciplined for not meeting deadlines).

BEST PRACTICES

business

Marshall Goldsmith

The more obnoxious the better: That's what Marshall Goldsmith is after when he looks for the clients he coaches to become better managers. Often brilliant, honest, and hardworking, managers can have low "emotional intelligence" and sometimes treat others with little respect. One man was known as a complete jerk at work and considered a hopeless case by his colleagues. Goldsmith opened the man's eyes to his behavior by asking how he treated his family. "Oh, I'm totally different at home," the manager replied. Picking up the telephone right then, Goldsmith asked the man's wife, who said "He's a jerk." The kids said, "Jerk," as well.

Goldsmith won't take on a client unless that person truly desires change, which allows the person to hear feedback and make adjustments in behavior. First, Goldsmith asks colleagues for comprehensive information on the leaders' strengths and weaknesses and confronts the client with data on what everybody *really* thinks. Then he advises them to apologize and ask for help on how to get better, focusing on future rather than past behaviors. The client is not allowed to explain or defend him- or herself in any way, but must act humbly and ask for forgiveness. Such behavior breaks down the ego and allows for self-reflection and examination.

Goldsmith advises clients to be happy now and not wait until the next promotion, or raise, or new house; to learn to see the ego as an obstacle to corporate and spiritual innovation. Habits, points of view, smugness, and past memories—all can get in the way. It is easier to change behavior than to try and understand how it came about in the first place—so why not just change the behavior? Goldsmith credits his own quality family life with applying his own principles at home. "How can I be a better dad?" he asks his children.

His work with individuals is the logical extension of the methods of encounter groups, which have the same purpose: the shocking revelations of how others see you can jolt you into becoming a humbler person. But instead of being used for psychological support, Goldsmith's 360° feedbacks are used for organizational effectiveness. Self-knowledge, humility, and sensitivity are seen as business assets.

"I've heard every excuse in the history of the world," Goldsmith says of people who blame mom, dad, and their CEO. He tells them, "Quit whining. Let it go."

SOURCE: Larissa MacFarquhar, "The Better Boss," *The New Yorker* (April 22, 2002), 114–136.

People's responses to stressors vary according to their personality, the resources available to help them cope, and the context in which the stress occurs. Thus, a looming deadline will feel different, depending on the degree to which the individual enjoys a challenge, the willingness of coworkers to team up and help each other succeed, and family members' understanding of an employee's need to work extra hours, among other factors.

When the level of stress is low relative to a person's coping resources, stress can be a positive force, stimulating desirable change and achievement. However, too much stress is associated with many negative consequences, including sleep disturbances, drug and alcohol abuse, headaches, ulcers, high blood pressure, and heart disease. People who are experiencing the ill effects of too much stress may withdraw from interactions with their coworkers, take excess time off for illnesses, and look for less stressful jobs elsewhere. They may become so irritable that they cannot work constructively with others; some employees may even explode in tantrums or violence. Clearly, too much stress is harmful to employees as well as to the organization.

In biological terms, the stress response follows a pattern known as the General Adaptation Syndrome. The **General Adaptation Syndrome (GAS)** is a physiological response to a stressor, which begins with an alarm response, continues to resistance, and may end in exhaustion if the stressor continues beyond a person's ability to cope.[48] As shown in Exhibit 11.10, the GAS begins when an individual first experiences a source of stress (called a stressor). The stressor triggers an *alarm* response; the person may feel panic and helplessness, wondering how to cope with the stressor. Occasionally, people simply give up,

General Adaptation Syndrome (GAS)

The physiological response to a stressor, beginning with an alarm response, continuing to resistance, and sometimes ending in exhaustion if the stressor continues beyond the person's ability to cope.

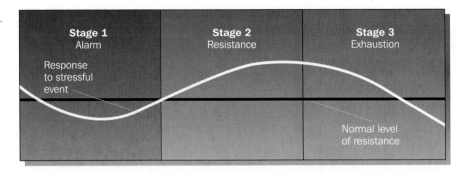

EXHIBIT 11.10

*The Stress Response: General
Adaptation Syndrome*

but more often they move to the next stage of the stress response, called *resistance*. At this stage, the person gathers strength and begins to decide how to cope. If exposure to the stressor continues past the person's ability to maintain resistance, the person enters the third stage: *exhaustion*.

Type A and Type B Behavior

Type A behavior

Behavior pattern characterized by extreme competitiveness, impatience, aggressiveness, and devotion to work.

Type B behavior

Behavior pattern that lacks Type A characteristics and includes a more balanced, relaxed lifestyle.

Researchers have observed that some people seem to be more vulnerable than others to the ill effects of stress. From studies of stress-related heart disease, they have categorized people as having behavior patterns called Type A and Type B.[49] The **Type A behavior** pattern includes extreme competitiveness, impatience, aggressiveness, and devotion to work. In contrast, people with a **Type B behavior** pattern exhibit less of these behaviors. They consequently experience less conflict with other people and a more balanced, relaxed lifestyle. Type A people tend to experience more stress-related illness than Type B people.

Most Type A individuals are high-energy people. L. Dennis Kozlowski, the chief executive of Tyco International, starts his day at dawn and goes for 16 hours, often traveling back and forth between time zones for meetings. "This is what it takes to be a CEO," Kozlowski says. "If you're not willing to do it, you should step out of the way so someone else can take your place."[50]

By pacing themselves and learning control and intelligent use of their natural high-energy tendencies, Type A individuals can be powerful forces for innovation and leadership within their organizations. However, many Type A personalities cause stress-related problems for themselves, and sometimes for those around them. Type B individuals typically live with less stress unless they are in high-stress situations. There are a number of factors that can cause stress in the workplace, even for people who are not naturally prone to high stress.

Causes of Work Stress

Work-related stress is on the rise. According to a recent study, the percentage of employees who report feeling burned out from job stress increased from 39 percent in 1995 to 53 percent in 1998. During the same time period, the amount of time employees reported missing work because of stress increased more than 35 percent.[51] Most people have a general idea of what a stressful job is like: difficult, uncomfortable, exhausting, even frightening. Managers can better cope with their own stress and establish ways for the organization to help employees cope if they define the conditions that tend to produce work stress. One way to identify work stressors is to place them in four categories: demands associated with job tasks, physical conditions, roles (sets of expected behaviors), and interpersonal pressures and conflicts.

Task demands are stressors arising from the tasks required of a person hold-ing a particular job. Some kinds of decisions are inherently stressful: those made under time pressure, those that have serious consequences, and those that must be made with incomplete information. For example, emergency room doctors are under tremendous stress as a result of the task demands of their jobs. They regularly have to make quick decisions, based on limited infor-mation, that may determine whether a patient lives or dies. Although not as extreme, many other jobs have task demands that lead to stress. Consider the task demands on Verizon's call center representatives.

Roland G. Collins, Jr. loves his job as a call-center representative for Verizon Communications. He enjoys connecting with customers; he makes good money and has good benefits. But he admits that it's not the job for everyone. About a third of the 100 or so calls a representative handles each day are stressful. Besides dealing with irate customers and handling calls regarding billing or other problems, representatives must be able to rattle off Verizon's string of prod-ucts and services, including terms and rates, and try to sell them to each and every caller. It does not matter how angry or rude the customer on the other end of the line—pushing new services is a key requirement of the job.

What makes matters worse is that representatives often have to do all this under observation. Managers routinely sit next to a representative or listen in on a call to check whether the rep has hit on nearly 80 different points required in every customer contact. Call center reps must meet precise performance spec-ifications, and managers defend the observation practice as a way to ensure consistency and better customer service. However, employees almost always find the experience adds to their stress level. For some employees, particu-larly inexperienced ones, an observation can create a panic situation, causing heart pounding and profuse sweating, which, in turn, creates even greater stress.[52]

Almost all jobs have some level of stress associated with task demands. For example, recall from Chapter 6 that managers frequently have to make *non-programmed decisions*—decisions that are characterized by incomplete infor-mation and have important consequences for the organization. Managers also experience stress from other factors, such as the responsibility of supervising or disciplining other people.

Physical demands are stressors associated with the setting in which an indi-vidual works. Some people must cope with work in a poorly designed setting, such as an office with inadequate lighting or little privacy. Some employees must maneuver in a cramped workspace; some have too little or too much heat for comfort. Some workplaces even present safety and health hazards, from greasy floors to polluted air. Work that involves repetitive movements, such as extensive computer work, also can lead to injury; thus this type of work inten-sifies stress for employees.

Role demands are challenges associated with a role—that is, the set of behav-iors expected of a person because of that person's position in the group. Some people encounter **role ambiguity**, meaning they are uncertain about what behaviors are expected of them. For example, one clinical psychologist who specializes in executive stress says that many upper-level executives, who grew up at a time when norms were different, do not understand what diversity requires of them—such as what women in the workplace view as appropriate

role ambiguity
Uncertainty about what behaviors are expected of a person in a particular role.

conduct. Consequently, some are fearful of inadvertently doing something that a woman will regard as sexual harassment.[53]

Although role ambiguity can be stressful, people who experience role conflict can feel as if they are being torn apart by conflicting expectations. **Role conflict** occurs when an individual perceives incompatible demands from others. Managers often feel role conflict because the demands of their superiors conflict with those of the employees in their department. For example, they may be expected to support employees and provide them with opportunities to experiment and be creative, while at the same time top executives are demanding a consistent level of output that leaves little time for creativity and experimentation. Filmmaker Doug Liman was hired because of his fresh creativity, but then confined at every turn with rules and structure of the big studio, causing conflict and high stress, which led to difficulties in working together, as described in the Focus on Collaboration box. In a company whose philosophy is "We're one big family," a manager who has to lay off employees would likely feel that this role conflicts with the expectation that she care about employees. These types of role conflict can create a high level of stress. Role conflict may also be experienced when the demands of the workplace conflict with demands from home. In the United States, the average number of hours worked per week is increasing, and almost 25 percent of employees report working an average of 50 hours or more per week.[54] For some, new technology such as e-mail and cell phones tie them to work and usurp their private lives around the clock. This means people have less time and energy to devote to family and friends, which may lead to role conflicts. A person's internalized values and beliefs may also collide with expectations in the workplace, leading to greater stress.

role conflict

Incompatible demands of different roles.

FOCUS ON COLLABORATION

The Bourne Identity

Colossal battles over the script and shooting locations, plus a continually delayed release date, plagued the production of Universal Pictures's $60 million *The Bourne Identity*, starring Matt Damon. Why all the drama? Most people point to inexperienced and idiosyncratic director Doug Liman, a self-proclaimed "paranoid," who stunned the film world with the low-budget $250,000 *Swingers*.

Bored with knock-offs and adaptation flicks, moviegoers have become critical, causing studios to hire new directors with fresh voices to supply creativity. Unfortunately, though, inexperienced and imaginative directors are not accustomed to the complexities of big-budget studio productions. Independent films have smaller crews and can make changes more easily. With a major-studio movie, though, changes can mean rewriting, destroying or building sets, or delays that typically cost millions per minute.

It all started when Universal tried to save money by filming the Paris scenes in Montreal. With shooting in seven countries, cutting costs in any location would make a big difference. Liman protested (though he now admits he was flippant and difficult): "What are they talking about?" he said. "Because

they speak French in Montreal, it's going to look like Paris? Nothing looks like Paris." He won that argument and then decided to hire a crew that spoke only French, so he could practice his collegiate French. That was only the beginning of the problems. When Matt Damon arrived, he didn't like recent changes to the script, so Liman tore apart the schedule.

"We wanted to be daring, to take risks," says Universal Chairman Stacey Snider. "But you can't just say 'Let's be bold and daring' without any parameters. Then it becomes reckless."

The studio and Liman continued to bicker, about locations, about the final action scene. "Doug came from a world where he had a lot more independence," says Snider. Because of all the conflicts, the film went $8 million over budget and took two weeks longer to shoot. Liman admits he had difficulty not only in delegating tasks, but also in managing the mammoth project, saying that the experience was a f—— nightmare." If he were asked, would he do another major studio movie? "I'd love to," he says.

SOURCE: Tom King, "'Bourne' to Be Wild," *The Wall Street Journal* (May 3, 2002), W1, W7.

Interpersonal demands are stressors associated with relationships in the organization. Although in some cases interpersonal relationships can alleviate stress, they also can be a source of stress when the group puts pressure on an individual or when there are conflicts. Interpersonal conflict occurs when two or more individuals perceive that their attitudes or goals are in opposition. Managers can work to resolve many interpersonal and intergroup conflicts, using techniques discussed in Chapter 15. A particularly challenging stressor is the personality clash. A personality clash occurs when two people simply cannot get along and do not see eye-to-eye on any issue. This type of conflict can be exceedingly difficult to resolve, and many managers have found that it is best to separate the two people so that they do not have to interact with one another.

Stress Management

Organizations that want to challenge their employees and stay competitive in a fast-changing environment will never be stress-free. But because many consequences of stress are negative, managers need to participate in stress management for themselves and for their employees. They can do so by identifying the major sources of stress, including the task, physical, role, and interpersonal demands of the job and organization. Does the overall level of these demands match the employee's taste for challenge and his or her coping resources? If so, the level of stress may be part of a successful person-job fit. If not, the organization and its employees should look for ways to reduce the stressors and increase employees' coping skills. Organizations can provide training or clearer directions so that employees feel able to handle their responsibilities. They can make the work environment safer and more comfortable. Individuals also can act on their own initiative to develop their knowledge and skills.

Individual Stress Management. A variety of techniques help individuals manage stress. Among the most basic strategies are those that help people stay healthy: exercising regularly, getting plenty of rest, and eating a healthful diet.

In addition, most people cope with stress more effectively if they lead balanced lives and are part of a network of people who support and encourage them. Family, relationships, friendships, and memberships in nonwork groups such as community or religious organizations are helpful for stress management, as well as for other benefits. People who don't take care of themselves physically and emotionally are more susceptible to stress in their personal as well as professional lives. Take the quick test in Exhibit 11.11 to rate your susceptibility to stress. Managers and employees in today's hectic, competitive work environment may sometimes think of these activities as luxuries. The study of organizational behavior, however, offers a reminder that employees are *human* resources with human needs.

New Workplace Responses to Stress Management. Although individuals can pursue stress management strategies on their own, today's enlightened companies support healthy habits to help employees manage stress and be more productive. Stress costs U.S. businesses an estimated $10,000 annually per employee in absenteeism, lower productivity, and higher health insurance and workers' compensation costs.[55] In the new workplace, taking care of employees has become a business as well as ethical priority.

Supporting employees can be as simple as encouraging people to take regular breaks and vacations. BellSouth, First Union, and Tribble Creative Group

Respond to the following on a 1-to-5 scale, with 1 meaning almost always and 5 meaning never. The higher the score, the higher your susceptibility to stress. If you have a high score (above 36), what will you do to reduce your susceptibility to stress?

1	2	3	4	5
Almost always				**Never**

1. I eat at least one balanced, hot meal a day and get at least seven hours of sleep a night. ____
2. I am in good health. ____
3. I exercise at least twice a week. ____
4. I regularly give and receive affection. ____
5. I have at least one relative within 50 miles on whom I can rely. ____
6. My income meets basic expenses. ____
7. I organize my time effectively. ____
8. I get strength from my religious beliefs. ____
9. I do something fun at least once a week. ____
10. I speak openly about my feelings. ____
11. I regularly take quiet time for myself. ____
12. I have an optimistic outlook on life. ____

Total Score: ____

EXHIBIT 11.11

The Stress Test

SOURCE: This is a portion of the Susceptibility Scale of the Personal Stress Navigator by Lyle H. Miller and Alma Dell Smith. Copyright by Stress Directions, Inc. 2000. Reprinted with permission.

are among the companies that have designated areas as quiet rooms or meditation centers where employees can take short, calming breaks at any time they feel the need.[56] The time off is a valuable investment when it allows employees to approach their work with renewed energy and a fresh perspective. Companies also develop other programs aimed specifically at helping employees reduce stress and lead healthier, more balanced lives. At the Seattle office of TPD Publications Inc., a custom publisher that has offices around the world, a masseuse is on site every Tuesday, and the company picks up half the bill.[57] Many companies offer wellness programs that provide access to nutrition counseling and exercise facilities. Others create broad work-life balance initiatives that may include flexible work options such as telecommuting and flexible hours, as well as benefits such as onsite day care, fitness centers, and personal services such as pick-up and delivery of dry cleaning. *Daily flextime* is considered by many employees to be the most effective work-life practice, which means giving employees the freedom to vary their hours as needed, such as leaving early to take an elderly parent shopping or taking time off to attend a child's school play.[58]

By acknowledging the personal aspects of employees' lives, work-life practices also communicate that managers and the organization care about employees as human beings. "When you help people find balance or work through difficult stretches in their lives, you say, 'We want to be partners for the long haul,'" says Rebecca Rhoads, CIO and vice president of Massachusetts-based defense contractor Raytheon.[59] Work-life balance initiatives help employees manage stress, improve productivity and quality of life, and enhance job satisfaction and organizational commitment. In addition, managers' attitudes make a tremendous difference in whether employees are stressed out and unhappy or relaxed, energetic, and productive.

Summary and Management Solution

The principles of organizational behavior describe how people as individuals and groups behave and affect the performance of the organization as a whole. Attitudes are evaluations that predispose people to behave in certain ways. Desirable work-related attitudes include job satisfaction and organizational commitment. Conflicts among attitudes create a state of cognitive dissonance, which people try to alleviate by shifting attitudes or behaviors. Attitudes affect people's perceptions and vice versa. Individuals often "see" things in different ways. The perceptual process includes perceptual selectivity and perceptual organization. Perceptual distortions, such as stereotyping, the halo effect, projection, and perceptual defense, are errors in judgment that can arise from inaccuracies in the perceptual process. Attributions are judgments that individuals make about whether a person's behavior was caused by internal or external factors.

Another area of interest is personality, the set of characteristics that underlie a relatively stable pattern of behavior. One way to think about personality is the Big Five personality traits of extroversion, agreeableness, conscientiousness, emotional stability, and openness to experience. Some important work-related attitudes and behaviors influenced by personality are locus of control, authoritarianism, Machiavellianism, and problem-solving styles. Four problem-solving styles are sensation-thinking, intuitive-thinking, sensation-feeling, and intuitive-feeling. Managers want to find a good person-job fit by ensuring that a person's personality, attitudes, skills, and abilities match the requirements of the job and the organizational environment.

New insight into personality has been gained through research in the area of emotional intelligence (EQ). Emotional intelligence includes the components of self-awareness, managing emotions, motivating oneself, empathy, and social skill. High emotional intelligence has been found to be important for success in a wide range of jobs and is particularly important for managers. EQ is not an in-born personality characteristic, but can be learned and developed. Vinita Gupta, described at the beginning of this chapter, needed to strengthen her emotional intelligence, particularly in the areas of self-awareness, empathy, and social skill, to improve morale and create a more positive work environment at Quick Eagle Networks. Gupta hired a corporate coach to help her learn more about herself and manage the personality characteristics and behaviors that could be contributing to decreased performance and higher turnover at Quick Eagle. Gupta worked on a series of exercises to help develop greater empathy and improve her social skills, including coaching employees, being more open and less defensive, and using humor to create a lighter atmosphere. Whereas before she rarely paused to speak to—or sometimes even glance at—anyone when she arrived at the office, she now makes a point of greeting people upon arrival, introducing herself to employees she's never met, and having lunch with colleagues. Gupta has learned that she cannot change some of her personality characteristics—for example, she will never score high on extroversion. However, she has learned to manage her attitudes and behaviors to make Quick Eagle a more pleasant, comfortable place to work. Employees have noticed that the atmosphere is lighter, and people are no longer afraid to speak up in meetings or if they have a concern. Turnover has decreased by 20 percent from a year earlier.[60]

Even though people's personalities may be relatively stable, individuals, like Vinita Gupta, can learn new behaviors. Learning refers to a change in behavior or performance that occurs as a result of experience. The learning process goes through a four-stage cycle, and individual learning styles differ. Four learning styles are Diverger, Assimilator, Converger, and Accommodator. Rapid changes in today's marketplace create a need for ongoing learning. They may also create greater stress for many of today's workers. Stress is a person's response to a stimulus that places a demand on that person. The causes of work stress include task demands, physical demands, role demands, and interpersonal demands. Individuals and organizations can alleviate the negative effects of stress by engaging in a variety of techniques for stress management.

Discussion Questions

1. Why is it important for managers to have an understanding of organizational behavior? Do you think a knowledge of OB might be more important at some managerial levels than at others? Discuss.

2. In what ways might the cognitive and affective components of attitude influence the behavior of employees who are faced with learning an entirely new set of computer-related skills in order to retain their jobs at a manufacturing facility?

3. What steps might managers at a company that is about to be merged with another company take to promote organizational commitment among employees?
4. In the Big Five personality factors, extroversion is considered a "good" quality to have. Why might introversion be an equally positive quality?
5. What is meant by *perceptual selectivity*? Explain some characteristics of the perceiver and of the stimuli that might affect perception.
6. Which of the five components of emotional intelligence do you consider most important to an effective manager in today's world? Why?
7. How might understanding whether an employee has an *internal* or an *external* locus of control help a manager better communicate with, motivate, and lead the employee?

8. Why is it important for managers to achieve person-job fit when they are hiring employees?
9. Review Exhibit 11.9. Which learning style type best characterizes you? How can you use this understanding to improve your learning ability? To improve your management skills?
10. Describe a time when you experienced role ambiguity or role conflict. What stress management techniques did you use to cope with the stress this created?
11. Do you think it is the responsibility of managers and organizations to help employees manage stress? Why or why not?

■ Manager's Workbook

Your personality is what you are. You have similarities and differences from other people. The differences measured here are not better or worse, merely different. Complete and score the inventory below to find out your personality type.

Personality Inventory
For each item, circle either a or b. If you feel both a and b are true, decide which one is more like you, even if it is only slightly more true.
1. When making a decision, the most important considerations are
   a. rational thoughts, ideas, and data.
   b. people's feelings and values.
2. When discussing a problem with colleagues, it is easy for me
   a. to see "the big picture."
   b. to grasp the specifics of the situation.
3. When I am working on an assignment, I tend to
   a. work steadily and consistently.
   b. work in bursts of energy with "down time" in between.
4. When I listen to someone talk on a subject, I usually try to
   a. relate it to my own experience and see if it fits.
   b. assess and analyze the message.
5. In work, I prefer spending a great deal of time on issues of
   a. ideas.
   b. people.
6. In meetings, I am most often annoyed with people who
   a. come up with many sketchy ideas.
   b. lengthen meetings with many practical ideas.
7. I would rather work for an organization where
   a. my job was intellectually stimulating.
   b. I was committed to its goals and mission.
8. I would rather work for a boss who is
   a. full of new ideas.
   b. practical.

In the following, choose the word in each pair that appeals to you more:
9. a. social
   b. theoretical
10. a. ingenuity
    b. practicality

Scoring Key
Count one point for each item listed below that you circled in the inventory.

Score for S	Score for N
2b	2a
3a	3b
6a	6b
8b	8a
10b	10a

Total S _____   Total N _____
Circle the one with more points: S or N

Score for T	Score for F
1a	1b
4b	4a
5a	5b
7a	7b
9b	9a

Total T_____   Total F _____
Circle the one with more points: T or F

Your score is:
S or N _____   T or F _____
S = Sensation
N = Intuitive
T = Thinking
F = Feeling
(see Exhibit 11.5)

■ Manager's Workshop

Applying What You Know about Perceptual Biases and Rater Errors

Scully and Mulder have to speak with a number of informants about a UFO sighting that occurred in Flatbush, Kansas. The informants are all poor, middle-aged farmers who have little education and strong rural accents. It appears that they don't bathe very often, and they also happen to have poor dental hygiene (many in fact are missing their teeth). Listed below are a number of perceptual biases and rater errors and examples of how Scully and Mulder may be susceptible to each of them when interacting with these people or evaluating the quality of their stories. Match each of the biases with the example that best reflects that error.

Primacy effect	Recency effect	Central traits
Implicit personality theory	Projection	Stereotyping
Contrast effects	Leniency	Harshness
Central tendency	Halo effect	Similar-to-me effect

1. At the beginning of her first interview, Scully discovers that the informant can't read and has very slow, drawn-out speech, which leads her to conclude that the person is probably mentally disabled. She conducts the rest of her interview based on that assumption.

   _____

2. Scully is a Christian, and her religion is very important to her. As a result, she is very skeptical about the whole UFO phenomenon and thinks that others are as well. Her interview questions are often phrased to reflect her skepticism: Do you think the light you saw might have been an airplane? You don't really believe that what you saw was visitors from another planet, do you?

   _____

3. Because Scully thinks that there is no such thing as UFOs, she has a tendency to invalidate the stories of all the farmers by finding flaws and inconsistencies in them.

   _____

4. Mulder has interviewed three people, all of whom fit the general description of the residents of this area. The fourth person who arrives is clean and well-dressed and very articulate. The difference is amazing and leads Mulder to put more weight on what this individual has to tell him.

   _____

5. On their way into town, Scully and Mulder nearly get into an accident with one of the local farmers. An argument ensues, and Mulder is tempted to arrest the man for obstruction of justice. When they meet later during one of the interview sessions, Mulder can't shake his negative impression of the guy and finds himself being very harsh.

   _____

6. At the conclusion of an interview that was going very well, an informant suddenly bursts into a medley of Broadway show tunes. Mulder is stunned by how nutty this person appears to be and forgets all the apparently rational things the individual has told him.

   _____

7. Because Mulder believes that UFOs are very real, he has a tendency to accept all of the farmers' stories as being highly accurate and valid.

   _____

8. The sheriff helped Mulder and Scully conduct the interviews. When it came time to evaluate them, however, he had a hard time distinguishing the good stories from the bad, so he classified them all as somewhat believable but flawed.

   _____

9. Scully thinks personal hygiene is extremely important; therefore, she concludes that if these people aren't very good at taking care of themselves, they are probably not very reliable as witnesses due to a lack of attention to detail.

   _____

10. One person whom Scully interviews is also a devout Christian, and she articulates many of the same concerns and skepticism that Scully has. Because of their obvious similarities, Scully is predisposed to like this woman and to believe her version of events.

    _____

11. Mulder thinks of farmers as having a strong work ethic and being very honest and forthright. Therefore, he is predisposed to believe everything that the informants tell him, even though the sheriff has told him that one of the farmers is a known liar and a convicted criminal.

    _____

12. Mulder thinks that people who are hard-working and make a lot of sacrifices are also generally honest. He therefore tends to believe the stories of the farmers who seem to be very hard-working and self-sacrificing.

    _____

SOURCE: Courtney Hunt, Northern Illinois University. Adapted from "Must See TV: The Timelessness of Television As a Teaching Tool," presented at the 60th Academy of Management Meeting, August, 2000. Used with permission.

■ Management in Practice: Ethical Dilemma

Should I Fudge the Numbers?

Sara MacIntosh recently joined MicroPhone, a large telecommunications company, to take over the implementation of a massive customer service training project. The program was created by Kristin Cole, head of human resources and Sara's new boss. According to the grapevine, Kristin was hoping this project alone would give her the "star quality" she needed to earn a coveted promotion. Industry competition was heating up, and MicroPhone's strategy called for being the very best at customer service. That meant having the most highly trained people in the industry, especially those who would work directly with customers. Kristin's new training program called for an average of one full week of intense customer service training for each of 3,000 people and had a price tag of about $40 million.

Kristin had put together a team of overworked staffers to develop the training program, but now she needed someone well qualified and dedicated to manage and implement the project, and Sara, with eight years of experience, a long list of accomplishments, and advanced degrees in finance and organizational behavior, seemed perfect for the job. However, during a thorough review of the proposal, Sara discovered some assumptions built into the formulas that raised red flags. She approached Dan Sotal, the team's coordinator, about her concerns, but the more Dan tried to explain how the financial projections were derived, the more Sara realized that Kristin's proposal was seriously flawed. No matter how she tried to work them out, the most that could be squeezed out of the $40 million budget was 20 hours of training per person, not the 40 hours everyone expected for such a high price tag.

Sara knew that, although the proposal had been largely developed before she came on board, it would bear her signature. As she carefully described the problems with the proposal to Kristin and outlined the potentially devastating conse-

quences, Kristin impatiently tapped her pencil. Finally, she stood up, leaned forward, and interrupted Sara, quietly saying, "Sara, make the numbers work so that it adds up to 40 hours and stays within the $40 million budget." Sara glanced up and replied, "I don't think it can be done unless we either change the number of employees who are to be trained or the cost figure. . . . " Kristin's smile froze on her face and her eyes began to snap as she again interrupted. "I don't think you understand what I'm saying. We have too much at stake here. *Make the previous numbers work.*" Stunned, Sara belatedly began to realize that Kristin was ordering her to fudge the numbers. She felt an anxiety attack coming on as she wondered what she should do.

What Do You Do?

1. Make the previous numbers work. Kristin and the entire team have put massive amounts of time into the project and they all expect you to be a team player. You don't want to let them down. Besides, this is a great opportunity for you in a highly visible position.
2. Stick to your principles and refuse to fudge the numbers. Tell Kristin you will work overtime to help develop an alternate proposal that stays within the budget by providing more training to employees who work directly with customers and fewer training hours for those who don't have direct customer contact.
3. Go to the team and tell them what you've been asked to do. If they refuse to support you, threaten to reveal the true numbers to the CEO and board members.

SOURCE: Adapted from Doug Wallace, "Fudge the Numbers or Leave," *Business Ethics* (May–June 1996), 58–59. Adapted with permission.

■ Surf the Net

1. **Emotional Intelligence.** Go to both sites listed below to assess your emotional intelligence quotient. After completing the tests and printing out the results at both sites, be prepared to discuss which of the two formats of results you preferred and your reasons for preferring one over the other.
   http://www.utne.com/azEq2.tmpl
   http://quiz.ivillage.com/health/tests/eqtest2.htm
2. **Machiavellianism.** Take a Machiavelli personality test found at one of the sites listed below, print out the results, write your name at the top, and submit the printout to your instructor.

   http://www.salon.com/books/it/1999/09/13/machtest/
   http://killeenroos.com/2/Machiavelli.htm
   http://www.humanlinks.com/personal/power_orientation.htm
3. **Stress Management.** Use a Web browser to locate stress management information using the following phrase: "stress management college students." Be prepared to share in a class discussion the three stress management techniques you located during your research that you thought were most helpful.

■ Case for Critical Analysis

Volkswagen's Ferdinand Piëch

Although many of today's organizations have shifted toward more democratic, participative types of management, one has not: Volkswagen. Ferdinand Piëch, who recently retired as CEO, ruled Volkswagen with an iron hand since 1993 and continues to wield enormous power behind the scenes. Immediately after he took the CEO job, Piëch centralized power in the organization, firing managers who questioned his ideas or who didn't follow his lead. He dove into engineering projects himself, proposing new projects, tinkering with designs. He presided over meetings with the demeanor of an autocrat, with the occasional result that important questions weren't asked because managers were fearful of presenting opposing points of view.

Even though he has now passed the reins to his hand-picked successor, Bernd Pischetsrieder, it is widely believed that Piëch will continue to call the shots at Europe's leading carmaker. After his retirement as CEO, Piëch was expected to step directly into a new role as chairman of VW's executive supervisory board, which will allow him to direct strategy, influence management and executive appointments, and perhaps block important decisions. Under German corporate law, the chairman of the supervisory board, not the CEO, appoints management board members. "Piëch could pull all the strings," said one VW executive. In fact, some believe the former CEO effectively put his trusted aides in key positions before his retirement to ensure that the company would continue to follow his vision and direction. Although some colleagues say Pischetsrieder is very much his own man, few expect him—or other top executives—to resist Piëch's continued influence.

There's no doubt that Piëch is a brilliant and forward-thinking businessman. Looking back over his years at VW, he can boast one of the great turnarounds in automotive history. He helped make models such as the Golf and the Passat all-time bestsellers and cemented VW's hold in the important U.S. market with the relaunch of the beloved VW Beetle. Volkswagen's four main worldwide brands—VW, Audi, Seat, and Skoda—have taken 19 percent of the European auto market, mostly at the expense of General Motors and Ford. VW vehicles account for one-quarter of all car sales in South America and one-half of all sales in China. In 2000, the company's profits nearly doubled, to $1.8 billion on sales of $76 billion.

Piëch (whose maternal grandfather was Ferdinand Porsche) came to VW with a vision of turning the company into the most powerful, most respected carmaker in the world, and he's well on the way to meeting that goal. Yet, rather than resting on his laurels, Piëch spent the final months of his tenure as CEO acting as if he were still trying to pull the company out of a major crisis. Part of the reason Piëch's management approach has been successful is his extensive knowledge of and passion for the cars themselves. From his days as an automotive engineer-

ing student at Zurich's Swiss Federal Institute of Technology, through his stint at Porsche, where he helped create world-class race cars, to his development of Audi's Quattro and the launch of the VW Beetle, Piëch could be found under the hood, tinkering. Thus, he knew his product and his customers and how to fit them together better than anyone else in the industry.

However, while he has excelled as an engineer, critics charge that Piëch's tight hold over the company has left VW with serious problems. "There is a lack of people equipped to be efficient managers," says one analyst in Germany. "No middle manager can make decisions because they haven't been used to doing so. All decisions have been pushed [to the top]." Piëch's retirement comes at a crucial time for VW, which is facing renewed competition from Ford and other carmakers in Europe. A recent push into upscale vehicles risks hurting existing sales. In addition, VW is still plagued by high labor costs and low productivity at many of its plants. Some colleagues believe Pischetsrieder is up to the challenge of keeping VW at the top of the heap, but analysts wonder if he can really do his job with Piëch looking over his shoulder.

Questions

1. What personality traits does Ferdinand Piëch exhibit? Do you think these contributed to a good person-job fit as CEO of Volkswagen? Why or why not?

2. Hardly anyone would argue that Piëch is not an authoritarian executive. Do you sense that he is Machiavellian as well? Do you think these characteristics will have a positive or negative impact on Volkswagen's future? Explain your answer.

3. Imagine that you are one of the "trusted" managers that Piech moved into a key position before his retirement. You are experiencing some cognitive dissonance about working long hours and investing significant resources in one of Piëch's pet projects, a new luxury car model about whose success you have doubts. How might you resolve your dissonance?

SOURCES: Christine Tierney, with Andrea Zammert, Joann Muller, and Katie Kerwin, "Volkswagen," *Business Week,* Industrial/Technology edition (July 23, 2001), 60–68; Wim Oude Weernick, Georg Auer, and Dorothee Ostle, "Pischetsrieder's In, But Piëch's Not Out," *Automotive News* (September 10, 2001), 1, 45; Scott Miller, "New VW Chief Assumes Post at Key Time—Stronger Rivals and Shadow of Piech May Make Life Hard for Pischetsrieder," *The Wall Street Journal* (September 7, 2001), A12; David Woodruff and Keith Naughton, "Hard-Driving Boss," *Business Week* (October 5, 1998), 82–87; and Christine Tierney with Katharine Schmidt, "Who's Behind the Wheel at Audi?" *Business Week,* Industrial/Technology edition (November 26, 2001), 50.

Leadership in Organizations

LEARNING OBJECTIVES

After studying this chapter, you should be able to

1 Define leadership and explain its importance for organizations.

2 Identify personal characteristics associated with effective leaders.

3 Explain the five sources of power and how each causes different subordinate behavior.

4 Describe the leader behaviors of initiating structure and consideration and when they should be used.

5 Describe Hersey and Blanchard's situational theory and its application to subordinate participation.

6 Explain the path-goal model of leadership.

7 Discuss how leadership fits the organizational situation and how organizational characteristics can substitute for leadership behaviors.

8 Describe transformational leadership and when it should be used.

9 Explain innovative approaches to leadership in the new workplace, such as Level 5 leadership, interactive leadership, virtual leadership, and servant leadership.

Management Challenge

Harvard President Lawrence Summers is in a pickle. The former U.S. Treasury Secretary had grown out of his interpersonal prickliness in Washington, D.C., but now seems to have gone back to his old ways. In his first semester as president, he managed to rattle faculty and students alike by blasting a generous grading system where half the grades were *A*s and nine-tenths of the students were honors graduates. Then after September 11, 2001, he criticized Harvard's longstanding ban of military on campus. To top it off, he had a nationally televised rift with African American scholar Cornel West, whose recent CD *Sketches of My Culture* was criticized by Summers as being unscholarly. Summers also said West was not publishing enough serious academic articles, focusing instead on popular books. West left for Princeton. Summers will have to improve his people skills if he wants to make the changes that he says out-of-date Harvard needs to retain its stature. Even though the venerable institution has doubled its endowment recently, to $18.3 billion, and has enough Nobel laureates to cause envy from any university, Summers is convinced his old alma mater needs more than fine tuning. Harvard does not provide undergraduates the kind of education this new-world economy requires, he says. He also wants the university to be instrumental in education reform, as well as a leader in medicine and bio-tech. Harvard's centuries-old preeminence results from its lack of complacency. "It has always been prepared to question the way things have been done," says Summers. But he fights against a system that allows almost total autonomy to the 12 deans, and where faculty are "narcisstic and self-serving," says Tufts University Provost Sol Gittleman.[1]

If you were Larry Summers, what kind of leadership would you exert to solve the problem and forge ahead with your new agenda? Do you believe a person can change his or her leadership style?

In the previous chapter, we explored differences in attitudes, personality, and so forth, that affect behavior. Different leaders behave in different ways, depending on their individual differences as well as their followers' needs and the organizational situation. Many different styles of leadership can be effective. For example, contrast the leadership style of Tom Siebel, CEO of Siebel Systems, with that of Herb Kelleher, recently retired president and CEO of Southwest Airlines. Siebel is known as a disciplined and dispassionate manager who likes to maintain control over every aspect of the business. He enforces a dress code, sets tough goals and standards, and holds people strictly accountable. Those who succeed are handsomely rewarded; those who don't are fired. "We go to work to realize our professional ambitions, not to have a good time," Siebel says.[2] Herb Kelleher, on the other hand, believes having a good time at work translates into higher productivity and better service. Kelleher was known for dressing up as Elvis or the Easter Bunny to entertain employees and for encouraging workers to have fun and let their own unique personalities come out in serving customers. Both Kelleher and Siebel are successful leaders, although their styles are quite different.

This chapter explores one of the most widely discussed and researched topics in management—leadership. Here we will define leadership, explore the differences between a leader and a manager, and discuss the sources of leader power. We will examine trait, behavioral, and contingency theories of leadership effectiveness, as well as discuss charismatic and transformational leadership. The final section of the chapter looks at new leadership approaches for today's workplace. Chapters 13 through 15 will look in detail at many of the functions of leadership, including employee motivation, communication, and encouraging teamwork.

The Nature of Leadership

There is probably no topic more important to business success today than leadership. The concept of leadership continues to evolve as the needs of organizations change. Among all the ideas and writings about leadership, three aspects stand out—people, influence, and goals. Leadership occurs among people, involves the use of influence, and is used to attain goals.[3] *Influence* means that the relationship among people is not passive. Moreover, influence is designed to achieve some end or goal. Thus, **leadership** as defined here is the ability to influence people toward the attainment of goals. This definition captures the idea that leaders are involved with other people in the achievement of goals.

leadership
The ability to influence people toward the attainment of organizational goals.

Leadership is reciprocal, occurring *among* people.[4] Leadership is a "people" activity, distinct from administrative paper shuffling or problem-solving activities. Leadership is dynamic and involves the use of power.

Leadership versus Management

Much has been written in recent years about the leadership role of managers. Management and leadership are both important to organizations. Effective managers have to be leaders, too, because there are distinctive qualities associated with management and leadership that provide different strengths for the organization, as illustrated in Exhibit 12.1. As shown in the exhibit, manage-

LEADER QUALITIES

MANAGER QUALITIES

SOUL
Visionary
Passionate
Creative
Flexible
Inspiring
Innovative
Courageous
Imaginative
Experimental
Initiates change
Personal power

MIND
Rational
Consulting
Persistent
Problem solving
Tough-minded
Analytical
Structured
Deliberate
Authoritative
Stabilizing
Position power

EXHIBIT 12.1

Leader and Manager Qualities

SOURCE: Based on Genevieve Capowski, "Anatomy of a Leader: Where Are the Leaders of Tomorrow?" *Management Review,* March 1994, 12.

ment and leadership reflect two different sets of qualities and skills that frequently overlap within a single individual. A person might have more of one set of qualities than the other, but ideally a manager develops a balance of both manager and leader qualities.

One of the major differences between manager and leader qualities relates to the source of power and the level of compliance it engenders within followers. **Power** is the potential ability to influence the behavior of others.[5] Management power comes from the individual's position in the organization. Because manager power comes from organizational structure, it promotes stability, order, and problem solving within the structure. Leadership power, on the other hand, comes from personal sources that are not as invested in the organization, such as personal interests, goals, and values. Leadership power promotes vision, creativity, and change in the organization. A good example of leadership power is Josh Raskin, a middle school teacher in upper Manhattan who became a mission-critical leader in the hours and days following the destruction of the World Trade Center towers in September 2001. Although he didn't have a formal position of authority, Raskin found himself in charge of coordinating a massive psych-clergy effort for crisis counseling, as well as guiding hundreds of other volunteers, based on his personal power. As he assigned a volunteer to guard a medical supply room, for example, Raskin infused the mundane chore with a higher vision and purpose by telling the young man everyone was counting on him to make sure no one stole drugs that would be desperately needed for the injured.[6]

Within organizations, there are typically five sources of power: legitimate, reward, coercive, expert, and referent.[7] Sometimes power comes from a person's position in the organization, while other sources of power are based on personal characteristics.

power

The potential ability to influence others' behavior.

Position Power

The traditional manager's power comes from the organization. The manager's position gives him or her the power to reward or punish subordinates in order to influence their behavior. Legitimate power, reward power, and coercive power are all forms of position power used by managers to change employee behavior.

Legitimate Power. Power coming from a formal management position in an organization and the authority granted to it is called **legitimate power**. For example, once a person has been selected as a supervisor, most workers understand that they are obligated to follow his or her direction with respect to work activities. Subordinates accept this source of power as legitimate, which is why they comply.

Reward Power. Another kind of power, **reward power**, stems from the authority to bestow rewards on other people. Managers may have access to formal rewards, such as pay increases or promotions. They also have at their disposal such rewards as praise, attention, and recognition. Managers can use rewards to influence subordinates' behavior.

Coercive Power. The opposite of reward power is **coercive power**: It refers to the authority to punish or recommend punishment. Managers have coercive power when they have the right to fire or demote employees, criticize, or withdraw pay increases. For example, if Paul, a salesman, does not perform as expected, his supervisor has the coercive power to criticize him, reprimand him, put a negative letter in his file, and hurt his chance for a raise.

Different types of position power elicit different responses in followers.[8] Legitimate power and reward power are most likely to generate follower compliance. *Compliance* means that workers will obey orders and carry out instructions, although they may personally disagree with them and may not be enthusiastic. Coercive power most often generates resistance. *Resistance* means that workers will deliberately try to avoid carrying out instructions or will attempt to disobey orders.

Thomas C. Graham, chairman of AK Steel, is a believer in position power. Unimpressed with new ideas about empowering workers, he prefers a military-style management, where cost cutting is rewarded and mistakes are quickly disciplined. His blunt views suggest that management in the steel industry has failed to push people and equipment hard enough. Graham's tough hierarchical approach has resulted in turnarounds for mills at LTV, U.S. Steel, and Washington Steel, but has also caused him to be ousted or passed over for promotion in the midst of his successes.[9]

Personal Power

In contrast to the external sources of position power, personal power most often comes from internal sources, such as a person's special knowledge or personality characteristics. Personal power is the tool of the leader. Subordinates follow a leader because of the respect, admiration, or caring they feel for the individual and his or her ideas. Personal power is becoming increasingly important as more businesses are run by teams of workers who are less tolerant of authoritarian management, as we discussed in Chapter 11.[10] Two types of personal power are expert power and referent power.

---

legitimate power

Power that stems from a formal management position in an organization and the authority granted to it.

reward power

Power that results from the authority to reward others.

coercive power

Power that stems from the authority to punish or recommend punishment.

Expert Power. Power resulting from a leader's special knowledge or skill regarding the tasks performed by followers is referred to as **expert power**. When the leader is a true expert, subordinates go along with recommendations because of his or her superior knowledge. Leaders at supervisory levels often have experience in the production process that gains them promotion. At top management levels, however, leaders may lack expert power because subordinates know more about technical details than they do. One top manager who benefits from expert power is Hector de Jesus Ruiz, president and COO of Advanced Micro Devices (AMD). Ruiz has a B.S. in electrical engineering and nearly 30 years of experience in all facets of the semiconductor industry, from top to bottom. Employees respect Ruiz's technical knowledge and operational expertise as a valuable strength as AMD battles Intel in the microprocessor wars. They appreciate having someone in top management who understands the nitty-gritty technical and production details that lower-level employees deal with every day.[11]

Referent Power. The last kind of power, **referent power**, comes from leader personality characteristics that command subordinates' identification, respect, and admiration so they wish to emulate the leader. When workers admire a supervisor because of the way she deals with them, the influence is based on referent power. Referent power depends on the leader's personal characteristics rather than on a formal title or position and is most visible in the area of charismatic leadership, which will be discussed later in this chapter. An example of referent power is Rachel Hubka, owner of Rachel's Bus Company (formerly Stewart's Bus Company). Hubka joined Stewart's as a dispatcher, set about learning every job in the business, and eventually bought the company. Today, as top leader of the school-bus operation, Hubka often hires people with marginal employment histories, gives them extensive training, and encourages them to follow their dreams. Nothing pleases her more than having an employee leave to start his or her own business.[12]

The follower reaction most often generated by expert power and referent power is commitment. *Commitment* means that workers will share the leader's point of view and enthusiastically carry out instructions. Needless to say, commitment is preferred to compliance or resistance. It is particularly important when change is the desired outcome of a leader's instructions, because change carries risk or uncertainty. Commitment assists the follower in overcoming fear of change.

Empowerment

A significant recent trend in corporate America is for top executives to *empower* lower employees. Fully 74 percent of executives in a survey claimed that they are more participatory, more concerned with consensus building, and more reliant on communication than on command compared with the past. Executives no longer hoard power.

Empowering employees works because total power in the organization seems to increase. Everyone has more say and hence contributes more to organizational goals. The goal of senior executives in many corporations today is not simply to wield power but also to give it away to people who can get jobs done.[13] For example, when Robin Landew Silverman and her husband made the decision to move their clothing store from downtown Grand Forks, North Dakota, to a suburban location, they knew they would need the full commitment

© Vito Aluia

Joanna B. Meiseles, president and founder of Snip-its Corp., a $1.5 million children's haircutting chain based in Natick, Massachusetts, demonstrates many of the personal traits associated with effective leadership. For example, she displayed intelligence, ability, knowledge, and judgment by knowing that to make her company successful, it had to be unique. Everything about Snip-its is tailored to children. Snip-its characters perch on a hot pink and lime green entry arch, games and stories are loaded on funky quasi-anthropomorphic computers at every cutting station, and the Magic Box dispenses a prize in exchange for a swatch of hair at the end of a visit.

of their staff. The Silvermans had been accustomed to calling the shots, but a new approach was needed to successfully accomplish the difficult transition. By giving up control of the operation, the Silvermans gave their employees opportunities to apply themselves in new ways. "Skills emerged that we didn't know people had," says Robin. For example, a timid secretary became a dynamic bid researcher, and a marketing manager showed a talent for interior design.[14]

The Focus on Collaboration box describes how one male manager is learning to become a better leader by incorporating some of the values associated with empowerment, such as personal humility, inclusion, relationship building, and caring.

Leadership Traits

traits

Distinguishing personal characteristics, such as intelligence, values, and appearance.

Early efforts to understand leadership success focused on the leader's personal characteristics or traits. **Traits** are the distinguishing personal characteristics of a leader, such as intelligence, values, and appearance. The early research focused on leaders who had achieved a level of greatness and hence was referred to as the *great man* approach. The idea was relatively simple: Find out what made these people great, and select future leaders who already exhibited the same traits or could be trained to develop them. Generally, research found only a weak relationship between personal traits and leader success.[15]

In addition to personality traits, physical, social, and work-related characteristics of leaders have been studied. Exhibit 12.2 summarizes the physical,

FOCUS ON COLLABORATION

Andy Pearson Transforms Himself As a Leader

When he was CEO of PepsiCo Inc., Andy Pearson was named one of the 10 toughest bosses in the United States by *Fortune* magazine. He was notorious for his brutal management style and the extreme, relentless demands he put on his subordinates. Twenty years later, as founding chairman and former CEO of Tricon Global Restaurants, Pearson is still tough, but he has learned that demanding high standards doesn't have to mean inflicting pain. Today, he leads not with fear, surprise, and intimidation but with humility, respect, and genuine caring.

Pearson began his transformation as a leader when he started asking himself what it would take to unleash the power of everyone in the organization. He had noticed how his coleader David Novak (now Tricon's CEO) inspired people throughout the company with his warmth, energy, and personal attention. He saw employees actually weep with gratitude in reaction to little more than a few words of praise from Novak. And gradually, he began to see how tapping into positive human emotions was the key driver of success at Tricon, which owns 30,000 KFC, Taco Bell, and Pizza Hut restaurants around the world. "I knew something was going on that was

very powerful," Pearson says. "If we could learn to harness that spirit with something systematic, then we would have something unique."

Pearson's new approach to leadership is not to issue orders but to seek answers from below. He talks and listens to people throughout the company and makes an enormous effort to let people know that their individual contribution is vital to the organization's success. If he disagrees with something, rather than beating people down and belittling their ideas, as the "old" Andy Pearson would have done, he will challenge them to think about the problem in a different light.

Most significantly, Pearson now considers caring about others and giving people recognition and approval a sign of leadership strength rather than weakness. "There's a human yearning for a certain amount of toughness," Pearson says. "But it can't be unmitigated toughness." What's his advice for successful leadership in today's workplace? "Ultimately, it's all about having more genuine concern for the other person," Pearson says. "There's an important aspect [of leadership] that has to do with humility."

SOURCE: David Dorsey, "Andy Pearson Finds Love," *Fast Company* (August 2001), 78–86.

Physical characteristics	**Personality**	**Work-related characteristics**
Energy	Self-confidence	Achievement drive, desire to excel
Physical stamina	Honesty and integrity	Conscientiousness in pursuit of goals
	Enthusiasm	Persistence against obstacles, tenacity
Intelligence and ability	Desire to lead	
Intelligence, cognitive ability	Independence	**Social Background**
Knowledge		Education
Judgment, decisiveness	**Social characteristics**	Mobility
	Sociability, interpersonal skills	
	Cooperativeness	
	Ability to enlist cooperation	
	Tact, diplomac	

SOURCE: Based on Bernard M. Bass, *Bass & Stogdill's Handbook of Leadership: Theory, Research, and Managerial Applications,* 3rd ed. (New York: Free Press, 1990), 80–81; and S. A. Kirkpatrick and E. A. Locke, "Leadership: Do Traits Matter?" *Academy of Management Executive 5,* no. 2 (1991), 48–60.

E X H I B I T *12.2*

Personal Characteristics of Leaders

social, and personal leadership characteristics that have received the greatest research support.[16] However, these characteristics do not stand alone. The appropriateness of a trait or set of traits depends on the leadership situation. The same traits do not apply to every organization or situation.

Further studies have expanded the understanding of leadership beyond the personal traits of the individual to focus on the dynamics of the relationship between leaders and followers.

Autocratic versus Democratic Leaders

One way to approach leader characteristics is to examine autocratic and democratic leaders. An **autocratic leader** is one who tends to centralize authority and rely on legitimate, reward, and coercive power. A **democratic leader** delegates authority to others, encourages participation, and relies on expert and referent power to influence subordinates.

The first studies on these leadership characteristics were conducted at the University of Iowa by Kurt Lewin and his associates.[17] These studies compared autocratic and democratic leaders and produced some interesting findings. The groups with autocratic leaders performed highly so long as the leader was present to supervise them. However, group members were displeased with the close, autocratic style of leadership, and feelings of hostility frequently arose. The performance of groups who were assigned democratic leaders was almost as good, and these were characterized by positive feelings rather than hostility. In addition, under the democratic style of leadership, group members performed well even when the leader was absent and left the group on its own.[18] The participative techniques and majority rule decision making used by the democratic leader trained and involved group members such that they performed well with or without the leader present. These characteristics of democratic leadership explain why the empowerment of lower employees is a popular trend in companies today.

This early work suggested that leaders were either autocratic or democratic in their approach. However, further work by Tannenbaum and Schmidt indicated that leadership could be a continuum reflecting different amounts of employee participation.[19] Thus, one leader might be autocratic (boss centered), another democratic (subordinate centered), and a third a mix of the two styles. The leadership continuum is illustrated in Exhibit 12.3.

autocratic leader

A leader who tends to centralize authority and rely on legitimate, reward, and coercive power to manage subordinates.

democratic leader

A leader who delegates authority to others, encourages participation, and relies on expert and referent power to manage subordinates.

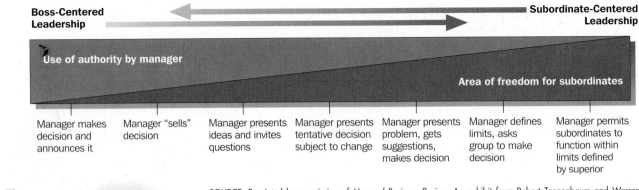

E X H I B I T *12.3*

The Leadership Continuum

SOURCE: Reprinted by permission of *Harvard Business Review*. An exhibit from Robert Tannenbaum and Warren Schmidt, "How to Choose a Leadership Pattern" (May–June 1973). Copyright © 1973 by the Harvard Business School Publishing Corporation, all rights reserved.

Most leaders have favored styles that they tend to use most often. For example, Jack Hartnett, president of D. L. Rogers Corp., which owns 54 Sonic franchises, almost always uses a highly autocratic style, whereas Patricia Gallup, PC Connection CEO, tends to use a more democratic style in many of her decisions.[20] However, while switching from autocratic to democratic or vice versa is not easy, leaders may adjust their styles depending on the situation. The Focus on Collaboration box describes how a school superintendent used participative leadership to launch a technological and educational revolution.

FOCUS ON COLLABORATION

Hunterdon High School

According to Ray Farley, "Once you put people in charge of their own destiny and say, 'Here's where you need to go if you want to be ready for the future,' the rest just happens." Farley has turned some of the traditional power of a school superintendent over to teams of students, teachers, and parents. Now, they decide what gets taught, who gets hired, and what the school calendar looks like. It was the school counselor, for example, who suggested running a grief program because so many students were self-medicating with drugs as a result of deep loss of loved ones.

One of the most important outcomes of this participative leadership has been a technological revolution at Hunterdon High School. The school's team found a way to equip the school with PCs, video facilities, ISDN lines, fiber-optic cables—the works—for $40,000 per classroom. Hunterdon also has a student-run FM radio station, a television studio, a telephone in every classroom, and a state-of-the-art instructional media center. Each classroom is linked to the school library, to the Internet, and to a host of other databases. The technology has led to a sort of virtual busing that links suburban, mostly white Hunterdon to four inner-city, mostly black New Jersey schools. Students at Hunterdon collaborate, for example, with their counterparts at Asbury Park to produce a poetry magazine in real time. With just a mouse click, a teacher can drop in and participate in the teamwork that is going on. Now, Asbury Park is increasing its technological edge as well. According to Dan Murphy, Asbury Park's principal, "One year ago we had two computers hooked up to the Internet. Right now, technicians are setting up 200 computers, providing them all with access. . . . And all of this is just the tip of the iceberg. It's unbelievable."

"Kids today live in a nanosecond world," Farley says. "You have to make available all the technology you can get your hands on. And then you have to do one more thing—you have to trust them." *http://www.hcrhs.hunterdon.k12.nj.us.*

SOURCES: Margo Nash, "The High School Where Grieving Is Part of the Curriculum," *New York Times* (October 22, 2000), 3; Nicholas Morgan, "Fast Times at Hunterdon High," *Fast Company* (February–March 1998), 42, 44.

Behavioral Approaches

The autocratic and democratic styles suggest that it is the "behavior" of the leader rather than a personality trait that determines leadership effectiveness. Perhaps any leader can adopt the correct behavior with appropriate training. The focus of research has shifted from leader personality traits toward the behaviors successful leaders display. Important research programs on leadership behavior were conducted at Ohio State University, the University of Michigan, and the University of Texas.

Ohio State Studies

Researchers at Ohio State University surveyed leaders to study hundreds of dimensions of leader behavior.[21] They identified two major behaviors, called *consideration* and *initiating structure*.

Consideration is the extent to which the leader is mindful of subordinates, respects their ideas and feelings, and establishes mutual trust. Considerate leaders are friendly, provide open communication, develop teamwork, and are oriented toward their subordinates' welfare.

Initiating structure is the extent to which the leader is task oriented and directs subordinate work activities toward goal attainment. Leaders with this style typically give instructions, spend time planning, emphasize deadlines, and provide explicit schedules of work activities.

Consideration and initiating structure are independent of each other, which means that a leader with a high degree of consideration may be either high or low on initiating structure. A leader may have any of four styles: high initiating structure–low consideration, high initiating structure–high consideration, low initiating structure–low consideration, or low initiating structure–high consideration. The Ohio State research found that the high consideration–high initiating structure style achieved better performance and greater satisfaction than the other leader styles. However, new research has found that effective leaders may be high on consideration and low on initiating structure or low on consideration and high on initiating structure, depending on the situation. Thus, the "high-high" style is not always the best.[22]

Michigan Studies

Studies at the University of Michigan at about the same time took a different approach by comparing the behavior of effective and ineffective supervisors.[23] The most effective supervisors were those who focused on the subordinates' human needs in order to "build effective work groups with high performance goals." The Michigan researchers used the term *employee-centered leaders* for leaders who established high performance goals and displayed supportive behavior toward subordinates. The less effective leaders were called *job-centered leaders;* these tended to be less concerned with goal achievement and human needs in favor of meeting schedules, keeping costs low, and achieving production efficiency.

The Leadership Grid

Blake and Mouton of the University of Texas proposed a two-dimensional leadership theory called **leadership grid** that builds on the work of the Ohio State

No longer leading a basketball team, Magic Johnson is now an entrepreneurial business leader. In 1995, Johnson, in partnership with Sony Retail Entertainment, opened the very successful Magic Johnson Theatres. Johnson describes his winning business leadership style as autocratic and centralized, "I've got a team of people who work for me and advise me. But I call my own shots . . . The team I built taught me how to get into business, how to run a business. They gave me the knowledge I needed to have. But now I'm on my own. Everybody knows they have to deal with me."

© Amy Cantrell

consideration

A type of leader behavior that describes the extent to which a leader is sensitive to subordinates, respects their ideas and feelings, and establishes mutual trust.

initiating structure

A type of leader behavior that describes the extent to which a leader is task oriented and directs subordinates' work activities toward goal achievement.

leadership grid

A two-dimensional leadership theory that measures a leader's concern for people and concern for production.

EXHIBIT *12.4*

The Leadership Grid® Figure

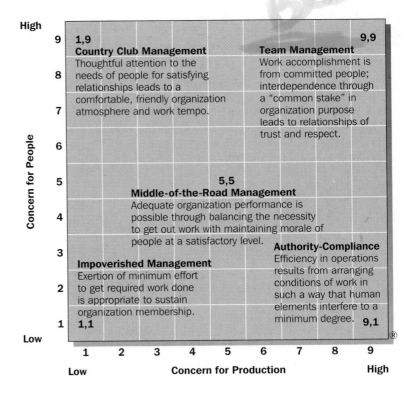

SOURCE: "The Leadership Grid®" figure, by Robert R. Blake and Anne Adams McCanse (formerly the Managerial Grid figure by Robert R. Blake and Jane S. Mouton), from *Leadership Dilemmas—Grid Solutions*, copyright © 1991 by Grid International, Inc., Austin, Texas.

and Michigan studies.[24] The two-dimensional model and five of its seven major management styles are depicted in Exhibit 12.4. Each axis on the grid is a 9-point scale, with 1 meaning low concern and 9 high concern.

Team management (9,9) often is considered the most effective style and is recommended for managers because organization members work together to accomplish tasks. *Country club management* (1,9) occurs when primary emphasis is given to people rather than to work outputs. *Authority-compliance management* (9,1) occurs when efficiency in operations is the dominant orientation. *Middle-of-the-road management* (5,5) reflects a moderate amount of concern for both people and production. *Impoverished management* (1,1) means the absence of a management philosophy; managers exert little effort toward interpersonal relationships or work accomplishment.

Contingency Approaches

contingency approach

A model of leadership that describes the relationship between leadership styles and specific organizational situations.

Several models of leadership that explain the relationship between leadership styles and specific situations have been developed. These are termed **contingency approaches** and include the leadership model developed by Fiedler and his associates, the situational theory of Hersey and Blanchard, the path-goal theory presented by Evans and House, and the substitutes-for-leadership concept.

Fiedler's Contingency Theory

An early, extensive effort to combine leadership style and organizational situation into a comprehensive theory of leadership was made by Fiedler and his associates.[25] The basic idea is simple: Match the leader's style with the situation most favorable for his or her success. By diagnosing leadership style and the organizational situation, the correct fit can be arranged.

Leadership Style. The cornerstone of Fiedler's contingency theory is the extent to which the leader's style is relationship oriented or task oriented. A *relationship-oriented leader* is concerned with people, as in the consideration style described earlier. A *task-oriented leader* is primarily motivated by task accomplishment, which is similar to the initiating structure style described earlier.

Leadership style was measured with a questionnaire known as the least preferred coworker (LPC) scale. The **LPC scale** has a set of 16 bipolar adjectives along an 8-point scale. Examples of the bipolar adjectives used by Fiedler on the LPC scale follow:

open	—	—	—	—	—	—	—	—	guarded
quarrelsome	—	—	—	—	—	—	—	—	harmonious
efficient	—	—	—	—	—	—	—	—	inefficient
self-assured	—	—	—	—	—	—	—	—	hesitant
gloomy	—	—	—	—	—	—	—	—	cheerful

LPC scale
A questionnaire designed to measure relationship-oriented versus task-oriented leadership style according to the leader's choice of adjectives for describing the "least preferred coworker."

If the leader describes the least preferred coworker using positive concepts, he or she is considered relationship oriented, that is, a leader who cares about and is sensitive to other people's feelings. Conversely, if a leader uses negative concepts to describe the least preferred coworker, he or she is considered task oriented, that is, a leader who sees other people in negative terms and places greater value on task activities than on people.

Situation. Leadership situations can be analyzed in terms of three elements: the quality of leader-member relationships, task structure, and position power.[26] Each of these elements can be described as either favorable or unfavorable for the leader.

1. *Leader-member relations* refers to group atmosphere and members' attitude toward and acceptance of the leader. When subordinates trust, respect, and have confidence in the leader, leader-member relations are considered good. When subordinates distrust, do not respect, and have little confidence in the leader, leader-member relations are poor.

2. *Task structure* refers to the extent to which tasks performed by the group are defined, involve specific procedures, and have clear, explicit goals. Routine, well-defined tasks, such as those of assembly-line workers, have a high degree of structure. Creative, ill-defined tasks, such as research and development or strategic planning, have a low degree of task structure. When task structure is high, the situation is considered favorable to the leader; when low, the situation is less favorable.

3. *Position power* is the extent to which the leader has formal authority over subordinates. Position power is high when the leader has the power to plan and direct the work of subordinates, evaluate it, and reward or punish them. Position power is low when the leader has little authority over subordinates and cannot evaluate their work or reward them. When position power is high, the situation is considered favorable for the leader; when low, the situation is unfavorable.

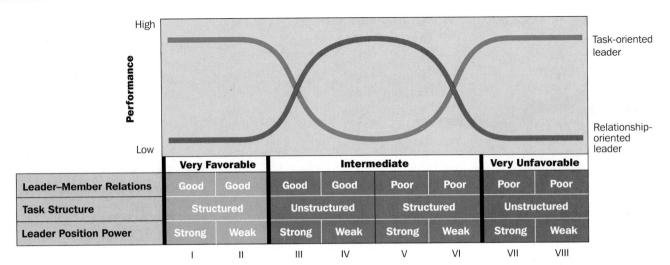

SOURCE: Based on Fred E. Fiedler, "The Effects of Leadership Training and Experience: A Contingency Model Interpretation," *Administrative Science Quarterly* 17 (1972), 455.

EXHIBIT *12.5*

How Leader Style Fits the Situation

Combining the three situational characteristics yields a list of eight leadership situations, which are illustrated in Exhibit 12.5. Situation I is most favorable to the leader because leader-member relations are good, task structure is high, and leader position power is strong. Situation VIII is most unfavorable to the leader because leader-member relations are poor, task structure is low, and leader position power is weak. All other octants represent intermediate degrees of favorableness for the leader.

Contingency Theory. When Fiedler examined the relationships among leadership style, situational favorability, and group task performance, he found the pattern shown in Exhibit 12.5. Task-oriented leaders are more effective when the situation is either highly favorable or highly unfavorable. Relationship-oriented leaders are more effective in situations of moderate favorability.

The task-oriented leader excels in the favorable situation because everyone gets along, the task is clear, and the leader has power; all that is needed is for someone to take charge and provide direction. Similarly, if the situation is highly unfavorable to the leader, a great deal of structure and task direction is needed. A strong leader defines task structure and can establish authority over subordinates. Because leader-member relations are poor anyway, a strong task orientation will make no difference in the leader's popularity.

The relationship-oriented leader performs better in situations of intermediate favorability because human relations skills are important in achieving high group performance. In these situations, the leader may be moderately well liked, have some power, and supervise jobs that contain some ambiguity. A leader with good interpersonal skills can create a positive group atmosphere that will improve relationships, clarify task structure, and establish position power.

A leader, then, needs to know two things in order to use Fiedler's contingency theory. First, the leader should know whether he or she has a relationship- or task-oriented style. Second, the leader should diagnose the situation and determine whether leader-member relations, task structure, and position power are favorable or unfavorable.

Fitting leader style to the situation can yield big dividends in profits and efficiency.[27] On the other hand, using an incorrect style for the situation can cause problems, as Alan Robbins discovered at Plastic Lumber Company.

Alan Robbins intentionally put his factory in a gritty downtown neighborhood in Akron, Ohio. He considers himself an enlightened employer who wants to give people—even those who have made serious missteps—a chance to prove themselves. Plastic Lumber Company, which converts old plastic milk and soda bottles into fake lumber, employs about 50 workers.

When he started the company, Robbins wanted to be both a boss and a friend to his workers. He would sometimes serve cold beers for everyone at the end of a shift or grant personal loans to employees in a financial bind. He stressed teamwork and spent lots of time running ideas by workers on the factory floor. He resisted the idea of drug testing, partly because of the expense and partly because it showed distrust. Besides, he couldn't imagine workers would show up drunk or on drugs when they knew they'd be operating dangerous machinery.

He was wrong. Robbins's relationship-oriented style didn't work in the situation in which he was operating. The low-skilled workers, many from low-income, drug-infested neighborhoods, weren't ready for the type of freedom Robbins granted them. Workers were frequently absent or late without calling, showed up under the influence, and started fights on the factory floor. The turning point came for Robbins when one worker was roaming the factory with an iron pipe in his hand, looking for a fight. Today, Robbins has given up his ideals of being a pal. "I'm too busy just trying to make sure they show up," he says.[28]

Robbins's leadership at Plastic Lumber was unsuccessful because he used a relationship-oriented style in an unfavorable situation. Because of their life circumstances, many of the employees he hired were naturally distrustful; thus, leader-member relations were poor. Although Robbins had high formal power, many workers had poor work ethics and little respect for authority. In their view, Robbins's failure to provide rules, guidelines, and direction weakened his authority. In the early days, workers believed they could get away with anything because of Robbins's easygoing style. Today, Robbins is developing a more task-oriented style, including putting together a comprehensive rules and policy manual and requiring drug tests of all new workers.

An important contribution of Fiedler's research is that it goes beyond the notion of leadership styles to show how styles fit the situation to improve organizational effectiveness. On the other hand, the model has also been criticized.[29] Using the LPC score as a measure of relationship- or task-oriented behavior seems simplistic, and how the model works over time is unclear. For example, if a task-oriented leader is matched with an unfavorable situation and is successful, the organizational situation is likely to improve and become more favorable to the leader. Thus, the leader might have to adjust his or her style or go to a new situation. For example, at Plastic Lumber Company, Alan Robbins is trying to shift to a task-oriented style, even though his natural inclination is to be a relationship-oriented leader.

Plastic Lumber Company

http://www.plasticlumber.com

Hersey and Blanchard's Situational Theory

The **situational theory** of leadership is an interesting extension of the behavioral theories described earlier and summarized in the leadership grid (Exhibit 12.4). More than previous theories, Hersey and Blanchard's approach focuses a great deal of attention on the characteristics of employees in determining appropriate leadership behavior. The point of Hersey and Blanchard is that subordinates vary in readiness level. People low in task readiness, because

situational theory

A contingency approach to leadership that links the leader's behavioral style with the task readiness of subordinates.

of little ability or training, or insecurity, need a different leadership style than those who are high in readiness and have good ability, skills, confidence, and willingness to work.[30]

According to the situational theory, a leader can adopt one of four leadership styles, based on a combination of relationship (concern for people) and task (concern for production) behavior, similar to the styles summarized earlier in Exhibit 12.4. The *telling style* reflects a high concern for production and a low concern for people. This is a very directive style. It involves giving explicit directions about how tasks should be accomplished. The *selling style* is based on a high concern for both people and production. With this approach, the leader explains decisions and gives subordinates a chance to ask questions and gain clarity and understanding about work tasks. The next leader behavior style, the *participating style,* is based on a combination of high concern for people and low concern for production. The leader shares ideas with subordinates, gives them a chance to participate, and facilitates decision making. The fourth style, the *delegating style,* reflects a low concern for both people and production. This leader style provides little direction and little support because the leader turns over responsibility for decisions and their implementation to subordinates.

The essence of Hersey and Blanchard's situational theory is to select a leader style that is appropriate for the readiness level of subordinates—their degree of education and skills, experience, self-confidence, and work attitudes. Followers may be at low, moderate, high, or very high levels of readiness.

Low Readiness Level. A telling style is appropriate when followers are at a low readiness level because of poor ability and skills, little experience, insecurity, or unwillingness to take responsibility for their own task behavior. When one or more subordinates exhibit very low levels of readiness, the leader is very specific, telling followers exactly what to do, how to do it, and when.

Moderate Readiness Level. A selling style works best for followers with moderate levels of readiness. These subordinates, for example, might lack some education and experience for the job, but they demonstrate high confidence, ability, interest, and willingness to learn. The selling style involves giving direction, but it also includes seeking input from others and clarifying tasks rather than simply instructing that they be performed.

High Readiness Level. When subordinates demonstrate a high readiness level, a participating style is effective. These subordinates might have the necessary education, experience, and skills but might be insecure in their abilities and need some guidance from the leader. The participating style enables the leader to guide followers' development and act as a resource for advice and assistance.

Very High Readiness Level. When followers have very high levels of education, experience, and readiness to accept responsibility for their own task behavior, the delegating style can effectively be used. Because of the high readiness level of followers, the leader can delegate responsibility for decisions and their implementation to subordinates, who have the skills, abilities, and positive attitudes to follow through. The leader provides a general goal and sufficient authority to do the task as followers see fit.

In summary, the telling style is best suited for subordinates who demonstrate very low levels of readiness to take responsibility for their own task behavior, the selling and participating styles work for subordinates with moderate-to-high readiness, and the delegating style is appropriate for employees with very high readiness. This contingency model is easier to understand than Fiedler's model, but it incorporates only the characteristics of followers, not those of the situation. The leader carefully diagnoses the readiness level of followers and adopts whichever style is necessary—telling, selling, participating, or delegating. For example, Phil Hagans, who owns two McDonald's franchises in northeast Houston, uses different styles as employees grow in their readiness level. Hagans gives many young employees their first job and he tells them every step to take during their first days, instructing them on everything from how to dress to how to clean the grill. As they grow in ability and confidence, he shifts to a selling or participating style. Hagans has had great success by carefully guiding young workers through each level of readiness.[31] A fast-food franchise leader would, however, probably need to take a different approach with a part-time worker who was retired after 40 years in the business world.

Path-Goal Theory

Another contingency approach to leadership is called the **path-goal** theory.[32] According to the path-goal theory, the leader's responsibility is to increase subordinates' motivation to attain personal and organizational goals. As illustrated in Exhibit 12.6, the leader increases their motivation by either (1) clarifying the subordinates' path to the rewards that are available or (2) increasing the rewards that the subordinates value and desire. Path clarification means that the leader works with subordinates to help them identify and learn the behaviors that will lead to successful task accomplishment and organizational rewards. Increasing rewards means that the leader talks with subordinates to learn which rewards are important to them—that is, whether they desire intrinsic rewards from the work itself or extrinsic rewards such as raises or promotions.

path-goal theory

A contingency approach to leadership specifying that the leader's responsibility is to increase subordinates' motivation by clarifying the behaviors necessary for task accomplishment and rewards.

EXHIBIT 12.6

Leader Roles in the Path–Goal Model

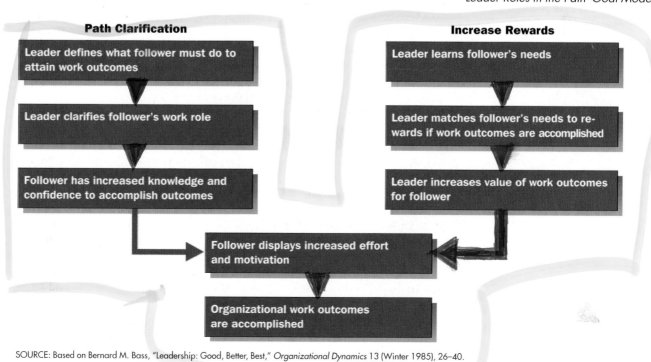

SOURCE: Based on Bernard M. Bass, "Leadership: Good, Better, Best," *Organizational Dynamics* 13 (Winter 1985), 26–40.

The leader's job is to increase personal payoffs to subordinates for goal attainment and to make the paths to these payoffs clear and easy to travel.[33]

This model is called a contingency theory because it consists of three sets of contingencies—leader behavior and style, situational contingencies, and the use of rewards to meet subordinates' needs.[34] Whereas in the Fiedler theory described earlier the assumption would be to switch leaders as situations change, in the path-goal theory leaders switch their behaviors to match the situation.

Leader Behavior. The path-goal theory suggests a fourfold classification of leader behaviors.[35] These classifications are the types of leader behavior the leader can adopt and include supportive, directive, achievement-oriented, and participative styles.

Supportive leadership involves leader behavior that shows concern for subordinates' well-being and personal needs. Leadership behavior is open, friendly, and approachable, and the leader creates a team climate and treats subordinates as equals. Supportive leadership is similar to the consideration leadership described earlier.

Directive leadership occurs when the leader tells subordinates exactly what they are supposed to do. Leader behavior includes planning, making schedules, setting performance goals and behavior standards, and stressing adherence to rules and regulations. Directive leadership behavior is similar to the initiating-structure leadership style described earlier.

Participative leadership means that the leader consults with his or her subordinates about decisions. Leader behavior includes asking for opinions and suggestions, encouraging participation in decision making, and meeting with subordinates in their workplaces. The participative leader encourages group discussion and written suggestions.

Achievement-oriented leadership occurs when the leader sets clear and challenging goals for subordinates. Leader behavior stresses high-quality performance and improvement over current performance. Achievement-oriented leaders also show confidence in subordinates and assist them in learning how to achieve high goals.

The four types of leader behavior are not considered ingrained personality traits as in the Fiedler theory; rather, they reflect types of behavior that every leader is able to adopt, depending on the situation.

Situational Contingencies. The two important situational contingencies in the path-goal theory are (1) the personal characteristics of group members and (2) the work environment. Personal characteristics of subordinates include such factors as ability, skills, needs, and motivations. For example, if employees have low ability or skill, the leader may need to provide additional training or coaching in order for workers to improve performance. If subordinates are self-centered, the leader must use rewards to motivate them. Subordinates who want clear direction and authority require a directive leader who will tell them exactly what to do. Craftworkers and professionals, however, may want more freedom and autonomy and work best under a participative leadership style.

The work environment contingencies include the degree of task structure, the nature of the formal authority system, and the work group itself. The task structure is similar to the same concept described in Fiedler's contingency theory; it includes the extent to which tasks are defined and have explicit job descriptions and work procedures. The formal authority system includes the amount of legitimate power used by managers and the extent to which policies and rules constrain employees' behavior. Work group characteristics are the educational level of subordinates and the quality of relationships among them.

Use of Rewards. Recall that the leader's responsibility is to clarify the path to rewards for subordinates or to increase the value of rewards to enhance satisfaction and job performance. In some situations, the leader works with subordinates to help them acquire the skills and confidence needed to perform tasks and achieve rewards already available. In others, the leader may develop new rewards to meet the specific needs of a subordinate.

Exhibit 12.7 illustrates four examples of how leadership behavior is tailored to the situation. In the first situation, the subordinate lacks confidence; thus, the supportive leadership style provides the social support with which to encourage the subordinate to undertake the behavior needed to do the work and receive the rewards. In the second situation, the job is ambiguous, and the employee is not performing effectively. Directive leadership behavior is used to give instructions and clarify the task so that the follower will know how to accomplish it and receive rewards. In the third situation, the subordinate is unchallenged by the task; thus, an achievement-oriented behavior is used to set higher goals. This clarifies the path to rewards for the employee. In the fourth situation, an incorrect reward is given to a subordinate, and the participative leadership style is used to change this. By discussing the subordinate's needs, the leader is able to identify the correct reward for task accomplishment. In all four cases, the outcome of fitting the leadership behavior to the situation produces greater employee effort by either clarifying how subordinates can receive rewards or changing the rewards to fit their needs.

Pat Kelly, founder and CEO of PSS World Medical, a specialty marketer and distributor of medical products, hires people who exhibit a desire to win and then keeps them motivated with his achievement-oriented leadership.

E x h i b i t   12.7

Path–Goal Situations and Preferred Leader Behaviors

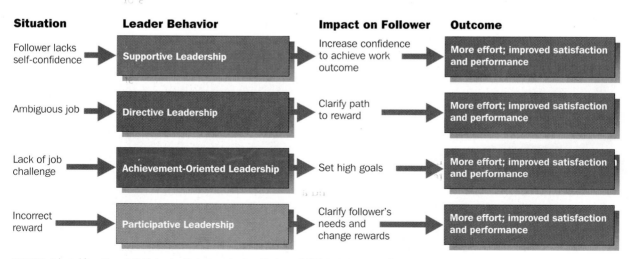

SOURCE: Adapted from Gary A. Yukl, *Leadership in Organizations* (Englewood Cliffs, N.J.: Prentice-Hall, 1981), 146–152.

PSS World Medical

http://www.pssworldmedical.com

Pat Kelly has always believed in establishing ambitious goals for his employees. He consistently sets higher financial and sales targets that challenge employees to perform at high levels. However, Kelly realizes that what gets people's juices flowing is not just reaching a new financial target, but winning. And Kelly makes sure employees have what they need to win and receive high rewards for their performance. PSS spends about 5 percent of its payroll budget each year on training, so that employees have the knowledge and skills they need to succeed. The company also emphasizes promotion from within. Moving people around to different divisions and different roles gives them opportunities for learning and advancement. If an employee does not do well in one position, PSS will help the person find another avenue to success.

Open communication plays an important role in Kelly's leadership. To meet high goals, employees have to know how they contribute and where they stand. Open book management is a cornerstone of corporate culture because Kelly believes people can succeed only when everyone knows the numbers and how they fit in. By setting high goals, providing people with the knowledge and skills to succeed, and running an open company, Kelly has created an organization full of people who think and act like CEOs. In fact, all delivery drivers have business cards with their names and "CEO" printed on them. As Kelly puts it, "when you're standing in front of the customer, you are the CEO."[36]

Kelly's achievement-oriented leadership is successful because the company's highly motivated professionals thrive on challenge, responsibility, and recognition. Path-goal theorizing can be complex, but much of the research on it has been encouraging.[37] Using the model to specify precise relationships and make exact predictions about employee outcomes may be difficult, but the four types of leader behavior and the ideas for fitting them to situational contingencies provide a useful way for leaders to think about motivating subordinates.

Substitutes for Leadership

The contingency leadership approaches considered so far have focused on the leaders' style, the subordinates' nature, and the situation's characteristics. The final contingency approach suggests that situational variables can be so powerful that they actually substitute for or neutralize the need for leadership.[38] This approach outlines those organizational settings in which a leadership style is unimportant or unnecessary.

Exhibit 12.8 shows the situational variables that tend to substitute for or neutralize leadership characteristics. A **substitute** for leadership makes the leadership style unnecessary or redundant. For example, highly professional subordinates who know how to do their tasks do not need a leader who initiates structure for them and tells them what to do. A **neutralizer** counteracts the leadership style and prevents the leader from displaying certain behaviors. For example, if a leader has absolutely no position power or is physically removed from subordinates, the leader's ability to give directions to subordinates is greatly reduced.

Situational variables in Exhibit 12.8 include characteristics of the group, the task, and the organization itself. For example, when subordinates are highly professional and experienced, both leadership styles are less important. The employees do not need much direction or consideration. With respect to task characteristics, highly structured tasks substitute for a task-oriented style, and

substitute

A situational variable that makes a leadership style unnecessary or redundant.

neutralizer

A situational variable that counteracts a leadership style and prevents the leader from displaying certain behaviors.

Variable		Task-Oriented Leadership	People-Oriented Leadership
Organizational variables:	Group cohesiveness	Substitutes for	Substitutes for
	Formalization	Substitutes for	No effect on
	Inflexibility	Neutralizes	No effect on
	Low positional power	Neutralizes	Neutralizes
	Physical separation	Neutralizes	Neutralizes
Task characteristics:	Highly structured task	Substitutes for	No effect on
	Automatic feedback	Substitutes for	No effect on
	Intrinsic satisfaction	No effect on	Substitutes for
Group characteristics:	Professionalism	Substitutes for	Substitutes for
	Training/experience	Substitutes for	No effect on

a satisfying task substitutes for a people-oriented style. With respect to the organization itself, group cohesiveness substitutes for both leader styles. Formalized rules and procedures substitute for leader task orientation. Physical separation of leader and subordinate neutralizes both leadership styles.

The value of the situations described in Exhibit 12.8 is that they help leaders avoid leadership overkill. Leaders should adopt a style with which to complement the organizational situation. For example, the work situation for bank tellers provides a high level of formalization, little flexibility, and a highly structured task. The head teller should not adopt a task-oriented style, because the organization already provides structure and direction. The head teller should concentrate on a people-oriented style. In other organizations, if group cohesiveness or previous training meet employees' social needs, the leader is free to concentrate on task-oriented behaviors. The leader can adopt a style complementary to the organizational situation to ensure that both task needs and people needs of the work group will be met.

EXHIBIT 12.8

Substitutes and Neutralizers for Leadership

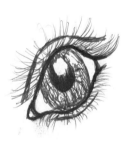

Change Leadership

In Chapter 1, we defined management to include the functions of leading, planning, organizing, and controlling. But recent work on leadership has begun to distinguish leadership as something more: a quality that inspires and motivates people beyond their normal levels of performance. Leadership is particularly important in companies trying to meet the challenges of a changing environment. Leaders in many organizations have had to reconceptualize almost every aspect of how they do business to meet the needs of increasingly demanding customers, keep employees motivated and satisfied, and remain competitive in a global, information-based business environment. As we discussed in Chapter 1, some are adopting e-business solutions and becoming learning organizations poised for constant change and adaptation.

Research has found that some leadership approaches are more effective than others for bringing about change in organizations. Two types of leadership that can have a substantial impact are charismatic and transformational. These types of leadership are best understood in comparison to *transactional leadership*.[39] **Transactional leaders** clarify the role and task requirements of subordinates, initiate structure, provide appropriate rewards, and try to be considerate to and meet the social needs of subordinates. The transactional leader's ability

transactional leader

A leader who clarifies subordinates' role and task requirements, initiates structure, provides rewards, and displays consideration for subordinates.

to satisfy subordinates may improve productivity. Transactional leaders excel at management functions. They are hardworking, tolerant, and fair minded. They take pride in keeping things running smoothly and efficiently. Transactional leaders often stress the impersonal aspects of performance, such as plans, schedules, and budgets. They have a sense of commitment to the organization and conform to organizational norms and values. Transactional leadership is important to all organizations, but leading change requires a different approach.

Charismatic and Visionary Leadership

charismatic leader

A leader who has the ability to motivate subordinates to transcend their expected performance.

vision

An attractive, ideal future that is credible yet not readily attainable.

Charismatic leadership goes beyond transactional leadership techniques. Charisma has been referred to as "a fire that ignites followers' energy and commitment, producing results above and beyond the call of duty."[40] The **charismatic leader** has the ability to inspire and motivate people to do more than they would normally do, despite obstacles and personal sacrifice. Followers transcend their own self-interests for the sake of the department or organization. The impact of charismatic leaders is normally from (1) stating a lofty vision of an imagined future that employees identify with, (2) shaping a corporate value system for which everyone stands, and (3) trusting subordinates and earning their complete trust in return.[41] Charismatic leaders tend to be less predictable than transactional leaders. They create an atmosphere of change, and they may be obsessed by visionary ideas that excite, stimulate, and drive other people to work hard.

© Alan Levenson

Co-chairmen of California Pizza Kitchen Inc. (CPK) restaurants, Rick Rosenfield and Larry Flax are leading their company through major changes. After PepsiCo Inc. bought 67 percent of CPK, the two leaders stayed as co-CEOs, managing a Pepsi-financed expansion that tripled the company's size to 90 restaurants. When Pepsi sold its restaurant business, Rosenfield and Flax bought their chain back at a profit. Now the co-leaders are sharpening their transformational leadership skills as they execute their vision to add 15 outlets a year and introduce frozen supermarket pizzas. "We always believed we could surpass Pizza Hut [a $4.7 billion chain]," says Flax, "We still believe we will."

Charismatic leaders are often skilled in the art of *visionary leadership.* A visionary leader speaks to the hearts of employees, letting them be part of something bigger than themselves. They see beyond current realities and help followers believe in a brighter future as well. A **vision** is an attractive, ideal future that is credible yet not readily attainable. For example, as principal of Harlem's Frederick Douglass School, Lorraine Monroe inspired teachers, students, and parents with her vision of transforming the school from one of the worst to one of the best in New York City. When she came to the school, it was known for excessive violence, poor attendance, and low achievement. Five years later, test scores of Frederick Douglass students ranked among the highest in New York City, and 96 percent of the school's graduates went on to college.[42]

Charismatic leaders have a strong vision for the future and can motivate others to help realize it.[43] They have an emotional impact on subordinates because they strongly believe in the vision and can communicate it to others in a way that makes the vision real, personal, and meaningful to others. The Focus on Skills box provides a short quiz to help you determine whether you have the potential to be a charismatic leader.

Charismatic leaders include Mother Theresa, Martin Luther King, Jr., Michael Jordan, and Adolf Hitler. Charisma can be used for positive outcomes that benefit the group, but it can also be used for self-serving purposes that lead to deception, manipulation, and exploitation of others. When charismatic lead-

FOCUS ON SKILLS

Are You a Charismatic Leader?

If you were the head of a major department in a corporation, how important would each of the following activities be to you? Answer yes or no to indicate whether you would strive to perform each activity.

1. Help subordinates clarify goals and how to reach them.
2. Give people a sense of mission and overall purpose.
3. Help get jobs out on time.
4. Look for the new product or service opportunities.
5. Use policies and procedures as guides for problem solving.
6. Promote unconventional beliefs and values.
7. Give monetary rewards in exchange for high performance from subordinates.
8. Command respect from everyone in the department.
9. Work alone to accomplish important tasks.
10. Suggest new and unique ways of doing things.
11. Give credit to people who do their jobs well.
12. Inspire loyalty to yourself and to the organization.
13. Establish procedures to help the department operate smoothly.
14. Use ideas to motivate others.
15. Set reasonable limits on new approaches.
16. Demonstrate social nonconformity.

The even-numbered items represent behaviors and activities of charismatic leaders. Charismatic leaders are personally involved in shaping ideas, goals, and direction of change. They use an intuitive approach to develop fresh ideas for old problems and seek new directions for the department or organization. The odd-numbered items are considered more traditional management activities, or what would be called *transactional leadership*. Managers respond to organizational problems in an impersonal way, make rational decisions, and coordinate and facilitate the work of others. If you answered yes to more even-numbered than odd-numbered items, you may be a potential charismatic leader.

SOURCES: Based on Bernard M. Bass, *Leadership and Performance beyond Expectations* (New York: Free Press, 1985); and Lawton R. Burns and Selwyn W. Becker, "Leadership and Managership," in *Health Care Management*, ed. S. Shortell and A. Kaluzny (New York: Wiley, 1986).

ers respond to organizational problems in terms of the needs of the entire group rather than their own emotional needs, they can have a powerful, positive influence on organizational performance.[44]

Transformational Leaders

Transformational leaders are similar to charismatic leaders, but are distinguished by their special ability to bring about innovation and change by recognizing followers' needs and concerns, helping them look at old problems in new ways, and encouraging them to question the status quo. Transformational leaders create significant change in both followers and the organization.[45] They have the ability to lead changes in the organization's mission, strategy, structure, and culture, as well as to promote innovation in products and technologies. Transformational leaders do not rely solely on tangible rules and incentives to control specific transactions with followers. They focus on intangible qualities such as vision, shared values, and ideas to build relationships, give larger meaning to diverse activities, and find common ground to enlist followers in the change process.[46]

A good example of a transformational leader is Richard Kovacevich, who steered mid-sized Norwest Corp. (now Wells Fargo & Co.) through numerous acquisitions to make it the fourth largest banking company in the United States. Kovacevich is known for spouting radical notions such as "Banking is necessary, banks are not." He has inspired his followers with a vision of becoming the Wal-Mart of financial services—and the company is well on its way. To

transformational leader

A leader distinguished by a special ability to bring about innovation and change.

motivate employees, Kovacevich leads with slogans such as, "Mind share plus heart share equals market share." Although some people might think it sounds hokey, Kovacevich and his employees don't care. It is the substance behind the slogans that matters. Employees are rewarded for putting both their hearts and minds into their work. Kovacevich constantly tells employees that they are the heart and soul of Wells Fargo, and that only through their efforts can the company succeed.[47]

Leading the New Workplace

The concept of leadership is also changing because of dramatic changes in today's environment and organizations. Globalization, e-commerce, virtual organizations and telecommuting, changes in employee interests and expectations, and increasing diversity have all contributed to a shift in how we think about and practice leadership. Four areas of particular interest for leadership in the new workplace are a new concept referred to as Level 5 leadership; women's ways of leading; virtual leadership; and servant leadership.

Level 5 Leadership. A recent five-year study conducted by Jim Collins and a group of 22 research associates identified the critical importance of what Collins calls *Level 5 leadership* in transforming companies from merely good to truly great organizations.[48] As described in his book, *Good to Great: Why Some Companies Make the Leap . . . and Others Don't,* Level 5 leadership refers to the highest level in a hierarchy of manager capabilities, as illustrated in Exhibit 12.9. A key characteristic of Level 5 leaders is an almost complete lack of ego. In contrast to the view of great leaders as "larger-than-life" personalities with strong egos and big ambitions, Level 5 leaders often seem shy and unpretentious. Although they accept full responsibility for mistakes, poor results, or failures, Level 5 leaders give credit for successes to other people. For example, Joseph F. Cullman III, former CEO of Philip Morris, staunchly refused to accept credit for the company's long-term success, citing his great colleagues, successors, and predecessors as the reason for the accomplishments.

EXHIBIT *12.9*

The Level 5 Leadership Hierarchy

Level 5: The Level 5 Leader
Builds an enduring great organization through a combination of personal humility and professional resolve.

Level 4: The Effective Executive
Builds widespread commitment to a clear and compelling vision; stimulates people to high performance.

Level 3: Competent Manager
Sets plans and organizes people for the efficient and effective pursuit of objectives.

Level 2: Contributing Team Member
Contributes to the achievement of team goals; works effectively with others in a group.

Level 1: Highly Capable Individual
Productive contributor; offers talent, knowledge, skills, and good work habits as an individual employee.

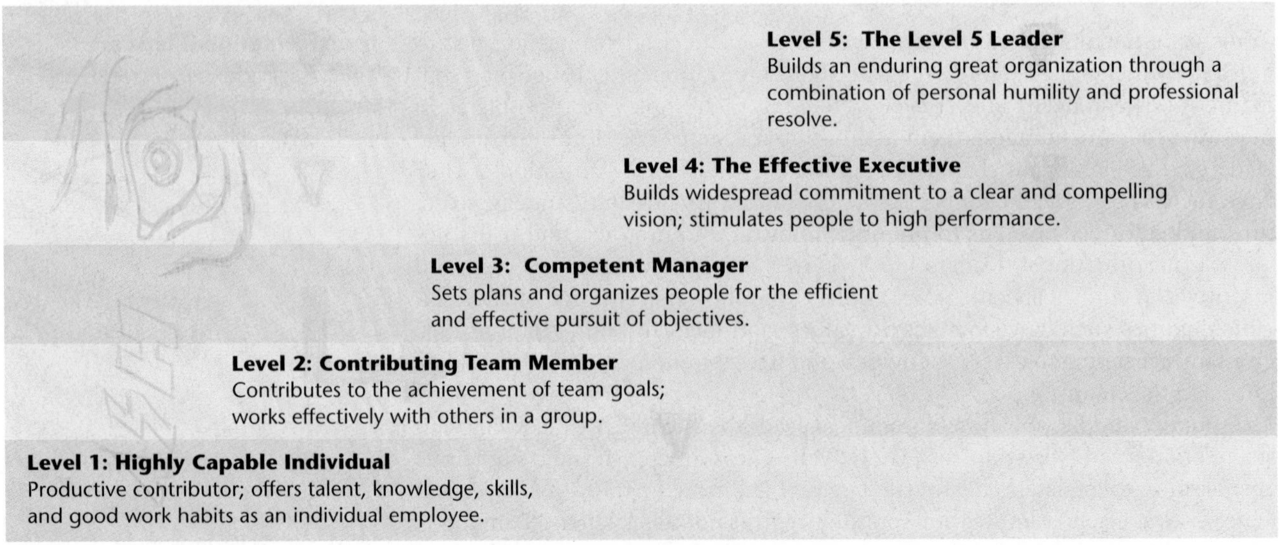

SOURCE: "The Level 5 Leadership Hierarchy" from *Good to Great: Why Some Companies Make the Leap and Others Don't,* by Jim Collins. Copyright © 2001 by Jim Collins. Reprinted by permission of HarperCollins Publishers, Inc.

Yet, despite their personal humility, Level 5 leaders have a fierce determination to do whatever it takes to produce great and lasting results for their organizations. They are extremely ambitious for their companies rather than for themselves. This becomes most evident in the area of succession planning. Level 5 leaders develop a solid corps of leaders throughout the organization, so that when they leave the company it can continue to thrive and grow even stronger. Egocentric leaders, on the other hand, often set their successors up for failure because it will be a testament to their own greatness if the company doesn't perform well without them. Rather than an organization built around "a genius with a thousand helpers," Level 5 leaders build an organization with many strong leaders who can step forward and continue the company's success. These leaders want everyone in the organization to develop to their fullest potential. D. Michael Abrashoff illustrates characteristics of both interactive and servant leadership, as well as the potential to become a Level 5 leader, showing that a leader can become more effective, as described in the Best Practices box.

Women's Ways of Leading. The focus on minimizing personal ambition and developing others has also been found to be common among female leaders. Recent research indicates that women's style of leadership is particularly suited to today's organizations.[50] Using data from actual performance evaluations, one study found that when rated by peers, subordinates, and bosses, female managers score significantly higher than men on abilities such as motivating others, fostering communication, and listening.[51] The Focus on Skills box lists these recent studies showing women as more effective leaders.

BEST PRACTICES

USS **Benfold**

Keeping good employees is tough for businesses, but for the U.S. Navy, it has been a nightmare in recent years. Forty percent of recruits wash out before their first four-year term is up. Considering it costs $35,000 to recruit one sailor and put him or her through nine weeks of boot camp, that's an expensive problem. In addition, only 30 percent of people who make it through their first tour reenlist for a second. When D. Michael Abrashoff took command of the destroyer USS *Benfold,* he came face to face with the biggest leadership challenge of his Navy career. Despite the fact that the *Benfold* was a technological marvel, most of its sailors could not wait to leave. People were so deeply unhappy and demoralized that walking aboard ship felt like entering a deep well of despair. Abrashoff knew that he needed to be a different kind of leader to turn things around and tap into the energy, enthusiasm, and creativity of his sailors.

To do so meant casting aside the long Navy tradition of relying on formal position power and authority. Abrashoff led with vision and values instead of command and control. Rather than issuing orders from the top, he started listening to ideas from below. He also made an effort to get to know each and every sailor as an individual. When the *Benfold's* sailors saw that Abrashoff was sincere, they responded with energy, enthusiasm, and commitment. Good ideas that came from the bottom up were implemented immediately, and many of them have now become standard throughout the U.S. Navy. Abrashoff also began handing over responsibility so that people could learn and grow. "If all you do is give orders, then all you get are order takers," he says. Abrashoff wanted to develop strong leaders at all levels and help people understand that they were the ones who made the ship successful. Under Abrashoff's leadership, the *Benfold* set all-time records for performance and retention. However, neither Abrashoff nor the crew are worried about what will happen when the captain moves on. "This crew . . . [knows] what results they get when they play an active role," Abrashoff says. "And they now have the courage to raise their hands and get heard. That's almost irreversible."[49]

SOURCES: D. Michael Abrashoff, "Retention through Redemption," *Harvard Business Review* (February 2001), 136–141; and Polly LaBarre, "The Most Important Thing a Captain Can Do Is to See the Ship from the Eyes of the Crew," *Fast Company* (April 1999), 115–126.

FOCUS ON SKILLS

Leading Women

Women started pouring into the workplace 30 years ago and soon discovered the glass ceiling. The solution many tried was to act more like men: talk sports, wear power suits, don't show too much emotion. Recent studies are shedding new light on the topic and suggest that men ought to be the ones doing the imitating. Their conclusions suggest: If you want a quality executive, hire a woman.

A wide range of studies of leaders in companies ranging from consumer products to high tech show that when bosses, colleagues, and employees are surveyed, they by-and-large give higher scores to females on many skills, from goal setting, to mentoring, to producing high-quality work. Though researchers weren't originally looking at gender issues, they discovered that women were rated higher on almost every index, in 42 of 52 skills measured. Women are more collaborative, think through issues more clearly, and are less inclined to seek personal glory, says the head of IBM's Global Services, Doug Elix. Management guru Rosabeth Moss Kanter says, "Women get high ratings on exactly those skills needed to succeed in the global Information Age, where teamwork and partnering are so important."

If women are so great, why aren't they running the world? Well, they are . . . almost, at the middle level, where they make up 45 percent of managers. At the CEO level, though,

there are only a handful. It's a pipeline problem, as a large cohort of women work their way up, but it is still compounded by the lack of mentors and being kept outside the inner communication circle. Also, too many women get stuck in HR or PR—career tracks that don't go anywhere. Because women's unique skills were underappreciated, they weren't even noticed much until recently. In fact, people skills were often seen as less important than so-called business skills. These dynamics have frustrated millions of capable women, who sometimes bail out of "corporate America" and start their own companies—9 million companies in the United States are female-owned, a 100 percent increase in 12 years. Another reason women haven't gotten ahead is that they are more team-focused, rather than looking for what makes *them* individually look better. "You should be looking out for yourself, not your people," one woman was told.

What makes the results of these studies compelling is that they come directly from bosses and coworkers in the corporations, not from a simulated situation in the research laboratory. Still, the investigators were not prepared for what they learned. Researcher Janet Irwin said, "We were startled by the results."

SOURCE: Rochelle Sharp, "As Leaders, Women Rule." *Business Week* (November 20, 2001), 74–84.

---

interactive leadership

A leadership style characterized by values such as inclusion, collaboration, relationship building, and caring.

This approach has been called **interactive leadership**.[52] This means that the leader favors a consensual and collaborative process, and influence derives from relationships rather than position power and formal authority. For example, Nancy Hawthorne, former chief financial officer at Continental Cablevision Inc., felt that her role as a leader was to delegate tasks and authority to others and to help them be more effective. "I was being traffic cop and coach and facilitator," Hawthorne says. "I was always into building a department that hummed."[53] It is important to note that men can be interactive leaders as well. The characteristics associated with interactive leadership are emerging as valuable qualities for both male and female leaders in the new workplace. A Finnish leader has learned how important interactive leadership is in sports, as described in the Digital, Inc. box.

Virtual Leadership. The virtual workplace, in which employees work remotely from each other and from leaders, is becoming more common in today's organizations, bringing new leadership challenges. In today's workplace, many people may work from home or other remote locations, wired to the office electronically. Sometimes people come together temporarily in virtual teams to complete a project and then disband, as we described in Chapter 7. In a virtual environment, leaders face a constant tension in trying to balance structure and accountability with flexibility.[54] They have to provide enough structure and direction so that people have a clear understanding of

DIGITAL, INC.

PK-35 Soccer Teams

Soccer coach Janne Viljamaa knows a thing or two about delegation. He lets 300 fans determine plays, using cell-phone text messages and the Internet. Finnish entrepreneur Jussi Rautavirta had an idea to give power to the fans. Searching for a coach who'd be willing to delegate some decisions to fans, he found his answer in amateur team PK-35, which had recently fallen from glory and its coach, Viljamaa. Started in 1935, PK-35 was split apart when its A-team was sold, leaving the remainder of players (students, factory workers, and postmen) to start over at the bottom of Division III.

Coach Viljamaa gives three to ten questions for fans to answer about team selection, training, and game tactics. The soccer friends get three minutes to answer the questions, and get responses back in another three minutes. Sometimes fan decisions bring dramatic results. Their recommendation to bring out substitute Hannu Takala resulted in a last-minute goal which won an end-of-season game.

Why would any coach agree to such an arrangement, to share his power and control? "Because it had never been done before, because I choose all the questions, and because it was a chance for PK-35 and me to share a little fame and income." He's learned lessons that apply for other businesses, as well: The more power you share with customers, vendors, and employees, the better the bottom line; don't share too much information—find a middle road; make the outcome very visible so information is meaningful; focus on the team, not individual goals.

As the new season starts, Rautavirta expects 1,000 fans to sign up for Club Manager, and have a say in more areas, such as which players to sign. The fans have proved that this concept is engaging. Additional backer Arturo Vallila notes the unique ability of Finland to foster such an experiment. "Because of our high rate of cell-phone usage," he says, "Finnish soccer can serve as a test-bed before taking the concept to the rest of the world."

SOURCE: Ian Wylie, "Who Runs This Team, Anyway?" *Fast Company* (April 2002), 32–33.

what is required of them, but they also have to trust that virtual workers will perform their duties responsibly without close control and supervision. Effective virtual leaders set clear goals and timelines and are very explicit about how people will communicate and coordinate their work. However, the details of day-to-day activities are left up to employees. This doesn't mean, however, that virtual workers are left on their own. Leaders take extra care to keep people informed and involved with one another and with the organization.

People who excel as virtual leaders tend to be open-minded and flexible, exhibit positive attitudes that focus on solutions rather than problems, and have superb communication, coaching, and relationship-building skills.[55] Good virtual leaders never forget that work is accomplished through *people*, not technology. Although they must understand how to select and use technology appropriately, leaders emphasize human interactions as the key to success. Building trust, maintaining open lines of communication, caring about people, and being open to subtle cues from others are essential in a virtual environment.[56]

Servant Leadership. In the new workplace, the best leaders operate from the assumption that work exists for the development of the worker as much as the worker exists to do the work.[57] Servant leadership, first described by Robert Greenleaf, is leadership upside down because leaders transcend self-interest to serve others and the organization.[58] **Servant leaders** operate on two levels: for the fulfillment of their subordinates' goals and needs and for the realization of the larger purpose or mission of their organization. Servant leaders give things away—power, ideas, information, recognition, credit for accomplishments. They truly value other people, encourage participation, share power, enhance others' self-worth, and unleash people's creativity, full commitment, and natural impulse to learn. Servant leaders bring the follower's higher motives to the

servant leader

A leader who works to fulfill subordinates' needs and goals as well as to achieve the organization's larger mission.

work and connect them to the organizational mission and goals. Frances Hesselbein, former CEO of the Girl Scouts, exhibits many of the qualities of a servant leader, as described below. Servant leaders bring the follower's higher motives to the work and connect them to the organizational mission and goals. They are devoted to building the organization rather than acquiring things for themselves. The leader who wants to be a single actor, a hero seeking personal recognition and resources, cannot build a learning organization.

The Girl Scout Way

http://www.gusa.org

Frances Hesselbein currently runs the Drucker Foundation, a small organization dedicated to sharing the leadership thinking of Peter Drucker. But she got her start more than 40 years ago as a volunteer scout leader. She eventually rose to CEO of the Girl Scouts, inheriting a troubled organization of 680,000 people, only 1 percent of whom were paid employees. By the time she retired in 1990, Hesselbein had turned around declining membership, dramatically increased participation by minorities, and replaced a brittle hierarchy with one of the most vibrant organizations in the nonprofit or business world.

How did she do it? By developing a leadership philosophy that emphasizes helping other people meet their needs. Hesselbein describes how she works with others as a circle in which everyone is included. Business and nonprofit leaders learn from Hesselbein's leadership style. George Sparks, manager of Hewlett-Packard's measuring-equipment business, says the time he spent following Hesselbein around was "the best two days of my career." As Sparks observed Hesselbein in action, he noted her ability to sense people's needs on an emotional level. Hesselbein listens carefully and then links people with matching needs and skills so that their personal needs are met at the same time they are serving the needs of the organization. She recognizes that the only way to achieve high performance is through the work of others, and she consistently treats people with care and respect. Hesselbein doesn't believe in forcing change on others. She draws her power from moral values, not from her position. For example, when she proposed that five-year-old girls from single-parent households be included as Girl Scout members (the minimum age was six), most of the councils opposed the plan. Even though the change was important because it would expand the Girl Scouts' reach into the minority community, Hesselbein didn't impose the change. She began working with the few councils who agreed with her and let the others continue their own way. Within a year, two-thirds of the councils had adopted the new age limit.

Hesselbein says her definition of leadership was "very hard to arrive at, very painful. . . . [It] is not a basket of tricks or skills. It is the quality and character and courage of the person who is the leader. It's a matter of ethics and moral compass, the willingness to remain highly vulnerable." To Frances Hesselbein, leadership means serving others, helping employees meet their personal needs at the same time they serve the organization.[59]

■ Summary and Management Solution

This chapter covered several important ideas about leadership. The early research on leadership focused on personal traits such as intelligence, energy, and appearance. Later, research attention shifted to leadership behaviors that are appropriate to the organizational situation.

Behavioral approaches dominated the early work in this area; consideration and initiating structure were suggested as behaviors that lead work groups toward high performance. The Ohio State and Michigan approaches and the managerial grid are in this category. Contingency approaches include Fiedler's theory, Hersey and Blanchard's situational theory, the path-goal model, and the substitutes-for-leadership concept.

Leadership concepts have evolved from the transactional approach to charismatic and transformational leadership behaviors. Charismatic leadership is the ability to articulate a vision and motivate followers to make it a reality. Transformational leadership extends charismatic qualities to guide and foster dramatic organizational change.

Four significant leadership concepts for the new workplace are Level 5 leadership, women's ways of leading, virtual leadership, and servant leadership. Level 5 leaders are characterized by personal humility combined with ambition to build a great organization that will continue to thrive beyond the leader's direct influence. Women's approach to leadership may be particularly suited to today's workplace because it emphasizes relationships and helping others develop to their highest potential. However, men as well as women can develop the characteristics associated with women's style of leadership, called *interactive leadership*. Managers in today's workplace also need to learn how to lead employees who may be working in a virtual environment and have little or no face-to-face contact with the leader. They may become servant leaders who facilitate the growth, goals, and development of others to liberate their best qualities in pursuing the organization's mission. In all of these new ways of leading, managers rely more on personal power than on position power.

Returning to our opening example, recall Harvard President Lawrence Summers's vision for a new Harvard, and the toes he has already stepped on in the process. Many people feel universities are not keeping up with the global information economy. A colleague says, "His real assignment is to create the kind of university to meet the needs of this very different society." And even competing universities want Summers to do well. The president of Yale called on Harvard to become a role model for change, saying, "All American education would be well served if Harvard devoted more attention to undergraduate education."

So how has Summer started? He's launched a battle on the status quo. Because Harvard's student-teacher ratio is abysmal, he is increasing the number of arts and sciences faculty from 642 to 700. At every opportunity, he will champion teaching, a priority of this former professor, who was known for being available to students. He will push the hiring of outstanding teachers, rather than brilliant scholars from outside. Tenure decisions will now be based on teaching evaluations, rather than primarily on publications. He will move for synthesis between various subjects in the undergraduate curriculum, to better reflect the world we live in. And he will push science knowledge, something for which Harvard grads aren't particularly known. His challenge in achieving these goals will be to learn to be collaborative, less autocratic and coercive, and more democratic, demonstrating better listening. He understands the structure of the changes, but now he needs to work on consideration. Only time will tell if he can learn fast enough.[60]

■ Discussion Questions

1. Do you think leadership style is fixed and unchangeable for a leader or flexible and adaptable? Discuss.
2. Suggest some personal traits that you believe would be useful to a leader. Are these traits more valuable in some situations than in others?
3. What is the difference between trait theories and behavioral theories of leadership?
4. Suggest the sources of power that would be available to a leader of a student government organization. To be effective, should student leaders keep power to themselves or delegate power to other students?
5. What skills and abilities does a manager need to effectively lead in a virtual environment? Do you believe a leader with a consideration style or an initiating-structure style would be more successful as a virtual leader? Explain your answer.
6. Consider Fiedler's theory as illustrated in Exhibit 12.5. How often do very favorable, intermediate, or very unfavorable situations occur in real life? Discuss.
7. What is transformational leadership? Differentiate between transformational leadership and transactional leadership. Give an example of each.
8. How does Level 5 leadership differ from the concept of servant leadership? Do you believe anyone has the potential to become a Level 5 leader? Discuss.
9. Do you think leadership is more important or less important in today's flatter, team-based organizations? Explain.
10. Consider the leadership position of a senior partner in a law firm. What task, subordinate, and organizational factors might serve as substitutes for leadership in this situation?

■ Manager's Workbook

T–P Leadership Questionnaire: An Assessment of Style

Some leaders deal with general directions, leaving details to subordinates. Other leaders focus on specific details with the expectation that subordinates will carry out orders. Depending on the situation, both approaches may be effective. The important issue is the ability to identify relevant dimensions of the situation and behave accordingly. Through this questionnaire, you can identify your relative emphasis on two dimensions of leadership: task orientation (T) and people orientation (P). These are not opposite approaches, and an individual can rate high or low on either or both.

Directions: The following items describe aspects of leadership behavior. Respond to each item according to the way you would most likely act if you were the leader of a work group. Circle whether you would most likely behave in the described way: always (A), frequently (F), occasionally (O), seldom (S), or never (N).

1. I would most likely act as the spokesperson of the group.	A	F	O	S	N
2. I would encourage overtime work.	A	F	O	S	N
3. I would allow members complete freedom in their work.	A	F	O	S	N
4. I would encourage the use of uniform procedures.	A	F	O	S	N
5. I would permit members to use their own judgment in solving problems.	A	F	O	S	N
6. I would stress being ahead of competing groups.	A	F	O	S	N
7. I would speak as a representative of the group.	A	F	O	S	N
8. I would needle members for greater effort.	A	F	O	S	N
9. I would try out my ideas in the group.	A	F	O	S	N
10. I would let members do their work the way they think best.	A	F	O	S	N
11. I would be working hard for a promotion.	A	F	O	S	N
12. I would tolerate postponement and uncertainty.	A	F	O	S	N
13. I would speak for the group if there were visitors present.	A	F	O	S	N
14. I would keep the work moving at a rapid pace.	A	F	O	S	N
15. I would turn the members loose on a job and let them go to it.	A	F	O	S•	N
16. I would settle conflicts when they occur in the group.	A	F	O	S	N
17. I would get swamped by details.	A	F	O	S	N
18. I would represent the group at outside meetings.	A	F	O	S	N
19. I would be reluctant to allow the members any freedom of action.	A	F	O	S	N
20. I would decide what should be done and how it should be done.	A	F	O	S	N
21. I would push for increased production.	A	F	O	S	N
22. I would let some members have authority that I could keep.	A	F	O	S	N
23. Things would usually turn out as I had predicted.	A	F	O	S	N
24. I would allow the group a high degree of initiative.	A	F	O	S	N
25. I would assign group members to particular tasks.	A	F	O	S	N
26. I would be willing to make changes.	A	F	O	S	N
27. I would ask the members to work harder.	A	F	O	S	N
28. I would trust the group members to exercise good judgment.	A	F	O	S	N
29. I would schedule the work to be done.	A	F	O	S	N
30. I would refuse to explain my actions.	A	F	O	S	N
31. I would persuade others that my ideas are to their advantage.	A	F	O	S	N
32. I would permit the group to set its own pace.	A	F	O	S	N
33. I would urge the group to beat its previous record.	A	F	O	S	N
34. I would act without consulting the group.	A	F	O	S	N
35. I would ask that group members follow standard rules and regulations.	A	F	O	S	N

T _____ P_____

The T–P Leadership Questionnaire is scored as follows:

a. Write the number 1 in front of a bolded question if you responded S (seldom) or N (never) to that item.

b. Also write a number 1 in front of an unbolded question if you responded A (always) or F (frequently).

c. Circle the number 1s that you have written in front of the following items: 3, 5, 8, 10, 15, 18, 19, 22, 24, 26, 28, 30, 32, 34, and 35.

d. *Count the circled number 1s.* This is your score for concern for people. Record the score in the blank following the letter P at the end of the questionnaire.

e. *Count uncircled number 1s.* This is your score for concern for task. Record this number in the blank following the letter T.

SOURCE: The T–P Leadership Questionnaire was adapted by J. B. Ritchie and P. Thompson in *Organization and People* (New York: West, 1984). Copyright 1969 by the American Educational Research Association. Adapted by permission of the publisher.

■ Manager's Workbook

Assumptions about Leaders

Complete the sentences below.

1. A leader must always . . .
2. Leaders should never . . .
3. The best leader I ever had did . . .
4. The worst leader I ever had did . . .
5. When I am doing a good job as a leader, I . . .
6. I am afraid of leaders who . . .
7. I would follow a leader who . . .
8. I am repelled by leaders who . . .
9. Some people think they are good leaders, but they are not because they . . .
10. I want to be the kind of leader who . . .

In groups of 4–6, discuss the following:

1. What did you learn about your own assumptions about leadership?
2. Trace those assumptions back to theories on leadership in this chapter.
3. What were common themes in your group?

Copyright © 2000 by Dorothy Marcic.

■ Management in Practice: Ethical Dilemma

Does Wage Reform Start at the Top?

Paula Smith has just been offered the opportunity of a lifetime. The chairman of the board of Resitronic Corporation has asked her to take the job as director of the troubled audio equipment manufacturing subsidiary. The first question Smith asked was, "Will the board give me the autonomy to turn this company around?" The answer was yes. Resitronic's problems were so severe that the board was desperate for change and ready to give Smith whatever it took to save the company.

Smith knows that she must cut costs. Labor expenses are too high, and product quality and production times are below industry standards. She sees that labor and management at Resitronic are two armed camps, but she needs cooperation at all levels to achieve a turnaround. Smith is energized. She knows she finally has the autonomy to try out her theories about an empowered workforce. Smith knows she must ask managers and workers to take a serious pay cut, with the promise of incentives to share in any improvements they might make. She also knows that everyone will be looking at her own salary as an indication of whether she walks her talk.

Smith is torn. She realizes she faces a year or two of complete hell, with long hours, little time for her family or outside interests, bitter resistance in subordinates, and no guarantees of success. Even if she comes in at the current director's salary, she will be taking a cut in pay. But if she takes a bigger cut coming in, with the promise of bonuses and stock options tied to her own performance, she sends a strong message to the entire subsidiary that they rise or fall together. She wonders what might happen if she fails. Many influences on the audio equipment subsidiary are beyond her control. Resitronic itself is in trouble. From her current vantage point, Smith believes she can turn things around, but what will she discover when she gets inside? What if the board undercuts her? Doesn't she owe it to herself and her family to be compensated at the highest possible level for the stress and risk they will be enduring? Can she afford to risk her own security to send a message of commitment to the plan she is asking others to follow?

What Do You Do?

1. Take the same salary as the current director for one year. Circulate the information that although you are taking a cut to come to Resitronic, you are confident that you can make a difference. Build in pay incentive bonuses for the following years if the subsidiary succeeds.
2. Take a bigger cut in pay with generous incentive bonuses. Ask the board and the entire workforce to do the same. Open the books and let the whole company know exactly where they stand.
3. Ask for the same salary you are making now. You know you are going to be worth it, and you don't want to ask your family to suffer monetarily as well as in their quality of life during this transition.

■ Surf the Net

1. **Marine Leadership Principles.** Locate and print out the "Marine Leadership Principles and Traits" available at either of the sites listed. Prepare for a class discussion or write a summary on the principles and traits and the way they contribute to leadership in any situation.
   http://www.cnet.navy.mil/cnet/nlpg2001/pdf/usmc_leadership.pdf
   http://millennium.fortunecity.com/redwood/352/usmc16.htm

2. **Leadership Training.** Visit one of following Web sites for organizations that provide leadership training to organizations and locate an item of interest related to leadership. Print it out and bring it to class to share during a classroom discussion.
   http://www.blanchardtraining.com
   http://www.tompeters.com
   http://www.franklincovey.com

■ Case for Critical Analysis

DGL International

When DGL International, a manufacturer of refinery equipment, brought in John Terrill to manage its Technical Services division, company executives informed him of the urgent situation. Technical Services, with 20 engineers, was the highest-paid, best-educated, and least-productive division in the company. The instructions to Terrill: Turn it around. Terrill called a meeting of the engineers. He showed great concern for their personal welfare and asked point blank: "What's the problem? Why can't we produce? Why does this division have such turnover?"

Without hesitation, employees launched a hail of complaints. "I was hired as an engineer, not a pencil pusher." "We spend over half our time writing asinine reports in triplicate for top management, and no one reads the reports."

After a two-hour discussion, Terrill concluded he had to get top management off the engineers' backs. He promised the engineers, "My job is to stay out of your way so you can do your work, and I'll try to keep top management off your backs too." He called for the day's reports and issued an order effective immediately that the originals be turned in daily to his office rather than mailed to headquarters. For three weeks, technical reports piled up on his desk. By month's end, the stack was nearly three feet high. During that time no one called for the reports. When other managers entered his office and saw the stack, they usually asked, "What's all this?" Terrill answered, "Technical reports." No one asked to read them.

Finally, at month's end, a secretary from finance called and asked for the monthly travel and expense report. Terrill responded, "Meet me in the president's office tomorrow morning."

The next morning the engineers cheered as Terrill walked through the department pushing a cart loaded with the enormous stack of reports. They knew the showdown had come.

Terrill entered the president's office and placed the stack of reports on his desk. The president and the other senior executives looked bewildered.

"This," Terrill announced, "is the reason for the lack of productivity in the Technical Services division. These are the reports you people require every month. The fact that they sat on my desk all month shows that no one reads this material. I suggest that the engineers' time could be used in a more productive manner, and that one brief monthly report from my office will satisfy the needs of other departments."

Questions

1. What leadership style did John Terrill use? What do you think was his primary source of power?
2. Based on the Hersey-Blanchard theory, should Terrill have been less participative? Should he have initiated more task structure for the engineers? Explain.
3. What leadership approach would you have taken in this situation?

Motivation in Organizations

LEARNING OBJECTIVES

After studying this chapter, you should be able to

1   Define motivation and explain the difference between current approaches and traditional approaches to motivation.

2   Identify and describe content theories of motivation based on employee needs.

3   Identify and explain process theories of motivation.

4   Describe reinforcement theory and how it can be used to motivate employees.

5   Discuss major approaches to job design and how job design influences motivation.

6   Discuss how empowerment heightens employee motivation.

Management Challenge

The clear, plastic bags in the produce department, the ones that unroll from a dispenser one at a time, began as a refugee's idea. Rafael Alvarado fled Nicaragua during the Sandanista revolution and escaped to Costa Rica, where he became general manager for a company that makes plastic liners for banana shipping crates. He emigrated to Houston in 1984, bringing with him a prototype for a new kind of plastic bag.

He and two partners pooled funds from their credit cards and started Better Bags to distribute plastic packaging and wrap. In the beginning, it was only the three of them with a forklift, working 16-hour days. Alvarado pushed himself so hard that he ended up with a herniated disk. Even so, he managed to save $150,000. In 1990 he invested his entire savings, plus $3 million in bank loans and venture capital, to start a solo business, manufacturing his patented pull-down dispensers and bags. He was very nervous about the future and unable to tell his wife he had risked their entire life savings. "At least one of us could sleep," he says.

Alvarado rented a 50,000-square-foot plant and planned to hire 30 workers. He knew, from personal experience, that there would be many eager immigrants willing to work for meager wages. But low wages would make it hard for these workers to support their families. He also knew that decent pay could be a motivating factor. Still, not only his business but also his life savings were on the line, and he had to keep costs down in the beginning to give the company a better chance to survive. If the company went bankrupt, he wouldn't be able to hire anyone.[1]

If you were Rafael Alvarado, what would you do? Would you pay the workers enough to motivate them, or would you try to get by with paying minimal wages now and promising better rewards as the company became more successful?

The problem for Better Bags is that unmotivated employees do the minimum amount of work, causing product quality to suffer and the company to lose its competitive edge. One secret for success in organizations is motivated and enthusiastic employees. The challenge for Better Bags and other companies is to keep employee motivation consistent with organizational goals. Motivation is a challenge for managers because motivation arises from within employees and typically differs for each person. For example, Janice Rennie makes a staggering $350,000 a year selling residential real estate in Toronto; she attributes her success to the fact that she likes to listen carefully to clients and then finds a house to meet their needs. Greg Storey is a skilled machinist who is challenged by writing programs for numerically controlled machines. After dropping out of college, he swept floors in a machine shop and was motivated to learn to run the machines. Frances Blais sells educational books and software. She is a top salesperson, but she does not care about the $50,000-plus commissions: "I'm not even thinking money when I'm selling. I'm really on a crusade to help children read well." In stark contrast, Rob Michaels gets sick to his stomach before he goes to work. Rob is a telephone salesperson who spends all day trying to get people to buy products they do not need, and the rejections are painful. His motivation is money; he earned $120,000 in the past year and cannot make nearly that much doing anything else.[2]

Rob is motivated by money, Janice by her love of listening and problem solving, Frances by the desire to help children read, and Greg by the challenge of mastering numerically controlled machinery. Each person is motivated to perform, yet each has different reasons for performing. With such diverse motivations, it is a challenge for managers to motivate employees toward common organizational goals.

This chapter reviews theories and models of employee motivation. First we will review several perspectives on motivation and cover models that describe the employee needs and processes associated with motivation. Then, we will discuss how *job design*—changing the structure of the work itself—can affect employee satisfaction and productivity. Finally, we will examine the trend of *empowerment*, where authority and decision making are delegated to subordinates to increase employee motivation.

The Concept of Motivation

motivation

The arousal, direction, and persistence of behavior.

Most of us get up in the morning, go to school or work, and behave in ways that are predictably our own. We respond to our environment and the people in it with little thought as to why we work hard, enjoy certain classes, or find some recreational activities so much fun. Yet all these behaviors are motivated by something. **Motivation** refers to the forces either within or external to a person that arouse enthusiasm and persistence to pursue a certain course of action. Employee motivation affects productivity, and part of a manager's job is to channel motivation toward the accomplishment of organizational goals.[3] The study of motivation helps managers understand what prompts people to initiate action, what influences their choice of action, and why they persist in that action over time.

A simple model of human motivation is illustrated in Exhibit 13.1. People have basic *needs*, such as for food, achievement, or monetary gain, that translate into an internal tension that motivates specific behaviors with which to fulfill the need. To the extent that the behavior is successful, the person is

NEED Creates desire to fulfill needs (food, friendship, recognition, achievement)	**BEHAVIOR** Results in actions to fulfill needs	**REWARDS** Satisfy needs; intrinsic or extrinsic rewards

FEEDBACK Reward informs person whether behavior was appropriate and should be used again.

rewarded in the sense that the need is satisfied. The reward also informs the person that the behavior was appropriate and can be used again in the future.

Rewards are of two types: intrinsic and extrinsic. **Intrinsic rewards** are the satisfactions a person receives in the process of performing a particular action. The completion of a complex task may bestow a pleasant feeling of accomplishment, or solving a problem that benefits others may fulfill a personal mission. For example, Frances Blais sells educational materials for the intrinsic reward of helping children read well. **Extrinsic rewards** are given by another person, typically a manager, and include promotions and pay increases. They originate externally, as a result of pleasing others. Rob Michaels, who hates his sales job, nevertheless is motivated by the extrinsic reward of high pay. Although extrinsic rewards are important, good managers strive to help people achieve intrinsic rewards, as well. Today's managers are finding that the most talented and innovative employees are rarely motivated exclusively by rewards such as money and benefits, or even praise and recognition. Instead, they seek satisfaction from the work itself.[4]

The importance of motivation as illustrated in Exhibit 13.1 is that it can lead to behaviors that reflect high performance within organizations. One recent study found that high employee motivation goes hand-in-hand with high organizational performance and profits.[5] Managers can use motivation theory to help satisfy employees' needs and simultaneously encourage high work performance. With the recent massive layoffs in many U.S. organizations, managers are struggling to keep remaining workers focused and motivated. In addition, as the economy improves, finding and keeping talented workers may

EXHIBIT 13.1

A Simple Model of Motivation

intrinsic reward

The satisfaction received in the process of performing an action.

extrinsic reward

A reward given by another person.

© Gregory Foster

Some employees at software developer SAS Institute in Cary, North Carolina, are motivated by the top-quality day care that is available for $250 per month for their young children. Other SAS employees are motivated by offerings such as a 35-hour week, a free on-site medical clinic, or 12 holidays a year plus a paid week off between Christmas and New Year's. These extrinsic rewards that help employees maintain a balance between work and personal life earned SAS third-place honors in Fortune *magazine' list of 100 best companies to work for in America.*

be a significant challenge because of weakened trust and commitment. Managers have to find the right combination of motivational techniques and rewards to keep workers satisfied and productive in a variety of organizational situations. Often inexperienced managers resort to ineffective methods, but can learn over time how to change their own behavior in order to motivate each person in the most effective way, as Gerald Chamales learned in his inkjet and laser printer manufacturing company.

Rhinotek Computer Products

http://www.rhinotek.com

When Gerald Chamales founded Rhinotek 20 years ago, he had no management experience and quickly fell into a dictatorial pattern, throwing temper tantrums and screaming at employees who did not follow orders or measure up to his standards. In addition, he would withhold his approval on an employee's work if he was angry at the employee for some minor infraction, such as showing up for work a few minutes late or taking a long break. Employees began to hate their jobs and dreaded coming to work every day. Performance declined, absenteeism increased, and turnover kept getting higher. "I was getting the opposite behavior from what I wanted," Chamales says.

Fortunately, Chamales was able to shift his own behavior and try other tactics. Rather than assuming people needed strict control and discipline, he started looking at employees as individuals, each of whom might be motivated by different things. Instead of issuing orders and demanding that employees do things a certain way, he tried to learn what employees enjoyed and could devote themselves to wholeheartedly. He started walking about the offices and plant floor talking to people and getting feedback. "I started to see that being a leader means playing off of people's strengths instead of reprimanding them for their weaknesses," he says.

The changes Chamales made have turned Rhinotek into a much happier place to work, and the job satisfaction of many employees has improved, reflected in a dramatically declining turnover rate.[6]

Foundations of Motivation

A manager's assumptions about employee motivation and use of rewards depend on his or her perspective on motivation. Four distinct perspectives on employee motivation have evolved: the traditional approach, the human relations approach, the human resources approach, and the contemporary approach.[7]

Traditional Approach

The study of employee motivation really began with the work of Frederick W. Taylor on scientific management. Recall from Chapter 1 that scientific management pertains to the systematic analysis of an employee's job for the purpose of increasing efficiency. Economic rewards are provided to employees for high performance. The emphasis on pay evolved into the notion of the *economic man*—people would work harder for higher pay. This approach led to the development of incentive pay systems, in which people were paid strictly on the quantity and quality of their work outputs.

Human Relations Approach

The economic man was gradually replaced by a more sociable employee in managers' minds. Beginning with the landmark Hawthorne studies at a Western Electric plant, as described in Chapter 1, noneconomic rewards, such as congenial work groups that met social needs, seemed more important than money as a motivator of work behavior.[8] For the first time, workers were studied as people, and the concept of *social man* was born.

Human Resource Approach

The human resource approach carries the concepts of economic man and social man further to introduce the concept of the *whole person*. Human resource theory suggests that employees are complex and motivated by many factors. For example, the work by McGregor on Theory X and Theory Y described in Chapter 1 argued that people want to do a good job and that work is as natural and healthy as play. Proponents of the human resource approach believed that earlier approaches had tried to manipulate employees through economic or social rewards. By assuming that employees are competent and able to make major contributions, managers can enhance organizational performance. The human resource approach laid the groundwork for contemporary perspectives on employee motivation.

Contemporary Approach

The contemporary approach to employee motivation is dominated by three types of theories, each of which will be discussed in the following sections. The first are *content theories,* which stress the analysis of underlying human needs. Content theories provide insight into the needs of people in organizations and help managers understand how needs can be satisfied in the workplace. *Process theories* concern the thought processes that influence behavior. They focus on how employees seek rewards in work circumstances. *Reinforcement theories* focus on employee learning of desired work behaviors. In Exhibit 13.1, content theories focus on the concepts in the first box, process theories on those in the second, and reinforcement theories on those in the third.

Content Perspectives on Motivation

Content theories emphasize the needs that motivate people. At any point in time, people have basic needs such as those for food, achievement, or monetary reward. These needs translate into an internal drive that motivates specific behaviors in an attempt to fulfill the needs. An individual's needs are like a hidden catalog of the things he or she wants and will work to get. To the extent that managers understand worker needs, the organization's reward systems can be designed to meet them and reinforce employees for directing energies and priorities toward attainment of organizational goals.

content theories

A group of theories that emphasize the needs that motivate people.

Hierarchy of Needs Theory

Probably the most famous content theory was developed by Abraham Maslow.[9] Maslow's **hierarchy of needs theory** proposes that humans are motivated by multiple needs and that these needs exist in a hierarchical order as illustrated in Exhibit 13.2. Maslow identified five general types of motivating needs in order of ascendance:

hierarchy of needs theory

A content theory that proposes that people are motivated by five categories of needs—physiological, safety, belongingness, esteem, and self-actualization—that exist in a hierarchical order.

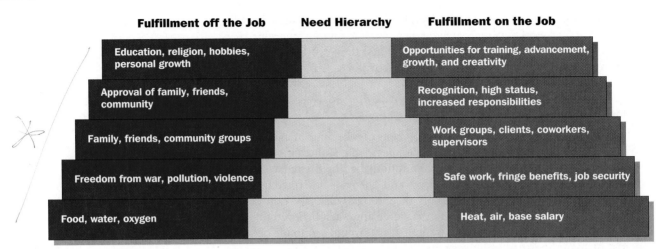

Fulfillment off the Job   **Need Hierarchy**   **Fulfillment on the Job**

Fulfillment off the Job	Fulfillment on the Job
Education, religion, hobbies, personal growth	Opportunities for training, advancement, growth, and creativity
Approval of family, friends, community	Recognition, high status, increased responsibilities
Family, friends, community groups	Work groups, clients, coworkers, supervisors
Freedom from war, pollution, violence	Safe work, fringe benefits, job security
Food, water, oxygen	Heat, air, base salary

E X H I B I T 13.2

Maslow's Hierarchy of Needs

1. *Physiological needs.* These are the most basic human physical needs, including food, water, and oxygen. In the organizational setting, these are reflected in the needs for adequate heat, air, and base salary to ensure survival.

2. *Safety needs.* These are the needs for a safe and secure physical and emotional environment and freedom from threats—that is, for freedom from violence and for an orderly society. In an organizational workplace, safety needs reflect the needs for safe jobs, fringe benefits, and job security.

3. *Belongingness needs.* These needs reflect the desire to be accepted by one's peers, have friendships, be part of a group, and be loved. In the organization, these needs influence the desire for good relationships with coworkers, participation in a work group, and a positive relationship with supervisors.

4. *Esteem needs.* These needs relate to the desire for a positive self-image and to receive attention, recognition, and appreciation from others. Within organizations, esteem needs reflect a motivation for recognition, an increase in responsibility, high status, and credit for contributions to the organization.

5. *Self-actualization needs.* These represent the need for self-fulfillment, which is the highest need category. They concern developing one's full potential, increasing one's competence, and becoming a better person. Self-actualization needs can be met in the organization by providing people with opportunities to grow, be creative, and acquire training for challenging assignments and advancement.

Mariposas de New Mexico recognized the primacy of basic survival needs when it began its programs.

Mariposas de New Mexico

Fleeing a husband who sexually abused her children, Maria Gonzales* moved from Mexico to Las Cruces, New Mexico. She arrived with two suitcases, three hundred dollars, three children, and no idea how she could support her family. Gonzalez is not alone in her predicament.

An awareness that poor Hispanic women often must support their families was one of the principles leading to the founding of Mariposas de New Mexico, a social and economic development project designed to employ poor Hispanic women. First the women are trained by Mujeres Mariposas, a program which provides day care and transportation to eligible women, who live primarily in areas lacking infrastructure such as sewage or water lines. Earning at least $7 per hour in a 14-week session, these women learn skilled trades in making high-end jewelry and scarves, which are then sold to vendors for department stores and boutiques. They learn how to make patterns, sew on sequins, how to do appliqué and sew invisible zippers, as well as how to make fringe, accents, and beads complement one another. The women who don't continue to work for Mariposas de New Mexico might find jobs with other small manufacturers. Others choose to start their own businesses, and can also learn computer skills, inventory management, and accounting, and apply for a revolving microcredit loan fund of $7,500.

Says Lupe Medina,* a Mariposas graduate, "I'm able to stop getting AFDC from the state with the pay that I'm receiving now. I'm hoping to have a little bit of time to start writing about what my life has been like, from as far back as I can remember to this point. I can pass it on to my family or help others realize that there is always hope if you believe in yourself."[10]

*names disguised

According to Maslow's theory, low-order needs take priority—they must be satisfied before higher-order needs are activated. The needs are satisfied in sequence: Physiological needs come before safety needs, safety needs before social needs, and so on. A person desiring physical safety will devote his or her efforts to securing a safer environment and will not be concerned with esteem needs or self-actualization needs. Once a need is satisfied, it declines in importance and the next higher need is activated. At All Metro Health Care in Lynbrook, New York, CEO Irving Edwards set up a special "customer service" department for his home health aides to help meet their basic needs, such as applying for food stamps and finding transportation and child care. Three employees are available solely to help workers with these issues. Once these lower-level needs are met, employees desire to have higher-level needs met in the workplace, so Irving developed programs such as an award for caregiver of the year, essay contests with prizes, and special recognition for high scores on quarterly training exercises.[11]

ERG Theory

Clayton Alderfer proposed a modification of Maslow's theory in an effort to simplify it and respond to criticisms of its lack of empirical verification.[12] His **ERG theory** identified three categories of needs:

1. *Existence needs.* These are the needs for physical well-being.

2. *Relatedness needs.* These pertain to the need for satisfactory relationships with others.

3. *Growth needs.* These focus on the development of human potential and the desire for personal growth and increased competence. Sandstrom faced a financial crisis that could spell doom, but instead learned to help its employees grow and thereby helped its own growth, as described below.

ERG theory

A modification of the needs hierarchy theory that proposes three categories of needs: existence, relatedness, and growth.

After 13 years at Sandstrom Products, a manufacturer of paints and coatings, Leo Henkelman was thinking about quitting. He had started as a paint runner, the lowest job in the plant, and worked his way up to a mill operator position.

Sandstrom products

http://www.sandstromproducts.com

Henkelman spent his days mixing paints in a giant blender, following formulas supplied by the lab. As he gained knowledge and experience, he came up with a lot of good ideas for improving formulas; yet the guys in the lab continually ignored his suggestions. "It was like they hired me from the neck down," he said. "Warm body, strong back, weak mind." Increasing pressure from quality-conscious customers multiplied the frustration he shared with most of the operators, who felt powerless to change anything. Some workers, including Henkelman, just stopped caring. Finding no challenge at work, he would show up with a hangover and just put in time until he could clock out and hit the bottle again. Top management knew the company had problems—for one thing, Sandstrom was hemorrhaging cash, losing money for the third year out of the last five. Things had to change, or Sandstrom would go broke. Then top management empowered workers by implementing open-book management. Henkelman was given the opportunity to take on more responsibility, learn new skills, and make improvements. He learned his own strengths and limitations in the process. While serving as a temporary plant manager, he found that delegation was not his strength—doing was. When a technician job opened up in the lab, he applied. Although he lacked the educational background normally required, the lab director gave him a chance. Now, using his experience, Henkelman guides the manufacturing process from beginning to end, working with customers to develop new products and refine old ones. As his skills and responsibilities increased, so did his pay, thanks to a proficiency pay system that based his pay on his skills and accomplishments and a gain-sharing plan that allowed him to share in the company's profits. By trusting and empowering workers, Sandstrom gave them a reason to care about the company and the knowledge and power to make personal contributions to organizational performance. Results were staggering, as Sandstrom rebounded from a loss of $100,000 to earnings of almost $800,000 two years later.[13]

frustration-regression principle

The idea that failure to meet a high-order need may cause a regression to an already satisfied lower-order need.

The ERG model and Maslow's need hierarchy are similar because both are in hierarchical form and presume that individuals move up the hierarchy one step at a time. However, Alderfer reduced the number of need categories to three and proposed that movement up the hierarchy is more complex, reflecting a **frustration-regression principle**, namely, that failure to meet a high-order need may trigger a regression to an already fulfilled lower-order need. Thus, a worker who cannot fulfill a need for personal growth may revert to a lower-order need and redirect his or her efforts toward making a lot of money. The ERG model therefore is less rigid than Maslow's need hierarchy, suggesting that individuals may move down as well as up the hierarchy, depending on their ability to satisfy needs.

Need hierarchy theory helps explain why organizations find ways to recognize employees and encourage their participation in decision making. Southwest Airlines emphasizes extensive employee training through its corporate university so that managers can push responsibility and decision making down the chain of command. "It's very validating and it taps into people's motivation for their jobs if they know that their opinion matters," says Peter Nelson, creative development manager for Southwest's University of People.[14] A recent survey found that employees who contribute ideas at work are more likely to feel valued, committed, and motivated. In addition, when employees' ideas are implemented and recognized, there tends to be a motivational ripple effect throughout the workforce.[15]

FOCUS ON COLLABORATION

Norsk Hydro: Working Better by Working Less

Norwegians have always had a very different attitude than Americans about the meaning of work and its place in one's life. Their view is rooted in the notion of balance, and the idea that working less often means working better. As one of Norway's dominant institutions, Norsk Hydro has long been involved in innovative work approaches that enable employees to live a balanced life. Hydro is involved in numerous businesses, from salmon farming, to fertilizers, to oil and metal. But despite its diverse businesses, the core values of the company haven't changed in its 95 years of operation. "What is deep in the culture of Hydro is to think in the long term, to think more holistically—to think about the connections between employees, the company, and society," says Roald Nomme, a consultant and former Hydro manager.

Today, Hydro is expanding its thinking about those connections further than ever before in a project called Hydroflex, which offers employees varying combinations of flexible hours, teamwork, home offices, new technology, and redesigned office space. For example, Atle Tærum, chief agronomist at Norsk Hydro, spends two days a week at home, where he tends to his farm and cares for his children. With his cell phone constantly within reach, Tærum may be consulting with customers from Africa or the Middle East while he's plowing a field or chaperoning his son's kindergarten class. Before the flexible arrangement, Tærum says he was tired and unhappy most of the time. "Now I can manage my day and my life a bit better. I think I'm doing a better job for Hydro." Another employee, Unni Foss, who works as a graphic artist at Hydro Media, was able to work at home full time during the months before her father's death, to be with him and help her mother. The arrangement enabled her to keep a job and salary she needed and enabled Hydro to get good work from a talented worker. "We used to focus on how many hours people were in the office," says Ole Johan Sagafos, the head of Hydro Media. "Now we focus on results. It doesn't really matter to me what my colleagues are doing as long as they deliver the results on time."

Hydro sees its work–life balance initiatives as critical strategic elements for remaining competitive. Offering people flexibility in terms of how, where, and when they work attracts better workers and makes them more productive. In addition, the initiatives promote flexibility and diversity of thinking that is critical for success in today's fast-paced world. Ragnhild Sohlberg, vice president of external relations and special projects, uses the analogy of an experienced farmer who knows better than to plant, harvest, plow, and reseed the same field season after season—he knows that the soil needs a period of time to rest and rejuvenate. Modern corporations, though, think nothing of working their most talented people ceaselessly until they burn out and leave. "And all their experience goes with them," she says. "It's lost. That practice is not good business."

SOURCE: Charles Fishman, "The Way to Enough," *Fast Company* (July–August 1999), 160–174.

Many companies are finding that creating a humane work environment that allows people to achieve a balance between work and personal life is also a great high-level motivator. At ClickAction Inc., an online direct-marketing firm based in Palo Alto, California, managers have created a culture of "working smarter and respecting people's time" to enhance motivation and productivity.[16] The Focus on Collaboration box introduces another company founded on the premise that people should have plenty of time and energy for a life outside the office. It describes how Norsk Hydro, a Norway-based organization that operates in 70 countries and employs 39,000 people, has gone to extraordinary lengths to demonstrate its commitment to people as the key source of competitive advantage.

Two-Factor Theory

Frederick Herzberg developed another popular theory of motivation called the *two-factor theory*.[17] Herzberg interviewed hundreds of workers about times when they were highly motivated to work and other times when they were dissatisfied and unmotivated at work. His findings suggested that the work characteristics associated with dissatisfaction were quite different from those

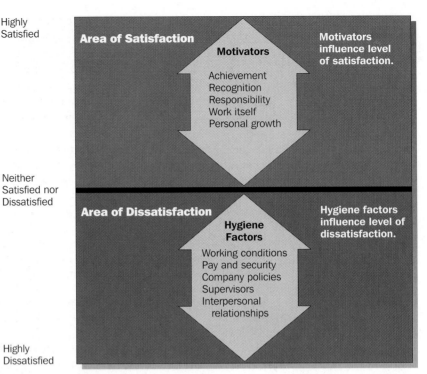

EXHIBIT 13.3

Herzberg's Two-Factor Theory

hygiene factors

Factors that involve the presence or absence of job dissatisfiers, including working conditions, pay, company policies, and interpersonal relationships.

motivators

Factors that influence job satisfaction based on fulfillment of high-level needs such as achievement, recognition, responsibility, and opportunity for growth.

pertaining to satisfaction, which prompted the notion that two factors influence work motivation.

The two-factor theory is illustrated in Exhibit 13.3. The center of the scale is neutral, meaning that workers are neither satisfied nor dissatisfied. Herzberg believed that two entirely separate dimensions contribute to an employee's behavior at work. The first, called **hygiene factors**, involves the presence or absence of job dissatisfiers, such as working conditions, pay, company policies, and interpersonal relationships. When hygiene factors are poor, work is dissatisfying. However, good hygiene factors simply remove the dissatisfaction; they do not in themselves cause people to be highly satisfied and motivated in their work.

The second set of factors does influence job satisfaction. **Motivators** are high-level needs and include achievement, recognition, responsibility, and opportunity for growth. Herzberg believed that when motivators are absent, workers are neutral toward work, but when motivators are present, workers are highly motivated and satisfied. Thus, hygiene factors and motivators represent two distinct factors that influence motivation. Hygiene factors work only in the area of dissatisfaction. Unsafe working conditions or a noisy work environment will cause people to be dissatisfied, but their correction will not lead to a high level of motivation and satisfaction. Motivators such as challenge, responsibility, and recognition must be in place before employees will be highly motivated to excel at their work.

The implication of the two-factor theory for managers is clear. Providing hygiene factors will eliminate employee dissatisfaction but will not motivate workers to high achievement levels. On the other hand, recognition, challenge, and opportunities for personal growth are powerful motivators and will promote high satisfaction and performance. The manager's role is to remove dissatisfiers—that is, to provide hygiene factors sufficient to meet basic needs—and then use motivators to meet higher-level needs and propel employees toward greater achievement and satisfaction. For example, A.W. Chesterton, a private, Massachusetts-based maker of seals and pumps, relies on both hygiene factors and motivators to try to prevent dissatisfaction and increase satisfaction among workers. In addition to adequate pay, good working conditions, and great benefits, Chesterton also incorporates high-level motivators such as a chance for employees to be involved in solving problems. Employees are provided with full information, including confidential data, and are challenged to come up with ideas to help the company survive in the face of increased competition. This open process is intrinsically motivating to employees, who appreciate the higher level of responsibility and the degree of trust placed in them. Employees have been known to go above and beyond the call of duty to solve a customer problem, even working voluntarily on weekends. Also at Chesterton, a profit-sharing plan and special awards to high performers increase satisfaction by providing a source of both achievement and recognition.[18]

At General Electric ebusiness, managers have found the combination of taking away dissatisfiers regarding working conditions, but still keeping the satisfiers in the form of chances for learning and growth, as described in the Digital, Inc. box.

Acquired Needs Theory

The final content theory was developed by David McClelland. The *acquired needs theory* proposes that certain types of needs are acquired during the individual's lifetime. In other words, people are not born with these needs but may learn them through their life experiences.[19] The three needs most frequently studied are these:

1. *Need for achievement.* The desire to accomplish something difficult, attain a high standard of success, master complex tasks, and surpass others.

2. *Need for affiliation.* The desire to form close personal relationships, avoid conflict, and establish warm friendships.

3. *Need for power.* The desire to influence or control others, be responsible for others, and have authority over others.

DIGITAL, INC.

General Electric Ebusiness

If an employee gets tired of eating free ice cream bars, watching the latest DVD movie, or playing foosball, the next thing to do is to put on inline skates and whiz through the office. Sound like a bunch of kids in a Silicon Valley start-up? Think again. It is the Atlanta office of General Electric's ebusiness, responsible for keeping up its Web site, a business-to-business exchange for its $40 million turbine business. It might be workplace-as-Space-Mountain, but the job is serious. It was inspired by Willy Wonka look-alike Alan Boehme, the CIO of GE's ebusiness center.

The fun isn't done just for fun. "It's a retention tool," says Boehme, who hasn't lost any of his 200 employees in over a year. The workplace itself has become a recruiting tool, as well, and most of his employees came from elsewhere in the company, lured by the lively atmosphere. But don't let the fun fool you. It's built on a hard-working culture that, in turn, shows high productivity. For every comfortable couch for lounging, there is a power strip and data jack within reach. You might think, though, that after a while all those whimsical goings on would get a bit tiring. IT Program Manager Dawn Griffin thought about lobbying for one of the rare private offices, but then decided otherwise. "I'd really miss this whole environment," she says. Maybe she meant the singing bass mounted on the wall.

SOURCE: Jason Kelly, "Who Says Work Isn't All Fun and Games?" http://www.business2.com (November 2000), 75.

Early life experiences determine whether people acquire these needs. If children are encouraged to do things for themselves and receive reinforcement, they will acquire a need to achieve. If they are reinforced for forming warm human relationships, they will develop a need for affiliation. If they get satisfaction from controlling others, they will acquire a need for power. For example, Jack Welch, former CEO of General Electric, has credited his mother for his ambition and achievement drive. Welch's mother was determined that he be successful, so she constantly encouraged and pushed him to do better in school.[20]

For more than 20 years, McClelland studied human needs and their implication for management. People with a high need for achievement are frequently entrepreneurs. They like to do something better than competitors and take sensible business risks. On the other hand, people who have a high need for affiliation are successful *integrators*, whose job is to coordinate the work of several departments in an organization.[21] Integrators include brand managers and project managers who must have excellent people skills. People high in need for affiliation are able to establish positive working relationships with others.

A high need for power often is associated with successful attainment of top levels in the organizational hierarchy. For example, McClelland studied managers at AT&T for 16 years and found that those with a high need for power were more likely to follow a path of continued promotion over time. More than half of the employees at the top levels had a high need for power. In contrast, managers with a high need for achievement but a low need for power tended to peak earlier in their careers and at a lower level. The reason is that achievement needs can be met through the task itself, but power needs can be met only by ascending to a level at which a person has power over others.

In summary, content theories focus on people's underlying needs and label those particular needs that motivate behavior. The hierarchy of needs theory, the ERG theory, the two-factor theory, and the acquired needs theory all help managers understand what motivates people. In this way, managers can design work to meet needs and hence elicit appropriate and successful work behaviors.

Process Perspectives on Motivation

process theories
A group of theories that explain how employees select behaviors with which to meet their needs and determine whether their choices were successful.

equity theory
A process theory that focuses on individuals' perceptions of how fairly they are treated relative to others.

Process theories explain how workers select behavioral actions to meet their needs and determine whether their choices were successful. There are two basic process theories: equity theory and expectancy theory.

Equity Theory

Equity theory focuses on individuals' perceptions of how fairly they are treated compared with others. Developed by J. Stacy Adams, equity theory proposes that people are motivated to seek social equity in the rewards they expect for performance.[22]

According to equity theory, if people perceive their compensation as equal to what others receive for similar contributions, they will believe that their treatment is fair and equitable. People evaluate equity by a ratio of inputs to outcomes. Inputs to a job include education, experience, effort, and ability. Outcomes from a job include pay, recognition, benefits, and promotions. The input-to-outcome ratio may be compared to another person in the work group or to a perceived group average. A state of **equity** exists whenever the ratio of one person's outcomes to inputs equals the ratio of another's outcomes to inputs.

Inequity occurs when the input/outcome ratios are out of balance, such as when a person with a high level of education or experience receives the same salary as a new, less-educated employee. Perceived inequity also occurs in the other direction. Thus, if an employee discovers she is making more money than other people who contribute the same inputs to the company, she may feel the need to correct the inequity by working harder, getting more education, or considering lower pay. Perceived inequity creates tensions within individuals that motivate them to bring equity into balance.[23]

The most common methods for reducing a perceived inequity are these:

- *Change inputs.* A person may choose to increase or decrease his or her inputs to the organization. For example, underpaid individuals may reduce their level of effort or increase their absenteeism. Overpaid people may increase effort on the job.

- *Change outcomes.* A person may change his or her outcomes. An underpaid person may request a salary increase or a bigger office. A union may try to improve wages and working conditions in order to be consistent with a comparable union whose members make more money. One company uses open information when someone requests a wage increase, as described in the Best Practices box.

- *Distort perceptions.* Research suggests that people may distort perceptions of equity if they are unable to change inputs or outcomes. They may artificially increase the status attached to their jobs or distort others' perceived rewards to bring equity into balance.

equity

A situation that exists when the ratio of one person's outcomes to inputs equals that of another's.

BEST PRACTICES

Romac Industries

The biggest secret in some workplaces is what everyone earns. But one 300-person Seattle company is the opposite of secretive. Waterworks manufacturer Romac Industries has workers who not only know what everyone else makes, but also vote on one another's raises. CEO Jim Larkin believes in openness and transparency, keeping all salaries an open book, and even subjecting the issue of pay to open debate.

When starting this process in 1974, Larkin viewed it as accepting reality. "The worst-kept secret in any plant is what people make," he says. "Everybody ends up finding out anyway, so we just post it."

If an employee wants more pay, the information goes up on a bulletin board: name, picture, current salary, and requested increase. All employees vote by secret ballot, indicating what raise they think the person deserves, from 0 to 100 percent. "You can get a raise every month if people vote for you," says Larkin.

Doesn't it become a popularity contest? Larkin thinks there's nothing wrong with giving employees a reason to get along with one another. There have been a few popular employees who didn't impress management as much as they did their coworkers, but those cases have been rare. The raises usually are what the managers would have given anyway.

In the beginning, employees could vote only yes or no for a fellow worker's raise, but they asked for the chance to give partial raises, and the percentage system was born. As Romac grew and employees knew less about one another, they started asking the person's foreman for advice. "So, now, foremen make recommendations, but employees don't have to listen," says Larkin.

SOURCE: Christopher Caggiano, "Raises by Democracy," *Inc.* (April 1999), 105.

- *Leave the job.* People who feel inequitably treated may decide to leave their jobs rather than suffer the inequity of being under- or overpaid. In their new jobs, they expect to find a more favorable balance of rewards.

The implication of equity theory for managers is that employees indeed evaluate the perceived equity of their rewards compared to others'. An increase in salary or a promotion will have no motivational effect if it is perceived as inequitable relative to that of other employees. A good example of equity theory comes from the J. Peterman Company, the trendy catalog company that eventually slid into bankruptcy before being acquired by another firm. John Peterman had created a comfortable, creative culture where employees were highly motivated to work together toward common goals. However, when the company began to grow rapidly, Peterman found himself having to hire people very quickly—and he often had to offer them higher salaries than those of his current employees to match what they were making elsewhere. In addition, when making important decisions, leaders tended to pay more attention to the ideas and thoughts of the new staff than they did the "old timers." Long-time employees felt slighted, and motivation declined significantly. Many employees began putting less energy and effort into their jobs. They were no longer willing to go the extra mile because of a perceived state of inequity.[24] Inequitable pay puts pressure on employees that is sometimes almost too great to bear. They attempt to change their work habits, try to change the system, or leave the job.[25]

Smart managers try to keep feelings of equity in balance in order to keep their workforces motivated.

Expectancy Theory

expectancy theory

A process theory that proposes that motivation depends on individuals' expectations about their ability to perform tasks and receive desired rewards.

Expectancy theory suggests that motivation depends on individuals' expectations about their ability to perform tasks and receive desired rewards. Expectancy theory is associated with the work of Victor Vroom, although a number of scholars have made contributions in this area.[26] Expectancy theory is concerned not with identifying types of needs but with the thinking process that individuals use to achieve rewards. Consider Bill Bradley, a university student with a strong desire for a B in his accounting course. Bill has a C+ average and one more exam to take. Bill's motivation to study for that last exam will be influenced by (1) the expectation that hard study will lead to an A on the exam and (2) the expectation that an A on the exam will result in a B for the course. If Bill believes he cannot get an A on the exam or that receiving an A will not lead to a B for the course, he will not be motivated to study exceptionally hard.

Elements of Expectancy Theory. Expectancy theory is based on the relationship among the individual's *effort,* the individual's *performance,* and the desirability of *outcomes* associated with high performance. These elements and the relationships among them are illustrated in Exhibit 13.4. The keys to expectancy theory are the expectancies for the relationships among effort, performance, and outcomes with the value of the outcomes to the individual.

E → P expectancy

Expectancy that putting effort into a given task will lead to high performance.

E → P expectancy involves whether putting effort into a task will lead to high performance. For this expectancy to be high, the individual must have the ability, previous experience, and necessary machinery, tools, and opportunity to perform. For Bill Bradley to get a B in the accounting course, the E → P expectancy is high if Bill truly believes that with hard work, he can get an A on the final exam. If Bill believes he has neither the ability nor the opportunity to achieve high performance, the expectancy will be low, and so will be his motivation.

P → O expectancy involves whether successful performance will lead to the desired outcome. In the case of a person who is motivated to win a job-related award, this expectancy concerns the belief that high performance will truly lead to the award. If the P → O expectancy is high, the individual will be more highly motivated. If the expectancy is that high performance will not produce the desired outcome, motivation will be lower. If an A on the final exam is likely to produce a B in the accounting course, Bill Bradley's P → O expectancy will be high. Bill might talk to the professor to see whether an A will be sufficient to earn him the B in the course. If not, he will be less motivated to study hard for the final exam.

Valence is the value of outcomes, or attraction for outcomes, for the individual. If the outcomes that are available from high effort and good performance are not valued by employees, motivation will be low. Likewise, if outcomes have a high value, motivation will be higher.

Expectancy theory attempts not to define specific types of needs or rewards but only to establish that they exist and may be different for every individual. One employee might want to be promoted to a position of increased responsibility, and another might have high valence for good relationships with peers. Consequently, the first person will be motivated to work hard for a promotion and the second for the opportunity for a team position that will keep him or her associated with a group.

A simple sales department example will explain how the expectancy model in Exhibit 13.4 works. If Alecia Adams, a salesperson at the Diamond Gift Shop, believes that increased selling effort will lead to higher personal sales, we can say that she has a high E → P expectancy. Moreover, if Alecia also believes that higher personal sales will lead to a promotion or pay raise, we can say that she has a high P → O expectancy. Finally, if Alecia places a high value on the promotion or pay raise, valence is high and Alecia will have a high motivational force. On the other hand, if either the E → P or P → O expectancy is low, or if the money or promotion has low valence for Alecia, the overall motivational force will be low. For an employee to be highly motivated, all three factors in the expectancy model must be high.[27]

© Barbara Laing

Circuit City managers are using expectancy theory principles to help meet employees' needs while attaining organizational goals. By creating an incentive program that is a commission-based plan designed to provide the highest compensation to sales counselors who are committed to serving every customer, Circuit City achieves its volume and profitability objectives. The incentive program is also used in other areas such as distribution, where employees are recognized for accomplishments in safety, productivity, and attendance.

P → O expectancy
Expectancy that successful performance of a task will lead to the desired outcome.

valence
The value or attraction an individual has for an outcome.

E X H I B I T *13.4*

Major Elements of Expectancy Theory

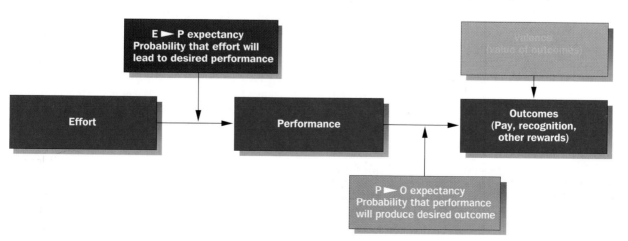

Effort →	Performance →	Outcomes (Pay, recognition, other rewards)

E ► P expectancy Probability that effort will lead to desired performance

Valence (value of outcomes)

P ► O expectancy Probability that performance will produce desired outcome

Implications for Managers. The expectancy theory of motivation is similar to the path-goal theory of leadership described in Chapter 12. Both theories are personalized to subordinates' needs and goals. Managers' responsibility is to help subordinates meet their needs and at the same time attain organizational goals. Managers must try to find a match between a subordinate's skills and abilities and the job demands. To increase motivation, managers can clarify individuals' needs, define the outcomes available from the organization, and ensure that each individual has the ability and support (namely, time and equipment) needed to attain outcomes.

Some companies use expectancy theory principles by designing incentive systems that identify desired organizational outcomes and give everyone the same shot at getting the rewards. The trick is to design a system that fits with employees' abilities and needs. Consider the following example from the restaurant industry.

Katzinger's Delicatessen

http://www.katzingers.com

When Steve and Diane Warren, co-owners of Katzinger's Delicatessen in Columbus, Ohio, instituted open-book management, they hoped it would help them cut costs and save money. The Warrens trained employees in how to read the financials and told them Katzinger's would share the rewards with employees if financial performance improved. However, because most of their workers were young and mobile, and not committed to a long-term career with the company, the vague long-range goals and rewards did not provide a high degree of motivation. Many of them felt that they could do little to improve overall performance and that doing so was the job of managers, anyway. Thus, both E → P expectancy and P → O expectancy were low. The Warrens needed a simple, short-term goal as a way to energize their young workers. They proposed a simple plan: If workers would help reduce food costs to below 35 percent of sales without sacrificing food quality or service, they would be rewarded with half the savings.

Katzinger's workers were well-trained and knew they had the skills and ability to meet the goal if they all worked together; thus, the E → P expectancy was high. Workers immediately began proposing ideas to reduce waste, such as matching perishable food orders more closely to expected sales. The P → O expectancy was also high because of the level of trust at the company; workers were highly motivated to cooperate to decrease food costs because they knew everyone would benefit from the savings. Since anyone could look at the financials, workers could actually track their progress toward meeting the goal. At the end of the first month, food costs had fallen nearly 2 percent and employees took home about $40 each from the savings. Later monthly payouts were as high as $95 per employee. By the end of the year, food consistency and service had improved and Katzinger's had indeed reduced its food costs to below 35 percent of total sales, saving the company $30,000. The Warrens gladly distributed $15,000 of that amount to their workers for helping to meet the goal. Now, the Warrens are working out a similar plan to increase sales at Katzinger's.[28]

Reinforcement Perspective on Motivation

The reinforcement approach to employee motivation sidesteps the issues of employee needs and thinking processes described in the content and process theories. **Reinforcement theory** simply looks at the relationship between behavior and its consequences. It focuses on changing or modifying the employees' on-the-job behavior through the appropriate use of immediate rewards and punishments.

reinforcement theory
A motivation theory based on the relationship between a given behavior and its consequences.

Reinforcement Tools

Behavior modification is the name given to the set of techniques by which reinforcement theory is used to modify human behavior.[29] The basic assumption underlying behavior modification is the **law of effect**, which states that behavior that is positively reinforced tends to be repeated, and behavior that is not reinforced tends not to be repeated. **Reinforcement** is defined as anything that causes a certain behavior to be repeated or inhibited. The four reinforcement tools are positive reinforcement, avoidance learning, punishment, and extinction. Each type of reinforcement is a consequence of either a pleasant or unpleasant event being applied or withdrawn following a person's behavior. The four types of reinforcement are summarized in Exhibit 13.5.

behavior modification
The set of techniques by which reinforcement theory is used to modify human behavior.

law of effect
The assumption that positively reinforced behavior tends to be repeated and unreinforced or negatively reinforced behavior tends to be inhibited.

reinforcement
Anything that causes a given behavior to be repeated or inhibited.

Positive Reinforcement. *Positive reinforcement* is the administration of a pleasant and rewarding consequence following a desired behavior. A good example of positive reinforcement is immediate praise for an employee who arrives on time or does a little extra in his or her work. The pleasant consequence will increase the likelihood of the excellent work behavior occurring again. As another example, Frances Flood, CEO of Gentner Communications, a manufacturer of high-end audioconferencing equipment based in Salt Lake City, offered engineers a stake in the company's profits if they met targets for getting new products to market faster. Within two years, product development time had been slashed by 30 percent.[30] Studies have shown that positive reinforcement does help to improve performance. In addition, nonfinancial reinforcements such as positive feedback, social recognition, and attention are just as effective as financial incentives.[31]

EXHIBIT 13.5

Changing Behavior with Reinforcement

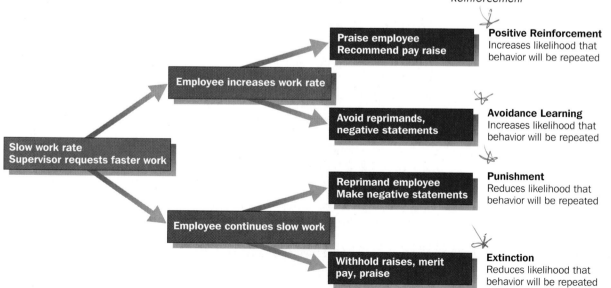

SOURCE: Based on Richard L. Daft and Richard M. Steers, *Organizations: A Micro/Macro Approach* (Glenview, Ill.: Scott, Foresman, 1986), 109.

Avoidance Learning. *Avoidance learning* is the removal of an unpleasant consequence following a desired behavior. Avoidance learning is sometimes called *negative reinforcement*. Employees learn to do the right thing by avoiding unpleasant situations. Avoidance learning occurs when a supervisor stops criticizing or reprimanding an employee once the incorrect behavior has stopped.

Punishment. *Punishment* is the imposition of unpleasant outcomes on an employee. Punishment typically occurs following undesirable behavior. For example, a supervisor may berate an employee for performing a task incorrectly. The supervisor expects that the negative outcome will serve as a punishment and reduce the likelihood of the behavior recurring. The use of punishment in organizations is controversial and often criticized because it fails to indicate the correct behavior. However, almost all managers report finding it necessary to occasionally impose forms of punishment ranging from verbal reprimands to employee suspensions or firings.[32]

Extinction. *Extinction* is the withdrawal of a positive reward. Whereas with punishment, the supervisor imposes an unpleasant outcome such as a reprimand, extinction involves withholding pay raises, praise, and other positive outcomes. The idea is that behavior that is not positively reinforced will be less likely to occur in the future. For example, if a perpetually tardy employee fails to receive praise and pay raises, he or she will begin to realize that the behavior is not producing desired outcomes. The behavior will gradually disappear if it is continually nonreinforced.

Some executives use reinforcement theory very effectively to shape employees' behavior. Jack Welch, former head of General Electric, was known as a master motivator. He used both positive and negative reinforcement through his famous handwritten notes either praising or prodding employees throughout the company. "The biggest job I have is to let people know how we feel about 'em," he once said. "You gotta tell them you love 'em and you gotta kick 'em in the [butt] when they're not doing their job. And you got to be able to hug 'em and kick 'em in the [butt] frequently."[33]

Schedules of Reinforcement

schedule of reinforcement

The frequency with which and intervals over which reinforcement occurs.

A great deal of research into reinforcement theory suggests that the timing of reinforcement has an impact on the speed of employee learning. **Schedules of reinforcement** pertain to the frequency with which and intervals over which reinforcement occurs. A reinforcement schedule can be selected to have maximum impact on employees' job behavior. There are five basic types of reinforcement schedules, which include continuous reinforcement and four types of partial reinforcement.

continuous reinforcement schedule

A schedule in which every occurrence of the desired behavior is reinforced.

Continuous Reinforcement. With a **continuous reinforcement schedule**, every occurrence of the desired behavior is reinforced. This schedule can be very effective in the early stages of learning new types of behavior, because every attempt has a pleasant consequence.

partial reinforcement schedule

A schedule in which only some occurrences of the desired behavior are reinforced.

Partial Reinforcement. However, in the real world of organizations, it is often impossible to reinforce every correct behavior. With a **partial reinforcement schedule**, the reinforcement is administered only after some occurrences of the correct behavior. There are four types of partial reinforcement schedules: fixed interval, fixed ratio, variable interval, and variable ratio.

1. *Fixed-Interval Schedule.* The *fixed-interval schedule* rewards employees at specified time intervals. If an employee displays the correct behavior each day, reinforcement may occur every week. Regular paychecks or quarterly bonuses are examples of a fixed-interval reinforcement. At Leone Ackerly's Mini Maid franchise in Marietta, Georgia, workers are rewarded with an attendance bonus each pay period if they have gone to work every day on time and in uniform.[34]

2. *Fixed-Ratio Schedule.* With a *fixed-ratio schedule,* reinforcement occurs after a specified number of desired responses, say, after every fifth. For example, paying a field hand $1.50 for picking 10 pounds of peppers is a fixed-ratio schedule. Most piece-rate pay systems are considered fixed-ratio schedules.

3. *Variable-Interval Schedule.* With a *variable-interval schedule,* reinforcement is administered at random times that cannot be predicted by the employee. An example would be a random inspection by the manufacturing superintendent of the production floor, at which time he or she commends employees on their good behavior.

4. *Variable-Ratio Schedule.* The *variable-ratio schedule* is based on a random number of desired behaviors rather than on variable time periods. Reinforcement may occur sometimes after 5, 10, 15, or 20 displays of behavior. One example is random monitoring of telemarketers, who may be rewarded after a certain number of calls in which they perform the appropriate behaviors and meet call performance specifications. Employees know they may be monitored but are never sure when checks will occur and when rewards may be given.

The schedules of reinforcement available to managers are illustrated in Exhibit 13.6. Continuous reinforcement is most effective for establishing new learning, but behavior is vulnerable to extinction. Partial reinforcement schedules are more effective for maintaining behavior over extended time periods. The most powerful is the variable-ratio schedule, because employee behavior will persist for a long time due to the administration of reinforcement only after a long interval.[35]

EXHIBIT *13.6*

Schedules of Reinforcement

Schedule of Reinforcement	Nature of Reinforcement	Effect on Behavior When Applied	Effect on Behavior When Withdrawn	Example
Continuous	Reward given after each desired behavior	Leads to fast learning of new behavior	Rapid extinction	Praise
Fixed-interval	Reward given at fixed time intervals	Leads to average and irregular performance	Rapid extinction	Weekly paycheck
Fixed-ratio	Reward given at fixed amounts of output	Quickly leads to very high and stable performance	Rapid extinction	Piece-rate pay system
Variable-interval	Reward given at variable times	Leads to moderately high and stable performance	Slow extinction	Performance appraisal and awards given at random times each month
Variable-ratio	Reward given at variable amounts of output	Leads to very high performance	Slow extinction	Sales bonus tied to number of sales calls, with random checks

One example of a small business that successfully uses reinforcement theory is Emerald Packaging in Union City, California.

Emerald Packaging

Emerald Packaging is a family-owned business that prints plastic bags for prepackaged salads and other vegetables. The company employs about 100 people and is the tenth-largest manufacturer in Union City, California, located about 30 miles southeast of San Francisco.

Kevin Kelly, vice president of operations for Emerald, and other top managers wanted to fire up employees by developing a positive reinforcement scheme that would motivate and reward workers. The plan at Emerald includes the following:

1. *Monthly quality award.* Each month, managers pick the best print job in the plant from samples submitted by printing press employees. The winning press operator gets $100 and the operator's helper wins $50.

2. *Safety program.* When the company has three or fewer minor accidents and no lost-time accidents during a quarter, leaders raffle off $1,000, provide workers with company shirts and jackets, and buy lunch for everyone. If employees make it through the entire year with only 12 minor accidents and no lost-time injuries, the company raffles a total of $10,000 to three winners and throws a party for all employees.

3. *Profit-sharing plan.* A certain percentage of operating profit is set aside into a bonus pool, which is shared among employees.

Has Emerald's plan for reinforcing correct behaviors worked? Kelly reports that customer returns for poor quality are down 75 percent over last year. The quality rewards of $50 to $100 are substantial enough to get employees' attention and make it worth their while to put increased effort into producing a high-quality print job. So far, safety results are also impressive. During the first five months of the program, the company had only one minor accident. Employees are much more careful about how they conduct themselves on the job because no one wants to derail the raffle.[36]

Reinforcement also works at such organizations as Campbell Soup Co., Emery Air Freight, Michigan Bell, and PSS World Medical, because managers reward appropriate behavior. They tell employees what they can do to receive reinforcement, tell them what they are doing wrong, distribute rewards equitably, tailor rewards to behaviors, and keep in mind that failure to reward deserving behavior has an equally powerful impact on employees. Communication is an important part of effective reinforcement because employees have to know what the rules are for getting rewards. At PSS World Medical, the bonus plan for sales representatives is communicated as a game, known as the "Field of Dreams," which has very clear rules and guidelines for how the bonus is calculated and what an employee must do to receive a bonus.[37]

Reward and punishment motivational practices dominate organizations, with as many as 94 percent of companies in the United States reporting that they use practices that reward performance or merit with pay.[38] In addition, a recent report by human resources consulting firm Towers Perrin indicates that incentive systems that reward employees with bonuses or other rewards for meeting certain goals are becoming increasingly popular. However, less than one-third of the companies reported seeing any noticeable impact of incentive

FOCUS ON SKILLS

The Carrot-and-Stick Controversy

Everybody thought Rob Rodin was crazy when he decided to wipe out all individual incentives for his sales force at Marshall Industries, a large distributor of electronic components based in El Monte, California. He did away with all bonuses, commissions, vacations, and other awards and rewards. All salespeople would receive a base salary plus the opportunity for profit sharing, which would be the same percent of salary for everyone, based on the entire company's performance. Six years later, Rodin says productivity per person has tripled at the company, but still he gets questions and criticism about his decision.

Rodin is standing right in the middle of a big controversy in modern management. Do financial and other rewards really motivate the kind of behavior organizations want and need? A growing number of critics say no, arguing that carrot-and-stick approaches are a holdover from the Industrial Age and are inappropriate and ineffective in today's economy. Today's workplace demands innovation and creativity from everyone—behaviors that rarely are inspired by money or other financial incentives. Reasons for criticism of carrot-and-stick approaches include the following:

1. *Extrinsic rewards diminish intrinsic rewards.* When people are motivated to seek an extrinsic reward, whether it be a bonus, an award, or the approval of a supervisor, generally they focus on the reward rather than on the work they do to achieve it. Thus, the intrinsic satisfaction people receive from performing their jobs actually declines. When people lack intrinsic rewards in their work, their performance stays just adequate to achieve the reward offered. In the worst case, employees may cover up mistakes, such as hiding an on-the-job accident in order to win a safety award.

2. *Extrinsic rewards are temporary.* Offering outside incentives may ensure short-term success, but not long-term high performance. When employees are focused only on the reward, they lose interest in their work. Without personal interest, the potential for exploration, creativity, and innovation disappears. Although the current deadline or goal may be met, better ways of working will not be discovered.

3. *Extrinsic rewards assume people are driven by lower-level needs.* Rewards such as bonuses, pay increases, and even praise presume that the primary reason people initiate and persist in behavior is to satisfy lower-level needs. However, particularly among today's knowledge workers, behavior also is based on yearnings for self-expression, and on feelings of self-esteem and self-worth. Offers of an extrinsic reward do not encourage the myriad behaviors that are motivated by people's need to express themselves and realize their higher needs for growth and fulfillment.

As Rob Rodin discovered at Marshall Industries, today's organizations need employees who are motivated to think, experiment, and continuously search for ways to solve new problems. Alfie Kohn, one of the most vocal critics of carrot-and-stick approaches, offers the following advice to managers regarding how to pay employees: "Pay well, pay fairly, and then do everything you can to get money off people's minds." Indeed, there is some evidence that money is not primarily what people work for. Managers should understand the limits of extrinsic motivators and work to satisfy employees' higher, as well as lower, needs. To be motivated, employees need jobs that offer self-satisfaction in addition to a yearly pay raise.

SOURCES: Alfie Kohn, "Incentives Can Be Bad for Business," *Inc.* (January 1998), 93–94; A. J. Vogl, "Carrots, Sticks, and Self-Deception" (an interview with Alfie Kohn), *Across the Board* (January 1994), 39–44; and Geoffrey Colvin, "What Money Makes You Do," *Fortune* (August 17, 1998), 213–214.

pay on business results.[39] Despite the testimonies of numerous organizations that enjoy successful incentive programs, there is growing criticism of these so-called carrot-and-stick methods, as discussed in the Focus on Skills box.

Job Design for Motivation

A *job* in an organization is a unit of work that a single employee is responsible for performing. A job could include writing tickets for parking violators in New York City or doing long-range planning for the Discovery cable television channel. Jobs are important because performance of their components may provide rewards that meet employees' needs. An assembly-line worker may install the same bolt over and over, whereas an emergency room physician may provide each trauma victim with a unique treatment package. Managers need to

job design

The application of motivational theories to the structure of work for improving productivity and satisfaction.

job simplification

A job design whose purpose is to improve task efficiency by reducing the number of tasks a single person must perform.

job rotation

A job design that systematically moves employees from one job to another to provide them with variety and stimulation.

know what aspects of a job provide motivation as well as how to compensate for routine tasks that have little inherent satisfaction. **Job design** is the application of motivational theories to the structure of work for improving productivity and satisfaction. Approaches to job design are generally classified as job simplification, job rotation, job enlargement, and job enrichment.

Job Simplification

Job simplification pursues task efficiency by reducing the number of tasks one person must do. Job simplification is based on principles drawn from scientific management and industrial engineering. Tasks are designed to be simple, repetitive, and standardized. As complexity is stripped from a job, the worker has more time to concentrate on doing more of the same routine task. Workers with low skill levels can perform the job, and the organization achieves a high level of efficiency. Indeed, workers are interchangeable, because they need little training or skill and exercise little judgment. As a motivational technique, however, job simplification has failed. People dislike routine and boring jobs and react in a number of negative ways, including sabotage, absenteeism, and unionization. Job simplification is compared with job rotation and job enlargement in Exhibit 13.7.

Job Rotation

Job rotation systematically moves employees from one job to another, thereby increasing the number of different tasks an employee performs without increasing the complexity of any one job. For example, an autoworker may install windshields one week and front bumpers the next. Job rotation still takes advantage of engineering efficiencies, but it provides variety and stimulation for employees. Although employees may find the new job interesting at first, the novelty soon wears off as the repetitive work is mastered.

Companies such as National Steel, Motorola, and Dayton Hudson have built on the notion of job rotation to train a flexible workforce. As companies break away from ossified job categories, workers can perform several jobs, thereby reducing labor costs and giving employees opportunities to develop new skills. At Home Depot, for example, workers scattered throughout the company's vast chain of stores can get a taste of the corporate climate by working at in-store support centers, while associate managers can dirty their hands out on the sales floor.[40] Job rotation also gives companies greater flexibility. One production worker might shift among the jobs of drill operator, punch operator, and assembler, depending on the company's need at the moment. Some unions have resisted the idea, but many now go along, realizing that it helps the company be more competitive.[41]

EXHIBIT *13.7*

Types of Job Design

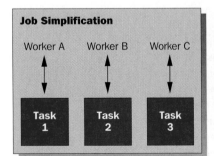
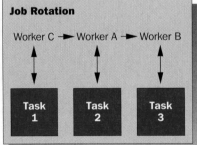
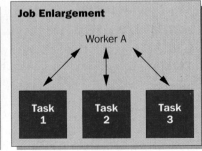

Job Enlargement

Job enlargement combines a series of tasks into one new, broader job. This is a response to the dissatisfaction of employees with oversimplified jobs. Instead of only one job, an employee may be responsible for three or four and will have more time to do them. Job enlargement provides job variety and a greater challenge for employees. At Maytag, jobs were enlarged when work was redesigned such that workers assembled an entire water pump rather than doing each part as it reached them on the assembly line. Similarly, rather than just changing the oil at a Precision Tune location, a mechanic changes the oil, greases the car, airs the tires, checks fluid levels, battery, air filter, and so forth. Then, the same employee is responsible for consulting with the customer about routine maintenance or any problems he or she sees with the vehicle.

job enlargement

A job design that combines a series of tasks into one new, broader job to give employees variety and challenge.

Job Enrichment

Recall the discussion of Maslow's need hierarchy and Herzberg's two-factor theory. Rather than just changing the number and frequency of tasks a worker performs, **job enrichment** incorporates high-level motivators into the work, including job responsibility, recognition, and opportunities for growth, learning, and achievement. In an enriched job, employees have control over the resources necessary for performing it, make decisions on how to do the work, experience personal growth, and set their own work pace. Many companies, including AT&T, Procter & Gamble, and Motorola, have undertaken job enrichment programs to increase employees' motivation and job satisfaction.

job enrichment

A job design that incorporates achievement, recognition, and other high-level motivators into the work.

Managers at Ralcorp's cereal manufacturing plant in Sparks, Nevada, enriched jobs by combining several packing positions into a single job and cross-training employees to operate all of the packing line's equipment. In addition, assembly line employees screen, interview, and train all new hires. They are responsible for managing the production flow to and from their upstream and downstream partners, making daily decisions that affect their work, managing quality, and contributing to continuous improvement. Enriched jobs have improved employee motivation and satisfaction, and the company has benefited from higher long-term productivity, reduced costs, and happier employees.[42] Half-Price Books took job enrichment to the limit by basing its planning and expansion on satisfying valued employees' managerial aspirations.

Half-Price Books
http://www.halfpricebooks.com

What's a CEO of a $100 million company doing driving a 1986 Volkswagen and earning only $50,000 per year? Sharon Wright, daughter of the founder of Dallas's Half-Price Books, is following in her late mother's footsteps, by keeping costs low in order to make the business flourish. "I still shop at garage sales," she says, "and I pick up a used newspaper at the airport. People laugh at me."

Everything in Wright's first store in 1972 was homemade or secondhand, and employees were hired for their eccentricities as well as their love of books. Most were well-educated, and they often had talents in display and promotion. Pat Anderson—Wright's mother—had a knack for pricing books low enough that they flew off the shelves at a profit.

Half-Price Books has a number of unusual practices. Perhaps the one that defies common business practice the most is its stubborn refusal to grow intentionally through a systematic plan or analysis of optimum market conditions. Instead, the company opened new stores in order to reward valuable employees who wanted to be managers. When Dallas became saturated with Half-Price stores, expansion took place in cities where employees had a desire to relocate. By 2002, Half-Price Books had 74 stores in ten states. But Wright recognized that a business must create benefits that emanate outward toward society. She encourages all 1,400 employees to be involved in some philanthropic pursuit. Wright also believes the firm must have an organizing principle: simpler is better. Her own principle? Providing livelihoods and career growth for friends and family. And finally, she understands it is better to track information than it is to control people, who, when allowed to be playful, can contribute to a more successful business.

After Pat Anderson died in 1995, many employees assumed Wright would sell off the business and start to live the good life. But Sharon never considered it. "Why would I want to sell?" she asks. "My family and friends all work here!"[43]

Job Characteristics Model

work redesign

The altering of jobs to increase both the quality of employees' work experience and their productivity.

job characteristics model

A model of job design that comprises core job dimensions, critical psychological states, and employee growth-need strength.

One significant approach to job design is the job characteristics model developed by Richard Hackman and Greg Oldham.[44] Hackman and Oldham's research concerned **work redesign**, which is defined as altering jobs to increase both the quality of employees' work experience and their productivity. Hackman and Oldham's research into the design of hundreds of jobs yielded the **job characteristics model**, which is illustrated in Exhibit 13.8. The model consists of three major parts: core job dimensions, critical psychological states, and employee growth-need strength.

Core Job Dimensions. Hackman and Oldham identified five dimensions that determine a job's motivational potential:

1. *Skill variety.* The number of diverse activities that compose a job and the number of skills used to perform it. A routine, repetitious, assembly line job is low in variety, whereas an applied research position that entails working on new problems every day is high in variety.

2. *Task identity.* The degree to which an employee performs a total job with a recognizable beginning and ending. A chef who prepares an entire meal has more task identity than a worker on a cafeteria line who ladles mashed potatoes.

3. *Task significance.* The degree to which the job is perceived as important and having impact on the company or consumers. People who distribute penicillin and other medical supplies during times of emergencies would feel they have significant jobs.

4. *Autonomy.* The degree to which the worker has freedom, discretion, and self-determination in planning and carrying out tasks. A house painter can determine how to paint the house; a paint sprayer on an assembly line has little autonomy.

5. *Feedback.* The extent to which doing the job provides information back to the employee about his or her performance. Jobs vary in their ability to let workers see the outcomes of their efforts. A football coach knows whether the team won or lost, but a basic research scientist may have to wait years to learn whether a research project was successful.

The job characteristics model says that the more these five core characteristics can be designed into the job, the more the employees will be motivated and the higher will be performance, quality, and satisfaction.

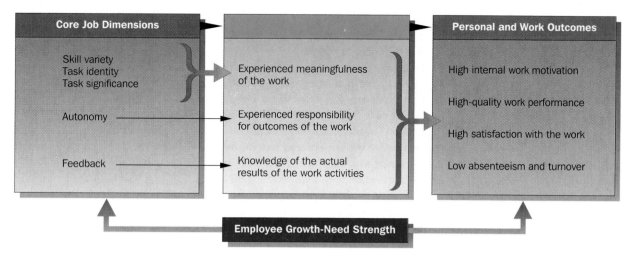

SOURCE: Adapted from J. Richard Hackman and G. R. Oldham, "Motivation through the Design of Work: Test of a Theory," *Organizational Behavior and Human Performance* 16 (1976), 256.

EXHIBIT 13.8

The Job Characteristics Model

Critical Psychological States. The model posits that core job dimensions are more rewarding when individuals experience three psychological states in response to job design. In Exhibit 13.8, skill variety, task identity, and task significance tend to influence the employee's psychological state of *experienced meaningfulness of work*. The work itself is satisfying and provides intrinsic rewards for the worker. The job characteristic of autonomy influences the worker's *experienced responsibility*. The job characteristic of feedback provides the worker with *knowledge of actual results*. The employee thus knows how he or she is doing and can change work performance to increase desired outcomes.

Personal and Work Outcomes. The impact of the five job characteristics on the psychological states of experienced meaningfulness, responsibility, and knowledge of actual results leads to the personal and work outcomes of high work motivation, high work performance, high satisfaction, and low absenteeism and turnover.

Employee Growth-Need Strength. The final component of the job characteristics model is called *employee growth-need strength*, which means that people have different needs for growth and development. If a person wants to satisfy low-level needs, such as safety and belongingness, the job characteristics model has less effect. When a person has a high need for growth and development, including the desire for personal challenge, achievement, and challenging work, the model is especially effective. People with a high need to grow and expand their abilities respond favorably to the application of the model and to improvements in core job dimensions.

One application of the job characteristics model that worked extremely well took place at Sequins International Inc.

Sequins International Inc., based in Woodside, New York, faces tough global competition, particularly from factories in China and India. Women and children in developing nations hand-sew sequins for meager wages, producing $100 million in wholesale goods annually. To compete, U.S. manufacturers use machines that were first developed in the 1940s. The machines save labor but

Sequins International Inc.
http://www.sequins.com

create other problems: The repetitive motions used in the process produce an array of muscle pains as well as mind-numbing boredom. With funding from the Ergonomics Project, administrated by the International Ladies Garment Workers Union, Sequins International redesigned the machines to reduce the physical stresses experienced by sequin makers. The use of adjustable chairs and machinery, along with automatic spooling devices, cut worker's compensation costs to $800 in 1999, down from $98,000 five years earlier. At the same time, skill variety was increased, as inspection jobs that were once performed separately were integrated into the manufacturing process. This gave workers increased task identity and a greater stake in quality control.

Because Sequins's workforce is 80 percent Hispanic and many workers have poor English skills, the company offers English lessons during lunch hours three times a week. Classes in mathematics and statistical process control are also available to train workers for a variety of new tasks. Two teams, one for product satisfaction and the other for customer support, monitor quality control and machine maintenance as part of the production process, as well as provide operators with ongoing feedback and training.

These improvements in job design and motivation dramatically increased worker satisfaction. As a result, absenteeism and costs are down and productivity has increased.[45]

Motivating in the New Workplace

Despite the controversy over carrot-and-stick motivational practices discussed in the Focus on Skills box earlier in this chapter, organizations are increasingly using various types of incentive compensation as a way to motivate employees to higher levels of performance. Exhibit 13.9 summarizes several methods of incentive pay. These programs can be effective if they are used appropriately and combined with motivational ideas that provide employees with intrinsic

EXHIBIT 13.9

New Motivational Compensation Programs

Program Name	Purpose
Pay for Performance	Rewards individual employees in proportion to their performance contributions. Also called merit pay.
Gain Sharing	Rewards all employees and managers within a business unit when predetermined performance targets are met. Encourages teamwork.
Employee Stock Ownership Plan (ESOP)	Gives employees part ownership of the organization, enabling them to share in improved profit performance.
Lump-Sum Bonuses	Rewards employees with a one-time cash payment based on performance.
Pay for Knowledge	Links employee salary with the number of task skills acquired. Workers are motivated to learn the skills for many jobs, thus increasing company flexibility and efficiency.
Flexible Work Schedule	Flextime allows workers to set their own hours. Job sharing allows two or more part-time workers to jointly cover one job. Telecommuting, sometimes called flex-place, allows employees to work from home or an alternate workspace.
Team-based Compensation	Rewards employees for behavior and activities that benefit the team, such as cooperation, listening, and empowering others.

rewards and meet higher-level needs. Effective organizations do not use incentive pay plans as the sole basis of motivation.

In addition, many organizations are giving employees a voice in how pay and incentive systems are designed, which increases motivation by increasing employees' sense of involvement and control.[46] At Premium Standard Farms' pork-processing plant, for example, managers hired a consultant to help slaughterhouse workers design and implement an incentive program. Annual payouts to employees for the year 2000 were around $1,000 per employee. More important, though, is that workers feel a greater sense of dignity and purpose in their jobs, which has helped to reduce turnover significantly. As one employee put it, "Now I have the feeling that this is my company, too."[47] The most effective motivational programs typically involve much more than money. Two recent motivational trends are empowering employees and designing work to have greater meaning.

eBay is growing 72 percent a year, and Wall Street is wild about the stock. How can a dot-com be this hot? One factor contributing to eBay's success is **empowerment**, the delegation of power and authority to the company's 2,400 employees. For example, CEO Meg Whitman, a onetime Procter & Gamble brand manager, Bain consultant, and Hasbro division manager, empowers her deputies to manage categories (toys, cars, collectibles) much as brand managers at P&G do Bounty or Tide. Highly motivated eBay employees have enabled the online auction site to attract 37 million customers with ever-increasing profits: $129 million in a recent year.

Empowerment

Empowerment is the delegation of power or authority to subordinates in an organization.[48] Increasing employee power heightens motivation for task accomplishment because people improve their own effectiveness, choosing how to do a task and using their creativity.[49] Most people come into an organization with the desire to do a good job, and empowerment releases the motivation that is already there. What about the motivation to be a better parent? Can empowering children, to give them a voice, become a motivator for a parent to change? The Focus on Leadership box shows how some executives are using 360° feedback as a means of empowering their children in how the family functions.

AES Corporation is an Arlington, Virginia, electricity producer with facilities all over the world. Every aspect of its organization is designed to give employees "the power and the responsibility to make important decisions, to engage with their work as businesspeople, not as cogs in a machine," as CEO Dennis Bakke puts it.[50] Empowerment at AES has released employee creativity, motivation, and energy by providing employees with challenging work and the information and power to make a difference every day for themselves and for the company.

Empowering employees means giving them four elements that enable them to act more freely to accomplish their jobs: information, knowledge, power, and rewards.[51]

empowerment

The delegation of power or authority to subordinates.

1. *Employees receive information about company performance.* In companies where employees are fully empowered, such as Semco, a Brazilian manufacturing company, all employees have access to all financial and operational information.

2. *Employees have knowledge and skills to contribute to company goals.* Companies use training programs to help employees acquire the knowledge and skills they need to contribute to organizational performance. For example, when DMC, which makes pet supplies, gave employee teams the authority and responsibility for assembly-line shutdowns, it provided extensive training

FOCUS ON LEADERSHIP

360°

Ben Porter was sitting through a tough performance review with seven associates. Though he was generally getting good marks, there were some sharp criticisms, such as not spending enough focused time and being too distracted. A charge of favoritism was so intense, it made the person giving it start to cry. Oh, yeah, one more thing—please spend more time playing Frisbee.

Porter was listening more carefully than he usually did at work, for these seven people were his wife and six kids. He was part of an experiment to use 360° to help executives become better spouses and parents. Daughter Jessica was the one who cried. "To see the tears in her eyes just killed me," says Porter. It turns out Porter had been shooting hoops with his sons, and had no idea that Jessica was feeling left out. Now he has regular "date nights" with her, and more Frisbee sessions with youngest son, six-year-old David.

Colorado-Springs's LeaderWorks developed the "Family 360" after its coaching experience with hundreds of top executives who couldn't seem to find a balance between their work and family lives. "These are guys who have made the money

several times over. More times than not, they've screwed up on the family side," says Porter, who sees this program as a way to accelerate improvement in family communication.

Avery Dennison President Dean Scarborough found Family 360 to be a useful wake-up call. "It was good, and sobering at the same time," he says. He got a lot of praise, but also heard family members asking for more patience from him, less traveling time, and more one-on-one time with each person. "At the end of the day, the best-balanced people are the best executives," he notes.

Family 360 is not an experiment for troubled families to try alone at home, as it might unearth painful issues that require a therapist's help to resolve. But it doesn't hurt to think about the process, and casually start asking what families want. Too many executives don't give their families anything close to the attention they give their work. Ellen Galinsky's book, *Ask the Children,* discusses the result of her 1,000-children survey. One of the most common messages to parents: "You need to spend more focused time with us."

SOURCE: Sue Shellenberger, "Frisbee, Favoritism and Tears: Scenes from a 'Corporate' Evaluation of Dad," *The Wall Street Journal* (July 11, 2002), D1.

on how to diagnose and interpret line malfunctions, as well as the costs related to shut-down and start-up. Employees worked through several case studies to practice decision making related to line shut-downs.[52]

3. *Employees have the power to make substantive decisions.* Workers have the authority to directly influence work procedures and organizational performance, often through quality circles or self-directed work teams. Semco pushes empowerment to the limits by allowing its 1,300 employees to choose what they do, how they do it, and even how they get compensated for it. Employees set their own pay by choosing from a list of 11 different pay options, such as set salary or a combination of salary and incentives.[53]

4. *Employees are rewarded based on company performance.* Organizations that empower workers often reward them based on the results shown in the company's bottom line. For example, at Semco, in addition to employee-determined compensation, a company profit-sharing plan gives each employee an even share of 23 percent of his or her department's profits each quarter.[54] Organizations may also use other motivational compensation programs described in Exhibit 13.9 to tie employee efforts to company performance.

Many of today's organizations are implementing empowerment programs, but they are empowering workers to varying degrees. At some companies, empowerment means encouraging workers' ideas while managers retain final authority for decisions; at others it means giving employees almost complete freedom and power to make decisions and exercise initiative and imagination.[55] Current methods of empowerment fall along a continuum, as illustrated

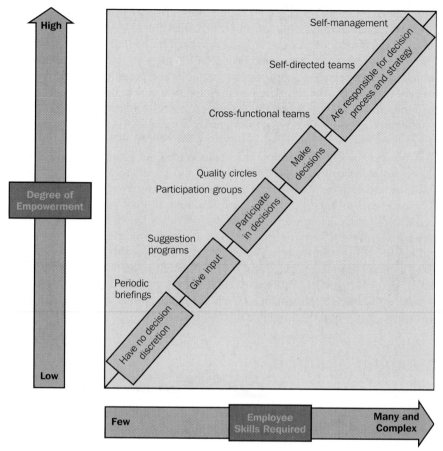

SOURCES: Based on Robert C. Ford and Myron D. Fottler, "Empowerment: A Matter of Degree," *Academy of Management Executive* 9, no. 3 (1995), 21–31; Lawrence Holpp, "Applied Empowerment," *Training* (February 1994), 39–44; and David P. McCaffrey, Sue R. Faerman, and David W. Hart, "The Appeal and Difficulties of Participative Systems," *Organization Science* 6, no. 6 (November–December 1995), 603–627.

in Exhibit 13.10. The continuum runs from a situation in which front-line workers have almost no discretion, such as on a traditional assembly line, to full empowerment, where workers even participate in formulating organizational strategy. An example of full empowerment is when self-directed teams are given the authority to hire, discipline, and dismiss team members and to set compensation rates.

Research indicates that most people have a need for self-efficacy, which is the capacity to produce results or outcomes, to feel that they are effective.[56] By meeting higher-level needs, empowerment can provide powerful motivation.

Giving Meaning to Work

The new workplace recognizes that the way to create engaged, motivated employees and high performance has less to do with extrinsic rewards such as pay and much more to do with fostering an environment in which people can flourish. There is a growing recognition that it is the behavior of managers that makes the biggest difference in employee motivation and whether people flourish in the workplace. A Gallup Organization study conducted over twenty-five years found that the single most important variable in whether employees feel good about their work is the relationship between employees and their direct supervisor.[57]

In the new workplace, the manager's role is not to control others but to organize the workplace in such a way that each person can learn, contribute, and grow. The most successful managers realize that they actually have less control than their subordinates—it is only through other people that managers can accomplish anything. Good managers channel employee motivation toward the accomplishment of goals by tapping into each individual's unique set of talents, skills, interests, attitudes, and needs. By treating each employee as an individual, managers can put people in the right jobs and provide intrinsic rewards to every employee every day. Then, managers make sure people have what they need to perform, clearly define the desired outcomes, and get out of the way.

One way to evaluate how a manager or a company is doing in meeting higher-level needs is a metric developed by the Gallup researchers called the Q12. When a majority of employees can answer a set of 12 questions positively, the organization enjoys a highly motivated and productive workforce. These questions are designed to examine and measure an employee's sense of control over their work and their progress, as well as their level of self-actualization.

Results of the Gallup study show that organizations where employees give high marks on the Q12 have less turnover, are more productive and profitable, and enjoy greater employee and customer loyalty. For example, among 400 Best Buy retail outlets, the store that scored the highest on the Q12 ranks in the top 10 percent, while the store with the lowest score ranks in the bottom 10 percent on financial performance.[58] When employees are more engaged and motivated, they—and their organizations—thrive.

■ Summary and Management Solution

This chapter introduced a number of important ideas about the motivation of people in organizations. The content theories of motivation focus on the nature of underlying employee needs. Maslow's hierarchy of needs, Alderfer's ERG theory, Herzberg's two-factor theory, and McClelland's acquired needs theory all suggest that people are motivated to meet a range of needs. Process theories examine how people go about selecting rewards with which to meet needs. Equity theory says that people compare their contributions and outcomes with others' and are motivated to maintain a feeling of equity. Expectancy theory suggests that people calculate the probability of achieving certain outcomes. Managers can increase motivation by treating employees fairly and by clarifying employee paths toward meeting their needs. Still another motivational approach is reinforcement theory, which says that employees learn to behave in certain ways based on the availability of reinforcements.

The application of motivational ideas is illustrated in job design and other motivational programs. Job design approaches include job simplification, job rotation, job enlargement, job enrichment, and the job characteristics model. Managers can change the structure of work to meet employees' high-level needs. The recent trend toward empowerment motivates by giving employees more information and authority to make decisions in their work while connecting compensation to the results. Managers create the environment that determines employee motivation. One way to measure the factors that determine whether people are engaged and motivated at work is the Q12, a list of 12 questions about the day-to-day realities of a person's job. Other motivational programs include pay for performance, gain sharing, ESOPs, lump-sum bonuses, pay for knowledge, flexible work schedules, and team-based compensation.

Recalling the case at the beginning of this chapter, Rafael Alvarado had to decide whether to pay his new workers well or promise higher wages in the future. Remembering how hard it was to make a go of it financially when he first came to the U.S., Alvarado decided to pay the 30 Hispanic immigrant employees decently, plus give them two weeks vacation, paid health insurance, and the chance to advance if they showed promise. "It's worked to his advantage," says business consultant Roy Serpa. "The folks on the factory floor are so motivated it's unbelievable."

Alvarado understood he had to sell his product differently, because it costs 20 percent more than the more common thin plastic bags on dispensers in grocery stores. His company focuses instead on better plastic, ease of use, less waste, and the ability to print a grocer's name in one of six colors on the bag. Something has worked, because Better Bags has grown 25 percent a year since 1996. The product that Alvarado envisioned while in Costa Rica now graces 7,000 stores in 49 states, and Alvarado expects to double output in the next four years. He couldn't do it without a highly motivated and committed workforce.[59]

Discussion Questions

1. In the aftermath of the September 11, 2001, terrorist attack, the U.S. government federalized airport security workers. Many argued that simply making screeners federal workers would not solve the root problem: bored, low-paid, and poorly trained security workers have little motivation to be vigilant. How might these employees be motivated to provide the security that travel conditions now demand?

2. One small company recognizes an employee of the month, who is given a parking spot next to the president's space near the front door. What theories would explain the positive motivation associated with this policy?

3. Campbell Soup Company reduces accidents with a lottery. Each worker who works 30 days or more without losing a day for a job-related accident is eligible to win prizes in a raffle drawing. Why has this program been successful?

4. One executive argues that managers have too much safety because of benefit and retirement plans. He rewards his managers for taking risks and has removed many guaranteed benefits. Would this approach motivate managers? Why?

5. If an experienced secretary discovered that she made less money than a newly hired janitor, how would she react? What inputs and outcomes might she evaluate to make this comparison?

6. Would you rather work for a supervisor high in need for achievement, need for affiliation, or need for power? Why? What are the advantages and disadvantages of each?

7. A survey of teachers found that two of the most important rewards were the belief that their work was important and a feeling of accomplishment. Is this consistent with Hackman and Oldham's job characteristics model?

8. The teachers in question 7 also reported that pay and benefits were poor, yet they continued to teach. Use Herzberg's two-factor theory to explain this finding.

9. What theories explain why employees who score high on the Q12 questionnaire are typically highly motivated and productive?

10. How can empowerment lead to higher motivation? Could a manager's empowerment efforts sometimes contribute to demotivation as well? Discuss.

11. What characteristics of individuals could determine the extent to which work redesign will have a positive impact on work satisfaction and work effectiveness?

Manager's Workbook

What Motivates You?

You are to indicate how important each characteristic is to you. Answer according to your feelings about the most recent job you had or about the job you currently hold. Circle the number on the scale that represents your feeling—1 (very unimportant) to 7 (very important).

	Unimportant					Important	
1. The feeling of self-esteem a person gets from being in that job	1	2	3	4	5	6	7
2. The opportunity for personal growth and development in that job	1	2	3	4	5	6	7
3. The prestige of the job inside the company (that is, regard received from others in the company)	1	2	3	4	5	6	7
4. The opportunity for independent thought and action in that job	1	2	3	4	5	6	7
5. The feeling of security in that job	1	2	3	4	5	6	7
6. The feeling of self-fulfillment a person gets from being in that position (that is, the feeling of being able to use one's own unique capabilities, realizing one's potential)	1	2	3	4	5	6	7
7. The prestige of the job outside the company (that is, the regard received from others not in the company)	1	2	3	4	5	6	7
8. The feeling of worthwhile accomplishment in that job	1	2	3	4	5	6	7
9. The opportunity in that job to give help to other people	1	2	3	4	5	6	7

	Unimportant						Important

10. The opportunity in that job for participation in the setting of goals

1	2	3	4	5	6	7

11. The opportunity in that job for participation in the determination of methods and procedures
12. The authority connected with the job
13. The opportunity to develop close friendships in the job

1	2	3	4	5	6	7
1	2	3	4	5	6	7
1	2	3	4	5	6	7

When you have completed the questionnaire, score it as follows:
Rating for question 5 = ____. Divide by 1 = security.
Rating for questions 9 and 13 = ____. Divide by 2 = ____ social.
Rating for questions 1, 3, and 7 = ____. Divide by 3 = ____ esteem.
Rating for questions 4, 10, 11, and 12 = ____. Divide by 4 = ____ autonomy.
Rating for questions 2, 6, and 8 = ____. Divide by 3 = ____ self-actualization.

The instructor has national norm scores for presidents, vice presidents, and upper middle-level, lower middle-level, and lower-level managers with which you can compare your *mean* importance scores. How do your scores compare with the scores of managers working in organizations?

SOURCE: Lyman W. Porter, *Organizational Patterns of Managerial Job Attitudes* (New York: American Foundation for Management Research, 1964), 17, 19. Used with permission.

■ Manager's Workshop

Hey, That's Not Fair!

Listed below are six vignettes depicting situations in which the Brady kids have perceived an unfair situation. For each vignette, identify the equity/justice concept that is best reflected in the description.

- Greg just found out that Tommy has been picked by the coach to be the new quarterback for the football team because his dad and the coach are old high school buddies. He is really bummed out, because that is the position he has been hoping to play ever since junior high.
- Marcia was upset about being turned down for the job of emcee for the school talent show, but she was even more bothered by the fact that the director of the show made her wait for half an hour and was rude and inconsiderate when giving her feedback about her tryout performance.
- Jan studied for about five hours for her geometry final, but her friend Sue only spent about 30 minutes cramming at the last minute. They just got back their test results today—much to Jan's surprise, she only got a B–, but Sue got an A!

- Peter has been working really hard at the malt shop for the last six months, doing extra chores and helping out other employees when they need it. The manager of the store just told him that he was going to give him a raise, but Peter is disappointed by the fact that it's only an extra 15¢ an hour. He thought that he deserved more.
- Bobby and his friend Dennis just finished doing a bunch of yard work for a neighbor, Mr. Wilson. Bobby worked nonstop, rarely taking a break, but Dennis kept goofing off and playing around. In the end Mr. Wilson gave them both the same amount of money, which Bobby didn't think was right.
- Cindy is upset because her science teacher selected three people to compete in the upcoming science fair without first asking if anybody wanted to volunteer to participate in it.

SOURCE: Courtney Hunt, Northern Illinois University. Adapted from "Must See TV: The Timelessness of Television As a Teaching Tool," presented at the 60th Academy of Management Meeting, August, 2000. Used with permission.

■ Management in Practice: Ethical Dilemma

Compensation Showdown

When Suzanne Lebeau, human resources manager, received a call from Bert Wilkes, comptroller of Farley Glass Works, she anticipated hearing good news to share with the Wage and Bonus Committee. She had already seen numbers to indicate that the year-end bonus plan, which was instituted by her committee in lieu of the traditional guaranteed raises of the past, was going to exceed expectations. It was a real relief to her, because the plan, devised by a committee representing all levels of the workforce, had taken 11 months to complete. It had also been a real boost to morale at a low point in the company's history. Workers at the glass shower production plant were bringing new effort and energy to their jobs, and Lebeau wanted to see them rewarded.

She was shocked to see Wilkes's face so grim when she arrived for her meeting. "We have a serious problem, Suzanne," Wilkes said to open the meeting. "We ran the numbers from third quarter to project our end-of-the-year figures and discovered that the executive bonus objectives, which are based on net operating profit, would not be met if we paid out the employee bonuses first. The executive bonuses are a major source of their income. We can't ask them to do without their salary to ensure a bonus for the workers."

Lebeau felt her temper rising. After all their hard work, she was not going to sit by and watch the employees be disappointed because the accounting department had not structured the employee bonus plan to work with the executive plan. She was afraid they would undo all the good that the bonus plan had done in motivating the plant workers. They had kept their end of the bargain, and the company's high profits were common knowledge in the plant.

What Do You Do?

1. Ask to appear before the executive committee to argue that the year-end bonus plan for workers be honored. Executives could defer their bonuses until the problem in the structure of the compensation plan is resolved.
2. Go along with the comptroller. It isn't fair for the executives to lose so much money. Begin to prepare the workers to not expect much this first year of the plan.
3. Go to the board of directors and ask for a compromise plan that splits the bonuses between the executives and the workers.

SOURCE: Based on Doug Wallace, "Promises to Keep," *What Would You Do?* (reprinted from *Business Ethics*), vol. II (July–August 1993), 11–12. Reprinted with permission from *Business Ethics Magazine*, P.O. Box 8439, Minneapolis, MN 55408 (612) 879–0695.

■ Surf the Net

1. **Acquired Needs Theory.** Take the motivation quiz at one of the sites listed (the same questions appear at both sites). *http://www.snc.edu/socsci/chair/333/motvquiz.htm http://www.pertinent.com/pertinfo/business/exercises/motivate.html* After following the scoring instructions at the site, print your scores in the spaces provided. The highest score indicates what your dominant need is and what motivates you most. Were you surprised by the results?
Achievement _____ Power _____ Affiliation _____

2. **Meaningful Workplace.** Go to the "Download Center" at *http://www.BetterWorkplaceNow.com* Locate an article of interest and print it out. As you read the article, highlight key points and submit the highlighted article to your instructor.

3. **Motivating in the New Workplace.** Go to *http://www. walmartstores.com,* find the "Benefits" link under "Careers." Check out the benefits offered to Wal-Mart employees and identify two benefits/motivators discussed in the section of the chapter "Motivating in the New Workplace."

■ Case for Critical Analysis

Kimbel's Department Store

Frances Patterson has been reading about a quiet revolution sweeping department store retailing and has decided to give it a try. At stores such as Bloomingdale's and Bergdorf Goodman, managers are using commission pay to motivate salespeople. At Bergdorf's, for example, a top-tier salesperson in women's apparel can earn nearly $200,000 a year.

Patterson wants to implement commission pay at Kimbel's, a regional chain of upscale department stores based in St. Louis. Kimbel's has long used commissions in departments such as electronics and appliances, where extra sales skill pays off, but Patterson believes extending the system storewide will attract better salespeople, increase motivation, and enable employees to earn more money. For example, under the old plan, a new salesclerk in women's wear would earn about $18,000 a year

based on hourly wages and a 0.5 percent commission on $500,000 in sales. Under the new plan, the annual pay would be $35,000 based on 7 percent commission on sales of $500,000. Patterson implemented the new system in two area stores first and plans to roll it out across the chain within the next six months.

Juan Santore, who works in the men's shoe salon, is enthusiastic about the changeover. His pay has increased an average of $150 per week. But in other departments, such as women's lingerie, employees are less enthusiastic. Making enough sales per week to earn their previous salary is nearly impossible, particularly when the economy slows down. Even during the holiday season, many employees saw their pay decrease an average of 8 percent.

Patterson is keeping a close eye on fluctuations in pay. She's becoming concerned that the commission system may not work as well for small-item purchases as it does for big-ticket items. In addition, one question is whether Kimbel's can meet its goal of creating more customer-oriented salespeople when they work on commission. Clerks may be less willing to handle complaints, make returns, and clean shelves, preferring instead to chase customers. Moreover, it will cost Kimbel's nearly $1 million per store to install the commission system because of training programs, computer upgrades, and increased pay in many departments. If the overall impact on service is negative, the increased efficiency might not seem worthwhile.

Questions

1. What theories about motivation underlie the switch from salary to commission pay?
2. Are high-level needs met under the commission system?
3. As a customer, would you prefer to shop where employees are motivated to make commissions?

SOURCES: Based on Francine Schwadel, "Chain Finds Incentives a Hard Sell," *The Wall Street Journal* (July 5, 1990), B4; Amy Dunkin, "Now Salespeople Really Must Sell for Their Supper," *Business Week* (July 31, 1989), 50–52; and Terry Pristin, "Retailing's Elite Keep the Armani Moving Off the Racks," *New York Times* (December 22, 2001), D1.

Communicating in Organizations

LEARNING OBJECTIVES

After studying this chapter, you should be able to

1 Explain why communication is essential for effective management and describe how nonverbal behavior and listening affect communication among people.

2 Explain how managers use communication to persuade and influence others.

3 Describe the concept of channel richness, and explain how communication channels influence the quality of communication in organizations.

4 Explain the difference between formal and informal organizational communications and the importance of each for organization management.

5 Identify how structure influences team communication outcomes.

6 Explain why open communication, dialogue, and feedback are essential approaches to communication in the new workplace.

7 Describe barriers to organizational communication, and suggest ways to avoid or overcome them.

Management Challenge

Bill Ernstrom faced a problem that is experienced by a lot of other CEOs in technology companies: He couldn't persuade his engineers at Colorado-based Voyant Technologies to listen to the marketing department. The lack of communication became obvious when the chief engineer mentioned that some customers wanted streaming media built into Voyant's flagship product, RediVoice. It sounded like a good idea, and Ernstrom gave the go-ahead. Four months later and $200,000 poorer, the CEO discovered his customers didn't care about streaming *anything*.

Realizing that this was a common problem didn't help Ernstrom, who couldn't see any way to bridge the Grand Canyon–sized gulf between the computer-savvy employees and the suits. Ernstrom had seen it happen again and again: In the early stages of a project, engineers have control. They design and manufacture elegant products that no one wants to buy.

Remember Apple's Newton, or their G4, or even Atari's Falcon?

Ernstrom realized he needed to solve this problem if his company was going to remain highly profitable. He tried hiring more businesspeople, redesigning floor plans to change office arrangements, and changing the compensation package. Finally, he hit on what he thought was a sure thing. He hired four product managers to head up each of the four product lines, thinking this would bring balance between engineering and marketing. But the engineers didn't trust the new managers, considering them as interlopers who had little knowledge about either the company's culture or technology. Ernstrom was at his wit's end. Nothing was working.[1]

If you were Bill Ernstrom, what would you do to help engineers better communicate with marketing and other business associates?

Bill Ernstrom at Voyant believed in communication, but faced problems in breaking down communication barriers. In today's intensely competitive environment, top managers at many companies are trying to improve communication. For example, managers at Boeing recruited employee volunteers to act as liaisons and encourage feedback from workers throughout the giant aerospace company. Deb Charnley, chief patient-care executive for Rochester General Hospital and the Genesee Hospitals, instituted "Deb Chats," regular, informal pow-wows that give overworked nurses a chance to ask questions, make suggestions, or just blow off steam.[2] At A. W. Chesterton Co., CEO Jim Chesterton holds quarterly meetings at which employees can ask him about anything and everything.[3] It isn't always easy when workers confront top managers with difficult questions or challenge them regarding management failings, but getting candid feedback from employees helps executives spot problems or recognize opportunities that might otherwise be missed.

To stay connected with employees and customers and shape company direction, managers must excel at personal communications. Nonmanagers often are amazed at how much energy successful executives put into communication. Consider this comment about Robert Strauss, former chairman of the Democratic National Committee and former ambassador to Russia, made by one of his friends:

> His network is everywhere. It ranges from bookies to bank presidents. . . . He seems to find time to make innumerable phone calls to "keep in touch"; he cultivates secretaries as well as senators; he will befriend a middle-level White House aide whom other important officials won't bother with. Every few months, he sends candy to the White House switchboard operators.[4]

This chapter explains why executives such as Robert Strauss, Jim Chesterton, and Deb Charnley are effective communicators. First we will see how managers' jobs require communication and describe a model of the communication process. Next we will consider the interpersonal aspects of communication, including communication channels, persuasion, and listening skills, that affect managers' ability to communicate. Then, we will look at the organization as a whole and consider formal upward and downward communications as well as informal communications. Finally, we will examine barriers to communication and how managers can overcome them.

Communication and the Manager's Job

How important is communication? Consider this: Managers spend at least 80 percent of every working day in direct communication with others. In other words, 48 minutes of every hour is spent in meetings, on the telephone, communicating online, or talking informally while walking around. The other 20 percent of a typical manager's time is spent doing desk work, most of which is also communication in the form of reading and writing.[5] Exhibit 14.1 illustrates the crucial position of management in the information network. Managers gather important information from both inside and outside the organization and then distribute appropriate information to others who need it.

Communication permeates every management function described in Chapter 1.[6] For example, when managers perform the planning function, they gather information; write letters, memos, and reports; and then meet with

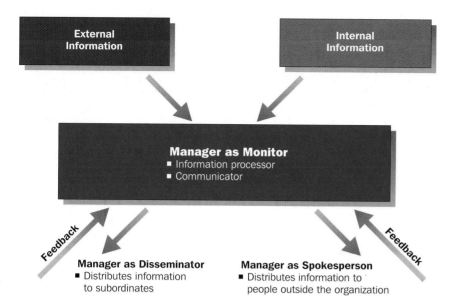

EXHIBIT 14.1

The Manager as Information Nerve Center

SOURCE: Adapted from Henry Mintzberg, *The Nature of Managerial Work* (New York: Harper & Row, 1973), 72.

other managers to explain the plan. When managers lead, they communicate to share a vision of what the organization can be and motivate employees to help achieve it. When managers organize, they gather information about the state of the organization and communicate a new structure to others. Communication skills are a fundamental part of every managerial activity.

What Is Communication?

A professor at Harvard once asked a class to define communication by drawing pictures. Most students drew a manager speaking or writing. Some placed "speech balloons" next to their characters; others showed pages flying from a laser printer. "No," the professor told the class, "none of you has captured the essence of communication." He went on to explain that communication means "to share"—not "to speak" or "to write."

Communication thus can be defined as the process by which information is exchanged and understood by two or more people, usually with the intent to motivate or influence behavior. Communication is not just sending information. This distinction between *sharing* and *proclaiming* is crucial for successful management. A manager who does not listen is like a used-car salesperson who claims, "I sold a car—they just did not buy it." Management communication is a two-way street that includes listening and other forms of feedback. Effective communication, in the words of one expert, is as follows:

> When two people interact, they put themselves into each other's shoes, try to perceive the world as the other person perceives it, try to predict how the other will respond. Interaction involves reciprocal role-taking, the mutual employment of empathetic skills. The goal of interaction is the merger of self and other, a complete ability to anticipate, predict, and behave in accordance with the joint needs of self and other.[7]

It is the desire to share understanding that motivates executives to visit employees on the shop floor, hold small informal meetings, or eat with employees in the company cafeteria. The things managers learn from direct communication with employees shape their understanding of the corporation.

communication

The process by which information is exchanged and understood by two or more people, usually with the intent to motivate or influence behavior.

EXHIBIT *14.2*

EXHIBIT *14.2*

A Model of the Communication Process

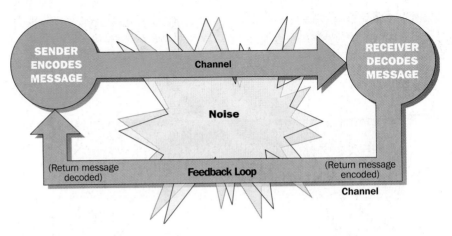

The Communication Process

Many people think communication is simple because they communicate without conscious thought or effort. However, communication usually is complex, and the opportunities for sending or receiving the wrong messages are innumerable. No doubt, you have heard someone say, "But that's not what I meant!" Have you ever received directions you thought were clear and yet still got lost? How often have you wasted time on misunderstood instructions?

To more fully understand the complexity of the communication process, note the key elements outlined in Exhibit 14.2. Two common elements in every communication situation are the sender and the receiver. The *sender* is anyone who wishes to convey an idea or concept to others, to seek information, or to express a thought or emotion. The *receiver* is the person to whom the message is sent. The sender **encodes** the idea by selecting symbols with which to compose a message. The **message** is the tangible formulation of the idea that is sent to the receiver. The message is sent through a **channel**, which is the communication carrier. The channel can be a formal report, a telephone call or e-mail message, or a face-to-face meeting. The receiver **decodes** the symbols to interpret the meaning of the message. Encoding and decoding are potential sources for communication errors, because knowledge, attitudes, and background act as filters and create "noise" when translating from symbols to meaning. Finally, **feedback** occurs when the receiver responds to the sender's communication with a return message. Without feedback, the communication is one-way; with feedback, it is *two-way*. Feedback is a powerful aid to communication effectiveness, because it enables the sender to determine whether the receiver correctly interpreted the message. Bruce Woolpert of Granite Rock used two-way communication to improve his companies profitability, as described below.

encode
To select symbols with which to compose a message.

message
The tangible formulation of an idea to be sent to a receiver.

channel
The carrier of a communication.

decode
To translate the symbols used in a message for the purpose of interpreting its meaning.

feedback
A response by the receiver to the sender's communication.

Granite Rock Company

http://www.graniterock.com

Granite Rock Co. of Watsonville, California, has been owned and operated by the Wilson/Woolpert family for over 100 years, but was hit with big changes 15 years ago. The threat of absorption into a conglomerate was added to California's tightening industrial regulations, while customers were clamoring for high-quality materials and more responsive service. Computer technology to automate quarry work was new and expensive. Granite Rock would have to find new ways of doing business admist a host of changes and well-financed predators.

Bruce Woolpert, a joint CEO with brother Steve, and eight-year veteran of Hewlett-Packard, wanted the company to be as efficient and customer-oriented as HP. First, he got maximum information flowing into the company. Instead of the industry standard of a dozen internal process controls, Granite Rock kept track of 100. Next, Bruce started asking customers to rate the company against competitors on "report cards."

Woolpert "benchmarked" within the company, identifying "best practices" by visiting cement plants and the quarry. By asking workers what they liked and disliked about their jobs and the company, he set up a model for two-way communication up and down the entire organization. He organized 100 highly focused, quality teams of managers and hourly workers to analyze problems. Both groups also attended many seminars together. Merging the two groups together increased input and united the company's now 736 employees.

Technology and training have made Granite Rock the region's low-cost producer of crushed rock with annual sales of more than $110 million. Quality and service levels are high enough to allow charging a 6 percent premium and still increase market share. To maintain high levels of quality, the company offers "short pay," the same as in a restaurant. If you don't like it, you don't pay for it.

The company has embraced many changes, including women truck drivers, a practice that was unheard of not long ago. One woman started driving trucks "because my dad said I couldn't." Granite Rock inspires fierce loyalty among workers. As a result, *Fortune* has listed it among its Top 100 places to work in the past few years, with its ranking moving up to number 16 in 2001. Former CEO Betsy Wilson Woolpert, Bruce's mother and daughter of founder Arthur Wilson, says, "Most Granite Rock people remain with us for their entire career. We like that and hope it can be maintained."[8]

Managers who are effective communicators understand and use the circular nature of communication. For example, at Nortel Networks, Dan Hunt, president of Caribbean and Latin American operations, and Emma Carrasco, vice president of marketing and communications, host a monthly television program called *Virtual Leadership Academy* that uses a talk-show format to spark corporate conversations. Employees from about 40 different countries watch the show from their regional offices and call in their questions and comments. "We're always looking for ways to break down barriers," says Carrasco. "People watch talk shows in every country, and they've learned that it's okay to say what's on their minds."[9] The television program is the channel through which Hunt and Carrasco send their encoded message. Employees decode and interpret the message and encode their feedback, which is sent through the channel of the telephone hookup. The communications circuit is complete.

Communicating among People

The communication model in Exhibit 14.2 illustrates the components that must be mastered for effective communication. Communications can break down if sender and receiver do not encode or decode language in the same way.[10] We all know how difficult it is to communicate with someone who does not speak our language, and managers in U.S. organizations today are often trying to communicate with people who speak many different native languages and have limited English skills. However, communication breakdowns can also occur between people who speak the same language.

FOCUS ON SKILLS

How to Be a Master Communicator

Communication is the manager's most important job, and for some it is also the most difficult. We have all had times when we've been misunderstood or tried to communicate something that goes unheard or unnoticed. Here are some tips on how to improve your communication effectiveness.

1. *Craft the message with a clear purpose in mind.* The content of a communication depends on the specific objectives. One common flaw is trying to cover too many issues at one time. Communication is always more successful when it is clearly focused on one or a few key points.

2. *To persuade and inspire people, aim for true intimacy.* When managers want to convey something really important, they should approach the communication openly, honestly, even vulnerably. One expert suggests that managers imagine they are talking to themselves, which enables them to share their deepest feelings. Listeners feel like they are sharing the speaker's unguarded thoughts and feelings, and they respond to that openness.

3. *Don't forget to listen.* Every communication should be structured to invite and encourage feedback. Open a communication with a question, because questions are more powerful than answers. A questioning approach also communicates that the manager cares about the other person's input and does not just want to give orders.

4. *Pay attention to timing.* Never make a difficult announcement or convey bad news and then leave town. Managers need to be visible and accessible, ready and willing to answer questions, provide clarification, and offer support.

5. *Be aware of body language and actions.* Particularly in times of rapid change or uncertainty, people are alert to any cue as to what is really going on in the organization. Facial expressions, moods, who the manager has lunch with, and whether the managers present at organizational events will all be interpreted by employees. Managers need to be aware that actions as well as words convey a message.

6. *Stay in touch with the grapevine.* In many organizations, informal communication channels such as the grapevine operate more effectively than formal channels. Successful managers develop their social networks so that they stay in touch with the rumor mill. Managers can also use the grapevine to their advantage by sharing important information with people they know will spread it to others.

SOURCES: Based on Patricia Wallington, "You Don't Say," *CIO* (October 1, 2000), 78–80; and Harriet Rubin, "Like the King, King David Knew How to Strum a Person Like an Instrument," *Fast Company* (November 2000), 410–413.

Many factors can lead to a breakdown in communications. For example, the selection of communication channels can determine whether the message is distorted by noise and interference. The listening skills of both parties and attention to nonverbal behavior can determine whether a message is truly shared. Thus, for managers to be effective communicators, they must understand how interpersonal factors such as communication channels, nonverbal behavior, and listening all work to enhance or detract from communication. This chapter's Focus on Skills box outlines some tips for effective manager communication.

Communication Channels

Managers have a choice of many channels through which to communicate to other managers or employees. A manager may discuss a problem face-to-face, use the telephone, send an e-mail, write a memo or letter, or put an item in a newsletter, depending on the nature of the message. Research has attempted to explain how managers select communication channels to enhance communication effectiveness.[11] The research has found that channels differ in their capacity to convey information. Just as a pipeline's physical characteristics limit the kind and amount of liquid that can be pumped through it, a communication channel's physical characteristics limit the kind and amount of information

Equipped with laptops, pagers, and cell phones, Intel employees can now communicate and collaborate on group projects from anywhere in the world. These forms of communication lack the channel richness found in face-to-face discussions. However, new technology such as instant messaging, groupware, and wireless Internet applications enable these devices to facilitate rapid feedback, thus increasing their value for organizational communication.

that can be conveyed among managers. The channels available to managers can be classified into a hierarchy based on information richness. **Channel richness** is the amount of information that can be transmitted during a communication episode. The hierarchy of channel richness is illustrated in Exhibit 14.3.

The capacity of an information channel is influenced by three characteristics: (1) the ability to handle multiple cues simultaneously; (2) the ability to facilitate rapid, two-way feedback; and (3) the ability to establish a personal focus for the communication. Face-to-face discussion is the richest medium, because it permits direct experience, multiple information cues, immediate feedback, and personal focus. Face-to-face discussions facilitate the assimilation of broad cues and deep, emotional understanding of the situation. For example, Tony Burns, CEO of Ryder Systems, Inc., likes to handle things face to face: "You can look someone in the eyes, and you can tell by the look in his eyes or the inflection in his voice what the real problem or question or answer is."[12] Telephone conversations are next in the richness hierarchy. Although eye

channel richness

The amount of information that can be transmitted during a communication episode.

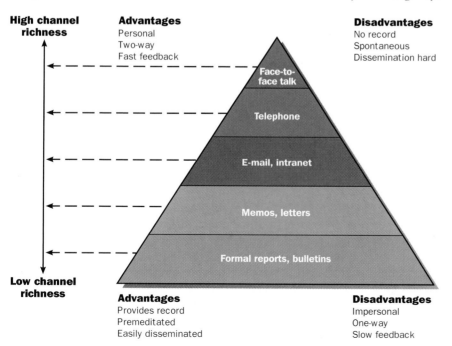

E X H I B I T 14.3

The Pyramid of Channel Richness

contact, posture, and other body language cues are missing, the human voice can still carry a tremendous amount of emotional information.

Electronic messaging, or e-mail, is increasingly being used for messages that were once handled via the telephone. A recent survey by Ohio State University researchers found that about half the respondents reported making fewer telephone calls since they began using e-mail. However, respondents also said they preferred the telephone or face-to-face conversation for communicating difficult news, giving advice, or expressing affection.[13] Because e-mail messages lack both visual and verbal cues, messages can sometimes be misunderstood. Recognizing the need for greater channel richness, many organizations are using interactive meetings over the Internet, sometimes adding video capabilities to provide visual cues as well. Following the September 11, 2001, terrorist attacks, many companies increased their reliance on virtual meetings to reduce employees' travel responsibilities. Masimo, a medical technology company in Irvine, California, decided to order an $8,000 videoconferencing system the day after the attacks.[14] Anxieties over anthrax-tainted mail have also led to greater use of e-mail and other forms of Web-based communication.

Still lower on the hierarchy of channel richness are written letters and memos. These can be personally focused, but they convey only the cues written on paper and are slow to provide feedback. Impersonal written media, including fliers, bulletins, and standard computer reports, are the lowest in richness. These channels are not focused on a single receiver, use limited information cues, and do not permit feedback.

It is important for managers to understand that each communication channel has advantages and disadvantages, and that each can be an effective means of communication in the appropriate circumstances.[15] Channel selection depends on whether the message is routine or nonroutine. *Nonroutine messages* typically are ambiguous, concern novel events, and impose great potential for misunderstanding. Nonroutine messages often are characterized by time pressure and surprise. Managers can communicate nonroutine messages effectively only by selecting rich channels. On the other hand, routine communications are simple and straightforward. *Routine messages* convey data or statistics or simply put into words what managers already agree on and understand. Routine messages can be efficiently communicated through a channel lower in richness. Written communications also should be used when the audience is widely dispersed or when the communication is "official" and a permanent record is required.[16]

Consider the executive director of the American Red Cross trying to work out a press release with public relations people to address charges that the organization intentionally misled the public about how it would use funds and blood donated in the weeks following September 11. An immediate response is critical, as the reputation of the organization is at stake. This type of nonroutine communication forces a rich information exchange. The group will meet face to face, brainstorm ideas, and provide rapid feedback to resolve disagreement and convey the correct information. If, on the other hand, the director is preparing a press release about a routine matter such as a policy change or new donation sites, less information capacity is needed. The CEO and public relations people might begin developing the press release with an exchange of memos, telephone calls, and e-mail messages.

The key is to select a channel to fit the message. During a major acquisition, one firm decided to send top executives to all major work sites of the acquired company, where 75 percent of the workers met the managers in person, heard about their plans for the company, and had a chance to ask questions. The results were well worth the time and expense of the personal, face-to-face meetings because the acquired workforce saw their new managers as understanding, open, and willing to listen.[17] Communicating their nonroutine message about the acquisition in person prevented damaging rumors and misunderstandings. The choice of a communication channel can also convey a symbolic meaning to the receiver. The firm's decision to communicate face to face with the acquired workforce signaled to employees that managers cared about them as individuals.

Persuasion and Influence

Communication is used not only to convey information, but to persuade and influence people. Managers use communication to sell employees on the vision for the organization and influence them to behave in such a way as to accomplish the vision. While communication skills have always been important to managers, the ability to persuade and influence others is more critical today than ever before. The command-and-control mindset of managers telling workers what to do and how to do it is gone. Businesses are run largely by cross-functional teams who are actively involved in making decisions. Issuing directives is no longer an appropriate or effective way to get things done.[18] Therefore, managers should understand how communication can be used to persuade and influence others. But what about when the influencing becomes overly controlling? The Focus on Collaboration box shows how two young musicians were able to collaborate in the highly complex world of music without letting themselves get bull-dozed.

Managers can enrich their communication encounters by paying attention to the language they use as well as the channels of communication they select to convey their messages. To persuade and influence, managers connect with

FOCUS ON COLLABORATION

Alicia Keys and India.Arie

Budding singers and musicians are entrepreneurs, and if they allow others to control too much of their careers, they sometimes can lose. How can a singer "make it," while working with the producers and backers who are needed, and at the same time not bowing to their often slick powers of persuasion?

Alicia Keys won several Grammys in 2001, including one for the best R&B album. Her song "A Woman's Worth" was acclaimed. The 22-year-old biracial singer has been writing songs since she was 15 years old. She has enough self-confidence to stand tall with the big guys, such as manager and producer Clive Davis. Her independence is part of a trend; along with other R&B singers, such as Macy Gray, Jill Scott, and Sunshine Anderson, she has taken control of her career at a young age.

Twenty-seven-year-old India.Arie has been nominated for some Grammys, and thinks one big reason for her success is

that she has connected with the many young women who don't like the perfectly sculpted bodies of the women seen in most music videos. Her hit single "Video" rejects those impossible-to-attain-without-surgery standards of beauty.

How did she manage to stand firm against the influences of an industry notorious for controlling younger artists? "I didn't have to do anything," Arie says, surprised that anyone would pose such a question, despite knowing about all the musicians who've been trampled by stronger forces in the industry. "Nobody can make you do anything you don't want—you're grown [up]. Sometimes people accept things just because they think they have to."

SOURCES: Randy Lewis, "Pop Beat: Doing It Her Way," *Los Angeles Times* (July 28, 2001), F1; Rozalyn S. Frazier, "A New Key—Alicia Chats with Essence," *Essence Magazine* (December 2001), 75–79.

others on an emotional level by using symbols, metaphors, and stories to express their messages. Joe Ford, chairman and CEO of Alltel Corp., tells the following story to every new group of employees to illustrate how customer service drives customer loyalty and company success. Alltel (then Allied Telephone) bought a group of tiny, independent phone companies back in 1948, including one in Amity, Arkansas, that had about 200 customers. One of those customers, Edna Nunn, operated the company's manual switchboard, collected all the bills, and handled customer complaints. After he became vice president and treasurer in 1963, Ford noticed something odd: Every single bill from Amity was paid on time, every month. Ford decided to drive to Amity and get a first-hand explanation for this miracle from Ms. Nunn, who told him shyly, "Well, they always pay me back." It's that kind of attitude, says Ford, that propelled Alltel from a small regional company to a communications empire.[19]

Using symbols and stories also helps managers make sense of a fast-changing environment in ways that members throughout the organization can understand. Managers help inspire desirable behaviors for change by tapping into the imaginations of their subordinates. If we think back to our early school years, we may remember that the most effective lessons often were couched in stories. Teresa Lever-Pollary, CEO of Nighttime Pediatrics Clinics, became concerned that employees were losing touch with the company's values in the face of rapid growth and the increasing strictures of managed care. She hired a consultant to collect stories from patients, doctors, nurses, clerks, and others and put them together in a collection called *Nighttime Stories*. For example, one story tells of a payroll employee who convinced managers to scrap an expensive investment in flawed software. Another focuses on a doctor who bent the rules to treat a disoriented elderly woman. Levar-Pollary believes stories help people stay grounded in the face of rapid change.[20]

Presenting hard facts and figures rarely has the same power as telling vivid stories. Evidence of the compatibility of stories with human thinking was demonstrated by a study at Stanford Business School.[21] The point was to convince MBA students that a company practiced a policy of avoiding layoffs. For some students, only a story was used. For others, statistical data were provided that showed little turnover compared to competitors. For other students, statistics and stories were combined, and yet other students were shown the company's official policy statements. Of all these approaches, the students presented with a vivid story alone were most convinced that the company truly practiced a policy of avoiding layoffs.

Nonverbal Communication

Managers also use symbols to communicate what is important. Managers are watched, and their behavior, appearance, actions, and attitudes are symbolic of what they value and expect of others.

nonverbal communication

A communication transmitted through actions and behaviors rather than through words.

Nonverbal communication refers to messages sent through human actions and behaviors rather than through words.[21] Although most nonverbal communication is unconscious or subconscious on our part, it represents a major portion of the messages we send and receive. Most managers are astonished to learn that words themselves carry little meaning. Major parts of the shared understanding from communication come from the nonverbal messages of facial expression, voice, mannerisms, posture, and dress.

Nonverbal communication occurs mostly face to face. One researcher found three sources of communication cues during face-to-face communication: the

FOCUS ON SKILLS

Voice Training for Managers

Voice quality makes up over one-third of the interpersonal communication process. It's not hard to see that managers with weak voice quality could enhance their relationships by working on their voices. Managers are also often called on to give presentations, and a good voice can be an important asset. By taking vocal training and learning the basic rudiments of breathing and sound production, they can work toward becoming excellent communicators.

Speakers, as well as singers and actors, would do well to master frontal placement of the voice. Frontal placement gets the voice up and out of the throat (where speech is muddy and muffled), and places it across the front of the face, where consonants are bright, crisp, and easily understood. Frontal placement keeps the spoken line alive and percussive, better holding the attention of the audience.

Nothing is worse than a speaker whose tone is placed too far down in the throat. This type of placement produces dark vowels; good enunciation is impossible. Every line sounds like a lullaby. The audience will soon be bored and less eager to learn, as they drift off to dreamland. This lifeless vocal sound produces clock-watchers, not eager participants ready to test the new material and techniques that are being introduced.

Once a manager becomes accustomed to speaking with good frontal resonance, his or her voice will have maximum power without effort. Gone will be the days of sore throats and hoarseness after long hours of speaking incorrectly at seminars, classes, and conventions. The speech will ring out. Every word will project well.

SOURCE: Ron Browning, voice coach, Nashville, Tennessee.

---

verbal, which are the actual spoken words; the vocal, which include the pitch, tone, and timbre of a person's voice; and facial expressions. According to this study, the relative weights of these three factors in message interpretation are as follows: verbal impact, 7 percent; vocal impact, 38 percent; and facial impact, 55 percent.[23] To improve verbal impact, managers can attend Toastmasters, International seminars or hire a voice coach, as described in the Focus on Skills box.

This research strongly implies that "it's not what you say but how you say it." A manager's tone of voice or glint in the eye may signal something entirely different from his or her words. Nonverbal messages convey thoughts and feelings with greater force than do our most carefully selected words. Body language often communicates our real feelings eloquently. Thus, while the conscious mind may be formulating vocal messages such as "I'm happy," or "Congratulations on your promotion," the body language may be signaling true feelings through blushing, perspiring, glancing, crying, or avoiding eye contact. When the verbal and nonverbal messages are contradictory, the receiver may be confused and usually will give more weight to behavioral actions than to verbal messages.[24]

A manager's office also sends powerful nonverbal cues. For example, what do the following seating arrangements mean if used by your supervisor? (1) She stays behind her desk, and you sit in a straight chair on the opposite side. (2) The two of you sit in straight chairs away from her desk, perhaps at a table. (3) The two of you sit in a seating arrangement consisting of a sofa and easy chair. To most people, the first arrangement indicates, "I'm the boss here," or "I'm in authority." The second arrangement indicates, "This is serious business." The third indicates a more casual and friendly, "Let's get to know each other."[25] Nonverbal messages can be a powerful asset to communication if they complement and support verbal messages. Managers should pay close attention to nonverbal behavior when communicating. They must learn to coordinate their verbal and nonverbal messages and at the same time be sensitive to what their peers, subordinates, and supervisors are saying nonverbally. One nonverbal cue relates to the role model the manager plays to employees. In the case of Rokenbok Toy Company, it had to do with making family important and making work a fun place for people to connect with each other.

The Rokenbok Magic

http//www.rokenbok.com

Paul Eichen wondered what a company would look like if its only aim was to promote a balanced, healthy, soulful life. Work had meant everything to Eichen, who had helped to start a successful technology company and grow it to sales of $100 million. However, this lifestyle was draining him, so he walked away from his lucrative, successful job and began pursuing his vision.

As a boy, Eichen had loved Legos, model kits, and machines, a love that would prove to be his salvation in a quest for a better life. "I think people tend to know what they need to do in their lives, and they can either ignore it or get on with it," Eichen says. He knew what he needed to do—start a toy company. But even more important, he wanted to create a new kind of business, one in which every company-defining decision was based on the way it would make work feel for the people who worked there. When Eichen opened the doors to Rokenbok Toy Co., it wasn't in an industrial park but in a village by the beach, in an old, rehabilitated warehouse just a short walk from the sand, with ethnic restaurants, sundries emporiums, coffee shops, and used-books stores as neighbors. The surroundings held a kind of magic for Eichen and his employees, who realized that where a company is located determines not only the commute, but also the richness of life outside the office.

The pattern of work at Rokenbok was also different from many other companies. As long as employees did their work, they were encouraged to set their own hours, dress as they liked, tend to their health, and put their families first. One Rokenbok engineer describes playing on the living-room floor with his child, surrounded by company toys, piecing together solutions to problems, working as he played, and playing as he worked. For most company employees, work became a source of reconnection with family, friends, and neighbors. "We're trying to make something classic, not disposable. Values that are important personally—quality, constructive fun, learning, design sophistication—are things we're trying to design right into the product, and that feels great," says Eichen. While designing lasting toys (one of them is a cross between a construction set and a motorized vehicle, similar to old-fashioned model trains), the best work design turned out to be teamwork. In a world where so many products are beyond the comprehension of anyone but engineers or scientists, Rokenbok was creating a product that everyone could understand. Employees could help make decisions about the color of a toy, the way it was packaged, or whether a bulldozer or truck was a better extension line.

In the five years of its existence, Rokenbok's employees have accomplished something noteworthy: They've created an independent American toy company, establishing a product that has won toy-industry accolades and climbed from sales of $2.6 million in 1997 to $10 million in 1999. And even though Eichen recalls that during the dot-com heyday, every one of his managers was recruited with the promise of "instant millions," none of them left. "Our executives have chosen quality of life over the seductiveness of . . . wealth," says Eichen.

Eichen does not kid himself that even the most balanced workplaces can prevent life from getting a little messy, but the Rokenbok work-style allows employees to have the energy and flexibility to pay attention to health, friends, family, and their dreams, as well as their work. "Look," Eichen says, "at a company like Rokenbok you still get to keep the good parts [of work]: intellectual stimulation, social activity, the fun of competing to win." Plus, you get to have a personal life, too. It's a winning combination.[26]

Listening

One of the most important tools of manager communication is listening, both to employees and customers. Most managers now recognize that important information flows from the bottom up, not the top down, and managers had better be tuned in.[27] In the communication model in Exhibit 14.2, the listener is responsible for message reception, which is a vital link in the communication process. **Listening** involves the skill of grasping both facts and feelings to interpret a message's genuine meaning. Only then can the manager provide the appropriate response. Listening requires attention, energy, and skill. Although about 75 percent of effective communication is listening, most people spend only 30 to 40 percent of their time listening, which leads to many communication errors.[28] Merrill Lynch superbroker Richard F. Green explained the importance of listening to organizational success: "If you talk, you'll like me. If I talk, I'll like you—but if I do the talking, my business will not be served."[29] However, listening involves much more than just "not talking." Many people do not know how to listen effectively. They concentrate on formulating what they are going to say next rather than on what is being said to them. Our listening efficiency, as measured by the amount of material understood and remembered by subjects 48 hours after listening to a 10-minute message, is, on average, no better than 25 percent.[30]

What constitutes good listening? Exhibit 14.4 gives ten keys to effective listening and illustrates a number of ways to distinguish a bad from a good listener. A good listener finds areas of interest, is flexible, works hard at listening, and uses thought speed to mentally summarize, weigh, and anticipate what the speaker says. Good listening means shifting from thinking about self to empathizing with the other person and thus requires a degree of emotional intelligence, as described in Chapter 11. An excellent example of good listening comes from some television talk shows. For example, Oprah Winfrey listens actively to guests or audience participants by blocking out distractions, focusing her full attention on the speaker, and using eye contact. Winfrey listens empathically without interrupting and then paraphrases the speaker's

listening
The skill of receiving messages to accurately grasp facts and feelings to interpret the genuine meaning.

EXHIBIT *14.4*

Ten Keys to Effective Listening

Keys	Poor Listener	Good Listener
1. Listen actively	Is passive, laid back	Asks questions, paraphrases what is said
2. Find areas of interest	Tunes out dry subjects	Looks for opportunities, new learning
3. Resist distractions	Is easily distracted	Fights or avoids distractions; tolerates bad habits; knows how to concentrate
4. Capitalize on the fact that thought is faster than speech	Tends to daydream with slow speakers	Challenges, anticipates, mentally summarizes; weighs the evidence; listens between the lines to tone of voice
5. Be responsive	Is minimally involved	Nods; shows interest, give and take, positive feedback
6. Judge content, not delivery	Tunes out if delivery is poor	Judges content; skips over delivery errors
7. Hold one's fire	Has preconceptions, starts to argue	Does not judge until comprehension is complete
8. Listen for ideas	Listens for facts	Listens to central themes
9. Work at listening	Shows no energy output; faked attention	Works hard, exhibits active body state, eye contact
10. Exercise one's mind	Resists difficult material in favor of light, recreational material	Uses heavier material as exercise for the mind

SOURCE: Adapted from Sherman K. Okum, "How to Be a Better Listener," *Nation's Business* (August 1975), 62; and Philip Morgan and Kent Baker, "Building a Professional Image: Improving Listening Behavior," *Supervisory Management* (November 1985), 34–38.

BEST PRACTICES

CEO Talk

What was CEO Jeffrey Skilling's defense, when asked over and over about Enron's improper financial transactions? "I didn't know." According to many experts, it is a death sentence for the top leader not to have a clue what is going on.

Take John Much of San Diego's HNC Software, who says his best source of information is informal conversations with employees. "As a leader, you need a network of people from the highest to the lowest levels who can be your trusted advisers, and who know that you are open to hearing any message, bad as well as good, they may send you," he says. One way he stimulates this network is to hold a weekly "Java with John" session for the first 20 employees who sign up, and he asks them to talk about their problems. Much also acts as a moral compass for his company in meetings, challenging proposed actions. "Maybe if a deal is at risk, we may think about a better pricing, but there are lines we don't cross—such as negotiating barter deals. We don't do that, and it's my job to remind people of our standards," he notes.

One CEO who sees his responsibility as knowing what is going on is U.K.-based Shire Pharmaceutical's Rolf Stahel, who is bombarded with mountains of data and reports. How does he know which are the most important to focus on? "It takes an enormous amount of energy and time to filter out what is critical and focus on essentials," he says. Using a "traffic light" system, he's learned to discriminate areas that need immediate attention versus those that need little oversight.

The former CEO of Honeywell, Michael Bonsignore, would spend half his time visiting various company sites around the world. "We encouraged straight talk and bad news," he says, so that employees could quickly find and solve problems before they erupted into crises. When going to a new location, he was careful to talk not only to executives, but to employees at the lowest levels, as well. "There's no substitute for skipping down management layers and finding out what lower-level employees think."

Even so, there are times when the CEO won't know everything. But the top leader certainly must try. "You have to delegate authority," says Bonsignore, "but at the end of the day, you are accountable for everything that happens."

SOURCE: Carol Hymowitz, "How CEOs Can Keep Informed Even As Work Stretches across Globe," *The Wall Street Journal* (March 12, 2002), B1.

---

comments and ideas to make sure she has understood. Her excellent listening skills make people feel welcomed, understood, and important.[31] Contrast that with talk shows characterized by yelling, cursing, and chair throwing.

Some organizations have created a culture that emphasizes active manager listening. For example, at Wal-Mart, top executives devote at least two days a week to visiting stores and listening to employee concerns. Listening may be one of the most important skills a leader has. Several CEOs note how important it is to a company's long-term success, as described in the Best Practices box.

Organizational Communication

Another aspect of management communication concerns the organization as a whole. Organizationwide communications typically flow in three directions— downward, upward, and horizontally. Managers are responsible for establishing and maintaining formal channels of communication in these three directions. Managers also use informal channels, which means they get out of their offices and mingle with employees.

Formal Communication Channels

formal communication channel
A communication channel that flows within the chain of command or task responsibility defined by the organization.

Formal communication channels are those that flow within the chain of command or task responsibility defined by the organization. The three formal channels and the types of information conveyed in each are illustrated in Exhibit 14.5.[32] Downward and upward communication are the primary forms

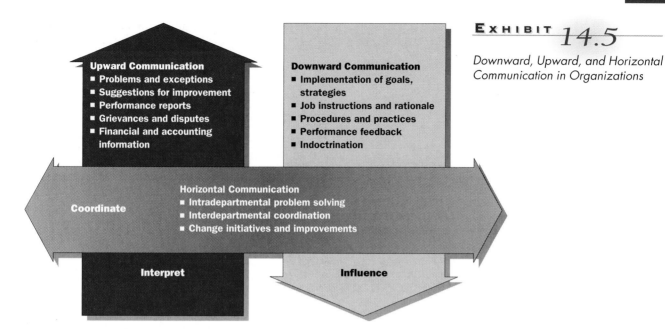

XHIBIT *14.5*

Downward, Upward, and Horizontal Communication in Organizations

SOURCE: Adapted from Richard L. Daft and Richard M. Steers, *Organizations: A Micro-Macro Approach*, 538. Copyright © 1986 by Scott, Foresman and Company. Used by permission.

of communication used in most traditional, vertically organized companies. However, the new workplace emphasizes horizontal communication, with people constantly sharing information across departments and levels.

Electronic communication such as e-mail and instant messaging have made it easier than ever for information to flow in all directions. For example, the U.S. Navy is using instant messaging to communicate within ships, across Navy divisions, and even back to the Pentagon in Washington. "Instant messaging has allowed us to keep our crew members on the same page at the same time," says Lieutenant Commander Mike Houston, who oversees the Navy's communications program. "Lives are at stake in real time, and we're seeing a new level of communication and readiness."[33]

Downward Communication. The most familiar and obvious flow of zformal communication, **downward communication**, refers to the messages and information sent from top management to subordinates in a downward direction. For example, StarMedia Network, a leading Internet portal for Spanish and Portuguese speakers, holds quarterly Web meetings in which CEO Fernando Espuelas and other top managers deliver quarterly results, communicate important news, announce strategic initiatives, or clarify goals. Because employees are scattered in 14 offices throughout 11 countries, the meetings are conducted in Spanish, Portuguese, and English. However, a local translator in each office recaps the entire meeting to ensure that no information gets lost in the translation.[34]

Managers sometimes use creative approaches to downward communication to be sure employees get the message. Mike Olson, plant manager at Ryerson Midwest Coil Processing, noticed that workers were dropping expensive power tools, so he hung price tags on the tools to show the replacement cost. Employees solved the problem by finding a way to hook up the tools so they wouldn't be dropped. Olson's communication helps workers see how their actions affect the entire company and creates a climate of working together for solutions.[35]

downward communication

Messages sent from top management down to subordinates.

Managers can communicate downward to employees in many ways. Some of the most common are through speeches, messages in company newsletters, e-mail, information leaflets tucked into pay envelopes, material on bulletin boards, and policy and procedure manuals. At VeriFone Inc., managers believe there's no such thing as giving employees too much information. They flood employees' home mailboxes with newsletters, total-compensation updates, benefit-program descriptions, and stock option plans. Since VeriFone is largely a "virtual" company, in which geographical dispersion is the operating principle, the company also makes extensive use of e-mail and the company intranet.[36]

Managers also have to decide what to communicate about. It is impossible for managers to communicate with employees about everything that goes on in the organization, so they have to make choices about the important information to communicate.[37] Downward communication in an organization usually encompasses these five topics:

1. *Implementation of goals and strategies.* Communicating new strategies and goals provides information about specific targets and expected behaviors. It gives direction for lower levels of the organization. Example: "The new quality campaign is for real. We must improve product quality if we are to survive."

2. *Job instructions and rationale.* These are directives on how to do a specific task and how the job relates to other organizational activities. Example: "Purchasing should order the bricks now so the work crew can begin construction of the building in two weeks."

3. *Procedures and practices.* These are messages defining the organization's policies, rules, regulations, benefits, and structural arrangements. Example: "After your first 90 days of employment, you are eligible to enroll in our company-sponsored savings plan."

4. *Performance feedback.* These messages appraise how well individuals and departments are doing their jobs. Example: "Joe, your work on the computer network has greatly improved the efficiency of our ordering process."

5. *Indoctrination.* These messages are designed to motivate employees to adopt the company's mission and cultural values and to participate in special ceremonies, such as picnics and United Way campaigns. Example: "The company thinks of its employees as family and would like to invite everyone to attend the annual picnic and fair on March 3."

The major problem with downward communication is *drop off,* the distortion or loss of message content. Although formal communications are a powerful way to reach all employees, much information gets lost—25 percent or so each time a message is passed from one person to the next. In addition, the message can be distorted if it travels a great distance from its originating source to the ultimate receiver. A tragic example is the following:

> A reporter was present at a hamlet burned down by the U.S. Army 1st Air Cavalry Division in 1967. Investigations showed that the order from the Division headquarters to the brigade was: "On no occasion must hamlets be burned down."
>
> The brigade radioed the battalion: "Do not burn down any hamlets unless you are absolutely convinced that the Viet Cong are in them."

The battalion radioed the infantry company at the scene: "If you think there are any Viet Cong in the hamlet, burn it down."

The company commander ordered his troops: "Burn down that hamlet."[38]

Information drop off cannot be completely avoided, but the techniques described in the previous sections can reduce it substantially. Using the right communication channel, consistency between verbal and nonverbal messages and active listening can maintain communication accuracy as it moves down the organization.

Upward Communication. Formal **upward communication** includes messages that flow from the lower to the higher levels in the organization's hierarchy. Most organizations take pains to build in healthy channels for upward communication. Employees need to air grievances, report progress, and provide feedback on management initiatives. Coupling a healthy flow of upward and downward communication ensures that the communication circuit between managers and employees is complete.[39] Wild Oats Market became successful because the founders began to understand the importance of upward communication.

upward communication
Messages transmitted from the lower to the higher levels in the organization's hierarchy.

Wild Oats Market
http://www.wildoats.com

From its beginnings, Wild Oats Market was offbeat, serving up health foods in a tiny market in Boulder, Colorado. Owners Libby Cook, Michael Gilliland, and Randy Clapp rang up sales and stocked the shelves themselves. It was easy back then to stay in touch with employees and customers. After four years, though, their success had exacted a price. With 11 stores scattered across three states, they found themselves managing a corporation rather than a tiny market. Employees' training and performance reviews had deteriorated. When they had worked side by side with shelf stockers and produce clerks, the founders could gauge employee morale. As Cook said, "In our business we need to keep our staff happy because they're the first line of defense when customers come into the store." But now, they not only could not work alongside employees, they couldn't even find time to visit them all. The three owners knew they had to devise some means of knowing what was happening in each store, to get feedback from each worker, so they could solve potential problems before customers shopped elsewhere.

Because Wild Oats staffers were known for their free-spirited attitudes, Cook, Gilliland, and Clapp developed a questionnaire to evaluate employee morale and satisfaction, using potential measures of "awful" and "remarkably bad" to "wonderful" and "terrific." Their "happiness index" rated respondents' sentiments, from "giddy" to "suicidal." Gilliland discovered that store managers were taking negative criticisms hard, even if their scores had a lot of "terrifics." To prevent this, he began reviewing the questionnaires to remove gratuitous or nonconstructive comments before going over them personally with each manager. The feedback has not only given a clear idea of work-force morale, but has also resulted in employee solutions to specific problems, such as employee participation in a stock-option program and a $200-per-worker wellness program allowance. Since the program began, turnover has dramatically decreased.

Communication and management practices at Wild Oats continue to be successful: The company now operates 105 stores nationwide and is up to yearly revenues of over $800 million.[40]

DIGITAL, INC.

Amazon.com Keeps Track of Employees' "Pulse Rate"

How do managers at Amazon.com keep in touch with employees' opinions and feelings about company decisions? By taking the organization's collective pulse twice a week.

Amazon works with eePulse, an Ann Arbor, Michigan-based application service provider, to electronically poll employees biweekly on their opinions and attitudes about various developments within the company. The electronic survey and communications tool uses a question format and asks employees to rate their "pulse," or energy level. Responses range from "not doing much, not having fun" to "overwhelmed by work and need help." Employees also have an opportunity for open comments about their work environment. These quick e-mail surveys, which take about two minutes to complete, provide feedback on a continuous basis, enabling managers to collect information and assess how things are going in real time. "Changes happen very quickly here," says one manager.

"By polling people this way, by e-mail, it's consistent and fast and provides the data we need." Employees are encouraged to talk to their manager about any specific concerns, and managers are trained to effectively use the eePulse and follow up on potential problems, such as low pulse rates or an employee whose pulse is about to go through the roof from overwork.

Whereas managers loved the new communications tool from the beginning, employees took a little longer to warm up to it. With typical management surveys, employees rarely see changes after results are compiled and publicized, and Amazon's workers expected this was just another useless poll. However, after numerous months in which Amazon's managers consistently reported back results to the employees and made sincere efforts to address concerns, attitudes toward eePulse have changed. Some people even enjoy regularly keeping tabs on the survey results and finding out what their coworkers are saying about their jobs and the company.

SOURCE: Teresa Welbourne, "New ASP Takes Workforce's 'Pulse'," *The New Corporate University Review* (July–August 2000), 20–21.

Many organizations make a great effort to facilitate upward communication. Mechanisms include suggestion boxes, employee surveys, open-door policies, management information system reports, and face-to-face conversations between workers and executives. At SoftChoice, a software reseller with 300 employees scattered across 23 offices, managers launched *SINews* (SoftChoice Internal News) to give employees a chance to speak their minds. Every page of the weekly online publication has a "Respond" bar that employees can click to ask questions, make comments, lodge complaints, or offer suggestions—anonymously, if they choose. Employees at Opus Event Marketing use bright-red Think cards to give feedback to managers.[41] This chapter's Digital, Inc. box describes one approach Amazon.com takes to find out what's on employees' minds.

Despite these efforts, however, barriers to accurate upward communication exist. Managers may resist hearing about employee problems, or employees may not trust managers sufficiently to push information upward.[42] Innovative companies search for ways to ensure that information gets to top managers without distortion. IBM's respected Speak Up program consists of anonymous employee letters or e-mails regularly channeled to management for action. Top managers at Golden Corral, a restaurant chain with headquarters in Raleigh, North Carolina, spend at least one weekend a year in the trenches—cutting steaks, rolling silverware, setting tables, and taking out the trash. By understanding the daily routines and challenges of waiters, chefs, and other employees at their restaurants, Golden Corral executives increase their awareness of how management actions affect others.[43]

horizontal communication

The lateral or diagonal exchange of messages among peers or coworkers.

Horizontal Communication. Horizontal communication is the lateral or diagonal exchange of messages among peers or coworkers. It may occur within or across departments. The purpose of horizontal communication is not only to inform but also to request support and coordinate activities. Horizontal communication falls into one of three categories:

1. *Intradepartmental problem solving.* These messages take place among members of the same department and concern task accomplishment. Example: "Betty, can you help us figure out how to complete this medical expense report form?"

2. *Interdepartmental coordination.* Interdepartmental messages facilitate the accomplishment of joint projects or tasks. Example: "Bob, please contact marketing and production and arrange a meeting to discuss the specifications for the new subassembly. It looks like we might not be able to meet their requirements."

3. *Change initiatives and improvements.* These messages are designed to share information among teams and departments that can help the organization change, grow, and improve. Example: "We are streamlining the company travel procedures and would like to discuss them with your department."

Horizontal communication is particularly important in learning organizations, where teams of workers are continuously solving problems and searching for new ways of doing things. Recall from Chapter 7 that many organizations build in horizontal communications in the form of task forces, committees, or even a matrix structure to encourage coordination. At Chicago's Northwestern Memorial Hospital, two doctors created a horizontal task force to solve a serious patient health problem.

Northwestern Memorial Hospital

http://www.nmh.org

We've all heard of it happening—a patient checks into the hospital for a routine procedure and ends up getting sicker instead of better. Hospital-borne infections afflict about two million patients—and kill nearly 100,000—each year. Greater antibiotic use causes the germs to develop greater resistance. The infection epidemic is growing worse worldwide, but a task force at Northwestern Memorial Hospital has reversed the trend by breaking down communication barriers.

When a cancer patient became Northwestern's first victim of a new strain of deadly bacteria, infectious-disease specialists Lance Peterson and Gary Noskin realized it would take everyone's help to defeat the insidious enemy. As infection spread throughout the hospital, they launched a regular Monday morning meeting to plot countermoves. Although some physicians and staff members were offended at having their procedures questioned, the goal of preventing needless deaths overrode their concerns. Absolute candor was the rule at the Monday morning meetings, which involved not only doctors and nurses, but also lab technicians, pharmacists, computer technicians, and admissions representatives. One pharmacist, for example, recognized that antibiotics act as fertilizers for many bacteria, which encouraged physicians to decrease their use of antibiotics in favor of alternative treatments. Computer representatives and admissions people got together to develop software to identify which returning patients might pose a threat for bringing infection back into the hospital. Eventually, the task force even included maintenance staff when studies showed that a shortage of sinks was inhibiting hand-washing.

Increasing horizontal communication paid off at Northwestern, saving millions in annual medical costs and at least a few lives. Over three years, Northwestern's rate of hospital-borne infections plunged 22 percent. In a recent fiscal year, such infections totaled 5.1 per 1,000 patients, roughly half the national average.[44]

Team Communication Channels

A special type of horizontal communication is communicating in teams. In many companies today, teams are the basic building block of the organization. Team members work together to accomplish tasks, and the team's communication structure influences both team performance and employee satisfaction.

Research into team communication has focused on two characteristics: the extent to which team communications are centralized and the nature of the team's task.[45] The relationship between these characteristics is illustrated in Exhibit 14.6. In a **centralized network**, team members must communicate through one individual to solve problems or make decisions. In a **decentralized network**, individuals can communicate freely with other team members. Members process information equally among themselves until all agree on a decision.[46]

In laboratory experiments, centralized communication networks achieved faster solutions for simple problems. Members could simply pass relevant information to a central person for a decision. Decentralized communications were slower for simple problems because information was passed among individuals until someone finally put the pieces together and solved the problem. However, for more complex problems, the decentralized communication network was faster. Because all necessary information was not restricted to one person, a pooling of information through widespread communications provided greater input into the decision. Similarly, the accuracy of problem solving was related to problem complexity. The centralized networks made fewer errors on simple problems but more errors on complex ones. Decentralized networks were less accurate for simple problems but more accurate for complex ones.[47]

The implication for organizations is as follows: In a highly competitive global environment, organizations use teams to deal with complex problems. When team activities are complex and difficult, all members should share information in a decentralized structure to solve problems. Teams need a free flow of communication in all directions.[48] At Microsoft, for example, teams hold "triage" meetings in the final months of a software development cycle. Everyone jumps in with their ideas and opinions and then "negotiates" to a decision.[49] However, teams who perform routine tasks spend less time processing information, and thus communications can be centralized. Data can be channeled to a supervisor for decisions, freeing workers to spend a greater percentage of time on task activities.

centralized network
A team communication structure in which team members communicate through a single individual to solve problems or make decisions.

decentralized network
A team communication structure in which team members freely communicate with one another and arrive at decisions together.

EXHIBIT 14.6

Effectiveness of Team Communication Network

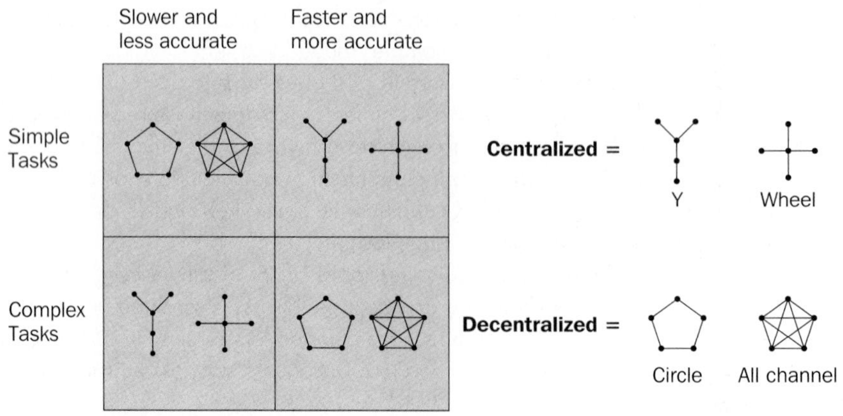

SOURCES: Adapted from A. Bavelas and D. Barrett, "An Experimental Approach to Organization Communication," *Personnel 27* (1951), 366–371; M. E. Shaw, *Group Dynamics: The Psychology of Small Group Behavior* (New York: McGraw-Hill, 1976); and E. M. Rogers and R. A. Rogers, *Communication in Organizations* (New York: Free Press, 1976).

Informal Communication Channels

Informal communication channels exist outside the formally authorized channels and do not adhere to the organization's hierarchy of authority. Informal communications coexist with formal communications but may skip hierarchical levels, cutting across vertical chains of command to connect virtually anyone in the organization. For example, to improve communication at OpenAir.com, a Boston-based provider of professional services software online, CEO Bill O'Farrell instituted the *morning huddle,* whereby the staff gathers for a big water-cooler chat in which each person shares a few anecdotes about his or her customer contacts from the day before. The "no chairs allowed" rule keeps things loose, informal, and fast. It gives people a great way to share information and get a jump on their day.[50] At SafeCard Services of Jacksonville, Florida, chief executive Paul Kahn opened up the "executives only" fitness center to all employees so people would have more opportunities for informal interaction and information exchange. Kahn believes providing greater opportunities for informal communications helped him turn the struggling company around.[51] An illustration of both formal and informal communications is given in Exhibit 14.7. Note how formal communications can be vertical or horizontal, depending on task assignments and coordination responsibilities.

Two types of informal channels used in many organizations are *management by wandering around* and the *grapevine.*

Management by Wandering Around. The communication technique known as **management by wandering around (MBWA)** was made famous by the books *In Search of Excellence* and *A Passion for Excellence.*[52] These books describe executives who talk directly with employees to learn what is going on. MBWA works for managers at all levels. They mingle and develop positive relationships with employees and learn directly from them about their department, division, or organization. For example, the president of ARCO had a habit of visiting a district field office. Rather than schedule a big strategic meeting with the district supervisor, he would come in unannounced and chat with the lowest-level employees. In any organization, both upward and downward communication are enhanced with MBWA. Managers have a chance to describe key ideas and values to employees and, in turn, learn about the problems and issues confronting employees.

informal communication channels

A communication channel that exists outside formally authorized channels without regard for the organization's hierarchy of authority.

management by wandering around (MBWA)

A communication technique in which managers interact directly with workers to exchange information.

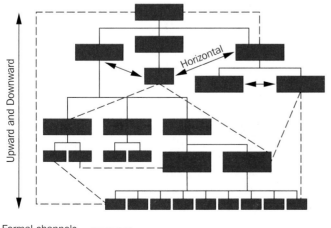

EXHIBIT *14.7*

Formal and Informal Organizational Communication Channels

Formal channels ————
Informal channels − − − −

When managers fail to take advantage of MBWA, they become aloof and isolated from employees. For example, Peter Anderson, president of Ztel, Inc., a maker of television switching systems, preferred not to personally communicate with employees. He managed at arm's length. As one manager said, "I don't know how many times I asked Peter to come to the lab, but he stayed in his office. He wasn't that visible to the troops." This formal management style contributed to Ztel's troubles and eventual bankruptcy.[53]

grapevine

An informal, person-to-person communication network of employees that is not officially sanctioned by the organization.

The Grapevine.   The **grapevine** is an informal, person-to-person communication network of employees that is not officially sanctioned by the organization.[54] The grapevine links employees in all directions, ranging from the president through middle management, support staff, and line employees. The grapevine will always exist in an organization, but it can become a dominant force when formal channels are closed. In such cases, the grapevine is actually a service because the information it provides helps makes sense of an unclear or uncertain situation. Employees use grapevine rumors to fill in information gaps and clarify management decisions. The grapevine tends to be more active during periods of change, excitement, anxiety, and sagging economic conditions. For example, when Jel, Inc., an auto supply firm, was under great pressure from Ford and GM to increase quality, rumors circulated on the shop floor about the company's possible demise. Management changes to improve quality—learning statistical process control, introducing a new compensation system, buying a fancy new screw machine from Germany—all started out as rumors, circulating days ahead of the actual announcements, and were generally accurate.[55]

Research suggests that a few people are primarily responsible for the grapevine's success. Exhibit 14.8 illustrates the two most typical grapevines.[56] In the *gossip chain,* a single individual conveys a piece of news to many other people. In a *cluster chain,* a few individuals each convey information to several others. Having only a few people conveying information may account for the accuracy of grapevines. If every person told one other person in sequence, distortions would be greater.

Surprising aspects of the grapevine are its accuracy and its relevance to the organization. About 80 percent of grapevine communications pertain to business-related topics rather than personal, vicious gossip. Moreover, from 70 to 90 percent of the details passed through a grapevine are accurate.[57] Many managers would like the grapevine to be destroyed because they consider its

E X H I B I T *14.8*

Two Grapevine Chains in Organizations

SOURCE: Based on Keith Davis and John W. Newstrom, *Human Behavior at Work: Organizational Behavior,* 7th ed. (New York: McGraw-Hill, 1985).

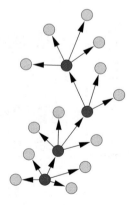

Gossip Chain
(One tells many)

Cluster Chain
(A few tell selected others)

rumors to be untrue, malicious, and harmful. Typically this is not the case; however, managers should be aware that almost five of every six important messages are carried to some extent by the grapevine rather than through official channels. In a survey of 22,000 shift workers in varied industries, 55 percent said they get most of their information via the grapevine.[58] Smart managers understand the company's grapevine. They recognize who's connected to whom and which employees are key players in the informal spread of information. In all cases, but particularly in times of crisis, executives need to manage communications effectively so that the grapevine is not the only source of information.[59]

Communicating in the New Workplace

Managers in today's leading companies put extraordinary emphasis on open and honest communication in all directions to build trust and promote learning and problem solving. In addition to encompassing the ideas and techniques discussed so far, the new workplace also focuses on open communication, dialogue, and feedback and learning.

Open Communication

A recent trend that reflects managers' increased emphasis on empowering employees, building trust and commitment, and enhancing collaboration is open communication. **Open communication** means sharing all types of information throughout the company, across functional and hierarchical levels. Many companies, such as Springfield Remanufacturing Corporation, Johnsonville Foods, and Quad/Graphics, are opening the financial books to workers at all levels so they understand how and why the company operates as it does. Wabash National Corporation, one of the nation's leading truck-trailer manufacturers, has employees complete several hours of business training and then holds regular meetings on the shop floor to review the company's financial performance. AES Corporation, a power producer, shares so much financial data with its employees that it has declared them all insiders for stock-trading purposes.[60]

Open communication runs counter to the traditional flow of selective information downward from supervisors to subordinates. By breaking down conventional hierarchical and departmental boundaries that may be barriers to communication, the organization can gain the benefit of all employees' ideas. The same ideas batted back and forth among a few managers do not lead to effective learning and change or to a network of relationships that keep companies thriving. New voices and conversations involving a broad spectrum of people revitalize and enhance organizational communication.[61]

The Great Harvest Bread Company uses both formal and informal communication channels to encourage the broad sharing of information and ideas among its franchisees, as described in the Focus on Collaboration box. Open communication also builds trust and a commitment to common goals, which is essential in organizations that depend on collaboration and knowledge-sharing to accomplish their purpose. Fifty percent of executives surveyed report that open communication is a key to building trust in the organization.[62]

open communication

Sharing all types of information throughout the company, across functional and hierarchical levels.

Dialogue

Another means of fostering trust and collaboration is through dialogue. The "roots of dialogue" are *dia* and *logos*, which can be thought of as "stream of

FOCUS ON COLLABORATION

Great Harvest Bread Company

Great Harvest Bread Company, a franchisor of retail bread bakeries, was founded on the philosophy that command-and-control management is downright wrong. Unlike most other franchisors, which dictate how their franchisees must operate, Great Harvest sets people free to run their stores as they see fit, encouraging bakery owners to be themselves, experiment, and, most important, share their ideas with others. By "putting freedom first," Great Harvest fully taps the creative energy of all franchisees.

At Great Harvest, ideas travel through both formal and informal channels. Informal ways of communication—what Great Harvest calls "management by shoptalk and gossip"—enable owners to profit from each other's experiences. When an owner tries something that works, he or she gets on the phone or sends an e-mail to tell another owner or owners, who can try the idea and spread the word. For example, "Baker for a Day" started in one store in Boulder, Colorado, spread to a bakery in Minnesota, and then gained momentum as word of the project's success spread via telephone and e-mail from one bakery owner to another. Baker for a Day opens the bakery for a special event on a Sunday (when the stores are usually closed) and donates the day's sales to a local charity, which promotes the event and helps staff it. Besides giving something to the community, the project also brings in potential new customers to taste Great Harvest's products.

Great Harvest founders Pete and Laura Wakeman also build in formal mechanisms to help ideas spread and guide owners to the best sources of help. One is the "learning community," which all owners are urged to join (most do). Those who participate in the learning community can hold nothing back from others in the community and must contribute information, sales figures, ideas, and observations whenever asked. Another formal mechanism is the Numbers Club, in which owners agree to open their books to the parent company and the other bakeries in the system. In return, members get a summary of where fellow owners are ranked by way of the stores' sales figures and performance in every category across the board. This enables franchisees to find stores with similar environments to theirs, such as bakery size, market, and level of labor, who may be more successful in some area of performance. With that information, the Numbers Club member can give the other store a call and establish a mentoring relationship. With the aid of Travel Match, which pays half the expenses, the store owner or an employee can visit the more successful store to learn how it is doing things better.

Great Harvest also uses other means of capturing and communicating ideas. For example, an internal Web site called "Breadboard" includes articles from staffers and outside press coverage; ongoing electronic chat discussions about anything from new recipes and equipment maintenance to tips on seasonal promotions; and archives that allow users to pull up information addressing specific concerns. Printed newsletters, field trips, annual conferences, and training sessions all serve to enable even the smallest ideas to travel, grow, and evolve.

SOURCES: Michael Hopkins, "Zen and the Art of the Self-Managing Company," *Inc.* (November 2000), 54–63.

dialogue

A group communication process aimed at creating a culture based on collaboration, fluidity, trust, and commitment to shared goals.

meaning." **Dialogue** is a group communication process in which people together create a stream of shared meaning that enables them to understand each other and share a view of the world.[63] People may start out at polar opposites, but by talking openly to one another, they discover common ground, common issues, and shared goals on which they can build a better future.

A useful way to describe dialogue is to contrast it with discussion. Exhibit 14.9 illustrates the differences between dialogue and discussion. The intent of discussion, generally, is to deliver one's point of view and persuade others to adopt it. A discussion is often resolved by logic or "beating down" opponents. Dialogue, on the other hand, asks that participants suspend their attachments to a particular viewpoint so that a deeper level of listening, synthesis, and meaning can evolve from the group. A dialogue's focus is to reveal feelings and build common ground. Both forms of communication—dialogue and discussion—can result in change. However, the result of discussion is limited to the topic being deliberated, whereas the result of dialogue is characterized by group unity, shared meaning, and transformed mindsets. As new and deeper solutions are developed, a trusting relationship is built among team members.[64]

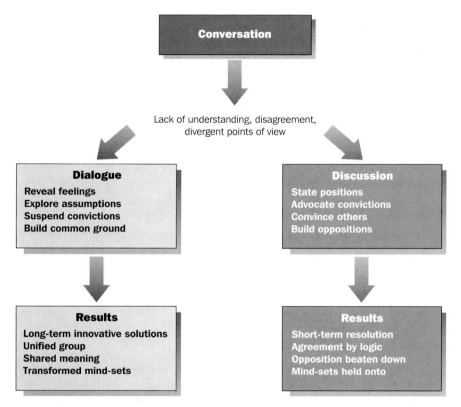

EXHIBIT 14.9

*Dialogue and Discussion:
The Differences*

SOURCE: Adapted from Edgar Schein, "On Dialogue, Culture and Organization Learning," *Organizational Dynamics* (Autumn 1993), 46.

Feedback and Learning

In the new workplace, **feedback** occurs when managers use evaluation and communication to help individuals and the organization learn and improve. Feedback enables manages to determine whether they have been successful or unsuccessful in communicating with others. It also helps them develop subordinates. At General Electric, managers are evaluated partly on their ability to give and receive effective feedback.[65] Recall from the communication model earlier in the chapter that feedback is an important part of the communication process. However, despite its importance, feedback is often neglected. One study found that although executives at a majority of companies agree that communication is a priority, less than half bother to tailor their messages to employees, customers, or suppliers, and even fewer seek feedback from those constituencies.[66] Using feedback can seem daunting because it potentially involves many sources. A single individual might receive feedback from supervisors, coworkers, customers, investors, suppliers, and members of partner organizations.

Successful managers focus feedback to help develop the capacities of subordinates and to teach the organization how to better reach its goals. Feedback is an important means by which individuals and organizations learn from their mistakes and improve their work. When managers enlist the whole organization in reviewing the outcomes of activities, they can quickly learn what works and what doesn't and use that information to improve the organization. Consider how the U.S. Army's feedback system promotes whole-system learning.

feedback

Using communication and evaluation to help the organization learn and improve.

U.S. Army

http://www.army.mil

At the National Training Center just south of Death Valley, U.S. Army troops engage in a simulated battle: The "enemy" has sent unmanned aerial vehicles (UAVs) to gather targeting data. When the troops fire on the UAVs, they reveal their location to attack helicopters hovering just behind a nearby ridge. After the exercise, unit members and their superiors hold an *after-action review* to review battle plans, discuss what worked and what didn't, and talk about how to do things better. General William Hertzog suggests that inexpensive decoy UAVs might be just the thing to make a distracted enemy reveal its location. The observation amounts to a "lesson learned" for the entire army.

In the U.S. Army, after-action reviews take just 15 minutes, and they occur after every identifiable event—large or small, simulated or real. The review involves asking four simple questions: What was supposed to happen? What actually happened? What accounts for any difference? What can we learn? It is a process of identifying mistakes, of innovating, and of continuously learning from experience. The lessons are based not only on simulated battles, but also on real-life experiences of soldiers in the field. The Center for Army Lessons Learned (CALL) sends experts into the field to observe after-action reviews, interview soldiers, and compile intelligence reports. The lessons learned are stockpiled and disseminated throughout the combat force. In Bosnia, a new list of lessons was distributed every 72 hours. Lessons are currently being disseminated in Afghanistan.[67]

In this example, the organization is learning by communicating feedback about the consequences of field operations and simulated battles. Compiling what is learned and using communication feedback create an improved organization. After-action reviews are used in corporate America. Steelcase Inc., an office furniture manufacturer, and BP are among the companies adapting the army's system to create a process of continuous learning and improvement. BP credits the feedback system for $700 million in cost savings and other gains.[68]

Managing Organizational Communication

Many of the ideas described in this chapter pertain to barriers to communication and how to overcome them. Barriers can be categorized as those that exist at the individual level and those that exist at the organizational level. First we will examine communication barriers; then we will look at techniques for overcoming them. These barriers and techniques are summarized in Exhibit 14.10.

Barriers to Communication

Barriers to communication can exist within the individual or as part of the organization.

Individual Barriers. First, there are *interpersonal barriers;* these include problems with emotions and perceptions held by employees. For example, rigid perceptual labeling or categorizing of others prevents modification or alteration of opinions. If a person's mind is made up before the communication starts, communication will fail. **Defense mechanisms,** such as rationalizing (self-serving explanations for behavior), distortion (reshaping reality), or intellectualization (excessive abstract thought) prevent open and authentic com-

defense mechanism

Emotional blocks that serve to minimize anxiety, protect the ego, and maintain repression of true feelings.

Barriers	How to Overcome
Individual	
Interpersonal dynamics	Active listening
Channels and media	Selection of appropriate channel
Defense mechanisms	Question underlying assumptions
Semantics	Knowledge of other's perspective
Inconsistent cues	MBWA
Organizational	
Status and power differences	Climate of trust, dialogue
Departmental needs and goals	Development and use of formal channels
Lack of formal channels	Encouragement of multiple channels, formal and informal
Communication network unsuited to task	Changing organization or group structure to fit communication needs
Poor coordination	Feedback and learning

EXHIBIT 14.10

Communication Barriers and Ways to Overcome Them

munication. Moreover, people with different backgrounds or knowledge may interpret a communication in different ways.

Second, *selecting the wrong channel or medium* for sending a communication can be a problem. For example, when a message is emotional, it is better to transmit it face to face rather than in writing. On the other hand, writing works best for routine messages but lacks the capacity for rapid feedback and multiple cues needed for difficult messages.

Third, *semantics* often causes communication problems. **Semantics** pertains to the meaning of words and the way they are used. A word such as *effectiveness* may mean achieving high production to a factory superintendent and employee satisfaction to a human resources staff specialist. Many common words have an average of 28 definitions; thus, communicators must take care to select the words that will accurately encode ideas.[69] Language differences can also be a barrier in today's organizations. At Semifreddi's, an artisan bread bakery in Emeryville, California, CEO Tom Frainier had to hire translators to help him communicate effectively with his employees, most of whom come from Mexico, Laos, China, Peru, Cambodia, Yemen, and Vietnam.[70]

Fourth, sending *inconsistent cues* between verbal and nonverbal communications will confuse the receiver. If one's facial expression does not reflect one's words, the communication will contain noise and uncertainty. The tone of voice and body language should be consistent with the words, and actions should not contradict words.

semantics
The meaning of words and the way they are used.

Organizational Barriers. Organizational barriers pertain to factors for the organization as a whole. First is the problem of *status and power differences*. Low-power people may be reluctant to pass bad news up the hierarchy, thus giving the wrong impression to upper levels.[71] High-power people may not pay attention or may think that low-status people have little to contribute.

Second, *differences across departments in terms of needs and goals* interfere with communications. Each department perceives problems in its own terms. The production department is concerned with production efficiency whereas the marketing department's goal is to get the product to the customer in a hurry.

Third, the *absence of formal channels* reduces communication effectiveness. Organizations must provide adequate upward, downward, and horizontal

The scoreboard at Colonial Mills, Inc., a $7 million specialty-rug manufacturer in Pawtucket, Rhode Island, overcomes communication barriers by helping all employees get involved in business targets and results. The board stretches 30 feet and covers most of the lunchroom wall. A big gold rocket ship in the middle shows the year-to-date company profit. Columns for winding, braiding, and the other production departments show monthly output—cans filled, square feet braided, etc.—all compared with the company's plan. The Colonial Mills scoreboard is a unique communication channel that encourages upward, downward, and horizontal communication. "Our targets aren't the powers-that-be coming down and saying, 'This shall be the number,'" says Colonial Mills CEO Don Scarlata. "They're numbers everybody has discussed and signed off on."

communication in the form of employee surveys, open-door policies, newsletters, memos, task forces, and liaison personnel. Without these formal channels, the organization cannot communicate as a whole.

Fourth, the *communication flow* may not fit the team's or organization's task. If a centralized communication structure is used for nonroutine tasks, there will not be enough information circulated to solve problems. The organization, department, or team is most efficient when the amount of communication flowing among employees fits the task.

A final problem is *poor coordination*, so that different parts of the organization are working in isolation without knowing and understanding what other parts are doing. Top executives are out of touch with lower levels, or departments and divisions are poorly coordinated so that people don't understand how the system works together as a whole.

Overcoming Communication Barriers

Managers can design the organization so as to encourage positive, effective communication. Designing involves both individual skills and organizational actions.

Individual Skills. Perhaps the most important individual skill is *active listening*. Active listening means asking questions, showing interest, and occasionally paraphrasing what the speaker has said to ensure that one is interpreting accurately. Active listening also means providing feedback to the sender to complete the communication loop.

Second, individuals should select the *appropriate channel* for the message. A complicated message should be sent through a rich channel, such as face-to-face discussion or telephone. Routine messages and data can be sent through memos, letters, or e-mail, because there is little chance of misunderstanding.

Third, senders and receivers should make a special effort to understand each other's *perspective*. Managers can sensitize themselves to the information receiver so that they will be better able to target the message, detect bias, and clarify missed interpretations. By communicators understanding others' perspectives, semantics can be clarified, perceptions understood, and objectivity maintained.

The fourth individual skill is *management by wandering around*. Managers must be willing to get out of the office and check communications with others. For example, John McDonnell of McDonnell Douglas always ate in the employee cafeteria when he visited far-flung facilities. Through direct observation and face-to-face meetings, managers develop an understanding of the organization and are able to communicate important ideas and values directly to others.

Organizational Actions. Perhaps the most important thing managers can do for the organization is to create a *climate of trust and openness*. Open communication and dialogue can encourage people to communicate honestly with one another. Subordinates will feel free to transmit negative as well as positive messages without fear of retribution. Efforts to develop interpersonal skills among employees can also foster openness, honesty, and trust.

Second, managers should develop and use *formal information channels* in all directions. Scandinavian Design uses two newsletters to reach employees. GM's Packard Electric plant is designed to share all pertinent information—financial, future plans, quality, performance—with employees. Dana Corporation has developed innovative programs such as the "Here's a Thought" board—called a HAT rack—to get ideas and feedback from workers. Other techniques include direct mail, bulletin boards, and employee surveys.

Third, managers should encourage the use of *multiple channels,* including both formal and informal communications. Multiple communication channels include written directives, face-to-face discussions, MBWA, and the grapevine. For example, managers at GM's Packard Electric plant use multimedia, including a monthly newspaper, frequent meetings of employee teams, and an electronic news display in the cafeteria. Sending messages through multiple channels increases the likelihood that they will be properly received.

Fourth, the structure should *fit communication needs.* For example, Harrah's created the Communication Team as part of its structure at the Casino/Holiday Inn in Las Vegas. The team includes one member from each department. It deals with urgent company problems and helps people think beyond the scope of their own departments to communicate with anyone and everyone to solve those problems. An organization can be designed to use teams, task forces, project managers, or a matrix structure as needed to facilitate the horizontal flow of information for coordination and problem solving. Structure should also reflect information needs. When team or department tasks are difficult, a decentralized structure should be implemented to encourage discussion and participation. A system of organizational *feedback and learning* can help to overcome problems of poor coordination, as well.

■ Summary and Management Solution

This chapter described several important points about communicating in organizations. Communication takes up 80 percent of a manager's time. Communication is a process of encoding an idea into a message, which is sent through a channel and decoded by a receiver. Communication among people can be affected by communication channels, nonverbal communication, and listening skills. Important aspects of management communication include persuasion and influence. Managers use communication to sell people on the vision for the organization and to influence them to behave in such a way as to accomplish the vision. To influence others, managers connect with people on an emotional level by using symbols, metaphors, and stories to communicate their messages.

At the organizational level, managers are concerned with managing formal communications in a downward, upward, and horizontal direction. Informal communications also are important, especially management by wandering around and the grapevine. Moreover, research shows that communication structures in teams and departments should reflect the underlying tasks. Open communication, dialogue, and feedback and learning are important communication mechanisms in the new workplace.

Finally, several barriers to communication were described. These barriers can be overcome by active listening, selecting appropriate channels, engaging in MBWA, using dialogue, developing a climate of trust, using formal channels, designing the correct structure to fit communication needs, and using feedback for learning.

At Voyant, Bill Ernstrom could not get the engineers to listen to the marketing department, although he tried many different options. After his other ideas failed, Ernstrom finally found one that worked. Because the product managers didn't have experience in the field, it was difficult for them to talk to the technology people who had worked at the company for years. Ernstrom created the position of chief product officer and hired John Guillame, with years of telecom experience, who was able to chat with the engineers as well as making sense to the businesspeople. Not one to let things be, Guillame had some radical ideas about how to unsettle Voyant's balkanized culture. "If I'd know what he was going to do up front, I would've been worried," says Ernstrom. First, Guillame gave higher profile to the product managers by giving them more visible tasks, such as presenting market research and writing definitions for products. Next, he asked two of Voyant's top engineers to head up the product group, which would give credibility to the product teams and allow the two groups to work together. As part of the whole restructuring, the executive team reconfigured seating arrangements, breaking up clumps of engineers and mixing with their product management teams. Finally, Guillame developed some systemic process for new ideas or changes to existing products. When someone has an idea, they put it on the company intranet, where engineers, accountants, and marketing people can review it and assess its financial potential and impact. It's nearly like an internal venture-capital process. And it works. Since instituting the changes, Voyant has kept all its engineers and increased sales by 25 percent, improved time to market by 40 percent, added three products to the line, and reduced R&D costs by 20 percent. All this was accomplished by figuring out new ways to communicate.[72]

Discussion Questions

1. How can electronic media such as e-mail improve communication in today's organizations? How might it also lead to poorer communication?
2. Describe the elements of the communication process. Give an example of each part of the model as it exists in the classroom during communication between teacher and students.
3. Why do you think stories are more effective than hard facts and figures in persuading others?
4. Try to recall an incident at school or work when information was passed primarily through the grapevine. How accurate were the rumors, and how did people react to them? How can managers control information that is processed through the grapevine?
5. What is the difference between a discussion and a dialogue? What steps might managers take to transform a discussion into a constructive dialogue?
6. What do you think are the major barriers to upward communication in organizations? Discuss.

7. What is the relationship between group communication and group task? For example, how should communications differ in a strategic planning group and a group of employees who stock shelves in a grocery store?
8. Some senior managers believe they should rely on written information and computer reports because these yield more accurate data than do face-to-face communications. Do you agree?
9. Why is management by wandering around considered effective communication? Consider channel richness and nonverbal communications in formulating your answer.
10. Is speaking accurately or listening actively the more important communication skill for managers? Discuss.
11. Assume that you have been asked to design a training program to help managers become better communicators. What would you include in the program?

Manager's Workbook

Listening Self-Assessment

Instructions: Choose one response for each of the items below. Base your choice on what you usually do, not on what you think a person *should* do.

1. When you are going to lunch with a friend, you:
   a. Focus your attention on the menu and then on the service provided
   b. Ask about events in your friend's life and pay attention to what's said
   c. Exchange summaries of what is happening to each of you while focusing attention on the meal
2. When someone talks nonstop, you:
   a. Ask questions at an appropriate time in an attempt to help the person focus on the issue
   b. Make an excuse to end the conversation
   c. Try to be patient and understand what you are being told

3. If a group member complains about a fellow employee who, you believe, is disrupting the group, you:
   a. Pay attention and withhold your opinions
   b. Share your own experiences and feelings about that employee
   c. Acknowledge the group member's feelings and ask the group member what options he or she has
4. If someone is critical of you, you:
   a. Try not to react or get upset
   b. Automatically become curious and attempt to learn more
   c. Listen attentively and then back up your position
5. You are having a very busy day and someone tells you to change the way you are completing a task. You believe the person is wrong, so you:
   a. Thank her or him for the input and keep doing what you were doing

b. Try to find out why she or he thinks you should change

c. Acknowledge that the other may be right, tell her or him you are very busy, and agree to follow up later

6. When you are ready to respond to someone else, you:

a. Sometimes will interrupt the person if you believe it is necessary

b. Almost always speak before the other is completely finished talking

c. Rarely offer your response until you believe the other has finished

7. After a big argument with someone you have to work with every day, you:

a. Settle yourself and then try to understand the other's point of view before stating your side again

b. Just try to go forward and let bygones be bygones

c. Continue to press your position

8. A colleague calls to tell you that he is upset about getting assigned to a new job. You decide to:

a. Ask him if he can think of options to help him deal with the situation

b. Assure him that he is good at what he does and that these things have a way of working out for the best

c. Let him know you have heard how badly he feels

9. If a friend always complains about her problems but never asks about yours, you:

a. Try to identify areas of common interest

b. Remain understanding and attentive, even if it becomes tedious

c. Support her complaints and mention your own complaints

10. The best way to remain calm in an argument is to:

a. Continue to repeat your position in a firm but even manner

b. Repeat what you believe is the other person's position

c. Tell the other person that you are willing to discuss the matter again when you are both calmer

Score each item of your Listening Self-Assessment

1. a = 0;	b = 10;	c = 5
2. a = 10;	b = 0;	c = 5
3. a = 5;	b = 0;	c = 5
4. a = 5;	b = 10;	c = 0
5. a = 0;	b = 10;	c = 5
6. a = 5;	b = 0;	c = 10
7. a = 10;	b = 5;	c = 0
8. a = 5;	b = 5;	c = 10
9. a = 0;	b = 10;	c = 5
10. a = 0;	b = 10;	c = 5

Add up your total score _____

80–100 **You are an active, excellent listener.** You achieve a good balance between listening and asking questions, and you strive to understand others.

50–75 **You are an adequate-to-good listener.** You listen well, although you may sometimes react too quickly to others before they are finished speaking.

25–45 **You have some listening skills but need to improve them.** You may often become impatient when trying to listen to others, hoping they will finish talking so you can talk.

0–20 **You listen to others very infrequently.** You may prefer to do all of the talking and experience extreme frustration while waiting for others to make their point.

SOURCE: Reprinted with permission of the publisher from *Managers As Facilitators: A Practical Guide to Getting Work Done in a Changing Workplace.* © 1997 by Richard G. Weaver and John D. Farrell. Berrett-Koehler Publishers, Inc. San Francisco, CA. All Rights Reserved. *http://www.bkconnection.com.*

■ Manager's Workbook

Do You Love Your Company?

Open, honest and authentic communcation can help create the kind of organization that employees love. Here's an instrument to determine which of five key principles your company does best.

	Agree Strongly				Disagree Strongly

Capture the Heart

	Agree Strongly				Disagree Strongly
1. We have a written vision that is known to all and lived every day.	1	2	3	4	5
2. We seek creative, low-cost ways to balance work and family.	1	2	3	4	5
3. We love to celebrate and find innovative ways to inject fun into the workplace.	1	2	3	4	5

Open Communication

	Agree Strongly				Disagree Strongly
1. It is obvious that management considers internal listening a priority.	1	2	3	4	5
2. Attention is given to using multiple communication channels—more than just using memos and e-mail.	1	2	3	4	5

	Agree Strongly			Disagree Strongly	

3. Employees received feedback in real time (immediate, direct, positive) rather than merely occasional performance appraisals.

| 1 | 2 | 3 | 4 | 5 |

Create Partnerships

1. There are few, if any, status barriers between employees (i.e., reserved parking, bonuses only for top management, special benefits).

| 1 | 2 | 3 | 4 | 5 |

2. We actively share financial numbers, ratios, and company performance measures with all employees.

| 1 | 2 | 3 | 4 | 5 |

3. Management visibly serves the front-line, customer-contact employee first (providing tools, resources, and training) before asking the front-line employee to serve us with reports, paperwork, etc.

| 1 | 2 | 3 | 4 | 5 |

Drive Learning

1. We guarantee lifelong employability (rather than lifetime employment) through offering extensive training, cross-training, and work variety.

| 1 | 2 | 3 | 4 | 5 |

2. Special attention is given to creating visible, activity-filled programs that help drive learning through all levels of the organization—up, down, and laterally.

| 1 | 2 | 3 | 4 | 5 |

3. We actively support a philosophy of lifelong learning for our employees that goes beyond focusing only on today's job needs.

| 1 | 2 | 3 | 4 | 5 |

Emancipate Action

1. We allow employees the freedom to fail and try again.

| 1 | 2 | 3 | 4 | 5 |

2. Constant attention is given to creating freedom from bureaucracy, unnecessary sign-offs, outdated procedures, and office politics.

| 1 | 2 | 3 | 4 | 5 |

3. All employees are encouraged to openly challenge the status quo to help find better, faster, more profitable ways to serve our customers.

| 1 | 2 | 3 | 4 | 5 |

Total Score _____

Summary score: The higher the score (on any of the five principles), the more you believe this principle is alive and well in your organization. The lower the score, the more your organization needs to adress this principle

SOURCE: Jim Harris, "The Partnership Facade: What's Your Love Quotient?" *Management Review* (April 1996), 45–48. Reprinted by permission.

■ Manager's Workshop

Defense Mechanism Exercise

1. **Preparation** Students form up to nine groups of 3–6 members. Instructor hands out a slip of paper with one of the defense mechanisms listed below to each group, which should not reveal its role to the other groups. Each group designs a role-play based on their assigned defense mechanism. If there are more than nine groups, more than one group can receive the same mechanism.
2. **Role Play** The role-plays are then presented to the entire class. Other groups guess which defense mechanism is represented.
3. **Class Discussion** Instructor will ask the class to address the following:

a. Did you recognize any behaviors that you have used? Provide examples.
b. Give examples of situations when these behaviors may have been used with you.

Behavioral Defense Mechanisms

Devaluation: Exaggerating negative attributes in self or others.
Distortion: Reshaping external reality to suit inner needs.
Idealization: Exaggerating positive qualities in self or others.
Intellectualization: Engaging in excessive abstract thought to avoid disturbing feelings.

Passive Aggressive: Expressing indirect and unassertive aggression toward others.

Projection: Attributing one's own feelings, impulses, or thoughts to others.

Rationalization: Devising reassuring or self-serving, but incorrect, explanations for one's behavior.

Reaction Formation: Substituting behaviors, thoughts, or feelings, which are opposed to one's true behaviors, thoughts, or feelings.

Repression: Inhibiting the ability to remember or be aware of disturbing thoughts, feelings, or experiences.

SOURCE: Adapted from an exercise by Dorothy A. Marcic (Vanderbilt University) and Susanne Fest (Vanderbilt University). Used with permission.

■ Management in Practice: Ethical Dilemma

The Voice of Authority

When Gehan Rasinghe was hired as an account assistant at Werner and Thompson, a business and financial management firm, he was relieved. He was overqualified for the job with his degree in accounting, but the combination of his accented English and his quiet manner had prevented him from securing any other position. Beatrice Werner, one of the managing partners of the firm, was impressed by his educational credentials and his courtly manner. She assured him he had advancement potential with the firm, but the account assistant position was the only one available. After months of rejections in his job hunt, Rasinghe accepted the position. He was committed to making his new job work at all costs.

Account Manager Cathy Putnam was Rasinghe's immediate superior. Putnam spoke with a heavy Boston accent, speaking at a lightning pace to match her enormous workload. She indicated to Rasinghe that he would need to get up to speed as quickly as possible to succeed in working with her. It was soon apparent that Putnam and Rasinghe were at odds. She resented having to repeat directions more than once to teach him his responsibilities. He also seemed resistant to making the many phone calls asking for copies of invoices, disputing charges on credit cards, and following up with clients' staff to get the information necessary to do his job. His accounting work was impeccable, but the public contact part of his job was in bad shape. Even his quiet answer of "No problem" to all her requests was starting to wear thin on Putnam. Before giving Rasinghe his three-month review, Putnam appealed to Beatrice Werner for help. Putnam was frustrated by their communication problems and didn't know what to do.

Werner had seen the problem coming. Although she had found Rasinghe's bank reconciliations and financial report preparations to be first-rate, she knew that phone work and client contact were a big part of any job in the firm. But as the daughter of German immigrants, Werner also knew that language and cultural barriers could be overcome with persistence and patience. Diversity was one of her ideals for her company, and it was not always easy to achieve. She felt sure that Rasinghe could become an asset to the firm in time. She worried that the time it would take was more than they could afford to give him.

What Do You Do?

1. Give Rasinghe his notice, with the understanding that a job that is primarily paperwork would be a better fit for him. Make the break now rather than later.
2. Place him with an account manager who has more time to help him develop his assertiveness and telephone skills and appreciates his knowledge of accounting.
3. Create a new position for him, where he could do the reports and reconciliations for several account managers, while their assistants concentrated on the public contact work. He would have little chance of future promotion, however.

■ Surf the Net

1. **Nonverbal Communication.** Read the section in the chapter on "Nonverbal Communication." Use one of the following sites to find information to add to the text's coverage of the topic. Be prepared to share two or three interesting facts in a classroom discussion on the topic.
   http://www.natcom.org/ctronline/nonverb.htm
   http://nonverbal.ucsc.edu
   http://euphrates.wpunj.edu/faculty/wagnerk/webagogy/hecht.htm

2. **Listening Skills.** The Cyber Listening Lab at *http://www.esl-lab.com/* is designed to be used for ESL (English as a Second Language) purposes. For this exercise, however, you will use the site to test your listening skills. Choose three different listening exercises to complete, record the title of each, listen to the audio clip (requires an audio player available to download at the site), take the listening quiz, and record your score for each. If you scored well on the quizzes (60 percent or better), list the keys from Exhibit 14.4 that you believe helped you listen effectively. If your score could have been better, identify the keys that you could have used to improve your score.

3. **Speaking Skills.** Use either of the following sites to access and print out an oral evaluation form:
   http://showcase.netins.net/web/bokat/rubricoral.htm
   http://www.phschool.com/professional_development/assessment/rub_oral_presentation.cfm

Use the form to evaluate an oral presentation as instructed by your professor. On the back side of the evaluation form, write a short paragraph describing the public-speaking prin-ciple you think contributes most to the success of an oral pres-entation and why you believe it is most important.

■ Case for Critical Analysis

Inter-City Manufacturing, Inc.

The president of Inter-City Manufacturing Inc., Rich Langston, wanted to facilitate upward communication. He believed an open-door policy was a good place to start. He announced that his own door was open to all employees and encouraged senior managers to do the same. He felt this would give him a way to get early warning signals that would not be filtered or redi-rected through the formal chain of command. Langston found that many employees who used the open-door policy had been with the company for years and were comfortable talking to the president. Sometimes messages came through about inadequate policies and procedures. Langston would raise these issues and explain any changes at the next senior managers' meeting.

The most difficult complaints to handle were those from people who were not getting along with their bosses. One employee, Leroy, complained bitterly that his manager had overcommitted the department and put everyone under too much pressure. Leroy argued that long hours and low morale were major problems. But he would not allow Rich Langston to bring the manager into the discussion nor to seek out other employees to confirm the complaint. Although Langston sus-pected that Leroy might be right, he could not let the matter sit and blurted out, "Have you considered leaving the company?" This made Leroy realize that a meeting with his immediate boss was unavoidable.

Before the three-party meeting, Langston contacted Leroy's manager and explained what was going on. He insisted that the manager come to the meeting willing to listen and without hos-tility toward Leroy. During the meeting, Leroy's manager lis-tened actively and displayed no ill will. He learned the problem from Leroy's perspective and realized he was over his head in his new job. After the meeting, the manager said he was relieved. He had been promoted into the job from a technical position just a few months earlier and had no management or planning experience. He welcomed Rich Langston's offer to help him do a better job of planning.

Questions

1. What techniques increased Rich Langston's communication effectiveness? Discuss.
2. Do you think that an open-door policy was the right way to improve upward communications? What other techniques would you suggest?
3. What problems do you think an open-door policy creates? Do you think many employees are reluctant to use it? Why?

SOURCE: Based on Everett T. Suters, "Hazards of an Open-Door Policy," *Inc.* (January 1987), 99–102.

Teamwork in Organizations

LEARNING OBJECTIVES

After studying this chapter, you should be able to

1 Identify the types of teams in organizations.

2 Discuss new applications of teams to facilitate employee involvement.

3 Identify roles within teams and the type of role you could play to help a team be effective.

4 Explain the general stages of team development.

5 Explain the concepts of team cohesiveness and team norms and their relationship to team performance.

6 Understand the causes of conflict within and among teams and how to reduce conflict.

7 Discuss the assets and liabilities of organizational teams.

"Poisonous" is the best word to describe the atmosphere in Millennium Teleservices IT department. CIO Lief Maiorini said, "No one looking at our department could tell we were ready to kill each other, but we were ready to kill each other." In the throes of a nervous breakdown, virtual-style, the 113-person technology department found its units warring with one another. Nine-tenths of the staff was ready to quit, revenues were flat, and productivity was at only 50 percent.

Founding partner Brian Pasch tried all sorts of methods to improve team functioning. He saw competent, professional people not getting along and tried saying, "Hey, you guys are adults. Go work it out." That was a dud. He encouraged the eight IT managers to attend various workshops, on topics such as communication. To enhance team spirit, he took them to New York Yankees baseball games and New Jersey Nets basketball games. Nothing worked.

The New Jersey company had been founded in the early 1990s by Dave Keezer and brothers Scott and Brian Pasch, and started having real problems in 1995 when Maiorini was hired by Scott Pasch to be vice president. Pasch had built up the IT department from scratch, but was ready to hand it over to someone else, so that he could focus on the company's overall growth.

Things got so bad that an IT manager came out of a meeting and said he felt like he'd been run over by a bus. Someone brought a toy bus to the next meeting, and "giving someone the bus" became slang for flaming a colleague. "For the first time in my career," says Maiorini, "I doubted my ability to have a positive effect on the situation."

Pasch and Maiorini knew if they didn't get the IT staff to work together, revenues would continue to suffer.[1]

If you were Pasch or Maiorini, how would you meet this challenge?

The problems facing Millennium Teleservices also confront many other companies. How can they learn to work together more effectively in an increasingly competitive environment? A quiet revolution has been taking place in organizations across the country and around the world as companies respond by using employee teams. From the assembly line to the executive office, from large corporations such as Ford Motor Company and 3M, to small businesses such as St. Louis plantscaping firm Growing Green, teams are becoming the basic building block of organizations. Recent data show that nearly half of *Fortune* 1000 companies make extensive use of teams, and 60 percent plan to increase their use of teams in the near future. A study of 109 Canadian organizations found that 42 percent reported widespread team-based activity, and only 13 percent reported little or no team activity. Teamwork has become the most frequent topic taught in company training programs.[2]

Teams are popping up in the most unexpected places. An electromechanical assembly plant found that both quality and productivity increased after it abandoned the traditional production line in favor of work teams.[3] At Mattel, a team of artists, toy designers, computer experts, and automobile designers slashed 13 months from the usual toy design process, creating Top Speed toy cars in only five months. Hecla Mining Company uses teams for company goal setting; a major telecommunications company uses teams of salespeople to deal with big customers with complex purchasing requirements; and Lassiter Middle School in Jefferson County, Kentucky, uses teams of teachers to prepare daily schedules and handle student discipline problems. Multinational corporations are now using international teams composed of managers from different countries.[4]

As we will see in this chapter, teams have emerged as a powerful management tool, because they involve and empower employees. Teams can cut across organizations in unusual ways. Hence workers are more satisfied, and higher productivity and product quality typically result. Moreover, managers discover a more flexible organization in which workers are not stuck in narrow jobs.

This chapter focuses on teams and their new applications within organizations. We will define various types of teams, explore their stages of development, and examine such characteristics as size, cohesiveness, and norms. We will discuss how individuals can make contributions to teams and review the benefits and costs associated with teamwork. Teams are an important aspect of organizational life, and the ability to manage them is an important component of manager and organization success.

Teams at Work

In this section, we will first define teams and then discuss a model of team effectiveness that summarizes the important concepts.

What Is a Team?

team

A unit of two or more people who interact and coordinate their work to accomplish a specific goal.

A **team** is a unit of two or more people who interact and coordinate their work to accomplish a specific goal.[5] This definition has three components. First, two or more people are required. Teams can be quite large, although most have fewer than 15 people. Second, people in a team have regular interaction. People who do not interact, such as when standing in line at a lunch counter or riding in an elevator, do not compose a team. Third, people in a team share a perfor-

Group	Team
• Has a designated strong leader	• Shares or rotates leadership roles
• Individual accountability	• Individual and mutual accountability (accountable to each other)
• Identical purpose for group and organization	• Specific team vision or purpose
• Individual work products	• Collective work products
• Runs efficient meetings	• Meetings encourage open-ended discussion and problem solving
• Effectiveness measured indirectly by influence on business (such as financial performance)	• Effectiveness measured directly by assessing collective work
• Discusses, decides, delegates work to individuals	• Discusses, decides, shares work

EXHIBIT 15.1

Differences between Groups and Teams

SOURCE: Adapted from Jon R. Katzenbach and Douglas K. Smith, "The Discipline of Teams," *Harvard Business Review* (March–April 1995), 111–120.

mance goal, whether it be to design a new handheld computer, build a car, or write a textbook. Students often are assigned to teams to do classwork assignments, in which case the purpose is to perform the assignment and receive an acceptable grade.

Although a team is a group of people, the two terms are not interchangeable. An employer, a teacher, or a coach can put together a *group* of people and never build a *team*. The team concept implies a sense of shared mission and collective responsibility. Exhibit 15.1 lists the primary differences between groups and teams. Pat Summitt, legendary coach of the University of Tennessee women's basketball team, is the second all-time winningest coach (male or female) of NCAA basketball. She has a talent for building solid teams rather than relying on top stars such as Chamique Holdsclaw. "You have to surrender the 'me' attitude for the good of the team," Summitt tells every new player. That philosophy is drummed into players from the recruiting process on, and veteran players usually push the team philosophy to new recruits just as hard as Summitt does.[6] The sports world provides many examples of successful teamwork. One manager learned valuable lessons about team-building by participating in the ten-month BT Global Challenge around-the-world race, as described in the Focus on Collaboration box.

Model of Work Team Effectiveness

Some of the factors associated with team effectiveness are illustrated in Exhibit 15.2. Work team effectiveness is based on two outcomes—productive

EXHIBIT 15.2

Work Team Effectiveness Model

FOCUS ON COLLABORATION

A High-Tech Executive Learns about Teamwork

Much of what Doug Webb knows about teamwork he learned during his ten months as a crew member on the yacht *Logica*, participating in the BT Global Challenge, an around-the-world race for amateurs, many of whom have never sailed before. Competitors put to sea in boats that are identical in every way, and crews are selected by race organizers to be as equal as possible. What makes the difference is the ability to quickly turn a group of diverse individuals into a high-performance team.

One key, Webb discovered, is to make sure everyone feels equal and to help each individual contribute to his or her full potential. In business, the tendency is often to identify the least dependable or weakest members of a team and replace them, but during the BT Global Challenge, that was not possible. Therefore, it was important to identify and understand every person's motivations, interests, and capabilities and use these to benefit the common good. With effective coaching, individuals who at first seemed less competent became key team members, with the leader enabling them to fill roles where they could make a maximum contribution and avoiding areas where they were likely to fail. Success breeds confidence, and as people grew in their roles, their contributions expanded. Another important aspect of building a team is communication. The *Logica* crew met with one another long before the race to get to know one another and set ground rules for how they would communicate, learning to accept both positive and negative feedback. The emphasis was on the ability to have open and frank conversations without crew members feeling hurt or insecure about their performance.

During the race itself, everyone engaged in evaluating and learning from mistakes, as well as celebrating each accomplishment. Conflicts were discussed openly instead of being allowed to fester and grow. The *Logica* team finished fourth out of a group of 12 racing teams. But the most important "win" for Webb was that as he returned to his job as CFO of Logica, a leading information technology company with more than 11,000 employees in 28 countries, he took with him the lessons of teamwork he learned at sea.

SOURCE: Doug Webb, "Rhyme of the Ancient Manager: A High-Tech Exec Takes a New Tack," *Forbes* (September 10, 2001), 76–79.

output and personal satisfaction.[7] *Satisfaction* pertains to the team's ability to meet the personal needs of its members and hence maintain their membership and commitment. *Productive output* pertains to the quality and quantity of task outputs as defined by team goals.

The factors that influence team effectiveness begin with the organizational context.[8] The organizational context in which the group operates is described in other chapters and includes such factors as structure, strategy, environment, culture, and reward systems. Within that context, managers define teams. Important team characteristics are the type of team, the team structure, and team composition. Factors such as the diversity of the team in terms of gender and race, as well as knowledge, skills, and attitudes, can have a tremendous impact on team processes and effectiveness.[9] Managers must decide when to create permanent teams within the formal structure and when to use a temporary task team. Team size and roles also are important. Managers must also consider whether a team is the best way to do a task. If costs outweigh benefits, managers may wish to assign an individual employee to the task.

These team characteristics influence processes internal to the team, which in turn affect output and satisfaction. Leaders must understand and manage stages of development, cohesiveness, norms, and conflict in order to establish an effective team. These processes are influenced by team and organizational characteristics and by the ability of members and leaders to direct these processes in a positive manner.

The model of team performance in Exhibit 15.2 is the basis for this chapter. In the following sections, we will examine types of organizational teams, team structure, internal processes, and team benefits and costs.

Types of Teams

Many types of teams can exist within organizations. The easiest way to classify teams is in terms of those created as part of the organization's formal structure and those created to increase employee participation.

Formal Teams

Formal teams are created by the organization as part of the formal organization structure. Two common types of formal teams are vertical and horizontal, which typically represent vertical and horizontal structural relationships, as described in Chapter 7. These two types of teams are illustrated in Exhibit 15.3. A third type of formal team is the special-purpose team.

formal team
A team created by the organization as part of the formal organization structure.

Vertical Team. A **vertical team** is composed of a manager and his or her subordinates in the formal chain of command. Sometimes called a *functional team* or a *command team,* the vertical team may in some cases include three or four levels of hierarchy within a functional department. Typically, the vertical team includes a single department in an organization. The third-shift nursing team on the second floor of St. Luke's Hospital is a vertical team that includes nurses and a supervisor. A financial analysis department, a quality control department, an accounting department, and a human resource department are all command teams. Each is created by the organization to attain specific goals through members' joint activities and interactions.

vertical team
A formal team composed of a manager and his or her subordinates in the organization's formal chain of command.

Horizontal Team. A **horizontal team** is composed of employees from about the same hierarchical level but from different areas of expertise.[10] A horizontal team is drawn from several departments, is given a specific task, and may be disbanded after the task is completed. The two most common types of horizontal teams are task forces and committees.

As described in Chapter 7, a *task force* is a group of employees from different departments formed to deal with a specific activity and existing only until the task is completed. Sometimes called a *cross-functional team,* the task force

horizontal team
A formal team composed of employees from about the same hierarchical level but from different areas of expertise.

EXHIBIT *15.3*

Horizontal and Vertical Teams in an Organization

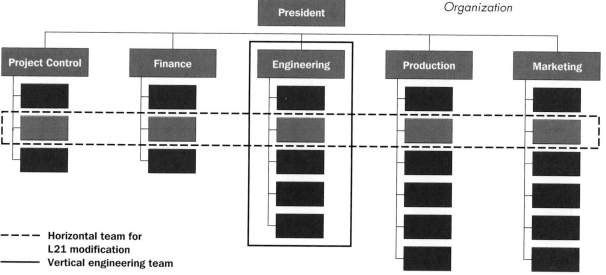

- - - - **Horizontal team for
L21 modification**
——— **Vertical engineering team**

might be used to create a new product in a manufacturing organization or a new history curriculum in a university. Several departments are involved, and many views have to be considered, so these tasks are best served with a horizontal team. For example, at GE Lighting Co., a cross-functional team with members from information technology, finance, and several other departments oversaw an ambitious systems-integration project that spanned operations in the United States and Canada.[11] Hallmark Cards uses cross-functional teams made up of artists, writers, lithographers, designers, and photographers to create new greeting cards for each major holiday.[12]

A **committee** generally is long-lived and may be a permanent part of the organization's structure. Membership on a committee usually is decided by a person's title or position rather than by personal expertise. A committee often needs official representation, compared with selection for a task force, which is based on personal qualifications for solving a problem. Committees typically are formed to deal with tasks that recur regularly. For example, a grievance committee handles employee grievances; an advisory committee makes recommendations in the areas of employee compensation and work practices; a worker-management committee may be concerned with work rules, job design changes, and suggestions for work improvement.[13]

As part of the horizontal structure of the organization, task forces and committees offer several advantages: (1) They allow organization members to exchange information; (2) they generate suggestions for coordinating the organizational units that are represented; (3) they develop new ideas and solutions for existing organizational problems; and (4) they assist in the development of new organizational practices and policies.

committee

A long-lasting, sometimes permanent team in the organization structure created to deal with tasks that recur regularly.

Special-Purpose Team. Special-purpose teams, sometimes called *project teams,* are created outside the formal organization structure to undertake a project of special importance or creativity. Special-purpose teams focus on a specific purpose and expect to disband once the specific project is completed.[14] Examples include the team that developed the first IBM ThinkPad, the project team for the original Ford Taurus, and the team that created Chicken McNuggets for McDonald's. A special-purpose team still is part of the formal organization and has its own reporting structure, but members perceive themselves as a separate entity.[15] Special purpose teams bring former foes together to work on creating a better environment, as the Focus on Collaboration box shows.

special-purpose team

A team created outside the formal organization to undertake a project of special importance or creativity.

Self-Directed Teams

Employee involvement through teams is designed to increase the participation of low-level workers in decision making and the conduct of their jobs, with the goal of improving performance. Employee involvement started out simply with techniques such as information sharing with employees or asking employees for suggestions about improving the work. Gradually, companies moved toward greater autonomy for employees, which led first to problem-solving teams and then to self-directed teams.[16]

Problem-solving teams typically consist of 5 to 12 hourly employees from the same department who voluntarily meet to discuss ways of improving quality, efficiency, and the work environment. Recommendations are proposed to management for approval. Problem-solving teams usually are the first step in a

problem-solving team

Typically 5 to 12 hourly employees from the same department who meet to discuss ways of improving quality, efficiency, and the work environment.

FOCUS ON COLLABORATION

Sustainable Northwest and Others

A few years ago, third-generation lumberjack Mike Mc-Mahon considered environmentalists his enemy. After all, he was cutting down the forests they were trying to sustain. These days, you might find him creating more breathing room for the tall Douglas firs in the Wallowa County area, by using a shredding machine to reduce thick shrubbery to pulp. Economics and severe logger layoffs in recent years have brought about new cooperative ventures in the woods.

Thanks to the nonprofit organization Sustainable Northwest, McMahon and other loggers are now working on the same goals as the environmentalists. With help from federal grants, the organization tries to pump up local economies with ecofriendly projects, creating over 100 "green" jobs in the process.

The Arizonan Sonoran Institute leads cattle ranchers away from soil-eroding grazing practices and into hosting ecotours,

while San Francisco Sustainable Conservation (SC) helped struggling strawberry farmers find work in helping to control steep-slope soil runoff. "To make these projects work," says SC's executive director Ashley Boren, "it has to benefit both sides."

Wallowa County's "greening" is one of the more visible successes in the sustainability movement. Unlike some confrontational environmentalists, this compromise-minded faction tries to turn foes into allies by offering jobs and incentives. Unemployed loggers are lining up to help. Mike McMahon, a 43-year-old burly lumberjack, finds himself in a new world. "This is sure a lot different from what I used to do," he says. "But at least it keeps me in the woods."

SOURCE: Jim Carlton, "A Quiet Truce in the Green Wars," *The Wall Street Journal* (November 15, 2001), B1–B4.

company's move toward greater employee participation. The most widely known application is quality circles, initiated by Japanese companies, in which employees focus on ways to improve quality in the production process. USX adopted this approach in several of its steel mills, recognizing that quality takes a team effort. Under the title All Product Excellence program (APEX), USX set up APEX teams of up to 12 employees who meet several times a month to solve quality problems.[17]

© Marc Houser

Highsmith Inc., a Fort Atkinson, Wisconsin, company, is the country's leading mail-order supplier of equipment such as book displays, audio-video tools, and educational software for schools and libraries. The company's employees work in a flat organization in which self-directed teams, along with a continuous-learning program and flextime, are manifest. According to CEO Duncan Highsmith, "We have a limited labor market, so I wanted to make the most of the people we had by helping them become decision makers, by providing them with information and the context to make good decisions." In the photo is a team of librarians (left to right, Oma Dixon, Lisa Guedea Carreño, and Genevieve Mecherly) who facilitate the culture of autonomy at Highsmith. "We're here to help people integrate information into their jobs as seamlessly as possible," says Carreño. "That way, they can keep doing their jobs."

As a company matures, problem-solving teams can gradually evolve into self-directed teams, which represent a fundamental change in how employee work is organized. Self-directed teams enable employees to feel challenged, find their work meaningful, and develop a strong sense of identity with the company.[18] **Self-directed teams** typically consist of 5 to 20 multiskilled workers who rotate jobs to produce an entire product or service or at least one complete aspect or portion of a product or service (e.g., engine assembly, insurance claim processing). The central idea is that the teams themselves, rather than managers or supervisors, take responsibility for their work, make decisions, monitor their own performance, and alter their work behavior as needed to solve problems, meet goals, and adapt to changing conditions.[19] Self-directed teams are permanent teams that typically include the following elements:

self-directed team

A team consisting of 5 to 20 multiskilled workers who rotate jobs to produce an entire product or service, often supervised by an elected member.

- The team includes employees with several skills and functions, and the combined skills are sufficient to perform a major organizational task. A team may include members from the foundry, machining, grinding, fabrication, and sales departments, with each member cross-trained to perform one another's jobs. The team eliminates barriers among departments, enabling excellent coordination to produce a product or service.

- The team is given access to resources such as information, equipment, machinery, and supplies needed to perform the complete task.

- The team is empowered with decision-making authority, which means that members have the freedom to select new members, solve problems, spend money, monitor results, and plan for the future.[20]

In a self-directed team, team members take over managerial duties such as scheduling or ordering materials. They work with minimum supervision, perhaps electing one of their own as supervisor, who may change each year. The most effective self-directed teams are those that are fully empowered, as described in the discussion of empowerment in Chapter 13. In addition to having increased responsibility and discretion, empowered teams are those that have a strong belief in their team's capabilities, find value and meaning in their work, and recognize the impact the team's work has on customers, other stakeholders, and organizational success.[21] Managers create the conditions that determine whether self-directed teams are empowered by giving teams true power and freedom, complete information, knowledge and skills, and appropriate rewards. Whole Foods Markets provides an excellent example of the use of self-directed teams.

Whole Foods Market

http://www.wholefoods.com

In 1991, Whole Foods Market had barely a dozen stores in three states. Today, it has the clout of a nationwide chain, with 126 stores throughout the United States and net profits that are typically double the national average.

The Whole Foods culture is based on decentralized teamwork. Each store is an autonomous profit center made up of an average of 10 self-directed teams—grocery, produce, and so forth. Teams—and only teams—have the power to approve new hires for full-time jobs. Store leaders screen candidates and recommend them for a job on a specific team, but it takes a two-thirds vote of the team to approve the hire. Team members deal directly with products, customers, and vendors, and everyone works together to identify and accomplish team goals.

> The company believes the first prerequisite of teamwork is trust. That trust starts with the hiring vote. In addition, Whole Foods supports teamwork with wide-open information on financial and operations systems. Sensitive figures on store sales, team sales, profit margins, and even yearly salaries and bonuses are available to any employee. According to CEO John Mackey, open information keeps everyone "aligned to the vision of shared fate. . . . If you're trying to create a high-trust organization, an organization where people are all-for-one and one-for-all, you can't have secrets."[22]

Self-directed teams such as those at Whole Foods Market can be highly effective. Another organization that succeeds with teamwork is Consolidated Diesel's engine factory in Whitakers, North Carolina. In its 20 or so years of operation as a team-based organization, the plant has had higher revenues, lower turnover, and significantly lower injury rates than the industry average. In addition, while most plants average 1 supervisor for every 25 workers, Consolidated Diesel has 1 for every 100 employees because the plant workers themselves handle many supervisory duties. The difference yields a savings of about $1 million a year.[23]

Teams in the New Workplace

Some exciting new approaches to teamwork have resulted from advances in information technology, shifting employee expectations, and the globalization of business. Two types of teams that are increasingly being used are virtual teams and global teams.

Virtual Teams. A **virtual team** is made up of geographically or organizationally dispersed members who are linked primarily through advanced information and telecommunications technologies.[24] Although some virtual teams may be made up only of organizational members, virtual teams often include contingent workers, members of partner organizations, customers, suppliers, consultants, or other outsiders. Team members use e-mail, voice mail, videoconferencing, Internet and intranet technologies, and various types of collaboration software to perform their work, although they may also sometimes meet face to face.

Virtual teams are highly flexible and dynamic. Some are temporary cross-functional teams pulled together to work on specific projects or problems, while others are long-term or permanent self-directed teams. Team leadership is typically shared or altered, depending on the area of expertise needed at each stage of the project.[25] In addition, team membership in virtual teams may change fairly quickly, depending on the tasks to be performed. One of the primary advantages of virtual teams is the ability to rapidly assemble the most appropriate group of people to complete a complex project, solve a particular problem, or exploit a specific strategic opportunity. The success of virtual teams depends on several factors, including selecting the right members, building trust, sharing information, and effectively using technology. VeriFone, described below, uses virtual teams in every aspect of its business.

> VeriFone, an equipment supplier for credit card verification and automated payments, started out as a virtual company over 15 years ago and today uses virtual teams in every aspect of its business. Teams of facility managers work

virtual team

A team that uses advanced information and telecommunications technologies so that geographically distant members can collaborate on projects and reach common goals.

VeriFone

http://www.verifone.com

together to determine how to reduce toxins in their offices. Marketing and development groups brainstorm new products. Sales reps pool information and customer testimonials.

VeriFone's concept of virtual teams is highly flexible. Some teams may include only VeriFone employees while others include outsiders, such as the employees of a customer or partner. Some are permanent, such as operational teams that run their companies virtually, while others are temporary. Any employee can organize a temporary virtual team to work on a specific problem. For example, one sales rep sent out an SOS when he saw a major sales prospect in Greece falling apart. Overnight, a team made up of sales, marketing, and technical-support staff from around the world came together online to provide data and testimonials that eventually helped the Greek representative make the sale.

Despite all this flexibility, VeriFone has some pretty strict "rules" to ensure that teams are not formed haphazardly. Employees complete a 40-hour training program in which they learn how to create a successful virtual team. In addition, leaders of virtual teams follow written procedures put together by the company's senior managers. VeriFone offers the following guidelines for successful virtual teams:

1. *Define the purpose.* A VeriFone team always starts by putting its purpose in writing. This keeps everyone on track and prevents misunderstandings.

2. *Recruit team members.* Most virtual teams should be between three and seven members. Also, the team should include people who represent a diversity of views and experiences. Selecting members in different time zones means productive work can be going on around the clock.

3. *Determine the duration of the team.* Decide whether the purpose and goals call for a short-term task force or problem-solving team or for a long-term operational team.

4. *Select the communications technology.* All VeriFone staffers are not only well-trained in how to use communications tools but also in when to use them. General guidelines are that for keeping in contact remotely, teams use beepers, cell phones, and voice mail; for disseminating information, fax, e-mail, and application sharing over the network. For brainstorming, discussion, and decision making, teams use e-mail, instant messaging, conference calls, and videoconferencing. Selecting the right tool is critical to the success of the virtual team.

VeriFone employees also are trained to understand the psychological pitfalls of communicating virtually. Some subtleties of meaning are always lost, and misunderstandings are more common than when teams work face to face. E-mail in particular can lead to misunderstandings, so team members communicate by phone or videoconference on sensitive or complicated issues.[26]

global team

A work team made up of members of different nationalities whose activities span multiple countries; may operate as a virtual team or meet face to face.

Global Teams. Virtual teams are also sometimes global teams. **Global teams** are cross-border work teams made up of members of different nationalities whose activities span multiple countries.[27] Generally, global teams fall into two categories: intercultural teams, whose members come from different countries or cultures and meet face to face, and virtual global teams, whose members remain in separate locations around the world and conduct their work electronically.[28] For example, lengthy phone calls, frequent e-mail, and weekly videoconferences provided the lifeline between global team members creating

Texas Instruments C82 digital signal processor.[29] The research department at BT Labs has 660 researchers spread across the United Kingdom and several other countries. The researchers work in global virtual teams that investigate virtual reality, artificial intelligence, and other advanced information technologies.[30]

Global teams can present enormous challenges for team leaders, who have to bridge gaps of time, distance, and culture. In some cases, members speak different languages, use different technologies, and have different beliefs about authority, time orientation, decision making, and so forth. Culture differences can significantly affect team-working relationships. Organizations using global teams invest the time and resources to adequately educate employees. They have to make sure all team members appreciate and understand cultural differences, are focused on goals, and understand their responsibilities to the team. For a global team to be effective, all team members must be willing to deviate somewhat from their own values and norms and establish new norms for the team.[31] As with virtual teams, carefully selecting team members, building trust, and sharing information are critical to success.

Team Characteristics

The next issue of concern to managers is designing the team for greatest effectiveness. One factor is team characteristics, which can affect team dynamics and performance. Characteristics of particular concern are team size and member roles.

Size

The ideal size of work teams often is thought to be 7, although variations of from 5 to 12 typically are associated with good team performance. These teams are large enough to take advantage of diverse skills, enable members to express good and bad feelings, and aggressively solve problems. They also are small enough to permit members to feel an intimate part of the group.

In general, as a team increases in size, it becomes harder for each member to interact with and influence the others. Ray Oglethorpe, president of AOL Technologies, which makes extensive use of teams, believes keeping teams small is the key to success. "If you have more than 15 or 20 people, you're dead," he says. "The connections between team members are too hard to make."[32] A summary of research on group size suggests the following:[33]

1. Small teams (2 to 4 members) show more agreement, ask more questions, and exchange more opinions. Members want to get along with one another. Small teams report more satisfaction and enter into more personal discussions. They tend to be informal and make few demands on team leaders.

2. Large teams (12 or more) tend to have more disagreements and differences of opinion. Subgroups often form, and conflicts among them occur, ranging from protection of "turf" to trivial matters such as "what kind of coffee is brewing in the pot." Demands on leaders are greater because there is more centralized decision making and less member participation. Large teams also tend to be less friendly. Turnover and absenteeism are higher in a large team, especially for blue-collar workers. Because less satisfaction is associated with specialized tasks and poor communication, team members have fewer opportunities to participate and feel an intimate part of the group.

As a general rule, large teams make need satisfaction for individuals more difficult; thus, there is less reason for people to remain committed to their goals. Teams of from 5 to 12 seem to work best. If a team grows larger than 20, managers should divide it into subgroups, each with its own members and goals.

Member Roles

For a team to be successful over the long run, it must be structured so as to both maintain its members' social well-being and accomplish its task. In successful teams, the requirements for task performance and social satisfaction are met by the emergence of two types of roles: task specialist and socioemotional.[34]

task specialist role

A role in which the individual devotes personal time and energy to helping the team accomplish its task.

People who play the **task specialist role** spend time and energy helping the team reach its goal. They often display the following behaviors:

- *Initiate ideas.* Propose new solutions to team problems.
- *Give opinions.* Offer opinions on task solutions; give candid feedback on others' suggestions.
- *Seek information.* Ask for task-relevant facts.
- *Summarize.* Relate various ideas to the problem at hand; pull ideas together into a summary perspective.
- *Energize.* Stimulate the team into action when interest drops.[35]

socioemotional role

A role in which the individual provides support for team members' emotional needs and social unity.

People who adopt a **socioemotional role** support team members' emotional needs and help strengthen the social entity. They display the following behaviors:

- *Encourage.* Are warm and receptive to others' ideas; praise and encourage others to draw forth their contributions.
- *Harmonize.* Reconcile group conflicts; help disagreeing parties reach agreement.
- *Reduce tension.* Tell jokes or in other ways draw off emotions when group atmosphere is tense.
- *Follow.* Go along with the team; agree to other team members' ideas.
- *Compromise.* Will shift own opinions to maintain team harmony.[36]

Exhibit 15.4 illustrates task specialist and socioemotional roles in teams. When most individuals in a team play a social role, the team is socially oriented. Members do not criticize or disagree with one another and do not forcefully offer opinions or try to accomplish team tasks, because their primary interest is to keep the team happy. Teams with mostly socioemotional roles can be very satisfying, but they also can be unproductive. At the other extreme, a team made up primarily of task specialists will tend to have a singular concern for task accomplishment. This team will be effective for a short period of time but will not be satisfying for members over the long run. Task specialists convey little emotional concern for one another, are unsupportive, and ignore team members' social and emotional needs. The task-oriented team can be humorless and unsatisfying.

dual role

A role in which the individual both contributes to the team's task and supports members' emotional needs.

As Exhibit 15.4 illustrates, some team members may play a dual role. People with **dual roles** both contribute to the task and meet members' emotional

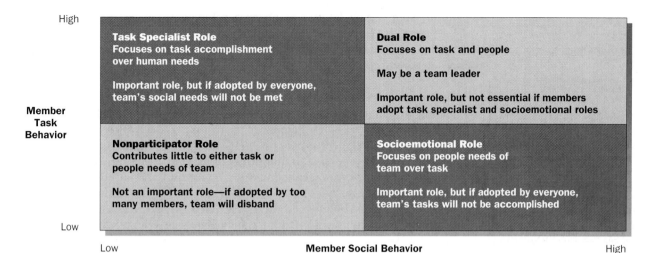

E X H I B I T *15.4*

Team Member Roles

nonparticipator role

A role in which the individual contributes little to either the task or members' socioemotional needs.

needs. Such people often become team leaders. A study of new-product-development teams in high-technology firms found that the most effective teams were headed by leaders who balanced the technical needs of the project with human interaction issues, thus meeting both task and socioemotional needs.[37] Exhibit 15.4 also shows the final type of role, called the **nonparticipator role**, in which people contribute little to either the task or the social needs of team members. They typically are held in low esteem by the team.

The important thing for managers to remember is that effective teams must have people in both task specialist and socioemotional roles. Humor and social concern are as important to team effectiveness as are facts and problem solving. Managers also should remember that some people perform better in one type of role; some are inclined toward social concerns and others toward task concerns. A well-balanced team will do best over the long term because it will be personally satisfying for team members and permit the accomplishment of team tasks.

Team Processes

Now we turn our attention to internal team processes. Team processes pertain to those dynamics that change over time and can be influenced by team leaders. In this section, we will discuss the team processes of stages of development, cohesiveness, and norms. The fourth type of team process, conflict, will be covered in the next section.

Stages of Team Development

After a team has been created, there are distinct stages through which it develops.[38] New teams are different from mature teams. Recall a time when you were a member of a new team, such as a fraternity or sorority pledge class, a committee, or a small team formed to do a class assignment. Over time the team changed. In the beginning, team members had to get to know one another, establish roles and norms, divide the labor, and clarify the team's task. In this way, members became parts of a smoothly operating team. The challenge for leaders is to understand the stage of the team's development and take action that will help the group improve its functioning.

EXHIBIT *15.5*

Five Stages of Team Development

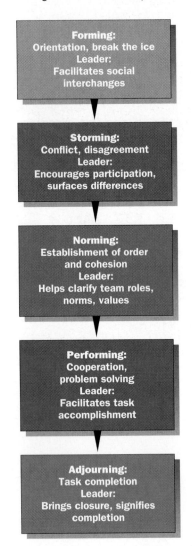

EXHIBIT *15.5*

Five Stages of Team Development

forming

The stage of team development characterized by orientation and acquaintance.

storming

The stage of team development in which individual personalities and roles, and resulting conflicts, emerge.

norming

The stage of team development in which conflicts developed during the storming stage are resolved and team harmony and unity emerge.

Research findings suggest that team development is not random but evolves over definitive stages. One useful model for describing these stages is shown in Exhibit 15.5. Each stage confronts team leaders and members with unique problems and challenges.[39]

Forming. The **forming** stage of development is a period of orientation and getting acquainted. Members break the ice and test one another for friendship possibilities and task orientation. Team members find which behaviors are acceptable to others. Uncertainty is high during this stage, and members usually accept whatever power or authority is offered by either formal or informal leaders. Members are dependent on the team until they find out what the ground rules are and what is expected of them. During this initial stage, members are concerned about such things as "What is expected of me?" "What is acceptable?" "Will I fit in?" During the forming stage, the team leader should provide time for members to get acquainted with one another and encourage them to engage in informal social discussions.

Storming. During the **storming** stage, individual personalities emerge. People become more assertive in clarifying their roles and what is expected of them. This stage is marked by conflict and disagreement. People may disagree over their perceptions of the team's mission. Members may jockey for positions, and coalitions or subgroups based on common interests may form. One subgroup may disagree with another over the total team's goals or how to achieve them. The team is not yet cohesive and may be characterized by a general lack of unity. Unless teams can successfully move beyond this stage, they may get bogged down and never achieve high performance. During the storming stage, the team leader should encourage participation by each team member. Members should propose ideas, disagree with one another, and work through the uncertainties and conflicting perceptions about team tasks and goals.

Norming. During the **norming** stage, conflict is resolved, and team harmony and unity emerge. Consensus develops on who has the power, who is the leader, and members' roles. Members come to accept and understand one another. Differences are resolved, and members develop a sense of team cohesion. This stage typically is of short duration. During the norming stage, the team leader should emphasize oneness within the team and help clarify team norms and values.

Performing. During the **performing stage**, the major emphasis is on problem solving and accomplishing the assigned task. Members are committed to the team's mission. They are coordinated with one another and handle disagreements in a mature way. They confront and resolve problems in the interest of task accomplishment. They interact frequently and direct discussion and influence toward achieving team goals. During this stage, the leader should concentrate on managing high task performance. Both socioemotional and task specialists should contribute.

Adjourning. The **adjourning** stage occurs in committees, task forces, and teams that have a limited task to perform and are disbanded afterward. During this stage, the emphasis is on wrapping up and gearing down. Task performance is no longer a top priority. Members may feel heightened emotionality,

© Pierre St. Jacques—Klixpix

They may be family, but the Ice.com management team, made up of the Gniwisches—brothers Shmuel, Mayer, and Pinny—along with father Isaac and brother-in-law Moshe Krasnanski, still had to go through the stages of team development to become effective. After creating Buyjewel.com in 1999, the team experienced a number of problems and conflicts in the forming and storming stages of development—not the least of which was Isaac's insistence on keeping a careful eye on the bottom line rather than going for rapid growth. Today, though, the team has reached the performing stage, running a successful business (renamed Ice.com) that sells affordable jewelry on the Internet, with $10 million in sales in one recent year.

strong cohesiveness, and depression or even regret over the team's disbandment. They may feel happy about mission accomplishment and sad about the loss of friendship and associations. At this point, the leader may wish to signify the team's disbanding with a ritual or ceremony, perhaps giving out plaques and awards to signify closure and completeness.

The five stages of team development typically occur in sequence. In teams that are under time pressure or that will exist for only a short period of time, the stages may occur quite rapidly. The stages may also be accelerated for virtual teams. For example, bringing people together for a couple of days of team building can help virtual teams move rapidly through the forming and storming stages. McDevitt Street Bovis, one of the country's largest construction management firms, uses an understanding of the stages of team development to put teams on a solid foundation.

performing
The stage of team development in which members focus on problem solving and accomplishing the team's assigned task.

adjourning
The stage of team development in which members prepare for the team's disbandment.

The team-building process at McDevitt Street Bovis is designed to take teams to the performing stage as quickly as possible by giving everyone an opportunity to get to know one another, explore the ground rules, and clarify roles, responsibilities, and expectations. The company credits this process for quickly and effectively unifying teams, circumventing damaging and time-consuming conflicts, and preventing lawsuits related to major construction projects.

Rather than the typical construction project characterized by conflicts, frantic scheduling, and poor communications, Bovis wants its collection of contractors, designers, suppliers, and other partners to function like a true team—putting the success of the project ahead of their own individual interests. The team is first divided into separate groups that may have competing objectives—such as the clients in one group, suppliers in another, engineers and architects in a third, and so forth—and asked to come up with a list of their goals for the project. Although interests sometimes vary widely in purely accounting terms, there are almost always common themes. By talking about conflicting goals and interests,

McDevitt Street Bovis

http://www.bovis.com

as well as what all the groups share, facilitators help the team gradually come together around a common purpose and begin to develop shared values that will guide the project. After jointly writing a mission statement for the team, each party says what it expects from the others, so that roles and responsibilities can be clarified. The intensive team-building session helps take members quickly through the forming and storming stages of development. "We prevent conflicts from happening," says facilitator Monica Bennett. Leaders at McDevitt Street Bovis believe building better teams builds better buildings.[40]

Team Cohesiveness

team cohesiveness

The extent to which team members are attracted to the team and motivated to remain in it.

Another important aspect of the team process is cohesiveness. **Team cohesiveness** is defined as the extent to which members are attracted to the team and motivated to remain in it.[41] Members of highly cohesive teams are committed to team activities, attend meetings, and are happy when the team succeeds. Members of less cohesive teams are less concerned about the team's welfare. High cohesiveness is normally considered an attractive feature of teams.

Determinants of Team Cohesiveness. Characteristics of team structure and context influence cohesiveness. First is *team interaction*. The greater the contact among team members and the more time spent together, the more cohesive the team. Through frequent interactions, members get to know one another and become more devoted to the team.[42] Second is the concept of *shared goals*. If team members agree on goals, they will be more cohesive. Agreeing on purpose and direction binds the team together. Third is *personal attraction to the team,* meaning that members have similar attitudes and values and enjoy being together. Mattel Inc. understands the importance of this cohesion in order to bring more creativity to the workplace, as described in the Focus on Collaboration box.

Two factors in the team's context also influence group cohesiveness. The first is the presence of competition. When a team is in moderate competition with other teams, its cohesiveness increases as it strives to win. Finally, team success and the favorable evaluation of the team by outsiders add to cohesiveness. When a team succeeds in its task and others in the organization recognize the success, members feel good, and their commitment to the team will be high.

Consequences of Team Cohesiveness. The outcome of team cohesiveness can fall into two categories—morale and productivity. As a general rule, morale is higher in cohesive teams because of increased communication among members, a friendly team climate, maintenance of membership because of commitment to the team, loyalty, and member participation in team decisions and activities. High cohesiveness has almost uniformly good effects on the satisfaction and morale of team members.[43]

With respect to team performance, research findings are mixed, but cohesiveness may have several effects.[44] First, in a cohesive team, members' productivity tends to be more uniform. Productivity differences among members are small because the team exerts pressure toward conformity. Noncohesive teams do not have this control over member behavior and therefore tend to have wider variation in member productivity.

With respect to the productivity of the team as a whole, research findings suggest that cohesive teams have the potential to be productive, but the degree

FOCUS ON COLLABORATION

Project Platypus

Throwing stuffed bunnies at team members and being part of a group cry might not seem like the average workplace behavior, but it is part of Mattel Inc.'s Project Platypus, designed to foster creativity through wild and crazy teamwork. Toy companies have been criticized for relying too much on movie or TV licenses in developing new toys. Mattel is out to change that.

The first product to hit the market from Platypus is Ello, a girls' construction activity. While coming up with the idea, the team observed five- to ten-year-old girls in play. Girls are interested in construction toys, says Mattel psychologist Michael Shore, but most building toys have boy themes, such as cars or trucks.

Between 20 and 30 employees from sales, engineering, design, and copyrighting participate in Project Platypus, in order to have time and permission to think up off-the-wall ideas. "We are such a machine in terms of what we deliver on an annual basis that it doesn't always allow time to think," says girls' division president Adrienne Fontanella.

Project Platypus was named after the animal because the platypus has various distinguishing characteristics, and the project is about "being able to think in an imaginative way and understand the sociology and psychology behind chil-

dren's patterns," says Fontanella. Platypus's guru Ivy Ross says that innovation requires employees to "cleanse their palates," leaving behind workplace rigidity. To do that, participants interact with an improvisationist, a Jungian psychologist, an expert in brain waves, and an architect. At the beginning, weeks are spent allowing group bonding time to achieve a collaborative sense of accomplishment. After the preliminaries, teams are formed that begin hatching and developing ideas. Group exercises include trying to prevent an egg from breaking when dropped 14 feet. The winner in that contest developed a bungee cord for eggs. The improvisationist had people throw stuffed bunnies at colleagues in order to release inhibitions. The group's brain waves were measured after a collective humming session, and later incorporated into a soundtrack.

During the entire process, the team continues to work with an idea and each person critiques and builds on other people's ideas, rather than following the more typical practice of passing the idea on to another design group.

"The whole sharing aspect brings you so much closer to the group," says Barbie designer Deborah Ava. Her colleague Kristie Scott piped in with, "We have the bond of a family."

SOURCE: Lisa Bannon, "Think Tank in Toyland," *The Wall Street Journal* (June 6, 2002), B1, B3.

of productivity depends on the relationship between management and the working team. Thus, team cohesiveness does not necessarily lead to higher team productivity. One study surveyed more than 200 work teams and correlated job performance with their cohesiveness.[45] Highly cohesive teams were more productive when team members felt management support and less productive when they sensed management hostility and negativism. Management hostility led to team norms and goals of low performance, and the highly cohesive teams performed poorly, in accordance with their norms and goals.

The relationship between performance outcomes and cohesiveness is illustrated in Exhibit 15.6. The highest productivity occurs when the team is cohesive and also has a high performance norm, which is a result of its positive relationship with management. Moderate productivity occurs when cohesiveness is low, because team members are less committed to performance norms. The lowest productivity occurs when cohesiveness is high and the team's performance norm is low. Thus, cohesive teams are able to attain their goals and enforce their norms, which can lead to either very high or very low productivity.

A good example of team cohesiveness combined with high performance norms comes from Nokia, the Finnish telecommunications giant. At Nokia, every job or project of any importance is assigned to a team rather than an individual manager or employee. Even though teams are often virtual and made up of people from all over the world, cohesiveness is typically high because Nokia's team-oriented culture and extensive training programs create a "meeting of minds among people," as CEO Jorma Ollila puts it. Nokia hires people

High	**Moderate Productivity** Weak norms in alignment with organization goals	**High Productivity** Strong norms in alignment with organization goals
Team Performance Norms	**Low/Moderate Productivity** Weak norms in opposition to organization goals	**Low Productivity** Strong norms in opposition to organization goals
Low		

Low   **Team Cohesiveness**   High

EXHIBIT 15.6

Relationship among Team Cohesiveness, Performance Norms, and Productivity

norm

A standard of conduct that is shared by team members and guides their behavior.

who demonstrate a commitment to working collaboratively, and the company's incentive programs reward teamwork. The combination of team cohesiveness and top management support has made the workforce highly productive and Nokia one of the most innovative companies around.[46]

Team Norms

A team **norm** is a standard of conduct that is shared by team members and guides their behavior.[47] Norms are informal. They are not written down, as are rules and procedures. Norms are valuable because they define boundaries of acceptable behavior. They make life easier for team members by providing a frame of reference for what is right and wrong. Norms identify key values, clarify role expectations, and facilitate team survival. For example, union members may develop a norm of not cooperating with management because they do not trust management's motives. In this way, norms protect the group and express key values.

Norms begin to develop in the first interactions among members of a new team.[48] Norms that apply to both day-to-day behavior and employee output and performance gradually evolve. Norms thus tell members what is acceptable and direct members' actions toward acceptable productivity or performance. Four common ways in which norms develop for controlling and directing behavior are illustrated in Exhibit 15.7.[49] Sometimes norms can develop that are not productive and need an intervention to bring change, as the Digital, Inc. box shows.

EXHIBIT 15.7

Four Ways Team Norms Develop

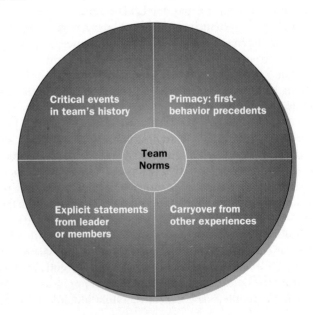

DIGITAL, INC.

Eze Castle Software

Sean McLaughlin realized it was time to take action when an employee approved paying $100 a month for a contractor to water Eze Castle Software's office plants. CEO McLaughlin's company had lost its entrepreneurial edge. When starting out in the securities trading software business six years ago, everyone took responsibility. If a package was sent Fedex, they knew what that cost the firm. Now, though, employees were acting with big-company sloppiness. One big bill was for overloaded access on the company's T1 line, because workers were downloading MP3 files. The entrepreneur was frustrated because employees didn't take responsibility for costs that negatively impacted the bottom line.

When both administrative assistants quit, McLaughlin saw a chance for change. It was a shock to lose the assistants' services as mail sorters and supply-room stockers. The refrigerator had no milk and the storeroom had no pens. While visiting his daughter's kindergarten class, McLaughlin noticed that the teacher divided classroom chores among children with a chore wheel. This method seemed just the thing to institute corporate responsibility.

COO Tom Gavin posts the eight tasks and the names of those responsible for each on the company intranet. Tasks rotate weekly and include maintaining the supply closet, stocking the kitchen with food, washing dishes, assigning tasks, and so on. At first, employees balked. They were already putting in 12-hour days. "I have to do all this stuff plus the dishes?" asked one. To reduce resistance, McLaughlin did dishes the first week and Gavin took the closet. McLaughlin announced that of the $100,000 saved in salary and benefits by not replacing the two employees, $20,000 would go to the employees and the rest to activities for workers. As the new system began to work, people started talking to each other more—about tasks, assignments, and improvements—and they got a greater sense of responsibility. Eze Castle's electrical bill went from the astronomical $4,000 per month to only $1,000 per month as workers became more conscious of turning off lights and computers.

Another problem was how little employees knew one another. So McLaughlin instituted another kindergarten tradition: milk and cookie breaks. "I wanted to build relationships among the employees, to make them feel more company morale," says the CEO. Every day at 2:30 people leave their cubicles for the kitchen—after turning out their lights.

SOURCE: Ilan Mochari, "It's All in the Details," *Inc.* (March 2002), 120–122.

Critical Events. Often, *critical events* in a team's history establish an important precedent. One example occurred when an employee at a forest products plant was seriously injured while standing too close to a machine being operated by a teammate. This led to a norm that team members regularly monitor one another to make sure all safety rules are observed.

Any critical event can lead to the creation of a norm. In one organization, a department head invited the entire staff to his house for dinner. The next day people discovered that no one had attended, and this resulted in a norm prohibiting outside entertaining.[50]

Managing Team Conflict

The final characteristic of team process is conflict. Of all the skills required for effective team management, none is more important than handling the conflicts that inevitably arise among members. Whenever people work together in teams, some conflict is inevitable. Conflict can arise among members within a team or between one team and another. **Conflict** refers to antagonistic interaction in which one party attempts to block the intentions or goals of another.[51] Competition, which is rivalry among individuals or teams, can have a healthy impact because it energizes people toward higher performance.[52] In addition, some conflict within teams may lead to better decision making because multiple viewpoints are considered. There is some research evidence that low conflict in top management teams is associated with poor decision making. Team

conflict

Antagonistic interaction in which one party attempts to thwart the intentions or goals of another.

members just go along with the strongest opinion, which often is that of the CEO, rather than consider alternate ideas and solutions.[53] However, too much conflict can be destructive, tear relationships apart, and interfere with the healthy exchange of ideas and information.[54]

Causes of Conflict

Several factors can cause people to engage in conflict:[55]

Scarce Resources. Resources include money, information, and supplies. In their desire to achieve goals, individuals may wish to increase their resources, which throws them into conflict. Whenever individuals or teams must compete for scarce or declining resources, conflict is almost inevitable. At the Levi Strauss blue jeans plant near Knoxville, Tennessee, a change in pay systems—in which employees were paid based on team output rather than on the old individual piecework system—led to severe conflict because some employees felt that slower team members hurt their pocketbooks. One worker says her hourly pay dropped nearly $2, while slower team members realized an increase over what they earned on the piecework system.[56]

Jurisdictional Ambiguities. Conflicts also emerge when job boundaries and responsibilities are unclear. When task responsibilities are well defined and predictable, people know where they stand. When they are unclear, people may disagree about who has responsibility for specific tasks or who has a claim on resources.

Communication Breakdown. Communication, as described in Chapter 14, sometimes is faulty. The potential for communication breakdown is even greater with virtual teams and global teams made up of members from different countries and cultures. Poor communication results in misperceptions and misunderstandings of other people and teams. In some cases, information is intentionally withheld, which can jeopardize trust among teams and lead to long-lasting conflict.

Personality Clashes. A personality clash occurs when people simply do not get along or do not see eye-to-eye on any issue. Personality clashes are caused by basic differences in personality, values, and attitudes. In one study, personality conflicts were the number-one reported cause preventing front-line management teams from working together effectively.[57] Some personality differences can be overcome. However, severe personality clashes are difficult to resolve. Often, it is a good idea to simply separate the parties so that they need not interact with one another.

Power and Status Differences. Power and status differences occur when one party has disputable influence over another. Low-prestige individuals or departments might resist their low status. People might engage in conflict to increase their power and influence in the team or organization.

Goal Differences. Conflict often occurs simply because people are pursuing conflicting goals. Goal differences are natural in organizations. Individual salespeople's targets may put them in conflict with one another or with the sales manager. Moreover, the sales department's goals might conflict with those of manufacturing.

Styles to Handle Conflict

Teams as well as individuals develop specific styles for dealing with conflict, based on the desire to satisfy their own concern versus the other party's concern. A model that describes five styles of handling conflict is in Exhibit 15.8. The two major dimensions are the extent to which an individual is assertive versus cooperative in his or her approach to conflict.

Effective team members vary their style of handling conflict to fit a specific situation. Each of these five styles is appropriate in certain cases.

1. The *competing style* reflects assertiveness to get one's own way, and should be used when quick, decisive action is vital on important issues or unpopular actions, such as during emergencies or urgent cost cutting.

2. The *avoiding style* reflects neither assertiveness nor cooperativeness. It is appropriate when an issue is trivial, when there is no chance of winning, when a delay to gather more information is needed, or when a disruption would be very costly.

3. The *compromising style* reflects a moderate amount of both assertiveness and cooperativeness. It is appropriate when the goals on both sides are equally important, when opponents have equal power and both sides want to split

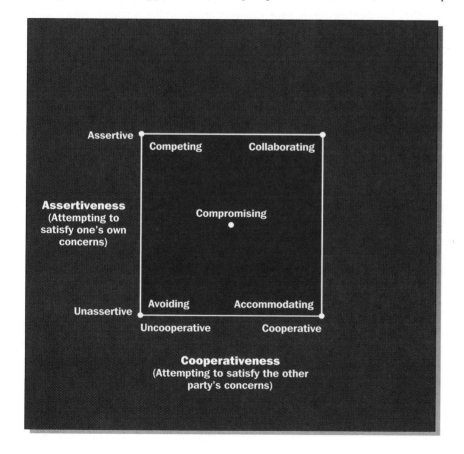

EXHIBIT 15.8

A Model of Styles to Handle Conflict

SOURCE: Adapted from Kenneth Thomas, "Conflict and Conflict Management," in *Handbook of Industrial and Organizational Behavior*, ed. M. D. Dunnette (New York: John Wiley, 1976), 900.

the difference, or when people need to arrive at temporary or expedient solutions under time pressure.

4. The *accommodating style* reflects a high degree of cooperativeness, which works best when people realize that they are wrong, when an issue is more important to others than to oneself, when building social credits for use in later discussions, and when maintaining harmony is especially important.

5. The *collaborating style* reflects both a high degree of assertiveness and cooperativeness. The collaborating style enables both parties to win, although it may require substantial bargaining and negotiation. The collaborating style is important when both sets of concerns are too important to be compromised, when insights from different people need to be merged into an overall solution, and when the commitment of both sides is needed for a consensus.[58]

The various styles of handling conflict can be used when an individual disagrees with others. But what does a manager or team leader do when a conflict erupts among others within a team or among teams for which the manager is responsible? Research suggests that several techniques can be used as strategies for resolving conflicts among people or departments. These techniques might also be used when conflict is formalized, such as between a union and management.

Superordinate Goals. The larger mission that cannot be attained by a single party is identified as a **superordinate goal**.[59] This is similar to the concept of *vision*. A powerful vision of where the organization wants to be in the future often compels employees to overcome conflicts and cooperate for the greater good. Similarly, a superordinate goal requires the cooperation of conflicting team members for achievement. People must pull together. To the extent that employees can be focused on team or organization goals, the conflict will decrease because they see the big picture and realize they must work together to achieve it.

Bargaining/Negotiation. Bargaining and negotiation mean that the parties engage one another in an attempt to systematically reach a solution. They attempt logical problem solving to identify and correct the conflict. This approach works well if the individuals can set aside personal animosities and deal with the conflict in a businesslike way.

Mediation. Using a third party to settle a dispute involves **mediation**. A mediator could be a supervisor, higher-level manager, or someone from the human resource department. The mediator can discuss the conflict with each party and work toward a solution. If a solution satisfactory to both sides cannot be reached, the parties might be willing to turn the conflict over to the mediator and abide by his or her solution.

Facilitating Communication. Managers can facilitate communication to ensure that conflicting parties hold accurate perceptions. Providing opportunities for the disputants to get together and exchange information reduces conflict. As they learn more about one another, suspicions diminish and improved teamwork becomes possible.

superordinate goal
A goal that cannot be reached by a single party.

mediation
The process of using a third party to settle a dispute.

Four guidelines can help facilitate communication and keep teams focused on substantive issues rather than on interpersonal conflicts.[60]

- *Focus on facts.* Keep team discussions focused on issues, not personalities. Working with more data and information rather than less can help keep team members focused on facts and prevent meetings from degenerating into pointless debates over opinions. At Star Electronics, the top management team meets daily, weekly, and monthly to examine a wide variety of specific operating measures. Looking at the details helps team members debate critical issues and avoid useless arguments.

- *Develop multiple alternatives.* Teams that deliberately develop many alternatives, sometimes considering four or five options at once, have a lower incidence of interpersonal conflict. Having a multitude of options to consider concentrates team members' energy on solving problems. In addition, the process of generating multiple choices is fun and creative, which sets a positive tone for the meeting and reduces the chance for conflict.

- *Maintain a balance of power.* Managers and team leaders should accept the team's decision as fair, even if they do not agree with it. Fairness requires a balance of power within the team.

- *Never force a consensus.* There will naturally be conflict over some issues, which managers find a way to resolve without forcing a consensus. When there are persistent differences of opinion, the team leader sometimes has to make a decision guided by input from other team members. At Andromeda Processing, the CEO insisted on consensus from his top management team, causing a debate to rage on for months. Eventually, most of the managers just wanted a decision, no matter whether it was the one they agreed with. Conflict and frustration mounted to the point where some top managers left the company. The group achieved consensus only at the price of losing several key managers.

Benefits and Costs of Teams

In deciding whether to use teams to perform specific tasks, managers must consider both benefits and costs. Teams may have positive impact on both the output productivity and satisfaction of members. On the other hand, teams may also create a situation in which motivation and performance actually are decreased.

Potential Benefits of Teams

Teams come closest to achieving their full potential when they enhance individual productivity through increased member effort, members' personal satisfaction, integration of diverse abilities and skills, and increased organizational flexibility.

Level of Effort. Employee teams often unleash enormous energy and creativity from workers who like the idea of using their brains as well as their bodies to accomplish an important goal. The shift to a team approach is an important component of the evolution to the learning organization as

social facilitation

The tendency for the presence of others to influence an individual's motivation and performance.

described in Chapter 1 and Chapter 7. To facilitate learning and problem solving, organizations are breaking down barriers, empowering workers, and encouraging employees to use their minds and creativity. Research has found that working in a team increases an individual's motivation and performance. **Social facilitation** refers to the tendency for the presence of others to enhance an individual's motivation and performance. Simply being in the presence of other people has an energizing effect.[61] Eileen Fisher runs her company in a way that facilitates people working together and having fun, with the idea that they will be happier people and more productive workers, as the Best Practices box describes.

Satisfaction of Members. As described in Chapter 13, employees have needs for belongingness and affiliation. Working in teams can help meet these needs. Participative teams reduce boredom and often increase employees' feeling of dignity and self-worth because the whole person is employed. People who have a satisfying team environment cope better with stress and enjoy their jobs.

Expanded Job Knowledge and Skills. The third major benefit of using teams is the empowerment of employees to bring greater knowledge and ability to the task. For one thing, multiskilled employees learn all of the jobs that the team performs. Teams gain the intellectual resources of several members who can suggest shortcuts and offer alternative points of view for team decisions.

BEST PRACTICES

Eileen Fisher, Inc.

When Eileen Fisher was in college, one assignment was designing a house. She told a few friends about her vision, and before long she had 40 people in her dorm room, wanting to contribute their ideas. She has brought this same vision-building and inspired team work into her women's apparel company (featured in Chapter 1). It all started in 1984 with her investment of $350 dollars in material, sewing some clothes, and taking them to a trade show. Now her company earns $130 million annually.

Great pains are taken to ensure that teamwork flourishes, while at the same time encouraging individual empowerment. Her 400 employees see her as a down-to-earth boss, one who promotes from within and knows everybody by name. To encourage teamwork and create justice, Fisher practices profit-sharing, giving 10 percent of the profits in year-end bonuses, which sometimes equals eight weeks' pay for each employee.

To develop a sense of belonging in the community, Fisher encourages all employees to volunteer—on company time. Community service includes assisting firefighters, redecorating the abused women's shelter, or working at the local Chamber of Commerce.

As CEO, Fisher is the head of the company's design team, but she says she spends most of her time keeping the staff happy and productive. Her management philosophy is based on values and human connection, whether it be through communication or teamwork. She encourages open and honest communication, to create a joyful and fun work environment, and to keep it simple.

"Keeping it simple" describes her design philosophy as well. Fisher designs clothes for women who want to get dressed in the morning and then not have to think about it again. The focus is not on the clothes, which are constructed with smooth, sleek lines. As she says, "I want people to notice the woman, not the clothes."

Fisher believes women are highly qualified to develop the kind of bonds that make an effective team. "Women have a unique way of approaching the world," she says. "The way we listen, the value we place on relationships, and our instinct to connect enhances out capacity to make a difference every day—whether we are running a company or running a home (or both!)"

SOURCES: Claudia Z. Carlin, "Eileen Fisher Simplifies," *Westchester Magazine* (May 2002), 44–45; Julie Szabo, "The Cutting Edge of Non-fashion," *Working Woman Magazine* (February 1995), 72–74.

Organizational Responsiveness. Employee teams enhance flexibility because workers can be reorganized and employees reassigned as needed. People work closely together, learn a variety of skills, and can exchange jobs as needed to accomplish the team's task. In addition, teams break down traditional organizational boundaries so that people collaborate across functional and hierarchical lines, which enables the organization to rapidly respond to changing customer needs.

Potential Costs of Teams

When managers decide whether to use teams, they must assess certain costs or liabilities associated with teamwork. When teams do not work very well, the major reasons usually are power realignment, free riding, coordination costs, or system revisions.

Power Realignment. When companies form front-line workers into teams, the major losers are low- and middle-level managers. These managers are reluctant to give up power. Indeed, when teams are successful, fewer supervisors are needed. This is especially true for self-directed teams, because workers take over supervisory responsibility. The adjustment is difficult for managers who fear the loss of status or even their job and who have to learn new, people-oriented skills to survive.[62]

© Eileen Fisher, Inc.

Free Riding. The term **free rider** refers to a team member who attains benefits from team membership but does not do a proportionate share of the work.[63] Free riding sometimes is called *social loafing,* because members do not exert equal effort. In large teams, some people are likely to work less. For example, research found that the pull exerted on a rope was greater by individuals working alone than by individuals in a group. Similarly, people who were asked to clap and make noise made more noise on a per person basis when working alone or in small groups than they did in a large group.[64] The problem of free riding has been experienced by people who have participated in student project groups. Some students put more effort into the group project than others, and often it seems that no members work as hard for the group as they do for their individual grades.

free rider
A person who benefits from team membership but does not make a proportionate contribution to the team's work.

Coordination Costs. The time and energy required to coordinate the activities of a group to enable it to perform its task are called **coordination costs.** Groups must spend time getting ready to do work and lose productive time in deciding who is to do what and when.[65] Once again, student project groups illustrate coordination costs. Members must meet after class just to decide when they can meet to perform the task. Schedules must be checked, telephone calls made, and meeting times arranged in order to get down to business. Hours may be devoted to the administration and coordination of the group. Students often feel they could do the same project by themselves in less time. Teams typically have frequent meetings throughout a project, so leaders have to know how to keep meetings focused and productive. This chapter's Focus on Skills box offers some tips for running a great meeting.

coordination costs
The time and energy needed to coordinate the activities of a team to enable it to perform its task.

FOCUS ON SKILLS

How to Run a Great Meeting

Many executives believe that meetings are a waste of time. Busy executives may spend up to 70 percent of their time in meetings at which participants doodle, drink coffee, and think about what they could be doing back in their offices.

However, successful meetings help people process important information and solve organizational problems. Good meetings don't just happen; they are designed through careful thought and planning. The success of a meeting depends on what is done in advance of, during, and after it.

Prepare in Advance. Advance preparation is the single most important tool for running an efficient, productive meeting. Advance preparation should include the following:

1. *Define the purpose.* The chairperson should be very explicit in setting goals and expressing them concisely and meaningfully.
2. *Prepare an agenda.* The agenda is a simple list of the topics to be discussed. It is important because it lets people know what to expect and keeps the meeting on track. The agenda provides order and logic and gives the chairperson a means of control during the meeting if the discussion starts to wander.
3. *Issue invitations selectively.* If the group gets too big, the meeting will not be productive. If everyone is expected to participate, keep membership between 4 and 12.
4. *Set a time limit.* A formal meeting should have a specified amount of time. The ending time should be announced in advance, and the agenda should require the meeting to move along at a reasonable pace.

During the Meeting. If the chairperson is prepared in advance, the meeting will go smoothly. Moreover, certain techniques will bring out the best in people and make the meeting even more productive:

5. *Start on time.* This sounds obvious—but do not keep busy people waiting. Starting on time has symbolic value, because it tells people that the topic is important.
6. *Outlaw cell phones.* Having the flow of discussion interrupted by the ringing of a cell phone can throw the meeting completely off-track. A chairperson who answers a cell phone signals that the meeting is not really important.
7. *State the purpose and review the agenda.* The chairperson should start the meeting by stating the explicit purpose and clarifying what should be accomplished by the time the meeting is over.

8. *Encourage participation.* Good meetings contain lots of discussion. If the chairperson merely wants to present one-way information to members, he or she should send a memo. A few subtle techniques go a long way toward increasing participation:
   a. *Draw out the silent.* This means saying, "Bob, what do you think of Nancy's idea?"
   b. *Control the talkative.* Some people overdo it and dominate the discussion. The chairperson's job is to redirect the discussion toward other people. One organization has a rule called NOSTUESO (No one speaks twice until everyone speaks once).
   c. *Encourage the clash of ideas.* A good meeting is not a series of dialogues but a crosscurrent of discussion and debate. The chairperson guides, mediates, stimulates, and summarizes this discussion.
   d. *Call on the most senior people last.* Sometimes junior people are reluctant to disagree with senior people, so it is best to get the junior people's ideas on the table first. This will provide wider views and ideas.
   e. *Listen.* The chairperson should not preach or engage in one-on-one dialogue with group members. The point is to listen and to facilitate discussion.
9. *Stick to the purpose.* Encouraging a free flow of ideas does not mean allowing participants to sidetrack the meeting into discussions of issues not on the agenda. This can waste valuable time and prevent the group from reaching its goals.

After the meeting. The actions following the meeting are designed to summarize and implement agreed-upon points. Postmeeting activities are set in motion by a call to action.

10. *End with a call to action.* The last item of the meeting's agenda is to summarize the main points and make sure everyone understands his or her assignments.
11. *Follow-up.* Mail minutes of the meeting to members. Use this memorandum to summarize the key accomplishments of the meeting, suggest schedules for agreed-upon activities, and start the ball rolling in preparation for the next meeting.

SOURCES: Based on Edward Michaels, "Business Meetings," *Small Business Reports* (February 1989), 82–88; Daniel Stoffman, "Waking Up to Great Meetings," *Canadian Business* (November 1986), 75–79; Antoney Jay, "How to Run a Meeting," *Harvard Business Review* (March–April 1976), 120–134; Jana Kemp, "Avoiding Agenda Overstack," *Corporate University Review* (May–June 1997), 42–43; and Jeffrey L. Seglin, "We've Got to Start Meeting Like This," *CIO* (March 1, 2001), 168–170.

Revising Systems. Implementing teams also requires changes in other parts of the organization. In particular, performance appraisal and reward systems have to be revised to reflect the new team approach; otherwise, teamwork will fail. Managers should be aware that a shift to teams requires that time and resources be invested to develop new systems that support and reinforce collaboration, sharing of information, and empowerment.

■ Summary and Management Solution

Several important concepts about teams were described in this chapter. Organizations use teams both to achieve coordination as part of the formal structure and to encourage employee involvement. Formal teams include vertical teams along the chain of command and horizontal teams such as cross-functional task forces and committees. Special-purpose teams are used for special, large-scale, creative organization projects. Employee involvement via teams is designed to bring low-level employees into decision processes to improve quality, efficiency, and satisfaction. Companies typically start with problem-solving teams, which may evolve into self-directed teams that take on responsibility for management activities. New approaches to teamwork include virtual teams and global teams. These teams may include contingent workers, customers, suppliers, and other outsiders. Although team members sometimes meet face to face, they use advanced information and telecommunications technology to accomplish much of their work.

Brian Pasch knew something drastic was needed to save Millennium Teleservices IT department from ruin. Having tried lots of strategies that didn't work, he decided to do something different. He called a shrink. Organizational psychologist Christine Truhe began a diagnosis intervention by assessing the relationship between groups and individuals, to understand better how the system interrelated. She convinced Maiorini that simply restructuring and moving boxes around in the organization chart would not solve the problem of connections between people. Truhe had helped other companies in similar situations, and knew that, in general, the problem was about competing authority figures.

The psychologist began by giving out surveys to the eight managers, asking them about the company's mission, their own responsibilities, and the strengths and weaknesses of Pasch and Maiorini. Answers were clear and straightforward. The managers saw Pasch as charm-ing, likable, and brilliant, while Maiorini was seen as a robot. Because Maiorini had been hired as a vice president, with the task of supervising managers hired by Pasch, suspicions were created around Maiorini, casting Pasch as the good guy and Maiorini as the bad guy. Perhaps the most important information was that the managers felt abandoned by Pasch.

Both Maiorini and Pasch agreed to share the survey results at a management meeting. Truhe diagnosed the problem at Millennium as authority dynamics, and helped them develop new ways of communicating with each other. They met once a week for three hours, working on intragroup conflict, anger over Maiorini's promotion, and job instability. The "treatment" was considered finished after a year. By all accounts, it worked. Efficiency and productivity are up, costs are down, retention has increased, and, to everyone's great relief, people can breathe again.[66]

Most teams go through systematic stages of development: forming, storming, norming, performing, and adjourning. Team characteristics that can influence organizational effectiveness are size, cohesiveness, norms, and members' roles. All teams experience some conflict because of scarce resources, ambiguous responsibility, communication breakdown, personality clashes, power and status differences, and goal conflicts. Techniques for resolving these conflicts include superordinate goals, bargaining, mediation, and communication. Techniques for facilitating team communication to minimize conflict are to focus on facts, develop multiple alternatives, maintain a balance of power, and never force a consensus. Advantages of using teams include increased motivation, diverse knowledge and skills, satisfaction of team members, and organizational responsiveness. Potential costs of using teams are power realignment, free riding, coordination costs, and revising systems.

■ Discussion Questions

1. Volvo went to self-directed teams to assemble cars because of the need to attract and keep workers in Sweden, where pay raises are not a motivator (due to high taxes) and many other jobs are available. Is this a good reason for using a team approach? Discuss.

2. How is a self-directed team different from a cross-functional team?

3. What factors in today's environment are contributing to an increasing use of virtual teams and global teams? Would you like to be part of a virtual team? Why or why not?

4. Suppose you are the leader of a team that has just been created to develop a new registration process at your college or university. How can you use an understanding of the stages of team development to improve your team's effectiveness?

5. Think of a work team or student project team of which you have been a member. Identify some of the team's unstated norms. How did these norms develop?

6. If you were the leader of a special-purpose team developing a new computer game, and conflicts arose related to power and status differences among team members, what would you do? How might you use the various conflict-resolution techniques described in the chapter?

7. When you are a member of a team, do you adopt a task specialist or socioemotional role? Which role is more important for a team's effectiveness? Discuss.

8. What is the relationship between team cohesiveness and team performance?

9. Describe the advantages and disadvantages of teams. In what situations might the disadvantages outweigh the advantages?

10. One company had 40 percent of its workers and 20 percent of its managers resign during the first year after reorganizing into teams. What might account for this dramatic turnover? How might managers ensure a smooth transition to teams?

■ Manager's Workbook

Is Your Group a Cohesive Team?

Think about a student group with which you have worked. Answer the questions below as they pertain to the functioning of that group.

	Disagree Strongly				Agree Strongly
1. Group meetings were held regularly and everyone attended.	1	2	3	4	5
2. We talked about and shared the same goals for group work and grade.	1	2	3	4	5
3. We spent most of our meeting time talking business, but discussions were open-ended and active.	1	2	3	4	5
4. We talked through any conflicts and disagreements until they were resolved.	1	2	3	4	5
5. Group members listened carefully to one another.	1	2	3	4	5
6. We really trusted each other, speaking personally about what we really felt.	1	2	3	4	5
7. Leadership roles were rotated and shared, with people taking initiative at appropriate times for the good of the group.	1	2	3	4	5
8. Each member found a way to contribute to the final work product.	1	2	3	4	5
9. I was really satisfied being a member of the group.	1	2	3	4	5
10. We freely gave each other credit for jobs well done.	1	2	3	4	5
11. Group members gave and received feedback to help the group do even better.	1	2	3	4	5
12. We held each other accountable; each member was accountable to the group.	1	2	3	4	5
13. Group members really liked and respected each other.	1	2	3	4	5

Total Score _____

The questions here are about team cohesion. If you scored 52 or greater, your group experienced authentic teamwork. Congratulations. If you scored between 39 and 51, there was a positive group identity that might have been developed even further. If you scored between 26 and 38, group identity was weak and probably not very satisfying. If you scored below 26, it was hardly a group at all, resembling a loose collection of individuals.

Remember, teamwork does not happen by itself. Individuals like you have to understand what a team is and then work to make it happen. What can you do to make a student group more like a team? Do you have the courage to take the initiative?

■ Manager's Workshop

Auntie Kate's Bakery Case Study

A group of management students is assigned to observe the operations at Auntie Kate's Bakery. Initial interviews show that employees identify with company values and practices; things always seem to work well. About 85 percent of the staff have been with the company for over 12 years. Supportive of her employees, the owner has an egalitarian attitude, respects workers, and continually refers to staff as "My family." Seen from the employee's perspective, Auntie Kate's Bakery is the perfect small business.

Class assignment: Observe the bakery's operations and suggest recommendations for improvement.

Results from class members: The task of bagging assorted cookies is inefficient. Eight staff members each stand in front of cartons filled with assorted cookies. The left hand holds a bag, while the right hand makes an extended reach to pick up cookies to place them in the bag. The staff works at a relaxed, informal pace. The tasks do not align with principles of motion economy, because the staff members do not use both hands simultaneously and each hand works in opposite directions. Nor are any materials pre-positioned for ease of reach.

After the students suggest highly structured changes to increase efficiency, the owner graciously rejects their recommendations. The students are confused.

1. In groups of 4–6 members answer the following questions:
   a. Why do you think the owner reject the recommendations?
   b. What elements regarding team motivation were overlooked by the students in the study?
   c. If you were the student group, what steps would you take if you were studying Auntie Kate's Bakery?
2. The class will discuss the answers of each group. What did you learn about team effectiveness?

■ Management in Practice: Ethical Dilemma

Consumer Safety or Team Commitment?

Nancy was part of a pharmaceutical team developing a product called loperamide, a liquid treatment for diarrhea for people unable to take solid medicine, namely infants, children, and the elderly. Loperamide contained 44 times the amount of saccharin allowed by the FDA in a 12-ounce soft drink, but there were no regulations governing saccharin content in medication.

Nancy was the only medical member of the seven-person project team. The team made a unanimous decision to reduce the saccharin content before marketing loperamide, so the team initiated a three-month effort for reformulation. In the meantime, management was pressuring the team to allow human testing with the original formula until the new formula became available. After a heated team debate, all the team members except Nancy voted to begin testing with the current formula.

Nancy believed it was unethical to test on old people and children a drug she considered potentially dangerous. As the only medical member of the team, she had to sign the forms allowing testing. She refused and was told that unless she signed, she would be removed from the project, demoted, and seen as a poor team player, nonpromotable, lacking in judgment, and unable to work with marketing people. Nancy was aware that no proof existed that high saccharin would be directly harmful to potential users of loperamide.

What Do You Do?

1. Refuse to sign. As a medical doctor, Nancy must stand up for what she believes is right.
2. Resign. There is no reason to stay in this company and be punished for ethically correct behavior. Testing the drug will become someone else's responsibility.
3. Sign the form. The judgment of other team members cannot be all wrong. The loperamide testing is not illegal and will move ahead anyway, so it would preserve team unity and company effectiveness to sign.

SOURCE: Based on Tom L. Beauchamp, *Ethical Theory and Business*, 2d ed. (Englewood Cliffs, N.J.: Prentice-Hall, 1983).

■ Surf the Net

1. **Teamwork and Your Career.** One of the most popular job sites, with more than 800,000 U.S. job listings, is located at *http://www.monster.com*. Choose the "Search Jobs" link, read the "Tips on Searching," and then conduct a job search in your career area and in geographical areas of your choice. If you're not finding what you need at monster.com, try other jobs sites such as
   http://www.thejobresource.com
   http://www.ajb.dni.us
   http://www.jobbankusa.com
   http://www.wetfeet.com/asp/home.asp
   Print out five job ads and then highlight any references to teams or teamwork on your printouts. Be prepared to discuss or submit your findings in class.

2. **Are You a Team Player?** Complete the team player assessment available at the following site. Print out the results, bring them to class, and be prepared to discuss your results during class.
   http://content.monster.com/tools/quizzes/teamplayer

3. **Conflict Management Style.** Complete an assessment to determine your own conflict management style. Print out the results of your assessment and be prepared to discuss what you learned about yourself and about conflict management from this exercise.
   http://www.mercer.edu/csil/leaps_resource_files.htm
   (Under heading "Organizational Success" choose "What's Your Conflict Management Style?")

■ Case for Critical Analysis

Acme Minerals Extraction Company

Several years ago, Acme Minerals Extraction Company introduced teams in an effort to solve morale and productivity problems at its Wichita plant. Acme used highly sophisticated technology, employing geologists, geophysicists, and engineers on what was referred to as the "brains" side of the business, as well as skilled and semi-skilled labor on the "brawn" side to run the company's underground extracting operations. The two sides regularly clashed, and when some engineers locked several operations workers out of the office in 100-degree heat, the local press had a field day. Suzanne Howard was hired to develop a program that would improve productivity and morale at the Wichita plant, with the idea that it would then be implemented at other Acme sites.

Howard had a stroke of luck in the form of Donald Peterson, a long-time Acme employee who was highly respected at the Wichita plant and was looking for one final, challenging project before he retired. Peterson had served in just about every possible line and staff position at Acme over his 39-year career, and he understood the problems workers faced on both the "brains" and the "brawn" sides of the business. Howard was pleased when Peterson agreed to serve as leader for the Wichita pilot project. There were three functional groups at the Wichita plant: operations, made up primarily of hourly workers who operated and maintained the extracting equipment; the "below ground" group, consisting of engineers, geologists, and geophysicists who determined where and how to drill; and the "above ground" group of engineers in charge of cursory refinement and transportation of the minerals. Howard and Peterson decided the first step was to get these different groups talking to one another and sharing ideas. They instituted a monthly "problem chat," an optional meeting to which all employees were invited to discuss unresolved problems. At

the first meeting, Howard and Peterson were the only two people who showed up. However, people gradually began to attend the meetings, and after about six months they had become lively problem-solving discussions that led to many improvements.

Next, Howard and Peterson introduced teams to "select a problem and implement a tailored solution," or SPITS. These were ad hoc groups made up of members from each of the three functional areas. They were formed to work on a specific problem identified in a chat meeting and were disbanded when the problem was solved. SPITS were given the authority to address problems without seeking management approval. There were some rocky moments, as engineers resented working with operations personnel and vice versa. However, over time, and with the strong leadership of Peterson, the groups began to come together and focus on the issues rather than spending most of their time arguing. Eventually, workers in Wichita were organized into permanent cross-functional teams that were empowered to make their own decisions and elect their own leaders. After a year and a half, things were really humming. The different groups weren't just working together; they had also started socializing together. At one of the problem chats, an operations worker jokingly suggested that the brains and the brawn should duke it out once a week to get rid of the tensions so they could focus all their energy on the job to be done. Several others joined in the joking, and eventually, the group decided to square off in a weekly softball game. Peterson had T-shirts printed up that said BRAINS AND BRAWN. The softball games were well attended, and both sides usually ended up having a few beers together at a local bar afterward. Productivity and morale soared at the Wichita plant, and costs continued to decline.

Top executives believed the lessons learned at Wichita should make implementing the program at other sites less costly and time-consuming. However, when Howard and her team attempted to implement the program at the Lubbock plant, things didn't go well. They felt under immense pressure from top management to get the team-based productivity project running smoothly at Lubbock. Because people weren't showing up for the problem chat meetings, attendance was made mandatory. However, the meetings still produced few valuable ideas or suggestions. Although a few of the SPITS teams solved important problems, none of them showed the kind of commitment and enthusiasm Howard had seen in Wichita. In addition, the Lubbock workers refused to participate in the softball games and other team-building exercises that Howard's team developed for them. Howard finally convinced some workers to join in the softball games by bribing them with free food and beer. "If I just had a Donald Peterson in Lubbock, things would go a lot more smoothly," Howard thought. "These workers don't trust us the way workers in Wichita trusted him." It seemed that no matter how hard Howard and her team tried to make the project work in Lubbock, morale continued to decline and conflicts between the different groups of workers actually seemed to increase.

Questions

1. What types of teams described in the chapter are represented in this case?
2. Why do you think the team project succeeded at Wichita but isn't working in Lubbock?
3. What advice would you give Suzanne Howard and her team for improving the employee involvement climate at the Lubbock plant?

SOURCE: Based on Michael C. Beers, "The Strategy That Wouldn't Travel," *Harvard Business Review*, (November–December 1996), 18–31.

Controlling

Harnessing creativity in the music business takes more than good songwriters and mellow vocals. Technology also plays a crucial role in the sounds played on radio and stored on CDs. Songs used to be recorded on analog tape, doing as many takes as necessary. Engineers would then splice tape together from different segments of the song in order to get the best sound. This not only took countless hours but a wrong cut meant the recording had to be redone. In addition, each time a song was transferred from tape to tape, it lost quality. Then came digital recording, which takes the sound and turns it into digital numbers on the computer. Tones can now be enhanced or corrected in a software program, reducing the number of recording sessions required. Songs can be recopied over and over without any deterioration of sound. Newer hard drives and software allow upward of 64 tracks to be used in the final process. Not only are there fewer hours needed for engineers, which reduces costs, but the cost of basic recording equipment is less than it used to be. That means someone can build a studio for a lot less money; digital recorders cost about 10 percent of what studio analog recorders cost. The smart use of technology in the recording business can produce high-quality sounds at a lower cost.

The Importance of Control

LEARNING OBJECTIVES

After studying this chapter, you should be able to

1 Define organizational control and explain why it is a key management function.

2 Describe differences in control focus, including feedforward, concurrent, and feedback control.

3 Explain the four steps in the control process.

4 Discuss the use of financial statements, financial analysis, and budgeting as management controls.

5 Contrast the bureaucratic and decentralized control approaches.

6 Define productivity and explain why and how managers seek to improve it.

7 Describe the concept of total quality management and major TQM techniques.

8 Identify current trends in financial control and discuss their impact on organizations.

9 Explain the value of open-book management and the balanced scorecard as new workplace approaches to control.

Management Challenge

When Richard Snyder took over as controller of Latt-Greene, an ailing knitting and converting operation with eight employees, he walked into a nest of problems: negative cash flow, a poor billing system that let some customers off scot-free, and a system so heavy with paper it was being crushed under its own weight. There was not a single computer on the premises, and the accountant kept records by hand, following an antiquated system. No records were kept that could be used to figure out how much yarn was knitted into unfinished textiles, nor the cost of making the final product. The owners operated on what they assumed to be the costs, rather than on hard data. And how could Snyder get employees to agree to drastic changes and reengineering, when those employees had been doing the same things for years and were, in fact, heavily invested in the current process?

As he introduced financial software to bring some order to the system, Snyder discovered that orders sometimes got lost in a paper file, that costs from vendors did not match the actual product, and that shipping orders did not correlate to any specific products. Knowing that reengineering was a scary word to employees, being viewed as a code word for "layoffs," Snyder had to find some way to bring about needed changes in order to save the company.[1]

How can Snyder use control systems and strategies to improve cost efficiency and save the company from bankruptcy? If you were Snyder, what would you do?

Control is a critical issue facing every manager in every organization today. At Samaritan, managers need to find new ways to cut costs, build morale, and increase productivity, or the organization will not survive. Other organizations face similar challenges, such as improving customer service, minimizing the time needed to resupply merchandise in retail stores, decreasing the number of steps needed to process an online merchandise order, or improving the tracking procedures for overnight package delivery. Control, including quality control, also involves office productivity, such as elimination of bottlenecks and reduction in paperwork mistakes. In addition, every organization needs basic systems for allocating financial resources, developing human resources, analyzing financial performance, and evaluating overall profitability.

This chapter introduces basic mechanisms for controlling the organization. It begins by summarizing the basic structure and objectives of the control process. Then it discusses controlling financial performance, including the use of budgets and financial statements. The next sections examine the changing philosophy of control, today's approach to total quality management, and recent trends such as ISO 9000 certification, economic value-added and market value-added systems, and activity based costing. The chapter concludes with a look at control in the new workplace, including the use of open-book management and the balanced scorecard.

The Meaning of Control

On a warm June day in 1999, the worst crisis in Coca-Cola's 113-year history began when hundreds of customers in Europe turned up sick after drinking "foul-smelling" Coke products. The failure of bottlers in Antwerp, Belgium, and Dunkirk, France, to follow quality-control procedures had gotten the company into a jam from which it is still trying to recover. Fourteen million cases of Coke products were recalled from five European countries, and the public relations nightmare raged for months. A lack of effective control can seriously damage an organization's health and threaten its future, as we saw in the opening case of Samaritan Medical Center. As another example, the Chrysler side of DaimlerChrysler is struggling to recover from financial problems that resulted partly from inadequate control mechanisms following the 1998 merger with Germany's Daimler Benz.[2]

organizational control

The systematic process through which managers regulate organizational activities to make them consistent with expectations established in plans, targets, and standards of performance.

Organizational control is the systematic process of regulating organizational activities to make them consistent with the expectations established in plans, targets, and standards of performance. In a classic article on the control function, Douglas S. Sherwin summarizes this concept as follows: "The essence of control is action which adjusts operations to predetermined standards, and its basis is information in the hands of managers."[3] Thus, effectively controlling an organization requires information about performance standards and actual performance, as well as actions taken to correct any deviations from the standards. Managers need to decide what information is essential, how they will obtain that information (and share it with employees), and how they can and should respond to it. Having the correct data is essential. Managers have to decide which standards, measurements, and metrics are needed to effectively monitor and control the organization and set up systems for obtaining that information. For example, an important metric for the Portland Trail Blazers basketball team is number of season tickets, which reduce the organization's

FOCUS ON SKILLS

E-Commerce Metrics

How do e-commerce organizations know how well their Web site is doing? It is not too difficult to find out how many people visit the site and how many pages they look at. But that's only the first step toward finding out how effective the site is in terms of achieving organizational goals. E-commerce managers have been struggling to identify metrics that will help them evaluate a company's performance and compare it to others. Although different companies often use different standards and measurements, some common e-commerce metrics are beginning to emerge:

- *Reach.* This refers to the number of potential customers, or the percentage of the possible audience that a Web site is able to reach. Many companies still use *hits* as the primary measure of Web site success, but that measure has evolved. *Eyeballs* refers to people who are habitual visitors to the company's site. *Unique users* are unduplicated visitors to the site.

- *Stickiness.* This is becoming one of the most important metrics in e-commerce because it measures how much attention the site gets over time. One formula for calculating the metric is

    Stickiness = Total Size Reach x Frequency x Duration

This means stickiness takes into account the total broad audience of potential customers, the frequency with which people come back to the site, and the length of time they spend at the site.

- *Conversion.* Conversion means the moment a customer buys, signs up for a seminar, subscribes to a newsletter, and so on. Cost per conversion is a critical number to track because it tells managers how much money they are spending to get one person to buy. Companies also track the conversion rate, which means the ratio of buyers to visitors, and the average order size.

- *Retention.* Companies want people to buy again and again, so it is important to track customer retention. The online auction site e-Bay has a high retention rate, because the same people keep coming back to the site to buy and sell merchandise.

E-commerce organizations track many other metrics. Tools are gradually being developed to help managers better measure, guide, and control e-commerce companies. Advanced data warehousing and data mining tools, for example, can cross-reference Web site data in multiple dimensions to help managers get a broader, clearer picture of customer activity so they can cut costs and maximize efficiency.

SOURCES: Jim Sterne, "Making Metrics Count," *Business2.com* (April 3, 2001), 72; Matt Cutler, "Emetrics: How to Measure Stickiness," *Business2.com* (March 20, 2001), 134; Ramin Jaleshgari, "The End of the Hit Parade," *CIO* (May 15, 2000), 183–190; and Thomas H. Davenport, "Sticky Business," *CIO* (February 1, 2000), 58–60.

dependence on more labor-intensive box-office sales.[4] One issue of current concern to many managers is how to track valuable metrics for e-commerce, as discussed in the Focus on Skills box.

Organizational Control Focus

Control can focus on events before, during, or after a process. For example, a local automobile dealer can focus on activities before, during, or after sales of new cars. Careful inspection of new cars and cautious selection of sales employees are ways to ensure high quality or profitable sales even before those sales take place. Monitoring how salespeople act with customers would be considered control during the sales task. Counting the number of new cars sold during the month or telephoning buyers about their satisfaction with sales transactions would constitute control after sales have occurred. These three types of control are formally called *feedforward*, *concurrent*, and *feedback* and are illustrated in Exhibit 16.1.

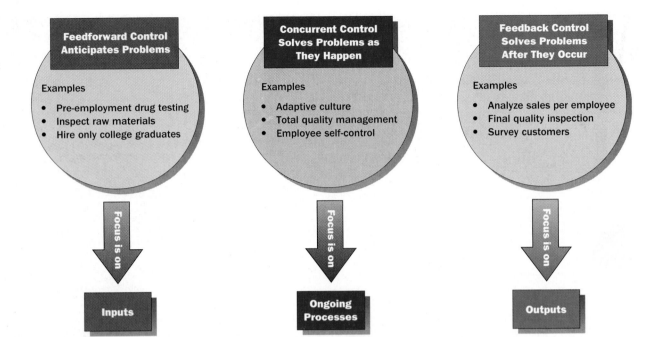

E X H I B I T 16.1

Organzational Control Focus

Feedforward Control

Control that attempts to identify and prevent deviations before they occur is called **feedforward control**. Sometimes called *preliminary* or *preventive control*, it focuses on human, material, and financial resources that flow into the organization. Its purpose is to ensure that input quality is high enough to prevent problems when the organization performs its tasks.

Feedforward controls are evident in the selection and hiring of new employees. Organizations attempt to improve the likelihood that employees will perform up to standards by identifying the necessary skills and using tests and other screening devices to hire people who have those skills. Many organizations also conduct drug screening to ensure that job candidates or employees do not impair their ability to work safely and effectively. Another type of feedforward control is to identify and manage risks. For example, banks typically require extensive documentation before approving major loans. Large accounting firms provide value to their clients by helping identify risks they have either knowingly or unknowingly taken on, rather than just evaluating financial performance after the fact.[5] Some organizations are using systems to reduce the risk of matching people together, such as in dorm rooms or for jobs, as described in the Digital, Inc. box.

Concurrent Control

Control that monitors ongoing employee activities to ensure they are consistent with performance standards is called **concurrent control**. Concurrent control assesses current work activities, relies on performance standards, and includes rules and regulations for guiding employee tasks and behaviors.

Many manufacturing operations include devices that measure whether the items being produced meet quality standards. Employees monitor the measurements; if they see that standards are not met in some area, they make a correction themselves or signal the appropriate person that a problem is occurring.

---

feedforward control

Control that focuses on human, material, and financial resources flowing into the organization; also caled *preliminary* or *preventive control*.

---

concurrent control

Control that consists of monitoring ongoing activities to ensure they are consistent with standards.

DIGITAL, INC.

Matchmaking for Dorms and Jobs

College students used to be randomly assigned roommates, and were expected to get along. Things are different now. With so many students starting college without having had the experience of sharing a bedroom, expectations are higher for the right match. University administrators are increasingly burdened with room changes when roommates don't get along. How can these problems be corrected before they occur?

As many as 1,500 colleges are letting computers do what has already been done with dating services: match up compatible pairs. Washington State University, for example, uses Cbord Group software that matches students by asking questions such as: "What is your level of interest in having intellectual discussions with your roommate?" Going a step further is the University of Texas, where a "Profiler" system allows students to learn about potential roommates online by reading their responses to a survey, and to e-mail the ones they like until they find someone they want to live with.

Colleges that use this type of software say it cuts down on dorm moves and is faster. Previously, one person would work full time for three weeks to get matches for 2,600 students at Washington State. The software does it in 18 minutes.

There are some bugs to work out in the system. North Carolina's Elon University paired up musician Will Duffy with another musician, who soon became the "roommate from hell"—staying out late, blasting Pink Floyd at all hours, and prone to throwing clothes on the floor. Another problem: Some schools report up to 25 percent of surveys are filled out by parents, who may not know all the dark secrets of their children. Even if the students fill the surveys out themselves, if they think Mom will read it, their answers will be less than honest.

Although matching roommates has uneven results in dorms, employers are having better luck. Oregon's application service provider Unicru has developed four different online employment questionnaires. The potential employee sits down at a computer at a mall for about 30 minutes, hits "send," and waits to hear from a hiring manager. Within ten minutes, the manager receives a report on the person that gives a green, yellow, or red light. Green means an automatic interview. This process has helped Unicru's customers cut the cycle time in hiring by seven days. Blockbuster has gotten it down to 72 hours and, with 4,300 hires per month, that means huge savings. Unicru's system also helped reduce employee turnover by about 30 percent. It appears that computers can, in fact, identify appropriate people.

Not bad for a matchmaking system.

SOURCES: Elizabeth Bernstein, "Matchmaking 101," *The Wall Street Journal* (August 30, 2002), W1 + W5; and Allison Overholt, "True or False, You're Hiring the Right People," *Fast Company* (February 2002), 110–114.

Technology advancements are adding to the possibilities for concurrent control in services as well. For example, retail stores such as Beall's, Sunglass Hut, and Saks use cash-register-management software to monitor cashiers' activities in real time and help prevent employee theft. Trucking companies like Schneider National and Covenant use computers to track the position of their trucks and monitor the status of deliveries.[6]

Other concurrent controls involve the ways in which organizations influence employees. An organization's cultural norms and values influence employee behavior, as do the norms of an employee's peers or work group. Concurrent control also includes self-control, through which individuals impose concurrent controls on their own behavior because of personal values and attitudes.

Feedback Control

Sometimes called *postaction* or *output control*, **feedback control** focuses on the organization's outputs—in particular, the quality of an end product or service. An example of feedback control in a manufacturing department is an intensive final inspection of a refrigerator at a General Electric assembly plant. In Kentucky, school administrators conduct feedback control by evaluating each school's performance every other year. They review reports of students' test scores as well as the school's dropout and attendance rates. The state rewards

feedback control

Control that focuses on the organization's outputs; also called *postaction* or *output control*.

schools with rising scores and brings in consultants to work with schools whose scores have fallen.[7]

Besides producing high-quality products and services, businesses need to earn a profit, and even nonprofit organizations need to operate efficiently to carry out their mission. Therefore, many feedback controls focus on financial measurements. Budgeting, for example, is a form of feedback control because managers monitor whether they have operated within their budget targets and make adjustments accordingly. Amazon.com has instituted a series of feedback controls to reach for profitability, as shown below.

Amazon.com

http://www.amazon.com

Gone are the free-wheeling days when Amazon was the darling of the dot-coms, had almost endless cash from investors, and could do no wrong. The idea was to grow big fast and figure out how to be profitable later. Well, later has arrived, and investors are tired of losses.

New employee Russell Algor, whose Massachusetts Institute of Technology Ph.D. is in quantitative productivity methods, attends numerous meetings to help Amazon start behaving like other companies: keep inventory low and shipping costs at a minimum, yet maintain customer satisfaction. That means not stocking many warehouses with different titles, which results in one customer receiving six different shipments to fulfill one order. Algor recommends getting rid of slow-selling titles, or at least only ordering them from distributors *after* the customer does. Warehouse VP Jim Miller is worried about reducing the number of items available within 24 hours. Searching for control models, the company built a computer program to calculate pretax profit on each item and then had a team spend six weeks weighing 30,000 products to come up with meaningful shipping costs.

Many such meetings and models have resulted in a list of actions to be taken for Amazon's increased productivity:

1. Eliminate unprofitable items—those that are too heavy, prone to breakage, or too bulky (such as rocks or big candleholders).

2. Improve the margin—either drop money-losing products, or get a better deal from the wholesaler, or raise prices.

3. Reduce warehouse errors—with six distribution centers, small problems can cost a lot of money, so Amazon will try new methods to increase conveyor speed or reduce packaging mix-ups.

4. Get others to do some of the work—Ingram and other distributors will ship books directly to customers.

5. Help customers to help themselves—make the Web site more self-managing, and offer more canned answers.

Harvard professor Ananth Raman says studying profitability can lead to an increase in profits of up to 19 percent. But these are difficult tactics. "There is no silver bullet," he says. "They are talking about doing the right things. But that doesn't mean they are doing them right."[8]

Feedback Control Model

All well-designed control systems involve the use of feedback to determine whether performance meets established standards. In this section, we will

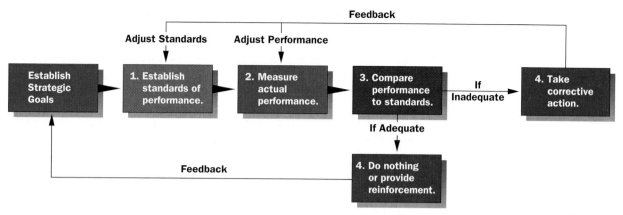

EXHIBIT 16.2

Feedback Control Model

examine the key steps in the feedback control model and then look at how the model applies to organizational budgeting.

Steps of Feedback Control

Managers set up control systems that consist of the four key steps illustrated in Exhibit 16.2: establish standards, measure performance, compare performance to standards, and make corrections as necessary.

Establish Standards of Performance. Within the organization's overall strategic plan, managers define goals for organizational departments in specific, operational terms that include a *standard of performance* against which to compare organizational activities. A standard of performance could include "reducing the reject rate from 15 to 3 percent," "increasing the corporation's return on investment to 7 percent," or "reducing the number of accidents to one per each 100,000 hours of labor."

Managers should carefully assess what they will measure and how they will define it. Especially when the organization will reward employees for the achievement of standards, these standards should reflect activities that contribute to the organization's overall strategy in a significant way. Standards should be defined clearly and precisely so that managers and workers can determine whether activities are on target.

Measure Actual Performance. Most organizations prepare formal reports of quantitative performance measurements that managers review daily, weekly, or monthly. These measurements should be related to the standards set in the first step of the control process. For example, if sales growth is a target, the organization should have a means of gathering and reporting sales data. If the organization has identified appropriate measurements, regular review of these reports helps managers stay aware of whether the organization is doing what it should be.

In most companies, managers do not rely exclusively on quantitative measures. They get out into the organization to see how things are going, especially for such goals as increasing employee participation and learning. Managers have to observe for themselves whether employees are participating in decision making and have opportunities to add to and share their knowledge.

Compare Performance to Standards. The third step in the control process is comparing actual activities to performance standards. When managers read computer reports or walk through the plant, they identify whether actual performance meets, exceeds, or falls short of standards. Typically, performance reports simplify such comparisons by placing the performance standards for the reporting period alongside the actual performance for the same period and by computing the variance—that is, the difference between each actual amount and the associated standard. To correct the problems that most require attention, managers focus on variances.

When performance deviates from a standard, managers must interpret the deviation. They are expected to dig beneath the surface and find the cause of the problem. If the sales goal is to increase the number of sales calls by 10 percent and a salesperson achieved an increase of 8 percent, where did she fail to achieve her goal? Perhaps several businesses on her route closed, additional salespeople were assigned to her area by competitors, or she needs training in making cold sales calls more effectively. Managers should take an inquiring approach to deviations in order to gain a broad understanding of factors that influenced performance. Effective management control involves subjective judgment and employee discussions, as well as objective analysis of performance data.

Take Corrective Action.   Managers also determine what changes, if any, are necessary. In a traditional top-down approach to control, managers exercise their formal authority to make necessary changes. Managers may encourage employees to work harder, redesign the production process, or fire employees. In contrast, managers using a participative control approach collaborate with employees to determine the corrective action necessary.

In some cases, managers may take corrective action to change performance standards. They may realize that standards are too high or too low if departments continually fail to meet or routinely exceed standards. If contingency factors that influence organizational performance change, performance standards may need to be altered to make them realistic and provide continued motivation for employees.

Managers may wish to provide positive reinforcement when performance meets or exceeds targets. They may reward a department that has exceeded its planned goals or congratulate employees for a job well done. Managers should not ignore high-performing departments at the expense of taking corrective actions elsewhere. The British express delivery and logistics company TNT UK provides a good illustration of the feedback control model.

TNT UK

http://www.tnt.co.uk

TNT UK's computerized management control systems track performance so regularly and in such detail that every manager is constantly aware of existing problems and every employee has the information to help correct them. TNT managers set performance targets each year and develop tight definitions of what quality service means for every aspect of the business, providing employees with clear guidelines that spell out how to make improvements.

One important measurement is customer satisfaction. When most delivery companies measure satisfaction, they simply look at whether packages are delivered on time, assuming that customers are happy when this standard is met. Not TNT—it tracks every aspect of the service it provides. One biannual customer satisfaction survey asks 4,000 randomly selected customers to rank key delivery attributes—such as reliability, price, staff professionalism, range of services, and so forth—in order of importance and to score the company's performance on each attribute. These measurements are then compared to the standards.

Far from feeling constrained by the tight measurements, employees are energized and motivated to meet performance targets. One reason is that managers are careful not to let number crunching get in the way of meeting the needs and goals of staff members. For example, Alan Jones, managing director of TNT UK, motivates van drivers with personal telephone calls or notes congratulating them when they meet or exceed standards. And low scores, rather than leading to a reprimand, bring a note encouraging the team to keep their chins up and work together with managers to determine the corrective actions needed. As Jones points out, without the data provided by computerized management information systems, he wouldn't be able to provide that level of continuous feedback to his employees.[9]

Application to Budgeting

Budgetary control, one of the most commonly used methods of managerial control, is the process of setting targets for an organization's expenditures, monitoring results and comparing them to the budget, and making changes as needed. As a control device, budgets are reports that list planned and actual expenditures for cash, assets, raw materials, salaries, and other resources. In addition, budget reports usually list the variance between the budgeted and actual amounts for each item.

A budget is created for every division or department within an organization, no matter how small, so long as it performs a distinct project, program, or function. The fundamental unit of analysis for a budget control system is called a responsibility center. A **responsibility center** is defined as any organizational department or unit under the supervision of a single person who is responsible for its activity.[10] A three-person appliance sales office in Watertown, New York, is a responsibility center, as is a quality control department, a marketing department, and General Electric's entire refrigerator manufacturing plant. The manager of each unit has budget "responsibility." Top managers use budgets for the company as a whole, and middle managers traditionally focus on the budget performance of their department or division. Budgets managers typically use expense budgets, revenue budgets, cash budgets, and capital budgets.

responsibility center
An organizational unit under the supervision of a single person who is responsible for its activity.

Expense Budget. An **expense budget** includes anticipated and actual expenses for each responsibility center and for the total organization. An expense budget may show all types of expenses or may focus on a particular category, such as materials or research and development expenses. When actual expenses exceed budgeted amounts, the difference signals the need for managers to identify whether a problem exists and take corrective action if needed. The difference may arise from inefficiency, or expenses may be higher because the organization's sales are growing faster than anticipated. Conversely, expenses below budget may signal exceptional efficiency or failure to meet some other standards, such as a desired level of sales or quality of service. Either way, expense budgets can help identify the need for further investigation but do not substitute for it.

expense budget
A budget that outlines the anticipated and actual expenses for a responsibility center.

Revenue Budget. A **revenue budget** lists forecasted and actual revenues of the organization. In general, revenues below the budgeted amount signal a need to investigate the problem to see whether the organization can improve

revenue budget
A budget that identifies the forecasted and actual revenues of the organization.

Entrepreneurs, as well as large corporations, use leveraged funds to finance their companies. Joshua Silver, a physics professor at England's Oxford University, needs $8 million for the manufacture and marketing of his glasses, which are the world's first adjustable-prescription specs. At a cost of only $10 per pair, the glasses could be a boon for the one-sixth of the world's population who are vision-impaired and cannot afford regular glasses.

cash budget

A budget that estimates and reports cash flows on a daily or weekly basis to ensure that the company has sufficient cash to meet its obligations.

capital budget

A budget that plans and reports investments in major assets to be depreciated over several years.

top-down budgeting

A budgeting process in which middle- and lower-level managers set departmental budget targets in accordance with overall company revenues and expenditures specified by top management.

bottom-up budgeting

A budgeting process in which lower-level managers budget their departments' resource needs and pass them up to top management for approval.

revenues. In contrast, revenues above budget would require determining whether the organization can obtain the necessary resources to meet the higher-than-expected demand for its products. Managers then formulate action plans to correct the budget variance.

Cash Budget. The **cash budget** estimates receipts and expenditures of money on a daily or weekly basis to ensure that an organization has sufficient cash to meet its obligations. The cash budget shows the level of funds flowing through the organization and the nature of cash disbursements. If the cash budget shows that the firm has more cash than necessary to meet short-term needs, the company can arrange to invest the excess to earn interest income. In contrast, if the cash budget shows a payroll expenditure of $20,000 coming at the end of the week but only $10,000 in the bank, the organization must borrow cash to meet the payroll.

Capital Budget. The **capital budget** lists planned investments in major assets such as buildings, heavy machinery, or complex information technology systems, often involving expenditures over more than a year. Capital expenditures not only have a large impact on future expenses, they are investments designed to enhance profits. Therefore, a capital budget is necessary to plan the impact of these expenditures on cash flow and profitability. Controlling involves not only monitoring the amount of capital expenditures but evaluating whether the assumptions made about the return on the investments are holding true. Managers should evaluate whether continuing investment in particular projects is advisable, as well as whether their procedures for making capital expenditure decisions are adequate. Some companies, including Boeing, Merck, Shell, United Technologies, and Whirlpool, evaluate capital projects at several stages to determine whether they still are in line with the company's strategy.[11]

Budgeting is an important part of organizational planning and control. Many traditional companies use **top-down budgeting**, which means that the budgeted amounts for the coming year are literally imposed on middle and lower-level managers.[12] These managers set departmental budget targets in accordance with overall company revenues and expenditures specified by top executives. Although there are some advantages to the top-down process, the movement toward employee empowerment, participation, and learning means that many organizations are adopting **bottom-up budgeting**, a process in which lower-level managers anticipate their departments' resource needs and pass them up to top management for approval.[13]

Budgeting is part of financial control, which can lead to sound financial footing. Other financial controls can indicate performance problems. For example, a sales decline may signal problems with products or customer service. In small start-ups, a frequent problem is too much success, which then requires the application of budgeting and financial controls to avoid complete breakdown, as described in the Focus on Skills box.

FOCUS ON SKILLS

Buckeye Beans & Herbs

Doug and Jill Smith had more success than they could handle. Their small Spokane, Washington, specialty food company was growing at an exponential rate for much of the 1990s. In one year alone, it grew 50 percent. But the work was so intense, they "got a hangover" from the rapid growth, and started to see increased revenues but declining profits.

Core customers were department stores, gourmet retailers and upscale grocery stores, but Buckeye Beans & Herbs started to sell to mass marketers and saw big volumes but low profit margins. Plus, there was increasing competition from the "big guys"—such as Quaker Oats and Hormel Foods. They refocused on core markets and let the big customers go. Revenues ultimately went down, but profits were up again.

They learned the truth of the saying "You can have too much of a good thing," and knew they had expanded their market past its optimal growth. The growth was too rapid and chaos prevailed: It became apparent when Buckeye moved into a larger facility and the Smiths found they were not running a little mom-and-pop business anymore. "We realized we needed people to take the order, to fill the order, to package the product, and so on," says Doug. Needing more control and structure than they were used to providing, the company was in crisis. "We just couldn't do it all, as we had done in the past, and we didn't have the people in place yet."

The Smiths were smart enough to realize they were in over their heads, so they hired a consultant (whom they referred to as a "pro-sultant," which Jills feels is not as negative as "consultant"). They now had an advisor who helped them look at the company's strengths and weaknesses, as well as providing ideas to restructure Buckeye and improve communications.

At first they resisted the advice of hiring a chief financial officer (CFO), because Doug was so good with numbers. But finally they succumbed, and now Jill says, "One of the smartest things we did was hire a CFO," who provided them with even more useful financial information (after all, that is a CFOs business) and improved their cash-flow management.

Even so, Buckeye became a little too secure in its growth and forgot to innovate, which caused sales to slow. In 1999, the Smiths sold out and the company lost its direction even further, with disastrous results.

The lessons entrepreneuers need to learn are: keep the focus, innovate, hire to delegate, and say "no" to certain customers. But as one business founder said, "Growth manages you if you let it. The challenge is to manage the growth."

SOURCE: "Jill & Doug Smith: Buckeye Beans," *Small Business School* (PBS, 2000); Kim Crompton, "Buckeye Beans Slashes Staff, Changes Direction," *Journal of Business* (March 11, 1999), A5; Sharon Nelton, "Coming to Grips with Growth," *Nation's Business* (February 1998), 26–32.

The Changing Philosophy of Control

Managers' approach to control is changing in many of today's organizations. In connection with the shift to employee participation and empowerment, many companies are adopting a *decentralized* rather than a *bureaucratic* control process. Bureaucratic control and decentralized control represent different philosophies of corporate culture, which was discussed in Chapter 2. Most organizations display some aspects of both bureaucratic and decentralized control, but managers generally emphasize one or the other, depending on the organizational culture and their own beliefs about control.

Bureaucratic control involves monitoring and influencing employee behavior through extensive use of rules, policies, hierarchy of authority, written documentation, reward systems, and other formal mechanisms.[14] In contrast, **decentralized control** relies on cultural values, traditions, shared beliefs, and trust to foster compliance with organizational goals. Managers operate on the assumption that employees are trustworthy and willing to perform effectively without extensive rules and close supervision.

Exhibit 16.3 contrasts the use of bureaucratic and decentralized methods of control. Bureaucratic methods define explicit rules, policies, and procedures for employee behavior. Control relies on centralized authority, the formal hierarchy, and close personal supervision. Responsibility for quality control rests

bureaucratic control

The use of rules, policies, hierarchy of authority, reward systems, and other formal devices to influence employee behavior and assess performance.

decentralized control

The use of organizational culture, group norms, and a focus on goals, rather than rules and procedures, to foster compliance with organziational goals.

*Bureaucratic and Decentralized
Methods of Control*

Bureaucratic Control	Decentralized Control
Uses detailed rules and procedures; formal control systems	Limited use of rules; relies on values, group and self-control, selection and socialization
Top-down authority, formal hierarchy, position power, quality control inspectors	Flexible authority, flat structure, expert power, everyone monitors quality
Task-related job descriptions; measurable standards define minimum performance	Results-based job descriptions; emphasis on goals to be achieved
Emphasis on extrinsic rewards (pay, benefits, status)	Extrinsic and intrinsic rewards (meaningful work, opportunities for growth)
Rewards given for meeting individual performance standards	Rewards individual and team; emphasis on equity across employees
Limited, formalized employee participation (e.g., grievance procedures)	Broad employee participation, including quality control, system design, and organizational governance
Rigid organizational culture; distrust of cultural norms as means of control	Adaptive culture; culture recognized as means for uniting individual, team, and organizational goals for overall control

SOURCES: Based on Richard E. Walton, "From Control to Commitment in the Workplace," *Harvard Business Review* (March–April 1985), 76–84; and Don Hellriegel, Susan E. Jackson, and John W. Slocum, Jr., *Management*, 8th ed. (Cincinnati, Ohio: South-Western College Publishing, 1999), 663.

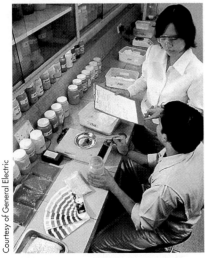

Courtesy of General Electric

For more than a decade, managers at General Electric have been dedicated to decentralized control through a program called "Work Out." Work Out is an ongoing effort to achieve what former CEO Jack Welch called "boundaryless behavior"—behavior that "ends all barriers of rank, function, geography, and bureaucracy in an endless pursuit of the best idea." With boundaries diminished, GE launched Six Sigma, a disciplined methodology that focuses on quality for every process that affects the GE customer. Cindy Lee and S. Mani were part of a Six Sigma team at the color lab of the GE Plastics plant in Singapore. The team reduced the lead time for matching colors of GE resins to customer requirements by 85 percent, providing a distinct competitive advantage in the fast-paced global market for plastics.

with quality control inspectors and supervisors rather than with employees. Job descriptions generally are specific and task related, and managers define minimal standards for acceptable employee performance. In exchange for meeting the standards, individual employees are given extrinsic rewards such as wages, benefits, and possibly promotions up the hierarchy. Employees rarely participate in the control process, with any participation being formalized through mechanisms such as grievance procedures. With bureaucratic control, the organizational culture is somewhat rigid, and managers do not consider culture a useful means of controlling employees and the organization. Technology often is used to control the flow and pace of work or to monitor employees, such as by measuring how long employees spend on phone calls or how many keystrokes they make at the computer.

Bureaucratic control techniques can enhance organizational efficiency and effectiveness. Many employees appreciate a system that clarifies what is expected of them, and they may be motivated by challenging, but achievable, goals.[15] However, although many managers effectively use bureaucratic control, too much control can backfire. Employees resent being watched too closely, and they may try to sabotage the control system. One veteran truck driver expressed his unhappiness with electronic monitoring to a *Wall Street Journal* reporter investigating the use of devices that monitor truck locations. According to the driver, "It's getting worse and worse all the time. Pretty soon they'll want to put a chip in the drivers' ears and make them robots." He added that he occasionally escapes the relentless monitoring by parking under an overpass to take a needed nap out of the range of the surveillance satellites.[16]

Decentralized control is based on values and assumptions that are almost opposite to those of bureaucratic control. Rules and procedures are used only when necessary. Managers rely instead on shared goals and values to control employee behavior. The organization places great emphasis on the selection and socialization of employees to ensure that workers have the appropriate values needed to influence behavior toward meeting company goals. No organization can control employees 100 percent of the time, and self-discipline and self-control are what keep workers performing their jobs up to standard. Empowerment of employees, effective socialization, and training all can contribute to internal standards that provide self-control.

With decentralized control, power is more dispersed and is based on knowledge and experience as much as position. The organizational structure is flat and horizontal, as discussed in Chapter 7, with flexible authority and teams of workers solving problems and making improvements. Everyone is involved in quality control on an ongoing basis. Job descriptions generally are results-based, with an emphasis more on the outcomes to be achieved than on the specific tasks to be performed. Managers use not only extrinsic rewards such as pay, but the intrinsic rewards of meaningful work and the opportunity to learn and grow. Technology is used to empower employees by giving them the information they need to make effective decisions, work together, and solve problems. People are rewarded for team and organizational success as well as their individual performance, and there is an emphasis on equity among employees. Employees participate in a wide range of areas, including setting goals, determining standards of performance, governing quality, and designing control systems.

With decentralized control, the culture is adaptive, and managers recognize the importance of organizational culture for uniting individual, team, and organizational goals for greater overall control. Ideally, with decentralized control, employees will pool their areas of expertise to arrive at procedures that are better than managers could come up with working alone.

Managing Productivity

Productivity is significant because it influences the well-being of the entire society as well as of individual companies. The only way to increase the output of goods and services to society is to increase organization productivity.

Measuring Productivity

What is productivity, and how is it measured? In simple terms, **productivity** is the organization's output of goods and services divided by its inputs. This means that productivity can be improved by either increasing the amount of output using the same level of inputs or reducing the number of inputs required to produce the output. Sometimes a company can even do both. Ruggieri & Sons, for example, invested in mapping software to help it plan deliveries of heating fuel. The software plans the most efficient routes based on the locations of customers and fuel reloading terminals, as well as the amount of fuel each customer needs. When Ruggieri switched from planning routes by hand to using the software, its drivers began driving fewer miles but making 7 percent more stops each day—in others words, burning less fuel in order to sell more fuel.[17]

The accurate measure of productivity can be complex. Two approaches for measuring productivity are total factor productivity and partial productivity. **Total factor productivity** is the ratio of total outputs to the inputs from labor, capital, materials, and energy:

productivity
The organization's output of products and services divided by its inputs.

total factor productivity
The ratio of total outputs to the inputs from labor, capital, materials, and energy.

$$\text{Total factor productivity} = \frac{Output}{Labor + Capital + Materials + Energy}$$

Total factor productivity represents the best measure of how the organization is doing. Often, however, managers need to know about productivity with respect

Harley-Davidson Motor Company is using capacity planning to keep pace with the growing, worldwide demand for its high-quality motorcycles. As the only major American-based motorcycle manufacturer, Harley-Davidson has brand names that are among the best known in the industry. All three of the company's manufacturing facilities have been extensively redesigned and reconfigured to improve productivity, work-flow, product quality, and the environment. Facilities such as this recently completed touring-motorcycle assembly line in York, Pennsylvania, have put Harley-Davidson a full year ahead in its production schedule, and the company plans to have the capacity to produce 115,000 units a year.

© James Schnepf

partial productivity

The ratio of total outputs to the inputs from a single major input category.

to certain inputs. **Partial productivity** is the ratio of total outputs to a major category of inputs. For example, many organizations are interested in labor productivity, which would be measured as follows:

$$\text{Labor Productivity} = \frac{Output}{Labor\ dollars}$$

Calculating this formula for labor, capital, or materials provides information on whether improvements in each element are occurring. However, managers often are criticized for relying too heavily on partial productivity measures, especially direct labor.[18] Measuring direct labor misses the valuable improvements in materials, manufacturing processes, and work quality. Labor productivity is easily measured, but may show an increase as a result of capital improvements. Thus, managers will misinterpret the reason for productivity increases.

Total Quality Management

total quality management

An organizationwide commitment to infusing quality into every activity through continuous improvement.

One popular approach based on a decentralized control philosophy is **total quality management (TQM)**, an organizationwide effort to infuse quality into every activity in a company through continuous improvement. TQM became attractive to U.S. managers in the 1980s because it had been successfully implemented by Japanese companies that were gaining market share—and an international reputation for high quality. The Japanese system was based on the work of such U.S. researchers and consultants as Deming, Juran, and Feigenbaum, whose ideas attracted U.S. executives after the methods were tested overseas.[19]

The TQM philosophy focuses on teamwork, increasing customer satisfaction, and lowering costs. Organizations implement TQM by encouraging managers and employees to collaborate across functions and departments, as well as with customers and suppliers, to identify areas for improvement, no matter how small. Each quality improvement is a step toward perfection, and meeting a goal of zero defects. Quality control becomes part of the day-to-day business of every employee, rather than being assigned to specialized departments.

The implementation of total quality management is similar to that of other decentralized control methods. Feedforward controls include training employees to think in terms of prevention, not detection, of problems and giving them the responsibility and power to correct errors, expose problems, and contribute to solutions. Concurrent controls include an organizational culture and employee commitment that favor total quality and employee participation. Feedback controls include targets for employee involvement and for zero defects.

TQM Techniques

The implementation of total quality management involves the use of many techniques, including quality circles, benchmarking, six sigma principles, reduced cycle time, and continuous improvement.

Quality Circles. One approach to implementing the decentralized approach of TQM is to use quality circles. A **quality circle** is a group of 6 to 12 volunteer employees who meet regularly to discuss and solve problems affecting the quality of their work.[20] At a set time during the workweek, the members of the quality circle meet, identify problems, and try to find solutions. Circle members are free to collect data and take surveys. Many companies train team members in team building, problem solving, and statistical quality control. The reason for using quality circles is to push decision making to an organization level at which recommendations can be made by the people who do the job and know it better than anyone else.

quality circle
A group of 6 to 12 volunteer employees who meet regularly to discuss and solve problems affecting the quality of their work.

Benchmarking. Introduced by Xerox in 1979, benchmarking is now a major TQM component. **Benchmarking** is defined as "the continuous process of measuring products, services, and practices against the toughest competitors or those companies recognized as industry leaders."[21] The key to successful benchmarking lies in analysis. Starting with its own mission statement, a company should honestly analyze its current procedures and determine areas for improvement. As a second step, a company *carefully* selects competitors worthy of copying. For example, Xerox studied the order fulfillment techniques of L. L. Bean and learned ways to reduce warehouse costs by 10 percent. Companies can emulate internal processes and procedures of competitors, but must take care to select companies whose methods are compatible. Once a strong, compatible program is found and analyzed, the benchmarking company can then devise a strategy for implementing a new program.

benchmarking
The continuous process of measuring products, services, and practices against major competitors or industry leaders.

Six Sigma. Six sigma quality principles were first introduced by Motorola, which started on a quality path in the mid-1980s, and were later popularized by General Electric, where former CEO Jack Welch regularly praised six sigma for quality and efficiency gains that saved the company billions of dollars. Based on the Greek letter *sigma*, which statisticians use to measure how far something deviates from perfection, **six sigma** is a highly ambitious quality standard that specifies a goal of no more than 3.4 defects per million parts. That essentially means being defect-free 99.9997 percent of the time.[22] However, six sigma has deviated from its precise definition to become a generic term for a quality-control approach that takes nothing for granted and emphasizes a

six sigma
A quality control approach that emphasizes a relentless pursuit of higher quality and lower costs.

disciplined and relentless pursuit of higher quality and lower costs. The discipline is based on a methodology referred to as *DMAIC* (Define, Measure, Analyze, Improve, and Control), which provides a structured way for organizations to approach and solve problems.[23]

General Electric has applied six sigma to almost every aspect of its business, from improving products, to increasing customer satisfaction, to fine-tuning delivery processes. For example, the company used six sigma methodologies and measurements to determine the best way to set up a Web-based system to arrange delivery of GE appliances bought at Home Depot. Six sigma helped managers determine that customers cared less about issues such as evening or Sunday delivery and more about having delivery personnel and installers who were knowledgeable, professional, and caring. Thus, GE invested heavily in training rather than costly changes in delivery schedules.[24] Other well-known companies that have embarked on six sigma programs include Ford Motor Company, Dow Chemical, DuPont, Nokia, Texas Instruments, and Merck.[25]

Reduced Cycle Time. In the book *Quality Alone Is Not Enough*, the authors refer to cycle time as the "drivers of improvement." **Cycle time** refers to the steps taken to complete a company process, such as teaching a class, publishing a textbook, or designing a new car. The simplification of work cycles, including the dropping of barriers between work steps and among departments and the removal of worthless steps in the process, enables a TQM program to succeed. Even if an organization decides not to use quality circles or other techniques, substantial improvement is possible by focusing on improved responsiveness and acceleration of activities into a shorter time. Reduction in cycle time improves overall company performance as well as quality.[26]

L. L. Bean, Inc., the Freeport, Maine, mail-order firm, is a recognized leader in cycle time control. Workers used flowcharts to track their movements, pinpoint wasted motions, completely redesign the order-fulfillment process. Today, a computerized system breaks down an order based on the geographic area of the warehouse in which items are stored. Items are placed on conveyor belts, where electronic sensors re-sort the items for individual orders. After orders are packed, they are sent to a FedEx facility on site. Improvements such as these have enabled L. L. Bean to process most orders within two hours after the order is received.[27]

Continuous Improvement. In North America, crash programs and designs have traditionally been the preferred method of innovation. Managers measure the expected benefits of a change and favor the ideas with the biggest payoffs. In contrast, Japanese companies have realized extraordinary success from making a series of mostly small improvements. This approach, called **continuous improvement**, is the implementation of a large number of small, incremental improvements in all areas of the organization on an ongoing basis. In a successful TQM program, all employees learn that they are expected to contribute by initiating changes in their own job activities. The basic philosophy is that improving things a little bit at a time, all the time, has the highest probability of success. Innovations can start simple, and employees can build on their success in this unending process.

TQM Success Factors

Despite its promise, total quality management does not always work. A few firms have had disappointing results. In particular, six sigma principles might

cycle time
The steps taken to complete a company process.

continuous improvement
The implementation of a large number of small, incremental improvements in all areas of the organization on an ongoing basis.

Positive Factors	Negative Factors
• Tasks make high skill demands on employees.	• Management expectations are unrealistically high.
• TQM serves to enrich jobs and motivate employees.	• Middle managers are dissatisfied about loss of authority.
• Problem-solving skills are improved for all employees.	• Workers are dissatisfied with other aspects of organizational life.
• Participation and teamwork are used to tackle significant problems.	• Union leaders are left out of QC discussions.
• Continuous improvement is a way of life.	• Managers wait for big, dramatic innovations.

EXHIBIT *16.4*

Quality Program Success Factors

not be appropriate for all organizational problems, and some companies have expended tremendous energy and resources for little payoff.[28] Many contingency factors (listed in Exhibit 16.4) can influence the success of a TQM program. For example, quality circles are most beneficial when employees have challenging jobs; participation in a quality circle can contribute to productivity because it enables employees to pool their knowledge and solve interesting problems. TQM also tends to be most successful when it enriches jobs and improves employee motivation. In addition, when participating in the quality program improves workers' problem-solving skills, productivity is likely to increase. Finally, a quality program has the greatest chance of success in a corporate culture that values quality and stresses continuous improvement as a way of life.

Trends in Quality and Financial Control

Many companies are responding to changing economic realities and global competition by reassessing organizational management and processes—including control mechanisms. Some of the major trends in quality and financial control include international quality standards, economic value-added and market value-added systems, and activity-based costing.

International Quality Standards

One impetus for total quality management in the United States is the increasing significance of the global economy. Many countries have endorsed a universal framework for quality assurance called **ISO 9000**, a set of international standards for quality management systems established by the International Organization for Standardization in 1987 and revised in late 2000.[29] By the end of 1999, more than 340,000 organization in 150 countries, including the United States, had been certified to demonstrate their commitment to quality. Europe continues to lead in the total number of ISO 9000 certifications, but the greatest number of new certifications in recent years have been in the United States. ISO 9000 has become the recognized standard for evaluating and comparing companies on a global basis, and more U.S. companies are feeling the pressure to participate in order to remain competitive in international markets. In addition, many countries and companies require ISO 9000 certification before they will do business with an organization.

ISO 9000

A set of international standards for quality management, setting uniform guidelines for processes to ensure that products conform to customer requirements.

New Financial Control Systems

In addition to traditional financial tools, managers in many organizations are using systems such as economic value added, market value added, and activity-based costing to provide effective financial control.

economic value added (EVA) system

A control system that measures performance in terms of after-tax profits minus the cost of capital invested in tangible assets.

Economic Value Added (EVA). Hundreds of companies, including AT&T, Quaker Oats, the Coca-Cola Company, and Philips Petroleum Company, have set up **economic value added (EVA)** measurement systems as a new way to gauge financial performance. EVA can be defined as a company's net (after-tax) operating profit minus the cost of capital invested in the company's tangible assets.[30] Measuring performance in terms of EVA is intended to capture all the things a company can do to add value from its activities, such as run the business more efficiently, satisfy customers, and reward shareholders. Each job, department, or process in the organization is measured by the value added.

market value added (MVA) system

A control system that measures the stock market's estimate of the value of a company's past and expected capital investment projects.

Market Value Added (MVA). Market value added (MVA) adds another dimension because it measures the stock market's estimate of the value of a company's past and projected capital investment projects. For example, when a company's market value (the value of all outstanding stock plus the company's debt) is greater than all the capital invested in it from shareholders, bondholders, and retained earnings, the company has a positive MVA, an indication that it has created wealth. A positive MVA usually goes hand-in-hand with a high EVA measurement.[31]

activity-based costing (ABC)

A control system that identifies the various activities needed to provide a product and allocates costs accordingly.

Activity-Based Costing (ABC). Managers measure the cost of producing goods and services so they can be sure they are selling those products for more than the cost to produce them. Traditional methods of costing assign costs to various departments or functions, such as purchasing, manufacturing, human resources, and so on. With a shift to more horizontal, flexible organizations has come a new approach called **activity-based costing** (ABC), which allocates costs across business processes. ABC attempts to identify all the various activities needed to provide a product or service and allocate costs accordingly. For example, an activity-based costing system might list the costs associated with processing orders for a particular product, scheduling production for that product, producing it, shipping it, and resolving problems with it. Because ABC allocates costs across business processes, it provides a more accurate picture of the cost of various products and services.[32] In addition, it enables managers to evaluate whether more costs go to activities that add value (meeting customer deadlines, achieving high quality) or to activities that do not add value (such as processing internal paperwork). They can then focus on reducing costs associated with non–value-added activities.

Control in the New Workplace

Changing organizational structures and the resulting management methods that emphasize information sharing, employee participation, learning, and teamwork have led to some new approaches to control in today's workplace. Two significant aspects of control in the new workplace are open-book management and use of the balanced scorecard.

Open-Book Management

In an organizational environment that touts information sharing, teamwork, and the role of managers as facilitators, executives cannot hoard financial data. They must admit employees throughout the organization into the loop of financial control and responsibility to encourage active participation and commitment to organizational goals. A growing number of managers are opting for full disclosure in the form of open-book management. **Open-book management** allows employees to see for themselves—through charts, computer printouts, meetings, and so forth—the financial condition of the company. Second, open-book management shows the individual employee how his or her job fits into the big picture and affects the financial future of the organization. Finally, open-book management ties employee rewards to the company's overall success. With training in interpreting the financial data, employees can see the interdependence and importance of each function. If they are rewarded according to performance, they become motivated to take responsibility for their entire team or function, rather than merely their individual jobs.[33] Cross-functional communication and cooperation are also enhanced.

The goal of open-book management is to get every employee thinking and acting like a business owner rather than like a hired hand. To get employees to think like owners, management provides them with the same information owners have: what money is coming in and where it is going. Open-book management helps employees appreciate why efficiency is important to the organization's success. Open-book management turns traditional control on its head. This chapter's Best Practices box describes how Ricardo Semler runs a successful company by being an "anti-control" freak.

open-book management

Sharing financial information and results with all employees in the organization.

BEST PRACTICES

Semco's Open Book Policy

When Ricardo Semler took over from his father as head of the family business, Brazil's Semco, he decided to manage based on a philosophy of "giving up control" by having faith in people and respect for their ideas. At Semco, employees have no set work schedules, no dress codes, no strict rules and regulations, and no employee manuals. About 30 percent of employees even set their own pay, and everyone in the company knows everyone else's salary. All workers receive the company's financial statements and are taught how to read them through classes set up by the labor union. Board meetings are open to all employees who want to attend. Self-managed teams have replaced the management hierarchy, and people have a chance to choose what they want to do based on how they can best make a contribution to the company. Top managers are voted in and evaluated on a regular basis by employees—with the outcomes posted for all to see.

The idea that ties all this together is Semler's belief in taking top management out of running the business, which led *Fortune* magazine to give him the title of "anti–control freak." Semler believes that if an organization gives people complete freedom and full information, they will act in their own, and consequently the company's, best interests. "It is only when you rein them in, when you tell them what to do and how to think, that they become inflexible, bureaucratic, and stagnant," says Semler. Despite all the freedom, organizational control at Semco is quite strong, based not on power and authority but on organizational vision and cultural values that emphasize self-initiative, self-control, and full disclosure of all types of information. Employees think like business owners because they can see how their jobs and actions fit in and contribute to the organization's—and their own—success or failure.

The approach must be working. In the past ten years, Semco has quadrupled its revenues and increased its workforce from 450 to 1,300 employees. Semler believes his company's success is a powerful reminder that it is possible to have an efficient business without strict rules and controls, guided by managers who lead rather than wield their power.

SOURCES: Geoffrey Colvin, "The Anti-Control Freak," *Fortune* (November 26, 2001), 60, 80; and Ricardo Semler, "How We Went Digital Without a Strategy," *Harvard Business Review* (September/October 2000), 51–58.

The Balanced Scorecard

Another recent innovation is to integrate the various dimensions of control, combining internal financial measurements and statistical reports with a concern for markets and customers as well as employees.[34] Whereas many managers once focused primarily on measuring and controlling financial performance, they are increasingly recognizing the need to evaluate other aspects of organizational performance to assess the value-creating activities of the contemporary organization.[35]

One fresh approach is the balanced scorecard. The **balanced scorecard** is a comprehensive management control system that balances traditional financial measures with operational measures relating to a company's critical success factors.[36] A balanced scorecard contains four major perspectives, as illustrated in Exhibit 16.5: financial performance, customer service, internal business processes, and the organization's capacity for learning and growth.[37] Within these four areas, managers identify key performance metrics the organization will track. The *financial perspective* reflects a concern that the organization's activities contribute to improving short- and long-term financial performance. It includes traditional measures such as net income and return on investment.

balanced scorecard

A comprehensive management control system that balances traditional financial measures with measures of customer service, internal business processes, and the organization's capacity for learning and growth.

EXHIBIT **16.5**

The Balanced Scorecard

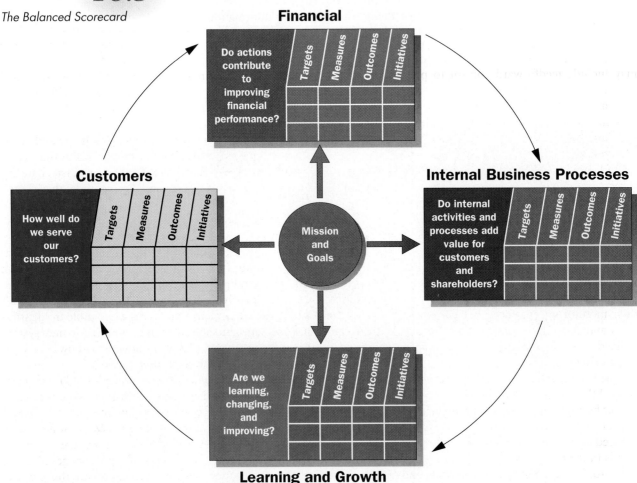

SOURCES: Based on Robert S. Kaplan and David P. Norton, "Using the Balanced Scorecard as a Strategic Management System," *Harvard Business Review* (January–February 1996), 75–85; and Chee W. Chow, Kamal M. Haddad, and James E. Williamson, "Applying the Balanced Scorecard to Small Companies," *Management Accounting* 79, no. 2 (August 1997), 21–27.

Customer service indicators measure such things as how customers view the organization, as well as customer retention and satisfaction. *Business process* indicators focus on production and operating statistics, such as order fulfillment or cost per order. The final component looks at the organization's *potential for learning and growth*, focusing on how well resources and human capital are being managed for the company's future. Metrics may include such things as employee retention, business process improvements, and the introduction of new products. The components of the scorecard are designed in an integrative manner, as illustrated in Exhibit 16.5. The balanced scorecard helps managers focus on key performance measures and communicate them clearly throughout the organization. The scorecard has become the core management control system for many organizations today. Well-known companies using the system include Bell Emergis (a division of Bell Canada), Mobil Oil Corp., AT&T Canada, and Cigna Insurance.[38]

■ Summary and Management Solution

This chapter introduced a number of important concepts about organizational control. Organizational control is the systematic process through which managers regulate organizational activities to meet planned goals and standards of performance. The focus of the control system may include feedforward control to prevent problems, concurrent control to monitor ongoing activities, and feedback control to evaluate past performance. Well-designed control systems include four key steps: establish standards, measure performance, compare performance to standards, and make corrections as necessary.

Budgeting is one of the most commonly used forms of managerial control. Managers might use expense budgets, revenue budgets, cash budgets, and capital budgets, for example. Other financial controls include use of the balance sheet, income statement, and financial analysis of these documents.

The philosophy of controlling has shifted to reflect changes in leadership methods. Traditional bureaucratic controls emphasized establishing rules and procedures, then monitoring employee behavior to make sure the rules and procedures have been followed. With decentralized control, employees assume responsibility for monitoring their own performance.

Besides monitoring financial results, organizations control the quality of their goods and services. They may do this by adopting total quality management (TQM) techniques such as quality circles, benchmarking, six sigma, reduced cycle time, and continuous improvement. Recent trends in control include the use of international quality standards, economic-value added (EVA) and market-value added (MVA) systems, and activity-based costing. Other important aspects of control in the new workplace are open-book management and use of the balanced scorecard.

The story of Latt-Greene, detailed at the beginning of the chapter, demonstrates the importance of control. Latt-Greene had huge problems of negative cash flow and ineffective billing system. Controller Richard Snyder knew everyone had to be included in decisions for changing the system. Even though he knew what needed to be done, Snyder realized the workers could add new perspective and ask important questions. After all, they knew the operation best.

During the process of change, Snyder talked to as many people as he could, soliciting ideas. But there were a few employees who were dead-set against changing "the way we've always done it." He had to let them know that the new system would be installed and they needed to learn it. Gradually, everyone came on board.

In order to get the very best system for Latt-Greene, Snyder talked to everyone inside and outside the company who was involved in the process of converting yarn into dyed and printed textiles. He looked at every piece of paper involved with the process during a past month and involved as many employees as possible in identifying problems and solutions. By the time the new system was developed, the employees already had ownership of it and the transition was relatively smooth.

The cost of the new system was $150,000, but Latt-Greene has saved that many times over. No downsizing occurred. The company has roughly the same number of staff, but now they know what comes in, what it is made into, and where it goes, and all invoices are collected. Snyder attributes the success of the change to three methods: be open with employees about the change; involve as many of them as possible in the change process; and know the new process thoroughly yourself, so that you don't have to rely as much on consultants.[39]

■ Discussion Questions

1. Why is it important for managers to understand the process of organizational control?
2. How might a public school system use feedforward control to identify the best candidates for its teaching positions?
3. Can you give examples of feedback control that might be used in a family-style restaurant? In a large hospital?
4. What standards of performance has your professor established for this class? How will your actual performance be measured? How will your performance be compared to the standards? Do you think the standards and methods of measurement are fair? Why or why not?
5. In what ways could a university benefit from bureaucratic control? In what ways might it benefit from decentralized control? Overall, which approach do you think would be best at your college or university? Why?
6. Why is benchmarking an important component of total quality management (TQM) programs? Do you believe a company could have a successful TQM program without using benchmarking?
7. How might activity-based costing provide better financial control tools for managers of a company such as Kellogg that produces numerous food products?
8. Why do you think today's managers would want to use the balanced scorecard to measure and control organizational performance?

■ Manager's Workbook

Is Your Budget in Control?

By the time you are in college, you are in charge of at least some of your own finances. How well you manage your personal budget may indicate how well you will manage your company's budget on the job. Respond to the following statements to evaluate your own budgeting habits. If the statement doesn't apply directly to you, respond the way you think you would behave in a similar situation.

1. I spend all my money as soon as I get it.	Yes	No
2. At the beginning of each week (or month, or term), I write down all my fixed expenses.	Yes	No
3. I never seem to have any money left over at the end of the week (or month).	Yes	No
4. I pay all my expenses, but I never seem to have any money left over for fun.	Yes	No
5. I am not putting any money away in savings right now; I'll wait until after I graduate from college.	Yes	No
6. I can't pay all my bills.	Yes	No
7. I have a credit card, but I pay the balance in full each month.	Yes	No

8. I take cash advances on my credit card.	Yes	No
9. I know how much I can spend on eating out, movies, and other entertainment each week.	Yes	No
10. I pay cash for everything.	Yes	No
11. When I buy something, I look for value and determine the best buy.	Yes	No
12. I lend money to friends whenever they ask, even if it leaves me short of cash.	Yes	No
13. I never borrow money from friends.	Yes	No
14. I am putting aside money each month to save for something that I really need.	Yes	No

Yes responses to statements 2, 9, 10, 13, and 14 point to the most disciplined budgeting habits; **yes** responses to 4, 5, 7, and 11 reveal adequate budgeting habits; **yes** responses to 1, 3, 6, 8, and 12 indicate the poorest budgeting habits. If you have answered honestly, chances are you'll have a combination of all three. Look to see where you can improve your budgeting.

■ Manager's Workshop

Organizational Control Mechanisms

1. Divide into groups of 5–6 members.
2. Each group examines the following university request form for a complimentary parking pass and identifies flaws with the design of the form.

3. After identifying basic design flaws, groups then answer the following questions:
   a. *Is the control cost-effective?* Are the costs associated with the control mechanism offset by the benefits derived?

b. *Is the control acceptable?* Do the people affected believe it is necessary?

c. *Is the control appropriate?* Are the steps involved commensurate with the activity?

d. *Is the process strategic?* Is it a critical activity in the operation of the university?

e. *Is the control reliable and effective?* Is it clear what criteria are necessary for the approval of the request and what will be construed as sufficient justification?

Request for Complimentary Campus Parking Permits

Requesting Department:	Person Requesting:
Phone:	Event:
Date(s):	Time(s):
Number of Persons for Event:	Number of Permits Requested:
Permits Mailed:	Justification for Waived Fee:
Dean Signature	Vice-President Signature
Approve: _____	Approve: _____
Disapprove: _____	Disapprove: _____

SOURCE: H. Eugene Baker III and Kenneth M. Jennings (1994). "An Out-of-Control Organizational Control Mechanism." *Journal of Management Education*, Vol. 18 (no. 3), 380–384. Reprinted by permission of Sage Publications.

■ Management in Practice: Ethical Dilemma

Go Along to Get Along?

As the home health care industry began to take off, Rhonda Gilchrist was presented with a terrific opportunity: a start-up home health care agency offered her a position managing its staff of visiting nurses. She supported home health care because patients were treated in the relaxed, comfortable atmosphere of their homes; home visits gave patients and nurses more independence; and home visits were intended to be much cheaper than hospital stays or doctor's office visits.

Most of the patients treated by Gilchrist's nurses were elderly, with a variety of complaints ranging from diabetes to hip injuries. At first, Gilchrist encouraged her staff to make their visits efficient and productive so that patients could be weaned from care in a timely manner. However, when she reported that one patient had recovered enough from a heart attack that he no longer needed three visits a week, the agency owner replied, "You should be looking for ways to increase the number of visits, not decrease them!" Gilchrist was shocked, but she soon understood that the only way to keep her job—and her nurses' jobs—was to go along with her company's wishes. Those extra visits, paid for by Medicare, were paying her salary.

Meanwhile, Gilchrist did some research on her own. She learned that the average home-care patient now gets 80 visits per year (nearly four times the number of a decade ago), for which Medicare pays up to $90 per visit. Rhonda knows home health care is extremely important to many patients, but she also realizes it is being abused by others, as well as by the agencies.

As she drove to the office, Rhonda considered her alternatives. She knew that some of her clients no longer needed care. But she also knew that she needed a job, and most patients were lonely and looked forward to the nurses' visits. She wondered if there was a better way to control costs and deliver the best care to her patients.

What Do You Do?

1. Go along with the status quo and forget about the abuses of the system—that's your boss's problem. Besides, Medicare has deep pockets.

2. Look for another job as soon as possible. You don't want to be associated with unethical, and potentially illegal, practices.

3. Approach the owner of the agency and suggest other ways the agency might make a profit and deliver high-quality care, such as innovative ways to attract new clients to replace those who leave the roster in better health.

SOURCE: Based on George Anders and Laurie McGinley, "Medical Morass: How Do You Tame a Wild U.S. Program?" *The Wall Street Journal* (March 6, 1997), A1, A8.

■ Surf the Net

1. **National Quality Award.** The Malcolm Baldrige National Quality Improvement Act of 1987 launched a national quality award program in the United States to help improve quality and productivity. This award helps to stimulate American companies to improve quality and productivity, recognizes the achievements of outstanding companies, provides an example to other organizations, establishes guidelines and criteria that can be widely used, and makes available to other organizations detailed information on how winning organizations were able to achieve outstanding quality. Go to *http://www.quality.nist.gov/* and find information to help you answer the following questions:
   a. In what three areas does the Baldrige National Quality Award (BNQA) provide *Criteria for Performance Excellence*?
   b. The first recipients of the BNQA were Globe Metallurgical Inc., Westinghouse Electric Corporation Commercial Nuclear Fuel Division, and Motorola Inc. What year did these three companies win the BNQA?
   c. Name the most recent recipients of the BNQA.
2. **Six Sigma.** As you learned from the chapter, General Electric is a well-known Six Sigma company. Visit the GE Six Sigma site at *http://www.ge.com/sixsigma/* and write a three-paragraph report on what further insights you gained about Six Sigma after visiting this Web site.
3. **SCORE.** The Service Corp of Retired Executives offers services to businesses. Go to *http://www.score.org* and find sample projects that include control mechanisms.

■ Case for Critical Analysis

Lincoln Electric

Imagine having a management system that is so successful people refer to it with capital letters—the Lincoln Management System—and other businesses benchmark their own systems by it. That is the situation of Ohio-based Lincoln Electric. For a number of years, other companies have tried to figure out Lincoln Electric's secret—how management coaxes maximum productivity and quality from its workers, even during difficult financial times.

Lincoln Electric is a leading manufacturer of welding products, welding equipment, and electric motors, with more than $1 billion in sales and six thousand workers worldwide. The company's products are used for cutting, manufacturing, and repairing other metal products. Although it is now a publicly traded company, members of the Lincoln family still own more than 60 percent of the stock.

Lincoln uses a diverse control approach. Tasks are rigidly defined, and individual employees must meet strict measurable standards of performance. However, the Lincoln system succeeds largely because of an organizational culture based on openness and trust, shared control, and an egalitarian spirit. Although the line between managers and workers at Lincoln is firmly drawn, managers respect the expertise of production workers and value their contributions to many aspects of the business. The company has an open-door policy for all top executives, middle managers, and production workers, and regular face-to-face communication is encouraged. Workers are expected to challenge management if they believe practices or compensation rates are unfair. Most workers are hired right out of high school, then trained and cross-trained to perform different jobs. Some eventually are promoted to executive positions, because Lincoln believes in promoting from within. Many Lincoln workers stay with the company for life.

One of Lincoln's founders felt that organizations should be based on certain values, including honesty, trustworthiness, openness, self-management, loyalty, accountability, and cooperativeness. These values continue to form the core of Lincoln's culture, and management regularly rewards employees who manifest them. Because Lincoln so effectively socializes employees, they exercise a great degree of self-control on the job. Production workers are paid on a piece-rate system, plus merit pay based on performance. Employees also are eligible for annual bonuses, which fluctuate according to the company's fortunes, and they participate in stock purchase plans. Bonuses are based on a number of factors, such as productivity, quality, dependability, and cooperation with others. Factory workers at Lincoln have been known to earn more than $100,000 a year. However, there also are other, less tangible rewards. Pride of workmanship and feelings of involvement, contribution, and esprit de corps are intrinsic rewards that flourish at Lincoln Electric. Cross-functional teams, empowered to make decisions, take responsibility for product planning, development, and marketing. Information about the company's operations and financial performance is openly shared with workers throughout the company.

Lincoln places emphasis on anticipating and solving customer problems. Sales representatives are given the technical training they need to understand customer needs, help customers understand and use Lincoln's products, and solve problems. This customer focus is backed up by attention to the production process through the use of strict accountability standards and formal measurements for productivity, quality, and innovation for all employees. In addition, a software program called Rhythm is used to streamline the flow of goods and materials in the production process.

Lincoln's system has worked extremely well in the United States. The cultural values, open communication, and formal control and reward systems interact to align the goals of managers, workers, and the organization as well as encourage learning and growth. Now Lincoln is discovering whether its system can hold up overseas. Although most of Lincoln's profits come from domestic operations, and a foreign venture in the 1990s lost a lot of money for the company, top managers want to expand globally because foreign markets are growing much more rapidly than domestic markets. Thus far, Lincoln managers have not developed a strategic control plan for global operations, relying instead on duplicating the domestic Lincoln system.

Questions

1. What types of control—feedforward, concurrent, or feedback—are illustrated in this case? Explain.
2. Based on what you've just read, what do *you* think makes the Lincoln System so successful?
3. Would you characterize Lincoln Electric as having a primarily bureaucratic or decentralized approach to control? Explain your answer.

SOURCE: Based on Joseph Maciariello, "A Pattern of Success: Can This Company Be Duplicated?" *Drucker Management* 1, no. 1 (Spring 1997), 7–11.

Le Meridien Managers Manage by Walking About

LE MERIDIEN IS A CHAIN OF 125 LUXURY HOTELS IN 55 countries around the globe. You can find Le Meridien hotels in the United States, throughout Europe, in Africa, Australia, India, Egypt, and other locations. Premium customer service is key to the success of a hotel chain, and a manager's skills can make or break a hotel. At Le Meridien Hotel in Boston, a manager's work is never done. Take a typical day for Bob van den Oord, assistant general manager of the hotel, which is part of a luxury chain owned by Great Eagle in Hong Kong and managed by Le Meridien in London. He arrives at the hotel before 8:00 A.M. and does a walk-through of the entire hotel, inspecting empty rooms, the kitchen, dining rooms, reservations desk, front lobby, and even the laundry, to be certain that everything is running smoothly. He may meet with other managers, such as Dutch-born Michiel Lugt, who runs room service and stewarding (restaurant and catering services) for the hotel, or the housekeeping or security managers if they have a specific issue to discuss. By 9:30, all managers—including Bob—are assembled for the daily operational meeting, in which everyone reports briefly on the hotel's activities for the past 24 hours. Managers for the information technology department, reservations, housekeeping, and human resource departments give thumbnail reports on problems currently needing solutions or ones that have already been dealt with—such as a brief lack of hot water in some of the building's guest rooms. By 9:45 the meeting is over, and all managers return to their posts.

Bob van den Oord fulfills all the four management functions every day he's on the job. As assistant general manager, he meets with the general manager to "set the overall goals for the hotel, so I take a more strategic role and provide the tools and resources to the other managers" so they can do their jobs. He functions in an organizational role, assigning responsibility to other managers—such as the head of security—to accomplish particular tasks or assignments, such as evaluating and updating security at the hotel. He leads and motivates workers by constantly keeping in touch with them—he manages by walking around. "It's a good tool to see what's going on," he says, from the kitchen to the plants out in front of the building. "Ninety percent of problems are because of management screw-ups," he notes candidly. "I like [walking around], the staff likes it, and guests like to see management around as well." Van den Oord admits that he asks a lot of his managers, but he devotes a lot of himself to the job, as well. "The hotel is a 24-hour operation," he explains. "We have to be here when other people are having fun." Finally, he fulfills the control function by monitoring activi-

ties and making necessary corrections. His daily walk-through is a prime example of this function. "Management is about constant feedback," van den Oord comments. "It allows people to improve their performance."

Michiel Lugt, the functional manager who runs room service—which is open 24 hours a day, 7 days a week—fully agrees with his boss's philosophy of management. He likes to lead by example and is always ready to help out when necessary, even if it means serving coffee to guests in one of the dining rooms. He believes that people skills are vitally important in the hotel industry, not only in dealing with staff but in dealing with guests as well. He remarks that, as a young manager, "Sometimes you have to manage people who are older than you are; that's a massive challenge. People should realize that experience is important." He makes a special effort to learn whatever he can from staff members who have been in the business longer than he has. "I try to be one of the gang, basically," he says of his relationship with his staff. "We have a hotel to run, and business and things have to be done, but that doesn't mean you have to be a tyrant." He encourages staff members to approach him with questions and concerns whenever possible.

Le Meridien in Boston—a single hotel in a huge organization—is a complex organization in itself, hosting more than 100,000 visitors each year. On any given day, Bob van den Oord and his staff may welcome honeymooners, international tourists, business travelers, groups for conventions or conferences, and college reunions. "It's hard work, but it's fun," notes van den Oord. Of his staff he says, "We're all in it together." That, in a nutshell, is the new paradigm of management at Le Meridien Hotel.

Questions

1. In addition to human skills, a hotel manager needs technical skills and conceptual skills. Identify what you think some of those technical skills and conceptual skills might be, either for a general manager or for a functional manager at a hotel.
2. Would you call Le Meridien Hotel in Boston a learning organization? Why or why not?
3. Describe at least one social force, political force, and economic force that may influence Le Meridien and its management practices.

SOURCE: Company Web site, *http://www.lemeridien-hotels.com*, accessed January 4, 2002.

Student Advantage Has the Advantage in the New Economy

THINK ABOUT IT: WHEN YOU GET TO COLLEGE, YOU WANT TO stay connected. You want news and information that's relevant to your life; you want to hear about events that you might want to attend; you want to be able to book your trip back home as easily as possible; you want to purchase CDs by your favorite music groups; and you need to buy books. What if you could do all those things—and much more—at a single Web site? You can. In fact, you may already have done so at CollegeClub.com, a division of Student Advantage.

Student Advantage was founded in 1992 to provide a "media, marketing, and commerce connection for millions of college students and the businesses and universities that serve them," says the company's Web site. Through its CollegeClub.com site, students can obtain financial aid information, use their university ID cards for off-campus purchases, find out about college sports, book trips, get discounts on advanced-level exams such as GMATs or LSATs, and much, much more. Student Advantage works on a membership basis. Students pay a fee for discounts on goods and services from 15,000 merchants, access to information, and other services. Universities and merchants also pay fees to be included in Student Advantage's various sites, including CollegeClub.com, CarePackages.com, FANS only.com, and others.

Student Advantage is a prime example of a new economy company that shares ideas, information, and knowledge throughout its network of student subscribers and business customers. It is also a company that would not be in business without the Internet and other information technology—it literally could not have existed a generation ago. Student Advantage is based on building relationships—relationships with other companies, universities, and students. Therefore, the company is involved in both business-to-business and business-to-consumer e-commerce. As founder and CEO Ray Sozzi says:

> Our student members decide where this company goes. For example, when students first told us they wanted some savings on travel, we developed that sector of our service and put in place a program with Greyhound bus service and some airlines. We structured it so there would be discounts on bus and air travel, as well as rental cars. When they wanted telecommunications services, they wanted savings; but they wanted quality even more, so we brought in AT&T as a partner.

These arrangements illustrate how important the relationships are—not only with the students but with the companies that agree to provide the discounted services through Student Advantage. The nature of Student Advantage's business also requires it to be flexible—able to change to meet the needs of businesses and consumers. When students indicate that they need or want a service such as the travel arrangements described earlier, Student Advantage moves quickly to provide it.

Currently, CollegeClub.com is rated the number one college-oriented site, having attracted 1.8 million new members in the year 2000 alone. Through CollegeClub.com, consumers and firms have a chance to foster positive exchanges with each other. Students have access to the goods and services from companies that range from Warner Brothers to State Farm Insurance. But CollegeClub.com is just one of Student Advantage's sites. CarePackages.com offers gift packages that are popular with both parents—the senders—and students—the recipients. Through the Internet, parents can send packages for just about any occasion, from Halloween to graduation. The program has worked so well that *The Wall Street Journal* voted CarePackages.com the "Best Overall" and "Best Value" in a review of college gift packages. Through its revenue-sharing partnerships, CarePackages.com actually helps campus organizations and business owners generate money with virtually no risk—a relationship that everyone can live with.

Student Advantage builds special relationships with universities and colleges around the country. The company uses existing university communication channels to inform students about Student Advantage, and its benefits, and remind them when their annual membership is due. Memberships can be sold through online and offline channels, including brochures, direct-mail flyers, an affiliate link on the school's Web site, or a link to Student Advantage's online enrollment system. Universities receive referral fees and other incentives for students who enroll with Student Advantage.

Student Advantage enjoys working with college students as customers, because they are Internet savvy consumers. "They go online to communicate, to research, and to buy," says Ray Sozzi, "and they want the best. They are the most scrutinizing and critical group out there." Ray Sozzi is talking about you.

Questions

1. In what ways do you think Student Advantage could use relationships and e-commerce to expand to different markets—either globally or beyond the college experience?
2. How important is the role of knowledge management in the way Student Advantage operates? Give reasons for your answer.
3. As a college student and consumer, would you be interested in the goods and services provided by a company like Student Advantage? Why or why not?

SOURCES: Company Web site, *http://www.studentadvantage.com*, accessed February 8, 2002; "Student Advantage, Inc.," company capsule, *Hoover's Online, http://www.hoovers.com*, accessed February 8, 2002; Seth Fineberg, "An Interview with Ray Sozzi, CEO of Student Advantage," *NewsBeat Channel 7*, January 13, 2000, *http://www.channelseven.com*.

Fallon Worldwide: Can Its Corporate Culture Be a Soul Survivor?

WHEN A CORPORATE GIANT TAKES OVER A SMALLER FIRM, THE question everyone asks is, What will happen to the culture of the small company? Will the quirks, the flexibility, and the creativity of the small fish be swallowed by the larger fish? When Paris-based Publicis Group SA announced its acquisition of Minneapolis-based advertising agency Fallon Worldwide, the worry was on every manager's, staffer's, and client's mind. "One of my greatest fears was that our people would think we sold out," recalls Pat Fallon, founder and chairman of the company. "People were worried that we would become more corporate and less like the home they knew. And if people feel as if a bond has been broken, then everything is up for grabs." Fallon had always been known for its high-energy, creative culture. People who worked there loved the atmosphere. Clients enjoyed Fallon's cozy, quirky, sometimes outrageous spirit. "It was a time of uncertainty," says Anne Bologna, planning director of Fallon's Minneapolis office. "There was this sense that we no longer had the freedom to be entrepreneurs." So Bologna made a call to action throughout the agency for new ideas. What began as hallway chat-fests turned into a full-scale company initiative bent on preserving Fallon's culture.

"People wanted proof that the soul of the company wasn't going to change," recalls Rob White, co-president of Fallon. "We had to show them that the acquisition [by Publicis] was a strategic move to help us achieve very ambitious goals that we probably couldn't achieve on our own." There's the catch: Fallon founders had to find a way to mesh the driving force of their company—its high level of energy, its creative spirit—with an external environment that included a sluggish economy, fierce competitors, and a new boss. "Staying energized is the only way to survive," insists Anne Bologna. "In a down economy, creativity as currency is needed more than ever." So, if Fallon could enhance its already-existing culture, the company might not just survive but actually thrive under the umbrella of Publicis. During the year after Bologna's initial call for new ideas, the agency launched Fallonet, an intranet that allows the free-flow of ideas, humor, and challenges. Fallon also established an interactive consulting group as a full-fledged company division.

One employee who took Anne Bologna's directive seriously was John King, a young media planner. He proposed a new program called Dream Catchers, in which Fallon would assist employees in funding their own "impossible" dreams, thus fueling their creativity. Employees who want to participate simply decide how much they want to deduct from their paychecks on a regular basis to set aside for their "dream" sabbatical. Fallon then matches their deductions up to $2,500. Once an employee has been there three years, he or she can take a two-week, paid sabbatical—in addition to vacation time—to pursue a dream. One staffer used the sabbatical to visit the Van Gogh Museum in Amsterdam while another ran with the bulls in Pamplona. "Dream Catchers gives you license to be selfish if you want to be," says program designer King. "So many people get caught up in day-to-day living and put their dreams on hold indefinitely. The program is supposed to be a kick in the [butt]." A company whose internal culture promotes creativity in a variety of ways is likely to see the impact in its products and services. Since Fallon instituted its new initiatives, the agency has won new clients as well as several prestigious advertising awards for its work.

Today, despite a tight labor market and a slow economy, Fallon has billings of more than $800 million per year and a client list that reads like a Who's Who of corporate giants: BMW of North America, Citibank, EDS, Holiday Inn, Nikon, Nordstrom, Nuveen Investments, PBS, Ralston Purina, Starbucks Coffee Company, Timex, and United Airlines to name a few. In selecting Fallon, United's director of Worldwide Marketing Communications, Jerry Dow, indicated the importance of Fallon's innovative culture to the decision. "In the end, Fallon showed United that the agency best understood the airline's brand vision, and had the tools to develop and deliver a hard-hitting, integrated global message and global brand platform."

There's no doubt that Fallon faces some tough challenges as it continues to try to integrate with Publicis without losing its own identity, trudges through an economic downturn, and looks for ways to keep employees energized, happy, and productive. But company founder Pat Fallon remains optimistic. "It comes down to one thing," he says. "Do you or don't you live by your values? Even in this tough economic climate, we can never invest enough in our people if we want them to do the best work of their lives." Pat Fallon intends his agency to be a soul survivor.

Questions

1. Imagine that you are a member of Fallon's staff. Write a brief paragraph proposing your own idea for sparking creativity at Fallon.
2. Why is maintaining Fallon's corporate culture so important?
3. How is Fallon's corporate culture linked to its external environment?

SOURCES: "Forecasters Predict Drop in Ad Spending," *The New York Times*, December 3, 2001, Christine Canabou, "Free to Innovate," *Fast Company*, November 2001, http://www.fastcompany.com; "United Selects Fallon Worldwide to Manage Its North American and International Advertising," United Airlines press release, January 22, 2001, http://www.ual.com.

Fallon Worldwide—Its Name Spells Global

EVEN BEFORE THE MINNEAPOLIS-BASED ADVERTISING AGENCY Fallon Worldwide was acquired by France's Publicis, Pat Fallon was on the hunt for alliances he could make with other companies around the world. Managing the global environment is more important than ever for companies, as technology expands boundaries or eliminates them altogether. In early 1999, Pat Fallon met Robert Senior in London for a cup of tea. Fallon was searching for his first foreign partners in Britain. Fallon Worldwide (then called Fallon McElligott) had already established a reputation for passion and independence. Senior and his colleagues were quick to jump on board. In less than a year, the Fallon London office had a dozen top clients and billings of $40 million. What made the international alliance work? Shared values, reported Britain's Senior. "Passion for great advertising is part of Pat Fallon's DNA," he enthused. "Part of exporting the Fallon brand is to find folks who share that ambition. You need those people who are going to get out there and push harder. You can try to dress up people in a set of beliefs and values, but it's much more potent if it is fueled from within."

Julie Thompson, Fallon's director of communications, said at the time, "It all comes down to relationships. We searched for two years to find our partners in London. We are very, very careful to find people of like mind. It has been a longtime goal of the partners to expand globally, but it will be a measured, well-planned expansion."

One aspect of global expansion is overcoming cultural and language barriers. As Fallon began to make plans for alliances farther afield, Julie Thompson explained how the agency would address this issue. "We suspect the models will vary in every city. Our values do seem to translate across the continents, but we'll ward off [language and other barriers to understanding] by partnering with local talent who can help us crack that code." Industry expert David Tree, who helped Young and Rubicam, Inc., open branches in Paris, Oslo, Tokyo, and Hong Kong, agreed with Fallon's approach. "There are certain cultural givens, certain global truths," he noted. "Every kid around the world wants a Coke. But there are cultural nuances that you would never understand like a national. The creative expertise you must leave up to the locals."

About a year after the London deal took place, Publicis acquired Fallon and the global focus intensified. Clients had been pressing the advertising industry in general to service them on a global basis; the only way Fallon could do that, reasoned its founders, was to partner with a larger organization. From the start, Publicis and Fallon intended to expand to up to a dozen other locations outside the United States. The company also faced the issue of e-commerce, which was mushrooming around the world. "It will take a new kind of branding communications company to succeed in the emerging worldwide digital economy, and with Publicis' support, we intend to be that company," said Pat Fallon of the merger and expansion plans. A year after the Publicis deal was finalized, Fallon Worldwide's expansion was well under way. The company announced the formation of three new "creativity centers" located on two continents, with six internationally known partners. Fallon would open agencies in São Paulo, Singapore, and Hong Kong. This strategy was formulated not only to overcome cultural, economic, and legal-political barriers in each region but also to maintain the flexible, innovative reputation that Fallon had built its business on. "The traditional agency network model is about distribution, which is fine for certain marketers," explained Pat Fallon. "But we believe there are clients who will get excited by the idea of a lean, agile network built around the power of creativity, not mass."

Fallon Worldwide chose the locations for the creativity centers carefully so that they would cover certain economic regions, giving multinational clients access to these markets without simply blanketing the globe with tiny agency outposts. Selecting partners to manage the centers would be crucial to the success of the entire endeavor. "Our philosophy is to find the best people in the world and give them a once-in-a-lifetime opportunity under a great brand name with collaborative support and resources from the other partners," remarked John Gerzema, Fallon's managing partner for international expansion. "Our network will be highly intimate—with people who know each other, respect each other, and share a passion for work that drives business results." These international partners share both risks and rewards based on an agreement that includes shared ownership and accountability.

Each of Fallon's top managers around the world has a global perspective on culture and on business. For instance, Calvin Soh, a creative partner for Fallon Singapore and Fallon Hong Kong, has worked in both New York and Singapore in the past. "As Asians, we found that Fallon's Midwestern values of humility, hard work, respect, and integrity weren't very different from ours. Particularly enlightening was Fallon's belief that to excel in Asia, you need to develop local talent and expose them to the world. For us, Fallon felt right." Fallon hopes to find such partners—and clients—the world over.

Questions

1. Do you think Fallon's approach to global expansion by establishing regional creativity centers will be an effective one? Why or why not?
2. How might ASEAN affect Fallon's business in Asia?
3. What are some of the personal challenges that Fallon's global managers might face?

SOURCES: Sandy Hunter, "Fallon Worldwide Expands," *Boards Magazine*, November 1, 2001, http://www.boardsmag.com; "Fallon Expands Global Network," *Business Wire*, October 9, 2001, http://www.hoovers.com; Jennifer Franklin, "Fallon's British Invasion," *City Business*, July 30, 1999, http://twincities.bizjournals.com; Christine Whitehouse, "The New Ad Ventures," *Time Europe*, April 3, 2000, http://www.time.com; "Publicis Scoops Up Fallon McElligott to Forge New Global Branding Network," *Media*, March 3, 2000, www.media.com; "Publicis Boosts Midwest Clout with Fallon Buy," *Chicago Tribune*, February 3, 2000, http://www.chicagotribune.com.

Timberland Walks the Walk of Social Responsibility

THE TIMBERLAND COMPANY DESIGNS, MANUFACTURES, AND sells premium boots, casual shoes, hiking boots, and boat shoes, as well as high-performance outdoor clothing and accessories. The New Hampshire–based company builds its products to last—"to withstand the elements of nature," as the company's Web site states. But Timberland is striving to build something more permanent than just high-quality footwear and clothing. It's trying to make the world a better, safer place to live and work—one person and one community at a time.

Along with the customers who buy its high-quality products, Timberland considers its other stakeholders in its business dealings. First, it recognizes its responsibility to be profitable for investors and employees. With yearly revenues of nearly $1.1 billion, the company recently reported 20 consecutive quarters of record revenue and improved earnings. Even in the face of a recent economic downturn, which hit retail establishments hard, CEO Jeffrey Schwartz said, "Timberland delivered record revenues for 2001 in a difficult environment" that included higher leather costs, increased competition, and softer U.S. sales. But he is not deterred from his goal of making Timberland a leading global lifestyle brand.

Timberland also considers its employee stakeholders as critical to its success. Once again, the company was listed on *Fortune* magazine's list of best companies to work for, ranked at number 65. The company is committed to diversity in its workforce, with 29 percent of its employees being non-Caucasian minorities and nearly half women. The company provides 22 hours of professional training per year to employees to improve their skills. Timberland is also concerned about its global manufacturing workforce. With repeated news reports about exploitation of foreign workers at other companies, Timberland instituted a year-long audit of all its manufacturing facilities and some of its licensee's facilities, including tanneries and other major suppliers. It hired Verit, a nonprofit nongovernmental organization, to check working conditions such as health and safety, air quality, noise, and lighting. The company also monitors its Asian factories every 8 to 12 weeks to ensure that workers are paid decent wages, provided periodic work breaks, and not required to work excessive overtime. It considers its commitment an ongoing process, requiring continual checks and improvements.

Companies often profess their belief in good corporate citizenship to their communities, but Timberland is an organization that literally considers what it is like to walk in someone else's shoes. From the CEO to office workers to sales associates on the floor, Timberland encourages all its employees to become involved in their communities. Through its long-standing Path of Service program, the company gives full-time employees 40 hours of paid time off for community volunteer service during regular working hours. The company also recently instituted a paid sabbatical program, allowing four employees each year to contribute their professional skills to nonprofit organizations for up to six months. And, it has long been involved in City Year, a national youth service organization for young people aged 17 to 24 years who serve different communities for a full year. The company serves as a City Year National Leadership Sponsor, and CEO Schwartz chairs the City Year board. In addition to these efforts, the company partners with many other service organizations, working on activities as wide-ranging as prevention of child hunger, skills training, eliminating exploitative working conditions, and closing the technology gap between organizations. The company's Web site also provides a link to SERVnet, an online news and events site listing needed community service projects.

Finally, Timberland considers the impact on the environment that its activities may have. It created an Environmental Affairs department to reduce the harmful effects of its production on the environment. The company is committed to recycling leather scraps and minimizing its use of toxic compounds and nonrenewable resources, as well as reducing carbon dioxide emissions to help curb global warming. Using innovative methods to reduce its energy consumption and conserve other resources, Timberland includes skylights at its sites to reduce power consumption and constructs some of its retail stores with furnishings and fixtures made from recycled materials, such as salvaged wood and bricks. Its shoe boxes are made entirely from recycled products and printed with environmentally friendly vegetable dyes.

Through its daily efforts to improve its operations while offering products with proven workmanship, Timberland certainly walks the walk when it comes to ethical and socially responsible behavior. Perhaps one incident can best capture Timberland's commitment to its communities: On September 11, 2001, CEO Schwartz and more than 100 other employees were volunteering at a school in the Bronx, New York City. After the World Trade Center crashes and collapse of the towers were reported, the Timberland employees were advised to evacuate the city. Instead, they chose to stay and finish their job of repairing windows, painting hallways, and doing various cleaning and repair jobs. No wonder *Fortune* magazine says of Timberland, "No one takes social responsibility more seriously."

Questions

1. Consider the three stages of ethical development. If Timberland were an individual, what level of moral development do you think the company has attained? Explain.
2. How much does Timberland's organizational culture influence its employees' socially responsible behavior?
3. Name some ways that Timberland demonstrates a high level of discretionary responsibility in its social performance. Would you like to work at Timberland?

SOURCES: Timberland company Web site, *http://www.timberland.com*, accessed March 29, 2002; "Best Companies to Work For," *Fortune*, *http://www.fortune.com*, accessed March 26, 2002; Marjorie Kelly, "Capitalism Has Its Shining Side," the *Corporate Social Responsibility Newswire*, *http://www.csrwire.com*, accessed March 26, 2002.

The Geek Squad: Providing Service That Makes You Smile

COMPUTERS AND TECHNOLOGY SEEM TO BE EVERYWHERE these days. From the office desktop to home Internet surfing to e-mail on cell phones, the computer chip has invaded our lives. But the simple fact is that most of us don't have a clue how any of that technology actually works—or even worse, why it *doesn't* work. Enter the Geek Squad, a computer-repair, technical assistance, and maintenance service based in Minneapolis, Los Angeles, Chicago, and San Francisco. The Geek Squad offers computer service—with a twist.

Founded by twenty-something Robert Stephens in the mid-1990s, the company has "special agents" who wear white shirts, clip-on ties, too-short pants, and pocket protectors. They drive to their on-site repairs, or "crime scenes," in Geekmobiles—black and white VW Beetles, renovated ice cream trucks, and even an old police squad car emblazoned with the Geek Squad logo. Stephens, who calls himself the Chief Inspector, got the idea for his company when he overheard two people in a grocery store checkout line discussing whether they were going to upgrade the RAM on their computer hard drives at home. At that time, the Internet was just beginning to take off. Stephens says of his vision, "That's a fundamental social shift that occurred, that you have normal people talking computers. I thought, 'This is going to blow big.'" So Stephens saw his window of opportunity, quit his computer programming job at the University of Minnesota, and started his company with $200 and a good dose of humor.

From its humble beginnings, the Geek Squad grew under Stephens's guidance (the company motto is "Creativity in the Absence of Capital") and through his personal connections. A lucky break came when a movie was being filmed in Minneapolis, and the crew's computers crashed. The Geek Squad repaired the damage. Soon, the company was known as "computer people for the movie industry in the Twin Cities," recalls Stephens. The company repaired computers for *Grumpy Old Men* and a Mighty Ducks hockey movie. The company also began to help rock bands with their computers. Over the years, they've helped U2, the Rolling Stones, Ice Cube, and Jonny Lang, among others. "You wouldn't think rock stars use computers," says Stephens. "But rock stars use laptops on the road, so actually they're the most finicky, demanding people. They're great practice for us." An added bonus for employees is getting great seats at concerts.

With customers' increasing dissatisfaction with the computer support provided by large hardware and software companies, the Geek Squad has found its niche by offering personalized carry-in, on-site, and emergency service 24 hours a day, seven days a week. The company prices its services by the job, not the hour, so customers know up front what the cost of the service will be. And the company will quote the cost of the service over the phone. Geek Squad employees maintain and repair everything from IBM-compatible and Macintosh hardware and software, to networks, printers, and even cell phones and personal digital assistants. They also give their customers set time frames for when a problem will be fixed.

Once a sole proprietorship owned by Stephens, the Geek Squad has now become a corporation with several million dollars in annual sales. The Geek Squad qualifies as a small business, currently employing fewer than 100 employees. Throughout the company's growth, Stephens has managed to maintain the fun work atmosphere for his employees, and he relies on their imaginations to play the role of computer nerd for sometimes-tense customers. The company dubs its carry-in service "counter intelligence." Flashing their badges before they begin work, employees quickly calm the fears and gain the trust of anxious customers, and the invoices they present carry the words, "Pay up, sucka!" All of this humor helps create not only fun for employees, but goodwill for the company, and referrals for future business.

Stephens has received offers to buy the company, but he says he isn't interested in selling. He takes those offers as evidence that he has created something unique and useful. In fact, Stephens has even extended his business by writing a book with coauthor Dale Burg called *The Geek Squad Guide to Solving Any Computer Glitch*, published by Simon & Schuster. The book is a compilation of useful tips, written in normal language that any nontechie can understand. Of his business, Stephens says, "I'm just having a lot of fun. I'm energized by that. For me, the Geek Squad is an artistic experiment."

Questions

1. Review the differnt types of business owners. Which type do you think Robert Stephens is?
2. How did Stephens come up with his business idea for the Geek Squad? What qualities have helped make the company a success?
3. At what stage of growth do you think the Geek Squad is currently? Explain.

SOURCES: The Geek Squad company Web site, *http://www.geeksquad.com*, accessed March 28, 2002; Bob Weinstein, "Company Builds on 'Geek' Image," *Chicago Sun-Times*, April 30, 2000, *http://www.suntimes.com*; "Geek Squad's Robert Stephens No Geek at Marketing," *Minnesota Entrepreneurs' Inc. Newsletter*, February 2000, *http://www.mn-entrepreneurs.org*; Jamie Allen, "'Geek Squad Guide' Offers Unique Computer Help," CNN, September 3, 1999, *http://www.cnn.com*.

Caribou Coffee Has a Mission

JOHN AND KIM PUCKETT LOVE THE OUTDOORS. THEY ALSO LOVE coffee. About a decade ago, they were hiking Sable Mountain in Alaska. When they reached the summit, they were inspired not only by the scenery surrounding them but also by the sight of a distant herd of caribou galloping through the valley below. No, the Pucketts didn't suddenly pull a coffeemaker out of a backpack and start brewing coffee on the mountaintop. But when they got home after their mountain trip, they wanted to find a way to re-create the sights and sounds of the Alaskan wilderness, preserving some of the feelings they had experienced. They wanted to establish a place where people could gather to share good and simple things: casual conversation with friends, time for the daily newspaper, a tasty cup of coffee, "an escape from the daily grind." They also wanted to start their own business. So they opened their first coffee shop in Minneapolis, in December of 1992.

Today, Caribou Coffee is the nation's second-largest specialty coffee company, with 160 stores and 2,000 employees across eight states. The Pucketts have remained true to their original vision of bringing the wilderness home: Each store is built and decorated to look like an Alaskan lodge, with knotty-pine cabinets, a rustic fireplace, and comfortable seating. "We still strive to make the Caribou experience adventurous, rewarding, and fun," says the company's Web site. "Our mission is to be the best neighborhood gathering place; fast and friendly service is at the heart of this goal."

A clear mission is the soul of an organization, but achievable goals and good planning are its heart and lungs. Caribou Coffee integrates all three, but its development and growth have not been without struggle. The Pucketts perfected the company's rustic image and style. With the help of Barry Judge, vice president of marketing, and the Carmichael Lynch advertising agency in Minneapolis, Caribou came up with buzzwords to capture the Caribou experience: "Outdoorsy. Leave smiling. Hand-made. Down to earth. Clever. Transformational."

People who had a Caribou shop in their area immediately became loyal customers. They seemed to prefer Caribou's brew to that of its largest competitor, Starbucks, and Caribou even debuted certain flavors and brewing methods that Starbucks followed later. Quality, service, satisfied customers—all were goals that Caribou could achieve. But the company had problems with setting more specific goals and planning for growth. For one thing, Caribou lacked the funds for the kind of expansion that the Pucketts envisioned. For another, their expansion from Minneapolis to other locations was driven by the competition—they simply went where Starbucks *wasn't* located, instead of establishing growth goals independently. By 1997, Caribou Coffee had 123 stores, with only Starbucks ahead of it. Caribou company president Jay Willoughby declared, "Our intent is to be a national player." But Starbucks had more than 2,000 stores, including nearly 190 overseas. Caribou wasn't even close. That doesn't mean being number two is necessarily bad. In fact, said Alan Hickok,

an industry analyst, "In markets where [Caribou] competes head-to-head with Starbucks, they've done just fine . . . There's no consumer category, with the exception of Microsoft, where consumers have been satisfied with having just one choice. Absolutely, there's room for a No. 2."

Caribou still wanted to grow—but they were having trouble coming up with a clear plan and the money to back it. Enter Don Dempsey, former head of McDonald's China division. Dempsey joined Caribou as its new CEO in 1999. Why would he make the leap from a giant like McDonald's to the small beans of Caribou Coffee? "When you're running an international company for McDonald's, you really have a lot of autonomy," he explained. "I wanted to take what I had learned at a large company and apply it to a small one." When one newswriter asked Dempsey about his goal for the company, he answered that he wanted to "reliably and consistently grow profits." But he needed a plan, and he needed a way to raise the money to achieve his overall goal.

Dempsey recalls that when he needed more money to fund a project at McDonald's, he just called up the CEO and asked for it. Funding wasn't so easy for Caribou. But eventually the Crescent Capital group of Atlanta agreed to purchase a percentage of the company, which would pump the needed growth dollars into the organization. Dempsey outlined a plan for expansion: stick with locations in which Caribou already had stores and strengthen the Caribou brand within those locations. Caribou's largest market is its hometown of Minneapolis-St. Paul, but other markets include Columbus and Cleveland, Ohio; Raleigh and Charlotte, North Carolina; Atlanta; Detroit; Chicago; and Washington, D.C. "We have to increase penetration and increase brand awareness in order to improve our economics," Dempsey said. Meanwhile, Caribou would continue to brew a good cup of coffee in a place where people can get away from the daily grind.

Questions
1. Write what you think would be an effective, updated mission statement for Caribou Coffee.
2. What is the relationship between Dempsey's goal and his plan for sticking with existing markets?
3. How important is the Pucketts' original vision to the company's identity today? Explain your answer.

SOURCES: Company Web site, http://www.cariboucoffee.com, accessed February 21, 2002; Jessica Griffith, "Caribou Coffee Brewing a Caffeine-Fueled Expansion," *Finance and Commerce*, December 26, 2001, http://www.finance-commerce.com; Eleni Chamis, "Sale Stalling Coffee Chain's Local Growth," *Washington Business Journal*, October 30, 2000, http://washington.bizjournals.com; Jim McCartney, "Caribou Coffee Taking on King of the Hill," *Shopping Centers Today*, May 1, 1999, http://www.icsc.org.

Caribou Coffee's Strategy: Worth More Than Beans

PICTURE DRINKING YOUR DAILY CUPPA JOE IN AN ALASKAN lodge. You have plenty of time to chat with friends, scan the daily paper, and imagine that when you step outside you'll have a sweeping view of Denali itself, with a few stray caribou grazing its foothills. That's what the folks at Caribou Coffee want you to feel, whether you're in Minneapolis, Ohio, or Washington, D.C. The rustic image conveyed by Caribou's 160 coffee shops is a major part of the company's strategy, which is to create a comfortable, attractive, unique atmosphere in which customers can relax and enjoy their coffee.

But the company's *grand* strategy is growth. At first, founders John and Kim Puckett followed a strategy of placing Caribou shops wherever their major competitor, Starbucks, didn't have shops. But that growth strategy lacked cohesiveness and planning. The company also tried to grow too fast, a pitfall of many young firms. "There's a lot of instability with rapid growth," says Jay Willoughby, a restaurant executive whom the Pucketts hired to be president of their company in 1997, five years after they opened their first shop in Minneapolis. Willoughby determined that before Caribou grew any more, it had to become more stable financially, without sacrificing value to its customers. In other words, every cup of coffee served by Caribou staff, from Kenya AA to Fireside Blend, had to be fresh, hot, and full of flavor. It also had to come at a reasonable price. To offer value and still make a profit, Willoughby had to make sure that the company's warehouse and field operations were functioning efficiently and cost-effectively, so that all coffee goods moved through the system quickly, remaining fresh. Only then would a grand strategy of growth make sense.

In 1999, Don Dempsey joined Caribou as its new CEO. After 20 years with McDonald's, Dempsey was ready for a new challenge. Like Willoughby, he examined the company's previous expansion strategy. "Their strategy was to go where Starbucks wasn't, and that was a flawed strategy," noted Dempsey. "They had a half-dozen stores here and a half-dozen there, but no strong brand awareness in any one market. Then, they ran out of money." First Dempsey had to come up with more backing for the company, then create a strategy of controlled growth. He found the backing he needed in the form of Crescent Capital of Atlanta, which agreed to purchase a portion of the company for $80 million, giving Caribou the funding it needed for growth. Dempsey has so far resisted franchising as a source of income or expansion, however. All Caribou stores are company owned. "Our stores run pretty well, and I like getting all of the profit from the stores," he explains. Also, the recapitalization from Crescent has given the company enough money to carry through its growth plans without franchising or making an offer of public stock. "I'd love to have a nice, big private company," Dempsey admits.

It was important to accomplish controlled growth while maintaining Caribou's woodsy, rustic, comfortable style. Everyone involved with Caribou—from its founders to its loyal customers—already knew that the Caribou shops performed well against Starbucks. In fact, claims Dempsey, "You can put us right next to a Starbucks. But our place cannot be less convenient or attractive than the Starbucks." Industry analyst Alan Hickok agrees with Dempsey. "Even in my little suburb, there are three Caribous within a couple of miles and a couple of Starbucks, and they are all doing quite well. Dempsey is a smart guy, and he knows exactly what he is doing." Minneapolis investor Jim Jundt concurs with Dempsey's strategic management. "He is using a strategy that has succeeded for him in the past," Jundt says.

Where can you go for a cup of Caribou? If you live in a few Midwestern states or Georgia, North Carolina, or Washington, D.C., you're in luck. If not, you can order coffee beans and other products through Caribou's catalog or online. If you visit the Web site, you can find out how much caffeine is in a cup of coffee, why you should use an oxygen-bleached filter, and why it's a *bad* idea to microwave a cooled cup of premium coffee. But you don't have to be a coffee aficionado to appreciate the aroma of success that seems to be wafting around Caribou Coffee. Don Dempsey had never sipped a cup of gourmet coffee before he came to Caribou. "I recently had some of the coffee I used to drink, and I was astounded at how bad it was," he recalls. "Once you've had good coffee . . . you can't go back."

Questions

1. Why was it important for Caribou to achieve stability before proceeding with further growth?
2. How would you define Caribou's core competence?
3. Identify two internal strengths and two internal weaknesses of Caribou's.

SOURCES: Company Web site, http://www.cariboucoffe.com, accessed February 21, 2002; Jessica Griffith, "Caribou Coffee Brewing a Caffeine-Fueled Expansion," *Finance and Commerce*, December 26, 2001, http://www.finance-commerce.com; Ashley Gibson, "The Uptown Coffee Buzz: More Starbucks, Caribous," *The Business Journal*, October 27, 2000, http://charlotte.bizjournals.com; Eleni Chamis, "Sale Stalling Coffee Chain's Local Growth," *Washington Business Journal*, October 27, 2000, http://washington.bizjournals.com; Jim McCartney, "Caribou Coffee Taking on King of the Hill," *Shopping Centers Today*, May 1, 1999, http://www.icsc.org.

Machado and Silvetti: A Business Based on Decisions

WHEN WAS THE LAST TIME YOU DESIGNED A BUILDING? MAYBE you cut a door in a large cardboard box when you were a child, painted on windows and crawled inside your new "house" with a couple of friends. Maybe you were one of those lucky kids who actually had a tree fort. Or perhaps an ambitious schoolteacher assigned you a project that involved planning and constructing an imaginary structure. Regardless of how simple or complex your building project was, it involved many decisions, from materials to dimensions. Harvard professors Rodolfo Machado and Jorge Silvetti, who also head up their own architectural firm, are examples of advanced design and architecture decision makers. In fact, almost everyone who works at Machado and Silvetti Associates makes decisions—whether programmed or nonprogrammed.

Machado and Silvetti Associates, based in Boston, specializes in creating housing and other structures for colleges and universities, as well as public buildings such as the Boston Public Library. The firm has an impressive roster of clients, including the J. Paul Getty Trust, the Utah Museum of Fine Arts, the Federal Reserve Bank of Boston, the City of Vienna, and, of course, Harvard University. Like most architectural firms, Machado and Silvetti is essentially organized around its projects, so that professionals such as associate Michael Yusem, a project manager, can focus on all the decisions related to a certain assignment. Since every project is different, many of these decisions are nonprogrammed, and much effort goes into reducing both uncertainty and risk. For instance, once initial design choices are made and a budget approved by a client, Yusem and his colleagues need to figure out how to deliver the design requirements within the budget, or risk losing money. Then come the building details, all of which must satisfy the customer while producing revenue for the firm. As the team develops a new graduate housing facility for a local university, they must consider the needs of future residents, the overall look or image of the complex, as well as the choice of quality materials including rugs, tiles, flooring, bathroom fixtures, and appliances. They need to determine the number and size of the rooms. They must be certain that the facility complies with local building and environmental codes. They must select and coordinate subcontractors for various phases of the project. And they must deliver the project on a schedule. All of this coordination is for just one of the firm's projects.

Across the country, another Machado and Silvetti team has undertaken the renovation of the Getty Villa, which is part of the J. Paul Getty Museum in southern California. The mission for the Getty Villa is entirely different from that of the graduate housing—its residents are works of art from the museum's Antiquities Collection, which contains roughly 50,000 objects ranging from statues to ancient tools. So the design team had to come up with a plan that incorporated the classical inspiration of the works themselves as well as the surrounding buildings of the museum. To achieve this, they chose pattern mosaic and terrazzo floors, coffered ceilings, and colorful plaster walls, with detailing in wood and bronze. But they also considered the modern needs of visitors and caretakers of the museum. In doing so, they added skylights and reopened some of the old windows to bring in natural light for better viewing, and added a variety of other modern amenities for comfort. Each of these decisions involved development of and selection among alternatives, along with feedback from the client. And all of the decisions had to contribute somehow to the mission of the project as a whole.

Machado and Silvetti enjoys a top-notch reputation for its designs around the world, both with clients and critics. "The new branch of the Boston Public Library in Allston is a delight: an airy, spacious place where the breeze seems to flow through uninterrupted. . . . This is the best new public building in Boston in years," writes architecture critic Robert Campbell of *The Boston Globe*. When the firm won the First Award in Architecture from the American Academy of Arts and Letters, the awards committee wrote, "In a series of boldly conceived and brilliantly executed urban projects completed over the past two decades Rodolfo Machado and Jorge Silvetti have pursued an extended and vigorous program of research through design. Their investigations . . . have been uncompromisingly dedicated to envisioning a meaningful architecture of the public realm." And it's all done one brick—and one decision—at a time.

Questions

1. How might project managers at Machado and Silvetti use the classical model of decision making to make a decision about what type of windows to install in a building?
2. What might be the consequences of using satisficing in a project like Getty Villa?
3. How might project managers at Machado and Silvetti use decision making to enhance performance beyond its current levels?

SOURCES: Company Web site, *http://www.machado-silvetti.com*, accessed February 5, 2002; Alex Ulam, "Harvard Inc.," *Metropolis Magazine*, February 2001, *http://www.metropolismag.com*; "The New Getty Villa," Getty Museum Web site, 2000, *http://www.getty.edu*.

Student Advantage Helps College Students Stay Organized

FOR ABOUT $20 A YEAR, COLLEGE STUDENTS CAN JOIN A CLUB that offers all kinds of services, from online purchase of textbooks to discounts on travel. Maybe most students don't have $20 in their pockets at any given time, but it's about the price of two large pizzas, and Student Advantage is committed to providing value to its members.

Massachusetts-based Student Advantage is made up of a number of divisions, each organized around a particular focus. Perhaps the most well-known of its departments is CollegeClub.com, a Web site that provides "one-stop shopping" for financial aid information, including comparisons of different student loans and opportunities for online application; a program that allows students to use their university ID cards for off-campus purchases; the nation's largest free newswire for college media; the largest site devoted entirely to college sports; online shopping for student-only values, and more. CollegeClub.com also provides marketing opportunities for companies promoting travel, events, and other services—as well as some administrative services for universities. And that's just one division of the company.

The SA Marketing Group, another Student Advantage department, develops and manages marketing programs for the college and youth markets on behalf of such clients at AT&T, Amtrak, New Balance, and Hotjobs.com. CarePackages.com a third Student Advantage operation, was founded in 1999 to establish relationships with more than 25 colleges and universities and related Internet sites such as Yahoo! Greetings and FTD.com florist service. Through CarePackages.com, parents, grandparents, and just about anyone else can select and send gift packages to students as they study for exams, or to make them laugh for Halloween. (There's even a special "ScarePackage.") CarePackages.com has created such a successful relationship between consumers and retail companies that *The Wall Street Journal* rated it one of the best such sites in business. In addition, CarePackages.com's revenue-sharing partnerships have helped associations, campus organizations, other nonprofits and business owners earn money without taking any risk.

For sports fans—and there are usually plenty of those on campus—Student Advantage's FANSonly Network provides online brand management, content delivery, consumer marketing, and business assistance to more than 120 colleges and universities around the nation. FANSonly works like a network hub for individual colleges' official athletic sites, so students and coaches can log on to get all kinds of information specific to their schools and team, from scores to schedules to merchandise. Finally, U-Wire is the country's largest free newswire for college media. The site delivers student-produced news and commentary to more U-Wire members, professional media outlets and syndication partners (including Yahoo! and USAToday.com).

Each of these sites is developed with a specific purpose to contribute to the company's overall mission of connecting students, universities, and businesses with each other in a positive relationship. If any does not fit the overall mission—or actually siphons off valuable resources from the company without contributing to it, then Student Advantage lets it go, keeping only the strongest divisions. One such business unit was Voice FX, which operated Campus Direct, a service that allowed students and alumni to access grades and order transcripts over the Internet and by phone. After reviewing the unit's performance relative to Student Advantage as a whole, CEO Ray Sozzi decided to sell Voice FX. "Our focus and our future are on the core enterprises on which the company's been built—our media properties, our membership program, including SA Cash, and our expanding online and offline commerce operations," explained Sozzi. In a sluggish economy, Student Advantage would retain only its "core" or central operations, and manage these as strategically as possible.

Student Advantage is structured on the consumer needs of college students. Such a well-defined focus makes it easier to structure the organization so that each department is related to students and the universities they attend. While some critics believe that targeting college students on the Web is too limiting, founder Ray Sozzi disagrees. He does, however, believe that a Web presence must be complemented by an offline presence. "The Internet is very important to college students, but it is not the end-all, be-all medium. There are plenty of transactions that happen offline; college students still go to local stores to buy books and CDs. The most limiting thing is if you *only* have an offline presence. You have to establish customer loyalty, and the most effective way is through an integrated approach. . . . That's the way we run our business."

Questions

1. Draw a diagram of Student Advantage as a network structure.
2. Do you see an advantage in a divisional structure at Student Advantage? Why or why not?
3. In what ways might Student Advantage benefit from the use of teams?

SOURCES: Company Web site, *http://www.studentadvantage.com*, accessed February 8, 2002; "Student Advantage Sheds Division," *Boston.internet.com*, November 8, 2001, *http://boston.internet.com;* Seth Fineberg, "An Interview with Ray Sozzi, CEO of Student Advantage," *NewsBeat Channel 7*, January 13, 2000, *http://www.channelseven.com*.

Machado and Silvetti: Building the Business of Building

AN ORGANIZATION IS A LOT LIKE A BUILDING: IT RELIES ON STRUCTURE just to stand up. It has a foundation, some system of support, pathways between areas, and a roof for protection. The Boston-based architectural firm of Machado and Silvetti, founded by Harvard professors Rodolfo Machado and Jorge Silvetti, knows plenty about structure. Without structure, there would be no building—and no firm. Because the two founders have spent so much of their careers in an academic setting, says associate Michael Yusem, "Our office is structured very similar to a typical academic studio configuration, where projects are developed through an intensive, workshop style environment."

This studio environment means that the Machado and Silvetti firm relies heavily on teams to develop the projects for which it has become famous—a new branch of the Boston Public Library, a renovation of the Getty Villa at the J. Paul Getty Museum, the South Boston waterfront, the Rockefeller Stone Barns, and a 365-bed graduate housing dormitory for a local university. "Team structure for specific projects is usually based on a principal-in-charge, a managing associate, and a team of designers," says Michael Yusem. Although many architectural firms are similarly organized on a project basis, Machado and Silvetti has a less hierarchical, more horizontal structure than more traditional firms. "By encouraging creative input at all staff levels, the system intends to encourage commitment and dedication among team members by creating opportunities for personal input and involvement," continues Yusem.

The team structure also contributes to decision making through meetings in which team members, associates, and principals gather to review the progress on each project and discuss problems and potential solutions. "We find that this approach encourages creative problem solving and minimizes the tendency for stagnation and repetition that more traditional bureaucracies may yield," explains Yusem. It also supports the concept of the learning organization.

Coordination among team members, between teams, and with outside groups and individuals is vital to the success of a firm like Machado and Silvetti. Since the firm does not specialize in designing a particular category of structure, each project team must address different demands related to the project. Many times, the firm will call in outside consultants who have expertise that applies to a certain project, and these individuals must be coordinated with the in-house architectural design team as well as the client's staff. "Once established, the architectural and consultant team works closely with the client, user group representatives, and construction managers to provide for the design, schedule, construction and budget of the project," says Yusem. "This involves an exhaustive review of program requirements, user-group demands, as well as the appropriateness of various design solutions which are tested throughout the process." All of this spells coordination. For instance, during the graduate housing project, the interests of the university and the surrounding community—including donor groups, trustees, facilities managers, faculty, student groups, and community organizations—all had to be addressed and coordinated.

This level of coordination requires patience from Machado and Silvetti's project managers. They must make sure everyone receives relevant information and has time to understand and respond to issues, and they must be able to anticipate and resolve conflicts. The firm tries to structure its contact with its clients in much the same way it is structured internally in order to achieve this coordination. "We have found that the particular circumstances of each project and client group differ, and our ability to hand-select the appropriate design team personalities and consultant group is paramount in creating an effective project delivery system," says Michael Yusem. "In this sense, we strive to establish a similar interactive, collaborative decision-making process with our client as we do with our own internal structure." In other words, they build each museum, library wing, or housing facility as if it were their own.

Questions

1. Can you see any possible downside to the way Machado and Silvetti is structured? If not, why not? If so, what is it?
2. If Machado and Silvetti was organized in a vertical structure, how would the approach to projects be different?
3. How important is open information to a firm like Machado and Silvetti?

SOURCES: Company Web site, http://www.machado-silvetti.com, accessed February 5, 2002; Alex Ulam, "Harvard Inc.," Metropolis Magazine, February 2001, http://www.metropolismag.com; "The New Getty Villa," Getty Museum Web Site, 2000, http://www.getty.edu.

Peter Pan Offers a Safe Ride

MANY ORGANIZATIONS HAVE TAKEN A SECOND LOOK AT THEIR safety and security procedures since the terrorist attacks of September 11, 2001. Financial institutions have updated security of their computer data; hotels have examined ways to make guests safer from intruders or unauthorized visitors; and every company operating modes of travel, from airlines to bus lines, has re-evaluated ways to ensure the safety and security of its passengers and staff. Re-evaluation and resulting changes are two positive actions that have come out of a great tragedy. Peter Pan Bus Lines, based in Springfield, Massachusetts, has been in business since 1933 and has undergone plenty of changes. But its attention to the details of safety and security post–September 11 is much more focused and intense.

"It is the policy of Peter Pan Bus Lines, Inc., to promote a safe and secure environment for all of our employees and customers," writes Peter A. Picknelly, president of the company. This policy extends to all of the company's 850 employees, 3.5 million passengers, 150 coaches (buses), and routes ranging from Concord, New Hampshire, to Washington, D.C. And it encompasses the entire Peter Pan Group, which includes the bus lines, Peter Pan World Travel, several hotels, and other affiliates. Some of the changes resulting from the new safety policy involve technology; others involve changes in people or culture, such as creating a heightened alertness to safety issues. Of course, it is important for the changes to be supported by the top of the organization, as they are at Peter Pan; otherwise, they will not receive the attention and resources they need for implementation.

As Christopher Crean, director of safety for the company, and other managers reviewed the company's safety procedures, they were happy to note that Peter Pan had instituted important safety measures long before September 11. For instance, bus drivers have had on-board computers (similar to the "black boxes" on airplanes) since 1989. Recently, Crean was presented with the first Safety Leader of the Year Award by the United Motorcoach Association (UMA) for his previous six years of work in the company's safety program. Under Crean's leadership, Peter Pan had achieved the highest safety rating from the Department of Defense for three years and the highest safety rating from the Department of Transportation for five years. But September 11 threw safety and security issues into a whole new arena, so Crean and his colleagues examined the company's practices from top to bottom.

When the review was complete, they decided to implement some changes in employee training and testing, and in policies and proce-dures. All employees, including the president of the company, would participate in a three-and-a-half hour safety and security training program to reinforce their existing knowledge, heighten their aware-ness of potential dangers or threats, and teach them how to make the best decisions for their safety and that of their passengers. Mean-while, Peter Pan would be implementing its "mystery rider" program, which operates much like the "mystery shopper" that restaurants or department stores might use. Mystery riders take Peter Pan buses sev-eral times each month and rate all aspects of service. In addition, according to Crean, all managers are required to ride a coach twice a month.

New policies and procedures for the company include the follow-ing: requiring identification of all passengers when they buy tickets, issuing company ID badges to all employees, instituting a new security plan, and implementing new security measures for the buses them-selves. Some of the additions to security on the buses include interior mirrors, which allow drivers greater visibility of passengers' activities, and plastic ties placed on all luggage hatches once they have been closed so no new items may be added. In addition, Peter Pan has worked with the Springfield, Massachusetts, police—the company's home base—to make sure that its emergency action plans are up-to-date and workable.

Change isn't easy, even for a company that already has a superior track record in the area of safety and security. People need to be re-educated and motivated to implement changes on a daily basis, and sometimes it takes weeks or months for the changes to settle into place. But when change begins at the top—as it has at Peter Pan—it is very likely to succeed. Peter Pan takes security seriously on every run because every passenger's safety is important to the company.

Questions

1. What characteristics of Peter Pan would identify it to you as a learning organization?
2. What might be some sources of resistance to the changes in Peter Pan's safety and security practices?
3. Of the implementation tactics discussed in the chapter, which seem to have been used successfully by Peter Pan?

SOURCE: Company Web site, http://www.peterpanbus.com.

Fannie Mae: A Superstar to American Home Buyers and Workers

WOULDN'T IT BE GREAT TO BE ABLE TO AFFORD TO BUY THE home you've always dreamed of owning? Wouldn't it be nice to work at a company that truly values your contribution to the organization? One corporation makes dreams like this come true every day, every year: the Federal National Mortgage Association, commonly known as Fannie Mae. Fannie Mae is a private corporation that works with primary lenders—such as banks, credit unions, mortgage companies, and government housing finance agencies—to ensure that there are enough funds available for mortgage loans. The company does this by buying mortgages from these primary lenders up to a loan limit of $300,700. With cash in hand from Fannie Mae, the primary lenders can turn around and lend more money to home buyers. Fannie Mae earns money through different investments, fees, and interest. Fannie Mae's overall mission is "to help more families achieve the American dream of home ownership."

With such wonderful goals to achieve, what is it like to work for Fannie Mae? How does the organization attract and develop an effective work force? Fannie Mae has established core values that include treating its employees with respect, giving them opportunities to perform and grow, compensating them fairly, helping them find ways to balance work and family life, and recognizing their achievements. As a result, the organization has received many awards for its positive work environment, among them being named one of the 100 Best Corporate Citizens by *Business Ethics* magazine, named one of 100 top companies for working mothers by *Working Mother* magazine, and listed on of *Fortune*'s 100 Best Companies to Work For. "Being a responsible corporate citizen is one of Fannie Mae's core commitments," notes Dan Mudd, Fannie Mae's vice chair and chief operating officer. "By ensuring at all times that Fannie Mae has a positive impact on the lives of our employees, the communities in which we live, and the nation we serve, we are better able to meet our unique public mission to reduce barriers, lower costs, and increase the opportunities for home ownership and affordable rental housing for all Americans."

Among the most important benefits offered to Fannie Mae employees are those designed to help them balance work and family obligations, including flexible work options, paid leave for new fathers, prenatal education, maternity leave phase-back, and Eldercare, a special program for assisting workers in their care of senior relatives. Eldercare's Elderkit includes information, resources, a summary of benefits, and assistance with paperwork pertaining to eldercare, from medical records to health insurance information. Employees can access Elderkit on the company's Web site or receive help at the human resource department. "By providing benefits that help employees balance their work and personal lives, we foster a committed workforce that is highly motivated to help us meet our critical housing mission and achieve our stretch business goals," says vice chair Jamie Gorelick.

Other benefits include an employee stock plan; a stock purchase plan; life insurance; free on-site annual health and fitness evaluations, including a "healthy living" day off; paid childbirth and adoption leave; exercise classes; housing assistance; and paid time off for volunteer activities. Fannie Mae's Crest of the WAVE Award acknowledges workers whose volunteer projects have helped to make a difference in their community. Fannie Mae also has an emergency child-care center at its Washington, D.C., office for employees whose regular caregivers are suddenly unavailable. Employees who live outside the Washington area are offered emergency child-care vouchers for up to 25 days.

Fannie Mae has a variety of programs designed to develop an effective workforce through job training, advanced education, and mentoring. The organization is "committed to retaining and expanding our outstanding workforce by encouraging employee development and career growth," states the company Web site. "We offer our employees a wide variety of opportunities to increase their productivity and further their careers." Its Assistance for Collegiate Education program offers financial assistance to staffers who want to continue their college education. A number of internal programs provide training in management and professional development, computer skills, and the secondary mortgage business. Career development programs and learning centers offer self-study opportunities. The Corporate Mentor Program helps establish mentoring as a core value at the company. This program is formal and structured, providing employees with the tools and opportunities to build and maintain relationships with managers who can help them grow in their careers.

Today, Fannie Mae is the third-largest U.S. corporation in terms of assets, and the nation's largest provider of home mortgage funds. In fact, with more than 12 million active mortgages, Fannie Mae is one of the largest financial institutions in the world. Each of its 4,000 employees is considered a contributing member to an important mission, and each is "encouraged to use good judgment in all that they say and do in the workplace." In sum, Fannie Mae sounds like the embodiment of the American dream—for people who want to purchase their own home, and for people who want a nice place to work.

Questions

1. In what ways do you think Fannie Mae's work/life benefits help maintain an effective workforce?
2. How might Fannie Mae's treatment of its workforce be considered part of its competitive strategy?
3. Write a brief statement outlining what you believe to be Fannie Mae's social contract with its workers.

SOURCE: Company Web site, accessed January 17, 2002, http://www. fanniemae.com.

Fannie Mae Promotes a Diverse Workforce

MANY COMPANIES TRY, WITH GREATER OR LESSER SUCCESS, TO recruit, develop, and promote a truly diverse workforce. Federal and local guidelines govern such areas as equal opportunity and affirmative action. But organizations that move beyond rules and regulations to embrace diversity as a core value can reap rewards in employee satisfaction and performance. At the Federal National Mortgage Association (Fannie Mae), which employs over 4,000 workers, diversity is a way of life. Fannie Mae's corporate culture is grounded in diversity. "In keeping with [our] values, our corporate philosophy on diversity is based on respect for one another and recognition that each person brings his or her own unique attributes to the corporation," states the company Web site. "We are committed to providing equal opportunity for all employees to reach their full potential; it is a fundamental value, and it makes good business sense. . . . We are committed to demonstrating that 'Diversity Works at Fannie Mae.'"

That said, how does Fannie Mae breathe life into its words? First, the diversity of American society as a whole is reflected at every level of the corporate structure. More than 47 percent of Fannie Mae's management group, including officers and directors, are minorities; nearly 54 percent of the company's employees are women; and 42 percent of the employees are minorities. In addition, the company is pledged to equal opportunity for workers with disabilities, older employees, and gay or lesbian workers. "Diversity is not just an initiative at Fannie Mae; it's a principle that permeates every aspect of how we do business," explains Maria Johnson, vice president of diversity, health, and work-life. "Diversity is codified as one of the company's core commitments."

Fannie Mae also supports diversity by awarding a significant number of outsourced contracts to minority-owned businesses, a practice for which it was named among the top 30 companies for achievements in increasing supplier diversity by *Working Woman* magazine. "More than 21 percent of the company's discretionary spending in 2000 went to minority- and women-owned businesses, proof that Fannie Mae's commitment to diversity extends to all areas of the organization," says Barbara Lang, Fannie Mae's vice president of corporate services. "We require minority contractors to be included on all bids, where possible, and also encourage our majority suppliers and customers to work with capable minority vendors." In addition, Fannie Mae provides diversity training to its lender customers and hosts regular benchmarking sessions for other employers who want to learn more about how diversity can contribute to a company's success.

Fannie Mae has established specific goals to increase the ratio of minorities at upper levels, ties certain compensation to promoting diversity, and has implemented a number of programs, such as mentoring, to make certain everyone gets equal opportunity for career growth. "Company leaders are urged to unleash the potential of all employees, promote a spectrum of perspectives, view differences as assets rather than liabilities, and help create a diverse, talented, and committed workforce," says Maria Johnson.

Promoting diversity within the workforce at Fannie Mae is good strategy not only because a diverse workforce can bring more strength and creativity to an organization but also because such a workforce reflects Fannie Mae's customer base. People of all backgrounds come to Fannie Mae's lenders in search of mortgage loans. In addition, Fannie Mae's philanthropic arm, the Fannie Mae Foundation, works to increase the supply of affordable housing to those who might not otherwise be able to find a home—to homeless individuals and families, immigrant communities, those in rural areas, and lower-income minority groups.

Diversity has been an integral part of Fannie Mae's corporate culture for at least 15 years, illustrating the importance of support from a company's senior managers. "Fannie Mae committed to incorporate diversity as part of its core culture back in the late 1980s," reports Maria Johnson. "Our program has been successful because top executives have had an ongoing relationship with our diversity initiatives from the onset." Because diversity programs have support at the very top of the organization, they are much more apt to be successful at lower levels. But Fannie Mae doesn't engage in these initiatives entirely out of socially responsible motives; instead, the company believes that being socially responsible is also good business. "The company's record of 14 consecutive years of double-digit growth in operating earnings shows that a company can act responsibly and still deliver value to its shareholders," says Jamie Gorelick, vice-chair of Fannie Mae. There's no arguing with success.

Questions

1. No one is perfect, including managers and workers at Fannie Mae. What are some of the challenges that mid-level managers at Fannie Mae might face in managing a diverse group of workers?
2. Based on what you have read in this case and the previous case on Fannie Mae, what type of initiatives can you identify that should prevent women from encountering the glass ceiling at Fannie Mae?
3. Using the chart in Exhibit 10.5, try to identify—honestly—your own level of diversity awareness. Based on your evaluation, do you think you would fit in as a manager at Fannie Mae? Why or why not?

SOURCES: Company Web site, accessed January 17, 2002, http://www. fanniemae.com; "Fannie Mae Foundation Receives New $300 Million Contribution from Fannie Mae," company press release, January 14, 2002.

CVS Stands for Consumer Value Store

WHEN THE FIRST CVS STORE OPENED IN LOWELL, MASSACHU-setts, in 1963, customers knew it as the Consumer Value Store. But as the store itself caught on with consumers, so did the abbreviation CVS. Today, CVS—which has acquired other stores such as Peoples Drug, Revco D.S., and Arbor Drugs—employs more than 80,000 workers nationwide, including 12,000 pharmacists in 4,200 stores. In addition, when CVS acquired Soma.com of Seattle, Washington, it became the first company in the nation to launch an Internet pharmacy site. One way that the company has managed to grow and continue to offer value to its customers is through a heavy emphasis on continuous learning throughout the organization.

Training is paramount at CVS. The company offers an Emerging Leaders Program several times a year for managerial candidates; but, perhaps more important, CVS considers every employee to have the potential to grow. Thus, employees at every level are offered opportunities to learn the skills they will need for their next job at CVS. With formal training programs, mentoring, and other methods of learning, CVS employees have a greater chance of achieving person-job fit as they move up in the company than they might have if they were simply promoted without preparation and support.

The Emerging Leaders Program is offered to about ninety district manager candidates and ten regional manager candidates at each session. According to CVS spokesperson Seth B. Kamen, candidates ideally enter the program about a year and a half before they are ready for a promotion. Participants gather at the company's Store Support Center for a two-day kickoff session; then they return to the field to complete twenty-three training activities. Participants receive regular feedback from their managers and communicate regularly with peers for continuous learning. Throughout the program, participants gain experience in planning and organizing, customer service, interviewing and selection, loss prevention, laptop skills, pharmacy regulations, merchandising, and more. During the first year of the program, twenty-one out of twenty-seven participants actually achieved their desired promotions. Response to the new program has been positive. "By working with the Emerging Leaders Program, I have learned new insights on my own job," says one participant. "The exposure I have to my regional manager has been great to help me understand expectations," reports another.

Kamen believes that the value of the program goes beyond the boundaries of its initial intention. Leader-led training blended with actual job experience—the field activities—creates a stronger result than might be achieved with one or the other alone. He observes that the program has influenced other programs and practices at CVS. "We developed a new process and tools for field managers to use to conduct store visits that are tied directly to the capability model we present through the program," he explains. And "when new projects, critical assignments, focus groups, and so forth come up, participants in the Emerging Leaders Program are among the first people the organization considers."

CVS also uses THINQ Training Server, a learning management system to help manage its training efforts. The system has helped CVS employees adapt to standardized training that is designed not only to help them advance but also to increase the consistency of customer service and improve their overall knowledge of the pharmacy industry and the company. With the help of the system, CVS employees have a pass rate of 97 percent on the national PTCB exam, which exceeds the national average of 81 percent.

CVS's commitment to learning extends throughout the company, at every level. Employees appreciate the opportunities available to them and work hard to perform their best. This is how loyalty is built: when learning never stops. One Emerging Leaders graduate sums it up this way: "CVS is very interested in my success!"

Questions

1. In what ways do you think the Emerging Leaders Program helps achieve good person-job fit at CVS?
2. How might CVS's training programs help develop positive work-related attitudes among employees?
3. How does the model of the learning process in Exhibit 11.8 apply to the Emerging Leaders Program?

SOURCES: Company Web site, *http://www.cvs.com*, accessed March 18, 2002; Don Steinberg, "The Smart Business 50," *Tech Update*, ZDNet, *http://techupdate. zdnet.com*, accessed March 18, 2002; "Case Study: CVS/Pharmacy," *Thinq*, *http://learning.thinq.com*, accessed March 18, 2002.

Donna Fernandes: She's the Leader of the Pack

DONNA FERNANDES ISN'T YOUR AVERAGE MBA. HER EXPERTISE lies in the behavior of slugs—real ones, not the human kind. She also holds a Doctor of Sciences degree from Princeton, she's worked at the Franklin Park Zoo in Boston, led wildlife tours through Kenya and Tanzania, hosted her own educational television show, and now she's the director of the Buffalo Zoo in upstate New York, where her clients include elephants, gorillas, hyenas, polar bears, and more.

When Fernandes arrived at the 23-acre zoo a couple of years ago, it was a mess. "Most of what I found about the current state of the zoo was negative," she recalls. The 125-year-old park, the third-oldest zoo in the country, was in a terrible state of disrepair and was in danger of losing its accreditation. The management and board of directors were considering moving the zoo from its home in the Delaware Park area of Buffalo and relocating it to an industrial neighborhood along the Buffalo River. But the community rallied against the move, and it was postponed. Still, something had to be done to bring the zoo back to life. Fernandes quickly found that her base of support as a leader would come from the community and from volunteers and workers at the zoo. "As soon as I walked through the gates of the zoo, I just felt at home," she says. "The people were really friendly. . . . It seemed like people all wanted to improve the zoo. The amount of grass roots support for this zoo is phenomenal."

Fernandes used her position power to put forth a vision for improvement, but she quickly developed personal power as well. People liked her and respected her from the outset. She immediately outlined plans to bring the zoo back up to the standards of the American Zoo and Aquarium Association, which were backed by a pledge of $350,000 from Governor George Pataki. More funding was needed, so the board undertook a massive fundraising effort. Fernandes noted that as the zoo was upgraded she would place more emphasis on children and education through programs at the zoo. "I will also focus on trying to increase family visitors by making exhibits the right height for children in strollers and people in wheelchairs." In addition, she planned to create more natural settings for the animals, with an emphasis on wildlife habitats rather than cages. "These are issues to which I am very sensitive," she explained.

With strong support for Fernandes's vision, plans to relocate the zoo were abandoned, though she was careful to say that she understood the reasons why the board had considered it. Today, visitors enjoy the giraffe feeding station, guided tours, and especially the WILD place, where curious—and brave—participants can wash an elephant or even watch one paint. (Daryl Hoffman, the elephant keeper and head of the animal training committee at the zoo, has instituted a program called Art Gone Wild, in which the zoo sells "art-work" created by elephants, primates, and big cats.) The zoo's outreach program includes the Zoomobile and Distance Learning, both of which take the zoo's mission outside the grounds to people who might not be able to visit the zoo in person.

Fernandes's democratic leadership style encourages input from staff, groundskeepers, volunteers, the community, and the board of directors. She likes people to stop by her office to give her feedback, suggestions, and even complaints. But this open atmosphere didn't exist before Fernandes arrived; she had to cultivate it. The change began almost by accident. In the days following the events of the September 11, 2001, attacks on the Pentagon and the World Trade Center, everyone around the zoo was shaken. On a whim, Fernandes decided to bring her new puppy into the office to cheer herself and others up. Pretty soon people were stopping by to see the puppy and have a chat. Before long, Fernandes was receiving valuable feedback from people who would never have otherwise felt comfortable providing it—and a whole new line of communication had opened up between Fernandes and her staff. The puppy, who is rapidly growing, now makes regular appearances at the office, and Fernandes lets everyone know that she likes her employees to visit whenever they want.

Fernandes is happy with her work and seems comfortable in her leadership role. Of the 186 accredited zoos in the country, only 20 have female directors; so she is aware of her mentoring role as well. "I believe this is probably the most important thing I will ever do, being in this position in a community at a juncture where they want to rebuild their zoo," she says. "When I interviewed for this job, I did a presentation to the board on my vision for the zoo. I told them it would take 10 to 25 years of a shared dream, rather than just my vision, to restore the Buffalo Zoo to its greatness." Fernandes truly believes that her zoo will enjoy a second golden age—within limits. "I won't promise the world in rebuilding this zoo, but if I promise a continent, you'll get a continent." Which is plenty of ground for everyone.

Questions

1. In what ways do you believe Fernandes exhibits both expert power and referent power?
2. Using Exhibit 12.2, create a profile of Fernandes's personal characteristics.
3. Would you characterize Fernandes's leadership style as appropriate for building a learning organization? Why or why not?

SOURCES: Buffalo Zoo Web site, http://www.buffalo.com, accessed March 20, 2002; Christina Abt, "Donna Fernandes, Director, Buffalo Zoological Society," *Eve Magazine*, pp. 26–27; "Governor Pataki Announces $350,000 for Buffalo Zoo," May 22, 2001, http://www.state.ny.us.

Motivation Is a Wild Experience at the Buffalo Zoo

AT THE BUFFALO ZOO IN UPSTATE NEW YORK, YOU CAN BUY A painting by an elephant, primate, or big cat. You can visit the giraffe feeding station, bathe an elephant, take a starlight safari, tour the conservation station, and take in the vanishing animals exhibit. You'll find renovated buildings, naturalized habitats, and clean grounds. You'll be one of 340,000 people annually to enjoy the zoo. Much of this is the work of zoo director Donna Fernandes, her staff, volunteers, and the community of Buffalo. How she got everyone to transform the run-down, sparsely visited zoo in the space of just a few years is a story of motivation.

Fernandes herself is a motivated leader who believes in empowering everyone—inside and outside the organization—to turn the Buffalo Zoo into the very best it can be. She believes that her plans are "a shared dream, rather than just my vision, to restore the Buffalo Zoo to its greatness." When Fernandes first arrived at the zoo, employees were unenthusiastic about their jobs. A senior manager had adopted an autocratic leadership style that had reduced morale. Employees were often reprimanded and threatened with suspension for minor infractions of strict rules. Many felt that they were not given the freedom and respect to do their jobs as well-educated, specialized experts in the care of animals. Communication was lacking, information and ideas were not shared, and the zoo had begun to languish.

Fernandes has a doctorate from Princeton in animal behavior; she's worked at several large zoos; she is interested in education; she can communicate with and relate to her staff, who know and care a great deal about animals. She also has a business degree, so she can understand the thinking and decisions of the zoo's board of directors. And when she arrived, she knew she had to motivate both staff and board members in order to save the zoo, which was in danger of losing its accreditation with the American Zoo and Aquarium Association. One of her first actions as president and CEO of the zoo was to dismiss the senior manager and abolish the rigid policies that actually interfered with workers' freedom to get their jobs done. "Things happen. Your car breaks down, your kid is sick, it's no big deal," she explains. "It's not like we have a real problem with [attendance] anyway." By removing rules that prevented people from caring for a sick child or accompanying a parent to the doctor's office, Fernandes showed employees that she respected them as individuals who were trying to balance their family lives with their jobs.

Fernandes believed that there was too little communication and knowledge sharing among the departments at the zoo. Under the old management, employees actually hoarded information because they were afraid they would not receive any recognition for their work. So Fernandes established weekly staff meetings with vets, animal keepers, and trainers from all parts of the zoo. Here people share ideas and knowledge, take part in training, and openly share concerns with management. Fernandes also includes staff demonstrations in the meetings to give employees an opportunity to showcase new projects and developments in their areas of expertise. Fernandes observes that these demonstrations not only give recognition for a job well done but also allow the valuable sharing of information. Fernandes expands her motivating leadership to the board of directors and the community at large, who have been engaged in fundraising to renovate the zoo. The board of directors, once considered a stagnant bunch, is now one of the most sought-after groups for community involvement in upstate New York.

These days, the atmosphere at the Buffalo Zoo is much more upbeat. Employees are happier in their jobs, they feel free to offer ideas, and they have the authority to make decisions in their jobs. They also enjoy communication with the "Top Dog" herself. After September 11, 2001, Fernandes began bringing her new puppy to the office just to make herself—and everyone else—feel better. It didn't take long for people to stop in, pet the puppy, and chat with Fernandes about whatever was going on around the zoo. Fernandes finds these puppy visits as valuable as the staff meetings. It's not surprising that she talks with people as easily as she talks with her animals.

Questions

1. What types of intrinsic rewards are workers now receiving from their jobs at the Buffalo Zoo?
2. In what ways might the human resource department at the Buffalo Zoo use job design to increase motivation among zoo workers?
3. How important is empowerment to motivation at the Buffalo Zoo?

SOURCES: Buffalo Zoo Web site, http://www.buffalozoo.org, accessed March 20, 2002; Christina Abt, "Donna Fernandes, Director, Buffalo Zoological Society," *Eve Magazine;* "Governor Pataki Announces $350,000 for Buffalo Zoo," May 22, 2001, http://www.state.ny.us.

Communication Is Paramount at Le Meridien

PERHAPS THE MOST IMPORTANT PART OF A MANAGER'S JOB IS communication. Bob van den Oord, assistant general manager at Boston's luxury Le Meridien hotel, would agree. Most of his job involves communicating—with department heads, staff, guests, suppliers, the general manager, and senior managers of the hotel chain, which is based in London. That's why he spends so much time developing both the formal and informal channels of communication at the hotel. "There are a number of things we've done to improve communication at Le Meridien," van den Oord notes. One of the most important parts of his day takes place between 9:30 and 9:45, during which he and his managers hold an operational meeting to discuss the day's events, timeline, and staffing requirements. "It's quite casual," says van den Oord. "Everyone has a cup of coffee and talks." In those fifteen minutes, a great deal of communication is accomplished because managers have learned how to present their messages clearly, listen, and help each other come to a resolution when necessary.

Daily operational meetings aren't the only communication channels at Le Meridien. Van den Oord also holds weekly departmental meetings, such as the food and beverage meeting, in which managers may discuss their schedule of events, supply needs, or paperwork for group dinners; interdepartmental meetings; and yearly staff meetings during which all employees in attendance have an opportunity to ask questions and learn about the hotel's future plans and to review results for the year. Van den Oord calls this annual gathering a team-building opportunity as well. Other channels include the daily briefing sheet—literally a sheet of paper—that staff members can pick up near the hotel lobby to learn about the day's VIP visitors or groups, special events, restaurant promotions, and the like. Also, all managers have access to e-mail on the hotel's intranet.

Clearly, Bob van den Oord prefers the channel richness of face-to-face communication. Although he concedes that e-mail is convenient—and necessary—he is quick to point out that it is not a substitute for personal interaction. If there is a conflict, he wants it resolved either by phone or in person so that both parties have the opportunity to listen and understand each other's words and gestures. Instead of relying on e-mail, van den Oord prefers what he calls "management by walk about," or simply walking through the hotel's different departments to see how things are going. "It gives the staff a chance to talk to me," he explains. "They like it. They like to see that the manager is not just sitting in his office. . . . All the one-on-one, constant feedback is important." Although his daily walk through the hotel is part of the organization's formal communication channels, it has many informal qualities—van den Oord can easily pick up on the grapevine during this journey.

Michiel Lugt, the hotel's room service and stewarding manager, wholeheartedly agrees. "E-mail facilitates the communication process, but it's not the solver of all problems," he says. Lugt notes that it's very easy for someone who sends an e-mail to assume that the recipient actually received and understood the message—and will act on it if necessary—when in fact the person might not have received or understood the message, or might have underestimated its importance. Lugt echoes van den Oord's concern with communication throughout the hotel. "We have so many departments, and they all need to perform. If one department doesn't communicate, everyone struggles." For instance, if the person taking dinner reservations oversells the restaurant so that people must wait for tables or the kitchen is not prepared with the right amount of food, all departments suffer. "Communication is key in our industry," Lugt concludes.

Van den Oord and Lugt understand well that part of their job as communicators is to influence their employees—to motivate them to perform at the highest level. One of the ways they do this is by setting an example of their own commitment and performance. "You need to be present," notes Lugt. "You are leading by example." Lugt is quick to help out wherever he is needed, whether it's filling in a service gap by serving morning coffee to guests at the restaurant or taking meal orders. By doing so, he communicates to his staff that they are all part of a team running the hotel together.

Van den Oord views good communication as part of good business. Good communication contributes to a happy staff, he believes. "A happy staff equals happy guests," he notes with a smile. "And happy guests help us meet our business objectives."

Questions

1. How important is nonverbal communication to a hotel manager such as Bob van den Oord or Michiel Lugt?
2. Why is feedback an important part of Bob van den Oord's daily process of management by walk about?
3. In the video, assistant general manager Bob van den Oord has to work with another manager to clear up a misunderstanding about the staff's vacation schedule. Put yourself in Bob's shoes and write a brief outline of how you would communicate with the manager to solve the problem. Hint: You might want to refer to the Focus on Skills box, "How to Be a Master Communicator," in Chapter 14 for ideas.

SOURCES: Company Web site, http://www.lemeridien-hotels.com, accessed January 4, 2002.

Cannondale: Teams Perform in the Race for the Perfect Bicycle

HIGH-PERFORMANCE BICYCLES ARE FINELY TUNED MACHINES that are tailored to their riders for peak performance. The search for the perfect bicycle is a never-ending race that pits a material's strength against its weight. Cannondale Corporation, based in Bethel, Connecticut, constantly runs that race and wins—through dedicated teamwork.

The company has come a long way from its beginnings in 1971 in a loft above a pickle factory. From the company's early efforts in manufacturing bicycle trailers and cycling apparel, it expanded to high-performance bicycle design and production in the 1980s. And it hasn't looked back since. The company became renowned early on for its innovative introduction of aluminum bicycle frames, combining strength, flexibility, and light weight. At the time, competitors constructed their frames of much heavier steel. Today, Cannondale is the leading manufacturer of aluminum bicycles, selling more than 80 models in 60-plus countries worldwide. And with the turn of the 21st century, the company ventured into the design and manufacture of motocross motorcycles and all-terrain vehicles. As Cannondale's Web site proudly proclaims, its "passion is to be the best cycling and off-road motorsports company in the world." Cycling experts would agree it is well on its way.

Maintaining its position in the competitive cycling market isn't easy. Cannondale must continually create new designs that boost performance. To do so, it relies on the best of art and science—the creativity of teams of engineers and experienced production craftsmen combined with the speed and precision of computer technology. The company forms special-purpose teams to create its designs. Design engineers for the teams are selected based on their particular areas of expertise—some are materials experts, others skilled at drawing, and still others experienced at proofing the designs to ensure that all the pieces fit, so that the bicycles can be built. Cannondale also encourages engineers to volunteer for projects based on their interest in the particular product being considered. For example, a carbon-fiber materials specialist may get involved in a project to contribute to the design because he or she wants to help or has a unique idea. The goal of these design teams is to work creatively to solve a particular design problem and produce innovative products. Usually two to four engineers team up for a design.

The design engineers also rely on technology to execute their ideas. Engineers draw their designs on a computer-aided design (CAD) system called Pro/Engineer and can generate a plastic prototype to check the overall design concept. From there, the engineers transmit their designs electronically to the production teams based in two company-owned factories in Bedford, Pennsylvania. John Horn, research and development project manager at Cannondale says, "The design and production teams are separated by roughly 400 miles, but the communication is instantaneous." Production teams can generate a single prototype bicycle using the CAD system and actual materials to test its performance—strength, durability, flexibility, and dimensions. Frames are at the heart of Cannondale bicycles, and they undergo 12 to 15 different tests before a design is approved for production.

With all of its high-tech capabilities, Cannondale doesn't ignore the human touch in its manufacturing process. The company relies on skilled craftspeople to weld, sand, paint, and finish its bikes. "Aluminum is not an easy material to weld," says Horn. "It's more difficult than steel." So the company hires, trains, and certifies its welders to perform at their peak. The welders' jobs are coveted at the company—they carry prestige and high pay. After the welds are completed, the weld joints are sanded smooth—a mark of quality that Cannondale bikes carry over their competition. Then frames are machined to finish edges and prepare them for additional parts such as cranks and wheels. After that, the bikes are hand painted, matte or gloss finish is applied, and decals are added to customer specifications or sales demand.

Cannondale believes in the quality of human workmanship and relies on assembly-line work teams, instead of robotic lines stamping out 10,000 copies at a time. Individual attention to each bicycle allows the company to monitor sales and be extremely flexible to meet customer demands—for a particular model, in a particular size, and in a particular color and finish. Such attention to detail creates pride in Cannondale's work teams—from design through production—and satisfies customers. As the company's Web site states, "We concentrate on detail, because the last 5 percent is often the difference between success and failure." Cannondale is proving that one bike and one rider at a time.

Questions

1. Cannondale uses special-purpose teams to design and produce its bicycles. What are some benefits to that approach?
2. What could be some drawbacks to Cannondale's team approach?
3. How does Cannondale make use of virtual teamwork to produce its products?

SOURCES: Interview with John Horn, research and development product manager at Cannondale Corporation, April 9, 2002; Cannondale Web site, *http://www.cannondale.com*, accessed March 22, 2002.

Cannondale Has Finely Tuned Control Processes

ORGANIZATIONS TODAY FACE THE CONSTANT CHALLENGE OF controlling their activities to reduce waste, shorten time frames, and maximize profits. Their very survival depends on how well they can streamline processes and produce high-quality products from the outset. The high-performance bicycle industry is no different; it is extremely competitive among the top handful of companies. Known for its innovative designs, Connecticut-based Cannondale Corporation believes in control before, during, and after its design and manufacturing processes. In fact, to remain a profitable, viable, business, the organization needs to run as a finely tuned machine, with all parts contributing to overall goals.

Creativity drives and inspires Cannondale's teams, but continual innovation also requires checks and balances to ensure quality. After new bicycle designs are created using a computer-aided design (CAD) software program, teams review them carefully. And before a bicycle design is approved for production, design engineers check its accuracy and feasibility through a proofing process, the first step in quality control. The goal of proofing is to answer the question, Can the design be built as envisioned? Once they feel confident in the new design, engineers send the CAD system's design to a rapid prototyping machine, which constructs a plastic model so that engineers can see in three dimensions what they have planned. Overseeing this design process is the research and development project manager, who keeps an eye on design timelines and prototyping schedules. John Horn, a Cannondale R&D project manager says, "Engineers are perfectionists, but the R&D project manager must make sure the product gets to market when it's needed."

Once the design engineers have perfected a design, they transmit it electronically to the production teams in Bedford, Pennsylvania. Production engineers at the factory use the computer design to develop working samples using actual materials. New designs undergo 12 to 15 different tests to ensure impact strength, durability of the materials, and performance. Testing includes actually riding the prototype, as well as destructive testing to check the design's limits.

Manufacturing processes are controlled through precision machinery and empowered teams. Cannondale uses computer-guided laser machines to cut the frame's aluminum tubes to precise dimensions. Then the company relies on its craftsmen's experience and training. Because the strength of a bicycle frame depends on the quality of its welds, welders undergo a training and certification program to ensure that they meet quality standards. During manufacturing, any employee on the assembly line can speak up and stop production at any time to fix problems immediately. Once a frame has been constructed, Cannondale's coordinate-measuring machine checks every measurement, and as a final control, a technician manually verifies the measurements. The frame is then sanded, cleaned, and hand painted, and protective finishes are applied.

Critical to bicycle design is actual testing of performance in the field. Cannondale seeks ideas from professional bicycle racers to maintain its cutting-edge designs. The company sponsors professional racing teams—two mountain-bike racing teams, three road-racing teams, and a triathlon team. The feedback that the racers supply is invaluable to the company's design and manufacturing processes. The company has won many quality awards through the years, among them *Bicycling* magazine's "Publisher's Award for Innovation," *VeloNews* magazine's "Technological Development of the Year Award," *Popular Science's* "Best of What's New" award, *Business Week's* "Best New Products of the Year Award," *Design News* magazine's "Computer-Aided Design Award," and *Popular Mechanics'* "Design and Engineering Award."

Even with such acclaim, Cannondale is not content to rest. The company can change product lines as often as every six months to remain at the forefront of bicycle design and competitive in its market. And it has been revamping its inventory and manufacturing processes to streamline them for profitability. It recently switched its materials control computer software from a time-consuming program that took 9 hours and much manual intervention to complete to one that performed profitability analyses in 2 hours and 12 minutes. With such timely information, the company was able to review its processes and reduce its inventory stock by roughly 25 percent, which freed up money and resources to be used elsewhere—such as research and development. Cannondale's purchasing manager says that the new system has eliminated not only the time involved but many headaches as well. "Before, it took so much effort to work through the mountain of computer printouts to find what you were looking for that you just wouldn't do it." Now the company can generate that information in seconds and feed it back to critical decision makers. That kind of speed record is as critical to Cannondale as awards and races won.

Questions

1. Review the three types of control outlined. From the information provided, categorize the types of control Cannondale uses in its design and manufacturing processes as feedforward, concurrent, or feedback.
2. Would you say that Cannondale relies more on bureaucratic control or decentralized control to ensure quality?
3. Does Cannondale practice total quality management? Explain.

SOURCES: Interview with John Horn, Cannondale research and development project manager, April 9, 2002; Cannondale company Web site, http://www.cannondale.com, accessed March 22, 2002; Nick Wreden, "Doing Wheelies," *Consumer Goods*, May 2000, http://www.consumergoods.com; David J. Bak, "Skin and Bones, but Plenty Tough: Cannondale Combines CAD and Composites for a Breakthrough Bike," *Design News*, March 2, 1998, accessed at http://www.findarticles.com.

Cannondale's Information Technology: From Office to Factory Floor—and Beyond

INFORMATION IS A VALUABLE RESOURCE FOR TODAY'S ORGANI-zations, and information technology can tap its potential. Cannondale Corporation, the leading designer and manufacturer of high-performance aluminum bicycles and cycling accessories, believes in the strategic use of information technology. The company employs computer systems for everything from bicycle design, precision manu-facturing, and quality control, to inventory and sales management. Cannondale's director of marketing and media relations, Tom Arm-strong, says the goal of using information technology is to move faster than competitors. "We have tried to do that by innovating not only on the product front but in every other aspect as well. A lot of our own production engineering is about getting inside the development cycle of our competitors."

Cannondale's design engineers, based in Connecticut, use a computer-aided design (CAD) system called Pro/Engineer, a three-dimensional modeling program. With the program, designers can execute an idea and nearly instantly generate the measurements and parts needed for prototyping and mold making for manufacturing. They can also automatically create many different sizes in the same model style—to fit cyclists of many different shapes and sizes. With more than 80 different bicycle models currently, the CAD system gives the company flexibility—and a competitive edge.

After a design is finalized, the CAD system relays the design elec-tronically to the production engineers in the company's Bedford, Penn-sylvania, factories. Several years ago, the company saw the promise of Internet technology and harnessed it to track its manufacturing process. It installed an intranet in its Pennsylvania manufacturing plants to reduce the complexity and costs of the manufacturing system. The company's application engineer installed Web browser software on personal computers on the factory floor and replaced the keyboards with bar-code scanners and mouses for ease of input. As employees on the assembly line finish a step, they swipe the scanner across a bar-code on each bicycle. The company's managers can then capture information and track the manufacturing processes to ensure that parts and supplies are available when needed.

Cannondale also uses the Internet's communications capability to relay product specifications to its subsidiaries in the Netherlands, Japan, and Australia, which do final product assembly and finishing for overseas products. Before the use of the Web, workers sent hard-copy drawings to the subsidiaries, and employees there placed them in binders, which had to be updated periodically. That process was time-consuming and unreliable. Now the company can instantly transmit its drawings electronically, complete with final paint colors. The result is consistency in product manufacturing, reduced time, and reduced costs.

Cannondale has focused most of its information technology system on personal computers running Windows software. This strategic deci-sion simplifies the company's hardware and software systems and allows employees in all divisions to share the information in word pro-cessing, spreadsheet, and other programs. Cannondale recently began working with AimNet Solutions to handle its network infrastruc-ture. AimNet will monitor the company's network and ensure it per-forms reliably. Cannondale's vice-president of information technology, Mike Dower, explains the strategic partnership this way: "Our strategy at Cannondale has been the same since our inception. We strive to cre-ate innovative, differentiated, high-performance products. With our passion for growth, . . . we couldn't afford to be distracted from that strategy. . . . We can stay focused on creating superior products" and let AimNet oversee the network infrastructure.

Cannondale has also reconstructed its inventory and sales man-agement systems with information technology. With its new PC-based system, the company is able to track supplies more accurately and, as a result, reduced inventory stocks by approximately one quarter. The system may eventually be used to tie Cannondale's information system with its suppliers'. Cannondale sales representatives also gather data from retail partners about which models are selling well. They relay that information to the company's information system, and managers can switch manufacturing to needed models. This quick response to customer needs is important to Cannondale's success. The company has also begun using its corporate Web site to inform prospective cus-tomers about tailor-made bicycles. Currently, the company allows the customer to choose from over eight million possible frame and color variations available on the CAAD5 road frame. Giving customers such wide choices and ensuring the product they want is in their local store helps solidify their relationships with the company. Cannondale's Web site says, "Our focus is people—employees, customers, retailers, and our vendors—working together to accomplish our mission." And Can-nondale uses sophisticated information technology systems to link those people into one big network.

Questions

1. What types of groupware does Cannondale use?
2. How important is Cannondale's information technology to its design and manufacturing?
3. Cannondale uses information technology in many ways to stream-line its business processes. What other ways could it use them in the future?

SOURCES: Cannondale company Web site, http://www.cannondale.com, accessed March 22, 2002; "Cannondale Signs with Genosys Technology Management," Busi-ness Wire, October 29, 2001; Blaise Zerega, "Cannondale Rides Web for Productiv-ity," InfoWorld, November 16, 1998, http://www. infoworld.com; David F. Carr, "Extending an Intranet to the Factory Floor," Internet World, September 21, 1998, accessed at http://www.findarticles. com.

Cannondale's Consuming Passion for Perfection

YOU'D EXPECT A COMPANY THAT PRODUCES PREMIUM BICYCLES to care about its manufacturing processes. After all, the company knows how gears must mesh perfectly and how lightweight and durable frames must fit their riders' bodies seamlessly to form a single unit built for speed. You'd expect the company to realize how each system must perform flawlessly. You'd expect that, and you'd be right. Cannondale Corporation pursues its mission of producing innovative, quality products with nothing short of passion.

Cannondale's manufacturing organization produces physical goods—bicycles, cycling accessories, and off-road vehicles. And its operations strategy lies at the very heart of the company—it must produce its products quickly, efficiently, and well to survive. But Cannondale has another goal in mind besides mere survival: it strives to be an innovator. That focus places additional pressure on its operations, not only to support the company but to provide a competitive advantage.

As the Internet became more widely used in the mid-1990s, Cannondale foresaw its potential for supply chain management. Rather than install complex systems, the company used the simplicity of Web technology to manage its manufacturing processes. It installed personal computers directly on the factory floor and used scanners and bar-code technology to track the stages of the manufacturing process. Workers simply swipe the scanner over a bar code attached to a bicycle frame, and the system automatically updates a database. The database serves as a gateway to the company's material requirements planning (MRP) application. The database can also be accessed by management and Cannondale's overseas subsidiaries for decision making and planning.

Cannondale revamped its inventory control system in the late 1990s to allow it more flexibility. The old system created a one-to three-week delay in analyzing design or order changes—too long a time frame for a company that can change its product line every six months. Frustrated with the system's pokiness, the company invited vendor WebPlan to demonstrate its system using actual corporate data. The new system allowed the company to do an MRP run in 2 hours and 12 minutes. Cannondale expanded the system's use to scheduling and planning in purchasing, finance, and other departments. Such efficiency allowed the company to reduce its inventory drastically and use the dollars previously tied up in inventory for other purposes, especially product design. The company is also planning to link its suppliers to the system via the Internet. As Cannondale's purchasing manager says, "If [suppliers] can see our requirements on the Internet as fast as we can, then a lot of time can be saved. Buyers and planners don't have to spend time communicating on every little detail, and parts production can begin when it's needed, not when it's communicated using a phone or fax." Integrating suppliers into the system provides a unified supply chain management system.

Cannondale's small production runs on its assembly lines allow the company to be more flexible in its manufacturing systems than other companies, which produce thousands of units at a time with robotics. Cannondale can quickly and easily change paint colors or customize decal designs to meet sales demand or customer preferences. It uses technology when appropriate for accuracy and consistency but also provides craftsmanship with skilled employees. Such flexibility enables Cannondale to ship a custom bicycle out of the factory within six weeks of a signed custom order. It can also meet its retail partners' specific demands more quickly.

Productivity is a key to Cannondale's success—through technology and its employees. From its Web-based factory floor software to its computer-aided design and manufacturing systems, the company has created a top-performing production line. With its redesigned production processes, the company expanded from manufacturing one product line of about 50 bike models to six lines with 120 models. But the constant push for design innovation and new materials keeps the company on its toes. Sophisticated bicycles must balance strength, flexibility, and weight for peak performance. Cannondale is meeting those challenges head on and aiming to change the bicycle world at the same time. As the company's Web site says, "We devise flexible manufacturing processes that enable us to deliver those innovative, quality products to the market quickly and then back them with excellent customer service." From its early beginnings in a loft above a pickle factory, Cannondale has been racing toward perfection for 30 years, and it hasn't tired yet.

Questions

1. From this video case and those for on pages AA-19 to AA-21, identify the inputs to Cannondale's manufacturing organization.
2. How does Cannondale's operations support its production of high-performance bicycles?

SOURCES: Interview with John Horn, Cannondale research and development project manager, April 9, 2002; Nick Wreden, "Doing Wheelies," *Consumer Goods*, May 2000, http://www.consumergoods.com; David F. Carr, "Extending an Intranet to the Factory Floor," *Internet World*, September 21, 1998, accessed at http://www.findarticles.com.

Part One: Ford Motor Company Makes History

THE HISTORY OF FORD MOTOR COMPANY EMBODIES THE history of American management itself. When Henry Ford began a manufacturing revolution with his company's mass production of automobiles, much of the country was still bouncing along in horse-drawn carriages. A hundred years later, despite many ups and downs, Ford Motor Company is firmly established as the world's largest pickup-truck manufacturer and the number-two maker of cars (behind General Motors). Ford has progressed from an offering of one color—black—to a wide range of makes, models, and hues from which consumers may choose, depending on their budget, lifestyle, and mood. In addition to the autos it produces under its own name, Ford's brands now include Jaguar, Lincoln, Mercury, and Volvo, a 33 percent stake in Mazda, BMW's Land Rover SUV, along with the Hertz rental agency. Ford has had hugely successful models, such as the Taurus, as well as duds that it would rather forget, such as the Pinto. In recent years, the company has been mired in a public-relations disaster surrounding its popular SUV, the Explorer, and the vehicle's standard tires, which were manufactured by Firestone/Bridgestone. Still, the company has managed to survive by making changes in leadership, improving efficiency and effectiveness of its management and manufacturing operations, and embracing new management competencies. As you study your course of management this semester, you'll follow the rises, dips, and turns of one of America's most well-known and enduring organizations.

Fast-forward from that original assembly line spewing out those black Model Ts and Model As to the end of the twentieth century, when a whirlwind known as Jacques (Jac) Nasser took over as CEO of Ford Motor Company and immediately began to change management practices that previously had included a complex bureaucracy bogged down by centralized decision making and an unwillingness to budge from the status quo.

Although Nasser didn't explicitly use the term *learning organization,* he set out to turn his company into one. He hired a group of skilled managers from different automakers around the world (including Volkswagen and BMW), lured a number of marketers and salespeople from consumer-goods manufacturers, and pushed the entire Ford workforce to get as close to customers as possible to find out what people really wanted in their automobiles. He encouraged information sharing with such initiatives as a venture with MSN's CarPoint Web site that would provide data from online purchases. Ford marketers and designers would learn which models, colors, and features certain buyers preferred. And he let managers know in no uncertain terms that Ford Motor Company was now on the move—with their help as empowered workers who were accountable for their own (and their employees') performance. "You've got to earn [a promotion,]" Nasser supposedly thundered in one meeting. "The days of entitlement at Ford Motor Company are gone forever." To that end, he instituted a forced-ranking system, under which a certain number of employees would be considered underperformers and laid off each year. The system, which worked something like a grading curve, drew much criticism and was eventually abandoned.

On a grand scale, Nasser announced an organizational shakeup that meant decentralizing authority and decision-making powers, and transferring them to semiautonomous business units around the world. "Jac learned to make decisions without a lot of bureaucratic oversight from [Ford headquarters at] Dearborn," recalled Robert Lutz, Nasser's former boss. Now Nasser was promoting this kind of independent decision making with a new generation of Ford managers.

All of these actions were part of Nasser's strategy to transform a century-old industrial giant into a nimble, flexible company that could rapidly meet consumers' wants and needs. Designers, engineers, and marketers were required to attend seminars at a Consumer Insight Center to learn how to listen to customers and engage them in conversations designed to reveal what products and features they would most likely buy. Then they were sent in small teams out into the field for eight weeks of "customer immersion." Nasser wasn't kidding. He wanted all managers at all levels to understand their customers, inside and out.

Nasser made some radical changes at Ford Motor Company, an organization that has long been a symbol of American business and ingenuity. The company has been around so long that it has passed through several historical phases of management, from scientific management to today's learning organization. In 1913, one of the first moving assembly lines was installed in the company's Highland Park plant, reducing production time by 50 percent. With this new system, a Ford Model T came off the assembly line every ten seconds. Today, Ford managers rely on teams, empowerment, the Internet, and high-speed technology to produce thousands of cars a day. Ford's ability to change when the environment demands it may be the single most important factor in its long-term survival.

Questions

1. How have the necessary skills for a successful manager changed at Ford over the decades?
2. Why was it important for Ford to become a learning organization?
3. Do you think that Jacques Nasser was an effective manager? Why or why not?

SOURCES: "Ford Motor Company," Hoover's Capsule, Hoover's Online (November 16, 2001), http://www.hoovers.com; "Profile—Ford Motor Company," Yahoo! Finance; Julie Cantwell, "Exec Changes Help Ford with Basics," *Automotive News* (November 12, 2001), http://www.autonews. com; Geoffrey Colvin, "We Can't All Be Above Average," *Fortune,* August 13, 2001, http://www.fortune.com; Kathleen Kerwin and Keith Naughton, "Remaking Ford," *Businessweek Online* (October 11, 1999), http://www.businessweek. com.

Part Two: Ford Operates in a Complex Environment

HENRY FORD WAS AN ENTREPRENEUR WHOSE COMPANY became an American icon over the course of a century. He never could have guessed that by late 2001, CEO Jacques Nasser, the aggressive, embattled Australian businessman who had been in Ford's driver's seat for only three years, would be standing by the side of the road, briefcase in hand. Nasser had shaken up Ford's stodgy, bureaucratic corporate culture and attempted to lead the organization through the worst crisis of its history—the Firestone tire debacle—but the company had suffered too many blows during his reign. During this period, Ford and its managers faced enormous challenges involving ethics, social responsibility, a change in culture, and a competitive, constantly changing environment both in the United States and abroad. Ultimately, Nasser was asked to step aside.

In August 2000, Ford's world blew apart as it became apparent that some of its standard tires, those manufactured by Bridgestone/Firestone and installed in Ford's top-selling Explorer SUV, were doing exactly that: the treads were separating from the tire's core, leading to injurious and fatal crashes. Although Nasser chose to endure public scrutiny and Bridgestone/Firestone's Japanese leaders remained in relative seclusion, neither company immediately took responsibility. Instead, they engaged in finger pointing, damaging a relationship that had gone back as far as Henry Ford and Harvey Firestone. Firestone recalled the 6 million tires it believed were faulty, but meanwhile accused Ford of poor automobile design. Ford announced that it would replace all 13 million of the Wilderness AT tires that were on its Explorers, even those that were presumed safe. Then Firestone severed its relationship with Ford. The recall program took so long that consumers and dealers became frustrated and fearful of the consequences—and increasingly distrustful of both companies. Ford and Firestone officials were called to testify before Congress. Meanwhile, as more accidents were investigated and analyzed, the death toll associated with the faulty tires rose to more than two hundred. Who was right, Ford or Firestone? Did Ford handle the situation ethically? Much has been written about the debacle, and the answers most likely will not be resolved for many years.

Meanwhile, Ford's general and task environments were continually changing. General Motors revamped its truck lineup, and Toyota opened up the throttle on its SUVs with its new Highlander and Sequoia models. Ford's quality was suffering, increasing the cost of its warranties and decreasing consumers' confidence in its products. Also, Ford had purchased several European brands, including Volvo and BMW Land Rover, and the economic downturn in Europe was of concern. Ford, along with other car manufacturers, tried to attract new buyers with innovative features and design. "It is a reflection of the market softening generally," explained Ford Europe's chairman and chief executive, David Thursfield. "We have to bring out more new innovative products to give the market a boost. That is what we are certainly doing at Ford." And the slowdown of the American economy, along with the $3 billion price tag attached to the tire recall, forced Ford to offer early retirement packages to nearly 5,000 man-agers in order to cut costs. Finally, relationships with dealers and suppliers, who continued to struggle with the tire recall, needed to be repaired. In this midst of all the turmoil, Ford's board of directors announced that Jacques Nasser would be leaving the company and that Bill Ford, Jr., would be taking over. Ford, in his mid-forties, was the first Ford family member to be CEO of the company since Henry Ford II resigned in 1979.

Bill Ford, known for his commitment to environmental issues, immediately pledged to make Ford Motor Company a leader in environmental protection as part of a company turnaround plan. A visit to the company's Web site reveals a whole host of environmentally friendly initiatives—not all introduced by Bill Ford, but indicative of the company's push toward social responsibility. For instance, Ford has teamed up with Environmental Defense to "provide automotive shoppers with comprehensive information about the environmental impact of automobiles sold in North America." Environmental Defense is a group that sponsors "For My World," a Web site that allows visitors to learn about the "Green Score" of particular vehicles. In addition, Ford is experimenting with water-based paints for its vehicles and working on ways to tackle pollution-producing manufacturing processes as well as traffic congestion.

Of course, these measures deal with only one facet of the overall environment in which Ford conducts its business. Bill Ford and his team of managers need to deal with quality issues, resolve the Firestone tire situation, and get new, more exciting autos into the pipeline. As he took the wheel of his family's company, Ford was closemouthed about his strategy for guiding the company into the future. "Everything is up for review—every asset, every piece of geography," he said. "We continue to review our mix of businesses." In November 2001, Ford announced that its Australian subsidiary would begin designing and manufacturing a new vehicle for the local Australian market, creating as many as 10,000 jobs there. Code-named Raptor, the new model would be poised to take on new cars introduced in Australia by General Motors. Despite the many roadblocks, Ford was showing signs of rolling forward again.

Questions

1. Add to your knowledge of the Firestone tire debacle by researching it on the Internet or at the library. Then prepare for a class discussion or written summary on whether or not you believe Ford acted ethically throughout the crisis and why.
2. Visit the Ford Web site and click on several of the company's pages dealing with socially responsible initiatives—the environment, education, and so forth. Then discuss the role you think these initiatives play in Ford's overall corporate culture.
3. Ford Motor Company was founded by an entrepreneur and was once a small business. Name three ways in which you think Ford has contributed to the American economy and culture over the last century.

SOURCES: Ford Motor Company Web site, *http://www.ford.com*, accessed January 8, 2002; Tim Burt, "Thursfield Champions Ford of Europe," *Financial Times*, November 28, 2001, *http://news.ft.com*; Virginia Marsh, "Ford Launch Could Create 10,000 Jobs in Australia," *Financial Times*, November 15, 2001, *http://news.ft.com*; Kathleen Kerwin and Joann Muller, "Bill Ford Takes the Wheel," *BusinessWeek Online*, November 1, 2001, *http://www.businesseek. com*; Charles Child and Mary Connelly, "Nasser Out; Bill Ford Takes Over," *Automotive News*, October 29, 2001, *http://www.autonews.com*; "Ford Concern on Europe Downturn," *BBC News*, September 10, 2001, *http://news.bbc.co.uk*; Jamie Butters, "Job Cuts at Ford Likely to Increase," Auto.com, August 10, 2001, *http://www.auto.com*; "Tire Trouble: The Ford-Firestone Blowout," *Forbes*, June 20, 2001, *http://www.forbes.com*.

Part Three: A Tale of Two Strategies

THE STORY OF BILL FORD AND JACQUES NASSER IS NOT ONLY the story of two leaders but also the story of two strategies marked by differing management styles, differing goals, and perhaps even differing views of the company's mission. When Nasser came to the top position at Ford, he had already worked for the company for thirty years. No one would argue that his sometimes harsh, autocratic decision-making style made him less than popular among Ford workers, managers, and media members. But Nasser arrived at the top in the late 1990s with bold plans to turn an aging, stumbling company into a streamlined, flexible contender in the auto industry. Ford's ventures into the financial services and defense industries in the 1980s had turned out to be disastrous. Nasser pledged that his new mission for the company, "to be the world's leading consumer company for automotive services and products," would be backed by solid strategic planning. "It's a world going through tremendous change," said Nasser early in his reign, "not just through economic events, but largely through technology. We're trying not to be left behind." So Nasser set a goal of hiring 20 percent new managers while also developing leaders from within the company. He also emphasized team building. He began to acquire other brands, in the United States and abroad, including Land Rover, Jaguar, and a chain of British auto-service centers called Kwik-Fit. He vowed to turn Ford's less profitable car lines around (the company was much stronger in the truck and SUV business): "In the past, we tried to do too much in the car business and dispersed our resources. Now we're simplifying the product line. And we're separating the models that remain and giving them better brand identities." He planned to jump into e-business with all four wheels. "Technology and networks in particular determine the shape of everything else," Nasser remarked. He began with a joint venture with Microsoft's CarPoint, which allowed consumers to build cars to order online (the site also provided Ford with data about car buyers).

How did Nasser's planning work out? Within a couple of years, Wall Street named Ford the most profitable and best-managed automaker of the Big Three (the other two are General Motors and DaimlerChrysler). Then came the Firestone tire recall, quality problems that began to surface, a sluggish economy, and other woes. Nasser's grand Internet plans didn't work out as he had hoped—the information technology department simply wasn't ready. In the summer of 2001, Ford's board of directors voted to give company chairman Bill Ford "a greater strategic role" in the company. In other words, Ford and Nasser would share power and responsibilities that would "focus on policy, strategy, key issues affecting the future direction of the company and other major business issues." For several months, the two men remained diplomatic in public, but there was no mistaking their differing management styles, visions for the company, or proposed strategies. Eventually, Nasser was voted out. Bill Ford had a huge task ahead of him.

First, Bill Ford created a triumvirate—a team of three top executives—to formulate a new vision and strategies for the company. He named Carl E. Reichardt vice-chairman and Nick Scheele chief operating officer. Scheele came from Ford's Jaguar division and Reichardt,

former head of a bank, from the board of directors. "I expect the three of us will have an easygoing relationship," noted Ford. Scheele began his term with a "back to basics" slogan that indicated the company's new strategy would focus on its core business: making and selling cars and trucks. Then came the massive restructuring plan, whose goal was to cut $3 billion to $5 billion in costs. Most experts believe that Nasser would have favored downsizing in order to meet Ford's shrinking share in the marketplace, but Bill Ford would likely favor other strategies. Still, he warned in an early press release that the company would have to take "tough action" to reverse its losses. "It is not going to surprise anyone that there will be some pretty dramatic changes," noted Greg Melich of Morgan Stanley Dean Witter. "The one area where you can do more quickly is in the managerial and administrative areas, whereas restructuring the manufacturing side is much more difficult." However, it was clear that there was surplus manufacturing capacity in North America that needed to be addressed. And before Nasser's departure, the company was considering laying off as much as 20 percent of its U.S. white-collar staff, or more than 8,000 salaried workers, as part of a strategic overhaul. Also, the company proposed delaying the release of certain new auto models, including the Ford Ranger. Another part of the plan involved using more shared parts to cut manufacturing costs, even in Ford's premium car lines such as Volvo and Jaguar. A "strategy board" was developed specifically to formulate plans for the Premier Automotive Group (PAG), which would open the door for more than shared parts—perhaps shared engineering, sales, and purchasing teams—while maintaining the individual identities of the brands. "We have developed a structure which will allow us to more effectively support all our PAG brands," announced Wolfgang Reitzle, chairman of the PAG. "Individually, the companies do not have the critical mass to compete on equal terms."

Finally, Bill Ford began to push for a reconciliation between his company and Firestone/Bridgestone; after all, there are Fords and Firestones in both families. Mending the relationship might indicate a return to normalcy on the road "back to the basics." What are Ford's basics? "It's not the Internet, junkyards, or auto parts," quips David E. Cole, director of the Center for Automotive Research in Ann Arbor, Michigan. "It's building cars and trucks." Now there's a plan.

Questions

1. Based on what you've read, formulate a brief mission statement for the "new" Ford Motor Company.
2. Imagine that you are part of Bill Ford's management team. Set a stretch goal either for the company as a whole or for the Premier group strategy board that you think would realistically help the company turn around. Explain why you chose this goal.
3. Describe the differences between Jacques Nasser and Bill Ford as decision makers.

SOURCES: John Griffiths and Tim Burt, "Moving to Drive the Premier Growth Machine Faster," *Financial Times*, November 23, 2001, http://news.ft.com; Tim Burt and Nikki Tait, "Ford May Axe 20 percent of U.S. White Collar Staff," *Financial Times*, November 6, 2001, http://news.ft.com; Kathleen Kerwin and Joann Muller, "Bill

Ford Takes the Wheel," *BusinessWeek Online*, November 1, 2001, *http://www. businessweek.com;* David Ibison, "New Ford Chief Edges Closer to Truce with Bridgestone," *Financial Times*, November 1, 2001, *http://news.ft.com;* Tim Burt, "Nasser Signals Further Cuts in Ford's U.S. Production," *Financial Times*, October 25, 2001, *http://news.ft.com;* Tim Burt, "Nasser Says Ford Has the Strategy to Confound Critics," *Financial Times*, September 13, 2001, *http://news.ft.com;* Jerry Flint, "Ford: A Distracted Driver," *Forbes.com*, September 6, 2001, *http://www.forbes.com;*

Tim Burt and Nikki Tait, "Getting Ford Around the Corner," *Financial Times*, July 30, 2001, *http://news.ft.com;* Jeff Moad, "Ford Rebuilds IT Engine," ZDNet News, January 28, 2001, *http://www.zdnet.com;* Amey Stone and Kathleen Kerwin, "Can Nasser Get Ford's Stock onto a Smoother Road?" *BusinessWeek Online*, October 11, 1999, *http://www.businessweek.com;* "Jac Nasser: In the Past, We Tried to Do Too Much," *BusinessWeek Online*, October 11, 1999, *http://www. businessweek.com.*

Part Four: Managing Organizational Changes at Ford

MOST OF US RESIST CHANGE: IT IS HUMAN NATURE TO WANT things to stay the same, even if the conditions of our lives are less than ideal. Changes within organizations are just as difficult for managers to implement and employees to accept. Whether it is learning a new technology, increasing or decreasing staff, expanding or downsizing manufacturing capabilities, adding or deleting products to the line, change can be stressful for everyone in the organization. Conceiving of and announcing the change may fall to upper-level executives, but implementing the change is usually the responsibility of managers, including human resource managers. When the restructuring plan put together by Bill Ford's new executive team began to unfold in late 2001 and early 2002, all of Ford Motor Company was on edge.

After announcing a series of management changes, including the retirement of the chief financial officer, the elevation of Nick Scheele to chief operating officer, and the appointment of three new group vice presidents, the team focused on massive restructuring of Ford's U.S. operations. In January 2002, the team announced that Ford would be closing key manufacturing plants in New Jersey, Missouri, Ohio, Michigan, and Ontario, citing too much capacity at those plants. In other words, the company was overproducing and did not need to build as many cars in a weak economy. In addition, Ford took several well-known but slow-selling models out of production—the Ford Escort, the Mercury Villager (a minivan), the Mercury Cougar, and the Lincoln Continental. Saying that former CEO Jacques Nasser had diversified the organization too much, the new group declared that Ford was now focusing on its core business of building cars and trucks. Overall, 35,000 Ford workers (10 percent of the total global workforce) would probably lose their jobs, at least temporarily. Although this sounds grim, managers and other experts believed that these massive changes would ultimately help Ford survive a weak economy and the costs incurred by the Firestone tire debacle and ultimately lead to its growth.

A company such as Ford naturally has a huge, diverse workforce to manage. Although diversity challenges most often relate to ensuring that a variety of people have equal job opportunity, rarely do we think of older, white male employees as needing protection by the law. But that is exactly what happened at Ford, when a class-action lawsuit was filed against the company for reverse discrimination. The suit alleged that the company's performance appraisal system was targeting those workers for dismissal or early retirement. How could this happen? Under a system instituted by former CEO Nasser, called the Performance Management Process, workers were given performance grades of A, B, or C. Those who received a C could lose their bonuses and raises; those who received two C grades in a row could be fired. If that sounds fair, here's the catch: Under the original plan, a quota of at least 10 percent of Ford employees were to receive C grades; later, the percentage was lowered to 5 percent. Many liken the ranking system, currently being used by a number of leading companies, to a grading curve because regardless of actual performance, a certain number of employees received high scores and a certain number received low

ones. As it turned out at Ford, many of the C grades were handed out to older white males. Ford's system was eventually changed to one designating top achievers, achievers, and those requiring improvement. But within a year and a half, Ford agreed to abandon the system, which affected about 18,000 managers. As Bill Ford took over the CEO spot in late 2001, negotiations in the lawsuits continued. However, it seemed clear that both sides wanted the cases settled as amicably as possible.

Compensating nearly half a million employees in different countries is another huge challenge for human resource managers at Ford. In the fall of 2001, the combination of sluggish car sales and the Firestone recall forced the human resource department to circulate a memo announcing that about 6,000 managers would not be receiving their typical yearly bonuses. The company simply did not have the pool of cash—about $440 million—it had had in the past to pay out the bonuses. Nasser's retirement package was also tied to the company's overall financial performance, but he still received a bonus worth more than $5 million.

It is doubtful that anyone would dispute that Ford's management team has had an extremely rocky ride during the past few years. Managers at every level have faced constant challenges as their organization has struggled with massive changes. However, Ford's is taking clear steps to survive and ultimately come out on top with its focus on producing new car models and perhaps even a retooled organization model.

Questions

1. What factors in the environment do you believe have affected Ford's structure in the past? What environmental factors do you believe will affect its structure in the future?
2. What internal forces for change has Ford faced in the last five years?
3. From a human resource management perspective, why do you think Jacques Nasser's performance appraisal system failed?

SOURCES: Ed Garsten, "Tentative Terms in Ford Bias Cases," Associated Press, (November 16, 2001), http://www.ford.com; "Ford Moving Closer to Settling Suits—WSJ," Reuters Limited (November 16, 2001); Ed Garsten, "Ford Announces Management Shuffle," Associated Press (November 15, 2001), http://dailynews.yahoo.com; August Cole, "Ford Shuffles Another Round of Execs," CBS MarketWatch.com (November 15, 2001), http://www.marketwatch.com; "Nasser's Retirement Package Tied to Ford's Performance," Auto.co (November 15, 2001), http://www.auto.com; "Exec Changes Help Ford with Basics," Automotive News (November 12, 2001), http://www.autonews.com; Nikki Tait, "Lincoln Bears Brunt of Ford Restructuring," Financial Times (November 11, 2001), http://news.ft.com; Tim Burt and Nikki Tait, "Ford May Axe 20 Percent of White Collar Staff," Financial Times (November 6, 2001), http://news.ft.com; John Gallagher, "No Bonuses This Year for Ford's Top Bosses," Detroit Free Press (August 29, 2001), http://www.freep.com; Tim Burt and Nikki Tait, "Ford Refines Chain of Command in U.S.," Financial Times (July 16, 2001), http://news.ft.com; Tim Burt, "Ford's White Knight Summoned to Aid of U.S. in Distress," Financial Times (July 15, 2001), http://news.ft.com.

Part Five: Ford Enters a New Era of Leadership

LEADERS COME IN ALL SHAPES AND SIZES. THEY MAY COME FROM different countries and cultures. They exhibit different personality traits. They practice different leadership styles. They may be team players or loners. They may have legitimate power, like Jacques Nasser and Bill Ford. They may practice coercive power, as Nasser did with his controversial performance appraisal system. They often have personal power, as demonstrated by Bill Ford in his commitment to good relationships with union workers. They may possess different visions for the same company, but they all want to motivate their managers and employees toward that vision. And they look for ways to communicate their goals.

Jacques Nasser's entire tenure as CEO of Ford Motor Company was driven by his goal for the company to become "the world's leading consumer company for automotive services and products." He began by slashing costs and reducing payrolls, earning the nickname "Jac the Knife." Then he diversified Ford's business activities around the world, to the dismay of critics who believed he was carrying the company too far afield from its core business of building and selling cars and trucks. (Some thought he invested too much time and money on the Internet prematurely.) He professed to be a believer in teams and open communication, stating in one interview, "You let your teams have room to work and give them air cover. I'm not a believer in telling people [exactly] what to do. If you start giving people a cookbook, you start to get very narrow solutions." Despite cutting a number of jobs, Nasser claimed to be looking for the best people within the company, to motivate them and move them up. "We are spending more time and effort developing leaders from inside the company," he said. "We're trying to strengthen the team. Like any sports team, if you stop recruiting, over time, you'd lose your competitiveness. If you look at the team we've got today, there's a tremendous mix of different backgrounds, even among the people who came up through Ford Motor Co." But Nasser also had a reputation for being an intimidating leader who kept tight controls on his managers—he had sixteen senior managers reporting directly to him instead of creating a team of top executives with the authority to make decisions.

Bill Ford is a completely different type of leader, one who actually sees himself on par with the rank and file workers instead of heir to a family dynasty. His personal power is partly expert—he not only grew up in the business (as did Nasser) but prepared to take over the chairmanship by heading up the company's finance committee—and partly referent. People at all levels of the organization genuinely like him. "You can't get mad at Bill Ford," says Lincoln-Mercury dealer Martin J. McInerney. "He's just too nice a guy." He truly believes that Ford Motor Co. can—and should—have a positive relationship with all its workers and associated unions. And he is passionate about the environment. He sees no reason why the company can't set an example as an environmentally friendly auto manufacturer. "I've staked much of my personal reputation on the environment," he says. "Sometimes I wake up wondering whether I'm taking the company on a diversionary course that won't pay off . . . but on other nights I wake up thinking we're not doing enough." Since taking over as CEO, Ford has redrawn the lines of communication within the company, estab-lishing an executive team that he believes will work well together. "I expect the three of us [Ford, Nick Scheele, and Carl Reichardt] will have an easygoing relationship," predicts Ford.

Ford had already tried to share the leadership role when he took over the chairmanship position while Jacques Nasser was still CEO. The company's board of directors urged the two men to hammer out an arrangement to share power to benefit the company. "You guys need each other," the directors said to each man in separate meetings. So the two tried to establish their roles. "We wanted to ensure that there was clear accountability and clarity with the roles so that we didn't confuse the organization," said Nasser at the time. The result was an arrangement that continued Nasser's primary responsibility for running the company's day-to-day operations and tied Ford more closely to management, but it only lasted for a few short months.

By November 2001, Nasser was out. Some reports say he resigned; others say he was fired. Chances are, both are true. Although Bill Ford certainly had a hand in Nasser's departure, he also takes responsibility for perhaps waiting too long to replace Nasser as the company was stumbling. "I'll always accept my share of the blame," he concedes. Although skeptics are waiting to see whether Bill Ford is tough enough to be the transformational leader that they believe the company now needs, he does have a vision for the company's role not only as a high-quality auto manufacturer, but also as an agent of change. "I'm in this for my children and my grandchildren," he explains. "I want them to inherit a legacy they're proud of. I don't want anybody, whether it's my grandchildren or any of our employees' grandchildren, to have to apologize for working for Ford Motor Co. In fact, I want the opposite. I want them to look and say, 'What a difference we made!'"

Questions

1. Using Exhibit 12.2, make a chart showing what you believe are the personal characteristics of leaders that Bill Ford and Jacques Nasser possess.
2. Do you think Bill Ford and Jacques Nasser are effective communicators? Explain your answer for each.
3. In what ways might Bill Ford use problem-solving teams to benefit his organization? Give one example describing a problem-solving team that might be effective at Ford Motor Co.

SOURCES: Alex Taylor, "Car Jacqued!" *Fortune*, November 26, 2001, http://www.fortune.com; David Booth, "FoMoCo on Firmer Ground with Family Back at Helm," *Financial Times*, November 16, 2001, http://globalarchive.ft.com; "Bill Ford Takes the Wheel," *BusinessWeek Online*, November 1, 2001, http://www.businessweek.com; Doron Levin, "Bill Ford Jr. Got His Wish, and Has Much to Prove," *Bloomberg.com*, October 31, 2001, http://quote.bloomberg.com; "Getting Ford Round the Corner," *Financial Times*, July 30, 2001, http://news.ft.com; Mary Connelly, "Where Jacques Nasser Went Wrong," *Automotive News*, October 15, 2001, www.autonews.com; Jeffrey E. Garten, "The Mind of the C.E.O.," *BusinessWeek Online*, February 5, 2001, http://www.businessweek.com; Keith H. Hammonds, "Grassroots Leadership—Ford Motor Company," *Fast Company*, April 2000, http://www.fastcompany.com; Alex Taylor, "The Fight at Ford," *Fortune*, April 3, 2000, www.fortune.com; Betsy Morris, "Idealist on Board," *Fortune*, April 3, 2000, www.fortune.com.

Part 6: At Ford, Quality Is Job 1—Again

A FEW YEARS AGO, FORD RAN AN ADVERTISING CAMPAIGN whose motto was "At Ford, Quality, Is Job 1." The company boasted top quality not only in the manufacture of its trucks and cars, but also in its service. In the summer of 2000, the old slogan came back to haunt the company, as it became evident that literally millions of tires—made by Firestone—on Ford's popular SUVs, including the Explorer, were separating and shredding, causing serious and even fatal accidents. Even though Ford didn't manufacture the tires, those tires were installed on Ford vehicles; and the press, general public, and even Congress had a hard time distinguishing between the two. The situation was exacerbated as Bridgestone/Firestone accused Ford of building inferior vehicles. Finger pointing between the two organizations, centered on quality issues, continued for months as the tires were recalled and replaced. A year later, the National Highway Traffic Safety Administration reported that the defective tires, not the Ford vehicles, were to blame for the crashes; but the damage was already done in the public's eyes. "I think as long as this battle is going on in the press nobody is going to win," noted Anne Sceia Klein, a public-relations expert in Philadelphia. "The general public will walk away from [the Ford Explorer] if they can't sort it out."

Maintaining the quality of goods and services is a major part of the controlling function in an organization. Unfortunately, even if a quality problem is only a perceived one—or is exaggerated by publicity—damage to the organization's reputation can occur, and ultimately sales can drop. Ford faced both real and perceived quality issues in its struggle with the tire/SUV problem. Former CEO Jacques Nasser disputed Firestone's charges that the Explorer was at least partially to blame for the rollover crashes. "If you happen to be in a vehicle that had a tread separation, and that vehicle happens to be a compact SUV, you'd be much safer in an Explorer," argued Nasser. "If those Firestone tires were on other SUVs, the rollover instance would be much worse."

Some experts believe that the right information technology, which would have allowed greater knowledge sharing between Bridgestone/Firestone and Ford, and better designed production systems could have prevented the mismatch of tires and vehicles. In fact, Ford already had in place its own Best Practices Replication Process, which was designed to improve the efficiency of various parts of the manufacturing process. In 1995, Dale McKeehan, then vice president of manufacturing, called together his vehicle operations people, including the heads of body construction, painting, and final assembly and said, "Figure out a way to share best practices." Stan Kwiecien, then head of a group working on plant productivity recalls, "So we figured it out. We're engineers." Around the same time, McKeehan met with another manager, Dar Wolford, who was using early information technology to improve efficiency at Ford plants. McKeehan introduced Wolford to Kwiecien, and Ford's Best Practices Replication Process was born. Within four years, more than 2,800 proven superior practices had been shared among Ford's widespread manufacturing facilities, at a total documented value of $850 million. But knowledge sharing did not extend outside the company, so Ford and Firestone never communicated with each other about potential problems with the pairing of their two products.

Around the time of the tire recall, Ford began training managers in a program called Six Sigma, which is a system for continuous improvement in quality and efficiency to help the organization avoid manufacturing mistakes. Six Sigma uses statistical analysis to find the root of a problem that other methods can't seem to locate. For instance, the company's new Lincoln LS sedan had trouble starting on the first try. Using Six Sigma, an engineering team traced the problem to a screw that wasn't properly tightened. How did so many of these screws come off the assembly line loose? Because workers were using the wrong power tool to tighten them. Ford managers claim that Six Sigma saved the company $52 million in errors the first year, with another $300 million projected for the following year.

Feedback is a vital component of control, and recently Ford faced a hard feedback fact: although customers who participated in marketing surveys consistently said they wanted more environmentally responsible vehicles, they are unwilling to pay a higher sticker price for them. Meanwhile, Ford received feedback from the Insurance Institute for Highway Safety in the form of poor results from low-speed crash tests designed to test bumper damage. Still, the Ford Explorer remains the most popular sport utility vehicle on the market, accounting for 20 percent of Ford Motor Company's sales. And Bill Ford remains firm in his commitment to improve the overall quality of his company's vehicles, including reducing their impact on the environment. As for his competitors, Ford notes, "If we didn't provide [the SUV], someone else would, and they wouldn't provide it as responsibly as we do." Already, Ford Motor Company voluntarily builds its SUVs to emit less tailpipe pollution than allowed by law. If Bill Ford has his way, quality will indeed be job 1 at the century-old company for the next one hundred years.

Questions

1. Do you think that Ford Motor Company would benefit from open-book management? Why or why not?
2. In what ways might Ford Motor Company further use information technology to manage knowledge and create a competitive strategy?
3. Which stage of operations strategy would you say is illustrated by Ford Motor Company in this case? Why?

SOURCES: Nedra Pickler, "Explorer Fender Benders Costly," *Auto.com*, November 30, 2002, http://www.auto.com; "Jacques Knifed," *The Economist*, November 3, 2001, http://www.economist.com; Alex Taylor III, "What's Behind Ford's Fall?" *Fortune*, October 29, 2001, http://www.fortune.com; Joann Muller, "Ford: Why It's Worse Than You Think," *BusinessWeek Online*, June 25, 2001, http://www.businessweek.com; "Ford Goes on Offensive to Explain Massive Tire Replacement Plan," *Fox News*, May 24, 2001, http://www.foxnews.com; Thomas A. Stewart, "Knowledge Worth $1.25 Billion," *Fortune*, November 27, 2001, http://www.fortune.com; Keith Bradsher, "Ford Is Conceding S.U.V. Drawbacks," *The New York Times*, May 12, 2000, http://www.serv.com.

What Is Entrepreneurship?

ENTREPRENEURSHIP IS THE PROCESS OF INITIATING A BUSINESS venture, organizing the necessary resources, and assuming the associated risks and rewards.[1] An entrepreneur is someone who engages in entrepreneurship. An entrepreneur recognizes a viable idea for a business product or service and carries it out. This means finding and assembling necessary resources—money, people, machinery, location—to undertake the business venture. Entrepreneurs also assume the risks and reap the rewards of the business. They assume the financial and legal risks of ownership and receive the business's profits.

For example, Vivian Jimenez, Lorraine Brennan O'Neil, and Karen Janson started a business called 10 Minute Manicure, which they hope to open in airports across the country.[2] Responding to the exploding number of female business travelers and the limited services available to women in airports, they thought of setting up inexpensive two-chair kiosks and offering travelers a luxury manicure while they wait for their boarding call. The three women have invested their own savings, cut back their hours or quit their jobs to devote time to building the business, and are lining up investors and selling the idea to airport officials. Jimenez, O'Neil and Janson spotted an opportunity and are willing to assume the risks of making it happen.

Successful entrepreneurs have many different motivations, and they measure rewards in different ways. A recent study classified small business owners in five different categories, as illustrated in Exhibit C.1. Some people are *idealists*, who like the idea of working on something that is new, creative, or personally meaningful. *Optimizers* are rewarded by the personal satisfaction of being a business owner. Entrepreneurs in the *sustainer* category like the chance to balance work and personal life and often don't want the business to grow too large, while *hard workers* enjoy putting in the long hours and dedication to build a larger, more profitable business. The *juggler* category includes entrepreneurs who like the chance a small business gives them to handle everything themselves. These are high-energy people who thrive on the pressure of paying bills, meeting deadlines, and making payroll.[3]

For decades, half the working population has been confiding secretly to pals and pollsters the desire to leave corporate America and go it alone or with a few partners, but, until recently, such dreams were often squashed in their infancy by worried parents, friends, and spouses. Clearly, times have changed. After growing steadily since the 1950s, America's largest companies began cutting their payrolls during the economic downturn of the late 1980s. Downsizing throughout the corporate world forced many employees to consider other options. Bob Kuenzig started a small business that makes while-you-wait hearing aids after he lost his job at one of the nation's largest home builders in 1990.[4] With the recent round of major layoffs, today's latent entrepreneurs also may get just the push they need to strike out on their own. "I don't think I would have had the nerve to have left on my own," said Robin Gorman Newman, who lost her job as vice president of a public relations firm due to a restructuring. Now Newman runs her own PR business, RGN Communications, and has also fashioned a whole new career as the "Love Coach," a separate business that offers counseling to singles.[5] Many experts actually believe an economic downturn is the best time to start a small business because it forces entrepreneurs to keep costs in line, enables them to hire good people, and gives them the time needed to build something of lasting value rather than struggle to keep pace with rapid growth.[6]

Many people also regard entrepreneurship as a better use of their time, talent, and energy. Women and minorities, who have sometimes found their opportunities limited in the corporate world, are often seeing entrepreneurship as the only way to go. The National Federation of Women Business Owners (NFWBO) reports that women owned 38 percent of all U.S. businesses in 1999, with about 13 percent of those companies owned by minority women.[7] Many of these are small businesses started by women and minority entrepreneurs who found limited opportunities in established firms. For instance, NFWBO reports that Hispanic women are starting companies at four times the national growth rate. "The [corporate] work environment is not friendly to Latinas," says Alma Morales Fiojas, CEO of Mana, a National Latina Organization. "Sometimes the best avenue . . . is to go into your own business, where there is more

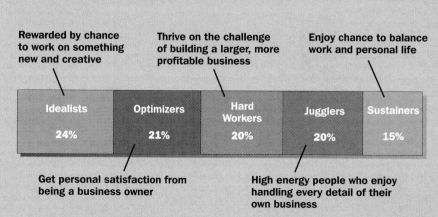

Rewarded by chance to work on something new and creative

Thrive on the challenge of building a larger, more profitable business

Enjoy chance to balance work and personal life

Idealists	Optimizers	Hard Workers	Jugglers	Sustainers
24%	21%	20%	20%	15%

Get personal satisfaction from being a business owner

High energy people who enjoy handling every detail of their own business

EXHIBIT *C.1*

Five Types of Small Business Owners

SOURCE: Study conducted by Yankelovich Partners, reported in Mark Henricks, "Type-Cast," *Entrepreneur* (March 2000), 14–16.

flexibility and you can accomplish more."[8] The National Urban League's 2001 annual review of black America also found that black-owned businesses have steadily increased and, significantly, more than two-thirds of those surveyed said they have entrepreneurial dreams for the future.[9]

Entrepreneurship and the Environment

Not so long ago, scholars and policy makers were worrying about the potential of small business to survive. The recent turbulence in the Internet economy and the demise of many dot-com start-ups again has some questioning whether small companies can compete with big business. However, entrepreneurship and small business are vital, dynamic, and increasingly important parts of the U.S. economy. There are an estimated 15 to 17 million small businesses in the United States, which account for a tremendous portion of the goods and services provided.[10] Another interesting finding is that there are approximately 10 million Americans who make their living as *solo professionals*, often working out of their homes providing services to other companies. Some popular businesses for solo professionals are insurance agencies and brokerages, real estate, legal or medical services, translation and interpretation, and technical, scientific, and professional services. Overall, about half of all small businesses or solo professionals are in the service sector, (including finance, insurance, and real estate).[11]

Entrepreneurship Today

There are a number of reasons small business is such a dynamic part of today's economy, including economic changes, globalization and increased competition, advancing technology, and new market niches.[12]

Economic Changes. Today's economy is fertile soil for entrepreneurs. The economy changes constantly, providing opportunities for new businesses. For example, the demand for services is booming, and 97 percent of service firms are small, with fewer than 100 employees. Since government deregulation removed restrictions that inhibited small business formation in the trucking industry, thousands of small trucking companies have been started. In addition, long-distance freight trucking has become the biggest industry for one-person businesses, accounting for about $12.5 billion.[13]

Globalization and Increased Competition. Even the largest of companies can no longer dominate their industry in a fast-changing global marketplace. Globalization demands entrepreneurial behavior—companies have to find ways to do things faster, better, and less expensively. Large companies are cutting costs by outsourcing work to smaller businesses or freelancers and selling off extraneous operations. Globalization and increased competition also give an advantage to the flexibility and fast response small business can offer rather than to huge companies with economies of scale.

Technology. Rapid advances and dropping prices in computer technology have spawned whole new industries, as well as entirely new methods of producing goods and delivering services. Unlike technological advances of the past, these are within the reach of companies of all sizes. The explosive growth of the Internet has created tremendous opportunities for entrepreneurs. For every story of a failed dot-com business, there are any number of small companies using the Web to sell products and services, to improve productivity, communications, and customer service, or to obtain information and market their services. Singer-songwriter Peter Breinholt recently started selling CDs, song books, and T-shirts on his Web site, and he reports that his sales have nearly doubled. Thos. Moser Cabinetmakers, a Maine-based business that makes and sells handcrafted furniture, uses the Web as an onsite catalog to build offsite sales. Visitors can take a virtual tour of how the furniture gets made and view contextual pictures of the furniture in a home. The Web site has enabled the small company to reach people it could never reach before the advent of the Internet—and that's led to lots of new buyers.[14] Of the 27 percent of companies with 50 or fewer employees that have a Web site, more than half report that the site has broken even or paid for itself in increased business.[15]

Other technological advances also provide opportunities for small business. Biotechnology, aided by recent work in genomics, is a growing field for small businesses. Research into microelectromechanical systems (MEMS), tiny machines used in numerous applications from biotechnology and telecommunications to the auto industry, is being conducted primarily by small companies.

New Opportunities and Market Niches. Today's entrepreneurs are taking advantage of the opportunity to meet changing needs in the marketplace. Sisters Dana Schulz and Jessica Taylor of Garland, Texas, started FunPhones to create interchangeable cell phone covers, ranging from stars and stripes to sporty bouncing balls to wild animal prints. Since cell phones have become almost as ubiquitous a part of a woman's outfit as her purse, the two spotted an opportunity to make them a fashion accessory. The demand for their designs catapulted FunPhones to around a million in sales in only its second year of operation.[16] Recognizing the need for a magazine to serve the United States' estimated 3 million educated, affluent Latina professionals, Anna Maria Arias founded *Latina Style*, a spicy mix of Hispanic cultural, business, and entertainment news.[17]

Definition of Small Business

The full definition of "small business" used by the Small Business Administration (SBA) is detailed and complex, taking up 37 pages of SBA regulations. Most people think of a business as small if it has fewer than 500 employees. This general definition works fine, but the SBA further defines it by industry. Exhibit C.2 gives a few examples of how the SBA defines small business for a sample of industries. It also illustrates the types of businesses most entrepreneurs start—retail, manufacturing, and service. Additional types of new small businesses are construction, agriculture, and wholesaling.

EXHIBIT *C.2*

Examples of SBA Definitions of Small Business

Manufacturing	
Computer terminals and peripheral equipment	Number of employees does not exceed 1,000
Motor vehicle parts and accessories	Number of employees does not exceed 750
Apparel and footwear	Number of employees does not exceed 500
Retail	
Department stores	Average annual receipts do not exceed 20.0 million
Computer and software stores	Average annual receipts do not exceed 6.5 million
Sporting goods stores and bicycle shops	Average annual receipts do not exceed 5.0 million
Services	
Business consulting services	Average annual receipts do not exceed 5.0 million
Architectural services	Average annual receipts do not exceed 2.5 million
Building cleaning and maintenance	Average annual receipts do not exceed 12.0 million
Miscellaneous	
Book, magazine, or newspaper publishing	Number of employees does not exceed 1,000
Banks and credit unions	Has no more than $100 million in assets

Impact of Entrepreneurial Companies

The impact of entrepreneurial companies on our economy is astonishing. According to the Internal Revenue Service, only about 16,000 businesses in the United States employ more than 500 people, and the majority employ fewer than 100. In addition, the 5.7 million U.S. businesses that have fewer than 100 employees generate 40 percent of the nation's output.[18] Small business formation is also at an all-time high. The U.S. Small Business Administration reports that 2.9 million companies were started between the years of 1989 and 1995.[19] Approximately 600,000 new businesses are started in the United States each year, and the status of the SBA administrator was recently elevated to a cabinet-level position in recognition of the importance of small business in the U.S. economy.[20] Many recent converts to entrepreneurship are corporate refugees (often middle management victims of corporate layoffs and downsizing) and corporate dropouts (those who prefer the uncertainty of self-employment to the corporate bureaucracy). In addition, growing numbers of executives are voluntarily leaving their big-company pay and perks at companies such as AT&T, IBM, and American Express to work for small start-up companies, citing the opportunity to do something new, creative, and exciting.[21]

Traditionally, new entrepreneurs most frequently start businesses in the areas of business services and restaurants. Today, inspired by the growth of companies such as Amazon.com, entrepreneurs are still flocking to the Internet to start new businesses. Demographic and lifestyle trends have created new opportunities in areas such as environmental services, children's markets, fitness, and home health care. Entrepreneurship and small business in the United States is an engine for job creation, innovation, and diversity.

Job Creation. Researchers disagree over what percentage of new jobs is created by small business. Research has found that the *age* of a company, more than its size, determines the number of jobs it creates. That is, virtually *all* of the net new jobs in recent years have come from new companies, which includes not only small companies but also new branches of huge, multinational organizations. However, small companies still are thought to create a large percentage of new jobs. According to the U.S. Small Business Administration, small companies created 76.5 percent of net new jobs from 1990 to 1995 and 75.8 percent from 1996 to 1997.[22] Jobs created by small businesses give the United States an economic vitality no other country can claim.

Innovation. According to Cognetics, Inc., a research firm run by David Birch that traces the employment and sales records of some 9 million companies, new and smaller firms have been responsible for 55 percent of the innovations in 362 different industries and 95 percent of all radical innovations. In addition, fast-growing businesses, which Birch calls "gazelles," produce twice as many product innovations per employee as do larger firms. Among the notable products for which small businesses can be credited are cellophane, the jet engine, and the ballpoint pen. Virtually every new business represents an innovation of some sort, whether a new product or service, how the product is delivered, or how it is made.[23] Entrepreneurial innovation often spurs larger companies to try new things. Lamaur, Inc., created a new shampoo for permanent-waved hair. Soon three giant competitors launched similar products. Small-business innovation keeps U.S. companies competitive, which is especially important in today's global marketplace.

Diversity. Entrepreneurship offers opportunities for individuals who may feel blocked in established corporations. Women-owned and minority-owned businesses may be the emerging growth companies of the next decade. There are approximately 9.1 million women-owned businesses that employ almost 30 million people and contribute $3.6 trillion to the U.S. economy.[24] Statistics for minorities are also impressive. Between 1987 and 1997, the number of Asian-owned companies in the United States increased a whopping 157 percent; Hispanic-owned businesses increased 144 percent. The number of black-owned businesses grew much slower, but still increased 27 percent over the 10 year period.[25] Exhibit C.3 illustrates the growth of minority-owned businesses in the United States. Michael and Barbara Turney started Mama Turney's Pie Company in Nashville in the mid-1990s. Mama Turney's is an example of a successful black-owned business that builds on family traditions. Using recipes handed down from Michael Turney's mother has led to tremendous success for the company, which sells pies to numerous restaurants as well as through Kroger stores and in vending machines.[26]

Who Are Entrepreneurs?

The heroes of American business—Fred Smith, Spike Lee, Henry Ford, Sam Walton, Mary Kay Ash, Bill Gates, Michael Dell—are almost always entrepreneurs. Entrepreneurs start with a vision. Often they are unhappy with their current jobs and see an opportunity to bring together the resources needed for a new venture. However, the image of entrepreneurs as bold pioneers probably is overly romantic. A survey of the CEOs of the nation's fastest-growing small firms found that these entrepreneurs could be best characterized as hardworking and practical, with great familiarity with their market and industry.[27] For example, Bobby Frost worked 22 years in the mirror-manufacturing industry before leaving his employer. He started a mirror and glass fabrication business to use technology that his former employer refused to try and that Frost believed would work. It did. Eight years after its founding, Consolidated Glass & Mirror Corp. had 600 employees and $36 million in sales.

Personality Traits

A number of studies have investigated the personality characteristics of entrepreneurs and how they differ from successful managers in established organizations. Some suggest that entrepreneurs in general want something different from life than do traditional managers. Entrepreneurs seem to place high importance on being free to achieve and maximize their potential. Some 40 traits have been identified as associated with entrepreneurship, but 6 have special importance.[28] These characteristics are illustrated in Exhibit C.4.

Internal Locus of Control. The task of starting and running a new business requires the belief that you can make things come out the way you want. The entrepreneur not only has a vision but also must be able to plan to achieve that vision and believe it will happen. An internal locus of control is the belief by individuals that their future is within their control and that external forces will have little influence. For entrepreneurs, reaching the future is seen as being in the hands of the individual. Many people, however, feel that the world is highly uncertain and that they are unable to make things come out the way they

E X H I B I T *C.3*

Growth of Minority-Owned Businesses in the United States, 1987–1997

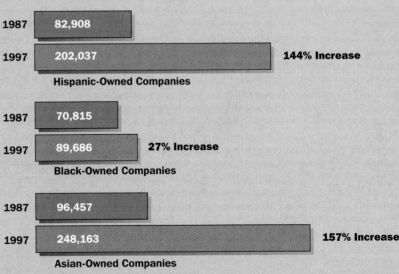

1987	82,908
1997	202,037 — 144% Increase

Hispanic-Owned Companies

1987	70,815
1997	89,686 — 27% Increase

Black-Owned Companies

1987	96,457
1997	248,163 — 157% Increase

Asian-Owned Companies

SOURCES: U.S. Small Business Administration, Office of Advocacy, *Minorities in Business* (Washington, D.C.: U.S. Government Printing Office, 1999); SBA, Office of Advocacy, *The Facts about Small Business 1999*, reported in "Tomorrow's Self-Employed American," *Inc.* (State of Small Business 2001), 46–48.

NOTE: Includes only businesses that have employees.

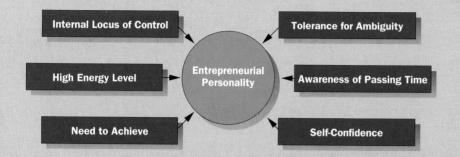

EXHIBIT *C.4*

Characteristics of Entrepreneurs

SOURCE: Adapted from Charles R. Kuehl and Peggy A. Lambing, *Small Business: Planning and Management* (Ft. Worth: The Dryden Press, 1994), 45.

want. An external locus of control is the belief by individuals that their future is not within their control but rather is influenced by external forces. Entrepreneurs are individuals who are convinced they can make the difference between success and failure; hence they are motivated to take the steps needed to achieve the goal of setting up and running a new business.

High Energy Level. A business start-up requires great effort. Most entrepreneurs report struggle and hardship. They persist and work incredibly hard despite traumas and obstacles. A survey of business owners reported that half worked 60 hours or more per week. Another reported that entrepreneurs worked long hours, but that beyond 70 hours little benefit was gained. The data in Exhibit C.5 show findings from a survey conducted by the National Federation of Independent Business. New business owners work long hours, with only 23 percent working fewer than 50 hours, which is close to a normal workweek for managers in established businesses.

Need to Achieve. Another human quality closely linked to entrepreneurship is the need to achieve, which means that people are motivated to excel and pick situations in which success is likely.[29] People who have high achievement needs like to set their own goals, which are moderately difficult. Easy goals present no challenge; unre-

alistically difficult goals cannot be achieved. Intermediate goals are challenging and provide great satisfaction when achieved. High achievers also like to pursue goals for which they can obtain feedback about their success.

Self-Confidence. People who start and run a business must act decisively. They need confidence about their ability to master the day-to-day tasks of the business. They must feel sure about their ability to win customers, handle the technical details, and keep the business moving. Entrepreneurs also have a general feeling of confidence that they can deal with anything in the future; complex, unanticipated problems can be handled as they arise.

Awareness of Passing Time. Entrepreneurs tend to be impatient; they feel a sense of urgency. They want things to progress as if there is no tomorrow. They want things moving immediately and seldom procrastinate. Entrepreneurs "seize the moment."

Tolerance for Ambiguity. Many people need work situations characterized by clear structure, specific instructions, and complete information. Tolerance for ambiguity is the psychological characteristic that allows a person to be untroubled by disorder and uncertainty. This is an important trait, because few situations present more uncertainty

EXHIBIT *C.5*

Reported Hours per Week Worked by Owners of New Businesses

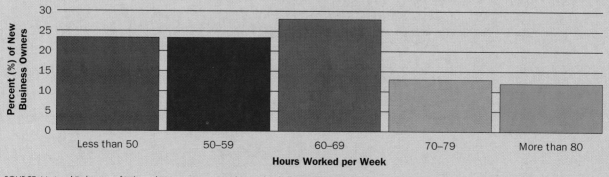

SOURCE: National Federation of Independent Business. Reported in Mark Robichaux, "Business First, Family Second," *The Wall Street Journal* (May 12, 1989), B1.

than starting a new business. Decisions are made without clear understanding of options or certainty about which option will succeed.

Demographic Factors

In addition to the six personality traits described so far, entrepreneurs often have background and demographic characteristics that distinguish them from other people. Entrepreneurs are more likely to be the first born within their families, and their parents are more likely to have been entrepreneurs. Children of immigrants also are more likely to be entrepreneurs, as are children for whom the father was absent for at least part of the childhood.[30]

Some research suggests that there are particular times during a person's career life cycle when the opportunities for entrepreneurship are particularly favorable. The two most obvious "windows of opportunity" are when a young person is just beginning a career and when a person is retiring from a career. Other windows present themselves along a continuum as a person grows in experience, industry knowledge, understanding of the marketplace, or financial ability. In addition, unplanned events such as the loss of a job, inheritance, or divorce may create opportunities for entrepreneurship. The important point is that entrepreneurship should be viewed as a career-long process, not something that has to be done at a certain time or age.[31]

In the past, most entrepreneurs launched their businesses between the ages of 25 and 40. Today, however, early retirement programs and corporate downsizing have created a whole new class of older entrepreneurs with high-level skills and years of experience. Many of these former managers have decided their chances are better in becoming entrepreneurs than in trying to reenter an overcrowded job market.[32] Today's successful entrepreneurs come in all ages and may have a combination of personality traits. No one should be discouraged from starting a business because he or she doesn't fit a specific profile. Michael Napoliello, Jr. and Jason Moskowitz launched their first business as college sophomores. While making summer plans at the Jersey Shore, they noticed that no newspaper catered to the numerous socially active young people. The two friends launched *The Wave*, a summer arts and entertainment publication that proved to be a huge hit. R.E. Coleberd, on the other hand, started his first business, Pacific West Oil Data, at the age of 51. Rumors of restructuring, downsizing, and potential layoffs, combined with his uncertainty about finding another job, convinced Coleberd to take the plunge. Now, he says he would pick cotton in Georgia before going back to work for a large corporation. "I have felt like a kid with a new red wagon ever since I started my business."[33]

Starting an Entrepreneurial Firm

The first step in pursuing an entrepreneurial dream is to start with a viable idea and plan like crazy. Once you have a new idea in mind, a business plan must be drawn and decisions must be made about legal structure, financing, and basic tactics, such as whether to start the business from scratch and whether to pursue international opportunities from the start.

New-Business Idea

To some people, the idea for a new business is the easy part. They do not even consider entrepreneurship until they are inspired by an exciting idea. Other people decide they want to run their own business and set about looking for an idea or opportunity. Exhibit C.6 shows the most important reasons people start a new business and the source of new-business ideas. Note that 37 percent of business founders got their idea from an in-depth understanding of the industry, primarily because of past job experience. Interestingly, almost as many—36 percent—spotted a market niche that wasn't being filled.[34]

EXHIBIT *C.6*

*Sources of Entrepreneurial
Motivation and New-Business Ideas*

Reasons for Starting a Business

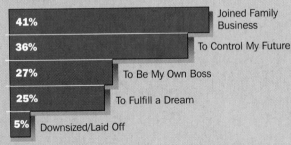

41% — Joined Family Business
36% — To Control My Future
27% — To Be My Own Boss
25% — To Fulfill a Dream
5% — Downsized/Laid Off

Source of New-Business Ideas

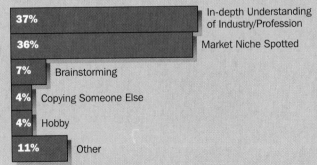

37% — In-depth Understanding of Industry/Profession
36% — Market Niche Spotted
7% — Brainstorming
4% — Copying Someone Else
4% — Hobby
11% — Other

SOURCE: "The Rewards," Inc. State of Small Business, 2001 (May 29, 2001), 50–51; and Leslie Brokow, "How to Start an Inc. 500 Company," Inc. 500 (1994), 51–65.

The trick for entrepreneurs is to blend their own skills and experience with a need in the marketplace. Acting strictly on one's own skills may produce something no one wants to buy. On the other hand, finding a market niche that you do not have the ability to fill does not work either. Both personal skill and market need typically must be present. Entrepreneur Roger Greene found a way to blend his skills and interests with a need in the marketplace to create a new kind of software company, as described in the Best Practices box.

The Business Plan

Once an entrepreneur is inspired by a new-business idea, careful planning is crucial. A business plan is a document specifying the business details prepared by an entrepreneur prior to opening a new business. Planning forces the entrepreneur to carefully think through all of the issues and problems associated with starting and developing the business. Most entrepreneurs have to borrow money, and a business plan is absolutely critical to persuading lenders and investors to participate in the business. Studies have shown that small businesses with a carefully thought out, written business plan are much more likely to succeed than those without one.[35]

The details of a business plan may vary, but successful business plans generally share several characteristics:[36]

- Demonstrate a clear, compelling vision that creates an air of excitement.
- Provide clear and realistic financial projections.
- Give detailed information about the target market.
- Include detailed information about the industry and competitors.
- Provide evidence of an effective entrepreneurial management team.
- Pay attention to good formatting and clear writing.

BEST PRACTICES

The Soft Touch Leads to Success at Ipswitch Software

In 1991, Roger Greene set out to use his skills and experience in software and the Internet to build a different kind of software company—one where he and his employees could live happy, balanced lives while producing innovative, low-cost products that would appeal to a broad market. Ipswitch, based in Lexington, Massachusetts, specializes in Windows-based software that makes the Internet and intranets accessible and manageable. In addition, the company is well known among programmers for its WS_FTP software that can move huge amounts of data across different computer platforms. Ipswitch has amassed a treasure trove of praise in the form of positive product reviews and awards, including *PC Magazine* Editors' Choice, *Internet Week* Approved, *Network Computing* Editors' Choice, and *VARBusiness* Editors' Choice.

In most software companies, employees work long hours under intense pressure to beat the competition. But Greene provides the foundation for high performance at Ipswitch by maintaining an easy-does-it attitude and a philosophy that puts employees ahead of profits. He is constantly encouraging people to take more personal days and vacation time. "A lot of people work really hard for 30 or 40 years and then they retire and try to do all the things they didn't do before," Greene says. "I'd much rather live life as it goes along and do neat things while you're working and enjoy every year of your life." To be sure employees have the time to "do neat things,"

Greene recently bumped up the three weeks' vacation time to five weeks—and he pushes people to take every minute of it. At Ipswitch, the idea of being a workaholic is downgraded, and no one ever gets rewarded for burning the midnight oil.

Ipswitch's worker-friendly environment is also reflected in other aspects of the workplace. For example, when an employee's boyfriend died, Greene hired a bereavement counselor to help her through the crisis. He believes people should be allowed to embrace the whole of human experience at work as well as in their personal lives. Greene's emphasis on treating people as whole human beings contributes directly to a low 9 percent turnover rate, roughly half the technology-company average. In addition, Greene and other managers have made a conscious decision to keep the organization small so people get to know one another on a more personal level. Betty Lang-Holmes, vice president of human resources, says, "I don't ever want to see a face here I don't know." The decision to stay small also means Ipswitch has been able to develop slowly and steadily rather than burning out because of the pressures of rapid growth.

Greene's formula of applying his skills to a market he understood, using a soft touch with employees, and plotting a slow and steady course for the future has led to success for Ipswitch and to better lives for many employees.

SOURCES: Based on Eleena DeLisser, "A Software Startup Attracts Staff with Ban on Midnight Oil," *The Wall Street Journal* (August 23, 2000), A1; and http://www.Ipswitch.com, assecced on August 8, 2001.

- Keep the plan short—no more than 50 pages long.
- Highlight critical risks that may threaten business success.
- Spell out the sources and uses of start-up funds and operating funds.
- Capture the reader's interest with a killer summary.

The business plan should indicate where the product or service fits into the overall industry and should draw on concepts that have been discussed throughout this book. For example, Chapter 5 described competitive strategies that entrepreneurs can use. Detailed suggestions for writing a business plan are provided in the Best Practices box.

Legal Form

Before entrepreneurs have founded a business, and perhaps again as it expands, they must choose an appropriate legal structure for the company. The three basic choices are proprietorship, partnership, or corporation.

Sole Proprietorship. A sole proprietorship is defined as an unincorporated business owned by an individual for profit. Proprietorships make up 70 percent of all businesses in the United States. This form is popular because it is easy to start and has few legal requirements. A proprietor has total ownership and control of the company and can make all decisions without consulting anyone. However, this type of organization also has drawbacks. The owner has unlimited liability for the business, meaning that if someone sues, the owner's personal as well as business assets are at risk. Also, financing can be harder to obtain because business success rests on one person's shoulders.

Partnership. A partnership is an unincorporated business owned by two or more people. Partnerships, like proprietorships, are relatively easy to start. Two friends may reach an agreement to start a pet store. To avoid misunderstandings and to make sure the business is well planned, it is wise to draw up and sign a formal partnership agreement with the help of an attorney. The agreement specifies how partners are to share responsibility and resources and how they will contribute their expertise. The disadvantages of partnerships are the unlimited liability of the partners and the disagreements that almost always occur among strong-minded people. A poll by *Inc.* magazine illustrated the volatility of partnerships. Fifty-nine percent of respondents considered partnerships a bad business move, citing reasons such as partner problems and conflicts. Partnerships often dissolve within 5 years. Respondents who liked partnerships pointed to the equality of partners (sharing of workload and emotional and financial burdens) as the key to a successful partnership.[37]

Corporation. A corporation is an artificial entity created by the state and existing apart from its owners. As a separate legal entity, the corporation is liable for its actions and must pay taxes on its income. Unlike other forms of ownership, the corporation has a legal life of its own; it continues to exist regardless of whether the owners live or die.

And the corporation, not the owners, is sued in the case of liability. Thus, continuity and limits on owners' liability are two principal advantages of forming a corporation. For example, a physician can form a corporation so that liability for malpractice will not affect his or her personal assets. The major disadvantage of the corporation is that it is expensive and complex to do the paperwork required to incorporate the business and to keep the records required by law. When proprietorships and partnerships are successful and grow large, they often incorporate to limit liability and to raise funds through the sale of stock to investors.

Financial Resources

A crucial concern for entrepreneurs is the financing of the business. An investment usually is required to acquire labor and raw materials and perhaps a building and equipment. The financing decision initially involves two options—whether to obtain loans that must be repaid (debt financing) or whether to share ownership (equity financing). A survey of successful growth businesses asked, "How much money was needed to launch the company?" Approximately one-third were started on less than $10,000, one-third needed from $10,000 to $50,000, and one-third needed more than $50,000. The primary source of this money was the entrepreneurs' own resources, but they often had to mortgage their homes, depend on credit cards, borrow money from the bank, or give part of the business to a venture capitalist.[38]

Debt Financing. Borrowing money that has to be repaid at a later date in order to start a business is debt financing. One common source of debt financing for a start-up is to borrow from family and friends. Another common source is a bank loan. Banks provide some 25 percent of all financing for small business. Sometimes entrepreneurs can obtain money from a finance company, wealthy individuals, or potential customers.

Another form of loan financing is provided by the Small Business Administration (SBA). The SBA supplies direct loans to some entrepreneurs who are unable to get bank financing because they are considered high risk. The SBA is especially helpful for people without substantial assets, providing an opportunity for single parents, minority group members, and others with a good idea. For example, in recent years the SBA has tripled the number of loans to women entrepreneurs.[39]

Equity Financing. Any money invested by owners or by those who purchase stock in a corporation is considered equity funds. Equity financing consists of funds that are invested in exchange for ownership in the company.

A venture capital firm is a group of companies or individuals that invests money in new or expanding businesses for ownership and potential profits. This is a potential form of capital for businesses with high earning and growth possibilities. For example, during 2000, venture capitalists invested $103 billion in 5,380 new companies. About 40 percent of those businesses were Internet-specific, but venture capitalists also invested heavily in communications, software, and

Helpful Hints for Writing the Business Plan

The Summary
- Make it no more than three pages.
- This is the most crucial part of your plan because it must capture the reader's interest.
- What, how, why, where, etc., must be summarized.
- Complete this part *after* the finished business plan has been written.

The Business Description Segment
- Name of the business.
- A background of the industry with history of the company (if any) should be covered here.
- The potential of the new venture should be described clearly.
- Any unique or distinctive features of the venture should be spelled out.

The Marketing Segment
- Convince investors that sales projections and competition can be met.
- Market studies should be used and disclosed.
- Identify target market, market position, and market share.
- Evaluate *all* competition and specifically cover why and how you will be better than the competitors.
- Identify all market sources and assistance used for this segment.
- Demonstrate pricing strategy, since your price must penetrate and maintain a market share to *produce profits*. Thus the lowest price is *not* necessarily the "best" price.
- Identify your advertising plans with cost estimates to validate the proposed strategy.

The Research, Design, and Development Segment
- Cover the *extent of* and *costs involved* in needed research testing, or development.
- Explain carefully what has been accomplished *already* (prototype, lab testing, early development).
- Mention any research or technical assistance provided for you.

The Manufacturing Segment
- Provide the advantages of your location (zoning, tax laws, wage rates).
- List the production needs in terms of facilities (plant, storage, office space) and equipment (machinery, furnishings, supplies).
- Describe the access to transportation (for shipping and receiving).
- Explain proximity to your suppliers.
- Mention the availability of labor in your location.
- Provide estimates of manufacturing costs—be careful; too many entrepreneurs underestimate their costs.

The Management Segment
- Provide résumés of all key people in the management of the venture.
- Carefully describe the legal structure of the venture (sole proprietorship, partnership, or corporation).
- Cover the added assistance (if any) of advisers, consultants, and directors.
- Provide information on how everyone is to be compensated (how much, also).

The Critical-Risks Segment
- Discuss potential risks *before* investors point them out. Some examples follow:
  - Price cutting by competitors
  - Potentially unfavorable industry-wide trends
  - Design or manufacturing costs in excess of estimates
  - Sales projections not achieved
  - Product development schedule not met
  - Difficulties or long lead times encountered in the procurement of parts or raw materials
  - Larger-than-expected innovation and development costs to stay competitive
- Name alternative course of action.

The Financial Segment
- Provide statements.
- Describe the needed sources for your funds and the uses you intend for the money.
- Provide a budget.
- Create stages of financing for the purpose of allowing evaluation by investors at various points.

The Milestone Schedule Segment
- Provide a timetable or chart to demonstrate when each phase of the venture is to be completed. This shows the relationship of events and provides a deadline for accomplishment.

SOURCES: Donald F. Kuratko, Ray V. Montagno, and Frank J. Sabatine, *The Entrepreneurial Decision* (Muncie, IN: The Midwest Entrepreneurial Education Center, Ball State University, 1997), 45–46. Reprinted with permission.

services.[40] Venture capital firms want new businesses that have the potential for an extremely high rate of return. This is reflected in the amount of financing provided to Internet ventures over the past few years. Investment slowed dramatically during the latter part of 2000 when Internet companies by the scores began going out of business. Venture capitalists also usually provide assistance, advice, and information to help the entrepreneur prosper.

Tactics

There are several ways an aspiring entrepreneur can become a business owner. These include starting a new business from scratch, buying an existing business, or starting a franchise. Another popular entrepreneurial tactic is to participate in a business incubator.

Start a New Business. One of the most common ways to become an entrepreneur is to start a new business from scratch. This is exciting because the entrepreneur sees a need for a product or service that has not been filled before and then sees the idea or dream become a reality. Jennifer and Brian Maxwell, both long-distance runners, founded PowerBar Inc. to give athletes a snack bar that would provide quick energy but be easy to digest. Jennifer, who studied nutrition and food science at the University of California, hit on the idea after Brian told her of losing the London Marathon largely because of a case of stomach cramps.[41] The advantage of starting a business is the ability to develop and design the business in the entrepreneur's own way. The entrepreneur is solely responsible for its success. A potential disadvantage is the long time it can take to get the business off the ground and make it profitable. The uphill battle is caused by the lack of established clientele and the many mistakes made by someone new to the business. Moreover, no matter how much planning is done, a start-up is risky; there is no guarantee that the new idea will work.

Buy an Existing Business. Because of the long start-up time and the inevitable mistakes, some entrepreneurs prefer to reduce risk by purchasing an existing business. This offers the advantage of a shorter time to get started and an existing track record. The entrepreneur may get a bargain price if the owner wishes to retire or has other family considerations. Moreover, a new business may overwhelm an entrepreneur with the amount of work to be done and procedures to be determined. An established business already has filing systems, a payroll tax system, and other operating procedures. Potential disadvantages are the need to pay for goodwill that the owner believes exists and the possible existence of ill will toward the business. In addition, the company may have bad habits and procedures or outdated technology, which may be why the business is for sale.

Buy a Franchise. Franchising is perhaps the most rapidly growing path to entrepreneurship. The International Franchise Association reports that about 1,500 franchises do business through 320,000 franchise outlets in the United States. Franchises account for an estimated one-third of the nation's annual retail sales.[42] According to some estimates, franchises account for 1 out of every 12 businesses in the United States, and a franchise opens every eight minutes of every business day.[43] Franchising is an arrangement by which the owner of a product or service allows others to purchase the right to distribute the product or service with help from the owner. The franchisee invests his or her money and owns the business but does not have to develop a new product, create a new company, or test the market. The franchisee typically pays a flat fee plus a percentage of gross sales. Franchises exist for weight-loss clinics, pet-sitting services, sports photography, bakeries, janitorial services, auto repair shops, real estate offices, and numerous other types of businesses. Exhibit C.7 lists the top 10 franchises in a recent year, based on financial strength and stability, growth rate, and size of the franchise system. The exhibit also shows the up-front fee required by each franchise. Fees typically range from $10,000 to $25,000, and that doesn't count the other start-up costs the entrepreneur will have to cover. A study by an economics professor found that the typical franchise costs $94,886 to open. For a company such as McDonald's, the cost is much higher, from about $400,000 to $500,000, depending on the restaurant location.[44]

The powerful advantage of a franchise is that management help is provided by the owner. For example, Burger King does not want a franchisee to fail and will provide the studies necessary to find a good location. The franchisor also provides an established name and

EXHIBIT C.7

Top Ten Franchises Based on Financial Strength, Growth Rate, and Size

Franchise	Number of Outlets	Year Founded	Up-Front Fee
1. Yogen Fruz Worldwide	4,722	1986	$25,000
2. McDonald's	16,319	1955	$45,000
3. Subway	13,395	1965	$10,000
4. Wendy's	4,032	1969	$25,000
5. Jackson Hewitt Tax Service	1,836	1960	$25,000
6. KFC	6,635	1930	$25,000
7. Mail Boxes, Etc.	3,655	1980	$29,950
8. TCBY Treats	2,913	1981	$5,000–$20,000
9. Taco Bell Corp.	2,927	1962	$45,000
10. Jani-King	7,038	1969	$6,500–$33,000

SOURCE: *Entrepreneur* magazine, 1998, reported in Lisa Benavides, "Linking Up with a Chain," *The Tennessean* (April 6, 1999), 1E.

national advertising to stimulate demand for the product or service. Potential disadvantages are the lack of control that occurs when franchisors want every business managed in exactly the same way. In some cases, franchisors require that franchise owners use certain contractors or suppliers which may cost more than others would. In addition, franchises can be very expensive, and the high start-up costs are followed with monthly payments to the franchisor that can run from 2 percent to 15 percent of sales.

Entrepreneurs who are considering buying a franchise should investigate the company thoroughly. The prospective franchisee is legally entitled to a copy of franchisor disclosure statements, which include information on 20 topics, including litigation and bankruptcy history, identities of the directors and executive officers, financial information, identification of any products the franchisee is required to buy, and from whom those purchases must be made.[45] The entrepreneur also should talk with as many franchise owners as possible, since they are among the best sources of information about how the company really operates. Wild Birds Unlimited lists 26 questions on its Web site (http://www.wbu.com) that it recommends interested franchise applicants ask current franchisees. The Internet has become franchising's hottest marketing tool, but entrepreneurs should be aware that there are few rules about what the company must disclose over the Web. Not all companies are as above-board as Wild Birds Unlimited about exploring the potential downside of the franchise.[46] Exhibit C.8 lists some specific questions entrepreneurs should ask about themselves and the company when considering buying a franchise. Answering such questions may improve the chances for a successful career as a franchisee.

Participate in a Business Incubator. An attractive innovation for entrepreneurs who want to start a business from scratch is to join a business incubator. The business incubator provides shared office space, management support services, and management advice to entrepreneurs. By sharing office space with other entrepreneurs, managers share information about local business, financial aid, and market opportunities.

This innovation arose two decades ago to nurture start-up companies. Business incubators have become a significant segment of the small business economy: the number of incubators nationwide jumped from 385 in 1990 to about 1,000 today.[47] Many of these are operated as not-for-profit organizations, including government agencies and universities, to boost the viability of small business and spur job creation. The big growth in more recent years, however, is in for-profit incubators in the United States, which jumped from only 24 in early 1999 to 213 by May 2000.[48] Spurred by dreams of dot-com riches and glory, ambitious entrepreneurs set up incubators to help other ambitious entrepreneurs start Internet-based companies. These high-profile incubators dominated headlines during the dramatic rise—and the even more dramatic fall—of the Internet market, and many of them are now going out of business. The incubators that are thriving are primarily not-for-profits and those that cater to niches or focus on helping women or minority entrepreneurs. The value of an incubator is the expertise of an in-house mentor, who serves as adviser, role model, and cheerleader. Incubators also give budding entrepreneurs a chance to network and learn from one another.[49]

Internet Start-Ups

As this textbook is being written, thousands of dot-com companies have crashed and technology stocks have taken a steep dive. Yet the Internet is still a growing part of our lives and businesses, and new companies are springing up every day. A well-known pet site, Pets.com, bombed, but the SitStay GoOut Store (http://www.sitstay.com), a small company that sells upscale dog toys and supplies

EXHIBIT *C.8*

Sample Questions for Choosing a Franchise

Questions about the Entrepreneur	Questions about the Franchisor	Before Signing on the Dotted Line
1. Will I enjoy the day-to-day work of this business?	1. What assistance does the company provide in terms of selection of location, set-up costs, and securing credit; day-to-day technical assistance; marketing; and ongoing training and development?	1. Do I understand the risks associated with this business, and am I willing to assume them?
2. Do my background, experience, and goals make this a good choice for me?		2. Have I had an advisor review the disclosure documents and franchise agreement?
3. Am I willing to work within the rules and guidelines established by the franchisor?	2. How long does it take the typical franchise owner to start making a profit?	3. Do I understand all the terms of the contract?
	3. How many franchises changed ownership within the past year, and why?	

SOURCE: Based on Thomas Love, "The Perfect Franchise," *Nation's Business* (April 1998), 59–65; and Roberta Maynard, "Choosing a Franchise," *Nation's Bsuness* (October 1996), 56–63.

on the Web, is still pulling in profits.[50] Garden.com bit the dust, but Etera (*http://www.etera.com*), an online plant seller based in Mount Vernon, Washington, is thriving, selling $30 million worth of plants a year.[51] A study by *The Industry Standard* found that at least half of all business-to-consumer dot-com companies survived the e-commerce bloodbath of late 2000 and early 2001.[52] Just as with other small companies, many of the Internet companies being started now will fail, but many others will go on to become highly successful businesses. Small business formation is the primary process by which an economy recreates and reinvents itself,[53] and the huge bubble of Internet start-ups—and the turbulence they face—is evidence of a shifting but thriving U.S. economy.

Launching an Internet Business

Internet start-ups face many of the same challenges as other small businesses. However, they may also face some unique issues and problems. People starting traditional small businesses, such as a hair salon, day-care center, or local delicatessen, might be able to get started using their own savings, borrowing money from family and friends, and relying on credit cards. They might build their businesses slowly, starting with only a few clients and gradually building a larger clientele. If there are problems with products or services, they are solved as the entrepreneurs learn from experience. Entrepreneurs starting Internet companies, on the other hand, often need big money up front to build a technology infrastructure before they can even begin doing business. In addition, because the Internet world moves so swiftly, dot-com entrepreneurs might not have the luxury of building slowly and learning from experience. If the Web site crashes too often, for example, a company may be doomed—there are too many other options on the Web for visitors to give the company a second chance. There's little time for trial and error. All the kinks must be ironed out before the company puts its offering before the customer. In this section, we will examine what's involved in launching an Internet start-up, based on what is known about these companies so far.

Starting with the Idea. As with any small company, an entrepreneur has to have a viable idea for the business, and one that is appropriate to the fast-changing world of the Internet. Cache Flow Inc. started because the founders had an idea for a way to help customers access frequently used Web pages more quickly by providing local storage, or *caching*, of frequently used Internet data.[54] Research has found that the chances are only six in one million that an idea for a high-tech business eventually turns into a successful public company.[55] A good idea for an Internet company has to be one that can grow in scale and adapt quickly. Start-ups have the advantage of being nimble, but the idea itself must be one that is flexible enough to allow rapid adaptation as the environment changes. In addition, there should be innovative Web-based marketing techniques to promote the idea. For example, HotMail grew rapidly because every customer became a way to advertise the product to friends and colleagues.[56]

Writing the Business Plan. With the lightning-fast pace of the Internet, a traditional business plan is usually obsolete by the time it is written. Internet entrepreneurs have to create a compelling story about why their idea is the seed of the next big Internet success. The entrepreneur has to convince venture capitalists and potential employees to join in a risky adventure that has huge potential but few guarantees. The plan should cover eight basic points:

1. A description of the business and why it is unique
2. A profile of potential customers and market needs
3. The key ingredient of the business that will attract millions of customers
4. Why customers will come to this site rather than competitors
5. What the company has accomplished so far, including partnerships or early customer relationships
6. The entrepreneur's background and role in the company
7. Specific data about where the company is located, key management people, and contact information
8. Essential information about funding received so far, funding and staffing needs, and expectations for growth of the business over the next year.[57]

Note that many of these topics are also covered by a traditional business plan as described in the Best Practices box earlier in this appendix. The key for the Internet start-up is to condense the essential information into a vivid, compelling story that can be told quickly and adapted quickly as the Internet world changes.

Getting Initial Financing. A vivid story, told with passion and enthusiasm, is crucial to obtaining needed up-front financing. As with other small business start-ups, the entrepreneur relies on numerous sources, including family, friends, personal savings, and credit. However, Internet start-ups often need a large amount of funding just to get started. Forrester Research estimates that the cost to get a business up and running on the Web typically ranges from $2 million to $40 million.[58] One typical source of first funds is through angel financing. Angels are wealthy individuals, typically with business experience and contacts, who believe in the idea for the start-up and are willing to invest their personal funds to help the business get started. This first round of financing is extremely important. It can enable the entrepreneur to quit another job to devote time to building a foundation for the new company, filing for necessary permits or patents, hiring technical consultants, marketing the new product or service, and so forth. Significantly, angels also provide advice and assistance as the entrepreneur is developing the company. The entrepreneur wants angels who can make business contacts, help find talented employees, and serve as all-around advisors.

Building and Testing the Product or Service. Once an entrepreneur has up-front financing, it is time to build and test the product. This stage may include hiring employees and consultants, buying or building the technological infrastructure, and perhaps securing office space or other needed facilities. Start-ups should also begin securing top-flight legal and financial assistance. The time to begin working with lawyers and bankers is early in the process, not after the company runs into trouble, needs specific legal or financial advice, or is ready to go public. Most experts agree, however, that the most critical hire in the early phases of the company is the system architect who can bring the entrepreneur's dream to life by putting together the hardware and software. Expert software engineers, Web site developers, product developers, and network administrators are also important to build the product or service and get it out to the public.[59] An indispensable part of this stage is making sure the idea and the basic technology to support it actually work.

Reliability is crucial in the world of e-business. For example, a string of crashes at eBay's Web site almost destroyed the company.[60] At one point, the site went down for more than 20 hours, leaving collectors as well as investors furious. EBay eventually hired a troubleshooter to make sure the problems never happened again, offering him a salary package that outstripped that of the CEO. Managers knew that having the technology right is a matter of life and death for an Internet-based company. Google's founders went through alpha and beta tests of their Web site before launching the official site, as described in the Digital, Inc., box.

Launching the Company. The launch phase is when the company's products and services are officially made available to the public over the Internet. Marketing is the most important focus at this stage of development. Internet start-ups cannot afford to take years to build a brand; they have to make a name for themselves virtually overnight.[61] A catchy logo and a visually appealing Web site are important in creating the "look" of the company. The name, if not yet selected, should be chosen with care or modified to give the company a distinctive personality that sticks in the mind of customers. For example, Ask.com, a Web site devoted to answering questions on just about anything, revised its brand name to Ask Jeeves, which proved to be a stroke of marketing genius.[62]

Hiring a competent public relations firm at this stage can help to create a buzz about the new company in the business community, which helps attract future investors as well as get the word out to customers. Just as important is creating buzz by building an interactive *community of customers* so that word about the new business spreads from person to person. Today's most popular Internet sites are those that give users a chance to share information about their common interests.[63]

Amazon.com encourages buyers or browsers to write online reviews of books for other customers and vote on how useful they find others' reviews. EBay members rate the quality of their buying and selling experiences with other members, and those ratings are aggregated into a symbol for each member that others can immediately recognize. Many members strive to develop a high status in the community by securing good ratings.[64] Other online features including chat rooms, message boards, and a customer newsletter have made eBay a round-the clock forum for people to share their passion for trading or for their various hobbies.[65] These community-building mechanisms work because people enjoy the chance to provide feedback and interact with others who share their interests.

DIGITAL, INC.

Getting Google Right

Larry Page and Sergey Brin met in 1995 while they were doctoral candidates at Stanford University, where they decided to collaborate on a search engine initally called Back-Rub. After polishing their technology, in the summer of 1998 the two put their academic careers on hold to bet everything on the Internet search engine they renamed Google (http://www.google.com).

In the early days, Page and Brin worked out of a friend's garage, conducting hi-tech meetings around a ping-pong table. They knew the perfect way to improve their product would be through various *alpha* testing stages, with continuous testing, feedback, and refining. The Stanford University community proved to be the perfect testing ground in which Google could evolve. Through this testing, testing, and retesting, Page and Brin were assured that the basic technolgy was solid enough to put before a wider public. However, they also wanted to do a further *beta* testing phase with the public before launching the official site. This beta phase gave much needed elbow room because it warned visitors that Google's technology was a work in progress. The company had to make sure its users knew the developers were "making things better not worse," as Page put it. Putting the search engine before the public forced Google to grow with the Web and meet the needs of actual users. An added benefit was that it earned the company a loyal following among users who appreciated the chance to act as testers and shape how the site would work. Google has relied almost entirely on word-of-mouth advertising. People who used the site had such a good experience that they told others, helping Google's traffic grow from the thousands to the millions by the time the official site was launched in September of 1999.

Simplicity of design is a key to Google's success. For example, Google uses only text-based advertising, which makes for a less-cluttered look and faster loading. The goal is to get the user to an answer as quickly, simply, and accurately as possible. Although the company is working on the next generation of technologies that will broaden search capabilities and present information in fresh ways across multiple platforms, the founders emphasize that "Google's charge will forever be to ensure that every search is a find."

SOURCE: Larry Page and Sergey Brin, "Merits of a Beta Launch," *Business 2.0* (March 2000), 180; "When Larry Met Sergey," http://www.up-mag.com/themag/feature1htm, accessed on July 31, 2001; http://www.google.com/press/overview.html; accessed on July 31, 2001; and http://www.google.com/press/milestones.html, accessed on July 31, 2001.

Securing Additional Financing. Almost every Internet start-up eventually has to secure further funding to support growth and expansion. The entrepreneur has to make sure salaries are paid, infrastructure is maintained, and marketing efforts are continued. In addition, as the company grows, it might need to add more staff, expand office space, or purchase new hardware and software to support growth. The most obvious source of funding at this stage is *venture capital.* As descrived earlier, venture capitalist firms are groups of companies or individuals that invest money in exchange for a stake in the company. For example, the top source of funding for Internet start-ups in 1999 was Softbank Venture Capital.[66] Another source of venture capital is large corporations that want to play an active role in the emerging Internet economy. Companies such as Microsoft, Cisco Systems, and Intel have invested huge sums in exchange for a stake in Internet start-ups. Many start-ups form a board of directors to lend a sense of stability and permanence to the new company and to help the business move to the next level. A board of directors can help the company stay focused on the core issues that will lead to success.[67]

Developing Partnerships. Another role the board often plays is to help a start-up create alliances with other companies, which are critical to helping the business grow. Partnerships for Internet start-ups are generally of two types.[68] A start-up that primarily needs exposure and marketing assistance will partner with a larger, well-established company that can help the smaller firm gain rapid market awareness. The second type involves partnering with a company that assists in actual operations such as customer service, logistics, or warehousing and shipping, and involves electronic linkages between the partners. The company might outsource some functions to focus on core strategic issues. Shoebuy.com established strategic alliances with several established Internet shopping sites and e-tailers to keep its marketing costs low. In addition, the entire Shoebuy concept is based on close partnerships with shoe manufacturers who will drop-ship shoes directly to Shoebuy customers from their own warehouses.[69]

Going Public. The final step in the start-up process is often the initial public offering (IPO), in which stock in the new company is sold to the public. The dream for many Internet entrepreneurs is to grow fast, go public, and get rich if the stock price increases. Although the "get rich quick" dreams have faded, the goal of most Internet entrepreneurs is to eventually take the company public and become a corporation rather than remain a sole proprietorship or partnership, as described earlier in this chapter. During this stage, the entrepreneur begins interviewing bankers who are interested in leading the IPO and puts together a team of bankers, lawyers, and other advisors who can steer the company through the process. The money generated from public investors can help grow the business further and help it become firmly established in its market.

Managing a Growing Business

Once an entrepreneurial business is up and running, how does the owner manage it? Often the traits of self-confidence, creativity, and internal locus of control lead to financial and personal grief as the enterprise grows. A hands-on entrepreneur who gave birth to the organization loves perfecting every detail. But after the start-up, continued growth requires a shift in management style. Those who fail to adjust to a growing business can be the cause of the problems rather than the solution.[70] In this section, we will look at the stages through which entrepreneurial companies move and then consider how managers should carry out their planning, organizing, leading, and controlling.

Stages of Growth

Entrepreneurial businesses go through distinct stages of growth, with each stage requiring different management skills. The five stages are illustrated in Exhibit C.9.

EXHIBIT *C.9*

Five Stages of Growth for an Entrepreneurial Company

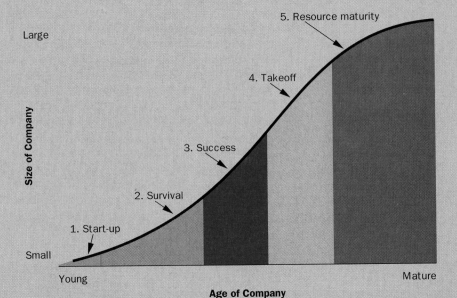

SOURCE: Based on Neil C. Churchill and Virginia L. Lewis, "The Five Stages of Small Business Growth," *Harvard Business Review* (May–June 1993), 30–50.

1. *Start-up*. In this stage, the main problems are producing the product or service and obtaining customers. Key issues facing managers are: Can we get enough customers? Will we survive? Do we have enough money? Many Internet companies are still in the start-up stage, although a few, such as Amazon.com and Yahoo!, have progressed to survival and are moving toward the success stage of growth.

2. *Survival*. At this stage, the business has demonstrated that it is a workable business entity. It is producing a product or service and has sufficient customers. Concerns here have to do with finances—generating sufficient cash flow to run the business and making sure revenues exceed expenses. The organization will grow in size and profitability during this period.

3. *Success*. At this point, the company is solidly based and profitable. Systems and procedures are in place to allow the owner to slow down if desired. The owner can stay involved or consider turning the business over to professional managers.

4. *Takeoff*. Here the key problem is how to grow rapidly and finance that growth. The owner must learn to delegate, and the company must find sufficient capital to invest in major growth. This is a pivotal period in an entrepreneurial company's life. Properly managed, the company can become a big business. However, another problem for companies at this stage is how to maintain the advantages of "smallness" as the company grows.

5. *Resource maturity*. At this stage, the company has made substantial financial gains, but it may start to lose the advantages of small size, including flexibility and the entrepreneurial spirit. A company in this stage has the staff and financial resources to begin acting like a mature company with detailed planning and control systems.

Planning

In the early start-up stage, formal planning tends to be nonexistent except for the business plan described earlier in this chapter. The primary goal is simply to remain alive. As the organization grows, formal planning usually is not instituted until around the success stage. Recall from Chapter 1 that planning means defining goals and deciding on the tasks and use of resources needed to attain them. Chapters 5 and 6 described how entrepreneurs can define goals and implement strategies and plans to meet them. It is important that entrepreneurs view their original business plan as a living document that evolves as the company grows or the market changes. Johann Verheem started a business called Application Technologies, which develops and licenses proprietary technology for packaging consumer products, based on a business plan he wrote as a student at San Diego State University. The professor gave the plan a B–, but he loved the concept and encouraged Verheem to take the plunge and start the business. Verheem and his student partner, now marketing manager for Application Technologies, kept shifting and fine-tuning their plans as they gathered input from venture capitalists, professors, and other experts.[71]

Organizing

In the first two stages of growth, the organization's structure is typically very informal with all employees reporting to the owner. At about

stage 3—success—functional managers often are hired to take over duties performed by the owner. A functional organization structure will begin to evolve with managers in charge of finance, manufacturing, and marketing. During the latter stages of entrepreneurial growth, managers must learn to delegate and decentralize authority. If the business has multiple product lines, the owner may consider creating teams or divisions responsible for each line. The organization must hire competent managers and have sufficient management talent to handle fast growth and eliminate problems caused by increasing size. As an organization grows, it might also be characterized by greater use of rules, procedures, and written job descriptions. For example, Tara Cronbaugh started a small coffeehouse in a college town, but its success quickly led to the opening of three additional houses. With the rapid growth, Cronbaugh found that she needed a way to ensure consistency across operations. She decided to put together an operations manual with detailed rules, procedures, and job descriptions so managers and employees at each coffeehouse would be following the same pattern.[72] Chapters 7 through 10 discussed organizing in detail.

Leading

The driving force in the early stages of development is the leader's vision. This vision, combined with the leader's personality, shapes corporate culture. The leader can signal cultural values of service, efficiency, quality, or ethics. Often entrepreneurs do not have good people skills but do have excellent task skills in either manufacturing or marketing. By the success stage of growth, the owner must either learn to motivate employees or bring in managers who can. Rapid takeoff is not likely to happen without employee cooperation.

Stepping from the self-absorption of the early days of a company to the more active communication necessary for growth can be tricky for entrepreneurs. Charles Barnard, the owner of Foot Traffic, a chain of specialty sock stores based in Kansas City, Missouri, believes leaders should focus on communication as a company grows. "A lot of the time," Barnard says, "you get to running real fast, and you don't think about the people around you. But you can never get anywhere if you're pulling your staff around behind you all the time."[73] The president of Foreign Candy Company of Hull, Iowa, saw his company grow rapidly when he concentrated more on employee needs and less on financial growth. He made an effort to communicate with employees, conducted surveys to learn how they were feeling about the company, and found ways to involve them in decision making. His leadership style allowed the company to enter the takeoff stage with the right corporate culture and employee attitudes to sustain rapid growth.

Leadership also is important because many small firms have a hard time hiring qualified employees. Labor shortages often hurt small firms that grow rapidly. A healthy corporate culture can help attract and retain good people.[74] You learned more about leadership in Chapters 11 through 15.

Controlling

Financial control is important in each stage of the entrepreneurial firm's growth. In the initial stages, control is exercised by simple accounting records and by personal supervision. By stage 3—success—operational budgets are in place, and the owner should start implementing more structured control systems. During the takeoff stage, the company will need to make greater use of budgets and standard cost systems and use computer systems to provide statistical reports. These control techniques will become more sophisticated during the resource maturity stage.

As Amazon.com has grown and expanded internationally, entrepreneur and CEO Jeff Bezos has found a need for increasingly sophisticated control mechanisms. For example, as the company struggled to standardize procedures and achieve profitability, Bezos hired a computer systems expert to develop a system to track and control all of the company's operations.[75]

Summary and Management Solution

This chapter explored entrepreneurship and small-business management. Entrepreneurs start new businesses, and entrepreneurship plays an important role in the economy by stimulating job creation, innovation, and opportunities for minorities and women. An entrepreneurial personality includes the traits of internal locus of control, high energy level, need to achieve, tolerance for ambiguity, awareness of passing time, and self-confidence.

Starting an entrepreneurial firm requires a new-business idea. At that point a comprehensive business plan should be developed and decisions made about legal structure and financing. Tactical decisions for the new venture include whether to start, buy, or franchise, and whether to participate in a business incubator.

A new kind of small business is the Internet start-up. These companies face the same challenges as other small businesses, but Internet entrepreneurs also encounter some unique issues. Based on what is known about Internet start-ups, entrepreneurs typically follow eight steps: (1) formulating the idea and concept for the company; (2) developing a business plan and a "story" to sell the idea; (3) securing up-front financing; (4) building and testing the product and service; (5) officially launching the Web site; (6) obtaining additional financing; (7) developing partnerships with other organizations; and (8) perhaps taking the company public through an initial public offering.

After a business is started, it generally proceeds through five stages of growth—start-up, survival, success, takeoff, and resource maturity. The management functions of planning, organizing, leading, and controlling should be tailored to each stage of growth.

Discussion Questions

1. Dan McKinnon started an airline with one airplane. To do so required filing more than 10,000 pages of manuals, ordering 50,000 luggage tags, buying more than $500 million in insurance, and spending more than $300,000 to train employees. A single inspection test cost $18,000. Evaluate whether you think this is a good entrepreneurial opportunity, and discuss why you think Dan McKinnon undertook it.
2. What do you think are the most important contributions of small business to our economy?
3. Why would small-business ownership have great appeal to immigrants, women, and minorities?
4. Consider the six personality characteristics of entrepreneurs. Which two traits do you think are most like those of managers in large companies? Which two are least like those of managers in large companies?
5. Why is purchasing an existing business or franchise less risky than starting a new business?
6. If you were to start a new business, would you have to search for an idea, or do you already have an idea to try? Explain.
7. Many entrepreneurs say they did little planning, perhaps scratching notes on a legal pad. How is it possible for them to succeed?
8. What is the difference between debt financing and equity financing? What are common sources of each type?
9. How does an entrepreneurial firm in the start-up stage differ from one in the success stage?
10. How does starting an online business differ from starting a small business such as a local auto repair shop or delicatessen? What is the role of alliances and partnerships in online versus traditional small businesses?
11. How might the management functions of planning and controlling differ for an online business as compared to a traditional business?

Manager's Workbook

What's Your Entrepreneurial IQ?

Rate yourself on the following 15 behaviors and characteristics, according to the following scale.

1 = Strongly disagree   3 = Agree
2 = Disagree   4 = Strongly agree

____ 1. I am able to translate ideas into concrete tasks and outcomes.
____ 2. When I am interested in a project, I tend to need less sleep.
____ 3. I am willing to make sacrifices to gain long-term rewards.
____ 4. Growing up, I was more of a risk-taker than a cautious child.
____ 5. I often see trends, connections, and patterns that are not obvious to others.
____ 6. I have always enjoyed spending much of my time alone.
____ 7. I have a reputation for being stubborn.
____ 8. I prefer working with a difficult but highly competent person to working with someone who is congenial but less competent.
____ 9. As a child, I had a paper route, lemonade stand, or other small enterprise.
____ 10. I usually keep New Year's resolutions.
____ 11. I'm not easily discouraged, and I persist when faced with major obstacles.
____ 12. I recover quickly from emotional setbacks.
____ 13. I would be willing to dip deeply into my "nest egg"—and possibly lose all I had saved—to go it alone.
____ 14. I get tired of the same routine day in and day out.
____ 15. When there is something I want, I keep the goal clearly in mind.

Scoring: Total your score for the 15 items. If you tallied 50–60 points, you have a very strong entrepreneurial IQ. A score of 30–50 indicates good entrepreneurial possibilities. Your chances of starting a successful entrepreneurial business are good if you have the desire and motivation. If you scored below 30, you probably do not have much entrepreneurial potential.

Go back over each question, thinking about changes you might make to become more or less entrepreneurial, depending on your career interests.

Manager's Workshop

1. In groups of 4 to 6 members, either select a local small business (one that is still run by the original entrepreneur) or the instructor will assign one.
2. Your job is to do as much research as you can about the small business. Look in the newspaper, trade journals, and so on. Find out when it started, how much business it does, some of its problems and successes.
3. Then go and interview the entrepreneur who started it. Find out what the experience of being an entrepreneur was like. What advice would that person have for someone starting out?
4. You will be asked to either write a paper or give a presentation on your company.

Management in Practice: Ethical Dilemma

As the new, heavily recruited CEO of an Internet start-up backed by several of Silicon Valley's leading venture capitalists, Chuck Campbell is flying high—great job, good salary, stock options, and a chance to be in on the ground floor and build one of the truly great e-commerce organizations. Just a few days into the job, Chuck helped make a presentation to a new group of potential investors for funding that could help the company expand marketing, improve its services, and invest in growth. By the end of the meeting, the investors had verbally committed $15 million in funding.

But things turned sour pretty fast. As Chuck was leaving around 9 P.M., the corporate controller, Betty Mars, who has just returned from an extended leave, cornered him. He was surprised to find her working so late, but before he could even open his mouth, Betty blurted out her problem: The numbers Chuck had presented to the venture capitalists were flawed. "The assumptions behind the revenue growth plan are absolutely untenable," she said. "Not a chance of ever happening." Chuck was stunned. He told Betty to get on home and he'd stay and take a look at the figures.

At 11 P.M., Chuck was still sitting in his office wondering what to do. His research showed that the numbers were indeed grossly exaggerated, but most of them were at least statistically possible (however remote that possibility was!). However, what really troubled him was that the renewal income figure was just flat-out false—and it was clear that one member of the management team who participated in the presentation knew this all along. To make matters worse, it was the renewal income figure that ultimately made the investment so attractive to the venture capital firm. Chuck knew what was at stake—no

less that the life or death of the company itself. If he told the truth about the deceptive numbers, the company's valuation would almost certainly be slashed and the $15 million possibly canceled.

What Do You Do?

1. Say nothing about the false numbers. Of course, the company will miss the projections and have to come up with a good explanation, but, after all, isn't that par for the course among fledgling e-businesses? Chances are the whole thing will blow over without a problem.
2. Go ahead and close the deal, but come clean later. Explain that the controller had been on an extended leave of absence and, because you had been on the job only a few days you had not had time to personally do an analysis of the numbers.
3. Take swift action to notify the venture capitalists of the truth of the situation—and start cleaning house to get rid of people who would knowingly lie to close a deal.

SOURCE: Adapted from Kent Weber, "The Truth Could Cost You $16 Million," *Business Ethics* (March–April 2001), 18.

Surf the Net

1. **Do You Have What It Takes?** Have you ever thought about starting your own business where you could be your own boss? Although there are many appealing aspects to starting your own business, you need to consider all aspects of being an entrepreneur carefully. The following site will give you a balanced perspective of what it will take for you to be successful in starting your own business. After completing the self-assessment be prepared to explain why the results suggest you either are or are not suited to fill the role of an entrepreneur.
   http://www.liraz.com/webquiz.htm
2. **SBA.** The U.S. Small Business Administration is "America's Small Business Resource." Visit the SBA's home page at *http://www.sba.gov*, list three links from the home page that you believe provided the most helpful or interesting information, and briefly explain what you found at each of the three links.
3. **Business Incubators.** The National Business Incubation Association, the world's leading organization advancing business incubation and entrepreneurship, provides a wealth of information about business incubation. Learn more by going to the NBIA Web site at *http://www.nbia.org*.

Find out where the incubators are located in your state or another state assigned by your instructor. Print out the page describing the state's incubators and bring it to class.

Case for Critical Analysis

Radiata Software

The founders of one of the hottest young software companies of the decade were meeting in Rob Larson's den to decide what to do. Radiata Software, founded by the three friends right after they graduated from college, makes financial software targeted to small professional service firms. Radiata had been an instant hit among solo professionals such as accountants and financial planners, as well as among small businesses that did not have the resources and equipment to run big, complex software programs. With a solid customer base, Radiata has been able to expand its product line and add a Web site providing customers with an all-in-one site for small business accounting and finance. One of the most popular features of the site is the electronic bulletin boards where solo professionals trade comments, seek advice, and share their stories of what it's like to be a free agent.

But Radiata's success had also come with some problems. Rapid growth left the founders struggling to keep pace with managing staff, handling development of new products and services, marketing, negotiating contracts, and so forth. Rob, who had come up with the idea for the company, served as CEO, and the other founders each had specific titles and duties, but all three were involved in essentially every aspect of the business. Whenever a major decision had to be made, they made it together, often after hours or days talking with one another to reach an agreement. Eventually, Susan Boyd, a representative from the venture capital firm that was Radiata's biggest source of funds, suggested they needed to bring in professional managers to help run the place. "You'll still have plenty of say in running the business," she said. "But after six years, Radiata is getting too big to manage as an entrepreneurial start-up. You need some professional help to take things to the next level." The founders agreed she was right, and Susan quickly recruited a chief operating officer, a chief information officer, and a chief financial officer to help Radiata through its growing pains. The three brought a tremendous wealth of knowledge and experience to the young company, and everyone seemed sure Radiata would grow even faster and be even more successful with a solid management team behind it.

"So, what went wrong?" Rob asks his co-founders now, after six months of working with the new management team. From the beginning, the three founders and the three new managers had seemed to segregate into two separate camps. The founders had been friends since their freshman year in college, had lived together until the last couple of years, and still partied together on the weekends. It came naturally for them to get together separately from the three newcomers and talk about the business, how the new managers were doing, and so forth. Feeling left out, the three seasoned managers gradually began turning to one another more and more, ignoring the younger trio. Although in the beginning the team of six had vowed to have regular Monday morning meetings, the meetings often got canceled for one reason or another. In addition, over time it became clear to the new managers that the three founders had already met and discussed issues prior to the formal meeting, so the three new managers began doing the same. By now, there were clearly two separate teams trying to run Radiata. Tomorrow, the group will be discussing whether to merge with a larger software company. "They'll swallow us," said Jessie. "Our dream of running our own business will be dead."

"Ha!" barked Thai. "You think it's not already dead? I expect our 'dream team' of senior managers are holed up somewhere right now discussing their strategy. They want this deal to go through, and you know they've got Susan in their back pocket. Who do you think is in charge of this company these days?"

"Look," said Rob. "We have to accept that a lot of this is our fault. It's always been us against them. We never made any effort to really make them a part of the company and share our ideas and vision with them. Almost every day, we find some way to meet without them and make some decision behind their backs—like when we signed that partnership agreement with an accounting services firm without even talking to them about it. It was an innocent mistake, but it clearly didn't sit well. Now they're meeting without us and maybe wanting to take the company in a direction we don't want to go. Also, I heard from our venture capital rep that our CIO is thinking of jumping ship. She's frustrated and miserable here, feels like she's spinning her wheels and wasting her time. If that happens, I don't think Susan and the venture capital team are going to be very happy. If we lose them, we're in serious trouble. Is there any way to get out of this mess?"

Questions

1. What is the underlying cause of the problems at Radiata? Can you think of ways to bring the two sides together and get the company back on the right track?
2. What management functions seem to be needed most at this point—planning, organizing, leading, or controlling? Discuss.
3. What do you think the founders need to do in this situation? What do you think the three new managers should do?

SOURCE: Based on Regina Fazio Maruca, "Entrepreneurs versus Executives at Socaba.com," *Harvard Business Review* (July–August 2000), 30–38.

Chapter 3

1. China (1.3 billion)
    India (1.0 billion)
    United States (278 million)
    Indonesia (228 million)
    Brazil (174 million)
    Russia (145 million)
2. 1. Mandarin (15.0%)
    2. English (5.5%)
    3. Spanish (5.0%)
    4. Arabic (3.3%)
    5. Hindi (3.2%)
    6. Bengali (3.0%)
3. c. 6,800
4. b. 191
5. 300%
6. 2 million
7. a. declined from 980 million in 1970 to 780 million in 2000.
8. c. $17 trillion
9. c. two-thirds
10. 66%
11. 50%
12. a. one-tenth
13. b. 20%
14. c. 35%
15. Mexico City
16. $42 trillion
17. 19,000% from 376,000 to 73.4 million
18. 20 percent in South Africa, 25 percent in Zimbabwe, and 36 percent in Botswana
19. 60 would be Asian
    80 would be non-white
    67 would be non-Christian
    25 Would live in substandard housing
    17 would be illiterate
    2 would have a college education
    4 would own a computer

SOURCE: United Nations Web site, 2002; Reka Balu, "Please Don't Forward This Email," *Fast Company* (June 2001), 58–59; World Watch Institute, *World Watch 2002* (New York: W. W. Norton).

Chapter 4

Ethics-Quiz Answers

Compare your answers with other Americans who were surveyed:

1. 34% said personal e-mail on company computers is wrong
2. 37% said using office equipment for schoolwork is wrong
3. 49% said playing computer games at work is wrong
4. 54% said Internet shopping at work is wrong
5. 61% said it's unethical to blame your error on technology
6. 87% said it's unethical to visit pornographic sites at work
7. 33% said $25 is the amount at which a gift from a supplier or client becomes troubling, while 33% said $50, and 33% said $100
8. 35% said a $50 gift to the boss is unacceptable
9. 12% said a $50 gift from the boss is unacceptable
10. 70% said it's unacceptable to take the $200 football tickets
11. 70% said it's unacceptable to take the $120 theater tickets
12. 35% said it's unacceptable to take the $100 food basket
13. 45% said it's unacceptable to take the $25 gift certificate
14. 40% said it's unacceptable to take the $75 raffle prize
15. 11% reported they lie about sick days
16. 4% reported they take credit for the work or ideas of others
17. 90% of Fortune 500 and 50% of all corporations
18. a.
19. b.
20. b.

Chapter 9

Answers: 1. F; 2. F; 3. T; 4. F; 5. T; 6. F; 7. F; 8. F; 9. T; 10. F.

Chapter 10

1. True–46%
2. False–59%
3. False–divorced=75%, married=63%
4. True
5. True
6. False, women's median earnings were $26, 324
7. False–with working wife=$60,000, without=$34,000
8. True
9. True
10. True
11. False–74 cents on the dollar
12. Lawyers
13. 47%
14. 20 million
    14 million
    9 million
15. 14%
    54%
16. 21%
    What percentage of male vs. female? 21% women age 25 and older, 25% men age 25 and older
    More info: 56% of all college students in 1998 were women. Women have represented the majority of college students since 1979.
17. 78%
18. New Mexico and California. The two least? Maine and Vermont
    20%
    48%

SOURCE: Copyright © 2002 by Dorothy Marcic.

Glossary

360-degree feedback A process that uses multiple raters, including self-rating, to appraise employee performance and guide development.

accountability The fact that the people with authority and responsibility are subject to reporting and justifying task outcomes to those above them in the chain of command.

activity-based costing (ABC) A control system that identifies the various activities needed to provide a product and allocates costs accordingly.

adjourning The stage of team development in which members prepare for the team's disbandment.

administrative model A decision-making model that describes how managers actually make decisions in situations characterized by nonprogrammed decisions, uncertainty, and ambiguity.

administrative principles A subfield of the classical management perspective that focused on the total organization rather than the individual worker, delineating the management functions of planning, organizing, commanding, coordinating, and controlling.

affirmative action A policy requiring employers to take positive steps to guarantee equal employment opportunities for people within protected groups.

ambiguity The goals to be achieved or the problem to be solved is unclear, alternatives are difficult to define, and information about outcomes is unavailable.

application form A device for collecting information about an applicant's education, previous job experience, and other background characteristics.

assessment center A technique for selecting individuals with high managerial potential based on their performance on a series of simulated managerial tasks.

attitude A cognitive and affective evaluation that predisposes a person to act in a certain way.

attributions Judgments about what caused a person's behavior—either characteristics of the person or of the situation.

authoritarianism The belief that power and status differences *should* exist within the organization.

authority The formal and legitimate right of a manager to make decisions, issue orders, and allocate resources to achieve organizationally desired outcomes.

autocratic leader A leader who tends to centralize authority and rely on legitimate, reward, and coercive power to manage subordinates.

B2B marketplaces An electronic marketplace set up by an intermediary where buyers and sellers meet.

balanced scorecard A comprehensive management control system that balances traditional financial measures with measures of customer service, internal business processes, and the organization's capacity for learning and growth.

behavior modification The set of techniques by which reinforcement theory is used to modify human behavior.

behavioral sciences approach A subfield of the humanistic management perspective that applies social science in an organizational context, drawing from economics, psychology, sociology, and other disciplines.

behaviorally anchored rating scale (BARS) A rating technique that relates an employee's performance to specific job-related incidents.

benchmarking The continuous process of measuring products, services, and practices against major competitors or industry leaders.

biculturalism The sociocultural skills and attitudes used by racial minorities to move back and forth between the dominant culture and their own ethnic or racial culture.

Big Five personality factors Dimensions that describe an individual's extroversion, agreeableness, conscientiousness, emotional stability, and openness to experience.

bottom-up budgeting A budgeting process in which lower-level managers budget their departments' resource needs and pass them up to top management for approval.

bounded rationality The concept that people have the time and cognitive ability to process only a limited amount of information on which to base decisions.

bureaucratic control The use of rules, policies, hierarchy of authority, reward systems, and other formal devices to influence employee behavior and assess performance.

bureaucratic organizations A subfield of the classical management perspective that emphasized management on an impersonal, rational basis through such elements as clearly defined authority and responsibility, formal recordkeeping, and separation of management and ownership.

capital budget A budget that plans and reports investments in major assets to be depreciated over several years.

cash budget A budget that estimates and reports cash flows on a daily or weekly basis to ensure that the company has sufficient cash to meet its obligations.

central planning department A group of planning specialists who develop plans for the organization as a whole and its major divisions and departments and typically report directly to the president or CEO.

centralization The location of decision authority near top organizational levels.

centralized network A team communication structure in which team members communicate through a single individual to solve problems or make decisions.

ceremony A planned activity that makes up a special event and is conducted for the benefit of an audience.

certainty All the information the decision maker needs is fully available.

chain of command An unbroken line of authority that links all individuals in the organization and specifies who reports to whom.

change agent An OD specialist who contracts with an organization to facilitate change.

changing The intervention stage of organizational development in which individuals experiment with new workplace behavior.

channel The carrier of a communication.

channel richness The amount of information that can be transmitted during a communication episode.

charismatic leader A leader who has the ability to motivate subordinates to transcend their expected performance.

chief ethics officer A company executive who oversees ethics and legal compliance.

classical model A decision-making model based on the assumption that managers should make logical decisions that will be in the organization's best economic interests.

classical perspective A management perspective that emerged during the nineteenth and early twentieth centuries that emphasized a rational, scientific approach to the study of management and sought to make organizations efficient operating machines.

coalition An informal alliance among managers who support a specific goal.

code of ethics A formal statement of the organization's values regarding ethics and social issues.

coercive power Power that stems from the authority to punish or recommend punishment.

cognitive dissonance A condition in which two attitudes or a behavior and an attitude conflict.

collectivism A preference for a tightly knit social framework in which individuals look after one another and organizations protect their members' interests.

committee A long-lasting, sometimes permanent team in the organization structure created to deal with tasks that recur regularly.

communication The process by which information is exchanged and understood by two or more people, usually with the intent to motivate or influence behavior.

compensation Monetary payments (wages, salaries) and nonmonetary goods/commodities (benefits, vacations) used to reward employees.

competitors Other organizations in the same industry or type of business that provide goods or services to the same set of customers.

concurrent control Control that consists of monitoring ongoing activities to ensure they are consistent with standards.

conflict Antagonistic interaction in which one party attempts to thwart the intentions or goals of another.

consideration A type of leader behavior that describes the extent to which a leader is sensitive to subordinates, respects their ideas and feelings, and establishes mutual trust.

content theories A group of theories that emphasize the needs that motivate people.

contingency approach A model of leadership that describes the relationship between leadership styles and specific organizational situations.

contingency plans Plans that define company responses to specific situations, such as emergencies, setbacks, or unexpected conditions.

contingent workers People who work for an organization, but not on a permanent or full-time basis, including temporary placements, contracted professionals, or leased employees.

continuous improvement The implementation of a large number of small, incremental improvements in all areas of the organization on an ongoing basis.

continuous process production A type of technology involving mechanization of the entire work flow and nonstop production.

continuous reinforcement schedule A schedule in which every occurrence of the desired behavior is reinforced.

coordination The quality of collaboration across departments.

coordination costs The time and energy needed to coordinate the activities of a team to enable it to perform its task.

core competence A business activity that an organization does particularly well in comparison to competitors.

corporate university An in-house training and education facility that offers broad learning opportunities for employees.

cost leadership A type of competitive strategy with which the organization aggressively seeks efficient facilities, cuts costs, and employs tight cost controls to be more efficient than competitors.

creativity The generation of novel ideas that may meet perceived needs or offer opportunities for the organization.

cross-functional team A group of employees from various departments that meets as a team to resolve mutual problems.

cultural leader A manager who uses signals and symbols to influence corporate culture.

culture The set of key values, beliefs, understandings, and norms that members of an organization share; the shared knowledge, beliefs, values, behaviors and ways of thinking among members of a society.

culture shock Feelings of confusion, disorientation, and anxiety that result from being immersed in a foreign culture.

culture/people change A change in employees' values, norms, attitudes, beliefs, and behavior.

customer relationship management (CRM) systems Systems that help companies track customers' interactions with the firm and allow employees to call up information on past transactions.

customers People and organizations in the environment who acquire goods or services from the organization.

cycle time The steps taken to complete a company process.

data Raw, unsummarized, and unanalyzed facts and figures.

decentralization The location of decision authority near lower organizational levels.

decentralized control The use of organizational culture, group norms, and a focus on goals, rather than rules and procedures, to foster compliance with organziational goals.

decentralized network A team communication structure in which team members freely communicate with one another and arrive at decisions together.

decentralized planning Managers work with planning experts to develop their own goals and plans.

decision A choice made from available alternatives.

decision making The process of identifying problems and opportunities and then resolving them.

decision style Differences among people with respect to how they perceive problems and make decisions.

decode To translate the symbols used in a message for the purpose of interpreting its meaning.

defense mechanism Emotional blocks that serve to minimize anxiety, protect the ego, and maintain repression of true feelings.

delegation The process managers use to transfer authority and responsibility to positions below them in the hierarchy.

democratic leader A leader who delegates authority to others, encourages participation, and relies on expert and referent power to manage subordinates.

departmentalization The basis on which individuals are grouped into departments and departments into the total organization.

descriptive An approach that describes how managers actually make decisions rather than how they should.

devil's advocate A decision-making technique in which an individual is assigned the role of challenging the assumptions and assertions made by the group to prevent premature consensus.

diagnosis The step in the decision-making process in which managers analyze underlying causal factors associated with the decision situation.

dialogue A group communication process aimed at creating a culture based on collaboration, fluidity, trust, and commitment to shared goals.

differentiation A type of competitive strategy with which the organization seeks to distinguish its products or services from competitors'.

digital technology Technology characterized by use of the Internet and other digital processes to conduct or support business operations.

direct investing An entry strategy in which the organization is involved in managing its production facilities in a foreign country.

discretionary responsibility Organizational responsibility that is voluntary and guided by the organization's desire to make social contributions not mandated by economics, law, or ethics.

discrimination The hiring or promoting of applicants based on criteria that are not job relevant.

diversity awareness training Special training designed to make people aware of their own prejudices and stereotypes.

downward communication Messages sent from top management down to subordinates.

dual role A role in which the individual both contributes to the team's task and supports members' emotional needs.

E → P expectancy Expectancy that putting effort into a given task will lead to high performance.

e-business Work an organization does by using electronic linkages; any business that takes place by digital processes over a computer network rather than in physical space.

e-commerce Business exchanges or transactions that occur electronically.

e-cruiting Recruiting job applicants online.

economic dimension The dimension of the general environment representing the overall economic health of the country or region in which the organization functions.

economic forces Forces that affect the availability, production, and distribution of a society's resources among competing users

economic value added (EVA) system A control system that measures performance in terms of after-tax profits minus the cost of capital invested in tangible assets.

effectiveness The degree to which the organization achieves a stated goal.

efficiency The use of minimal resources—raw materials, money, and people—to produce a desired volume of output.

electronic data interchange (EDI) A network that links the computer systems of buyers and sellers to allow the transmission of structured data primarily for ordering, distribution, and payables and receivables.

employee network groups Groups based on social identity, such as race or gender, and organized by employees to focus on concerns of employees from that group.

employment test A written or computer-based test designed to measure a particular attribute such as intelligence or aptitude.

empowerment The delegation of power or authority to subordinates.

encode To select symbols with which to compose a message.

enterprise resource planning (ERP) Systems that unite a company's major business functions—order processing, product design, purchasing, inventory, etc.

equity A situation that exists when the ratio of one person's outcomes to inputs equals that of another's.

equity theory A process theory that focuses on individuals' perceptions of how fairly they are treated relative to others.

ERG theory A modification of the needs hierarchy theory that proposes three categories of needs: existence, relatedness, and growth.

escalating commitment Continuing to invest time and resources in a failing decision.

ethical dilemma A situation that arises when all alternative choices or behaviors have been deemed undesirable because of potentially negative consequence, making it difficult to distinguish right from wrong.

ethics The code of moral principles and values that govern the behaviors of a person or group with respect to what is right or wrong.

ethics committee A group of executives assigned to oversee the organization's ethics by ruling on questionable issues and disciplining violators.

ethics training Training programs to help employees deal with ethical questions and values.

ethnocentrism The belief that one's own group or subculture is inherently superior to other groups or cultures.

ethnorelativism The belief that groups and subcultures are inherently equal.

euro A single European currency that replaced the currencies of 11 European nations.

exit interview An interview conducted with departing employees to determine the reasons for their termination.

expatriates Employees who live and work in a country other than their own.

expectancy theory A process theory that proposes that motivation depends on individuals' expectations about their ability to perform tasks and receive desired rewards.

expense budget A budget that outlines the anticipated and actual expenses for a responsibility center.

expert power Power that stems from special knowledge of or skill in the tasks performed by subordinates.

exporting An entry strategy in which the organization maintains its production facilities within its home country and transfers its products for sale in foreign countries.

extranet A company communications system that uses the Internet and gives access to suppliers, partners, and others outside the company.

extrinsic reward A reward given by another person.

feedback A response by the receiver to the sender's communication; using communication and evaluation to help the organization learn and improve.

feedback control Control that focuses on the organization's outputs; also called *postaction* or *output control*.

feedforward control Control that focuses on human, material, and financial resources flowing into the organization; also called *preliminary* or *preventive control*.

femininity A cultural preference for cooperation, group decision making, and quality of life.

flat structure A management structure characterized by an overall broad span of control and relatively few hierarchical levels.

focus A type of competitive strategy that emphasizes concentration on a specific regional market or buyer group.

force-field analysis The process of determining which forces drive and which resist a proposed change.

formal communication channel A communication channel that flows within the chain of command or task responsibility defined by the organization.

formal team A team created by the organization as part of the formal organization structure.

forming The stage of team development characterized by orientation and acquaintance.

franchising A form of licensing in which an organization provides its foreign franchisees with a complete package of materials and services.

free rider A person who benefits from team membership but does not make a proportionate contribution to the team's work.

frustration-regression principle The idea that failure to meet a high-order need may cause a regression to an already satisfied lower-order need.

fundamental attribution error The tendency to underestimate the influence of external factors on another's behavior and to overestimate the influence of internal factors.

General Adaptation Syndrome (GAS) The physiological response to a stressor, beginning with an alarm response, continuing to resistance, and sometimes ending in exhaustion if the stressor continues beyond the person's ability to cope.

general environment The layer of the external environment that affects the organization indirectly.

glass ceiling Invisible barrier that separates women and minorities from top management positions.

global outsourcing Engaging in the international division of labor so as to obtain the cheapest sources of labor and supplies regardless of country; also called *global sourcing*.

global team A work team made up of members of different nationalities whose activities span multiple countries; may operate as a virtual team or meet face to face.

goal A desired future state that the organization attempts to realize

grand strategy The general plan of major action by which an organization intends to achieve its long-term goals.

grapevine An informal, person-to-person communication network of employees that is not officially sanctioned by the organization.

halo effect A type of rating error that occurs when an employee receives the same rating on all dimensions regardless of his or her performance on individual ones; an overall impression of a person or situation based on one attribute, either favorable or unfavorable.

Hawthorne studies A series of experiments on worker productivity begun in 1924 at the Hawthorne plant of Western Electric Company in Illinois; attributed employees' increased output to managers' better treatment of them during the study.

hero A figure who exemplifies the deeds, character, and attributes of a strong corporate culture.

hierarchy of needs theory A content theory that proposes that people are motivated by five categories of needs—physiological, safety, belongingness, esteem, and self-actualization—that exist in a hierarchical order.

high-context culture A culture in which communication is used to enhance personal relationships.

horizontal communication The lateral or diagonal exchange of messages among peers or coworkers.

horizontal team A formal team composed of employees from about the same hierarchical level but from different areas of expertise.

human capital The economic value of the knowledge, experience, skills, and capabilities of employees.

human relations movement A movement in management thinking and practice that emphasized satisfaction of employees' basic needs as the key to increased worker productivity.

human resource information system An integrated computer system designed to provide data and information used in HR planning and decision making.

human resource management (HRM) Activities undertaken to attract, develop, and maintain an effective workforce within an organization.

human resource planning The forecasting of human resource needs and the projected matching of individuals with expected job vacancies.

human resources perspective A management perspective that suggests jobs should be designed to meet higher-level needs by allowing workers to use their full potential.

humanistic perspective A management perspective that emerged around the late nineteenth century that emphasized understanding human behavior, needs, and attitudes in the workplace.

hygiene factors Factors that involve the presence or absence of job dissatisfiers, including working conditions, pay, company policies, and interpersonal relationships.

idea champion A person who sees the need for and champions productive change within the organization.

idea incubator An in-house program that provides a safe harbor where ideas from employees throughout the organization can be developed without interference from company bureaucracy or politics.

implementation The step in the decision-making process that involves using managerial, administrative, and persuasive abilities to translate the chosen alternative into action.

individualism A preference for a loosely knit social framework in which individuals are expected to take care of themselves.

individualism approach The ethical concept that acts are moral when they promote the individual's best long-term interests, which ultimately leads to the greater good.

informal communication channels A communication channel that exists outside formally authorized channels without regard for the organization's hierarchy of authority.

information Data that have been converted into a meaningful and useful context for the receiver.

information technology The hardware, software, telecommunications, database management, and other technologies used to store, process, and distribute information.

infrastructure A country's physical facilities that support economic activities.

initiating structure A type of leader behavior that describes the extent to which a leader is task oriented and directs subordinates' work activities toward goal achievement.

instant messaging Technology that provides a way to send quick notes from PC to PC over the Internet so two people who are online at the same time can communicate instantly.

interactive leadership A leadership style characterized by values such as inclusion, collaboration, relationship building, and caring.

internal environment The environment within the organization's boundaries.

international dimension Portion of the external environment that represents events originating in foreign countries as well as opportunities for American companies in other countries.

international management The management of business operations conducted in more than one country.

Internet A global collection of computer networks linked together for the exchange of data and information.

intranet An internal communications system that uses the technology and standards of the Internet but is accessible only to people within the organization.

intrinsic reward The satisfaction received in the process of performing an action.

intuition The immediate comprehension of a decision situation based on past experience but without conscious thought.

ISO 9000 A set of international standards for quality management, setting uniform guidelines for processes to ensure that products conform to customer requirements.

job analysis The systematic process of gathering and interpreting information about the essential duties, tasks, and responsibilities of a job.

job characteristics model A model of job design that comprises core job dimensions, critical psychological states, and employee growth-need strength.

job description A concise summary of the specific tasks and responsibilities of a particular job.

job design The application of motivational theories to the structure of work for improving productivity and satisfaction.

job enlargement A job design that combines a series of tasks into one new, broader job to give employees variety and challenge.

job enrichment A job design that incorporates achievement, recognition, and other high-level motivators into the work.

job evaluation The process of determining the value of jobs within an organization through an examination of job content.

job rotation A job design that systematically moves employees from one job to another to provide them with variety and stimulation.

job satisfaction A positive attitude toward one's job.

job simplification A job design whose purpose is to improve task efficiency by reducing the number of tasks a single person must perform.

job specification An outline of the knowledge, skills, education, and physical abilities needed to adequately perform a job.

joint venture A variation of direct involvement in which an organization shares costs and risks with another firm to build a manufacturing facility, develop new products, or set up a sales and distribution network.

justice approach The ethical concept that moral decisions must be based on standards of equity, fairness, and impartiality.

knowledge management The efforts to systematically find, organize, and make available a company's intellectual capital and to foster a culture of continuous learning and knowledge sharing.

labor market The people available for hire by the organization.

large-group intervention An approach that brings together participants from all parts of the organization (and may include key outside stakeholders as well) to discuss problems or opportunities and plan for major change.

law of effect The assumption that positively reinforced behavior tends to be repeated and unreinforced or negatively reinforced behavior tends to be inhibited.

leadership The ability to influence people toward the attainment of organizational goals.

leadership grid A two-dimensional leadership theory that measures a leader's concern for people and concern for production.

learning A change in behavior or performance that occurs as a result of experience.

learning organization An organization in which everyone is engaged in identifying and solving problems, enabling the organization to continuously experiment, improve, and increase its capability.

legal–political dimension The dimension of the general environment that includes federal, state, and local government regulations and political activities designed to influence company behavior.

legitimate power Power that stems from a formal management position in an organization and the authority granted to it.

licensing An entry strategy in which an organization in one country makes certain resources available to companies in another in order to participate in the production and sale of its products abroad.

line authority A form of authority in which individuals in management positions have the formal power to direct and control immediate subordinates.

listening The skill of receiving messages to accurately grasp facts and feelings to interpret the genuine meaning.

locus of control The tendency to place the primary responsibility for one's success or failure either within oneself (internally) or on outside forces (externally).

long-term orientation A greater concern for the future and high value on thrift and perseverance.

low-context culture A culture in which communication is used to exchange facts and information.

LPC scale A questionnaire designed to measure relationship-oriented versus task-oriented leadership style according to the leader's choice of adjectives for describing the "least preferred coworker."

Machiavellianism The tendency to direct much of one's behavior toward the acquisition of power and the manipulation of others for personal gain.

management The attainment of organizational goals in an effective and efficient manner through planning, organizing, leading, and controlling organizational resources.

management by objectives A method of management whereby managers and employees define goals for every department, project, and person and use them to monitor subsequent performance.

management by wandering around (MBWA) A communication technique in which managers interact directly with workers to exchange information.

management information system (MIS) A computer-based system that provides information and support for effective managerial decision making.

management science perspective A management perspective that emerged after World War II and applied mathematics, statistics, and other quantitative techniques to managerial problems.

market entry strategy An organizational strategy for entering a foreign market.

market value added (MVA) system A control system that measures the stock market's estimate of the value of a company's past and expected capital investment projects.

masculinity A cultural preference for achievement, heroism, assertiveness, work centrality, and material success.

mass production A type of technology characterized by the production of a large volume of products with the same specifications.

matching model An employee selection approach in which the organization and the applicant attempt to match each other's needs, interests, and values.

mediation The process of using a third party to settle a dispute.

mentor A higher-ranking, senior organizational member who is committed to providing upward mobility and support to a protégé's professional career.

message The tangible formulation of an idea to be sent to a receiver.

mission The organization's reason for existence.

mission statement A broadly stated definition of the organization's basic business scope and operations that distinguishes it from similar types of organizations.

modular approach A manufacturing company uses outside suppliers to provide large components of the product, which are then assembled into a final product by a few workers.

monoculture A culture that accepts only one way of doing things and one set of values and beliefs.

moral-rights approach The ethical concept that moral decisions are those that best maintain the rights of those people affected by them.

most favored nation A term describing a GATT clause that calls for member countries to grant other member countries the most favorable treatment they accord any country concerning imports and exports.

motivation The arousal, direction, and persistence of behavior.

motivators Factors that influence job satisfaction based on fulfillment of high-level needs such as achievement, recognition, responsibility, and opportunity for growth.

multicultural teams Teams made up of members from diverse national, racial, ethnic, and cultural backgrounds.

multinational corporation (MNC) An organization that receives more than 25 percent of its total sales revenues from operations outside the parent company's home country; also called *global corporation* or *transnational corporation*.

network structure An organization structure that disaggregates major functions into separate companies that are brokered by a small headquarters organization.

neutralizer A situational variable that counteracts a leadership style and prevents the leader from displaying certain behaviors.

new-venture team A unit separate from the mainstream of the organization that is responsible for developing and initiating innovations.

nonparticipator role A role in which the individual contributes little to either the task or members' socioemotional needs.

nonprogrammed decision A decision made in response to a situation that is unique, is poorly defined and largely unstructured, and has important consequences for the organization.

nonverbal communication A communication transmitted through actions and behaviors rather than through words.

norm A standard of conduct that is shared by team members and guides their behavior.

normative An approach that defines how a decision maker should make decisions and provides guidelines for reaching an ideal outcome for the organization.

norming The stage of team development in which conflicts developed during the storming stage are resolved and team harmony and unity emerge.

office automation systems Systems that combine modern hardware and software to handle the tasks of publishing and distributing information.

on-the-job training (OJT) A type of training in which an experienced employee "adopts" a new employee to teach him or her how to perform job duties.

open communication Sharing all types of information throughout the company, across functional and hierarchical levels.

open-book management Sharing financial information and results with all employees in the organization.

operational goals Specific, measurable results expected from departments, work groups, and individuals within the organization.

operational plans Plans developed at the organization's lower levels that specify action steps toward achieving operational goals and that support tactical planning activities.

operations information system A computer-based information system that supports a company's day-to-day operations.

opportunity A situation in which managers see potential organizational accomplishments that exceed current goals.

organization A social entity that is goal directed and deliberately structured.

organization chart The visual representation of an organization's structure.

organization structure The framework in which the organization defines how tasks are divided, resources are deployed, and departments are coordinated.

organizational behavior An interdisciplinary field dedicated to the study of how individuals and groups tend to act in organizations.

organizational change The adoption of a new idea or behavior by an organization.

organizational citizenship Work behavior that goes beyond job requirements and contributes as needed to the organization's success.

organizational commitment Loyalty to and heavy involvement in one's organization.

organizational control   The systematic process through which managers regulate organizational activities to make them consistent with expectations established in plans, targets, and standards of performance.

organizational development (OD)   The application of behavioral science techniques to improve an organization's health and effectiveness through its ability to cope with environmental changes, improve internal relationships, and increase problem-solving capabilities.

organizational environment   All elements existing outside the organization's boundaries that have the potential to affect the organization.

organizing   The deployment of organizational resources to achieve strategic goals.

P → O expectancy   Expectancy that successful performance of a task will lead to the desired outcome.

partial productivity   The ratio of total outputs to the inputs from a single major input category.

partial reinforcement schedule   A schedule in which only some occurrences of the desired behavior are reinforced.

path-goal theory   A contingency approach to leadership specifying that the leader's responsibility is to increase subordinates' motivation by clarifying the behaviors necessary for task accomplishment and rewards.

pay-for-performance   Incentive pay that ties at least part of compensation to employee effort and performance.

peer-to-peer (P2P) file sharing   File sharing that allows PCs to communicate directly with one another over the Internet, bypassing central databases, servers, control points, and Web pages.

perception   The cognitive process people use to make sense out of the environment by selecting, organizing, and interpreting information.

perceptual defense   The tendency of perceivers to protect themselves by disregarding ideas, objects, or people that are threatening to them.

perceptual distortions   Errors in perceptual judgment that arise from inaccuracies in any part of the perception process.

perceptual selectivity   The process by which individuals screen and select the various stimuli that vie for their attention.

performance   The organization's ability to attain its goals by using resources in an efficient and effective manner.

performance appraisal   The process of observing and evaluating an employee's performance, recording the assessment, and providing feedback to the employee.

performance gap   A disparity between existing and desired performance levels.

performing   The stage of team development in which members focus on problem solving and accomplishing the team's assigned task.

permanent team   A group of participants from several functions who are permanently assigned to solve ongoing problems of common interest.

personality   The set of characteristics that underlie a relatively stable pattern of behavior in response to ideas, objects, or people in the environment.

person-job fit   The extent to which a person's ability and personality match the requirements of a job.

plan   A blueprint specifying the resource allocations, schedules, and other actions necessary for attaining goals.

planning   The act of determining the organization's goals and the means for achieving them.

planning task force   A group of managers and employees who develop a strategic plan.

pluralism   The organization accommodates several subcultures, including employees who would otherwise feel isolated and ignored.

point-counterpoint   A decision-making technique in which people are assigned to express competing points of view.

political forces   The influence of political and legal institutions on people and organizations.

political instability   Events such as riots, revolutions, or government upheavals that affect the operations of an international company.

political risk   A company's risk of loss of assets, earning power, or managerial control due to politically based events or actions by host governments.

power   The potential ability to influence others' behavior.

power distance   The degree to which people accept inequality in power among institutions, organizations, and people.

pressure group   An interest group that works within the legal–political framework to influence companies to behave in socially responsible ways.

problem   A situation in which organizational accomplishments have failed to meet established goals.

problem-solving team   Typically 5 to 12 hourly employees from the same department who meet to discuss ways of improving quality, efficiency, and the work environment.

process   An organized group of related tasks and activities that work together to transform inputs into outputs and create value.

process theories   A group of theories that explain how employees select behaviors with which to meet their needs and determine whether their choices were successful.

product change   A change in the organization's product or service output.

productivity   The organization's output of products and services divided by its inputs.

programmed decision   A decision made in response to a situation that has occurred often enough to enable decision rules to be developed and applied in the future.

project manager   A person responsible for coordinating the activities of several departments on a full-time basis for the completion of a specific project.

projection The tendency to see one's own personal traits in other people.

quality circle A group of 6 to 12 volunteer employees who meet regularly to discuss and solve problems affecting the quality of their work.

realistic job preview (RJP) A recruiting approach that gives applicants all pertinent and realistic information about the job and the organization.

recruiting The activities or practices that define the desired characteristics of applicants for specific jobs.

reengineering The radical redesign of business processes to achieve dramatic improvements in cost, quality, service, and speed.

referent power Power that results from characteristics that command subordinates' identification with, respect and admiration for, and desire to emulate the leader.

refreezing The reinforcement stage of organizational development in which individuals acquire a desired new skill or attitude and are rewarded for it by the organization.

reinforcement Anything that causes a given behavior to be repeated or inhibited.

reinforcement theory A motivation theory based on the relationship between a given behavior and its consequences.

responsibility The duty to perform the task or activity an employee has been assigned.

responsibility center An organizational unit under the supervision of a single person who is responsible for its activity.

revenue budget A budget that identifies the forecasted and actual revenues of the organization.

reward power Power that results from the authority to reward others.

risk A decision has clear-cut goals and good information is available, but the future outcomes associated with each alternative are subject to chance.

risk propensity The willingness to undertake risk with the opportunity of gaining an increased payoff.

role A set of expectations for one's behavior.

role ambiguity Uncertainty about what behaviors are expected of a person in a particular role.

role conflict Incompatible demands of different roles.

satisficing To choose the first solution alternative that satisfies minimal decision criteria regardless of whether better solutions are presumed to exist.

schedule of reinforcement The frequency with which and intervals over which reinforcement occurs.

scientific management A subfield of the classical management perspective that emphasized scientifically determined changes in management practices as the solution to improving labor productivity.

search The process of learning about current developments inside or outside the organization that can be used to meet a perceived need for change.

selection The process of determining the skills, abilities, and other attributes a person needs to perform a particular job.

self-directed team A team consisting of 5 to 20 multiskilled workers who rotate jobs to produce an entire product or service, often supervised by an elected member.

self-serving bias The tendency to overestimate the contribution of internal factors to one's successes and the contribution of external factors to one's failures.

semantics The meaning of words and the way they are used.

servant leader A leader who works to fulfill subordinates' needs and goals as well as to achieve the organization's larger mission.

service technology Technology characterized by intangible outputs and direct contact between employees and customers.

short-term orientation A concern with the past and present and a high value on meeting social obligations.

situation analysis Analysis of the strengths, weaknesses, opportunities, and threats (SWOT) that affect organizational performance.

situational theory A contingency approach to leadership that links the leader's behavioral style with the task readiness of subordinates.

Six Sigma A quality control approach that emphasizes a relentless pursuit of higher quality and lower costs.

skunkworks A separate small, informal, highly autonomous, and often secretive group that focuses on breakthrough ideas for the business.

slogan A phrase or sentence that succinctly expresses a key corporate value.

small-batch production A type of technology that involves the production of goods in batches of one or a few products designed to customer specifications.

social facilitation The tendency for the presence of others to influence an individual's motivation and performance.

social forces The aspects of a culture that guide and influence relationships among people—their values, needs, and standards of behavior.

social responsibility The obligation of organization management to make decisions and take actions that will enhance the welfare and interests of society as well as the organization.

sociocultural dimension The dimension of the general environment representing the demographic characteristics, norms, customs, and values of the population within which the organization operates.

socioemotional role A role in which the individual provides support for team members' emotional needs and social unity.

span of management The number of employees who report to a supervisor; also called *span of control.*

special-purpose team A team created outside the formal organization to undertake a project of special importance or creativity.

staff authority A form of authority granted to staff specialists in their areas of expertise.

stakeholder Any group within or outside the organization that has a stake in the organization's performance.

stereotyping Placing an employee into a class or category based on one or a few traits or characteristics; the tendency to assign an individual to a group or broad category and then attribute generalizations about the group to the individual.

storming The stage of team development in which individual personalities and roles, and resulting conflicts, emerge.

story A narrative based on true events that is repeated frequently and shared by organizational employees.

strategic goals Broad statements of where the organization wants to be in the future; pertain to the organization as a whole rather than to specific divisions or departments.

strategic management The set of decisions and actions used to formulate and implement strategies that will provide a competitively superior fit between the organization and its environment so as to achieve organizational goals.

strategic plans The action steps by which an organization intends to attain strategic goals.

strategy The plan of action that prescribes resource allocation and other activities for dealing with the environment and helping the organization attain its goals.

strategy formulation The stage of strategic management that involves the planning and decision making that lead to the establishment of the organization's goals and of a specific strategic plan.

strategy implementation The stage of strategic management that involves the use of managerial and organizational tools to direct resources toward achieving strategic outcomes.

stress A physiological and emotional response to stimuli that place physical or psychological demands on an individual.

structural changes Any change in the way in which the organization is designed and managed.

substitute A situational variable that makes a leadership style unnecessary or redundant.

superordinate goal A goal that cannot be reached by a single party.

suppliers People and organizations who provide the raw materials the organization uses to produce its output.

survey feedback A type of OD intervention in which questionnaires on organizational climate and other factors are distributed among employees and the results reported back to them by a change agent.

symbol An object, act, or event that conveys meaning to others.

synergy The condition that exists when the organization's parts interact to produce a joint effect that is greater than the sum of the parts acting alone.

tactical goals Goals that define the outcomes that major divisions and departments must achieve in order for the organization to reach its overall goals.

tactical plans Plans designed to help execute major strategic plans and to accomplish a specific part of the company's strategy.

tall structure A management structure characterized by an overall narrow span of management and a relatively large number of hierarchical levels.

task environment The layer of the external environment that directly influences the organization's operations and performance.

task force A temporary team or committee formed to solve a specific short-term problem involving several departments.

task specialist role A role in which the individual devotes personal time and energy to helping the team accomplish its task.

team A group of participants from several departments who meet regularly to solve ongoing problems of common interest; a unit of two or more people who interact and coordinate their work to accomplish a specific goal.

team building A type of OD intervention that enhances the cohesiveness of departments by helping members learn to function as a team.

team cohesiveness The extent to which team members are attracted to the team and motivated to remain in it.

team-based structure Structure in which the entire organization is made up of teams that coordinate their work and work directly with customers to accomplish the organization's goals.

technical complexity The degree to which complex machinery is involved in the production process to the exclusion of people.

technological dimension The dimension of the general environment that includes scientific and technological advancements in the industry and society at large.

technology The knowledge, tools, techniques, and activities used to transform the organization's inputs into outputs.

technology change A change that pertains to the organization's production process.

telecommuting Using computers and telecommunications equipment to perform work from home or another remote location.

time-based competition A strategy of competition based on the ability to deliver products and services faster than competitors.

top-down budgeting A budgeting process in which middle- and lower-level managers set departmental budget targets in accordance with overall company revenues and expenditures specified by top management.

total factor productivity The ratio of total outputs to the inputs from labor, capital, materials, and energy.

total quality management (TQM) A concept that focuses on managing the total organization to deliver quality to customers. Four significant elements of TQM are employee involvement, focus on the customer, benchmarking, and continuous improvement. Also, an organizationwide commitment to infusing quality into every activity through continuous improvement.

traits Distinguishing personal characteristics, such as intelligence, values, and appearance.

transaction-processing system A type of operations information system that records and processes data resulting from routine business transactions such as sales, purchases, and payroll.

transactional leader A leader who clarifies subordinates' role and task requirements, initiates structure, provides rewards, and displays consideration for subordinates.

transformational leader A leader distinguished by a special ability to bring about innovation and change.

Type A behavior Behavior pattern characterized by extreme competitiveness, impatience, aggressiveness, and devotion to work.

Type B behavior Behavior pattern that lacks Type A characteristics and includes a more balanced, relaxed lifestyle.

uncertainty Managers know which goal they wish to achieve, but information about alternatives and future events is incomplete.

uncertainty avoidance A value characterized by people's intolerance for uncertainty and ambiguity and resulting support for beliefs that promise certainty and conformity.

unfreezing The stage of organizational development in which participants are made aware of problems in order to increase their willingness to change their behavior.

upward communication Messages transmitted from the lower to the higher levels in the organization's hierarchy.

utilitarian approach The ethical concept that moral behaviors produce the greatest good for the greatest number.

valence The value or attraction an individual has for an outcome.

validity The relationship between an applicant's score on a selection device and his or her future job performance.

vertical team A formal team composed of a manager and his or her subordinates in the organization's formal chain of command.

virtual organization An organization that has few on-site employees and does most of its interactions online.

virtual team A team that uses advanced information and telecommunications technologies so that geographically distant members can collaborate on projects and reach common goals.

vision An attractive, ideal future that is credible yet not readily attainable.

Vroom-Jago model A model designed to help managers gauge the amount of subordinate participation in decision making.

wage and salary surveys Surveys that show what other organizations pay incumbents in jobs that match a sample of "key" jobs selected by the organization.

whistle-blowing The disclosure by an employee of illegal, immoral, or illegitimate practices by the organization.

work redesign The altering of jobs to increase both the quality of employees' work experience and their productivity.

work specialization The degree to which organizational tasks are subdivided into individual jobs; also called division of labor.

workforce diversity Hiring people with different human qualities who belong to various cultural groups.

World Wide Web (WWW) A collections of central servers for accessing information on the Internet.

Chapter 1
Managing the New Workplace

1. Michael Chazin, "Have it Your Way," *Upholstery Design & Management* (February 2001), 16–21; Thomas Petzinger, *The New Pioneers* (New York: Simon & Schuster, 1999).

2. Nicholas Imparato and Oren Harari, *Jumping the Curve: Innovation and Strategic Choice in an Age of Transition* (San Francisco: Jossey-Bass Publishers, 1994); Tom Broersma, "In Search of the Future," *Training and Development* (January 1995), 38–43; Rahul Jacob, "The Struggle to Create an Organization for the Twenty-First Century," *Fortune* (April 3, 1995) 90–99; and Charles Handy, *The Age of Paradox* (Boston: Harvard Business School Press, 1994).

3. Keith H. Hammonds, "The Monroe Doctrine," *Fast Company* (October 1999), 230–236; and David Beardsley, "This Company Doesn't Brake for (Sacred) Cows," *Fast Company* (August 1998), 66–68.

4. John Jurgensen, "After Garcia's Death, Dead's Legacy Thrives," Associated Press story in *Johnson City Press* (August 9, 2000), 16; David E. Bowen and Caren Siehl, "Sweet Music: Grateful Employees, Grateful Customers, 'Grate' Profits," *Journal of Management Inquiry* (June 1992), 154–156; and Leslie Brokaw, "The Dead Have Customers, Too," *Inc.* (September 1994), 90–92.

5. James A. F. Stoner and R. Edward Freeman, *Management,* 4th ed. (Englewood Cliffs, N.J.: Prentice-Hall, 1989).

6. Peter F. Drucker, *Management Tasks, Responsibilities, Practices* (New York: Harper & Row, 1974).

7. Kathleen Collins, "E-Publishing Through the Ages," *Working Woman* (Special Internet Issue, 2000), 22; Curtis Sittenfeld, "Hope Is a Weapon," *Fast Company* (February–March 1999), 179–184.

8. Martha Brannigan and Eleena De Lisser, "Cost Cutting at Delta Raises the Stock Price But Lowers the Service," *The Wall Street Journal* (June 20, 1996), A1.

9. Robert L. Katz, "Skills of an Effective Administrator," *Harvard Business Review* 52 (September–October 1974), 90–102.

10. Heath Row, "Force Play" (Company of Friends column), *Fast Company* (March 2001), 46.

11. Charles Fishman, "Sweet Company," *Fast Company* (February 2001), 136–145.

12. Henry Mintzberg, *The Nature of Managerial Work* (New York: Harper & Row, 1973); and Mintzberg, "Rounding Out the Manager's Job," *Sloan Management Review* (Fall 1994), 11–26.

13. Robert E. Kaplan, "Trade Routes: The Manager's Network of Relationships," *Organizational Dynamics* (Spring 1984), 37–52; Rosemary Stewart, "The Nature of Management: A Problem for Management Education," *Journal of Management Studies* 21 (1984), 323–330; John P. Kotter, "What Effective General Managers Really Do," *Harvard Business Review* (November–December 1982), 156–167; and Morgan W. McCall, Jr., Ann M. Morrison, and Robert L. Hannan, "Studies of Managerial Work: Results and Methods" (Technical Report No. 9, Center for Creative Leadership, Greensboro, N.C., 1978).

14. Jennifer Couzin, "Tick, Tick, Tick," *The Industry Standard* (April 16, 2001), 62–67.

15. Henry Mintzberg, "Managerial Work: Analysis from Observation," *Management Science* 18 (1971), B97–B110.

16. Based on Carol Saunders and Jack William Jones, "Temporal Sequences in Information Acquisition for Decision Making: A Focus on Source and Medium," *Academy of Management Review* 15 (1990), 29–46; Kotter, "What Effective General Managers Really Do"; and Mintzberg, "Managerial Work."

17. Mintzberg, "Managerial Work."

18. Anita Lienert, "A Day in the Life: Airport Manager Extraordinaire," *Management Review* (January 1995), 57–61.

19. Lance B. Kurke and Howard E. Aldrich, "Mintzberg Was Right!: A Replication and Extension of *The Nature of Managerial Work,*" *Management Science* 29 (1983), 975–984; Cynthia M. Pavett and Alan W. Lau, "Managerial Work: The Influence of Hierarchical Level and Functional Specialty," *Academy of Management Journal* 26 (1983), 170–177; and Colin P. Hales, "What Do Managers Do? A Critical Review of the Evidence," *Journal of Management Studies* 23 (1986), 88–115.

20. Mintzberg, "Rounding out the Manager's Job."

21. Edward O. Welles, "There Are No Simple Businesses Anymore," *The State of Small Business* (1995), 66–79.

22. This section is based largely on Peter F. Drucker, *Managing the Non-Profit Organization: Principles and Practices* (New York: HarperBusiness, 1992); and Thomas Wolf, *Managing a Nonprofit Organization* (New York: Fireside/Simon & Schuster, 1990).

23. Christine W. Letts, William P. Ryan, and Allen Grossman, *High Performance Nonprofit Organizations* (New York: John Wiley & Sons, 1999), 30–35.

24. Toby J. Tetenbaum, "Shifting Paradigms: From Newton to Chaos," *Organizational Dynamics* (Spring 1998), 21–32. The following section is based on Tetenbaum, "Shifting Paradigms," John A. Byrne, "Management By Web," *Business Week* (August 28, 2000), 84–96, and Mark Gimein, "CEOs Who Manage Too Much," *Fortune* (September 4, 2000), 235–242.

25. Nancy B. Kurland and Diane E. Bailey, "Telework: The Advantages and Challenges of Working Here, There, Anywhere, Anytime," *Organizational Dynamics* (Autumn 1999), 53–67; and Thomas H. Davenport and Keri Pearlson, "Two Cheers for the Virtual Office," *Sloan Management Review* (Summer 1998), 51–65.

26. Clare Ansberry, "In the New Workplace, Jobs Morph to Suit Rapid Pace of Change," *The Wall Street Journal* (March 22, 2002), A1, A7.

27. American Electronics Association, 2000, reported in "The Great Migration (in Numbers), compiled and edited by Jill Kirschenbaum, *Fast Company* (July 2000), 199–206.

28. Randy Myers, "E-commerce, Unplugged," *eCFO* (Summer 2001), 53–57.

29. Faith Keenan, General Electric profile in "Giants Can Be Nimble," *Business Week E.Biz* (September 18, 2000), EB98–EB104.

30. Jon Pareles, David Bowie, "21st Century Entrepreneur," *The New York Times* (June 9, 2002), Section 2, 1.

31. Gail Edmondson, with Kerry Capell, Pamela L. Moore, and Peter Burrows, "See the World, Erase Its Borders," *Business Week* (August 28, 2000), 113–114.

32. G. Pascal Zachary, "Mighty Is the Mongrel," *Fast Company* (July 2000), 270–284.

33. Tetenbaum, "Shifting Paradigms: From Newton to Chaos."

34. Ibid.

35. Christopher A. Bartlett and Sumantra Ghoshal, "The Myth of the Generic Manager: New Personal Competencies for New Management Roles," *California Management Review* 40, no. 1 (Fall 1997), 92–116.

36. Tom Pohlmann with Bobby Cameron, Emily Jastrzembski, and Mary Lynn Pulley, "Building e-Business Leadership" (Forrester Research 2001), from the *Wharton Leadership Digest,* Wharton Center for Leadership and Change Management, *http://leadership.wharton.upenn.edu/digest/index.shtml.*

37. Byrne, "Management By Web."

38. Scott Kirsner, "Every Day, It's a New Place," *Fast Company* (April–May 1998), 130–134; Peter Coy, "The Creative Economy," *Business Week* (August 28, 2000), 76–82; and Jeremy Main, "The Shape of the New Corporation," *Working Woman* (October 1998), 60–63.

39. Quoted in James Sterngold, "Power Crisis Abates, But It Hounds Gov. Davis," *The New York Times* (October 5, 2001), A16.

40. This section is based on Leslie Wayne and Leslie Kaufman, "Leadership, Put to a New Test," *The New York Times* (September 16, 2001), Section 3, 1, 4; Jerry Useem, "What It Takes," *Fortune* (November 12, 2001), 126–132; and Andy Bowen, "Crisis Procedures that Stand the Test of Time," *Public Relations Tactics* (August 2001), 16.

41. Susan Orenstein, "'Our Focus Had to Be on People,'" *Business 2.0* (November 2001), 30–31.

42. Peter Senge, *The Fifth Discipline: The Art and Practice of Learning Organizations* (New York: Doubleday/Currency, 1990).

43. Jeffrey Pfeffer, "Producing Sustainable Competitive Advantage through the Effective Management of People," *Academy of Management Executive* 9, no. 1 (1995), 55–69.

44. Alex Markels, "The Wisdom of Chairman Ko," *Fast Company* (November 1999), 258–276.

45. Edward O. Welles, "Mind Gains," *Inc.* (December 1999), 112–124.

46. Kevin Kelly, *New Rules for the New Economy: 10 Radical Strategies for a Connected World* (New York: Viking Penguin, 1998).

47. Wayne Kawamoto, "Click Here for Efficiency," *Business Week Enterprise* (December 7, 1998), 12–14.

48. Nick Wingfield, "In the Beginning. . . ," *The Wall Street Journal* (May 21, 2001), R18.

49. Andy Reinhardt, "From Gearhead to Grand High Pooh-Bah," *Business Week* (August 28, 2000), 129–130.

50. Matt Murray and Jathon Sapsford, "GE Reshuffles Its Dot-Com Strategy to Focus on Internal 'Digitizing,'" *The Wall Street Journal* (May 4, 2001) B1, B4; Daniel Lyons, "Lion in Winter," *Forbes* (April 30, 2001), 68–70.

51. William J. Holstein and Edward Robinson, "The Re-Education of Jacques Nasser," *Business2.Com* (May 29, 2001), 60–73.

52. Bernard Wysocki, Jr., "Corporate Caveat: Dell or Be Delled," *The Wall Street Journal* (May 10, 1999), A1.

53. Andy Reinhardt, "From Gearhead to Grand High Pooh-Bah," *Business Week* (August 28, 2000), 129–130.

54. Quoted in Colvin, "Managing in the Info Era."

55. Jeffrey Zygmont, "The Ties That Bind," *Inc. Tech* no. 3, (1998), 70–84; and Nancy Ferris, "ERP: Sizzling or Stumbling?" *Government Executive* (July 1999), 99–102.

56. Harrington, "The Big Ideas." Also see Peter Drucker, *Post-Capitalist Society* (Oxford: Butterworth Heinemann, 1993), 5.

57. Based on Andrew Mayo, "Memory Bankers," *People Management* (January 22, 1998), 34–38; William Miller, "Building the Ultimate Resource," *Management Review* (January 1999), 42–45; and Todd Datz, "How to Speak Geek," *CIO Enterprise,* Section 2 (April 15, 1999), 46–52.

58. Louisa Wah, "Behind the Buzz," *Management Review* (April 1999), 17–26.

59. Eric Abrahamson, "Management Fashion," *Academy of Management Review* 21, no. 1 (January 1996), 254–285. Also see "75 Years of Management Ideas and Practice," a supplement to the *Harvard Business Review* (September–October 1997), for a broad overview of historical trends in management thinking.

60. "Of Water Coolers and Coffee Breaks," timeline in Matthew Boyle, "How the Workplace Was Won," *Fortune* (January 22, 2001), 139+.

61. Daniel A. Wren, *The Evolution of Management Thought,* 2d ed. (New York: Wiley, 1979), 6–8. Much of the discussion of these forces comes from Arthur M. Schlesinger, *Political and Social History of the United States,* 1829–1925 (New York: Macmillan, 1925); and Homer C. Hockett, *Political and Social History of the United States,* 1492–1828 (New York: Macmillan, 1925).

62. Alison Wellner, "Get Ready for Generation Next," *Training* (February 1999), 42+; Roger Herman, "Gen X Won't Like What Their Parents Did," *American Drycleaner* (February 2001), 184; and Julie Wallace, "After X Comes Y," *HRMagazine* (April 2001), 192.

63. The discussion of trends is based on Marnie E. Green, "Beware and Prepare: The Government Workforce of the Future," *Public Personnel Management* (Winter 2000), 435+.

64. Robin Wright and Doyle McManus, *Flashpoints: Promise and Peril in a New World* (New York: Alfred A. Knopf, 1991).

65. This section is based heavily on Thomas Petzinger, Jr., "So Long Supply and Demand," *The Wall Street Journal* (January 1, 2000), R31.

66. Petzinger, "So Long Supply and Demand."

67. Daniel A. Wren, "Management History: Issues and Ideas for Teaching and Research," *Journal of Management* 13 (1987), 339–350.

68. Business historian Alfred D. Chandler, Jr., quoted in Jerry Useem, "Entrepreneur of the Century," *Inc.* (20th Anniversary Issue, 1999), 159–174.

69. Useem, "Entrepreneur of the Century."
70. The following is based on Wren, *Evolution of Management Thought,* Chapters 4, 5; and Claude S. George, Jr., *The History of Management Thought* (Englewood Cliffs, N.J.: Prentice-Hall, 1968), Chapter 4.
71. Charles D. Wrege and Ann Marie Stoka, "Cooke Creates a Classic: The Story behind F. W. Taylor's Principles of Scientific Management," *Academy of Management Review* (October 1978), 736–749; Robert Kanigel, *The One Best Way: Frederick Winslow Taylor and the Enigma of Efficiency* (New York: Viking, 1997); and Alan Farnham, "The Man Who Changed Work Forever," *Fortune* (July 21, 1997), 114.
72. Quoted in Ann Harrington, "The Big Ideas," *Fortune* (November 22, 1999), 152–154.
73. Wren, *Evolution of Management Thought,* 171; and George, *History of Management Thought,* 103–104.
74. Geoffrey Colvin, "Managing in the Info Era," *Fortune* (March 6, 2000), F-5–F-9.
75. Max Weber, *General Economic History,* trans. Frank H. Knight (London: Allen & Unwin, 1927); Max Weber, *The Protestant Ethic and the Spirit of Capitalism,* trans. Talcott Parsons (New York: Scribner, 1930); and Max Weber, *The Theory of Social and Economic Organizations,* ed. and trans. A. M. Henderson and Talcott Parsons (New York: Free Press, 1947).
76. "UPS," *The Atlanta Journal and Constitution* (April 26, 1992), H1; Richard L. Daft, *Organization Theory and Design,* 3rd ed. (St. Paul, Minn.: West, 1989), 181–182; and Kathy Goode, Betty Hahn, and Cindy Seibert, "United Parcel Service: The Brown Giant" (unpublished manuscript, Texas A&M University, 1981).
77. Henri Fayol, *Industrial and General Administration,* trans. J. A. Coubrough (Geneva: International Management Institute, 1930); Henri Fayol, *General and Industrial Management,* trans. Constance Storrs (London: Pitman and Sons, 1949); and W. J. Arnold and the editors of *Business Week, Milestones in Management* (New York: McGraw-Hill, vol. I, 1965; vol. II, 1966).
78. Mary Parker Follett, *The New State: Group Organization: The Solution of Popular Government* (London: Longmans, Green, 1918); and Mary Parker Follett, *Creative Experience* (London: Longmans, Green, 1924).
79. Henry C. Metcalf and Lyndall Urwick, eds., *Dynamic Administration: The Collected Papers of Mary Parker Follett* (New York: Harper & Row, 1940); Arnold, *Milestones in Management.*
80. Follett, *The New State*; Metcalf and Urwick, *Dynamic Administration* (London: Sir Isaac Pitman, 1941).
81. Martha E. Mangelsdorf, "Managing the New Workforce," *Inc.com.* (April 24, 2002); Jennifer Gormanous Burke, "A Sweet Deal," *Bostonia* (Spring 2000); Ben Strohehecker, "A Business Built on Trust," *Guideposts* (August 1996), pp. 6–9; Leslie Brokaw, "Like Money for Chocolate: Harbor Sweets," *Hemisphere* (December 1995), 35–38; Anne Driscoll, "Candy Man of the People," *Boston Globe* (March 29, 1992); Tracy E. Benson, "In Trust We Manage," *Industry Week* (March 4, 1991), 26–27; Martha Mangelsdorf, "Managing the New Workforce," *Inc.com* (January), 78–83. Company sources.
82. William B. Wolf, *How to Understand Management: An Introduction to Chester I. Barnard* (Los Angeles: Lucas Brothers, 1968); and David D. Van Fleet, "The Need-Hierarchy and Theories of Authority," *Human Relations* 9 (Spring 1982), 111–118.
83. Gregory M. Bounds, Gregory H. Dobbins, and Oscar S. Fowler, *Management: A Total Quality Perspective* (Cincinnati: South-Western Publishing, 1995), 52–53.
84. Curt Tausky, *Work Organizations: Major Theoretical Perspectives* (Itasca, Ill.: F. E. Peacock, 1978), 42.
85. Charles D. Wrege, "Solving Mayo's Mystery: The First Complete Account of the Origin of the Hawthorne Studies—The Forgotten Contributions of Charles E. Snow and Homer Hibarger" (paper presented to the Management History Division of the Academy of Management, August 1976).
86. Ronald G. Greenwood, Alfred A. Bolton, and Regina A. Greenwood, "Hawthorne a Half Century Later: Relay Assembly Participants Remember," *Journal of Management* 9 (Fall/Winter 1983), 217–231.
87. F. J. Roethlisberger, W. J. Dickson, and H. A. Wright, *Management and the Worker* (Cambridge, Mass.: Harvard University Press, 1939).
88. H. M. Parson, "What Happened at Hawthorne?" *Science* 183 (1974), 922–932; John G. Adair, "The Hawthorne Effect: A Reconsideration of the Methodological Artifact," *Journal of Applied Psychology* 69, no. 2 (1984), 334–345; and Gordon Diaper, "The Hawthorne Effect: A Fresh Examination," *Educational Studies* 16, no. 3 (1990), 261–268.
89. Greenwood, Bolton, and Greenwood, "Hawthorne a Half Century Later," 219–221.
90. F. J. Roethlisberger and W. J. Dickson, *Management and the Worker.*
91. Ramon J. Aldag and Timothy M. Stearns, *Management,* 2nd ed. (Cincinnati, Ohio: South-Western Publishing, 1991), 47–48.
92. Tausky, *Work Organizations: Major Theoretical Perspectives,* 55.
93. Douglas McGregor, *The Human Side of Enterprise* (New York: McGraw-Hill, 1960), 16–18.
94. Gina Imperato, "Dirty Business, Bright Ideas," *Fast Company* (February–March 1997), 89–93.
95. Mansel G. Blackford and K. Austin Kerr, *Business Enterprise in American History* (Boston: Houghton Mifflin, 1986), Chapters 10, 11; and Alex Groner and the editors of *American Heritage and Business Week, The American Heritage History of American Business and Industry* (New York: American Heritage Publishing, 1972), Chapter 9.
96. Larry M. Austin and James R. Burns, *Management Science* (New York: Macmillan, 1985).
97. Marcia Stepanek, "How an Intranet Opened Up the Door to Profits," *Business Week E.Biz* (July 26, 1999), EB32–EB38.
98. Matt Vilano, "A Lead-Pipe Cinch," *CIO,* Section 1 (March 15, 1999), 51–59.
99. Samuel Greengard, "25 Visionaries Who Shaped Today's Workplace," *Workforce* (January 1997), 50–59; and Harrington, "The Big Ideas."
100. Mauro F. Guillen, "The Age of Eclecticism: Current Organizational Trends and the Evolution of Managerial Models," *Sloan Management Review* (Fall 1994), 75–86.
101. Jeremy Main, "How to Steal the Best Ideas Around," *Fortune* (October 19, 1992), 102–106.
102. Chazin, "Have It Your Way"; Petzinger, *The New Pioneers.*

Chapter 2

The Environment and Corporate Culture

1. Emily Barker, "Cheap Executive Officer," *The Whole New Business Catalog* (April 1, 2002); and Rusty Cawley, "Rick Sapio Banks on 1–800–MUTUALS Concept," *Dallas Business Journal* (October 22, 1999), 22–23.

2. Lucette Lagnado, "Strained Peace: Gerber Baby Food, Grilled by Greenpeace, Plans Swift Overhaul," *The Wall Street Journal* (July 30, 1999), A1, A6, and "Group Sows Seeds of Revolt Against Genetically Altered Foods in U.S.," *The Wall Street Journal* (October 12, 1999), B1, B4.

3. Seth Lubove, "Dial-a-Mess," *Forbes* (January 24, 2000), 68–70.

4. Warren St. John, "Barnes & Noble's Epiphany," *Wired* (June 1999), 132–144; Patrick M. Reilly, "In the Age of the Web, a Book Chain Flounders," *The Wall Street Journal* (February 22, 1999), B1, B4.

5. Chuck Hutchcraft, "Fiscal Worries Pain La Rabida in Its 100th Year," *Chicago Tribune* (March 17, 1996), Sec. 5, 1, 6.

6. Richard L. Daft, *Organization Theory and Design,* 5th ed. (St. Paul, Minn.: West, 1995).

7. L. J. Bourgeois, "Strategy and Environment: A Conceptual Integration," *Academy of Management Review* 5 (1980), 25–39.

8. Jim Milliott, "Leapfrog IPO Looks to Raise $150 Million," *Publisher's Weekly* (May 6, 2002), 13; and Miguel Helft, "Leapfrogging the Competition," *The Industry Standard* (April 9, 2001), 68–75.

9. Ann Carrns, "Point Taken: Hit Hard by Imports, American Pencil Icon Tries to Get a Grip," *The Wall Street Journal* (November 24, 1999), A1, A6.

10. Lawrence Chimerine, "The New Economic Realities in Business," *Management Review* (January 1997), 12–17; Ram Charan, "The Rules Have Changed," *Fortune* (March 16, 1998), 159–162; and Lisa Benavides, "Handful of Tennessee Companies Feel a Pinch," *The Tennessean* (September 5, 1998), 1E, 2E.

11. Darlene Superville, "Gadget-Giddy Americans Love Communicating," AP story, *The Johnson City Press* (July 7, 2001), 7; Janet Guyon, "The World Is Your Office," *Fortune* (June 12, 2000), 227–234.

12. Gene Bylinsky, "Mutant Materials," *Fortune* (October 13, 1997), 140–147.

13. William B. Johnston, "Global Work Force 2000: The New World Labor Market," *Harvard Business Review* (March–April 1991), 115–127.

14. Statistics reported in Peter Coy, "The Creative Economy," *Business Week* (August 28, 2000), 76–82.

15. U.S. Census, http://www.census.gov.

16. Marc Gunter, "God & Business," *Fortune* (July 9, 2001), 58–80.

17. Linda Himelstein and Laura Zinn, with Maria Mallory, John Carey, Richard S. Dunham, and Joan O'C. Hamilton, "Tobacco: Does It Have a Future?" *Business Week* (July 4, 1994), 24–29; Bob Ortega, "Aging Activists Turn, Turn, Turn Attention to Wal-Mart Protests," *The Wall Street Journal* (October 11, 1994), A1, A8.

18. Louise Lee, "Can Levi's Be Cool Again?" *Business Week* (March 13, 2000), 144, 148.

19. John Simons, "Stop Moaning About Gripe Sites and Log On," *Fortune* (April 2, 2001), 181–182.

20. Sarah Moore, "On Your Markets," *Working Woman* (February 2001), 26; and Simons, "Stop Moaning about Gripe Sites and Log On."

21. Rick Brooks, "Home Depot Turns Copycat in Its Efforts to Stoke New Growth," *The Wall Street Journal* (November 21, 2000), A1; Dan Sewell, "Home Depot, Lowe's Building Up Competition," *Lexington Herald-Leader,* Business Profile supplement (December 8, 1997), 3.

22. Robert B. Duncan, "Characteristics of Organizational Environment and Perceived Environmental Uncertainty," *Administrative Science Quarterly* 17 (1972), 313–327; and Daft, *Organization Theory and Design.*

23. Scott Bernard Nelson, "FleetBoston Executives Discuss Ways to Improve Its Customer Service Record," *Knight-Ridder Tribune Business News* (April 18, 2002), 1; and Lotte Bailyn, "Fleet Financial and Radcliffe Explore Paths of Work/Life Integration," *Journal of Organizational Excellence* (Summer 2001), 49–64.

24. Yoash Wiener, "Forms of Value Systems: A Focus on Organizational Effectiveness and Culture Change and Maintenance," *Academy of Management Review* 13 (1988), 534–545; V. Lynne Meek, "Organizational Culture: Origins and Weaknesses," *Organization Studies* 9 (1988), 453–473; John J. Sherwood, "Creating Work Cultures with Competitive Advantage," *Organizational Dynamics* (Winter 1988), 5–27; and Andrew D. Brown and Ken Starkey, "The Effect of Organizational Culture on Communication and Information," *Journal of Management Studies* 31, no. 6 (November 1994), 807–828.

25. Ralph H. Kilmann, Mary J. Saxton, and Roy Serpa, "Issues in Understanding and Changing Culture," *California Management Review* 28 (Winter 1986), 87–94; and Linda Smircich, "Concepts of Culture and Organizational Analysis," *Administrative Science Quarterly* 28 (1983), 339–358.

26. Based on Edgar H. Schein, *Organizational Culture and Leadership,* 2d ed. (San Francisco: Jossey-Bass, 1992), 3–27.

27. James C. Collins, "Change is Good—But First Know What Should Never Change," *Fortune* (May 29, 1995), 141.

28. Charles A. O'Reilly III and Jeffrey Pfeffer, "Star Makers," *CIO* (September 15, 2000), 225–246.

29. Christine Canabou, "Here's the Drill," *Fast Company* (February 2001), 58.

30. Melanie Warner, "Confessions of a Control Freak," *Fortune* (September 4, 2000), 130–140.

31. Elizabeth Weil, "Every Leader Tells a Story," *Fast Company* (June–July 1998), 38–39; and Robert Specter, "The Nordstom Way," *Corporate University Review* (May–June 1997), 24–25, 60.

32. Robert E. Quinn and Gretchen M. Spreitzer, "The Road to Empowerment: Seven Questions Every Leader Should Consider," *Organizational Dynamics* (Autumn 1997), 37–49.

33. Terrence E. Deal and Allan A. Kennedy, *Corporate Cultures: The Rites and Rituals of Corporate Life* (Reading, Mass.: Addison-Wesley, 1982).

34. Barbara Ettorre, "Retooling People and Processes," *Management Review* (June 1995), 19–23.

35. Patricia Jones and Larry Kahaner, *Say It and Live It: 50 Corporate Mission Statements That Hit the Mark* (New York: Currency Doubleday, 1995).

36. Harrison M. Trice and Janice M. Beyer, "Studying Organizational Cultures through Rites and Ceremonials," *Academy of Management Review* 9 (1984), 653–669.

37. Alan Farnham, "Mary Kay's Lessons in Leadership," *Fortune* (September 20, 1993), 68–77.

38. Jennifer A. Chatman and Karen A. Jehn, "Assessing the Relationship Between Industry Characteristics and Organizational Culture: How Different Can You Be?" *Academy of Management Journal* 37, no. 3 (1994), 522–553.

39. John P. Kotter and James L. Heskett, *Corporate Culture and Performance* (New York: The Free Press, 1992).

40. This discussion is based on Paul McDonald and Jeffrey Gandz, "Getting Value from Shared Values," *Organizational Dynamics* 21, no. 3 (Winter 1992), 64–76; Daniel R. Denison and Aneil K. Mishra, "Toward a Theory of Organizational Culture and Effectiveness," *Organization Science* 6, no. 2 (March–April 1995), 204–223; and Richard L. Daft, *The Leadership Experience* (Fort Worth: Dryden, 2002), 524–528.

41. Robert Hooijberg and Frank Petrock, "On Cultural Change: Using the Competing Values Framework to Help Leaders Execute a Transformational Strategy," *Human Resource Management* 32, no. 1 (1993), 29–50.

42. Warner, "Confessions of a Control Freak."

43. Charles Fishman, "Sanity Inc.," *Fast Company* (January 1999), 85–96; and Sharon Overton, "And to All a Goodnight," *Sky* (October 1996), 37–40.

44. Rekha Balu, "Pacific Edge Projects Itself," *Fast Company* (October 2000), 371–381.

45. Jeffrey Pfeffer, *The Human Equation: Building Profits by Putting People First* (Boston, Mass.: Harvard Business School Press, 1998).

46. Jeremy Kahn, "What Makes a Company Great?" *Fortune* (October 26, 1998), 218; James C. Collins and Jerry I. Porras, *Built to Last: Successful Habits of Visionary Companies* (New York: HarperCollins, 1994); and James C. Collins, "Change is Good—But First Know What Should Never Change," *Fortune* (May 29, 1995), 141.

47. Jenny C. McCune, "Exporting Corporate Culture," *Management Review* (December 1999), 52–56.

48. Charlene Marmer Solomon, "Managing Virtual Teams," *Workforce* (June 2001), 60.

49. Mark Gimein, "Smart Is Not Enough," *Fortune* (January 8, 2001), 124–136.

50. Charles A. O'Reilly III and Jeffrey Pfeffer, "Star Makers."

51. Jenny C. McCune, "Exporting Corporate Culture," *Management Review* (December 1999), 52–56.

52. Thomas H. Davenport, "Two Cheers for the Virtual Office," *Sloan Management Review* (Summer 1998), 51–65.

53. Nancy B. Kurland and Diane E. Bailey, "Telework: The Advantages and Challenges of Working Here, There, Anywhere, Anytime," *Organizational Dynamics* (Autumn 1999), 53–68.

54. Solomon, "Managing Virtual Teams."

55. Thomas J. Peters and Robert H. Waterman, Jr., *In Search of Excellence* (New York: Warner, 1988).

56. McCune, "Exporting Corporate Culture."

57. Stephanie Gruner, "Lasting Impressions," *Inc.* (July 1998), 126.

58. Jill Rosenfeld, "MTW Puts People First," *Fast Company* (December 1999), 86–88.

59. Excerpt from Peter B. Grazier, "Before It's Too Late: Employee Involvement . . . An Idea Whose Time Has Come," *Pete's Corner* by Peter B. Grazier, *http://www.teambuilding.com*.

60. McCune, "Exporting Corporate Culture."

61. Emily Barker, "Cheap Executive Officer," *The Whole New Business Catalog* (April 1, 2002); and Rusty Cawley, "Rick Sapio Banks on 1-800-MUTUALS Concept," *Dallas Business Journal* (October 22, 1999), 22–23.

62. Lagnado, "Strained Peace."

Chapter 3

Managing in a Global Environment

1. Howard LaFranchi, "Women Have Their Cake (and E-commerce, Too)," *Christian Science Monitor* (June 13, 2000), 1; Stockholm Challenge Award results.

2. David Kirkpatrick, "One World—For Better or Worse," *Fortune* (November 26, 2001), 74–75; Andy Grove quoted in Brian O'Keefe, "Global Brands," *Fortune* (November 26, 2001), 102–110.

3. Nilly Ostro-Landau and Hugh D. Menzies, "The New World Economic Order," in *International Business 97/98, Annual Editions,* Fred Maidment, ed. (Guilford, Conn.: Dushkin Publishing Group, 1997), 24–30; and Murray Weidenbaum, "American Isolationism Versus the Global Economy," in *International Business 97/98, Annual Editions,* Fred Maidment, ed. (Guilford Conn.: Dushkin Publishing Group, 1997), 12–15.

4. Joseph B. White, "There Are No German or U.S. Companies, Only Successful Ones," *The Wall Street Journal* (May 7, 1998), A1.

5. Pete Engardio, with Robert D. Hof, Elisabeth Malkin, Neil Gross, and Karen Lowry Miller, "High-Tech Jobs All Over the Map," *Business Week/21st Century Capitalism* (November 18, 1994), 112–117.

6. Raju Narisetti and Jonathan Friedland, "Diaper Wars of P&G and Kimberly-Clark Now Heat Up in Brazil," *The Wall Street Journal* (June 4, 1997), and Stephen Baker, "The Bridges Steel Is Building," *Business Week* (June 2, 1997), 39.

7. Figures provided by CXO Media, reported in Steve Ulfelder, "All the Web's a Stage," *CIO* (October 1, 2000), 133–142.

8. Eric Matson, "How to Globalize Yourself," *Fast Company* (April–May 1997), 133–139; and Gunnar Beeth, "Multicultural Managers Wanted," *Management Review* (May 1997), 17–21.

9. "Slogans Often Lose Something in Translation," *The New Mexican* (July 3, 1994), F1, F2.

10. Jim Holt, "Gone Global?" *Management Review* (March 2000), 13.

11. Ibid.

12. "Slogans Often Lose Something in Translation."

13. Louis S. Richman, "Global Growth is on a Tear," in *International Business 97/98, Annual Editions,* Fred Maidment, ed. (Guilford, Conn.: Dushkin Publishing Group, 1997), 6–11.

14. International Data Corporation, reported in Ian Katz and Elisabeth Malkin, "Battle for the Latin American Net," *Business Week* (November 1, 1999), 194–200.

15. Katz and Malkin, "Battle for the Latin American Net"; Pamela Drukerman and Nick Wingfield, "Lost in Translation: AOL's Big Assault on Latin America Hits Snags in Brazil," *The Wall Street Journal* (July 11, 2000), A1.

16. Amal Kumar Jaj, "United Technologies Looks Far from Home for Growth," *The Wall Street Journal* (May 26, 1994), B4.

17. Kathleen Deveny, "McWorld?" *Business Week* (October 13, 1986), 78–86; and Andrew E. Serwer, "McDonald's Conquers the World," *Fortune* (October 17, 1994), 103–116.

18. Bruce Kogut, "Designing Global Strategies: Profiting from Operational Flexibility," *Sloan Management Review* 27 (Fall 1985), 27–38.

19. Mark Fitzpatrick, "The Definition and Assessment of Political Risk in International Business: A Review of the Literature," *Academy of Management Review* 8 (1983), 249–254.

20. "Multinational Firms Act to Protect Overseas Workers from Terrorism," *The Wall Street Journal* (April 29, 1986), 31; Robert J. Bowman, "Are You Covered?" *World Trade* (March 1995), 100–104; and Frederick Stapenhurst, "Political Risk Analysis in North American Multinationals: An Empirical Review and Assessment," *The International Executive* (March–April, 1995), 127–145.

21. O'Keefe, "Global Brands."

22. Alan Charles Raul, "World to America: Zip It!" *eCompany Now* (July 2001), 26–29.

23. Michael R. Czinkota, Ilkka A., Ronkainen, Michael H. Moffett, and Eugene O. Moynihan, *Global Business* (Fort Worth, Texas: The Dryden Press, 1995), 151; and Robert D. Gatewood, Robert R. Taylor, and O. C. Ferrell, *Management* (Burr Ridge, Ill.: Irwin, 1995), 131–132.

24. This discussion of WTO is based on William J. Kehoe, "GATT and WTO Facilitating Global Trade," *Journal of Global Business* (Spring 1998), 67–76.

25. Justin Fox, "Introducing the Euro," *Fortune* (December 19, 2001), 229–236.

26. Barbara Rudolph, "Megamarket," *Time* (August 10, 1992), 43–44.

27. J. S. McClenahan, "NAFTA Works," *IW* (January 10, 2000), 5–6.

28. Mei Fong, "For a Muslim Woman from Two Cultures, Swimsuits are Tricky—Born in Pakistan, Raised in U.S., Neelam Nourani Nervously Dips into Beauty Pageants," *The Wall Street Journal* (March 22, 2002), A1, A6.

29. Geert Hofstede, "The Interaction between National and Organizational Value Systems," *Journal of Management Studies* 22 (1985), 347–357; and Geert Hofstede, "The Cultural Relativity of the Quality of Life Concept," *Academy of Management Review* 9 (1984), 389–398.

30. Geert Hofstede, "Cultural Constraints in Management Theory," *Academy of Management Executive* 7 (1993): 81–94; and G. Hofstede and M. H. Bond, "The Confucian Connection: From Cultural Roots to Economic Growth," *Organizational Dynamics* 16 (1988): 4–21.

31. Chantell E. Nicholls, Henry W. Lane, and Mauricio Brehm Brechu, "Taking Self-Managed Teams to Mexico," *Academy of Management Executive* 13, no. 2 (1999), 15–27; Ellen F. Jackofsky, John W. Slocum, Jr., and Sara J. McQuaid, "Cultural Values and the CEO: Alluring Companions?" *Academy of Management Executive* 2 (1988), 39–49.

32. Carol Hymowitz, "Companies Go Global, But Many Managers Just Don't Travel Well," (In the Lead column) *The Wall Street Journal* (August 15, 2000), B1.

33. Orla Sheehan, "Managing a Multinational Corporation: Tomorrow's Decision Makers Speak Out," *Fortune* (August 24, 1992), 233.

34. Richard Gibson and Matt Moffett, "Why You Won't Find Any Egg McMuffins for Breakfast in Brazil," *The Wall Street Journal* (October 23, 1997), A1, A8; and Kenneth Labich, "America's International Winners," *Fortune* (April 14, 1986), 34–46.

35. Robert Frank, "Big Boy's Adventures in Thailand," *The Wall Street Journal* (April 12, 2000), B1, B4.

36. Jonathan Moore with Bruce Einhorn, "A Business-to-Business E-Boom," *Business Week* (October 25, 1999), 62.

37. Elisabeth Malkin, "Backlash," *Business Week* (April 24, 2000), 38–44.

38. Jean Kerr, "Export Strategies," *Small Business Reports* (May 1989), 20–25.

39. Robert S. Greenberger, "As U.S. Exports Rise, More Workers Benefit," *The Wall Street Journal* (September 10, 1997), A1.

40. Kathryn Rudie Harrigan, "Managing Joint Ventures," *Management Review* (February 1987), 24–41; and Therese R. Revesz and Mimi Cauley de Da La Sierra, "Competitive Alliances: Forging Ties Abroad," *Management Review* (March 1987), 57–59.

41. Julia Flynn with Richard A. Melcher, "Heineken's Battle to Stay Top Bottle," *Business Week* (August 1, 1994), 60–62; and "Importing Can Help a Firm Expand and Diversify," *Nation's Business* (January 1995), 11.

42. Katz and Malkin, "Battle for the Latin American Net."

43. "How Revenues of the Top Ten Global Companies Compare with Some National Economies," *Fortune* (July 27, 1992), 16.

44. Friedland and Lee, "The Wal-Mart Way Sometimes Gets Lost in Translation Overseas."

45. Robert T. Moran and John R. Riesenberger, *The Global Challenge* (London: McGraw-Hill, 1994), 260.

46. James L. Gibson, John M. Ivancevich, and James H. Donnelly, Jr., *Organizations*, 8th ed. (Burr Ridge, Ill.: Irwin, 1994), 83.

47. Joann S. Lublin, "Younger Managers Learn Global Skills," *The Wall Street Journal* (March 31, 1992), B1.

48. Moran and Riesenberger, *The Global Challenge,* 251–262.

49. Patricia M. Carey, "Culture Club," *Working Woman* (July/August 1999), 71–72.

50. Valerie Frazee, "Keeping Up on Chinese Culture," *Global Workforce* (October 1996), 16–17; and Jack Scarborough, "Comparing Chinese and Western Cultural Roots: Why 'East is East and . . .'" *Business Horizons* (November-December 1998), 15–24.

51. Fons Trompenaars, *Riding the Waves of Culture: Understanding Diversity in Global Business* (Burr Ridge, Ill.: Irwin, 1994).

52. Randall S. Schuler, Susan E. Jackson, Ellen Jackofsky, and John W. Slocum, Jr., "Managing Human Resources in Mexico: A

Cultural Understanding," *Business Horizons* (May–June 1996), 55–61.

53. Shari Caudron, "Lessons from HR Overseas," *Personnel Journal* (February 1995), 88.

54. Moran and Riesenberger, *The Global Challenge,* 255; and Caudron, "Lessons from HR Overseas."

55. Brenton R. Schlender, "Matsushita Shows How to Go Global," *Fortune* (July 11, 1994), 159–166.

56. LaFranchi, "Women Have Their Cake (and E-commerce, Too)" 1; Stockholm Challenge Award results.

Chapter 4
Managerial Ethics and Corporate Social Responsibility

1. Helene Cooper, Rachel Zimmerman, and Laurie McGinley, "Patents Pending: AIDS Epidemic Traps Drug Firms in a Vise: Treatment vs. Profits," *The Wall Street Journal* (March 2, 2001), A1, A6.

2. Bethany McLean, "Why Enron Went Bust," *Fortune* (December 24, 2001), 58–68; Jeffrey L. Seglin, "Dot.com," *Forbes ASAP* (February 21, 2000), 135; Jerry Useem, "New Ethics . . . or No Ethics?" *Fortune* (March 20, 2000), 82–86; and Jeremy Kahn, "Presto Chango! Sales Are Huge!" *Fortune* (March 20, 2000), 90–96.

3. Amy Zipkin, "Getting Religion on Corporate Ethics," *The New York Times* (October 18, 2000), C1, C10; Steve Liesman, "Inside the Race to Profit from Global Warming," *The Wall Street Journal* (October 19, 1999), B1, B4.

4. "The Socially Correct Corporate Business," segment in Leslie Holstrom and Simon Brady, "The Changing Face of Global Business," special advertising section, *Fortune* (July 24, 2000), S1–S38.

5. Dale Kurschner, "Tying Executive Pay to Social Responsibility," *Business Ethics* (September–October 1995), 47.

6. Gordon F. Shea, *Practical Ethics* (New York: American Management Association, 1988); and Linda K. Treviño, "Ethical Decision Making in Organizations; A Person-Situation Interactionist Model," *Academy of Management Review* 11 (1986), 601–617.

7. Thomas M. Jones, "Ethical Decision Making by Individuals in Organizations: An Issue-Contingent Model," *Academy of Management Review* 16 (1991), 366–395.

8. Dan Goodin, "Can Napster Change Its Tune?" *The Industry Standard* (February 26, 2001), 39–42.

9. Rushworth M. Kidder, "The Three Great Domains of Human Action," *Christian Science Monitor* (January 30, 1990).

10. Ralph Blumenthal, "Charges of Payola over Radio Music," *The New York Times* (May 25, 2002), 7; Craig Havignurt, Labels Say Radio Needs 'New Set of Rules,'" *Tennessean* (June 3, 2002), E1.

11. Jones, "Ethical Decision Making."

12. This discussion is based on Gerald F. Cavanagh, Dennis J. Moberg, and Manuel Velasquez, "The Ethics of Organizational Politics," *Academy of Management Review* 6 (1981), 363–374; Justin G. Longenecker, Joseph A. McKinney, and Carlos W. Moore, "Egoism and Independence: Entrepreneurial Ethics,"

Organizational Dynamics (Winter 1988), 64–72; Carolyn Wiley, "The ABCs of Business Ethics: Definitions, Philosophies, and Implementation," *IM* (February 1995), 22–27; and Mark Mallinger, "Decisive Decision Making: An Exercise Using Ethical Frameworks," *Journal of Management Education* (August 1997), 411–417.

13. Michael J. McCarthy, "Now the Boss Knows Where You're Clicking," and "Virtual Morality: A New Workplace Quandary," *The Wall Street Journal* (October 21, 1999), B1, B4; and Jeffrey L. Seglin, "Who's Snooping on You?" *Business 2.0* (August 8, 2000), 202–203.

14. John Kekes, "Self-Direction: The Core of Ethical Individualism," *Organizations and Ethical Individualism,* ed. Konstanian Kolenda (New York: Praeger, 1988), 1–18.

15. Tad Tulega, *Beyond the Bottom Line* (New York: Penguin Books, 1987).

16. Doug Cahn, "Reebok Takes the Sweat out of Sweatshops," *Business Ethics* (January–February 2000), 9.

17. Lynn Sharp Paine, "Managing for Organizational Integrity," *Harvard Business Review* (March–April 1994), 106–117.

18. This discussion is based on Treviño, "Ethical Decision Making in Organizations."

19. L. Kohlberg, "Moral Stages and Moralization: The Cognitive-Developmental Approach," in *Moral Development and Behavior: Theory, Research, and Social Issues,* ed. T. Lickona (New York: Holt, Rinehart & Winston, 1976) 31–83; L. Kohlberg, "Stage and Sequence: The Cognitive-Developmental Approach to Socialization," in *Handbook of Socialization Theory and Research,* ed. D. A. Goslin (Chicago: Rand McNally, 1969); and Jill W. Graham, "Leadership, Moral Development, and Citizenship Behavior," *Business Ethics Quarterly* 5, no. 1 (January 1995), 43–54.

20. Carol Gilligan, *In a Different Voice: Psychological Theory and Women's Development* (Cambridge, Mass.: Harvard University Press, 1982).

21. See Thomas Donaldson and Thomas W. Dunfee, "When Ethics Travel: The Promise and Peril of Global Business Ethics," *California Management Review* 41, no. 4 (Summer 1999), 45–63.

22. Andrew W. Singer, "Ethics: Are Standards Lower Overseas?" *Across the Board* (September 1991), 31–34; and David Vogel, "Is U.S. Business Obsessed with Ethics?" *Across the Board* (November–December 1993), 31–33.

23. The Global Compact Web site *http://www.unglobalcompact.org,* accessed on July 18, 2001; and Zipkin, "Getting Religion on Corporate Ethics."

24. Duane M. Covrig, "The Organizational Context of Moral Dilemmas: The Role of Moral Leadership in Administration in Making and Breaking Dilemmas," *The Journal of Leadership Studies* 7, no. 1 (2000), 40–59; and James Weber, "Influences Upon Organizational Ethical Subclimates: A Multi-Departmental Analysis of a Single Firm," *Organizational Science* 6, no. 5 (September–October 1995), 509–523.

25. Alan Schwarz, "Scoring Hits, Runs, and Asterisks," *The New York Times* (June 9, 2002), 4, 5, and Amy Shipley, Baseball Player Says Steroid Use Is Heavy, *The Washington Post,* May 29, 2002, p. 1.

26. This discussion is based on Linda Klebe Treviño, "A Cultural Perspective on Changing and Developing Organizational

Ethics," in *Research and Organizational Change and Development,* ed. R. Woodman and W. Pasmore (Greenwich, Conn.: JAI Press, 1990), 4.

27. Ibid.; John B. Cullen, Bart Victor, and Carroll Stephens, "An Ethical Weather Report: Assessing the Organization's Ethical Climate," *Organizational Dynamics* (Autumn 1989), 50–62; and Bart Victor and John B. Cullen, "The Organizational Bases of Ethical Work Climates," *Administrative Science Quarterly* 33 (1988), 101–125.

28. Russell Mitchell with Michael Oneal, "Managing by Values," *Business Week* (August 1, 1994), 46–52; and Alan Farnham, "State Your Values, Hold the Hot Air," *Fortune* (April 19, 1993), 117–124.

29. Eugene W. Szwajkowski, "The Myths and Realities of Research on Organizational Misconduct," in *Research in Corporate Social Performance and Policy,* ed. James E. Post (Greenwich, Conn.: JAI Press, 1986), 9:103–122; and Keith Davis, William C. Frederick, and Robert L. Blostrom, *Business and Society: Concepts and Policy Issues* (New York: McGraw-Hill, 1979).

30. Nancy C. Roberts and Paula J. King, "The Stakeholder Audit Goes Public," *Organizational Dynamics* (Winter 1989), 63–79; and Thomas Donaldson and Lee E. Preston, "The Stakeholder Theory of the Corporation: Concepts, Evidence, and Implications," *Academy of Management Review* 20, no. 1 (1995), 65–91.

31. Jeffrey S. Harrison and Caron H. St. John, "Managing and Partnering with External Stakeholders," *Academy of Management Executive* 10, no. 2 (1996), 46–60.

32. Max B. E. Clarkson, "A Stakeholder Framework for Analyzing and Evaluating Corporate Social Performance," *Academy of Management Review* 20, no. 1 (1995), 92–117.

33. Erika Rasmusson, "Doing Well, Doing Good: Inspiring Ways to Share the Wealth," *Working Woman* (December/January 2001), 42, 44.

34. Elizabeth Roberts, "From Soap to Soapbox," *Working Woman* (December–January 2001), 22–25.

35. Mark A. Cohen, "Management and the Environment," *The Owen Manager* 15, no. 1 (1993), 2–6.

36. Zipkin, "Getting Religion on Corporate Ethics."

37. Liesman, "Inside the Race to Profit from Global Warming."

38. Jeffrey Ball, "Warming Trend: Auto Makers Juggle Substance and Style in New Green Policies," *The Wall Street Journal* (May 15, 2001), A1, A6.

39. Ed Garsten, "GM Calls Fuel Cells 'Holy Grail,'" Associated Press (January 18, 2002), accessed at *http://www.yahoo.com.*

40. R. E. Freeman, J. Pierce, and R. Dodd, *Shades of Green: Business Ethics and the Environment* (New York: Oxford University Press, 1995).

41. Greg Toppo, "Company Agrees to Pay Record Pollution Fine," Associated Press, *Johnson City Press* (July 21, 2000), 9.

42. Andrew C. Revkin, "7 Companies Agree to Cut Gas Emissions," *The New York Times* (October 18, 2000), C1, C6.

43. Gwen Kinkead, "In the Future, People Like Me Will Go to Jail," *Fortune* (May 24, 1999), 190–200; Charles Fishman, "I Want to Pioneer the Company of the Next Industrial Revolution," *Fast Company* (April–May 1998), 136–142; Thomas Petzinger, Jr., "Business Achieves Greatest Efficiency When at Its Greenest," *The Wall Street Journal* (July 11, 1997), B1; and

Catherine Arnst, "When Green Begets Green," *Business Week* (November 10, 1997), 98–106.

44. Archie B. Carroll, "A Three-Dimensional Conceptual Model of Corporate Performance," *Academy of Management Review* 4 (1979), 497–505. For a discussion of various models for evaluating corporate social performance, also see Diane L. Swanson, "Addressing a Theoretical Problem by Reorienting the Corporate Social Performance Model," *Academy of Management Review* 20, no. 1 (1995), 43–64.

45. Milton Friedman, *Capitalism and Freedom* (Chicago: University of Chicago Press, 1962), 133; and Milton Friedman and Rose Friedman, *Free to Choose* (New York: Harcourt Brace Jovanovich, 1979).

46. Eugene W. Szwajkowski, "Organizational Illegality: Theoretical Integration and Illustrative Application," *Academy of Management Review* 10 (1985), 558–567.

47. David J. Fritzsche and Helmut Becker, "Linking Management Behavior to Ethical Philosophy—An Empirical Investigation," *Academy of Management Journal* 27 (1984), 165–175.

48. Saul W. Gellerman, "Managing Ethics from the Top Down," *Sloan Management Review* (Winter 1989), 73–79.

49. This discussion is based on Linda Klebe Treviño, Laura Pincus Hartman, and Michael Brown, "Moral Person and Moral Manager: How Executives Develop a Reputation for Ethical Leadership," *California Management Review* 42, no. 4 (Summer 2000), 128–142.

50. "Corporate Ethics: A Prime Business Asset," *The Business Roundtable,* 200 Park Avenue, Suite 2222, New York, New York, 10166, February 1988.

51. Michael Barrier, "Doing the Right Thing," *Nation's Business* (March 1998), 33–38.

52. Joseph L. Badaracco, Jr., and Allen P. Webb, "Business Ethics: A View from the Trenches," *California Management Review* 37, no. 2 (Winter 1995), 8–28.

53. Linda Klebe Treviño, Gary R. Weaver, David G. Gibson, and Barbara Ley Toffler, "Managing Ethics and Legal Compliance: What Works and What Hurts?" *California Management Review* 41, no. 2 (Winter 1999), 131–151.

54. Linda Klebe Treviño and Katherine A. Nelson, *Managing Business Ethics: Straight Talk About How to Do It Right,* 2nd ed. (New York: John Wiley & Sons, 1999), 274–283.

55. Treviño, Hartman, and Brown, "Moral Person and Moral Manager."

56. "Corporate Ethics."

57. Treviño et al., "Managing Ethics and Legal Compliance."

58. Carolyn Wiley, "The ABC's of Business Ethics: Definitions, Philosophies, and Implementation," *IM* (January–February 1995), 22–27; Badaracco and Webb, "Business Ethics: a View from the Trenches"; and Ronald B. Morgan, "Self- and Co-Worker Perceptions of Ethics and Their Relationships to Leadership and Salary," *Academy of Management Journal* 36, no. 1 (February 1993), 200–214.

59. "Setting the Standard," *http://www.lockheedmartin.com/about/ethics/standard.html,* accessed on August 9, 2002.

60. Cassandra Kegler, "Holding Herself Accountable," *Working Woman* (May 2001), 13; and Louisa Wah, "Treading the Sacred Ground," *Management Review* (July–August, 1998), 18–22.

61. Alan Yuspeh, "Do the Right Thing," *CIO* (August 1, 2000), 56–58.

62. Zipkin, "Getting Religion on Corporate Ethics."

63. Beverly Geber, "The Right and Wrong of Ethics Offices," *Training* (October 1995), 102–118.

64. Zipkin, "Getting Religion on Corporate Ethics."

65. John A. Byrne, "The Best Laid Ethics Programs. . . ," *Business Week* (March 9, 1992), 67–69.

66. Marcia Parmarlee Miceli and Janet P. Near, "The Relationship among Beliefs, Organizational Positions, and Whistle-Blowing Status: A Discriminant Analysis," *Academy of Management Journal* 27 (1984), 687–705.

67. Eugene Garaventa, "*An Enemy of the People* by Henrik Ibsen: The Politics of Whistle-Blowing," *Journal of Management Inquiry* 3, no. 4 (December 1994), 369–374; Marcia P. Miceli and Janet P. Near, "Whistleblowing: Reaping the Benefits," *Academy of Management Executive* 8, no. 3 (1994), 65–74.

68. Patricia Kiger, "Truth and Consequences," *Working Woman* (May 2001), 56–61.

69. Philip L. Cochran and Robert A. Wood, "Corporate Social Responsibility and Financial Performance," *Academy of Management Journal* 27 (1984), 42–56.

70. Dale Kurschner, "5 Ways Ethical Business Creates Fatter Profits," *Business Ethics* (March–April 1996), 20–23.

71. Mark Schapiro, "All Over the Board," *grok* (February–March 2001), 110–112.

72. Reported in "The Socially Correct Corporate Business."

73. Jean B. McGuire, Alison Sundgren, and Thomas Schneeweis, "Corporate Social Responsibility and Firm Financial Performance," *Academy of Management Journal* 31 (1988), 854–872; and Louisa Wah, "Treading the Sacred Ground," *Management Review* (July–August 1998), 18–22.

74. George Anders, "Honesty is the Best Policy," *Fast Company* (August 2000), 262–266.

75. This discussion is based on Seglin, "Who's Snooping on You?"

76. Ibid.

77. Jeffery L. Seglin, "Dot.Con", *Forbes ASAP* (February 21, 2000), 135; and Edward C. Baig, Marcia Stepanek, and Neil Gross, "Privacy," *Business Week* (April 5, 1999), 84–90.

78. Glenn R. Simpson, "The Battle Over Web Privacy," *The Wall Street Journal* (March 21, 2001), B1, B4; and Jason Sykes and Glenn R. Simpson, "Some Big Sites Back P3P Plan; Others Wait," *The Wall Street Journal* (March 21, 2001), B1, B4.

79. Lori Hinnant, "Company Lowers HIV-Drug Prices for Africa, Others," Associated Press, *Johnson City Press* (March 8, 2001), 16.

Chapter 5

Organizational Planning and Goal Setting

1. Peter G. Martin, "Heroes of U.S. Manufacturing," *Fortune* (March 18, 2002), 130A–130L.

2. Oren Harari, "Good/Bad News about Strategy," *Management Review* (July 1995), 29–31.

3. Amitai Etzioni, *Modern Organizations* (Englewood Cliffs, N.J.: Prentice-Hall, 1984), 6.

4. Max D. Richards, *Setting Strategic Goals and Objectives,* 2d ed. (St. Paul, Minn.: West, 1986).

5. C. Chet Miller and Laura B. Cardinal, "Strategic Planning and Firm Performance: A Synthesis of More than Two Decades of Research," *Academy of Management Journal* 37, no. 6 (1994), 1649–1685.

6. This discussion is based on Richard L. Daft and Richard M. Steers, *Organizations: A Micro/Macro Approach* (Glenview, Ill.: Scott, Foresman, 1986), 319–321; Herbert A. Simon, "On the Concept of Organizational Goals," *Administrative Science Quarterly* 9 (1964), 1–22; and Charles B. Saunders and Francis D. Tuggel, "Corporate Goals," *Journal of General Management* 5 (1980), 3–13.

7. David Whitford, "A Human Place to Work," *Fortune* (January 8, 2001), 108–121.

8. Steven L. Marks, "Say When," *Inc.* (February 1995), 19–20.

9. David Pearson, "Breaking Away," *CIO,* Section 1 (May 1, 1998), 34–46.

10. Peter Galuszka and Ellen Neuborne with Wendy Zellner, "P&G's Hottest New Product: P&G," *Business Week* (October 5, 1998), 92, 96.

11. Frank Rose, "Now Quality Means Service Too," *Fortune* (April 22, 1991), 99–108.

12. Mary Klemm, Stuart Sanderson, and George Luffman, "Mission Statements: Selling Corporate Values to Employees," *Long-Range Planning* 24, no. 3 (1991), 73–78; John A. Pearce II and Fred David, "Corporate Mission Statements: The Bottom Line," *Academy of Management Executive* (1987), 109–116; Jerome H. Want, "Corporate Mission: The Intangible Contributor to Performance," *Management Review* (August 1986), 46–50; and Alan Farnham, "Brushing Up Your Vision Thing," *Fortune* (May 1, 1995), 129.

13. Paul Haschak, *Corporate Statements: The Official Missions, Goals, Principles, and Philosophies of Over 900 Companies* (Jefferson, N.C.: McFarland & Company, 1998), 63.

14. Charles A. O'Reilly III and Jeffrey Pfeffer, "Star Makers," (book excerpt from *From Hidden Value: How Great Companies Achieve Extraordinary Results with Ordinary People,* Boston, Mass.: Harvard University Press, 2000), in *CIO* (September 15, 2000), 226–246.

15. "Strategic Planning: Part 2," *Small Business Report* (March 1983), 28–32.

16. Paul Meising and Joseph Wolfe, "The Art and Science of Planning at the Business Unit Level," *Management Science* 31 (1985), 773–781.

17. Jenny C. McCune, "On the Train Gang," *Management Review* (October 1994), 57–60.

18. Mark Fischetti, "Team Doctors, Report to ER!" *Fast Company* (February/March 1998), 170–177.

19. Gina Imperato, "Dirty Business, Bright Ideas," *Fast Company* (February/March, 1997), 89–93.

20. John O. Alexander, "Toward Real Performance: The Circuit-Breaker Technique," *Supervisory Management* (April 1989), 5–12.

21. Mark J. Fritsch, "Balanced Scorecard Helps Northern States Power's Quality Academy Achieve Extraordinary Performance," *Corporate University Review* (September–October 1997), 22.

22. Joy Riggs, "Empowering Workers by Setting Goals," *Nation's Business* (January 1995), 6.

23. Joel Hoekstra, "3M's Global Grip," *WorldTraveler* (May 2000), 31–34; and Thomas A. Stewart, "3M Fights Back," *Fortune* (February 5, 1996), 94–99.

24. Edwin A. Locke, Garp P. Latham, and Miriam Erez, "The Determinants of Goal Commitment," *Academy of Management Review* 13 (1988), 23–39.

25. George S. Odiorne, "MBO: A Backward Glance," *Business Horizons* 21 (October 1978), 14–24.

26. Jan P. Muczyk and Bernard C. Reimann, "MBO as a Complement to Effective Leadership," *The Academy of Management Executive* 3 (1989), 131–138; and W. Giegold, *Objective Setting and the MBO Process*, vol. 2 (New York: McGraw-Hill, 1978).

27. "Corporate Planning: Drafting a Blueprint for Success," *Small Business Report* (August 1987), 40–44.

28. Bernard Wysocki Jr., "Soft Landing or Hard? Firm Tests Strategy on 3 Views of Future," *The Wall Street Journal* (July 7, 2000), A1, A6.

29. Ian Mitroff with Gus Anagnos, *Managing Crises Before They Happen* (New York: AMACOM, 2001).

30. This discussion is based largely on W. Timothy Coombs, *Ongoing Crisis Communication: Planning, Managing, and Responding* (Thousand Oaks, Calif.: Sage Publications, 1999).

31. Coombs, *Ongoing Crisis Communication*, 28–29.

32. Ian I. Mitroff, "Crisis Leadership," *Executive Excellence* (August 2001), 19; Andy Bowen, "Crisis Procedures That Stand the Test of Time," *Public Relations Tactics* (August 2001), 16.

33. Kirstin Downey Grimsley, "Many Firms Lack Plans for Disaster," *The Washington Post* (October 3, 2001), E1.

34. "Disaster Planning," *Ioma's Report on Controlling Law Firm Costs* (October 2001), 9.

35. Kirstin Downey Grimsley, "Many Firms Lack Plans for Disaster," *The Washington Post* (October 3, 2001), E1; "Girding Against New Risks: Global Executives Are Working to Better Protect Their Employees and Businesses from Calamity," *Time* (October 8, 2001), B8+.

36. Ian I. Mitroff, "Crisis Leadership," *Executive Excellence* (August 2001), 19.

37. Ian I., Mitroff, Christine M. Pearson, and L. Katharine Harrington, *The Essential Guide to Managing Corporate Crises: A Step-by-Step Handbook for Surviving Major Catastrophes* (New York: Oxford University Press, 1996), 13–17.

38. "Delayed Anthrax Treatments? Postal Workers Angered, Health Officials Admit Surprise," (October 23, 2001), accessed at *http://abcnews.go.com/sections/us/DailyNews/anthrax_postal.html* on January 29, 2002.

39. "Girding Against New Risks."

40. Harari, "Good News/Bad News about Strategy."

41. Jay Finegan, "Everything According to Plan," *Inc.* (March 1995), 78–85; and Art Kleiner, "Jack Stack's Story Is an Open Book," *Strategy & Business* (Third Quarter 2001), 76–85.

42. Gerald E. Ledford, Jr., Jon R. Wendenhof, and James T. Strahley, "Realizing a Corporate Philosophy," *Organizational Dynamics* (Winter 1995), 5–18. James C. Collins, "Building Companies to Last," *The State of Small Business* (1995), 83–86; James C. Collins and Jerry I. Porras, "Building a Visionary Company," *California Management Review* 37, no. 2 (Winter 1995), 80–100; James C. Collins and Jerry I. Porras, "The Ultimate Vision," *Across the Board* (January 1995), 19–23.

43. See Kenneth R. Thompson, Wayne A. Hockwarter, and Nicholas J. Mathys, "Stretch Targets: What Makes Them Effective?" *Academy of Management Executive* 11, no. 3 (August 1997), 48.

44. Gary Hamel, "Avoiding the Guillotine," *Fortune* (April 2, 2001), 139–144.

45. Henry Mintzberg, "The Fall and Rise of Strategic Planning," *Harvard Business Review* (January–February, 1994), 107–114.

46. Jeffrey A. Schmidt, "Corporate Excellence in the New Millennium," *Journal of Business Strategy* (November–December 1999), 39–43.

47. Polly LaBarre, "The Company Without Limits," *Fast Company* (September 1999), 160–186.

48. Keith H. Hammonds, "Michael Porter's Big Ideas," *Fast Company* (March 2001), 150–156.

49. John E. Prescott, "Environments as Moderators of the Relationship between Strategy and Performance," *Academy of Management Journal* 29 (1986), 329–346; John A. Pearce II and Richard B. Robinson, Jr., *Strategic Management: Strategy, Formulation, and Implementation*, 2d ed. (Homewood, Ill.: Irwin, 1985); and David J. Teece, "Economic Analysis and Strategic Management," *California Management Review* 26 (Spring 1984), 87–110.

50. Markides, "Strategic Innovation."

51. K. Oanh Ha, "Cupertino, Calif. Woman Answers Telephones for Small Businesses," *Knight Ridder Tribune Business News* (February 9, 2002), 1.

52. Michael E. Porter, "What Is Strategy?" *Harvard Business Review* (November–December 1996), 61–78.

53. Arthur A. Thompson, Jr., and A. J. Strickland III, *Strategic Management: Concepts and Cases*, 6th ed. (Homewood, Ill.: Irwin, 1992); and Briance Mascarenhas, Alok Baveja, and Mamnoon Jamil, "Dynamics of Core Competencies in Leading Multinational Companies," *California Management Review* 40, no. 4 (Summer 1998), 117–132.

54. Ronald B. Lieber, "Smart Science," *Fortune* (June 23, 1997), 73.

55. Mascarenhas, Baveja, and Jamil, "Dynamics of Core Competencies."

56. Paul Roberts, "Live! From Your Office! It's . . ." *Fast Company* (October 1999), 151–170.

57. Betsy Morris, "Can Michael Dell Escape The Box?" *Fortune* (October 16, 2000), 93–110; and Stewart Deck, "Fine Line," *CIO* (February 1, 2000), 88–92.

58. Michael Goold and Andrew Campbell, "Desperately Seeking Synergy," *Harvard Business Review* (September–October 1998), 131–143.

59. John A. Byrne, "PepsiCo's New Formula," *Business Week* (April 10, 2000), 172–184.

60. Cathy Olofson, "No Place Like Home," *Fast Company* (July 2000), 328–329.

61. Bethany McLean, "Growing Up Gallo," *Fortune* (August 14, 2000), 211–220.

62. Hitt, Ireland, and Hoskisson, *Strategic Management*.

63. Milton Leontiades, "The Confusing Words of Business Policy," *Academy of Management Review* 7 (1982), 45–48.

64. Lawrence G. Hrebiniak and William F. Joyce, *Implementing Strategy* (New York: Macmillan, 1984).

65. James E. Svatko, "Analyzing the Competition," *Small Business Reports* (January 1989), 21–28; and Brian Dumaine, "Corpo-

rate Spies Snoop to Conquer," *Fortune* (November 7, 1988), 68–76.

66. Mascarenhas, Baveja, and Jamil, "Dynamics of Core Competencies."

67. Nanette Byrnes, "Old Stores, New Rivals, and Changing Trends Have Hammered Toys 'R' Us," *Business Week* (December 4, 2000), 128–140.

68. Michael E. Porter, *Competitive Strategy* (New York: Free Press, 1980), 36–46; Danny Miller, "Relating Porter's Business Strategies to Environment and Structure: Analysis and Performance Implementations," *Academy of Management Journal* 31 (1988), 280–308; and Michael E. Porter, "From Competitive Advantage to Corporate Strategy," *Harvard Business Review* (May–June 1987), 43–59.

69. Michael E. Porter, "Strategy and the Internet," *Harvard Business Review* (March 2001), 63–78.

70. Jim Kerstetter and Spencer E. Ante, "IBM vs. Oracle: It Could Get Bloody," *Business Week* (May 28, 2001), 65–66.

71. Erik Sherman, "Happy in Harleysville," *CIO* (October 15, 2000), 84–86.

72. Thomas L. Wheelen and J. David Hunger, *Strategic Management and Business Policy* (Reading, Mass.: Addison-Wesley, 1989).

73. Andrew Park and Peter Burrows, "Dell, the Conqueror," *Business Week* (September 24, 2001), 92–102; and Thompson and Strickland, *Strategic Management.*

74. Greg Burns, "It Only Hertz When Enterprise Laughs," *Business Week* (December 12, 1994), 44.

75. Joshua Rosenbaum, "Guitar Maker Looks for a New Key," *The Wall Street Journal* (February 11, 1998), B1, B5.

76. Porter, "Strategy and the Internet"; and Hammonds, "Michael Porter's Big Ideas."

77. Based on John Burton, "Composite Strategy: The Combination of Collaboration and Competition," *Journal of General Management* 21, No. 1 (Autumn 1995), 1–23; and Roberta Maynard, "Striking the Right Match," *Nation's Business* (May 1996), 18–28.

78. Elizabeth Jensen and Eben Shapiro, "Time Warner's Fight with News Corp. Belies Mutual Dependence," *The Wall Street Journal* (October 28, 1996), A1, A6.

79. Don Tapscott, "Rethinking Strategy in a Networked World," *Strategy & Business,* Issue 24 (Third Quarter 2001), 34–41.

80. Byrnes, "Old Stores, New Rivals, and Changing Trends."

81. Burton, "Composite Strategy: The Combination of Collaboration and Competition."

82. L. J. Bourgeois III and David R. Brodwin, "Strategic Implementation: Five Approaches to an Elusive Phenomenon," *Strategic Management Journal* 5 (1984), 241–264; Anil K. Gupta and V. Govindarajan, "Business Unit Strategy, Managerial Characteristics, and Business Unit Effectiveness at Strategy Implementation," *Academy of Management Journal* (1984), 25–41; and Jeffrey G. Covin, Dennis P. Slevin, and Randall L. Schultz, "Implementing Strategic Missions: Effective Strategic, Structural, and Tactical Choices," *Journal of Management Studies* 31, no. 4 (1994), 481–505.

83. Rainer Feurer and Kazem Chaharbaghi, "Dynamic Strategy Formulation and Alignment," *Journal of General Management* 20, no. 3 (Spring 1995), 76–90; and Henry Mintzberg, *The Rise and Fall of Strategic Planning* (Toronto: Maxwell Macmillan Canada, 1994).

84. Jay R. Galbraith and Robert K. Kazanjian, *Strategy Implementation: Structure, Systems and Process,* 2d ed. (St. Paul, Minn.: West, 1986); and Paul C. Nutt, "Selecting Tactics to Implement Strategic Plans," *Strategic Management Journal* 10 (1989), 145–161.

85. Morris, "Can Michael Dell Escape the Box?"

86. James E. Skivington and Richard L. Daft, "A Study of Organizational 'Framework' and 'Process' Modalities for the Implementation of Business-Level Strategies" (unpublished manuscript, Texas A&M University, 1987).

87. Roger Thurow, "A Sports Icon Regains Its Footing by Using the Moves of the Past," *The Wall Street Journal* (January 21, 1998), A1, A10.

88. Martin, "Heroes of U.S. Manufacturing."

Chapter 6
Managerial Decision Making

1. Jeanne Cummings and Gary Fields, "For Two Tense Days, Bush Team Wrestled with Vague Threat," *The Wall Street Journal* (May 17, 2002), 1.

2. Richard A. Melcher, "Dusting Off the *Britannica*," *Business Week* (October 21), 1997, 143, 146; and Pui-Wing Tam, "One for the History Books: The Tale of How Britannica is Trying to Leap from the Old Economy Into the New One," *The Wall Street Journal* (December 11, 2000), R32.

3. Kim Girard, "Cozone in the Ozone," *Business 2.0* (June 27, 2000), 90–95.

4. "Tickling a Child's Fancy," *The Tennessean* (February 6, 1997), 1E, 4E; and John R. Emshwiller and Michael J. McCarthy, "Coke's Soda Fountain for Offices Fizzles, Dashing High Hopes," *The Wall Street Journal* (June 14, 1993), A1, A6.

5. Dean Takahashi, "How the Competition Got Ahead of Intel in Making Cheap Chips," *The Wall Street Journal* (February 12, 1998), A1.

6. Linda Yates and Peter Skarzynski, "How Do Companies Get to the Future First?" *Management Review* (January 1999), 16–22.

7. Ronald A. Howard, "Decision Analysis: Practice and Promise," *Management Science* 34 (1988), 679–695.

8. Herbert A. Simon, *The New Science of Management Decision* (Englewood Cliffs, N.J.: Prentice-Hall, 1977), 47.

9. Gregory L. White, "Why GM Rewound Its Product Strategy, Delaying New Cavalier," *The Wall Street Journal* (July 30, 1999), A1, A6.

10. Samuel Eilon, "Structuring Unstructured Decisions," *Omega* 13 (1985), 369–377; and Max H. Bazerman, *Judgment in Managerial Decision Making* (New York: Wiley, 1986).

11. James G. March and Zur Shapira, "Managerial Perspectives on Risk and Risk Taking," *Management Science* 33 (1987), 1404–1418; and Inga Skromme Baird and Howard Thomas, "Toward a Contingency Model of Strategic Risk Taking," *Academy of Management Review* 10 (1985), 230–243.

12. J. G. Higgins, "Planning for Risk and Uncertainty in Oil Exploration," *Long Range Planning* 26, no. 1 (February 1993),

111–122; Alex Taylor III, "Wrong Turn at Saturn," *Fortune* (July 24, 2000), 371–372.

13. Eilon, "Structuring Unstructured Decisions"; and Philip A. Roussel, "Cutting Down the Guesswork in R&D," *Harvard Business Review* 61 (September–October 1983), 154–160.

14. Russell Wild, "Think Fast!" *Working Woman* (September 2000), 89–90.

15. Michael Masuch and Perry LaPotin, "Beyond Garbage Cans: An AI Model of Organizational Choice," *Administrative Science Quarterly* 34 (1989), 38–67; and Richard L. Daft and Robert H. Lengel, "Organizational Information Requirements, Media Richness and Structural Design," *Management Science* 32 (1986), 554–571.

16. David M. Schweiger, William R. Sandberg, and James W. Ragan, "Group Approaches for Improving Strategic Decision Making: A Comparative Analysis of Dialectical Inquiry, Devil's Advocacy, and Consensus," *Academy of Management Journal* 29 (1986), 51–71; and Richard O. Mason and Ian I. Mitroff, *Challenging Strategic Planning Assumptions* (New York: Wiley Interscience, 1981).

17. Michael Pacanowsky, "Team Tools for Wicked Problems," *Organizational Dynamics* 23, no. 3 (Winter 1995), 36–51.

18. Boris Blai, Jr., "Eight Steps to Successful Problem Solving," *Supervisory Management* (January 1986), 7–9; and Earnest R. Archer, "How to Make a Business Decision: An Analysis of Theory and Practice," *Management Review* 69 (February 1980), 54–61.

19. Stacie McCullough, "On the Front Lines," Section 1, *CIO*, (October 15, 1999), 78–81.

20. Anna Muoio, "Decisions, Decisions" (Unit of One column), *Fast Company* (October 1998), 93–101.

21. Thomas M. Cook, SABRE Soars," *OR/MS Today* (June 1998), 26–35.

22. Herbert A. Simon, *The New Science of Management Decision* (New York: Harper & Row, 1960), 5–6; and Amitai Etzioni, "Humble Decision Making," *Harvard Business Review* (July–August 1989), 122–126.

23. James G. March and Herbert A. Simon, *Organizations* (New York: Wiley, 1958).

24. Herbert A. Simon, *Models of Man* (New York: Wiley, 1957), 196–205; and Herbert A. Simon, *Administrative Behavior,* 2d ed. (New York: Free Press, 1957).

25. John Taylor, "Project Fantasy: A Behind-the-Scenes Account of Disney's Desperate Battle against the Raiders," *Manhattan* (November 1984).

26. Weston H. Agor, "The Logic of Intuition: How Top Executives Make Important Decisions," *Organizational Dynamics* 14 (Winter 1986), 5–18; and Herbert A. Simon, "Making Management Decisions: The Role of Intuition and Emotion," *Academy of Management Executive* 1 (1987), 57–64.

27. Lisa A. Burke and Monica K. Miller, "Taking the Mystery Out of Intuitive Decision Making," *Academy of Management Executive* 13, no. 4 (1999), 91–99.

28. Bill Breen, "What's Your Intuition?" *Fast Company* (September 2000), 290–300.

29. Alden M. Hayashi, "When to Trust Your Gut," *Harvard Business Review* (February 2001), 59–65.

30. Chris Smith, "Chao, Baby," *New York* (October 18, 1993), 66–75; and "Chao in Charge," *Cablevision* (November 29, 1999), 24.

31. William B. Stevenson, Jon L. Pierce, and Lyman W. Porter, "The Concept of 'Coalition' in Organization Theory and Research," *Academy of Management Review* 10 (1985), 256–268.

32. Jonathan Harris, "Why Speedy Got Stuck in Reverse," *Canadian Business* (September 26, 1997), 87–88.

33. James W. Fredrickson, "Effects of Decision Motive and Organizational Performance Level on Strategic Decision Processes," *Academy of Management Journal* 28 (1985), 821–843; James W. Fredrickson, "The Comprehensiveness of Strategic Decision Processes: Extension, Observations, Future Directions," *Academy of Management Journal* 27 (1984), 445–466; James W. Dean, Jr., and Mark P. Sharfman, "Procedural Rationality in the Strategic Decision-Making Process," *Journal of Management Studies* 30, no. 4 (July 1993), 587–610; Nandini Rajagopalan, Abdul M. A. Rasheed, and Deepak K. Datta, "Strategic Decision Processes: Critical Review and Future Directions," *Journal of Management* 19, no. 2 (1993), 349–384; and Paul J. H. Schoemaker, "Strategic Decisions in Organizations: Rational and Behavioral Views," *Journal of Management Studies* 30, no. 1 (January 1993), 107–129.

34. Marjorie A. Lyles and Howard Thomas, "Strategic Problem Formulation: Biases and Assumptions Embedded in Alternative Decision-Making Models," *Journal of Management Studies* 25 (1988), 131–145; and Susan E. Jackson and Jane E. Dutton, "Discerning Threats and Opportunities," *Administrative Science Quarterly* 33 (1988), 370–387.

35. Anita Lienert, "Can Liz Wetzel's Baby Save Buick?" *Working Woman* (May 2001), 33–36, 78.

36. Richard L. Daft, Juhani Sormunen, and Don Parks, "Chief Executive Scanning, Environmental Characteristics, and Company Performance: An Empirical Study" (unpublished manuscript, Texas A&M University, 1988).

37. C. Kepner and B. Tregoe, *The Rational Manager* (New York: McGraw-Hill, 1965).

38. Mylene Mangalindan and Suein L. Hwang, "Gang of Six: Coterie of Early Hires Made Yahoo! A Hit But an Insular Place," *The Wall Street Journal* (March 9, 2001), A1, A6.

39. Paul C. Nutt, "Surprising But True: Half the Decisions in Organizations Fail," *Academy of Management Executive* 13, 4 (1999), 75–90.

40. Lienert, "Can Liz Wetzel's Baby Save Buick?"

41. Peter Mayer, "A Surprisingly Simple Way to Make Better Decisions," *Executive Female* (March–April 1995), 13–14; and Ralph L. Keeney, "Creativity in Decision-Making with Value-Focused Thinking," *Sloan Management Review* (Summer 1994), 33–41.

42. Robert Levering and Milton Moskowitz, "The 100 Best Companies to Work For: The Best in the Worst of Times," *Fortune* (February 4, 2002), 60.

43. Gregory L. White and Joseph B. White, "GM Appoints An Industry Guru To Fix Its Lineup," *The Wall Street Journal* (August 3, 2001), B1, B6; Ian Springsteel, "Paul J. Liska" profile in "The Class of 2000," *CFO* (October 2000), 72–74.

44. Jenny C. McCune, "Making Lemonade," *Management Review* (June 1997), 49–53, 51.

45. Based on A. J. Rowe, J. D. Boulgaides, and M. R. McGrath, *Managerial Decision Making* (Chicago: Science Research Associates, 1984); and Alan J. Rowe and Richard O. Mason, *Managing with Style: A Guide to Understanding, Assessing, and Improving Your Decision Making* (San Francisco: Jossey-Bass, 1987).

46. Peter Elkind, "Vulgarians at the Gate," *Fortune* (June 21, 1999), 133–145.

47. Victor H. Vroom, "A New Look at Managerial Decision Making," *Organizational Dynamics* (Spring 1972), 66–80.

48. V. H. Vroom and Arthur G. Jago, *The New Leadership: Managing Participation in Organizations* (Englewood Cliffs, N.J.: Prentice-Hall, 1988).

49. Victor H. Vroom, "Leadership and the Decision-Making Process," *Organizational Dynamics* 28, no. 4 (Spring 2000), 82–94.

50. R. H. G. Field, "A Test of the Vroom-Yetton Normative Model of Leadership," *Journal of Applied Psychology* (October 1982), 523–532; and R. H. G. Field, "A Critique of the Vroom-Yetton Contingency Model of Leadership Behavior," *Academy of Management Review* 4 (1979), 249–257.

51. Vroom, "Leadership and the Decision Making Process"; Jennifer T. Ettling and Arthur G. Jago, "Participation under Conditions of Conflict: More on the Validity of the Vroom-Yetton Model," *Journal of Management Studies* 25 (1988), 73–83; Madeline E. Heilman, Harvey A. Hornstein, Jack H. Cage, and Judith K. Herschlag, "Reactions to Prescribed Leader Behavior as a Function of Role Perspective: The Case of the Vroom-Yetton Model," *Journal of Applied Psychology* (February 1984), 50–60; and Arthur G. Jago and Victor H. Vroom, "Some Differences in the Incidence and Evaluation of Participative Leader Behavior," *Journal of Applied Psychology* (December 1982), 776–783.

52. Based on a decision problem presented in Victor H. Vroom, "Leadership and the Decision-Making Process," *Organizational Dynamics* 28, 4 (Spring 2000), 82–94.

53. Kathleen M. Eisenhardt, "Strategy as Strategic Decision Making," *Sloan Management Review* (Spring 1999), 65–72.

54. See Katharine Mieskowski, "Digital Competition," *Fast Company* (December 1999), 155–162; Thomas A. Stewart, "Three Rules for Managing in the Real-Time Economy," *Fortune* (May 1, 2000), 333–334; and Colvin, "How to Be a Great eCEO," *Fortune* (May 24, 1999), 104–110.

55. Michael V. Copeland, "Mistakes Happen," *Red Herring* (May 2000), 346–354.

56. Ibid.

57. Joshua Klayman, Richard P. Larrick, and Chip Heath, "Organizational Repairs," *Across the Board* (February 2000), 26–31.

58. The discussion of collective intuition is based on Eisenhardt, "Strategy as Strategic Decision Making."

59. Ettling and Jago, "Participation under Conditions of Conflict."

60. Eisenhardt, "Strategy as Strategic Decision Making"; and David A. Garvin and Michael A. Roberto, "What You Don't Know about Making Decisions," *Harvard Business Review* (September 2001), 108–116.

61. David M. Schweiger and William R. Sandberg, "The Utilization of Individual Capabilities in Group Approaches to Strategic Decision-Making," *Strategic Management Journal* 10 (1989),

31–43; and "The Devil's Advocate," *Small Business Report* (December 1987), 38–41.

62. Eisenhardt, "Strategy as Strategic Decision Making."

63. Garvin and Roberto, "What You Don't Know About Making Decisions."

64. Christopher Palmeri, "Believe in Yourself, Believe in the Merchandise," *Continental* (December 1997), 49–51.

65. Derek Slater, "Chain Commanders," *CIO Enterprise* (August 15, 1998), 29–30+.

66. Jane Linder and Drew Phelps, "Call to Action," *CIO* (April 1, 2000), 166–174.

67. John P. Mello Jr., "Fly Me To the Web," *CFO* (March 2000), 79–84.

68. Heather Harreld, "Pick-Up Artists," *CIO* (November 1, 2000), 148–154.

69. Roger Fillion, "No Receptionist Necessary," *Inc. Technology* (2001), no. 2, 23.

70. Jim Turcotte, Bob Silveri, and Tom Jobson, "Are You Ready for the E-Supply Chain?" *APICS—The Performance Advantage* (August 1998), 56–59.

71. Steve Hamm with David Welch, Wendy Zellner, Faith Keenan, and Peter Engardio, "E-Biz: Down But Hardly Out," *Business Week* (March 26, 2001), 126–130.

72. Marie-Claude Boudreau, Karen D. Loch, Daniel Robey, and Detmar Straud, "Going Global: Using Information Technology to Advance the Competitiveness of the Virtual Transnational Organization," *Academy of Management Executive* 12, no. 4 (1998), 120–128.

73. Based on Ranjay Gulati and Jason Garino, "Get the Right Mix of Bricks and Clicks," *Harvard Business Review* (May–June 2000), 107–114.

74. Kris Frieswick, "You've Got to Have Friends," *CFO* (August 2001), 50–53.

75. This discussion is based on Pamela Barnes-Vieyra and Cindy Claycomb, "Business-to-Business E-Commerce: Models and Managerial Decisions," *Business Horizons* (May–June 2001), 13–20.

76. Reported in Hamm et. al., "E-Biz: Down But Hardly Out."

77. Ibid.

78. Eric Young, "Web Marketplaces That Really Work," *Fortune/CNET Tech Review* (Winter 2001), 78–86.

79. Brian Caulfield, "Facing Up to CRM," *Business 2.0* (August–September 2001), 149–150.

80. Meg Mitchell Moore, "Thinking Small," *Darwin Magazine* (May 2001), 71–78.

81. Anthony Scaturro, "All in the Family," *Inc. Technology,* no. 1 (1998), 25–26.

82. Stephanie Overby, "Paving over Paperwork," *CIO* (February 1, 2002), 82–82.

83. Liz Thach and Richard W. Woodman, "Organizational Change and Information Technology: Managing on the Edge of Cyberspace," *Organizational Dynamics* (Summer 1994), 30–46.

84. Greg Jaffe, "Tug of War: In the New Military, Technology May Alter Chain of Command," *The Wall Street Journal* (March 30, 2001), A3, A6.

85. Joseph McCafferty, "Coping with Infoglut," *CFO* (September 1998), 101–102.

86. Leonard M. Fuld, "The Danger of Data Slam," *CIO,* Section 2 (September 15, 1998), 28–33.

87. Stewart Deck, "New Connections," *CIO* (February 1, 2001), 130–132.

88. Joanne Lee-Young and Megan Barnett, "Furiously Fast Fashions," *The Industry Standard* (June 11, 2001), 72–79.

89. Spencer E. Ante, with Amy Borrus and Robert D. Hof, "In Search of the Net's Next Big Thing," *Business Week* (March 26, 2001), 140–141.

90. Robert Poe, "Instant Messaging Goes to Work," *Business2.com* (July 10, 2001), 36.

91. Ante et. al., "In Search of the Net's Next Big Thing."

92. Susannah Patton, "The Wisdom of Starting Small," *CIO* (March 15, 2001), 80–86.

93. Ante et al., "In Search of the Net's Next Big Thing"; Amy Cortese, "Peer to Peer," *The Business Week 50* (Spring 2001), 194–196.

94. Mark Roberti, "Peer-to-Peer Isn't Dead," *The Industry Standard* (April 23, 2001), 58–59.

95. Cummings and Fields, "For Two Tense Days, Bush Team Wrestled with Vague Threat."

Chapter 7
Fundamentals of Organizing

1. Roger O. Crockett, "A New Company Called Motorola," *Business Week* (April 17, 200), 86.

2. Karen Chan, "From Top to Bottom," *The Wall Street Journal* (May 21, 2001), R12.

3. Peter Burrows, "The Radical," *Business Week* (February 19, 2001), 70–80.

4. John Child, *Organization: A Guide to Problems and Practice,* 2d ed. (London: Harper & Row, 1984).

5. Adam Smith, *The Wealth of Nations* (New York: Modern Library, 1937).

6. Glenn L. Dalton, "The Collective Stretch," *Management Review* (December 1998), 54–59.

7. This discussion is based on Richard L. Daft, *Organization Theory and Design,* 4th ed. (St. Paul, Minn.: West, 1992), 387–388.

8. C. I. Barnard, *The Functions of the Executive* (Cambridge, Mass.: Harvard University Press, 1938).

9. Thomas A. Stewart, "CEOs See Clout Shifting," *Fortune* (November 6, 1989), 66.

10. Michael G. O'Loughlin, "What Is Bureaucratic Accountability and How Can We Measure It?" *Administration & Society* 22, no. 3 (November 1990), 275–302.

11. Carrie R. Leana, "Predictors and Consequences of Delegation," *Academy of Management Journal* 29 (1986), 754–774.

12. Curtis Sittenfeld, "Powered By the People," *Fast Company* (July–August 1999), 178–189.

13. Paul D. Collins and Frank Hull, "Technology and Span of Control: Woodward Revisited," *Journal of Management Studies* 23 (March 1986), 143–164; David D. Van Fleet and Arthur G. Bedeian, "A History of the Span of Management," *Academy of Management Review* 2 (1977), 356–372; and C. W. Barkdull, "Span of Control—A Method of Evaluation," *Michigan Business Review* 15 (May 1963), 25–32.

14. Brian Dumaine, "What the Leaders of Tomorrow See," *Fortune* (July 3, 1989), 48–62.

15. Charles Haddad, "How UPS Delivered Through the Disaster," *Business Week* (October 1, 2001), 66.

16. Brian O'Reilly, "J&J Is on a Roll," *Fortune* (December 26, 1994), 178–191; and Joseph Weber, "A Big Company That Works," *Business Week* (May 4, 1992), 124–132.

17. Clay Chandler and Paul Ingrassia, "Just as U.S. Firms Try Japanese Management, Honda Is Centralizing," *The Wall Street Journal* (April 11, 1991), A1, A10.

18. The following discussion of structural alternatives draws heavily on Jay R. Galbraith, *Designing Complex Organizations* (Reading, Mass.: Addison-Wesley, 1973); Jay R. Galbraith, *Organization Design* (Reading, Mass.: Addison-Wesley, 1977); Robert Duncan, "What Is the Right Organization Structure?" *Organizational Dynamics* (Winter 1979), 59–80; and J. McCann and Jay R. Galbraith, "Interdepartmental Relations," in *Handbook of Organizational Design,* ed. P. Nystrom and W. Starbuck (New York: Oxford University Press, 1981), 60–84.

19. Sandra N. Phillips, "Team Training Puts Fizz in Coke Plant's Future," *Personnel Journal* (January 1996), 87–92.

20. John Hillkirk, "Challenging Status Quo Now in Vogue," *USA Today* (November 9, 1993); and Thomas A. Stewart, "The Search for the Organization of Tomorrow," *Fortune* (May 18, 1992), 92–98.

21. Charles Fishman, "Total Teamwork: Imagination Ltd.," *Fast Company* (April 2000), 156–168.

22. Raymond E. Miles and Charles C. Snow, "The New Network Firm: A Spherical Structure Built on a Human Investment Philosophy," *Organizational Dynamics* (Spring 1995), 5–18; and Raymond E. Miles, Charles C. Snow, John A. Matthews, Grant Miles, and Henry J. Coleman, Jr., "Organizing in the Knowledge Age: Anticipating the Cellular Form," *Academy of Management Executive* 11, no. 4 (1997), 7–24.

23. Raymond E. Miles and Charles C. Snow, "Organizations: New Concepts for New Forms," *California Management Review* 28 (Spring 1986), 62–73; and "Now, The Post-Industrial Corporation," *Business Week* (March 3, 1986), 64–74.

24. N. Anand, "Modular, Virtual, and Hollow Forms of Organization Design," Working paper, London Business School, 2000; Don Tapscott, "Rethinking Strategy in a Networked World," *Strategy & Business,* Issue 24 (Third Quarter 2001), 34–41.

25. John Case, "The Age of the Specialist," *Inc.* (August 1995), 15–16.

26. Heath Row, "This 'Virtual' Company is for Real," *Fast Company* (December–January 1998), 48–50; Evan Ramstad, "A PC Maker's Low-Tech Formula: Start with the Box," *The Wall Street Journal* (December 29, 1997), B1, B8; and http://www.monorail.com/company/company.htm accessed on February 19, 2002.

27. Gregory G. Dess, Abdul M. A. Rasheed, Kevin J. McLaughlin, and Richard L. Priem, "The New Corporate Architecture," *Academy of Management Executive* 9, no. 3 (1995), 7–20.

28. Kathleen Kerwin, "GM: Modular Plants Won't Be a Snap," *Business Week* (November 9, 1998), 168, 172.

29. Raymond E. Miles, "Adapting to Technology and Competition: A New Industrial Relations System for the Twenty-First Cen-

tury," *California Management Review* (Winter 1989), 9–28; and Miles and Snow, "The New Network Firm."

30. Dess et al., "The New Corporate Architecture."

31. Melissa A. Schilling, "Industry Determinants of the Adoption of Modular Organizational Forms: An Empirical Test," *Academy of Management Journal,* forthcoming.

32. John Byrne, "The Virtual Corporation," *Business Week* (February 8, 1993), 99–103; Dess et al., "The New Corporate Architecture," and Anand, "Modular, Virtual, and Hollow Forms."

33. M. Lynne Markus, Brook Manville, and Carole E. Agres, "What Makes a Virtual Organization Work?" *Sloan Management Review* (Fall 2000), 13–26.

34. Keith H. Hammonds, "This Virtual Agency Has Big Ideas," *Fast Company* (November 1999), 70–72.

35. Adam Lashinsky, "It Worked in Kindergarten," *Fortune* (April 2, 2001), 174.

36. N. Anand, "Modular, Virtual, and Hollow Forms," and Markus et al., "What Makes a Virtual Organization Work?"

37. Thomas H. Davenport and Keri Pearlson, "Two Cheers for the Virtual Office," *Sloan Management Review* (Summer 1998), 51–65.

38. Laurie P. O'Leary, "Curing the Monday Blues: A U.S. Navy Guide for Structuring Cross-Functional Teams," *National Productivity Review* (Spring 1996), 43–51; and Alan Hurwitz, "Organizational Structures for the 'New World Order,'" *Business Horizons* (May–June 1996), 5–14.

39. Richard L. Daft, *Organization Theory and Design,* 7th ed. (Cincinnati, Ohio: South-Western College Publishing, 2001).

40. Michelle Conlin, "Write Your Own Title," *Business Week* (August 28, 2000), 148.

41. "Job Titles of the Future" column in *Fast Company* (December 1999), 92.

42. Lee Iacocca with William Novak, *Iacocca: An Autobiography* (New York: Phantom Books, 1984), 152–153.

43. Alan Webber, "The Best Organization is No Organization," *USA Today* (March 6, 1997), 13A.

44. William J. Altier, "Task Forces: An Effective Management Tool," *Management Review* (February 1987), 52–57.

45. "Task Forces Tackle Consolidation of Employment Services," *Shawmut News,* Shawmut National Corp. (May 3, 1989), 2.

46. Michael Brody, "Can GM Manage It All?" *Fortune* (July 8, 1985), 22–28.

47. Henry Mintzberg, *The Structure of Organizations* (Englewood Cliffs, N.J.: Prentice-Hall, 1979).

48. Barbara Ettorre, "Simplicity Cuts a New Pattern," *Management Review* (December 1993), 25–29; and Jeffrey Ball, "A Car Veteran Explains Why IPC = (A + W + P – I) x S," *The Wall Street Journal* (June 8, 1999), B1, B20.

49. Paul R. Lawrence and Jay W. Lorsch, "New Managerial Job: The Integrator," *Harvard Business Review* (November–December 1967), 142–151.

50. Ronald N. Ashkenas and Suzanne C. Francis, "Integration Managers: Special Leaders for Special Times," *Harvard Business Review* (November–December 2000), 108–116.

51. Jeffrey A. Tannenbaum, "Why Are Companies Paying Close Attention to This Toilet Maker?" (The Front Lines column), *The Wall Street Journal* (August 20, 1999), B1.

52. This discussion is based on Michael Hammer and Steven Stanton, "How Process Enterprises *Really* Work," *Harvard Business Review* (November–December 1999), 108–118; Richard L. Daft, *Organization Theory and Design,* 5th ed. (Minneapolis, Minn.: West Publishing Company, 1995), 238; Raymond L. Manganelli and Mark M. Klein, "A Framework for Reengineering," *Management Review* (June 1994), 9–16; and Barbara Ettorre, "Reengineering Tales from the Front," *Management Review* (January 1995), 13–18.

53. Hammer and Stanton, "How Process Enterprises *Really* Work."

54. Michael Hammer, definition quoted in "The Process Starts Here," *CIO* (March 1, 2000), 144-156; and David A. Garvin, "The Processes of Organization and Management," *Sloan Management Review* (Summer 1998), 33–50.

55. Hammer and Stanton, "How Process Enterprises *Really* Work."

56. Ibid.

57. Richard Koonce, "Reengineering the Travel Game," *Government Executive* (May 1995), 28–34, 69–70.

58. John A. Byrne, "The Horizontal Corporation," *Business Week* (December 20, 1993), 76–81.

59. Erik Brynjolfsson, Amy Austin Renshaw, and Marshall Van Alstyne, "The Matrix of Change," *Sloan Management Review* (Winter 1997), 37–54.

60. Frank Ostroff, *The Horizontal Organization: What the Organization of the Future Looks Like and How It Delivers Value to Customers* (New York: Oxford University Press, 1999).

61. Julie Carrick Dalton, "Between the Lines: The Hard Truth about Open Book Management," *CFO* (March 1999), 58–64; Alex Markels, "The Wisdom of Chairman Ko," *Fast Company* (November 1999), 258–276.

62. E. C. Nevis, A. J. DiBella, and J. M. Gould, "Understanding Organizations as Learning Systems," *Sloan Management Review* (Winter 1995), 73–85; and G. Hamel, "Strategy as Revolution," *Harvard Business Review* (July–August 1996), 69–82.

63. Marc S. Gerstein and Robert B. Shaw, "Organizational Architectures for the Twenty-First Century," in David A. Nadler, Marc S. Gerstein, Robert B. Shaw and Associates, eds., *Organizational Architecture: Designs for Changing Organizations* (San Francisco: Jossey-Bass, 1992), 263–274.

64. Thomas A. Stewart, "Three Rules for Managing in the Real-Time Economy," *Fortune* (May 1, 2000), 333–334.

65. Scott Kirsner, "Every Day, It's a New Place," *Fast Company* (April–May 1998), 130–134.

66. Jeffrey Pfeffer, "Producing Sustainable Competitive Advantage Through the Effective Management of People," *Academy of Management Executive* 9, no. 1 (1995), 55–69.

67. Mary Anne Devanna and Noel Tichy, "Creating the Competitive Organization of the Twenty-First Century: The Boundaryless Corporation," *Human Resource Management* 29 (Winter 1990), 455–471; and Fred Kofman and Peter M. Senge, "Communities of Commitment: The Heart of Learning Organizations," *Organizational Dynamics* (Autumn 1993), 4–23.

68. Chuck Salter, "This is One Fast Factory," *Fast Company* (August 2001), 32–33.

69. Dorothy Leonard-Barton, "The Factory as a Learning Laboratory," *Sloan Management Review* (Fall 1992), 23–38.

70. Michael E. Porter, *Competitive Strategy* (New York: Free Press, 1980), 36–46.

71. Kerry Capell, "MTV's World," *Business Week* (February 18, 2002), 81–84.

72. Pam Black, "Finally, Human Rights for Motorists," *Business Week* (May 1, 1995), 45.

73. Paul R. Lawrence and Jay W. Lorsch, *Organization and Environment* (Homewood, Ill.: Irwin, 1969).

74. Robert B. Duncan, "Characteristics of Organizational Environments and Perceived Environmental Uncertainty," *Administrative Science Quarterly* 17 (1972), 313–327; W. Alan Randolph and Gregory G. Dess, "The Congruence Perspective of Organization Design: A Conceptual Model and Multivariate Research Approach," *Academy of Management Review* 9 (1984), 114–127; and Masoud Yasai-Ardekani, "Structural Adaptations to Environments," *Academy of Management Review* 11 (1986), 9–21.

75. Robert Pool, "In the Zero Luck Zone," *Forbes ASAP* (November 27, 2000), 85+.

76. Ibid.

77. Denise M. Rousseau and Robert A. Cooke, "Technology and Structure: The Concrete, Abstract, and Activity Systems of Organizations," *Journal of Management* 10 (1984), 345–361; Charles Perrow, "A Framework for the Comparative Analysis of Organizations," *American Sociological Review* 32 (1967), 194–208; and Denise M. Rousseau, "Assessment of Technology in Organizations: Closed versus Open Systems Approaches," *Academy of Management Review* 4 (1979), 531–542.

78. Joan Woodward, *Industrial Organizations: Theory and Practice* (London: Oxford University Press, 1965); and Joan Woodward, *Management and Technology* (London: Her Majesty's Stationery Office, 1958).

79. Woodward, *Industrial Organizations,* vi.

80. Peter K. Mills and Thomas Kurk, "A Preliminary Investigation into the Influence of Customer-Firm Interface on Information Processing and Task Activity in Service Organizations," *Journal of Management* 12 (1986), 91–104; Peter K. Mills and Dennis J. Moberg, "Perspectives on the Technology of Service Operations," *Academy of Management Review* 7 (1982), 467–478; and Roger W. Schmenner, "How Can Service Businesses Survive and Prosper?" *Sloan Management Review* 27 (Spring 1986), 21–32.

81. Richard B. Chase and David A. Tansik, "The Customer Contact Model for Organization Design," *Management Science* 29 (1983), 1037–1050; and Gregory B. Northcraft and Richard B. Chase, "Managing Service Demand at the Point of Delivery," *Academy of Management Review* 10 (1985), 66–75.

82. Michael Hammer in "The Process Starts Here"; and Emelie Rutherford, "End Game" (an interview with David Weinberger, coauthor of *The Cluetrain Manifesto*), *CIO* (April 1, 2000), 98–104.

83. Stewart, "Three Rules for Managing in the Real-Time Economy."

84. Crockett, "A New Company Called Motorola."

Chapter 8
Change and Development

1. Ilan Mochari, "Climbing Back Up," *Inc.* (March 1, 2002), 92–100; "Ladder Inventors Win Design Case," *The New York Times* (August 19, 2001), 1.

2. George Anders, "Hard Cell," *Fast Company* (May 2001), 108–122.

3. Stuart F. Brown, "The Automaker's Big-Time Bet on Fuel Cells," *Fortune* (March 30, 1998), 122(B)–122(D); and Geeta Anand, "Inventor Struggles to Breathe Life Into Cancer Vaccine," *The Wall Street Journal* (May 22, 2001), B1, B4.

4. Richard L. Daft, "Bureaucratic vs. Nonbureaucratic Structure in the Process of Innovation and Change," in *Perspectives in Organizational Sociology: Theory and Research,* ed. Samuel B. Bacharach (Greenwich, Conn.: JAI Press, 1982), 129–166.

5. This discussion is based on Richard L. Daft, *Organization Theory and Design,* 5th ed. (St. Paul, Minn.: West, 1995); and Don Hellriegel and John W. Slocum, Jr., *Management,* 7th ed. (Cincinnati, Ohio: South-Western, 1996).

6. Tom Broersma, "In Search of the Future," *Training and Development* (January 1995), 38–43.

7. Andre L. Delbecq and Peter K. Mills, "Managerial Practices That Enhance Innovation," *Organizational Dynamics* 14 (Summer 1985), 24–34.

8. Paul M. Barrett, "A Once-Stodgy Firm Makes a Flashy Return, But at What Cost?" *The Wall Street Journal* (August 17, 1998), A1, A6.

9. Carol Hymowitz, "Managing in a Crisis Can Bring Better Ways to Conduct Business" (In the Lead column), *The Wall Street Journal* (October 23, 2001), B1.

10. John P. Kotter, *Leading Change* (Boston: Harvard University Press, 1996), 20–25; and "Leading Change: Why Transformation Efforts Fail," *Harvard Business Review* (March–April, 1995), 59–67.

11. Almar Latour, "Trial by Fire: A Blaze in Albuquerque Sets Off Major Crisis for Cell-Phone Giants," *The Wall Street Journal* (January 29, 2001), A1, A8.

12. Attributed to Gregory Bateson in Andrew H. Van de Ven, "Central Problems in the Management of Innovation," *Management Science* 32 (1986), 595.

13. Teresa M. Amabile, "Motivating Creativity in Organizations: On Doing What You Love and Loving What You Do," *California Management Review* 40, no. 1 (Fall 1997), 39–58; and Timothy A. Matherly and Ronald E. Goldsmith, "The Two Faces of Creativity," *Business Horizons* (September/October 1985), 8.

14. Gordon Vessels, "The Creative Process: An Open-Systems Conceptualization," *Journal of Creative Behavior* 16 (1982), 185–196.

15. Robert J. Sternberg, Linda A. O'Hara, and Todd I. Lubart, "Creativity as Investment," *California Management Review* 40, no. 1 (Fall 1997), 8–21; Teresa M. Amabile, "Motivating Creativity in Organizations"; and Ken Lizotte, "A Creative State of Mind," *Management Review* (May 1998), 15–17.

16. James Brian Quinn, "Managing Innovation: Controlled Chaos," *Harvard Business Review* 63 (May–June 1985), 73–84; Howard H. Stevenson and David E. Gumpert, "The Heart of Entrepreneurship," *Harvard Business Review* 63 (March–April 1985),

85–94; and Marsha Sinetar, "Entrepreneurs, Chaos, and Creativity—Can Creative People Really Survive Large Company Structure?" *Sloan Management Review* 6 (Winter 1985), 57–62.

17. Cynthia Browne, "Jest for Success," *Moonbeams* (August 1989), 3–5; and Rosabeth Moss Kanter, *The Change Masters* (New York: Simon and Schuster, 1983).

18. Cathy Olofson, "Play Hard, Think Big," *Fast Company* (January 2001), 64.

19. "Hands On: A Manager's Notebook," *Inc.* (January 1989), 106.

20. Robert I. Sutton, "The Weird Rules of Creativity," *Harvard Business Review* (September 2001), 94–103.

21. Katy Koontz, "How to Stand Out from the Crowd," *Working Woman* (January 1988), 74–76.

22. Anders, "Hard Cell."

23. Sutton, "The Weird Rules of Creativity."

24. C. K. Bart, "New Venture Units: Use Them Wisely to Manage Innovation," *Sloan Management Review* (Summer 1988), 35–43; and Michael Tushman and David Nadler, "Organizing for Innovation," *California Management Review* 28 (Spring 1986), 74–92.

25. Peter F. Drucker, *Innovation and Entrepreneurship* (New York: Harper & Row, 1985).

26. Christopher Hoenig, "Skunk Works Secrets," *CIO* (July 1, 2000), 74–76; and Tom Peters and Nancy Austin, *A Passion for Excellence: The Leadership Difference* (New York: Random House, 1985).

27. Hoenig, "Skunk Works Secrets."

28. Sutton, "The Weird Rules of Creativity."

29. Eng, "Hatching Schemes."

30. Ibid.

31. J. P. Kotter and L. A. Schlesinger, "Choosing Strategies for Change," *Harvard Business Review* 57 (March–April 1979), 106–114.

32. James McNair, "Workers Take Case to Federated," *Cincinnati Enquirer* (February 9, 2002), B1.

33. G. Zaltman and Robert B. Duncan, *Strategies for Planned Change* (New York: Wiley Interscience, 1977).

34. Leonard M. Apcar, "Middle Managers and Supervisors Resist Moves to More Participatory Management," *The Wall Street Journal* (September 16, 1985), 25.

35. Dorothy Leonard-Barton and Isabelle Deschamps, "Managerial Influence in the Implementation of New Technology," *Management Science* 34 (1988), 1252–1265.

36. Kurt Lewin, *Field Theory in Social Science: Selected Theoretical Papers* (New York: Harper & Brothers, 1951).

37. Paul C. Nutt, "Tactics of Implementation," *Academy of Management Journal* 29 (1986), 230–261; Kotter and Schlesinger, "Choosing Strategies"; R. L. Daft and S. Becker, *Innovation in Organizations: Innovation Adoption in School Organizations* (New York: Elsevier, 1978); and R. Beckhard, *Organization Development: Strategies and Models* (Reading, Mass.: Addison-Wesley, 1969).

38. Rob Muller, "Training for Change," *Canadian Business Review* (Spring 1995), 16–19.

39. Taggart F. Frost, "Creating a Teamwork-Based Culture within a Manufacturing Setting," *IM* (May–June 1994), 17–20.

40. Dean Foust with Gerry Khermouch, "Repairing the Coke Machine," *Business Week* (March 19, 2001), 86–88.

41. Jeremy Main, "The Trouble with Managing Japanese-Style," *Fortune* (April 2, 1984), 50–56.

42. J. Hyatt, "Guaranteed Growth," *Inc.* (September 1995), 69–78.

43. Daft, *Organization Theory and Design*; and Tom Burns and G. M. Stalker, *The Management of Innovation* (London: Tavistock Publications, 1961).

44. Thomas Petzinger, Jr., "The Front Lines: Bread Store Chain Tells Its Franchisees: Do Your Own Thing," *The Wall Street Journal* (November 21, 1997), B1.

45. Harold J. Leavitt, "Applied Organizational Change in Industry: Structural, Technical, and Human Approaches," in *New Perspectives in Organization Research,* ed. W. W. Cooper, H. J. Leavitt, and M. W. Shelly II (New York: Wiley, 1964), 55–74.

46. Glenn Rifkin, "Competing through Innovation: The Case of Broderbund," *Strategy & Business Issue* 11 (Second Quarter, 1998), 48–58; and Deborah Dougherty and Cynthia Hardy, "Sustained Product Innovation in Large, Mature Organizations: Overcoming Innovation-to-Organization Problems," *Academy of Management Journal* 39, no. 5 (1996), 1120–1153.

47. Robert McMath, *What Were They Thinking? Marketing Lessons I've Learned from Over 80,000 New Product Innovations and Idiocies* (New York: Times Business, 1998); Paul Lukas, "The Ghastliest Product Launches," *Fortune* (March 16, 1998), 44.

48. Melissa A. Schilling and Charles W. L. Hill, "Managing the New Product Development Process," *Academy of Management Executive* 12, no. 3 (1998), 67–81.

49. Andrew H. Van de Ven, "Central Problems in the Management of Innovation," *Management Science* 32 (1986), 590–607; Daft, *Organization Theory;* and Science Policy Research Unit, University of Sussex, *Success and Failure in Industrial Innovation* (London: Centre for the Study of Industrial Innovation, 1972).

50. William L. Shanklin and John K. Ryans, Jr., "Organizing for High-Tech Marketing," *Harvard Business Review* 62 (November–December 1984), 164–171; and Arnold O. Putnam, "A Redesign for Engineering," *Harvard Business Review* 63 (May–June 1985), 139–144.

51. Faith Keenan, "Opening the Spigot," *Business Week E.biz* (June 4, 2001), EB17–EB20.

52. Susan Caminiti, "A Quiet Superstar Rises in Retailing," *Fortune* (October 23, 1989), 167–174.

53. Fariborz Damanpour, "The Adoption of Technological, Administrative, and Ancillary Innovations: Impact of Organizational Factors," *Journal of Management* 13 (1987), 675–688.

54. McGee, M. K. "Lessons from a Cultural Revolution." *Information Week,* Oct. 25, 1999, pp. 46–53.

55. Daft, "Bureaucratic vs. Nonbureaucratic Structure."

56. Nanette Byrnes, "Avon: The New Calling," *Business Week* (September 18, 2000), 136–148; and Katrina Brooker, "It Took a Lady to Save Avon," *Fortune* (October 15, 2001), 203–208.

57. E. H. Schein, "Organizational Culture," *American Psychologist* 45 (February 1990), 109–119; and A. Kupfer, "An Outsider Fires Up a Railroad," *Fortune* (December 18, 1989), 133–146.

58. Michelle Conlin, "Tough Love for Techie Souls," *Business Week* (November 29, 1999), 164–170.

59. M. Sashkin and W. W. Burke, "Organizational Development in the 1980s," *General Management* 13 (1987), 393–417; and Richard Beckhard, "What Is Organization Development?" in *Organization Development and Transformation: Managing*

Effective Change, Wendell L. French, Cecil H. Bell, Jr., and Robert A. Zawacki, eds. (Burr Ridge, Ill.: Irwin McGraw-Hill, 2000), 16–19.

60. Wendell L. French and Cecil H. Bell, Jr., "A History of Organizational Development," in French, Bell, and Zawacki, *Organization Development and Transformation,* 20–42.

61. Paul F. Buller, "For Successful Strategic Change: Blend OD Practices with Strategic Management," *Organizational Dynamics* (Winter 1988), 42–55; and Robert M. Fulmer and Roderick Gilkey, "Blending Corporate Families: Management and Organization Development in a Postmerger Environment," *The Academy of Management Executive* 2 (1988), 275–283.

62. W. Warner Burke, "The New Agenda for Organizational Development," *Organizational Dynamics* (Summer 1997), 7–19.

63. This discussion is based on Kathleen D. Dannemiller and Robert W. Jacobs, "Changing the Way Organizations Change: A Revolution of Common Sense," *The Journal of Applied Behavioral Science* 28, no. 4 (December 1992), 480–498; and Barbara Benedict Bunker and Billie T. Alban, "Conclusion: What Makes Large Group Interventions Effective?" *The Journal of Applied Behavioral Science* 28, no. 4 (December 1992), 570–591.

64. Bunker and Alban, "What Makes Large Group Interventions Effective?"

65. J. Quinn, "What a Work-Out!" *Performance* (November 1994), 58–63; and B. B. Bunker and B. T. Alban, "Conclusion: What Makes Large Group Interventions Effective?" *The Journal of Applied Behavioral Science* 28, no. 4 (December 1992), 572–591.

66. Thomas Petzinger Jr., *The New Pioneers: The Men and Women Who Are Transforming the Workplace and the Marketplace* (New York: Simon & Schuster, 1999), 27–32.

67. Kurt Lewin, "Frontiers in Group Dynamics: Concepts, Method, and Reality in Social Science," *Human Relations* 1 (1947), 5–41; and E. F. Huse and T. G. Cummings, *Organization Development and Change.* St. Paul: West Publishing, 1985.

68. Carol Lavin Bernick, "When Your Culture Needs a Makeover," *Harvard Business Review* (June 2001), 53–61.

69. Based on John Kotter's eight-step model of planned change, which is described in John Kotter, *Leading Change* (Boston: Harvard Business School Press, 1996), 20–25, and "Leading Change: Why Transformation Efforts Fail," *Harvard Business Review* (March–April, 1995), 59-67.

70. Mochari, "Climbing Back Up"; "Ladder Inventors Win Design Case," *New York Times* (August 19, 2001), 1.

Chapter 9

Human Resource Management

1. Joyce Gannon, "Hash Out Succession Plans for Family Business before There's a Crisis," *Knight Ridder Tribune Business News* (March 30, 2002), 1; Ray Marano, "When Employees Come First," *Small Business News* (February 1, 1999), 14.

2. Robert L. Mathis and John H. Jackson, *Human Resource Management: Essential Perspectives,* 2nd ed. (Cincinnati, Ohio: South-Western Publishing, 2002), 1.

3. Jonathan Poet, "Schools Looking Overseas for Teachers," *Johnson City Press* (April 20, 2001), 6; and Jill Rosenfeld, "How's This for a Tough Assignment?" *Fast Company* (November 1999), 104–106.

4. Mark A. Huselid, Susan E. Jackson, and Randall S. Schuler, "Technical and Strategic Human Resource Management Effectiveness as Determinants of Firm Performance," *Academy of Management Journal* 40, no. 1 (1997), 171–188; and John T. Delaney and Mark A. Huselid, "The Impact of Human Resource Management Practices on Perceptions of Organizational Performance," *Academy of Management Journal* 39, no. 4 (1996), 949–969.

5. D. Kneale, "Working at IBM: Intense Loyalty in a Rigid Culture," *The Wall Street Journal* (April 7, 1986), 17.

6. Jeffrey Pfeffer, "Producing Sustainable Competitive Advantage through the Effective Management of People," *Academy of Management Executive* 9, no. 1 (1995), 55–72.

7. James N. Baron and David M. Kreps, "Consistent Human Resource Practices," *California Management Review* 41, no. 3 (Spring 1999), 29–53.

8. Cynthia D. Fisher, "Current and Recurrent Challenges in HRM," *Journal of Management* 15 (1989), 157–180.

9. See Dave Ulrich, "A New Mandate for Human Resources," *Harvard Business Review* (January–February 1998), 124–134; Philip H. Mirvis, "Human Resource Management: Leaders, Laggards, and Followers," *Academy of Management Executive* 11, no. 2 (1997), 43–56; Richard McBain, "Attracting, Retaining, and Motivating Capable People," *Manager Update* (Winter 1999), 25–36; and Oren Harari, "Attracting the Best Minds," *Management Review* (April 1998), 23–26.

10. Floyd Kemske, "HR 2008: A Forecast Based on Our Exclusive Study," *Workforce* (January 1998), 46–60.

11. This definition and discussion is based on George Bollander, Scott Snell, and Arthur Sherman, *Managing Human Resources* 12th ed. (Cincinnati, Ohio: South-Western Publishing, 2001), 13–15.

12. Jennifer J. Laabs, "It's OK to Focus on Heart and Soul," *Workforce* (January 1997), 60–69.

13. Judith Neal, personal communication, June 2002.

14. Rich Wellins and Sheila Rioux, "The Growing Pains of Globalizing HR," *Training and Development* (May 2000), 79–85.

15. Ibid.

16. Alison Stein Wellner, "Click Here for HR," *Business Week Frontier* (April 24, 2000), F24–F26; and Esther Shein, "Requiem for a Paperweight," *eCFO* (Winter 2000), 81–83.

17. Deidre A. Depke, "Picking Up the Tab for Bias at Shoney's," *Business Week* (November 6, 1992), 50.

18. Section 1604.1 of the EEOC Guidelines based on the Civil Rights Act of 1964, Title VII.

19. Brigid McMenamin, "Payroll Paternalism," *Fortune* (April 16, 2001), 114–120.

20. Charles F. Falk and Kathleen A. Carlson, "Newer Patterns in Management for the Post–Social Contract Era," *Midwest Management Society Proceedings* (1995), 45–52.

21. Richard Pascale, "The False Security of 'Employability,'" *Fast Company* (April–May 1996), 62, 64; and Louisa Wah, "The New Workplace Paradox," *Management Review* (January 1998), 7.

22. Douglas T. Hall and Jonathan E. Moss, "The New Protean Career Contract: Helping Organizations and Employees Adapt," *Organizational Dynamics* (Winter 1998), 22–37.

23. Wal-Mart employee data from "Inside the Fortune 500: How the Companies Stack Up," *Fortune* (April 16, 2001), F29–F32.

24. The discussion of temporary employment agencies is based on David Wessel, "Capital: Temp Workers Have a Lasting Effect," *The Wall Street Journal* (February 1, 2001), A1.

25. Brenda Paik Sunoo, "Temp Firms Turn Up the Heat on Hiring," *Workforce* (April 1999), 50–54.

26. Hall and Moss, "The New Protean Career Contract," and John Challenger, "There Is No Future for the Workplace," *Public Management* (February 1999), 20–23.

27. Jaclyn Fierman, "The Contingency Workforce," *Fortune* (January 24, 1994), 30–31.

28. Nancy B. Kurland and Diane E. Bailey, "Telework: The Advantages and Challenges of Working Here, There, Anywhere, Anytime," *Organizational Dynamics* (Autumn 1999), 53–68.

29. Kevin Voigt, "For 'Extreme Telecommuters,' Remote Work Means Really Remote," *The Wall Street Journal* (January 31, 2001), B1.

30. Ibid.

31. Challenger, "There Is No Future for the Workplace."

32. Sean Donahue, "New Jobs for the New Economy," *Business 2.0* (July 1999), 102–109.

33. James G. March and Herbert A. Simon, *Organizations* (New York: Wiley, 1958).

34. Richard McBain, "Attracting, Retaining, and Motivating Capable People: A Key to Competitive Advantage," *Manager Update* (Winter 1999), 25–36.

35. Dennis J. Kravetz, *The Human Resources Revolution* (San Francisco, Calif.: Jossey-Bass, 1989).

36. David E. Ripley, "How to Determine Future Workforce Needs," *Personnel Journal* (January 1995), 83–89.

37. J. W. Boudreau and S. L. Rynes, "Role of Recruitment in Staffing Utility Analysis," *Journal of Applied Psychology* 70 (1985), 354–366.

38. Brian Dumaine, "The New Art of Hiring Smart," *Fortune* (August 17, 1987), 78–81.

39. This discussion is based on Mathis and Jackson, *Human Resource Management*, Chapter 4, 49–60.

40. Victoria Griffith, "When Only Internal Expertise Will Do," *CFO* (October 1998), 95–96, 102.

41. J. P. Wanous, *Organizational Entry* (Reading, Mass.: Addison-Wesley, 1980).

42. Samuel Greengard, "Technology Finally Advances HR," *Workforce* (January 2000), 38–41; and Scott Hays, "Hiring on the Web," *Workforce* (August 1999), 77–84.

43. Marlene Piturro, "The Power of E-Cruiting," *Management Review* (January 2000), 33–37.

44. Jerry Useem, "For Sale Online: You," *Fortune* (July 5, 1999), 67–78.

45. George Bohlander, Scott Snell, and Arthur Sherman, *Managing Human Resources*, 12th ed. (Cincinnati, Ohio: South-Western College Publishing, 2001), 145.

46. Kathryn Tyler, "Employees Can Help Recruit New Talent," *HR Magazine* (September 1996), 57–60.

47. Carol Leonetti Dannhauser, "Putting the Ooh in Recruiting," *Working Woman* (March 2000), 32–34.

48. Ann Harrington, "Anybody Here Want a Job?" *Fortune* (May 15, 2000), 489–498.

49. "Bank of America to Hire 850 Ex-Welfare Recipients," *Johnson City Press* (January 14, 2001), 29.

50. E. Blacharczyk, "Recruiters Challenged by Economy, Shortages, Unskilled," *HRNews* (February 1990), B1.

51. Victoria Rivkin, "Visa Relief," *Working Woman* (January 2001), 15.

52. P. W. Thayer, "Somethings Old, Somethings New," *Personnel Psychology* 30 (1977), 513–524.

53. J. Ledvinka, *Federal Regulation of Personnel and Human Resource Management* (Boston: Kent, 1982); and Civil Rights Act, Title VII, 42 U.S.C. Section 2000e et seq. (1964).

54. Bohlander, Snell, and Sherman, *Managing Human Resources*, 202.

55. Ibid.

56. "Assessment Centers: Identifying Leadership through Testing," *Small Business Report* (June 1987), 22–24; and W. C. Byham, "Assessment Centers for Spotting Future Managers," *Harvard Business Review* (July–August 1970), 150–167.

57. Mike Thatcher, "'Front-line' Staff Selected by Assessment Center," *Personnel Management* (November 1993), 83.

58. Bernard Keys and Joseph Wolfe, "Management Education and Development: Current Issues and Emerging Trends," *Journal of Management* 14 (1988), 205–229.

59. William J. Rothwell and H. C. Kazanas, *Improving On-The-Job Training: How to Establish and Operate a Comprehensive OJT Program* (San Francisco, Calif.: Jossey-Bass, 1994).

60. Matt Murray, "GE Mentoring Program Turns Underlings into Teachers of the Web," *The Wall Street Journal* (February 15, 2000), B1, B16.

61. Jeanne C. Meister, "The Brave New World of Corporate Education," *The Chronicle of Higher Education* (February 9, 2001), B10–B11.

62. Meister, "The Brave New World of Corporate Education"; and Meryl Davids Landau, "Corporate Universities Crack Open Their Doors," *The Journal of Business Strategy* (May–June 2000), 18–23.

63. John Byrne, "The Search for the Young and Gifted," *Business Week* (October 4, 1999), 108–116.

64. Eileen M. Garger, "Goodbye Training, Hello Learning," *Workforce* (November 1999), 35–42.

65. Ibid.

66. Walter W. Tornow, "Editor's Note: Introduction to Special Issue on 360-Degree Feedback," *Human Resource Management* 32, no. 2/3 (Summer/Fall 1993), 211–219; and Brian O'Reilly, "360 Feedback Can Change Your Life," *Fortune* (October 17, 1994), 93–100.

67. Kris Frieswick, "Truth & Consequences," *CFO* (June 2001), 56–63.

68. Carol A. L. Dannhauser, "How'm I Doing?" *Working Woman* (December–January 1999), 38.

69. This discussion is based on Matthew Boyle, "Performance Reviews: Perilous Curves Ahead," *Fortune* (May 28, 2001), 187–188; Carol Hymowitz, "Ranking Systems Gain Popularity

But Have Many Staffers Riled" (In the Lead column), *The Wall Street Journal* (May 15, 2001), B1; and Frieswick, "Truth & Consequences."

70. Boyle, "Performance Reviews."

71. Hymowitz, "Ranking Systems Gain Popularity," and Boyle, "Performance Reviews."

72. V. R. Buzzotta, "Improve Your Performance Appraisals," *Management Review* (August 1988), 40–43; and H. J. Bernardin and R. W. Beatty, *Performance Appraisal: Assessing Human Behavior at Work* (Boston: Kent, 1984).

73. Ibid.

74. Richard I. Henderson, *Compensation Management: Rewarding Performance,* 4th ed. (Reston, Va.: Reston, 1985).

75. L. R. Gomez-Mejia, "Structure and Process Diversification, Compensation Strategy, and Firm Performance," *Strategic Management Journal* 13 (1992), 381–397; and E. Montemayor, "Congruence Between Pay Policy and Competitive Strategy in High-Performing Firms," *Journal of Management* 22, no. 6 (1996), 889–908.

76. Renée F. Broderick and George T. Milkovich, "Pay Planning, Organization Strategy, Structure and 'Fit': A Prescriptive Model of Pay" (paper presented at the 45th Annual Meeting of the Academy of Management, San Diego, August 1985).

77. E. F. Lawler, III, *Strategic Pay: Aligning Organizational Strategies and Pay Systems* (San Francisco: Jossey-Bass, 1990); and R. J. Greene, "Person-Focused Pay: Should It Replace Job-Based Pay?" *Compensation and Benefits Management* 9, no. 4 (1993), 46–55.

78. L. Wiener, "No New Skills? No Raise," *U.S. News and World Report* (October 26, 1992), 78.

79. Data from Hewitt Associates, Bureau or Labor Statistics, reported in Michelle Conlin and Peter Coy, with Ann Therese Palmer, and Gabrielle Saveri, "The Wild New Workforce," *Business Week* (December 6, 1999), 39–44.

80. *Employee Benefits,* 1997 (Washington, D.C.: U. S. Chamber of Commerce, 1997), 7.

81. Frank E. Kuzmits, "Communicating Benefits: A Double-Click Away," *Compensation and Benefits Review* 30, no. 5 (September–October 1998), 60–64; and Lynn Asinof, "Click and Shift: Workers Control Their Benefits Online," *The Wall Street Journal* (November 27, 1997), C1.

82. Robert S. Catapano-Friedman, "Cafeteria Plans: New Menu for the '90s," *Management Review* (November 1991), 25–29.

83. "Exit Interviews: An Overlooked Information Source," *Small Business Report* (July 1986), 52–55.

84. Yvette Debow, "GE: Easing the Pain of Layoffs," *Management Review* (September 1997), 15–18.

85. "In contact," *Naval History* (October 2001), 8; Greg Jaffe, "After the Ax Falls, A Plant's Workers find Good News in the Bad," *The Wall Street Journal* (November 30, 1999), A1 + A6.

86. Gannon, "Hash Out Succession Plans for Family Business Before There's a Crisis"; 1; Ray Marano, "When Employees Come First," *Small Business News* (February 1, 1999), 14.

Chapter 10
Managing Diverse Employees

1. Kenneth Labich, "No More Crude at Texaco," *Fortune* (September 6, 1999), 205–212.

2. Aaron Bernstein with Michael Arndt, "Racism in the Workplace," *Business Week* (July 30, 2001); Reed Abelson, "Can Respect Be Mandated? Maybe Not Here," *The New York Times* (September 10, 2000), BU1.

3. M. Fine, F. Johnson, and M. S. Ryan, "Cultural Diversity in the Workforce," *Public Personnel Management* 19 (1990), 305–319.

4. Taylor H. Cox, "Managing Cultural Diversity: Implications for Organizational Competitiveness," *Academy of Management Executive* 5, no. 3 (1991), 45–56; and Faye Rice, "How to Make Diversity Pay," *Fortune* (August 8, 1994), 78–86.

5. G. Pascal Zachary, "Mighty Is the Mongrel," *Fast Company* (July 2000), 270–284.

6. Reported in "Keeping Your Edge: Managing a Diverse Corporate Culture," Special Advertising Section, *Fortune* (June 3, 2001).

7. Roy Harris, "The Illusion of Inclusion," *CFO* (May 2001), 42–50.

8. "Keeping Your Edge."

9. "Valuing Diversity, Part I: Making the Most of Cultural Differences at the Workplace," *Personnel* (June 1988), 52–60.

10. Lennie Copeland, "Learning to Manage a Multicultural Workforce," *Training* (May 25, 1988), 48–56; and D. Farid Elashmawi, "Culture Clashes: Barriers to Business," *Managing Diversity* 2, no. 11 (August 1993), 1–3.

11. Marilyn Loden and Judy B. Rosener, *Workforce America!* (Homewood, Ill.: Business One Irwin, 1991); and Marilyn Loden, *Implementing Diversity* (Homewood, Ill.: Irwin, 1996).

12. N. Songer, "Workforce Diversity," *B&E Review* (April–June 1991), 3–6.

13. Robert Doktor, Rosalie Tung, and Mary Ann von Glinow, "Future Directions for Management Theory Development," *Academy of Management Review* 16 (1991), 362–365; and Mary Munter, "Cross-Cultural Communication for Managers," *Business Horizons* (May–June 1993), 69–78.

14. Renee Blank and Sandra Slipp, "The White Male: An Endangered Species?" *Management Review* (September 1994), 27–32; Michael S. Kimmel, "What Do Men Want?" *Harvard Business Review* (November–December 1993), 50–63; and Sharon Nelton, "Nurturing Diversity," *Nation's Business* (June 1995), 25–27.

15. M. Bennett, "A Developmental Approach to Training for Intercultural Sensitivity," *International Journal of Intercultural Relations* 10 (1986), 179–196.

16. Keith H. Hammonds, "Difference Is Power," *Fast Company* (July 2000), 258–266.

17. Vanessa J. Weaver, "What These CEOs and Their Companies Know about Diversity," in "Winning with Diversity," special advertising section, *Business Week* (September 10, 2001).

18. C. Keen, "Human Resource Management Issues in the '90s," *Vital Speeches* 56, no. 24 (1990), 752–754.

19. Zachary, "Mighty Is the Mongrel."

20. "Keeping Your Edge"; Steven Greenhouse, N.Y. Times News Service, "Influx of Immigrants Having Profound Impact on

Economy," *Johnson City Press* (September 4, 2000), 9; Richard W. Judy and Carol D'Amico, *Workforce 2020: Work and Workers in the 21st Century* (Indianapolis, Ind.: Hudson Institute, 1997).

21. Stephanie N. Mehta, "What Minority Employees Really Want," *Fortune* (June 10, 2000), 181–186.

22. Harris, "The Illusion of Inclusion."

23. Mehta, "What Minority Employees Really Want."

24. Robert Hooijberg and Nancy DiTomaso, "Leadership In and Of Demographically Diverse Organizations," *Leadership Quarterly* 7, no. 1 (1996): 1–19.

25. Harris, "The Illusion of Inclusion."

26. Copeland, "Valuing Diversity, Part I: Making the Most of Cultural Differences at the Workplace"; and Judy and D'Amico, *Workforce 2020;* and S. Hutchins, Jr., "Preparing for Diversity: The Year 2000," *Quality Process* 22, no. 10 (1989), 66–68.

27. Leon E. Wynter, "Allstate Rates Managers on Handling Diversity," *The Wall Street Journal* (Business and Race column) (October 1, 1997), B1; Louisa Wah, "Diversity at Allstate: A Competitive Weapon," *Management Review* (July–August 1999), 24–30; Joan Crockett, "Diversity: Winning Competitive Advantage through a Diverse Workforce," *HR Focus* (May 1999), 9–10; and Joan Crockett, "Diversity as a Business Strategy," *Management Review* (May 1999), 62.

28. Roosevelt Thomas, Jr., "From Affirmative Action to Affirming Diversity," *Harvard Business Review* (March–April 1990), 107–117; and Nicholas Lemann, "Taking Affirmative Action Apart," *The New York Times Magazine* (July 11, 1995), 36–43.

29. Madeline E. Heilman, Caryn J. Block, and Peter Stathatos, "The Affirmative Action Stigma of Incompetence: Effects of Performance Information Ambiguity," *Academy of Management Journal* 40, no. 1 (1997), 603–625.

30. Robert J. Grossman, "Is Diversity Working?" *HR Magazine* (March 2000), 47–50.

31. Cora Daniels, "Too Devout for Our Own Good?" *Fortune* (July 9, 2001), 116.

32. Jack Gordon, "Different from What? Diversity as a Performance Issue," (Training) May 1995, 25–33; and Leon E. Wynter, "Diversity Is Often All Talk, No Affirmative Action," *The Wall Street Journal* (December 21, 1994), B1.

33. "Keeping Your Edge."

34. Annie Finnigan, "Different Strokes," *Working Woman* (April 2001), 42–48.

35. Debra E. Meyerson and Joyce K. Fletcher, "A Modest Manifesto for Shattering the Glass Ceiling," *Harvard Business Review* (January–February 2000), 127–136; Finnegan, "Different Strokes."

36. "The Wage Gap," National Women's Law Center, *http://www. infoplease.com,* The Learning Network, 2001.

37. Deborah L. Jacobs, "Back from the Mommy Track," *The New York Times* (October 9, 1994), F1, F6; Lisa Cullen, "Apple Pie, My Eye," *Working Woman* (May–June 2001), 19–20; and Michelle Conlin, "The New Debate Over Working Moms," *Business Week* (September 18, 2000), 102–104.

38. Cullen, "Apple Pie, My Eye"; and Ann Crittenden, *The Price of Motherhood* (New York: Metropolitan Books, 2001).

39. Barbara Presley Noble, "A Quiet Liberation for Gay and Lesbian Employees," *The New York Times* (June 13, 1993), F4.

40. "Diversity in the New Millennium," special advertising section, *Working Woman* (March 2000).

41. C. Soloman, "Careers under Glass," *Personnel Journal* 69, no. 4 (1990), 96–105.

42. Belle Rose Ragins, Bickley Townsend, and Mary Mattis, "Gender Gap in the Executive Suite: CEOs and Female Executives Report on Breaking the Glass Ceiling," *Academy of Management Executive* 12, no. 1 (1998), 28–42.

43. Julie Amparano Lopez, "Study Says Women Face Glass Walls as Well as Ceilings," *The Wall Street Journal* (March 3, 1992), B1, B2; and Ida L. Castro, "Q: Should Women Be Worried About the Glass Ceiling in the Workplace?" *Insight* (February 10, 1997), 24–27; Meyerson and Fletcher, "A Modest Manifesto for Shattering the Glass Ceiling."

44. Sheila Wellington with Betty Spence, *Be Your Own Mentor: Strategies from Top Women on the Secrets of Success* (New York: Random House, 2001).

45. Anne B. Fisher, "When Will Women Get to the Top?" *Fortune* (September 21, 1992), 44–56.

46. Finnigan, "Different Strokes."

47. Mark Schilder, *http://www.pphq.net/forums/viewthread.php? tid=361,* accessed 12/4/2002; Sara Lyle, "Goosehead Guide to Life," *YM* (August 2001), 60; Jennifer Pendelton, "Web Site for Girls Turns Creator into Top Executive at 15," *Los Angeles Times* (July 25, 2000), 4.

48. Abelson, "Can Respect Be Mandated?"

49. Jacqueline A. Gilbert and John M. Ivancevich, "Valuing Diversity: A Tale of Two Organizations," *Academy of Management Executive* 14, no. 1 (2000), 93–105; and Weaver, "What These CEOs and Their Companies Know about Diversity."

50. Copeland, "Learning to Manage a Multicultural Workforce."

51. Geber, "Managing Diversity," *Training* 27, no. 7 (1990), 23–30.

52. Reported in "Strength Through Diversity for Bottom-Line Success," special advertising section, *Working Woman* (March 1999).

53. Finnigan, "Different Strokes."

54. "Diversity in a Affiliated Company," in Vanessa J. Weaver, "Winning with Diverity," special advertising section, *Business Week* (September 10, 2001).

55. B. Ragins, "Barriers to Mentoring: The Female Manager's Dilemma," *Human Relations* 42, no. 1 (1989), 1–22; and Ragins et al., Gender Gap in the Executive Suite."

56. David A. Thomas, "The Truth about Mentoring Minorities—Race Matters," *Harvard Business Review* (April 2001), 99–107.

57. Mary Zey, "A Mentor for All," *Personnel Journal* (January 1988), 46–51.

58. "Keeping Your Edge."

59. "Ernst & Young LLP: An Aggressive Approach," in "Diversity Today: Developing and Retaining the Best Corporate Talent," special advertising section, *Fortune* (June 21, 1999); and Leveraging Diversity: Opportunities in the New Market," Part III of "Diversity: The Bottom Line," special advertising section, *Forbes* (November 13, 2000).

60. J. Black and M. Mendenhall, "Cross-Cultural Training Effectiveness: A Review and a Theoretical Framework for Future Research," *Academy of Management Review* 15 (1990), 113–136.

61. E. G. Collins, "Managers and Lovers," *Harvard Business Review* 61 (1983), 142–153.

62. Sharon A. Lobel, Robert E. Quinn, Lynda St. Clair, and Andrea Warfield, "Love without Sex: The Impact of Psychological Intimacy between Men and Women at Work," *Organizational Dynamics* (Summer 1994), 5–16.

63. William C. Symonds with Steve Hamm and Gail DeGeorge, "Sex on the Job," *Business Week* (February 16, 1998), 30–31.

64. Carol Hymowitz and Ellen Joan Pollock, "The One Clear Line in Interoffice Romance Has Become Blurred," *The Wall Street Journal* (February 4, 1998), A1, A8.

65. Linda Bryant and Paul DeWitt, "Romance in the Workplace" *The Tennessean* (May 31, 2002), E1–E2; "Few Employers Have Workplace Romance Policies: SHRM Survey," *HR Focus* (April 2002), 9.

66. "Sexual Harassment: Vanderbilt University Policy." Nashville: Vanderbilt University, 1993.

67. Joanne Cole, "Sexual Harassment: New Rules, New Behavior," *HR Focus* (March 1999), 1, 14–15. Also see EEOC charge complaints at *http://www.eeoc.gov*.

68. Jack Corcoran, "Of Nice and Men," *Success* (June 1998), 65–67.

69. Barbara Carton, "At Jenny Craig, Men Are Ones Who Claim Sex Discrimination," *The Wall Street Journal* (November 29, 1994), A1, A11.

70. Jennifer J. Laabs, "Sexual Harassment: HR Puts Its Questions on the Line," *Personnel Journal* (February 1995), 35–45; Sharon Nelton, "Sexual Harassment: Reducing the Risks," *Nation's Business*, March 1995, 24–26; and Gary Baseman, "Sexual Harassment: The Inside Story," *Working Woman* (June 1992), 47–51, 78.

71. Judy and D'Amico, *Workforce 2020.*

72. Joann S. Lublin, "Companies Use Cross-Cultural Training to Help Their Employees Adjust Abroad," *The Wall Street Journal* (August 4, 1992), B1, B9.

73. "Leveraging Diversity."

74. Gilbert Fuchsberg, "As Costs of Overseas Assignments Climb, Firms Select Expatriates More Carefully," *The Wall Street Journal* (January 9, 1992), B3, B4.

75. J. Kennedy and A. Everest, "Put Diversity in Context," *Personnel Journal* (September 1991), 50–54.

76. "Impact of Diversity Initiatives on the Bottom Line: A SHRM Survey of the Fortune 1000," pp. S12–S14, in *Fortune,* special advertising section, "Keeping Your Edge: Managing a Diverse Corporate Culture," produced in association with the Society for Human Resource Management.

77. Joseph J. Distefano and Martha L. Maznevski, "Creating Value with Diverse Teams in Global Management," *Organizational Dynamics* 29, no. 1 (Summer 2000), 45–63; and Finnigan, "Different Strokes."

78. W. E. Watson, K. Kumar, and L. K. Michaelsen, "Cultural Diversity's Impact on Interaction Process and Performance: Comparing Homogeneous and Diverse Task Groups," *Academy of Management Journal* 36 (1993), 590–602; G. Robinson and K. Dechant, "Building a Business Case for Diversity," *Academy of Management Executive* 11, no. 3 (1997), 21–31; and D. A. Thomas and R. J. Ely, "Making Differences Matter: A New Paradigm for Managing Diversity," *Harvard Business Review* (September–October 1996), 79–90.

79. Marc Hequet, Chris Lee, Michele Picard, and David Stamps, "Teams Get Global," *Training* (December 1996), 16–17.

80. Chiori Santiago, "Culture Club," *Working Woman* (April 2001), 46–47, 78.

81. Lionel Laroche, "Teaming Up," *CMA Management* (April 2001), 22–25.

82. G. Pascal Zachary, "The Rage for Global Teams," *Technology Review* (July–August 1998), 33.

83. See Distefano and Maznevski, "Creating Value with Diverse Teams" for a discussion of the advantages of multicultural teams.

84. Watson, Kumar, and Michaelsen, "Cultural Diversity's Impact on Interaction Process and Performance."

85. Distefano and Maznevski, "Creating Value with Diverse Teams."

86. This definition and discussion is based on Raymond A. Friedman, "Employee Network Groups: Self-Help Strategy for Women and Minorities," *Performance Improvement Quarterly* 12, no. 1 (1999), 148–163.

87. "Leveraging Diversity."

88. Finnigan, "Different Strokes."

89. Raymond A. Friedman, Melinda Kane, and Daniel B. Cornfield, "Social Support and Career Optimism: Examining the Effectiveness of Network Groups Among Black Managers," *Human Relations* 51, no. 9 (1998), 1155–1177; "Diversity in the New Millennium," special advertising supplement, *Working Woman* (March 2000).

90. Labich, "No More Crude at Texaco."

Chapter 11
Foundations of Behavior in Organizations

1. Julia Lawlor, "Personality 2.0," *Red Herring* (April 1, 2001), 98–103.

2. John W. Newstrom and Keith Davis, *Organizational Behavior: Human Behavior at Work,* 11th ed. (Burr Ridge, Ill.: McGraw-Hill Irwin, 2002), Chapter 9.

3. A. Feuerstein, "E-marketing Firm Lands Hotshot CEO," *San Francisco Business Times* (January 17, 2000), 1–2; and J. Kaufman, "What Happens When a 20-Something Whiz Is Suddenly the Boss," *The Wall Street Journal* (October 8, 1999), A1, A10.

4. S. J. Breckler, "Empirical Validation of Affect, Behavior, and Cognition as Distinct Components of Attitude," *Journal of Personality and Social Psychology* (May 1984), 1191–1205; and J. M. Olson and M. P. Zanna, "Attitudes and Attitude Change," *Annual Review of Psychology* 44 (1993), 117–154.

5. M. T. Iaffaldano and P. M. Muchinsky, "Job Satisfaction and Job Performance: A Meta-Analysis," *Psychological Bulletin* (March 1985), 251–273; C. Ostroff, "The Relationship between Satisfaction, Attitudes, and Performance: An Organizational Level Analysis," *Journal of Applied Psychology* (December 1992), 963–974; and M. M. Petty, G. W. McGee, and J. W. Cavender, "A Meta-Analysis of the Relationship between Individual Job Satisfaction and Individual Performance," *Academy of Management Review* (October 1984), 712–721.

6. Sue Shellenbarger, "Companies Are Finding Real Payoffs in Aiding Employee Satisfaction" (Work & Family column), *The Wall Street Journal* (October 11, 2000), B1.

7. Tony Schwartz, "The Greatest Sources of Satisfaction in the Workplace Are Internal and Emotional," *Fast Company* (November 2000), 398–402.

8. William C. Symonds, "Where Paternalism Equals Good Business," *Business Week* (July 20, 1998), 16E4, 16E6.

9. Aaron Bernstein, "We Want You to Stay. Really," *Business Week* (June 22, 1998), 67–68+.

10. Jennifer Laabs, "They Want More Support—Inside and Outside of Work," *Workforce* (November 1998), 54–56.

11. For a discussion of cognitive dissonance theory, see Leon A. Festinger, *Theory of Cognitive Dissonance* (Stanford, Calif.: Stanford University Press, 1957).

12. D. A. Kravitz and S. L. Klineberg, "Reactions to Two Versions of Affirmative Action Among Whites, Blacks, and Hispanics," *Journal of Applied Psychology* 85 (2000), 597–611; and Robert J. Grossman, "Race in the Workplace" *HR Magazine* (March 2000), 41–45.

13. J. A. Deutsch, W. G. Young, and T. J. Kalogeris, "The Stomach Signals Satiety," *Science* (April 1978), 22–33.

14. Richard B. Chase and Sriram Dasu, "Want to Perfect Your Company's Service? Use Behavioral Science," *Harvard Business Review* (June 2001), 79–84.

15. H. H. Kelley, "Attribution in Social Interaction," in E. Jones et al. (eds.), *Attribution: Perceiving the Causes of Behavior* (Morristown, N.J.: General Learning Press, 1972).

16. See J. M. Digman, "Personality Structure: Emergence of the Five-Factor Model," *Annual Review of Psychology* 41 (1990), 417–440; M. R. Barrick and M. K. Mount, "Autonomy as a Moderator of the Relationships Between the Big Five Personality Dimensions and Job Performance," *Journal of Applied Psychology* (February 1993), 111–118; and J. S. Wiggins and A. L. Pincus, "Personality: Structure and Assessment," *Annual Review of Psychology* 43 (1992), 473–504.

17. Kortney Stringer, "People Who Need People," *The Wall Street Journal* (Monday, May 21, 2001), R14.

18. Michelle Leder, "Is That Your Final Answer?" *Working Woman* (December–January 2001), 18; "Can You Pass the Job Test?" *Newsweek* (May 5, 1986), 46–51.

19. Alan Farnham, "Are You Smart Enough to Keep Your Job?" *Fortune* (January 15, 1996), 34–47.

20. Cora Daniels, "Does This Man Need a Shrink?" *Fortune* (February 5, 2001), 205–208.

21. Daniel Goleman, *Emotional Intelligence: Why It Can Matter More than IQ* (New York: Bantam Books, 1995); Sharon Nelton, "Emotions in the Workplace," *Nation's Business* (February 1996), 25–30; and Lara E. Megerian and John J. Sosik, "An Affair of the Heart: Emotional Intelligence and Transformational Leadership," *The Journal of Leadership Studies* 3, no. 3 (1996), 31–48.

22. Farnham, "Are You Smart Enough to Keep Your Job?"

23. Hendrie Weisinger, *Emotional Intelligence at Work* (San Francisco, Calif.: Jossey-Bass, 2000); D. C. McClelland, "Identifying Competencies with Behavioral-Event Interviews," *Psychological Science* (Spring 1999), 331–339; Daniel Goleman, "Leadership That Gets Results," *Harvard Business Review* (March–April 2000), 78–90; D. Goleman, *Working with Emotional Intelligence* (New York: Bantam Books, 1999); and Lorie Parch, "Testing . . . 1, 2, 3," *Working Woman* (October 1997), 74–78.

24. Pamela Kruger, "A Leader's Journey," *Fast Company* (June 1999), 116–129.

25. Goleman, "Leadership That Gets Results."

26. J. B. Rotter, "Generalized Expectancies for Internal versus External Control of Reinforcement," *Psychological Monographs* 80, no. 609 (1966).

27. Andy Serwer, "There's Something about Cisco," *Fortune* (May 15, 2000); Stephanie N. Mehta, "Cisco Fractures Its Own Fairy Tale," *Fortune* (May 14, 2001), 104–112.

28. See P. E. Spector, "Behavior in Organizations as a Function of Employee's Locus of Control," *Psychological Bulletin* (May 1982), 482–497.

29. T. W. Adorno, E. Frenkel-Brunswick, D. J. Levinson, and R. N. Sanford, *The Authoritarian Personality* (New York: Harper & Row, 1950).

30. Mike Freeman, "A New Breed of Coaches Relates Better to Players," *The New York Times* (August 19, 2001), Y36.

31. Niccolo Machiavelli, *The Prince,* trans. George Bull (Middlesex, United Kingdom: Penguin, 1961).

32. Richard Christie and Florence Geis, *Studies in Machiavellianism* (New York: Academic Press, 1970).

33. R. G. Vleeming, "Machiavellianism: A Preliminary Review," *Psychological Reports* (February 1979), 295–310.

34. Christie and Geis, *Studies in Machiavellianism.*

35. Carl Jung, *Psychological Types* (London: Routledge and Kegan Paul, 1923).

36. Quentin Hardy, "All Carly, All the Time," *Forbes* (December 13, 1999), 138–144.

37. Charles A. O'Reilly III, Jennifer Chatman, and David F. Caldwell, "People and Organizational Culture: A Profile Comparison Approach to Assessing Person-Organization Fit," *Academy of Management Journal* 34, no. 3 (1991), 487–516.

38. Anna Muoio, "Should I Go .Com?" *Fast Company* (July 2000), 164–172.

39. Leder, "Is That Your Final Answer?"

40. David A. Kolb, "Management and the Learning Process," *California Management Review* 18, no. 3 (Spring 1976), 21–31.

41. De' Ann Weimer, "The Houdini of Consumer Electronics," *Business Week* (June 22, 1998), 88, 92.

42. See David A. Kolb, I. M. Rubin, and J. M. McIntyre, *Organizational Psychology: An Experimental Approach*, 3rd ed. (Englewood Cliffs, N.J.: Prentice-Hall, 1984), 27–54.

43. Stephanie Gruner, "Our Company, Ourselves," *Inc.* (April 1998), 127–128.

44. Simon Williams, "In Review: Melbourne," *Opera News* (November 2001), 79–81; Eleena de Lisser, "Start-ups Are Tough, Even When Mozart Created the Product," *The Wall Street Journal* (September 3, 1999), B1.

45. Ira Sager, "Big Blue's Blunt Bohemian," *Business Week* (June 14, 1999), 107–112.

46. Paul Roberts, "The Best Interest of the Patient Is the Only Interest to be Considered," *Fast Company* (April 1999), 149–162.

47. T. A. Beehr and R. S. Bhagat, *Human Stress and Cognition in Organizations: An Integrated Perspective* (New York: Wiley, 1985).

48. Hans Selye, *The Stress of Life* (New York: McGraw-Hill, 1976).

49. M. Friedman and R. Rosenman, *Type A Behavior and Your Heart* (New York: Knopf, 1974).

50. Carol Hymowitz, "How Some CEOs Get the Energy to Work Those Endless Days," *The Wall Street Journal* (March 20, 2001), B1.

51. Laabs, "They Want More Support."

52. Kris Maher, "At Verizon Call Center, Stress Is Seldom On Hold," *The Wall Street Journal* (January 16, 2001), B1, B12.

53. Anne Fisher, "Why Are You So Paranoid?" *Fortune* (September 8, 1997), 171–172.

54. Louisa Wah, "The Emotional Tightrope," *Management Review* (January 2000), 38–43; Laabs, "They Want More Support."

55. Andrea Higbie, "Quick Lessons in the Fine Old Art of Unwinding," *The New York Times* (February 25, 2001), BU–10.

56. Leslie Gross Klass, "Quiet Time at Work Helps Employee Stress," *Johnson City Press* (January 28, 2001), 30.

57. Stephanie Gruner, "A Relaxed Workforce," *Inc.* (September 1998), 129.

58. David T. Gordon, "Balancing Act," *CIO* (October 15, 2001), 58–62.

59. Ibid.

60. Lawlor, "Personality 2.0."

Chapter 12

Leadership in Organizations

1. Chester E. Finn, Jr., "An Open Letter to Lawrence H. Summers," *Policy Review* (July 2002), 75–86; William C. Symonds and Rich Miller, "Harvard," *Business Week* (February 18, 2002), 71–78.

2. Melanie Warner, "Confessions of a Control Freak," *Fortune* (September 4, 2000), 130–140.

3. Gary Yukl, "Managerial Leadership: A Review of Theory and Research," *Journal of Management* 15 (1989), 251–289.

4. James M. Kouzes and Barry Z. Posner, "The Credibility Factor: What Followers Expect from Their Leaders," *Management Review* (January 1990), 29–33.

5. Henry Mintzberg, *Power In and Around Organizations* (Englewood Cliffs, N.J.: Prentice-Hall, 1983); and Jeffrey Pfeffer, *Power in Organizations* (Marshfield, Mass.: Pitman, 1981).

6. Andy Raskin, "The Accidental Leader," *Business 2.0* (November 2001), 32.

7. J. R. P. French, Jr., and B. Raven, "The Bases of Social Power," in *Group Dynamics,* ed. D. Cartwright and Alvin F. Zander (Evanston, Ill.: Row, Peterson, 1960), 607–623.

8. G. A. Yukl and T. Taber, "The Effective Use of Managerial Power," *Personnel* (March–April 1983), 37–44.

9. Erle Norton, "Chairman of AK Steel Tries to Shake Off Tag of 'Operating Man,'" *The Wall Street Journal* (November 25, 1994), A1, A5.

10. Jay A. Conger, "The Necessary Art of Persuasion," *Harvard Business Review* (May–June 1998), 84–95.

11. Andy Reinhardt, "Meet AMD's Rags-to-Riches Heir Apparent," *Business Week* (October 2, 2000), 112–117.

12. Michael E. McGill and John W. Slocum, Jr., "A Little Leadership, Please?" *Organizational Dynamics* (Winter 1998), 39–49.

13. Thomas A. Stewart, "New Ways to Exercise Power," *Fortune* (November 6, 1989), 52–64; and Thomas A. Stewart, "CEOs See Clout Shifting," *Fortune* (November 6, 1989), 66.

14. Robin Landew Silverman, "A Moving Experience," *Inc.* (August 1996), 23–24.

15. G. A. Yukl, *Leadership in Organizations* (Englewood Cliffs, N.J.: Prentice-Hall, 1981); and S. C. Kohs and K. W. Irle, "Prophesying Army Promotion," *Journal of Applied Psychology* 4 (1920), 73–87.

16. R. Albanese and D. D. Van Fleet, *Organizational Behavior: A Managerial Viewpoint* (Hinsdale, Ill.: The Dryden Press, 1983).

17. K. Lewin, "Field Theory and Experiment in Social Psychology: Concepts and Methods," *American Journal of Sociology* 44 (1939), 868–896; K. Lewin and R. Lippitt, "An Experimental Approach to the Study of Autocracy and Democracy: A Preliminary Note," *Sociometry* 1 (1938), 292–300; and K. Lewin, R. Lippitt, and R. K. White, "Patterns of Aggressive Behavior in Experimentally Created Social Climates," *Journal of Social Psychology 10* (1939), 271–301.

18. R. K. White and R. Lippitt, *Autocracy and Democracy: An Experimental Inquiry* (New York: Harper, 1960).

19. R. Tannenbaum and W. H. Schmidt, "How to Choose a Leadership Pattern," *Harvard Business Review* 36 (1958), 95–101.

20. Marc Ballon, "Equal Parts Old-Fashioned Dictator and New Age Father Figure, Jack Hartnett Breaks Nearly Every Rule of the Enlightened Manager's Code," *Inc.* (July 1998), 60+; Esther Wachs Book, "Leadership for the Millennium," *Working Woman* (March 1998), 29–34.

21. C. A. Schriesheim and B. J. Bird, "Contributions of the Ohio State Studies to the Field of Leadership," *Journal of Management* 5 (1979), 135–145; and C. L. Shartle, "Early Years of the Ohio State University Leadership Studies," *Journal of Management* 5 (1979), 126–134.

22. P. C. Nystrom, "Managers and the High-High Leader Myth," *Academy of Management Journal* 21 (1978), 325–331; and L. L. Larson, J. G. Hunt, and Richard N. Osborn, "The Great High-High Leader Behavior Myth: A Lesson from Occam's Razor," *Academy of Management Journal* 19 (1976), 628–641.

23. R. Likert, "From Production- and Employee-Centeredness to Systems 1–4," *Journal of Management* 5 (1979), 147–156.

24. Robert R. Blake and Jane S. Mouton, *The Managerial Grid III* (Houston: Gulf, 1985).

25. Fred E. Fiedler, "Assumed Similarity Measures as Predictors of Team Effectiveness," *Journal of Abnormal and Social Psychology* 49 (1954), 381–388; F. E. Fiedler, *Leader Attitudes and Group Effectiveness* (Urbana, Ill.: University of Illinois Press, 1958); and F. E. Fiedler, *A Theory of Leadership Effectiveness* (New York: McGraw-Hill, 1967).

26. Fred E. Fiedler and M. M. Chemers, *Leadership and Effective Management* (Glenview, Ill.: Scott, Foresman, 1974).

27. Fred E. Fiedler, "Engineer the Job to Fit the Manager," *Harvard Business Review* 43 (1965), 115–122; and F. E. Fiedler, M. M. Chemers, and L. Mahar, *Improving Leadership Effectiveness: The Leader Match Concept* (New York: Wiley, 1976).

28. Timothy Aeppel, "Personnel Disorders Sap a Factory Owner of His Early Idealism," *The Wall Street Journal* (January 14, 1998), A1, A14.

29. R. Singh, "Leadership Style and Reward Allocation: Does Least Preferred Coworker Scale Measure Tasks and Relation Orientation?" *Organizational Behavior and Human Performance* 27 (1983), 178–197; and D. Hosking, "A Critical Evaluation of Fiedler's Contingency Hypotheses," *Progress in Applied Psychology* 1 (1981), 103–154.

30. Paul Hersey and Kenneth H. Blanchard, *Management of Organizational Behavior: Utilizing Human Resources,* 4th ed. (Englewood Cliffs, N.J.: Prentice-Hall, 1982).

31. Jonathon Kaufman, "A McDonald's Owner Becomes a Role Model for Black Teenagers," *The Wall Street Journal* (August 23, 1995), A1, A6.

32. M. G. Evans, "The Effects of Supervisory Behavior on the Path-Goal Relationship," Organizational Behavior and Human Performance 5 (1970), 277–298; M. G. Evans, "Leadership and Motivation: A Core Concept," *Academy of Management Journal* 13 (1970), 91–102; and B. S. Georgopoulos, G. M. Mahoney, and N. W. Jones, "A Path-Goal Approach to Productivity," *Journal of Applied Psychology* 41 (1957), 345–353.

33. Robert J. House, "A Path-Goal Theory of Leader Effectiveness," *Administrative Science Quarterly* 16 (1971), 321–338.

34. M. G. Evans, "Leadership," in *Organizational Behavior,* ed. S. Kerr (Columbus, Ohio: Grid, 1974), 230–233.

35. Robert J. House and Terrence R. Mitchell, "Path-Goal Theory of Leadership," *Journal of Contemporary Business* (Autumn 1974), 81–97.

36. Charles A. O'Reilly III and Jeffrey Pfeffer, "Star Makers," book excerpt from *From Hidden Value: How Great Companies Achieve Extraordinary Results with Ordinary People* (Harvard Business School Press, 2000), published in *CIO* (September 15, 2000), 226–246.

37. Charles Greene, "Questions of Causation in the Path-Goal Theory of Leadership," *Academy of Management Journal* 22 (March 1979), 22–41; and C. A. Schriesheim and Mary Ann von Glinow, "The Path-Goal Theory of Leadership: A Theoretical and Empirical Analysis," *Academy of Management Journal* 20 (1977), 398–405.

38. S. Kerr and J. M. Jermier, "Substitutes for Leadership: Their Meaning and Measurement," *Organizational Behavior and Human Performance* 22 (1978), 375–403; and Jon P. Howell and Peter W. Dorfman, "Leadership and Substitutes for Leadership among Professional and Nonprofessional Workers," *Journal of Applied Behavioral Science* 22 (1986), 29–46.

39. The terms *transactional* and *transformational* come from James M. Burns, *Leadership* (New York: Harper & Row, 1978); and Bernard M. Bass, "Leadership: Good, Better, Best," *Organizational Dynamics* 13 (Winter 1985), 26–40.

40. Katherine J. Klein and Robert J. House, "On Fire: Charismatic Leadership and Levels of Analysis," *Leadership Quarterly* 6, no. 2 (1995), 183–198.

41. Jay A. Conger and Rabindra N. Kanungo, "Toward a Behavioral Theory of Charismatic Leadership in Organizational Settings," *Academy of Management Review* 12 (1987), 637–647; Walter Kiechel III, "A Hard Look at Executive Vision," *Fortune* (October 23, 1989), 207–211; and William L. Gardner and Bruce J. Avolio, "The Charismatic Relationship: A Dramaturgical Perspective," *Academy of Management Review* 23, no. 1 (1998), 32–58.

42. Keith Hammonds, "The Monroe Doctrine," *Fast Company* (October 1999), 230–236.

43. Robert J. House, "Research Contrasting the Behavior and Effects of Reputed Charismatic vs. Reputed Non-Charismatic Leaders" (paper presented as part of a symposium, "Charismatic Leadership: Theory and Evidence," Academy of Management, San Diego, 1985).

44. Robert J. House and Jane M. Howell, "Personality and Charismatic Leadership," *Leadership Quarterly* 3, no. 2 (1992), 81–108; and Jennifer O'Connor, Michael D. Mumford, Timothy C. Clifton, Theodore L. Gessner, and Mary Shane Connelly, "Charismatic Leaders and Destructiveness: A Historiometric Study," *Leadership Quarterly* 6, no. 4 (1995), 529–555.

45. Bernard M. Bass, "Theory of Transformational Leadership Redux," *Leadership Quarterly* 6, no. 4 (1995), 463–478; Noel M. Tichy and Mary Anne Devanna, *The Transformational Leader* (New York: John Wiley & Sons, 1986); and Badrinarayan Shankar Pawar and Kenneth K. Eastman, "The Nature and Implications of Contextual Influences on Transformational Leadership: A Conceptual Examination," *Academy of Management Review* 22, no. 1 (1997), 80–109.

46. Richard L. Daft and Robert H. Lengel, *Fusion Leadership: Unlocking the Subtle Forces that Change People and Organizations* (San Francisco: Berrett-Koehler, 1998).

47. Bethany McLean, "Is This Guy the Best Banker in America?" *Fortune* (July 6, 1998), 126–128; and Jacqueline S. Gold, "Bank to the Future," *Institutional Investor* (September 2001), 54–63.

48. Jim Collins, "Level 5 Leadership: The Triumph of Humility and Fierce Resolve," *Harvard Business Review* (January 2001), 67–76; Collins, "Good to Great," *Fast Company* (October 2001), 90–104; A. J. Vogl, "Onward and Upward" (an interview with Jim Collins), *Across the Board* (September–October 2001), 29–34; and Jerry Useem, "Conquering Vertical Limits," *Fortune* (February 19, 2001), 84–96.

49. Abrashoff, "Retention through Redemption," and LaBarre, "The Most Important Thing a Captain Can Do."

50. Judy B. Rosener, *America's Competitive Secret: Utilizing Women as a Management Strategy* (New York: Oxford University Press, 1995); Rosener, "Ways Women Lead," *Harvard Business Review* (November–December 1990), 119–125; Sally Helgesen, *The Female Advantage: Women's Ways of Leadership* (New York: Currency/Doubleday, 1990); and Bernard M. Bass and Bruce J. Avolio, "Shatter the Glass Ceiling: Women May Make Better Managers," *Human Resource Management* 33, no. 4 (Winter 1994), 549–560.

51. Rochelle Sharpe, "As Leaders, Women Rule," *Business Week* (November 20, 2000), 75–84.

52. Rosener, *America's Competitive Secret.* 129–135.

53. Sharpe, "As Leaders, Women Rule."

54. Deborah L. Duarte and Nancy Tennant Snyder, *Mastering Virtual Teams: Strategies, Tools, and Techniques That Succeed* (San Francisco: Jossey-Bass, 1999).

55. This discussion is based on Wayne F. Cascio, "Managing a Virtual Workplace," *Academy of Management Executive* 14, no. 3

(August 2000), 81–90, and Charlene Marmer Solomon, "Managing Virtual Teams," *Workforce* (June 2001), 60–65.

56. Nancy Chase, "Learning to Lead a Virtual Team," *Quality* (August 1999), 76.

57. Daft and Lengel, *Fusion Leadership.*

58. Robert K. Greenleaf, *Servant Leadership: A Journey into the Nature of Legitimate Power and Greatness* (Mahwah, N.J.: Paulist Press, 1977).

59. Fred Andrews, "Thinking Great Thoughts without Great Money," *The New York Times* (January 12, 2000), C10; Stratford Sherman, "How Tomorrow's Best Leaders Are Learning Their Stuff," *Fortune* (September 27, 1995), 90–102.

60. Finn, Jr., "An Open Letter to Lawrence H. Summers"; Symonds and Miller, "Harvard."

Chapter 13
Motivation in Organizations

1. Kate Murphy, "A Better Mousetrap? For This Immigrant, It's a Plastic Bag," *The New York Times* (May 20, 2001), 7.

2. David Silburt, "Secrets of the Super Sellers," *Canadian Business* (January 1987), 54–59; "Meet the Savvy Supersalesmen," *Fortune* (February 4, 1985), 56–62; Michael Brody, "Meet Today's Young American Worker," *Fortune* (November 11, 1985), 90–98; and Tom Richman, "Meet the Masters. They Could Sell You Anything . . . ," *Inc.* (March 1985), 79–86.

3. Richard M. Steers and Lyman W. Porter, eds., *Motivation and Work Behavior,* 3d ed. (New York: McGraw-Hill, 1983); Don Hellriegel, John W. Slocum, Jr., and Richard W. Woodman, *Organizational Behavior,* 7th ed. (St. Paul, Minn.: West, 1995), 170; and Jerry L. Gray and Frederick A. Starke, *Organizational Behavior: Concepts and Applications,* 4th ed. (New York: Macmillan, 1988), 104–105.

4. Carol Hymowitz, "Readers Tell Tales of Success and Failure Using Rating Systems" (in the Lead column), *The Wall Street Journal* (May 29, 2001), B1.

5. Linda Grant, "Happy Workers, High Returns," *Fortune* (January 12, 1998), 81.

6. Carol Hymowitz, "Bosses Need to Learn Whether They Inspire, or Just Drive, Staff," *The Wall Street Journal* (August 14, 2001), B1.

7. Steers and Porter, *Motivation.*

8. J. F. Rothlisberger and W. J. Dickson, *Management and the Worker* (Cambridge, Mass.: Harvard University Press, 1939).

9. Abraham F. Maslow, "A Theory of Human Motivation," *Psychological Review* 50 (1943), 370–396.

10. Greg Bloom, "Mujeres Mariposas: Helping Women Work in the Colonias," *Frontera NorteSur,* New Mexico State University, February 2002. Accessed November 2002 at *http://www.nmsu.edu/~frontera/feb02/main.html.*

11. Roberta Maynard, "How to Motivate Low-Wage Workers," *Nation's Business* (May 1997), 35–39.

12. Clayton Alderfer, *Existence, Relatedness and Growth* (New York: Free Press, 1972).

13. David Whitford, "Before & After," *Inc.* (June 1995), 44–50.

14. Jeff Barbian, "C'mon, Get Happy," *Training* (January 2001), 92–96.

15. Ibid.

16. Pamela Kruger, "Stop the Insanity," *Fast Company* (July 2000), 240–254.

17. Frederick Herzberg, "One More Time: How Do You Motivate Employees?" *Harvard Business Review* (January–February 1968), 53–62.

18. William C. Symonds, "Where Paternalism Equals Good Business," *Business Week* (July 20, 1998), 16E4–16E6.

19. David C. McClelland, *Human Motivation* (Glenview, Ill.: Scott, Foresman, 1985).

20. Carol Hymowitz, "For Many Executives, Leadership Lessons Started with Mom" (in the Lead column), *The Wall Street Journal* (May 16, 2000), B1.

21. David C. McClelland, "The Two Faces of Power," in *Organizational Psychology,* ed. D. A. Colb, I. M. Rubin, and J. M. McIntyre (Englewood Cliffs, N.J.: Prentice-Hall, 1971), 73–86.

22. J. Stacy Adams, "Injustice in Social Exchange," in *Advances in Experimental Social Psychology,* 2d ed., ed. L. Berkowitz (New York: Academic Press, 1965); and J. Stacy Adams, "Toward an Understanding of Inequity," *Journal of Abnormal and Social Psychology* (November 1963), 422–436.

23. Ray V. Montagno, "The Effects of Comparison to Others and Primary Experience on Responses to Task Design," *Academy of Management Journal* 28 (1985), 491–498; and Robert P. Vecchio, "Predicting Worker Performance in Inequitable Settings," *Academy of Management Review* 7 (1982), 103–110.

24. John Peterman, "The Rise and Fall of the J. Peterman Company," *Harvard Business Review* (September–October 1999), 59–66.

25. James E. Martin and Melanie M. Peterson, "Two-Tier Wage Structures: Implications for Equity Theory," Academy of Management Journal 30 (1987), 297–315.

26. Victor H. Vroom, *Work and Motivation* (New York: Wiley, 1964); B. S. Gorgopoulos, G. M. Mahoney, and N. Jones, "A Path-Goal Approach to Productivity," *Journal of Applied Psychology* 41 (1957), 345–353; and E. E. Lawler III, *Pay and Organizational Effectiveness: A Psychological View* (New York: McGraw-Hill, 1981).

27. Richard L. Daft and Richard M. Steers, *Organizations: A Micro/Macro Approach* (Glenview, Ill.: Scott, Foresman, 1986).

28. Mike Hofman, "Everyone's a Cost Cutter," *Inc.* (July 1998), 117; and Abby Livingston, "Gain-Sharing Encourages Productivity," *Nation's Business* (January 1998), 21–22.

29. Alexander D. Stajkovic and Fred Luthans, "A Meta-Analysis of the Effects of Organizational Behavior Modification on Task Performance, 1975–95," *Academy of Management Journal* (October 1997), 1122–1149; H. Richlin, *Modern Behaviorism* (San Francisco: Freeman, 1970); and B. F. Skinner, *Science and Human Behavior* (New York: Macmillan, 1953).

30. Lea Goldman, "Over the Top," *Forbes* (October 29, 2001), 146–147.

31. Stajkovic and Luthans, "A Meta-Analysis of the Effects of Organizational Behavior Modification on Task Performance, 1975–95," and Fred Luthans and Alexander D. Stajkovic, "Reinforce for Performance: The Need to Go Beyond Pay and Even Rewards," *Academy of Management Executive* 13, no. 2 (1999), 49–57.

32. Kenneth D. Butterfield and Linda Klebe Trevino, "Punishment from the Manager's Perspective: A Grounded Investigation and Inductive Model," *Academy of Management Journal* 39, no. 6 (December 1996), 1479–1512; and Andrea Casey, "Voices from the Firing Line: Managers Discuss Punishment in the Workplace," *Academy of Management Executive* 11, no. 3 (1997), 93–94.

33. Pamela L. Moore with Diane Brady, "Running the House That Jack Built," *Business Week* (October 2, 2000), 130–138.

34. Roberta Maynard, "How to Motivate Low-Wage Workers."

35. L. M. Sarri and G. P. Latham, "Employee Reaction to Continuous and Variable Ratio Reinforcement Schedules Involving a Monetary Incentive," *Journal of Applied Psychology* 67 (1982), 506–508; and R. D. Pritchard, J. Hollenback, and P. J. DeLeo, "The Effects of Continuous and Partial Schedules of Reinforcement on Effort, Performance, and Satisfaction," *Organizational Behavior and Human Performance* 25 (1980), 336–353.

36. Kevin Kelly, "Firing Up the Team," *Business Week Frontier* (May 24, 1999), F32.

37. Charles A. O'Reilly III and Jeffrey Pfeffer, "Star Makers," book excerpt from *From Hidden Value: How Great Companies Achieve Extraordinary Results with Ordinary People* (Harvard Business School Press, 2000), published in *CIO* (September 15, 2000), 226–246.

38. A. J. Vogl, "Carrots, Sticks, and Self-Deception" (an interview with Alfie Kohn), *Across the Board* (January 1994), 39–44.

39. Hilary Rosenberg, "Building a Better Carrot," *CFO* (June 2001), 64–70.

40. Barbian, "C'mon, Get Happy."

41. Norm Alster, "What Flexible Workers Can Do," *Fortune* (February 13, 1989), 62–66.

42. Glenn L. Dalton, "The Collective Stretch," *Management Review* (December 1998), 54–59.

43. Jason Lynch and Gabrielle Cosgroff, "Shelf Help," *People Weekly* (May 20, 2002), 127–128; Thomas Petzinger, Jr., "In Search of the New World (of Work)," *Fast Company* (April 1999), 219–226.

44. J. Richard Hackman and Greg R. Oldham, *Work Redesign* (Reading, Mass.: Addison-Wesley, 1980); and J. Richard Hackman and Greg Oldham, "Motivation through the Design of Work: Test of a Theory," *Organizational Behavior and Human Performance* 16 (1976), 250–279.

45. Barbara Ettorre, "Retooling People and Processes," *Management Review* (June 1995), 19–23; and Albert R. Karr, "A Special News Report about Life on the Job—and Trends Taking Shape There," *The Wall Street Journal* (November 16, 1999), A1.

46. Ann Podolske, "Giving Employees a Voice in Pay Structures," *Business Ethics* (March–April 1998), 12.

47. Rekha Balu, "Bonuses Aren't Just For the Bosses," *Fast Company* (December 2000), 74–76.

48. Edwin P. Hollander and Lynn R. Offermann, "Power and Leadership in Organizations," *American Psychologist* 45 (February 1990), 179–189.

49. Jay A. Conger and Rabindra N. Kanungo, "The Empowerment Process: Integrating Theory and Practice," *Academy of Management Review* 13 (1988), 471–482.

50. Bradley L. Kirkman and Benson Rosen, "Powering Up Teams," *Organizational Dynamics* (Winter 2000), 48–66.

51. David E. Bowen and Edward E. Lawler III, "The Empowerment of Service Workers: What, Why, How, and When," *Sloan Management Review* (Spring 1992), 31–39; and Ray W. Coye and James A. Belohav, "An Exploratory Analysis of Employee Participation," *Group and Organization Management* 20, no. 1, (March 1995), 4–17.

52. Russ Forrester, "Empowerment: Rejuvenating a Potent Idea," *Academy of Management Executive* 14, No. 3 (2000), 67–80.

53. Ricardo Semler, "How We Went Digital Without a Strategy," *Harvard Business Review* (September–October 2000), 51–58.

54. Podolske, "Giving Employees a Voice in Pay Structures."

55. This discussion is based on Robert C. Ford and Myron D. Fottler, "Empowerment: A Matter of Degree," *Academy of Management Executive* 9, no. 3 (1995), 21–31.

56. Jay A. Conger and Rabindra N. Kanungo, "The Empowerment Process: Integrating Theory and Practice," *Academy of Management Review* 13 (1998), 471–482.

57. This discussion is based on Tony Schwartz, "The Greatest Sources of Satisfaction in the Workplace are Internal and Emotional," *Fast Company* (November 2000), 398–402; and Marcus Buckingham and Curt Coffman, *First, Break All the Rules: What the World's Greatest Managers Do Differently* (New York: Simon & Schuster, 1999).

58. Polly LaBarre, "Marcus Buckingham Thinks Your Boss Has an Attitude Problem" *Fast Company* (August 2001), 88–98.

59. Kate Murphy, "A Better Mousetrap?," 7.

Chapter 14
Communicating in Organizations

1. Stephanie Clifford, "How to Get the Geeks and the Suits to Play Nice," *Business 2.0* (May 2002), 92–93.

2. Christina Le Beau, "Bad Vibes," *Working Woman* (November 2000), 30–32.

3. Jenny C. McCune, "That Elusive Thing Called Trust," *Management Review* (July–August 1998), 10–16.

4. Elizabeth B. Drew, "Profile: Robert Strauss," *The New Yorker* (May 7, 1979), 55–70.

5. Henry Mintzberg, *The Nature of Managerial Work* (New York: Harper & Row, 1973).

6. Fred Luthans and Janet K. Larsen, "How Managers Really Communicate," *Human Relations* 39 (1986), 161–178; and Larry E. Penley and Brian Hawkins, "Studying Interpersonal Communication in Organizations: A Leadership Application," *Academy of Management Journal* 28 (1985), 309–326.

7. D. K. Berlo, *The Process of Communication* (New York: Holt, Rinehart and Winston, 1960), 24.

8. Robert Levering and Milton Moskowitz, "100 Best Companies to Work For: The Best in the Worst of Times," *Fortune* (February 2002), 60–61; Nancy Austin, "Rock through the Ages," *Inc.* (May 16, 2000), 68–76.

9. Paul Roberts, "Live! From Your Office! It's . . . ," *Fast Company* (October 1999), 150–170.

10. Bruce K. Blaylock, "Cognitive Style and the Usefulness of Information," *Decision Sciences* 15 (Winter 1984), 74–91.

11. Robert H. Lengel and Richard L. Daft, "The Selection of Communication Media as an Executive Skill," *Academy of Management Executive* 2 (August 1988), 225–232; Richard L. Daft and Robert H. Lengel, "Organizational Information Requirements, Media Richness and Structural Design," *Managerial Science* 32 (May 1986), 554–572; and Jane Webster and Linda Klebe Trevino, "Rational and Social Theories as Complementary Explanations of Communication Media Choices: Two Policy-Capturing Studies," *Academy of Management Journal* 38, no. 6 (1995), 1544–1572.

12. Ford S. Worthy, "How CEOs Manage Their Time," *Fortune* (January 18, 1988), 88–97.

13. "E-mail Can't Mimic Phone Calls," *Johnson City Press* (September 17, 2000), 31.

14. Thomas E. Weber, "After Terror Attacks, Companies Rethink Role of Face-to-Face," *The Wall Street Journal* (September 24, 2001), B1.

15. Ronald E. Rice, "Task Analyzability, Use of New Media, and Effectiveness: A Multi-Site Exploration of Media Richness," *Organizational Science* 3, no. 4 (November 1992), 475–500; and M. Lynne Markus, "Electronic Mail as the Medium of Managerial Choice," *Organizational Science* 5, no. 4 (November 1994), 502–527.

16. Richard L. Daft, Robert H. Lengel, and Linda Klebe Trevino, "Message Equivocality, Media Selection and Manager Performance: Implication for Information Systems," *MIS Quarterly* 11 (1987), 355–368.

17. Mary Young and James E. Post, "Managing to Communicate, Communicating to Manage: How Leading Companies Communicate with Employees," *Organizational Dynamics* (Summer 1993), 31–43.

18. Jay A. Conger, "The Necessary Art of Persuasion," *Harvard Business Review* (May–June 1998), 84–95.

19. Steve Barnes, "Everyone Now Hears Once-Quiet Company," New York Times News Service in *Johnson City Press* (September 10, 2000), 33.

20. Thomas A. Stewart, "The Cunning Plots of Leadership," *Fortune* (September 7, 1998), 165–166.

21. J. Martin and M. Powers, "Organizational Stories: More Vivid and Persuasive than Quantitative Data," in B. M. Staw, ed., *Psychological Foundations of Organizational Behavior* (Glenview, Ill.: Scott Foresman, 1982), 161–168.

22. I. Thomas Sheppard, "Silent Signals," *Supervisory Management* (March 1986), 31–33.

23. Albert Mehrabian, *Silent Messages* (Belmont, Calif.: Wadsworth, 1971); and Albert Mehrabian, "Communicating without Words," *Psychology Today* (September 1968), 53–55.

24. Sheppard, "Silent Signals."

25. Arthur H. Bell, *The Complete Manager's Guide to Interviewing* (Homewood, Ill.: Richard D. Irwin, 1989).

26. Danielle Reed, "Toy Trouble," *The Wall Street Journal* (December 14, 2001), W1; Michael Hopkins, "The Pursuit of Happiness," *Inc.* (August 2000), 72–89.

27. C. Glenn Pearce, "Doing Something about Your Listening Ability," *Supervisory Management* (March 1989), 29–34; and Tom Peters, "Learning to Listen," *Hyatt Magazine* (Spring 1988), 16–21.

28. M. P. Nichols, *The Lost Art of Listening* (New York: Guilford Publishing, 1995).

29. Monci Jo Williams, "America's Best Salesman," *Fortune* (October 26, 1987), 122–134.

30. Gerald M. Goldhaber, *Organizational Communication,* 4th ed. (Dubuque, Iowa: Wm. C. Brown, 1980), 189.

31. John M. Ivancevich and Michael T. Matteson, *Organizational Behavior and Management,* 6th ed. (Boston, Ill.: McGraw-Hill Irwin, 2002), 507.

32. Richard L. Daft and Richard M. Steers, *Organizations: A Micro/Macro Approach* (New York: HarperCollins 1986); and Daniel Katz and Robert Kahn, *The Social Psychology of Organizations,* 2d ed. (New York: Wiley, 1978).

33. Aaron Pressman, "Business Gets the Message," *The Industry Standard* (February 26, 2001), 58–59.

34. Cathy Olofson, "What We Have Here Is No Failure to Communicate," *Fast Company* (July 2000), 76.

35. Roberta Maynard, "It Can Pay to Show Employees the Big Picture," *Nation's Business* (December 1994), 10.

36. William C. Taylor, "At VeriFone, It's a Dog's Life (And They Love It)," *Fast Company* (November 1995), 12–15; and William R. Pape, "Relative Merits," *Inc. Technology* 1 (1998), 23.

37. Phillip G. Clampitt, Robert J. DeKoch, and Thomas Cashman, "A Strategy for Communicating about Uncertainty," *Academy of Management Executive* 14, no. 4 (2000), 41–57.

38. J. G. Miller, "Living Systems: The Organization," *Behavioral Science* 17 (1972), 69.

39. Michael J. Glauser, "Upward Information Flow in Organizations: Review and Conceptual Analysis," *Human Relations* 37 (1984), 613–643; and "Upward/Downward Communication: Critical Information Channels," *Small Business Report* (October 1985), 85–88.

40. Joann S. Lublin, "Ex-chief of Ben & Jerry's to Join Wild Oats," *The Wall Street Journal* (March 7, 2001), B6; "Wild Oats Markets to Buy 13 Stores from Competitors," *The Los Angeles Times* (November 1, 1999), 3; Michele Conklin, "Wild Oats to Sow Expansion," *Rocky Mountain News* (October 9, 1996), 2b.

41. Carol Leonetti Dannhauser, "Shut Up and Listen," *Working Woman* (May 1999), 41.

42. Mary P. Rowe and Michael Baker, "Are You Hearing Enough Employee Concerns?" *Harvard Business Review* 62 (May–June 1984), 127–135; W. H. Read, "Upward Communication in Industrial Hierarchies," *Human Relations* 15 (February 1962), 3–15; and Daft and Steers, *Organizations.*

43. Barbara Ettorre, "The Unvarnished Truth," *Management Review* (June 1997), 54–57; and Roberta Maynard, "Back to Basics, From the Top," *Nation's Business* (December 1996), 38–39.

44. Thomas Petzinger, "A Hospital Applies Teamwork to Thwart An Insidious Enemy," *The Wall Street Journal* (May 8, 1998), B1.

45. E. M. Rogers and R. A. Rogers, Communication in Organizations (New York: Free Press, 1976); and A. Bavelas and D. Barrett, "An Experimental Approach to Organization Communication," *Personnel* 27 (1951), 366–371.

46. This discussion is based on Daft and Steers, *Organizations.*

47. Bavelas and Barrett, "An Experimental Approach"; and M. E. Shaw, *Group Dynamics: The Psychology of Small Group Behavior* (New York: McGraw-Hill, 1976).

48. Richard L. Daft and Norman B. Macintosh, "A Tentative Exploration into the Amount and Equivocality of Information Processing in Organizational Work Units," *Administrative Science Quarterly* 26 (1981), 207–224.

49. Matt Goldberg, "Microsoft Knows How to Operate—Fast," *Fast Company* (April–May 1998), 76.

50. Erika Germer, "Huddle Up!" *Fast Company* (December 2000), 86.

51. Nancy K. Austin, "The Skill Every Manager Must Master," *Working Woman* (May 1995), 29–30.

52. Thomas J. Peters and Robert H. Waterman Jr., *In Search of Excellence* (New York: Harper & Row, 1982); and Tom Peters and Nancy Austin, *A Passion for Excellence: The Leadership Difference* (New York: Random House, 1985).

53. Lois Therrien, "How Ztel Went from Riches to Rags," *Business Week* (June 17, 1985), 97–100.

54. Keith Davis and John W. Newstrom, *Human Behavior at Work: Organizational Behavior,* 7th ed. (New York: McGraw-Hill, 1985).

55. Joshua Hyatt, "The Last Shift," *Inc.* (February 1989), 74–80.

56. Goldhaber, *Organizational Communication;* and Philip V. Louis, *Organizational Communication,* 3d ed. (New York: Wiley, 1987).

57. Donald B. Simmons, "The Nature of the Organizational Grapevine," *Supervisory Management* (November 1985), 39–42; and Davis and Newstrom, *Human Behavior.*

58. Barbara Ettorre, "Hellooo. Anybody Listening?" *Management Review* (November 1997), 9.

59. "They Hear It through the Grapevine," in Michael Warshaw, "The Good Guy's Guide to Office Politics," *Fast Company* (April–May 1998), 157–178 (page 160); Carol Hildebrand, "Mapping the Invisible Workplace," *CIO Enterprise,* Section 2 (July 15, 1998), 18–20; and David I. Bradford and Allan R. Cohen, *Power Up: Transforming Organizations Through Shared Leadership* (New York: Wiley, 1998).

60. John Case, "Opening the Books," *Harvard Business Review,* (March–April 1997), 118–127.

61. Gary Hamel, "Killer Strategies That Make Shareholders Rich," *Fortune* (June 23, 1997), 70–84.

62. "What Is Trust?" results of a survey by Manchester Consulting, reported in Jenny C. McCune, "That Elusive Thing Called Trust," *Management Review* (July–August 1998), 10–16.

63. David Bohm, *On Dialogue* (Ojai, Calif.: David Bohm Seminars, 1989).

64. The discussion is based on Glenna Gerard and Linda Teurfs, "Dialogue and Organizational Transformation," in *Community Building: Renewing Spirit and Learning in Business,* ed. Kazinierz Gozdz (New Leaders Press, 1995), 142–153; and Edgar H. Schein, "On Dialogue, Culture, and Organizational Learning," *Organizational Dynamics* (Autumn 1993), 40–51.

65. Carol Hymowitz, "How to Tell Employees All the Things They Don't Want to Hear" (in the Lead column), *The Wall Street Journal* (August 22, 2000), B1.

66. Peter Lowry and Byron Reimus, "Ready, Aim, Communicate," *Management Review* (July 1996).

67. Thomas E. Ricks, "Army Devises System to Decide What Does, and Does Not, Work," *The Wall Street Journal* (May 23, 1997), A1, A10; Stephanie Watts Sussman, "CALL: A Model for Effective Organizational Learning," *Strategy* (Summer 1999), 14–15; and Thomas A. Stewart, "Listen Up, Maggots! You Will Deploy a More Humane and Effective Managerial Style!" *Ecompany* (July 2001), 95.

68. Stewart, "Listen Up, Maggots!"

69. James A. F. Stoner and R. Edward Freeman, *Management,* 4th ed. (Englewood Cliffs, N.J.: Prentice-Hall, 1989).

70. Mike Hofman, "Lost in the Translation," *Inc.* (May 2000), 161–162.

71. Janet Fulk and Sirish Mani, "Distortion of Communication in Hierarchical Relationships," in *Communication Yearbook,* vol. 9, ed. M. L. McLaughlin (Beverly Hills, Calif.: Sage, 1986), 483–510.

72. Clifford, "How to Get the Geeks and the Suits to Play Nice," 92–93.

Chapter 15

Teamwork in Organizations

1. Stephanie Overby, "Corporate Angst," *CIO* (April 1, 2002), 78–84.

2. James Wallace Bishop and K. Dow Scott, "How Commitment Affects Team Performance," *HR Magazine* (February 1997), 107–111; Patricia Booth, "Embracing the Team Concept," *Canadian Business Review* (Autumn 1994), 10–13; and "Training in the 1990s," *The Wall Street Journal* (March 1), 1990, B1.

3. Rajiv D. Banker, Joy M. Field, Roger G. Schroeder, and Kingshuk K. Sinha, "Impact of Work Teams on Manufacturing Performance: A Longitudinal Field Study," *Academy of Management Journal* 39, no. 4 (1996), 867–890.

4. Eric Schine, "Mattel's Wild Race to Market," *Business Week* (February 21, 1994), 62–63; Frank V. Cespedes, Stephen X. Dole, and Robert J. Freedman, "Teamwork for Today's Selling," *Harvard Business Review* (March–April 1989), 44–55; Victoria J. Marsick, Ernie Turner, and Lars Cederholm, "International Managers as Team Leaders," *Management Review* (March 1989), 46–49; and "Team Goal-Setting," *Small Business Report* (January 1988), 76–77.

5. Carl E. Larson and Frank M. J. LaFasto, *TeamWork* (Newbury Park, Calif.: Sage, 1989).

6. Erika Rasmusson, "One for All," *Working Woman* (March 2001), 68.

7. Eric Sundstrom, Kenneth P. De Meuse, and David Futrell, "Work Teams," *American Psychologist* 45 (February 1990), 120–133.

8. Deborah L. Gladstein, "Groups in Context: A Model of Task Group Effectiveness," *Administrative Science Quarterly* 29 (1984), 499–517.

9. Dora C. Lau and J. Keith Murnighan, "Demographic Diversity and Faultlines: The Compositional Dynamics of Organizational Groups," *Academy of Management Review* 23, no. 2 (1998), 325–340.

10. Thomas Owens, "Business Teams," *Small Business Report* (January 1989), 50–58.

11. Laton McCartney, "A Team Effort," *IW* (December 18, 1995), 65–72.

12. John Grossmann, "The Kiss," *Sky* (January 1998), 62–67.

13. "Participation Teams," *Small Business Report* (September 1987), 38–41.

14. Susanne G. Scott and Walter O. Einstein, "Strategic Performance Appraisal in Team-Based Organizations: One Size Does Not Fit All," *Academy of Management Executive* 15, no. 2 (2001), 107–116.

15. Larson and LaFasto, *TeamWork*.

16. James H. Shonk, *Team-Based Organizations* (Homewood, Ill.: Business One Irwin, 1992); and John Hoerr, "The Payoff from Teamwork," *Business Week* (July 10, 1989), 56–62.

17. Gregory L. Miles, "Suddenly, USX Is Playing Mr. Nice Guy," *Business Week* (June 26, 1989), 151–152.

18. Jeanne M. Wilson, Jill George, and Richard S. Wellings, with William C. Byham, *Leadership Trapeze: Strategies for Leadership in Team-Based Organizations* (San Francisco: Jossey-Bass, 1994).

19. Ruth Wageman, "Critical Success Factors for Creating Superb Self-Managing Teams," *Organizational Dynamics* (Summer 1997), 49–61.

20. Thomas Owens, "The Self-Managing Work Team," *Small Business Report* (February 1991), 53–65.

21. "Powering Up Teams," *Organizational Dynamics* (Winter 2000), 48–66.

22. Charles Fishman, "Whole Foods is All Teams," *Fast Company* (April–May 1996), 102–109.

23. Curtis Sittenfeld, "Powered by the People," *Fast Company* (July–August 1999), 178–189.

24. The discussion of virtual teams is based on Anthony M. Townsend, Samuel M. DeMarie, and Anthony R. Hendrickson, "Virtual Teams: Technology and the Workplace of the Future," *Academy of Management Executive* 12, No. 3 (August 1998), 17–29; and Deborah L. Duarte and Nancy Tennant Snyder, *Mastering Virtual Teams* (San Francisco: Jossey-Bass, 1999).

25. Jessica Lipnack and Jeffrey Stamps, "Virtual Teams: The New Way to Work," *Strategy & Leadership* (January–February 1999), 14–19.

26. William R. Pape, "Group Insurance," *Inc. Technology* (1997), no. 2, 29, 31.

27. Vijay Govindarajan and Anil K. Gupta, "Building an Effective Global Business Team," *MIT Sloan Management Review* 42, no. 4 (Summer 2001), 63–71.

28. Charlene Marmer Solomon, "Building Teams Across Borders," *Global Workforce* (November 1998), 12–17.

29. James Daly, "Digital Cowboys," *Forbes ASAP* (February 26, 1996), 62.

30. Jane Pickard, "Control Freaks Need Not Apply," *People Management* (February 5, 1998), 49.

31. Sylvia Odenwald, "Global Work Teams," *Training and Development* (February 1996), 54–57; and Debby Young, "Team Heat," *CIO*, Section 1 (September 1, 1998), 43–51.

32. Ray Oglethorpe in Regina Fazio Maruca, ed., "What Makes Teams Work" (Unit of One column), *Fast Company* (November 2000), 109–140.

33. For research findings on group size, see M. E. Shaw, *Group Dynamics*, 3d ed. (New York: McGraw-Hill, 1981); and G. Manners, "Another Look at Group Size, Group Problem-Solving and Member Consensus," *Academy of Management Journal* 18 (1975), 715–724.

34. George Prince, "Recognizing Genuine Teamwork," *Supervisory Management* (April 1989), 25–36; K. D. Benne and P. Sheats, "Functional Roles of Group Members," *Journal of Social Issues* 4 (1948), 41–49; and R. F. Bales, *SYMLOG Case Study Kit* (New York: Free Press, 1980).

35. Robert A. Baron, *Behavior in Organizations*, 2d ed. (Boston: Allyn & Bacon, 1986).

36. Ibid.

37. Avan R. Jassawalla and Hemant C. Sashittal, "Strategies of Effective New Product Team Leaders," *California Management Review* 42, no. 2 (Winter 2000), 34–51.

38. Kenneth G. Koehler, "Effective Team Management," *Small Business Report* (July 19, 1989), 14–16; and Connie J. G. Gersick, "Time and Transition in Work Teams: Toward a New Model of Group Development," *Academy of Management Journal* 31 (1988), 9–41.

39. Bruce W. Tuckman and Mary Ann C. Jensen, "Stages of Small-Group Development Revisited," *Group and Organizational Studies* 2 (1977), 419–427; and Bruce W. Tuckman, "Developmental Sequences in Small Groups," *Psychological Bulletin* 63 (1965), 384–399. See also Linda N. Jewell and H. Joseph Reitz, *Group Effectiveness in Organizations* (Glenview, Ill.: Scott, Foresman, 1981).

40. Thomas Petzinger Jr., "Bovis Team Helps Builders Construct a Solid Foundation" (the Front Lines column), *The Wall Street Journal* (March 21, 1997), B1.

41. Shaw, *Group Dynamics*.

42. Daniel C. Feldman and Hugh J. Arnold, *Managing Individual and Group Behavior in Organizations* (New York: McGraw-Hill, 1983).

43. Dorwin Cartwright and Alvin Zander, *Group Dynamics: Research and Theory*, 3d ed. (New York: Harper & Row, 1968); and Elliot Aronson, *The Social Animal* (San Francisco: W. H. Freeman, 1976).

44. Peter E. Mudrack, "Group Cohesiveness and Productivity: A Closer Look," *Human Relations* 42 (1989), 771–785. Also see Miriam Erez and Anit Somech, "Is Group Productivity Loss the Rule or the Exception? Effects of Culture and Group-Based Motivation," *Academy of Management Journal* 39, no. 6 (1996), 1513–1537.

45. Stanley E. Seashore, *Group Cohesiveness in the Industrial Work Group* (Ann Arbor, Mich.: Institute for Social Research, 1954).

46. S. R. Crockett and N. Gross, "Can CEO Ollila Keep the Cellular Superstar Flying High?" *Business Week* (August 10, 1998), 48–55; and J. Fox, "Nokia's Secret Code," *Fortune* (May 1, 2000), 161–174.

47. J. Richard Hackman, "Group Influences on Individuals," in *Handbook of Industrial and Organizational Psychology*, ed. M. Dunnette (Chicago: Rand McNally, 1976).

48. Kenneth Bettenhausen and J. Keith Murnighan, "The Emergence of Norms in Competitive Decision-Making Groups," *Administrative Science Quarterly* 30 (1985), 350–372.

49. The following discussion is based on Daniel C. Feldman, "The Development and Enforcement of Group Norms," *Academy of Management Review* 9 (1984), 47–53.

50. Hugh J. Arnold and Daniel C. Feldman, *Organizational Behavior* (New York: McGraw-Hill, 1986).

51. Stephen P. Robbins, *Managing Organizational Conflict: A Nontraditional Approach* (Englewood Cliffs, N.J.: Prentice-Hall, 1974).

52. Daniel Robey, Dana L. Farrow, and Charles R. Franz, "Group Process and Conflict in System Development," *Management Science* 35 (1989), 1172–1191.

53. Kathleen M. Eisenhardt, Jean L. Kahwajy, and L. J. Bourgeois III, "Conflict and Strategic Choice: How Top Management Teams Disagree," *California Management Review* 39, no. 2 (Winter 1997), 42–62.

54. Koehler, "Effective Team Management"; and Dean Tjosvold, "Making Conflict Productive," *Personnel Administrator* 29 (June 1984), 121.

55. This discussion is based in part on Richard L. Daft, *Organization Theory and Design* (St. Paul, Minn.: West, 1992), Chapter 13; and Paul M. Terry, "Conflict Management," *The Journal of Leadership Studies* 3, no. 2 (1996), 3–21.

56. Ralph T. King, Jr., "Levi's Factory Workers Are Assigned to Teams, And Morale Takes a Hit," *The Wall Street Journal* (May 20, 1998), A1.

57. Clinton O. Longenecker and Mitchell Neubert, "Barriers and Gateways to Management Cooperation and Teamwork," *Business Horizons* (September-October 2000), 37–44.

58. This discussion is based on K. W. Thomas, "Towards Multidimensional Values in Teaching: The Example of Conflict Behaviors," *Academy of Management Review* 2 (1977), 487.

59. Robbins, *Managing Organizational Conflict*.

60. Based on Kathleen M. Eisenhardt, Jean L. Kahwajy, and L. J. Bourgeois III, "How Management Teams Can Have a Good Fight," *Harvard Business Review* (July–August 1997), 77–85.

61. R. B. Zajonc, "Social Facilitation," *Science* 149 (1965), 269–274; and Erez and Somech, "Is Group Productivity Loss the Rule or the Exception?"

62. Aaron Bernstein, "Detroit vs. the UAW: At Odds over Teamwork," *Business Week* (August 24, 1987), 54–55.

63. Robert Albanese and David D. Van Fleet, "Rational Behavior in Groups: The Free-Riding Tendency," *Academy of Management Review* 10 (1985), 244–255.

64. Baron, *Behavior in Organizations*.

65. Harvey J. Brightman, *Group Problem Solving: An Improved Managerial Approach* (Atlanta: Georgia State University, 1988).

66. Stephanie Overby, "Corporate Angst," 78–84.

Chapter 16
The Importance of Control

1. Richard H. Snyder, "How I Engineered a Small Business," *Strategic Finance* (May 1999), 26–30.

2. Nikhil Deogun, James R. Hagerty, Steve Stecklow, and Laura Johannes, "Anatomy of a Recall: How Coke's Controls Fizzled Out in Europe," *The Wall Street Journal* (June 29,1999), A1; Christine Tierney and Jeff Green, "Can Schrempp Stop the Careening at Chrysler?" *Business Week* (December 4, 2000), 40.

3. Douglas S. Sherwin, "The Meaning of Control," *Dunn's Business Review* (January 1956).

4. Russ Banham, "Nothin' But Net Gain," *eCFO* (Fall 2001), 32–33.

5. Jeannie Cameron, "Death of Traditional Accounting Will Prove to Be a Boon," *The Asian Wall Street Journal* (April 27, 1998), 16.

6. Jennifer S. Lee, "Tracking Sales and the Cashiers," *The New York Times* (July 11, 2001), C1, C6; Anna Wilde Mathews, "New Gadgets Track Truckers Every Move," *The Wall Street Journal* (July 14, 1997), B1, B10.

7. Steve Stecklow, "Kentucky's Teachers Get Bonuses, but Some Are Caught Cheating," *The Wall Street Journal* (September 2, 1997), p. A1, A5.

8. Saul Hansell, "Listen Up! It's Time for a Profit," *The Wall Street Journal* (May 20, 2002), BU 1 &14.

9. Trevor Merriden, "Measured for Success," *Management Review* (April 1999), 27–32.

10. Sumantra Ghoshal, *Strategic Control* (St. Paul, Minn.: West, 1986), Chapter 4; and Robert N. Anthony, John Dearden, and Norton M. Bedford, *Management Control Systems*, 5th ed. (Homewood, Ill.: Irwin, 1984).

11. John A. Boquist, Todd T. Milbourn, and Anjan V. Thakor, "How Do You Win the Capital Allocation Game?" *Sloan Management Review* (Winter 1998), pp. 59–71.

12. Anthony, Dearden, and Bedford, *Management Control Systems*.

13. Participation in budget setting is described in a number of studies, including Neil C. Churchill, "Budget Choice: Planning versus Control," *Harvard Business Review* (July–August 1984), 150–164; Peter Brownell, "Leadership Style, Budgetary Participation, and Managerial Behavior," *Accounting Organizations and Society* 8 (1983), 307–321; and Paul J. Carruth and Thurrell O. McClandon, "How Supervisors React to 'Meeting the Budget' Pressure," *Management Accounting* 66 (November 1984), 50–54.

14. William G. Ouchi, "Markets, Bureaucracies, and Clans," *Administrative Science Quarterly* 25 (1980), 129–141; and B. R. Baligia and Alfred M. Jaeger, "Multinational Corporations: Control Systems and Delegation Issues," *Journal of International Business Studies* (Fall 1984), 25–40.

15. Sherwin, "The Meaning of Control."

16. Mathews, "New Gadgets Trace Truckers' Every Move," B10.

17. Emily Esterson, "First-Class Delivery," *Inc. Technology* (September 15, 1998), 89.

18. W. Bouce Chew, "No-Nonsense Guide to Measuring Productivity," *Harvard Business Review* (January–February 1988), 110–118.

19. A. V. Feigenbaum, *Total Quality Control: Engineering and Management* (New York: McGraw-Hill, 1961); John Lorinc, "Dr. Deming's Traveling Quality Show," *Canadian Business* (September 1990), 38–42; Mary Walton, *The Deming Management Method* (New York: Dodd-Meade & Co., 1986); and J. M. Juran and Frank M. Gryna, eds., *Juran's Quality Control Handbook*, 4th ed. (New York: McGraw-Hill, 1988).

20. Edward E. Lawler III and Susan A. Mohrman, "Quality Circles after the Fad," *Harvard Business Review* (January–February 1985), 65–71; and Philip C. Thompson, *Quality Circles: How to Make Them Work in America* (New York: AMACOM, 1982).

21. Howard Rothman, "You Need Not Be Big to Benchmark," *Nation's Business* (December 1992), 64–65.

22. Tom Rancour and Mike McCracken, "Applying 6 Sigma Methods for Breakthrough Safety Peformance," *Professional Safety* 45, no. 10 (October 2000), 29–32; G. Hasek, "Merger Marries Quality Efforts," *Industry Week* (August 21, 2000), 89–92; and Lee Clifford, "Why You Can Safely Ignore Six Sigma," *Fortune* (January 22, 2001), 140.

23. Michael Hammer and Jeff Goding, "Putting Six Sigma in Perspective," *Quality* (October 2001), 58–62.

24. Claudia H. Deutsch, "New Economy, Old-School Rigor," *The New York Times* (June 12, 2000), C1, C2.

25. Norihiko Shirouzu, "Gadget Inspector: Why Toyota Wins Such High Marks on Quality Surveys," *The Wall Street Journal* (March 15, 2001), A1, A11; Cynthia Challenger, "Six Sigma: Can the GE Model Work in the Chemical Industry?" *Chemical Market Reporter* (July 16, 2001); FR6–FR10.

26. Philip R. Thomas, Larry J. Gallace, and Kenneth R. Martin, *Quality Alone Is Not Enough (AMA Management Briefing),* New York: American Management Association, August 1992.

27. Kate Kane, "L. L. Bean Delivers the Goods," *Fast Company* (August–September 1997), 104–113.

28. Clifford, "Why You Can Safely Ignore Six Sigma"; and Hammer and Goding, "Putting Six Sigma in Perspective."

29. Frank C. Barnes, "ISO 9000 Myth and Reality: A Reasonable Approach to ISO 9000," *SAM Advanced Management Journal* (Spring 1998), 23–30; and Thomas H. Stevenson and Frank C. Barnes, "Fourteen Years of ISO 9000: Impact, Criticisms, Costs, and Benefits," *Business Horizons* (May-June 2001), 45–51.

30. Don L. Bohl, Fred Luthans, John W. Slocum Jr., and Richard M. Hodgetts, "Ideas That Will Shape the Future of Management Practice," *Organizational Dynamics* (Summer 1996), 7–14.

31. K. Lehn and A. K. Makhija, "EVA and MVA as Performance Measures and Signals for Strategic Change," *Strategy & Leadership* (May-June 1996), 34–38;

32. Terence C. Pare, "A New Tool for Managing Costs," *Fortune* (June 14, 1993), 124–129; and Don L. Bohl, Fred Luthans, John W. Slocum Jr., and Richard M. Hodgetts, "Ideas that Will Shape the Future of Management Practice," *Organizational Dynamics* (Summer 1996), 7–14.

33. Perry Pascarella, "Open the Books to Unleash Your People," *Management Review* (May 1998), 58–60.

34. This discussion is based on a review of the balanced scorecard in Richard L. Daft, *Organization Theory and Design,* 7th ed. (Cincinnati, Ohio: South-Western College Publishing, 2001), 300–301.

35. "On Balance," a CFO Interview with Robert Kaplan and David Norton, *CFO* (February 2001), 73–78.

36. Robert Kaplan and David Norton, "The Balanced Scorecard: Measures that Drive Performance," *Harvard Business Review* (January–February, 1992), 71–79; and Chee W. Chow, Kamal M. Haddad, and James E. Williamson, "Applying the Balanced Scorecard to Small Companies," *Management Accounting* 79, no. 2 (August 1997), 21–27.

37. Based on Kaplan and Norton, "The Balanced Scorecard"; Chow, Haddad, and Williamson, "Applying the Balanced Scorecard"; and Cathy Lazere, "All Together Now," *CFO* (February 1998), 28–36.

38. "On Balance," and Debby Young, "Score It a Hit," *CIO Enterprise* (November 15, 1998), 26–32.

39. Snyder, "How I Engineered a Small Business," 26–30.

Appendix C
Entreprenuership and Small Business Management

1. Donald F. Kuratko and Richard M. Hodgetts, *Entrepreneurship: A Contemporary Approach*, 4th ed. (Fort Worth: The Dryden Press, 1998), 30.

2. Karen Dillon, "Three Women and a Kiosk," *Inc.* (January 2000), 60–62.

3. Study conducted by Yankelovich Partners, reported in Mark Henricks, "Type-Cast," *Entrepreneur* (March 2000), 14–16.

4. Christina Le Beau, "Kick in the Pants," *The Wall Street Journal* (May 14, 2001), R8.

5. Ibid.

6. Hilary Stout, "Start Low," *The Wall Street Journal* (May 14, 2001), R8.

7. Statistics from the Small Business Administration and the National Foundation for Women Business Owners, reported in "Tomorrow's Self-Employed American," *Inc.*, State of Small Business 2001 (May 29, 2001), 46–48.

8. Kathleen Collins, "¡La Vida Próspera! Latin-Owned Businesses Explode," *Working Woman* (October 2000), 13.

9. National Urban League, *http://www.nul.org*. Statistics also reported in Gina Holland, "Black America," Associated Press story, *The Johnson City Press* (July 22, 2001), 6.

10. Reported in John Case, "Counting Companies," *Inc.*, State of Small Business 2001 (May 29, 2001), 21–23.

11. Based on information in "Market Share," *Inc.* State of Small Business 2001 (May 29, 2001), 25–26; and "The Soloists," *Inc.*, State of Small Business 2001 (May 29, 2001), 37–39.

12. This section is based on John Case, "The Wonderland Economy," *The State of Small Business* (1995), 14–29; and Richard L. Daft, *Management*, 3d ed. (Fort Worth, Texas: The Dryden Press, 1992).

13. U. S. Census Bureau, 1997 Economic Census: Nonemployer Statistics, reported in "The Soloists," *Inc.* State of Small Business 2001 (May 29, 2001), 37–39.

14. George Mannes, "Don't Give Up on the Web," Fortune Small Business section, *Fortune* (March 5, 2001), 184[B]–184[L].

15. Ibid.

16. Jane Shealy, "Designing Women," *Success* (July/August 2000), 52–53.

17. Marc Ballon, "Start-up Mambos to Beat of Booming Market," *Inc.*, September 1997, 23; and Collins, "¡La Vida Próspera!"

18. Bill Meyers, "Worker Shortage Forces Small Businesses into Creative Hiring," *USA Today* (October 30, 1998), 1B, 2B.

19. Reported in Gene Koretz, "Cycles of Death and Rebirth," *Business Week* (November 16, 1998), 26.

20. Barbara Benham, "Big Government, Small Business," *Working Woman* (February 2001), 24.

21. Jerry Useem, "The New Entrepreneurial Elite," *Inc.* (December 1997), 50–68.

22. Research and statistics reported in "The Job Factory," *Inc.* State of Small Business 2001 (May 29, 2001), 40–43.

23. Kuratko and Hodgetts, *Entrepreneurship: A Contemporary Approach*, 4th ed., 11; and "100 Ideas for New Businesses," *Venture* (November 1988), 35–74.

24. Behham, "Big Government, Small Business."

25. Reported in "Tomorrow's Self-Employed American," *Inc.*, State of Small Business 2001 (May 29, 2001), 46–48.

26. Lisa Benavides, "Success Easy as Pie," *The Tennessean* (November 2, 1997), 3E.

27. John Case, "The Origins of Entrepreneurship," *Inc.* (June 1989), 51–63.

28. This discussion is based on Charles R. Kuehl and Peggy A. Lambing, *Small Business: Planning and Management*, 3d ed. (Ft. Worth: The Dryden Press, 1994).

29. David C. McClelland, *The Achieving Society* (New York: Van Nostrand, 1961).

30. Robert D. Hisrich, "Entrepreneurship-Intrapreneurship," *American Psychologist* (February 1990), 209–222.

31. Michael Harvey and Rodney Evans, "Strategic Windows in the Entrepreneurial Process," *Journal of Business Venturing* 10 (1995), 331–347.

32. "Downsized Chickens Come Home to Roost," *Managing Office Technology*, January 1994, 68.

33. Ron MacLean, "Big Manager on Campus," *Inc. 500* (1999), 62–66; R. E. Coleberd, "The Business Economist at Work: The Economist as Entrepreneur," *Business Economics* (October, 1994), 54–57.

34. Leslie Brokaw, "How to Start an *Inc.* 500 Company," *Inc. 500* 1994, 51–65.

35. Paul Reynolds, "The Truth about Start-ups," *Inc.* (February 1995), 23; Brian O'Reilly, "The New Face of Small Business," *Fortune* (May 2, 1994) 82–88.

36. Based on Linda Elkins, "Tips for Preparing a Business Plan," *Nation's Business* (June 1996), 60R–61R; Carolyn M. Brown, "The Do's and Don'ts of Writing a Winning Business Plan," *Black Enterprise* (April 1996), 114–116; and Kuratko and Hodgetts, *Entrepreneurship*, 4th ed., 295–297. For a clear, thorough step-by-step guide to writing an effective business plan, see Linda Pinson and Jerry Jinnett, *Anatomy of a Business Plan*, 5th ed. (Virginia Beach, Va: Dearborn, 2001).

37. The INC. FAXPOLL, *Inc.* (February 1992), 24.

38. "Venture Capitalists' Criteria," *Management Review* (November 1985), 7–8.

39. Benham, "Big Government, Small Business."

40. Statistics from Venture Economics and Venture Capital Association, reported in "Cash Flow," *Inc.*, State of Small Business 2001, 76–77.

41. Jennifer Maxwell profile in Betsy Wiesendanger, "Labors of Love," *Working Woman* (May 1999), 43–56.

42. Small Business Administration statistics, reported in Henry Weil, "Business in a Box," *Working Woman* (September 1999), 59–64.

43. Echo Montgomery Garrett, "The Twenty-First-Century Franchise," *Inc.* (January 1995), 79–88; Lisa Benavides, "Linking Up with a Chain," *The Tennessean* (April 6, 1999), 1E.

44. Weil, "Business in a Box."

45. Roberta Maynard, "Choosing a Franchise," *Nation's Business* (October 1996), 56–63.

46. Richard Gibson, "Richard Gibson on Franchising: Make Sure to Read Between the Web Lines," *The Wall Street Journal* (May 14, 2001), R12.

47. Dale Buss, "Bringing New Firms Out of Their Shell," *Nation's Business* (March 1997), 48–50; and Amy Oringel, "Sowing Success," *Working Woman* (May 2001), 72.

48. Harvard Business School statistics, reported in Kimberly Weisul, "Incubators Lay an Egg," *Business Week Frontier* (October 9, 2000), F14.

49. Oringel, "Sowing Success."

50. Jill Hecht Maxwell, "Sit! Stay! Make Money! Good Company!," *Inc. Tech* No. 1 (2001), 43–44.

51. Miguel Helft, "Dot-Com Survivors," *The Industry Standard* (July 9–16, 2001), 30–39.

52. Ibid.

53. John Case, "Who's Looking at Start-Ups?" *Inc.*, State of Small Business 2001 (May 29, 2001), 60.

54. Suzanne McGee, "CacheFlow: The Life Cycle of a Venture-Capital Deal," *The Wall Street Journal* (February 22, 2000), C1.

55. Reported in "Did You Know?" sidebar in J. Neil Weintraut, "Told Any Good Stories Lately?" *Business 2.0* (March 2000), 139–140.

56. Steve Jurvetson and Andreas Stavropoulos, "Does Your Idea Make Sense?" *Business 2.0* (March 2000), 138–139.

57. J. Neil Weintraut, "Told Any Good Stories Lately?" *Business 2.0* (March 2000), 139–140.

58. Reported in H. M. Dietel, P. J. Dietel, and K. Steinbuhler, *e-Business and e-Commerce for Managers* (Upper Saddle River, NJ: Prentice Hall, 2001), 58.

59. Jeff Green, "Employees by the Round," *Business 2.0* (March 2000), 168–169.

60. Julie Pitta, "Webb Master," *Forbes* (December 13, 1999), 322–324.

61. This section is based on Glen Rifkin and Ken Lambert, "Marketing Your Startup," *Business 2.0* (March 2000), 181–184.

62. Clay Timon, "10 Tips for Naming," *Business 2.0* (March 2000), 151–152.

63. Queena Sook Kim, "People Like Us," *The Wall Street Journal* (February 12, 2001), R34.

64. Katherine Mieszkowski, "Community Standards," *Fast Company* (September 2000), 368+.

65. Rosabeth Moss Kanter, "A More Perfect Union," *Inc.* (February 2001), 92–98.

66. Bob Kagle, "The VC Meeting," *Fast Company* (March 2000), 147–148.

67. Bruce Golden, "Forming a Board," *Fast Company* (March 2000), 171.

68. Wendy Lea, "Dancing with a Partner," *Fast Company* (March 2000), 159–161.

69. Christopher Caggiano, "E-tailing by the Numbers," *Inc. Tech* No. 1, (2001), 46–49.

70. Carrie Dolan, "Entrepreneurs Often Fail as Managers," *The Wall Street Journal* (May 15, 1989), B1.

71. Michael Warshaw, "Plan B-minus," *Inc.* (January 2000), 56–58.

72. Amanda Walmac, "Full of Beans," *Working Woman* (February 1999), 38–40.

73. Michael Barrier, "The Changing Face of Leadership," *Nation's Business* (January 1995), 41–42.

74. Udayan Gupta and Jeffrey A. Tannenbaum, "Labor Shortages Force Changes at Small Firms," *The Wall Street Journal* (May 22, 1989), B1, B2; "Harnessing Employee Productivity," *Small Business Report* (November 1987), 46–49; and Molly Klimas, "How to Recruit a Smart Team," *Nation's Business* (May 1995), 26–27.

75. Saul Hansell, "Listen Up! It's Time for a Profit: A Front Row Seat as Amazon Gets Serious," *The New York Times* (May 20, 2001), Section 3, 1.

Name Index

Company Index

Subject Index

Functional departments, 253, 268
Functional team. *See* Vertical team
Fundamental attribution error, 386

Gallup study, 472
Gay men, 350
General Adaptation Syndrome (GAS), 399–400
General Agreement on Tariffs and Trade (GATT), 89–90
General and Industrial Management (Fayol), 33
General environment, 53, 54–58, 74. *See also* Environment
Generation X, 19, 28, 356
Generation Y, 19, 28, 57, 356
Germany, 88, 93
Glass ceiling, 350, 365
Global contact, 140
Global dispersion, 71
Global diversity, 361–363
Global environment, 57–58
Globalization
    corporate strategies for, 119–121, 421
    employment and, 41, 52, 82, 83–84, 102, 362 (*See also* World trade)
    and ethical conduct, 120
    and human resource management, 309
    international quality standards, 565
    language and, 84
    leadership and, 100–101
    manufacturing and, 83–84
    stages of, 84
Global learning, 101–102, 103
Global outsourcing, 95
Global team, 524–525
Global technology, 18
Goal, 146, 152, 153–154, 163. *See also* Planning; Plans
    criteria for, 153–154
    hierarchy, 153
    setting of, 154–155, 182
Good to Great: Why Some Companies Make the Leap . . . and Others Don't (Collins), 432
Gossip chain, 500
Government red tape, 52
Grand strategy, 165
Grapevine, 500–501, 507
Great Britain, 93
Greece, 93
Greenhouse gases, 126
Green standards, 126, 127
Group as compared to team, 517
Gun manufacturers, 57

Halo effect, 328, 384–385
Hawthorne effect, 36
Hawthorne studies, 35–36, 446–447
Headhunters, 317
Health foods, 57
Health Insurance Portability and Accountability Act (HIPPA), 311

Heroes, 65–66, 75
Hersey-Blanchard situational theory, 423–425
Hierarchy of needs theory, 37, 447–449, 450, 472
High-context culture, 362, 363
High performance, 41
Hiring practices, 71–72, 315–324. *See also* Recruiting
    interview process, 321–322
    and organizational needs, 317–318
    selection, 321–324
Hispanic-Americans, 344. *See also* Diversity; Minorities
Home-based business, 314
Homeless, hiring of, 321
Horizontal communication, 496–497, 507
Horizontal coordination, 250–251, 251, 269
Horizontal linkage, 298
Horizontal organization, 249–255
Horizontal structure, 253, 255–256, 277, 520
Horizontal team, 519–520
Human behavior, 37, 296
Human capital, 308, 333
Human embryonic stem cells, 115
Human genome, 56
Humanistic perspective, 29, 35–39, 41
Human Relations Movement, 35, 36–38
Human resource information system, 309–310
Human resource management (HRM), 304–337, 333
    federal laws and, 311
    hiring employees, 315–324, 315–324
    strategic role of, 306–307
    and workforce, 307
Human resource managers, 306, 361–362
Human resource perspective, 37
Human resource planning, 316–317
Human Resources, 179
Human skills, 10, 11, 19
Hydrogen fuel cells, 126
Hygiene factors, 452

Idea champions, 281–282
Idea incubator, 282–283, 298
Immigrants, 443
Implementation, 177–178, 200
Incremental change, 277
India, 93, 94, 96
Individualism, 93, 137
Individualism approach, 116–117
Informal communication channels, 499–501
Informal organization, 35
Information, 210–211
Information evaluation, 393
Information Fatigue Syndrome, 221
Information overload, 221
Information sharing, 277
Information technology (IT), 40, 224, 309–310

for decision making, 209–211
    departments of, 249
    e-business and, 210
    efficiency of, 220–221
    management implications for, 219–220
    and new workplace, 222–223
Infrastructure, 87–88
Initiating structure, 419
Instant messaging, 222–223, 493
Integrators, 453–454
Interactive leadership, 434, 437
Internal dimension, 74
Internal environment, 54, 63–65, 67
Internal incubator, 283
Internal organization, 75
Internal recruiting, 317
International dimension, 54–55
International environment, 86
International management, 84, 86
International monetary fund, 58
International quality standards, 565, 569
International Standards Organization, 133
Internet, 18, 19, 26, 29. *See also* Computers
    customer privacy, 136
    customers and, 20, 59–60, 269
    e-business and, 95–96, 224, 269
    e-commerce and, 17
    globalization and, 83
    legal issues, 140
    and partnership strategies, 176–177
    resources on, 45, 77, 182, 228, 271, 301, 336, 369, 408, 440, 475, 511, 544, 572
    wireless, 223
Interview process, 71, 321–322, 323
Intranet, 18, 25, 215, 485, 486
Intrinsic reward, 445
Intuition, 193–195, 393, 394
Inventory systems, 286–287
ISO 9000, 565
Italy, 260

Japan, 40, 93
Job analysis, 318
Job-based pay, 329–330
Job characteristics model, 466–468
Job description, 318
Job design, 464, 473
Job enlargement, 464, 465
Job enrichment, 465
Job evaluation, 330
Job knowledge, 538–539
Job performance, 390
Job posting, 327
Job rotation, 464
Job satisfaction, 379, 380
Job simplification, 464
Job specification, 318
Job termination, 332
Joint venture, 98
Justice approach, 118, 137
Just-in-time (JIT) inventory control system, 286–287